2002

CANADIAN DIRECTORY OF SEARCH FIRMS

RÉPERTOIRE CANADIEN DES AGENCES DE PLACEMENT

MEDIACORP CANADA INC.
TORONTO

Canadian Directory of Search Firms
Mediacorp Canada Inc.
21 New Street
Toronto, Ontario
M5R 1P7

Telephone	(416) 964-6069
Fax	(416) 964-3202

E-mail	info@mediacorp2.com
Web Site	http://www.mediacorp2.com

5th edition. 1st edition: 1997.
ISBN 1-894450-04-3

To purchase this directory on CD-ROM, telephone (416) 964-6069. The price is $99.95.

Printed in Canada by Webcom.

Répertoire canadien des agences de placement
Mediacorp Canada Inc.
21, rue New
Toronto (Ontario)
M5R 2S2

Téléphone	*(416) 964-6069*
Télécopieur	*(416) 964-3202*

Courriel	*info@mediacorp2.com*
Site Internet	*http://www.mediacorp2.com*

5iem édition. 1er edition: 1997.
ISBN 1-894450-04-3

Pour se procurer ce répertoire en CD-ROM, veuillez téléphoner au (416) 964-6069. Le prix est 99,95$.

Imprimé au Canada par Webcom.

TABLE OF CONTENTS

TABLE DES MATIÈRES

HOW TO USE
THIS DIRECTORY

Firms listed in this directory are engaged in the business of locating career-level candidates for employer clients. This includes traditional search firms paid on a retainer or contingency basis, as well as consulting firms with established search practices.

Also included in this directory are accounting firms and management consultants that do occasional search work for clients, and a number of personnel agencies that place career-level candidates such as engineers and accountants.

This directory does not include temporary help agencies or firms that typically provide clerical or industrial workers. Nor does it include career counselling firms or companies that charge job-seekers any type of fee. (If you discover such a firm, please let us know and we will delete their listing from future editions.)

Search firms are listed in alphabetical order by name. To find all the recruitment firms in your field:

1. Start with the **Detailed List of Occupations** on page 274. Find the occupational category that best describes your line of work.

2. Then turn to the appropriate **Occupational Index** for your field. Here you'll see all the search firms that specialize in your occupational category. Highlight the firms in the city or region that interests you.

3. Then refer to the **Firm Listings** section at the front of the book to find more information on the firms you selected. Each firm listing includes full contact information, practice specialties, fee information (for employers), year founded, number of employees and the level of position typically recruited.

In addition to the Occupational Index, four topical indexes let you find search firms by other criteria:

✔ The **Geographic Index** (p. 347) lets you find all the agencies in a particular city or province. Included here is a special international section that lists over 200 search firms in USA, Asia and

COMMENT UTILISER
CE RÉPERTOIRE

Les firmes que l'on retrouve dans ce répertoire ont comme priorité l'embauche de candidats à la recherche d'une carrière auprès de leurs employeurs-clients. Il peut s'agir de firmes qui font de la recherche de personnel selon une méthode traditionnelle payée sur la base d'un plan de relance ou de prévoyance tel que les firmes de consultants exerçant selon des normes reconnues.

Vous retrouverez aussi des firmes comptables et consultants en gestion qui offrent le service de recherche de candidats pour leur clientèle, et un certain nombre d'agences de personnel qui font du placement de candidats pour des carrières telles que les ingénieurs et les comptables.

Ce répertoire ne comprend pas les agences qui offrent ou recherchent des candidats à des postes temporaires dans les secteurs administratifs ou industriels. Il ne comprend pas non plus des firmes de counselling ou des entreprises de recherche de candidats qui exigent des frais de tous genres. (Si vous découvrez de telle firme dans le répertoire, faites-le nous savoir et nous radierons son nom à la prochaine édition.)

Les firmes sont énumérées par ordre alphabétique. Pour trouver tous les agences dans votre domaine:

1. Commencer avec la **Liste détaillée des occupations** à la page 274. Trouver la catégorie qui décrit votre spécialité professionnelle.

2. Ensuite, voir l'**Index occupationnel** et trouver votre catégorie occupationnelle. Vous verrez toute firme qui fait de la recherche de personnel qui spécialise dans votre domaine. Choisir les firmes d'une ville ou d'une région qui vous intéressent.

3. Ensuite, voir la section des **Agences** au début du livre pour trouver de l'information sur les firmes que vous avez choisies. Chaque inscription inclut des renseignements concernant des contacts, des spécialités, des frais (pour employeur), l'année fondée, nombre d'employés et niveau de positions recruté.

En plus de l'Index occupationnel, quatres indexes topiques vous permittent de trouver des firmes par d'autres critères:

✔ Vous trouverez toute agence d'une ville ou province en particulier dans l'**Index géographique** (p. 347). L'Index géographique inclut une section spéciale internationale qui indique plus de 200 firmes aux États-Unis, en Asie et en Europe qui recrutent souvent

Europe that actively recruit in Canada and locate international staff.

✔ The **Minimum Salary Index** (p. 366) lets you find agencies that recruit staff above a particular salary level.

✔ The **Fee Basis Index** (p. 370) lets you find agencies according to whether they are paid by employers on a retainer or contingent basis.

✔ The **Who's Who Index** (p. 377) lists over 4200 recruitment professionals across Canada and shows you the firms that employ them.

The information in this directory is compiled from a variety of sources, including listing forms supplied by most of the firms. While every effort has been taken to ensure that the information is accurate and up-to-date, we assume no responsibility for errors or omissions.

If you find information that is out-of-date or inaccurate, use the form at back to let us know and we will update the information in the next edition.   ❧

au Canada et trouvent de personnel international.

✔ *L'Index salaire minimum* (p. 366) vous permet de trouver des agences qui recrutent au-dessus d'un niveau de salaire en particulier.

✔ *L'Index frais* (p. 370) vous permet de trouver des agences qui sont payées par honoraire ou dans une manière relative.

✔ Le bottin des *personnes-ressources* (p. 377) comprend plus de 4200 recruteurs professionels autour du Canada et vous indique les firmes qui les emploient.

L'information contenue dans ce répertoire provient de différentes sources, incluant les reseignements fournis sur une base volontaire par la majorité des firmes. Quoique tous les efforts ont été faits pour s'assurer de l'exactitude des informations et de leur mise à jour, nous devons décliner toute responsabilité quant aux erreurs ou omissions.

Si vous trouvez une information erronnée ou périmée, vous pouvez utiliser l'avis de changement à la fin du répertoire afin que nous puissions apporter les corrections nécessaires à la prochaine édition.   ❧

WHAT YOU NEED TO KNOW ABOUT USING A RECRUITMENT FIRM

While working on this directory each year, we speak to hundreds of job-seekers who are interested in learning more about the recruitment industry and how to find a recruiter in their field. We have gathered the 11 most common questions to help you make the best use of search firms and recruiters:

1. Does a recruiter work for the employer or the job-seeker?

Recruiters work for the employers that hire them. Many job-seekers mistakenly believe that a recruiter can help them find a new job, or even a new career. Recruiters can only recommend you for particular assignments they have been engaged to work on by employers.

2. Who pays a recruiter's fees and how much do they charge?

The cardinal rule is that the candidate never pays. Employers pay each of the search firms listed in this directory. (If you encounter a firm that charges job-seekers any kind of fee, let us know and we will take them out of the next edition.)

You should be aware that there are a variety of career counselling firms and resume writing companies that do charge candidates to improve their job hunting skills. Also keep in mind that there are outplacement firms paid by employers to assist recently-terminated employees in finding new positions. None of these organizations is paid by an employer to fill a vacant position and, as such, none has been included in this directory.

Recruitment firms usually set their fee as a percentage of a candidate's first-year salary. For mid-level and junior positions, the fee will typically range from 20% to 25%. For more senior-level assignments, which require more time and effort, the range is from 30% to as high as 35%.

3. What is the difference between retainer and contingency firms?

On a retainer assignment, the recruiter has an exclusive engagement to find a suitable candidate, and is paid whether or not a successful placement is made. Generally,

QUE DEVRIEZ-VOUS SAVOIR AU MOMENT DE FAIRE APPEL À UNE AGENCE DE PLACEMENT?

Lorsque nous préparons ce répertoire chaque année, nous parlons à des centaines d'individus qui cherchent activement du travail et qui veulent apprendre davantage sur le marché de recrutement ainsi que sur la façon de se trouver un agent de placement dans leur domaine respectif. Nous avons réuni les onze questions les plus courantes afin de vous aider à bénéficier pleinement des contacts avec les agences et les agents de recrutement:

1. L'agent de placement travaille-t-il pour l'employeur ou pour l'individu qui cherche du travail?

Les agents de placement travaillent pour les employeurs qui les engagent. Plusieurs individus qui cherchent du travail croient, par erreur, qu'un agent de placement est en mesure de les aider à trouver un nouvel emploi, voire une nouvelle carrière. Les agents de placement ne font que vous recommander à des employeurs afin que vous travailliez sur certaines tâches dont l'accomplissement ceux-là sont responsables étant donné qu'ils ont été engagés par les employeurs.

2. Qui doit payer les frais de services des agents de placement et combien peuvent s'élever ces montants?

Selon la règle directrice, le candidat ne débourse jamais les montants en question. Les employeurs paient les frais de chacune des agences de placement qui font partie de ce répertoire. S'il vous arrive de faire affaire avec une agence où l'on vous demande de payer les frais de services, veuillez nous en prévenir afin que nous enlevions du répertoire, lors de sa prochaine édition, le nom de l'agence en question.

Vous devriez savoir qu'il y a une variété d'agences de planification de carrière et de compagnies spécialisées en rédaction de curriculum vitae où vous devrez payer pour apprendre à améliorer vos techniques de recherche d'emploi.

N'oubliez pas qu'il existe des compagnies de placement externe engagées par des employeurs afin d'aider des employés qui viennent d'être mis à pieds à trouver de nouveaux postes. Aucune de ces organisations n'est engagée par un employeur quelconque afin de trouver le bon candidat pour un poste libre: par conséquent, elles ne figurent pas dans ce répertoire.

Le calcul des frais relatifs aux services des agences de placement est basé sur un pourcentage du salaire d'un candidat pendant sa première année de travail. Les frais peuvent généralement varier de 20% à 25% du salaire annuel d'un individu qui occupe un poste de niveau moyen et subalterne. Les pourcentages vont de 30% jusqu'à 35% dans les cas des

senior-level and executive searches are done on a retainer basis since they require more time and effort. In retainer assignments, the employer usually sets a time limit (between 60 days and six months) for the assignment, after which the search may be offered to other recruiters.

Contingency assignments are non-exclusive and recruiters are paid only if one of their candidates is hired for the position. An employer will usually offer a contingency assignment to several recruitment firms at once. The recruiter who fills the position is the one who receives the fee.

In this directory, you will also see some search firms described as "sometimes contingent." This means that they accept both retainer and contingency assignments. Usually, their mid-level assignments are contingency, while senior-level searches are done on a retainer basis.

4. How much industry experience do I need before I can use a recruiter?

Candidates should have a reasonable amount of experience before using a search firm or recruiter. The experience required will vary by industry and the level of position you seek. In some fields (such as computing and technical sales), candidates with as little as two years of experience are encouraged to contact recruiters. In most fields, however, recruiters will consider you only if you have at least four or five years of industry experience.

5. How many search firms or recruiters should I contact?

The answer depends on the level of position you are seeking and your industry. For junior- and mid-level assignments (i.e. having an annual salary under $65,000), you should contact dozens of recruiters — as many as 50 to 100. If you are a more senior-level candidate, fewer firms specialize in assignments at this level and you will find yourself dealing with only 10 to 15 at the most.

The exception to this rule is if you work in an industry that has developed a specialized recruitment community. In the Occupational Index at the back of this directory, you will find certain fields (e.g. Plastics, Public Relations or Hospitality) have a relatively small number of recruiters who work exclusively in that field.

individus qui occupent un poste de niveau supérieur dont les tâches exigent plus de temps et d'effort.

3. Quelle est la différence entre les agences à honoraires et celles dites relatives?

Lors d'une tâche à honoraires, l'agent de placement s'engage de façon exclusive à trouver le candidat approprié à un poste donné. Celui-là se fait payer indépendamment de la réussite du placement. Généralement, les recherches de niveaux supérieur et exécutif se réalisent selon le modèle à honoraires puisqu'elles demandent plus de temps et d'effort. Lorsqu'il s'agit d'une tâche à honoraires, l'employeur fixe un délai (de 60 jours à 6 mois) pour son accomplissement. Au cas où le but ne soit pas atteint dans le délai prévu, on demande à d'autres agents de recrutement de s'en occuper.

Les tâches relatives ne sont pas réalisées de manière exclusive. Les agents de recrutement ne sont payés qu'au cas où l'un de leurs candidats soit engagé pour occuper le poste. L'employeur confie généralement une tâche relative à plusieurs agents de placement à la fois. L'agent de placement qui arrive à trouver le bon candidat pour le poste se fait payer les frais de service.

Dans ce répertoire vous trouverez également quelques agences de placement qui sont décrites en tant que "parfois relatives". Cela veut dire qu'elles acceptent les deux types de tâches: à honoraires et relatives. Généralement leurs tâches de niveau moyen sont relatives tandis que les recherches de niveau supérieur sont à honoraires.

4. Quel est le niveau d'expérience dans le marché dont j'ai besoin afin de bénéficier pleinement des services d'un agent de placement?

Tout candidat devrait avoir un niveau d'expérience considérable avant de faire appel aux services d'une agence de placement. Le niveau d'expérience requis dépendra du domaine et du niveau de responsabilité du poste visé. Dans certains domaines, tels que l'informatique et les ventes techniques, les candidats ayant tout au plus deux ans d'expérience sont encouragés à prendre contact avec des agents de placement. Cependant, dans la plupart des domaines, les agents de placement ne vous accepteront en tant que client que si vous avez au moins quatre ou cinq ans d'expérience dans le marché.

5. Combien d'agents de placement devrais-je aborder?

La réponse à cette question dépend du niveau de responsabilité du poste que vous souhaitez occuper et de votre domaine d'activité. Dans le cas de tâches de niveaux subalterne et moyen (dont le revenu ne dépasse pas $65 000 par année), vous devriez contacter des dizaines d'agents de recrutement: de 50 à 100 agents. Toutefois, si vous êtes candidat à un poste de niveau supérieur, vous ne ferez affaire qu'avec un maximum de dix à quinze agences car celles qui sont spécialisées en tâches de ce niveau ne sont pas nombreuses.

6. How do I make sure two recruiters don't send my resume to the same employer? How do I ensure my current employer doesn't find out that I'm looking around?

A good recruiter will always call you and ask before sending your resume to a client. The last thing the recruiter wants is for you to decline an invitation to meet their client! If you are dealing with a firm that works on a contingency basis (or is listed as "sometimes contingent"), in your cover letter ask the recruiter to contact you before sending your resume to employers.

7. What is the best way to contact a recruiter?

Almost every search firm in this directory prefers that you contact them by telephone before sending your resume. When you call, ask to speak with the person who specializes in placements in your field (e.g. *"Can you tell me who at your firm specializes in placing pharmaceutical people?"*). When you have the right person on the telephone, ask if they have a moment to speak with you. If they are busy, find out when would be a better time to call.

If the recruiter can speak with you, provide them with a short three or four sentence summary of your background (e.g. *"My name is Janice Leblanc, I'm 35 years old and have five years' experience as a marketing representative in the pharmaceutical industry. I'm looking for a position in the Montreal area with a salary around $95,000."*)

If the recruiter is interested in your background, they will ask you to send your resume. Above all, job-seekers should not request an interview in the initial telephone interview. This will come only after the recruiter has reviewed your resume.

8. What happens after I send a recruiter my resume?

If you do not hear anything from the recruiter for a few weeks, call them to make sure they received your resume. Usually, the recruiter will confirm that they have your resume on file and say they will contact you if something comes up.

Some recruiters will invite you in for an initial interview shortly after receiving your resume. This "getting acquainted" session is just an opportunity for the recruiter to become familiar with you. At this stage, the recruiter likely does not have a particular assignment for you. The

L'exception à cette règle se présente si vous travaillez dans un domaine où l'on ait développé une communauté de spécialisée. Vous trouverez, dans la liste alphabétique de professions à la fin de ce répertoire, certains domaines, comme celui du plastique, des affaires publiques ou de l'hospitalité, avec lesquels ne travaillent en exclusivité qu'un nombre relativement réduit d'agents de placement.

6. Comment puis-je éviter que deux agents distincts de placement envoient mon curriculum vitae au même employeur? Comment puis-je suis être sûr et certain que mon employeur courant n'apprendra pas que je cherche du travail ailleurs?

Tout agent de placement compétent vous appellera toujours pour vous demander la permission avant d'envoyer votre curriculum vitae à un client. L'agent de placement a intérêt à éviter à tout prix que vous refusiez de rencontrer un de ses clients! Au cas où vous fassiez affaire avec une agence où l'on travaille sur une base relative ou qui est classée en tant que "parfois relative", marquez clairement dans votre lettre de présentation que vous voudriez que l'agent vous contacte avant d'envoyer votre curriculum vitae à des employeurs.

7. Quel est le moyen le plus efficace pour entrer en contact avec un agent de placement?

Presque tous les agents de placement faisant partie de ce répertoire préfèrent que vous les contactiez par téléphone avant de leur envoyer votre curriculum vitae. Lorsque vous faites l'appel, demandez à parler avec l'individu spécialisé en placements dans votre domaine d'activité. (Par exemple: "Pourriez-vous me dire le nom du professionnel dans votre agence qui s'occupe du placement de personnel dans le domaine pharmaceutique?") Lorsque vous aurez la bonne personne au bout du fil, demandez-lui s'il peut vous parler. S'il est occupé, demandez-lui à quel moment votre appel serait opportun.

Au cas où l'agent puisse vous parler, présentez-vous succinctement avec trois ou quatre phrases qui résument bien votre expérience dans le domaine d'activité. (Par exemple: "Je m'appelle Janice Leblanc. J'ai 35 ans. J'ai cinq ans d'expérien ce en tant que représentante commerciale dans le domaine pharmaceutique. Je cherche un poste à occuper dans la région de Montréal, avec un salaire de $95 000.")

L'agent vous demandera de lui envoyer votre curriculum vitae s'il est intéressé en votre profil professionnel. Les individus qui cherchent du travail ne devraient surtout pas demander une entrevue lors du premier contact par téléphone. La bonne occasion pour faire cette demande ne se présentera qu'après que l'agent de placement aura étudié votre curriculum vitae.

8. Que se passe-t-il après que j'aurai envoyé mon curriculum vitae à un agent de placement?

recruiter is trying to determine if you measure up in person to the candidate described in your resume. Most recruiters will use this initial meeting to get a better understanding of your career objectives and salary expectations.

After the initial interview, it is good form to send the recruiter a short "thank you" note. (Generally in your job search, send "thank you" notes to everyone who takes the time to meet with you — even if you are not chosen for the position.) In your "thank you" note, be polite, to the point and avoid being solicitous — nobody appreciates an insincere gladhander.

If the recruiter has a suitable position you, the recruiter will generally invite you back for a more extensive interview before you meet the employer. By the time you meet the employer, you should be confident — the recruiter has already passed judgement on you and believes you are a suitable candidate for the position.

9. Will a recruiter help me negotiate the job offer?

The short answer is no. Generally, the offer stage is not the time to be discussing issues like salary. A good recruiter should know your salary expectations from your initial "getting acquainted" meeting. As well, remember that the recruiter and employer agreed on the salary level when the recruiter initially accepted the search assignment.

If there are complicated aspects of the employment offer — such as severance periods or non-competition clauses — it is best to consult a lawyer (or a friend who understands these things), rather than place the recruiter in a conflict-of-interest.

10. I've just landed a job through a recruiter. What's next?

After you have accepted the offer of employment, send the recruiter a short "thank you" note for the time they spent with you. Then contact the other recruiters you approached and let them know that you have a new assignment and thank them for their assistance.

Remember that the recruiter usually guarantees your placement for a period of time — usually from one to six months, depending on your level of seniority (i.e. a longer guarantee is usually provided for more senior placements). If you leave during this period or are dismissed with

Appelez l'agent de placement si vous n'en avez pas de nouvelle au bout de quelques semaines afin de lui demander s'il a bien reçu votre curriculum vitae. Normalement, l'agent vous dira que votre curriculum vitae se trouve dans leurs dossiers et que l'on vous appellera au moment où une offre se présentera.

Il est possible que certains agents vous invitent à passer une entrevue initiale peu après la réception de votre curriculum vitae. Cette première rencontre n'est qu'une occasion pour l'agent de mieux vous connaître. À cette étape, il est fort probable que l'agent n'ait pour vous aucune offre en vue. L'agent essaye simplement de vérifier si la personne qu'il rencontre est à la hauteur de la description faite dans le curriculum vitae.

La plupart des agents profiteront de cette rencontre initiale pour mettre au clair vos objectifs de carrière et vos attentes en ce qui concerne le revenu.

Suite à la rencontre initiale, il est recommandable d'envoyer à l'agent un mot de remerciement. Pendant votre processus de recherche d'emploi, envoyez des mots de remerciement à tous ceux qui prennent le temps de vous rencontrer, même si vous n'avez pas été choisi pour occuper le poste. Lorsque vous écrivez des remerciements, soyez poli, succinct et surtout évitez la sollicitude. Personne n'apprécie le manque de sincérité!

Au cas où l'agent de recrutement ait pour vous une offre, vous serez invité à revenir à son bureau afin de passer une entrevue plus approfondie avant de rencontrer l'employeur. Vous devriez faire preuve d'assurance au moment de rencontrer l'employer puisque l'agent de placement vous aura déjà donné sa rétroaction ainsi que son évaluation et il vous en aura fait part s'il croit que vous êtes le candidat idéal pour le poste.

9. L'agent de placement m'aidera-t-il lors des négociations de l'offre d'emploi?

La réponse la plus directe à cette question est "non". Généralement, l'étape de l'offre d'emploi n'est pas le meilleur moment pour parler de questions comme le salaire. Tout agent compétent devrait bien connaître vos attentes en ce qui concerne le revenu depuis la rencontre initiale entre vous deux. De plus, n'oubliez pas que l'agent et l'employeur se sont mis d'accord quant à l'échelle salariale au moment où l'agent a accepté la tâche de recherche.

Finalement, si vous devez faire face à des aspects compliqués de l'offre d'emploi, tels que des périodes d'interruption ou des clauses de non compétitivité, il vaut mieux faire appel à un avocat ou à un ami qui s'y connaisse plutôt que de mettre l'agent de placement dans une position de conflit d'intérêts.

10. Je viens de trouver un emploi grâce à un agent de placement. Quelle est-elle, la prochaine étape?

Suite à l'acceptation d'une offre d'emploi, envoyez à l'agent un petit mot de remerciement pour le temps qu'il vous a consacré. Ensuite, contactez les autres agents avec qui vous faisiez également affaire et

cause, the recruiter must find a replacement candidate at no cost to the employer.

Once you are settled in your new position, keep in touch with the key recruiters that you met or spoke with during your job search. At least once a year, call them and let them know where you are and what you are doing. (A good Christmas card also works wonders.) A well-cultivated relationship with a recruiter can pay handsome dividends both in your new job and your own career for years to come.

11. What else do recruiters do besides finding suitable candidates?

It really depends on the scope of the recruiter's engagement. Retainer firms generally spend a lot more time working with an employer to draw up the job description and determine the appropriate salary level. Contingency firms do not have the luxury of time — they are paid only if they make a placement — and generally work with the requirements established by the employer.

Both types of recruiters will use their extensive network of contacts to locate prospective candidates. This is what employers are really paying for when they engage a recruiter's services. In addition to their in-house database of candidates, recruiters will often advertise assignments on their websites or in newspapers and trade magazines.

Today, many search firms are moving beyond traditional recruitment and selection work and also offer more general human resources consulting. These services include coaching, compensation studies, performance management, employee satisfaction surveys and management training. A few recruitment firms now even "rent" mid- and senior-level managers on a contract basis for employers that can't commit to longer-term employment arrangements. The line between management consultant and recruiter is blurring as search firms broaden the range of services they offer employers.

informez-les au sujet de votre nouvel emploi tout en les remerciant pour l'assistance qu'ils vous ont prêtée.

Rappelez-vous que l'agent garantit normalement votre placement pendant une certaine période de temps: généralement, cela peut aller de un à six mois, selon votre niveau de placement (veuillez remarquer que les garanties les plus étendues ne sont offertes qu'aux placements de niveau supérieur). Si vous donnez votre démission ou si vous êtes mis à pied pour une raison spécifique pendant cette période, l'agent de placement doit trouver un candidat remplaçant sans qu'il y ait aucun coût additionnel pour l'employeur.

Pensez à garder le contact avec les principaux agents de placement que vous avez rencontrés ou à qui vous avez parlé pendant votre recherche d'emploi. Appelez-les au moins une fois par année et dites-leur où vous vous trouvez et ce que vous faites. Veuillez noter qu'une belle carte de Noël fait de vrais miracles!

En conclusion, cultiver une bonne relation avec un agent de placement peut sans doute vous être très profitable en ce qui concerne votre nouvel emploi ainsi que votre propre carrière dans les années à venir.

11. Que font-ils d'autre, les agents de placement, à part trouver des candidats convenables?

Cela dépend vraiment de l'étendue de l'engagement de l'agent. Généralement, les agences à honoraires passent beaucoup plus de temps à travailler avec un employeur afin de concevoir la description des tâches de travail et déterminer l'échelle salariale appropriée. Les agences dites relatives ne peuvent pas se permettre un tel luxe (car on les paye seulement si un placement est réalisé) et on y travaille généralement selon les exigences de l'employeur.

Les deux types d'agents se servent de leurs vastes réseaux de contacts afin de repérer d'éventuels candidats. Voici ce pour quoi paient en réalité les employeurs lorsqu'ils font demande aux services d'un agent. À part l'utilisation de leur banques privées de candidats, les agents placent des annonces dans leurs sites Internet ou dans les journaux et ils échangent des magazines.

Actuellement, plusieurs agences de placement vont au-delà de leur travail de recrutement traditionnel et de sélection afin d'offrir des services plus globaux de conseil-expert en ressources humaines. Les services en questions comprennent le monitorat, les études d'indemnité, la gestion de la performance, les enquêtes sur la satisfaction des employés et la formation de l'administration.

Présentement, certaines agences de placement "louent" des administrateurs de niveaux moyen et supérieur sur des bases contractuelles à des employeurs qui ne peuvent pas s'engager à des ententes d'emploi à plus long terme. La frontière entre expert-conseil en administration et agent de placement devient de plus en plus floue au fur et à mesure que les agences élargissent l'éventail de services offerts aux employeurs.

FIRM LISTINGS

AGENCES

180 CONSULTING INC.
1 Dundas Street West
Suite 2500, PO Box 84
Toronto, ON M5G 1Z3

Telephone 416-260-4722
Fax 416-204-1939
E-mail jobs@180consulting.
com
Website www.180consulting.
com

Specialties Computing

Level Mid-Level

Description 180 Consulting Inc. is a high tech recruiting and consulting firm.

180 CONSULTING INC.
165 Commerce Valley Drive West
Suite 110
Thornhill, ON L3T 7V8

Telephone 905-882-4454
Fax 905-882-0192
E-mail jobs@180consulting.
com
Website www.180consulting.
com

Specialties Computing

Level Mid-Level

Description 180 Consulting Inc. is a high tech recruiting and consulting firm.

1ST CHOICE PERSONNEL
10730 Pacific Street, Suite 111
Omaha, NE 68114
USA

Telephone 402-392-0747
Fax 402-392-0774
E-mail jobs@
1stChoicePersonnel.com
Website www.1stchoice
personnel.com

Specialties Administrative
Accounting
Finance
Marketing
Sales
Computing
International

Level Mid-Level

Contact Willa Siemek,
Managing Director

Description 1st Choice Personnel recruits skilled and qualified employees for positions in administrative, accounting, finance, sales, marketing and IT markets.

1ST CHOICE STAFFING LTD.
6541 Mississauga Road North
Mississauga, ON L5N 1A6

Telephone 905-814-7782
E-mail 1stchoicestaffing@
on.aibn.com

Specialties Logistics
Administrative

Level Mid-Level

500 SERVICES DE SELECTION LTÉE
CP 508
Val-d'Or, QC J9P 4P5

Téléphone 819-825-5500
Télécopieur 819-825-5090
Courriel apa500@lino.com

Fondée 1984
Employés 3

Spécialités Comptabilité
Ressources humaines
Gestion
Marketing
Achat
Ventes

Échelon Direction
Intermédiaire

Contact Jean-Yves Gonthier

Description 500 Services de Selection specialise dans le recrutement et location de personnel à court et à long terme et la sélection et évaluation de candidats.

55 PLUS PERSONNEL PLACEMENT
1405 King Street East
Rockway Centre for Active Living
Kitchener, ON N2G 2N9

Telephone 519-741-2509
Fax 519-741-2650
E-mail lvplus@golden.net
website www.kwmc.on.ca/
directory/55+.html

Specialties General Practice

Contact Norma Sims

Description Specializing in placing personnel 55 years and over.

A.B. SCHWARTZ & ASSOCIATES INC.
92 Whitehorn Crescent
Toronto, ON M2J 3B2

Telephone 416-482-1854
Fax 416-491-3046
E-mail aschwart@ican.net

Founded 1986
Employees 5

Specialties Telecom
Engineering

Level Senior
Mid-Level

Fee Basis Sometimes contingent

Contact Arthur B. Schwartz,
President

Description A.B. Schwartz & Associates Inc. is a consulting firm in the telecom industry that is occasionally involved in placement.

A.E. HARRISON & PARTNERS INC.
190 Robert Speck Parkway
Suite 209
Mississauga, ON L4Z 3K3

Telephone 905-615-1577
Fax 905-615-0436
E-mail resumes@
aeharrison.com
Website www.aeharrison.com

Founded 1971
Employees 2

Specialties Sales
Marketing

Level Mid-Level
Senior

Fee Basis Retainer Only

Recruiters Betty-Anne Davis
Rick Harrison

Contact Rick Harrison

Description A.E. Harrison is a retainer-based search company specializing in all areas of sales and marketing management, with over 25 years experience.

A. LAWRENCE ABRAMS & ASSOCIATES
267 Shakespeare Drive
Waterloo, ON N2L 2T8

Telephone 519-886-5034
Fax 519-743-3303

Specialties Accounting
Finance
Management
Operations

Level Mid-Level

Contact A. Lawrence Abrams

A.O. MANAGEMENT SERVICES LTD.
3311 - 58th Street, Suite 43
Edmonton, AB T6L 6X3

Fax 780-465-1035
E-mail aomgnt@
telusplanet.com

Specialties Govt/Nonprofit

Level Mid-Level

A.R. BEADLE & ASSOCIATES LTD.
4199 Gallagher's Crescent
Kelowna, BC V1W 3Z9

Telephone 250-868-8909
Fax 250-868-8963
E-mail art@arbeadle.com
Website www.arbeadle.com

Founded 1990

Specialties Health/Medical

Level Mid-Level

Contact A.R. (Art) Beadle, CHRP

Description Since 1990, A.R. Beadle & Associates has been providing human resource management services throughout British Columbia.

A.W. FRASER & ASSOCIATES / PSA INTERNATIONAL
10303 Jasper Avenue, Suite 2660
Edmonton, AB T5J 3N6

Telephone 780-428-8578
Fax 780-426-2933
E-mail edmonton@
awfraser.com
Website www.awfraser.com

Founded 1963
Employees 5

Specialties	Management
	Human Resource
	Marketing
	Construction
	Forestry
	Purchasing
	Engineering
Level	Mid-Level
	Senior
Min. Salary	$30,000
Fee Basis	Retainer Only
Recruiters	Ross Hill
	Dr. Gerald Long
	Larry Pelensky CMC
Contact	Larry Pelensky CMC

Description Strategic recruiting, psychological assessment for selection and development; coaching for management and top executives. Outplacement and career planning. Member PSA International.

A.W. FRASER & ASSOCIATES / PSA INTERNATIONAL
540 - 5th Avenue SW, Suite 900
Calgary, AB T2P 0M2

Telephone	403-264-4480
Fax	403-264-4489
E-mail	jroshak@awfraser.com
Website	www.awfraser.com
Founded	1963
Specialties	Management
	Marketing
	Engineering
	Finance
	Sales
	Operations
Level	Mid-Level
	Senior
Fee Basis	Retainer Only
Contact	John Roshak, CMC

Description Industrial psychologists. Strategic recruiting, psychological assessment for selection and development; personal coaching for management and top executives; outplacement and career planning/management. Member PSA International.

ABANE & ASSOCIATES
16715 - 12 Yonge Street, Suite 269
Newmarket, ON L3X 1R2

Telephone	905-836-9764
Fax	905-836-1259
E-mail	abane-associates@home.com
Specialties	Computing
	Engineering
Level	Mid-Level
Fee Basis	Always contingent
Contact	Lucille Abate

Description Abane & Associates specializes in the placement of intermediate to senior technical candidates in the advanced technology arena.

ABC CORRIES (CANADA) LTD.
521 - 3rd Avenue SW, Suite 380
Calgary, AB T2P 3T3

Fax	403-269-1050
E-mail	advert@abccorries.com
Website	www.abccorries.com
Specialties	Construction
	Engineering
	Oil & Gas
	Trade Shows
Level	Mid-Level
	Senior

Description ABC Corries (Canada) Ltd. is an international manpower supply company that specializes in placing engineering personnel in oil and gas, energy, petrochemical, shipbuilding, offshore and commercial construction industries.

ABECASSIS CONSEIL EN RECHERCHES DE CADRES INC.
507 Place d'Armes, Bureau 240
Montréal, QC H2Y 2W8

Telephone	514-842-8213
Fax	514-842-8128
E-mail	abecassis@aci.ca
Website	www.abecassis.com
Founded	1994
Employees	3
Specialties	Finance
	General Practice
	Engineering
	Human Resource
	Management
	Marketing
	Telecom
	Logistics
Level	Mid-Level
Fee Basis	Retainer Only
Recruiters	Pauline P. Abecassis
	Anne-Marie Medeirda
Contact	Pauline P. Abecassis, Directrice

Description Abecassis relies on its focus and efficiency in exploring the employment market to find the right person.

ABEL PLACEMENT CONSULTANTS, INC. / APC
7030 Woodbine Avenue, Suite 100
Markham, ON L3R 6G2

Telephone	905-513-1515
Fax	905-513-2769
E-mail	ja@abelplacement.com
Website	www.abelplacement.com
Founded	1987
Employees	3
Specialties	Accounting
	Administrative
	Computing
	Management
	Marketing
	Sales
Level	Senior
	Mid-Level
Min. Salary	$40,000

Fee Basis	Always contingent
Recruiters	John M. Abel
	Jason Abel BA
	Claire Schwass
Contact	John M. Abel, President

Description APC provides permanent staffing solutions to clients in the manufacturing, wholesaling, distribution, service, high-tech, e-commerce, real estate, construction and engineering industries.

ABOUT STAFFING
10130 - 103 Street, Suite 105
Edmonton, AB T5J 3R2

Telephone	780-429-4473
Fax	780-429-3299
E-mail	infoedmonton@aboutstaffing.com
Website	www.aboutstaffing.com
Founded	2000
Specialties	General Practice
Contact	Coralee Beet, President

ABOUT STAFFING LTD.
1300 - 8th Street SW, Suite 150
Calgary, AB T2R 1B2

Telephone	403-508-1000
Fax	403-508-1010
E-mail	infocalgary@aboutstaffing.com
Website	www.aboutstaffing.com
Founded	1996
Specialties	General Practice
Level	Junior
	Mid-Level
Recruiters	Sharlene Massey
	Mary Schoenthaler
Contact	Sharlene Massie, CEO

ABP PERSONNEL CONSULTANTS INC.
4333, rue St-Catherine O.
Bureau 640
Westmount, QC H3Z 1P9

Telephone	514-939-3399
Fax	514-939-0241
E-mail	abppersonnel@sympatico.ca
Founded	1994
Employees	2
Specialties	Sales
	Marketing
	Direct Mktng.
Contact	Gilbert Pigeon

Description ABP is a search firm specializing in finding special individuals that will make the difference in your organization.

ACCENTURE
5458 Dundas Street West, Suite 290
Toronto, ON M9B 6E3

Fax	800-762-5796
E-mail	jobs.canada@accenture.com

Website   www.accenture.com

Specialties   Computing

Level   Mid-Level
Senior

Description Accenture (formerly Andersen Consulting) is a management consulting firm that occasionally does recruitment for clients.

ACCESS CAREER SOLUTIONS INC.
2 County Court Blvd., Suite 440
Brampton, ON   L6W 3W8

Telephone   905-866-6616
Fax   905-866-6683
E-mail   allisonbailey@
accesscareers.com
Website   www.accesscareers.com

Specialties   Accounting
Purchasing
Operations
Engineering

Level   Mid-Level

Recruiters   Allison Bailey
Linda Ford
Lori Robinson

Contact   Linda Ford, President

ACCESS HUMAN RESOURCES INC. / ACCESSHR
130 Albert Street, Suite 414
Ottawa, ON   K1P 5G4

Telephone   613-236-6114
Fax   613-236-5552
E-mail   careers@accesshr.com
Website   www.accesshr.com

Specialties   General Practice

Recruiters   Alison Davis
Susanna Rodriguez

Contact   Alison Davis, Principal

Description AccessHR provides businesses and human resource professionals with the resources and support needed to run their companies in a cost efficient manner.

ACCLAIM CAREER & COMMUNICATION SERVICES
280 Smith Street, Suite 301
Winnipeg, MB   R3C 1K2

Telephone   204-947-9470
Fax   204-947-9479
E-mail   acclaim@escape.ca
Website   www.escape.ca/
~acclaim

Specialties   General Practice

ACCOUNT ABILITY
2 Sheppard Avenue E., Suite 503
Toronto, ON   M2N 5Y7

Telephone   416-224-0770
Fax   416-224-0813

Specialties   Accounting
Finance

Level   Mid-Level
Junior

Contact   Ivan Markiet, Director

ACCOUNTANTS ON CALL / AOC FINANCIAL EXECUTIVE SEARCH
505 Burrard Street, Suite 1730
Vancouver, BC   V7X 1M4

Telephone   604-669-9096
Fax   604-669-9196
E-mail   vancouver@aocnet.com
Website   www.aocnet.com

Founded   1979
Employees   6

Specialties   Accounting
Finance

Level   Mid-Level

Min. Salary $25,000
Fee Basis   Always contingent

Recruiters   Paula Hollander
Christine Horodyskj
Emma Skillen
Pamela Tennant

Contact   Paula Hollander

Description With over 120 offices in North America, AOC specializes in providing qualified accounting and finance professionals on a contract and permanent basis.

ACCOUNTANTS ON CALL / AOC FINANCIAL EXECUTIVE SEARCH
20 Eglinton Avenue West
Suite 1101, Yonge Eglinton Centre
Toronto, ON   M4R 1K8

Telephone   416-932-1566
Fax   416-932-2766
E-mail   toronto@oacnet.com
Website   www.aocnet.com

Founded   1979
Employees   14

Specialties   Accounting
Finance

Level   Senior
Mid-Level

Min. Salary $40,000
Fee Basis   Always contingent

Recruiters   Thomas Byun
Katherine Cicciarella
Sharon Clements
Sara Cooper
Rocchina Furgher
Bethany LaMorre
Karen Markesini
Luciane Nallli
Vic Rock
Faye Traiforos
Marc Viola

Contact   Katherine Cicciarella

Description With over 120 offices in North America, AOC specializes in providing qualified accounting and finance professionals on a contract and permanent basis.

ACCOUNTEMPS FINANCIAL STAFFING
1055 Dunsmuir Street, Suite 1274
Vancouver, BC   V7X 1L4

Telephone   604-685-4253
Fax   604-687-7533
E-mail   vancouver.bc@
accountemps.com

Website   www.accountemps.com

Specialties   Accounting
Finance
Human Resource

Level   Mid-Level

Contact   Sandra Reder, Branch
Manager

Description Accountemps is the world's first and largest specialized contract staffing service for accounting, finance and bookkeeping professionals, with over 280 offices worldwide.

ACCOUNTEMPS FINANCIAL STAFFING
15127 - 100th Avenue, Suite 302
Surrey, BC   V3R 0N9

Telephone   604-581-4254
Fax   604-581-4225
E-mail   fraser.valley@
accountemps.com
Website   www.accountemps.com

Specialties   Accounting
Finance
Human Resource

Level   Mid-Level

Description Accountemps is the world's first and largest specialized contract staffing service for accounting, finance and bookkeeping professionals, with over 280 offices worldwide.

ACCOUNTEMPS FINANCIAL STAFFING
10180 - 101 Street, Suite 1280
Edmonton, AB   T5J 3S4

Telephone   780-423-1466
Fax   780-423-1581
E-mail   edmonton@
accountemps.com
Website   www.accountemps.com

Specialties   Accounting
Finance
Human Resource

Level   Mid-Level

Description Accountemps is the world's first and largest specialized contract staffing service for accounting, finance and bookkeeping professionals, with over 280 offices worldwide.

ACCOUNTEMPS FINANCIAL STAFFING
421 - 7th Avenue SW, Suite 1515
Calgary, AB   T2P 4K9

Telephone   403-269-5387
Fax   403-264-0934
E-mail   calgary@
accountemps.com
Website   www.accountemps.com

Specialties   Accounting
Finance
Human Resource

Level   Mid-Level

Contact   Janis Bradley

Description Accountemps is the world's first and largest specialized contract staffing service for accounting, finance and bookkeeping professionals, with over 280 offices worldwide.

ACCOUNTEMPS FINANCIAL STAFFING
201 Portage Avenue, Suite 902
Winnipeg, MB R3B 3K6

Telephone	204-957-5400
Fax	204-957-5385
E-mail	winnipeg@ accountemps.com
Website	www.accountemps.com
Specialties	Accounting Finance Human Resource
Level	Mid-Level

Description Accountemps is the world's first and largest specialized contract staffing service for accounting, finance and bookkeeping professionals, with over 280 offices worldwide.

ACCOUNTEMPS FINANCIAL STAFFING
181 Bay St., Suite 820, PO Box 824
Toronto, ON M5J 2T3

Telephone	416-365-9140
Fax	416-350-3573
E-mail	toronto@ accountemps.com
Website	www.accountemps.com
Specialties	Accounting Finance Human Resource
Level	Mid-Level

Description Accountemps is the world's largest specialized contract staffing service for accounting, finance and bookkeeping professionals, with over 280 offices worldwide.

ACCOUNTEMPS FINANCIAL STAFFING
5140 Yonge Street, Suite 1500
Toronto, ON M2N 6L7

Telephone	416-226-4570
Fax	416-226-4498
E-mail	north.york@ accountemps.com
Website	www.accountemps.com
Specialties	Accounting Finance Human Resource
Level	Mid-Level

Description Accountemps is the world's largest specialized contract staffing service for accounting, finance and bookkeeping professionals, with over 280 offices worldwide.

ACCOUNTEMPS FINANCIAL STAFFING
5575 North Service Road
Burlington, ON L7L 6M1

Telephone	905-319-9384
Fax	905-319-2095
E-mail	burlington@ accountemps.com
Website	www.accountemps.com
Specialties	Accounting Finance Human Resource
Level	Junior

Description Accountemps is the world's first and largest specialized contract staffing service for accounting, finance and bookkeeping professionals, with over 280 offices worldwide.

ACCOUNTEMPS FINANCIAL STAFFING
1 Robert Speck Parkway, Suite 940
Mississauga, ON L4Z 3M3

Telephone	905-273-6524
Fax	905-273-6217
E-mail	mississauga@ accountemps.com
Website	www.accountemps.com
Specialties	Accounting Finance Human Resource
Level	Mid-Level

Description Accountemps is the world's first and largest specialized contract staffing service for accounting, finance and bookkeeping professionals, with over 280 offices worldwide.

ACCOUNTEMPS FINANCIAL STAFFING
100 York Blvd., 1st Floor
Markham, ON L4B 1J8

Telephone	905-709-8009
Fax	905-709-3664
E-mail	markham@ accountemps.com
Website	www.accountemps.com
Specialties	Accounting Finance Human Resource
Level	Mid-Level

Description Accountemps is the world's first and largest specialized contract staffing service for accounting, finance and bookkeeping professionals, with over 280 offices worldwide.

ACCOUNTEMPS FINANCIAL STAFFING
427 Laurier Avenue W., Suite 1400
Ottawa, ON K1R 7Y2

Telephone	613-236-4253
Fax	613-236-2159
E-mail	ottawa@ accountemps.com
Website	www.accountemps.com
Specialties	Accounting Finance Human Resource
Level	Mid-Level

Description Accountemps is the world's first and largest specialized contract staffing service for accounting, finance and bookkeeping professionals, with over 280 offices worldwide.

ACCOUNTEMPS FINANCIAL STAFFING
1 Place Ville Marie, Suite 2838
Montréal, QC H3B 4G4

Telephone	514-875-8585
Fax	514-875-8066
E-mail	montreal@ accountemps.com
Website	www.accountemps.com
Specialties	Accounting Finance Human Resource
Level	Mid-Level

Description Accountemps is the world's first and largest specialized contract staffing service for accounting, finance and bookkeeping professionals, with over 280 offices worldwide.

ACCOUNTING MACHINE PERSONNEL
330 Bay Street, Suite 1304
Toronto, ON M5H 2S8

Telephone	416-364-5275
Fax	416-364-1204
Specialties	Accounting Finance
Level	Mid-Level Junior
Contact	Lynne D. Delfs, Manager

ACCU-STAFF RESOURCE SYSTEMS / TECHNICAL GROUP
3703 Walker Road
Windsor, ON N8W 3S9

Telephone	519-966-8888
Fax	519-966-8072
E-mail	vicky@accu-staff.com
Website	www.accu-staff.com
Founded	1990
Specialties	Automotive Engineering
Level	Mid-Level
Contact	Paul Chernish, President

Description Accu-Staff specializes in technical recruiting, especially in the automotive field.

ACE RECRUITERS CANADA INC.
3300 Highway 7 West, Suite 320
Vaughan, ON L4K 4M3

Telephone	905-760-1174
Fax	905-760-9774
Specialties	General Practice

ACORN CONSULTING GROUP INC.
7777 Keele Street, Suite 204
Concord, ON L4K 1Y7

Telephone	905-738-9447
Fax	905-567-5021
Specialties	Computing
Level	Mid-Level
Contact	David J. Aquilina

ACTION INFO-TRAVAIL INC.
787, rue de la Madone
Mont-Laurier, QC J9L 1T3

Téléphone	819-623-9491
Télécopieur	819-623-9564
Courriel	info@ action-info-travail.qc.ca
Fondée	1991
Employés	16
Spécialités	Généralistes Administratif Ressources humaines
Recruteurs	Lucie Dorval Ph.D. Jacques Drolet B.A. Stéphan Dugrosprez Johanne Lefebvre Daniel Moreau M.Sc. Louise Pollender Chantale Robidoux
Contact	Daniel Moreau, Président

Description Service-conseil en ressources humaines: recrutement, sélection, réaffectation, orientation professionnelle, entrepreneurship, évaluations psychométriques. Développement commercial; gestion des ressources humaines formations.

ACTION MANUTENTION LASALLE INC.
378 rue Lafleur
Lasalle, QC H8R 3H6

Telephone	514-363-1531
Fax	514-363-3930
Founded	1992
Employees	7
Specialties	Transport Logistics
Level	Junior Mid-Level
Fee Basis	Always contingent
Recruiters	Daniel Cavigueur Eric Cayer Steve McFall
Contact	Steve McFall

ACTION PERSONNEL SERVICES
PO Box 6853, Stn Main
Peace River, AB T8S 1S6

Telephone	780-624-5340
Specialties	Accounting
Contact	Patsy McLure

AD-LINK ADVERTISING INC.
478 Queen Street East, Suite 201
Toronto, ON M5A 1T7

Telephone	416-366-6181
Fax	416-366-6200
E-mail	resume@adlink.on.ca
Website	www.adlink.on.ca
Founded	1988
Specialties	Operations General Practice Banking Purchasing
Level	Senior Mid-Level

Description Ad-Link is a full-service advertising agency specializing in recruitment advertising and employee communication services.

ADDITION 2000 INC.
500 Sherbrooke West, Suite 590
Montréal, QC H3A 3C6

Telephone	514-842-1021
Fax	514-842-3458
E-mail	m.p.allard@ addition2000.com
Specialties	Sales Marketing
Level	Mid-Level
Fee Basis	Always contingent
Contact	Marie-Pier Allard

Description Addition 2000 Inc. specializes in professional sales recruitment.

ADDMORE PERSONNEL INC.
5799 Yonge Street, Suite 500
Toronto, ON M2M 3V3

Telephone	416-229-6868
Fax	416-229-0757
E-mail	resumes@ addmorepersonnel.com
Website	www.addmore personnel.com
Founded	1992
Specialties	Computing
Level	Mid-Level
Contact	Gary Marks

Description Addmore Personnel Inc. is a specialty IT recruitment firm.

ADECCO CANADA INC.
730 View Street, Suite 420
Victoria, BC V8W 3Y7

Telephone	250-386-4422
Fax	250-386-4154
E-mail	beverly.arts@ adecco.com
Website	www.adecco.ca
Specialties	Accounting Engineering Computing Sales Bilingual Construction Health/Medical
Level	Mid-Level

	Junior
Contact	Beverly Arts, Branch Manager

Description Adecco Canada Inc. provides clerical, industrial and technical staffing in 60 countries around the world.

ADECCO CANADA INC.
505 Burrard Street
Suite 1650, Bentall One
Vancouver, BC V7X 1M4

Telephone	604-669-1203
Fax	604-682-3078
E-mail	Vancouver.DT@ adecco.com
Website	www.adecco.ca
Specialties	Accounting Engineering Finance
Contact	Joan Fradera, Branch Manager

Description Adecco Canada Inc. provides clerical, industrial and technical staffing in 60 countries around the world.

ADECCO CANADA INC.
5900 No. 3 Road, Suite 880
Richmond, BC V6X 3P7

Telephone	604-273-8761
Fax	604-270-4298
E-mail	richmond.canada@ adecco.com
Website	www.adecco.ca
Specialties	Accounting Finance Engineering
Contact	Glenna Edwards, Branch Manager

Description Adecco Canada Inc. provides clerical, industrial and technical staffing in 60 countries around the world.

ADECCO CANADA INC.
9600 Cameron Street, Suite 307
Burnaby, BC V3J 7N3

Telephone	604-421-3005
Fax	604-421-3088
E-mail	burnaby.canada@ adecco.com
Website	www.adecco.ca
Specialties	Accounting Forestry Engineering
Contact	Debbie Thompson

Description Adecco Canada Inc. provides clerical, industrial and technical staffing in 60 countries around the world.

ADECCO CANADA INC.
19916 - 64th Avenue, Suite 104
Langley, BC V2Y 1A2

Telephone	604-514-5567
Fax	604-514-5574

E-mail	langley.canada@ adecco.com
Website	www.adecco.ca
Specialties	Accounting Finance Engineering
Recruiters	Marlene Lyons Jennifer MacDougall
Contact	Jennifer MacDougall

Description Adecco Canada Inc. provides clerical, industrial and technical staffing in 60 countries around the world.

ADECCO CANADA INC.
10279 Jasper Avenue
Edmonton, AB T5J 1X9

Telephone	780-428-1266
Fax	780-426-0031
E-mail	hilary.predy@ adeccona.com
Website	www.adecco.ca
Employees	15
Specialties	Management Administrative Computing Human Resource
Level	Mid-Level Junior
Recruiters	Ann Connelly Greg McNeil Mickie Roesch
Contact	Hilary Predy

Description Adecco Canada Inc. provides clerical, industrial and technical staffing in 60 countries around the world.

ADECCO CANADA INC.
8500 Macleod Trail SE
145N Heritage Square
Calgary, AB T2H 2N1

Telephone	403-261-0860
Fax	403-266-3640
E-mail	calgary.downtown@ adecco.com
Website	www.adecco.ca
Employees	7
Specialties	Accounting Bilingual Engineering Govt/Nonprofit Human Resource Management Consulting
Level	Mid-Level Junior
Fee Basis	Always contingent
Recruiters	Raymond Biggs Nicole Blondie Greg MacNeil
Contact	Raymond Biggs, Branch Manager

Description Adecco Canada Inc. provides clerical, industrial and technical staffing in 60 countries around the world.

ADECCO CANADA INC.
201 - 21st Street East, Suite 1000
Saskatoon, SK S7K 0B8

Telephone	306-975-7170
Fax	306-975-1021
E-mail	saskatoon.sk.canada@ adecco.com
Website	www.adecco.ca
Employees	4
Specialties	Accounting Human Resource Management Administrative Trade Shows Sales
Level	Mid-Level Junior
Fee Basis	Always contingent
Contact	Karen Baynton, Staffing Coordinator

Description Adecco Canada Inc. provides clerical, industrial and technical staffing in 60 countries around the world.

ADECCO CANADA INC.
1844 Scarth Street
Regina, SK S4P 2G3

Telephone	306-359-9720
Fax	306-359-9722
E-mail	regina.sk.office@ adecco.com
Website	www.adecco.ca
Employees	4
Specialties	Accounting Banking Bilingual Human Resource Management Administrative
Level	Mid-Level Junior
Fee Basis	Always contingent
Contact	Sue Ceulemans, Manager

Description Adecco Canada Inc. provides clerical, industrial and technical staffing in 60 countries around the world.

ADECCO CANADA INC.
200 Graham Avenue, Main Floor
Winnipeg, MB R3C 4L5

Telephone	204-956-5454
Fax	204-956-4590
E-mail	winnipeg.mt.mgr@ adecco.com
Website	www.adecco.ca
Specialties	Accounting Computing
Level	Junior Mid-Level
Fee Basis	Always contingent
Recruiters	Michelle Gowdar Karen Pooley
Contact	Michelle Gowdar, Branch Manager

Description Adecco Canada Inc. provides clerical, industrial and technical staffing in 60 countries around the world.

ADECCO CANADA INC.
562 Wellington Street, Main Floor
London, ON N6A 3R5

Telephone	519-667-7774
Fax	519-667-7017
E-mail	london.ontario@ adecco.com
Website	www.adecco.ca
Specialties	Insurance Management Operations
Level	Mid-Level Junior
Recruiters	Carol Gilcrist Bev Makins
Contact	Bev Makins, Branch Manager

Description Adecco Canada Inc. provides clerical, industrial and technical staffing in 60 countries around the world.

ADECCO CANADA INC.
73 King Street West, Main Floor
Kitchener , ON N2G 1A7

Telephone	519-741-5559
Fax	519-741-5578
E-mail	kitchener.ki.on.office@ adecco.ca
Website	www.adecco.ca
Specialties	Insurance Management Operations Administrative Finance
Level	Mid-Level Junior
Recruiters	Debora Ritchie Cassandra Sheen Heidi Solway
Contact	Debora Ritchie, Branch Manager

Description Adecco Canada Inc. provides clerical, industrial and technical staffing in 60 countries around the world.

ADECCO CANADA INC.
46 Cork Street
Guelph, ON N1H 2W8

Telephone	519-763-9698
Fax	519-763-6494
E-mail	suzanne.mckolskey@ adecco.com
Website	www.adecco.com
Specialties	Accounting Engineering
Level	Mid-Level Junior
Recruiters	Suzanne McKolskey Elaine Uhleman
Contact	Suzanne McKolskey

Description Adecco Canada Inc. provides clerical, industrial and technical staffing in 60 countries around the world.

ADECCO CANADA INC.
1243 Islington Avenue, Suite 100
Toronto, ON M8X 1Y9

Telephone	416-231-4600
Fax	416-231-3779
E-mail	elaine.bartelli@ adecco.com
Website	www.adecco.ca
Specialties	Administrative Trades/Technicians
Level	Mid-Level Junior
Contact	Britt Wiethe

Description Adecco Canada Inc. provides clerical, industrial and technical staffing in 60 countries around the world.

ADECCO CANADA INC.
3200 Dufferin Street, Suite 200B
Toronto, ON M6A 2T3

Telephone	416-256-3577
Fax	416-256-4553
E-mail	downsview.on.office@ adecco.com
Website	www.adecco.ca
Specialties	Administrative Office Support/Clerical Accounting Human Resource
Level	Mid-Level Junior
Fee Basis	Always contingent

Description Adecco Canada Inc. provides clerical, industrial and technical staffing in 60 countries around the world.

ADECCO CANADA INC.
175 Bloor Street East
Suite 608, North Tower
Toronto, ON M5W 3R8

Telephone	416-964-9100
Fax	416-964-0355
E-mail	grace.rivers@ adecco.com
Website	www.adecco.ca
Specialties	Administrative Trades/Technicians
Level	Mid-Level Junior
Contact	Grace Rivers, Branch Manager

Description Adecco Canada Inc. provides clerical, industrial and technical staffing in 60 countries around the world.

ADECCO CANADA INC.
161 Bay Street, BCE Place
Suite 4310, Canada Trust Tower
Toronto, ON M5J 2S1

Telephone	416-214-2244
Fax	416-214-0969
E-mail	kimberley.clarke@ adecco.com
Website	www.adecco.ca
Specialties	Management Accounting Computing Engineering
Level	Mid-Level Junior
Contact	Desrine Nelson

Description Adecco Canada Inc. provides clerical, industrial and technical staffing in 60 countries around the world.

ADECCO CANADA INC.
10 Bay Street
14th Floor, WaterPark Place
Toronto, ON M5J 2R8

Telephone	416-364-2020
Fax	416-368-4199
E-mail	info@adecco.ca
Website	www.adecco.ca
Specialties	Management
Level	Senior Mid-Level
Contact	Deborah Forster, Executive Assistant

Description Adecco Canada Inc. provides clerical, industrial and technical staffing in 60 countries around the world.

ADECCO CANADA INC.
100 Consilium Place, Suite 310
Toronto, ON M1H 3E3

Telephone	416-296-0822
Fax	416-296-0829
E-mail	joan.hayes@ adecco.com
Website	www.adecco.ca
Founded	1957
Employees	7
Specialties	Administrative Packaging Accounting Bilingual Management Sales
Level	Mid-Level Junior
Recruiters	Lynn Barrett Cathy Doomernik Rose Hills Julie Stewart Brenda Wilson
Contact	Lynne Barrett

Description Adecco Canada Inc. provides clerical, industrial and technical staffing in 60 countries around the world.

ADECCO CANADA INC.
21 Nelson Street West, Unit 3
Brampton, ON L6X 4B6

Telephone	905-796-1550
Fax	905-796-1544
E-mail	trevor.stewart@ adecco.com
Website	www.adecco.ca
Specialties	Accounting Computing Engineering
Level	Mid-Level Junior
Contact	Ellen Bell

Description Adecco Canada Inc. provides clerical, industrial and technical staffing in 60 countries around the world.

ADECCO CANADA INC.
700 Dorval Drive, Suite 111
Oakville, ON L6K 3V3

Telephone	905-842-5173
Fax	905-842-6468
E-mail	charla.temeriski@ adecco.com
Website	www.adecco.com
Specialties	Accounting Computing Engineering
Level	Mid-Level Junior
Contact	Vici Prosser, Branch Manager

Description Adecco Canada Inc. provides clerical, industrial and technical staffing in 60 countries around the world.

ADECCO CANADA INC.
675 Cochrane Drive
Suite 304, Pillsbury Tower
Markham, ON L3R 0B8

Telephone	905-474-9555
Fax	905-474-1860
E-mail	chris.vergucht@ adecco.com
Website	www.adecco.ca
Specialties	Accounting Computing Engineering Sales
Level	Mid-Level Junior
Recruiters	Maria Carchidi Darlene Klemchuck
Contact	Darlene Klemchuck

Description Adecco Canada Inc. provides clerical, industrial and technical staffing in 60 countries around the world.

ADECCO CANADA INC.
1885 Glenanna Road, Suite 114
Pickering, ON L1V 6R6

Telephone	905-831-7359
Fax	905-831-4922
E-mail	pickering.on.office@ adecco.com
Website	www.adecco.ca
Specialties	Computing Engineering Sales

Level	Mid-Level
	Junior
Contact	Melanie Seymour,
	Branch Manager

Description Adecco Canada Inc. provides clerical, industrial and technical staffing in 60 countries around the world.

ADECCO CANADA INC.
150 Isabella Street, Suite 300
Ottawa, ON K1S 1V7

Telephone	613-230-7777
Fax	613-230-3411
E-mail	alean.alkoutsi@
	adeccona.com
Website	www.adecco-ottawa.com
Founded	1983
Employees	8
Specialties	Computing
	Design
	Engineering
	Govt/Nonprofit
	Human Resource Management
	Multimedia
	Purchasing
	Telecom
Level	Mid-Level
	Junior
Fee Basis	Always Contingent
Contact	· Alean Alkoutsi

Description Adecco Canada Inc. provides clerical, industrial and technical staffing in 60 countries around the world.

ADECCO CANADA INC.
126 Sparks Street
Ottawa, ON K1P 5B6

Telephone	613-563-7555
Fax	613-541-1643
E-mail	work@adeccocr.com
Website	www.adecco.ca
Specialties	Accounting
	Computing
	Finance
	Govt/Nonprofit
	Hospitality
	Marketing
	Sales
Level	Mid-Level
Contact	Joanne Stewart

Description Adecco Canada Inc. provides clerical, industrial and technical staffing in 60 countries around the world.

ADECCO CANADA INC.
5657 Spring Garden Road
Box 233, Suite 601
Park Lane Terraces
Halifax, NS B3J 3R4

Telephone	902-423-3344
Fax	902-420-0039
E-mail	ypcstaff@
	ns.sympatico.ca
Website	www.adecco.ca

Specialties	Administrative
	Trades/Technicians
Level	Mid-Level
	Junior
Contact	Lisa DeYoung, Branch Manager

Description Adecco Canada Inc. provides clerical, industrial and technical staffing in 60 countries around the world.

ADECCO - COMPAQ CANADA NATIONAL HIRING CENTRE
5700 Yonge Street, Suite 190
Toronto, ON M5M 4K2

Telephone	416-226-1516
Fax	416-226-5711
E-mail	wendy.wells@
	adecco.com
Website	www.adecco.ca
Specialties	Accounting
	Sales
	Administrative
	Computing
Level	Mid-Level
	Junior
Contact	Wendy Wells

Description This Adecco location does the recruiting for Compaq Canada.

ADECCO LPI
3100, Côte Vertu, Bureau 260
Saint-Laurent, QC H4R 2J8

Téléphone	514-333-5551
Télécopieur	514-333-1325
Courriel	adecco.vsl@
	sympatico.ca
Site Internet	www.adecco.ca
Employés	6
Spécialités	Comptabilité
	Administratif
	Affaires de banque
	Santé/médical
	Ressources humaines
	Marketing
	Achat
Échelon	Intermédiaire
	Débutant
Recruteurs	Marie Girard
	Annick Vinet
Contact	Annick Vinet, Branch Manager

Description Firme de recruitment de personnel permanent et temporaire dans les secteurs professionels et industriel.

ADECCO PERSONNEL TECHNIQUE
65, rue Belvedere Nord
Bureau 300
Sherbrooke, QC J1H 4A7

Téléphone	819-346-9922
Télécopieur	819-346-1567
Courriel	adecco@abacom.com
Site Internet	www.adecco.ca
Spécialités	Comptabilité
	Informatique

	Ingénierie
	Ventes
Échelon	Intermédiaire
Contact	Caroline Fredette, Branch Manager

Description Adecco Personnel Technique offrant des services de gestion de paie, impartition et évènements spéciaux dans les secteurs professionnel et industriel.

ADECCO QUÉBEC
370, chemin Chambly, Bureau 110
Longueuil, QC J4H 3Z6

Téléphone	450-674-8787
Télécopieur	450-674-3126
Courriel	adeccolong@sprint.ca
Site Internet	www.adecco.ca
Fondée	1995
Employés	6
Spécialités	Bilingue
	Informatique
	Marketing direct
	Finance
	Ressources humaines
	Logistique
	Emballage
Échelon	Intermédiaire
	Débutant
Recruteurs	Marie-Josée Boucher
	Julie Munger
	Julie Nachon
	Ginette Rocheleau
	Mariane Villemure
Contact	Mariane Villemure, Branch Manager

Description Firme de recrutement de personnel permanent et temporaire offrant des services dans les secteurs du secrétariate, de l'administration et industriel/technique.

ADECCO QUÉBEC INC.
200, rue Racine Est, Bureau 30
Chicoutimi, QC G7H 1S1

Téléphone	418-549-8787
Télécopieur	415-549-7022
Courriel	adeccochicoutimi@
	sympatico.ca
Site Internet	www.adecco.ca
Fondée	1989
Employés	6
Spécialités	Comptabilité
	Informatique
	Ingénierie
	Finance
	Gouvt/OSBL
	Ressources humaines
	Gestion
	Exploitation
	Emballage
	Plastique
	Ventes
Échelon	Intermédiaire
Contact	Nicole Girard, Branch Manager

Description Recrutement et placement de personel dans les secteurs de l'administration, industrie, secretariat, service a la clientele et centres d'appels.

ADECCO QUÉBEC INC.
635, Grande Allée est
Québec, QC G1R 2K4

Téléphone   418-523-9922
Télécopieur 418-523-8697
Courriel   adecco@
            globetrotter.net
Site Internet www.adecco.ca

Fondée   1989
Employés   6

Spécialités Comptabilité
            Administratif
            Bilingue
            Ingénierie
            Ressources humaines
            Gestion
            Ventes

Recruteurs Sophie Bazinet
            Pascale Jacques
            Christian Lorte
            Michael Louchard
            Nadiah Smith

Contact   Rémi Tremblay, Senior
            Vice-President

Description Recrutement et placement de personel dans les secteurs
de l'administration, industrie, secretariat, service a la clientele et centres d'appels.

ADECCO QUÉBEC INC. (LAVAL)
2550 boul. Daniel-Johnson, bur. 120
Laval, QC H7T 2L1

Téléphone   450-682-8700
Télécopieur 450-602-7606
Courriel   adeccolaval@sprint.ca
Site Internet www.decouvrez.qc.ca

Fondée   1991
Employés   8

Spécialités Comptabilité
            Administratif
            Informatique
            Ingénierie
            Exploitation
            Achat
            Scientifique

Échelon   Intermédiaire
            Débutant

Recruteurs Suzanne Dorval
            Mireille Dumontet
            Sylvie Rodrigue
            Natalie Tourville
            Yvan Tremblay

Contact   Sylvie Rodrigue,
            Directrice

Description Adecco Quebec Inc. offre
des services de gestion de paie,
impartition et évènements spéciaux
dans le secteur professionnel et
industriel.

ADECCO QUÉBEC INC. (VIEUX-MONTREAL)
465, rue McGill, Rez-de-chaussee
Montréal, QC H2Y 2H1

Téléphone   514-287-0187
Télécopieur 514-287-0481
Courriel   adeccovm@
            globetrotter.qc.ca
Site Internet www.decouvrez.qc.ca

Spécialités Administratif

            Métiers/techniciens

Échelon   Intermédiaire
            Débutant

Contact   Michel Lestage, Manager

Description Adecco Quebec Inc. offre
des services de gestion de paie, impartition et évènements spéciaux
dans le secteur professionnel et industriel.

ADIRECT RECRUITING CORP.
468 Queen Street East
Suite 206, PO Box 22
Toronto, ON M5A 1T7

Telephone   416-365-9889
Fax   416-365-3123
E-mail   resumes@
            adirectrecruiting.com
Website   www.adirect
            recruiting.com

Founded   1983

Specialties Management
            Accounting
            Finance
            Human Resource
            Marketing
            Pharmaceutical
            Publishing/Media

Level   Senior
            Mid-Level

Min. Salary $50,000
Fee Basis   Retainer Only

Contact   Bob Copp

Description Adirect Recruiting Corporation is a non-contingent, fee-
based management recruiting firm.

ADLER RECRUITMENT
71 Friar Street, Droitwich Spa
Worcestershire, WR9 8ED
UNITED KINGDOM

Telephone   44-1905-795388
Fax   44-1905-795009
E-mail   info@ adler-
            recruitment.co.uk
Website   www.adler-
            recruitment.co.uk

Specialties Engineering
            International
            Purchasing

Description Adler Recruitment is an
employment agency for the construction industry.

ADMINISTRATION GESPRO
1080, cote du Beaver Hall
Bureau 1810
Montréal, QC H2Z 1S8

Téléphone   514-878-3535

Specialties Accounting
            Finance

Level   Mid-Level

Contact   Noelle Hayes

ADMINISTRATIVE FUNDAMENTALS INC.
71 King Street East, 2nd Floor
Toronto, ON M5C 1G3

Telephone   416-601-2226
Fax   416-601-1695
E-mail   afi@aficap.com
Website   www.aficap.com

Specialties Administrative
            Finance

Level   Mid-Level
            Junior

Recruiters Robert Boyd
            Patricia Spice

Contact   Robert Boyd, Senior
            Manager

Description Administrative Fundamentals Inc. provides management
consulting for the financial industry.
Part of their services include providing offsite administrative staff for
various data processing projects in
the finance sector.

ADV ADVANCED TECHNICAL SERVICES INC.
1037 McNicoll Avenue, Suite 200
Toronto, ON M1W 3W6

Telephone   416-502-2545
Fax   416-502-2544
E-mail   contact@
            advtechnical.com
Website   www.advtechnical.com

Specialties Computing
            Engineering
            Aerospace
            Telecom

Level   Senior
            Mid-Level

Min. Salary $40,000
Fee Basis   Sometimes contingent

Contact   Paul Guy Hill

Description ADV Advanced Technical Services Inc. specializes in placing high-tech engineers, including
those in real-time embedded software, firmware, hardware, digital,
ASIC, IC, FPGA, manufacturing,
SMT and test.

ADVANCED DESIGN & DRAFTING
365 Watline Avenue, Unit 4
Mississauga, ON L4Z 1P3

Telephone   905-890-4566
Fax   905-890-0707
E-mail   addmiss@addplus.com
Website   www.addplus.com

Founded   1987
Employees   28

Specialties Design
            Engineering

Contact   Darren McRae

Description Advanced Design &
Drafting is a computer-aided drafting and design service provider.

ADVANCED TECHNOLOGY PARTNERS INC.
777 Dunsmuir Street, Suite 1850
Vancouver, BC V7Y 1K5

Telephone   604-683-6400
Fax   604-683-6440
E-mail   jobs@atpstaff.com

Website   www.atpstaff.com
Specialties Computing
             Engineering
             Telecom
Level   Senior
             Mid-Level

Description Advanced Technology
Partners Inc. provides full-time and
contract staffing for IT professionals. The company is now a division
of The Design Group.

ADVANCED TECHNOLOGY PARTNERS INC.

10155 - 102nd Street
Suite 2595, Commerce Place
Edmonton, AB T5J 4G8

Telephone   780-448-5850
Fax   780-420-6040
E-mail   edmonton@
             atpstaff.com
Website   www.atpstaff.com
Founded   1996
Employees   5

Specialties Computing
             Engineering
             Telecom
Level   Senior
             Mid-Level
Fee Basis   Always contingent
Contact   M. Russnak

Description Advanced Technology
Partners Inc. provides full-time and
contract staffing for IT professionals. The company is now a division
of The Design Group.

ADVANCED TECHNOLOGY PARTNERS INC.

1110 Center Street North, Suite 401
Calgary, AB T2E 2R2

Telephone   403-233-2788
Fax   403-266-5203
E-mail   sgroening@atpstaff.com
Website   www.atpstaff.com
Founded   1996
Employees   5

Specialties Computing
             Engineering
             Telecom
Level   Senior
             Mid-Level
Fee Basis   Always contingent
Contact   Recruiting Manager

Description Advanced Technology
Partners Inc. provides full-time and
contract staffing for IT professionals. The company is now a division
of The Design Group.

ADVANCED TECHNOLOGY PARTNERS INC.

195 The West Mall, Suite 903
Toronto, ON M9C 5K1

Telephone   416-621-5552
Fax   416-620-1632
E-mail   toronto@atpstaff.com
Website   www.atpstaff.com

Founded   1996
Employees   5

Specialties Computing
             Engineering
             Telecom
Level   Senior
             Mid-Level
Fee Basis   Always contingent
Contact   M. Scheibli

Description Advanced Technology
Partners Inc. provides full-time and
contract staffing for IT professionals. The company is now a division
of The Design Group.

ADVANTAGE GROUP, THE

2130 Lawrence Ave. East, Suite 310
Toronto, ON M1R 3A6

Telephone   416-288-0368
Fax   416-288-8893
E-mail   advscarb@istar.ca
Website   www.onyourteam.com

Specialties Transport
Recruiters   Pauline Harris
             Karen LeBlanc
             Melanie Moore
             Ann-Marie Strzelczyk
             John Turnbull

Contact   Karen LeBlanc,
             Manager

Description Advantage Group specializes in qualified AZ and DZ
driver recruitment.

ADVANTAGE GROUP, THE

7015 Tranmere Drive, Unit 14
Mississauga, ON L5S 1M2

Telephone   905-677-9767
Fax   905-677-9082
E-mail   tnguyen@
             onyourteam.com
Website   www.onyourteam.com

Specialties Transport
Level   Junior
             Mid-Level

Recruiters   Penny Crane
             Rick Karl
             Luben Kouchlev
             Tram Nguyen
             Bruce Rogers
             Luke Sebben
             Sukhi Sidhu
             Gary Warren
             John Weeks

Contact   Tram Nguyen,
             Office Coordinator

Description Advantage Group specializes in qualified AZ and DZ
driver recruitment.

ADVANTAGE GROUP, THE

605 Brock Street North, Unit 5
Whitby, ON L1N 8R2

Telephone   905-430-2120
Fax   905-430-6469
E-mail   advwhi@istar.ca
Website   www.onyourteam.com
Founded   1986

Specialties Transport
Recruiters   Karen Downer
             Peter Kazmer
             Matt Saunders
Contact   Peter Kazmer, Manager

Description Advantage Group specializes in qualified AZ and DZ
driver recruitment.

ADVANTAGE GROUP, THE

22 Antares Drive, Suite 101
Nepean, ON K2E 7Z6

Telephone   613-723-7788
Fax   613-723-1889
E-mail   nepean@
             onyourteam.com
Website   www.onyourteam.com
Founded   1987
Employees   3

Specialties Transport
Level   Mid-Level
             Junior

Recruiters   Peggy Emond
             Daniel Lavallee
             Dianne Liberty
             Peter Valdstyn

Contact   Peter Valdstyn,
             Manager

Description Advantage Group specializes in qualified AZ and DZ
driver recruitment.

ADVANTAGE GROUP, THE

3767 Thimens, Suite 260
Saint-Laurent, QC H4R 1W4

Telephone   514-335-3774
Fax   514-335-0465
E-mail   persadv@istar.ca
Website   www.onyourteam.com
Founded   1987

Specialties Transport
Level   Mid-Level
             Junior

Recruiters   Normand Langlois
             Paul Lessard

Contact   Paul Lessard, Manager

Description Advantage Group specializes in qualified AZ and DZ
driver recruitment.

ADVANTAGE GROUP, THE

27 Expansion Avenue
Saint John, NB E2R 1A6

Telephone   506-652-2186
Fax   506-652-2107
E-mail   advaserv@nbnet.nb.ca
Website   www.onyourteam.com
Founded   1987
Employees   3

Specialties Transport
Level   Mid-Level
             Junior

Recruiters   Dianne Cochrane
             Mary MacNeill
             Kim Pierce
             Peter Smith

Contact Peter Smith, General Manager, Maritimes

Description Advantage Group specializes in qualified AZ and DZ driver recruitment.

ADVANTAGE GROUP, THE
175 Champlain Street
Moncton, NB E1A 1N9

Telephone	506-383-8880
Fax	506-383-1849
E-mail	advmonc@istar.ca
Website	www.onyourteam.com
Founded	1987
Specialties	Transport
Level	Mid-Level Junior
Recruiters	Fred Chiswell Joyce Leblanc Susan Smith Seretha Spinney
Contact	Fred Chiswell, Manager

Description Advantage Group specializes in qualified AZ and DZ driver recruitment.

ADVANTAGE GROUP, THE
25 Macdonald Avenue
Dartmouth, NS B3B 1C6

Telephone	902-468-5624
Fax	902-468-6294
E-mail	advhal@istar.ca
Website	www.onyourteam.com
Founded	1987
Specialties	Transport
Level	Mid-Level Junior
Recruiters	John Cotterill Jay-J Crowe Dave Ettinger Krista Murphy Dave Patton
Contact	John Cotterill, Manager

Description Advantage Group specializes in qualified AZ and DZ driver recruitment.

ADVANTAGE GROUP, THE
31 Peet Street, Unit 217
St. John's, NF A1B 3W8

Telephone	709-579-4990
Fax	709-579-4992
E-mail	advantnt@nfld.com
Website	www.onyourteam.com
Founded	1987
Employees	3
Specialties	Transport
Level	Mid-Level Junior
Recruiters	Jeannie Colombe Todd Williams
Contact	Todd Williams, Branch Manager

Description Advantage Group specializes in qualified AZ and DZ driver recruitment.

ADVANTAGE TECH INC.
400 - 3rd Avenue SW
Suite 500, Canterra Tower
Calgary, AB T2P 3R7

Telephone	403-237-8855
Fax	403-265-2704
E-mail	info@advantagetech.com
Website	www.advantagetech.com
Founded	1982
Employees	10
Specialties	Computing Geology/Geography Human Resource Oil & Gas Packaging Telecom
Level	Senior Mid-Level
Fee Basis	Sometimes contingent
Contact	Dana Tremblay

Description Advantage Tech Inc. (The Advantage Tech Group) is headquartered in Calgary with affiliates and associates operating in 41 countries through 68 offices, including Canadian offices in Vancouver, Toronto, Montreal, Quebec City and Ottawa.

ADVOCATE PLACEMENT LTD.
1200 Bay Street, Suite 902
Toronto, ON M5R 2A5

Telephone	416-927-9222
Fax	416-927-8772
E-mail	contact@advocateplacement.com
Website	www.advocateplacement.com
Founded	1989
Employees	4
Specialties	Law
Level	Mid-Level Senior
Min. Salary	$60,000
Fee Basis	Sometimes contingent
Recruiters	William B. Dickson Anita Lerek LL.B.
Contact	Anita Lerek

Description Advocate Placement Ltd. is Canada's oldest lawyer placement agency, offering contract and permanent placements as well as web-based recruiting.

ADVOCATE PLACEMENT LTD.
7030 Woodbine Avenue, Suite 500
Markham, ON L3R 6G2

Telephone	905-470-6430
Fax	416-927-8772
E-mail	contact@advocateplacement.com
Website	www.advocateplacement.com
Specialties	Law
Level	Senior Mid-Level
Min. Salary	$60,000

Contact Anita Lerek

Description Advocate Placement Ltd. is Canada's longest running lawyer placement agency, offering contract and permanent placements as well as web-based recruiting.

AEROPERSONNEL INTERNATIONAL
9501, avenue Ryan, Bureau 201
Dorval, QC H9P 1A2

Telephone	514-636-3737
Fax	514-636-3388
E-mail	cv@aeropersonnel.com
Founded	1997
Employees	12
Specialties	Aerospace
Level	Senior Mid-Level
Min. Salary	$40,000
Fee Basis	Sometimes contingent
Recruiters	André Allard Joanne Francoeur Yolande Frigault Paul Lalancette Jim McLarnon Glory Z. Valois John Watson
Contact	André Allard

Description AeroPersonnel International recruits in the aviation and aerospace sector.

AES RECRUITMENT ADVERTISING
120 Carlton Street, Suite 301
Toronto, ON M5A 4K2

Telephone	416-924-1818
Fax	416-924-1030
Website	www.aescompany.com
Specialties	Operations Sales Human Resource Accounting Health/Medical
Level	Mid-Level

Description AES is an ad agency specializing in recruitment advertising.

AFFILIATES, THE
888 - 3rd Street SW, Suite 4200
Calgary, AB T2P 5C5

Telephone	403-262-5553
Fax	403-264-0934
E-mail	calgary@affiliates.com
Website	www.affiliates.com
Specialties	Law
Level	Mid-Level Junior
Contact	Koula Vasilopoulos, Branch Manager

Description The Affiliates, the legal staffing division of Robert Half International Inc., places law office and corporate legal professionals.

AFFILIATES, THE
181 Bay Street, Suite 820, Box 824
Toronto, ON M5J 2T3

Telephone	416-365-3153
Fax	416-350-3573
E-mail	toronto@affiliates.com
Website	www.affiliates.com
Founded	1948
Specialties	Law
Level	Mid-Level
	Junior
Fee Basis	Always contingent
Recruiters	Lesley Gunn
	Sharon Hindley-Smith
	Lesley Perry
Contact	Carol A. Cameron

Description The Affiliates, the legal staffing division of Robert Half International Inc., places law office and corporate legal professionals.

AFFILIATES, THE
427 Laurier Ave. West, Suite 1400
Ottawa, ON K1R 7Y2

Telephone	613-565-4606
Fax	613-236-2159
E-mail	ottawa@affiliates.com
Website	www.affiliates.com
Specialties	Law
Level	Mid-Level
	Junior

Description The Affiliates, the legal staffing division of Robert Half International Inc., places law office and corporate legal professionals.

AFFILIATES, THE
1 Place Ville Marie, Suite 2838
Montréal, QC H3B 4R4

Telephone	514-875-0750
Fax	514-875-8066
E-mail	montreal@ affiliates.com
Website	www.affiliates.com
Specialties	Law
Level	Mid-Level
	Junior

Description The Affiliates, the legal staffing division of Robert Half International Inc., places law office and corporate legal professionals.

AFFORDABLE PERSONNEL SERVICES INC.
1750 Steeles Ave. West, Suite 219
Concord , ON L4K 2L7

Telephone	905-761-0415
Fax	905-761-0413
Specialties	Administrative
	Trades/Technicians
Contact	John C. Rich

AGCALL HUMAN RESOURCES
251 Midpark Blvd. SE, Suite 150
Calgary, AB T2X 1S3

Telephone	403-256-1229
Fax	403-254-2371
E-mail	gbutcher@agcall.com
Website	www.agcall.com

Founded	1988
Employees	6
Specialties	Agriculture/Fisheries
Level	Senior
	Mid-Level
Min. Salary	$35,000
Fee Basis	Sometimes contingent
Recruiters	Kim Bedard
	Gordon Butcher PAg
	Jennifer Maier
	Kerry Mitchell
	Steve Peddie BComm
	Ken Robertson
	Angela Waite
Contact	Gordon Butcher, PAg

Description AgCall Human Resources is a premier placement agency specializing in the agricultural industry.

AGCALL HUMAN RESOURCES
PO Box 145
St. Jean, MB R0G 2B0

Telephone	204-746-5041
Fax	204-758-3836
E-mail	bmanikel@agcall.com
Website	www.agcall.com
Specialties	Agriculture/Fisheries
Contact	Barrie Manikel

Description AgCall Human Resources is a premier placement agency specializing in the agricultural industry.

AGCALL HUMAN RESOURCES
80 McCarty Crescent
Markham, ON L3P 4R7

Telephone	905-472-6384
Fax	905-294-7910
Website	www.agcall.com
Specialties	Agriculture/Fisheries
Level	Senior
	Mid-Level
Min. Salary	$40,000
Fee Basis	Sometimes contingent
Contact	Don Tod

Description AgCall Human Resources is a premier placement agency specializing in the agricultural industry.

AGENCE DE PERSONNEL ABITIBI INC.
595 - 8e Rue, CP 508
Val-d'Or, QC J9P 4P5

Téléphone	819-825-7350
Télécopieur	819-825-5090
Courriel	apa500@lino.com
Site Internet	www.lino.com/ ~apa.com
Fondée	1986
Employés	3
Spécialités	Comptabilité
	Bilingue
	Gouvt/OSBL
	Mines
	Transport

Échelon	Intermédiaire
	Débutant
Contact	Lucie B. Turmel

Description Abitibi specialise dans la location de personnel a court et a long terme et la recherche d'emploi. Service de paie, curriculum vitae, secretariat et traduction.

AGENCE DE PERSONNEL ROUTIER
8143, rue Pascal Gagnon
Saint-Léonard, QC H1P 1Y5

Téléphone	514-326-2000
Spécialités	Transport
Échelon	Intermédiaire
	Débutant

AGENCE DE PERSONNEL YOTT
5488 boul. Henri-Bourassa Est
Montréal, QC H1G 2S9

Téléphone	514-328-0713
Spécialités	Généralistes
Contact	Gary Yott

AGENCE DE PLACEMENT ET SERVICES
137 - 2 Avenue
Notre-Dame-des-Prairies, QC J6E 1R5

Téléphone	450-755-2945
Télécopieur	450-755-2185
Spécialités	Généralistes
	Administratif
	Métiers/techniciens
Échelon	Intermédiaire
	Débutant
Contact	Denise Vandenbroucke

AGENCE DE PLACEMENT HÉLÈNE ROY LTÉE / SUR APPEL
1275 Blanchette
Saint-Hyacinthe, QC J2S 1J9

Téléphone	450-261-0101
Courriel	richelieu@ surappelinc.com
Site Internet	www.surappelinc.com
Fondée	1985
Spécialités	Administratif
	Affaires de banque
	Finance
Échelon	Intermédiaire
	Débutant

Description L'Agence de placement Hélène Roy Ltée / Sur Appel offre un service de remplacement de personnel courant, conseil et administratif dans les Caisses Desjardins.

AGENCE DE PLACEMENT HÉLÈNE ROY LTÉE / SUR APPEL
605 Atwater
Montréal, QC H3J 2T8

Téléphone	514-932-1055

Télécopieur 514-932-8843
Courriel admin@surappelinc.com
Site Internet www.surappelinc.com
Fondée 1985
Spécialités Administratif
Affaires de banque
Finance
Échelon Intermédiaire
Débutant

Description L'Agence de placement Hélène Roy Ltée / Sur Appel offre un service de remplacement de personnel courant, conseil et administratif dans les Caisses Desjardins.

AGENCE DE PLACEMENT HÉLÈNE ROY LTÉE / SUR APPEL
3330 chemin Ste Foy
Sainte-Foy, QC G1X 1S5

Téléphone 418-650-9950
Courriel admin@surappelinc.com
Site Internet www.surappelinc.com
Fondée 1985
Spécialités Administratif
Affaires de banque
Finance
Échelon Intermédiaire
Débutant

Description L'Agence de placement Hélène Roy Ltée / Sur Appel offre un service de remplacement de personnel courant, conseil et administratif dans les Caisses Desjardins.

AGINOVE INC.
620, ch. Bord-du-Lac, Bureau 206
Dorval, QC H9S 2B6

Téléphone 514-631-4224
Télécopieur 514-631-4665
Courriel lucl@aginove.com
Site Internet www.aginove.com
Fondée 1989
Employés 2
Spécialités Informatique
Ingénierie
Échelon Intermédiaire
Salaire min. 35 000 $
Frais Toujours relative
Contact Luc Laparé

Description Aginove Inc. se spécialise, depuis les 6 dernières années, dans le recrutement d'effectifs des technologies de l'information.

AIDE TECHNIQUE
45 Place Charles Lemoyne
Bureau 100
Longueuil, QC J4K 5G5

Telephone 450-651-7001
Fax 450-651-7007
Specialties Computing
Engineering
Level Mid-Level
Contact Hugh LeBlanc,
President

AIM PERSONNEL SERVICES INC.
55 Metcalfe Street, Suite 1470
Ottawa, ON K1P 6L5

Telephone 613-230-6991
Fax 613-230-7183
E-mail info@aim-personnel.com
Website www.aim-personnel.com
Founded 1988
Employees 14
Specialties Computing
Accounting
Engineering
Management
Bilingual
Telecom
Fee Basis Sometimes contingent
Contact Meredith Egan

Description AIM Personnel Services Inc. is a Canadian-owned, ISO-certified company that provides engineering, information technology and administrative personnel to government and private industry.

AIMCO PERSONNEL RESOURCES
700 Dundas Street East, Suite 11
Mississauga, ON L4Y 3Y5

Telephone 905-896-7732
Fax 905-848-1466
E-mail jbyrne@aimco.ca
Website www.aimco.ca
Founded 1984
Specialties Administrative
Level Mid-Level
Junior

Description Aimco Staffing Solutions provides personnel services to Fortune 500 companies in the Greater Toronto Area.

AIMCO STAFFING SOLUTIONS
96 Rexdale Blvd., Suite 201
Toronto, ON M9W 1N7

Telephone 416-740-7330
Fax 416-748-6892
E-mail rexdale@aimco.ca
Website www.aimco.ca
Founded 1984
Specialties Administrative
Level Mid-Level
Junior

Description Aimco Staffing Solutions provides personnel services to Fortune 500 companies in the Greater Toronto Area.

AIMCO STAFFING SOLUTIONS
2100 Ellesmere Road, Suite 208
Toronto, ON M1H 3H7

Telephone 416-439-4106
Fax 416-439-7597
E-mail scarborough@aimco.ca
Website www.aimco.ca
Founded 1984
Specialties Administrative

Level Mid-Level
Junior

Description Aimco Staffing Solutions provides personnel services to Fortune 500 companies in the Greater Toronto Area.

AIMCO STAFFING SOLUTIONS
3060 Mainway Drive, Suite 104
Burlington, ON L7M 1A3

Telephone 905-336-6664
Fax 905-336-3377
E-mail burlington@aimco.ca
Website www.aimco.ca
Founded 1984
Specialties Administrative
Level Mid-Level
Junior

Description Aimco Staffing Solutions provides personnel services to Fortune 500 companies in the Greater Toronto Area.

AIMCO STAFFING SOLUTIONS
85 Kennedy Road South, Suite 33
Brampton, ON L6W 3P3

Telephone 905-454-4972
Fax 905-454-8333
E-mail brampton@aimco.ca
Website www.aimco.ca
Founded 1984
Specialties Administrative
Level Mid-Level
Junior

Description Aimco Staffing Solutions provides personnel services to Fortune 500 companies in the Greater Toronto Area.

AIMCO STAFFING SOLUTIONS
700 Dundas Street East, Suite 10
Mississauga, ON L4Y 3Y5

Telephone 905-896-3181
Fax 905-896-2589
E-mail mississauga@aimco.ca
Website www.aimco.ca
Founded 1984
Specialties Administrative
Level Mid-Level
Junior

Description Aimco Staffing Solutions provides personnel services to Fortune 500 companies in the Greater Toronto Area.

AIME CONSULTANTS INC.
1155 Robson Street
Suite 407, John Robson Place
Vancouver, BC V6E 1B2

Telephone 604-685-2004
Fax 604-685-2005
E-mail info@aimemployment.com
Website www.aimemployment.com
Specialties Health/Medical
Marketing

Computing
Sales

Level Mid-Level
Senior

Description AIME Consultants Inc. is a professional consulting group specializing in career management services for industrial and vocational psychology, marketing and e-commerce industries.

AJILON CANADA
543 Granville Street, Suite 701
Vancouver, BC V6C 1X8

Telephone 604-689-8717
Fax 604-629-1182
E-mail vancouver@ajilon.ca
Website www.ajilon.ca

Specialties Computing

Level Mid-Level

Contact Ruth Clark

Description Ajilon Canada (formerly DGS Information Consultants and IMI Ward) is a leading provider of recruitment services in the IT industry.

AJILON CANADA
550 - 6th Avenue SW
Suite 520, Calgary House
Calgary, AB T2P 0S2

Telephone 403-261-5927
Fax 403-264-8161
E-mail calgary@ajilon.ca
Website www.ajilon.ca

Specialties Computing

Level Mid-Level

Contact Ron Alltree

Description Ajilon Canada (formerly DGS Information Consultants and IMI Ward) is a leading provider of recruitment services in the IT industry.

AJILON CANADA
701 Evans Avenue, Suite 408
Toronto, ON M9C 1A3

Telephone 416-367-2020
Fax 416-366-2001
Website www.ajilon.ca

Specialties Computing

Level Mid-Level

Contact Mona M. Agius, General Manager

Description Ajilon Canada (formerly DGS Information Consultants and IMI Ward) is a leading provider of recruitment services in the IT industry.

AJILON CANADA
10 Bay Street
7th Floor, Waterpark Place
Toronto, ON M5J 2R8

Telephone 416-367-2020
Fax 416-366-2001
E-mail toronto@ajilon.ca

Website www.ajilon.ca
Specialties Computing
Level Mid-Level
Senior

Contact Brian Keyes

Description Ajilon Canada (formerly DGS Information Consultants and IMI Ward) is a leading provider of recruitment services in the IT industry.

AJILON CANADA
60 Columbia Way, Suite 300
Markham, ON L3R 0C9

Telephone 416-367-2020
Fax 416-366-2001
Website www.ajilon.ca

Specialties Computing

Level Mid-Level

Description Ajilon Canada (formerly DGS Information Consultants and IMI Ward) is a leading provider of recruitment services in the IT industry.

AJILON CANADA
155 Queen Street, Suite 1206
Ottawa, ON K1P 6L1

Telephone 613-786-3106
Fax 613-567-3341
E-mail ottawa@ajilon.ca
Website www.ajilon.ca

Specialties Computing

Level Mid-Level
Senior

Contact Andrew German

Description Ajilon Canada (formerly DGS Information Consultants and IMI Ward) is a leading provider of recruitment services in the IT industry.

AJILON CANADA
1155 University Street, Suite 1410
Montréal, QC H3B 3A7

Telephone 514-875-9520
Fax 514-875-9241
E-mail montreal@ajilon.ca
Website www.ajilon.ca

Specialties Computing

Level Mid-Level

Recruiters Patrick Guest
Marc Labbé

Contact Patrick Guest

Description Ajilon Canada (formerly DGS Information Consultants and IMI Ward) is a leading provider of recruitment services in the IT industry.

AJILON CANADA
1959 Upper Water Street, Suite 407
Halifax, NS B3J 3N2

Telephone 902-421-2025
Fax 902-422-8686
E-mail halifax@ajilon.ca

Website www.ajilon.ca
Founded 1978
Employees 400
Specialties Computing
Level Mid-Level
Senior

Contact Mike Sabourin

Description Ajilon Canada (formerly DGS Information Consultants and IMI Ward) is a leading provider of recruitment services in the IT industry.

AJILON CANADA
47 New Gower Street
St. John's, NF A1C 1J4

Telephone 709-754-4240
Fax 709-722-1871
E-mail stjohns@ajilon.ca
Website www.ajilon.ca

Specialties Computing

Description Ajilon Canada (formerly DGS Information Consultants and IMI Ward) is a leading provider of recruitment services in the IT industry.

AJILON CANADA, INTERNATIONAL DIVISION
10 Bay Street, 7th Floor
Toronto, ON M5J 2R8

Telephone 416-367-2020
Fax 416-366-2001
E-mail international@ajilon.ca
Website www.ajilon.ca

Specialties Computing
International

Level Mid-Level

Description Ajilon Canada (formerly DGS Information Consultants and IMI Ward) is a leading provider of recruitment services in the IT industry.

AJJA INFORMATION TECHNOLOGY CONSULTANTS INC.
785 Carling Avenue, Suite 800
Ottawa, ON K1S 5H4

Telephone 613-563-2552
Fax 613-563-3438
E-mail adam.jasek@ajja.com
Website www.ajja.com

Founded 1980

Specialties Computing

Level Mid-Level

Contact Adam Jasek, CEO

Description AJJA Information Technology Consultants Inc. is an IT consulting firm that also recruits computing professionals for contract assignments.

AL-KHALEEJ COMPUTERS & ELECTRONIC SYSTEMS
PO Box 16091
Riyadh, 11464
SAUDI ARABIA

Telephone	966-1-463-2143
Fax	966-1-463-3230
E-mail	info@al-khaleej.net
Website	www.al-khaleej.net
Founded	1979
Employees	250
Specialties	Computing
	Banking
	Education
	Govt/Nonprofit
	Human Resource
	Telecom
	Oil & Gas
	International
Level	Mid-Level
	Senior
Contact	Zafar A. Khan

Description Al-Khaleej Computers & Electronic Systems is an IT consulting company that also provides computer, communications consultants and trainers to large multinational oil companies.

ALAN DAVIS & ASSOCIATES INC.
155 Queen Street, Suite 900
Ottawa, ON K1P 6L1

Telephone	613-224-9950
Fax	613-225-6818
E-mail	info@alandavis.com
Website	www.alandavis.com
Founded	1983
Employees	21
Specialties	Aerospace
Level	Senior
	Mid-Level
Fee Basis	Retainer Only
Contact	Tom Bursey, Managing Director

Description Alan Davis & Associates provides radical recruiting solutions to complex challenges in global recruiting. They are best known for their recruitment services for the Canadian Space Agency.

ALAN DAVIS & ASSOCIATES INC.
538 Main Road
Hudson Heights, QC J0P 1J0

Telephone	450-458-3535
Fax	450-458-3530
E-mail	mailbox@alandavis.com
Website	www.alandavis.com
Founded	1983
Employees	21
Specialties	Management
	Computing
	Aerospace
	Telecom
	Pharmaceutical
	Engineering
	General Practice
Level	Mid-Level
	Senior
Fee Basis	Retainer Only
Recruiters	Diane Bates
	Dianne Bradshaw
	Linda Constant
	Alan Davis

Contact	Alan Davis, President

Description Alan Davis & Associates provides radical recruiting solutions to complex challenges in global recruiting. They are best known for their recruitment services for the Canadian Space Agency.

ALBERTA RECRUITING GROUP
407 - 2nd Street SW, Suite 1220
Calgary, AB T2P 2Y3

Telephone	403-262-0334
Fax	403-262-4252
E-mail	arg-jobsearch@cadvision.com
Specialties	Oil & Gas
Level	Mid-Level
Contact	Leah A. Klock

ALCONSULT INTERNATIONAL LTD.
734 - 7th Avenue SW, Suite 1720
Calgary, AB T2P 3P8

Telephone	403-262-5886
Fax	403-262-3544
E-mail	alconsult@nucleus.com
Website	www.alconsult.net
Founded	1986
Specialties	Oil & Gas
Contact	Fred G. Rayer, President

Description Alconsult is a consulting engineering firm specializing in oil and gas projects. They occasionally do recruitment for oil & gas clients.

ALDER CENTRE, THE
2625 Danforth Avenue
Toronto, ON M4C 1L4

Telephone	416-693-2922
Fax	416-698-6453
E-mail	ld@aldercentre.org
Website	www.aldercentre.org
Specialties	Disabled
Contact	Sheri Cohen

Description The Alder Centre assists individuals with learning disabilities secure workplace accommodation and employment.

ALDONNA BARRY MANAGEMENT CONSULTANTS
18 King Street East
Bolton, ON L7E 1E8

Telephone	905-951-3434
Fax	905-951-3638
Specialties	Management
	Finance
	Marketing
	Sales
Level	Mid-Level
	Senior
Contact	Aldona Barry

ALL HEALTH SERVICES INC.
46 St. Clair Avenue East, 3rd Floor
Toronto, ON M4T 1M9

Telephone	416-515-1151
Fax	416-515-0889
Specialties	Health/Medical
Level	Mid-Level
Contact	Marilyn Anden

ALLEGIANCE GROUP, THE
325 Crossways Park Drive
Woodbury, NY 11797
USA

Telephone	516-921-0100
Fax	516-921-3489
E-mail	recruit@allegiance.com
Website	www.allegiance.com
Specialties	Computing
	International
Level	Mid-Level
	Senior
Recruiters	Dan Greenburg
	Audrey S. Perlman
Contact	Dan E. Greenburg, President

Description The Allegiance Group is a full-service IT consulting and staffing firm that places computing professionals in the tri-state area (NY, NJ & CT).

ALLEMBY MANAGEMENT GROUP INC.
45 Sheppard Avenue E.
Suite 900, Sheppard Centre
Toronto, ON M2N 5W9

Telephone	416-783-1881
Fax	416-783-0831
E-mail	info@allemby.com
Website	www.allemby.com
Founded	1989
Employees	4
Specialties	Marketing
Level	Senior
	Mid-Level
Fee Basis	Retainer Only
Recruiters	Patricia Favret
	Melissa Schafer
Contact	Melissa Schafer, President

Description Allemby specializes in recruiting senior managers and executives in the marketing research industry.

ALLEN AUSTIN LOWE & POWERS
4543 Post Oak Place, Suite 217
Houston, TX 77027
USA

Telephone	713-355-1900
Fax	713-355-1901
E-mail	randrews@aalpsearch.com
Website	www.aalpsearch.com
Founded	1996
Employees	31
Specialties	Accounting
	Computing
	Finance
	Hospitality

Law
Management
Marketing
Purchasing
Sales
International
Advertising
Construction
Banking
Franchising
Geology/Geography
Logistics

Level	Senior
Min. Salary	$60,000
Fee Basis	Retainer Only
Recruiters	Robert L. Andrews
	Dick Babcock
	Jake Baker
	Richard C. Costin
	Chris Hallard
	Rebecca Harlein
	Dana Houston
	Judy Hutcheson
	Jerry Leatherman
	John F. Marr PhD
	Morgan McCain
	Dave Salmons
	Mark Spillard
	Brenda Welling
	King D. White
	Ylonka Wiggins
Contact	Robert L. Andrews, President

Description Allen Austin Lowe & Powers is one of the top 100 retainer-based executive search firms in North America.

ALLEN BALLACH ASSOCIATES INC.
11 Parkview Blvd, Suite 100
Whitby, ON L1N 3M8

Telephone	905-725-0314
Fax	905-725-3418
E-mail	allen@aballach.com
Website	www.aballach.com
Founded	1978
Employees	3
Specialties	Management
	Computing
	Engineering
	Aerospace
	Automotive
	Marketing
	Pulp & Paper
	Telecom
Level	Senior
Min. Salary	$80,000
Recruiters	Allen Ballach
	Sonya DaCosta
Contact	Allen Ballach

Description Allen Ballach Associates specializes in hi-tech, senior-level searches.

ALLEN ETCOVITCH ASSOCIATES LTD. / PSA INTERNATIONAL
666 Sherbrooke St. W., Suite 1707
Montréal, QC H3A 1E7

Telephone	514-287-9933
Fax	514-287-9940
E-mail	etcoall@total.net

Founded	1969
Employees	5
Specialties	Apparel
	Management
	Operations
	Finance
	Retail
	Marketing
	General Practice
Level	Senior
	Mid-Level
Min. Salary	$40,000
Fee Basis	Sometimes contingent
Recruiters	Marie-Josée Demers
	Allen Etcovitch
Contact	Allen Etcovitch

Description Allen Etcovitch Associates Ltd. / PSA International provides recruitment, assessment, career planning, outplacement and general human resource consulting services.

ALLEN PERSONNEL SERVICES
181 Wellington Street
London , ON N6B 2K9

Telephone	519-672-7040
Fax	519-672-7044
E-mail	allen.jobs@ sympatico.ca
Website	www.allenpersonnel. com
Founded	1970
Employees	20
Specialties	Accounting
	Administrative
	Automotive
	Computing
	Engineering
	Logistics
	Management
Level	Mid-Level
Min. Salary	$30,000
Recruiters	Jim Dimitropoulos
	Linda Disik
	Shawn McEwen
	Cindy McPherson
	Cathy Monchamp
	Lorry Pace
	Paul Soutiere
	John Sumilas
	Gerri Teal CPC
Contact	Cindy McPherson

Description Allen Personnel Services is a full-service agency offering contract and full-time placement services and staffing solutions.

ALLEN PERSONNEL SERVICES
1425 Bishop Street North, Suite 5A
Cambridge, ON N1R 6J9

Telephone	519-623-5510
Fax	519-623-1513
Website	www.allenpersonnel. com
Founded	1970
Employees	40
Specialties	Accounting
	Computing
	Engineering

Marketing
Sales

Level	Mid-Level
Contact	Pat Paddock

Description Allen Personnel Services is a full-service agency offering contract and full-time placement services and staffing solutions.

ALLIANCE HUMAN RESOURCES INC.
525A Dundas Street East
Belleville, ON K8N 1G4

Telephone	613-969-1010
Fax	613-969-7404
Specialties	General Practice
Contact	Sharon Bray

ALLIANCE PERSONNEL GROUP, THE
10109 - 106 Street NW, Suite 1202
Edmonton, AB T5J 3L7

Telephone	780-413-9110
Fax	780-487-4893
Website	www.tag-4staff.com
Specialties	Transport
	Operations
	Logistics
	Administrative
	Purchasing
Level	Mid-Level
	Junior
Contact	Carl Joosse

Description Alliance Personnel Group is a professional employer organization that offers a full complement of specialized people in driver, warehouse and management / administrative services.

ALLIANCE PERSONNEL GROUP, THE
2892 Portland Road
Oakville, ON L6H 5W8

Telephone	905-829-1444
Fax	905-829-9664
E-mail	tapg@tag-4staff.com
Website	www.tag-4staff.com
Specialties	Transport
	Operations
	Logistics
	Administrative
	Purchasing
Level	Mid-Level
	Junior

Description Alliance Personnel Group is a professional employer organization that offers a full complement of specialized people in driver, warehouse and management / administrative services.

ALLIANCE SEARCH GROUP INC.
20 Maud Street, Suite 307
Toronto, ON M8V 2M5

Telephone	416-203-9393
Fax	416-203-9494
E-mail	peter@ alliancesearch.net
Founded	1998

Specialties	Computing
	Multimedia
Recruiters	Roy Andrade
	Peter Cho
Contact	Peter Cho

ALLIANCE SEARCH INC.
1066 West Hastings St., Suite 2000
Vancouver, BC V6E 3X2

Telephone	604-801-5298
Fax	604-801-5257
E-mail	jobs@teksource.net
Website	www.teksource.net
Specialties	Computing

ALLMAT & ASSOCIATES LTD.
995A William Street
Cobourg, ON K9A 5J3

Fax	705-725-1285
E-mail	rjallmat@hotmail.com
Specialties	Finance
Level	Mid-Level
	Senior

ALPHA JOB CONSULTING INC.
67 Yonge Street, Suite 1508
Toronto, ON M5E 1J8

Telephone	416-366-5562
Fax	416-366-8899
E-mail	contact@alphajob.com
Website	www.alphajob.com
Specialties	Computing

Description Alpha Job Consulting Inc. provides specialist recruitment services in the IT field.

ALPHASOURCE INC.
20 Bay Street
Suite 1205, Waterpark Place
Toronto, ON M5J 2N8

Telephone	416-365-2001
Fax	416-214-2043
E-mail	dthib@
	alphasourceinc.com
Website	www.alpha
	sourceinc.com
Specialties	Computing

Description AlphaSource Inc. specializes in information technology placements, primarily in the Southern Ontario market area.

ALTERNATIVE RESOURCES CORPORATION / ARC
20 Bay Street, Suite 1205
Toronto, ON M5J 2N8

Telephone	416-777-0188
Fax	416-777-0411
E-mail	info@arcnow.com
Website	www.arcnow.com
Specialties	Computing
	Sales
Level	Senior
	Mid-Level

Description ARC is a US-based company and a leading provider of IT staffing and technology management services to clients across North America.

ALTIS HUMAN RESOURCES
330 Bay Street, Suite 1508
Toronto, ON M5H 2S8

Telephone	416-214-9280
Fax	416-214-9479
E-mail	lara@altishr.com
Website	www.altishr.com
Founded	1989
Employees	8
Specialties	Accounting
	Administrative
	Bilingual
	Computing
	Govt/Nonprofit
Level	Mid-Level
	Junior
Recruiters	Larissa Abrera
	Tara Azulay
	Lara Creber
	Stacey Jessome
	Keltie Neville
Contact	Tara Azulay

Description Altis Human Resources is a growing full-service staffing firm, placing candidates in permanent careers in administration, accounting, computer support, HR and marketing since 1989.

ALTURA GROUP LIMITED
45 Sheppard Ave. East, Suite 900
Toronto, ON M2N 5W9

Telephone	416-642-1696
Fax	416-642-1698
E-mail	info@alturagroup.com
Website	www.alturagroup.com
Founded	2000
Employees	4
Specialties	Sales
	Human Resource
Level	Senior
	Mid-Level
Min. Salary	$40,000
Fee Basis	Sometimes contingent
Contact	Mark Toren, President
	& CEO

Description Altura Group is a management consulting firm that places senior-level sales management and HR placements.

ALUMNI-NETWORK RECRUITMENT CORPORATION
3065 Keynes Cres.
Mississauga, ON L5N 2Z9

Telephone	905-785-0844
Fax	905-785-0877
E-mail	karen@ alumni-
	network.com
Website	www.alumni-
	network.com
Founded	1998
Employees	1
Specialties	Accounting
	Automotive
	Computing
	Engineering
	Health/Medical
	Telecom
Level	Senior
	Mid-Level
Fee Basis	Always contingent
Contact	Karen Berends

Description Alumni-Network recruits hi-tech engineering, SAP / ERP / BAAN / Peoplesoft, E-Commerce / Internet professionals for clients worldwide.

AMAC CONSULTANTS INC.
1066 West Hastings St., 20th Floor
Vancouver, BC V6E 3X2

Fax	604-669-3844
E-mail	amac@execcentre.com
Specialties	Insurance
Level	Mid-Level
Contact	John C. McArthur, FCIP

AMBRIDGE MANAGEMENT CORP.
36 Toronto Street, Suite 850
Toronto, ON M5C 2C5

Telephone	416-367-3810
Fax	416-367-9458
E-mail	ambridge@caspar.net
Founded	1986
Employees	3
Specialties	Banking
	Finance
Level	Senior
	Mid-Level
Min. Salary	$50,000
Fee Basis	Sometimes contingent
Contact	Gordon Sherwin

Description Ambridge Management Corp. specializes in banking, corporate finance, project finance and commercial lending, including leasing and inventory finance in Canada and the USA.

AMROP INTERNATIONAL
Oxtorget 3, S-111
Stockholm, 57 SWEDEN

Telephone	46-8-5450-4530
Fax	46-8-5450-4540
E-mail	stockholm@amrop.com
Website	www.amrop.se
Specialties	International
Level	Senior
Contact	Ulf Assargard

Description Amrop Hever Group is the largest global senior-level search partnership of its kind, operating 78 offices in 45 countries.

AMROP INTERNATIONAL
Bergstrasse 109
Zurich, 8032
SWITZERLAND

Telephone	41-1-267-60-10
Fax	41-1-267-60-19
E-mail	zurich@amrop.com
Website	www.amrop.ch
Specialties	International
Level	Senior
Fee Basis	Retainer Only
Contact	Nanno J.H. de Vries

Description Amrop Hever Group is the largest global senior-level search partnership of its kind, operating 78 offices in 45 countries.

AMROP INTERNATIONAL

Ebulula Caddesi, Caglayan Sitesi A
Blok No 26/9 Levent
Istanbul,   80630
TURKEY

Telephone	90-212-351-0909
Fax	90-212-351-0908
E-mail	yesim.toduk.akis@ amrop.com
Website	www.amrop.com
Specialties	International
Level	Senior
Contact	Yesim Toduk Akis

Description Amrop Hever Group is the largest global senior-level search partnership of its kind, operating 78 offices in 45 countries.

AMROP INTERNATIONAL / PMC

Rua do Rocio, 220, 8 andar
São Paulo, SP,   04552-000
BRAZIL

Telephone	55-11-822-9077
Fax	55-11-822-0781
E-mail	pmc@pmcamrop. com.br
Website	www.pmcamrop. com.br
Specialties	International
Level	Senior
Fee Basis	Retainer Only
Contact	Guilherme Velloso

Description Amrop Hever Group is the largest global senior-level search partnership of its kind, operating 78 offices in 45 countries.

AMROP INTERNATIONAL / SEELIGER Y CONDE

Calle Provenza, 267-269 Pral
Barcelona,   08008
SPAIN

Telephone	34-93-215-0505
Fax	34-93-215-7887
E-mail	mail.bcn@syc.es
Website	www.syc.es
Specialties	International
Level	Senior
Contact	Luis Conde

Description Amrop Hever Group is the largest global senior-level search partnership of its kind, operating 78 offices in 45 countries.

ANDERSEN

401 West Georgia Street, Suite 2000
Vancouver, BC   V6B 5A1

Telephone	604-643-2500
Fax	604-688-5205
E-mail	kate.l.richards@ ca.arthurandersen.com
Website	www.arthur andersen.com
Specialties	Accounting Finance Management
Level	Mid-Level Senior
Contact	Kate L. Richards

Description Andersen (formerly Arthur Andersen) is a global professional services organization consisting of over 100 member firms in 81 countries, and over 70,000 employees.

ANDERSEN

355 - 4th Avenue SW, Suite 2100
Calgary, AB   T2P 0J1

Telephone	403-298-5900
Fax	403-298-5990
E-mail	canada@ arthurandersen.com
Website	www.arthur andersen.com
Specialties	Management
Level	Mid-Level
Contact	Karyn K. Marklinger

Description Andersen (formerly Arthur Andersen) is a global professional services organization consisting of over 100 member firms in 81 countries, and over 70,000 employees.

ANDERSEN

330 St. Mary Avenue, 5th Floor
Winnipeg, MB   R3C 3Z5

Telephone	204-942-6541
Fax	204-956-0830
E-mail	canada@ arthurandersen.com
Website	www.arthur andersen.com
Specialties	Accounting Finance Management
Level	Mid-Level Senior
Contact	Todd Temple

Description Andersen (formerly Arthur Andersen) is a global professional services organization consisting of over 100 member firms in 81 countries, and over 70,000 employees.

ANDERSEN

79 Wellington Street West
Suite 1900, PO Box 29, T-D Centre
Toronto, ON   M5K 1B9

Telephone	416-863-1540
Fax	416-947-7878

E-mail	canada@ arthurandersen.com
Website	www.arthur andersen.com
Specialties	Accounting Finance Management
Level	Mid-Level Senior

Description Andersen (formerly Arthur Andersen) is a global professional services organization consisting of over 100 member firms in 81 countries, and over 70,000 employees.

ANDERSEN

4 King Street West, Suite 1050
Toronto, ON   M5H 1B6

Telephone	416-814-7214
Fax	416-947-7788
E-mail	canada@ arthurandersen.com
Website	www.arthur andersen.com
Specialties	Accounting Finance Management
Level	Mid-Level Senior

Description Andersen (formerly Arthur Andersen) is a global professional services organization consisting of over 100 member firms in 81 countries, and over 70,000 employees.

ANDERSEN

1 City Centre Drive, Suite 500
Mississauga, ON   L5B 1M2

Telephone	905-949-3900
Fax	905-949-3911
E-mail	canada@ arthurandersen.com
Website	www.arthur andersen.com
Specialties	Accounting Finance Management
Level	Mid-Level Senior

Description Andersen (formerly Arthur Andersen) is a global professional services organization consisting of over 100 member firms in 81 countries, and over 70,000 employees.

ANDERSEN

360 Albert Street
12th Floor, Constitution Square
Ottawa, ON   K1R 7X7

Telephone	613-787-8200
Fax	613-787-8242
E-mail	canada@ arthurandersen.com
Website	www.arthur andersen.com
Specialties	Accounting Finance Management

Level   Mid-Level
            Senior

Description Andersen (formerly Arthur Andersen) is a global professional services organization consisting of over 100 member firms in 81 countries, and over 70,000 employees.

ANDERSEN
5 Place Ville-Marie, Suite 1000
Montréal, QC H3B 4X3

Telephone 514-871-8559
Fax   514-871-1997
E-mail   canada@
             arthurandersen.com
Website   www.arthur
             andersen.com

Specialties Accounting
               Finance
               Computing
Level   Mid-Level
               Senior

Contact   Francis Pallascio

Description Andersen (formerly Arthur Andersen) is a global professional services organization consisting of over 100 member firms in 81 countries, and over 70,000 employees.

ANDERSEN
5 Tache Blvd. East, Suite 200
Montmagny, QC G5V 1B6

Telephone 418-248-5777
Fax   418-248-9631
E-mail   canada@
             arthurandersen.com
Website   www.arthur
             andersen.com

Specialties Management
Level   Mid-Level
               Senior

Description Andersen (formerly Arthur Andersen) is a global professional services organization consisting of over 100 member firms in 81 countries, and over 70,000 employees.

ANDERSEN
2954 Laurier Blvd.
Suite 400, Place Iberville IV
Sainte-Foy, QC G1V 4T2

Telephone 418-653-4431
Fax   418-656-0800
E-mail   canada@
             arthurandersen.com
Website   www.arthur
             andersen.com

Specialties Accounting
               Finance
               Management
Level   Mid-Level
               Senior

Description Andersen (formerly Arthur Andersen) is a global professional services organization of over 100 member firms in 81 countries, and over 70,000 employees.

ANDERSON ASSOCIATES
1200 Eglinton East, Suite 306
Toronto, ON M3C 1H9

Telephone 416-444-3837
Fax   416-444-8765
E-mail   bd@andersoncareers.
             com
Website   www.andersoncareers.
             com

Founded   1986
Employees 10

Specialties Management
               Sales
               Finance
               Engineering
               Computing
Level   Mid-Level
               Senior

Recruiters   Bryon Dunscombe
               Chris Fernandes
               Ken Fisico
               Tim Gray
               Roberta Miggiani
               Peter Olo

Contact   Bryon Dunscombe,
               Partner

Description Anderson Associates has been providing top-quality executives and future executives for a broad range of corporate clients since 1986.

ANDREW CAMPBELL & ASSOCIATES INC.
268 Lakeshore Road East, Suite 523
Oakville, ON L6J 7S4

Telephone 905-845-0318
Specialties Management
               Operations
Level   Mid-Level

ANDREW DUNCAN ASSOCIATES
Pytel House
Winkfield Lane, Winkfield
Windsor, SL4 4QU
UNITED KINGDOM

Fax   44-1344-891552
E-mail   adasearch@
             btinternet.com

Specialties International
               Finance
               Banking
               Human Resource
Level   Senior
               Mid-Level

ANGUS EMPLOYMENT LIMITED
1100 Burloak Drive
5th Floor, Royal Bank Building
Burlington, ON L7L 6B2

Telephone 905-319-0773
Fax   905-336-9445
E-mail   resumes@
             angusemployment.com
Website   www.angus
             employment.com

Founded   1966
Employees 5

Specialties Aerospace
               Automotive
               Telecom
               Computing
               Engineering
               Finance
               Management
Level   Mid-Level

Fee Basis   Sometimes contingent

Recruiters   Brenda Ferguson
               Dawn Lukish
               John Stewart
               Evan Stewart

Contact   John Stewart, Director

Description Angus Employment Limited provides recruitment services across Canada and the USA.

ANGUS ONE PROFESSIONAL RECRUITMENT LTD.
777 Hornby Street, Suite 1240
Vancouver, BC V6Z 1S4

Telephone 604-682-8367
Fax   604-682-4664
E-mail   info@angusmiles.com
Website   www.angusmiles.com

Founded   1986
Employees 10

Specialties Operations
               Management
               Computing
               Finance
               Sales
Level   Mid-Level
               Senior

Recruiters   Karen Fraser
               Lynn Gerbrandt
               Jennifer Main CPC

Contact   Karen Fraser

Description Angus One Professional Recruitment serves the recruitment needs of the Vancouver and Victoria business community, from high tech and industrial companies to financial institutions and governments.

ANNE WHITTEN BILINGUAL HUMAN RESOURCES INC.
438 University Avenue, Suite 308
Toronto, ON M5G 2K8

Telephone 416-595-5974
Fax   416-598-5127
E-mail   awhitten@istar.ca
Website   www.annewhitten.com

Specialties Bilingual
Contact   Anne Whitten

Description Anne Whitten Bilingual Human Resources Inc. specializes in placing bilingual personnel.

ANOKIIWIN EMPLOYMENT SOLUTIONS, INC.
260 St. Mary Avenue, Suite 106
Winnipeg, MB R3C 0M6

Telephone 204-925-2760
Fax   204-943-1352
E-mail   work@anokiiwin.com

Website	www.anokiiwin.com
Specialties	General Practice
Contact	Elaine Cowan, President

Description An aboriginal owned and operated employment agency, recruiting in all industries at all levels.

APEX SEARCH INC.
45 Sheppard Ave. East, Suite 900
Toronto, ON M2N 5W9

Telephone	416-226-2828
Fax	416-226-1417
E-mail	joanne@apexsearch.com
Website	www.apexsearch.com
Founded	1994
Employees	3
Specialties	Computing
Level	Mid-Level Senior
Fee Basis	Always contingent
Recruiters	Karen Agulnik Joanne Bloye
Contact	Karen Agulnik, Manager

Description Apex Search Inc. specializes in the selection and placement of IT professionals for contract and permanent opportunities.

APPLE MANAGEMENT CORP.
31 Ames Circle
Toronto, ON M3B 3B9

Telephone	416-441-0670
Fax	416-441-0671
E-mail	lawrieapple@applemanagement.com
Website	www.applemanagement.com
Specialties	Finance Management Accounting Law
Level	Mid-Level Senior
Recruiters	Lawrie Apple CA Carol Good Bill Sedgwick Keith Southey
Contact	Lawrie Apple, CA

Description Apple Management Corporation is a management consulting firm that occasionally offers recruitment services to its clients.

APPLE ONE EMPLOYMENT SERVICES
3331 Bloor Street West
Toronto, ON M8X 1E7

Telephone	416-236-4000
Fax	416-236-0422
E-mail	ggregg@mail.appleone.com
Website	www.appleone.com
Specialties	Accounting Computing

	Human Resource Operations Sales Administrative
Recruiters	Gary Gregg Anne Middleton
Contact	Gary Gregg

Description Supplier of full-time and contract employees.

APPLICANT TESTING SERVICES INC. / ATS
1764 Oxford Street East, Suite J12
London, ON N5V 3R6

Telephone	519-569-8686
Fax	519-659-8787
E-mail	atsi@odyssey.on.ca
Website	www.applicanttesting.com
Specialties	Law
Level	Mid-Level
Contact	Greg Currie, President

Description ATS is an independent firm that specializes in recruiting law enforcement applicants for positions in the field of policing.

APPLICANTS INC.
41 River Road East, Unit B-2
Kitchener, ON N2B 2G3

Telephone	888-548-8897
Fax	888-834-5855
E-mail	harlick@applicantsinc.com
Website	www.applicantsinc.com
Founded	1996
Employees	6
Specialties	Engineering Accounting Quality Control Purchasing Operations Computing Logistics Design
Level	Mid-Level
Min. Salary	$35,000
Fee Basis	Always contingent
Recruiters	Martin J. Harlick Emily Wiles Colin Wright
Contact	Martin J. Harlick

Description Applicants Inc. places managers, supervisors and support staff in various industries, including engineering, accounting, operations, productions, purchasing and IT.

APPLIED MANAGEMENT CONSULTANTS
150 Eglinton Ave. East, Suite 803
Toronto, ON M4P 1E8

Telephone	416-487-2855
Fax	416-487-4851
E-mail	bryan@appliedmanagement.ca
Website	www.appliedmanagement.ca

Specialties	Health/Medical
Level	Mid-Level
Contact	Bryan Ferguson

Description Applied Management Consultants is a management consulting firm specializing in the healthcare field that occasionally does search work for clients.

APPLIED MANAGEMENT CONSULTANTS
151 Brunswick Street
Fredericton, NB E3B 1G7

Telephone	506-458-8370
Fax	506-452-7883
E-mail	lamont@appliedmanagement.ca
Website	www.appliedmanagement.ca
Specialties	Health/Medical
Level	Mid-Level

Description Applied Management Consultants is a management consulting firm specializing in the healthcare field that occasionally does search work for clients.

APPLIED TECHNOLOGY SOLUTIONS INC. / ATS
55 York Street, Suite 1100
Toronto, ON M5J 1R7

Telephone	416-369-0008
Fax	416-369-0199
E-mail	info@atsglobal.com
Website	www.atsglobal.com
Founded	1989
Employees	16
Specialties	Computing Management
Level	Mid-Level Senior
Min. Salary	$30,000
Fee Basis	Always contingent
Recruiters	Shawn Armstrong Dave Chanchlani Tim Diardichuk Gayla Goshulak William Jackson Lorne Kastner Victor Munro Joe Sassine Helen Stankova John Tapp Diane Tichbourne Deepak Tiku
Contact	Joe Sassine, VP Business Development

Description ATS is a multifaceted IT consulting firm specializing in the placement of quality contract and full-time IT professionals.

APTUS PERSONNEL CARE SERVICES
29 Throgmorton Street
Unit 45 - 46, Warnford Court
London, ECN 2AT
UNITED KINGDOM

Telephone	44-20-7374-4301

Fax   44-20-7588-3532
Website   www.aptus-
             personnel.com

Founded   1963

Specialties International

Level   Mid-Level

Description Aptus Personnel is one of the UK's top 50 recruitment companies, providing contract and permanent staff and innovative personnel services to more than 5,000 clients each year.

AQUENT PARTNERS
815 Hornby Street, Suite 606
Vancouver, BC V6Z 2E6

Telephone 604-669-5600
Fax   604-669-5665
E-mail   van@aquent.com
Website   www.aquent.com

Specialties Computing
             Design
             Multimedia
             Graphic Arts
             Printing

Level   Senior
             Mid-Level

Fee Basis Always contingent

Recruiters Darren Hull
             Michal Suchanek

Contact   Mr. Michal Suchanek

Description For 15 years, Aquent Partners has been placing print and web designers, production staff, graphic designers and technical staff in freelance and permanent positions. Aquent has offices in 12 countries and 4 continents.

AQUENT PARTNERS
77 Bloor Street West
Suite 1205
Toronto, ON M5S 1M2

Telephone 416-323-0600
Fax   416-323-9866
E-mail   mwales@aquent.com
Website   www.aquent.com

Founded   1986
Employees 7

Specialties Computing
             Design
             Graphic Arts
             Printing
             Multimedia

Level   Senior
             Mid-Level

Fee Basis Always contingent

Recruiters Marie Boal
             Mandy Gilbert
             Stephen Hodges
             Christopher Plommer
             Debra Sharp
             Michelle Wales

Contact   Michelle Wales,
             Director of Canadian
             Operations

Description For 15 years, Aquent Partners has been placing print and web designers, production staff,

graphic designers and technical staff in freelance and permanent positions. Aquent has offices in 12 countries and 4 continents.

AQUENT PARTNERS
1350 Sherbrooke St. W., Suite 1105
Montréal, QC H3G 1J1

Telephone 514-289-9009
Fax   514-289-1003
Website   www.aquent.com

Specialties Computing
             Design
             Multimedia
             Graphic Arts
             Printing

Level   Senior
             Mid-Level

Fee Basis Always contingent

Contact   Sophie Dereveanko

Description For 15 years, Aquent Partners has been placing print and web designers, production staff, graphic designers and technical staff in freelance and permanent positions. Aquent has offices in 12 countries and 4 continents.

ARABIAN CAREERS LIMITED
Berkeley Square House, 7th Floor
Berkeley Square
London, W1X 5LB
UNITED KINGDOM

Telephone 44-20-495-3285
Fax   44-20-681-2901
E-mail   recruiter@
             arabiancareers.com
Website   www.arabian
             careers.com

Specialties International
             Health/Medical
             Oil & Gas
             Education
             Computing

Contact   Margaret Peers

Description Specializes in the recruitment of healthcare professionals for hospitals in Saudi Arabia, where career opportunities exist for all professionals.

ARAMCO SERVICES COMPANY
9009 West Loop South
Houston, TX 77096
USA

Telephone 713-432-4000
Website   www.aramco
             services.com

Specialties Oil & Gas
             International
             Engineering
             Health/Medical

Contact   Ahmed K. Al-Arnaout,
             President & CEO

Description Aramco Services Company recruits for Saudi Aramco, the state oil company responsible for all refining, international marketing and distribution of petroleum products from Saudi Arabia.

ARCHER ASSOCIATES
629 Broadview Avenue
Toronto, ON M4K 2N9

Telephone 416-463-7904

Specialties Accounting
             Finance

Fee Basis Always contingent

Contact   Jennifer Toliver

Description Retained searches for a stable client base in the fields of accounting and finance.

ARCHER RESOURCE SOLUTIONS INC.
6725 Airport Road, 6th Floor
Mississauga, ON L4V 1V2

Telephone 905-405-8652
Fax   905-405-1738
E-mail   archinfo@archer.ca
Website   www.archer.ca

Specialties Aerospace
             Automotive
             Biotech/Biology
             Design
             Engineering
             Logistics

Level   Senior
             Mid-Level

Fee Basis Always contingent

Recruiters Bratati Bhattacharjee
             Susan Corazzola
             Laura Sullivan
             Glen Thompson
             Vaina Wang

Contact   Susan Corazzola,
             Manager

Description Archer Resource Solutions Inc. is a total service contract and permanent placement agency focusing on the engineering and information technology industries.

ARES CONSULTING SERVICES LTD.
1835 Yonge Street, Suite 603
Toronto, ON M4S 1X8

Telephone 416-480-2700
Fax   416-480-2886
E-mail   resumes@
             aresconsulting.com
Website   www.ares
             consulting.com

Specialties Computing
             Multimedia

Level   Mid-Level

Contact   Claire Colley

ARGENTUS INC.
47 Colborne Street, Suite 300
Toronto, ON M5e 1P8

Telephone 416-364-9919
Fax   416-364-0100
E-mail   recruit@argentus.com
Website   www.argentus.com

Specialties Computing
             Accounting
             Finance
             Management

Recruiters	Adele Casciaro
	Gabriella Cristofoli
	Darrell Hines
	Linda Stober
Contact	Linda Stober, Managing
	Director

Description Argentus is a diversified recruitment firm placing people in the IT, accounting, finance and management fields.

ARGUS GROUP CORPORATION, THE
249 Roehampton Ave., 2nd Floor
Toronto, ON M4P 1R4

Telephone	416-932-9321
Fax	416-932-9387
E-mail	cdn.directory@
	argusgroupcorp.com
Website	www.argus
	groupcorp.com
Founded	1994
Employees	5
Specialties	Sales
	Marketing
	Computing
	Telecom
Fee Basis	Always contingent
Recruiters	Sandra Gregoire
	Lisa Marcos
	Michelle McKay
	Alec Reed
Contact	Alec Reed, President

Description The Argus Group Corporation are sales and marketing specialists focusing on the IT industry.

ARIE SHENKAR & ASSOCIATES INC.
401 Bay Street, Suite 2315
Toronto, ON M5H 2Y4

Telephone	416-860-0233
Fax	416-860-0817
E-mail	ashenkar@
	pathcom.com
Founded	1986
Specialties	Computing
Level	Mid-Level
	Senior
Recruiters	Ned Manalili
	Arie Shenkar
Contact	Arie Shenkar

Description Specializes in IT placements.

ARIEL GROUP INTERNATIONAL
20 Holly Street, Suite 203
Toronto, ON M4S 3B1

Telephone	416-322-3091
Fax	416-322-5499
Specialties	Management
	Sales
	Marketing
	Engineering
Level	Senior

Description Ariel Group International specializes in executive searches in management, sales, marketing and technical areas.

ARLYN PERSONNEL AGENCIES LTD.
625 Howe Street, Suite 1160
Vancouver, BC V6C 2T6

Telephone	604-681-4432
Fax	604-681-4418
Specialties	Accounting
Level	Mid-Level
	Junior
Contact	Darlene Foster

Description Arlyn Personnel specializes in financial placements.

ARMITAGE ASSOCIATES LTD.
885 West Georgia Street, Suite 1500
Vancouver, BC V6C 3E8

Telephone	604-683-6790
Fax	604-683-6023
E-mail	info@
	armitagesearch.com
Website	www.armitage
	search.com
Founded	1976
Specialties	Computing
	Finance
	Management
Level	Senior
Min. Salary	$80,000
Fee Basis	Retainer Only
Contact	Jade Bourelle

Description Armitage handles complex, sensitive senior-level searches and has over 30 years of experience working with business leaders in Canadian industry.

ARMITAGE ASSOCIATES LTD.
151 Yonge Street, Suite 1210
Toronto, ON M5C 2W7

Telephone	416-863-0576
Fax	416-863-0092
E-mail	info@
	armitagesearch.com
Website	www.armitage
	search.com
Founded	1976
Employees	3
Specialties	Computing
	Management
	Finance
Level	Senior
Min. Salary	$80,000
Fee Basis	Retainer Only
Recruiters	John D. Armitage
	Ron Cuperfain
	Karen Wood
Contact	John D. Armitage,
	President

Description Armitage handles complex, sensitive senior-level searches and has over 30 years of experience working with business leaders in Canadian industry.

ARMITAGE ASSOCIATES LTD.
279, boul. Rosmere
Rosmere, QC J7A 2T1

Telephone	450-965-1441

Fax	450-990-8989
E-mail	info@
	armitagesearch.com
Website	www.armitage
	search.com
Specialties	Computing
	Finance
	Management
Level	Senior
Min. Salary	$80,000
Fee Basis	Retainer Only
Contact	Daniel Lacoste

Description Armitage handles complex, sensitive senior-level searches and has over 30 years of experience working with business leaders in Canadian industry.

ARMOR PERSONNEL
66 Broadway
Orangeville, ON L9W 1J9

Telephone	519-940-4921
Fax	519-940-9230
E-mail	info@
	armorpersonnel.com
Website	www.armor
	personnel.com
Founded	1971
Specialties	Administrative
	Accounting
	Sales
Level	Mid-Level
Recruiters	Cody-Lynn Abbot
	Dell Heaney
Contact	Dell Heaney

Description Armor supplies permanent staffing, recruitment services, creative and flexible personnel solutions and HR consulting.

ARMOR PERSONNEL
181 Queen Street East
Brampton, ON L6W 2B3

Telephone	905-459-1617
Fax	905-459-1704
E-mail	info@
	armorpersonnel.com
Website	www.armor
	personnel.com
Specialties	Accounting
	Administrative
	Sales
Level	Mid-Level
	Junior
Recruiters	Brenda Cowie
	Cynthia Kirlew
	Christopher McLaughlin
	Ann Ragobar
Contact	Brenda Cowie

Description Armor supplies permanent staffing, recruitment services, creative and flexible personnel solutions and HR consulting.

ARMOR PERSONNEL
165 Dundas Street West, Suite 109
Mississauga, ON L5B 2N6

Telephone	905-566-4591
Fax	905-566-9783
E-mail	info@armorpersonnel.com
Website	www.armorpersonnel.com
Specialties	Administrative Accounting Sales
Level	Mid-Level
Recruiters	Bruce Callaghan C. Wilding
Contact	C. Wilding

Description Armor Personnel is a leading supplier of permanent staffing, recruitment services, creative and flexible personnel solutions and human resources consulting.

ARMOR PERSONNEL
36 Bessemer Court, Units 1 and 2
Vaughan, ON L4K 3C9

Telephone	905-660-7888
Fax	905-660-0874
E-mail	info@armorpersonnel.com
Website	www.armorpersonnel.com
Specialties	Administrative Accounting Sales
Level	Mid-Level
Recruiters	Winfield Brown Maria Manuele
Contact	Linda Ford

Description Armor Personnel is a leading supplier of permanent staffing, recruitment services, creative and flexible personnel solutions and human resources consulting.

ARON PRINTZ & ASSOCIATES LTD.
688 West Hastings Street, Suite 580
Vancouver, BC V6B 1P1

Telephone	604-687-3121
Fax	604-687-3122
E-mail	vci@mindlink.net
Website	mindlink.net/vci/apahp.htm
Specialties	Management Operations
Level	Mid-Level
Recruiters	Bob Guns Aron Printz Linda Thorp
Contact	Aron Printz

Description Provides a complete range of human resources consulting services, including testing and recruitment.

ASHLAR-STONE MANAGEMENT CONSULTANTS INC.
50 Burnhamthorpe Road West
Suite 401
Mississauga, ON L5B 3C2

Telephone	905-615-0900
Fax	905-615-0917
E-mail	info@ashlar-stone.com
Website	www.ashlar-stone.com
Founded	1991
Employees	3
Specialties	Automotive Finance Human Resource Logistics Marketing Operations Sales
Level	Senior
Min. Salary	$70,000
Fee Basis	Retainer Only
Recruiters	Robert Bonnell Robert Chisholm Stuart Moore
Contact	Stuart Moore

Description Ashlar-Stone is a direct sourcing executive search practice that does not advertise. Their client base is located in Canada, US and the UK.

ASHTEAD MANAGEMENT CONSULTANTS LTD.
11 Church Road, Gothic Lodge
Great Bookham, PO Box 32
Surrey, KT23 3PD
UNITED KINGDOM

Fax	44-1372-278015
E-mail	royj@ashteadman.co.uk
Website	www.ashteadman.co.uk
Founded	1982
Specialties	International Construction Oil & Gas Engineering
Level	Mid-Level Senior
Contact	Roy James

Description Supplies technical professionals for overseas assignments in construction, highways, mechanical and electrical contracting, petrochemicals, oil & gas, power generation, desalination, airports and hospitals.

ASHTON COMPUTER PROFESSIONALS INC. / ACP
15-C Chesterfield Place
Lonsdale Quay
North Vancouver, BC V7M 3K3

Telephone	604-904-0304
Fax	604-904-0305
E-mail	info@acprecruit.com
Website	www.acprecruit.com
Founded	1984
Employees	3
Specialties	Computing Management Telecom
Level	Mid-Level Senior
Min. Salary	$30,000
Fee Basis	Always contingent
Recruiters	Barbara L. Ashton

Peter Birt
Mike Woodhouse

Contact	Peter Birt

Description Specializes in IT professional recruitment services. Member of National Personnel Association.

ASSET COMPUTER PERSONNEL LTD.
48 Yonge Street, Suite 500
Toronto, ON M5E 1G6

Telephone	416-777-1717
Fax	416-777-0647
E-mail	asset@asset.ca
Website	www.asset.ca
Founded	1985
Employees	36
Specialties	Computing
Level	Mid-Level
Fee Basis	Always contingent
Recruiters	Lisa Ardito BA Gene Balfour BSc Fiona Bryan BEng Randy Clemens BA Laura Colley BA Ray Corlett HMD Anita D'Costa Mark Dooley MA
Contact	Jerry Rumack PEng, MBA

Description Asset Computer Personnel Ltd. specializes in attracting and placing qualified computer personnel into permanent and contract positions.

ASSISTANCE TEKNICA LTD.
York House, Borough Road
Middlesbrough, TS1 2HJ
UNITED KINGDOM

Telephone	44-1642-224545
Fax	44-1642-243514
E-mail	eng.ser@teknica.co.uk
Website	www.teknica.co.uk
Founded	1980
Specialties	Engineering International Metals

Description Assistance Teknica is a privately-owned management and operational consultancy specializing in capital industrial projects.

ASSOCIATED RECRUITMENT CONSULTANTS
35 Wynford Heights Crescent
Suite 1502
Toronto, ON M3C 1L1

Telephone	416-446-0496
Fax	416-446-7404
E-mail	ken@torontojobsource.com
Website	www.torontojobsource.com
Specialties	Real Estate
Level	Mid-Level Senior

Contact   Ken Roulston

Description Associated Recruitment Consultants is a recruitment firm specializing in the placement of real estate professionals in the Greater Toronto Area.

ASSOCIATES GROUP OF COMPANIES, THE
222 Somerset Street West, Suite 700
Ottawa, ON K2P 2G3

Telephone	613-567-0222
Fax	613-567-6441
E-mail	recruiting@the associatesgroup.com
Website	www.theassociates group.com
Founded	1988
Employees	14
Specialties	Accounting
	Computing
	Banking
	Engineering
	Finance
	Govt/Nonprofit
	Insurance
	International
	Law
	Management
	Marketing
Level	Mid-Level
Contact	Recruiter

Description The Associates Group of Companies is a full-service recruiting and placement consulting company.

ASSOCIATION MANAGEMENT CONSULTANTS INC.
409 Granville Street, Suite 523
Vancouver, BC V6C 1T2

Telephone	604-669-5344
Fax	604-669-5343
E-mail	amc@amcdirectory.com
Website	www.amcdirectory.com
Founded	1987
Specialties	Govt/Nonprofit
Level	Senior
Contact	Tom Abbott

Description AMC is the only management consulting firm in BC that specializes in recruitment for non-profit and public sector clients.

ASSOCIATION RESOURCE CENTRE INC., THE
2 Bloor Street West, Suite 100
Toronto, ON M4W 3E2

Telephone	416-926-8780
Fax	905-842-8275
E-mail	info@association consultants.com
Website	www.association consultants.com
Founded	1997
Employees	8
Specialties	Administrative
	Banking
	Finance
	Govt/Nonprofit
	Management
	Marketing
	Trade Shows
Level	Senior
Min. Salary	$50,000
Fee Basis	Always contingent
Recruiters	Jack Shand CAE
	Ken Thacker MBA
Contact	Jack Shand, Managing Partner

Description The Association Resource Centre provides recruitment services for not-for-profit organizations and businesses servicing the association sector.

ASSOCIATION STRATEGY GROUP
90 Sparks Street, Suite 1127
Ottawa, ON K1P 5B4

Telephone	613-233-4789
Fax	613-235-5866
E-mail	chris@association strategygroup.com
Website	www.association strategygroup.com
Specialties	Govt/Nonprofit
Contact	Christopher LeClair, Managing Partner

Description Association Strategy Group provides executive search and recruitment to regional and national associations.

ASSOCIES DE DESSINS MECANIQUES
180, boul. René-Lévesque E.
Bureau 112
Montréal, QC H2X 1N5

Telephone	514-861-2341
Fax	514-861-0307
E-mail	mda@noramtec.com
Specialties	Engineering
	Design
	Computing
	Telecom
Level	Mid-Level
Recruiters	Brian Holland
	Glen Holland
Contact	Glen Holland

ASSOCIUM CONSULTANTS
1 Yonge Street, Suite 2201
Toronto, ON M5E 1E5

Telephone	416-867-9350
Fax	416-867-9139
E-mail	admin@associum.com
Website	www.associum.com
Specialties	Govt/Nonprofit
	Administrative
	Human Resource
Level	Mid-Level
Contact	Adrian C. Johnson

Description Associum Consultants provides a full range of human resources consulting services, including recruitment.

ASTRA MANAGEMENT CORP.
1281 West Georgia Street, Suite 700
Vancouver, BC V6E 3J7

Telephone	604-682-3141
Fax	604-688-5749
E-mail	astra@wood-west.com
Website	www.wood-west.com
Founded	1996
Employees	9
Specialties	Engineering
	Telecom
	Accounting
	Finance
	Computing
	Design
Level	Mid-Level
	Senior
Min. Salary	$50,000
Fee Basis	Sometimes contingent
Recruiters	Jim Black
	John Jaye
	Sash Prasad
	Don Sturgess
	Cliff Tang
	Andrea York
Contact	Fred West, P.Eng., MCP

Description ASTRA Management specializes in recruiting for the consulting engineering, telecommunications, accounting, finance and IT sectors.

AT KEARNEY EXECUTIVE SEARCH
130 Adelaide St. West, Suite 2710
Toronto, ON M5H 3P5

Telephone	416-947-1990
Fax	416-947-0255
E-mail	baker_harris@ atkearney.com
Website	www.atkearney.com
Founded	1947
Employees	15
Specialties	Finance
	Management
	Human Resource
	Marketing
	General Practice
	Pharmaceutical
	Telecom
Level	Senior
Min. Salary	$120,000
Fee Basis	Retainer Only
Recruiters	Gerry Baker
	Rosemary Duff
	Jack Harris
	Virginia Murray
	Richard Wajs
Contact	Rosemary Duff

Description AT Kearney is a leading international search firm that conducts senior-level searches in all industry sectors.

ATI CONSULTING CORP. INC.
1505 Barrington Street
Maritime Centre, 11th Floor South
PO Box 2045, Station M
Halifax, NS B3J 2Z1

Telephone	902-422-1617
Fax	902-423-7593

E-mail ati@mgnet.ca
Website www.mgnet.ca/ati

Specialties Management
Govt/Nonprofit
Health/Medical

Level Senior

Recruiters George Hall
John M. Heseltine
Tom McGuire BA, MA
Armand Pinard
Debra Sherwood
Diana H. Whalen

Contact John M. Heseltine,
Vice-President

Description ATI Consulting Corporation Inc. is a management consulting firm serving primarily the public-sector that occasionally provides recruitment services for clients.

ATS RELIANCE INDUSTRIAL GROUP
150 Consumers Road, Suite 401
Toronto, ON M2J 1P9

Telephone 416-498-9494
Fax 416-498-0094
E-mail industrial@
atsrecruitment.com
Website www.ats
recruitment.com

Specialties Aerospace
Automotive
Design
Computing
Engineering

Level Mid-Level

Description ATS is a leading North American recruitment specialist of engineers and other technical personnel for companies in the consulting, manufacturing, service and construction industries.

ATS RELIANCE TECHNICAL GROUP
1501 West Broadway, Suite 300
Vancouver, BC V6J 4Z6

Telephone 604-915-9333
Fax 604-915-9339
E-mail van.bc@
atsrecruitment.com
Website www.ats
recruitment.com

Founded 1975

Specialties Engineering
Aerospace
Design
Trades/Technicians
Computing
Oil & Gas

Level Senior
Mid-Level

Description ATS is a leading North American recruitment specialist of engineers and other technical personnel for companies in the consulting, manufacturing, service and construction industries.

ATS RELIANCE TECHNICAL GROUP
8711 West 50th Avenue, Suite 201
Edmonton, AB T6E 5H4

Telephone 780-462-1815
Fax 780-461-9968
E-mail edmonton@
atsrecruitment.com
Website www.ats
recruitment.com

Specialties Aerospace
Computing
Design
Engineering
Oil & Gas
Plastics

Level Mid-Level
Senior

Description ATS is a leading North American recruitment specialist of engineers and other technical personnel for companies in the consulting, manufacturing, service and construction industries.

ATS RELIANCE TECHNICAL GROUP
1305 - 11th Avenue SW, Suite 408
Calgary, AB T3C 3P6

Telephone 403-261-4600
Fax 403-265-2909
E-mail calgary@
atsrecruitment.com
Website www.ats
recruitment.com

Founded 1975

Specialties Engineering
Design
Computing
Aerospace
Oil & Gas
Plastics

Level Mid-Level
Senior

Description ATS is a leading North American recruitment specialist of engineers and other technical personnel for companies in the consulting, manufacturing, service and construction industries.

ATS RELIANCE TECHNICAL GROUP
171 Queens Avenue, Suite 601
London, ON N6A 5J7

Telephone 519-679-2886
Fax 519-679-1483
E-mail london@
atsrecruitment.com
Website www.ats
recruitment.com

Founded 1975
Employees 12

Specialties Engineering
Automotive
Computing
Design
Logistics
Oil & Gas
Quality Control

Level Senior

Mid-Level

Recruiters Mike Abbott
Jeff Collier
Mark Gillies
Charlotte Pickersgill
John Rose
Christine Verwagen

Contact John Rose

Description ATS is a leading North American recruitment specialist of engineers and other technical personnel for companies in the consulting, manufacturing, service and construction industries.

ATS RELIANCE TECHNICAL GROUP
2323 Yonge Street, Suite 700
Toronto, ON M4P 2C9

Telephone 416-482-8002
Fax 416-482-1210
E-mail ats@
atsrecruitment.com
Website www.ats
recruitment.com

Founded 1975

Specialties Computing
Engineering
Aerospace
Automotive
Oil & Gas
Plastics

Level Mid-Level
Senior

Fee Basis Always contingent

Recruiters Brad Austin
Jenn Chorney
Louie Deligianis
Graham Gies
Dave Gilmour
John Gilmour
David Jackson
Catherine Jull
Dave Maynard
Dave McDougall
Phil McDougall
Jason Wahl

Contact David Jackson

Description ATS is a leading North American recruitment specialist of engineers and other technical personnel for companies in the consulting, manufacturing, service and construction industries.

ATS RELIANCE TECHNICAL GROUP
3310 South Service Road, Suite 307
Burlington, ON L7N 3M6

Telephone 905-333-9632
Fax 905-333-9326
E-mail burlington@
atsrecruitment.com
Website www.ats
recruitment.com

Specialties Engineering
Aerospace
Design
Trades/Technicians
Computing
Oil & Gas
Plastics

Level	Mid-Level
	Senior

Description ATS is a leading North American recruitment specialist of engineers and other technical personnel for companies in the consulting, manufacturing, service and construction industries.

ATTICUS RESOURCES
250 - 6th Avenue SW
Suite 1500, Bow Valley IV
Calgary, AB T2P 3H7

Telephone	403-547-2405
Specialties	Computing
Level	Mid-Level

AUDAX CORPORATION
3300 Bloor St. W., Centre Tower
11th Floor, Suite 3140
Toronto, ON M8X 2X3

Telephone	416-231-1819
Fax	416-231-7007
E-mail	careerinfo@audaxcorporation.com
Website	www.audaxcorporation.com
Founded	1989
Specialties	Consulting
	Finance
	Human Resource
	Management
	Marketing
	Operations
	Purchasing
Level	Senior
	Mid-Level
Min. Salary	$50,000
Fee Basis	Retainer Only
Contact	Patricia Langmuir Taylor

Description Audax Corporation assists organizations to recruit and select management and executive-level staff. Thorough research and assessment techniques are our hallmark.

AUGMENT PRESTIGE SERVICES
704 Mara Street, Suite 115
DMI Professional Building
Point Edward, ON N7V 1X4

Telephone	519-336-6433
Fax	519-336-5874
E-mail	vbergin@ebtech.net
Specialties	Administrative
	Automotive
	Engineering
Contact	Marilyn Soulard

AUSTIN MARLOWE INTERNATIONAL INC.
151 Yonge Street, Suite 1401
Toronto, ON M5C 2W7

Telephone	416-368-9469
Fax	416-368-1815
E-mail	allisonmackellar@austinmarlowe.com
Website	www.austinmarlowe.com
Employees	5
Specialties	Finance
	Actuarial
	Management
	Human Resource
	Sales
	Marketing
Level	Senior
Min. Salary	$75,000
Fee Basis	Retainer Only
Recruiters	Stanley Braithwaite
	Allison MacKellar
Contact	Allison MacKellar

Description Austin Marlowe International Inc. is a retainer-based search firm whose consultants have successfully completed assignments in most functional areas and industries.

AUSTIN PARK MANAGEMENT GROUP INC.
40 Eglinton Avenue East, Suite 207
Toronto, ON M4P 3A2

Telephone	416-488-9565
Fax	416-488-9601
E-mail	austin@austinpark.com
Website	www.austinpark.com
Founded	1986
Employees	12
Specialties	Computing
	Banking
	Insurance
	Telecom
	Engineering
	Finance
Level	Senior
	Mid-Level
Min. Salary	$40,000
Fee Basis	Sometimes contingent
Recruiters	Michael Crawford
	Earl Gardner
	Lynn Gardner
	Howard Prince
Contact	L. Gardener, New Business Development

Description Austin Park is the number one UNIX recruiter in Canada, offering career and contract staffing in software development and technical support for emerging technologies.

AVIATION PERSONNEL SUPPORT INC. / APS
968 Wilson Avenue, Suite 102
Toronto, ON M3K 1E7

Telephone	416-635-6211
Fax	416-635-0311
E-mail	hr@thepersonnelco.com
Website	www.thepersonnelco.com
Specialties	Aerospace
Level	Mid-Level
Recruiters	Michael Dickinson
	Ian Hendrie
Contact	Ian Hendrie

Description APS, in partnership with RAS Completions Limited (Aviation Division), supplies engineering personnel to the aerospace industry.

AXIOM INTERNATIONAL REFERENCE CHECKING SERVICES
2343 Brimley Road, Suite 250
Toronto, ON M1S 3L6

Telephone	416-291-0903
Fax	416-291-3493
Specialties	General Practice
Contact	Roger Clements

Description Axiom provides reference-checking services to recruiters and search firms.

AXXES TECHNOLOGIES INC.
3333 Cote Vertu Blvd., Suite 215
Saint-Laurent, QC H4R 2N1

Telephone	514-856-6800
Fax	514-856-6849
E-mail	resume@axxes-tech.com
Website	www.axxes-tech.com
Founded	1997
Employees	12
Specialties	Computing
	Telecom
Level	Mid-Level
	Junior
Contact	Silvin Langlois

Description Axxes is a recruiting firm specializing in the information technology and telecom industry.

AXXES TECHNOLOGIES INC.
1126 chemin St. Louis, Bureau 702
Sillery, QC G1S 1E5

Telephone	418-688-8785
Fax	418-688-7057
E-mail	axxes@axxes-tech.com
Website	www.axxes-tech.com
Founded	1997
Employees	12
Specialties	Computing
	Telecom
	Multimedia
	Engineering
	Quality Control
	Human Resource
	Management
	Marketing
Level	Mid-Level
Fee Basis	Sometimes contingent
Recruiters	François Du Sablon
	François Jetté
Contact	Francois Du Sablon

Description Axxes is a recruiting firm specializing in the information technology and telecom industry.

AYRSHIRE GROUP, THE
67 Yonge Street, Suite 808
Toronto, ON M5E 1J8

Telephone	416-364-6388
Fax	416-364-5302
E-mail	resume@ ayrshiregroup.com
Website	www.ayrshiregroup.com
Employees	5
Specialties	Finance Computing Accounting Insurance Operations

Description The Ayrshire Group provides a wide range of clients with strategic recruitment consultation.

AZTECH RECRUITMENT CO.
4131 North 24th Street, Suite A122
Phoenix, AZ 85016 USA

Telephone	602-955-8080
Fax	602-955-9639
E-mail	resumes@ aztechjobs.com
Website	www.aztechjobs.com
Founded	1993
Employees	8
Specialties	Engineering Computing International Aerospace Design Telecom
Level	Senior Mid-Level
Min. Salary	$40,000
Fee Basis	Retainer Only
Recruiters	Charles Bohm Lionel R. Eras Chris John Lidia John Allen Kelly David Ketterer Tony Tomko
Contact	Lionel Eras

Description Aztech provides retained recruiting services for US, Canadian and European employers.

AZUR RESSOURCES HUMAINES LTÉE
259 boul. St-Joseph, Bureau 303B
Hull, QC J8Y 6T1

Téléphone	819-772-8080
Télécopieur	819-595-3728
Courriel	hr@azurhr.com
Site Internet	www.azurhr.com
Spécialités	Généralistes Gouvt/OSBL
Échelon	Intermédiaire

Description AZUR Ressources Humaines Ltée s'engage à offrir les services des personnes les plus qualifiées de l'industrie pour le gouvernement fédéral et provincial ainsi que le groupe T.L.C.

B.B. CONSULTANTS GROUP
704 Mara Street, Suite 201
DMI Professional Building
Point Edward, ON N7V 1X4

Telephone	519-337-9950
Fax	519-337-9178
E-mail	bbbailey@ebtech.net
Website	www.sarnia.com/bb
Specialties	Administrative Engineering Construction Design Trades/Technicians Computing Management
Recruiters	Laura Bailey Cecily Mills-Gordon
Contact	Laura Bailey

Description B.B. Consultants Group specializes in supplying skilled technical personnel to clients across North America.

B & L CONSULTANTS INC. / AUTORECRUIT INC.
720 Arrow Road
Toronto, ON M9M 2M1

Telephone	416-748-1547
Fax	416-748-6992
E-mail	info@blconsultants.com
Website	www.blconsultants.com
Founded	1994
Employees	9
Specialties	Automotive Transport
Level	Mid-Level Senior
Fee Basis	Sometimes contingent
Recruiters	Farid Ahmad RPR Chris MacMillan RPR Paul Martin RPR Kim McLeod RPR
Contact	Chris MacMillan

Description B & L Consultants Inc. / Autorecruit Inc. is a recruitment firm specializing in all aspects of the automobile industry and car rental field.

B WYZE INC.
45B West Wilmot
Richmond Hill, ON L4B 2P3

Telephone	905-881-0555
Fax	905-881-3520
Website	www.bwyze.com
Specialties	Computing
Level	Mid-Level Senior
Recruiters	Rick Beaudry Liz Chilton Jason Cull Virginia Kandilogianakis John Peco John Towsley
Contact	John Peco

Description B Wyze Inc. provides innovative IT and project management staffing and placement services for mid- and large-sized organizations.

BACH ASSOCIATES
5735 Hampton Place, Suite 208
Vancouver, BC V6T 2G8

Telephone	604-221-9979
Fax	604-221-9970
E-mail	lbach@ bach-associates.com
Website	www.bach-associates.com
Specialties	Computing Multimedia
Level	Senior
Min. Salary	$75,000
Fee Basis	Retainer Only
Contact	Leora Bach

BAILEY PROFESSIONAL SEARCH
1604 - 21A Street NW
Calgary, AB T2N 2M6

Telephone	403-289-5802
Fax	403-282-7912
E-mail	nairb@bailey search.com
Founded	1990
Employees	3
Specialties	Computing Engineering Management Marketing Oil & Gas Sales Telecom
Level	Mid-Level
Min. Salary	$35,000
Fee Basis	Sometimes contingent
Recruiters	Nair H. Bailey Jeanette L. Vosburgh
Contact	Nair H. Bailey, General Manager

Description Bailey Professional Search recruits sales and engineering professionals for industrial manufacturers, distributors and engineering companies in Western Canada.

BAINES GWINNER LIMITED
30 Eastcheap
London, EC3M 1HD
UNITED KINGDOM

Telephone	44-20-7623-1414
Fax	44-20-7623-1100
E-mail	jftb@baine.co.uk
Website	www.baines.co.uk
Specialties	International Finance Accounting
Level	Senior
Recruiters	Jonathan F.T. Baines Karin Barnick Sarah Dudney Hugo Eddis Vanessa Eertmans Victoria Evans Nick Hedley Richard Ker Lynda Knill Nadine Lewis Rebecca Longley Caroline Lor

Anthony May
Jennifer O'Connell
Richard Phillips
Martyn Pocock
Amy Russo
Renee Sohanpal
Sonia Thomas
Jennifer Walker
Leonie Wykes

Contact Jonathan F.T. Baines

Description Baines Gwinner is an executive search firm specializing in placing people in the financial and professional services industry.

BAKER CONSULTING INC.
51 University Avenue
Financial Building
Charlottetown, PE C1A 4K8

Telephone	902-892-9000
Fax	902-628-8100
E-mail	baker.consulting@ pei.sympatico.ca
Website	www.bcinc.pe.ca
Founded	1992
Specialties	General Practice
Recruiters	Don Baker Kathryn Coll David Knight Allison MacDougall
Contact	Kathryn Coll

Description Baker is a management consulting firm that also provides recruitment services for clients.

BALDOCK & ASSOCIATES LTD.
145 King Street W., Suite 1000
Toronto, ON M5H 1J8

Telephone	416-947-9484
Fax	416-947-0231
E-mail	crsi@sprint.ca
Founded	1952
Employees	4
Specialties	Banking Finance Accounting Computing Management Marketing
Level	Senior Mid-Level
Fee Basis	Retainer Only
Contact	Robert Baldock

Description Baldock & Associates provides diversified executive recruiting services. Their clients include financial institutations, senior corporations, small/medium enterprises and government.

BALDWIN STAFFING GROUP LTD.
550 - 17th Avenue SW, Main Floor
Calgary, AB T2S 0B1

Telephone	403-228-1999
Fax	403-228-5533
E-mail	info@baldwinstaffing. com
Website	www.baldwinstaffing. com

Founded	1987
Employees	10
Specialties	Accounting Administrative Law Oil & Gas Sales Engineering Computing
Level	Mid-Level Senior
Fee Basis	Sometimes contingent
Contact	Stephen Baldwin, President

Description BSG and its affiliate company, SearchCorp International, provide national and international companies with contract, permanent and executive search staffing solutions.

BARCON CONSULTING INC.
PO Box 1308
New Hamburg, ON N0B 2G0

Telephone	519-662-4432
Fax	519-662-4435
E-mail	vanandel@orc.ca
Specialties	Govt/Nonprofit
Level	Mid-Level
Contact	Connie Van Andel

BARR LEGAL PERSONNEL
120 Eglinton Ave. East, Suite 1100
Toronto, ON M4P 1E2

Telephone	416-322-7810
Fax	416-322-5075
Specialties	Law
Level	Mid-Level Junior
Min. Salary	$25,000
Contact	Margaret F. Barr, MA

Description Barr Legal Personnel provides legal secretaries and law clerks to a client base of large downtown Toronto law firms.

BARRETT ROSE & LEE INC.
55 University Avenue, Suite 1700
Toronto, ON M5S 2H7

Telephone	416-363-9700
Fax	416-363-8999
E-mail	info@barrettrose.com
Website	www.barrettrose.com
Founded	1988
Employees	10
Specialties	Management Computing Marketing Sales
Level	Mid-Level Senior
Min. Salary	$60,000
Fee Basis	Sometimes contingent
Recruiters	Arthur Clark H. Peter Heinemann
Contact	Arthur Clark

Description Barrett Rose & Lee Inc. is a mid-market search firm specializing in recruiting managers in the IT field.

BARRY BLOSTEIN RECRUITMENT
97 Heatherton Way
Thornhill, ON L4J 3E7

Telephone	905-763-0728
Fax	905-763-0099
E-mail	bblostein@ sympatico.ca
Founded	1990
Specialties	Accounting Finance Operations Human Resource Telecom Logistics Purchasing
Level	Mid-Level
Fee Basis	Sometimes contingent
Contact	Barry Blostein

Description Barry Blostein has been in practice for a decade, recruiting mid- and senior-level people in a variety of industries, including IPO telecom companies.

BARRY HULTS CONSULTANTS LTD.
20 Crown Steel Drive, Suite 10
Markham, ON L3R 9X9

Telephone	905-475-9161
Fax	905-475-8736
Specialties	Administrative Accounting Sales
Level	Mid-Level
Contact	Barry Hults, President

Description Barry Hults Consultants Ltd. provides management consulting services for the promotional products industry, including occasional recruitment work.

BASSETT LAUDI PARTNERS INC.
2 Bloor Street West
Suite 2600, Box 4
Toronto, ON M4W 2G7

Telephone	416-935-0855
Fax	416-935-1106
E-mail	careers@ bassettlaudi.com
Website	www.bassettlaudi.com
Specialties	Computing Management Marketing Telecom
Level	Senior Mid-Level
Min. Salary	$35,000
Fee Basis	Always contingent
Contact	Martyn Bassett

Description Bassett Laudi brings together the best in intellectual capital and corporations in North America, specializing in IT positions.

BAY STREET PLACEMENT
11 Thames Court
Richmond Hill, ON L4B 1N5

Telephone	416-368-0113
Specialties	Finance Accounting
Contact	Sam Dixon

Description Bay Street Placement specializes in placements in the financial services industry.

BAY3000 CONSULTING INC.
140 Allstate Parkway, Suite 506
Markham, ON L3R 5Y8

Telephone	905-947-8562
Fax	905-947-8563
E-mail	info@bay3000.com
Website	www.bay3000.com
Specialties	Operations

Description Bay3000 Consulting Inc. is a management consulting firm specializing in project management work that also does recruitment work for clients.

BC HEALTH SERVICES LTD. / BCHS
1380 Burrard Street, Suite 700
Vancouver, BC V6Z 2H3

Telephone	604-488-0600
Fax	604-488-0665
E-mail	resumes@bchs.bc.ca
Website	www.bchs.bc.ca
Specialties	Health/Medical
Recruiters	G. Fred Pearson CEO Georgina Pon
Contact	G. Fred Pearson

Description BCHS offers consulting and professional services to healthcare organizations, including executive search.

BCB CANDIDATES BANK INC.
378 LaFleur
Lasalle, QC H8R 3H6

Telephone	514-363-3649
Fax	514-363-3930
Specialties	Administrative
Level	Junior Mid-Level
Contact	Shirley Blainey

BDO DUNWOODY & ASSOCIATES LIMITED
305 King Street West, Suite 401
Kitchener, ON N2G 1B9

Telephone	519-576-5220
Fax	519-576-5471
E-mail	tsothern@bdo.ca
Website	www.kitchener.bdo.ca
Employees	35
Specialties	Accounting Finance Management
Level	Mid-Level Senior
Contact	Tim Sothern, HR Specialist

Description BDO Dunwoody, with 80 offices across Canada, is an accounting and consulting firm concentrating on the needs of independent business and community-based organizations.

BDO DUNWOODY & ASSOCIATES LIMITED
505 York Boulevard, Suite 2
Hamilton, ON L8R 3K4

Telephone	905-525-6800
Fax	905-525-6841
E-mail	cjerome@bdo.ca
Website	www.bdo.ca
Specialties	Accounting Finance
Level	Mid-Level
Contact	Chuck Jerome, Vice-President, Corporate IT Consulting

Description BDO Dunwoody, with 80 offices across Canada, is an accounting and consulting firm concentrating on the needs of independent business and community-based organizations.

BDO DUNWOODY & ASSOCIATES LIMITED
60 Columbia Way, Suite 400
Markham, ON L3R 0C9

Telephone	905-946-1066
Fax	905-946-9524
Website	www.bdo.ca
Employees	90
Specialties	Accounting Finance
Level	Mid-Level
Contact	John Trainor CA, Vice-President

Description BDO Dunwoody, with 80 offices across Canada, is an accounting and consulting firm concentrating on the needs of independent business and community-based organizations.

BDO DUNWOODY EXECUTIVE SEARCH
191 Broadway, 5th Floor
Wawanesa Building
Winnipeg, MB R3C 3T8

Telephone	204-956-7200
Fax	204-926-7201
E-mail	mrivard@bdo.ca
Website	www.bdo.ca
Employees	35
Specialties	Accounting Finance
Level	Senior Mid-Level
Contact	Marc Rivard, CA

Description BDO Dunwoody, with 80 offices across Canada, is an accounting and consulting firm concentrat-

ing on the needs of independent business and community-based organizations.

BDO DUNWOODY LLP
175 Hargrave Street, Suite 600
Winnipeg, MB R3C 3R8

Telephone	204-944-8720
Fax	204-947-3468
E-mail	inquiries@sill.ca
Website	www.sill.ca
Founded	1990
Employees	40
Specialties	Accounting Finance Management Health/Medical
Level	Mid-Level Senior
Fee Basis	Sometimes contingent
Recruiters	David Anderson CA W.D. "Bill" Bodman Doug Einarson CA
Contact	W.D. Bill Bodman

Description BDO Dunwoody LLP (formerly Sill & Company) is accounting firm that also does search work for clients.

BDO DUNWOODY LLP
265 Exmouth Street, PO Box 730
Sarnia, ON N7T 7J7

Telephone	519-336-9900
Fax	519-332-4828
E-mail	fjorourke@sarnia.bdo.ca
Website	www.sarnia.bdo.ca
Specialties	Accounting Finance
Contact	F. Joseph O'Rourke, Managing Partner

Description BDO Dunwoody, with 80 offices across Canada, is an accounting and consulting firm concentrating on the needs of independent business and community-based organizations.

BDO DUNWOODY LLP
200 Bay Street, Royal Bank Plaza
PO Box 32, South Tower
Toronto, ON M5J 2J8

Telephone	416-865-0200
Fax	416-865-0887
E-mail	jbonnell@bdo.ca
Website	www.bdo.ca
Specialties	Accounting Finance
Level	Mid-Level Senior
Contact	Peter E. Held

Description BDO Dunwoody is an accounting and consulting firm, serving independent business clients and community-based organizations, with 80 offices across Canada.

BDO DUNWOODY LLP
38 Toronto Street North
PO Box 1648
Uxbridge, ON L9P 1N7

Telephone	905-852-9714
Fax	905-852-9898
E-mail	uxbridge@bdo.ca
Website	www.bdo.ca
Specialties	Accounting
	Finance
Contact	Randy J. Hickey

Description BDO Dunwoody, with 80 offices across Canada, is an accounting and consulting firm concentrating on the needs of independent business and community-based organizations.

BDO DUNWOODY LLP
471 Counter Street, Suite 301
Kingston, ON K7M 8S8

Telephone	613-544-2903
Fax	613-544-6151
E-mail	kingston@bdo.ca
Website	www.kingston.bdo.ca
Specialties	Accounting
	Finance
Level	Mid-Level
Contact	Brian D. Mann

Description BDO Dunwoody is an accounting and consulting firm, serving independent business clients and community-based organizations, with 80 offices across Canada.

BDO DUNWOODY LLP
301 Moodie Drive, Suite 400
Nepean, ON K2H 9C4

Telephone	613-820-8010
Fax	613-820-0465
E-mail	ottawa.recruiting@ bdo.ca
Website	www.bdo.ca
Employees	90
Specialties	Accounting
	Finance
Level	Mid-Level
Recruiters	Robert W.C. Rock CA
	Mildred Verhallen
Contact	Robert W.C. Rock, CA

Description BDO Dunwoody, with 80 offices across Canada, is an accounting and consulting firm concentrating on the needs of independent business and community-based organizations.

BDO DUNWOODY LLP
475 Main Street, PO Box 390
Winchester, ON K0C 2K0

Telephone	613-774-2854
Fax	613-744-2586
E-mail	bmann@ winchester.bdo.ca
Website	www.winchester.bdo.ca
Specialties	Accounting
	Finance

Recruiters	Jeffrey Jackson
	Brian D. Mann CA
Contact	Brian D. Mann

Description BDO Dunwoody, with 80 offices across Canada, is an accounting and consulting firm concentrating on the needs of independent business and community-based organizations.

BDO DUNWOODY LLP
4150 St. Catherine Street West
Suite 600
Montréal, QC H3Z 2Y5

Telephone	514-931-0841
Fax	514-931-9491
E-mail	plussier@bdo.ca
Website	www.montreal.bdo.ca
Specialties	Accounting
	Finance
Level	Mid-Level
Contact	Pierre Lussier,
	Managing Partner

Description BDO Dunwoody, with 80 offices across Canada, is an accounting and consulting firm for independent business and community-based organizations.

BDS CHALLENGE INTERNATIONAL
80 Tribune Street, South Brisbane
Queensland, 4101
AUSTRALIA

Telephone	61-7-3844-8093
Fax	61-7-3844-2140
E-mail	aallebone@ bdschall.com.au
Website	www.bdstech.com.au
Founded	1964
Specialties	International
	Engineering
Contact	Alan Allebone,
	Manager International
	Recruitment

Description BDS Challenge International is an international recruitment agency dedicated to assisting professional engineering personnel secure positions worldwide.

BEALLOR & PARTNERS LLP
28 Overlea Boulevard
Toronto, ON M4H 1B6

Telephone	416-423-0707
Fax	416-423-7000
E-mail	mbeallor@beallor.com
Website	www.beallor.com
Specialties	Accounting
	Finance
Contact	Morley Beallor

Description Beallor & Partners LLP is an accounting firm that also does some search work for its clients.

BECKY JONES & ASSOCIATES LTD.
890 Yonge Street, Suite 402
Toronto, ON M4W 3P4

Telephone	416-413-4995
Fax	416-413-4996
E-mail	bjones@ beckyjones.com
Website	www.beckyjones.com
Founded	1981
Specialties	Management
Level	Mid-Level
Recruiters	Veronica Davies
	Mary Francis Fox
	Vera Hall
	Becky Jones
	Brian Reevie
	David Tollefson
Contact	Becky Jones, President

Description Becky Jones & Associates Ltd. provides a range of human resources consulting services, including placement and outplacement counseling.

BEDARD RESSOURCES INC.
5115 Trans-Island, Bureau 238
Montréal, QC H3W 2Z9

Telephone	514-482-0444
Fax	514-482-6464
E-mail	sarah@bedres.com
Website	www.bedres.com
Founded	1996
Specialties	Pharmaceutical
Recruiters	Yvonne Bédard
	Carole Bédard
	Caroline Brassard
	Catherine Brissette
Contact	Yvonne Bédard CRHA,
	President

BEDFORD CONSULTING GROUP INC., THE
60 Bedford Road, Bedford House
Toronto, ON M5R 2K2

Telephone	416-963-9000
Fax	416-963-9998
E-mail	search@ bedfordgroup.com
Website	www.bedfordgroup.com
Founded	1979
Employees	14
Specialties	Banking
	Computing
	Mining
	Pharmaceutical
	Pulp & Paper
	Telecom
	Retail
Level	Senior
Min. Salary	$60,000
Fee Basis	Retainer Only
Recruiters	G. Russell Buckland
	Steven G. Pezim
	Howard J. Pezim
Contact	Steven G. Pezim,
	President

Description Bedford provides global search capabilities for positions at senior and middle management levels in diverse industries. Partner in TranSearch International.

BEDFORD CONSULTING GROUP INC., THE
132 Reynolds Street
Oakville, ON L6J 3K5

Telephone	905-338-7008
Fax	905-338-0662
E-mail	search@ bedfordgroup.com
Website	www.bedfordgroup.com
Specialties	Banking Computing Mining Pharmaceutical Pulp & Paper Retail Telecom
Level	Senior
Min. Salary	$60,000
Fee Basis	Retainer Only
Contact	Steven G. Pezim, President

Description Bedford provides global search capabilities for positions at senior and middle management levels in diverse industries. Partner in TranSearch International.

BEECHWOOD RECRUITMENT LIMITED
219 High Street
London, W3 9BY
UNITED KINGDOM

Telephone	44-20-992-8647
Fax	44-20-993-5658
E-mail	cv@beechwood recruit.com
Website	www.beechwood recruit.com
Specialties	International Engineering
Contact	Richard Hickson

Description Beechwood Recruitment Limited specializes in professional and experienced graduate recruitment throughout the UK, Europe and overseas.

BELANGER PARTNERS LIMITED
2012 John Street
Thornhill, ON L3T 1Z1

Telephone	905-709-0909
Fax	905-762-9178
E-mail	belanger@belanger partners.com
Website	www.belanger partners.com
Founded	1981
Employees	5
Specialties	Computing Telecom Management Marketing Sales International
Level	Senior Mid-Level
Min. Salary	$40,000
Fee Basis	Sometimes contingent
Recruiters	Rick Belanger Roy Willcocks

Contact	Rick Belanger, President

Description Belanger are placement specialists for companies that sell computer and communication products, hardware and software.

BELLE ISLE DJANDJI BRUNET, INC.
1555, rue Peel, Bureau 1200
Les Cours Mont Royal
Montréal, QC H3A 3L8

Telephone	514-844-1012
Fax	514-844-0539
E-mail	reception@bidi.com
Website	www.bidi.com
Employees	6
Specialties	General Practice
Level	Senior Mid-Level
Fee Basis	Retainer Only
Recruiters	Charles Belle Isle Michel S. Brunet CA Guy N. Djandji
Contact	Guy N. Djandji, Associé

Description Belle Isle Djandji Brunet is a search practice affiliated with Charles Belle-Isle Inc and Michel Brunet & Associates.

BERESFORD BLAKE THOMAS LTD.
14 Buckingham Palace Rd., Victoria
London SW1W 0QP
UNITED KINGDOM

Telephone	44-20-828-1555
Fax	44-20-828-1941
E-mail	recruit@bbt.co.uk
Website	www.bbt.co.uk
Founded	1989
Employees	75
Specialties	Engineering International Health/Medical
Contact	Steve Thomas

Description Beresford Blake Thomas specializes in placing engineering and healthcare professionals.

BERKELEY CONSULTING GROUP
380 Esna Park Drive, Suite 100
Markham, ON L3R 1H5

Telephone	905-475-2525
Fax	905-479-9211
E-mail	bcg@berkeley consulting.com
Specialties	Govt/Nonprofit
Level	Mid-Level Senior

Description Berkeley is a management consulting firm specializing in government consulting, including occasional recruitment work.

BERKELEY STREET AGENCY
15 Langholm Road, Langton Green
Royal Tunbridge Wells
Kent, TN3 0EY
UNITED KINGDOM

Telephone	44-1892-863377
Fax	44-1892-863971
E-mail	support@ipta.co.uk
Website	www.ipta.co.uk/ berkeley-street/
Specialties	International Hospitality
Level	Mid-Level Junior

Description Berkeley Street Agency specialises in the recruitment of qualified domestic staff for the UK.

BERLYS INC., SERVICE DE PERSONNEL
1500, rue du College, Bureau 315
Saint-Laurent, QC H4L 5G6

Téléphone	514-855-1311
Télécopieur	514-855-1312
Courriel	berlys@cedep.com
Fondée	1986
Employés	7
Spécialités	Aérospatial Automobile Sylviculture Plastique Affaires publiques Télécommunications
Frais	Parfois relative
Recruteurs	Lise Bergeron Nadia Deegan Anny Filion Benoît Gosselin Alain Quesnel
Contact	Lise Bergeron, President

Description Service personnalisé. Disponibilité bilinguisme (division anglophones). Sélection organisationelle de tous nos candidats.

BERNARD FRIGON & ASSOCIÉS INC.
1155, boul. René-Lévesque O.
Bureau 2500
Montréal, QC H3B 2K4

Telephone	514-393-8145
Fax	450-444-4349
E-mail	bfrigon@ globetrotter.net
Founded	1984
Employees	4
Specialties	General Practice Computing Management Sales Telecom
Level	Senior Mid-Level
Contact	Bernard Frigon, President

Description Bernard Frigon & Associés Inc. specializes in information technology placements at all levels, including telecommunications, consulting and sales.

BERNARD HODES GROUP
2445 West 41st Avenue
Vancouver, BC V6M 2A5

Telephone	604-266-7350
Fax	604-266-7420
Website	www.hodes.com
Specialties	General Practice
Contact	Lisa Benjamin

Description Bernard Hodes Group is a recruitment advertising firm. They do not accept unsolicited resumes.

BERNARD HODES GROUP
2 Adelaide Street West, 4th Floor
Toronto, ON M5H 1L6

Telephone	416-362-7999
Fax	416-367-9895
E-mail	camail@to.hodes.com
Website	www.hodes.com
Specialties	General Practice
Contact	Helen Tom

Description Bernard Hodes Group is a recruitment advertising firm. They do not accept unsolicited resumes.

BERNHARD CONSULTING INC.
1215 Henderson Highway
Suite 201, Kingsford Building
Winnipeg, MB R2G 1L8

Telephone	204-338-4777
Fax	204-338-4222
E-mail	berncons@ mb.sympatico.ca
Specialties	Management Marketing Operations Finance
Level	Mid-Level
Contact	Barry L. Bernhard

BERNIER & ASSOCIÉS RECHERCHE ET SELECTION
1155 boul Rene Levesque O.
Bureau 2500
Montréal, QC H3B 2K4

Telephone	519-879-5944
Fax	519-879-5940
E-mail	cchauvin@bernier.com
Website	www.bernier.com
Founded	1992
Specialties	Computing
Level	Mid-Level
Contact	Caroline Chouier

Description Bernier & Associés recruits highly skilled professionals for high technology industries.

BERTRAND, ELBAZ C.R.H.
1212 St. Mathieu
Montréal, QC H3H 2H7

Telephone	514-393-9991
Fax	514-393-1236
E-mail	elbaza@ibm.net
Specialties	Computing Engineering Human Resource

Level	Mid-Level Senior
Contact	Alain Elbaz

BESSNER GALLAY KREISMAN / BGK
215 Redfern Avenue, Suite 300
Westmount, QC H3Z 3L5

Telephone	514-908-3600
Fax	514-908-3630
E-mail	hr@bgsk.com
Website	www.bgsk.com
Specialties	Accounting Finance
Level	Mid-Level Senior
Contact	Philip C. Levi

Description BGK is an accounting firm that also does occasional search work for clients.

BEST PERSONNEL SERVICES
251 Campbell Street
Sarnia, ON N7T 2H2

Telephone	519-336-7962
Fax	519-336-4769
E-mail	reception@ best-personnel.com
Website	www.best-personnel.com
Specialties	Engineering Operations
Level	Mid-Level Junior
Contact	Don Callum, President

Description Best Personnel has been supplying contract and long-term personnel to businesses in the Lambton County for over 17 years.

BEST PERSONNEL SERVICES
48 Front Street East, Suite 5
Strathroy, ON N7G 1Y6

Telephone	519-245-7997
Fax	519-245-1448
E-mail	strathroy@ best-personnel.com
Website	www.best-personnel.com
Specialties	Engineering Operations
Level	Mid-Level Junior

Description Best Personnel Services has been supplying contract and long-term personnel to businesses in the Lambton county for over 17 years.

BEST-NEWMAN PERSONNEL SERVICES INC. / BNPS
2065 Dundas Street East, Suite 113
Mississauga, ON L4X 2W1

Telephone	905-629-4274
Fax	905-629-3591
Founded	1978
Employees	10
Specialties	General Practice

Level	Mid-Level Junior
Contact	Nancy Samuels

Description BNPS is a full-service firm providing quality staffing to all business sectors.

BESTARD AGRICULTURAL PLACEMENTS
Box 3247
St. Marys, ON N4X 1A8

Telephone	519-284-4400
Fax	519-284-4158
E-mail	bestard@bestard.on.ca
Website	www.bestard.on.ca
Specialties	Agriculture/Fisheries
Level	Senior Mid-Level
Recruiters	Michael Bachner Brian Bestard
Contact	Brian Bestard

Description Bestard Agricultural Placements specializes in placements in the agribusiness industry, including feed, crop, animal health, seed, banking, credit, fertilizer, crop protection, advertising agencies, retail and equipment.

BETTY STEINHAUER & ASSOCIATES LIMITED
150 Balmoral Avenue
Toronto, ON M4V 1J4

Telephone	416-921-4342
Specialties	Govt/Nonprofit
Contact	Betty Steinhauer

BEVERTEC CST INC.
191 The West Mall, Suite 700
Toronto, ON M9C 5K8

Telephone	416-695-7525
Fax	416-695-7526
E-mail	resumes@bevertec.com
Website	www.bevertec.com
Founded	1981
Specialties	Computing
Level	Senior Mid-Level
Contact	Manager, Recruitment Practice

Description Bevertec is an IT recruiting and consulting firm that provides software professionals for the financial services, manufacturing, communications and transportation sectors.

BEYONDTECH SOLUTIONS INC.
3665 Kingsway, Suite 300
Vancouver, BC V5R 5W2

Fax	604-433-0627
E-mail	careers@ beyond-tech.com
Website	www.beyond-tech.com
Specialties	Computing Engineering

Architecture
Design
Multimedia

Level   Mid-Level

Description BeyondTech Solutions Inc. provides technical recruitment services to clients across industry sectors.

BIALECKI INC.
780 Third Avenue, Suite 4203
New York, NY 10017
USA

Telephone	212-755-1090
Fax	212-755-1130
Website	www.bialecki.com
Specialties	International
	Finance
Level	Senior
Recruiters	Linda Bialecki MBA
	Kathryn Williams
Contact	Linda Bialecki, MBA

Description Bialecki Inc. is a retainer executive search firm specializing exclusively in recruiting senior Wall Street talent for a few select clients.

BILINGUAL SOURCE
30 St. Clair Avenue West, Suite 302
Toronto, ON M4V 3A1

Telephone	416-515-8880
Fax	416-515-9819
E mail	info@
	bilingualsource.com
Website	www.bilingual
	source.com
Founded	1984
Employees	10
Specialties	Administrative
	Banking
	Bilingual
	Finance
	Human Resource
	Insurance
	Pharmaceutical
	Sales
Min. Salary	$30,000
Fee Basis	Always contingent
Contact	Tony Troiano

Description Bilingual Source is a full-service bilingual staffing firm.

BILINGUAL-JOBS.COM
1001 West Broadway
Suite 101, Department 185
Vancouver, BC V6H 4E4

Telephone	604-688-8363
Fax	604-608-3214
E-mail	manager@
	bilingual-jobs.com
Website	www.bilingual-jobs.com
Founded	1996
Employees	5
Specialties	Bilingual
	International
	Education
Level	Mid-Level
Min. Salary	$40,000

Contact   Wilson Lee

Description Bilingual-Jobs.com is a recruitment service operated by International Consulting Group Incorporated.

BILL KELLIE CONSULTING
23 Main Street East, PO Box 1027
Norwich, ON N0J 1P0

Telephone	519-863-3492
Fax	519-863-3493
E-mail	kellieb@execulink.com
Specialties	Consulting
	Human Resource
Contact	Bill Kellie

Description Call toll-free: 1-888-755-7755.

BIRCH & ASSOCIÉS
2155, rue Guy, Bureau 740
Montréal, QC H3H 2R9

Telephone	514-846-1878
Fax	514-846-9395
E-mail	info@ birch-protocole.com
Website	www.birch-protocole.com
Founded	1985
Employees	6
Specialties	Management
	Marketing
	Retail
	Sales
	Finance
Level	Mid-Level
	Senior
Recruiters	Jerry Birch
	Stan Birch
Contact	Jerry Birch, President

Description Birch & Associés are experts in the field of executive recruitment.

BLACK TALON SERVICES LTD.
3610 Hill View Crescent NW
Edmonton, AB T6L 1C4

Telephone	780-970-5128
Fax	780-970-5105
E-mail	resumes@ blacktalon.com
Website	www.blacktalon.com
Specialties	Computing
Level	Mid-Level

Description Black Talon Services Ltd. recruits IT professionals to fill permanent and contract positions in all high-tech disciplines.

BLACKSHIRE RECRUITING SERVICES INC.
713 Columbia Street, Suite 103
New Westminster, BC V3M 1B2

Telephone	604-517-3551
Fax	604-526-1295
E-mail	information@ blackshire.com
Website	www.blackshire.com

Specialties	Engineering
	Computing
Fee Basis	Always contingent

Description Blackshire Recruiting Services Inc. provides IT recruiting services for software companies, systems engineering firms, systems consulting companies, hardware companies, technology vendors and data processing departments.

BLOOMING HUMANS
1325 King's Road
Victoria, BC V8R 2N6

Telephone	250-592-4011
Fax	250-592-4011
E-mail	patj@tnet.net
Website	www.direct.ca/orw/ source/job/ blooming.htm
Specialties	Disabled
Contact	Pat Johnstone

Description Places people with physical disabilities.

BMA INTERNATIONAL
3460 rue Peel
Montréal, QC H3A 2M1

Telephone	514-932-0120
Founded	1986
Employees	5
Specialties	Aerospace
	Bilingual
	Engineering
	Finance
	Logistics
	Multimedia
	Telecom
Level	Mid-Level
	Senior
Min. Salary	$40,000
Fee Basis	Sometimes contingent

Description BMA International specializes in the search of highly-qualified professionals who understand international markets and have fluent English, French and often a third language.

BMA INTERNATIONAL
1115 Sherbrooke West
Montréal, QC H3A 1H3

Telephone	514-287-9033
Fax	514-285-1890
Founded	1986
Employees	5
Specialties	Aerospace
	Bilingual
	Engineering
	Finance
	Logistics
	Multimedia
	Telecom
Level	Mid-Level
	Senior
Min. Salary	$40,000
Fee Basis	Sometimes contingent
Recruiters	Micheline Brunet

Jean-Bernard Fabre
Dean McDougall

Contact   Micheline Brunet,
President

Description BMA specializes in placing highly-qualified professionals who understand international markets and have fluent English, French and often a third language.

BMB / MAXSYS
142 Guigues Street
Ottawa, ON K1N 5H9

Telephone 613-562-9943
Fax   613-241-6742
E-mail   hr@maxsys.ca
Website   www.maxsys.ca

Specialties Computing
Engineering
Consulting
Level   Mid-Level
Senior
Recruiters Bryan Brulotte
Ian Murray
Louis Nadeau
Contact   Bryan Brulotte,
President

Description BMB / MaxSys, an affiliate of BMB Management Consulting, is a professional staffing and solutions firm.

BONDWELL STAFFING
2171 Avenue Road, Suite 100
Toronto, ON M5M 4B4

Telephone 416-489-8009
Fax   416-489-5136
E-mail   bondwellstaffing@
primus.ca

Specialties Finance
Accounting

BONGARD MARSH ASSOCIATES INC.
39 Roehampton Avenue
Toronto, ON M4P 1P9

Telephone 416-482-0744
Fax   416-482-2070
E-mail   bmai@interlog.com
Website   www.lifeinsurance
brokers.com/bmai

Founded   1993
Employees 7

Specialties Automotive
Plastics
Engineering
Insurance
Marketing
Administrative
Design
Level   Mid-Level
Recruiters Susan Bongard
Deborah Long
Malcolm Marsh
Contact   Susan Bongard

Description Specializing in mid-level placements in the automotive, food and plastics industries.

BOOKE & PARTNERS
5 Donald Street, Suite 500
Winnipeg, MB R3L 2T4

Telephone 204-284-7060
Fax   204-284-7105

Specialties Accounting
Finance
Contact   David Devere, CA

Description Booke & Partners is an accounting firm that also does search work for clients.

BOOTH INTERNATIONAL MANAGEMENT CONSULTANTS
290 North Queen Street, Suite 120
Toronto, ON M9C 5L2

Telephone 416-695-7111
Fax   416-695-3635

Specialties Computing
Human Resource
Level   Senior
Mid-Level
Fee Basis   Retainer Only
Recruiters Richard W. Booth
Tim Hutchins
Contact   Richard W. Booth

Description Booth International specializes in placing human resources, payroll and HRIS (including implementations, sales and support) personnel.

BOSCAN CONSULTANTS INC.
R.R. #1
Marysville, ON K0K 2N0

Telephone 613-396-6784
Fax   613-396-6785
E-mail   boscan@kos.net
Founded   1989

Specialties Computing
Engineering
Management
Marketing
Telecom
Level   Mid-Level
Senior
Min. Salary $40,000
Contact   Mike Bossio

Description Specialize in the placement of management, engineering and marketing professionals in the telecommunications industry.

BOSWORTH FIELD ASSOCIATES
111 Richmond St. W., Suite 404
Richmond-Adelaide Building
Toronto, ON M5H 2S8

Telephone 416-362-2151
Fax   416-362-2195
E-mail   amohammed@
bosworthfieldassoc.com

Specialties Finance
Accounting
Computing
Level   Mid-Level

Fee Basis   Always contingent
Recruiters Diane Armstrong
Mark Keller
Anisa Mohammed
Contact   Adrienne Tidy, Office
Manager

Description Bosworth Field Associates specializes in the placement of finance and accounting professionals and middle managers.

BOTRIE ASSOCIATES / STANTON CHASE INTERNATIONAL
20 Adelaide Street East, Suite 401
Toronto, ON M5C 2T6

Telephone 416-868-0118
Fax   416-868-0121
E-mail   toronto@
stantonchase.com
Website   www.toronto.stanton
chase.com
Founded   1985
Employees 18

Specialties Finance
Management
Operations
Sales
Computing
Telecom
Health/Medical
Pharmaceutical
Level   Mid-Level
Senior
Min. Salary $60,000
Fee Basis   Retainer Only
Recruiters James Botrie
Peter Caven
Randy De Piero
David Nirenberg
Contact   James Botrie,
Managing Director

Description Botrie Associates is affiliated with Stanton Chase International, which has provided retainer executive search services for Fortune 500 organizations for over 15 years.

BOURASSA, BRODEUR & ASSOCIÉS
7175, boul. Marion, Bureau 312
Trois-Rivières, QC G9A 5Z9

Téléphone 819-373-5300
Télécopieur 819-373-0612
Courriel   bbda@netrover.com

Spécialités Administratif
Informatique
Éducation
Ingénierie
Ressources humaines
Gestion
Exploitation
Échelon   Intermédiaire
Contact   Bruno Bourassa,
President

Description Orientation et gestion de carrière, gestion des ressources humaines, évaluation psychométrique.

BOURIS, WILSON LLP
1701 Woodward Drive, 2nd Floor
Ottawa, ON K2C 0R4

Telephone	613-727-8500
Fax	613-727-8585
E-mail	sholtom@ bouriswilson.com
Website	www.bouriswilson.com
Specialties	Accounting Finance
Level	Mid-Level
Contact	Susan Holtom

Description Bouris Wilson LLP is a chartered accounting firm that also does occasional search work for clients.

BOWEN STAFFING
525 - 7th Avenue SW, Suite 101
Calgary, AB T2P 3V5

Telephone	403-262-1156
Fax	403-269-7107
E-mail	info@bowen staffing.com
Website	www.bowen staffing.com
Specialties	Management Oil & Gas
Level	Mid-Level
Recruiters	Shannon Bowen-Smed Terry Davey CPC
Contact	Shannon Bowen-Smed, CPC, President

Description Bowen Staffing is a single-source human resource provider.

BOWER NG STAFF SYSTEMS INC.
750 West Pender Street, Suite 1205
Vancouver, BC V6C 2T8

Telephone	604-688-8282
E-mail	careers@ staffsystems.ca
Website	www.staffsystems.bc.ca
Founded	1991
Employees	6
Specialties	Accounting Administrative Computing Finance Management Real Estate
Level	Mid-Level Junior
Recruiters	Jamie Bower Pauline Ng
Contact	Pauline Ng

Description Placement specialists in the areas of administration, secretarial, accounting, finance, technology and management.

BOYD PETROSEARCH
800 - 6th Avenue SW, Suite 1200
Calgary, AB T2P 3G3

Telephone	403-233-2455
Fax	403-262-4344
E-mail	info@boydpetro.com
Website	www.boydpetro.com
Specialties	Oil & Gas Geology/Geography
Contact	John P. Boyd, President

Description Boyd PetroSearch is a geophysical consulting company that occasionally does search work for clients.

BOYD-LAIDLER & ASSOCIATES INC.
44 Charles Street West, Suite 2519
Toronto, ON M4Y 1R7

Telephone	416-922-9947
Fax	416-922-3467
E-mail	slaidler@interlog.com
Specialties	Banking Finance Accounting
Recruiters	Jolae Fuller Sandra Laidler Diana Lombardi
Contact	Sandra Laidler

BOYDEN GLOBAL EXECUTIVE SEARCH
601 - 10th Avenue SW, Suite 145
Calgary, AB T2R 0B2

Telephone	403-237-6603
Fax	403-237-5551
E-mail	calgary@boyden.com
Website	www.boyden calgary.com
Founded	1982
Employees	4
Specialties	Computing Engineering Human Resource Marketing Oil & Gas Packaging Sales Telecom
Level	Senior Mid-Level
Fee Basis	Retainer Only
Recruiters	Chantel Maloney Samuel L. Travis Robert S. Travis
Contact	Robert Travis, Managing Partner

Description Boyden, Global Executive Search is a generalist executive search firm with experience over a wide range of industries, functional areas and professions.

BOYDEN GLOBAL EXECUTIVE SEARCH
1250, boul. René-Lévesque O.
Bureau 4110
Montréal, QC H3B 4W8

Telephone	514-935-4601
Fax	514-935-4530
E-mail	montreal@boyden.ca
Website	www.boyden.ca
Founded	1974
Employees	4
Specialties	General Practice

Level	Senior Mid-Level
Min. Salary	$75,000
Fee Basis	Retainer Only
Recruiters	Sonya Bilodeau Paul J. Bourbeau Sophie Sollings
Contact	Paul J. Bourbeau CHRP, President

Description A generalist executive search firm with experience over a wide range of industries, functional areas and professions.

BP FLOATER STAFFING INC.
5940 Macleod Trail SW, Suite 207
Calgary, AB T2H 2G4

Telephone	403-252-1987
Fax	403-252-2847
E-mail	floaters@ floaterstaffing.com
Website	www.floater staffing.com
Founded	1983
Specialties	Administrative Hospitality Trades/Technicians
Level	Mid-Level Junior
Recruiters	John Kaye Anne Laver CPC Barbara Premdas CPC
Contact	Barbara Premdas, CPC

Description BP specializes in office, industrial, technical, professional and hospitality placements.

BRAD LAKE CONSULTING / BLC
5929 Jean d'Arc, Suite 178
Orleans, ON K1C 7K2

Telephone	613-834-7959
Fax	613-834-0721
E-mail	resume@blc.on.ca
Website	www.blc.on.ca
Specialties	Computing
Level	Mid-Level
Contact	Brad Lake

Description BLC is a Canadian computer systems consulting firm providing EDP and information consulting services to the public and private sectors.

BRADFORD BACHINSKI LIMITED
173 Heath Street
Ottawa, ON K1H 5E6

Telephone	613-247-9600
Fax	613-247-7514
E-mail	bradski@sympatico.ca
Founded	1993
Employees	3
Specialties	Management Govt/Nonprofit International Human Resource Multimedia Scientific Telecom

Level	Mid-Level
	Senior
Min. Salary	$50,000
Fee Basis	Retainer Only
Contact	Anne Bachinski

Description Bradford Bachinski Limited is a management consulting firm offering a full range of services, including recruitment.

BRADSON HOME HEALTH CARE INC.
260 Hearst Way, Suite 103
Kanata, ON K2L 3H1

Telephone	613-592-1182
Fax	613-592-7987
E-mail	homehealthcare@
	bradson.com
Founded	1957
Specialties	Health/Medical
Contact	Stacy Brown, Branch Manager

Description Bradson Home Health Care Inc. has been matching people with opportunity for over 40 years.

BRADSON HOME HEALTH CARE INC.
440 Laurier Ave. West, Suite 100
Ottawa, ON K1R 7X6

Telephone	613-782-2244
Fax	613-782-2903
E-mail	homehealthcare@
	bradson.com
Founded	1957
Employees	20
Specialties	Health/Medical
Level	Mid-Level
	Junior
Contact	Allayne Evans

Description Bradson Home Health Care Inc. has been matching people with opportunity for over 40 years.

BRADSON HOME HEALTH CARE INC.
1400 Blair Place, Suite 707
Gloucester, ON K1J 9B8

Telephone	613-748-5308
Fax	613-745-2092
E-mail	homehealthcare@
	bradson.com
Founded	1957
Specialties	Health/Medical
Level	Mid-Level
	Junior
Contact	Cheryl Baldwin

Description Bradson Home Health Care Inc. has been matching people with opportunity for over 40 years.

BRADSON TECHNOLOGY PROFESSIONALS
2300 Yonge Street
Suite 1902, Box 2439
Toronto, ON M4P 1E4

Telephone	416-932-1700
Fax	416-932-2776
E-mail	toronto@sps-it.com
Website	www.sps-it.com
Founded	1992
Employees	30
Specialties	Computing
Level	Senior
	Mid-Level
Contact	Tony Gilchrist, Branch Manager

Description Bradson Technology Professionals (formerly SPS Information Technology) is an international firm specializing in staffing of IT positions in public and private sectors.

BRADSON TECHNOLOGY PROFESSIONALS
1791 Barrington Street, Suite 1130
Halifax, NS B3J 3K9

Telephone	902-422-1701
Fax	902-420-0156
E-mail	halifax@sps-it.com
Website	www.sps-it.com
Founded	1998
Specialties	Computing
Level	Mid-Level
Contact	Sharon Rutland

Description Bradson Technology Professionals (formerly SPS Information Technology) is an international firm specializing in staffing of IT positions in public and private sectors.

BRADSON TECHNOLOGY PROFESSIONALS
83 South King Street, Suite 205
Seattle, WA 98104
USA

Telephone	206-903-6810
Fax	203-903-6821
E-mail	seattle@sps-it.com
Website	www.sps-it.com
Specialties	Computing
	International
Level	Mid-Level

Description Bradson Technology Professionals (formerly Programming Resource Organization) is an international firm specializing in staffing of IT positions in public and private sectors.

BRAINHUNTER.COM
99 Atlantic Avenue, Suite 200
Toronto, ON M6K 3J8

Telephone	416-588-7111
Fax	416-588-9239
E-mail	seekersupport@
	brainhunter.com
Website	www.brainhunter.com
Specialties	Computing
	Engineering
	Finance
	Sales
	Marketing
	Administrative
	Human Resource
Level	Mid-Level
Recruiters	Neil King
	Raj Singh
Contact	Raj Singh, CEO

Description Brainhunter is the first web-based recruitment firm, filling both permanent and contract positions across all job disciplines.

BRAINHUNTER.COM
168 Dalhousie Street
Ottawa, ON K1N 7C4

Telephone	613-562-2323
Fax	613-562-1237
E-mail	seekersupport@
	brainhunter.com
Website	www.brainhunter.com
Specialties	Computing
	Engineering
	Finance
	Sales
	Marketing
	Administrative
	Human Resource
Level	Mid-Level

Description Brainhunter is the first web-based recruitment firm, filling both permanent and contract positions across all job disciplines.

BRANT & ASSOCIATES
370 Elm Street
Winnipeg, MB R3M 3P3

Telephone	204-488-1942
Fax	204-487-0469
E-mail	brant@
	brantconsulting.com
Website	www.brant
	consulting.com
Founded	1992
Employees	5
Specialties	Computing
	Management
	Hospitality
	Sales
	Administrative
	Human Resource
	Oil & Gas
Level	Mid-Level
	Senior
Recruiters	Suzanne Mancer
	Jim Swackhamer
Contact	Jim Swackhamer, President

Description Brant & Associates provides executive and general recruitment, including placements of skilled foreign information technology professionals.

BRASSARD & ASSOCIÉS RECHERCHE DE CADRES INC.
1155, boul. René-Lévesque O
Bureau 3430
Montréal, QC H3B 2K4

Telephone	514-875-9123
Fax	514-875-4205

E-mail   sberube@brassard.ca
Website   www.brassard.ca

Founded   1981
Employees   4

Specialties   General Practice

Level   Mid-Level
                Senior

Min. Salary $70,000
Fee Basis   Retainer Only

Contact   Sylvie Bérubé,
                Recherchiste

Description Brassard & Associés is a small boutique operation offering its clients executive search services.

BRAUN-VALLEY ASSOCIATES LTD.
373 Vidal Street South
Suite D2, PO Box 2168
Sarnia, ON N7T 7L7

Telephone   519-336-4590
Fax   519-336-8164
E-mail   mbraun@mnsi.net

Founded   1968
Employees   58

Specialties   Automotive
                Design
                Human Resource
                Logistics
                Pharmaceutical
                Oil & Gas
                Scientific
                Engineering
                Computing

Level   Mid-Level

Min. Salary $40,000
Fee Basis   Always contingent

Recruiters   Mark Braun
                Kathy Furlotte
                Shelley Weir

Contact   Mark Braun,
                Contracts Manager

Description Braun-Valley provides technical staffing on an "as needed" basis, and permanent or contract personnel for specific requirements.

BRAY, LAROUCHE ET ASSOCIÉS INC.
2000, rue Peel, Bureau 5050
Montréal, QC H3A 2W5

Téléphone   514-845-2114
Télécopieur   514-845-3808
Courriel   bray.larouche.ass@
                videotron.net

Fondée   1991
Employés   11

Spécialités   Comptabilité
                Administratif
                Informatique
                Ingénierie
                Finance
                Ressources humaines
                Assurance
                Gestion
                Marketing
                Exploitation
                Achat
                Ventes

Échelon   Intermédiaire
                Débutant

Contact   Sylvie Larouche

Description Une équipe dynamique et professionelle prête à vous offrir un personnel méthodiquement sélectionné et à s'assurer d'un suivi attentif de son service.

BRENDAN WOOD INTERNATIONAL
17 Prince Arthur Avenue
Toronto, ON M5R 1B2

Telephone   416-924-8110
Fax   416-924-2293
E-mail   mail@brendan
                wood.com
Website   www.brendan
                wood.com

Specialties   Management
                Banking
                Finance

Level   Senior

Fee Basis   Retainer Only

Contact   Nora Turkevics

Description BWI is a management consulting firm offering research and other services to the finance industry, including occasional senior-level recruitment for clients.

BRETHET, BARNUM & ASSOCIATES INC.
703 Evans Avenue, Suite 300
Toronto, ON M9C 5E9

Telephone   416-621-4900
Fax   416-621-9818
E-mail   brethet@wwonline.com

Founded   1980
Employees   3

Specialties   Biotech/Biology
                Health/Medical
                Pharmaceutical
                Sales
                Marketing
                Management

Level   Senior
                Mid-Level

Min. Salary $40,000
Fee Basis   Sometimes contingent

Recruiters   Anne Brethet
                Phyllis Chrzan
                Robert A. (Bob) Shiley

Contact   Robert A. (Bob) Shiley
                CPC, Associate

Description Brethet, Barnum specializes in pharmaceutical, medical, diagnostic and biotechnology sales and marketing placements.

BRIAN HETHERINGTON & ASSOCIATES
10130 - 103 Street, Suite 1410
Edmonton, AB T5J 3N9

Telephone   780-428-6459
Fax   780-420-1230
E-mail   bhapr@bhapr.com
Website   www.bhapr.com

Specialties   Education

Contact   Brian Hetherington,
                President

Description Brian Hetherington & Associates is a full service public relations and government affairs firm that occasionally does recruitment for clients.

BRIDGE INFORMATION TECHNOLOGY INC.
916 West Broadway, Suite 369
Vancouver, BC V5Z 1K7

Telephone   604-739-4383
Fax   604-736-7453
E-mail   info@bridgerecruit.com
Website   www.bridgerecruit.com

Specialties   Computing
                Engineering
                Telecom

Recruiters   Ben Lamprecht
                Louisa van Niekerk

Contact   Ben Lamprecht, Senior
                Partner

Description Bridge Information Technology Inc. specializes in placing people with software, engineering and technical communications experience for contract or permanent positions in BC, Canada and the USA.

BRIDGEMOUNT SOLUTIONS INC.
21 Antares Drive, Unit 113
Ottawa, ON K2E 7T8

Telephone   613-224-8677
E-mail   gary@bridgemount.
                com
Website   www.bridgemount.com

Specialties   Computing

Level   Mid-Level

Description Bridgemount Solutions Inc. is a Canadian-based IT staffing company.

BRIDGES CONSULTING
200 First Avenue, Suite 204
Ottawa, ON K1S 2G6

Telephone   613-231-3804
Fax   613-231-6018
E-mail   consulting@
                bridgescanada.com

Specialties   Govt/Nonprofit
                Public Relations

Level   Mid-Level

Contact   David Kardish, Senior
                Partner

Description Bridges Consulting is an Ottawa-based communications and human resources consultancy.

BROCK PLACEMENT GROUP INC.
1370 Don Mills Road, Suite 300
Toronto, ON M3B 3N7

Telephone   416-642-3992
Fax   416-642-3982
E-mail   resume@
                brockplacement.com
Website   www.brockplacement.
                com

Employees   4

Specialties	Sales
	Marketing
	Administrative
	Management
	Health/Medical
	Operations
	Pharmaceutical
Level	Senior
	Mid-Level
Fee Basis	Sometimes contingent
Recruiters	Julie Andrews
	Eric Fobert
	Shelley Rosner
	Jeff Steele
Contact	Jeff Steele

Description Brock is a Canadian-owned firm with 10 years of recruitment and staffing experience. Specialties include sales, marketing, management, engineering and operations.

BROWNLOW & ASSOCIATES
259 Wilson Street East
Ancaster, ON L9G 2B8

Telephone	905-648-0404
Fax	905-648-0403
E-mail	samantha@
	brownlowcas.com
Specialties	Accounting
	Finance
Level	Junior
	Mid-Level
Contact	Samantha Stewart

BRUCE COWAN & ASSOCIATES
4214 Dundas Street West, Suite 202
Toronto, ON M8X 1Y6

Telephone	416-207-0115
Fax	416-207-0789
E-mail	brucowan@idirect.com
Founded	1998
Employees	2
Specialties	Sales
	Marketing
	Telecom
	Computing
	Management
Level	Senior
	Mid-Level
Min. Salary	$60,000
Fee Basis	Sometimes contingent
Recruiters	Bruce Cowan
	Marge Cowan
Contact	Bruce Cowan, President

Description Bruce Cowan & Associates specializes in search and placement in the Canadian computer, data-telecom and software vendor industry.

BRUCE HILL & ASSOCIATES / INTERNATIONAL EDUCATION CONSULTANTS INC.
298 Lonsdale Road
Toronto, ON M4V 1X2

Fax	416-483-7085
E-mail	bwhill@bconnex.net
Specialties	Education
	International

BRUCE R. DUNCAN & ASSOCIATES LTD.
8 King Street East, Suite 709
Toronto, ON M5C 1B5

Telephone	416-361-1451
Fax	416-361-1225
E-mail	staff@bruceduncan.com
Website	www.bruceduncan.com
Specialties	Accounting
	Finance
	Marketing
	Administrative
Level	Mid-Level
Recruiters	Laura Da Silva
	Jim Gordon
	Joan Perry
	Tom Rainey
	Mira Sharma
Contact	Mira Sharma

Description Over 30 years of successful search and placement expertise for accounting, finance and brokerage clients.

BRUCE WARD PARTNERS INC.
150 King Street West
Suite 2414, Sun Life Centre
Toronto, ON M5H 1J9

Telephone	416-979-0663
Fax	416-979-7743
E-mail	brwpi@aol.com
Specialties	Management
	Education
	Finance
	Law
	General Practice
	Aerospace
	Automotive
	Human Resource
	Mining
	Retail
	Operations
Level	Senior
Min. Salary	$80,000
Fee Basis	Retainer Only
Contact	Bruce Ward

Description Bruce Ward Partners Inc. is a boutique, retainer-based search firm offering high-quality individualized service.

BRYAN JASON & ASSOCIATES INC.
111 Richmond St. West, Suite 1200
Toronto, ON M5H 2G4

Telephone	416-867-9295
Fax	416-867-3067
E-mail	rbryan@bryan-jason.ca
Website	www.bryan-jason.ca
Founded	1971
Employees	10
Specialties	Accounting
	Finance
	Real Estate
	Bilingual
	Human Resource
	Administrative
Level	Senior
	Mid-Level
Fee Basis	Always contingent
Recruiters	Rickie Bryan
	Bonnie Jason
	Chantal Lebel
Contact	Rickie Bryan

Description Bryan Jason & Associates Inc. is a boutique agency specializing in real estate, accounting / finance and bilingual positions.

BTSN, INC.
PO Box 909
St. George, ON N0E 1N0

Telephone	519-448-4035
Fax	519-448-3103
E-mail	search@btsn.com
Website	www.btsn.com
Specialties	Biotech/Biology
	Telecom
	Computing
	Engineering
Level	Mid-Level
	Senior
Contact	Leslie Stallard, CEO

Description Btsn, inc. specializes in placing experienced people in the biotechnology, telecommunications, semiconductor and networks sectors. Also has office in California.

BUCKLEY SEARCH INC.
100 Adelaide Street West, Suite 410
Toronto, ON M5H 1S3

Telephone	416-865-0695
Fax	416-865-9747
E-mail	kevin@buckleysearch.com
Website	www.buckleysearch.com
Founded	1990
Specialties	Logistics
	Management
	Transport
Level	Senior
	Mid-Level
Fee Basis	Sometimes contingent
Recruiters	Kevin Buckley CPC
	Anna Buckley BA
Contact	Kevin Buckley CPC, President

Description Buckley specializes in recruitment in the areas of transportation, customs and logistics.

BUREAU DE PLACEMENT D'ANJOU
3235 rue Granby
Montréal, QC H1N 2Z7

Telephone	514-254-9925
Fax	514-254-1759
Specialties	Administrative
	Trades/Technicians
Level	Mid-Level
	Junior
Contact	Denise Marino

BURKE GROUP, THE
14 Hughson Street South
Hamilton, ON L8N 4H3

Fax	905-317-4861
E-mail	tbg@theburke group.com
Website	www.theburke group.com
Founded	1979
Employees	15
Specialties	Management Engineering Consulting Administrative Finance Human Resource
Level	Mid-Level Senior
Fee Basis	Sometimes contingent
Contact	Wendy Boyea

Description The Burke Group offers executive to contract recruitment services, along with outsourcing, consulting and outplacement services.

BURKE GROUP, THE
63 Church Street, Suite 204
St. Catharines, ON L2R 3C4

Telephone	905-641-3070
Fax	905-641-0478
E-mail	roser@theburke group.com
Website	www.theburke group.com
Founded	1979
Employees	15
Specialties	Management Engineering Consulting Administrative Finance Human Resource
Level	Mid-Level Senior
Fee Basis	Sometimes contingent
Recruiters	Anne Charette Sandra Nugent-Rooney Rose Raso
Contact	Rose Raso

Description Burke Group is a leading provider of staffing and human resources consulting services throughout Southern Ontario.

BUSINESS & PROFESSIONAL APPOINTMENTS
163 / 164 London Wall
Suite 123 / 124, Salisbury House
London, EC2M 5ST
UNITED KINGDOM

Telephone	44-207-628-1464
Fax	44-207-628-2577
E-mail	enquiries@ bpappointments.co.uk
Website	www.bpappoint ments.co.uk
Specialties	Accounting Finance International

Contact	A.B. Osman

Description Business & Professional Appointments specializes in the recruitment of accountancy and taxation personnel for firms in the UK and overseas.

BUSINESS RESCUE ASSOCIATES LTD.
262 Woodroffe Avenue
PO Box 5432, Station F
Ottawa, ON K2A 3V4

Telephone	613-725-1579
Fax	613-725-9031
E-mail	brescue@cmw.ca
Specialties	Administrative
Level	Junior Mid-Level
Contact	Mary Craddock, President

Description Business Rescue Associates provides a range of administrative staffing services.

C & E CONN & ASSOCIATES LTD.
100 City Centre Drive
PO Box 2154, Square One
Mississauga, ON L5B 3C7

Telephone	905-949-2569
Fax	905-276-8368
E-mail	econn@ceconn.com
Website	www.ceconn.com
Founded	1994
Employees	2
Specialties	General Practice
Level	Mid-Level Senior
Min. Salary	$40,000
Fee Basis	Always contingent
Recruiters	Erika Conn Charles Conn
Contact	Erika Conn

Description C & E Conn & Associates recruits mid- to executive-level jobs for high and low tech assignments across Canada.

C.G. THOMSON & COMPANY
235 Yorkland Blvd., Suite 300
Toronto, ON M2J 4Y8

Telephone	416-495-9327
Fax	416-495-7031
E-mail	cgt@home.com
Founded	1973
Specialties	Accounting Engineering Health/Medical Human Resource Marketing Operations Sales
Level	Senior Mid-Level
Min. Salary	$30,000
Recruiters	Ronald Blair Tony Mendes
Contact	Ronald Blair

C.J. RICHARDSON RESOURCES
2984 Folkway Drive, Streetsville
Mississauga, ON L5L 1Z6

Telephone	905-828-4128
Specialties	General Practice
Contact	Jill Richardson

C.J. STAFFORD & ASSOCIATES
2323 Yonge Street, Suite 501
Toronto, ON M4P 2C9

Telephone	416-484-1960
Fax	416-484-0626
E-mail	cjstaff@cjstafford.com
Website	www.cjstafford.com
Founded	1981
Employees	6
Specialties	Mining Construction Architecture Engineering Metals Pharmaceutical
Level	Mid-Level Senior
Fee Basis	Sometimes contingent
Recruiters	Vince Keenan Chris J. Stafford Tara Wooller
Contact	Chris J. Stafford, President

Description C.J. Stafford & Associates specializes in recruiting engineering and technical management for building and construction, heavy industrial, engineering and mining sectors.

C.N. TAYLOR CONSULTING INC.
1160 Bedford Highway
Suite 303, Bayswater Place
Bedford, NS B4A 1C1

Telephone	902-461-1616
Fax	902-435-6300
E-mail	globalsearch@ cntaylor.com
Website	www.cntaylor.com
Founded	1975
Specialties	Accounting Computing Management Engineering Sales Finance Health/Medical Oil & Gas Pulp & Paper Telecom
Level	Mid-Level Senior
Min. Salary	$50,000
Fee Basis	Sometimes contingent
Recruiters	Tara Shaw Clifford N. Taylor Heather Yaschuk
Contact	Clifford N. Taylor, President

Description C.N. Taylor Consulting Inc. is an executive and technical search firm.

C. PRICE & ASSOCIATES
181 University Avenue, Suite 401
Toronto, ON M5H 3M7

Telephone	416-362-1892
Fax	416-362-8084
E-mail	heather@cprice.on.ca

Employees 7

Specialties	Human Resource
	Accounting
	Banking
	Finance
Level	Senior
	Mid-Level
Contact	Charlotte Price, President

C. SCOTT & ASSOCIATES INC.
70 York Street, Suite 1510
Toronto, ON M5J 1S9

Telephone	416-214-9822
Fax	416-214-9820
E-mail	info@cscottinc.com
Website	www.cscottinc.com

Founded 1993
Employees 1

Specialties	Finance
	Insurance
	Computing
	Banking
Level	Mid-Level
Min. Salary	$40,000
Fee Basis	Always contingent
Contact	Christina Scott, President

Description C. Scott & Associates Inc. specializes in the recruitment, selection, and placement of information technology professionals for the financial services sector.

C. SNOW & ASSOCIATES
1 Yonge Street, Suite 1801
Toronto, ON M5E 1W7

Telephone	416-465-8735
Fax	416-369-0515
E-mail	c.snow@netcom.ca

Founded 1992

Specialties	Finance
	Accounting
	Marketing
	Telecom
Level	Senior
	Mid-Level
Fee Basis	Always contingent
Contact	Christine Snow

Description C. Snow & Associates specializes in placing accountants/finance, marketing and telecom candidates. CPC designate, member of HRPAO and NPA (H.D. Michigan).

C. STEVENSON CONSULTING INC.
PO Box 1009
Pointe-Claire, QC H9S 4H9

E-mail	stevenson@ qc.aibn.com

Specialties Human Resource

Level	Mid-Level
Contact	C. Stevenson, Managing Director

C.W. CLASEN RECRUITING SERVICES
3030 Lincoln Avenue, Suite 211
Coquitlam, BC V3B 6B4

Telephone	604-942-1314
Fax	604-464-4122
E-mail	colinc@ clasenrecruiting.com

Founded 1985

Specialties	Forestry
	Management
	Trades/Technicians
	Quality Control
	Human Resource
	Engineering
	Pulp & Paper
Level	Senior
	Mid-Level
Fee Basis	Always contingent
Contact	Colin Clasen

Description C.W. Clasen Recruiting Services specializes in placements at all levels in the forestry industry, including sawmills, plywood / composite board, pulp and paper.

C. WOLFE & ASSOCIATES
36 Eglinton Avenue W., Suite 408
Toronto, ON M4R 1A1

Telephone	416-484-4317
Fax	416-484-4318

Founded 1976

Specialties	Sales
	Marketing
	Engineering
	Bilingual
	Automotive
	Telecom
	Printing
Level	Mid-Level
Contact	Claus Wolfe

CADILLAC CAREER CENTRE INC.
335 Bay Street, Suite 503
Toronto, ON M5H 2R3

Telephone	416-363-0101

Founded 1972

Specialties	Insurance
	Management
	Accounting
	Banking
	Computing
	Bilingual
	Administrative
Level	Mid-Level
	Junior
Contact	Todd Wilson

Description Cadillac Career Centre Inc. specializes in administrative and management-level recruiting, particularly in insurance and finance.

CADMAN CONSULTING GROUP INC.
666 Burrard Street
Suite 500, Park Place
Vancouver, BC V6C 3J8

Telephone	604-689-4345
Fax	604-689-4348
E-mail	info@cadman.ca
Website	www.cadman.ca

Founded 1993

Specialties	Engineering
	Computing
	Human Resource
Level	Senior
	Mid-Level
Min. Salary	$40,000
Fee Basis	Retainer Only
Contact	Gary Cadman

Description Cadman Consulting Group is a leading provider of IT consultants in the Lower Mainland.

CALDWELL INTERNATIONALE, LA SOCIETE
1840 Sherbrooke Street West
Montréal, QC H3H 1E4

Téléphone	514-935-6969
Télécopieur	514-935-7402
Courriel	montreal@caldwell.ca
Site Internet	www.caldwell partners.com

Fondée 1970
Employés 9

Spécialités	Généralistes
	Gestion
	Marketing
	Exploitation
Échelon	Direction
	Intermédiaire
Salaire min.	80 000 $
Frais	Honoraire seulement
Contact	Guy Hébert

Description Firme de recrutement de cadres supérieurs et de membres de conseil d'administration.

CALDWELL PARTNERS, THE
999 West Hastings Street, Suite 750
Vancouver, BC V6C 2W2

Telephone	604-669-3550
Fax	604-669-5095
E-mail	vancouver@caldwell.ca
Website	www.caldwell partners.com

Founded 1970
Employees 10

Specialties	General Practice
	Management
	Finance
	Govt/Nonprofit
	Forestry
	Human Resource
	Mining
	Pulp & Paper
Level	Senior
Min. Salary	$80,000
Contact	Kevin McBurney

Description Caldwell Partners' search practice includes executive search, board search, team-building and interim (contract) executive placements.

CALDWELL PARTNERS, THE
400 - 3rd Avenue SW, Suite 3450
Calgary, AB T2P 4H2

Telephone	403-265-8780
Fax	403-263-6508
E-mail	calgary@caldwell.ca
Website	www.caldwell.ca
Founded	1970
Employees	6
Specialties	Management Marketing Human Resource International Law Oil & Gas Public Relations
Level	Mid-Level Senior
Min. Salary	$75,000
Contact	Tim Hamilton

Description Caldwell Partners' search practice includes executive search, board search, team-building and interim (contract) executive placements.

CALDWELL PARTNERS, THE
64 Prince Arthur Avenue
Toronto, ON M5R 1B4

Telephone	416-920-7702
Fax	416-922-8646
E-mail	resumes@caldwell.ca
Website	www.caldwell.ca
Founded	1970
Employees	58
Specialties	Management
Level	Senior
Min. Salary	$80,000
Fee Basis	Retainer Only
Contact	Heather Scott

Description Caldwell Partners' search practice includes executive search, board search, team-building and interim (contract) executive placements.

CALDWELL PARTNERS, THE
5657 Spring Garden Road
Suite 500, Park Lane Box 247
Halifax, NS B3J 3R4

Telephone	902-429-5909
Fax	902-429-5606
E-mail	halifax@caldwell.ca
Website	www.caldwell.ca
Founded	1998
Specialties	General Practice
Level	Senior
Fee Basis	Retainer Only
Contact	Jeff Sommerville

Description Caldwell's search practice includes executive search, board search, team-building and interim (contract) executive placements.

CALIAN TECHNOLOGY SERVICES LTD.
1 City Centre Drive, 7th Floor
Mississauga, ON L5B 1M2

Telephone	905-848-2818
Fax	905-848-4944
E-mail	info@calian.com
Website	www.calian.com
Specialties	Computing Engineering Telecom Administrative
Level	Mid-Level Junior
Contact	Robert Suwary, Director Greater Toronto Area, Staffing Services

Description Calian Technology Services is an IT consulting company that also offers recruitment and placement services to clients.

CALIAN TECHNOLOGY SERVICES LTD.
80 Hines Road
Ottawa, ON K2K 2T8

Telephone	613-599-8600
Fax	613-599-0956
E-mail	info@calian.ca
Website	www.calian.ca
Specialties	Computing Engineering Telecom Administrative
Level	Mid-Level Junior

Description Calian Technology Services is an IT consulting company that also offers recruitment and placement services to clients.

CALIAN TECHNOLOGY SERVICES LTD.
2 Beaverbrook Road, Calian Centre
Kanata, ON K2K 1L1

Telephone	613-599-8600
Fax	613-599-8842
E-mail	careers@calian.com
Website	www.calian.com
Specialties	Computing Engineering Telecom Administrative
Level	Mid-Level Junior
Recruiters	Carol Chamerland Keeley Durocher
Contact	Keeley Durocher, Technical Recruiter

Description Calian Technology Services is an IT consulting company that also offers recruitment and placement services to clients.

CALIAN TECHNOLOGY SERVICES LTD.
130 Albert Street
Ottawa, ON K1P 5G4

Telephone	613-238-2600
Fax	613-238-3831
E-mail	info@calian.com
Website	www.calian.com
Specialties	Computing

Description Calian Technology Services is an IT consulting company that also offers recruitment and placement services to clients.

CALVIN PARTNERS INTERNATIONAL
22 College Street, Suite 488
Toronto, ON M5G 1K2

Telephone	416-925-9566
Fax	416-968-0232
Founded	1979
Employees	15
Specialties	Banking Finance
Level	Senior Mid-Level
Min. Salary	$65,000
Fee Basis	Sometimes contingent
Contact	Ron Simpson

CAMBRIDGE MANAGEMENT PLANNING INC.
2323 Yonge Street, Suite 203
Toronto, ON M4P 2C9

Telephone	416-484-8408
Fax	416-484-0151
E-mail	admin@cambridge mgmt.com
Website	www.cambridge mgmt.com
Founded	1976
Employees	12
Specialties	Operations Sales Accounting
Level	Senior Mid-Level
Min. Salary	$80,000
Fee Basis	Retainer Only
Recruiters	Timothy Caley Graham Carver Debra Clinton David W. Howes E.J. May Igor Poliakov C.J. (Chris) Poole
Contact	Graham Carver, President

Description Cambridge Management Planning is an established executive search firm, specializing in senior management recruitment requirements of manufacturing businesses.

CAMERON CONSULTING GROUP
38 Alexandra Crescent
Brampton, ON L6T 1N3

Telephone	905-799-6080
Fax	905-792-1764
E-mail	dsinnett99@home.com
Founded	1998
Employees	2

Specialties	Accounting
	Bilingual
	Finance
	Marketing
	Pharmaceutical
	Sales
	Telecom
	Computing
Level	Senior
	Mid-Level
Min. Salary	$35,000
Fee Basis	Sometimes contingent
Recruiters	Jack Cameron
	Diane Sinnett
Contact	Diane Sinnett

Description Cameron Consulting Group recruits professionals in the fields of finance, accounting, IT, and sales & marketing. Works on both retainer and contingency assignments.

CAMERON MANAGEMENT SERVICES GROUP / CMSG
10020 - 101A Avenue, Suite 520
Edmonton, AB T5J 3G2

Telephone	780-414-5448
Fax	780-414-5451
E-mail	kiersten@
	telusplanet.net
Website	www.cmsg.ca
Founded	1983
Employees	20
Specialties	Accounting
	Human Resource
	Law
Level	Senior
	Mid-Level
Recruiters	Janice Batiuk
	Kiersten McDonald
Contact	Kiersten McDonald

Description CMSG provides a variety of consulting and other services to professional firms (such as law and accounting), including recruitment.

CAMERON MANAGEMENT SERVICES GROUP / CMSG
633 - 6th Avenue SW, Suite 1200
Calgary, AB T2P 2Y5

Telephone	403-290-0878
Fax	403-269-4926
E-mail	bnimmo@cmsg.ca
Website	www.cmsg.ca
Founded	1983
Employees	20
Specialties	Accounting
	Human Resource
	Law
Level	Senior
	Mid-Level
Recruiters	Lyla Brown
	H. Allen Cameron
	Daunine G. Fraser
	John Hamilton
	Sharon Harris
	Stan J. Martin
	Bryce K. Nimmo
	Carol Sparks

Contact	H. Allen Cameron,
	CMC, CMA

Description CMSG provides a variety of consulting and other services to professional firms (such as law and accounting), including recruitment.

CAMPA & ASSOCIATES
1 Yonge Street, Suite 2203
Toronto, ON M5E 1E5

Telephone	416-407-7777
Fax	416-214-5764
E-mail	carl@campasearch.com
Employees	3
Specialties	Engineering
	Management
	Operations
	Design
	Automotive
	Metals
Level	Mid-Level
	Senior
Min. Salary	$75,000
Fee Basis	Retainer Only
Recruiters	Carl Campa
	Kim Dowhanick
Contact	Carl Campa

Description CAMPA & Associates have provided search services for industrial technology leaders for over 20 years. The firm recruits for all functions in high tech engineered products manufacturing.

CAMPBELL CLARK INC.
4275 Village Centre Court
Suite 100
Mississauga, ON L4Z 1V3

Telephone	905-897-9666
Fax	905-897-9306
E-mail	info@campbell
	clark.com
Website	www.campbell
	clark.com
Specialties	Sales
	Marketing
	Operations
	Human Resource
Level	Senior
	Mid-Level

Description Campbell Clark Inc. specializes in recruiting executives for sales and marketing, operations and human resource positions.

CAMPBELL EDGAR INC.
4940 No. 3 Road, Suite 212
Richmond, BC V6X 3A5

Telephone	604-273-8515
Fax	604-278-3005
E-mail	info@retailcareers.com
Website	www.retailcareers.com
Founded	1993
Employees	4
Specialties	Retail
	Management
	Sales
	Apparel
	Marketing

	Human Resource
	Logistics
Level	Senior
	Mid-Level
Min. Salary	$25,000
Fee Basis	Always contingent
Contact	Elaine Hay, President

Description Campbell Edgar Inc. is one of the largest recruitment firms in Canada dedicated to the retail industry.

CAMPBELL EDGAR INC.
4388 - 49 Street
Delta, BC V4K 2S7

Telephone	604-946-8535
Fax	604-946-2384
E-mail	info@retailcareers.com
Website	www.retailcareers.com
Founded	1993
Employees	3
Specialties	Retail
	Management
	Sales
	Apparel
	Marketing
	Human Resource
	Logistics
Level	Senior
	Mid-Level
Min. Salary	$25,000
Fee Basis	Always contingent
Recruiters	Ashley Anderson
	Elaine Hay
	Michael Reeves
	Rosalie Wald
Contact	Elaine Hay

Description Campbell Edgar Inc. is one of the largest recruitment firms in Canada dedicated to the retail industry.

CAMPBELL MORDEN INC.
480 University Avenue, Suite 1010
Toronto, ON M5G 1V2

Telephone	416-598-4020
Fax	416-598-3963
E-mail	cm@campbell
	morden.com
Website	www.mordendesigns.
	com/campbellmorden
Founded	1984
Employees	6
Specialties	Finance
	Management
	Operations
	Engineering
	Sales
	Marketing
	Insurance
	Health/Medical
Level	Mid-Level
	Senior
Recruiters	Tanya Bassil
	Colin Campbell
	Peggy De Oliveira
	Peter Kennedy
	John Morden
Contact	Colin Campbell

Description Specialists in recruiting senior-level positions in Finance, General Management, Manufacturing, Engineering, Sales & Marketing, Insurance and Health Care.

CAN-TECH SERVICES
45 Baldwin Street, PO Box 629
Brooklin, ON L0B 1C0

Telephone	905-655-8441
Fax	905-655-8443
E-mail	pgeissler@cantechservices.com
Website	www.cantechservices.com
Founded	1974
Specialties	Engineering
	Aerospace
	Automotive
	Logistics
	Trades/Technicians
	Transport
	Computing
Level	Mid-Level
Recruiters	Valerie Davis
	Jorg Geissler
	Paul Geissler
Contact	Paul Geissler

Description Can-Tech Services supplies personnel to the aeronautical and related technical industries, including automotive, marine, computer and manufacturing.

CAN-TECH SERVICES
5929 Transcanada Highway
Suite 120
Saint-Laurent, QC H4T 1Z6

Telephone	514-744-2121
Fax	514-744-1616
E-mail	gmnixon@cantechservices.com
Website	www.cantechservices.com
Specialties	Aerospace
	Automotive
	Computing
	Engineering
	Operations
	Logistics
	Trades/Technicians
Level	Mid-Level
Contact	Geoff Nixon, Manager

Description Can-Tech Services supplies personnel to the aeronautical and related technical industries, including automotive, marine, computer and manufacturing.

CANADAIT VENTURES INC.
13065 - 19th Avenue
Surrey, BC V4A 7S5

Telephone	604-538-6015
E-mail	admin@canadait.com
Website	www.canadait.com
Founded	1996
Specialties	Computing
	Multimedia
Level	Mid-Level

Contact   Peter Standeven, President

Description CanadaIT Ventures is an online service matching qualified candidates in the IT and Internet sectors with over 1,700 companies.

CANADIAN CAREER PARTNERS
112 - 4th Avenue SW, Suite 800
Calgary, AB T2P 0H3

Telephone	403-290-0466
Fax	403-294-7240
E-mail	opportunities@career-partners.com
Website	www.career-partners.com
Founded	1996
Employees	43
Specialties	General Practice
	Hospitality
	Oil & Gas
Level	Mid-Level
Fee Basis	Retainer Only
Recruiters	Gary Agnew
	Jane Bathurst
	Irene Berglund
	Myles Bollman
	Ed Bownes
	Mary K. Bull
	Ed Burdon
	Victoria Calvert
	Debbie Chisholm
	Barbara Dodd-Jones
	Everett Gratix
	Bruce Green
	Wilf Heibert
	Sherry-Lynn Irving
	Christine Jansen
	Debra Johnstone
	Neal Jones
	John Knight
	Sherry Knight
	Carol Laurich
	Elaine Macfarlane
	Clive MacRaild
	Adonica Marchand
	Kelly Maurer
	Cam McRae
	Crystal Munroe
	Jan Nighswander
	Drina Nixon
	Derek Norman
	Kathleen O'Hare
	Pamela Rowe
	Andrea Scheelar
	Meagan Schroeder
	Jerry Stilson
	Debra Strong
	Leigh Tracy
	Murray Vines
	Bruce Wade
Contact	Debra Johnstone

Description CCP is part of Career Partners International, the world's largest alliance of independently-owned, international providers of human resources and career and management consulting services.

CANADIAN CAREER PARTNERS / CBD NETWORK INC.
2033 Gordon Drive, Suite 201
Kelowna, BC V1Y 3J2

Telephone	250-717-1821
Fax	250-717-3686
E-mail	opportunities@career-partners.com
Website	www.career-partners.com
Specialties	General Practice

Description Canadian Career Partners provides fully-integrated HR services, including career transition, career management and coaching, executive search / recruitment and executive coaching.

CANADIAN EXECUTIVE CONSULTANTS INC.
1111 Finch Ave. West, Suite 400
Toronto, ON M3J 2E5

Telephone	416-665-7577
Fax	416-665-8509
E-mail	info@cdnexec.com
Website	www.cdnexec.com
Founded	1983
Employees	20
Specialties	Accounting
	Administrative
	Computing
	Finance
	Health/Medical
	Human Resource
	Sales
Level	Senior
	Mid-Level
Fee Basis	Sometimes contingent
Recruiters	Jay Averbach
	Marion Baran
	Lisa Barkin
	Lisa Cohen
	Lyn Gill
	Carol Haberman
	Jay Herberman
	Eric King
	Caroline Klians
	Linda Madden
	Fiona Marshall
	Jennifer Mitchell
	Caroline Nielsen
	Amanda Rigby
	Lee Shemuel
	Toni Spadone
Contact	Jay Herberman, President

Description Canadian Executive Consultants handles mergers and acquisitions, executive search, executive outplacement, organizational development, large administrative division handling support staff, telestaffing and call centre management.

CANADIAN EXECUTIVE RECRUITMENT
2400 Dundas Street West
Unit 6, Suite 243
Mississauga, ON L5K 2R8

Telephone	905-569-1906
Fax	905-569-1449
E-mail	careers@cdnexec.net
Website	www.cdnexec.net
Founded	1993
Employees	2

Specialties	Engineering
	Operations
	Management
	Logistics
	Plastics
	Automotive
Level	Mid-Level
	Senior
Min. Salary	$40,000
Fee Basis	Sometimes contingent
Recruiters	Brian J. Connors
	L.A. Young
Contact	Brian J. Connors,
	Consultant

Description Canadian Executive Recruitment recruit engineering, operations, management and logistics positions in the chemical, consumer goods, electronics, plastics, automotive and heavy industries.

CANADIAN FINDINGS LTD.
439 Wellington St. W., Studio 222
Toronto, ON M5V 1E7

Telephone	416-205-9909
Fax	416-977-6645
E-mail	info@canadian findings.com
Website	www.canadian findings.com
Founded	1986
Employees	1810
Specialties	Bilingual
	Finance
	Packaging
	Plastics
	Purchasing
	Transport
Level	Senior
	Mid-Level
Fee Basis	Sometimes contingent
Recruiters	Ostyne Alambo
	Huw Davies
	Marcela de la Torre
	Ed Gornak
	Alex Grigonis
	Carl Hamilton
	Daniel King
	Daphne Kotsopoulos
	Lola Lipsey
	Jack Milczynski
	Desh Minwalla
	Shannon Pountney
	Jon Saulnier
	Jeff Tabone
	Harold Tabone
	Patricia Tabone
	William Wallace
	Rishma Wallani
Contact	Harold Tabone,
	Consultant

Description Canadian Findings is a progressive personnel search agency serving North American clients.

CANADIAN LOGISTICS RECRUITERS
5014 New Street, Suite 435
Burlington, ON L7L 6E8

E-mail	canlog87a@home.com
Specialties	Transport
	Logistics

Level	Mid-Level
	Junior

CANADIAN MEDICAL PLACEMENT SERVICE
148 York Street
London, ON N6A 1A9

Telephone	519-672-0777
Fax	519-672-0830
E-mail	info@cmps.ca
Website	www.cmps.ca
Specialties	Health/Medical
Level	Mid-Level
	Senior
Fee Basis	Sometimes contingent
Contact	Brian J. Tibbet, MBA,
	CHE, President

Description Canadian Medical Placement Service is a healthcare consulting firm specializing in physician recruitment.

CANADIAN NURSE & PHYSICIAN RECRUITERS
48 St. Francis Street North
Kitchener, ON N2H 5B5

Telephone	519-585-0722
Fax	519-585-0394
E-mail	information@ canadian-nurse- recruiter.com
Website	www.canadian-nurse- recruiter.com
Specialties	Health/Medical
Level	Mid-Level
	Senior
Contact	Lisa Filipowitsch,
	Director of Healthcare
	Recruitment

Description Canadian Nurse & Physician Recruiters specializes in the placement of Canadian nurses and physicians in US hospitals.

CANADIAN PATHFINDER CONSULTING SERVICES INC.
29 Gervais Drive, Suite 200
Toronto, ON M3C 1Y9

Telephone	416-645-3016
Fax	416-385-3839
E-mail	contact@pathfinder canada.com
Website	www.pathfinder canada.ca
Founded	2000
Specialties	General Practice
Level	Mid-Level
	Junior
Contact	Robert Vickers

Description Canadian Pathfinder Consulting Services Inc. provides employment consulting services for new immigrants.

CANADIANRETAIL.CA
2309 West 41st Avenue, Suite 306
Vancouver, BC V6M 2A3

Telephone	604-269-2820
Fax	604-269-2822
E-mail	info@canadian retail.com
Website	www.canadianretail.ca
Specialties	Retail
Contact	Brenda Dumont

Description Canadianretail.ca is an online agency specializing in positions in the retail industry.

CANATRADE INTERNATIONAL INC.
151, boul. Jean Leman
Canatrade House
Candiac, QC J5R 4V5

Telephone	450-444-4691
Fax	450-444-5780
E-mail	psagar@canatrade.com
Website	www.canatrade.com
Specialties	Computing
	Finance
	Management
	Consulting
	Marketing
Level	Mid-Level
	Senior
Contact	Pradeep K. Sagar, CMC

Description Canatrade is a management consulting firm offering services in information technology, training and personal and business relocation.

CANDIDATECH INC., SERVICE DE PLACEMENT
CP 125
Sainte-Julie, QC J3E 1X5

Téléphone	450-922-6460
Télécopieur	450-649-3724
Courriel	resume@ candidatech.qc.ca
Site Internet	www.candidatech.qc.ca
Fondée	1997
Employés	2
Spécialités	Informatique
	Télécommunications
Frais	Parfois relative
Recruteurs	Jean-Paul April
	Frederic April
Contact	Jean-Paul April

Description Spécialistes dans le recruitment de personnel spécialisé en informatique pour le Canada et l'international.

CANJOBS.COM INC.
512 Woolwich Street, Suite 2
Guelph, ON N1H 3X7

Telephone	519-763-9660
Fax	519-837-3408
E-mail	info@canjobs.com
Website	www.canjobs.com
Specialties	General Practice
Level	Mid-Level
	Junior
Recruiters	Graham Dyer
	Darren Marsland

Contact Graham Dyer, Chief Operating Officer

Description Canjobs.com Inc. aims to be the leading Canadian-only recruitment site, by providing the most comprehensive list of high-quality Canadian job postings.

CANMED CONSULTANTS INC.
659 Mississauga Crescent
Mississauga, ON L5H 1Z9

Telephone 905-274-0707
Fax 905-274-0067
E-mail info@canmed.com
Website www.canmed.com

Founded 1982
Employees 5

Specialties Health/Medical
Pharmaceutical
Biotech/Biology

Level Senior
Mid-Level

Min. Salary $50,000
Fee Basis Sometimes contingent

Recruiters Dr. Marc C. Raheja
Maggie Ugryn

Contact Dr. Marc C. Raheja, President

Description CanMed Consultants Inc. are recruitment specialists for the pharmaceutical, biotechnology and healthcare industries.

CANPRO EXECUTIVE SEARCH
7321 Victoria Park Ave., Suite 302
Markham, ON L3R 2Z8

Telephone 905-475-3115
Fax 905-475-2849
E-mail aboyle@canpro.com
Website www.canpro.com

Founded 1975
Employees 4

Specialties Marketing
Finance
Apparel
General Practice
Engineering
Human Resource
Logistics
Management
Operations
Sales
Packaging
Pharmaceutical

Level Senior
Mid-Level

Min. Salary $45,000
Fee Basis Retainer Only

Contact Art Boyle, President

Description Canpro is a search firm operating on behalf of Canada's premier corporations and specializing in consumer packaged goods and the food / beverage industry.

CAPITAL CONSULTING & RESEARCH
51 Locust Avenue, 12th Floor
New Canaan, CT 06840-4739
USA

Telephone 203-966-3200
Fax 203-966-8131

Specialties Computing
International

Level Mid-Level

Contact Peg Toomey, Recruiter

CAPITAL EXECUTIVE LTD.
441 - 5th Avenue SW, Suite 1010
Calgary, AB T2P 3A8

Telephone 403-266-2020
Fax 403-237-7929
E-mail alison@capital executive.com
Website www.capital executive.com

Founded 1983

Specialties Computing
Engineering
Accounting
Oil & Gas
Design

Level Senior
Mid-Level

Recruiters Patrick Gallant
Alison Goodchild
Lee Harris
Trish Mueller
Tanya Ring
Jan Ross

Contact Alison Goodchild

Description Capital Executive Ltd. is a professional recruitment agency specializing in information technology, oil and gas, accounting and engineering / design drafting on a permanent and contract basis.

CAPITAL RESOURCES INTERNATIONAL INC. / CRI
2085 Hurontario St., Suite 300
Southgate Executive Centre
Mississauga, ON L5A 4G1

Telephone 905-272-4330
Fax 905-272-4371
E-mail admin@capresources intl.com
Website www.capresources intl.com

Specialties General Practice

Level Mid-Level
Senior

Description CRI provides full-time staffing and recruitment for small- and mid-sized businesses.

CAPP EMPLOYMENT SERVICES INC.
5155 Spectrum Way, Building 38
Mississauga, ON L4W 5A1

Telephone 905-625-4400
Fax 905-625-4433
E-mail employ@cappcon.com
Website www.cappcon.com/ cappconsultant

Founded 1982
Employees 4

Specialties Sales
Purchasing
Management
Accounting
Logistics
Operations
Real Estate

Level Mid-Level

Recruiters Marni D'Arcy
Laura Laboni

Contact Marni D'Arcy

Description CAPP specializes in placements in several vertical markets, including distribution, manufacturing and real estate development / property management.

CAREER ADVANCEMENT EMPLOYMENT SERVICES INC. / CAES
522 Burlington Avenue, Suite 200
Burlington, ON L7S 1R8

Telephone 905-681-8240
Fax 905-639-4601
E-mail info@career advancement.on.ca
Website www.career advancement.on.ca

Founded 1999
Employees 3

Specialties Administrative
Engineering
Finance
Management
Sales
Environmental

Level Mid-Level

Min. Salary $30,000
Fee Basis Always contingent

Contact Jim Gilchrist, President

Description CAES recruits permanent positions for the environmental, manufacturing, financial and consulting industries.

CAREER CENTRE, THE
4211 Yonge Street, Suite 205
Toronto, ON M2P 2A9

Telephone 416-221-5666
Fax 416-221-5845

Founded 1983

Specialties Administrative

Level Mid-Level
Junior

Contact Murray Chant

Description Serving clients in the Greater Toronto Area, The Career Centre offers recruiting and placement for permanent positions in an office setting.

CAREER CONNECTIONS
398 - 28th Street West
Prince Albert, SK S6C 4S9

Telephone 306-922-3212
Fax 306-922-6333
E-mail mpete@inet2000.com

Specialties General Practice

Contact Marilyn Peterson

CAREER CONNECTIONS INC.
710 - 3rd Street
Brandon, MB R7A 3C8

Telephone	204-728-9594
Fax	204-725-0105
Specialties	Disabled

CAREER MANAGEMENT SOLUTIONS INC. / CMS
20 Eglinton Ave. West, Suite 1901
Toronto, ON M4R 1K8

Telephone	416-487-1441
Fax	416-487-5771
E-mail	info@cmsrecruit.com
Website	www.cmsrecruit.com
Specialties	Computing
Fee Basis	Always contingent
Contact	Elena Rozneberg, Office Manager

Description CMS specializes in contingency search and recruitment for contract and permanent positions in the information technology field. They are affiliated with the TIMS Group, an immigration service for professionals.

CAREER PARTNERS / HARRISON ASSOCIATES
135 James Street South
Suite 500, Alexandra Square
Hamilton, ON L8P 2Z6

Telephone	905-527-1071
Fax	905-527-1211
E-mail	resumes@cpi-hamilton.com
Website	www.cpi-hamilton.com
Founded	1975
Employees	6
Specialties	Accounting
	Administrative
	Computing
	Engineering
	Finance
	Management
	Sales
Level	Senior
	Mid-Level
Min. Salary	$35,000
Fee Basis	Sometimes contingent
Recruiters	Don Harrison
	Fred Hopkinson
	Carol Lyn Sauberli
	Peter Soderquest
Contact	Fred Hopkinson, President

Description CPI has provided quality executive search services.

CAREER PATH PERSONNEL
15 Toronto Street, Suite 500
Toronto, ON M5C 2E2

Telephone	416-366-6000
Fax	416-366-6165
E-mail	cpp@wiznet.ca
Specialties	General Practice
	Human Resource
	Pharmaceutical
Level	Mid-Level
	Junior
Recruiters	Brian Brown
	Donna Morettin
Contact	Donna Morettin

CAREERS & PROFESSIONS INC.
555 Rene-Levesque Blvd. West
Suite 550
Montréal, QC H2Z 1B1

Telephone	514-866-7000
Fax	514-866-7008
E-mail	carrieres@professions.ca
Website	www.professions.ca
Specialties	Accounting
	Finance
Level	Mid-Level
	Senior
Recruiters	Laurie Kathleen Fox
	Josée Laliberté
Contact	Laurie Kathleen Fox

CARION RESOURCE GROUP INC.
6790 Davand Drive, Unit 2
Mississauga, ON L5T 2G5

Telephone	905 795-9187
Fax	905-795-1074
E-mail	jobs@carionresource.com
Website	www.carionresource.com
Founded	1995
Employees	6
Specialties	Automotive
	Plastics
	Accounting
	Finance
	Operations
	Pharmaceutical
	Engineering
Level	Mid-Level
Min. Salary	$30,000
Fee Basis	Always contingent
Contact	Harvey Carey, CMA

Description Carion Resource specializes in recruiting for all functional positions in manufacturing industries, including operations, sales, accounting, QA, HR and logistics.

CARMICHAEL BIRRELL & CO. INC.
15 Allstate Parkway, Suite 210
Toronto, ON L3R 5B4

Telephone	416-495-8887
Fax	416-495-8270
E-mail	info@carmichaelbirrell.com
Website	www.carmichaelbirrell.com
Founded	1990
Employees	8
Specialties	General Practice
	Management
Level	Senior
	Mid-Level
Min. Salary	$60,000
Fee Basis	Retainer Only
Recruiters	David Birrell
	Colin Carmichael
Contact	Colin Carmichael, Managing Director

Description Carmichael Birrell & Co. is a retained, research-based executive search firm that specializes in placing middle management to senior executive candidates.

CARON EXECUTIVE SEARCH
841 Wellington Road S., Unit 4C
London, ON N6E 3R5

Telephone	519-681-4400
Fax	519-681-7050
E-mail	info@caronexecutive.com
Website	www.caronexecutive.com
Founded	1976
Specialties	Automotive
	Engineering
	Pharmaceutical
	Scientific
	Metals
	Plastics
Level	Mid-Level
	Senior
Recruiters	Ed Lauterbach
	Carrie Lauterbach
	Aaron Lauterbach
	Stan Meksula
Contact	Ed Lauterbach

Description Caron Executive Search recruits senior and middle management professionals for positions in OEM, automotive, food, pharmaceutical, chemical, metal fabrication, plastics and high-tech industries.

CARRIÈRES AVENIR INC.
385 Place d'Youville, Bureau 212
Montréal, QC H2Y 2B7

Téléphone	514-844-0400
Télécopieur	514-984-9703
Courriel	cavenir@total.net
Spécialités	Informatique
Échelon	Intermédiaire
Contact	Manon Latulipe

CARSCARP CONSULTING
47 Eastpark Drive
Gloucester, ON K1B 3Z6

Telephone	613-824-6547
Fax	613-837-6206
E-mail	digger@magi.com
Specialties	General Practice
	Printing
	Sales
Contact	J. Robert MacDougall

Description Carscarp specializes in career transition and management services, including recruitment.

CARTEL INC.
1 First Canadian Place
Suite 5100, Box 24
Toronto, ON M5X 1K2

Telephone 416-359-9000
Fax 416-359-9500
E-mail info@cartelinc.com
Website www.cartelinc.com

Founded 1975

Specialties Law

Level Mid-Level
Junior

Contact Jennifer Mulligan

Description Cartel has been supplying permanent and contract legal support staff to corporations and law firms throughout Toronto since 1975.

CATALYST CONSULTING
2474 Point Grey Road, Suite 201
Vancouver, BC V6K 1A2

Telephone 604-689-1776
Fax 604-689-1792
E-mail catalyst@catalystlegal.com
Website www.catalystlegal.com

Founded 1994

Specialties Law

Level Senior
Mid-Level

Contact Patricia M. Byrne

Description Catalyst Consulting provides management consulting services to Canadian law firms and law departments, including occasional recruitment.

CATALYST CONSULTING
70 York Street, Suite 730
Toronto, ON M5J 1S9

Telephone 416-367-4447
Fax 416-367-4449
E-mail catalyst@catalystlegal.com
Website www.catalystlegal.com

Founded 1997
Employees 4

Specialties Law

Level Senior
Mid-Level

Contact Lori D. Brazier

Description Catalyst Consulting provides management consulting services to Canadian law firms and law departments, including occasional recruitment.

CATALYST CONSULTING
1000 St. Antoine Street West
Suite 725
Montréal, QC H3C 3R7

Telephone 514-284-0637
Fax 514-874-0006
E-mail catalyst@catalystlegal.com
Website www.catalystlegal.com

Founded 1997
Employees 4

Specialties Law

Level Senior

Mid-Level

Min. Salary $50,000

Contact Richard G. Stock

Description Catalyst offers management consulting services to Canadian law firms and law departments, including occasional recruitment.

CATHERINE M. THOMAS & PARTNERS INC.
657 Carlaw Avenue
Toronto, ON M4K 3K6

Telephone 416-461-9923
Fax 905-803-1024
E-mail cmthom@netcom.ca

Specialties Accounting
Human Resource

Contact Catherine M. Thomas

CATHRYN LOHRISCH & CO. INC.
3266 Yonge Street, Suite 1201
Toronto, ON M4N 3P6

Telephone 416-222-3063
Fax 416-222-2430
E-mail lohrisch@sympatico.ca

Specialties General Practice
Education
Finance
Govt/Nonprofit
Human Resource
International
Management

Level Mid-Level
Senior

Fee Basis Retainer Only

Contact Cathryn Lohrisch

Description Cathryn Lohrisch & Co. Inc. specializes in searches for organizations in the private, public and not-for-profit sectors.

CBM PROJECTS INC.
609 - 14th Street NW, Suite 400
Calgary, AB T2N 2A1

Telephone 403-270-3444
Fax 403-270-3822
E-mail hr@cbmprojects.com
Website www.cbmprojects.com

Specialties Oil & Gas

Level Mid-Level
Senior

Recruiters Miles Byrne
Alan Chan
Brien McDonald

Contact Brien McDonald,
President

Description CBM Projects Inc. is a project management company specializing in the recruitment and placement of highly skilled technical professionals for the petrochemical industry.

CCG MANAGEMENT CONSULTANTS
2810 Matheson Blvd. E., Suite 505
Mississauga, ON L4W 4X7

Telephone 905-602-8577
Fax 905-238-5087
E-mail mread@cuco.on.ca
Website www.cuco.on.ca

Founded 1991
Employees 12

Specialties Finance
Banking
Consulting
Human Resource
Management
Accounting

Level Mid-Level
Senior

Min. Salary $70,000
Fee Basis Retainer Only

Contact Alan G. Small,
Executive Vice
President

Description CCG specializes in senior-level assignments in the financial services industry, primarily in HR, finance and information technology.

CCT INC.
151 York Street
London, ON N6A 1A8

Telephone 519-858-8369
Fax 519-743-5305
E-mail people@cntrcadd.com
Website www.cctinc.org

Founded 1993
Employees 30

Specialties Engineering
Computing
Design

Level Mid-Level

Fee Basis Always contingent

Contact Robert Van Slyck,
President

Description CCT Inc. (formerly Contract CADD Technologies) specializes in providing engineering and technical personnel to manufacturing companies in southern Ontario.

CCT INC.
1770 King Street E.
Kitchener, ON N2G 2P1

Telephone 519-743-4894
Fax 519-743-5305
E-mail people@cctinc.org
Website www.cctinc.org

Founded 1993
Employees 67

Specialties Engineering
Consulting
Design

Level Mid-Level
Junior

Fee Basis Always contingent

Contact Robert Van Slyk,
President

Description CCT Inc. (formerly Contract CADD Technologies) specializes in providing engineering and technical personnel to manufacturing companies in southern Ontario.

CCT INC.
3425 Harvester Road, Suite 202
Burlington, ON L7N 3N1

Telephone	905-632-7617
Fax	519-743-5305
Website	www.cctinc.org
Founded	1993
Employees	25
Specialties	Engineering
	Computing
	Design
Level	Mid-Level
Fee Basis	Always contingent
Contact	Bob Van Slyck, President

Description CCT Inc. (formerly Contract CADD Technologies) specializes in providing engineering and technical personnel to manufacturing companies in southern Ontario.

CCT INC.
2550 Argentia Road, Suite 119
Mississauga, ON L5N 5R1

Telephone	905-858-1481
Fax	800-546-4483
Website	www.cctinc.org
Founded	1993
Employees	25
Specialties	Engineering
	Computing
	Design
Level	Mid-Level
Recruiters	Al Hull RPR
	Rob Van Slyck CPC
Contact	Robert Van Slyck, CET, RPR, President

Description CCT Inc. (formerly Contract CADD Technologies) specializes in providing engineering and technical personnel to manufacturing companies in southern Ontario.

CDI TECHNICAL SERVICES LTD.
736 - 8th Avenue SW, Suite 330
Calgary, AB T2P 1H4

Telephone	403-266-1009
Fax	403-264-1961
E-mail	calgary@cdicorp.com
Website	www.cdicorp.com
Founded	1951
Employees	10
Specialties	Engineering
	Computing
	Oil & Gas
	Design
	Construction
	Telecom
	International
Level	Mid-Level
	Senior
Recruiters	Robb Adams
	Rob Cutforth
	Jason Landa
	Ken Melnychuk
	Kerry Muenchrath
	Scott Willis
Contact	Ken Melnychuk

Description CDI Technical Services Ltd., a division of CDI Corporation, is North America's largest provider of engineering and engineering support staff.

CDI TECHNICAL SERVICES LTD.
710 Dorval Drive, Suite 220
Oakville, ON L6K 3V7

Telephone	905-338-3100
Fax	905-338-9951
E-mail	oakville@cdicorp.com
Website	www.cdicorp.com
Founded	1951
Specialties	Engineering
	Computing
	Design
Level	Mid-Level
Recruiters	Catherine Belgrave
	W. Wong
Contact	Doug Prince

Description CDI Technical Services Ltd., a division of CDI Corporation, is North America's largest provider of engineering and engineering support staff.

CDI TECHNICAL SERVICES LTD.
1000 St-Jean Boulevard, Suite 200
Pointe-Claire, QC H9R 5P1

Telephone	514-697-9212
Fax	514-697-9011
E-mail	pointclaire@cdicorp.com
Website	www.cdicorp.com
Specialties	Engineering
	Computing
	Design
Level	Mid-Level
Contact	Annie-Marie Labrecque

Description CDI Technical Services Ltd., a division of CDI Corporation, is North America's largest provider of engineering and engineering support staff.

CDM & ASSOCIATES
672 Broadview Avenue
Toronto, ON M4K 2P1

Telephone	416-462-3031
Fax	416-462-3024
E-mail	cdm@consultant.com
Website	www.cdmassociates.com
Specialties	Hospitality
	Publishing/Media
	Multimedia
	Marketing
	Public Relations
	Finance
	Banking
Level	Senior
	Mid-Level
Fee Basis	Always contingent
Contact	Colleen McCullough

Description CDM is a unique, personalized employment agency serving the Greater Toronto Area.

Description CDI Technical Services Ltd., a division of CDI Corporation, is North America's largest provider of engineering and engineering support staff.

CENTRAL MANAGEMENT CONSULTANTS INC.
57 Widdicombe Hill Blvd.
Suite 703
Toronto, ON M9R 1Y4

Telephone	416-248-9669
Fax	416-243-2027
E-mail	centralmgt@on.aibn.com
Founded	1985
Employees	4
Specialties	Accounting
	Finance
	Automotive
	Construction
	Operations
	Sales
	Management
Level	Senior
	Mid-Level
Min. Salary	$30,000
Fee Basis	Sometimes contingent
Contact	Robert D. Chelew CA, President

Description Central Management Consultants provides personalized, professional services and empathetic outplacement counselling to clients and candidates.

CENTRE FOR ABORIGINAL HUMAN RESOURCE DEVELOPMENT
181 Higgins, Suite 304
Winnipeg, MB R3B 3G1

Telephone	204-989-7110
Fax	204-988-7113
E-mail	staffing@abcentre.org
Website	www.cahrd.org
Specialties	Govt/Nonprofit
	General Practice

Description CAHRD is a non-profit organization that assists employers in recruiting aboriginal candidates.

CENTRE FOR CORPORATE RESOURCES, THE
133 Richmond St. West, Suite 615
Toronto, ON M5H 2L3

Telephone	416-364-2900
Fax	416-364-0493
E-mail	resumes@ccragent.com
Website	www.ccragent.com
Founded	1990
Employees	30
Specialties	Accounting
	Finance
	Operations
	Automotive
	Telecom
	Pharmaceutical
	Computing
Level	Senior
	Mid-Level
Min. Salary	$30,000
Fee Basis	Sometimes contingent
Recruiters	Gordon Diver
	Richard C. Fernandes
	Brad Grant
Contact	Richard C. Fernandes, President & CEO

Description Centre for Corporate Resources is a human management company, providing high-calibre candidates to leading corporate clients through a group of professional, highly dedicated staff.

CENTREX HUMAN RESOURCE CENTRE
124 James Street South, Suite 200
Hamilton, ON L8P 2Z4

Telephone   905-528-5141
Fax   905-528-5147
E-mail   centrex@netcom.ca
Website   members.attcanada.ca/
            ~centrex/

Founded   1987
Employees   3

Specialties Accounting
            Computing
            Finance
            Management
            Marketing
            Operations
            Purchasing
            Sales
            Human Resource
            Administrative

Level   Junior
            Mid-Level

Fee Basis   Sometimes contingent

Contact   Suzanne Davidson,
            President

Description Centrex is a full-service placement company, servicing Halton, Hamilton-Wentworth and Niagara regions.

CEO INC.
589 Fairway Road South, Unit 6
Kitchener, ON N2C 1X4

Telephone   519-895-0004
Fax   519-895-2636
E-mail   sales@ceoemp.com
Website   www.ceoemp.com

Specialties General Practice

Description CEO Inc. is an employment consulting service that also does recruitment and candidate screening for clients.

CES & ASSOCIATES
PO Box 52006,
Edmonton Trail RPO
Calgary, AB T2E 8K9

Fax   403-206-0663

Specialties Govt/Nonprofit

Level   Mid-Level

CFT TRAINING AND HUMAN RESOURCES
1600, rue Notre Dame Ouest
Bureau 203
Montréal, QC H3J 1S6

Telephone   514-935-7277
Fax   514-935-6118
E-mail   information@cfthr.com
Website   www.cfthr.com

Specialties Computing
            Engineering

Level   Senior
            Mid-Level

Recruiters Marie-Josée Laberge
            Carolyn-Fe Trinidad

Contact   Marie Josée Laberge

Description CFT recruits information technology personnel for clients in the high-tech industry.

CG CONSULTING GROUP
29A Stafford Street
Toronto, ON M6J 2R7

Telephone   416-977-2727
Fax   416-209-9599
E-mail   carlos@cgconsulting
            group.com
Website   www.cgconsulting
            group.com

Founded   1991

Specialties Computing
            Multimedia
            Telecom

Level   Mid-Level
            Senior

Contact   Carlos Goncalves

Description CG Consulting Group specializes in recruiting IT and MIS professionals for full-time or contract placements for clients throughout Ontario.

CHACRA, BELLIVEAU & ASSOCIATES INC.
1550 de Maisonneuve Ouest
Bureau 805
Montréal, QC H3G 1N2

Telephone   514-931-8801
Fax   514-931-1940
E-mail   info@chacra.com
Website   www.chacra.com

Founded   1976
Employees   22

Specialties Computing
            Management
            Sales
            Engineering

Level   Mid-Level
            Senior

Min. Salary $30,000
Fee Basis   Sometimes contingent

Recruiters Benoît Campeau
            Steven Chacra

Contact   Benoît Campeau

Description Chacra, Belliveau & Associates is an information technology services firm specializing in the recruitment and staffing of permanent and contract IT professionals.

CHAD MANAGEMENT GROUP
21 St. Clair Avenue E., Suite 1000
Toronto, ON M4T 1L9

Telephone   416-968-1000
Fax   416-968-7754
E-mail   jobs@chadman.com
Website   www.chadman.com

Founded   1985
Employees   12

Specialties Marketing
            Sales
            Graphic Arts
            Finance
            Advertising
            Accounting
            Public Relations

Level   Senior
            Mid-Level

Contact   Rick Chad, President

Description One of Canada's leading executive recruitment consulting agencies. Large database of marketing, direct marketing, sales, advertising, promotion, media, buying and technology candidates and companies for above.

CHANCELLOR PARTNERS, THE
1111 West Georgia St., Suite 1700
Vancouver, BC V6E 4M3

Telephone   604-687-8141
Fax   604-689-3348
E-mail   ewhite@axion.net

Employees   15

Specialties Management
            Govt/Nonprofit

Level   Mid-Level
            Senior

Contact   Eric White

Description The Chancellor Partners is a management consulting firm that occasionally does recruitment work for clients.

CHAPMAN & ASSOCIATES
555 Burrard Street
Suite 1065, Two Bentall Centre
Vancouver, BC V7X 1M8

Telephone   604-682-7764
Fax   604-682-8746
E-mail   resumes@
            chapmanassoc.com
Website   www.chapman
            assoc.com

Founded   1958
Employees   5

Specialties Engineering
            Human Resource
            Marketing
            Purchasing
            Sales
            Finance
            Scientific

Level   Mid-Level

Min. Salary $30,000
Fee Basis   Sometimes contingent

Recruiters Lynn Armstrong
            Gary Fumano
            Bruce J. MacKenzie
            Bryce Stacey

Contact   Lynn Armstrong

Description Chapman & Associates is one of Western Canada's longest serving and most respected search and recruitment companies.

CHARTER MANAGEMENT GROUP

Box 129
Winnipeg, MB R3C 2G1

Telephone	204-944-1400
Fax	204-942-8600
E-mail	lhoeppnr@ mbnet.mb.ca
Website	biznet.maximizer.com/ cmg1
Specialties	Accounting
Contact	Ben Hoeppner, Consultant

Description CMG is provides a range of HR consulting services, including recruitment.

CHASE CONSULTANTS INC.

151 City Centre Drive, Suite 400
Mississauga, ON L5B 1M7

Telephone	905-566-9448
Fax	905-566-9606
E-mail	careers@ chaseconsultants.com
Website	www.chase consultants.com
Founded	1994
Employees	6
Specialties	Marketing Sales Computing Accounting Engineering Management Operations Telecom Transport Banking
Level	Senior Mid-Level
Fee Basis	Sometimes contingent
Recruiters	Ted Gushev Richard Ryan
Contact	Ted Gushev

Description Chase Consultants Inc. provides executive search and consulting services in sales and marketing and information systems.

CHERYL CRAIG CAREERS CORP.

4145 North Service Road, Suite 102
Burlington, ON L7L 6A3

Telephone	905-332-1600
Fax	905-332-7993
E-mail	info@ cherylcraigcareers.com
Website	www.cherylcraig careers.com
Founded	1981
Specialties	Accounting Human Resource Administrative Trades/Technicians
Level	Mid-Level Junior
Contact	Cheryl Craig

Description Cheryl Craig Careers recruits contract and permanent positions in a variety of fields in the Mississauga - Burlington area.

CHISHOLM & PARTNERS INTERNATIONAL INC.

40 King Street West
Suite 4900, Scotia Plaza
Toronto, ON M5H 4A2

Telephone	416-777-6800
Fax	416-777-6777
E-mail	tjc@chisintl.com
Founded	1997
Employees	3
Specialties	Finance Accounting Marketing Management Sales Telecom Human Resource Pharmaceutical
Level	Senior
Min. Salary	$50,000
Fee Basis	Sometimes contingent
Recruiters	Timothy J. Chisholm Sherilynn Chisholm Jayne Richards
Contact	Timothy J. Chisholm, Principal

Description Chisholm & Partners is a senior-level executive search practice.

CHRIS GREEN & ASSOCIATES

2463 Bellevue Avenue
Vancouver, BC V7V 1E1

Telephone	604-926-4445
Fax	604-987-9650
E-mail	cgavan@idirect.ca
Specialties	Education Govt/Nonprofit

Description Chris Green & Associates is a management consulting firm that also does recruitment work for clients.

CHRISTIAN & TIMBERS

25825 Science Park Drive
1 Corporate Exchange, Suite 400
Cleveland, OH 44122 USA

Telephone	216-464-8710
Fax	216-464-6160
E-mail	resume@ctnet.com
Website	www.ctnet.com
Founded	1980
Specialties	International Computing Biotech/Biology Finance Oil & Gas
Level	Senior
Recruiters	Jeffrey E. Christian David Kinley Stephen Moore BA Mark Ross LLB, BA
Contact	Jeffrey E. Christian, Chairman & CEO

Description Christian & Timbers recruits CEO-level candidates in several fields, including IT, venture capital, financial services, consumer goods, biotech, professional services, energy and industrial areas.

CHRISTMAS, MCIVOR & ASSOCIATES INC.

33 City Centre Drive, Suite 551
Mississauga, ON L5B 2N5

Telephone	905-270-0405
Fax	905-270-0406
E-mail	recruiters@ globalserve.net
Founded	1990
Employees	6
Specialties	Accounting Automotive Computing Engineering Finance Logistics Marketing Management Metals Purchasing Sales
Fee Basis	Always contingent
Contact	Jim McIvor

CHRISTOPHER VINCENT & ASSOCIATES LTD.

250 - 6th Avenue SW, Suite 1500
Calgary , AB T2P 3H7

Telephone	403-233-7700
Fax	403-264-1262
Founded	1985
Specialties	Accounting Computing Banking Forestry Human Resource International Mining Oil & Gas Pulp & Paper Transport
Level	Senior Mid-Level
Min. Salary	$60,000
Fee Basis	Retainer Only
Contact	Christopher P. Vincent, CMC

Description Christopher Vincent & Associates is a professional search practice focusing on significant corporate and operational resource developers. Affiliated with Research Associates Ltd. in Edmonton.

CHURCHILL GROUP, THE

1 Yonge Street, Suite 1801
Toronto, ON M5E 1W7

Telephone	416-368-1358
Fax	416-369-0515
E-mail	churchill@bmts.com
Founded	1991
Specialties	Management General Practice Accounting Automotive Engineering Human Resource Telecom
Fee Basis	Sometimes contingent
Contact	Murray Fullerton

Description An executive search firm specializing in human resources, manufacturing, engineering, accounting, and sales positions in the industrial, telecom, and computing sectors.

CLA PERSONNEL
424 Queen Street, Suite C
Ottawa, ON K1R 5A8

Telephone	613-567-0045
Fax	613-567-0049
E-mail	jobs@clapersonnel.ca
Website	www.clapersonnel.ca
Founded	1988
Employees	6
Specialties	Accounting
	Administrative
	Banking
	Bilingual
	Govt/Nonprofit
	Graphic Arts
	Health/Medical
	Finance
Level	Mid-Level
	Junior
Recruiters	Carole B. Joanisse
	Eric Joanisse
	Chantal Lorrain
	Rachel Proulx CPC
Contact	Carole B. Joanisse, President

Description CLA Personnel specializes in placing administrative support and informatics personnel.

CLARENDON PARKER MIDDLE EAST
City Tower 2, Sheikh Zayed Road
Suite 1402, PO Box 26359
Dubai
UNITED ARAB EMIRATES

Telephone	971-4-3317092
Fax	971-4-3315668
E-mail	gm@clarendon parker.com
Website	www.clarendon parker.com
Specialties	Oil & Gas
	Computing
	Accounting
	Finance
	Engineering
	International
Contact	Patrick Luby, General Manager

Description Clarendon Parker Middle East, now part of the US-based CDI Group, is a search firm providing recruitment opportunities across the Middle East.

CLARK, POLLARD & GAGLIARDI
490 Dutton Drive, Suite C1
Waterloo, ON N2L 6H7

Telephone	519-744-6120
Fax	519-744-6226
E-mail	info@cpandg.com
Website	www.cpandg.com
Specialties	Accounting
	Finance
Level	Mid-Level
	Senior
Recruiters	Bob Clark
	Nino Gagliardi
	Mike Pollard
Contact	Bob Clark

Description CP&G is an accounting firm that does some search work.

CLARKE, HENNING LLP
10 Bay Street, Suite 801
Toronto, ON M5J 2R8

Telephone	416-364-4421
Fax	416-367-8032
E-mail	ch@clarkehenning.com
Website	www.clarke henning.com
Founded	1915
Employees	61
Specialties	Accounting
	Finance
Level	Mid-Level
	Senior
Contact	Jim Blue

Description Clarke, Henning LLP is a well established accounting firm that also does some search work and recruitment for clients.

CLARKE MANAGEMENT SERVICES, INC.
250 - 6th Avenue SW, Suite 940
Calgary, AB T2P 3H7

Telephone	403-290-1469
Fax	403-264-3310
Specialties	General Practice
Contact	Brad Clarke

CLASSIC CONSULTING GROUP INC.
706 - 7th Avenue SW, Suite 607
Calgary, AB T2P 0Z1

Telephone	403-233-8388
Fax	403-233-8755
E-mail	classic@classic consulting.com
Website	www.classic consulting.com
Employees	5
Specialties	Engineering
	Accounting
	Computing
	Finance
	Scientific
	Geology/Geography
	Oil & Gas
Level	Mid-Level
	Senior
Fee Basis	Always contingent
Recruiters	Janine Gowans
	Doreen Leggett
	Karen McGrath
	Karen Ryan
Contact	Karen Ryan

Description Classic Consulting Group specializes in oil and gas executive search for technical, finance and IS professionals for all industries.

CLASSIFIED CANADA CONFIDENTIAL REPLY
922 Kamato Road
Mississauga, ON L4W 2R6

Telephone	905-206-1811
Fax	905-625-5727
Specialties	Govt/Nonprofit
	Management
	Accounting
	Finance
Level	Senior
	Mid-Level

Description Classified Canada is an advertising agency that specializes in recruitment advertising.

CLAUDE GUEDJ & ASSOCIÉS
1555, rue Peel, Bureau 901
Montréal, QC H3A 3L8

Téléphone	514-499-1245
Courriel	cguedj@proxyma.net
Fondée	1991
Employés	2
Spécialités	Comptabilité
	Consultatif
	Finance
	Ressources humaines
	Gestion
	Marketing
	Vente au détail
Échelon	Direction
	Intermédiaire
Salaire min.	60 000 $
Frais	Honoraire seulement
Contact	Claude Guedj, Président

Description Psychologie industrielle et organisationnelle.

CLAYMORE SEARCH GROUP
140 Fullarton
London, ON N6A 5P2

Telephone	519-433-9099
Fax	519-663-1165
Specialties	General Practice
	Sales

CLEMENTS CONSULTING GROUP
222 - 58th Avenue SW, Suite 204
Calgary, AB T2H 2S3

Telephone	403-296-0155
Fax	403-296-0159
E-mail	info@clements group.com
Website	www.clements group.com
Specialties	Sales
Level	Mid-Level
	Senior
Recruiters	Wayne Clements
	Kim Pettigrew
Contact	Wayne Clements, CEO

Description Clements Consulting Group provides training sessions to improve the skills of sales managers, in addition to occasional recruitment services for clients.

CM INC.
2800 John Street, Suite 19
Markham, ON L3R 2W4

Telephone	905-475-2248
Fax	905-475-2275
E-mail	info@interlog.com
Website	www.cmigroup.com
Founded	1982
Employees	15
Specialties	Computing
	Human Resource
	Management
Level	Senior
	Mid-Level
Recruiters	Gordon Chillcott
	Jeff Ivers
	Robin Traboulay
Contact	Robin Traboulay

Description CM Inc. specializes in the delivery of IT consulting, systems development / integration, training and placement services.

CMP SELECT
2323 Yonge Street, Suite 203
Toronto, ON M4P 2C9

Telephone	416-484-8408
Fax	416-484-0151
E-mail	careers@cmpselect.com
Website	www.cambridge mgmt.com
Founded	1976
Employees	12
Specialties	Operations
	Sales
	Accounting
	Management
Level	Senior
Min. Salary	$80,000
Fee Basis	Retainer Only
Contact	Graham Carver, Partner

Description CMP is a division of Cambridge Management Planning Inc., an executive search firm specializing in senior-level recruiting for manufacturing businesses.

CNC GLOBAL
1090 West Georgia Street, Suite 420
Vancouver, BC V6C 3V7

Telephone	604-687-5919
Fax	604-687-5397
E-mail	vancouver@ cncglobal.com
Website	www.cncglobal.com
Specialties	Computing
Level	Mid-Level
Contact	Melanie Taylor

Description CNC Global provides highly skilled IT professionals on a contract and permanent basis to organizations across North America.

CNC GLOBAL
10180 - 101st Street
Suite 1150, Manulife Place
Edmonton, AB T5J 3S4

Telephone	780-497-7750
Fax	780-497-7760
E-mail	edmonton@ cncglobal.com
Website	www.cncglobal.com
Specialties	Computing

Description CNC Global provides highly-skilled IT professionals on a contract and permanent basis to organizations across North America.

CNC GLOBAL
700 - 9th Avenue SW, South Tower
Ste. 2910, Western Canadian Place
Calgary, AB T2P 3V4

Telephone	403-263-4501
Fax	403-263-4502
E-mail	calgary@cncglobal.com
Website	www.cnc.ca
Founded	1987
Employees	130
Specialties	Computing
Level	Mid-Level
	Senior
Contact	Lori Free

Description CNC Global provides highly-skilled IT professionals on a contract and permanent basis to organizations across North America.

CNC GLOBAL
60 Bloor Street West, Suite 1400
Toronto, ON M4W 3B8

Telephone	416-962-9262
Fax	416-962-9709
E-mail	toronto@cncglobal.com
Website	www.cncglobal.com
Specialties	Computing
Level	Mid-Level
	Senior
Contact	Heather Gouin, VP Marketing

Description CNC Global provides highly-skilled IT professionals on a contract and permanent basis to organizations across North America.

CNC GLOBAL
3 Robert Speck Parkway, Suite 280
Mississauga, ON L4Z 2G5

Telephone	905-277-9111
Fax	905-896-8901
E-mail	mississauga@ cncglobal.com
Website	www.cncglobal.com
Founded	1981
Employees	100
Specialties	Computing
Level	Senior
	Mid-Level
Fee Basis	Always contingent
Contact	Duncan Pursell

Description CNC Global provides highly-skilled IT professionals on a contract and permanent basis to organizations across North America.

CNC GLOBAL
1 West Pearce Street, Suite 308
Richmond Hill, ON L4B 3K3

Telephone	905-882-1044
Fax	905-882-1230
E-mail	richmondhill@ cncglobal.com
Website	www.cncglobal.com
Specialties	Computing
Contact	Sergio Mateus

Description CNC Global provides highly-skilled IT professionals on a contract and permanent basis to organizations across North America.

CNC GLOBAL
350 Albert Street, Suite 1825
Ottawa, ON K1R 1A4

Telephone	613-786-3220
Fax	613-567-2659
E-mail	ottawa@cncglobal.com
Website	www.cncglobal.com
Founded	1986
Employees	17
Specialties	Computing
Level	Mid-Level
	Senior
Recruiters	Brenda Bernardo
	Terry Brown
	Neil Campbell
	John Chapatis
	Arlene Hall
	Liz McCourt
	Dan Murphy
	Keith O'Reilly
	Brennan Senos
	Janice Webster
	Jennifer Wright
Contact	John Maur

Description CNC Global is one of North America's leading information technology staffing companies.

CNC GLOBAL
1470 Peel Street, Suite 720
Montréal, QC H3A 1T1

Telephone	514-845-5775
Fax	514-845-0774
E-mail	montreal@ cncglobal.com
Website	www.cncglobal.com
Specialties	Computing
Level	Mid-Level
	Senior
Contact	James La

Description CNC Global provides highly-skilled IT professionals on a contract and permanent basis to organizations across North America.

CNC GLOBAL
2501 Blue Ridge Road
Suite 250, Research Triangle Park
Raleigh, NC 27607 USA

Telephone	919-510-9770
Fax	919-510-4647
E-mail	raleigh@cncglobal.com
Website	www.cncglobal.com

Specialties Computing
International

Level Mid-Level
Senior

Description CNC Global provides highly-skilled IT professionals on a contract and permanent basis to organizations across North America.

COAKWELL CRAWFORD CAIRNS
318 Centre Street S.
High River, AB T1V 1N7

Telephone 403-652-3032
Fax 403-652-7051
E-mail inquire@coakwell.com
Website www.coakwell.com
Founded 1986
Specialties Agriculture/Fisheries
Finance
Management
Accounting

Level Mid-Level

Min. Salary $50,000
Fee Basis Retainer Only

Recruiters Cam Crawford
Donald C. Phillips

Contact Cam Crawford, FCA,
CMC

Description Coakwell Crawford Cairns is an accounting and consulting firm that also does occasional search work for clients.

COAPE STAFFING NETWORK
885 Dunsmuir Street, Suite 370
Vancouver, BC V6C 1N5

Telephone 604-687-2226
Fax 604-687-2251
E-mail vancouver@
coapestaffing.com
Website www.coapestaffing.com
Specialties Administrative
Accounting
Computing
Sales

Description Coape Staffing Network specializes in the placement of skilled IT and other professionals.

COAPE STAFFING NETWORK
4501 North Road, Unit 217
Burnaby, BC V3N 4R7

Telephone 604-420-4533
Fax 604-420-4542
E-mail burnaby@
coapestaffing.com
Website www.coapestaffing.com
Specialties Administrative
Accounting
Computing
Sales

Description Coape Staffing Network specializes in the placement of skilled IT and other professionals.

COAPE STAFFING NETWORK
10264 - 100 Street, Suite 800
Edmonton, AB T5J 0H1

Telephone 780-424-1088
Fax 780-421-0055
E-mail edmonton@
coapestaffing.com
Website www.coapestaffing.com
Specialties Computing
Administrative
Accounting
Sales

Description Coape Staffing Network specializes in the placement of skilled professionals in all job placements.

COAPE STAFFING NETWORK
665 - 8th Street SW, Suite 800
Calgary, AB T2P 3K7

Telephone 403-509-0100
Fax 403-509-0114
E-mail calgary@
coapestaffing.com
Website www.coapestaffing.com
Founded 1998
Employees 5
Specialties Administrative
Accounting
Computing
Sales

Level Mid-Level
Junior

Recruiters Clint Belcourt
Kurt Johnson
Debbie Read

Contact Debbie Read

Description Coape Staffing Network specializes in the placement of skilled professionals in all job placements.

COAST PERSONNEL SERVICES LTD.
PO Box 2313, Station A
Nanaimo, BC V9R 6E8

Telephone 250-758-1828
Fax 250-758-8244
E-mail vwcoast@island.net
Website www.island.net/~work
Founded 1986
Employees 1
Specialties Computing
Pulp & Paper
Forestry
Management
Sales
Accounting
Engineering

Level Mid-Level

Min. Salary $35,000
Fee Basis Sometimes contingent

Contact Vincent G.B. Willden,
CPC

Description Coast Personnel Services Ltd. provides professional and technical employees in western Canada and all employment categories of the forest industry.

CODEV INTERNATIONAL INC.
1929 Tupper Street
Montréal, QC H3H 1N6

Telephone 514-939-6400
Fax 514-939-1548
Specialties General Practice
Level Mid-Level
Senior

Contact Raymond Lapierre,
President

COE & COMPANY INTERNATIONAL INC.
400 - 3rd Avenue SW, Suite 2600
Calgary, AB T2P 4H2

Telephone 403-232-8833
Fax 403-237-0165
E-mail coe@coeand
company.com
Website www.coeand
company.com
Employees 6
Specialties Telecom
Sales
Marketing
Human Resource
Finance
Operations
Oil & Gas

Level Senior
Mid-Level

Min. Salary $75,000
Fee Basis Retainer Only

Recruiters Kalyna Bilinski BA
Karen J. Coe Ph.D.
Jill Couillard
Rosemary Penelhum
Andy Sharman CMA
Valerie Silbernagel

Contact Kalyna Bilinski, Senior
Research Consultant

Description Coe & Company International, a member EMA International, is an executive search management consulting firm.

COFFEY & ASSOCIATES
195 James St. S., Basement Unit
Hamilton, ON L8P 3A8

Telephone 905-546-5503
Fax 905-546-1578
E-mail tjcoffey@istar.ca
Employees 5
Specialties Insurance
Engineering
Computing
Design

Level Mid-Level
Fee Basis Always contingent
Contact Tommy Joe Coffey,
President

Description Coffey & Associates specializes in engineering, design and insurance personnel.

COKE & ASSOCIATES LTD.
FRANCHISE RECRUITERS LTD.
20 Holly Street, Suite 203
Toronto, ON M4S 3B1

Telephone 416-322-5730
Fax 416-322-0648

E-mail   gkinzie@netcom.ca
Website   www.starpages.com/
                coke-associates

Founded   1984
Employees   2

Specialties   General Practice
                Franchising
                Hospitality
                Management
                Retail
                Sales
                Human Resource

Level   Mid-Level
                Senior

Min. Salary $40,000
Fee Basis   Sometimes contingent

Recruiters   Sheila Aiawick
                George A. Kinzie

Contact   George A. Kinzie CPC,
                President

Description Since 1984, executive search and placement in management and sales. Franchise recruiters since 1986.

COLES ASSOCIATES LTD.
197 Malpeque Road, PO Box 695
Charlottetown, PE C1A 7L3

Telephone   902-368-2300
Fax   902-566-3768
E-mail   hcoles@caltech.ca
Website   www.cole
                sassociates.com

Specialties   Architecture
                Engineering
                International

Level   Mid-Level
                Senior

Contact   Howard Coles, MRAIC,
                PEng

Description Coles Associates is a consulting engineering and architectural firm that also provides management consulting services, including some recruitment work for clients.

COLINTEX AGENCIES LTD.
23 Swansdown Drive
Toronto, ON M2L 2N2

Telephone   416-449-3100
Fax   416-449-9001
E-mail   colintex@home.com
Website   www.colintex.com

Specialties   Apparel
                Marketing
                Direct Mktng.
                Design
                Retail
                Sales

Level   Mid-Level
                Junior

Fee Basis   Always contingent

Recruiters   Lori Layton
                Colin Lewis
                Shari Stancer

Contact   Colin Lewis

Description Colintex is recruitment placement firm specializing in the textile and fashion industries.

COLLINS BARROW
777 - 8th Avenue SW, Suite 1400
Calgary, AB T2P 3R5

Telephone   403-298-1500
Fax   403-298-5814
E-mail   cambridge@
                collinsbarrow.com
Website   www.collinsbarrow.com

Founded   1922
Employees   110

Specialties   Accounting
                Finance

Level   Mid-Level
                Senior

Recruiters   Lynn Cyr
                Merv Manthey

Contact   Merv Manthey

Description Collins Barrow is a chartered accounting firm that occasionally provides recruitment services for clients.

COMFACT CORPORATION
710 Dorval Drive, Suite 300
Oakville, ON L6K 3V7

Telephone   905-339-3404
Fax   905-339-3407
E-mail   comfact@
                comfactcorp.com
Website   www.comfactcorp.com

Founded   1926
Employees   15

Specialties   Aerospace
                Design
                Engineering
                Health/Medical
                Oil & Gas
                Telecom
                International

Level   Senior
                Mid-Level

Fee Basis   Always contingent

Recruiters   Matthew Tyre
                Gary Woods

Contact   Matthew Tyre

Description ComFact supplies qualified personnel to offshore marine shipbuilding/oil rig companies, and to the aerospace/aviation industries.

COMIDIC INC.
4470, rue Beaubien Est, Bureau 109
Montréal, QC H1T 3Y8

Téléphone   514-593-4690
Spécialités   Santé/médical
Échelon   Intermédiaire
                Débutant
Contact   Lili Desbiens, Directrice

COMMUNICATION DYNAMIQUE INC.
186 Sutton Place, Suite 116
Beaconsfield, QC H9W 5S3

Telephone   514-693-1311
E-mail   communication.
                dynamics@qc.aibn.com

Specialties   Engineering
                Public Relations

Level   Senior
                Mid-Level

Contact   Elaine Creighton

Description Communication Dynamique Inc. is a public relations consulting firm that occasionally does recruitment for clients.

COMMUNITY LIVING SOUTH MUSKOKA / CLSM
23 Balls Drive, Unit 3
Bracebridge, ON P1L 1T1

Telephone   705-645-5494
Fax   705-645-4621
E-mail   clsm@think.iprimus.ca
Website   www.clsm.on.ca

Specialties   Disabled

Description CLSM provides employment opportunities to disabled people in the South Muskoka region.

COMPETITIVE EDGE
21 King Street, Suite 118
London, ON N6A 5H3

Telephone   519-679-8607
Fax   519-679-8607

Specialties   General Practice

COMPTON GRAHAM INTERNATIONAL INC.
21 St. Clair Ave. East, Suite 1400
Toronto, ON M4T 2T7

Telephone   416-944-2000
Fax   416-944-2020
E-mail   inquiry@compton
                graham.com
Website   www.compton
                graham.com

Founded   1992

Specialties   Management
                General Practice

Level   Senior

Min. Salary $100,000
Fee Basis   Retainer Only

Contact   Jo Ann L. Compton,
                CMC, CHRP

Description Compton Graham provides quality executive search and research services in Canada and the USA.

COMPUFORCE INC.
101 - 6th Avenue SW, Suite 1220
Calgary, AB T2P 3P4

Telephone   403-233-7871
Fax   403-205-4460
E-mail   general@compuforce
                inc.com
Website   www.compuforce
                inc.com

Founded   1986
Employees   30

Specialties   Computing
                Human Resource

Fee Basis   Always contingent

Contact   Walter Ilenseer

Description CompuForce is a leading supplier of information systems professionals for contract and permanent information technology assignments.

COMPUTER ACTION COMPANY
100 - 4th Avenue SW, Suite 803
Calgary, AB T2P 3N2

Telephone 403-262-4111
Fax 403-263-2716
E-mail careers.canada@ modisit.com
Website www.modisit.com
Specialties Computing
Level Mid-Level
Contact Deb Ingram

Description Computer Action Company is the consulting branch of Modis, one of the world's leading providers of IT consulting services and solutions.

COMPUTER ACTION COMPANY
195 Dufferin Street, Suite 602
London, ON N6A 1K7

Telephone 519-663-4330
Fax 519-663-4277
E-mail london.consulting@ modisit.com
Website www.modisit.com
Specialties Computing
Level Mid-Level
Senior
Contact Roger Weese

Description Computer Action Company is the consulting branch of Modis, one of the world's leading providers of IT consulting services and solutions.

COMPUTER ACTION COMPANY
2 Lansing Square, Suite 800
Toronto, ON M2J 4P8

Telephone 416-492-5656
Fax 416-492-3561
E-mail toronto.consulting@ modisit.com
Website www.modisit.com
Founded 1980
Employees 24
Specialties Computing
Level Mid-Level
Senior
Recruiters Kyra Bellis
Billi Damjanovic
Stephen Garrette
Colette O'Neil-Taylor
Marnie Pertsinidis
Jane Varghese
Contact Colette O'Neil Taylor, Branch Manager

Description Computer Action Company is the consulting branch of Modis, one of the world's leading providers of IT consulting services and solutions.

COMPUTER CONSULTANTS INC.
2050 Sheppard Avenue East
Toronto, ON M2J 5B3

Telephone 416-498-6644
Fax 416-498-6508
E-mail ccincorp@interlog.com
Specialties Computing
Contact Simon Lagopoulos

Description CCI specializes in AS/400 programmers and analysts.

COMPUTER HORIZONS ISG
734 - 7th Avenue SW, Suite 420
Calgary, AB T2P 3P8

Telephone 403-265-3380
Fax 403-265-3301
E-mail calgary@isgjobs.com
Website www.isgjobs.com
Specialties Computing
Level Mid-Level
Recruiters Andrea Guinn
Suzanne Hall
Contact Andrea Guinn, VP, Staffing Services

Description Computer Horizons ISG provides IT professionals for permanent and contract assignments with client organizations.

COMPUTER HORIZONS ISG
5045 Orbitor Drive
Building 7, Suite 200
Mississauga, ON L4W 4Y4

Telephone 905-602-6085
Fax 905-602-6091
E-mail resumes@isgjobs.com
Website www.isgjobs.com
Specialties Computing
Level Mid-Level
Senior
Contact Frank Vrabel, VP Staffing Services

Description Computer Horizons ISG provides IT professionals for permanent and contract assignments with client organizations.

COMPUTER HORIZONS ISG
180 Elgin Street, Suite 801
Ottawa, ON K2P 2K3

Telephone 613-688-0918
Fax 613-688-0917
E-mail ottawa@isgjobs.com
Website www.isgjobs.com
Specialties Computing
Level Mid-Level
Contact Mark Cohen, VP Staffing Services

Description Computer Horizons ISG provides IT professionals for permanent and contract assignments with client organizations.

COMPUTER PEOPLE COMPANY, THE
1235 Bay Street, Suite 500
Toronto, ON M5R 3K4

Telephone 416-955-9131
Fax 416-934-5021
E-mail cpcint@attglobal.net
Specialties Computing
Level Mid-Level

COMPUTER TASK GROUP / CTG
1 Yonge Street, Suite 1902
Toronto, ON M5E 1E5

Telephone 416-868-1212
Fax 416-868-9449
Website www.ctg.com
Founded 1967
Employees 100
Specialties Computing
Level Senior
Mid-Level
Fee Basis Always contingent
Recruiters Douglas C. Burgess
Monica Chen
Geoff Webb
Contact Geoff Webb

Description CTG provides IT professionals to large corporations where IT is critical to corporate strategies.

COMTECH PROFESSIONAL SERVICES INC.
3200 Deziel Drive, Suite 411
Windsor, ON N8W 5K8

Telephone 519-944-6335
Fax 519-944-3955
E-mail hr@comtech international.com
Founded 1994
Specialties Engineering
Management
Scientific
Design
Level Senior
Mid-Level
Contact Jason Claxton

Description Comtech Professional Services Inc. specializes in contract engineering and engineering recruitment.

COMUNITY SYSTEMS CONSULTANTS INC.
888 - 3rd Street SW
1500 Bankers Hall West
Calgary, AB T2P 5C5

Telephone 403-216-6999
Fax 403-216-6995
E-mail resumes@comunity.net
Website www.comunity.net
Founded 1996
Specialties Computing
Multimedia
Level Mid-Level
Contact Allan Jones , Director, Consulting

Description ComUnity Systems Consultants is a technical outsourcing firm specializing in ERP systems and Internet development personnel.

CONCEPT II EMPLOYMENT SERVICES

236 St. George Street
Suite 412, Commerce House
Moncton, NB E1C 8M9

Telephone	506-388-9675
Fax	506-388-9674
E-mail	info@concept2 employment.com
Website	www.concept2 employment.com
Founded	1997
Specialties	Administrative
Level	Junior Mid-Level
Contact	Robert Snider, Manager

Description Concept II is a leading small business recruitment and staffing service in Atlantic Canada.

CONCORD CONSULTING CORPORATION

9343 - 50th Street, Suite 5
Edmonton, AB T6B 2L5

Telephone	780-463-6060
Fax	780-463-6170
E-mail	concord@oanet.com
Website	www.concord consulting.com
Specialties	General Practice

Description Concord Consulting Corporation is an HR consulting firm that also provides occasional recruitment services.

CONESTOGA PERSONNEL RESOURCES INC.

421 Greenbrook Drive
Forest Hill Plaza
Kitchener, ON N2M 4K1

Telephone	519-570-1226
Fax	519-570-9530
E-mail	glogel@conestoga personnel.com
Website	www.conestoga personnel.com
Specialties	Engineering Operations Insurance Accounting
Level	Mid-Level Senior
Recruiters	Garry Logel Ben Logel
Contact	Garry Logel, President

Description Conestoga Personnel Resources Inc. is a professional placement and personnel search facility.

CONLIN PERSONNEL

789 West Pender Street, Suite 670
Vancouver, BC V6C 1H2

Telephone	604-685-1400
Fax	604-685-1425
E-mail	fwhite@conlin.bc.ca
Website	www.conlin personnel.com
Founded	1988
Specialties	Insurance
Level	Mid-Level
Recruiters	Hayley Ireland Freyja White
Contact	Freyja White

Description Conlin Personnel is BC's largest supplier of insurance staff. Now part of Ian Martin Limited.

CONNAUGHT CLARK & COMPANY INC.

2085 Hurontario Street, Suite 300
Mississauga, ON L5A 4G1

Telephone	905-270-5767
Fax	905-270-5755
E-mail	info@ connaughtclark.com
Website	www.connaught clark.com
Specialties	General Practice
Level	Senior Mid-Level
Min. Salary	$60,000
Fee Basis	Retainer Only
Contact	Peter J. Jacek

Description Connaught Clark & Co. is a leading retained executive search firm recruiting across a wide range of industries and functions.

CONNECTSTAFF SOLUTIONS CORP.

350 - 7th Avenue SW, Suite 3000
Calgary, AB T2P 3N6

Telephone	403-263-0039
Fax	403-263-0776
E-mail	gary.bozek@hvld.com
Website	www.connectstaff.com
Founded	1995
Employees	2
Specialties	Computing Human Resource Engineering
Level	Senior
Fee Basis	Sometimes contingent
Contact	Gary Bozek

Description Connectstaff Solutions specializes in IT, consulting, human resources and engineering discipline, with special attention to matching soft skills to client needs.

CONNOR CLARK & ASSOCIATES

43A Cross Street
Dundas, ON L9H 2R5

Telephone	905-627-3357
Fax	905-627-4787
E-mail	resumes@ connorclark.com
Website	www.connorclark.com
Founded	1998
Specialties	Marketing Sales Telecom
Level	Mid-Level
Min. Salary	$50,000
Fee Basis	Sometimes contingent
Recruiters	Jane Clark Carolyn Connor Perry Stuart
Contact	Jane Clark

Description Connor Clark & Associates specializes in recruiting sales and marketing professionals in the telecom and high tech industries.

CONNORS, LOVELL & ASSOCIATES INC.

260 Holiday Inn Drive, Suite 22
Cambridge, ON N3C 4E8

Telephone	519-651-1004
Fax	519-651-2083
E-mail	careers@conlov.com
Website	www.conlov.com
Founded	1996
Employees	9
Specialties	Accounting Engineering Health/Medical Human Resource Marketing Operations Purchasing Sales Automotive
Level	Senior Mid-Level
Min. Salary	$35,000
Fee Basis	Sometimes contingent
Recruiters	Barry Connors Virginia Grant Greg McKeown Ian Roberts Jim Vanderleeuw Jane Ward Ivan Zupanic
Contact	Barry Connors

Description Connors, Lovell & Associates Inc. is a full-service recruiting firm that meets and evaluates each and every candidate prior to a client presentation.

CONNORS, LOVELL & ASSOCIATES INC.

4 Robert Speck Parkway, Suite 280
Mississauga, ON L4Z 1S1

Telephone	905-566-4051
Fax	905-566-1038
E-mail	mississauga@ conlov.com
Website	www.conlov.com
Founded	1988
Employees	10
Specialties	Accounting Engineering Finance Health/Medical Human Resource International Management Marketing Operations Purchasing Sales Automotive Computing
Level	Mid-Level

Min. Salary $30,000
Fee Basis Sometimes contingent

Recruiters Frank Attard
Kevin Babinger
Lynn Beechey CPC
Randy Burke
Jon Hayhurst
Sharman Keddy
Nat La Rosa
Andrée Lovell CPC

Contact Andrée Lovell, CPC

Description Connors, Lovell & Associates Inc. is a full-service recruiting firm that meets and evaluates each and every candidate prior to a client presentation.

CONROY PARTNERS LIMITED
255 - 5th Avenue SW
Suite 830, Bow Valley Square 3
Calgary, AB T2P 3G6

Telephone 403-261-8080
Fax 403-261-8085
E-mail mail@conroy
partners.com
Website www.conroy
partners.com

Founded 1994
Specialties Oil & Gas
Management
Finance
Telecom
International
Geology/Geography

Level Senior
Min. Salary $75,000
Fee Basis Retainer Only

Recruiters M.J. (Jim) Conroy
Noranne Dickin
Scott S. Doupe
Peter Edwards
Mark Hopkins
Rick Lancaster

Contact M.J. (Jim) Conroy,
Managing Partner

Description Based in the center of Canada's oil and gas industry, about half Conroy Partners' search assignments are in this sector. Affiliated internationally with IIC Partners.

CONSEILLERS EN ADMINISTRATION FORMA, LES
3425, rue St. Hubert
Montréal, QC H2L 3Z8

Téléphone 514-521-7988
Télécopieur 514-521-4417
Courriel forma.inc@
sympatico.ca

Spécialités Généralistes
Aérospatial
Agriculture/pêches
Éducation
Ressources humaines
Gestion
Scientifique
Transport

Échelon Direction
Intermédiaire

Frais Honoraire seulement

CONSEILLERS EN PERSONNEL JACQUES CARTIER, LES
666 Sherbrooke West, 19th Floor
Montréal, QC H3A 1E7

Telephone 514-861-1511
Fax 514-861-7901
E-mail conseillers@
jacquescartier.com
Website www.jacques
cartier.com

Founded 1978
Specialties Management
Sales
Accounting
Computing
Engineering
Scientific
Bilingual

Level Mid-Level
Senior

Contact Linda Olivier

Description Les Conseillers en Personnel Jacques Cartier specializes in the recruitment and placement of permanent and contract personnel.

CONSULPRO
4141, rue Sherbrooke O.
Bureau 650
Westmount, QC H3Z 1B8

Telephone 514-932-9523
Fax 514-933-9192

Employees 80
Specialties Pharmaceutical
Biotech/Biology
Marketing
Sales

Level Senior
Mid-Level

Fee Basis Sometimes contingent
Recruiters David Browne
Maximilian Hoyos

Contact David Browne,
President

CONSULPRO EXECUTIVE SEARCH & RECRUITING
470 Somerset Street West
Ottawa, ON K1R 5J8

Telephone 613-236-3417
Fax 613-236-7964
E-mail conslpro@istar.ca

Founded 1967
Employees 5

Specialties Computing
Engineering
Management
Marketing
Sales

Level Senior
Min. Salary $40,000

Contact Mel Spotswood CPC,
President

Description ConsulPRO specializes in high tech placements — engineers to project management; sales & marketing to VP level; Presidents,

COO and CEO. National and international searches.

CONSULTANT'S CHOICE, INC.
1900 North Loop West, Suite 205
Houston, TX 77018 USA

Telephone 713-263-1400
Fax 713-263-1375
E-mail mmueller@cocho.com
Website www.consultants
choice.com

Founded 1982
Specialties International
Computing

Recruiters Gwen Bartley
Jerry Longsworth
Peter White
John Wise

Contact Mary Raymond

Description Consultant's Choice, Inc. places IT professionals on contract assignments in SAP, object-oriented programming, client server, Peoplesoft and Internet fields.

CONSULTATION DELAN INC.
750 Marcel-Laurin Street, Suite 128
Saint-Laurent, QC H4M 2M4

Telephone 514-744-3000
Fax 514-744-9941
E-mail info@delan.qc.ca
Website www.delan.qc.ca

Founded 1997
Employees 4

Specialties Computing
Level Senior
Mid-Level

Recruiters Anne-Marie Deslauriers
Lucie Houde
Laniel Louis
Diana Mackenzie

Contact Anne- Marie
Deslauriers

Description Consultation Delan Inc. is a search firm specializing in the recruitment of computer and high-tech professionals.

CONSULTATIONS GASTON BRAULT, LES
10 Shannon Street
Valleyfield, QC J6T 5V7

Téléphone 514-377-4494
Télécopieur 450-377-4494
Courriel gbrault@rocler.qc.ca

Spécialités Scientifique
Échelon Direction
Intermédiaire

Contact Gaston Brault

Description Les Consultations Gaston Brault offre un service conseil en gestion des ressources humaines et en relations industrielles.

CONTEMPORARY PERSONNEL INC.
808 Nelson Street, Suite 509
Vancouver, BC V6Z 2H2

Telephone   604-689-7775
Fax   604-689-1998
E-mail   van@contemporary.ca
Website   www.contemporary.ca

Employees   5

Specialties Accounting
             Administrative
             Banking

Level   Mid-Level
             Junior

Fee Basis   Always contingent

Contact   Leigh-Anne Stitt

Description Contemporary Personnel Inc. is a full-service personnel agency providing contract and permanent placement.

CONTEMPORARY PERSONNEL, INC.
4950 Yonge Street
Suite 202, Madison Centre
Toronto, ON M2N 6K1

Telephone   416-250-1500
Fax   416-250-1760
E-mail   stephw@
             contemporary.ca
Website   www.contemporary.ca

Specialties Computing
             Engineering
             Finance
             Administrative

Level   Mid-Level
             Junior

Fee Basis   Always contingent

Contact   Matt Coveart, Vice-President

Description Contemporary Personnel is a Canadian, full-service employment agency providing employees in all segments of the workforce.

CONTEMPORARY PERSONNEL INC.
7700 Hurontario Street, Suite 411
Brampton, ON L6Y 4M3

Telephone   905-457-8970
Fax   905-457-9651
E-mail   bramp@
             contemporary.ca
Website   www.contemporary.ca

Specialties Administrative
             Operations

Level   Junior

Fee Basis   Always contingent

Contact   Marianne Fraresso

Description Contemporary Personnel is a Canadian, full-service provider of staffing solutions focusing on the human resource sector.

CONTEMPORARY PERSONNEL INC.
11 Victoria Street, Suite 218
Barrie, ON L4N 6T3

Telephone   705-739-1238
Fax   705-739-0533
E-mail   barrie@
             contemporary.ca
Website   www.contemporary.ca

Specialties Administrative
             Operations

Level   Junior

Fee Basis   Always contingent

Contact   John Sudol, Manager

Description Contemporary Personnel is a Canadian, full-service provider of staffing solutions focusing on the human resource sector.

CONTEMPORARY PERSONNEL INC.
17665 Leslie Street, Suite 32
Newmarket, ON L3Y 3E3

Telephone   905-895-7001
Fax   905-895-0553
E-mail   newmrkt@
             contemporary.ca
Website   www.contemporary.ca

Specialties Automotive
             Administrative

Level   Junior

Fee Basis   Always contingent

Contact   John Sudol, Regional Manager

Description Contemporary Personnel is a Canadian, full-service provider of staffing solutions focusing on the human resource sector.

CONTEMPRA PERSONNEL
955 St-Jean Boulevard, Suite 206
Pointe-Claire, QC H9R 5K3

Telephone   514-694-1505
Fax   514-694-4330
E-mail   info@contempra
             personnel.com
Website   www.contempra
             personnel.com

Founded   1975

Specialties Engineering
             Sales
             Pharmaceutical

Level   Mid-Level

Recruiters   Michele Joly
             Karen Lester

Contact   Michele Joly

CONTRACTS CONSULTANCY LTD.
162 - 164 Upper Richmond Road
Putney, London SW15 2SL
UNITED KINGDOM

Telephone   44-208-333-4141
Fax   44-208-333-4151
E-mail   ccl@ccl.uk.com
Website   www.ccl.uk.com

Founded   1981

Specialties Engineering
             International
             Oil & Gas
             Mining
             Construction

Recruiters   David Giles
             Peter Maltby

Contact   David Giles,
             Operations Director

Description CCL provides contract and permanent staff to companies practically anywhere in the world. They have a database of over 24,000

professionals and annual sales of over $10 million.

CORE GROUP, THE
1200 Eglinton Ave. East, Suite 708
Toronto, ON M3C 1H9

Telephone   416-445-7855
Fax   416-445-7853
E-mail   info@corecareer.com
Website   www.corecareer.com

Specialties Computing
             Engineering
             Finance
             Sales

Level   Mid-Level

Contact   Ramil Navidad,
             Director

Description The Core Group specializes in the placement of mid-management to executive positions in IT, engineering, finance and sales.

CORE-STAFF INCORPORATED
2255 Sheppard Ave. E., Suite A133
Toronto, ON M2J 5C4

Telephone   416-498-4444
Fax   416-498-0378

Employees   3

Specialties Accounting
             Administrative
             Bilingual
             Human Resource
             Printing

Level   Junior
             Mid-Level

Fee Basis   Always contingent

Contact   Judith Crawley,
             Manager

Description Core-Staff Incorporated provides all levels of permanent and contract administrative support staff across the Greater Toronto Area.

CORNELL CONSULTING CORP.
3050 Harvester Road, Suite 104
Burlington, ON L7N 3J1

Telephone   905-333-8947
Fax   905-333-6606
E-mail   consult@sprint.ca

Specialties Computing
             Engineering
             Design

Contact   Gerald Cornell,
             Resource Manager

CORPORATE & CAREER DEVELOPMENT INC.
800 West Pender Street, Suite 220
Vancouver, BC V6C 2V6

Telephone   604-685-5094
Fax   604-685-6597
E-mail   proact@uniserve.com

Specialties Accounting
             Hospitality
             Sales
             Computing

Contact   A. McPherson

CORPORATE COACH, THE
303 Mount Lorette Place SE
Calgary, AB T2Z 2L8

Telephone	403-257-8125
Fax	403-257-8126
E-mail	corpcoach@ cybersurf.net
Specialties	General Practice
Level	Mid-Level
Contact	Marilyn Hanner

Description The Corporate Coach provides HR, training and development and pre-screening services to small/medium-sized businesses.

CORPORATE CONSULTANTS
155 University Avenue, Suite 1910
Toronto, ON M5H 3B7

Telephone	416-862-1259
Fax	416-862-7926
E-mail	corpcon@istar.ca
Founded	1976
Employees	10
Specialties	Accounting
	Computing
	Engineering
	Finance
	International
	Management
	Marketing
	Operations
	Purchasing
	Sales
	Scientific
	Aerospace
	Biotech/Biology
	Health/Medical
Level	Mid-Level
	Senior
Fee Basis	Sometimes contingent
Contact	Gordon Brown

Description Corporate Consultants operate in the financial, operations, marketing and technology / scientific sectors, finding solutions to clients' recruiting problems.

CORPORATE CONTROLLERS INC.
1454 Dresden Row, Suite 104
Halifax, NS B3J 3G6

Telephone	902-425-8975
Fax	902-492-3758
E-mail	cci@istar.ca
Founded	1996
Employees	3
Specialties	Accounting
	Finance
Level	Mid-Level
Contact	David Flewwelling
	CMA

Description Corporate Controllers Inc. provides professional management accountants on contract or permanent assignments.

CORPORATE EXPRESSIONS INC.
41 Spruce Street, Unit 4
Toronto, ON M5A 2H8

Telephone	416-922-6701
Fax	416-366-4747
Specialties	Accounting
	Human Resource
Contact	Anne Perdue

CORPORATE HUMAN RESOURCE COMMUNICATIONS LTD.
280 Smith Street, 2nd Floor
Winnipeg, MB R3C 1K2

Telephone	204-943-3312
Fax	204-943-6192
E-mail	llicharson@chrc.mb.ca
Founded	1985
Employees	11
Specialties	Finance
	Accounting
	Human Resource
	Health/Medical
	General Practice
	Engineering
	Banking
Contact	Larry Licharson, President

Description Corporate HR Communications specializes in recruitment advertising.

CORPORATE RECRUITERS INC.
48 Hayden Street
Toronto, ON M4Y 1V8

Telephone	416-362-6111
Fax	416-362-1041
E-mail	info@ corporate-recruiters.com
Website	www.corporate-recruiters.com
Specialties	Insurance
	Finance

Description Corporate Recruiters Inc. specializes in recruiting professionals in the insurance and financial sectors.

CORPORATE RECRUITERS LTD.
1140 West Pender Street, Suite 490
Vancouver, BC V6E 4G1

Telephone	604-687-5993
Fax	604-687-2427
E-mail	jobs@corporate.bc.ca
Website	www.corporate.bc.ca
Founded	1980
Employees	12
Specialties	Engineering
	Marketing
	Sales
	Computing
	Telecom
Level	Senior
	Mid-Level
Min. Salary	$40,000
Fee Basis	Sometimes contingent
Recruiters	Doug Anderson
	Kimberllay Brooks
	Charles Brooks
	Julie Clark
	Amanda Du Toit
	Bruce Edmond
	Robbie Herd
	Ivan Hnatiuk
	Albert Pflug
	Marvin Pon
	Don Safnuk
	Chantal St-Lauren
	Raymond To
Contact	Roanne Liew

Description Corporate Recruiters is Western Canada's largest high-tech and technical sales recruitment specialist.

CORPORATE RESOURCES (HERTFORD) LTD.
28 Waterdale, Hertford SG13 8DU
UNITED KINGDOM

Telephone	44-1992-422022
Fax	44-1992-558661
E-mail	mark.tizard@ lineone.net
Specialties	Accounting
	Finance
	International
	Oil & Gas
Contact	Mark Tizard

CORPORATE RESOURCES INC.
145 King Street West, Suite 1000
Toronto, ON M5H 1J8

Telephone	416-368-2333
Fax	416-947-0231
E-mail	crsi@sprint.ca
Specialties	Finance
	Accounting
	Architecture
Level	Mid-Level

CORTEX HR INC.
340 Lonsdale Road, Suite 206
Toronto, ON M5P 1R2

Telephone	877-6CORTEX
Fax	416-784-4023
E-mail	info@cortexhr.com
Website	www.cortexhr.com
Specialties	Scientific
	Biotech/Biology
	Pharmaceutical
Level	Mid-Level
Contact	Michael A. Kalchman, BSc, PhD

Description Cortex HR Inc. provides consulting and recruiting services for the biotechnology and pharmaceutical industries.

COSIER ASSOCIATES, INC.
520 - 5th Avenue SW, Suite 2300
Calgary, AB T2P 3R7

Telephone	403-232-8350
Fax	403-781-5885
E-mail	cosierb@cadvision.com
Founded	1997
Employees	3
Specialties	Oil & Gas
	Engineering
	Geology/Geography
	Finance
Level	Mid-Level

Min. Salary $70,000
Fee Basis Sometimes contingent

Contact Brian L. Cosier

Description Cosier Associates, Inc. places men and women in Canada's oil and gas industry.

COUNSEL NETWORK, THE
400 Burrard Street, Suite 1400
Vancouver, BC V6C 3G2

Telephone 604-240-7457
Fax 604-685-3148
E-mail dal@inhousecounsel.ca
Website www.inhouse
counsel.ca

Founded 1988
Employees 4

Specialties Law

Level Senior
Mid-Level

Min. Salary $40,000
Fee Basis Sometimes contingent

Recruiters Dalvinder Bhathal
Karen Maki

Contact Dal Bhathal

Description Counsel Network is an international lawyer recruitment and career consulting firm.

COUNSEL NETWORK, THE
888 - 3rd Street SW
Suite 1500, Bankers Hall West
Calgary, AB T2P 5C5

Telephone 403-264-3838
Fax 403-264-3819
E-mail snash@headhunt.com
Website www.headhunt.com

Specialties Law

Level Senior
Mid-Level

Min. Salary $40,000

Recruiters Sean Dunnigan QC
Stephen Nash
Leslie Weekes

Contact G. Sean Dunnigan,
Managing Director

Description The Counsel Network is an international lawyer recruitment and career consulting firm, with offices in Canada and the USA.

COUNSEL NETWORK, THE
110 - 110th Avenue NE
Suite 503, PO Box 90015
Bellevue, WA 98004 USA

Telephone 206-292-4797
Fax 206-292-4798
E-mail snash@headhunt.com
Website www.headhunt.com

Founded 1988

Specialties Law
International

Level Senior
Mid-Level

Min. Salary $40,000

Contact Stephen Nash

Description The Counsel Network primarily focuses on the legal markets in western Canada, the Pacific Northwest and the western USA.

COUNTY PERSONNEL SERVICES
1506 Greenwood Road, PO Box 253
Ruthven, ON N0P 2G0

Telephone 519-326-2974
Fax 519-326-7073
E-mail cps@wincom.net

Founded 1997
Employees 1

Specialties General Practice

Contact Kathryn Bates

COURTNEY PERSONNEL INC.
201 County Court Blvd., Suite 501A
Brampton, ON L6W 4L2

Telephone 905-452-9555
Fax 905-452-7762
E-mail courtneypers@sprint.ca

Founded 1987
Employees 5

Specialties Accounting
Finance
Health/Medical
Management
Marketing
Operations
Purchasing
Bilingual

Level Mid-Level

Fee Basis Always contingent

Contact Helen Watkinson

Description Career specialists. Permanent and contract positions. Outplacement consultants. Human resources experts.

COWAN & ASSOCIATES
400 - 5th Avenue SW, Suite 300
Calgary, AB T2P 0L6

Telephone 403-303-2849
Fax 403-264-9218
E-mail gordon.cowan@
internode.net

Specialties Accounting
Automotive

Level Mid-Level

Contact Gordon Cowan

Description Cowan & Associates is an executive recruiting and human resources management firm.

COWAN PERSONNEL CONSULTANTS LTD.
4141, rue Sherbrooke O.
Bureau 303
Montréal, QC H3Z 1B8

Telephone 514-842-8311
Fax 514-842-8313
E-mail info@cowan
personnel.com
Website www.cowan
personnel.com

Founded 1954

Specialties International
Management
Accounting
Engineering
Human Resource
Geology/Geography
Mining
Pulp & Paper

Level Mid-Level
Senior

Fee Basis Sometimes contingent

Recruiters Andrew Harris
Cathy Harris
Christiane St-Amour

Contact Andrew Harris

Description Canada's longest-established executive search and recruitment company. Over 46 years of experience in the recruitment of highly trained personnel for the international mining industry. Many assignments in Africa.

COWAN WRIGHT LTD.
100 Regina Street South
Suite 270, PO Box 96
Waterloo, ON N2J 3Z8

Telephone 519-886-1690
Fax 519-886-0829
E-mail info@cowanwright.com
Website www.cowanwright.com

Founded 1980
Employees 70

Specialties Insurance

Level Mid-Level

Contact E. Robert Pyatt CA CHRP

Description Cowan Wright Ltd. (formerly Wright Mogg & Associates Ltd.) is a management consulting firm, specializing in human resources. Their services include recruitment in the insurance industry.

COX, MERRITT & CO. LLP
308 Palladium Drive, Suite 106
Kanata, ON K2V 1A1

Telephone 613-591-7605
Fax 613-591-7607
E-mail cox.merritt@
sympatico.ca

Specialties Accounting
Finance

Level Mid-Level

Description Cox, Merritt & Co. LLP is a firm of chartered accountants that provides a full range of services, including search services, to clients throughout Ottawa-Carleton.

CPC HUMAN RESOURCES INC.
4385 Jean-Brillant
Montréal, QC H3T 1P2

Specialties General Practice

Level Mid-Level

CRAIG DAVIES COLLINS
5913 - 50th Avenue, 2nd Floor
Red Deer, AB T4N 4C4

Telephone	403-346-4134
Fax	403-341-4242
E-mail	cdcca@telusplanet.net
Specialties	Finance
	Accounting
Level	Mid-Level
Contact	W.G. Craig CA

Description Craig Davies Collins is an accounting firm that also does occasional search work for clients.

CRAWFORD DE MUNNIK EXECUTIVE SEARCH
130 Adelaide St. West, Suite 2000
Toronto, ON M5H 3P5

Telephone	416-863-0153
Fax	416-863-1390
E-mail	toronto@crawford demunnik.com
Founded	2001
Employees	4
Specialties	General Practice
	Finance
	Mining
	Automotive
	International
	Oil & Gas
	Publishing/Media
Level	Senior
	Mid-Level
Min. Salary	$90,000
Fee Basis	Retainer Only
Recruiters	John D. Crawford
	N. Lynne de Munnik
Contact	N. Lynne de Munnik

Description Crawford de Munnik Executive Search (former Boyden Global 's Toronto office) is a generalist executive search firm with experience in a wide range of industries, functional areas and professions.

CREATIVE FINANCIAL STAFFING
1190 Hornby Street, Suite 1000
Vancouver, BC V6Z 2W2

Telephone	604-669-9525
Fax	604-687-5617
E-mail	bcjobs@cfstaffing.com
Website	www.cfstaffing.com
Founded	1997
Employees	1
Specialties	Accounting
	Finance
Level	Mid-Level
Fee Basis	Always contingent
Contact	Wendi Hinton

Description CFS is a contract and direct-hire staffing company specializing in accounting and financial placements.

CREATIVE FINANCIAL STAFFING
595 Bay Street, Suite 303
Toronto, ON M5G 2C2

Telephone	416-596-7075
Fax	416-596-1456
E-mail	cfsadmin@hto.com
Website	www.cfstaffing.com

Founded	1995
Employees	13
Specialties	Accounting
	Finance
Level	Mid-Level
	Junior
Fee Basis	Always contingent
Contact	Jeff Silver

Description CFS is a contract and direct-hire staffing company specializing in accounting and financial placements. This office is managed by the accounting firm of Horwath Orenstein LLP.

CREATIVE FINANCIAL STAFFING
45 Sheppard Avenue East
Suite 900
Toronto, ON M2N 5W9

Telephone	416-218-4261
Fax	416-218-4262
E-mail	cfsadmin@hto.com
Website	www.cfstaffing.com
Founded	1994
Specialties	Accounting
	Finance
Level	Mid-Level

Description CFS is a contract and direct-hire staffing company specializing in accounting and financial placements.

CREATIVE FINANCIAL STAFFING
201 City Centre Drive, Suite 900
Mississauga, ON L5B 2T4

Telephone	905-306-7733
Fax	905-306-7716
E-mail	cfsadmin@hto.com
Website	www.cfstaffing.com
Founded	1994
Specialties	Accounting
Level	Mid-Level
Contact	Daren Radford

Description CFS is a contract and direct-hire staffing company specializing in accounting and financial placements.

CREATIVE FORCE NETWORK LTD.
150 Eglinton Ave. East, Suite 303
Toronto, ON M4P 1E8

Telephone	416-932-3830
Fax	416-932-3506
E-mail	creative@ cforcenet.com
Specialties	Graphic Arts
	Design
	Multimedia
	Advertising
Level	Senior
	Mid-Level
Recruiters	Dorothea Kanga
	Laura McCormick
Contact	Laura McCormick

Description Creative Force Network Ltd. specializes in placing graphic designers, copywriters, multimedia specialists, coordinators and proofreaders in freelance and full-time opportunities.

CRODEN PERSONNEL CONSULTING SERVICES INC.
1090 West Georgia Street, Suite 830
Vancouver, BC V6E 3V7

Telephone	604-683-9691
Fax	604-683-2285
E-mail	staff@croden personnel.com
Website	www.croden personnel.com
Founded	1975
Employees	4
Specialties	Computing
	Health/Medical
	Scientific
Level	Mid-Level
Recruiters	Irene Croden CHRP
	Debby McKenzie
	Jill Shea
Contact	Irene Croden, President

Description Croden Personnel Consulting specializes in recruiting for permanent, contract, IT and healthcare staffing positions.

CROMARK INTERNATIONAL INC.
6507D Mississauga Road
Mississauga, ON L5N 1A6

Telephone	905-816-9090
Fax	905-816-9077
E-mail	resume@cromark.com
Website	www.cromark.com
Founded	1973
Specialties	Transport
	Automotive
	Retail
Level	Mid-Level
	Senior
Recruiters	Clive Crowe
	Ian McEwen
	Steve Munro
Contact	Clive Crowe, CEO

Description Cromark International has been a leading Canadian search firm for opportunities within the automotive and retail industries since 1973.

CROSS COUNTRY TRAVCORPS
6551 Park of Commerce Blvd.
Suite 200
Boca Raton, FL 33487-8247
USA

Telephone	800-530-6125
Fax	561-998-8533
E-mail	info@cctcmail.com
Website	www.crosscountry travcorps.com
Specialties	Health/Medical
	International
Level	Mid-Level

Description Cross Country TravCorps has thousands of nationwide opportunities for nurses, technicians, therapists, advanced practitioners, and other medical professionals in a variety of settings.

CROSSLINK CONSULTING
1500 West Georgia St., Suite 1400
Vancouver, BC V6G 2Z6

Telephone	604-689-0155
Fax	604-821-1004
E-mail	lightfoot@wwdb.org
Specialties	Computing
Contact	Jolyane A. Lightfoot

Description CrossLink is an IT consulting firm that recruits various computer professionals, including Peoplesoft and Unix programmers.

CRYSTAL PERSONNEL SERVICES
909 Simcoe North
Oshawa, ON L1G 4W1

Telephone	905-579-0252
Fax	905-579-0667
Specialties	General Practice

CSI CONSULTING
150 York Street, Suite 1820
Toronto, ON M5H 3S5

Telephone	416-364-6376
Fax	416-364-2735
E-mail	csi@csican.com
Website	www.csican.com
Specialties	Computing
Level	Mid-Level
	Senior
Contact	Shylee Holla

Description CSI is an IT consulting practice providing customized project resourcing and technology solutions addressing the unique needs of clients across North America.

CTC COMPUTER-TECH CONSULTANTS LTD.
355 Burrard Street, Suite 880
Vancouver, BC V6C 2G8

Telephone	604-689-2900
Fax	604-689-2905
E-mail	vancouver@ ctctech.com
Website	www.ctctech.com
Founded	1985
Specialties	Computing
Level	Senior
	Mid-Level
Recruiters	Faye Cardenas
	Nidal Haley
	Judy Norraine
Contact	Paul Woodhouse, President

Description CTC Computer-Tech Consultants Ltd. is one of western Canada's largest providers of information technology resources. Now part of Ajilon Canada Inc.

CTC COMPUTER-TECH CONSULTANTS LTD.
Edmonton Centre
1824 Merrill Lynch Tower
Edmonton, AB T5J 2Z1

Telephone	780-421-8937
Fax	780-425-0700
E-mail	edmonton@ ctctech.com
Website	www.ctctech.com
Founded	1985
Employees	50
Specialties	Computing
Level	Mid-Level
	Senior
Contact	Deborah Horn

Description CTC Computer-Tech Consultants Ltd. is one of western Canada's largest providers of information technology professionals. Now part of Ajilon Canada Inc.

CTC COMPUTER-TECH CONSULTANTS LTD.
101 - 6th Avenue SW, Suite 2420
Calgary, AB T2P 3G2

Telephone	403-233-7233
Fax	403-233-7343
E-mail	calgary@ctctech.com
Website	www.ctctech.com
Founded	1985
Specialties	Computing
Level	Mid-Level
Recruiters	Griff Hawkins
	Jeanne Lefebvre
	Sandra Major
	Patrick Saunderson
Contact	Paul Woodhouse, President

Description CTC Computer-Tech Consultants Ltd. is one of western Canada's largest providers of information technology resources. Now part of Ajilon Canada Inc.

CTC COMPUTER-TECH CONSULTANTS LTD.
1777 Victoria Avenue, Suite 1000
Regina, SK S4P 4K5

Telephone	306-757-3119
Fax	306-757-3732
E-mail	regina@ctctech.com
Website	www.ctctech.com
Founded	1985
Specialties	Computing
Level	Senior
	Mid-Level
Recruiters	Charles Hoppe
	Paul Woodhouse
Contact	Charles Hoppe

Description CTC Computer-Tech Consultants Ltd. is one of western Canada's largest providers of information technology professionals on a permanent or contract basis. Now part of Ajilon Canada Inc.

CTC COMPUTER-TECH CONSULTANTS LTD.
177 Lombard Avenue, Suite 401
Winnipeg, MB R3B 0W5

Telephone	204-942-6699
Fax	204-942-8833
E-mail	winnipeg@ctctech.com
Website	www.ctctech.com
Founded	1985
Specialties	Computing
Level	Mid-Level
Fee Basis	Sometimes contingent
Contact	Renée Sierra, Manager

Description CTC Computer-Tech Consultants Ltd. is one of western Canada's largest providers of information technology professionals on a permanent or contract basis. Now part of Ajilon Canada Inc.

CTEW EXECUTIVE PERSONNEL SERVICES INC.
409 Granville Street, Suite 1207
Vancouver, BC V6C 1T2

Telephone	604-682-3218
Fax	604-683-3211
E-mail	ctew@imag.net
Founded	1989
Employees	12
Specialties	Hospitality
	General Practice
Level	Senior
	Mid-Level
Min. Salary	$35,000
Fee Basis	Always contingent
Recruiters	Shaula Evans
	Hayley Lau
Contact	Hayley Lau, Manager

Description CTEW is a full-service recruitment firm providing junior-to executive-level placement services, particularly in the hospiatlity industry.

CTS INTERNATIONAL, INC.
11100 - 8th Street NE, Suite 510
Bellevue, WA 98004-4441
USA

Telephone	425-451-0051
Fax	425-451-0052
E-mail	recruiting@ ctsinternational.com
Website	www.ctstech.com
Specialties	Computing
	Aerospace
	International
	Telecom
Level	Senior
	Mid-Level
Recruiters	David Chalmers
	Stephen Dworkin
	Eli Grayevsky
	Charles Mosher
Contact	Stephen Dworkin, President

Description CTS International, Inc. provides highly-skilled technical personnel to the information technology, telecommunications and aerospace industries.

CV THEQUE
1800 boul. le Corbusier, bur. 120
Laval, QC H7S 2K1

Téléphone 450-686-1333
Télécopieur 450-686-1722
Courriel resume@cvtheque.com
Site Internet www.cvtheque.com

Spécialités Biotechnologie/biologie
Informatique
Ingénierie
Métiers/techniciens

Échelon Direction
Intermédiaire

Contact Jean-Luc Archambealt

Description CVTHÈQUE est une banque centrale de CV et d'emplois spécialisés en TGCA (technologie, génie, chimie, administration).

CYBERNA ASSOCIATES LIMITED
999, boul. de Maisonneuve Ouest
Bureau 650
Montréal, QC H3A 3L4

Telephone 514-843-8349
Fax 514-843-6993
E-mail wbrown@
optioncyberna.com

Founded 1970
Employees 6

Specialties Accounting
Engineering
Finance
Human Resource
Logistics
Pharmaceutical
Marketing

Level Senior
Mid-Level

Min. Salary $50,000
Fee Basis Sometimes contingent

Recruiters Wanda Brown
Jean-François Deslisle
Jean-Marc Robitaille
Hanna Vineberg

Contact Wanda Brown, VP &
General Manager

Description Cyberna Associates is an HR consulting firm offering recruitment and executive search as well as interim management, contract placement and outsourcing services.

CYR & ASSOCIATES
5069 Cedar Springs Court
Campbellville, ON L0P 1B0

Fax 416-946-1353
E-mail acyr@home.com

Specialties Finance
Management

Level Mid-Level
Senior

D.C. POWERS & ASSOCIATES LTD.
900 West Hastings Street, 4th Floor
Vancouver, BC V6C 1E6

Telephone 604-622-5555
Fax 604-622-5556
E-mail dhalley@dcpowers.com
Website www.dcpowers.com

Founded 1986

Specialties Insurance
Disabled

Contact Dean Powers

Description D.C. Powers & Associates Ltd. specializes in directing people with disabilities toward suitable employment opportunities.

D & G DUDAR CONSULTANTS
148 Springbrooke Crescent
Mississauga, ON L5R 2L2

Telephone 905-890-9968
Fax 905-890-8579
E-mail ddudar@sympatico.ca
Website www3.sympatico.ca/
ddudar

Specialties General Practice

Description D & G Dudar Consultants provides HR consulting services, including occasional recruiting for clients.

D & H GROUP
1441 Creekside Drive, Suite 500
Vancouver, BC V6J 4S7

Telephone 604-731-5881
Fax 604-731-9923
E-mail mlouie@dhgroup.ca
Website www.dhgroup.ca

Founded 1952
Employees 40

Specialties Accounting
Finance
Real Estate

Level Mid-Level

Min. Salary $35,000
Fee Basis Retainer Only

Contact Michael E. Louie

Description D&H Group is an accounting firm that also does search work for clients on an as-needed basis.

D.J. MACADAM & ASSOCIATES INC.
103 - 2609 Westview Dr., Box 202
North Vancouver, BC V7N 4N2

Telephone 604-929-6852
Fax 604-929-8655
E-mail deb@djmacadam.com

Specialties Govt/Nonprofit
Computing
Engineering

Contact Deborah Macadam

Description D.J. Macadam & Associates Inc. provides technical recruitment and HR consulting.

D.J. SIMPSON ASSOCIATES INC.
1900 Minnesota Court, Suite 118
Mississauga, ON L5N 3C9

Telephone 905-821-2727
Fax 905-821-3800

E-mail djsai@inforamp.net
Specialties Management
Level Mid-Level
Senior

Contact David J. Simpson,
Principal

D.P. GROUP, THE
1 - 7 Fulham High Street
Nightingale House
London, SW6 3JH
UNITED KINGDOM

Telephone 44-20-460-7900
Fax 44-20-460-8030
E-mail enquiries@
thedpgroup.com
Website www.thedpgroup.com

Founded 1987
Employees 25

Specialties Computing
Banking
International
Accounting
Management
Telecom

Level Senior

Min. Salary $80,000
Fee Basis Sometimes contingent

Recruiters Nigel Connell
Julie Harrington
Colette Harrison
David Jones
Conor O'Dwyer
Tom Owen

Contact Rosalyn Dwan

Description The D.P. Group is an established recruitment consultancy, resourcing the needs of the management, information technology and telecom marketplace.

D.R. NOLAN ASSOCIATES INC.
320 Bay St., Suite 1510, PO Box 16
Toronto, ON M5H 4A6

Telephone 416-868-9991
Fax 416-868-9394
E-mail drnolan@sympatico.ca

Founded 1996

Specialties Finance
Banking
Human Resource
Management

Level Senior

Min. Salary $80,000
Fee Basis Retainer Only

Contact D.R. Nolan

Description D.R. Nolan Associates Inc. does not accept unsolicited resumes outside their practice area (senior-level placements).

DAN MCNAMARA & ASSOCIATES
1147 Mohawk Street
Woodstock, ON N5T 1B1

Fax 519-421-2353
E-mail mcnamara@oxford.net
Website www.execulink.com/
~mcnamara

Specialties	Engineering Operations General Practice
Recruiters	George Hodgins Dan McNamara Shannon McNamara Craig Ryan
Contact	Dan McNamara, President

Description Dan McNamara & Associates is a management consulting firm specializing in HR assignments, including search and placement.

DANA CONSULTANTS
3532 Griffith Street
Saint-Laurent, QC H4T 1A7

Telephone	514-731-6836
Specialties	Operations Scientific
Level	Junior
Contact	M. Daniel Salem, Président

Description Dana Consultants provides consulting services within the chemical industry, including occasional recruitment services.

DANA STEHR & ASSOCIATES INC.
21 St. Clair Ave. East, Suite 1400
Toronto, ON M4T 1L9

Telephone	416-515-7100
Fax	416-515-0003
E-mail	dana@pmds-search.com
Employees	4
Specialties	Govt/Nonprofit Management Health/Medical
Level	Mid-Level Senior
Fee Basis	Retainer Only
Recruiters	Paul Michaelis Dana Stehr
Contact	Dana Stehr

Description Dana Stehr & Associates is a boutique search practice specializing in social service, healthcare and not-for-profit sectors.

DANEK ANTHONY INC.
14774 Goggs Avenue
White Rock, BC V4B 2N2

Telephone	604-542-0131
Fax	604-542-0138
E-mail	domdomin@ uniserve.com
Founded	1998
Specialties	Human Resource Management General Practice
Level	Senior Mid-Level
Fee Basis	Retainer Only
Contact	Don Dominczuk

Description Danek Anthony Inc. provides professional, executive and technical search and employee resource management services.

DANEK ANTHONY INC.
250 The Esplanade, Suite 402
Toronto, ON M5A 1J2

Telephone	416-214-9938
Fax	416-214-9004
Founded	1998
Specialties	Human Resource Management General Practice
Level	Senior Mid-Level
Fee Basis	Retainer Only

Description Danek Anthony Inc. provides professional, executive and technical search and employee resource management services.

DANETTE MILNE CORPORATE SEARCH INC.
4981 Hwy.7 E., Unit 12A, Suite 205
Markham, ON L1S 7A8

Telephone	416-410-1814
Fax	905-426-2552
E-mail	danette@ dmcorpsearch.com
Founded	1990
Employees	3
Specialties	Computing Engineering Finance Human Resource Sales
Level	Senior Mid-Level
Min. Salary	$35,000
Fee Basis	Always contingent
Recruiters	Danette Milne Evette Milne Carole Milne
Contact	Danette Milne

DANILUCK & ASSOCIATES INTERNATIONAL
5555 Calgary Trail
Suite 1435, Weber Centre
Edmonton, AB T6H 5P9

Telephone	780-448-1717
Fax	780-448-0127
E-mail	search@daniluck.com
Website	www.daniluck.com
Founded	1982
Employees	5
Specialties	Sales Marketing Accounting Computing Engineering Management General Practice Logistics
Level	Mid-Level Senior
Fee Basis	Retainer Only

Recruiters	Bruce Daniluck Vanore Voaklander
Contact	Bruce Daniluck CMC, CHRP

Description Daniluck & Associates International is an HR consulting firm specializing in executive searches on a regional, national and international basis.

DARE HUMAN RESOURCES CORPORATION
275 Slater Street, Suite 900
Ottawa, ON K1P 5H9

Telephone	613-238-4485
Fax	613-236-3754
E-mail	jvitanza@darehr.com
Website	www.darehr.com
Founded	1987
Employees	200
Specialties	Trades/Technicians Administrative Health/Medical Law Accounting Sales
Level	Junior Mid-Level
Fee Basis	Always contingent
Contact	Jocelyne Vitanza

Description Dare Human Resources Corporation (formerly Dare Personnel Inc.) specialize in technical, administrative, medical, legal and industrial recruitment.

DATALIST
55 Eglinton Avenue East, Suite 605
Toronto, ON M4P 1G8

Telephone	416-483-7424
Fax	416-483-7676
E-mail	info@datalist.com
Website	www.datalist.com
Founded	1983
Employees	25
Specialties	Computing Management
Level	Mid-Level Senior
Recruiters	Fiona Adams Theresa Adrusko Diane Archer Derek Bailey Kerry Bryski Tony Damourakis Fiorenzo Di Biase Rachel Di Natale Sherri Dmyterko Val Freedman Sheryl Hamilton Lisa Kamerling Terry King Dave Mann Victor Munroe Richard Smith Lisa Titian Rachel Whittington Angeline Yuen-Pitre
Contact	Rita Leyderman, Office Manager

Description Datalist specializes in the recruitment and placement of IT professionals within local and national markets.

DATAWARE CONSULTING INC.
423 Bedford Park Avenue
PO Box 54544
Toronto, ON M5M 1K2

Telephone	416-784-4322
Fax	416-784-3333
E-mail	it@dataware consulting.com
Website	www.dataware consulting.com
Founded	1988
Specialties	Computing
Level	Mid-Level

Description Dataware Consulting Inc. is a highly specialized IT recruitment and consulting firm focused on Unix, Windows and client-server technologies.

DATPRO PERSONNEL INC.
7368 Yonge Street, Suite 300
Toronto, ON L4J 8H9

Telephone	905-763-0989
Fax	905-763-6141
E-mail	info@datpro.com
Website	www.datpro.com
Founded	1995
Specialties	Computing
Level	Mid-Level
Contact	Victor Visconti

Description DatPro specializes in IT placements, with a database of over 20,000 IT professionals and clients in the Toronto area.

DAVE WHITE PERSONNEL INC.
1400 Mary Street
Ottawa, ON L1G 7B6

Telephone	905-432-9655
Fax	905-432-9657
E-mail	dwhitepernsl@ home.com
Specialties	Banking Finance
Contact	Dave White

DAVID APLIN & ASSOCIATES
10235 - 101st Street
Suite 2300, Oxford Tower
Edmonton, AB T5J 3G1

Telephone	780-428-6663
Fax	780-421-4680
E-mail	adedm@aplin.com
Website	www.aplin.com
Founded	1975
Employees	23
Specialties	Oil & Gas Pharmaceutical Telecom Engineering Finance Accounting Computing

Level	Mid-Level Senior
Min. Salary	$30,000
Fee Basis	Always contingent
Recruiters	David Aplin Mike Bacchus JoAnn Beliveau Michael Clark Mike Corbett Margie Graham Susanne Hoffmann Lorraine Krahn Burke Linttell Denise Mondor Terri Nobert Tricia Penton Diane Rolin Jennifer Ward
Contact	David Aplin, President

Description David Aplin & Associates, a 25-year old firm, specializes in providing mid-level technical professionals for companies in Western Canada.

DAVID APLIN & ASSOCIATES
777 - 8th Avenue SW
Suite 1600, First Alberta Place
Calgary, AB T2P 3R5

Telephone	403-261-5903
Fax	403-266-7195
E-mail	adcgy@aplin.com
Website	www.aplin.com
Founded	1974
Employees	16
Specialties	Computing Accounting Management Sales Telecom Engineering Human Resource
Level	Mid-Level Senior
Min. Salary	$30,000
Fee Basis	Always contingent
Recruiters	Michelle Cariou Daphne Harris Ken Hergert Andrew Horton Kathryn Lock Kieran Longworth Denise Richards Janice Smith Laura Strachan Kim Strba Stacey Tennant
Contact	Kieran Longworth

Description David Aplin & Associates, a 25-year old firm, specializes in providing mid-level technical professionals for companies in Western Canada.

DAVID BELL EXECUTIVE SEARCH
277 Richmond Street West
Toronto, ON M5V 1X1

Telephone	416-410-6060
Fax	416-597-0432
E-mail	info@davidbell search.com
Website	www.pub-rels.com
Specialties	Public Relations
Level	Senior Mid-Level
Recruiters	David Bell Roxanne Cramer
Contact	David Bell

Description David Bell is the only executive search firm in Canada that specializes exclusively in all facets of public relations/public affairs.

DAVID TAYLOR MANUFACTURING SEARCH INC.
50 Birch Avenue
Toronto, ON M4V 1C8

Telephone	416-963-8002
Fax	416-364-2733
E-mail	dave@taylorsearch.com
Founded	1999
Employees	2
Specialties	Engineering Management Operations
Level	Mid-Level Senior
Min. Salary	$60,000
Fee Basis	Retainer Only
Contact	David Taylor

DAVID WARWICK KENNEDY & ASSOCIATES / DWK
666 Burrard Street
Suite 3400, Park Place
Vancouver, BC V6C 2X8

Telephone	604-685-9494
Fax	604-669-5156
E-mail	dwksearch@ lightspeed.bc.ca
Website	www.biznet. maximizer.com/ dwksearch
Founded	1984
Employees	1
Specialties	Finance Accounting Sales Computing Forestry Mining
Level	Mid-Level Senior
Min. Salary	$50,000
Fee Basis	Retainer Only
Contact	David W. Kennedy

Description We perform daring acts of human resource larceny throughout business and the professions. We particularly relish assignments which involve headhunting financial, sales or IT professionals.

DAVIES KIDD
1 Temple Ave., Hamilton House
Victoria Embankment
London, EC4Y 0HA
UNITED KINGDOM

Telephone	44-20-7489-2053

Fax 44-20-7353 0612
E-mail careers@ davies-
kidd.co.uk
Website www.erisk.co.uk
Specialties Accounting
Finance
International
Contact Jeff Davies
Description Davies Kidd is a global
recruitment consultancy which of-
fers a service dedicated exclusively
to the practice and consultancy.

DAVIES PARK
10235 - 101st Street
Suite 904, Oxford Tower
Edmonton, AB T5J 3G1
Telephone 780-420-9900
Fax 780-426-2936
E-mail search@
daviespark.ab.ca
Website www.daviespark.ab.ca
Founded 1989
Employees 8
Specialties Management
Govt/Nonprofit
Accounting
Human Resource
General Practice
Health/Medical
Marketing
Level Senior
Mid-Level
Min. Salary $60,000
Fee Basis Retainer Only
Recruiters K. Darwin CMC
A. Gerry Davies CMC
Elizabeth Hurley
K. Darwin Park CMC
Anurag Shourie MBA
Pam Sprague
Lourens van Rensburg
Contact K. Darwin, CMC
Description Davies Park is dedicated
to executive search on a full-time
basis, working in every area of in-
dustry and the public sector.

DAVIES PARK
300 - 5th Avenue SW, Suite 2930
Calgary , AB T2P 3C4
Telephone 403-263-0600
Fax 403-269-1080
E-mail consult@
daviespark.ab.ca
Website www.daviespark.ab.ca
Founded 1989
Employees 4
Specialties General Practice
Management
Oil & Gas
Geology/Geography
Education
Human Resource
Health/Medical
Marketing
Accounting
Level Senior
Mid-Level
Min. Salary $50,000

Fee Basis Retainer Only
Recruiters Mike Kerr
Bonnie Michaels
Allan C. Nelson CMA
Carolina J. Walls
Laura Youngberg MBA
Contact Allan C. Nelson, CMA
Description Davies Park provides ex-
ecutive search services to every area
of industry and the private sector.

DAVIS, DAIGNAULT, SCHICK & CO.
665 - 8th Street SW, Suite 400
Calgary, AB T2P 3K7
Telephone 403-262-3394
Fax 403-269-3540
E-mail kstephens@dds.ab.ca
Specialties Finance
Accounting
Management
Level Mid-Level
Contact Ken Stephens
Description Davis, Daignault, Schick
& Co. is a medium-sized accounting
firm that also does occasional search
work for clients.

DAVIS SEARCH GROUP
75 Dufflaw Road, Unit 201
Toronto, ON M6A 2W4
Telephone 416-782-7191
Fax 416-782-2842
E-mail requests@
davissearch.com
Website www.davissearch.com
Specialties Computing
Telecom
Level Mid-Level
Contact Jason Davis
Description Davis Search Group is a
specialized recruiting firm working
within the North American high
tech and telecom industries.

DAVITECH CONSULTING INC.
6815 - 8th Street NE, Suite 103
Calgary, AB T2A 5P6
Telephone 403-274-5774
Fax 403-547-8523
E-mail bhealy@davitech.com
Specialties Management
Biotech/Biology
Hospitality
Level Mid-Level
Contact Bruce Healey,
President
Description Davitech Consulting Inc.
is a management consulting firm
that also does recruitment work for
clients.

DAY ADVERTISING GROUP INC.
1920 Yonge Street, Suite 501
Toronto, ON M4S 3E6
Telephone 416-480-6560
Fax 416-487-6121

E-mail mail@
dayadvertising.com
Specialties General Practice
Govt/Nonprofit
Management
Level Senior
Contact Helen Assad
Description Day Advertising Group is
an advertising agency specializing in
recruitment advertising.

DDP CONSULTING GROUP
3640 East Hastings Street, Suite 7
Vancouver, BC V5K 2A9
Telephone 604-294-9193
Fax 604-294-9155
E-mail ddp_info@ddp.ca
Website www.ddp.ca
Founded 1981
Specialties Computing
Telecom
Description DDP Consulting Group
is an IT consulting firm that offers
contract opportunities in Western
Canada.

DEAN & ASSOCIATES
360 Bay Street, Suite 700
Toronto, ON M5H 2V6
Telephone 416-368-6446
Fax 416-368-6463
Specialties Finance
Accounting
Administrative
Level Mid-Level
Junior
Contact Peggy Dean
Description Dean & Associates spe-
cializes in the placement of perma-
nent and contract positions for the
financial services industry.

DEAN TOWER & ASSOCIATES
307 Richmond Road, Unit C
Ottawa, ON K1Z 6X3
Telephone 613-722-6102
Employees 1
Specialties Management
Level Mid-Level
Contact Dean Tower
Description General human re-
sources consulting firm that does
occasional search work.

DECISIONAIDE CANADA LTD.
355 West Principale Street
Unit 100
Magog, QC J1X 2B1
Telephone 819-868-3304
Fax 819-868-3303
E-mail dcl@abacom.com
Specialties Management
Hospitality

DEEVAN TECHNOLOGY MANAGEMENT
111 Granton Drive, Suite 401
Richmond Hill, ON L4B 1L5

Telephone	905-882-6993
Fax	905-882-8367
E-mail	sales@deevan.com
Website	www.deevan.com
Founded	1989
Specialties	Computing
Level	Mid-Level Senior
Fee Basis	Sometimes contingent
Contact	Vince Forrestall, President

Description Deevan Technology Management (formerly Deevan IT Placements) offers contract opportunities for skilled IT professionals.

DÉFI-CHANGEMENT
2500 boul. Jean Perrin
Québec, QC G2C 1X1

Téléphone	418-681-6390
Spécialités	Généralistes
Contact	André Gosselin

DELOITTE CONSULTING
5140 Yonge Street, Suite 1700
Toronto, ON M2N 6L7

Telephone	416-229-2100
Fax	416-601-6185
E-mail	vabennet@deloitte.ca
Website	www.dc.com
Specialties	Accounting Finance
Level	Mid-Level Senior
Contact	Val Bennett

Description Deloitte Consulting is the management consulting arm of Deloitte & Touche, one of Canada's largest professional services firms. Their assignments occasionally include recruiting work for clients.

DELOITTE CONSULTING
1 Place Ville Marie
Suite 3000
Montréal, QC H3B 4T9

Telephone	514-393-7115
Fax	514-390-4111
E-mail	cchoquet@deloitte.ca
Website	www.dc.com
Specialties	Accounting Finance
Level	Mid-Level Senior
Contact	Celine Choquet

Description Deloitte Consulting is the management consulting arm of Deloitte & Touche, one of Canada's largest professional services firms. Their assignments occasionally include recruiting work for clients.

DELOITTE TOUCHE TOHMATSU
152 - 158 St. George's Terrace
16th Floor, Central Park
GPO Box A46, Perth, WA 6837
AUSTRALIA

Telephone	61-8-9365-7250
Fax	61-8-9365-7004
E-mail	info@deloitte.com.au
Website	www.deloitte.com.au
Specialties	International Management
Level	Senior
Contact	Terry Swift

Description Deloitte Touche Tohmatsu provides service in all aspects of strategic and operational human resource consulting.

DELORME ET ASSOCIÉS INC.
1220, boul. Le Bourgneuf
Bureau 150
Québec, QC G2K 2G4

Telephone	418-626-0554
Fax	418-626-5798
E-mail	p.delorme@ delorme.qc.ca
Website	www.delorme.qc.ca
Founded	1980
Employees	4
Specialties	Accounting Engineering Finance Human Resource Management Marketing Operations Purchasing Sales Scientific
Level	Mid-Level Senior
Recruiters	Pierre Delorme Johanne Lehouillier
Contact	Pierre Delorme

Description Delorme et Associés inc., specializing in the recruitment and evaluation of executives and specialized personnel, fills positions in upper management, marketing, sales, production, engineering, research and development, finance, human resources in all types of industry in Canada and the USA.

DELTA MANAGEMENT OPTIONS GROUP / DMO
1 First Canadian Place
Suite 5100, Box 24
Toronto, ON M5X 1K2

Telephone	416-360-6555
Fax	416-360-6620
E-mail	options@dmo group.com
Website	www.dmogroup.com
Specialties	Actuarial Insurance

Description DMO specializes in actuarial recruitment, including life and health, pensions and casualty assignments.

DELTON PERSONNEL LTD.
14 Ribblesdale Place
Ribblesdale House
Preston, PR1 3NA
UNITED KINGDOM

Telephone	44-1772-884545
Fax	44-1772-885005
E-mail	delton_preston@ ibm.net
Specialties	Oil & Gas International

DELYNN PERSONNEL
2 Bloor Street West, Suite 700
Toronto, ON M4W 3R1

Telephone	416-921-3703
Specialties	General Practice
Level	Mid-Level
Contact	Debbie Itegi

DENISE WALTERS & ASSOCIATES
5308 - 187 Street
Edmonton, AB T6M 2K5

Telephone	780-481-4755
Fax	780-481-8030
Specialties	Govt/Nonprofit
Level	Mid-Level
Contact	Denise Walters

DENTAL CAREERS
7400 Minoru Boulevard, Unit 30
Richmond, BC V6Y 3J5

Telephone	604-270-1210
Specialties	Health/Medical
Level	Mid-Level Junior
Contact	David Gregg

DENTAL-AID / MEDICAL-AID PERSONNEL
550 - 6th Street
New Westminster, BC V3L 3B7

Telephone	604-524-3904
Fax	604-925-9223
Specialties	Health/Medical
Level	Mid-Level Junior
Contact	Glennie Attrell

Description Dental-Aid specializes recruitment for medical and dental assistants.

DERHAK IRELAND & PARTNERS LTD.
65 International Boulevard
Suite 100
Toronto, ON M9W 6L9

Telephone	416-675-7600
Fax	416-675-7833
E-mail	dvschaik@ derhak- ireland.com
Website	www.derhak- ireland.com
Founded	1989
Employees	8

Specialties	Engineering
	Management
	Marketing
	Sales
	Health/Medical
	Pharmaceutical
	Biotech/Biology
Level	Mid-Level
	Senior
Fee Basis	Retainer Only
Recruiters	Murray W. Clarke
	Allen R. Derhak
	William M. Derhak
	Howard Kleiman
	Vincent J. McKnight
	Wayne Percy
	David E. Van Schalk
Contact	Allen R. Derhak,
	Partner

Description Derhak Ireland & Partners Ltd. concentrates on the selective placement of middle and senior personnel.

DERKITT & HERBERT EXECUTIVE SEARCH INC.
717 - 7th Avenue SW, Suite 577
Calgary, AB T2P 0Z3

Telephone	403-266-8800
Fax	403-266-8801
E-mail	rob@derkittand
	herbert.com
Website	www.rjderkitt
	associates.com
Founded	1992
Employees	2
Specialties	Oil & Gas
	Engineering
	Geology/Geography
	Marketing
	Logistics
	Finance
Level	Senior
	Mid-Level
Min. Salary	$65,000
Fee Basis	Retainer Only
Contact	Robert J. Derkitt

Description Derkitt & Herbert provides independent, knowledgeable, efficient and personalized executive search services to all types and sizes of operation companies.

DESCHENEAUX RECRUITMENT SERVICES LTD.
750 West Pender St., Suite 1700
Vancouver, BC V6C 2T8

Telephone	604-669-9787
Fax	604-688-2130
E-mail	info@insurance
	headhunters.com
Website	www.insurance
	headhunters.com
Specialties	Insurance
Level	Mid-Level
	Senior
Fee Basis	Sometimes contingent
Recruiters	Pat Descheneaux
	Allison Young
Contact	Ms Pat Descheneaux,
	President

Description Specializing in the insurance industry for over 20 years.

DESIGN GROUP STAFFING SERVICES INC., THE
1066 West Hastings, Suite 760
Vancouver, BC V6E 3X2

Telephone	604-687-2788
Fax	604-669-3540
E-mail	resumevan@
	tdgstaff.com
Website	www.tdgstaff.com
Founded	1976
Employees	4
Specialties	Engineering
	Design
	Computing
	Construction
	Mining
	Oil & Gas
	Pulp & Paper
Level	Mid-Level
Fee Basis	Sometimes contingent
Contact	Graham Compton,
	Manager

Description Design Group specializes in contract and permanent technical placement for engineers, designers/drafters, project control personnel and IS/IT personnel.

DESIGN GROUP STAFFING SERVICES INC., THE
10155 - 102 Street
Suite 2380, Commerce Place
Edmonton, AB T5J 4G8

Telephone	780-428-1505
Fax	780-428-7095
E-mail	resumeedm@
	tdgstaff.com
Website	www.tdgstaff.com
Founded	1976
Specialties	Engineering
	Design
	Oil & Gas
	Computing
Level	Mid-Level

Description Design Group specializes in contract and permanent technical placement for engineers, designers/drafters, project control personnel and IS/IT personnel.

DESIGN GROUP STAFFING SERVICES INC., THE
4915 - 54th Street, 3rd Floor
Red Deer, AB T4N 2G7

Telephone	403-309-0757
Fax	403-309-0852
E-mail	resumered@
	tdgstaff.com
Website	www.tdgstaff.com
Founded	1976
Specialties	Design
	Computing
	Engineering
Level	Mid-Level

Contact	Melanie Regear

Description Design Group specializes in contract and permanent technical placement for engineers, designers/drafters, project control personnel and IS/IT personnel.

DESIGN GROUP STAFFING SERVICES INC., THE
1110 Centre Street North, Suite 401
Calgary, AB T2E 2R2

Telephone	403-233-2788
Fax	403-262-0549
E-mail	resumecal@
	tdgstaff.com
Website	www.tdgstaff.com
Founded	1976
Employees	17
Specialties	Engineering
	Design
	Oil & Gas
	Construction
	Operations
	Accounting
	Computing
Level	Mid-Level
Fee Basis	Always contingent
Recruiters	Josie Fisher
	Shawn Lawler
	Jack Watson
Contact	Graham Wake, VP
	Business Development

Description Design Group specializes in contract and permanent technical placement for engineers, designers/drafters, project control personnel and IS/IT personnel.

DESIGN GROUP STAFFING SERVICES INC., THE
255 Queens Avenue, Suite 1800
London, ON N6A 5R8

Telephone	519-673-6272
Fax	519-679-8409
E-mail	resumelon@
	tdgstaff.com
Website	www.tdgstaff.com
Founded	1976
Specialties	Computing
	Design
	Engineering
Level	Mid-Level

Description Design Group specializes in contract and permanent technical placement for engineers, designers/drafters, project control personnel and IS/IT personnel.

DESIGN GROUP STAFFING SERVICES INC., THE
195 The West Mall, Suite 903
Toronto, ON M9C 5K1

Telephone	416-620-5577
Fax	416-620-1632
E-mail	resumetor@
	tdgstaff.com
Website	www.tdgstaff.com
Founded	1976

Specialties Engineering
             Design
             Construction
             Operations
             Accounting
             Computing
             Management

Level   Mid-Level

Fee Basis   Always contingent

Contact   Joe Caputi

Description Design Group specializes in contract and permanent technical placement for engineers, designers/drafters, project control personnel and IS/IT personnel.

DESIGN TEAM INCORPORATED
100 W. Beaver Creek Rd., Units 8 & 9
Richmond Hill, ON L4B 1H4

Telephone   905-707-8480
Fax   905-707-8483
E-mail   mail@dti.ca
Website   www.dti.ca

Specialties Engineering
             Design

Recruiters   John Ingold
             Yvonne Jhu
             Paul Shelk

Contact   Paul Shelk

Description Design Team is dedicated to meeting the staffing needs of their clients from product design services to Pro / Engineer modeling and FEA.

DEVONWOOD PARTNERS INC.
1404 Bancroft Drive
Mississauga, ON L5V 1M2

Telephone   905-821-7000
Fax   905-821-7006
E-mail   resumes@
             devonwood.com
Website   www.devonwood.com

Founded   1989

Specialties Insurance

Level   Mid-Level
             Senior

Contact   Debbie Trainor-
             McCubbin, Senior
             Partner

Description Devonwood is the largest recruiting firm in Canada specializing exclusively in life insurance.

DHR CANADA INC.
2 Robert Speck Parkway, Suite 750
Mississauga, ON L4Z 1H8

Fax   905-306-3451

Specialties Human Resource
             Engineering
             Govt/Nonprofit

Contact   Doug Colling, President

DIAL A-1 RESOURCES
4936 Yonge Street, Suite 253
Toronto, ON M2N 6S3

Telephone   416-730-9969

Fax   416-730-9967
E-mail   melrooke@aol.com
Website   www.diala-1.com

Founded   1986

Specialties Advertising
             Graphic Arts
             Multimedia

Contact   Morgan White

Description Dial A-1 is an agency that provides the services of technical writers, trainers, web designers, advertising / marketing specialists, illustrators, and graphic artists.

DIAL STAFFING SOLUTIONS
777 - 8th Avenue SW, Suite 1505
Calgary, AB T2P 3R5

Telephone   403-265-6544
Fax   403-264-9086
E-mail   ddial@dialstaffing.com
Website   www.dialstaffing.com

Specialties Sales
             Administrative
             Accounting
             Computing
             Marketing
             Management

Level   Mid-Level
             Junior

Description Dial Staffing Solutions is a full-service recruiting organization working with clients in western Canada and the Pacific Northwest.

DICK COOK SCHULLI
999 - 8th Street SW, Suite 555
Calgary, AB T2R 1J5

Telephone   403-245-1717
Fax   403-244-9306
E-mail   mail@dcs-ca.com
Website   www.dcs-ca.com

Specialties Accounting
             Finance

Level   Mid-Level

Description Dick Cook Schulli is a chartered accounting firm that does occasional search work for clients.

DIGITAL POWER CORP. LTD.
4037 - 42nd Street NW, Suite 236
Calgary, AB T3A 2M9

Telephone   403-247-1222

Specialties Computing
             Sales
             Marketing
             Management

Contact   Don West

Description Digital Power specializes in permanent and contract assignments in software development, real-time systems, infrastructure, technology planning, technical writing, user support, sales / marketing, consulting and management.

DIGITAL STAFFING
208 South LaSalle St., Suite 1276
Chicago, IL 60604 USA

Telephone   312-357-1012
Fax   312-357-1005
E-mail   loop@digital
             staffing.com
Website   www.digital
             staffing.com

Specialties Computing
             International

Level   Mid-Level

Contact   Bryan Ray

Description Digital Staffing specializes in recruitment in the information technology field.

DILBERT GROUP, THE
12 Cumberland Street, Suite 301
Toronto, ON M4W 1J5

Telephone   416-929-0299
Fax   416-929-9960
E-mail   dilbertgroup@
             globalserve.net

Specialties Computing

DINGLE & ASSOCIATES INC.
150 King Street West
Suite 2414, Sun Life Centre
Toronto, ON M5H 1J9

Telephone   416-979-1233
Fax   416-979-7743
E-mail   tdingle@
             dingleassoc.com

Specialties Management
             Banking
             Finance

Level   Senior

Fee Basis   Retainer Only

Contact   D. Terence Dingle,
             Partner

Description Dingle & Assoc. recruits board- and senior-level executives.

DION MANAGEMENT EXECUTIVE SEARCH
885 West Georgia Street, Suite 1500
Vancouver, BC V6C 3E8

Telephone   604-683-7330
E-mail   contact@dion-
             management.com
Website   www.dion-
             management.com

Founded   1990

Specialties General Practice

Level   Mid-Level
             Senior

Fee Basis   Retainer Only

Description Dion is a retainer-based firm recruiting senior-level candidates and is affiliated with International Search Associates.

DION MANAGEMENT EXECUTIVE SEARCH
145 King Steet West, Suite 1000
Toronto, ON M5H 3X6

Telephone   416-867-1176
E-mail   contact@dion-
             management.com

Website	www.dion-management.com
Founded	1990
Specialties	Human Resource
	Marketing
	Operations
	Scientific
	Biotech/Biology
	Health/Medical
	Finance
Level	Senior
	Mid-Level
Min. Salary	$60,000
Fee Basis	Retainer Only
Contact	Jacques Clairoux

Description Dion is a retainer-based firm recruiting senior-level candidates and is affiliated with International Search Associates.

DION MANAGEMENT GROUPE CONSEIL INC.
615 Rene-Levesque Blvd. West
Suite 1200
Montréal, QC H3B 1P5

Telephone	514-861-3331 ext. 25
Fax	514-861-3657
E-mail	contact@dion-management.com
Website	www.dion-management.com
Founded	1990
Employees	4
Specialties	Consulting
	Finance
	Human Resource
	Management
	Marketing
	Operations
	Scientific
Level	Senior
	Mid-Level
Min. Salary	$60,000
Fee Basis	Retainer Only
Contact	Marlene Harris

Description Dion is a retainer-based firm recruiting senior-level candidates and is affiliated with International Search Associates.

DION MANAGEMENT GROUPE CONSEIL INC.
2600, boul. Laurier
Bureau 2240, Tour Belle Coeur
Sainte-Foy, QC G1V 4M6

Telephone	418-657-6693
E-mail	contact@dion-management.com
Website	www.dion-management.com
Founded	1990
Specialties	Management
	Consulting
	Finance
	Marketing
	Operations
	Scientific
	Biotech/Biology
	Pharmaceutical
	Human Resource

Level	Senior
Min. Salary	$60,000
Fee Basis	Retainer Only
Contact	Marcelle Rheaume

Description Dion is a retainer-based firm recruiting senior-level candidates and is affiliated with International Search Associates.

DIRECT CAREER CONCEPTS INC.
93 Woodbridge Ave., PO Box 56548
Woodbridge, ON L4L 8V3

Telephone	905-264-7999
Fax	905-850-7937
Founded	1991
Employees	4
Specialties	Automotive
	Management
	Metals
	Pharmaceutical
	Plastics
	Logistics
	Operations
Level	Mid-Level
	Senior
Min. Salary	$50,000
Fee Basis	Sometimes contingent
Contact	Louie Romano

Description Direct Career Concepts Inc. provides recruitment and selection services to a wide range of manufacturing-based companies.

DISTINCT DIRECTIONS INC.
1255 Saginaw Crescent
Mississauga, ON L5H 1X4

Telephone	905-278-7711
Fax	905-271-1660
E-mail	gj@distinctdirections.com
Website	www.distinctdirections.com
Founded	1995
Employees	1
Specialties	Telecom
Level	Mid-Level
Fee Basis	Sometimes contingent
Contact	George Johnston

Description Distinct Directions Inc. specialized in staffing for companies that are in, or service, the telecom carrier industry.

DIVERSIFIED STAFFING SERVICES LTD.
10909 Jasper Avenue, Main Floor
Edmonton, AB T5J 3L9

Telephone	780-429-9058
Fax	780-425-7419
E-mail	dssedm@diversifiedstaffing.com
Website	www.diversifiedstaffing.com
Founded	1978
Specialties	Oil & Gas
	Govt/Nonprofit
	Law
	Construction
	Real Estate
	Health/Medical
	Education

Description Diversified Staffing is a full-service placement agency providing placements in a number of industries, including oil & gas.

DIVERSIFIED STAFFING SERVICES LTD.
840 - 6 Avenue SW, Main Floor
Calgary, AB T2P 3E5

Telephone	403-237-5577
Fax	403-269-1428
E-mail	dsscal@diversifiedstaffing.com
Website	www.diversifiedstaffing.com
Founded	1978
Specialties	Oil & Gas
	Govt/Nonprofit
	Law
	Construction
	Real Estate
	Health/Medical
	Education

Description A full-service placement agency with offices in Calgary and Edmonton providing placements in a number of industries, including Oil & Gas.

DON MILES PERSONNEL CONSULTANTS INC.
PO Box 275
Toronto, ON M9A 4X2

Telephone	416-231-1676
Fax	416-231-1672
Founded	1977
Employees	2
Specialties	Construction
Level	Senior
	Mid-Level
Min. Salary	$50,000
Fee Basis	Always contingent
Recruiters	Don Miles
	Hughes Miles
Contact	Don Miles

Description Don Miles Personnel provides the construction industry and contractors with skilled estimators, project managers, coordinators and supers.

DONALD GIVELOS & ASSOCIATES INC. / DGA
335 Bay Street, Suite 810
Toronto, ON M5H 2R3

Telephone	416-868-6711
Fax	416-868-6329
E-mail	resume@dgacareers.com
Website	www.dgacareers.com
Founded	1986
Specialties	Insurance
Level	Senior
	Mid-Level

Recruiters   Don Givelos
Collett Ricketts
Michelle Straka

Contact   Don Givelos, President

Description Aims to be the definitive recruiting organization for property and casualty insurance in Canada.

DONALD L. HART & ASSOCIATES / TALENT IN MOTION
3 Church Street, Suite 604
Toronto, ON   M5E 1M2

Telephone	416-862-7104
Fax	416-862-7139
E-mail	info@dlhart.com
Website	www.dlhart.com
Founded	1981
Employees	4
Specialties	Computing
	Management
	Marketing
	Sales
Level	Mid-Level
	Senior
Recruiters	Donald L. Hart
	S. Moco
Contact	Donald L. Hart

Description Donald L. Hart & Associates specializes in recruiting IT professionals for: general management; sales management; technical management; sales; and marketing.

DONATI & ASSOCIATES
33 Belmont Crescent
Maple, ON   L6A 1L5

Telephone	905-303-0504
Fax	905-303-0505
Specialties	Management
	Marketing
	Sales
Level	Mid-Level
Contact	Morris Donati

DORÉ LIAISON INC.
277, boul. Churchill
Bureau 301, Édifice Concorde
Greenfield Park, QC   J4V 2M8

Telephone	450-465-6620
Fax	450-465-3080
E-mail	info@doreliaison.com
Website	www.doreliaison.com
Founded	1969
Employees	8
Specialties	Accounting
	Banking
	Computing
	Engineering
	Finance
	International
	Law
	Management
	Marketing
	Operations
	Purchasing
	Sales
Level	Mid-Level
	Senior

Recruiters   Joseph L. Doré
André H.J. Doré
Vincent Doré
Nancy Rooke
Marc Tremblay

Contact   Joseph L. Doré, Président

Description Doré Liaison has helped many international corporations and organizations in attracting quality people, who become the basis of their success.

DOTEMTEX EXECUTIVE SEARCH
5000, Jean-Talon West, Bureau 260
Montréal, QC   H4P 1W9

Telephone	514-736-1000
Fax	514-736-0371
E-mail	info@dotemtex.com
Website	www.dotemtex.com
Founded	1995
Employees	20
Specialties	Human Resource
	Engineering
	Finance
	Administrative
	Accounting
	Banking
	Aerospace
	Telecom
Level	Senior
	Mid-Level
Min. Salary	$45,000
Fee Basis	Retainer Only
Recruiters	Jean-François Aboud
	Lyn Babin
	Benoît Beaulieu
	Lysanne Bernier
	Roxanne Blaise
	Nancy Dion
	Mélanie Gendron
	Suzette Gravel
	Kim Laliberté
	Patricia Lavalée
	Yves Lesieur
	Jean-Marc Léveillé
	Isabelle Sarne
	Ginette Séguin
	Brian Tansey
Contact	Patricia Lavalée

Description Dotemtex Executive Search provides recruitment services in most industry sectors.

DOTEMTEX EXECUTIVE SEARCH
1303 McGuire Avenue
Sillery, QC   G1T 1Z2

Telephone	800-736-6160
Fax	418-681-4338
E-mail	dotemtex@dotemtex.com
Website	www.dotemtex.com
Employees	1994
Specialties	General Practice
	Aerospace
	Computing
	Govt/Nonprofit
	Pharmaceutical
	Biotech/Biology
	Retail

Description Dotemtex Executive Search provides recruitment services in most industry sectors.

DOUG MORLEY & ASSOCIATES
6980 - 78th Street NW
Calgary, AB   T3B 4Z2

Fax	403-247-5113
E-mail	dougmorleyassociates@home.com
Specialties	Oil & Gas
	International
Contact	Doug J. Morley, CHRP

DRAKE EXECUTIVE
400 Burrard Street, 14th Floor
Vancouver, BC   V6C 3G2

Telephone	604-601-2800
Fax	604-682-8523
E-mail	emcdonald@drakeintl.com
Website	www.drakeintl.com
Specialties	Management
Level	Senior
	Mid-Level

Description Drake Executive is a division of Drake International, a recruitment, consulting and training organization with over 250 offices around the world.

DRAKE EXECUTIVE
9940 Lougheed Highway, Suite 360
Burnaby, BC   V3J 1N3

Telephone	604-601-2800
Fax	604-682-8523
E-mail	mcoutu@drakeintl.com
Website	www.drakeintl.com
Specialties	Accounting
	Finance
	Management
Level	Mid-Level
	Senior
Contact	Larry Hill, Regional Manager

Description Drake Executive is a division of Drake International, a recruitment, consulting and training organization based in Toronto with over 250 offices around the world.

DRAKE EXECUTIVE
101 - 6th Avenue SW, Suite 420
Calgary, AB   T2P 3P4

Telephone	403-266-8971
Fax	403-262-1045
E-mail	calgary@na.drakeintl.com
Website	www.drakeintl.com
Founded	1951
Employees	20
Specialties	General Practice
Fee Basis	Always contingent
Contact	Karen Strong

Description Drake Executive is a division of Drake International, a recruitment, consulting and training organization based in Toronto with over 250 offices around the world.

DRAKE EXECUTIVE
444 St. Mary Avenue, Suite 780
Winnipeg, MB R3C 3T1

Telephone	204-947-0077
Fax	204-947-5678
E-mail	winnipeg@na.drakeintl.com
Website	www.drakeintl.com
Founded	1951
Specialties	Management Accounting Finance
Recruiters	Terry Cyr Maria Mathews Kevin O'Leary Michele Rich
Contact	Kevin O'Leary, Manager

Description Drake Executive is a division of Drake International, a recruitment, consulting and training organization based in Toronto with over 250 offices around the world.

DRAKE EXECUTIVE
27 Cedar Street, Suite 203
Sudbury, ON P3E 1A1

Telephone	705-674-8367
Fax	705-674-8951
E-mail	drakesud@isys.ca
Website	www.drakeintl.com
Specialties	Accounting Finance Management
Level	Mid-Level
Contact	Darla Scott, General Manager

Description Drake Executive is a division of Drake International, a recruitment, consulting and training organization based in Toronto with over 250 offices around the world.

DRAKE EXECUTIVE
171 Queen Avenue, Suite 602
London, ON N6A 5J7

Telephone	519-645-8862
Fax	519-645-1404
E-mail	meng@drakeintl.com
Website	www.drakeintl.com
Specialties	Accounting Finance Management
Level	Mid-Level

Description Drake Executive is a division of Drake International, a recruitment, consulting and training organization based in Toronto with over 250 offices around the world.

DRAKE EXECUTIVE
2323 Bloor Street West, Suite 218A
Toronto, ON M6S 1P2

Telephone	416-762-4414
Fax	416-763-0823

E-mail	islington@na.drakeintl.com
Website	www.drakeintl.com
Specialties	Accounting Finance Management Aerospace Bilingual Human Resource Administrative
Level	Mid-Level
Fee Basis	Sometimes contingent
Recruiters	Kimberly Bain Brenda Siversen
Contact	Kimberly Bain

Description Drake Executive is a division of Drake International, a recruitment, consulting and training organization based in Toronto with over 250 offices around the world.

DRAKE EXECUTIVE
181 Bay Street
BCE Place, Suite 2030
Toronto, ON M5J 2T3

Telephone	416-216-1000
Fax	416-216-1109
E-mail	bceplace@na.drakeintl.com
Website	www.drakeintl.com
Specialties	Management
Level	Mid-Level
Recruiters	M.E. Bell Lisa Bobeldyk

Description Drake Executive is a division of Drake International, a recruitment, consulting and training organization based in Toronto with over 250 offices around the world.

DRAKE EXECUTIVE
1155 University Street, Suite 1212
Montréal, QC H3B 3A7

Telephone	514-395-9595
Fax	514-395-9922
E-mail	resaulnier@na.drakeintl.com
Website	www.drakeintl.com
Specialties	Accounting Finance Management Administrative
Level	Junior Mid-Level
Recruiters	Barbara Bell Hela Diamond Mary MacArthur Roxanne Saulnier
Contact	Roxanne Saulnier

Description Drake Executive is a division of Drake International, a recruitment, consulting and training organization based in Toronto with over 250 offices around the world.

DRAKE INDUSTRIAL
405 Columbia Street
New Westminster, BC V3L 1A9

Telephone	604-519-8700

Fax	604-519-8648
E-mail	newwestminster@na.drakeintl.com
Website	www.drakeintl.com
Specialties	Trades/Technicians

Description Drake Industrial is a division of Drake International, a recruitment, consulting and training organization with over 250 offices around the world.

DRAKE INDUSTRIAL
11822A St. Albert Trail
Edmonton, AB T5L 5B5

Telephone	780-414-6341
Fax	780-488-1678
E-mail	edmonton@na.drakeintl.com
Website	www.drakeintl.com
Specialties	Trades/Technicians
Level	Junior Mid-Level

Description Drake Industrial is a division of Drake International, a recruitment, consulting and training organization with over 250 offices around the world.

DRAKE INDUSTRIAL
2323 Bloor Street West, Suite 218A
Toronto, ON M6S 1P2

Telephone	416-762-4414
Fax	416-763-0823
E-mail	islington@na.drakeintl.com
Website	www.drakeintl.com
Specialties	Trades/Technicians
Level	Mid-Level Junior
Fee Basis	Always contingent

Description Drake Industrial is a division of Drake International, a recruitment, consulting and training organization based in Toronto with over 250 offices around the world.

DRAKE INDUSTRIAL
181 Bay Street
Suite 2030, BCE Place
Toronto, ON M5J 2T3

Telephone	416-216-1000
Fax	416-216-1109
E-mail	bceplace@na.drakeintl.com
Website	www.drakeintl.com
Specialties	Trades/Technicians
Level	Mid-Level Junior
Fee Basis	Always contingent

Description Drake Industrial is a division of Drake International, a recruitment, consulting and training organization based in Toronto with over 250 offices around the world.

DRAKE INDUSTRIAL
55 Town Centre Court, Suite 700
Toronto, ON M1P 4X4

Telephone	416-279-1333
Fax	416-279-0021
E-mail	bceplace@na.drakeintl.com
Website	www.drakeintl.com
Specialties	Trades/Technicians
Level	Mid-Level Junior
Fee Basis	Always contingent

Description Drake Industrial is a division of Drake International, a recruitment, consulting and training organization based in Toronto with over 250 offices around the world.

DRAKE INTERNATIONAL
400 Burrard Street, 14th Floor
Vancouver, BC V6C 3G2

Telephone	604-601-2800
Fax	604-682-8523
E-mail	vancouver@na.drakeintl.com
Website	www.drakeintl.com
Specialties	General Practice
Level	Mid-Level

Description Drake International provides a comprehensive range of services and products that focus on human resource outsourcing.

DRAKE INTERNATIONAL
9940 Lougheed Highway, Suite 360
Burnaby, BC V3J 1N3

Telephone	604-439-0828
Fax	604-439-6757
E-mail	gkikot@drakeintl.com
Website	www.drakeintl.com
Specialties	Administrative Trades/Technicians
Level	Mid-Level Junior

Description Drake International provides a comprehensive range of services and products that focus on human resource outsourcing.

DRAKE INTERNATIONAL
Edmonton Centre
Suite 412, Merrill Lynch Tower
Edmonton, AB T5J 2Z2

Telephone	780-426-5955
Fax	780-426-4324
E-mail	edmonton@na.drakeintl.com
Website	www.drakeintl.com
Employees	12
Specialties	Accounting Finance Management Human Resource Quality Control Marketing Consulting
Level	Mid-Level
Fee Basis	Sometimes contingent
Recruiters	Heidi Roberts Carrie Warkentin
Contact	Susan Hazelwood

Description Drake International provides executive and permanent recruiting for all areas of industry.

DRAKE INTERNATIONAL
112 Lakeshore Drive, Main Floor
North Bay, ON P1A 2A8

Telephone	705-495-2458
Fax	705-495-2472
E-mail	drakenby@vianet.on.ca
Website	www.drakeintl.com
Founded	1951
Specialties	Accounting Finance Management
Level	Mid-Level
Contact	Linda Taylor, Branch Manager

Description Drake International provides a comprehensive range of services and products that focus on human resource outsourcing.

DRAKE INTERNATIONAL
685 Richmond Street, Suite 201
London, ON N6A 5M1

Telephone	519-433-3151
Fax	519-673-3770
E-mail	london@na.drakeintl.com
Website	www.drakeintl.com
Founded	1951
Specialties	Accounting Finance Management
Level	Mid-Level
Contact	Bonnie Pierotti, Branch Supervisor

Description Drake International provides a comprehensive range of services and products that focus on human resource outsourcing.

DRAKE INTERNATIONAL
181 Bay Street, Suite 2030
PO Box 760, BCE Place
Toronto, ON M5J 2T3

Telephone	416-216-1000
Fax	416-216-1109
E-mail	bceplace@na.drakeintl.com
Website	www.drakeintl.com
Specialties	Management Finance Accounting Operations Retail Sales Marketing
Level	Mid-Level Senior
Min. Salary	$70,000
Fee Basis	Sometimes contingent
Recruiters	Raj Chaterji Christie Collett Simonne De Gannes Hugh Grzela Julie Hucker Seandra Mathews Jennifer Mensah Karen Meredith David Newton
Contact	Simonne De Gannes

Description Drake International is a recruitment, consulting and training organization based in Toronto with over 250 offices around the world.

DRAKE INTERNATIONAL
25 Main Street West, Suite 1610
Hamilton, ON L8P 1H1

Telephone	905-528-9855
Fax	905-528-0014
E-mail	hamilton@na.drakeintl.com
Website	www.drakeintl.com
Employees	6
Specialties	Accounting Finance Management
Level	Mid-Level
Fee Basis	Always contingent
Contact	Julia Peterson

Description Drake International provides a comprehensive range of services and products that focus on human resource outsourcing.

DRAKE INTERNATIONAL
1275 North Service Road West
Suite 609
Oakville, ON L6M 3G4

Telephone	905-469-9022
Fax	905-469-9019
E-mail	oakville@na.drakeintl.com
Website	www.drakeintl.com
Founded	1951
Specialties	Management Accounting Finance
Level	Mid-Level
Contact	Jan Moyer, Recruiter

Description Drake International provides a comprehensive range of services and products that focus on human resource outsourcing.

DRAKE INTERNATIONAL
1275 North Service Road, Suite 609
Oakville, ON L6M 3G4

Telephone	905-469-9022
Fax	905-469-9019
E-mail	oakville@na.drakeintl.com
Website	www.drakeintl.com
Specialties	General Practice
Level	Mid-Level

Description Drake International provides a comprehensive range of services and products that focus on human resource outsourcing.

DRAKE INTERNATIONAL
1 City Centre Drive, Suite 306
Mississauga, ON L5B 3C2

Telephone	905-279-9000
Fax	905-279-1915
E-mail	mississauga@ na.drakeintl.com
Website	www.drakeintl.com
Specialties	Administrative Trades/Technicians
Contact	Wendy Mcaleer

Description Drake International is a recruitment, consulting and training organization. The company has over 250 offices worldwide.

DRAKE INTERNATIONAL
13 Collier Street
Barrie , ON L4M 1G5

Telephone	705-721-1002
Fax	705-721-1003
E-mail	barrie@ na.drakeintl.com
Website	www.drakeintl.com
Specialties	Accounting Finance Management
Contact	John Chiles, Manager

Description Drake International provides a comprehensive range of services and products that focus on human resource outsourcing.

DRAKE INTERNATIONAL
199 Front Street, Suite 214
Belleville, ON K8N 5H5

Telephone	613-966-7283
Fax	613-966-0421
E-mail	belleville@ na.drakeintl.com
Website	www.drakeintl.com
Specialties	Accounting Management Consulting Engineering
Level	Mid-Level
Contact	Hazel Lloyst, Manager

Description Drake International provides a comprehensive range of services and products that focus on human resource outsourcing.

DRAKE INTERNATIONAL
1096 Princess Street, Suite 1040
Kingston, ON K7L 1H2

Telephone	613-542-3790
Fax	613-542-6335
E-mail	kingston@ drakeintl.com
Website	www.drakeintl.com
Specialties	Accounting Finance Management
Level	Mid-Level
Recruiters	David Burkey David Clarke Stephanie Sambey
Contact	D. Clarke

Description Drake International provides a comprehensive range of

services and products that focus on human resource outsourcing.

DRAKE INTERNATIONAL
3000 Marleau Avenue
Cornwall, ON K6H 6B5

Telephone	613-938-4777
Fax	613-936-1780
E-mail	r_cornwall@ na.drakeintl.com
Website	www.drakeintl.com
Specialties	General Practice
Level	Mid-Level

Description Drake International provides a comprehensive range of services and products that focus on human resource outsourcing.

DRAKE INTERNATIONAL
151 Slater Street, Suite 800
Ottawa, ON K1P 5H3

Telephone	613-237-3370
Fax	613-237-2901
E-mail	ottawa@ na.drakeintl.com
Website	www.drakeintl.com
Specialties	Accounting Finance Management
Level	Mid-Level
Contact	Gerrie Trotman, Branch Manager

Description Drake International provides a comprehensive range of services and products that focus on human resource outsourcing.

DRAKE INTERNATIONAL
50 Place Cremazie, Bureau 417
Montréal, QC H2P 2T1

Telephone	514-384-9340
Fax	514-384-5182
E-mail	cremazie@ na.drakeintl.com
Website	www.drakeintl.com
Specialties	Management Operations Human Resource Accounting Finance
Level	Mid-Level Senior
Contact	Hela Diamond

Description Drake International provides a comprehensive range of services and products that focus on human resource outsourcing.

DRAKE INTERNATIONAL
320, rue St. Joseph Est, Bureau 35
Québec, QC G1K 8G5

Telephone	418-529-9371
Fax	418-529-9364
E-mail	quebeccity@ na.drakeintl.com
Website	www.drakeintl.com
Founded	1951
Specialties	Accounting

	Finance Management
Level	Mid-Level
Contact	Denis Malo, Gérant

Description Drake International provides a comprehensive range of services and products that focus on human resource outsourcing.

DRAKE INTERNATIONAL
95 Foundry Street, Suite 103
Moncton, NB E1C 5H7

Telephone	506-862-1893
Fax	506-862-1808
E-mail	moncton@ na.drakeintl.com
Website	www.drakeintl.com
Founded	1951
Specialties	Accounting Finance Management
Contact	Leona LeBlanc, Branch Manager

Description Drake International provides a comprehensive range of services and products that focus on human resource outsourcing.

DRAKE INTERNATIONAL
1718 Argyle Street, Suite 550
Halifax, NS B3J 3N6

Telephone	902-429-2490
Fax	902-429-2408
E-mail	halifax@ na.drakeintl.com
Website	www.drakeintl.com
Founded	1951
Specialties	Accounting Finance Management
Level	Mid-Level
Recruiters	Colleen Conway Lynne Pottie
Contact	Lynne Pottie, Branch Manager

Description Drake International provides a comprehensive range of services and products that focus on human resource outsourcing.

DRAKE MEDOX
557 Johnson Street
Victoria, BC V8W 1M2

Telephone	250-388-7388
Fax	250-388-5815
E-mail	mcarroll@ na.drakeintl.com
Website	www.drakeintl.com
Founded	1951
Specialties	Health/Medical
Level	Mid-Level
Contact	James McKenna

Description Drake Medox is a health services division of Drake International, a recruitment, consulting and training firm based in Toronto with over 250 offices around the world.

DRAKE MEDOX
4699 Marine Avenue
Powell River, BC V8A 2K2

Telephone	604-485-2508
Fax	604-485-6858
E-mail	aaron@prcn.org
Website	www.drakeintl.com
Specialties	Health/Medical
	Administrative
	Consulting
Level	Mid-Level

Description Drake Medox is a health services division of Drake International, a recruitment, consulting and training organization based in Toronto with over 250 offices around the world.

DRAKE MEDOX
535 - 10th Avenue West, Suite 200
Vancouver, BC V5Z 1K9

Telephone	604-420-7110
Fax	604-876-9875
E-mail	vancouver@
	na.drakeintl.com
Website	www.drakeintl.com
Specialties	Health/Medical
Level	Mid-Level

Description Drake Medox is a health services division of Drake International, a recruitment, consulting and training organization based in Toronto with over 250 offices around the world.

DRAKE MEDOX
2025 Croydon Avenue, Suite 116
Winnipeg, MB R2P 0N5

Telephone	204-452-8600
Fax	204-477-1645
E-mail	
	ssmith@mb.sympatico.ca
Website	www.drakeintl.com
Specialties	Health/Medical

Description Drake Medox is a health services division of Drake International, a recruitment, consulting and training organization based in Toronto with over 250 offices around the world.

DRAKE MEDOX
181 Bay Street, Suite 2030
Toronto, ON M5J 2T3

Telephone	416-216-1110
Fax	416-216-1119
E-mail	bceplace@
	na.drakeintl.com
Website	www.drakeintl.com
Specialties	Health/Medical
Level	Mid-Level

Description Drake Medox is a health services division of Drake International, a recruitment, consulting and training organization based in Toronto with over 250 offices around the world.

DRAKE OFFICE OVERLOAD
9940 Lougheed Highway, Suite 360
Burnaby, BC V3J 1N3

Telephone	604-439-0828
Fax	604-439-6757
E-mail	toram@drakeintl.com
Website	www.drakeintl.com
Specialties	Administrative
Level	Junior
	Mid-Level

Description Drake Office Overload is a division of Drake International, a recruitment, consulting and training organization based in Toronto with over 250 offices around the world.

DRAKE OFFICE OVERLOAD
2323 Bloor Street West, Suite 218A
Toronto, ON M6S 1P2

Telephone	416-762-4414
Fax	416-763-0823
E-mail	islington@
	na.drakeintl.com
Website	www.drakeintl.com
Specialties	Administrative
Level	Junior
	Mid-Level
Fee Basis	Always contingent

Description Drake Industrial is a division of Drake International, a recruitment, consulting and training organization based in Toronto with over 250 offices around the world.

DRAKE OFFICE OVERLOAD
181 Bay St., Suite 2030, BCE Place
Toronto, ON M5J 2T3

Telephone	416-216-1000
Fax	416-216-1109
E-mail	bceplace@
	na.drakeintl.com
Website	www.drakeintl.com
Specialties	Administrative
Level	Junior
	Mid-Level

Description Drake Office Overload is a division of Drake International, a recruitment, consulting and training organization based in Toronto with over 250 offices around the world.

DRAKE OFFICE OVERLOAD
5650 Yonge Street, Suite 1500
Toronto, ON M2M 4G3

Telephone	416-512-6206
Fax	416-512-9604
E-mail	bceplace@
	na.drakeintl.com
Website	www.drakeintl.com
Specialties	Administrative
Level	Junior
	Mid-Level

Description Drake Office Overload is a division of Drake International, a recruitment, consulting and training organization based in Toronto with over 250 offices around the world.

DRAKKAR HUMAN RESOURCES
1137 Derry Road East
Mississauga, ON L5T 1P3

Telephone	905-795-1397
Fax	905-795-1391
E-mail	mississauga@drakkar.ca
Website	www.drakkar.ca
Founded	1991
Employees	10
Specialties	Automotive
	Construction
	Consulting
	Human Resource
	Logistics
	Plastics
	Trades/Technicians
Level	Mid-Level
	Junior
Fee Basis	Retainer Only
Recruiters	Elaine Antonel
	Jennifer Baz
	Nancy Smith
	Deb Vance
Contact	Deb Vance

Description Drakkar provides value-added human resources consulting, executive search, personnel recruitment and placement services.

DRAKKAR HUMAN RESOURCES
8746 Côte-de-Liesse
Saint-Laurent, QC H4T 1H2

Telephone	514-733-6655
Fax	514-733-2828
E-mail	elacroix@drakkar.ca
Website	www.drakkar.ca
Founded	1991
Employees	50
Specialties	Aerospace
	Biotech/Biology
	Consulting
	Finance
	Human Resource
	Management
	Operations
Level	Senior
	Mid-Level
Fee Basis	Retainer Only
Recruiters	Michel Blaquière
	Eric Lacroix
	Sandra Savoy
	Catherine Tessier
Contact	Eric Lacroix

Description Drakkar provides value-added human resources consulting, executive search, personnel recruitment and placement services.

DRAKKAR HUMAN RESOURCES
1200 ave. McGill College, bur. 1650
Montréal, QC H3B 4G7

Telephone	514-871-0300
Fax	514-871-0916
E-mail	shuppee@drakkar.ca
Website	www.drakkar.ca
Founded	1991
Employees	50
Specialties	Accounting
	Administrative

Engineering
Logistics
Marketing
Sales
Transport

Level	Senior Mid-Level
Fee Basis	Retainer Only
Recruiters	Sussanne Huppee Joanne Marleau Johanne Petruzzelli Michel Tremblay
Contact	Sussanne Huppee

Description Drakkar provides value-added human resources consulting, executive search, personnel recruitment and placement services.

DRAKKAR HUMAN RESOURCES
766 Rene-Levesque Boulevard West
Québec, QC G1S 1T2

Telephone	800-667-1988
Website	www.drakkar.ca
Founded	1991
Employees	50
Specialties	Accounting Administrative Engineering Logistics Marketing Sales Transport
Level	Senior Mid-Level
Fee Basis	Retainer Only

Description Drakkar provides value-added human resources consulting, executive search, personnel recruitment and placement services.

DRIVER CARRIER PLACEMENT DEPOT
7 Greensboro Drive
Toronto, ON M9W 1C7

Telephone	416-249-0484
Fax	416-249-3039
E-mail	info@fordrivers.com
Website	www.fordrivers.com
Founded	1976
Specialties	Transport Consulting Human Resource Logistics
Level	Mid-Level
Min. Salary	$35,000
Fee Basis	Sometimes contingent
Contact	George Iacono

Description Driver Carrier Placement Depot specializes in truck driver recruitment and training for the private motor carrier industry throughout North America.

DRIVER'S CONNECTION, THE
3515 - 32 Street NE, Suite 202
Calgary, AB T1Y 5Y9

Telephone	403-250-1131
Fax	403-250-1191

E-mail	DriveCon@ IHorizons.net
Website	www.geocities.com/ Eureka/Enterprises/ 4118/
Specialties	Transport
Contact	Andrea

Description The Driver's Connection recruits long distance truck drivers who have a Class 'A' (1) Licence with air endorsement 'Z' . Call toll-free: 1-888-285-2103.

DRIVER'S CONNECTION, THE
268 Newburg Road
Napanee, ON K7R 1C6

Telephone	613-354-9359
Fax	613-354-0870
E-mail	DriveCon@ IHorizons.net
Website	www.geocities.com/ Eureka/Enterprises/ 4118/
Specialties	Transport
Contact	Sue or Carol

Description The Driver's Connection recruits long distance truck drivers who have a Class 'A' (1) Licence with air endorsement 'Z' . Call toll-free: 1-800-432-3995.

DRUMMOND & ASSOCIATES
50 Broadway , Suite 1201
New York, NY 10004 USA

Telephone	212-248-1120
Fax	212-248-1171
E-mail	chetdas@aol.com
Specialties	Computing International Finance
Level	Senior Mid-Level
Recruiters	Chester Feinberg Don Mochwart
Contact	Chester Feinberg, President

Description Drummond & Associates do senior-level recruitment in the IT, finance and investment banking fields.

DUCHARME GROUP INC.
157 Bowood Avenue
Toronto, ON M4N 1Y3

Telephone	416-481-7221
Fax	416-481-5641
E-mail	ducharmegroup@ sympatico.ca
Founded	1998
Specialties	General Practice Accounting Consulting Finance Human Resource Management Marketing Govt/Nonprofit
Level	Senior Mid-Level

Min. Salary	$60,000
Fee Basis	Retainer Only
Contact	Lynda Ducharme

Description Ducharme Group Inc. recruits mid- to senior-level management positions in the public/private sector.

DUKE BLAKEY, INC.
240 Duncan Mill Road, Suite 103
Toronto, ON M3B 1Z4

Telephone	416-447-6730
Fax	416-447-6757
E-mail	blakey@ dukeengineering.com
Website	www.dukeblakey.com
Founded	2000
Specialties	Engineering Oil & Gas
Level	Mid-Level
Contact	Robin D. Blakey, CEO and Vice-President

Description Duke Blakey, Inc. (formerly Blakey & Blakey Engineering Staffing) recruits in the IT, manufacturing, telecommunications, petrochemical and utilities industries.

DUMONT & ASSOCIATES RETAIL RECRUITMENT LTD.
1681 Chestnut Street, Suite 400
Vancouver, BC V7G 1V2

Telephone	604-733-8133
Fax	604-924-1754
E-mail	info@retailheadhunter. com
Website	www.retailheadhunter. com
Founded	1993
Employees	3
Specialties	Retail Purchasing Apparel
Level	Mid-Level Senior
Min. Salary	$35,000
Fee Basis	Sometimes contingent
Recruiters	Paul V.M. Iannacone Jackie Ross
Contact	Brenda A. Dumont

Description Dumont & Associates provides specialized expertise in all areas of the retail profession in Western Canada. Website posts positions weekly.

DUMONT & ASSOCIATES RETAIL RECRUITMENT LTD.
2057 Panorama Drive
North Vancouver, BC V7G 1V2

Telephone	604-924-1753
Fax	604-924-1754
E-mail	info@retailheadhunter. com
Website	www.retailheadhunter. com
Founded	1993
Employees	2

Specialties	Retail
	Purchasing
	Apparel
	Human Resource
	Marketing
Level	Mid-Level
	Senior
Min. Salary	$35,000
Fee Basis	Sometimes contingent
Contact	Brenda A. Dumont

Description Dumont & Associates provides specialized expertise in all areas of the retail profession in Western Canada. Website posts positions weekly.

DUNCAN & ASSOCIATES
1235 Bay Street, Suite 808
Toronto, ON M5R 3K4

Telephone	416-324-9963 ext 225
Fax	416-324-1151
E-mail	duncanx@idirect.com
Founded	1994
Employees	8
Specialties	Insurance
	Sales
	Computing
Level	Mid-Level
	Senior
Contact	Mike Cooper

DUNHILL CONSULTANTS (NORTH YORK) LTD.
5650 Yonge Street
Suite 1500, Xerox Tower
Toronto, ON M2M 4G3

Telephone	905-771-6241
Website	www.dunhillstaff.com
Founded	1952
Specialties	Accounting
	Finance
Level	Senior
	Mid-Level
Min. Salary	$25,000
Contact	Peter Pollock, President

Description This office specializes in finance and accounting placements across Canada.

DUNHILL PERSONNEL OF LONDON
159 Albert Street
London, ON N6A 1L9

Telephone	519-673-6684
Fax	519-673-6792
E-mail	dps@odyssey.on.ca
Website	www.dunhillstaff.com
Founded	1952
Employees	10
Specialties	Management
	Computing
	Accounting
Level	Mid-Level
	Senior
Min. Salary	$40,000
Fee Basis	Always contingent

Recruiters	Penny Coulter
	Lynn Lindsay
Contact	Lynn Lindsay, President

Description Dunhill Staffing Systems is North America's premier Search and Staffing service, with offices throughout the continental United States, Hawaii and Canada.

DUNHILL PROFESSIONAL SEARCH
1681 Chestnut Street, Suite 400
Vancouver, BC V6J 4M6

Telephone	604-739-0100
Fax	604-730-9974
E-mail	dunvan@home.com
Website	www.dunhillstaff.com
Founded	1952
Employees	3
Specialties	Sales
	Engineering
	Telecom
	Finance
	Management
Level	Mid-Level
	Senior
Min. Salary	$50,000
Fee Basis	Sometimes contingent
Contact	Peter Hamilton, President

Description For over 25 years, Dunhill Professional Search has served the needs of high-technology, manufacturing and distribution, and professional and engineering clients.

DUO MEGA INC.
2015, rue Peel, Bureau 1080
Montréal, QC H3A 1T8

Telephone	514-844-7988
Fax	514-288-1831
E-mail	bruno.gendron@ duomega.com
Founded	1991
Employees	3
Specialties	Computing
	Multimedia
	Telecom
	Bilingual
Level	Senior
	Mid-Level
Min. Salary	$40,000
Fee Basis	Sometimes contingent
Contact	Bruno Gendron

Description Duo Mega Inc. specializes in IT placements in the francophone and anglophone communities around Montreal.

DUTTON GROUP
4141 Yonge Street, Suite 207
Toronto, ON M2P 2A8

Telephone	416-250-5665
Fax	416-250-0093
E-mail	careers@dutton.com
Website	www.dutton.com
Specialties	General Practice
Level	Mid-Level
	Senior
Contact	Pam Young, Managing Director

Description Dutton Group is a recruitment advertising agency.

DYMAR MANAGEMENT CONSULTANTS INC.
6790 Century Avenue, Suite 30
Mississauga, ON L5N 2V8

Telephone	905-812-1900
Fax	905-812-1551
E-mail	dymar@istar.ca
Website	www.dymar consultants.com
Specialties	Govt/Nonprofit
	Management
	Marketing
	Direct Mktng.
	Finance
Level	Mid-Level
Fee Basis	Retainer Only
Contact	Mariann da Silva

Description Dymar is an HR consulting firm that also offers recruitment services. Typical fees for employers are hourly, not commission based.

DYNAMIC EMPLOYMENT SOLUTION INC.
197 County Court Blvd., Suite 101
Brampton, ON L6W 4P6

Telephone	905-796-3300
Fax	905-796-0043
E-mail	helenec@dynamic employment.com
Website	www.dynamic employment.com
Founded	1996
Employees	12
Specialties	Administrative
	Banking
	Bilingual
	Computing
	Insurance
	Logistics
	Operations
	Pharmaceutical
	Plastics
	Retail
	Telecom
Level	Mid-Level
Recruiters	Sylvie Hyndman
	Nancy Wiesner

Description Dynamic Employment Solution Inc. specializes in recruitment in administration and accounting, distribution, executive, management and professional markets. Also has executive division.

DYNAMIC EMPLOYMENT SOLUTION INC.
700 Balmoral Drive
Unit 6B, Southgate Plaza
Brampton, ON L6T 1X2

Telephone	905-790-9880
Fax	905-790-0347

E-mail	helenec@dynamic employment.com
Website	www.dynamic employment.com
Specialties	Computing Bilingual Banking Administrative Logistics Insurance Retail Plastics Pharmaceutical Operations Telecom
Level	Mid-Level

Description Dynamic Employment Solution Inc. specializes in recruitment in administration and accounting, distribution, executive, management and professional markets. Also has executive division.

DYNAMIC PERSONNEL CONSULTANTS
222 Somerset St. West, Suite 710
Ottawa, ON K2P 2G3

Telephone	613-567-8886
Fax	613-567-6441
E-mail	recruiting@ dynamicpersonnel.com
Website	www.dynamic personnel.com
Founded	1995
Specialties	Administrative
Level	Junior Mid-Level

Description Dynamic Personnel Consultants is a full service recruiting and placement consulting company.

E.H. SCISSONS & ASSOCIATES INC. / PSA INTERNATIONAL
123 - 2nd Avenue South
Suite 806, PO Box 263
Saskatoon, SK S7K 7E6

Telephone	306-652-2551
Fax	306-665-2584
E-mail	psa@sk.sympatico.ca
Specialties	Management Human Resource Accounting Finance
Level	Senior Mid-Level
Contact	Dr. E.H. Scissons

Description Dr. E.H. Scissons & Associates Inc. is a member of PSA International.

E.L. SHORE & ASSOCIATES
2 St. Clair Avenue East, Suite 1201
Toronto, ON M4T 2T5

Telephone	416-928-9399
Fax	416-928-6509
E-mail	info@elshore.com
Founded	1968
Employees	4
Specialties	Marketing

	Finance Management Aerospace Human Resource Logistics Retail
Level	Senior
Min. Salary	$75,000
Fee Basis	Retainer Only
Recruiters	Roz Baker Marty Collis Earl L. Shore
Contact	Earl L. Shore, Founder

Description E.L. Shore & Associates s a senior-level retainer search firm. Part of the Globe Search Group internationally.

E-SEARCH CONSULTING
20 Adelaide Street East, Suite 401
Toronto, ON M5C 2T6

E-mail	info@ esearchconsulting.com
Website	www.e-searchconsulting.com
Specialties	Human Resource Purchasing Marketing Finance Accounting Computing Multimedia
Level	Mid-Level

Description E-Search, a division of Botrie Associates and Stanton Chase International, is an Internet recruiting service specializing in Internet and e-search strategies.

EAE INFO STAFF LTD.
Wellheads Way, Offshore House,
Dyce, Aberdeen AB21 7GD
UNITED KINGDOM

Telephone	44-1224-428505
Fax	44-1224-428500
E-mail	cvs@eaegroup.com
Specialties	International Telecom
Contact	Ewan Stevenson

EAGLE PROFESSIONAL RESOURCES INC.
700 West Georgia St., Suite 690
Pacific Centre, PO Box 10008
Vancouver, BC V7Y 1A1

Telephone	604-899-1130
Fax	604-899-1150
E-mail	vancouver@ eagleonline.com
Website	www.eagleonline.com
Founded	1996
Employees	4
Specialties	Computing Consulting Automotive
Level	Senior Mid-Level
Min. Salary	$40,000
Fee Basis	Always contingent

Recruiters	Julia Ford Cindy Hogan
Contact	Cindy Hogan

Description Eagle Professional Resources Inc. is a Canadian-owned staffing agency specializing in IT placements on a contract basis.

EAGLE PROFESSIONAL RESOURCES INC.
205 - 5th Avenue SW, Suite 2920
Calgary, AB T2P 2V7

Telephone	403-205-3770
Fax	403-205-3774
E-mail	calgary@ eagleonline.com
Website	www.eagleonline.com
Founded	1996
Employees	6
Specialties	Computing Consulting
Level	Senior Mid-Level
Min. Salary	$40,000
Fee Basis	Always contingent
Recruiters	Sharon Blaskovits Bill Hanniman Cameron McCallum
Contact	Bill Hanniman

Description Eagle Professional Resources Inc. is a Canadian-owned staffing agency specializing in IT placements on a contract basis.

EAGLE PROFESSIONAL RESOURCES INC.
67 Yonge Street, Suite 510
Toronto, ON M5E 1J8

Telephone	416-861-0636
Fax	416-861-9275
E-mail	toronto@ eagleonline.com
Website	www.eagleonline.com
Founded	1996
Employees	15
Specialties	Computing Consulting
Level	Senior Mid-Level
Min. Salary	$40,000
Fee Basis	Always contingent
Recruiters	Rishma Ahmed Ainsley Allen Andrew Demmery Jason Noon Fakhera Ravji
Contact	Andrew Demmery

Description Eagle Professional Resources Inc. is a Canadian-owned staffing agency specializing in IT placements on a contract basis.

EAGLE PROFESSIONAL RESOURCES INC.
67 Yonge Street, Suite 200
Toronto, ON M5E 1J8

Telephone	416-861-1492
Fax	416-861-8401

E-mail	international@ eagleonline.com
Website	www.eagleonline.com
Founded	1996
Employees	2
Specialties	Computing Consulting
Level	Senior Mid-Level
Min. Salary	$40,000
Fee Basis	Always contingent
Recruiters	Leah Cosgrove Frances McCart
Contact	Frances McCart

Description Eagle Professional Resources Inc. is a Canadian-owned staffing agency specializing in information technology (IT) placements on a contract basis.

EAGLE PROFESSIONAL RESOURCES INC.
170 Laurier Ave. West, Suite 902
Ottawa, ON K1P 5Y5

Telephone	613-234-1810
Fax	613-234-0797
E-mail	ottawa@ eagleonline.com
Website	www.eagleonline.com
Founded	1996
Employees	15
Specialties	Computing Consulting
Level	Senior Mid-Level
Min. Salary	$40,000
Fee Basis	Always contingent
Recruiters	Jennifer Arkell Eric Brown Karin Brown Heather McKendry
Contact	Eric Brown

Description Eagle Professional Resources Inc. is a Canadian-owned staffing agency specializing in information technology (IT) placements on a contract basis.

EAGLE PROFESSIONAL RESOURCES INC.
1 Place Ville Marie, Bureau 1526
Montréal, QC H3B 2B5

Telephone	514-396-6594
Fax	514-396-6596
E-mail	montreal@ eagleonline.com
Website	www.eagleonline.com
Founded	1996
Employees	4
Specialties	Computing Consulting
Level	Senior Mid-Level
Min. Salary	$40,000
Fee Basis	Always contingent
Recruiters	Andrea Di Domenico François Laganière Axelle Ligot

Contact	Michelle Robertson

Description Eagle Professional Resources Inc. is a Canadian-owned staffing agency specializing in information technology (IT) placements on a contract basis.

EAGLE PROFESSIONAL RESOURCES INC.
1969 Upper Water St., 22nd Floor
Purdy's Wharf, Tower II
Halifax, NS B3J 3R7

Telephone	902-491-4275
Fax	902-429-5018
E-mail	halifax@ eagleonline.com
Website	www.eagleonline.com
Founded	1996
Employees	2
Specialties	Computing Consulting
Level	Senior Mid-Level
Min. Salary	$40,000
Fee Basis	Always contingent
Recruiters	Michelle Murray Shelley Reyno
Contact	Michelle Murray

Description Eagle Professional Resources Inc. is a Canadian-owned staffing agency specializing in information technology (IT) placements on a contract basis.

EASTGATE CONSULTANTS INC.
36 Toronto Street, Suite 850
Toronto, ON M5C 2C5

Telephone	416-366-2007
Fax	416-366-0481
Specialties	Banking Finance

EASTLEIGH PERSONNEL LTD.
20641 Logan Avenue, Suite 206
Langley, BC V3A 7R3

Telephone	604-533-1911
Fax	604-533-0115
Founded	1984
Employees	5
Specialties	Accounting Computing Management
Level	Mid-Level Junior
Contact	Diane Shepherd

Description Eastleigh Personnel Ltd. provides placement services and training for companies in the Lower Mainland.

EASTRIDGE INFOTECH TECHNOLOGY STAFFING
311 California Street, Sixth Floor
San Francisco, CA 94104 USA

Telephone	415-616-9724
Fax	415-616-9740

E-mail	sanfrancisco@ eastridgeinfotech.com
Website	www.eastridge infotech.com
Specialties	Computing Telecom Multimedia International

Description Eastridge Infotech is a technology staffing leader with over 25 years of placement experience.

EDAN SEARCH GROUP
95 King Street East, Suite 100
Toronto, ON M5C 1G4

Telephone	416-367-4591
Fax	416-367-1577
E-mail	pparedes@ edansearchgroup.com
Website	www.edansearch group.com
Founded	1997
Specialties	Accounting Finance
Contact	Pauline Parades

Description Edan Search Group specializes in placing accounting and finance professionals.

EDGE CONSULTING GROUP, THE
2677 Hammond Road, Suite 100
Mississauga, ON L5K 2M5

Fax	905-823-8230
Specialties	General Practice

EDGETECH SERVICES INC.
18 Wynford Drive, Suite 615
Toronto, ON M3C 3S2

Telephone	416-441-4046
Fax	416-441-0697
E-mail	jobs@ edgetechservices.com
Website	www.edgetech services.com
Founded	1995
Specialties	Computing

Description EdgeTech Services Inc. is an IT consulting firm that also provides contract assignments.

EDIE BENCH PERSONNEL CONSULTANTS
82 Dell Park Avenue
Toronto, ON M6B 2T8

Telephone	416-785-3933
Fax	416-782-9935
Founded	1984
Specialties	Marketing General Practice Accounting Construction Management Real Estate Administrative
Level	Senior Mid-Level
Contact	Edie Bench

EDPS INC.
1930 Yonge Street, Suite 1200
Toronto, ON M4S 1Z4

Telephone	416-439-3335
E-mail	edps@home.com
Website	www.edps.net
Specialties	Computing

Description EDPS provides CIO, VP, director, manager-level IT professionals and hard-to-find IT experts for permanent and contract assignments.

EDS EXECUTIVE STAFFING
2695 Granville Street, Suite 204
Vancouver, BC V6H 3H4

Telephone	604-730-5776
Fax	604-730-5710
E-mail	administrator@resscan.com
Website	www.resscan.com
Specialties	Finance
	Computing
	Administrative
Contact	Larry Ranger

Description EDS Executive Staffing is a technology-based staffing firm that assists professional financial, administrative and information systems staff in advancing their careers.

EFFECTIVE PERSONNEL SOLUTIONS, INC.
400 - 5th Avenue SW, Suite 300
Calgary, AB T2P 0L6

Telephone	403-205-6620
Fax	403-205-4324
E-mail	ckee@effectivepersonnel.com
Website	www.effectivepersonnel.com
Founded	1998
Specialties	General Practice
Level	Mid-Level
	Junior
Recruiters	Marc Bourdeau
	Colan Kee
Contact	Colan Kee

Description Effective Personnel provides a progressive and cost-effective approach for the human resource needs of small to medium-sized companies in all industries.

EGON ZEHNDER INTERNATIONAL INC.
181 Bay Street, BCE Place
Suite 2900, PO Box 810
Toronto, ON M5J 2T3

Telephone	416-364-0222
Fax	416-364-0955
E-mail	ezitoronto@ezi.net
Website	www.zehnder.com
Founded	1964
Employees	11
Specialties	General Practice
	Management
Level	Senior
Min. Salary	$100,000
Fee Basis	Retainer Only
Recruiters	Kenneth W. Purdy
	Jan J. Stewart MBA
	Rashid Wasti
Contact	Jan J. Stewart, Managing Partner

Description Egon Zehnder International is a leader in senior executive search, board search and management appraisal services, with over 300 consultants in more than 50 offices in 35 countries.

EGON ZEHNDER INTERNATIONAL INC.
1 Place Ville-Marie
Bureau 3310, 33rd Floor
Montréal, QC H3B 3N2

Telephone	514-876-4249
Fax	514-866-0853
E-mail	ezi-mon-research@ezi.net
Website	www.zehnder.com
Founded	1964
Employees	13
Specialties	Management
Level	Senior
Min. Salary	$100,000
Fee Basis	Retainer Only
Recruiters	Hélène Cyr MBA
	Andre LeComte
	Pierre Payette
	Christian Robertson
	J. Robert Swidler
Contact	J. Robert Swidler, Managing Partner

Description Egon Zehnder International is a leader in senior executive search, board search and management appraisal services, with over 300 consultants in more than 50 offices in 35 countries.

ÉLAN PERSONNEL
755 Hillside Avenue, Suite 100
Victoria, BC V8T 5B3

Telephone	250-383-2226
Fax	250-383-8018
E-mail	victoria@elandatamakers.com
Website	www.elandatamakers.com/personnel.html
Specialties	Administrative
	Computing
	Finance
Level	Mid-Level
	Junior

Description Élan Personnel specializes in permanent and contract staffing of office and computer professionals.

ÉLAN PERSONNEL
788 Beatty Street, Suite 307
Vancouver, BC V6B 2M1

Telephone	604-688-8521
Fax	604-669-0171

E-mail	vancouver@elandatamakers.com
Website	www.elandatamakers.com/personnel.html
Founded	1972
Specialties	Administrative
	Computing
	Finance
Level	Mid-Level
	Junior

Description Élan Personnel specializes in permanent and contract staffing of office and computer professionals.

ÉLAN PERSONNEL
700 - 4 Avenue SW, Suite 260
Calgary, AB T2P 3J4

Telephone	403-290-1661
Fax	403-263-5038
E-mail	calgary@elandatamakers.com
Website	www.elandatamakers.com/personnel.html
Founded	1972
Employees	10
Specialties	Accounting
	Computing
	Finance
Level	Mid-Level
Contact	Matt Gibson

Description Élan specializes in permanent and contract staffing of office and computer professionals.

ELIASSEN GROUP, INC.
30 Audubon Road
Wakefield, MA 01880 USA

Telephone	781-246-1600
Fax	781-245-6537
E-mail	jmarx@eliassen.com
Website	www.eliassen.com
Founded	1989
Specialties	Computing
	International
Contact	Michael McBrierty, Recruiting Manager

Description Eliassen Group, Inc. specializes in providing experts in state-of-the-art computer technology for short-term, long-term and regular staffing needs.

ELLIOT ASSOCIATES
49 Wheeler Avenue
Toronto, ON M4L 3V3

Telephone	416-691-6619
Fax	416-691-9407
E-mail	elliot.associates@sympatico.ca
Specialties	Marketing
	Sales
	Health/Medical
Level	Mid-Level
	Senior
Contact	Joanne Elliot

ELLIS FOSTER
1650 - 1st Avenue West
Vancouver, BC V6J 1G1

Telephone	604-734-1112
Fax	604-734-1502
E-mail	generaldelivery@ ellisfoster.com
Website	www.ellisfoster.com
Founded	1961
Employees	90
Specialties	Accounting Finance
Level	Mid-Level

Description Ellis Foster is an accounting and management consulting firm that occasionally provides recruitment services for clients.

EMEX SYSTEMS INC.
1220 Sheppard Ave. East, Suite 410
Toronto, ON M2K 2S5

Telephone	416-494-4466
Fax	416-490-0407
E-mail	info@emexsys.com
Website	www.emexsys.com
Founded	1984
Specialties	Computing
Level	Senior Mid-Level
Recruiters	Jutta Holder Mel Kent
Contact	Mel Kent, President

Description Emex Systems Inc. specializes in recruiting and placing IT professionals.

EMPLOIS COMPETENCES INC.
356 rue Principale, Bureau 5
Granby, QC J2G 2W6

Téléphone	450-360-0558
Spécialités	Administratif Métiers/techniciens
Échelon	Intermédiaire Débutant

Description Emplois Competences Inc. recrute surtout dans le secteur de l'industrie.

EMPLOIS COMPETENCES INC.
65, rue Belvedere N, Bureau 140
Sherbrooke, QC J1H 4A7

Téléphone	819-566-4070
Télécopieur	819-566-6484
Spécialités	Administratif Métiers/techniciens
Échelon	Intermédiaire Débutant

Description Emplois Competences Inc. recrute surtout dans le secteur de l'industrie.

EMPLOIS PLUS, SERVICE DE PRE-SÉLECTION
410, avenue Lafleur, Bureau 50
Lasalle, QC H8R 3H6

Téléphone	514-595-7587

Télécopieur	514-367-5462
Fondée	1992
Employés	3
Spécialités	Assurance Exploitation Achat Ventes
Échelon	Intermédiaire Débutant
Recruteurs	Zahia Agsous Silvianne Tchouanguem
Contact	Zahia Agsous

Description Service de présélection de la main d'oeuvre, s'adressant à tout type d'entreprise, offert gratuitement aux employeurs de Montréal et sa région.

EMPLOYER'S CHOICE, THE
197 County Court Boulevard
Suite 302
Brampton, ON L6W 4P6

Telephone	905-874-1035
Fax	905-874-0280
E-mail	info@theemployers choice.com
Website	www.theemployers choice.com
Specialties	Administrative Law
Level	Mid-Level
Recruiters	David Chondon Susan Crawford Francine Mullen
Contact	Francine Mullen, Principal

Description The Employers' Choice provides human resources recruitment, systems and training.

EMPLOYER'S OVERLOAD
5 Clarence Square
Toronto, ON M5V 1H1

Telephone	416-596-1018
Fax	416-596-6525
Specialties	Administrative
Level	Junior Mid-Level
Contact	Ms Lumen Gonzalo

EMPLOYMENT NETWORK INC.
4625 Albert Street, Suite 1
Regina, SK S4S 6B6

Telephone	306-585-7244
Fax	306-584-3544
E-mail	recruit@ employment-netcanada.com
Website	www.employment-netcanada.com
Founded	1996
Employees	4
Specialties	Management Agriculture/Fisheries Administrative Computing Design Finance International

---

Fee Basis	Always contingent
Contact	Linda Langelier, Owner

Description Employment Network Inc. is dedicated to bridging the gap between companies searching for top candidates and individuals looking for challenging opportunities.

EMPLOYMENT PARTNERSHIP INC.
32 King Street
Suite 5-D, PO Box 2700
Saint John, NB E2L 1G3

Telephone	506-652-7431
Fax	506-634-1874
E-mail	epinc@nbnet.nb.ca
Website	www.employment partnership.com
Specialties	Accounting Law Management Engineering
Level	Mid-Level Junior
Contact	Adele Townsend, Manager

Description Employment Partnership offers recruitment services to employers including culture assessment, screening, reference checks, follow-up, pre-employment coaching for candidates, security clearance and related documentation.

ENCORE EXECUTIVES INC.
188 Redpath Avenue, Suite 410
Toronto, ON M4P 3J2

Telephone	416-485-8548
Fax	416-485-3516
E-mail	encore-executives@ home.com
Founded	1991
Specialties	Computing
Level	Mid-Level
Fee Basis	Always contingent
Contact	Gary Petch

Description Encore Executives specializes in placing permanent and contract IT professionals in Canada and the US.

ENNS & ENNS CONSULTING
444 St. Mary Avenue, Suite 1070
Winnipeg, MB R3C 3T1

Telephone	204-943-0804
Fax	204-944-9252
E-mail	KLJREnns@escape.ca
Website	www.escape.ca/ ~kljrenns
Employees	3
Specialties	Management
Contact	Dr. Kenneth Enns

Description Dr. Enns practices consulting and clinical psychology and human resources consulting through his private practice on a full-time basis.

ENNS HEVER INC.
100 University Avenue
Suite 601, Box 134, South Tower
Toronto, ON M5J 1V6

Telephone	416-598-0012
Fax	416-598-4328
E-mail	info@ennshever.com
Website	www.ennshever.com
Founded	1983
Employees	12
Specialties	Marketing
	Finance
	Human Resource
	Operations
Level	Senior
Min. Salary	$100,000
Fee Basis	Retainer Only
Recruiters	Alan Burns
	George Enns
	Rita Eskudt
	Jock McGregor
	Morris Tambor
	Hilda Tzavaras
Contact	George Enns, Partner

Description Enns Hever, formerly the Enns Partners, focuses on senior-level searches for top management ranks in areas including marketing, finance, human resources and operations.

ENS GROUP INC., THE
294 Albert Street, Suite 404
Ottawa, ON K1P 6E6

Telephone	613-235-0299
Fax	613-235-5929
E-mail	hr@ensgroup.com
Website	www.ensgroup.com
Specialties	Computing
	Telecom
	Engineering
Level	Mid-Level
	Senior

Description ENS Group is a leading professional services and recruiting firm specializing in the provision of comprehensive technology consulting, recruitment and managed network services.

EPERSONNEL INC.
8975 Maurice Duplessis, Suite 1
Montréal, QC H1E 6V9

Telephone	514-494-2650
Fax	514-494-9597
E-mail	kamelc@e-personnel.net
Website	www.e-personnel.net
Specialties	Apparel
	Finance
	Retail
	Accounting
Level	Mid-Level
Contact	Kamel Charfeddine, Eng., President

Description ePersonnel Inc. recruits financial and accounting specialists for the textile and apparel industry.

EPW & ASSOCIATES
150 Millford Crescent, SS 4
Elora, ON N0B 1S0

Telephone	519-846-0682
Fax	519-846-5571
E-mail	gene@wasylciw.com
Founded	1979
Employees	2
Specialties	Computing
Level	Senior
	Mid-Level
Fee Basis	Sometimes contingent
Recruiters	Eugene (Gene) Wasylciw
	Lene Wasylciw
Contact	Eugene (Gene) Wasylciw

Description All contact by email or fax please.

ERC MANAGEMENT GROUP LTD., THE
PO Box 29007
Mission Postal Station
Kelowna, BC V1W 4A7

E-mail	gleier@home.com
Specialties	Telecom
	Management
	Automotive
	Operations
	Banking

Description ERC Management Group Ltd. is an executive search firm in the Okanagan Valley.

ERIC TURNER & ASSOCIATES LTD.
33 City Center Drive, Suite 555
Mississauga, ON L5B 2N5

Telephone	905-566-1616
Fax	905-566-9755
E-mail	search@macdougalturner.com
Specialties	Administrative
Contact	Cathy McCabe

Description Eric Turner & Associates Ltd. are placement specialists.

ERIE PERSONNEL CORPORATION
3550 Schmon Parkway, Suite 2
Thorold, ON L2V 4Y6

Telephone	905-684-8222
Fax	905-684-3888
E-mail	employment@eriepersonnel.com
Website	www.eriepersonnel.com
Founded	1992
Employees	10
Specialties	General Practice
	Management
	Human Resource
	Operations
	Engineering
	Accounting
	Aerospace
Fee Basis	Retainer Only
Contact	Marina Butler

Description Erie Personnel Corporation is a full-service employment agency providing a complete line of human resource services to businesses throughout Niagara Region.

ERIE PERSONNEL CORPORATION
1202 Garrison Road, Unit 1
Fort Erie, ON L2A 1P1

Telephone	905-871-2627
Fax	905-871-4696
E-mail	employment@eriepersonnel.com
Website	www.eriepersonnel.com
Founded	1992
Employees	10
Specialties	General Practice
	Management
	Human Resource
	Operations
	Engineering
	Accounting
	Aerospace
Level	Mid-Level
Fee Basis	Retainer Only
Recruiters	Ron Butler
	Marina Butler
	Maria Wallace
Contact	Marina Butler

Description Erie Personnel Corporation is a full-service employment agency providing a complete line of human resource services to businesses throughout Niagara Region.

ERLAND INTERNATIONAL
288 Fairlawn Avenue
Toronto, ON M5M 1T1

Telephone	416-489-3645
Fax	416-487-7624
E-mail	erland@istar.ca
Founded	1994
Specialties	Arts & Culture
Level	Senior
Fee Basis	Retainer Only
Contact	Kristin V. Ferguson

Description Erland International specializes in recruiting executives for cultural institutions, managing complex national and international projects and supporting the work of search committees.

ERNST DAVID INTERNATIONAL INC.
1 Lombard Place, Suite 1610
Winnipeg, MB R3B 0X3

Telephone	204-947-9922
Fax	204-942-2742
Founded	1985
Employees	4
Specialties	Finance
	Health/Medical
	Management
	Marketing
	Operations
	Agriculture/Fisheries
	Publishing/Media
Level	Senior

Min. Salary $60,000

Recruiters   Claude Chapman
             Ernest D. Warkentin

Contact   Adrienne Newbury

ERNST & YOUNG
515 Riverbend Drive
PO Box 9458, Station C
Kitchener, ON N2G 4W9

Telephone   519-744-1171
Fax   519-744-9604
E-mail   lisa.a.voll@ca.eyi.com
Website   www.eycan.com

Specialties Accounting
             Finance

Level   Mid-Level
             Senior

Recruiters Keturah Leonforde
             Lisa Voll

Contact   Lisa Voll

Description Ernst & Young is a leading professional services firm. This
office also provides recruitment and
search services.

ERNST & YOUNG
100 New Gower Street
Suite 800, Cabot Place
St. John's, NF A1C 6K3

Telephone   709-722-5593
Fax   709-722-1758
E-mail   jan.dicks@ca.eyi.com
Website   www.eycan.com

Founded   1864
Employees   60

Specialties General Practice
             Management

Level   Senior
             Mid-Level

Min. Salary $50,000
Fee Basis   Retainer Only

Recruiters Jan Dicks
             Catherine Squire

Contact   Jan Dicks, Manager

Description Ernst & Young is a leading professional services firm. This
office also provides recruitment and
search services.

ERNST & YOUNG
Al Faisaliah Office Tower
PO Box 2732
Riyadh, 11461
SAUDI ARABIA

Telephone   966-1-477-6272 x 412
Fax   966-1-477-6352
E-mail   phil.gandier@
             sa.eyi.com
Website   www.ey.com

Founded   1923
Employees   126

Specialties International
             Finance
             Accounting
             Consulting
             Human Resource
             Management
             Marketing

Level   Senior
             Mid-Level

Contact   Phil Gandier

Description Ernst & Young is a leading professional services firm. This
office also provides recruitment and
search services.

ERP STAFFING SOLUTIONS INC.
1829 Ranchlands Blvd. NW,
Suite 220
Calgary, AB T3G 2A7

Fax   403-208-8201
E-mail   jobs@erpstaffing.com
Website   www.erpstaffing.com

Specialties Computing
             Logistics
             Operations

Description ERP Staffing Solutions
Inc. specializes in placing IT professionals in enterprise resource planning (ERP), logistics and supply
chain management assignments.

ERP STAFFING SOLUTIONS INC.
11 Barr Crescent, Suite 2
Brampton, ON L6Z 3C3

Telephone   905-846-0373
Fax   905-840-0454
E-mail   jobs@erpstaffing.com
Website   www.erpstaffing.com

Founded   1998
Employees   5

Specialties Telecom
             Logistics
             Computing
             Operations

Level   Senior
             Mid-Level

Min. Salary $60,000
Fee Basis   Sometimes contingent

Description ERP Staffing Solutions
Inc. specializes in placing IT professionals in enterprise resource planning (ERP), logistics and supply
chain management assignments.

ETALENT GROUP INC.
214 King Street West, Suite 414
Toronto, ON M5H 3S6

Telephone   416-345-1777
E-mail   info@etalentgroup.com
Website   www.etalentgroup.com

Specialties Computing
             Multimedia

Level   Mid-Level
             Senior

Description eTalent Group Inc.
proactively recruits top e-commerce
and Internet talent for professional
career opportunities.

EUREKA RECRUITMENT
250 - 6th Avenue SW, Suite 1500
Calgary, AB T2P 3H7

Telephone   403-705-5388
Fax   403-705-5399

E-mail   info@eureka
             recruitment.com
Website   www.eureka
             recruitment.com

Founded   1988

Specialties Sales
             Accounting
             Management

Level   Mid-Level

Recruiters Andrea Lee
             Karen Strong

Contact   Karen Strong

Description We find positive people
in a wide variety of industries with
a wide variety of experiences, including accounting, sales, administration, management and other senior executives.

EURO-WEST CONSULTING LTD.
1130 West Pender Street, Suite 325
Vancouver, BC V6E 4A4

Telephone   604-688-9903
Fax   604-688-9961

Specialties Accounting
             Finance
             Franchising

Level   Mid-Level

EVANCIC, PERRAULT, ROBERTSON / EPR
5202 - 52nd Avenue, Box 7677
Drayton Valley, AB T7A 1S8

Telephone   780-542-2820 Ext 25
Fax   780-436-1994
E-mail   carlap@fleming-iss.com
Website   www.epr.ca

Specialties Accounting
             Finance

Level   Mid-Level

Contact   Carla Perry

Description EPR is an accounting
firm that occasionally does search
work for clients.

EVANS SEARCH GROUP
16 The Links Road, Suite 312
Toronto, ON M2P 1T5

Telephone   416-224-2277
Fax   416-229-1973

Founded   1982
Employees   3

Specialties Transport
             Logistics
             Accounting
             Administrative
             Bilingual
             Management
             Marketing

Level   Mid-Level
             Senior

Min. Salary $40,000
Fee Basis   Always contingent

Contact   Ray Evans

Description Evans Search Group specializes in the transportation, distri-

bution, third-party logistics, customs and traffic industries.

EVEREST MANAGEMENT NETWORK INC.
390 Bay Street, Suite 2410
Toronto, ON M5H 2Y2

Telephone	416-363-9798
Fax	416-363-3930
E-mail	info@everest management.com
Website	www.everest management.com
Founded	1990
Specialties	Accounting Banking Finance Human Resource Operations Real Estate Sales
Fee Basis	Sometimes contingent
Recruiters	Vanessa Disspain Donna Khawaja Barry Marcus Julius Spetter Matthew J. Standish
Contact	Vanessa Disspain

Description Everest provides recruitment and consultative services to clients.

EVEREST SYSTEMS NETWORK
235 Yorkland Blvd., Suite 300
Toronto, ON M5H 2Y2

Telephone	416-497-7817
Fax	416-497-7881
E-mail	systems@everest management.com
Website	www.everest management.com
Specialties	Computing Consulting
Contact	Stephen Johnstone, Consulting Services Manager

Description Everest Systems Network specializes in the permanent and contract placement of IT professionals.

EXCALIBUR CAREERS INC.
60 Columbia Way, Suite 300
Markham, ON L3R 0C9

Telephone	905-940-9335
Fax	905-707-8551
E-mail	excalibur.careers@ home.com
Website	www.nvo.com/ excalibur
Founded	1993
Employees	3
Specialties	Sales Marketing
Level	Senior Mid-Level
Min. Salary	$50,000
Fee Basis	Sometimes contingent

Recruiters	Esmond D'Cunha MBA Jean Houston
Contact	Jean Houston

Description Excalibur Careers Inc. specializes in placing sales professionals in office products, information technology and software.

EXCEL HUMAN RESOURCES CONSULTANTS
890 Yonge Street, Suite 1002
Toronto, ON M4W 3P4

Telephone	416-967-6654
Fax	416-967-7393
E-mail	hsl@pathcom.com
Founded	1977
Employees	12
Specialties	Computing Banking Govt/Nonprofit Finance Consulting Quality Control Management
Level	Mid-Level Senior
Recruiters	Russell Gynp Robert A. Sydia Robert W. Sydia
Contact	Robert A. Sydia, Partner

Description Excel Human Resources (formerly Hutchinson Smiley Limited) specializes in the recruitment of high-quality professionals in high technology, administrative and professional positions.

EXCEL HUMAN RESOURCES CONSULTANTS
102 Bank Street, Suite 300
Ottawa, ON K1P 5N4

Telephone	613-230-5393
Fax	613-230-1623
E-mail	excel@excelhr.com
Website	www.excelhr.com
Founded	1989
Employees	25
Specialties	Computing Govt/Nonprofit Administrative
Level	Mid-Level
Contact	Lynda Connerty

Description Excel Human Resources specializes in the recruitment of high-quality professionals in high technology, contracting, administrative and professional fields.

EXCEL PERSONNEL INC.
418 St. Paul Street, Suite 200
Kamloops, BC V2C 2J6

Telephone	250-374-3853
Fax	250-374-3854
E-mail	temphelp@excel.bc.ca
Website	www.excel.bc.ca
Founded	1992
Specialties	Accounting Computing

	Govt/Nonprofit Human Resource Law Management Administrative
Level	Mid-Level Junior
Fee Basis	Sometimes contingent
Recruiters	Cheryl Lemasurier Suzanne Skene Karen A. Watt CPC
Contact	Karen A. Watt, CPC

Description Excel provides professional office and industrial assistance, from clerical and accounting to management and IT Techs.

EXCEL PERSONNEL INC.
3737 Notre Dame Ouest
Montréal, QC H4C 1P8

Telephone	514-931-4251
E-mail	excel.personnel@ sympatico.ca
Specialties	Administrative
Contact	Robert Ziziam

EXECUCOUNSEL INC
2 Bloor Street West, Suite 700
Toronto, ON M4W 3R1

Telephone	416-928-3025
Fax	416-928-1292
Founded	1995
Specialties	Finance Health/Medical Accounting Insurance Human Resource
Level	Senior
Fee Basis	Retainer Only
Recruiters	Dick Marty Nick Williams
Contact	Dick Marty

Description ExecuCounsel Inc. are recuitment advisors to boards and senior management.

EXECUPLACE INC.
3535 St-Charles, Suite 456
Kirkland, QC H9H 5V9

Telephone	514-694-2512
Fax	514-355-9088
E-mail	info@execu-place.com
Website	www.execu-place.com
Specialties	Computing Engineering
Contact	Mike Lattimore

Description ExecuPlace Inc. is a recruitment firm that specializes in providing a range of technical resources and hard-to-find skills.

EXECUSEARCH, A DIVISION OF EXECUSERVE PLUS INC.
1003 - 4th Avenue South
Lethbridge, AB T1J 0P7

Telephone	403-320-5604

Fax	403-327-8577
E-mail	execuserv@ connect.ab.ca
Founded	1988
Employees	3
Specialties	Govt/Nonprofit Hospitality Management Tourism Administrative Marketing Trades/Technicians
Level	Mid-Level
Fee Basis	Retainer Only
Contact	Gillian Nish, President

Description Execusearch specializes in tourism/hospitality placements.

EXECUSOURCE STAFFING INTERNATIONAL
430 Pelissier Street, Suite 1111
Windsor, ON N9A 4K9

Telephone	519-250-9333
Fax	519-971-0567
E-mail	careers@execusource staffing.com
Website	www.execusource staffing.com
Founded	1998
Employees	4
Specialties	Automotive Computing Engineering Marketing Sales
Level	Senior Mid-Level
Fee Basis	Sometimes contingent
Contact	Naheed Ahmed-Salman

Description Execusource Staffing International is a full-service permanent placement firm.

EXECUTIVE 2000 INSTITUTE
255 Duncan Mill Road, Suite 702
Toronto, ON M3B 3H9

Telephone	416-447-0307
Fax	416-447-6943
E-mail	resume@executive2000 institute.com
Founded	1987
Specialties	Retail
Level	Mid-Level Senior
Recruiters	Omar Benidir Kevin McIntosh
Contact	Kevin McIntosh, Executive Director

Description Executive 2000 provides bilingual services in recruitment, training & development and organizational consulting to retail clients.

EXECUTIVE ASSISTANCE INC.
25 Adelaide Street East, Suite 1711
Toronto, ON M5C 1Y7

Telephone	416-368-8700

Fax	416-368-0555
E-mail	resumes@exec assistance.com
Website	www.exec assistance.com
Founded	1994
Employees	5
Specialties	Finance Trade Shows Accounting
Level	Mid-Level
Min. Salary	$25,000
Fee Basis	Sometimes contingent
Recruiters	Ann Binsted Gayle Mead Susan Pepper Melissa Roberts
Contact	Ann Binsted

Description Executive Assistance Inc. is a professional recruitment firm providing placement services in the financial services and event management sectors.

EXECUTIVE FACTS INC.
357 Bay Street, Suite 501
Toronto, ON M5H 2T7

Telephone	416-363-7200
Fax	416-363-6464
Employees	4
Specialties	Management Operations
Level	Mid-Level Senior
Contact	Chad M. Dakin

EXECUTIVE HOUSE INC.
40 Centre Street
Suite 301, 40 Centre Square
Chatham, ON N7M 5W3

Telephone	519-351-4622
Fax	519-351-4623
E-mail	exechous@kent.net
Website	www.kent.net/ executive-house
Founded	1988
Employees	12
Specialties	Automotive Operations
Level	Senior Mid-Level
Recruiters	Jennifer Highgate Joe Kehn Garda Markham Gary Nettleton Betty Smith
Contact	Gary Nettleton, General Manager

Description Executive House Inc. is a full-service organization specializing in permanent and contract placements in the automotive industry at all levels.

EXECUTIVE NETWORK, THE
612 View Street, 2nd Floor
Victoria, BC V8W 1J5

Telephone	250-389-2848

Fax	250-389-0194
E-mail	executivenetwork@ map-xn.com
Founded	1986
Employees	4
Specialties	Management Education Human Resource Retail Sales Accounting Hospitality International
Level	Senior Mid-Level
Min. Salary	$50,000
Fee Basis	Retainer Only
Recruiters	Brad Colbert Walter Donald
Contact	Walter Donald, CMP, CHRP

Description The Executive Network is primarily interested in recruiting for management and professional positions across Canada and Pacific Rim countries.

EXECUTIVE RECRUITERS
135 Albert Street
London, ON N6A 1L9

Telephone	519-679-2950
Fax	519-679-3454
E-mail	execrec@ lon.hookup.net
Founded	1984
Employees	5
Specialties	Marketing Health/Medical Sales Management
Level	Mid-Level
Contact	Nancy Howett, Sr. Partner

Description Call toll-free at 1-800-317-4473.

EXECUTIVE REGISTRY / RESSOURCES HUMAINES ER
1200 McGill College Avenue
Suite 1900, Capitol Centre
Montréal, QC H3B 2L1

Telephone	514-866-7981
Fax	514-866-7093
E-mail	hns@ executive-registry.net
Website	www.executive-registry.net
Employees	8
Specialties	Management Operations Sales Law
Level	Senior Mid-Level
Contact	Harvey N. Stewart

Description The Executive Registry conducts management and professional recruitment on a regional and national basis.

EXECUTIVE RESOURCES INTERNATIONAL

437 Argyle, CP 632, Succ. Victoria
Montréal, QC H3Y 3B3

Telephone	514-935-3695
Fax	514-931-2495
E-mail	eri@istar.ca
Founded	1976
Employees	2
Specialties	Agriculture/Fisheries
Biotech/Biology
Geology/Geography
Management
Oil & Gas
Pulp & Paper
Trades/Technicians
Level	Mid-Level
Senior
Min. Salary	$25,000
Fee Basis	Sometimes contingent
Recruiters	Michael Berger
G.P. Creighton
Contact	G.P. Creighton

Description An executive search organization specializing in the recruitment of management and technical personnel for service in developing areas as well as North America.

EXECUTIVE SERVICES PLUS LTD.

16 Germain Street
Suite 14, PO Box 434
Saint John, NB E2L 4L9

Telephone	506-633-1909
Fax	506-646-9920
E-mail	exec11@nbnet.nb.ca
Specialties	Management
Recruiters	Lynn Bell
Lisa Gallagher
Pat Pond
Contact	Lynn Bell, Owner

EXECUTIVE SOURCE, THE

2201 - 11th Avenue, Suite 401
Regina, SK S4P 0J8

Telephone	306-359-2550
Fax	306-359-2555
E-mail	search@theexecutive
source.com
Website	www.theexecutive
source.com
Founded	1997
Employees	3
Specialties	Management
Human Resource
Govt/Nonprofit
Accounting
Education
Logistics
Telecom
Level	Senior
Mid-Level
Fee Basis	Always contingent
Recruiters	Holly Hetherington
Rick McCormick
Sandra Merk
Valerie Smith
Contact	Sandra Merk, Manager,
Search Services

Description Executive Source is a Saskatchewan-owned and based executive recruitment firm committed to providing professional services to clients filling senior-level positions.

EXECUTIVES AVAILABLE

189, boul Hymus, Bureau 405
Pointe-Claire, QC H9R 1E9

Telephone	514-697-2227
Fax	514-697-7837
E-mail	eacd@total.net
Website	www.total.net/~eacd
Founded	1977
Employees	5
Specialties	General Practice
Accounting
Bilingual
Engineering
Human Resource
Marketing
Sales
Contact	Martin Shaw

Description Executives Available is a non-profit service that supplies candidates to agencies and employers.

EXECUTRADE CONSULTANTS LTD.

10123 - 99th Street
Suite 520, Sun Life Place
Edmonton, AB T5J 3H1

Telephone	780-944-1122
Fax	780-424-0106
E-mail	gawlik@
executrade.com
Website	www.executrade.com
Founded	1974
Employees	10
Specialties	Accounting
Management
Operations
Transport
Engineering
Human Resource
Marketing
Sales
Computing
Actuarial
Administrative
Banking
Level	Mid-Level
Senior
Fee Basis	Sometimes contingent
Recruiters	Marilyn Chorney CPC
Ron Egan CPC
Patricia Gawlik
Richard Stoppler
Scott Stoppler CPC
Contact	Patricia Gawlik

Description Executrade Consultants is a full-service agency that is ISO 9002-1994 certified.

EXPERT RECRUITERS INC.

1055 West Hastings St., Suite 300
Vancouver, BC V6E 2E9

Telephone	604-609-6176
Fax	604-684-6024
E-mail	jobs@expert
recruiters.com
Website	www.expert
recruiters.com
Employees	7
Specialties	Finance
Accounting
Administrative
Level	Mid-Level
Junior
Recruiters	Darcia Bower
Beverley I. Hart
Linsey Ross
Antoine Sajous
Sarah-Jane Thomson
Contact	Darcia Bower, Founder

Description We offer over eight years of experience and a reputation for delivering results.

EXPERTECH PERSONNEL SERVICES INC.

800 Rene Levesque W., Bur. 1501
Montréal, QC H3B 1X9

Telephone	514-876-8818
Fax	514-876-0523
E-mail	personnel@
expertech.ca
Website	www.expertech.ca
Founded	1993
Employees	10
Specialties	Accounting
Computing
Design
Level	Mid-Level
Fee Basis	Sometimes contingent
Recruiters	Patrick Pépin
Chrisanthopoulos Themis
Richard Wabha
Contact	Chrisanthopoulos Themis

Description Expertech Personnel Services Inc. specializes in IT recruiting, outsourcing, payroll staff and computer-based testing.

EXPERTS CONSEILS 2000

9386 Joseph Melancon
Montréal, QC H2M 2H8

Telephone	514-382-7939
E-mail	expertsconseils2000@
qc.aira.com
Specialties	General Practice
Contact	Joanne Chapdelaine

EXPRESS PERSONNEL SERVICES

1175 Johnson Street, Suite 208
Port Coquitlam, BC V3B 7K1

Telephone	604-944-8530
Fax	604-944-0897
E-mail	jobs@coquitlambc.
expresspersonnel.com
Website	www.express
personnel.com
Specialties	Administrative
Marketing
Sales
Human Resource

Level   Mid-Level
Junior

Contact   Brad Braekevelt

Description Express Personnel is a division of Express Services, Inc., a full-service staffing company.

EXPRESS PERSONNEL SERVICES
2825 Lauzon Parkway, Suite 213
Windsor, ON N8T 3H5

Telephone   519-251-1115
Fax   510 251 1118
E-mail   jobs.windsoron@
expresspersonnel.com
Website   www.expresspersonnel.
com

Specialties   Administrative
Human Resource
Sales
Marketing

Level   Mid-Level
Junior

Recruiters   Colleen Gaudette
Deborah Zsebak

Contact   Deborah Zsebak

Description Express Personnel is a division of Express Services, Inc., a full-service staffing company.

EXPRESS PERSONNEL SERVICES
150 Dufferin Avenue
Suite 604, Richmond Court
London, ON N6A 5N6

Telephone   519-672-7620
Fax   519-672-7694
E-mail   jobs.londonon@
expresspersonnel.com
Website   www.express
personnel.com

Founded   1980
Employees   30

Specialties   Administrative
Human Resource
Sales
Marketing

Level   Junior
Mid-Level

Fee Basis   Always contingent

Contact   Tracey Cross

Description Express Personnel is a division of Express Services, Inc., a full-service staffing company.

EXPRESS PERSONNEL SERVICES
50 Queen Street North, Suite 704
Kitchener, ON N2H 6P4

Telephone   519-578-9030
Fax   519-578-1121
E-mail   jobs.kitcheneron@
expresspersonnel.com
Website   www.express
personnel.com

Specialties   Administrative
Human Resource
Marketing
Sales

Level   Mid-Level
Junior

Contact   Judy Cawley

Description Express Personnel is a division of Express Services, Inc., a full-service staffing company.

EXPRESS PERSONNEL SERVICES
45 Speedvale Avenue East, Suite 1
Guelph, ON N1H 1J2

Telephone   519-821-4275
Fax   519-821-8054
E-mail   jobs.guelphon@
expresspersonnel.com
Website   www.express
personnel.com

Specialties   Administrative
Human Resource
Marketing
Sales

Level   Mid-Level
Junior

Contact   Terry Hanka

Description Express Personnel is a division of Express Services, Inc., a full-service staffing company.

EXPRESS PERSONNEL SERVICES
100 James Street South, Suite 201
Hamilton, ON L8P 2Z2

Telephone   905-528-7744
Fax   905-528-7289
E-mail   jobs.hamiltonon@
expresspersonnel.com
Website   www.express
personnel.com

Specialties   Administrative
Human Resource
Marketing
Sales

Level   Mid-Level
Junior

Contact   Alice Preston, Owner

Description Express Personnel is a division of Express Services, Inc., a full-service staffing company.

EXPRESS PERSONNEL SERVICES
440 Elizabeth Street, Suite 300
Burlington, ON L7R 2M1

Telephone   905-639-7117
Fax   905-639-8606
E-mail   jobs.burlington@
expresspersonnel.com
Website   www.expresspersonnel.com

Specialties   Administrative
Marketing
Sales
Human Resource

Level   Junior
Mid-Level

Contact   Terry Hanka

Description Express Personnel is a division of Express Services, Inc., a full-service staffing company.

EXPRESS PERSONNEL SERVICES
220 Laurier Ave. West, Suite 560
Ottawa, ON K1P 5Z9

Telephone   613-233-5988
Fax   613-233-4651
E-mail   jobs.ottawaon@
expresspersonnel.com
Website   www.express
personnel.com

Specialties   Marketing
Administrative
Bilingual
Sales
Human Resource

Level   Junior
Mid-Level

Fee Basis   Retainer Only

Recruiters   Joe Beauchamp
Catherine Laforce
Janet Moore
Eliane Rjeili

Contact   Catherine Laforce

Description Express Personnel is a division of Express Services, Inc., a full-service staffing company.

F.E.R. EXECUTIVE SEARCH
625 Howe Street, Suite 350
Vancouver, BC V6C 2T6

Telephone   604-683-8071
Fax   604-683-8152
E-mail   resume@feres.com
Website   www.feres.com

Specialties   Management
Bilingual

Level   Mid-Level

Contact   Rachel Yamamoto

Description F.E.R. Executive Search is one of the leading international professional search firms specializing with executive, senior, andmid-management placements in North America, Japan, Asia-Pacific Rim.

F.J. GALLOWAY ASSOCIATES INC.
350 Oxford Street West, Suite 203
London, ON N6H 1T3

Telephone   519-641-1325
Fax   519-472-9354

Specialties   Management
Architecture
Engineering

Contact   Fred Galloway

Description F.J. Galloway Associates Inc. is a management consulting firm that also does recruitment work for clients.

FACILITÉ INFORMATIQUE
360, rue St-Jacques Ouest
Bureau 1915
Montréal, QC H2Y 1P5

Telephone   514-284-5636
Fax   514-284-9529
E-mail   info@facilite.com
Website   www.facilite.com

Founded   1992
Employees   90

Specialties   Computing
International

Level   Mid-Level

Fee Basis   Retainer Only

Recruiters   Judith Brunelle
Gary Butler
Nathalie Gonnet
Julie Laroche
Josée Laroche
Bernard Laye
Luc Letendre

Contact   Julie Laroche

Description Facilité Informatique specializes in systems integration and consulting services in Canada, USA and Europe.

FAIRVIEW MANAGEMENT
338 - 5th Avenue E.
Prince Rupert, BC V8J 1R9

Telephone   250-627-4748
Fax   250-624-2044
E-mail   acompagn@citytel.net
Website   www.fms.bc.ca

Founded   1990

Specialties   Disabled

Level   Mid-Level

Contact   Alice Compagnon

Description Fairview Management assists disabled people find assisted work in the Prince Rupert area.

FAR WEST GROUP
2383 King George Highway
Suite 206
Surrey, BC V4A 5A4

Telephone   604-538-2079
Fax   604-536-1618
E-mail   cv@grpwest.com
Website   www.grpwest.com

Specialties   Computing

Contact   Charles van Veen

Description Far West Group is an IT consulting company that also recruits systems professionals for clients.

FARLEY LAW & ASSOCIATES
8500 Leslie Street
Thornhill, ON L3T 7M8

Telephone   905-771-8655
Fax   905-771-8659

Founded   1979

Specialties   Computing
Marketing
Sales
Finance

Level   Mid-Level

Fee Basis   Sometimes contingent

Recruiters   Ted Farley
Bill Law
Peter Law

Contact   Bill Law

FAS RESOURCES
4261 - A14 Highway No. 7
Suite 183
Markham, ON L3R 9W6

Telephone   905-470-1871

Fax   905-470-8767
E-mail   job@fasresources.com
Website   www.fasresources.com

Founded   1995

Specialties   Computing

Level   Mid-Level
Senior

Contact   Peter Chen

Description FAS Resources is a placement agency specializing in computer professionals.

FCM INC.
651 Notre-Dame Road W., Suite 200
Montréal, QC H3C 1H9

Telephone   514-393-1415
Fax   514-393-9092
E-mail   recrutement@
fcminc.qc.ca

Specialties   International
Human Resource

FELDMAN GRAY & ASSOCIATES INC.
45 St. Clair Avenue West, Suite 700
Toronto, ON M4V 1K9

Telephone   416-515-7600
Fax   416-515-7595
E-mail   general@feldman-
gray.com
Website   www.feldman-gray.com

Founded   1978
Employees   10

Specialties   Sales
Management
Computing
Insurance
Finance
Human Resource
Marketing
Operations

Level   Mid-Level
Senior

Min. Salary $60,000
Fee Basis   Retainer Only

Recruiters   Evelyn Bebby
Dennis Breault
Corey Daxon
Fred Feldman
Frank Gray
John Hierlihy
Jennifer Johnson
Vickie Kalles
Warren M. Lundy
Hugh R. MacMillan
Ron Meyers
Fred R. Nogas
Catherine VanderBerg
Kristina Vohma

Contact   Vickie Kalles

Description Feldman Gray & Associates specializes in retainer executive search, outplacement and career transition programs for groups and individuals at all levels.

FENTON LOCKHART ASSOC. INC.
451 Parkview Crescent SE
Calgary, AB T2J 4N8

Telephone   403-237-0244

Specialties   Management

Level   Mid-Level

Contact   David Fenton

FERN STEVENS & ASSOCIATES
2 Bloor Street East, Suite 2910
Toronto, ON M4W 1A8

Telephone   416-928-1212
Fax   416-928-0555
E-mail   office@fernstevens.com
Website   www.fernstevens.com

Founded   1986

Specialties   Computing

Level   Mid-Level
Senior

Contact   Fern Stevens

Description Fern Stevens & Assoc. is a leading search firm specializing in the placement of IT professionals.

FHG INTERNATIONAL INC.
14 Glengrove Avenue West
Toronto, ON M4R 1N4

Telephone   416-489-6996
Fax   416-489-7792
E-mail   info@fhgi.com
Website   www.fhgi.com

Founded   1984

Specialties   Hospitality
Franchising
Restaurant
Retail

Level   Senior

Min. Salary $100,000

Recruiters   Douglas P. Fisher
Peter Goffe
Elizabeth Hollyer
Domenic Zoffranieri

Contact   Douglas P. Fisher,
President

Description Management consulting firm specializing in franchise, retail and food service with demand for occasional high-profile recruitment.

FIALA CONSULTING GROUP, INC., THE
1112 West Pender Street, Suite 810
Vancouver, BC V6E 3X5

Telephone   604-684-1022
Fax   604-684-8010
E-mail   gfiala@qrtz.com

Specialties   Sales
Education

Level   Mid-Level

Contact   George Fiala

Description The Fiala Consulting Group, Inc. is a management consulting firm specializing in public sector assignments, including occasional recruitment work for clients.

FICELLES
49, rue St-Jean-Baptiste O.
Rimouski, QC G5L 4J2

Téléphone   418-723-2205

Télécopieur   418-723-4586
Courriel   ficelles@
globetrotter.net
Site Internet   www.libertel.org/
ficelles

Fondée   1985

Spécialités   Généralistes

Échelon   Intermédiaire
Débutant

Contact   Diane Vallières

Description   Services de placement pour les femmes qui veuillent retourner à travail.

FICELLES
1572, boul. Jacques-Cartier
Mont-Joli, QC G5H 2W2

Téléphone   418-775-2226
Télécopieur   418-775-1704
Courriel   ficelles@
globetrotter.net
Site Internet   www.libertel.org/
ficelles

Spécialités   Généralistes

Échelon   Intermédiaire
Débutant

Contact   Diane Vallières

Description   Services de placement pour les femmes qui veuillent retourner à travail.

FIFTH OPTION, THE
3701 Hastings Street, Suite 210
Burnaby, BC V5C 2H6

Telephone   604-659-1300
Fax   604-294-8283
E-mail   tfo@uniserve.com
Website   www.fifthoption.com

Founded   1989
Employees   7

Specialties   Accounting
Computing
Engineering
Finance
Health/Medical
Human Resource
Management
Marketing
Sales
Operations

Level   Senior
Mid-Level

Fee Basis   Sometimes contingent

Recruiters   George Coghlan
Daniel Leigh
Diane Rowland

Contact   George Coghlan

Description   The Fifth Option provides a number of unique HR consulting services, including "offsite" HR management and recruitment services.

FINACC EXECUTIVE SEARCH INC.
1013 Wilson Avenue, Suite 201
Toronto, ON M3K 1G1

Fax   416-636-8485
E-mail   finacc@netcom.ca

Specialties   Accounting
Finance

Description   Finacc Executive Search Inc. recruits finance professionals.

FINANCE DEPARTMENT LTD., THE
4576 Yonge Street, Suite 408
Toronto, ON M2N 6N4

Telephone   416-512-9119
Fax   416-512-9316
E-mail   info@tfdl.com
Website   www.tfdl.com

Founded   1996

Specialties   Finance
Accounting

Contact   John M. Huxtable,
Managing Director

Description   The Finance Department Ltd. specializes in contract and permanent placement of accounting professionals in Southern Ontario, Bermuda and the Cayman Islands.

FINNEY-TAYLOR CONSULTING GROUP LTD.
706 - 7th Avenue SW, Suite 900
Calgary, AB T2P 0Z1

Telephone   403-264-4001
Fax   403-264-4057
E-mail   mailbox@finney-
taylor.com
Website   jobs.finney-taylor.com

Founded   1967
Employees   6

Specialties   Computing

Level   Mid-Level
Senior

Min. Salary $37,000
Fee Basis   Always contingent

Recruiters   Ron Balachandra
David Skode
Martha Taylor
Traci Zeller

Contact   Davod Skode, GM

Description   Finney-Taylor is an IT resourcing and recruitment firm.

FIRST CHOICE PERSONNEL
655 Dixon Road
Suite 50, International Plaza
Toronto, ON M9W 1J4

Telephone   416-241-8611
Fax   416-241-4152
E-mail   mail@firstchoice
personnel.com
Website   www.firstchoice
personnel.com

Founded   1989
Employees   11

Specialties   Accounting
Computing
Engineering
Human Resource
Insurance
Marketing
Operations
Sales
Administrative
Automotive
Bilingual
Direct Mktng.
Graphic Arts
Logistics
Management
Transport
Telecom
Purchasing
Publishing/Media

Level   Mid-Level
Junior

Fee Basis   Always contingent

Recruiters   Brenda Cooke
Virginia Howatt
Lynn Hurlbut
John McFee
Lawton Osler
Helen Perruzza
Micheline Pesheau
Kaye Rees
Beverley Wood
Laura Youngs

Contact   John McFee

Description   With over 50 years of combined industry experience, First Choice Personnel specializes in permanent and contract service in all aspects of employment.

FIRST STEP RECRUITMENT
1 Yonge Street, Suite 1801
Toronto, ON M5E 1J9

Telephone   416-698-6473
Fax   416-698-5291

Specialties   Human Resource
General Practice

Level   Mid-Level

Contact   Sharon Nevard

Description   First Step Recruitment runs ads and conducts interviews on behalf of employers.

FISHER GROUP EXECUTIVE SEARCH
250 - 6th Avenue SW
Suite 1500, Bow Valley Square IV
Calgary, AB T2P 3H7

Telephone   403-251-3040
Fax   403-238-5732
E-mail   fishergroupexec@
aol.com

Founded   1984

Specialties   Finance
Management
Oil & Gas
Pharmaceutical
Printing
Sales
Telecom

Level   Mid-Level
Senior

Min. Salary $50,000
Fee Basis   Sometimes contingent

Contact   Mel V. Fisher CMC,
Principal

Description   Fisher Group provides executive search services to major multi-national, national and regional companies in high tech, IT, telecom, IS and oil and gas industries.

FLORIO GOSSET GROUP INC.
45 Kingsbridge Garden Circle
Suite 2207
Mississauga, ON L5R 3K4

Telephone 416-410-0099
Fax 905-501-1181
E-mail info@floriogosset
group.com
Website www.floriogosset
group.com

Founded 1991

Specialties Computing
Telecom

Contact John G. Florio,
President

Description Florio Gosset Group Inc.
is a Canadian recruitment firm specializing in IT and the wireless communications sectors.

FORBES & GUNN CONSULTANTS LTD.
1166 Alberni Street, Suite 1650
Vancouver, BC V6E 3Z3

Telephone 604-688-6461
Fax 604-681-6401
E-mail jobs@forbes-gunn.com
Website www.forbes-gunn.com

Specialties Computing

Level Senior
Mid-Level

Recruiters Lee Brebber
Mike Brown
Mark Budworth
Damian McElgunn
Sarita Naidu
Judy Woo

Contact Lee Brebber

Description Forbes & Gunn Consultants Ltd. is a professional recruitment and consulting firm with a focus on information technology.

FORBES & GUNN CONSULTANTS LTD.
1420 - 5th Avenue, Suite 2200
Seattle, WA 98101 USA

Telephone 206-523-7480
Fax 206-523-7412
E-mail jobs@forbes-gunn.com
Website www.forbes-gunn.com

Specialties Computing
International

Level Senior
Mid-Level

Fee Basis Always contingent

Contact Lee Brebber

Description Forbes & Gunn specializes in the recruitment and selection of IT personnel for full-time and contract opportunities.

FORBES & GUNN CONSULTANTS LTD.
1200 NE 8th Street, Suite 205
Bellevue, WA 98005 USA

Telephone 425-455-0130
Fax 425-455-0312

E-mail jobs@forbes-gunn.com
Website www.forbes-gunn.com

Specialties Computing
International

Level Senior
Mid-Level

Fee Basis Always contingent

Recruiters Eric Bartels
Lisa Booth
Jason Carl

Contact Jason Carl, Senior
Technical Recruiter

Description Forbes & Gunn Consultants Ltd. is a professional recruitment and consulting firm with a focus on information technology.

FORCE RECRUITING SERVICES
250 - 6th Avenue SW
1500 Bow Valley Square IV
Calgary, AB T2P 3H7

Telephone 403-237-6666
Fax 403-686-4544
E-mail inquiries@
forcerecruiting.com
Website www.force
recruiting.com

Specialties Finance
Computing
Administrative

Level Mid-Level

Contact Teresa Quintieri

Description Force Recruiting Services specializes in the recruitment, selection and placement of highly-skilled, knowledge-based employees in financial, technical, IT and business support service areas.

FOREFRONT INFORMATION STRATEGIES GROUP, INC.
396 Cooper Street, Suite 418
Ottawa, ON K2P 2H7

Telephone 613-234-4534
Fax 613-234-7642
E-mail hr@forefront.ca
Website www.forefront.ca

Founded 1991

Specialties Computing
International

Level Mid-Level

Contact Leon Dykler, President

Description ForeFront is an IT consulting firm that provides experienced consultants to clients in federal government, Crown corporations and private industry in Canada and the USA.

FOREST PEOPLE INTERNATIONAL SEARCH LTD.
1100 Melville Street, Suite 800
Vancouver, BC V6E 4A6

Telephone 604-669-5635
Fax 604-684-4972
E-mail people@forestpeople.
com
Website www.forestpeople.com

Founded 1992
Employees 6

Specialties Forestry
Pulp & Paper

Level Senior
Mid-Level

Fee Basis Always contingent

Recruiters Ron Hogg
Ian McFall
Bill Waschuk
Janice Waschuk
Nelia Yelle

Contact Ron Hogg, President

Description Forest People International Search Ltd. is a forest industry specialist, offering management, technical and professional placements in sawmills, panel board plants, woodlands and the pulp & paper industry.

FOUNTAINHEALTH RECRUITMENT
553 Merton Street
Toronto, ON M4S 1B4

Telephone 416-481-7969
Fax 416-201-9173
E-mail jobs@fountain
head.on.ca
Website www.fountain
health.com

Specialties Finance
Health/Medical

Recruiters Jim Anderson
Tony Andras

Contact Tony Andras,
Managing Partner

Description Fountainhealth Recruitment specializes in placements in the areas of healthcare and finance.

FRANCIS & ASSOCIATES
80 Dorset Road
Toronto, ON M1M 2S7

Telephone 416-267-5626
Fax 416-267-9446
E-mail generalinfo@francis-associates.com
Website www.francis-associates.com

Specialties Health/Medical

Description Francis & Associates is a Toronto-based personnel agency specializing in the placement of rehabilitation healthcare professionals throughout Canada.

FRAPPIER, ST-DENIS ET ASSOC.
410, rue St-Nicholas, Bureau 504
Montréal, QC H2Y 2P5

Téléphone 514-499-0997
Télécopieur 514-499-3646
Courriel frappier_st_denis@
videotron.ca

Spécialités Gestion
Marketing

Échelon Direction
Intermédiaire

Description Cabinet de gestion.

FRED D. LITMAN & ASSOCIATES
120 Eglinton Avenue E., Suite 1000
Toronto, ON M4P 1E2

Telephone	416-480-1515
Fax	416-322-6371
Founded	1993
Specialties	Advertising
	Graphic Arts
Level	Mid-Level
	Senior
Fee Basis	Sometimes contingent
Contact	Fred D. Litman

Description Fred D. Litman & Associates specializes in senior and mid-level media executives for the advertising industry.

FREELANCERS UNLIMITED INC.
1055 Yonge Street, Suite 200
Toronto, ON M4W 2L2

Telephone	416-969-9088
Fax	416-969-8965
E-mail	info@freelancers
	unlimited.com
Website	www.freelancers
	unlimited.com
Founded	1986
Specialties	Advertising
	Graphic Arts
	Marketing
	Multimedia
	Direct Mktng.
	Publishing/Media
Level	Senior
	Mid-Level
Recruiters	Nancy Arbic
	Beverly Gray
	James Gray
Contact	Beverly Gray

Description Freelancers Unlimited Inc. is a specializes in the freelance, contract and permanent placement of creative, marketing and advertising specialists.

FREELANDT CALDWELL REILLY
17 Frood Road, Suite 2
Sudbury, ON P3C 4Y9

Telephone	705-675-2200
Fax	705-675-2515
Specialties	Accounting
Level	Mid-Level

Description Freelandt Caldwell Reilly is an accounting firm that occasionally does search work for clients.

FRIDAY PERSONNEL INC.
808 Nelson Street
Suite 509, Box 12133
Vancouver, BC V6Z 2H2

Telephone	604-689-7775
Fax	604-689-1998
E-mail	van@friday.ab.ca
Website	www.friday.ab.ca
Founded	1987
Specialties	Finance
	Accounting
	Human Resource
	Engineering
	Marketing
	Computing
	Administrative
Level	Mid-Level
	Junior

Description Friday Personnel Inc. was formed in 1987 to provide professional and technical expertise to a wide range of industries.

FRIDAY PERSONNEL INC.
703 - 6th Avenue SW, Suite 120
Calgary, AB T2P 0T9

Telephone	403-233-0499
Fax	403-266-3731
E-mail	friday@friday.ab.ca
Website	www.friday.ab.ca
Founded	1987
Specialties	Finance
	Accounting
	Human Resource
	Engineering
	Marketing
	Computing
	Administrative
Level	Mid-Level
	Junior
Contact	Barb Janman, President

Description Friday Personnel Inc. was formed in 1987 to provide professional and technical expertise to a wide range of industries.

FRIEDMAN & FRIEDMAN
8000 Decarie Boulevard, Suite 500
Montréal, QC H4P 2S4

Telephone	514-731-7901
Fax	514-731-2923
E-mail	friedman@friedman.ca
Website	www.friedman.ca
Specialties	Accounting
	Management
	Finance
Level	Mid-Level
	Senior
Contact	Marvin Minkoff

Description Friedman & Friedman is an accounting firm that also performs search services.

FROMM & ASSOCIATES PERSONNEL LTD.
65 Queen Street West, Suite 500
Toronto, ON M5H 2M5

Telephone	416-368-0050
Fax	416-368-2858
E-mail	admin@fromm.net
Website	www.fromm.net
Founded	1987
Specialties	Accounting
	Finance
	Administrative
Level	Mid-Level
Contact	Naomi Fromm, President

Description Fromm & Associates is a privately-owned Canadian search firm specializing in accounting, financial and administrative staffing.

FSK ASSOCIATES INC.
622 East Oak Island Drive
PO Box 1078
Long Beach, NC 28465 USA

Telephone	910-278-1080
Fax	910-278-5353
E-mail	sfennell@fsk.com
Website	www.fsk.com
Specialties	Engineering
	Computing
	Telecom
	International
Level	Mid-Level
	Senior
Recruiters	Sharon Fennell
	Ken Fennell
	Mitsy Porter
Contact	Sharon Fennell

Description FSK Associates Inc. provides high-quality staff augmentation and staffing services for engineering, technical, computer consulting and administrative industry needs.

FULLER LANDAU
1010, rue de la Gauchetiere O.
Bureau 200, Place du Canada
Montréal, QC H3B 2N2

Telephone	514-875-2865
Fax	514-866-0247
E-mail	info.mtl@
	fullerlandau.com
Website	www.fullerlandau.com
Specialties	Accounting
	Finance
Level	Mid-Level
Contact	Ted Greenfield, CA

Description Fuller Landau is a chartered accounting firm that occasionally does search work for clients.

FUNDAMENTAL SOLUTIONS GROUP / FSG CONSULTANTS
5 Laval Street, Suite 204
Hull, QC J8X 3G6

Telephone	819-776-6374
Fax	819-776-4605
E-mail	info@fsg.ca
Website	www.fsg.ca
Founded	1993
Employees	50
Specialties	Computing
Level	Mid-Level

Description FSG Consultants offers consulting and placement services for information technology and information management positions.

FUTURE EXECUTIVE PERSONNEL INC.
300 International Drive, Suite 100
Williamsville, NY 14221 USA

Telephone	716-626-3451
Fax	716-626-3001
E-mail	staff@futureexec.com
Website	www.futureexec.com
Founded	1975
Employees	50
Specialties	Engineering
	Accounting
	Finance
	Computing
	Automotive
	Packaging
	Plastics
	International
Level	Mid-Level
	Senior

Description Future Executive Personnel Inc. is a technical recruitment firm operating in 6 divisions: accounting and finance, engineering, information technology, FEP automotive, packaging and plastics.

FUTURE EXECUTIVE PERSONNEL LTD.
425 University Avenue, Suite 800
Toronto, ON M5G 1T6

Telephone	416-979-7575
Fax	416-979-3030
E-mail	caneng@
	futureexec.com
Website	www.futureexec.com
Founded	1975
Employees	50
Specialties	Management
	Engineering
	Accounting
	Aerospace
	Banking
	Bilingual
	Finance
	Plastics
	Sales
Level	Senior
	Mid-Level
Min. Salary	$50,000
Fee Basis	Always contingent
Contact	Mike Mehta, President

Description Future Executive Personnel is a leading North American search and placement firm with offices in Toronto and New York.

FUTURESTEP
20 Queen Street West, Suite 3308
Toronto, ON M5H 3R3

Telephone	416-640-5470
Fax	416-640-5490
Website	www.futurestep.com
Founded	1998
Employees	10
Specialties	Finance
	Management
	Banking
	Marketing
	Accounting
	Sales
Level	Senior
	Mid-Level
Min. Salary	$75,000

Fee Basis	Retainer Only
Recruiters	Michael Adams
	Frances Arthur
	Brad Beveridge
	Linda Blair
	Lisa Butler
	Kent Flint
	Glenda Goodman
	David Pask
	Noelle Pepperall
Contact	Glenda Goodman

Description Futurestep is an executive recruiting service that combines traditional search expertise with Internet technology and proprietary assessment methodologies.

FWJ COMMUNICATIONS LTD.
639 - 5th Avenue SW, Suite 620
Calgary, AB T2P 0M9

Telephone	403-266-7061
Fax	403-269-4022
E-mail	confidential@fwj.com
Website	www.fwj.com
Founded	1954
Employees	40
Specialties	General Practice
	Advertising
	Public Relations
Level	Senior
	Mid-Level
Contact	Brad Stevens

Description FWJ is a recruitment advertising firm and does not accept unsolicited resumes. Inquiries from employers are welcome.

G.L. PENNEY & ASSOCIATES INC.
8830 - 60th Avenue
Edmonton, AB T6E 6A6

Telephone	780-944-1100
Fax	780-944-1111
E-mail	resumes@
	glpenney.com
Website	www.glpenney.com
Specialties	Forestry
	Operations
	Engineering
	Accounting
	Sales
	Pulp & Paper
	Management
	Oil & Gas
Level	Senior
	Mid-Level
Fee Basis	Always contingent
Recruiters	Mr. Lynn Kurach
	Darci Macht
	Greg L. Penney
Contact	Darci Macht

Description G.L. Penney consults on executive searches for middle and senior level positions.

G.W. GOUDREAU PERSONNEL SERVICES LTD.
555 Tecumseh Road East
Windsor, ON N8X 2S1

Telephone	519-977-7300
Fax	519-977-0300
E-mail	jobs@gwgoudreau.com
Specialties	Engineering
	Computing
Level	Mid-Level
	Junior
Contact	Gary W. Goudreau

Description Specializing in placements in the industrial and manufacturing sector.

G-P PERSONNEL INC.
413, rue Racine est, Bureau 205
Chicoutimi, QC G7H 1S8

Téléphone	418-545-1881
Télécopieur	418-545-0898
Fondée	1980
Employés	3
Spécialités	Comptabilité
	Ingénierie
	Ressources humaines
	Gestion
	Marketing
	Exploitation
	Ventes
Échelon	Direction
	Intermédiaire
Frais	Honoraire seulement
Recruteurs	Julie Gilbert
	Richard Giroux
	Madeleine Poirier
	Marie-Chantale St-Germain
Contact	Richard Giroux

Description Recrutement, évaluation et selection de personnel. Developpement organisationnel. Gestion de carrière.

G-TECH PROFESSIONAL STAFFING, INC.
17101 Michigan Avenue
Dearborn, MI 48126-2736 USA

Telephone	313-441-3600
Fax	313-441-3001
E-mail	gtsjobs@gogtech.com
Website	www.gogtech.com
Employees	380
Specialties	Engineering
	International
	Automotive
	Construction
	Logistics
	Packaging
Fee Basis	Retainer Only
Recruiters	Louis B. Ghafari
	Theresa Ghafari
Contact	Theresa Ghafari,
	President & COO

Description G-Tech Professional Staffing is a supplier to the automotive industry and utilities.

GAAP INC.
1524, avenue Summerhill
Montréal, QC H3H 1B9

Telephone	514-935-3253
Fax	514-935-0852

E-mail	ehughes@gaap search.com
Website	www.gaapsearch.com
Founded	1972
Employees	10
Specialties	Finance
	Human Resource
	Logistics
	Public Relations
	Biotech/Biology
	Insurance
	International
Level	Mid-Level
	Senior
Fee Basis	Retainer Only
Recruiters	Shawn Davidson
	Emerson Hughes
	Steve Johnstone
Contact	Emerson Hughes,
	Senior Partner

Description An executive search firm conducting searches coast to coast in the US and Canada, with offices in Toronto, Boston and Montreal.

GALLANT SEARCH GROUP INC.
431 Boler Road, PO Box 20086
London, ON N6K 2K0

Telephone	519-663-1070
Fax	519-663-1074
E-mail	gallant@automotive careers.com
Website	www.automotive careers.com
Founded	1988
Specialties	Automotive
	Management
	Engineering
	Design
	Plastics
	Logistics
	Purchasing
	Human Resource
Level	Mid-Level
	Senior
Min. Salary	$40,000
Fee Basis	Always contingent
Contact	Andrew Gallant,
	President

Description Gallant Search Group is a professional recruiting firm specializing in search and placement for the manufacturing community in North America.

GALLOWAY AND ASSOCIATES
55 St. Clair Avenue West, Suite 265
Toronto, ON M4V 2Y7

Telephone	416-969-8989
Fax	416-969-9498
E-mail	glenn@galloway search.com
Website	www.galloway search.com
Founded	1984
Employees	2
Specialties	Sales
	Marketing
	Computing
	Operations

Level	Senior
	Mid-Level
Min. Salary	$50,000
Fee Basis	Sometimes contingent
Recruiters	Robert Brenton
	Lionel Crabtree
	Glenn E. Galloway
	Edward Marlowe
	Terry Thornton
Contact	Glenn E. Galloway

Description Galloway and Associates specializes in recruiting in sales, marketing, IT and manufacturing positions.

GALT GLOBAL RECRUITING
595 Howe Street, Suite 1205
Vancouver, BC V6C 2T5

Telephone	604-685-0609
Fax	604-689-5981
E-mail	info@galtglobal.com
Website	www.galtglobal.com
Specialties	Computing
	Marketing
	Sales
	Management
	Accounting
Recruiters	Ian Doyle
	Peter Meingast CHRP
	Samantha Stone
Contact	Peter Meingast CHRP,
	CEO

Description Galt Global specializes in placing people in information technology, marketing, accounting, management positions with companies and organizations of merit.

GALT GLOBAL RECRUITING
425 - 1 Street SW, Suite 3400
Calgary, AB T2P 3L8

Telephone	403-266-7052
E-mail	info@galtglobal.com
Website	www.galtglobal.com
Specialties	Computing
	Marketing
	Sales
	Accounting
	Management
Contact	Shelley Nemeth

Description Galt Global specializes in placing people in information technology, marketing, accounting, management positions with companies and organizations of merit.

GARDNER & COOMBS
9 Church Hill, Box 455, Station C
St. John's, NF A1C 5K4

Telephone	709-753-3283
Fax	709-753-0707
Specialties	Accounting
	Finance
Level	Mid-Level
Contact	Eric L. Coombs CA,
	Partner

Description Gardner & Coombs is an accounting firm that also does occasional search work for clients.

GARRISON GROUP, THE
15 Toronto Street, Suite 502
Toronto, ON M5C 2E3

Telephone	416-956-4861
Fax	416-954-4861
E-mail	garrisongroup@ compuserve.com
Specialties	Accounting
	Finance
Level	Mid-Level
Contact	Ronald J. McGee

GARYMCCRACKEN EXECUTIVE SEARCH INC.
145 King Street West, Suite 1000
Toronto, ON M5H 1J8

Telephone	416-363-8900
E-mail	info@gary mccracken.com
Website	www.gary mccracken.com
Specialties	General Practice
Level	Senior
Min. Salary	$125,000
Fee Basis	Retainer Only
Recruiters	Keith J. Labbett
	Gary W. McCracken
Contact	Gary W. McCracken
	MBA

Description GaryMcCracken Executive Search Inc. is an independent, retained executive search firm, blending extensive search experience with senior executive operating experience.

GASPAR & ASSOCIATES
439 University Avenue, Suite 849
Toronto, ON M5G 1Y8

Telephone	416-598-5552
Fax	416-598-5556
E-mail	andrew@gaspar.ca
Specialties	Finance
	Accounting
Level	Mid-Level
	Senior
Min. Salary	$65,000
Fee Basis	Retainer Only
Contact	Andrew Gaspar

Description Gaspar & Associates has 28 years specialization in financial search at professional, management and executive levels for major organizations.

GAUDRY, SHINK, LEVASSEUR
1155, rue University, Bureau 505
Montréal, QC H3B 3A7

Telephone	514-878-1199
Fax	514-878-1940
E-mail	gsl@gslexec.com
Founded	1997
Employees	4
Specialties	Marketing
	Human Resource
	Finance
	Engineering

	Operations
	Sales
	Purchasing
Level	Senior
Min. Salary	$60,000
Fee Basis	Retainer Only
Recruiters	Jean Gaudry
	Marc Levasseur
	Gilles Shink
Contact	Jean Gaudry

Description Consultants in executive search for middle and senior-level positions.

GAUTHIER CONSEILS

1001, rue Sherbrooke E., bur. 510
Montréal, QC H2L 1L3

Telephone	514-528-9089
Fax	514-274-2242
E-mail	info@gauthier.com
Website	www.gauthier.com
Founded	1980
Employees	3
Specialties	Accounting
	Banking
	Engineering
	Finance
	Human Resource
	Management
	Marketing
	Operations
	Purchasing
	Sales
Level	Mid-Level
	Senior
Min. Salary	$35,000
Contact	Jean R. Gauthier

Description A member of the Order of Industrial Relations Consultants (C.R.I.), the firm offers over 20 years of recruitment and selection services to firms in Canada and abroad.

GBL RESOURCES INC.

6966 Crooks Road, Suite 20
Troy, MI 48098-1798 USA

Telephone	248-813-9595
Fax	248-813-9599
E-mail	LindaU@GBLres.com
Website	www.gblres.com
Founded	1994
Specialties	Automotive
	Engineering
	International
Level	Senior
	Mid-Level
Recruiters	Gil Bates
	Bob Scheper
	Linda Updike
Contact	Linda Updike,
	President

Description GBL Resources Inc. specializes in automotive engineering recruitment.

GEDDES JEFFERSON & ASSOC.

843 Yates Street
Victoria, BC V8W 1M1

Telephone	250-361-3264
Fax	250-361-3105
E-mail	laurie@geddes jefferson.com
Website	www.islandnet.com/~ thefirm/homepage.htm
Founded	1991
Specialties	Govt/Nonprofit
	Health/Medical
Level	Senior
	Mid-Level
Recruiters	Laurie Geddes
	Larry Jefferson
	Karen Thompson
Contact	Laurie Geddes

Description Geddes Jefferson & Associates provides management consulting and HR consulting services to private and public sector organizations.

GENERATIONJOBS.COM

873 Decarie Boulevard
Saint-Laurent, QC H4L 3M2

Telephone	514-748-1211
Fax	514-744-2163
E-mail	sales@generation jobs.com
Website	www.generation jobs.com
Specialties	General Practice

Description GenerationJobs.com is an online recruitment service.

GENESIS CORPORATE SEARCH LTD.

520 - 5th Avenue SW, Suite 1800
Calgary, AB T2P 3R7

Telephone	403-237-8622
Fax	403-233-7622
E-mail	genesis@genesis corporatesearch.com
Website	www.genesis corporatesearch.com
Founded	1983
Employees	7
Specialties	Engineering
	Accounting
	Finance
	Management
	Operations
	Oil & Gas
	Geology/Geography
Level	Mid-Level
	Senior
Min. Salary	$60,000
Fee Basis	Retainer Only
Recruiters	Vern Casey
	P.F. (Trish) Hines
Contact	Vern Casey

Description Genesis Corporate Search provides search services to the oil and gas industry, placing professionals in geoscience, engineering, and finance.

GENESIS GROUP LTD., THE

4915 - 48th Street
Suite 17, Panda II Centre
Yellowknife, NT X1A 3S4

Telephone	867-873-3456
Fax	867-873-8311
E-mail	genesis@theedge.ca
Website	www.genesisgroup.ca
Specialties	Govt/Nonprofit
	Management
Recruiters	Steve Bearss
	Kirsty Knudson
	Jamie MacKenzie
	Tom O'Connor
	John Simpson
	Deb Simpson
	Ali Simpson
	Amy Simpson
Contact	John Simpson,
	President

Description The Genesis Group Ltd. is an HR consulting firm that also provides recruitment services.

GÉNISA CONSEIL INC.

353, rue St. Nicolas, Bureau 401
Montréal, QC H2Y 2P1

Telephone	514-286-5188
Fax	514-286-8206
E-mail	info@genisa conseil.com
Founded	1993
Employees	1
Specialties	Engineering
Level	Mid-Level
Contact	Isabelle Berubé

Description Génisa Conseil Inc. specializes in engineering recruitment.

GENOVESE VANDERHOOF & ASSOCIATES

27 Carlton Street, Suite 1103
Toronto, ON M5B 2J7

Telephone	416-340-2762
E-mail	gva@aol.com
Specialties	Govt/Nonprofit
	Arts & Culture
Level	Mid-Level
Recruiters	Margaret Genovese
	Rob Lamb
	Dory Venderhoof
Contact	Margaret Genovese,
	Senior Partner

Description Genovese Vanderhoof & Associates is a management consulting firm in the arts and cultural community that also does occasional search work for clients.

GENS INC., LA

1650 Michelin Street
Laval, QC H7L 4R3

Telephone	450-973-1881
Fax	450-973-3386
E-mail	info@lagens.qc.ca
Website	www.lagens.qc.ca
Specialties	Trades/Technicians
	Administrative
Level	Mid-Level
	Junior

Description La Gens Inc., a member of the Association of Canadian Search, Employment and Staffing Services, provides recruitment services for temporary and permanent assignments.

GENTIVA HEALTH SERVICES
101 Queensway West, Suite 300
Mississauga, ON L5B 2P7

Telephone	905-896-0200
Fax	905-896-8353
E-mail	norma.tomlin@ gentiva.com
Website	www.gentiva.com
Specialties	Health/Medical
Contact	Neil McIntosh

Description Gentiva Health Services, formerly Olsten Health Services, is a leading provider of community-based home healthcare staff.

GEODE CONSULTING GROUP
2628 Granville Street, Suite 224
Vancouver, BC V6H 3H8

Telephone	604-730-1150
E-mail	geode@portal.ca
Specialties	Human Resource
Level	Mid-Level

GEORGE PREGER & ASSOCIATES INC.
41 MacPherson Avenue
Toronto, ON M5R 1W7

Telephone	416-922-6336
Fax	416-922-4902
E-mail	consult@george preger.com
Website	www.georgepreger.com
Founded	1977
Employees	2
Specialties	Management
Level	Senior Mid-Level
Min. Salary	$60,000
Fee Basis	Retainer Only
Contact	George A. Preger, President

Description George Preger & Associates Inc. concentrates on searches for company presidents, vice-presidents, general managers and their closest reports.

GEORGE STEWART CONSULTANTS LTD.
193 Burbank Drive
Toronto, ON M2K 1P5

Telephone	416-730-0920
Fax	416-730-0920
E-mail	sales@knowres.on.ca
Website	www.knowres.on.ca/gsc
Specialties	Banking Finance Insurance Management Operations
Level	Senior Mid-Level
Fee Basis	Retainer Only
Contact	George Stewart

Description George Stewart Consultants Ltd. is a Canadian management consulting firm specializing in executive and professional searches and placements.

GEORGIAN STAFFING SERVICES
50 Hume Street
Collingwood, ON L9Y 1V2

Telephone	705-444-1645
Fax	705-443-4026
E-mail	gsvws@georgian staffing.on.ca
Website	www.georgian staffing.on.ca
Specialties	Accounting Administrative Sales
Level	Mid-Level Junior
Recruiters	Brenda Hewgill Paul Newton
Contact	Brenda Hewgill

Description A division of Employment and Resource Services of Georgian Bay Area Incorporated, Georgian Staffing provides permanent and outplacement services to businesses in the Georgian Triangle area.

GERALD WALSH RECRUITMENT SERVICES INC.
1801 Hollis Street, Suite 220
Halifax, NS B3J 3N4

Telephone	902-421-1676
Fax	902-491-1300
E-mail	info@geraldwalsh.com
Website	www.geraldwalsh.com
Founded	1989
Employees	10
Specialties	Accounting Finance Management Marketing Operations Human Resource Law
Level	Mid-Level Senior
Recruiters	Rose Marie Gallant Jane Skiffington Patty Sypher Gerald Walsh
Contact	Gerald Walsh

Description Gerald Walsh Recruitment Services provides comprehensive staffing and recruitment solutions to clients and job candidates throughout Atlantic Canada.

GERI RAMSAY & ASSOCIATES
1055 West Hastings Street
Suite 300, Guinness Tower
Vancouver, BC V6E 2E9

Telephone	604-609-6176
Fax	604-684-6024
E-mail	cindybrannan@look.ca
Specialties	Accounting
Recruiters	Cindy Brannan Geri Ramsay
Contact	Cindy Brannan

GESTION CONSEILS DLT INC.
5345 Hilltop Drive
Manotick, ON K4M 1G4

Fax	613-692-0359
Specialties	Accounting Retail
Contact	Danielle Leblanc

GESTION ORION LTÉE
800 Place Victoria, Bureau 4700
Montréal, QC H4Z 1H6

Fax	514-878-1865
Specialties	Accounting
Level	Mid-Level

GESTION-CONSEIL GILLES RICHER INC.
1770 Rene Levesque Boul. West
Montréal, QC H3H 2S9

Telephone	514-933-1122
Fax	514-367-7346
Specialties	Purchasing
Level	Mid-Level

GIBSON KENNEDY & COMPANY
16 Maxwell Avenue
Toronto, ON M5P 2B5

Telephone	416-932-9923
Fax	416-932-9924
Specialties	Banking Computing Law Management
Level	Senior
Recruiters	David R. Gibson Alan Kennedy CMC
Contact	Alan Kennedy, Managing Partner

Description Gibson Kennedy & Company is a management consulting company focusing on strategic advice that occasionally does search work for clients.

GILLIGAN & ASSOCIATES INC.
145 King Street West, Suite 1000
Toronto, ON M5J 1J8

Telephone	416-363-9296
Fax	416-360-6436
Specialties	Banking Finance
Level	Mid-Level Senior
Min. Salary	$50,000
Fee Basis	Sometimes contingent
Contact	Irene Gilligan, Owner

GINSBERG GLUZMAN FAGE & LEVITZ, LLP
287 Richmond Road
Ottawa, ON K1Z 6X4

Telephone	613-225-9250
Fax	613-728-8085
E-mail	jb@ggfl.ca
Website	www.ggfl.ca
Specialties	Finance
	Accounting
Recruiters	John Baldwin
	Cheryl Banks
	Jeffery Miller
Contact	John Baldwin, CA

Description Ginsberg Gluzman Fage & Levitz, LLP is an accounting firm that also does occasional search work for clients.

GIRARDIN & ASSOCIATES INC.
444 St. Mary Avenue, Suite 1505
Winnipeg, MB R3C 3T1

Telephone	204-947-2500
Fax	204-947-2323
E-mail	ngirardin@home.com
Founded	1986
Employees	4
Specialties	Accounting
	Engineering
	Human Resource
	Management
	Operations
Level	Mid-Level
	Senior
Min. Salary	$40,000
Contact	Norbert B. Girardin

Description Girardin & Associates specializes in human resources consulting and industrial psychology.

GIVENS HAMILTON LAIN
12220 Stony Plain Road
Suite 300, West Chambers
Edmonton, AB T5N 3Y4

Telephone	780-482-7337
E-mail	edmonton@
	porterhetu.com
Specialties	Accounting
	Finance
Contact	J.E. Logan

Description Givens Hamilton Lain is an accounting (CGA) firm that also does search work for clients.

GLAZIN GROUP, THE
350 - 7th Avenue SW, Suite 3000
Calgary, AB T2P 3N9

Telephone	403-215-2680
E-mail	search@glazin.com
Specialties	General Practice
Level	Mid-Level
	Senior
Fee Basis	Retainer Only
Contact	Lynne Glazin

Description Glazin Group is a retainer-based, full-service executive search firm.

GLAZIN / SISCO EXECUTIVE SEARCH CONSULTANTS INC.
1066 West Hastings, Suite 2300
Vancouver, BC V6E 3X1

Telephone	604-687-3828
Fax	604-687-3875
E-mail	search@glazin.com
Website	www.glazinsisco.com
Founded	1993
Employees	5
Specialties	Hospitality
	Retail
	Real Estate
	Human Resource
	Management
	Marketing
Level	Senior
Min. Salary	$100,000
Fee Basis	Retainer Only
Recruiters	Lynne Glazin
	Sue Hall
	Shelly Silbernagel
Contact	Sue Hall

Description Glazin / Sisco is a retainer-based, full-service executive search firm with offices in Toronto and Vancouver, specializing in the hospitality, resorts, real estate, retail and food service industries.

GLAZIN / SISCO EXECUTIVE SEARCH CONSULTANTS INC.
95 King Street East, Suite 500
Toronto, ON M5C 1G4

Telephone	416-203-3004
Fax	416-203-3007
E-mail	search@glazin.com
Website	www.glazinsisco.com
Founded	1993
Employees	2
Specialties	Hospitality
	Retail
	Real Estate
	Human Resource
	Management
	Marketing
Level	Senior
Min. Salary	$100,000
Fee Basis	Retainer Only
Contact	Carol Sisco

Description Glazin / Sisco is a retainer-based, full-service executive search firm with offices in Toronto and Vancouver, specializing in the hospitality, resorts, real estate, retail and food service industries.

GLEN ABBEY EXECUTIVE SEARCH INC.
1155 North Service Rd. W., Unit 11
Glen Abbey Executive Suites
Oakville, ON L6M 3E3

Telephone	905-847-0560
Fax	905-847-9592
E-mail	art@execuprolink.com
Website	www.execuprolink.com
Founded	1990
Employees	2
Specialties	Sales

Management
Engineering
Finance
Human Resource
Marketing

Level	Mid-Level
	Senior
Min. Salary	$40,000
Fee Basis	Sometimes contingent
Recruiters	Thérèse Edwards
	Arthur Rivard
Contact	Arthur Rivard CMC,
	MBA, CHRP

Description Glen Abbey Executive Search specializes in the recruitment and selection of technical sales (chemical, civil, mechanical engineers) and non-technical sales and marketing professionals.

GLOBAL CAREER SERVICES INC.
84 Laguana Parkway
RR 1, Site 2, Box 136
Brechin, ON L0K 1B0

Telephone	705-484-5271
Fax	705-484-5440
Specialties	Health/Medical

GLOBAL CONSULTING GROUP INC.
195 Main Street North
Markham, ON L3P 1Y4

Telephone	905-472-9677
Fax	905-472-9671
E-mail	info@globalrecruit.com
Website	www.globalrecruit.com
Founded	1991
Employees	10
Specialties	Computing
	Engineering
	Sales
	Scientific
	Management
	Marketing
	Bilingual
Level	Senior
	Mid-Level
Min. Salary	$45,000
Fee Basis	Sometimes contingent
Recruiters	Patricia Chambers
	Judy Chambers
	Shawn McEween
	Don Musthill
Contact	Patricia Chambers

Description Global Consulting is an experienced executive and technology recruitment firm offering assistance to business partners in growing their human resources infrastructure.

GLOBAL HOSPITALITY SEARCH CONSULTANTS
2430 Meadowpine Blvd., Suite 107
Mississauga, ON L5N 6S2

Telephone	905-814-5701
Fax	905-814-5702
E-mail	mail@globalhospto.com
Website	www.globalhospto.com

Founded 1982
Employees 12

Specialties Hospitality

Level Senior
Mid-Level

Min. Salary $30,000

Recruiters David Eaton
Doug Henderson
Richard Mirosolin
Stephen Shanahan
Bill Swerdon

Contact Richard Mirosolin

Description Global Hospitality is dedicated to quality searches within the hospitality industry.

GLOBAL HOSPITALITY SEARCH CONSULTANTS
4170 Marlowe
Montréal, QC H4A 3M2

Telephone 514-488-4842
Fax 514-485-3975
E-mail mail@globalhospto.com
Website global.hcareers.ca

Specialties Hospitality

Level Senior
Mid-Level

Contact Denis Pairault, General Manager

Description Global Hospitality is an executive search firm serving the hospitality industry exclusively.

GLOBAL HOSPITALITY SEARCH CONSULTANTS
64 Atlantic View Dr., Sambro Head
Halifax, NS B3V 1L2

Telephone 902-868-1500
Fax 902-484-6691
E-mail halifax@globalhospto.com
Website global.hcareers.ca

Specialties Hospitality

Level Senior
Mid-Level

Contact Julie Marks, Managing Partner

Description Global Hospitality is an executive search firm serving the hospitality industry exclusively.

GLOBAL HOSPITALITY SEARCH CONSULTANTS
3579 East Foothill Blvd., Suite 229
Pasadena, CA 91107 USA

Telephone 626-836-1222
Fax 626-836-1223
E-mail mail@globalhospla.com
Website global.hcareers.ca

Specialties Hospitality
International

Level Senior
Mid-Level

Description Global Hospitality is an executive search firm serving the hospitality industry exclusively.

GLOBAL HUMAN RESOURCE CENTER INC.
776 Dundas Street East
Mississauga, ON L4Y 2B6

Telephone 905-281-8958
Fax 905-281-8959

Specialties General Practice

GLOBAL OPTIONS INC. / IT INTELLECT, INC.
1026 Towne Lake Hills East
Woodstock, GA 30189 USA

Telephone 770-926-1674
Fax 770-926-8764
E-mail jobs@itintellect.net
Website www.globaloptions-inc-usa.com

Founded 1997
Employees 2

Specialties Computing
International

Level Senior
Mid-Level

Contact Gordon Bell

Description Global Options Inc. / IT Intellect, Inc. services companies and consultants in the IT Industry throughout the world.

GLOBAL PERSONNEL
40 Eglinton Avenue East, Suite 204
Toronto, ON M4P 3A2

Telephone 416-482-5115
Fax 416-482-8998
E-mail marilyns@globalpersonnel.com
Website www.globalpersonnel.com

Founded 1992

Specialties Accounting
Advertising
Banking
Computing
Insurance
Law
Health/Medical
Real Estate
Telecom

Level Mid-Level
Junior

Contact Marilyn Schoenberg

Description Global Personnel provides timely employment solutions for Fortune 1000 employers, primarily in the Greater Toronto area.

GLOBAL PLACEMENT SERVICES
7025 Tomken Road, Suite 233
Mississauga, ON L5S 1R6

Telephone 905-565-0310
Fax 905-565-0311
E-mail cpanke@gpscanada.com
Website www.gpscanada.com

Founded 1995

Specialties Computing
Accounting
Engineering
Health/Medical
Marketing
Sales
Telecom

Description Global Placement Services is a division of Worldwide Immigration Consultancy Services Inc. (WWICS), a large international immigration firm specializing in immigration to Canada.

GLOBAL RECRUITMENT SPECIALISTS
501 Westport Avenue, Suite 285
Norwalk, CT 06851 USA

Telephone 203-899-0499
Fax 206-374-5455
E-mail GlobeR@CompuServe.com

Specialties International
Govt/Nonprofit

Contact Patrick Shields, President

Description Placing people in assignments in lesser developed countries around the world. In the last 5 years, GRS has filled 500+ positions.

GLOBAL SOFTECH INC.
1071 King Street West, Suite 326
Toronto, ON M6K 3K2

Telephone 416-879-8723
Fax 416-450-3732
E-mail resumes@gsoftech.com
Website www.gsoftech.com

Founded 1997

Specialties Computing
International

Level Mid-Level
Junior

Fee Basis Always contingent

Contact Amit Mathur

Description Global Softech provides consulting services and recruitment solutions to the IT industry.

GLOBAL STAFFING SPECIALISTS INC.
368 Broadway Avenue
Toronto, ON M4P 1X2

Telephone 416-487-7627
Fax 416-487-5470
E-mail gsjk@home.com

Specialties Computing

Contact Joe Kennedy

Description Global Staffing Specialists specializes in recruiting network engineers, system administrators, database administrators, IT security, network managers.

GLOBALTECH RECRUITING INC.
1246 Duchess Avenue
Vancouver, BC V7T 1H4

Telephone 604-913-0006
Fax 604-913-0014
E-mail resumes@globaltech.bc.ca
Website www.globaltech.bc.ca

Specialties   Computing

Description Globaltech Recruiting Inc. specializes in the recruitment of experienced Information Technology professionals.

GODBOUT MARTIN GODBOUT & ASSOCIATES
133 Wellington Street
Hull, QC J8X 2J1

Telephone	819-773-4224
Fax	819-773-3258
E-mail	gmgconseil@ gmgconseil.com
Website	www.gmgconseil.com
Founded	1989
Employees	6
Specialties	Management Plastics General Practice Computing Human Resource Operations Real Estate
Fee Basis	Sometimes contingent
Recruiters	Raul Apablaza Roch Fortin Latifa B. Fortin Alain J. Godbout Johannes Godbout Guillaume Godbout Gilbert G. Gougeon Glenn Grega Margaret Kirk Jacques Lauzon Michel Rancourt Pierre Tourigny Jeanne Veneranda
Contact	Alain J. Godbout, CMC

Description Godbout Martin Godbout & Associates is a HR consulting firm that also does recruitment work for clients.

GOLDBECK RECRUITING INC.
789 West Pender Street, Suite 855
Vancouver, BC V6C 1H2

Telephone	604-684-1428
Fax	604-684-1429
E-mail	henry@goldbeck.com
Website	www.goldbeck.com
Founded	1997
Employees	3
Specialties	General Practice Computing Human Resource Management Marketing Operations Sales
Level	Mid-Level Junior
Fee Basis	Always contingent
Recruiters	Henry Goldbeck CPC Phil Pacaud Terry Wilson Jeff Wood
Contact	Henry Goldbeck, CPC

Description Goldbeck Recruiting specializes in the recruitment and placement of professionals for companies in every major industry.

GOLDEN MILE MANAGEMENT CONSULTING SERVICES
2630 Eglinton Avenue East, Suite 3
Toronto, ON M1K 2S3

Telephone	416-266-4434
E-mail	careers@gmmcs.com
Website	www.gmmcs.com
Specialties	Sales Management Operations Human Resource
Level	Mid-Level Senior

Description Golden Mile Management Consulting Services provides human resource consulting services to Canadian business.

GOLDJOBS.COM
1 - 7 Fulham High Street
Nightingale House
London, SW6 3JH
UNITED KINGDOM

Telephone	44-20-7598-3050
Fax	44-20-7598-3055
E-mail	admin@goldjobs.com
Website	www.goldjobs.com
Specialties	General Practice International Management
Level	Senior
Min. Salary	$150,000
Contact	Rosalyn Dwan

Description Goldjobs.com is a high-profile online recruitment agency that specializes in senior international placements with salaries of $150,000 and up.

GOLDSMITH MILLER HERSH
1411 Fort Street, Suite 200
Montréal, QC H3H 2N6

Telephone	514-933-8611
Fax	514-933-1142
E-mail	jrosenthal@gmhca.com
Website	www.gmhca.com
Specialties	Accounting
Level	Mid-Level
Contact	Jack Rosenthal, CA

Description Goldsmith Miller Hersh is an accounting firm that does search work for clients.

GORDON WELCH CONSULTING INC.
98 Glencoe Place
Sherwood Park, AB T8A 5L2

Telephone	780-416-0704
E-mail	gwconsulting@ home.com
Specialties	Education
Contact	Gordon Welch

GR SEARCH INC.
10 Bay Street
Suite 1500, Waterpark Place
Toronto, ON M5J 2R8

Telephone	416-365-7770
Fax	416-365-7669
E-mail	mp@grsearch.com
Website	www.grsearch.com
Founded	1989
Employees	14
Specialties	Aerospace Finance Human Resource Mining Operations Purchasing Govt/Nonprofit
Level	Senior Mid-Level
Min. Salary	$60,000
Fee Basis	Retainer Only
Recruiters	Murray Geddes MBA Ron Rubin
Contact	Murray Geddes, Managing Partner

Description GR Search Inc. (formerly Geddes + Rubin Management Inc.) is an executive search firm providing professional solutions to their clients' selection and development process.

GRADUATE CONSULTING SERVICES, THE
100 Alexis Nihon Blvd, Bureau 408
Montréal, QC H4M 2N9

Telephone	514-748-9373
Fax	514-748-2117
E-mail	ecap@thegraduate.ca
Founded	1976
Specialties	Engineering Management Computing Scientific Accounting Pharmaceutical Human Resource
Level	Mid-Level Senior
Recruiters	Ewald Cap Rolf Voigt John Zukauskas
Contact	Ewald Cap, Co-founder

GRAHAM, ELLIOTT & ASSOCIATES
278 Bloor Street East, Suite 510
Toronto, ON M4W 3M4

Telephone	416-921-5144
Fax	416-921-6015
E-mail	bob.graham2@ sympatico.ca
Specialties	Sales
Level	Senior Mid-Level
Contact	Bob Graham

Description Graham, Elliott & Associates is an executive-level search firm.

GRAHAM MATTHEW & PARTNERS LLP
150 Pinebush Road, PO Box 880
Cambridge, ON N1R 5X9

Telephone	519-623-1870
Fax	519-623-9490
E-mail	admin@gmpca.com
Website	www.gmpca.com
Specialties	Accounting Finance
Contact	Richard Mathew, Managing Partner

Description Graham Matthew & Partners LLP is an accounting firm that also does occasional search work for clients.

GRAND RIVER PERSONNEL LTD.
842 Victoria Street North, Suite 16
Kitchener, ON N2B 3C1

Telephone	519-576-0920
Fax	519-576-0099
E-mail	grp@grpedge.com
Website	www.grpedge.com
Specialties	Computing Engineering Management Accounting Administrative Automotive Quality Control
Level	Mid-Level Senior
Fee Basis	Always contingent
Recruiters	Linda Dancey CHRP Bob Dancey Bernadette Lemos Chris Perkins CPC Ximena Schallenberg
Contact	Chris Perkins CPC, Manager

Description Based in Kitchener-Waterloo, GRP has been providing technical and professional searches for over 23 years.

GRANT MARTIN & ASSOCIATES (1996) INC.
120 W. Beaver Creek Rd., Unit 18
Richmond Hill, ON L4B 1L2

Telephone	905-709-3201
Fax	905-709-3206
E-mail	resumes@ grantmartin.com
Website	www.grantmartin.com
Founded	1988
Specialties	Computing Engineering Automotive
Level	Mid-Level Senior
Min. Salary	$35,000
Contact	Paul Martin

Description Grant Martin & Associates specializes in the recruitment and placement of professional engineers and management positions in the automotive industry.

GRANT SEARCH GROUP INC., THE
2275 Lakeshore Blvd. W., Suite 514
Toronto, ON M8V 3Y3

Telephone	416-252-5656
Fax	416-252-8511
E-mail	info@gsginc.on.ca
Website	www.gsginc.on.ca
Founded	1992
Specialties	Telecom Multimedia Marketing Direct Mktng.
Level	Mid-Level Senior
Min. Salary	$45,000
Fee Basis	Sometimes contingent
Contact	David Bodnaryk, President

Description Specializes in recruitment for telecommunications, websites, consumer and industrial marketing positions.

GRANT THORNTON INTERNATIONAL
888 Fort Street, 3rd Floor
Victoria, BC V8W 1H8

Telephone	250-383-4191
Fax	250-381-4623
E-mail	victoria@ grantthornton.ca
Website	www.grantthornton.ca
Specialties	Accounting Finance Hospitality
Level	Mid-Level
Contact	Peter Lloyd, CA

Description Grant Thornton is a national chartered accounting firm that also does occasional recruitment work for clients.

GRANT THORNTON INTERNATIONAL
5811 Cooney Road
Suite 602, North Tower
Richmond, BC V6X 3M1

Telephone	604-278-7159
Fax	604-278-0359
E-mail	richmond@ grantthornton.ca
Website	www.grantthornton.ca
Specialties	Accounting Finance
Level	Mid-Level
Contact	Mervyn Louis, CA

Description Grant Thornton is a national chartered accounting firm that also does occasional recruitment work for clients.

GRANT THORNTON INTERNATIONAL
1055 West Georgia Street
Suite 2800, PO Box 11177
Royal Centre
Vancouver, BC V6E 4N3

Telephone	604-687-2711
Fax	604-685-6569
E-mail	vancouver@ grantthornton.ca
Website	www.grantthornton.ca
Specialties	Accounting Finance
Level	Mid-Level Senior
Contact	Phil Noble, CA

Description Grant Thornton is a national chartered accounting firm that also does occasional recruitment work for clients.

GRANT THORNTON INTERNATIONAL
604 Columbia Street, 4th Floor
New Westminster, BC V3M 1A6

Telephone	604-521-3761
Fax	604-521-8170
E-mail	newwestminster@ grantthornton.ca
Website	www.grantthornton.ca
Specialties	Accounting Finance
Level	Mid-Level
Contact	Rick Mudie, CA

Description Grant Thornton is a national chartered accounting firm that also does occasional recruitment work for clients.

GRANT THORNTON INTERNATIONAL
6323 - 197th Street, Suite 200
Langley, BC V2Y 1K8

Telephone	604-532-3761
Fax	604-532-8130
E-mail	langley@ grantthornton.ca
Website	www.grantthornton.ca
Specialties	Accounting Finance
Level	Mid-Level
Contact	Graeme Davis, CA

Description Grant Thornton is a national chartered accounting firm that also does occasional recruitment work for clients.

GRANT THORNTON INTERNATIONAL
247 Lawrence Avenue
Kelowna, BC V1Y 6L2

Telephone	250-762-4434
Fax	250-762-8896
E-mail	kelowna@ grantthornton.ca
Website	www.grantthornton.ca
Specialties	Accounting Finance
Level	Mid-Level
Contact	Frank Milan, CA

Description Grant Thornton is a national chartered accounting firm that also does occasional recruitment work for clients.

GRANT THORNTON INTERNATIONAL
5108 - 51st Avenue
Wetaskiwin, AB T9A 0V2

Telephone	780-352-1679
Fax	780-352-2451
E-mail	wetaskiwin@ grantthornton.ca
Website	www.grantthornton.ca
Specialties	Accounting Finance
Level	Mid-Level
Contact	Tim Bolivar, CA

Description Grant Thornton is a national chartered accounting firm that also does occasional recruitment work for clients.

GRANT THORNTON INTERNATIONAL
10012 - 101st Street, Box 6030
Peace River, AB T8S 1S1

Telephone	780-624-3252
Fax	780-624-8758
E-mail	peaceriver@ grantthornton.ca
Website	www.grantthornton.ca
Specialties	Accounting Finance
Level	Mid-Level
Contact	Brian Rolling, CA

Description Grant Thornton is a national chartered accounting firm that also does occasional recruitment work for clients.

GRANT THORNTON INTERNATIONAL
10060 Jasper Avenue NW
Suite 2400, Scotia Place 1
Edmonton, AB T5J 3R8

Telephone	780-422-7114
Fax	780-426-3208
E-mail	edmonton@ grantthornton.ca
Website	www.grantthornton.ca
Founded	1936
Employees	45
Specialties	Accounting Finance Management
Level	Senior Mid-Level
Contact	J. Albert Mondor, CA

Description Grant Thornton is a national chartered accounting firm that also does occasional recruitment work for clients.

GRANT THORNTON INTERNATIONAL
500 - 4th Avenue SW, Suite 2800
Calgary, AB T2P 2V6

Telephone	403-260-2500
Fax	403-260-2571
E-mail	calgary@ grantthornton.ca
Website	www.grantthornton.ca

Specialties	Accounting Finance
Level	Mid-Level
Recruiters	Al Menzies CA Paul Takalo CA
Contact	Al Menzies, CA

Description Grant Thornton is a national chartered accounting firm that also does occasional recruitment work for clients.

GRANT THORNTON INTERNATIONAL
1 Lombard Place, Suite 900
Winnipeg, MB R3B 0X3

Telephone	204-944-0100
Fax	204-957-5442
E-mail	winnipeg@ grantthornton.ca
Website	www.grantthornton.ca
Specialties	Accounting Finance
Level	Mid-Level
Recruiters	D.H. Magnus CA Jeff Thomas CA
Contact	D.H. Magnus, CA

Description Grant Thornton is a national chartered accounting firm that also does occasional recruitment work for clients.

GRANT THORNTON INTERNATIONAL
421 Bay Street, 5th Floor
Sault Ste. Marie, ON P6A 1X3

Telephone	705-945-9700
Fax	705-945-9705
E-mail	saultstemarie@ grantthornton.ca
Website	www.grantthornton.ca
Specialties	Accounting Finance
Level	Mid-Level
Contact	Barry Magill, CA

Description Grant Thornton is a national chartered accounting firm that also does occasional recruitment work for clients.

GRANT THORNTON INTERNATIONAL
222 McIntyre St. West, Suite 200
North Bay, ON P1B 2Y6

Telephone	705-472-6500
Fax	705-472-7760
E-mail	northbay@ grantthornton.ca
Website	www.grantthornton.ca
Specialties	Accounting Finance
Level	Mid-Level
Contact	Glen Weckwerth, CA

Description Grant Thornton is a national chartered accounting firm that also does occasional recruitment work for clients.

GRANT THORNTON INTERNATIONAL
17 Wellington Street, PO Box 2170
New Liskeard, ON P0J 1P0

Telephone	705-647-8100
Fax	705-647-7026
E-mail	newliskeard@ grantthornton.ca
Website	www.grantthornton.ca
Specialties	Accounting Finance
Level	Mid-Level
Contact	Rheo Hacquard, CA

Description Grant Thornton is a national chartered accounting firm that also does occasional recruitment work for clients.

GRANT THORNTON INTERNATIONAL
150 Dufferin Avenue, Suite 902
London, ON N6A 5N6

Telephone	519-672-2930
Fax	519-672-6455
E-mail	london@ grantthornton.ca
Website	www.grantthornton.ca
Specialties	Accounting Finance
Level	Mid-Level
Contact	Bruce H. Estabrooks, CA

Description Grant Thornton is a national chartered accounting firm that also does occasional recruitment work for clients.

GRANT THORNTON INTERNATIONAL
200 Bay Street, 19th Floor
South Tower, Royal Bank Plaza
Toronto, ON M5J 2P9

Telephone	416-366-0100
Fax	416-360-4949
E-mail	toronto@ grantthornton.ca
Website	www.grantthornton.ca
Specialties	Finance Accounting
Level	Mid-Level
Contact	Al MacLean, CA

Description Grant Thornton is a national chartered accounting firm that also does occasional recruitment work for clients.

GRANT THORNTON INTERNATIONAL
120 King Street West
Suite 1040, Standard Life Centre
Hamilton, ON L8P 4V2

Telephone	905-525-1930
Fax	905-527-4413
E-mail	hamilton@ grantthornton.ca
Website	www.grantthornton.ca
Specialties	Accounting Finance

Level   Mid-Level

Contact   George Benton, CA

Description Grant Thornton is a national chartered accounting firm that also does occasional recruitment work for clients.

GRANT THORNTON INTERNATIONAL
350 Burnhamthorpe Road West
Suite 401
Mississauga, ON L5B 3J1

Telephone 905-804-0905
Fax   905-804-0509
E-mail   mississauga@grantthornton.ca
Website   www.grantthornton.ca
Specialties Accounting
             Finance
Level   Mid-Level
Contact   Gerry Popp, CA

Description Grant Thornton is a national chartered accounting firm that also does occasional recruitment work for clients.

GRANT THORNTON INTERNATIONAL
5 Bayfield Street, Unit 205
Barrie, ON L4M 3A7

Telephone 705-730-6574
Fax   705-730-6575
E-mail   barrie@grantthornton.ca
Website   www.grantthornton.ca
Specialties Accounting
             Finance
Level   Mid-Level
Contact   R. D. Woodman, CA

Description Grant Thornton is a national chartered accounting firm that also does occasional recruitment work for clients.

GRANT THORNTON INTERNATIONAL
279 Coldwater Road West
Orillia, ON L3V 3M1

Telephone 705-326-7605
Fax   705-326-0837
E-mail   orillia@grantthornton.ca
Website   www.grantthornton.ca
Specialties Accounting
             Finance
Level   Mid-Level
Contact   David Woodman, CA

Description Grant Thornton is a national chartered accounting firm that also does occasional recruitment work for clients.

GRANT THORNTON INTERNATIONAL
15 Allstate Parkway, Suite 200
Markham, ON L3R 5B4

Telephone 905-475-1100

Fax   905-475-8906
E-mail   markham@grantthornton.ca
Website   www.grantthornton.ca
Specialties Accounting
             Finance
Level   Mid-Level
Contact   Allister Byrne, FCA

Description Grant Thornton is a national chartered accounting firm that also does occasional recruitment work for clients.

GRANT THORNTON INTERNATIONAL
92 Charlotte Street
PO Box 336, Ste. B
Port Colborne, ON L3K 5W1

Telephone 905-834-3651
Fax   905-834-5095
E-mail   portcolborne@grantthornton.ca
Website   www.grantthornton.ca
Specialties Accounting
             Finance
Level   Mid-Level
Contact   Alex MacBeath, CA

Description Grant Thornton is a national chartered accounting firm that also does occasional recruitment work for clients.

GRANT THORNTON INTERNATIONAL
55 King Street
PO Box 2011, Suite 304
St. Catharines, ON L2R 7R7

Telephone 905-688-4822
Fax   905-688-4837
E-mail   stcatharines@grantthornton.ca
Website   www.grantthornton.ca
Specialties Accounting
             Finance
Level   Mid-Level

Description Grant Thornton is a national chartered accounting firm that also does occasional recruitment work for clients.

GRANT THORNTON INTERNATIONAL
570 Queen Street, Ste. 500
PO Box 1054, Barker House
Fredericton, NB E3B 5C2

Telephone 506-458-8200
Fax   506-453-7029
E-mail   fredericton@grantthornton.ca
Website   www.grantthornton.ca
Specialties Accounting
             Finance
Level   Mid-Level
Contact   G. Brian Trenholm CA

Description Grant Thornton is a national chartered accounting firm that also does occasional recruitment work for clients.

GRANT THORNTON INTERNATIONAL
55 Union Street, Suite 600
Saint John, NB E2L 5B7

Telephone 506-634-2900
Fax   506-634-4569
E-mail   saintjohn@grantthornton.ca
Website   www.grantthornton.ca
Founded   1932
Specialties Accounting
             Finance
             Consulting
             Operations
Level   Mid-Level
             Senior
Min. Salary $40,000
Fee Basis Retainer Only
Contact   Peter Meier, CA

Description Grant Thornton is a national chartered accounting firm that also does occasional recruitment work for clients.

GRANT THORNTON INTERNATIONAL
275 Main St., Harbourview Place
PO Box 220, Ste. 500
Bathurst, NB E2A 3Z2

Telephone 506-546-6616
Fax   506-548-5622
E-mail   bathurst@grantthornton.ca
Website   www.grantthornton.ca
Specialties Accounting
             Finance
Level   Mid-Level
Contact   Rob Lovesey, CA

Description Grant Thornton is a national chartered accounting firm that also does occasional recruitment work for clients.

GRANT THORNTON INTERNATIONAL
135 Henry Street
Miramichi, NB E1V 2N5

Telephone 506-622-0637
Fax   506-622-5174
E-mail   miramichi@grantthornton.ca
Website   www.grantthornton.ca
Specialties Accounting
             Finance
Level   Mid-Level
Contact   Hal Raper, CA

Description Grant Thornton is a national chartered accounting firm that also does occasional recruitment work for clients.

GRANT THORNTON INTERNATIONAL
633 Main Street
PO Box 1005, Ste. 500
Moncton, NB E1C 8P2

Telephone 506-857-0100

Fax	506-857-0105
E-mail	moncton@ grantthornton.ca
Website	www.grantthornton.ca
Specialties	Accounting Finance
Level	Mid-Level
Contact	Peter Worth, FCA

Description Grant Thornton is a national chartered accounting firm that also does occasional recruitment work for clients.

GRANT THORNTON INTERNATIONAL
220 Water Street, PO Box 1660
Summerside, PE C1N 2V5

Telephone	902-436-9155
Fax	902-436-6913
E-mail	summerside@ grantthornton.ca
Website	www.grantthornton.ca
Specialties	Accounting Finance
Level	Mid-Level
Contact	L. Byron Murray, CA

Description Grant Thornton is a national chartered accounting firm that also does occasional recruitment work for clients.

GRANT THORNTON INTERNATIONAL
199 Grafton St., Ste. 501, Box 187
Polyclinic Professional Centre
Charlottetown, PE C1A 7K4

Telephone	902-892-6547
Fax	902-566-5358
E-mail	charlottetown@ grantthornton.ca
Website	www.grantthornton.ca
Specialties	Accounting Finance Management
Level	Mid-Level Senior
Recruiters	Wayne Fudge CA J. Alan Long CA
Contact	Wayne Fudge, CA

Description Grant Thornton is a national chartered accounting firm that also does occasional recruitment work for clients.

GRANT THORNTON INTERNATIONAL
328 Main Street, PO Box 297
Yarmouth, NS B5A 4B2

Telephone	902-742-7842
Fax	902-742-0224
E-mail	yarmouth@ grantthornton.ca
Website	www.grantthornton.ca
Specialties	Accounting Finance
Level	Mid-Level

Contact	Martin Rutherford, CA

Description Grant Thornton is a national chartered accounting firm that also does occasional recruitment work for clients.

GRANT THORNTON INTERNATIONAL
166 North Street, PO Box 220
Bridgewater, NS B4V 2W8

Telephone	902-543-8115
Fax	902-543-7707
E-mail	bridgewater@ grantthornton.ca
Website	www.grantthornton.ca
Specialties	Accounting Finance
Level	Mid-Level
Contact	Robert Oakley, CA

Description Grant Thornton is a national chartered accounting firm that also does occasional recruitment work for clients.

GRANT THORNTON INTERNATIONAL
15 Webster Street, PO Box 68
Kentville, NS B4N 3V9

Telephone	902-678-7307
Fax	902-679-1870
E-mail	kentville@ grantthornton.ca
Website	www.grantthornton.ca
Specialties	Accounting Finance
Level	Mid-Level
Recruiters	Gordon B. Caldwell Harvey Nickerson CA
Contact	Harvey Nickerson, CA

Description Grant Thornton is a national chartered accounting firm that also does occasional recruitment work for clients.

GRANT THORNTON INTERNATIONAL
2000 Barrington Street, Ste. 1100
PO Box 426, Cogswell Tower
Halifax, NS B3J 2P8

Telephone	902-421-1734
Fax	902-420-1068
E-mail	halilfax@ grantthornton.ca
Website	www.grantthornton.ca
Employees	70
Specialties	Accounting Finance Management
Level	Mid-Level Senior
Contact	Glenn Williams, FCA

Description Grant Thornton is a national chartered accounting firm that also does occasional recruitment work for clients.

GRANT THORNTON INTERNATIONAL
238A Brownlow Ave., Ste. 301
PO Box 38049, Park Place II
Dartmouth, NS B3B 1X2

Telephone	902-463-4900
Fax	902-469-2860
E-mail	dartmouth@ grantthornton.ca
Website	www.grantthornton.ca
Specialties	Accounting Finance
Level	Mid-Level
Contact	Roland Jamieson, FCA

Description Grant Thornton is a national chartered accounting firm that also does occasional recruitment work for clients.

GRANT THORNTON INTERNATIONAL
35 Commercial Street, Ste. 400
Box 725, Bank of Montreal Bldg.
Truro, NS B2N 5E8

Telephone	902-893-1150
Fax	902-893-9757
E-mail	truro@grantthornton.ca
Website	www.grantthornton.ca
Specialties	Accounting Finance
Level	Mid-Level
Contact	Jerry Hutchings, CA

Description Grant Thornton is a national chartered accounting firm that also does occasional recruitment work for clients.

GRANT THORNTON INTERNATIONAL
610 East River Road
PO Box 427, Aberdeen Mall
New Glasgow, NS B2H 5E5

Telephone	902-752-8393
Fax	902-752-4009
E-mail	newglasgow@ grantthornton.ca
Website	www.grantthornton.ca
Specialties	Accounting Finance
Level	Mid-Level
Contact	Terry Kelly, CA

Description Grant Thornton is a national chartered accounting firm that also does occasional recruitment work for clients.

GRANT THORNTON INTERNATIONAL
257 Main Street, PO Box 1480
Antigonish, NS B2G 2L7

Telephone	902-863-4587
Fax	902-863-0917
E-mail	antigonish@ grantthornton.ca
Website	www.grantthornton.ca
Specialties	Accounting Finance

Level   Mid-Level

Contact   Ben Cullen, CA

Description Grant Thornton is a national chartered accounting firm that also does occasional recruitment work for clients.

GRANT THORNTON INTERNATIONAL
500 George Street
Suite 200, George Place
Sydney, NS B1P 1K6

Telephone   902-562-5581
Fax   902-562-0073
E-mail   sydney@
granttthornton.ca
Website   www.grantthornton.ca

Specialties   Accounting
Finance

Level   Mid-Level

Contact   Wayne MacIntosh, CA

Description Grant Thornton is a national chartered accounting firm that also does occasional recruitment work for clients.

GRANT THORNTON INTERNATIONAL
68 Water St.,Box 848, Basin Place
Digby, NS B0V 1A0

Telephone   902-245-2553
Fax   902-245-6161
E-mail   digby@
granttthornton.ca
Website   www.grantthornton.ca

Specialties   Accounting
Finance

Level   Mid-Level

Description Grant Thornton is a national chartered accounting firm that also does occasional recruitment work for clients.

GRANT THORNTON INTERNATIONAL
51 Park Street, Box 356, Suite 49
Corner Brook, NF A2H 6K2

Telephone   709-634-4382
Fax   709-634-9158
E-mail   cornerbrook@
granttthornton.ca
Website   www.grantthornton.ca

Specialties   Accounting
Finance

Level   Mid-Level

Contact   Rob Flynn, CA

Description Grant Thornton is a national chartered accounting firm that also does occasional recruitment work for clients.

GRANT THORNTON INTERNATIONAL
9 High Street, PO Box 83
Grand Falls-Windsor, NF A2A 2J3

Telephone   709-489-6622
Fax   709-489-6625

E-mail   grandfalls@
granttthornton.ca
Website   www.grantthornton.ca

Specialties   Accounting
Finance

Level   Mid-Level

Contact   Derrick Anthony, CA

Description Grant Thornton is a national chartered accounting firm that also does occasional recruitment work for clients.

GRANT THORNTON INTERNATIONAL
187 Kenmount Rd.
PO Box 8037, ICON Bldg.
St. John's, NF A1B 3M7

Telephone   709-722-5960
Fax   709-722-7892
E-mail   stjohns@
granttthornton.ca
Website   www.grantthornton.ca

Specialties   Accounting
Finance

Level   Mid-Level

Contact   Bill Brushett, CA

Description Grant Thornton is a national chartered accounting firm that also does occasional recruitment work for clients.

GRANT THORNTON INTERNATIONAL
2 Queen Street, PO Box 518
Marystown, NF A0E 2M0

Telephone   709-279-2300
Fax   709-279-2340
E-mail   marystown@
granttthornton.ca
Website   www.grantthornton.ca

Specialties   Accounting
Finance

Level   Mid-Level

Contact   Harvey Lunnen, CA

Description Grant Thornton is a national chartered accounting firm that also does occasional recruitment work for clients.

GRANT THORNTON INTERNATIONAL, NATIONAL OFFICE
200 Bay Street, 10th Floor
North Tower, Royal Bank Plaza
Toronto, ON M5J 2P9

Telephone   416-366-0100
Fax   416-360-4944
E-mail   careers@
granttthornton.ca
Website   www.grantthornton.ca

Specialties   Finance
Management
Accounting

Level   Mid-Level

Description Grant Thornton is a national chartered accounting firm that also does occasional recruitment work for clients.

GRAPEVINE EXECUTIVE RECRUITERS INC.
260 Richmond Street W., Suite 405
Toronto, ON M5V 1W5

Telephone   416-581-1445
Fax   416-581-1335
E-mail   darren@grapevine
recruiters.com
Website   www.grapevine
recruiters.com

Founded   1982
Employees   7

Specialties   Advertising
Direct Mktng.
Public Relations
Graphic Arts
Marketing
Health/Medical
Pharmaceutical

Level   Senior
Mid-Level

Min. Salary $30,000

Recruiters   Michael Hayward
Ray Kruszynski
Darren Kruszynski
Jeff Pollard
Patti Sanderson

Contact   Ray Kruszynski

Description Grapevine Executive Recruiters Inc. recruits middle and senior executives for the advertising, direct, promotions, public relations, graphics, marketing, healthcare and pharmaceutical industries.

GRAPHIC ASSISTANTS
239 McRae Drive, Upper Level
Toronto, ON M4G 1T7

Telephone   416-425-4601
Fax   416-425-6956

Specialties   Design
Graphic Arts

Level   Mid-Level
Junior

Contact   Susan Boudreau,
President

GRASSLANDS GROUP INC.
1002A Allowance Street SE
Medicine Hat, AB T1A 3G8

Telephone   403-527-9728
Fax   403-529-1805
E-mail   ggroup@
grasslands.sk.ca
Website   www.grasslands.sk.ca

Founded   1991
Employees   6

Specialties   Agriculture/Fisheries
Engineering
Management
Oil & Gas
Operations

Level   Senior
Mid-Level

Fee Basis   Sometimes contingent

Contact   Orest Tkachyk

Description Incorporated in 1993, Grasslands Group provides training, personal development, consulting and employment services to the agribusiness, plant maintenance and oil & gas sectors in Western Canada.

GRASSLANDS GROUP INC.
244 - 1st Avenue NE, Unit 5
Swift Current, SK S9H 2B4

Telephone	306-778-0570
Fax	306-778-6403
E-mail	ggroup@grasslands.sk.ca
Website	www.grasslands.sk.ca
Founded	1991
Employees	6
Specialties	Agriculture/Fisheries Engineering Management Oil & Gas Operations
Level	Senior Mid-Level
Fee Basis	Sometimes contingent
Recruiters	Blair Clark Erin Thiessen
Contact	Blair Clark

Description Incorporated in 1993, Grasslands Group provides training, personal development, consulting and employment services to the agribusiness, plant maintenance and oil & gas sectors in Western Canada.

GRH CONSULTANTS INC., LES
225, boul. Charest E., Bureau 100
Québec, QC G1K 3G9

Téléphone	418-648-8414
Télécopieur	418-648-9814
Courriel	grh@grh.qc.ca
Site Internet	www.grh.qc.ca
Fondée	1989
Spécialités	Comptabilité Informatique Éducation Ingénierie Finance Ressources humaines Assurance Gestion Marketing Exploitation Achat Ventes Scientifique
Échelon	Intermédiaire Débutant
Contact	Karine Scalabrini

Description GRH Consultants Inc. dessert des entreprises manufacturières et de services partout au Québec à travers ses trois bureaux.

GRIFFIN SPROSTON
55 Bloor St. W., Suite 228, Box 401
Toronto, ON M4W 1A5

Telephone	416-922-7777
Fax	416-922-3061
E-mail	info@griffinsproston.com
Website	www.griffinsproston.com
Founded	1973
Specialties	General Practice
Contact	Dana Wright

Description Griffin Sproston is a service-based recruitment firm handling everything from administrative to executive-level appointments.

GROOM & ASSOCIÉS LTÉE
755 St-Jean Blvd., Suite 600
Pointe-Claire, QC H9R 5M9

Telephone	514-630-7349
Fax	514-630-0935
E-mail	info@groomassocies.com
Website	www.groomassocies.com
Specialties	Computing Pharmaceutical Administrative Telecom
Level	Mid-Level
Fee Basis	Always contingent
Recruiters	Julie-Anne Conway Susie Groom De Mizio Manon Morin Charley Roberts
Contact	Charley Roberts

Description In business for over 10 years, Groom & Associés provides staffing solutions in administrative, professional, IT, telecom and pharmaceutical fields.

GROUP FOUR MANAGEMENT CONSULTANTS
126 Hazelton Avenue
Toronto, ON M5R 2E5

Telephone	416-961-4555
Fax	416-961-3223
E-mail	mail@groupfour.net
Website	www.groupfour.net
Founded	1973
Employees	10
Specialties	Law Management Human Resource Accounting Administrative
Level	Mid-Level Senior
Min. Salary	$30,000
Fee Basis	Always contingent
Recruiters	Michael L. Cooper Teena Ferguson Erin Goldberg Sherri Goldwater Carolyn Taylor
Contact	Michael L. Cooper

Description Group Four Management Consultants recruits for Canada's largest law firms, as well as medium-sized and boutique firms.

GROUPE CONSEIL LAMARCHE & DESROCHES INC.
329 Louis-Hébert
Granby, QC J2G 4P8

Téléphone	450-776-6126
Télécopieur	450-776-7900
Courriel	andree-lamarche@qc.aira.com
Fondée	1990
Employés	2
Spécialités	Comptabilité Administratif Ressources humaines Exploitation Ventes
Échelon	Direction Intermédiaire
Frais	Honoraire seulement
Contact	Andrée Lamarche

Description Groupe conseil Lamarche offre gestion conseil en ressources humaines et administration pour besoins ponctuels et suivis périodiques.

GROUPE CONSEIL STANTE INC.
6433 Jarry E.
Saint-Léonard, QC H1P 1W1

Telephone	514-955-3030
Fax	514-955-5506
Specialties	Sales Hospitality
Level	Mid-Level Junior
Contact	Michael Stante

GROUPE CONSULT AFFAIRE, LE
1170, boul. Lebourgneuf
Bureau 400
Québec, QC G2K 2E3

Téléphone	418-622-6522
Télécopieur	418-622-7167
Courriel	conaff@mediom.qc.ca
Fondée	1996
Employés	2
Spécialités	Affaires de banque Consultatif Finance Gestion
Échelon	Intermédiaire
Frais	Toujours relative
Contact	Claude Goulet, AdmA, CMC

Description Gestion et financement d'entreprises.

GROUPE GAGNE-LANGEVIN INC., LE
6375, boul. Henri Bourassa
Charlesbourg, QC G1H 3B5

Téléphone	418-626-3830
Télécopieur	418-626-3837
Courriel	jllangevin@gagnelangevin.com
Site Internet	www.gagnelangevin.com
Fondée	1981
Spécialités	Généralistes
Contact	Jean-Louis Langevin, CMC

Description Le Groupe Gagne-Langevin inc. est une entreprise-réseau qui associe des consultants seniors, des professionnels et des fournisseurs aux compétences diverses, au service du client engagé dans l'évolution de son organisation et de son management.

GROUPE LJL, LE
17870, rue Foster
Pierrefonds, QC H9J 3N6

Telephone	514-696-4884
Fax	514-696-5782
E-mail	info@ljlgroup.com
Website	www.ljlgroup.com
Founded	1982
Employees	3
Specialties	Pulp & Paper
	Forestry
	Mining
	Engineering
Level	Mid-Level
	Senior
Fee Basis	Sometimes contingent
Contact	Germain Laniel

Description Specializing in placements in the pulp and paper industry, and forestry in general.

GROUPE LSOFT INC., LE
1 Place Ville Marie, Suite 2821
Montréal, QC H3B 4R4

Telephone	514-334-1325
Fax	514-334-5970
E-mail	hr@lsoftgroup.com
Website	www.lsoftgroup.com
Specialties	Computing
Level	Mid-Level
	Senior
Contact	Eric Landriau

Description Specializes in IT recruitment for the high-tech sector.

GROUPE MCS, LE
1255 rue University, Bureau 1500
Montréal, QC H3B 3X2

Telephone	514-399-1142
Fax	514-399-1146
E-mail	cv@groupemcs.com
Website	www.groupemcs.com
Specialties	Computing
	Multimedia
Level	Mid-Level
	Senior
Contact	Stephanie Sauve

Description Groupe MCS specializes in recruitment for the IT and multimedia industries.

GROUPE PCA INC.
6850, rue Sherbrooke E., bur. 300
Montréal, QC H1N 1E1

Téléphone	514-256-8000
Télécopieur	514-256-8007
Courriel	nlachance@groupe-pca.com

Fondée	1982
Employés	21
Spécialités	Informatique
Frais	Toujours relative
Contact	Nathalie Lachance, Directrice

Description Courtier en emploi permanent et contractuel, specialisé en informatique.

GROUPE PLURIDIS INC.
3460 Peel Street, Suite 116
Montréal, QC H3A 2M1

Telephone	514-282-9674
Fax	514-282-9675
E-mail	pluridis@pluridis.qc.ca
Website	www.pluridis.qc.ca
Founded	1999
Employees	10
Specialties	General Practice
	Administrative
	Management
	Computing
	Finance
	Operations
	Engineering
Level	Senior
	Mid-Level
Fee Basis	Retainer Only
Recruiters	Claude P. Arcand
	Peter Cerminara
	Hélène Perreault
	Don Smith
Contact	Peter Cerminara

Description Groupe Pluridis is a Montreal-based firm comprised of senior multi-disciplined management professionals specializing in recruitment at intermediate and senior levels.

GROUPE PRIMACOR, LE
61 rue St. Charles Ouest
Longueuil, QC J4H 1C5

Telephone	514-875-1909
Fax	514-879-8967
E-mail	legroupeprimacor@ibm.net
Employees	4
Specialties	Pharmaceutical
	Computing
	Telecom
	Biotech/Biology
	Marketing
	Sales
Level	Mid-Level
	Senior
Min. Salary	$50,000
Fee Basis	Sometimes contingent
Contact	Dany Lebel

Description Groupe Primacor specializes in recruiting for management, marketing and sales talent.

GROUPE RANGER
2045 Stanley Street, 14th Floor
Montréal, QC H3A 2V4

Telephone	514-844-1746

Fax	514-844-6996
E-mail	lsdubois@groupe-ranger.com
Website	www.groupe-ranger.com
Founded	1980
Employees	15
Specialties	International
	Computing
	Mining
	Forestry
	Telecom
	Finance
	Aerospace
Level	Senior
	Mid-Level
Min. Salary	$50,000
Recruiters	Serge Bolduc
	Maryse Brouillard
	Louis-Stephane Dubois
	Lise Hebert
	Manon Lamontagne
	Rachel Lehouillier
	Jean-Jacques Ranger
	Sophie Valade
	Cathy Vo Buu
Contact	Louis-Stephane Dubois

Description Groupe Ranger recruits middle and upper-level managers for administrative and operational assignments.

GROUPE RESSOURCES (D.G.O.) INC., LE
1253, boul. des Forges
Trois-Rivières, QC G8Z 1T7

Téléphone	819-373-0154
Télécopieur	819-373-2051
Courriel	gr_dgo@marche.com
Site Internet	www.marche.com/gr_dgo
Fondée	1984
Employés	7
Spécialités	Sylviculture
	Mines
	Papeterie
Contact	Marc-André Verrette

Description Cabinet-conseil en developpement des Ressources Humaines: recrutement et sélection, santé-sécurité du travail, service d'orientation.

GROUPE SFP
3343, rue Foucher
Trois-Rivières, QC G8Z 1M8

Téléphone	819-373-8208
Télécopieur	819-373-8165
Courriel	resshum@groupe-sfp.com
Site Internet	www.groupe-sfp.com
Fondée	1981
Employés	18
Spécialités	Comptabilité
	Administratif
	Informatique
	Ingénierie
	Marketing
	Exploitation
	Achat

Échelon   Intermédiaire
            Débutant

Contact   Fernande Boisvert

Description Depuis plus de 15 ans, nous offrons des services sur mesure repondant aux besoins des entreprises de la région. Locations, recrutement, évaluation de personnel et consultation en ressources humaines.

GROUPE TELE RESSOURCES
2021 Union Avenue, Suite 915
Montréal, QC H3A 2S9

Telephone 514-842-0066, ext 278
Fax   514-842-7461
E-mail   info@tele
             ressources.com
Website   www.tele
             ressources.com

Specialties Administrative
              Accounting

Level   Mid-Level
             Junior

Contact   Marie-Andrée Beaudoin

GROVE PERSONNEL LTD.
46 - 48 Southbourne Grove
Bournemouth, BH6 3RB
UNITED KINGDOM

Telephone 44-1202-417533
Fax   44-1202-421746

Specialties Design
              International

GROVES & PARTNERS INTERNATIONAL
1401 Daniel Creek Road
Mississauga, ON L5V 1V3

Telephone 905-567-9247
Fax   905-567-9469
E-mail   barry@grovesintl.com
Website   www.grovesintl.com

Founded   1989

Specialties Logistics
              Transport

Level   Mid-Level
             Senior

Fee Basis Retainer Only

Contact   Barry Groves

Description Groves & Partners International is one of North America's leading experts in logistics and transportation recruitment.

GRUBER ASSOCIATES
1603 Boyer Road, PO Box 230
Orleans, ON K1C 1S7

Telephone 613-837-9605
Fax   613-837-9605
E-mail   gruber@ottawa.com
Website   www.magma.ca/
             ~gruber/about_us.htm

Founded   1988

Specialties Law

Contact   Gerald P. Gruber, M.A.

Description Gruber provides HR consulting services in the field of policing and law enforcement, including personnel selection for clients.

GSA SEARCH CONSULTANTS INC.
200 Waterfront Drive, Suite 100
Bedford, NS B4A 4J4

Telephone 902-492-2802
Fax   902-422-6675
E-mail   jobs@gsa-search.com
Website   www.gsa-search.com

Employees 6

Specialties Computing
              Engineering
              Sales

Level   Senior
             Mid-Level

Fee Basis Retainer Only

Contact   Brad Smith

Description GSA (formerly Gosine Sulley & Associates) offers flexible staffing solutions to premier organizations on contract, contract-to-hire or a full-time basis.

GSG PARTNERS
2200 Yonge Street, Suite 1210
Toronto, ON M5S 2C6

Telephone 416-943-1234
Fax   416-943-0065
E-mail   info@gsgpartners.com
Website   www.gsgpartners.com

Founded   1990

Specialties Law
              General Practice
              Computing
              International
              Telecom

Level   Senior
             Mid-Level

Fee Basis Retainer Only

Contact   David Laws

Description Generalist, retainer-based firm with expertise in professional services sector.

GSI INTERNATIONAL CONSULTING GROUP
55 University Avenue, Suite 1601
Toronto, ON M5J 2H7

Telephone 416-777-2525
Fax   416-777-2547
E-mail   rm@gsigroup.com
Website   www.gsigroup.com

Founded   1990
Employees 25

Specialties Computing
              Consulting
              Govt/Nonprofit
              Health/Medical
              Multimedia

Level   Senior
             Mid-Level

Min. Salary $35,000
Fee Basis Always contingent

Recruiters Attila Ban
             Melinda Ban
             Bob Bansal
             Rob Black
             Donna Carito
             Jamie Laird
             Nancy Lau
             John Moss
             Gord Murray
             Sid Preece
             Brian Preece
             Jane Raroso
             Steve Rowe
             Sharad Sood
             Ivars Vitols
             Garnet Waldron
             Marcia Walter
             Kyle West
             Phil White
             Bianca Wong

Contact   Sid Preece

Description GSI brings together top IT professionals and organizations that need their talents on a contract or permanent basis.

GSI INTERNATIONAL CONSULTING GROUP
427 Laurier Ave. West, Suite 910
Ottawa, ON K1R 7Y2

Telephone 613-782-2361
Fax   613-782-2228
E-mail   rmo@gsigroup.com
Website   www.gsigroup.com

Specialties Computing

Contact   Merv Patterson

Description GSI brings together top IT professionals and organizations that need their talents on a contract or permanent basis.

GSW MANAGEMENT CONSULTING
710 Dorval Drive, Suite 108
Oakville, ON L6K 3V7

Telephone 905-338-9701
Fax   905-338-9716
E-mail   contact-us@gsw
             consultants.com
Website   www.gsw
             consultants.com

Founded   1979
Employees 40

Specialties General Practice

Description GSW is an HR consulting firm that also does recruitment work for clients.

GSW MANAGEMENT CONSULTING
3585 Delson Drive
Ottawa, ON K4B 1K6

Telephone 613-835-4291
Fax   613-835-9195
E-mail   contact-us@gsw
             consultants.com
Website   www.gsw
             consultants.com

Founded   1979
Employees 40

Specialties General Practice

Description GSW is an HR consulting firm that also does recruitment work for clients.

GUAY, LABELLE & ASSOCIÉS INC.
442, rue Saint-Gabriel, Bureau 101
Montréal, QC H2Y 2Z9

Téléphone	514-875-6889
Spécialités	Marketing Ventes
Échelon	Intermédiaire
Contact	Danielle Laurinaitis

GUILDWOOD GROUP
24 Taylor Road
Ajax, ON L1S 2X4

Telephone	905-683-1973
Fax	905-683-1926
E-mail	gwg@sympatico.ca
Website	www.guildwood.com
Founded	1989
Specialties	Pulp & Paper Metals Mining
Level	Mid-Level Senior

Description Guildwood Group is an executive search firm for Canada's heavy process industries.

GULCO INTERNATIONAL RECRUITING SERVICES
23854 Highway 59 North, Suite 338
Kingwood, TX 77339-1531
USA

Fax	285-358-2120
E-mail	gulcointl@ worldnet.att.net
Specialties	Oil & Gas Engineering International
Level	Senior Mid-Level
Contact	Rod Gullo

H.R. ALLIANCE INC.
333 - 7th Avenue SW, Suite 2300
Calgary, AB T2P 2Z1

Fax	403-265-2412
E-mail	jsherlock@ dbmwest.com
Specialties	Finance
Level	Mid-Level

Description H.R. Alliance Inc. is affiliated with the outplacement firm Drake Beam Morin.

HAINS & ASSOCIATES
520 Dunedin Street, Suite 310
Victoria, BC V8T 2L6

Telephone	250-361-4819
Specialties	Automotive Sales

HALLMARK PERSONNEL LIMITED
700 Dorval Drive, Suite 503
Oakville, ON L6K 3V3

Telephone	905-842-3753
Fax	905-842-3680
E-mail	hallmark@ globalserve.net
Website	www.globalserve.net/ ~hallmark
Founded	1971
Specialties	Engineering Operations Logistics Administrative
Level	Mid-Level
Contact	Gerry Sibbald

Description Hallmark Personnel specializes in the recruitment of technical, engineering, materials, production, logistics and administrative personnel at all levels.

HAMILTON & SHERWOOD EMPLOYMENT SERVICES, INC.
1500 Main Street
Weymouth, MA 02190 USA

Telephone	800-863-0076
Fax	781-340-5257
E-mail	rcudmore@ hamsher.com
Website	www.hamsher.com
Founded	1991
Specialties	International Human Resource

Description Hamilton & Sherwood has been recruiting candidates from Canada for employment in the human service field for over four years.

HARBOUR EXECUTIVE RESOURCES INC.
151 Yonge Street, Suite 1400
Toronto, ON M5C 2W7

Telephone	416-306-9848
Fax	416-368-3464
Website	www.austin marlowe.com
Specialties	General Practice
Level	Senior

HARCOURT & ASSOCIATES
10180 - 101 Street
520 Manulife Place
Edmonton, AB T5J 3S4

Telephone	780-425-5555
Fax	780-990-1891
E-mail	recruiter@harcourt.ca
Website	www.harcourt.ab.ca
Founded	1976
Employees	14
Specialties	Computing Sales Management Operations Accounting Engineering Finance Health/Medical Hospitality Insurance International Marketing Purchasing Scientific Banking General Practice
Level	Senior Mid-Level
Min. Salary	$35,000
Recruiters	Kathryn Camire Peter Harcourt CPC Judy Harcourt CPC Barb Perkins CPC Don Unger
Contact	Judy Harcourt, President

Description Harcourt & Associates recruits professionals for growth companies in Alberta, northeastern BC and Saskatchewan.

HARCOURT & ASSOCIATES
444 - 5th Avenue SW, Suite 1600
Calgary, AB T2P 2T8

Telephone	403-263-5445
Fax	403-263-5467
E-mail	calgary@harcourt.ab.ca
Website	www.harcourt.ab.ca
Founded	1976
Employees	2
Specialties	Computing Sales Management Operations Accounting Engineering Finance Health/Medical Hospitality Insurance International Marketing Purchasing Scientific Banking General Practice
Level	Senior Mid-Level
Min. Salary	$35,000
Contact	Glen McGillvray

Description Harcourt & Associates are recruiting professionals for growth companies throughout Alberta, northeastern BC and Saskatchewan.

HARCOURT MATTHEWS GROUP INC., THE
10020 - 101A Avenue, Suite 1900
Phipps McKinnon Building
Edmonton, AB T5J 3G2

Telephone	780-423-4392
Fax	780-429-0046
E-mail	hmgumc@ planet.eon.net
Specialties	Accounting Hospitality
Contact	Bruce Hertz

HARRINGTON STAFFING SERVICES & INFORMATICS RESOURCES
164 Metcalfe Street
Ottawa, ON K2P 1P2

Telephone	613-236-4600
Fax	613-236-2192
E-mail	it@harringtonhr.com
Website	www.harringtonhr.com
Founded	1973
Specialties	Computing Engineering Telecom Administrative Bilingual Sales
Level	Mid-Level
Recruiters	Christine Audet Aimée Cheng Isabelle Copeland Linda Eburne Garry Harrington
Contact	Isabelle Copeland, General Manager

Description Harrington Staffing Services and Informatics Resources specializes in placing IT professionals on contract or permanent placements.

HARRIS CONSULTING CORPORATION, THE
444 St. Mary Avenue, Suite 1400
Winnipeg, MB R3C 3T1

Telephone	204-942-8735
Fax	204-944-8941
E-mail	resumes@ harrisconsult.com
Website	www.harrisconsult.com
Founded	1981
Employees	11
Specialties	Accounting Aerospace Banking Finance Health/Medical Insurance Management Marketing Pharmaceutical Operations Packaging Plastics Purchasing Logistics
Level	Mid-Level Senior
Min. Salary	$50,000
Fee Basis	Retainer Only
Recruiters	Corina Alexander Russell May C.M.C. Lori May B.N. Ken Poole B.A. Alan Thorlakson Donald Vernon C.A.
Contact	Russell H. May, BA, CMC, President

Description Harris offers a full range of human resource management programs and services, including recruitment and executive search.

HARRISON, CARLSON, CRIMINISI
3532 Commerce Court
Burlington, ON L7N 3L7

Telephone	905-639-0788
Fax	905-333-5221
E-mail	joanne@hccca.com
Website	www.hccca.com
Specialties	Accounting Finance
Recruiters	Irene Bucher Ted Carlson Carm Criminisi Trevor Gaskin Joe Harrison Ana Mancini Joanne Wood CGA
Contact	Joanne Wood, CGA, Manager

Description Harrison, Carlson, Criminisi is an accounting firm that also does search work for clients.

HARRISON JONES ASSOCIATES
Buckingham House East
The Broadway, Stanmore
Middlesex, HA7 4EB
UNITED KINGDOM

Telephone	44-20-8385-7881
Fax	44-20-8385-7882
E-mail	hjajobs@hja.co.uk
Website	www.hjajobs.net
Specialties	International Agriculture/Fisheries Management

Description For over 10 years, Harrison Jones Associates have specialised in recruiting Western expatriates for positions internationally.

HART & ASSOCIATES LTD.
5 Donald Street, Suite 200
Winnipeg, MB R3L 2T4

Telephone	204-475-5756
Specialties	Marketing Sales Pharmaceutical
Contact	Randy Hart

HARVARD GROUP, THE
7030 Woodbine Avenue, Suite 100
Markham, ON L3R 6G2

Telephone	905-513-6911
Fax	905-513-7349
E-mail	kzweep@ harvard- group.on.ca
Specialties	Computing General Practice
Contact	Mr. Kelly Zweep

HARVEY NASH PLC
13 Bruton St., London W1X 7AH
UNITED KINGDOM

Telephone	44-20-333-0033
Fax	44-20-333-0032
E-mail	harveynash@ harveynash.com
Website	www.harveynash.com
Founded	1988
Specialties	Computing International
Level	Senior Mid-Level
Recruiters	Nicholas Armstrong David Bradford Helen Chastney Caroline Edwards Chris Elridge Joanne Gribben Geoff Hornsby John Murray Susan O'Leary Collins
Contact	Nicholas Armstrong, Candidate Manager

Description Harvey Nash plc is a leading European recruitment group, specializing in IT, providing blue-chip clients with executive, middle management and technical professionals.

HASTINGS GROUP
111 Richmond St. West, Suite 400
Toronto, ON M5H 2G4

Telephone	416-362-5959
Fax	416-214-1632
Specialties	Banking Finance
Contact	Nancy Casola

HAWN & ASSOCIATES, INC.
421 Bay Street, 5th Floor
Sault Ste. Marie, ON P6A 1X3

Telephone	705-649-2496
Fax	705-649-1860
E-mail	paulr.hawn@ sympatico.ca
Specialties	Govt/Nonprofit
Level	Mid-Level
Contact	Paul R. Hawn

Description Hawn & Associates, Inc. is a human resource consulting and recruitment agency.

HAYHURST CONSULTING
79 Ridout Street South, Suite 102
London, ON N6C 3X2

Telephone	519-660-6380
Fax	519-660-8563
E-mail	steve@hayhurst consulting.com
Website	www.hayhurst annetts.com
Specialties	Engineering Operations Accounting Sales Automotive Human Resource Logistics
Level	Mid-Level Senior
Min. Salary	$45,000
Fee Basis	Retainer Only
Recruiters	Stephen A. Hayhurst Kerry Provost
Contact	Steve Hayhurst CMC

Description Hayhurst is a professional recruitment firm with 10+ years experience sourcing middle management and technical professionals for manufacturing clients.

HAYSZMB
37 Sun Street
London,   EC2M 2PL
UNITED KINGDOM

Telephone	44-20-523-3800
Fax	44-20-523-3881
E-mail	london@zmb.co.uk
Website	www.zmb.co.uk
Specialties	Law
	International
	Human Resource
	Marketing
	Finance
Level	Senior
	Mid-Level
Recruiters	Fiona Bennett
	Amanda Berg
	Jonathan Brenner
	Simon Calver
	Tamara Cohen
	Bhavisha Jolopara
	Justin Kopelowitz
	Kirsty McLeod
	Amanda Mukerjee
	Andrew Russell
	Yvonne Smythe
	Camilla Squirrel
	Joanne Street
	Stephen Watkins
	Dan Wilins
Contact	Andrew Russell

Description HaysZMB (formerly Zarak Macrae Brenner) is a leading specialist recruitment consultancy sourcing positions for lawyers, HR, marketing and finance professionals.

HCCA CANADA INC.
6553A Mississauga Road
Mississauga, ON L5N 1A6

Telephone	905-816-0101
Fax	905-816-0202
E-mail	canada@hccaintl.com
Website	www.hccaintl.com
Founded	1973
Specialties	Health/Medical
	International
Level	Mid-Level
Contact	Lisa Boniface, Director

Description HCCA Canada Inc. is a leader in the recruitment industry, specializing in the placement of medical professionals in overseas assignments.

HCR PERSONNEL SOLUTIONS INC.
19 Four Seasons Place, Suite 200
Toronto, ON M9B 6E7

Telephone	416-622-1427
Fax	416-622-7258
E-mail	info@hcrpsi.com
Website	www.hcrpsi.com
Founded	1996
Employees	15
Specialties	Trades/Technicians
	Plastics

Description HCR specializes in skilled trades, industrial and injection molding personnel.

HCR PERSONNEL SOLUTIONS INC.
325 Milner Avenue, Suite 1602
Toronto, ON M1B 5N1

Telephone	416-321-2697
Fax	416-321-2042
E-mail	info@hcrpsi.com
Website	www.hcrpsi.com
Specialties	Trades/Technicians
	Plastics

Description HCR specializes in skilled trades, industrial and injection molding personnel.

HCR PERSONNEL SOLUTIONS INC.
615 Davis Drive, Suite 301
Newmarket, ON L3Y 2R2

Telephone	905-954-0210
Fax	905-954-0214
E-mail	info@hcrpsi.com
Website	www.hcrpsi.com
Specialties	Trades/Technicians
	Plastics
Level	Junior
	Mid-Level
Fee Basis	Sometimes contingent
Recruiters	Tanja Hutahajan
	Barbara Jack
	Sue Sparkes
Contact	Barbara Jack

Description HCR specializes in skilled trades, industrial and injection molding personnel.

HE@D2HEAD.COM INC.
2439A Yonge St., Headland House
Toronto, ON M4P 2E7

Telephone	416-440-0097
E-mail	contact.he@d2head.com
Website	www.d2head.com
Specialties	Human Resource
Level	Mid-Level
	Senior
Recruiters	Paul Dodd
	Stan Hamersak
Contact	Paul Dodd, President

Description He@d2Head is an unusual recruitment firm — they recruit headhunters for permanent and contract assignments. Call toll-free: 1-877-609-4323.

HEALE & ASSOCIATES LTD.
67 Yonge Street, Suite 1500
Toronto, ON M5E 1J8

Telephone	416-360-7333
Fax	416-360-5616
E-mail	heale@cpol.com
Website	www.healejobsearch.com
Founded	1989
Employees	7
Specialties	Management
	Bilingual
	Finance
	Insurance
	Law
	Marketing
Level	Mid-Level
	Junior
Fee Basis	Always contingent
Recruiters	Maryanne Heale
	Sharon Heale
Contact	Rosemary Heale, President

Description Heale & Associates recruits for the financial, legal, accounting and corporate sectors. Member ACSESS.

HEALTH MATCH BC
1333 Broadway West, Suite 200
Vancouver, BC V6H 4C6

Telephone	604-736-5920
Fax	604-736-5963
E-mail	recruit@healthmatchbc.org
Website	www.healthmatchbc.org
Specialties	Health/Medical
Level	Mid-Level
Recruiters	Ethel Davis
	Jan Goode
	Susan Hill
	Tara McAteer
	Kam Sein Yee
Contact	Ethel Davis, Director

Description Health Match BC is a government-funded agency that recruits for permanent and locum physicians in rural hospitals and clinics throughout BC.

HEC GROUP, THE
911 Golf Links Road, Suite 207
Ancaster, ON L9K 1H9

Telephone	905-648-0013
Fax	905-648-7016
E-mail	info@hec-group.com
Website	www.hec-group.com
Founded	1976
Employees	10
Specialties	Engineering
	Automotive
	Management
	Sales
	Accounting
	Computing
	Human Resource
	Operations
Level	Mid-Level
	Senior
Min. Salary	$40,000
Fee Basis	Sometimes contingent
Contact	Robert M. Leek, General Manager

Description The HEC Group specializes in identifying top talent in the manufacturing sector.

HEENAN CONSULTING
25 Maitland St., Suite 505
Toronto, ON M4Y 2W1

Telephone	416-923-4088
E-mail	heenans@home.com
Founded	1997

Employees	5
Specialties	Computing
	Aerospace
	Management
	Telecom
Level	Senior
	Mid-Level
Fee Basis	Sometimes contingent
Contact	Sharon Heenan

Description Heenan Consulting recruits senior information technology staff, including technical, sales, marketing, and management personnel, for the Toronto area.

HEIDRICK & STRUGGLES CANADA INC.
161 Bay Street, BCE Place
Suite 2310, Box 601
Toronto, ON M5J 2S1

Telephone	416-361-4700
Fax	416-361-4770
E-mail	toronto@h-s.com
Website	www.heidrick.com
Founded	1953
Employees	24
Specialties	Govt/Nonprofit
	Education
	Finance
	Health/Medical
	Management
Level	Senior
Min. Salary	$150,000
Fee Basis	Retainer Only
Recruiters	Anne Brayley
	Heather Connelly
	Charlene Davis
	Hart Hillman
	Robert Hines
	John Koopman
	Jack Nederpelt
	Susan Sticlioff
	Dora Vell
Contact	Jack Nederpelt,
	Managing Partner

Description Heidrick & Struggles provides senior-level executive search services to Fortune 500 companies, universities, hospitals and not-for-profit organizations.

HEIDRICK & STRUGGLES CANADA INC.
1800 McGill College Avenue
Suite 2112, Place Montreal Trust
Montréal, QC H3A 3J6

Telephone	514-285-8900
Fax	514-285-8812
E-mail	montreal@h-s.com
Website	www.h-s.com
Founded	1953
Employees	5
Specialties	Management
	Operations
	Finance
	Education
	Govt/Nonprofit
	Health/Medical
Level	Senior

Min. Salary	$150,000
Fee Basis	Retainer Only
Contact	Jack Nederpelt,
	Managing Partner

Description Heidrick & Struggles provides senior-level executive search services to Fortune 500 companies, universities, hospitals and not-for-profit organizations.

HEIDRICK & STRUGGLES INTERNATIONAL, INC.
Na Rybnicku 5, 120 00
Prague 2
CZECH REPUBLIC

Telephone	420-2-96-36-8800
Fax	420-2-96-36-8801
E-mail	prague@h-s.com
Website	www.h-s.com
Specialties	International
Level	Senior
Contact	Irena Brichta

Description Heidrick & Struggles provides senior-level executive search services to Fortune 500 companies, universities, hospitals and not-for-profit organizations.

HEIDRICK & STRUGGLES INTERNATIONAL, INC.
112 avenue Kleber, Cedex 16
Paris 75784
FRANCE

Telephone	33-1-44-34-17-00
Fax	33-1-44-34-17-17
E-mail	paris@h-s.com
Website	www.h-s.com
Specialties	International
Level	Senior
Contact	Jean-Phillippe Saint-Geours, Office Managing Partner

Description Heidrick & Struggles provides senior-level executive search services to Fortune 500 companies, universities, hospitals and not-for-profit organizations.

HEIDRICK & STRUGGLES INTERNATIONAL, INC.
Corso Venezia, 16
Milan 20121
ITALY

Telephone	39-0-2-76-2521
Fax	39-0-2-76-0801
E-mail	milan@h-s.com
Website	www.h-s.com
Specialties	International
	Health/Medical
Level	Senior
Fee Basis	Retainer Only
Contact	Maurizia Villa, Office Managing Partner

Description Heidrick & Struggles provides senior-level executive search services to Fortune 500 companies, universities, hospitals and not-for-profit organizations.

HEIDRICK & STRUGGLES INTERNATIONAL, INC.
Kasumigaseki Building, 31 Fl.
3-2-5 Kasumigaseki, Chiyoda-ku
Tokyo 100 JAPAN

Telephone	81-3-5510-6800
Fax	81-3-3500-5350
E-mail	tokyo@heidrick.com
Website	www.h-s.com
Specialties	International
	Computing
	Health/Medical
Level	Senior
Fee Basis	Retainer Only
Recruiters	Kevin Kelly
	Tomoyuki Satoh
Contact	Kevin Kelly, Co-Managing Partner

Description Heidrick & Struggles provides senior-level executive search services to Fortune 500 companies, universities, hospitals and not-for-profit organizations.

HEIDRICK & STRUGGLES INTERNATIONAL, INC.
100 Piccadilly
London W1V 9FN
UNITED KINGDOM

Telephone	44-20-7491-31-24
Fax	44-20-7734-95-81
E-mail	london@h-s.com
Website	www.h-s.com
Specialties	International
Level	Senior
Contact	Johann Redlinghuys, Office Managing Partner

Description Heidrick & Struggles provides senior-level executive search services to Fortune 500 companies, universities, hospitals and not-for-profit organizations.

HEIDRICK & STRUGGLES INTERNATIONAL, INC.
1 California Street, Suite 2400
San Francisco, CA 94111 USA

Telephone	415-981-2854
Fax	415-982-0482
E-mail	sanfrancisco@h-s.com
Website	www.h-s.com
Specialties	International
Level	Senior
Fee Basis	Retainer Only
Contact	Jeff Hodge

Description With over 75 locations throughout North and South America, Europe, the Middle East, Africa and Asia, Heidrick & Struggles International, Inc. is a senior-level executive search firm.

HEIDRICK & STRUGGLES INTERNATIONAL, INC.
2740 Sand Hill Road
Menlo Park, CA 94025-7096
USA

Telephone	650-234-1500
Fax	650-854-4191
E-mail	menlopark@h-s.com
Website	www.h-s.com
Specialties	International Computing
Level	Senior
Fee Basis	Retainer Only
Contact	Mark Lonergan

Description Heidrick & Struggles provides senior-level executive search services to Fortune 500 companies, universities, hospitals and not-for-profit organizations.

HEIDRICK & STRUGGLES INTERNATIONAL, INC.
5950 Sherry Lane, Suite 400
Dallas, TX 75225 USA

Telephone	214-706-7700
Fax	214-987-4047
E-mail	dallas@h-s.com
Website	www.h-s.com
Founded	1953
Specialties	International
Level	Senior
Contact	David Pasahow

Description Heidrick & Struggles provides senior-level executive search services to Fortune 500 companies, universities, hospitals and not-for-profit organizations.

HEIDRICK & STRUGGLES INTERNATIONAL, INC.
233 South Wacker Drive
Suite 7000, Sears Tower
Chicago, IL 60606-6402
USA

Telephone	312-496-1000
Fax	312-496-1046
E-mail	chicago@h-s.com
Website	www.h-s.com
Specialties	Scientific International
Level	Senior
Fee Basis	Retainer Only
Contact	Linda Heagy

Description Heidrick & Struggles provides senior-level executive search services to Fortune 500 companies, universities, hospitals and not-for-profit organizations.

HEIDRICK & STRUGGLES INTERNATIONAL, INC.
245 Park Avenue, Suite 4300
New York, NY 10167-0152 USA

Telephone	212-867-9876
Fax	212-370-9035
E-mail	newyork@h-s.com
Website	www.h-s.com
Founded	1953
Specialties	International
Level	Senior
Contact	Marvin Berenblum

Description Heidrick & Struggles provides senior-level executive search services to Fortune 500 companies, universities, hospitals and not-for-profit organizations.

HEIDRICK & STRUGGLES INTERNATIONAL, INC.
Avenida Tamanaco, Piso 7
Torre Extebandes, El Rosal
Caracas, 1070 A VENEZUELA

Telephone	58-2-951-4663
Fax	58-2-951-6185
E-mail	h-s.vzla@h-s.com.ve
Website	www.h-s.com
Specialties	International
Level	Senior
Fee Basis	Retainer Only
Recruiters	Jorge Cardiad Alain Couturier Tony Egui
Contact	Nestor Osvaldo D'Angelo

Description Heidrick & Struggles provides senior-level executive search services to Fortune 500 companies, universities, hospitals and not-for-profit organizations.

HEIDRICK & STRUGGLES INTERNATIONAL
Frankfurt Airport Center 1
Hugo-Eckener Ring
Frankfurt 60549 GERMANY

Telephone	49-69-69-70-02-0
Fax	49-69-69-70-02-99
E-mail	frankfurt@h-s.com
Website	www.h-s.com
Specialties	International
Level	Senior
Contact	Dr. Florian Schilling, Office Manager

Description Heidrick & Struggles provides senior-level executive search services to Fortune 500 companies, universities, hospitals and not-for-profit organizations.

HEIGHWAY PERSONNEL LTD.
330 Central Avenue
London, ON N6B 2C8

Telephone	519-672-5620
Fax	519-672-6156
Specialties	Administrative Accounting
Level	Junior

Description Heighway Personnel Ltd. specializes in placing administrative staff, including medical and legal secretaries.

HEIN & COMPANY
1505 Laperriere Avenue, Suite 200
Ottawa, ON K1Z 7T1

Telephone	613-725-9900
Fax	613-725-9950
E-mail	info@heinco.on.ca
Website	www.heinco.on.ca
Specialties	Accounting Finance
Level	Mid-Level
Contact	Sharon Alger

Description Hein & Company is a chartered accounting firm that also does search work for clients.

HELEN ZIEGLER AND ASSOCIATES INC.
180 Dundas St. West, Suite 2403
Toronto, ON M5G 1Z8

Telephone	416-977-6941
Fax	416-977-6128
E-mail	hza@hziegler.com
Website	www.hziegler.com
Employees	11
Specialties	Health/Medical International
Level	Mid-Level Senior
Contact	Helen Ziegler

Description The largest recruiter in North America for international medical positions. Call 1-800-387-4616 in North America.

HELIX MANAGEMENT CONSULTING SERVICES INC.
1420 Youville Drive, Suite 7
Orleans, ON K1C 7B3

Telephone	613-830-3644
Fax	613-830-2983
E-mail	office@hmcs.on.ca
Website	www.hmcs.on.ca
Employees	50
Specialties	Computing
Level	Mid-Level
Recruiters	Richard Dicks Mark Garbe Dave Mouchet
Contact	Dave Mouchet, General Manager

Description HMCS is a Canadian-owned IT consulting firm that provides highly-skilled personnel to fill roles ranging from project manager to programmer.

HEMMERICH, FLANAGAN & ASSOCIATES
62 Regina North
Waterloo, ON N2J 3A5

Telephone	519-886-0084
Fax	519-886-8095
Specialties	Accounting Finance

Description Hemmerich, Flanagan is an accounting firm that also does occasional search work for clients.

HENRY HILL & ASSOCIATES INC.
2000 Argentia Road
Plaza 4, Suite 480
Mississauga, ON L5N 1W1

Telephone	905-814-1114

Fax	905-814-1110
E-mail	info@henryhill associates.com
Website	www.henryhill associates.com
Specialties	Pharmaceutical Health/Medical Advertising Biotech/Biology
Contact	Henry Hill

Description Henry Hill & Associates Inc. is a search firm serving the pharmaceutical and medical industries, as well as the businesses that supply them (such as advertising and technology).

HERMAN SMITH SEARCH INCORPORATED
161 Bay St., First Canadian Place
Suite 3600, Box 629
Toronto, ON M5J 2S1

Telephone	416-862-8830
Fax	416-869-1809
E-mail	info@herman smith.com
Founded	1974
Employees	7
Specialties	Management Finance General Practice Aerospace Automotive Banking Computing Publishing/Media Operations Govt/Nonprofit Human Resource Sales Trade Shows Logistics
Level	Senior
Min. Salary	$65,000
Fee Basis	Retainer Only
Contact	Herman M. Smith, President

Description Herman Smith Search, a member of the EMA Partners worldwide, conducts retainer-based senior searches in the private, public and not-for-profit sectors.

HERRMANN GROUP LIMITED, THE
60 Bloor Street W., Suite 1100
Toronto, ON M4W 3B8

Telephone	416-922-4242
Fax	416-922-4366
E-mail	info@herrmann group.com
Website	www.herrmann group.com
Founded	1985
Employees	6
Specialties	General Practice
Level	Mid-Level Senior
Min. Salary	$60,000
Fee Basis	Retainer Only
Contact	Gerlinde Herrmann

Description Herrmann Group has provided search and management to a range of businesses in Canada for over 15 years.

HESS ASSOCIATES EXECUTIVE SEARCH
1500 Don Mills Road, Suite 712
Toronto, ON M3B 3K4

Telephone	416-447-3355
Fax	416-447-3595
E-mail	hr@hessjobs.com
Website	www.hessjobs.com
Founded	1976
Specialties	Computing Biotech/Biology Pharmaceutical
Level	Mid-Level

Description Hess Associates Executive Search specializes in placing information systems and bioinformatics professionals in contract and permanent assignments.

HEYWOOD HOLMES & PARTNERS
4911 - 51 Street, Suite 500
Red Deer, AB T4N 6V4

Telephone	403-347-2226
E-mail	hhp@cnnet.com
Specialties	Accounting Finance
Level	Mid-Level
Fee Basis	Retainer Only
Contact	Patrick J. Blair

Description Heywood Holmes & Partners is an accounting firm that also does search work for clients.

HI TECH INTERNATIONAL CONSULTING GROUP
40 Gerrard Street East, Suite 305
Toronto, ON M5B 2E8

Telephone	416-593-7474
Fax	416-821-9251
E-mail	info@hicg.com
Website	www.hicg.com
Specialties	Computing

Description Hi Tech International provides IT consultants on a contract or permanent basis in USA and Canada.

HIGGINS INTERNATIONAL INC.
51 Falconer Bay
Winnipeg, MB R2M 4R6

Telephone	204-257-9929
Fax	204-257-9707
E-mail	bhiggins@ higginsinc.com
Website	www.higginsinc.com
Specialties	General Practice
Level	Mid-Level Senior
Fee Basis	Sometimes contingent
Recruiters	Brenda Higgins Barb McMahon Gwen A. Reid Sonia Smith
Contact	Brenda Higgins, Principal

Description Higgins International is a recruitment firm with 15 years progressive human resource management experience throughout Canada.

HIGH ROAD PERSONNEL
562 Maple Avenue
Burlington, ON L7S 1M6

Telephone	905-632-5870
Fax	905-632-5454
E-mail	info@highroad personnel.com
Website	www.highroad personnel.com
Founded	1970
Employees	5
Specialties	Administrative Accounting Computing Engineering Human Resource Management Operations
Level	Mid-Level Junior
Contact	Connie Mussell

HIGHER VISION RECRUITMENT STRATEGIES INCORPORATED
84 Yorkville Avenue, 3rd Floor
Toronto, ON M5R 1B9

Telephone	416-927-7272
Fax	416-927-7474
E-mail	information@ hirevision.com
Website	www.hirevision.com
Specialties	Accounting Administrative Computing Finance Human Resource Management
Min. Salary	$30,000
Fee Basis	Always contingent
Recruiters	Paul Kesler Jo Anne Phillips G.V. (Jim) Singh
Contact	Joanne Phillips, President

Description Higher Vision offers over 50 years experience in human resources staffing in managerial, sales, administrative and IT positions.

HILAND RESEARCH CONSULTANTS INC.
R.R. #2, Lakefield, ON K0L 2H0

Telephone	705-877-9000
Fax	705-877-9001
E-mail	hiland@peterboro.com
Founded	1987
Employees	2
Specialties	General Practice
Level	Senior

Min. Salary $100,000

Contact   Rick Hiland, Partner

Description Provides background research for search firms in Canada and the USA.

HIRE CHOICE INC.
1235 Bay Street, Suite 400
Toronto, ON M5R 3K4

Telephone 416-934-9811
Fax   416-934-9807
E-mail   hoconnor@
             hirechoice.com
Website   www.hirechoice.com

Founded   1999
Employees 15

Specialties Telecom
              Bilingual
              Administrative
              Finance

Level   Mid-Level

Min. Salary $30,000
Fee Basis   Always contingent

Recruiters Doug Gunn
              Shane Miner
              Helen O'Connor
              Shawn Parsons
              Scott Strickland

Contact   Helen O'Connor

Description Hire Choice is a recruiting company specializing in permanent and contract placements in the telecom industry.

HIRE PURPOSE INC., THE
460 Brant Street, Suite 26
Burlington, ON L7R 4B6

Telephone 905-681-2203
Fax   905-681-2894
E-mail   hirepurpose@
             on.aibn.com
Website   www.hirepurpose.com

Specialties Trades/Technicians
              Operations
              Logistics

Level   Mid-Level
              Junior

Contact   Nicole Quesnel

Description The Hire Purpose Inc. specializes in recruiting skilled tradespeople.

HIRE TECHNOLOGY
65 Front Street West , Suite 116
Toronto, ON M5J 1E6

Telephone 416-365-7797
Fax   416-484-4544
E-mail   sheila@
             hiretechnology.ca
Website   www.hiretechnology.ca

Specialties Telecom
              Computing

Level   Senior
              Mid-Level

Description Hire Technology offers executive search and strategic personnel planning specifically for technology-based companies such as

software development, services and hardware.

HIRELOGIX INC.
3800 Steeles Ave. West, Suite 100E
Woodbridge, ON L4L 4G9

Telephone 416-927-1010
Fax   416-927-1615
E-mail   info@hirelogix.com
Website   www.hirelogix.com

Founded   1982

Specialties Computing

Level   Mid-Level

Contact   Marcello Perry

Description HIRElogix Inc. recruits hardware and software positions in the IT field.

HIREPOWER
2795 Bathurst Street, PO Box 41060
Toronto, ON M6B 4J6

Telephone 416-635-6408
Fax   416-635-7548
E-mail   contact@
             hirepower.on.ca
Website   www.hirepower.on.ca

Founded   1992

Specialties General Practice
              Management

Level   Senior
              Mid-Level

Description Hirepower (formerly M.R. Strategic Recruitment) specializes in executive recruitment.

HIREPOWER
1096 Queen Street, Suite 217
Halifax, NS B3H 2R9

Telephone 902-634-4132
Fax   902-634-4216
E-mail   scherrio@
             hirepower.on.ca
Website   www.hirepower.on.ca

Specialties General Practice
              Management

Level   Senior

Description Hirepower (formerly M.R. Strategic Recruitment) specializes in executive recruitment.

HODGINS KOENIG & ASSOCIATES
803 CN Tower
Saskatoon, SK S7K 1J5

Telephone 306-934-1743
Fax   306-934-1641
E-mail   kkuse@quadrant.net
Website   www3.sk.sympatico.ca/
             martal/Koenig/
             hkhome.htm

Specialties Education
              Management
              Agriculture/Fisheries

Level   Mid-Level

Recruiters Karen Carlson
              Kendra Kuse

Contact   Kendra Kuse

HOFFMAN LEGAL SEARCH
5 Ajax Place
Berkeley, CA 94708   USA

Telephone 510-981-9800
Fax   510-981-9417
E-mail   clhoffman@msn.com

Specialties Law
              International

Level   Mid-Level
              Senior

Description Lawyer recruiters for some of the leading Bay Area law firms and corporations.

HOLLOWAY SCHULZ & PARTNERS INC.
1188 West Georgia St., Suite 1500
Vancouver, BC V6E 4A2

Telephone 604-688-9595
Fax   604-688-3608
E-mail   holloway@
             recruiters.com
Website   www.recruiters.com

Founded   1972
Employees 23

Specialties Accounting
              Computing
              Sales
              Operations
              Management
              Marketing
              Human Resource

Level   Mid-Level
              Senior

Fee Basis   Always contingent

Recruiters Lorna Court
              Terry Dusome CPC
              Karen Epp CPC
              Gabrielle Hawkins
              Clive Holloway
              James Hughes BA
              Catherine Jagger
              Dawn Longshaw
              Malcolm McGowan
              Bill Schulz
              James Seidel CPC
              Anna Shojania CPC
              Jean Wong BA

Contact   Terry Dusome, Senior
              Consultant

Description Holloway Schulz & Partners is a leader in professional recruitment on the West Coast, with affiliates throughout North America, Europe and Southeast Asia.

HORIZON RESOURCES INTERNATIONAL INC.
1700 Varsity Estates Drive NW
Varsity Execucentre
Calgary, AB T3B 2W9

Telephone 403-286-2193
Fax   403-286-9845
E-mail   resources@home.com

Founded   1978
Employees 8

Specialties Oil & Gas
              Engineering
              Design
              Accounting
              Finance

	Management Geology/Geography
Level	Senior Mid-Level
Fee Basis	Sometimes contingent
Contact	Gary Couzens

Description Horizon Resources International Inc. specializes in recruitment, staffing and contract consulting within the oil and gas and technology sectors.

HORWATH APPEL
1 Westmount Square, Suite 900
Montréal, QC H3Z 2P9

Telephone	514-932-4115
Fax	514-932-6766
E-mail	info@horwath appel.com
Website	www.horwath appel.com
Specialties	Accounting Finance
Level	Mid-Level Senior

Description Howarth Appel is an accounting firm that also does occasional search work for clients.

HOSPITALITY CANADA INC.
1575 Lawrence Ave. W., Suite 201
Toronto, ON M6L 1C3

Telephone	416-247-4687
Fax	416-247-4965
E-mail	hospitality@ sympatico.ca
Specialties	Hospitality
Level	Mid-Level Junior
Recruiters	Sharda Etkins Rajin Rasram
Contact	Sharda Etkins

HOSPITALITY PERSONNEL CONSULTANTS
8 Appledale Road
Toronto, ON M9B 5G4

Telephone	416-207-9543
Fax	416-207-0264
E-mail	info@hpeople.com
Website	www.hpeople.com
Founded	1986
Specialties	Hospitality
Contact	David Chun

Description Hospitality Personnel Consultants are specialists in the hospitality staffing industry.

HOTEL & RESTAURANT MANAGEMENT RESOURCES INC.
600 Bay Street, Suite 303
Toronto, ON M5G 1M6

Telephone	416-971-8813
Fax	416-971-8814
E-mail	103436.3524@ compuserve.com
Founded	1988

Employees	10
Specialties	Hospitality
Level	Mid-Level
Min. Salary	$25,000
Contact	David Jolly, President

Description Executive search for hotels, restaurants, food service, retail and entertainment industries.

HOUSTON PERSONNEL GROUP, THE
330 St. Mary Avenue, Suite 800
Winnipeg, MB R3C 3Z5

Telephone	204-947-6751
Fax	204-944-0177
E-mail	mhouston@ houstongrp.com
Website	www.houstongrp.com
Founded	1982
Specialties	Management Accounting Hospitality Human Resource Sales Computing
Level	Senior Mid-Level
Recruiters	Kevin Branch Beth Dykes Marilyn Houston RPR Kelly Scrivener Rae Staniloff
Contact	Marilyn Houston, RPR

Description The Houston Personnel Group is one of Winnipeg's largest full-service privately-owned recruiting firm offering executive, sales, accounting / finance, human resource and IT recruiting.

HR BUSINESS PARTNERS
222 Riverfront Avenue SW
Calgary, AB T2P 0A5

Telephone	403-266-8852
Fax	403-269-4040
E-mail	hrbp@telusplanet.net
Founded	1990
Employees	4
Specialties	Marketing Accounting Computing Human Resource Sales Oil & Gas Engineering
Level	Mid-Level Senior
Min. Salary	$80,000
Fee Basis	Retainer Only
Recruiters	Cindy Bruntjen Leslie Nadeau Sharon Spasoff Diana Walls
Contact	Cindy Bruntjen

HR IMPACT
1540 Cornwall Road, Suite 300
Toronto, ON L6J 7W5

Telephone	905-337-0293

Fax	905-339-1896
E-mail	info@hrimpact.net
Website	www.hrimpact.net
Specialties	Marketing General Practice
Level	Mid-Level Senior
Recruiters	Fiorella Callocchia Michael Ramsay CMC
Contact	Fiorella Callocchia, Principal

Description HR Impact provides a full range of HR consulting services, including executive recruitment.

HR RECRUITING & EMPLOYMENT SERVICES INC.
26534 Township Road 384, Suite 14
Red Deer, AB T4E 1A1

Telephone	403-347-7756
Fax	403-347-7271
E-mail	employment@ hrrecruit.com
Website	www.hrrecruit.com
Specialties	Engineering General Practice
Contact	Lesley Bateman

Description HR Recruiting & Employment Services Inc. provides permanent and contract staffing services for skilled individuals.

HR / RH INC.
3545, Côte-des-Neiges, Bureau 024
Montréal, QC H3H 1V1

Telephone	514-932-6500
Fax	514-932-6542
E-mail	info@hrrhinc.com
Website	www.hrrhinc.com
Founded	1971
Employees	7
Specialties	Management Marketing Finance Human Resource Operations Sales Logistics
Level	Senior Mid-Level
Min. Salary	$70,000
Fee Basis	Retainer Only
Recruiters	Marianne Bellmore-Donaldson Sylvie Desautels Marianne B. Donaldson Michel Labre Raymond Leduc Jean F. Morrissette Jacques Perreault
Contact	Marianne Bellmore-Donaldson, Sr. Partner

Description HR / RH provides general practice in executive search. Call toll-free 1-877-982-4774.

HR VISION CORPORATION, THE
152 Trafalgar Road, 2nd Floor
Oakville, ON L6J 3G6

Telephone	905-338-8555
Fax	905-338-0409
E-mail	hrvision@interlog.com
Specialties	Finance Accounting
Level	Mid-Level
Contact	Laurie Nadeau

HRMAX
33 Harbour Square, Suite 1213
Toronto, ON M5J 2G2

Telephone	416-862-9898
Fax	416-862-1996
E-mail	resumes@hrmax.com
Specialties	Computing
Level	Senior
Contact	Simon K. Anthony, VP Business Development

Description HRmax (formerly Kinetic Agency Services) is a headhunter that recruits high-tech professionals.

HT SEARCH COMPANY LTD.
6 Antares Drive, Unit 4, Phase 1
Nepean, ON K2E 8A9

Telephone	613-226-3321
Fax	613-226-6125
E-mail	jobs@htsearch.com
Website	www.htsearch.com
Founded	1995
Employees	12
Specialties	Computing Purchasing Logistics
Level	Senior Mid-Level
Fee Basis	Always contingent
Contact	Tony Zacconi

Description HT Search places IT professionals with ERP skills (PeopleSoft, SAP, Oracle, BaaN and JD Edwards).

HTC GLOBAL SERVICES INC.
28588 Northwestern Hwy., Ste. 450
Southfield, MI 4803   USA

Telephone	248-355-2500
Fax	248-355-3366
E-mail	itopps@htcinc.com
Website	www.htcinc.com
Specialties	Computing International

Description HTC is a global IT solution provider with an impressive array of customers including Fortune 500 companies.

HUGHES LEBEL
185 Somerset St. West, Suite 204
Ottawa, ON K3P 0J2

Telephone	613-567-5010
Fax	613-567-5021
Specialties	Accounting Finance
Level	Mid-Level

Contact	Rick G. Hughes, CA

Description Hughes LeBel is an accounting firm that also does occasional search work for clients.

HUMAN CAPITAL SOLUTIONS
5805 Whittle Road, Suite 102
Mississauga, ON L4Z 2J1

Telephone	905-507-9708
Fax	905-507-9718
E-mail	hroi@hroi.com
Website	www.hroi.com
Founded	1994
Employees	23
Specialties	Engineering Operations Computing

Description Their client list spans all industries, from manufacturing and engineering to hi-tech and service sectors.

HUMAN EDGE CONSULTING
1595 - 16th Avenue, Suite 301
Richmond Hill, ON L3B 4N9

Telephone	905-709-7412
Fax	905-709-7413
E-mail	humanedge@msn.com
Specialties	Sales Aerospace Engineering Finance Purchasing Human Resource Marketing
Level	Mid-Level Senior
Min. Salary	$45,000
Fee Basis	Always contingent
Contact	Tony Martin

HUMAN RESOURCE GROUP MANAGEMENT CONSULTANTS
4990 - 92 Avenue, Suite 105
Edmonton, AB T6B 2V4

Telephone	780-944-9194
Fax	780-466-6262
E-mail	hrgroup@oanet.com
Specialties	Operations Purchasing Govt/Nonprofit
Contact	Dimitri Pojidaeff, Partner

Description Call toll-free: 1-888-474-5463.

HUMAN RESOURCE INITIATIVES
5555 Turney Drive
Mississauga, ON L5M 1A2

Fax	905-819-9458
E-mail	kboyle@eol.ca
Specialties	General Practice
Level	Mid-Level
Contact	Kimberly Boyle

HUMAN RESOURCE MANAGEMENT GROUP
178 Main Street, Suite 104
Unionville, ON L3R 2G9

Telephone	905-477-2272
Fax	905-477-1074
Specialties	Human Resource Sales Administrative
Level	Mid-Level
Contact	Ron Sleeth, President

HUMAN RESOURCES CONSULTING GROUP
2291 Woking Crescent
Mississauga, ON L5K 1Z5

Telephone	905-822-9330
Fax	905-822-2520
E-mail	jud.newell@ sympatico.ca
Founded	1993
Specialties	Management Sales Marketing Accounting Human Resource Telecom Plastics
Level	Mid-Level Senior
Fee Basis	Sometimes contingent
Contact	Harry Garner, CHRP

Description Human Resources Consulting provides recruiting and consulting services in the areas of human resources management, organization development and training.

HUMAN RESOURCES MANAGEMENT CANADA INC.
2405 Lakeshore Blvd. W., Suite 403
Toronto, ON M8V 1C6

Telephone	416-259-4777
Fax	416-259-4757
E-mail	info@hrm.ca
Website	www.hrm.ca
Specialties	Management Engineering Computing
Level	Senior Mid-Level

Description HRM is a full-service recruitment organization specializing in recruitment for executive, management and technical positions.

HUMANETICS INC.
55 Elm Drive W.
Mississauga, ON L5B 3Z3

Telephone	905-949-8900
Fax	905-949-8279
E-mail	humanetx@istar.ca
Employees	2
Specialties	Advertising Telecom Sales Logistics

Level   Mid-Level

Contact   Margaret Cermel-Watson

HUNT TECHNICAL PERSONNEL
789 West Pender Street, Suite 760
Vancouver, BC V6C 1H2

Telephone   604-688-2555
Fax   604-688-6437
E-mail   people@
            hunttempyours.com
Website   www.hunt.ca
Founded   1967

Specialties Accounting
            Banking
            Computing
            Engineering
            Retail
            Sales

Recruiters Peggy Blumenthal
            Rick Colborne

Contact   Peggy Blumenthal

Description Hunt Technical is a
franchised agency serving clients
and applicants for over 30 years.

HUNT TECHNICAL PERSONNEL
717 - 7th Avenue SW
Suite 170, Elveden House
Calgary, AB T2P 0Z3

Telephone   403-269-6786
Fax   403-237-9016
E-mail   huntab@cadvision.com
Website   www.hunt.ca
Founded   1975

Specialties Accounting
            Banking
            Engineering
            Retail
            Sales
            Computing

Contact   Ilona Braun

Description Hunt Technical is a
franchised agency serving clients
and applicants for over 30 years.

HUNT TECHNICAL PERSONNEL
330 Bay St., Suite 403
Toronto, ON M5H 2S8

Telephone   416-860-0016
Fax   416-860-0029
E-mail   tordt@hunt.ca
Website   www.hunt.ca

Specialties Accounting
            Banking
            Engineering
            Retail
            Sales
            Computing

Contact   Anne Speirs

Description Hunt Technical is a
franchised agency serving clients
and applicants for over 30 years.

HUNT TECHNICAL PERSONNEL
6 Lansing Square, Suite 214
Toronto, ON M2J 1T5

Telephone   416-492-8500

Fax   416-492-2275
E-mail   info@hunt.ca
Website   www.hunt.ca
Founded   1967
Employees   8

Specialties Administrative
            Accounting
            Management
            Sales
            Engineering
            Computing

Level   Mid-Level
            Junior

Fee Basis   Always contingent

Recruiters Nadeen David
            Jane Eves
            McLean Hayes
            Lynn Jackson
            Patrick Kelly
            Janet Morrison
            Heather Phair
            Diane Ramster

Contact   Diane Ramster,
            Manager

Description Hunt Technical is a
franchised agency serving clients
and applicants for over 30 years.

HUNT TECHNICAL PERSONNEL
50 Burnhamthorpe Road West
Suite 204
Mississauga, ON L5B 3C2

Telephone   905-273-3221
Fax   905-273-6487
E-mail   torwest@hunt.ca
Website   www.hunt.ca
Founded   1967

Specialties Accounting
            Bilingual
            Design
            Marketing
            Computing
            Engineering

Level   Mid-Level
            Junior

Fee Basis   Always contingent

Recruiters Teresa Menna
            Anne Speirs
            Ida Warren

Contact   Anne Speirs, Owner

Description Hunt Technical is a
franchised agency serving clients
and applicants for over 30 years.

HUNT TECHNICAL PERSONNEL
220 Laurier Ave. West, Suite 1420
Ottawa, ON K1P 5Z9

Telephone   613-238-8801
Fax   613-238-5586
E-mail   apply@hunt-
            ottawa.com
Website   www.hunt-ottawa.com
Founded   1967
Employees   6

Specialties Banking
            Computing
            Govt/Nonprofit
            Librarians
            Bilingual
            Printing

            Administrative
            Engineering
Level   Mid-Level
            Junior

Contact   P. Brousseau

Description Hunt Technical is a
franchised agency serving clients
and applicants for over 30 years.

HUNT TECHNICAL PERSONNEL
935 Décarie Blvd.
Saint-Laurent, QC H4L 3M3

Telephone   514-744-8400
Fax   514-744-2264
E-mail   hunt-stlaurent@
            videotron.ca
Website   www.hunt
            personnel.net

Specialties Accounting
            Bilingual
            Banking
            Engineering
            Sales
            Computing

Contact   Richard Dugré

Description Hunt Technical is a
franchised agency serving clients
and applicants for over 30 years.

HUNT TECHNICAL PERSONNEL
666 rue Sherbrooke Ouest
Bureau 1702
Montréal, QC H3A 1E7

Telephone   514-842-4691
Fax   514-842-2997
E-mail   cv@huntpersonnel.net
Website   www.hunt
            personnel.net
Founded   1967
Employees   23

Specialties Accounting
            Engineering
            Computing
            Banking
            Retail
            Sales

Level   Mid-Level
            Junior

Fee Basis   Always contingent

Contact   Pauline Beaudry,
            Directrice

Description Hunt Technical is a
franchised agency serving clients
and applicants for over 30 years.

HUNTECH CONSULTANTS INC.
5160 Yonge Street
Suite 1005, PO Box 36
Toronto, ON M2N 6L9

Telephone   416-730-9188
Fax   416-730-9185
E-mail   careers@huntech.com
Website   www.huntech.com
Founded   1982

Specialties Computing
            Engineering

Level   Mid-Level
            Senior

Contact   Patrick Delaney,
          Manager

Description Huntech Consultants Inc. are search specialists in the advanced technology field.

HUNTECH CONSULTANTS INC.
440 Laurier Ave. West, Suite 200
Ottawa, ON K1R 7X6

Telephone	613-755-2723
Fax	613-755-2724
E-mail	careers@huntech.com
Website	www.huntech.com
Founded	1982
Specialties	Computing
	Engineering
Level	Mid-Level
	Senior

Description Huntech Consultants Inc. are advanced technology search specialists.

HUNTER INTERNATIONAL EXECUTIVE SELECTION SERVICES INC.
2 Bloor Street West, Suite 700
Toronto, ON M4W 3R1

Telephone	800-873-7172
Fax	905-873-2203
E-mail	sdhunter@idirect.com
Specialties	Hospitality
Level	Senior
Contact	Sean Hunter, President

Description Recruits senior-level managers for hotels.

HUNTINGTON GROUP, THE
6527 Main Street
Trumbull, CT 06611 USA

Telephone	203-261-1166
Fax	203-452-9153
E-mail	hg@huntington-group.com
Website	www.hgllc.com
Specialties	Computing
	International
Level	Mid-Level
	Senior
Contact	Emil Occhiboi, Managing Director

Description The Huntington Group is a national, full-service search firm specializing in the recruitment of executives for the information technology industries.

HUTCHINSON GROUP INC., THE
250 Consumers Road, Suite 603
Toronto, ON M2J 4V6

Telephone	416-499-6621
Fax	416-499-7953
E-mail	info@hutchgroup.com
Website	www.hutchgroup.com
Founded	1982
Employees	3
Specialties	Computing
	Management

Sales	Govt/Nonprofit
Level	Senior
Min. Salary	$150,000
Fee Basis	Retainer Only
Recruiters	Hamilton B. Hutchinson
	H. David Hutchinson
	Philip J.W. Smith
Contact	David Hutchinson, Vice President

Description The Hutchinson Group provides professional and search services.

IAN MARTIN LIMITED
789 West Pender Street, Suite 670
Vancouver, BC V6C 1H2

Telephone	604-637-1400
Fax	604-685-1425
E-mail	johnsonp@ianmartin.com
Website	www.iml.com
Specialties	Engineering
	Computing
Level	Mid-Level
	Senior
Contact	Phil Johnson

Description Ian Martin Limited recruits engineering, computing and technical professionals for over 1,000 of North America's largest corporations.

IAN MARTIN LIMITED
400 - 3rd Avenue SW
Suite 1400, Canterra Tower
Calgary, AB T2P 4H2

Telephone	403-262-2600
Fax	403-262-2670
E-mail	johnsonp@ianmartin.com
Website	www.iml.com
Specialties	Engineering
	Computing
Level	Mid-Level
	Senior
Contact	Phil Johnson

Description Ian Martin Limited recruits engineering, computing and technical professionals for over 1,000 of North America's largest corporations.

IAN MARTIN LIMITED
1940 Oxford Street East, Unit 7
London, ON N5V 4L8

Telephone	519-457-3420
Fax	519-457-3419
E-mail	macmillan@ianmartin.com
Website	www.ianmartin.com
Founded	1957
Specialties	Computing
	Engineering
Level	Mid-Level
	Senior
Contact	Victoria MacMillan

Description Ian Martin Limited recruits engineering, computing and technical professionals for over 1,000 of North America's largest corporations.

IAN MARTIN LIMITED
72 Victoria Road South, Suite 101
Kitchener, ON N2G 4Y9

Telephone	519-568-8300
Fax	519-568-8165
E-mail	smith@ianmartin.com
Website	www.ianmartin.com
Specialties	Computing
	Engineering
Level	Mid-Level
	Senior
Contact	Neil Smith

Description Ian Martin Limited recruits engineering, computing and technical professionals for over 1,000 of North America's largest corporations.

IAN MARTIN LIMITED
111 Grangeway Avenue, Suite 500
Toronto, ON M1H 3E9

Telephone	416-439-6400
Fax	416-439-6922
E-mail	byrne@iml.com
Website	www.iml.com
Founded	1957
Employees	9
Specialties	Computing
	Engineering
Level	Mid-Level
	Senior
Min. Salary	$35,000
Fee Basis	Sometimes contingent
Recruiters	Suzanne Byrne
	Hoda Nicholas
Contact	Hoda Nicholas

Description Ian Martin Limited recruits engineering, computing and technical professionals for over 1,000 of North America's largest corporations.

IAN MARTIN LIMITED
47 Grant Avenue
Hamilton, ON L8N 2X4

Telephone	905-522-4689
Fax	905-522-4680
E-mail	youngson@ianmartin.com
Website	www.the500.com
Specialties	Computing
	Engineering
Contact	Cameron Youngson

Description Ian Martin Limited recruits engineering, computing and technical professionals for over 1,000 of North America's largest corporations.

IAN MARTIN LIMITED
485 Morden Road, 2nd Floor
Oakville, ON L6K 3W6

Telephone	905-815-1600
Fax	905-815-1010
E-mail	recruit@iml.com
Website	www.iml.com
Specialties	Engineering
	Computing
Level	Senior
	Mid-Level
Fee Basis	Always contingent
Recruiters	Paul Baillie
	Jim Clarke
	Loree Gamble
	Stephen Hime
	Brad Lawrie
	John Moniz
	Trevor Rudd
	Nancy Ruddy
	Paul Thompson
Contact	Loree Gamble

Description Ian Martin Limited recruits engineering, computing and technical professionals for over 1,000 of North America's largest corporations.

IAN MARTIN LIMITED
275 Slater Street, Suite 203
Ottawa, ON K1P 5H9

Telephone	613-237-0155
Fax	613-237-2070
E-mail	oconnor@iml.com
Website	www.iml.com
Specialties	Engineering
	Computing
Level	Senior
	Mid-Level
Contact	Matthew O'Connor,
	Technical Recruiter

Description Ian Martin Limited recruits engineering, computing and technical professionals for over 1,000 of North America's largest corporations.

IAN MARTIN LIMITED
615, boul. René-Lévesque O.
Bureau 600
Montréal, QC H3B 1P6

Telephone	514-338-3800
Fax	514-338-1492
E-mail	hehn@ianmartin.com
Website	www.iml.com
Founded	1957
Employees	1200
Specialties	Engineering
	Management
	Computing
	Aerospace
Level	Mid-Level
	Senior
Contact	Peter Hehn

Description Ian Martin recruits engineering, computing and technical professionals for over 1,000 of North America's largest corporations.

IAN MARTIN LIMITED
979, de Bourgogne, Bureau 430
Sainte-Foy, QC G1W 2L4

Telephone	418-657-3832
Fax	418-657-7493
E-mail	stpierre@
	ianmartin.com
Website	www.ianmartin.com
Specialties	Computing
	Engineering
Level	Senior
	Mid-Level
Contact	Lyne St-Pierre

Description Ian Martin Limited recruits engineering, computing and technical professionals for over 1,000 of North America's largest corporations.

IAN MARTIN LIMITED
2800 - 156th Avenue SE, Suite 120
Bellevue, WA 98007
USA

Telephone	425-401-5282
E-mail	ellis@ianmartin.com
Website	www.iml.com
Specialties	Computing
	Engineering
	International
Level	Mid-Level
	Senior
Contact	Glen Ellis

Description Ian Martin recruits engineering, computing and technical professionals for over 1,000 of North America's largest corporations.

IAN MARTIN LIMITED
4819 Emperor Boulevard, 4th Floor
Durham, NC 27703 USA

Telephone	919-313-4690
Fax	919-313-4690
E-mail	murphy@
	ianmartin.com
Website	www.iml.com
Specialties	Computing
	Engineering
	International
Level	Mid-Level
	Senior
Contact	Meta Murphy

Description Ian Martin recruits engineering, computing and technical professionals for over 1,000 of North America's largest corporations.

IAN SCOTT & ASSOCIATES
1370 Hurontario Street
Mississauga, ON L5G 3H4

Telephone	905-278-3194
Fax	905-278-0507
E-mail	info@iandscott.com
Website	www.iandscott.com
Specialties	Hospitality
	Management
Contact	Ian Scott

Description Ian Scott & Associates is a management consulting firm that specializes in overseas market development. They occasionally do recruitment work for clients.

IBISKA TELECOM INC.
130 Albert Street, Suite 1810
Ottawa, ON K1P 5G4

Telephone	613-234-4434
Fax	613-234-4356
E-mail	info@ibiska.com
Website	www.ibiska.com
Specialties	Telecom
	International
Level	Mid-Level
Recruiters	Wayde Carter
	Dave Dexter
	Richard Doiron
	Helen Hayes
	Narindar Khabra
	Kelly Mattice
	Kelly Sokolowski
	Jim Winder
Contact	Narindar Khabra,
	President

Description IBISKA is an IT consulting firm specializing in recruiting telecom and networking personnel for mission-critical projects in Canada, USA, Europe, South America, Caribbean and the Far East.

ICAP MANAGEMENT INC.
461 King Street, Suite 202
Fredericton, NB E3B 1E5

Telephone	506-455-2420
Fax	506-455-2421
E-mail	masterson@icap
	management.com
Website	www.icap
	management.com
Employees	3
Specialties	Accounting
	Finance
	Banking
	Bilingual
	Computing
	Govt/Nonprofit
	Law
Level	Mid-Level
	Senior
Min. Salary	$30,000
Fee Basis	Sometimes contingent
Recruiters	Heather Doherty
	Paul Masterson
	Shelley Rankin
Contact	Paul Masterson,
	Managing Partner

Description A New Brunswick based recruitment and HR consulting firm specializing in matching human skills to business needs with a focus on finding the "right fit". Now part of Adecco Canada.

IDEAL PERSONNEL
55 City Centre Drive, Suite 307
Mississauga, ON L5B 1M4

Telephone	905-279-8050
Fax	905-279-0901
E-mail	resume@
	idealpersonnel.com
Website	www.ideal
	personnel.com
Founded	1965

Specialties Sales
Marketing
Accounting

Level Mid-Level

Contact Jan Delville,
Senior Consultant

ILLICO HODES ADVERTISING
130 Slater Street, Suite 750
Ottawa, ON K1P 6E2

Telephone 613-598-4677
Fax 613-594-8705
E-mail info@illicohodes.com
Website www.illicohodes.com

Specialties General Practice

Description Illico Hodes Advertising
is a recruitment advertising agency.

ILLICO HODES ADVERTISING
281 Saint-Paul St. E., 3rd Floor
Montréal, QC H2Y 1H1

Telephone 514-861-5450
Fax 514-874-0527
E-mail apoissant@
illicohodes.com
Website www.illicohodes.com

Specialties General Practice

Description Illico Hodes Advertising
is a recruitment advertising agency.

IMPACT STAFFING INC.
3410 Walker Road
Windsor, ON N8W 3S3

Telephone 519-972-8932
Fax 519-972-8128
E-mail staff@impact-
staffing.com
Website www.impact-
staffing.com

Founded 1995
Employees 5

Specialties Insurance
Accounting
Sales
Management
Mold & Die
Engineering
Health/Medical

Level Junior
Mid-Level

Fee Basis Sometimes contingent

Recruiters Cathy Beaupré
Rita Olivito

Contact Rita Olivito, President

Description Impact Staffing Inc. is a
placement agency specializing in
office and industrial recruitment.

IMS / INNOVATIVE MANAGEMENT SOLUTIONS GROUP
1881 Yonge Street, Suite 708
Toronto, ON M4S 3C4

Telephone 416-515-2939
Fax 416-515-2938
E-mail careers@imsgroup.net
Website www.imsgroup.net

Founded 1996

Employees 20

Specialties Computing
Management
Marketing
Sales

Level Mid-Level
Senior

Min. Salary $30,000
Fee Basis Always contingent

Contact Michael P. Grady,
President

Description IMS provides recruiting
services in all major job classifica-
tions for the IT, sales and marketing
fields.

IN PLACE SELECTIVE RECRUITMENT SERVICES
18 Beck Street
Toronto, ON M4C 4L5

Telephone 416-691-7102

Specialties Administrative
Banking
Graphic Arts
Human Resource
Marketing
Sales
Transport

Level Mid-Level
Junior

Min. Salary $30,000
Fee Basis Sometimes contingent

Contact Sandra Gravel

Description In Place is a boutique
agency that offers a-la-carte recruitment services to small to mid-sized
corporations.

IN TRANSIT PERSONNEL
7025 Tomken Road, Unit 27
Mississauga, ON L5S 1R6

Telephone 905 564-9424
Fax 905 564-8970
E-mail mississauga@ in-
transit.com
Website www.in-transit.com

Specialties Transport

Level Mid-Level
Junior

Description In Transit Personnel is a
leading recruitment and staffing
firm for the transportation industry.

INFO-TEK CONSULTING & TRAINING INC.
259 Burton Road
Edmonton, AB T6R 1P7

Telephone 780-448-5862
Fax 780-988-8960
E-mail infotekcom@cs.com
Website www.infotekcorp.com

Founded 1994
Employees 10

Specialties Computing
Engineering
Health/Medical
Scientific
Telecom

Level Mid-Level

Min. Salary $40,000

Contact Dr. Raj Ulagaraj

Description INFO-TEK Consulting &
Training Inc. provides three major
services in the human resources
field: consulting, educational training and research & development.

INFOCYBEX
15 Viewmount Crescent
Brampton, ON L6Z 4P4

Telephone 416-930-5323
Fax 905-840-0025
E-mail hrstaff@infocybex.com
Website www.infocybex.com

Founded 1991
Employees 25

Specialties Computing

Level Mid-Level

Min. Salary $30,000
Fee Basis Sometimes contingent

Contact Rafal Urbanczyk,
President

Description Infocybex is a staffing
company specializing in placing
computer experts on short and long
term assignments.

INFORMATION BUSINESS CONSULTING (IBC) GROUP INC.
10060 Jasper Avenue
Suite 2200, Tower 1, Scotia Place
Edmonton, AB T5J 3R8

Telephone 780-420-6422
Fax 780-417-3148
E-mail hr@ibcgrp.com
Website www.ibcgrp.com

Specialties Computing
Design
Engineering
Management
Publishing/Media
Quality Control

Contact Almas Murani, VP
Markerting

Description IBC Group Inc. specializes in the placement of computer
professionals and ISO 9000 quality
consulting.

INFORMATION RESOURCES CENTER
PO Box 876, Al-Khobar 31952
SAUDI ARABIA

Telephone 966-3-893-0850
Fax 966-3-893-0851
E-mail hr@arabianjobs.com
Website www.arabianjobs.com

Founded 1994
Employees 6

Specialties International
Computing
Engineering
Telecom
Oil & Gas

Level Senior
Mid-Level

Fee Basis   Always contingent

Contact   Ramzi Beidas

Description Information Resources Center specializes in searches for well-established professionals to fill IT, telecom and oil & gas positions in the Arab Gulf and Middle East.

INFORMATION SYSTEMS CONSULTING GROUP CORP. / ISC
9940 - 106th Street, Suite 220
Edmonton, AB T5K 2N2

Telephone	780-428-3069
Fax	780-702-1438
E-mail	hr@isc-group.com
Website	www.isc-group.com
Founded	1995
Employees	20
Specialties	Computing
	Consulting
Level	Mid-Level
	Junior
Recruiters	Ruheen Rajan
	Tameeza Ratansi

Description ISC is an information technology consulting firm based in Edmonton.

INFORMATION TECHNOLOGIES, INC.
9712 Pierce Street
Crown Point, IN 46307 USA

Telephone	219-662-7496
E-mail	support@
	infotechnologies.com
Website	www.infotechnologies.
	com
Founded	1990
Specialties	Computing
	International
Level	Mid-Level
Contact	Norma Lewis,
	Recruiting Director

Description Information Technologies, Inc. provides consultants for a wide range of IT projects.

INFORMATION TECHNOLOGY RECRUITING LTD. / ITR
200 Consumers Road
Suite 220
Toronto, ON M2J 4R4

Telephone	416-502-3400
Fax	416-502-9666
E-mail	resumes@
	itrlimited.com
Website	www.itrlimited.com
Specialties	Computing
Recruiters	Fernao Ferreira
	Dan Ferreira
	Simone Ferrier
Contact	Fernao Ferreira,
	President

Description ITR is an established information technology recruitment organization specializing in the placement of IT system professionals.

INFORMATION TECHNOLOGY RESOURCES INC. / ITR
5650 Yonge Street, Suite 1500
Toronto, ON M2M 4G3

Telephone	416-633-7072
Fax	416-633-7532
E-mail	rubbi@itr.net
Website	www.itr.net
Founded	1992
Specialties	Computing
Level	Senior
	Mid-Level
Fee Basis	Sometimes contingent
Contact	Rupinder Ubbi

Description ITR specializes in the recruitment of information technology professionals.

INGENIUS ENGINEERING INC.
30 Rosemount Avenue, Suite 200
Ottawa, ON K1Y 1P4

Telephone	613-729-6400
Fax	613-729-6770
E-mail	recruit@ingenius
	engineering.com
Website	www.ingenius
	engineering.com
Founded	1986
Employees	110
Specialties	Computing
	Engineering
	Govt/Nonprofit
	Human Resource
	Telecom
Level	Senior
	Mid-Level
Min. Salary	$35,000
Fee Basis	Always contingent
Recruiters	Paul Dogra
	Gina Etstathio
	Danny Faust
	Christine Methot
	Pierre Quinn
	Jim Shewan
	Marek Skrobecki
Contact	Pierre Quinn, Vice
	President, Business
	Development

Description InGenius Engineering Inc. is a high tech / IT staffing and consulting company specializing in software engineering, hardware engineering, telecom and IT professionals.

INITIAL EDUCATION PERSONNEL
7280 Victoria Park Avenue
Markham, ON L3R 2M5

Telephone	905-947-4553
Fax	905-947-4551
E-mail	shill@
	rentokilinitial.com
Website	www.initialps.
	co.uk/education
Specialties	Education
	International
Contact	Shawna Hill

Description Initial Education Personnel is committed to providing teachers of the highest quality and strictly to exacting requirements and needs of individual schools.

INITIAL HEALTHCARE
7280 Victoria Park Avenue
Markham, ON L3R 2M5

Telephone	905-943-9802
Fax	905-947-4551
E-mail	dmclenachan@
	rentokilinitial.com
Website	www.rentokilinitial.
	com
Specialties	Health/Medical
Level	Mid-Level
	Junior
Contact	Gary Buxton

Description Initial Healthcare provides permanent and contract staff to a range of healthcare clients.

INSIGHT TECHNOLOGY CORPORATION
839 - 5th Avenue SW, Suite 200
Calgary, AB T2P 3C8

Telephone	403-266-4463
Fax	403-266-5050
E-mail	insightk@insight
	technology.com
Website	www.insight
	technology.com
Specialties	Computing
Level	Mid-Level
Min. Salary	$35,000
Fee Basis	Always contingent
Contact	Karen Hartley, BA
	Comm

Description Insight Technology specializes in recruiting and placing information technology specialists in the Calgary marketplace.

INSURANCE CONSULTING GROUP
10 King Street E., Suite 1400
Toronto, ON M5C 1C3

Telephone	416-363-6767
Fax	416-366-7085
Specialties	Insurance
Level	Mid-Level
Contact	Ms. Pat Halferty

INSURANCE OVERLOAD SYSTEMS LTD.
130 King Street West
Suite 1800, Box 427
Toronto, ON M5X 1E3

Telephone	416-945-6610
Fax	416-945-6605
Website	www.insurance
	overload.com
Founded	1983
Specialties	Insurance
Level	Mid-Level
	Junior
Recruiters	Dan Canfield
	Jennifer McCallum

Contact   Dan Canfield, Branch Manager

Description Insurance Overload Systems Ltd. is an insurance-specific staffing service with 58 offices throughout the US and Canada.

INSURANCE OVERLOAD SYSTEMS LTD.
27777 Franklin Road, Suite 1575
Southfield, MI 48034 USA

Telephone	248-355-1940
Fax	248-355-0633
Website	www.insurance overload.com
Founded	1983
Specialties	Insurance International
Contact	Theresa Shari, Branch Manager

Description Insurance Overload Systems Ltd. has grown to be the largest insurance-specific staffing business in North America, with 58 offices throughout the US and Canada. Call us toll-free at 1-800-722-1983.

INSURANCEWORKS.COM INC.
335 Bay Street, Suite 809
Toronto, ON M5H 2R3

Telephone	416-603-6604
Fax	801-881-1301
E-mail	info@insurance works.com
Website	www.insurance works.com
Specialties	Insurance
Level	Mid-Level
Contact	Don Givelos

Description An online recruitment firm for insurance professionals.

INTEC RECRUITMENT SERVICES
41 High Street, Frimley
Surrey, GU16 5HJ
UNITED KINGDOM

Telephone	44-1276-709000
Fax	44-1276-709001
E-mail	frimley@ intec-recruitment.co.uk
Website	www.intec-recruitment.co.uk
Founded	1979
Specialties	International Engineering Computing
Recruiters	Les Allen Gordon Davies Stuart Wood
Contact	Gordon Davies

Description Intec Recruitment specializes in permanent and contract IT and engineering appointments in southern England and London.

INTEGRA IT PARTNERS INC.
40 Eglinton Avenue East, Suite 601
Toronto, ON M4P 3A2

Telephone	416-487-3301
Fax	416-440-4025
E-mail	recruiting@ integrait.com
Website	www.integrait.com
Specialties	Computing
Level	Mid-Level
Contact	Robyn Merizzi

Description Integra IT Partners is a professional recruiting firm specializing in the placement of IT professionals in the GTA for over 11 years.

INTEGRATED DATA SERVICES INC.
255 Albert Street, Suite 904
Ottawa, ON K1P 6A9

Telephone	613-233-9554
Fax	613-236-6203
E-mail	wexlerc@ compuserve.com
Website	www.nexusworld.com/ idsinc
Founded	1984
Specialties	Accounting Finance
Recruiters	Kathleen Holst Charles Wexler CA
Contact	Charles Wexler, C.A.

Description Integrated Data Services Inc. is a consulting firm that specializes in ACCPAC-related accounting consulting, as well as placement of accounting staff.

INTELLIGENT TECHNOLOGY SOLUTIONS INC.
203 Colonnade Road, Suite 201
Ottawa, ON K2E 7K3

Telephone	613-727-1212
Fax	613-727-9248
E-mail	webapply@ intelligentinc.com
Website	www.intelligentinc.com
Specialties	Computing Engineering
Level	Mid-Level

Description Intelligent Technology Solutions Inc. is a leading provider of full-time and project-based technical recruitment and consulting services.

INTER-TEK, INC.
3000 Ocean Park Blvd., Suite 1000
Santa Monica, CA 90405 USA

Telephone	310-452-9428
Fax	310-452-9468
E-mail	resume@ intertekinc.com
Website	www.intertekinc.com
Specialties	International Computing

Description Intertek, Inc. is a recruiting company with contract and permanent position opportunities in computer programming and many other highly technical areas.

INTERACTIVE BUSINESS SYSTEMS, INC. / IBS INC.
1 Yonge Street, Suite 1801
Toronto, ON M5E 1W7

Telephone	416-304-0008
Fax	416-369-0515
E-mail	afitz-gerald@ibs.com
Website	www.ibs.com
Specialties	Computing
Contact	Adrian Fitz-Gerald

Description IBS is one of North America's largest, privately-held IT consulting firms servicing Fortune 500 clients.

INTERCHANGE PERSONNEL INC.
1403 Joliet Avenue SW
Calgary, AB T2T 1S3

Telephone	403-216-1520
Fax	403-216-1522
Founded	1992
Employees	1
Specialties	Oil & Gas Engineering Geology/Geography Real Estate Marketing Computing Accounting
Level	Mid-Level Senior
Min. Salary	$30,000
Fee Basis	Sometimes contingent
Contact	Karen Aiken

Description Interchange Personnel provides search services at the management and board level.

INTERCOM RECRUITMENT LTD.
47 Colborne Street, Suite 301
Toronto, ON M5E 1P8

Telephone	416-364-5338
Fax	416-214-2043
E-mail	intercom@torweb.com
Website	www.intercom placement.com
Founded	1993
Employees	8
Specialties	Advertising Direct Mktng. Marketing Public Relations
Level	Senior Mid-Level
Min. Salary	$40,000
Fee Basis	Sometimes contingent
Recruiters	Tamara Bonar Ed Martin Iris Rosenblum Harry Teitelbaum Mark Wicken Gary Williams
Contact	Harry Teitelbaum, Partner

Description InterCom Recruitment specializes in contract and full-time placement of advertising, marketing and marketing communications professionals.

INTERIM MANAGEMENT RESOURCES INC. / IMR
420 Brittania Rd. E., Suite D-208
Mississauga, ON L4Z 3L5

Telephone 905-507-4662
Fax 905-507-4644
E-mail quality1@idirect.com
Website www.imrjobs.com

Specialties Aerospace
Direct Mktng.
Marketing
Printing
Graphic Arts
Telecom

Level Mid-Level
Senior

Min. Salary $50,000
Fee Basis Sometimes contingent

Recruiters D.C. Crosbie MBA
Sharon Foster
Nick Hogya MA
Susan Jennings BA
Barb Marsh CHRP
Robert J. (Bob) Nicholls
Moira Robinson CHRP

Contact D.C. Crosbie, MBA

Description IMR specializes in placements in the aerospace, printing, publishing / graphics and telecom industries.

INTERIM PLUS INC.
85, rue d'Ottawa
Granby, QC J2G 2R9

Téléphone 450-375-6486
Télécopieur 450-375-4258

Fondée 1985
Employés 5

Spécialités Comptabilité
Ingénierie
Ressources humaines
Gestion
Exploitation

Contact Claude Laverdière

INTERLAKE EMPLOYMENT SERVICES
326 Main Street
Stonewall, MB R0C 2Z0

Telephone 204-467-2061
Fax 204-467-7125

Founded 1990

Specialties Disabled

Contact Cheryl Fidler

Description We support adults with developmental disabilities to work in the community.

INTERMARK MANAGEMENT INC.
7895 Tranmere Drive, Suite 212
Mississauga, ON L5S 1V9

Fax 905-678-6414
E-mail marie.cafarelli@ sympatico.ca

Specialties Accounting
Finance
Human Resource

Level Mid-Level

INTERNATIONAL AGENCY GROUP
36 Eglinton Avenue West, Suite 401
Toronto, ON M4R 1A1

Telephone 416-480-1545
Fax 416-480-0772

Specialties Banking
Finance

Level Mid-Level

Contact Robert Hausman, Director

INTERNATIONAL BUSINESS PARTNERS
221 Baillol Street, Suite 1714
Toronto, ON M1S 1C8

Telephone 416-322-3324
Fax 416-322-3360
E-mail searchptnr@primus.ca

Specialties Engineering
Marketing
Logistics

Level Mid-Level
Senior

Contact Les Keremelvich, President

Description International Business Partners (formerly Search Partners International) provides executive search and consulting services, with clients across Canada and affiliates in the USA and Pacific Rim.

INTERNATIONAL BUSINESS SEARCH INC.
9030 Leslie Street, Suite 308
Richmond Hill, ON L4B 1G2

Telephone 905-889-9391
E-mail jobs@intbizsearch.com

Specialties Computing

Level Mid-Level
Senior

Contact Nikki Thomson

Description International Business Search Inc. provides leading organizations with qualified information systems personnel.

INTERNATIONAL CAREER SPECIALISTS / ICS
1041 McNicoll Avenue
Toronto, ON M1W 3W6

Telephone 416-492-3333
Fax 416-492-3339
E-mail kbadeski@icsjobs.org

Founded 1980
Employees 30

Specialties Computing

Level Senior
Mid-Level

Fee Basis Sometimes contingent

Contact Kathlene Badeski

Description ICS specializes in placing people in various full-time and contract IT positions.

INTERNATIONAL HEALTH EXCHANGE
134 Lower Marsh
London SE1 7AE
UNITED KINGDOM

Telephone 44-207-620-3333
Fax 44-207-620-2277
E-mail info@ihe.org.uk
Website www.ihe.org.uk

Specialties Health/Medical
International

Contact Patrick Brooke

Description International Health Exchange specialises in the recruitment, training and support of health workers working in international relief and development programmes.

INTERNATIONAL HOSPITAL RECRUITMENTS
2300 Yonge Street, Suite 2403
Toronto, ON M4P 1E4

Telephone 416-221-2761
Fax 416-222-6220
E-mail ihr@ihrcanada.com
Website www.ihrcanada.com

Founded 1994

Specialties International
Health/Medical

Contact Gus Abraham

Description International Hospital Recruitments specializes in healthcare recruitment for positions in Saudi Arabia and the Gulf states.

INTERNATIONAL SEARCH ASSOCIATES INC.
9 Hannaford Street
Toronto, ON M4E 3G6

Telephone 416-691-2325
Fax 416-691-3164
E-mail isa.greer@sympatico.ca

Founded 1991
Employees 4

Specialties Computing

Level Mid-Level

Fee Basis Always contingent

Contact Wayne Greer

Description IT recruitment specialists, particularly in the ERP and CRM fields.

INTERNATIONAL STAFFING CONSULTANTS, EUROPE
PO Box 124, Eastleigh
Hampshire, SO50 8ZE
UNITED KINGDOM

Telephone 44-1703-651-281
Fax 44-1703-620-877
E-mail isceurope@aol.com
Website www.iscworld.com

Founded 1979

Specialties International
Management
Engineering
Sales

Computing
Accounting

Level	Senior
	Mid-Level
Fee Basis	Always contingent
Recruiters	Michael L. Comer
	James R. Gettys
	Ian C. Smith
Contact	Ian C. Smith, President

Description International Staffing Consultants, Europe specializes in hiring Europeans to work in North America.

INTERNATIONAL TECHNICAL RECRUITING
380 Pelissier Street, Suite 213
Windsor, ON   N9A 6W8

Telephone	519-258-8318
Fax	519-258-4269
E-mail	itr@mnsi.net
Website	www.mnsi.net/~itr
Specialties	Computing
	Automotive
	Engineering
	Operations
Contact	Scott Murray

Description International Technical Recruiting provides technical job placements for the Manufacturing, Engineering and Information Systems industries.

INTEROCEAN PERSONNEL SERVICES (UK) LTD.
24a High Street, Interocean House
Stockton-on-Tees
Cleveland, TS18 1SP
UNITED KINGDOM

Telephone	44-1642-618995
Fax	44-1642-611916
E-mail	stockton@
	ipspersonnel.nl
Website	www.ipspersonnel.nl/
	stockton
Specialties	International
	Engineering
	Oil & Gas
	Transport
Recruiters	Alison Davis
	Bruce Davis

Description Interocean Personnel Services (UK) Ltd. is one of the leading suppliers of manpower to the international dredging, marine, offshore and petrochemical industries.

INTERSEARCH CANADA / CORSO, MIZGALA + FRENCH
90 Eglinton Avenue East, Suite 404
Toronto, ON M4P 2Y3

Telephone	416-488-4111
Fax	416-488-3111
E-mail	cmf@intersearch
	canada.com
Website	www.intersearch
	canada.com
Founded	1992
Employees	6

Specialties	Bilingual
	Govt/Nonprofit
	General Practice
	Finance
	Management
	Marketing
Level	Senior
Min. Salary	$90,000
Fee Basis	Retainer Only
Recruiters	John J. Corso
	Guy P. French
	Ralph G. Hansen
	Anthony B. Mizgala
Contact	Ralph Hansen

Description Corso, Mizgala + French is part of InterSearch Worldwide, an executive search organization with 80+ offices worldwide and 4 partner offices in Canada (Halifax, Montreal, Calgary and Vancouver).

INTERSEARCH CANADA / LENNOX PARTNERSHIP, THE
500 - 4th Avenue SW, Suite 1500
Calgary, AB T2P 2V6

Telephone	403-265-4222
Fax	403-264-8523
E-mail	info@lennox.net
Website	www.lennox.net
Founded	1975
Employees	11
Specialties	Marketing
	Management
	Operations
	Finance
	Human Resource
Level	Mid-Level
	Senior
Min. Salary	$50,000
Fee Basis	Retainer Only
Recruiters	Verna Baldwin
	Julie Ball
	Iruen Barter
	Coralie Braum
	Mike Kelly
	Gaye Knopf
	Rudy Krueger
	Kevin Powell
	David Waymouth
Contact	David Waymouth,
	Managing Partner

Description Lennox Partnership has affiliates in Toronto, Vancouver, Halifax, Montreal and InterSearch Internationally.

INTERSEARCH CANADA / STAFFING STRATEGISTS INTERNATIONAL
5945 Spring Garden Road
Halifax, NS B3H 1Y4

Telephone	902-423-1657
Fax	902-423-0277
E-mail	info@ staffing
	strategists.com
Website	www.staffing
	strategists.com
Founded	1990
Employees	18
Specialties	Oil & Gas
	Accounting

Engineering
Finance
Management
Purchasing
Telecom

Level	Senior
	Mid-Level
Min. Salary	$75,000
Fee Basis	Sometimes contingent
Recruiters	Christine Birchall
	David Delaney
	Sonja Erman
	Victoria Hebb
	John Landry
	Chris Schulz
	Jim Wilson
Contact	Jim Wilson,
	President & CEO

Description Staffing Strategists International provides executive search, executive selection, Internet recruitment and employee retention consulting services.

INTERSEARCH CANADA / WESTERN EXECUTIVE SELECTION INC.
700 West Georgia St., Suite 1450
Box 10015, Pacific Centre
Vancouver, BC V7Y 1A1

Telephone	604-684-2228
Fax	604-683-6345
E-mail	western@telus.net
Website	www.intersearch
	canada.com
Founded	1997
Employees	4
Specialties	Education
	Govt/Nonprofit
	Human Resource
	Marketing
	Telecom
	Biotech/Biology
Level	Senior
Min. Salary	$75,000
Fee Basis	Sometimes contingent
Recruiters	Michael Bailey
	Eric Denhoff
	Karin MacMillan
Contact	Eric Denhoff

Description Western Executive Selection Inc. is part of InterSearch Worldwide, an executive search organization with 81 offices worldwide and 4 partner offices in Canada.

INTERSTATE TECHNICAL SERVICES, INC.
2 Wellman Avenue, PO Box 901
Nashua, NH 03601   USA

Telephone	603-889-8440
Fax	603-882-3588
E-mail	nashstaff@
	itsstaffing.com
Website	www.itsstaffing.com
Founded	1980
Specialties	Computing
	International
	Design
	Engineering

Level	Mid-Level
	Senior

Description Interstate Technical Services, Inc. is a leading technical staffing firm, serving contract employment needs throughout the New England area.

INVITECH CORPORATION
67 Yonge Street
Toronto, ON M5E 1J8

Telephone	416-363-4700
Fax	416-363-5973
Specialties	Computing
Contact	Amit Deodhar

Description InviTech Corporation specializes in placing IT professionals, particularly AS400 people.

IRONSIDE CONSULTING SERVICES INC.
155 Ironside Drive
Sault Ste. Marie, ON P6A 6K4

Telephone	705-779-3223
Fax	705-779-9982
E-mail	bluntad@on.aibn.com
Specialties	Management
Contact	Antoinette Blunt

Description Ironside Consulting Services is a management consulting firm that also does occasional search work.

IRVING PERSONNEL PLUS INC.
245 Union Street
Saint John, NB E2L 1B2

Telephone	506-202-4744
Fax	506-202-4740
E-mail	ippi@nbnet.nb.ca
Specialties	General Practice
Level	Mid-Level
	Junior
Contact	Margo Rankin,
	General Manager

ISG INTERNATIONAL
PO Box 28165
London, ON N6H 5R2

Telephone	519-471-9212
Fax	519-657-0935
E-mail	info@isg-intl.com
Website	www.isg-intl.com
Specialties	General Practice

Description ISG International is an independent recruiting organization specializing in targeted searches conducted on a highly-customized and confidential basis.

ISOMERIC INC.
235 Yorkland Blvd., Suite 105
Toronto, ON M2J 4Y8

Telephone	416-491-5655
Fax	416-491-5355
E-mail	jobs@isomeric.net
Website	www.isomeric.net
Specialties	Computing
Level	Mid-Level
	Senior
Contact	Dean Edwards,
	President

Description Isomeric Inc. (formerly System Search Group Inc.) is a full-service IT staffing organization specializing in placing computer professionals at all levels.

IT PEOPLE LTD.
250 - 6th Avenue SW
Suite 700, Bow Valley Sq. 4
Calgary, AB T2P 3H7

Telephone	403-205-4860
Fax	403-205-4862
E-mail	lydiattj@cadvision.com
Founded	1997
Specialties	Computing
Level	Mid-Level
	Senior
Min. Salary	$40,000
Fee Basis	Sometimes contingent
Contact	Jay Lydiatt, President

Description IT People Ltd. provides IT professionals on a contract basis and, occasionally, on permanent placements.

IT PROSPECTS
525 University Avenue, Suite 835
Toronto, ON M5G 2L3

Telephone	416-596-1777
Fax	416-596-8364
E-mail	cdonaldson@
	itprospects.com
Website	www.itprospects.com
Specialties	Computing
Recruiters	Marilyn Croghan
	Arlene King
Contact	Marilyn Croghan,
	President

Description IT Prospects is a full-service consulting company, specializing in the recruitment and placement of IT professionals.

IT RESOURCES LTD.
25 Valleywood Drive, Suite 10
Markham, ON L3R 5L9

Telephone	905-415-1800
Fax	905-415-8111
E-mail	resumes@itrgroup.com
Website	www.itrgroup.com
Founded	1996
Employees	12
Specialties	Computing
	Banking
	Engineering
	Management
	Telecom
Fee Basis	Always contingent
Recruiters	John Danells
	Victoria Greco
	Janet Simpson
Contact	Victoria Greco, President

Description IT Resources Ltd. provides contract and permanent career opportunities for accomplished IT professionals with leading corporations in Canada and the US.

IT SELECT INC.
2 St. Clair Avenue East, Suite 800
Toronto, ON M4T 2T5

Telephone	416-921-1220
Fax	416-921-5537
E-mail	info@itselect.on.ca
Website	www.itselect.on.ca
Specialties	Computing

Description IT Select Inc. is a Toronto-based firm specializing in the recruitment of IT professionals. They have over 11 years experience in the recruitment business.

ITBANX TECHNOLOGY RECRUITERS
67 Mowat Avenue
Toronto, ON M6K 3E3

Telephone	416-533-7000
Fax	416-533-3888
E-mail	info@itbanx.com
Website	www.itbanx.com
Specialties	Computing
Level	Mid-Level
Contact	Mary-Leigh Brown

Description ITbanx is a full range staffing company with a sole focus on the IT marketplace, providing the services of candidates on a permanent, contract, or contract-to-hire basis.

ITECC CONSULTING
1 Yonge Street, Suite 1801
Toronto, ON M5E 1W7

Telephone	416-366-3200
Fax	416-369-0515
E-mail	recruiting@itecc.com
Website	www.itecc.com
Founded	1995
Employees	10
Specialties	Computing
Level	Mid-Level
	Senior
Contact	John McMillan,
	General Manager

Description ITECC specializes in contract and permanent placements of IT, engineering and management professionals.

ITNMOTION
4950 Yonge Street, Suite 208
Toronto, ON M2N 6K1

Telephone	416-250-2604
Fax	416-250-2629
E-mail	info@itnmotion.com
Website	www.itnmotion.com
Specialties	Computing
Contact	Lisa Sherman, Manager,
	Recruitment Services

Description ITnmotion, a division of Contemporary Personnel, specializes in IT recruitment.

ITPLACEMENTS.COM
201 Whitehall Drive, Unit 4
Markham, ON L3R 9Y3

Telephone	905-513-9999
Fax	905-513-9995
E-mail	information@itplacements.com
Website	www.itplacements.com
Specialties	Computing
Level	Mid-Level
Contact	Vince Forrestall

Description ITPlacements.com is an online recruitment service specializing in computing placements.

ITSUPERSTARS RECRUITING COMPANY
163 Sterling Road, Suite 5
Toronto, ON M6R 2B2

Telephone	416-537-5329
Fax	416-227-0988
E-mail	info@itsuperstars.com
Website	www.itsuperstars.com
Founded	1994
Specialties	Computing
Contact	Robert C. Cecil, CEO

Description ITSuperstars is the principal hub for several thousand active IT professionals seeking new career opportunities.

ITSUPERSTARS RECRUITING COMPANY
396 Queenston Road
Hamilton, ON L8K 1J2

Telephone	905-543-8955
E-mail	info@itsuperstars.com
Website	www.itsuperstars.com
Specialties	Computing
Contact	Robert C. Cecil

Description ITSuperstars is the principal hub for several thousand active IT professionals seeking new career opportunities.

J.E. COULTER ASSOCIATES LIMITED
1210 Sheppard Ave. East, Suite 211
Toronto, ON M2K 1E3

Telephone	416-502-8598
Fax	416-502-3473
E-mail	jcoulter@idirect.com
Specialties	Engineering
Contact	John Coulter, President

Description J.E. Coulter is a consulting engineering firm that occasionally does recruitment work for clients in acoustical engineering.

J. EDGAR & ASSOCIATES INC.
4 Whittaker Crescent
Toronto, ON M2K 1K8

Telephone	416-222-1909
Fax	416-222-9862
Website	jedgarcareers.com
Specialties	Computing Engineering Sales Operations
Level	Mid-Level Senior
Fee Basis	Always contingent
Recruiters	Jason Edgar Cris Murray
Contact	Joan Edgar

Description J. Edgar and Associates Inc. is a private search firm dedicated to sourcing candidates in the areas of information systems and technical manufacturing.

J.G. FLYNN & ASSOCIATES INC.
885 West Georgia Street, Suite 1500
Vancouver, BC V6C 3E8

Telephone	604-689-7205
Fax	604-689-2676
E-mail	recruit@jgflynn.com
Website	www.jgflynn.com
Founded	1983
Employees	3
Specialties	General Practice Management Mining Engineering Pulp & Paper Construction Computing International
Level	Senior
Min. Salary	$80,000
Fee Basis	Retainer Only
Recruiters	John English MBA Jerry G. Flynn Harry Parslow Holly Symons
Contact	Jerry Flynn

Description J.G. Flynn & Associates Inc. is an independent search firm specializing in global recruitment for clients with operations or projects in developing countries.

J.O. BUSH & ASSOCIATES
29 Nixon Street, Suite 210
Mindemoya, ON P0P 1S0

Telephone	705-377-4324
Fax	705-377-4324
E-mail	kk@jewellconlink.net
Founded	1985
Specialties	Engineering Human Resource Accounting Sales Pulp & Paper Mining
Level	Senior Mid-Level
Min. Salary	$50,000
Fee Basis	Sometimes contingent
Contact	Jim Bush

Description J.O. Bush is a retainer search firm with associates in Toronto and Montreal serving a select clientele in the manufacturing and service industries.

J.P. ANDERSON & ASSOCIATES INC.
360 Torrance Street, Suite 407
Burlington, ON L7R 2R9

Telephone	905-634-3222
Fax	905-634-3850
E-mail	careers@jpanderson.com
Website	www.jpanderson.com
Founded	1996
Employees	1
Specialties	Engineering Operations Logistics Transport Computing
Level	Mid-Level Senior
Min. Salary	$35,000
Fee Basis	Always contingent
Contact	Jeff Anderson

Description J.P. Anderson & Associates Inc., part of a 7-member Canadian cooperative search group, specializes in recruiting for logistics, engineering, information technology and operations management positions.

J.R. BECHTLE & COMPANY
112 Water Street, Suite 500
Boston, MA 02109   USA

Telephone	617-722-9980
Fax	617-722-4130
E-mail	jrbech@jrbechtle.com
Website	www.jrbechtle.com
Founded	1979
Employees	15
Specialties	International Management Bilingual Automotive Engineering Finance Operations Sales
Level	Senior
Min. Salary	$100,000
Fee Basis	Retainer Only
Recruiters	Max Thomiak Peter Witt
Contact	Peter Witt

Description J.R. Bechtle & Company specializes in retained executive-level searches for German, Swiss and Austrian companies. German speakers preferred.

JACQUELINE A. LECKIE MEDICAL CONSULTANTS, INC.
250 - 6th Avenue SW, Suite 240
Calgary, AB T2P 3H7

Telephone	403-237-5762
Fax	403-781-7567

E-mail   jleckie@
         telusplanet.net

Specialties   Health/Medical

Level   Mid-Level

Contact   Jacqueline A. Leckie

Description Jacqueline A. Leckie Medical Consultants, Inc. is a healthcare consulting company that also recruits doctors and nurses for client organizations.

JAMES E. THOMAS & ASSOCIATES INC.
383 Richmond Street, Suite 1110
London, ON   N6A 3C4

Telephone   519-661-0476
Fax   519-661-0478
E-mail   jethomas@
            odyssey.on.ca
Website   www.thomas-
            hrconsultants.com

Founded   1988

Specialties   Engineering
              Management
              Operations
              Govt/Nonprofit
              Accounting
              Human Resource

Level   Mid-Level
        Senior

Contact   James E. Thomas

Description Thomas & Associates specializes in executive search for manufacturing companies on a Canada-wide basis.

JAMES PARTNERSHIP, THE
5 Reid St., Kitson Building
PO Box HM 463
Hamilton, HM BX   BERMUDA

Telephone   441-292-9987
Fax   441-295-1025
E-mail   tjp@ibl.bm
Website   www.thejames
            partnership.bm

Founded   1991

Specialties   Computing
              Accounting
              Insurance
              Banking
              International

Level   Senior
        Mid-Level

Min. Salary $45,000
Fee Basis   Sometimes contingent

Recruiters   Angela Birk
             Louisa Bussey
             Britt Gardiner
             Kathy-Anne Paynter
             Sarah Reynolds

Contact   Angela Birk, Senior IT
          Recruitment Consultant

Description The James Partnership is a Bermuda-based executive search and selection recruitment agency, specializing in the IT, insurance / reinsurance, accounting and banking sectors.

JAMES T. BOYCE & ASSOCIATES
2161 Yonge Street, Suite 200
Toronto, ON M4S 3A6

Telephone   416-322-0192
Fax   416-322-9590

Founded   1990

Specialties   Accounting
              Finance
              International
              Health/Medical
              Human Resource
              Marketing
              Management

Level   Senior
        Mid-Level

Fee Basis   Always contingent

Recruiters   Paul M. Balabanowicz
             James T. (Jim) Boyce
             Carl E. Cox

Contact   James T. (Jim) Boyce,
          President

Description James T. Boyce & Associates are search and placement consultants to the financial marketplace, specializing in the life insurance and employee benefit fields.

JAMICH TECHNOLOGY GROUP, INC.
2720 Queensview Drive, Suite 1114
Ottawa, ON K2B 1A5

Telephone   613-726-1734
Fax   613-726-8995
E-mail   estephen@jamich.com
Website   www.jamich.com

Founded   1996

Specialties   Computing

Level   Mid-Level

Description Jamich Technology Group, Inc. provides IT consulting services to the high-tech sector and the federal government for both short- and long-term assignments, with offices in Tampa, Indianapolis and Ottawa.

JAN HOWARD & ASSOCIATES LTD.
220 Yonge St., Eaton Centre
Suite 115, Box 515
Toronto, ON M5B 2H1

Telephone   416-598-1775
Fax   416-598-0363
E-mail   jan.howard@
            sympatico.ca

Founded   1976

Specialties   Marketing
              Administrative
              Accounting
              Bilingual
              Engineering
              Computing
              Operations

Level   Mid-Level
        Junior

Fee Basis   Always contingent

Contact   Jan Howard

Description Specializes in the recruitment of marketing, administrative, accounting, bilingual, technical personnel in the manufacturing and service industries throughout Ontario.

JANET WRIGHT & ASSOCIATES INC.
21 Bedford Road, Suite 300
Toronto, ON M5R 2J9

Telephone   416-923-3008
Fax   416-923-8311
E-mail   jwassoc@total.net

Founded   1995
Employees 11

Specialties   Education
              Health/Medical
              Govt/Nonprofit
              Arts & Culture
              Human Resource

Level   Senior

Fee Basis   Retainer Only

Recruiters   Dan Birch
             Jack Dimond
             Colleen Keenan
             Gerri Woodford
             Janet Wright

Contact   Janet Wright

Description JWA assists public-sector and not-for-profit organizations and institutions with senior-level search assignments.

JANKAR HUMAN RESOURCES INC.
2289 Fairview Street, Suite 205
Burlington, ON L7R 2E3

Telephone   905-333-3699
Fax   905-333-5580

Specialties   General Practice
              Hospitality

Contact   Barbara J. Gloyd,
          Manager

Description Jankar Human Resources does general placements, particularly in the travel industry.

JAWABY OIL SERVICE
15-17 Lodge Road, St. John's Wood
London, NW8 7JA
UNITED KINGDOM

Telephone   44-17-1314-6000
Fax   44-20-7314-6136
E-mail   pnicholls@
            jawaby.co.uk
Website   www.jawaby.co.uk

Specialties   Oil & Gas
              International
              Engineering
              Geology/Geography

Level   Mid-Level
        Senior

Recruiters   May Mohamed
             Peter Nicholls

Contact   Peter Nicholls

Description Recruits for oil-related positions in Libya.

JCOR HUMAN RESOURCE SERVICES INC.
5920 - 1A Street SW, Suite 507
Calgary, AB T2H 0G3

Telephone	403-543-6040
Fax	403-543-6045
E-mail	resumes@jcorhr.com
Specialties	Engineering
	Design
	International
Level	Mid-Level
Contact	David Soles

JEFFERY GROUP LTD., THE
133 Richmond St. West, Suite 506
Toronto, ON M5H 3B7

Telephone	416-361-1475
Fax	416-361-1652
E-mail	executivesearch@
	thejefferygroup.com
Website	www.thejeffery
	group.com
Founded	1995
Specialties	Public Relations
Level	Senior
	Mid-Level
Recruiters	Kristina Filmer
	Christopher Holz
	Pam Jeffery
	Caroline Pinto
Contact	Pam Jeffery

Description Public affairs executive
search.

JENEREAUX & ASSOCIATES INC.
33 City Centre Drive, Suite 577
Mississauga, ON L5B 2N5

Telephone	905-270-0020
Fax	905-270-9327
E-mail	mail@jenereaux.com
Website	www.jenereaux.com
Founded	1984
Specialties	Finance
	Health/Medical
	Accounting
	Management
	Computing
	Sales
	Public Relations
	Printing
	Telecom
	Direct Mktng.
Level	Mid-Level
Min. Salary	$40,000
Fee Basis	Always contingent
Recruiters	Doralee Azure
	Phyllis Ellis
	Catherine Jenereaux
	Robin Paddley
	Kirsten Rogers
Contact	Catherine Jenereaux

Description Jenereaux & Associates
Inc. recruits for Fortune 500 clients
in the high tech, healthcare, biomedical, manufacturing, printing,
telecom, distribution, financial, call
centre and public affairs fields.

JENEX TECHNOLOGY PLACEMENT INC.
1260 Hornby Street, Suite 104
Vancouver, BC V6Z 1W2

Telephone	604-687-3585
Fax	604-687-5432
E-mail	jobs@jenex.bc.ca
Website	www.jenex.bc.ca
Founded	1994
Employees	4
Specialties	Computing
	Scientific
	Telecom
Level	Mid-Level
Fee Basis	Always contingent
Recruiters	Anita Chan
	Allison Guld
	Jennifer Rigal
Contact	Allison Guld

Description JENEX specializes in
placing advanced-technology professionals, including software developers, programmers, database designers, systems architects and other
technical specialists.

JERRY ADEL & COMPANY
3266 Yonge Street, Suite 1202
Toronto, ON M4N 3P6

Telephone	416-488-7585
Fax	416-481-4065
E-mail	jerry@jerryadel.com
Website	www.jerryadel.com
Founded	1982
Employees	5
Specialties	Engineering
	Sales
	Accounting
	Automotive
	Direct Mktng.
	Health/Medical
	Marketing
	Operations
Level	Senior
	Mid-Level
Min. Salary	$40,000
Fee Basis	Retainer Only
Contact	Jerry Adel

Description Jerry Adel & Company is
a management consulting firm
whose services include executive
recruitment.

JOANNE STARR CONSULTANTS LTD.
287 Richmond St. East, Suite 103
Toronto, ON M5A 1P2

Telephone	416-360-1855
Fax	416-360-1884
E-mail	resumes@
	compuserve.com
Website	www.jostarr.com
Specialties	Insurance
Contact	Joanne Starr

Description A placement agency specializing in the insurance industry.

JOB BORN CANDIDATE SELECTION BUREAU
370 Main Street East, Suite 305
Hamilton, ON L8N 1J7

Telephone	905-522-7551
Fax	905-522-2952
E-mail	resumes@job-
	bornrecruiting.com
Website	www.job-
	bornrecruiting.com
Founded	1984
Specialties	Accounting
	Engineering
	Human Resource
	Insurance
	Management
	Sales
Level	Mid-Level
Recruiters	Sue Barns
	Dominique Tselepaki
	Mary Ann Vaughn CPC
Contact	Mary Ann Vaughn,
	President

Description Job Born Candidate Selection Bureau is a leading placement and recruiting firm that recruits high-calibre employees for
their clients.

JOHN DOUCETTE MANAGEMENT SERVICES
13025 Yonge Street, Suite 201
Richmond Hill, ON L4E 1Z5

Telephone	416-346-1174
Fax	905-773-0395
E-mail	doucettesan@sprint.ca
Founded	1987
Specialties	Computing
Level	Senior
Min. Salary	$50,000
Fee Basis	Sometimes contingent
Recruiters	John Doucette
	Matthew San
Contact	John Doucette

JOHN STOTEN CONSULTING
10104 - 103rd Avenue
Suite 2201, Canada Trust Tower
Edmonton, AB T5J 0H8

Telephone	780-448-9151
Fax	780-425-0530
E-mail	srussell@
	planet.eon.net
Specialties	Management
Fee Basis	Retainer Only
Recruiters	Suzanne Russell
	John Stoten CMC
Contact	Suzanne Russell

JOHNSTONE ASSOCIATES PROFESSIONAL SEARCH INC.
421 - 7th Avenue SW, Suite 1200
Calgary, AB T2P 4K9

Telephone	403-264-6806
Fax	403-264-6812
E-mail	trevor@johnstone.ab.ca
Website	www.johnstone.ab.ca
Specialties	Oil & Gas
	Computing
Level	Mid-Level
	Senior
Contact	Trevor Johnstone

Description Johnstone Associates is a recruitment agency specializing in the oil & gas and IT fields.

JONATHAN
157 rue des Chenes O., Bureau 275
Québec, QC G1L 1K6

Téléphone	418-622-4822
Télécopieur	418-622-7593
Courriel	jonathan@ videotron.net
Employés	6
Spécialités	Généralistes
Échelon	Intermédiaire Débutant
Contact	Louise Lambert, Directrice

Description Centre d'aide à l'emploi pour femmes.

JSG GROUP MANAGEMENT CONSULTANTS
178 Main Street, Suite 400
Unionville, ON L3R 2G9

Telephone	905-477-3625
Fax	905-477-8211
E-mail	rick@jsggroup.com
Website	www.jsggroup.com
Founded	1984
Employees	3
Specialties	Accounting Marketing Telecom Computing Management Operations Automotive
Level	Senior
Fee Basis	Retainer Only
Recruiters	Richard W. Birarda Rick Birarda Brian Sweeney
Contact	Rick Birarda, Managing Partner

Description JSG Group specializes in management assessment and executive search services for Fortune 500 manufacturers, distributors of automobiles, auto parts, computers, software and related services companies.

JSL SEARCH LEADERS INC.
120 Eglinton Avenue East
Suite 200
Toronto, ON M4P 1E2

Telephone	416-545-1465
Fax	416-545-1466
E-mail	info@emailyour resume.com
Website	www.jslsearch leaders.com
Founded	1997
Employees	8
Specialties	Computing Banking Finance Logistics Telecom

	Insurance Management
Level	Senior Mid-Level
Min. Salary	$50,000
Fee Basis	Always contingent
Contact	Janet Levenstadt, President

Description JSL Search Leaders are specialists in information technology recruitment, focusing on professionals who are in the "top ten percentile."

JUNO SYSTEMS INC.
1-9 On Hing Terrace
Unit D, 9/F, On Hing Building
Hong Kong, Central
CHINA

Telephone	852-2801-5988
Fax	852-2801-5818
E-mail	info@ junosystems.com.hk
Website	www.junosystems.com
Specialties	Computing International
Level	Mid-Level
Fee Basis	Always contingent
Contact	Verda Ak

Description Juno Systems is a global organization specializing in IT staffing, project management and management consulting.

JURISSEC INC.
510 boul. Saint-Laurent, bur. 300
Montréal, QC H2Y 2Y9

Téléphone	514-845-1212
Télécopieur	514-845-9424
Courriel	info@jurissec.com
Site Internet	www.jurissec.com
Fondée	1979
Employés	4
Spécialités	Droit
Échelon	Intermédiaire Débutant
Recruteurs	Renée A. Pépin Lise G. Tremblay
Contact	Renée A. Pépin

Description Agence spécialisée dans le recrutement de personnel juridique (secrétaires ou techniciens juridiques).

JWT SPECIALIZED COMMUNICATIONS
160 Bloor Street East, 8th Floor
Toronto, ON M4W 3P7

Telephone	416-926-7300
Fax	416-926-7316
E-mail	confidential@ jwtworks.com
Website	www.jwtworks.com
Specialties	General Practice
Level	Mid-Level

Description JWT Specialized Communications is a recruitment adver-

tising agency that provides advertising and communications solutions to an array of high-profile clients.

K.B. LYE & ASSOCIATES
207 Adelaide Street East, Suite 104
Toronto, ON M5A 1M8

Telephone	416-365-0408
Fax	416-365-1759
E-mail	kblye@interlog.com
Employees	6
Specialties	Engineering Operations Scientific
Level	Mid-Level
Contact	Brett Lye

K-INTERNATIONAL GROUP LTD.
5650 Yonge Street
Suite 1500, Xerox Tower
Toronto, ON M2M 4G3

Telephone	416-736-1308
Fax	416-663-1968
E-mail	careers@k-international group.com
Website	www.k-international group.com
Founded	1989
Specialties	International Accounting Finance Banking Insurance Computing
Level	Senior Mid-Level
Min. Salary	$49,000
Fee Basis	Sometimes contingent
Contact	Marleine R. Kay

Description X-International specializes in international accounting, finance and IT positions, with a main focus on 2-year and extended contracts in Bermuda / Caribbean.

KARABUS MANAGEMENT INC.
2 Tippett Road, Suite 100
Toronto, ON M3H 2V2

Telephone	416-222-6408
Fax	416-222-3263
E-mail	contactus@netcom.ca
Website	www.karabus.com
Specialties	Law Computing Management Retail
Level	Mid-Level
Contact	Robert Logan

Description Karabus Management is a leading management consulting firm, specializing in the retail and consumer product industries.

KAS PERSONNEL SERVICES INC.
4 Commerce Crescent
North Bay, ON P1B 8G4

Telephone	705-475-0421

E-mail   northbay@
           kasstaffing.com
Website   www.kas.on.ca

Specialties Transport
              Accounting
              Engineering
              Operations
              Computing

Level   Mid-Level
           Junior

Description KAS Personnel is a placement agency that also does professional-level recruitment in the fields
of transport, accounting, engineering, manufacturing and IT.

KAS PERSONNEL SERVICES INC.
100 Victoria Street North, Suite E
Kitchener, ON N2H 6R5

Telephone 519-578-7398
E-mail   kitchener@
            kasstaffing.com
Website   www.kas.on.ca

Specialties Transport
              Accounting
              Engineering
              Operations
              Computing

Level   Mid-Level
           Junior

Description KAS Personnel is a placement agency that also does professional-level recruitment in the fields
of transport, accounting, engineering, manufacturing and IT.

KAS PERSONNEL SERVICES INC.
21 Surrey Street West, Suite 303
Guelph, ON N1H 3R3

Telephone 519-767-3304
E-mail   guelph@
            kasstaffing.com
Website   www.kas.on.ca

Specialties Transport
              Accounting
              Engineering
              Operations
              Construction

Level   Mid-Level
           Junior

Description KAS Personnel is a placement agency that also does professional-level recruitment in the fields
of transport, accounting, engineering, manufacturing and IT.

KAS PERSONNEL SERVICES INC.
2304 Islington Avenue, Suite 301
Toronto, ON M9W 3W9

Telephone 416-740-7658
E-mail   rexdale@
            kasstaffing.com
Website   www.kas.on.ca

Specialties Transport
              Accounting
              Engineering
              Computing
              Operations

Level   Mid-Level
           Junior

Description KAS Personnel is a placement agency that also does professional-level recruitment in the fields
of transport, accounting, engineering, manufacturing and IT.

KAS PERSONNEL SERVICES INC.
2555 Eglinton Ave. East, Suite 201
Toronto, ON M1K 5J1

Telephone 416-269-0033
E-mail   scarborough@
            kasstaffing.com
Website   www.kas.on.ca

Specialties Transport
              Accounting
              Engineering
              Operations
              Computing

Level   Mid-Level
           Junior

Description KAS Personnel is a placement agency that also does professional-level recruitment in the fields
of transport, accounting, engineering, manufacturing and IT.

KAS PERSONNEL SERVICES INC.
1022 Barton Street East
Hamilton, ON L8L 3E4

Telephone 905-545-4656
Fax   905-545-2116
E-mail   hamilton@
            kasstaffing.com
Website   www.kas.on.ca
Founded   1987

Specialties Transport
              Accounting
              Engineering
              Operations
              Computing

Level   Mid-Level
           Junior

Description KAS Personnel is a placement agency that also does professional-level recruitment in the fields
of transport, accounting, engineering, manufacturing and IT.

KAS PERSONNEL SERVICES INC.
4043 New Street
Burlington, ON L7L 1S8

Telephone 905-637-9755
E-mail   burlington@
            kasstaffing.com
Website   www.kas.on.ca

Specialties Transport
              Accounting
              Engineering
              Operations
              Computing

Level   Mid-Level
           Junior

Description KAS Personnel is a placement agency that also does professional-level recruitment in the fields
of transport, accounting, engineering, manufacturing and IT.

KAS PERSONNEL SERVICES INC.
270 Orenda Road
Brampton, ON L6T 4X6

Telephone 905-454-0751
E-mail   brampton@
            kasstaffing.com
Website   www.kas.on.ca

Specialties Transport
              Accounting
              Engineering
              Operations
              Computing

Level   Mid-Level
           Junior

Description KAS Personnel is a placement agency that also does professional-level recruitment in the fields
of transport, accounting, engineering, manufacturing and IT.

KAS PERSONNEL SERVICES INC.
1945 Dundas Street East, Suite 210
Mississauga, ON L4X 2T8

Telephone 905-282-9199
E-mail   mississauga@
            kasstaffing.com
Website   www.kas.on.ca

Specialties Transport
              Accounting
              Engineering
              Operations
              Computing

Level   Mid-Level
           Junior

Contact   Costa Schizas

Description KAS Personnel is a placement agency that also does professional-level recruitment in the fields
of transport, accounting, engineering, manufacturing and IT.

KAS PERSONNEL SERVICES INC.
511 Welham Road, Suite 2
Barrie, ON L4N 8Z6

Telephone 705-737-3134
E-mail   barrie@kasstaffing.com
Website   www.kas.on.ca

Specialties Transport
              Accounting
              Engineering
              Operations
              Computing

Level   Mid-Level
           Junior

Description KAS Personnel is a placement agency that also does professional-level recruitment in the fields
of transport, accounting, engineering, manufacturing and IT.

KAS PERSONNEL SERVICES INC.
200 North Front Street, Unit 1
Belleville, ON K8P 3C2

Telephone 613-966-3895
E-mail   belleville@
            kasstaffing.com
Website   www.kas.on.ca

Specialties Transport
              Accounting
              Engineering

Operations
Computing

Level   Mid-Level
           Junior

Description KAS Personnel is a placement agency that also does professional-level recruitment in the fields of transport, accounting, engineering, manufacturing and IT.

KATE COWHIG INTERNATIONAL RECRUITMENT LTD.
41 Dawson Street
Dublin 2 IRELAND

Telephone   353-1-671-5557
Fax   353-1-671-5965
E-mail   cowhig@iol.ie
Website   www.kcr.ie

Founded   1990
Employees   12

Specialties Health/Medical
           International

Level   Mid-Level

Fee Basis   Always contingent

Contact   Kate Cowhig

Description Kate Cowhig International Recruitment Ltd. specializes in placing healthcare professionals to leading teaching hospitals throughout England, Ireland, the Channel Islands and Middle East.

KATHERINE HOLT ENTERPRISES LTD.
27 Broadbridge Drive
Toronto, ON M1C 3K5

Telephone   416-208-0139
Fax   416-208-0141
E-mail   kholtltd@idirect.com
Website   www.pm-online.com/
           ~holt

Employees   3

Specialties Real Estate
           Construction

Level   Mid-Level

Min. Salary $30,000
Fee Basis   Sometimes contingent

Contact   Katherine Holt

Description Katherine Holt Enterprises Ltd. is a search firm with broad experience in the recruitment, screening and placement of candidates in all areas of the Real Estate Industry.

KATHY JACKSON ASSOCIATES
900 Howe Street, Suite 330
Vancouver, BC V6Z 2M4

Telephone   604-688-4506
Fax   604-801-5201
E-mail   kja@direct.ca

Specialties Law

Level   Mid-Level

Recruiters Kathy Jackson
           Tom Reid

Contact   Kathy Jackson

Description Specializes in the placement of paralegals.

KAYMAC & ASSOCIATES
120 Eglinton Ave. East, Suite 303
Toronto, ON M4P 1E2

Telephone   416-322-8111
Fax   416-322-8110
E-mail   search@kaymac.com

Employees   24

Specialties Accounting
           Finance
           Management

Level   Senior
           Mid-Level

Min. Salary $45,000
Fee Basis   Sometimes contingent

Contact   Mary A. Kaye

KEE TRANSPORT GROUP INC.
6760 Davand Drive, Unit 9
Mississauga, ON L5T 2L9

Telephone   905-670-0835
Fax   905-670-5513
E-mail   admin@
           keetransport.com
Website   www.keetransport.com

Specialties Transport

Contact   Kieran O'Brian,
           President

Description Kee Transport Group Inc. places people in the transport field.

KEELEY CONSULTING INC.
54A Scollard Street
Toronto, ON M5R 1E9

Telephone   416-924-2552
Fax   416-924-7601
Website   www.keeley
           consulting.com

Employees   2

Specialties Finance
           Accounting
           Banking

Level   Mid-Level
           Senior

Fee Basis   Retainer Only

Recruiters Stephanie Brooks Keeley
           Ann H. Chamberlain
           Timothy J. Keeley

Contact   Timothy J. Keeley,
           Principal

Description Keeley Consulting Inc. is an executive search firm that provides search and consulting services to client firms in the financial services industry exclusively.

KEITH BAGG & ASSOCIATES INC.
85 Richmond Street W., Suite 700
Toronto, ON M5H 2C9

Telephone   416-863-1800
Fax   416-350-9600
E-mail   info@bagg.com
Website   www.bagg.com

Founded   1971

Specialties General Practice
           Management
           Marketing
           Engineering
           Sales
           Accounting

Level   Mid-Level
           Senior

Min. Salary $35,000
Fee Basis   Sometimes contingent

Recruiters Alan Alderton
           Simon E. Bois
           Larry Bowen
           Joanne Bowers
           Shanna U'Ren
           Melanie Wyndowe

Contact   Geoffrey Bagg, VP,
           Operations

Description Keith Bagg & Associates provides executive search and recruitment and offers staffing solutions at the mid-management and senior level on a full-time, and contract basis. 25+ years of experience, and over 14,000 placements.

KEITH BAGG INFORMATION TECHNOLOGY SEARCH INC.
85 Richmond Street West, Suite 700
Toronto, ON M5H 2C9

Telephone   416-863-1800
Fax   416-350-9600
E-mail   resumes@bagg.com
Website   www.kbits.com

Founded   1996
Employees   4

Specialties Computing

Recruiters Tim Bullen
           Sandra Kim
           Sarah Mitchell
           Sean Siman

Contact   Sarah Mitchell

Description KBITS provides search and recruitment for full-time and contract IT professionals with an emphasis on client-server, networks and mainframe technology areas.

KEITH BAGG STAFFING (REGIONAL) INC.
33 City Centre Drive, Suite 580
Mississauga, ON L5B 2N5

Telephone   905-276-6109
Fax   416-350-9634
E-mail   resumes@bagg.com
Website   www.bagg.com

Specialties Management
           Administrative

Contact   Keith Bagg

Description Providing full-time and contract placements in accounting, administration, call-centre, customer service, operations and financial services.

KEITH BAGG STAFFING (REGIONAL) INC.
2900 Steeles Ave. East, Suite 219
Thornhill, ON L3T 4X1

Telephone 905-709-3917
Fax 416-350-9600
E-mail resumes@bagg.com
Website www.bagg.com
Specialties Accounting
Administrative
Banking
Bilingual
Computing
Management
Marketing
Level Mid-Level
Junior
Recruiters Hogarthe Browne
Angela Papps
Maria Teotico
Contact Sarah Mitchell
Description Providing full-time and
contract placements in accounting,
administration, call-centre, cus-
tomer service, operations and finan-
cial services.

**KEITH BAGG STAFFING
RESOURCES INC.**
85 Richmond Street West, Suite 700
Toronto, ON M5H 2C9
Telephone 416-863-1800
Fax 416-350-9614
E-mail andrewp@bagg.com
Website www.bagg.com
Specialties Accounting
Administrative
Bilingual
Banking
Computing
Fee Basis Always contingent
Recruiters Mary Bagg
Luann Bagg CPC
Jacqueline Chua CPC
Joanne Hickey CPC
Michele Lown
Jenny Szulc
Contact Sarah Mitchell
Description Keith Bagg Staffing Re-
sources Inc. provides full-time and
contract placements in accounting,
administration, call-centre, cus-
tomer service, operations and finan-
cial services.

KEITH-MURRAY PARTNERSHIP
17 Sword Street
Toronto, ON M5A 3N3
Telephone 416-926-0491
Fax 416-924-0688
E-mail info@kmpsearch.com
Founded 1988
Employees 3
Specialties General Practice
Direct Mktng.
Management
Marketing
Mining
Human Resource
Level Senior
Mid-Level
Fee Basis Retainer Only
Contact Marnie Keith-Murray,
CMC

Description Keith-Murray Partnership is a research-based executive
search firm with a policy of working with only one firm of a kind in
an industry.

**KELLMAN MANAGEMENT
RESOURCES**
7030 Woodbine Avenue, Suite 100
Markham, ON L3R 6G2
Telephone 905-946-8541
Fax 905-946-0548
E-mail peter@kellman
mgmt.com
Specialties Engineering
Automotive
Level Mid-Level
Description Kellman Management
Resources places candidates with
automotive clients.

KELLY, LES SERVICES
155, rue Saint-Jacques, Bureau 301
Granby, QC J2G 9A7
Téléphone 450-378-6371
Télécopieur 450-378-2232
Site Internet www.kellyservices.com
Spécialités Comptabilité
Informatique
Ingénierie
Échelon Intermédiaire
Contact Hélène Girard,
Directrice

KELLY, LES SERVICES
755, boul. St-Jean, Bureau 501
Pointe-Claire, QC H9R 5M9
Telephone 514-695-7955
Fax 514-695-8353
E-mail ks7815@
kellyservices.com
Website www.kellyservices.ca
Specialties Administrative
Accounting
Finance
Engineering
Level Mid-Level
Junior
Contact Mike Iacovelli

KELLY, LES SERVICES
999, de Maisonneuve Ouest
Bureau 570
Montréal, QC H3A 3L4
Telephone 514-284-0323
Fax 514-284-2470
E-mail ks7811@
kellyservices.com
Website www.kellyservices.ca
Specialties Administrative
Trades/Technicians
Level Mid-Level
Junior

KELLY, LES SERVICES
1000 Sherbrooke O., Bureau 2000
Montréal, QC H3A 3G4

Telephone 514-284-0323
Fax 514-284-2470
Website www.kellyservices.com
Specialties Computing
Engineering
Level Mid-Level
Recruiters Maude Boivin CPC
Isabelle Tremblay
Contact Maude Boivin
Description Kelly Services has been
a global leader in the staffing serv-
ices industry for over 50 years.

KELLY, LES SERVICES
110, boul. Crémazie Ouest
Bureau 500
Montréal, QC H2P 1B9
Téléphone 514-389-8787
Télécopieur 514-389-0161
Courriel ks7813@
kellyservices.com
Site Internet www.kellyservices.ca
Spécialités Administratif
Métiers/techniciens
Échelon Intermédiaire
Débutant

KELLY, LES SERVICES
5400, boul. des Galeries, bur. 220
Québec, QC G2K 2B4
Téléphone 418-621-0061
Télécopieur 418-621-5750
Courriel kellys@tactik.com
Site Internet www.kellyservices.ca
Spécialités Comptabilité
Ingénierie
Finance
Échelon Intermédiaire
Débutant
Contact Kathleen Harding

**KELLY PERMANENT
RECRUITMENT**
33 Bloor Street East, Suite 800
Toronto, ON M4W 3H1
Telephone 416-967-3509
Fax 416-967-0051
E-mail ks7629@
kellyservices.com
Website www.kellyservices.ca
Founded 1996
Employees 3
Specialties Sales
Administrative
Accounting
Human Resource
Purchasing
Management
Level Mid-Level
Junior
Min. Salary $28,000
Fee Basis Always contingent
Contact Suzanne Hague,
Branch Manager
Description Kelly Permanent pro-
vides a professional, consistent and
convenient partnership for meeting
full-time placement needs.

KELLY PERMANENT RECRUITMENT
300 Consilium Place, Suite 302
Toronto, ON M1H 3G2

Telephone	416-290-0362
Fax	416-290-0363
E-mail	kelly291@netcom.ca
Website	www.kellyservices.ca
Founded	1996
Employees	3
Specialties	Sales
	Administrative
	Accounting
	Human Resource
	Purchasing
	Management
Level	Mid-Level
	Junior
Min. Salary	$28,000
Fee Basis	Always contingent
Recruiters	Ruth Griffiths
	Jocelyn Ware
Contact	Suzanne Hague,
	Branch Manager

Description Kelly Permanent provides a professional, consistent and convenient partnership for meeting full-time placement needs.

KELLY PERMANENT RECRUITMENT
50 Burhamthorpe Rd. W., Suite 803
Mississauga, ON L5L 2R3

Telephone	905-276-4441
Fax	905-949-9994
E-mail	ks7629@
	kellyservices.com
Website	www.kellyservices.ca
Founded	1996
Employees	5
Specialties	Sales
	Administrative
	Accounting
	Human Resource
	Purchasing
	Management
Level	Mid-Level
	Junior
Min. Salary	$28,000
Fee Basis	Always contingent
Recruiters	Deborah Bertucci
	Dawn Stinson
Contact	Suzanne Hague, Branch Manager

Description Kelly Permanent provides a professional, consistent and convenient partnership for meeting full-time placement needs.

KELLY PROFESSIONAL & TECHNICAL SERVICES
1175 Douglas Street, Suite 900
Victoria, BC V8W 2E1

Telephone	250-384-2121
Fax	250-385-3144
E-mail	ks7120@
	kellyservices.com
Website	www.kellyservices.ca

Specialties	Computing
	Engineering
	Accounting
	Management
Level	Mid-Level
	Junior

Description Kelly Services has been a global leader in the staffing services industry for over 50 years.

KELLY PROFESSIONAL & TECHNICAL SERVICES
555 Burrard Street
Suite 255, Two Bentall Centre
Vancouver, BC V7X 1M7

Telephone	604-669-1236
Fax	604-669-1270
E-mail	ks7111@
	kellyservices.com
Website	www.kellyservices.ca
Specialties	Computing
	Consulting
	Engineering
	Accounting
	Management
Level	Mid-Level
	Junior
Contact	Joan Page, CPC

Description Kelly Services has been a global leader in the staffing services industry for over 50 years.

KELLY PROFESSIONAL & TECHNICAL SERVICES
10020 - 101A Avenue, Suite 850
Edmonton, AB T5J 3G2

Telephone	780-421-7777
Fax	780-426-5355
E-mail	ks7021@
	kellyservices.com
Website	www.kellyservices.com
Specialties	Computing
	Engineering
	Administrative
Level	Junior
	Mid-Level
Contact	Leona Yurkoski

Description Kelly Services has been a global leader in the staffing services industry for over 50 years.

KELLY PROFESSIONAL & TECHNICAL SERVICES
119 - 4th Avenue South, Suite 6
Saskatoon, SK S7K 5X2

Telephone	306-931-4787
Fax	306-934-8847
E-mail	ks7911@
	kellyservices.com
Website	www.kellyservices.ca
Specialties	Computing
	Engineering
Level	Mid-Level

Description Kelly Services has been a global leader in the staffing services industry for over 50 years.

KELLY PROFESSIONAL & TECHNICAL SERVICES
1801 Hamilton Street, Suite 480
Regina, SK S4P 4B4

Telephone	306-359-7449
Fax	306-525-6071
E-mail	ks7920@
	kellyservices.com
Website	www.kellyservices.ca
Specialties	Computing
	Engineering
Level	Mid-Level

Description Kelly Services has been a global leader in the staffing services industry for over 50 years.

KELLY PROFESSIONAL & TECHNICAL SERVICES
240 Graham Avenue
Suite 816, Cargill Building
Winnipeg, MB R3C 0J7

Telephone	204-944-1114
Fax	204-943-1737
E-mail	ks7211@
	kellyservices.com
Website	www.kellyservices.ca
Specialties	Computing
	Engineering
Level	Mid-Level
	Junior

Description Kelly Services has been a global leader in the staffing services industry for over 50 years.

KELLY PROFESSIONAL & TECHNICAL SERVICES
2224 Walker Road, Suite 320
Windsor, ON N8W 3P6

Telephone	519-254-2562
Fax	519-254-1070
E-mail	ks7660@
	kellyservices.com
Website	www.kellyservices.ca
Founded	1969
Employees	12
Specialties	Accounting
	Computing
	Marketing
	Human Resource
	Hospitality
	Health/Medical
	Finance
Level	Mid-Level
	Junior
Contact	Patricia Morris

Description Kelly Services has been a global leader in the staffing services industry for over 50 years.

KELLY PROFESSIONAL & TECHNICAL SERVICES
101 Kiel Drive South, Suite 2
Chatham, ON N7M 3H2

Telephone	519-351-8747
Fax	519-354-5282
E-mail	ks7655@
	kellyservices.com
Website	www.kellyservices.ca

Specialties   Operations
            Accounting
            Engineering
            Computing

Level   Junior
        Mid-Level

Description Kelly Services has been a global leader in the staffing services industry for over 50 years.

KELLY PROFESSIONAL & TECHNICAL SERVICES
380 Wellington Street
City Centre Mall
London, ON N6A 5B5

Telephone   519-673-0345
Fax   519-673-1479
E-mail   kellylon@netcom.ca
Website   www.kellyservices.ca

Specialties   Operations
            Accounting
            Engineering

Level   Junior
        Mid-Level

Description Kelly Services has been a global leader in the staffing services industry for over 50 years.

KELLY PROFESSIONAL & TECHNICAL SERVICES
538 Talbot Street
St. Thomas, ON N5P 1C5

Telephone   519-633-1252
Fax   519-631-7380
Website   www.kellyservices.com

Specialties   Operations
            Accounting
            Engineering
            Computing

Level   Junior
        Mid-Level

Description Kelly Services has been a global leader in the staffing services industry for over 50 years.

KELLY PROFESSIONAL & TECHNICAL SERVICES
44 King Street West, Suite 201
Brantford, ON N3T 3C7

Telephone   519-759-8150
Fax   519-759-6344
E-mail   ks7652@
            kellyservices.com
Website   www.kellyservices.ca

Specialties   Computing
            Engineering
            Accounting
            Management

Level   Mid-Level
        Junior

Description Kelly Services has been a global leader in the staffing services industry for over 50 years.

KELLY PROFESSIONAL & TECHNICAL SERVICES
101 Frederick Street, Scott Tower
Kitchener, ON N2H 6R2

Telephone   519-578-9640
Fax   519-570-4249
E-mail   kelly650@netcom.ca
Website   www.kellyservices.ca

Founded   1946
Employees   25

Specialties   Operations
            Accounting
            Engineering
            Automotive
            Human Resource
            Management
            Computing

Level   Junior
        Mid-Level

Contact   Yvonne Tennenbaum

Description Kelly Services has been a global leader in the staffing services industry for over 50 years.

KELLY PROFESSIONAL & TECHNICAL SERVICES
1400 Bishop Street, Suite 101
Cambridge, ON N1R 6W8

Telephone   519-622-1410
Fax   519-622-3559
E-mail   ks7653@
            kellyservices.com
Website   www.kellyservices.ca

Specialties   Operations
            Accounting
            Engineering

Level   Junior
        Mid-Level

Description Kelly Services has been a global leader in the staffing services industry for over 50 years.

KELLY PROFESSIONAL & TECHNICAL SERVICES
42 Wyndham Street N., Suite 103
Guelph, ON N1H 4E6

Telephone   519-836-6460
Fax   519-767-0523
E-mail   ks7651@
            kellyservices.com
Website   www.kellyservices.ca

Specialties   Operations
            Accounting
            Engineering
            Computing

Level   Junior
        Mid-Level

Description Kelly Services has been a global leader in the staffing services industry for over 50 years.

KELLY PROFESSIONAL & TECHNICAL SERVICES
1 University Avenue, Suite 300
Toronto, ON M5J 2P1

Telephone   416-368-1058
Fax   416-368-3987
Website   www.kellyservices.ca

Specialties   Computing
            Management
            Telecom

Level   Mid-Level
        Junior

Fee Basis   Sometimes contingent

Recruiters   Arnold Chan
            Elly Mrozek
            Steve Oldfield

Contact   Steve Oldfield, Systems
            Manager

Description Kelly Services has been a global leader in the staffing services industry for over 50 years.

KELLY PROFESSIONAL & TECHNICAL SERVICES
33 Bloor Street East, Suite 800
Toronto, ON M4W 3H1

Telephone   416-967-4182
Fax   416-967-4297
E-mail   croftsd@netcom.ca
Website   www.kellyservices.ca

Specialties   Engineering
            Trades/Technicians
            Computing

Description Kelly Services has been a global leader in the staffing services industry for over 50 years.

KELLY PROFESSIONAL & TECHNICAL SERVICES
1120 Finch Avenue West, Suite 105
Downsview, ON M3J 3H7

Telephone   416-650-5617
Fax   416-650-9375
Website   www.kellyservices.ca

Specialties   Engineering
            Computing
            Trades/Technicians

Description Kelly Services has been a global leader in the staffing services industry for over 50 years.

KELLY PROFESSIONAL & TECHNICAL SERVICES
300 Consilium Place
Suites 100 & 303
Toronto, ON M1H 3G2

Telephone   416-290-6790
Fax   416-290-6604
E-mail   ks7695@
            kellyservices.com
Website   www.kellyservices.ca

Specialties   Engineering
            Computing
            Trades/Technicians

Level   Mid-Level
        Junior

Description Kelly Services has been a global leader in the staffing services industry for over 50 years.

KELLY PROFESSIONAL & TECHNICAL SERVICES
4 Hughson Street South, 2nd Floor
Hamilton, ON L8N 3Z1

Telephone   905-525-9422
Fax   905-572-9105
E-mail   ks7612@
            kellyservices.com
Website   www.kellyservices.ca

Specialties   Operations

Accounting	
Engineering	

Level Junior
Mid-Level

Description Kelly Services has been a global leader in the staffing services industry for over 50 years.

KELLY PROFESSIONAL & TECHNICAL SERVICES
3027 Harvester Road, Suite 302
Burlington, ON L7N 3G7

Telephone 905-639-0597
Fax 905-333-0558
Website www.kellyservices.ca

Specialties Computing
Engineering
Accounting
Management

Level Mid-Level
Junior

Description Kelly Services has been a global leader in the staffing services industry for over 50 years.

KELLY PROFESSIONAL & TECHNICAL SERVICES
18 King Street, Suite 6A
Bolton, ON L7E 1E8

Telephone 905-857-9860
Fax 905-857-9554
Website www.kellyservices.ca

Specialties Engineering
Computing
Trades/Technicians

Level Mid-Level
Junior

Description Kelly Services has been a global leader in the staffing services industry for over 50 years.

KELLY PROFESSIONAL & TECHNICAL SERVICES
20 Nelson Street West, Suite 404
Brampton, ON L6X 2M6

Telephone 905-457-7006
Fax 905-450-9632
E-mail ks7666@
kellyservices.com
Website www.kellyservices.ca

Specialties Computing
Engineering
Accounting
Management

Level Mid-Level
Junior

Description Kelly Services has been a global leader in the staffing services industry for over 50 years.

KELLY PROFESSIONAL & TECHNICAL SERVICES
710 Dorval Drive, Suite 105
Oakville, ON L6K 3V7

Telephone 905-842-4402
Fax 905-842-7436
Website www.kellyservices.ca

Specialties Computing
Engineering
Accounting
Management

Level Mid-Level
Junior

Description Kelly Services has been a global leader in the staffing services industry for over 50 years.

KELLY PROFESSIONAL & TECHNICAL SERVICES
17360 Yonge Street, Suite 101
Newmarket, ON L3Y 7R6

Telephone 905-898-3447
Fax 905-898-2350
E-mail ks7615@netcom.ca
Website www.kellyservices.ca

Specialties Engineering
Computing
Trades/Technicians

Level Mid-Level
Junior

Description Kelly Services has been a global leader in the staffing services industry for over 50 years.

KELLY PROFESSIONAL & TECHNICAL SERVICES
7100 Woodbine Avenue, Suite 113
Markham, ON L3R 5J2

Telephone 905-477-5748
Fax 905-477-8205
E-mail ks7696@
kellyservices.com
Website www.kellyservices.ca

Specialties Engineering
Computing
Trades/Technicians

Description Kelly Services has been a global leader in the staffing services industry for over 50 years.

KELLY PROFESSIONAL & TECHNICAL SERVICES
8 Church Street, 3rd Floor
St. Catharines, ON L2R 3B3

Telephone 905-685-7338
Fax 905-687-8611
E-mail kellytem@
mergetel.com
Website www.kellyservices.com

Specialties Operations
Accounting
Engineering
Computing

Level Junior
Mid-Level

Description Kelly Services has been a global leader in the staffing services industry for over 50 years.

KELLY PROFESSIONAL & TECHNICAL SERVICES
419 King St. W., Suite 203
Oshawa Executive Tower
Oshawa, ON L1J 2K5

Telephone 905-434-5425
Fax 905-434-1965
E-mail ks7622@
kellyservices.com
Website www.kellyservices.ca

Specialties Computing
Engineering
Accounting
Management

Level Mid-Level
Junior

Description Kelly Services has been a global leader in the staffing services industry for over 50 years.

KELLY PROFESSIONAL & TECHNICAL SERVICES
257 Pinnacle Street, Suite 101
Belleville, ON K8N 3B2

Telephone 613-962-8647
Fax 613-962-9753
E-mail ks7691@
kellyservices.com
Website www.kellyservices.ca

Specialties Accounting
Computing
Sales
Marketing

Level Mid-Level
Junior

Description Kelly Services has been a global leader in the staffing services industry for over 50 years.

KELLY PROFESSIONAL & TECHNICAL SERVICES
797 Princess Street, Suite 203
Kingston, ON K7L 1G1

Telephone 613-548-3116
Fax 613-548-7527
E-mail ks7692@
kellyservices.com
Website www.kellyservices.ca

Specialties Operations
Accounting
Engineering

Level Junior
Mid-Level

Description Kelly Services has been a global leader in the staffing services industry for over 50 years.

KELLY PROFESSIONAL & TECHNICAL SERVICES
200 Kent Street, Centennial Towers
Ottawa, ON K2P 2J8

Telephone 613-236-5001
Fax 613-230-0130
E-mail ks7630@
kellyservices.com
Website www.kellyservices.ca

Specialties Computing
Administrative
Engineering
Finance
Govt/Nonprofit
Management

Level Mid-Level
Junior

Contact   Laura Landry, Branch
             Manager
Description Kelly Services has been
a global leader in the staffing services industry for over 50 years.

KELLY PROFESSIONAL & TECHNICAL SERVICES
65 Regent Street, Suite 140
Fredericton, NB E3B 7H9

Telephone 506-459-5686
Fax   506-459-5681
Website   www.kellyservices.ca

Specialties Accounting
             Computing
             Engineering
Level   Mid-Level
             Junior

Description Kelly Services has been
a global leader in the staffing services industry for over 50 years.

KELLY PROFESSIONAL & TECHNICAL SERVICES
75 Prince William Street, Suite 405
Saint John, NB E2L 2B2

Telephone 506-658-0285
Fax   506-653-9310
E-mail   kellysvc@nb.aibn.com
Website   www.kellyservices.ca

Specialties Accounting
             Computing
             Engineering
Level   Mid-Level
             Junior
Contact   Maria Jimenez

Description Kelly Services has been
a global leader in the staffing services industry for over 50 years.

KELLY PROFESSIONAL & TECHNICAL SERVICES
633 Main Street, Suite 130
Moncton, NB E1C 9X9

Telephone 506-383-2042
Fax   506-383-2946
E-mail   kellyser@nbnet.nb.ca
Website   www.kellyservices.ca

Specialties Accounting
             Computing
             Engineering
Level   Mid-Level
             Junior

Description Kelly Services has been
a global leader in the staffing services industry for over 50 years.

KELLY PROFESSIONAL & TECHNICAL SERVICES
1809 Barrington Street, Main Floor
Halifax, NS B3J 3K8

Telephone 902-425-8770
Fax   902-466-7990
E-mail   ks7311@
             kellyservices.com
Website   www.kellyservices.ca

Specialties Accounting
             Computing

             Engineering
Level   Mid-Level
             Junior

Contact   Dawn Webb-Titchmarsh

Description Kelly Services has been
a global leader in the staffing services industry for over 50 years.

KELLY SCIENTIFIC RESOURCES
50 Burnhamthorpe Road West
Suite 803
Mississauga, ON L5B 3C2

Telephone 905-949-0428
Fax   905-949-2289
E-mail   ksr7677@
             kellyservices.com
Website   www.kellyservices.ca
Employees 4

Specialties Biotech/Biology
             Pharmaceutical
             Quality Control
             Scientific
Level   Mid-Level
             Senior
Recruiters Kasey Butler
             Paula McKay
Contact   Penny Henderson

Description KSR is the scientific division of Kelly Services, the world's
largest scientific staffing company.
KSR recruits individuals at all levels
in most scientific disciplines.

KELLY SCIENTIFIQUE
110, boul. Crémazie Ouest
Bureau 505
Montréal, QC H2P 1B9

Téléphone 514-388-9779
Télécopieur 514-388-9155
Courriel   ksr7877@
             kellyservices.com
Site Internet www.kellyservices.ca
Employés   2

Spécialités Biotechnologie/biologie
             Pharmaceutique
             Contrôl de qualité
             Scientifique
Échelon   Direction
             Intermédiaire
Contact   Sylvie Grenier,
             Branch Manager

Description Kelly Scientifique, une
division des Services Kelly, est la
plus grande agence de placement
scientifique au monde. Kelly offre
des postes a tous niveaux d'experience dans tous disciplines scientifiques.

KELLY SELECT
2 - 408 Dundas St., Ste. 204, Upper
Woodstock, ON N4S 1B9

Telephone 519-539-0448
Fax   519-421-1232
Website   www.kellyservices.com

Specialties Operations
Level   Mid-Level
             Junior

Contact   Marilyn Moore,
             Branch Manager

KELLY SERVICES
324 - 8th Avenue SW
Suite 700, Home Oil Tower
Calgary, AB T2P 2Z2

Telephone 403-269-2586
Fax   403-269-5976
E-mail   ks7011@
             kellyservices.com
Website   www.kellyservices.ca

Specialties Computing
             Engineering
Level   Mid-Level
             Junior
Contact   Sheila Musgrove,
             Provinicial Manager

Description Kelly Services has been
a global leader in the staffing services industry for over 50 years.

KENNETH MURPHY & ASSOCIATES / KMA
5112 Prince Street
Halifax, NS B3J 1L3

Telephone 902-425-4495
Fax   902-425-6691
E-mail   jobs@kma.ns.ca
Website   www.kma.ns.ca
Founded   1992

Specialties Computing
             Management
             Operations
             Sales
             Finance
             Accounting
Level   Senior
Min. Salary $45,000
Fee Basis Always contingent
Recruiters Karin Dobson
             Kenneth Murphy
Contact   Kenneth Murphy

Description KMA specializes in recruitment for executive and senior
management positions in IT, sales,
marketing, HR and large scale
project staffing.

KENNIFF DENIS INC.
2000 Mansfield, Bureau 1020
Montréal, QC H3A 2Z7

Telephone 514-844-8338
Fax   514-285-5550
E-mail   kenniff@cam.org
Founded   1997
Employees 3

Specialties Banking
             Finance
             Law
             Mining
             Logistics
             Telecom
             Pharmaceutical
Level   Senior
             Mid-Level
Min. Salary $65,000
Fee Basis Retainer Only

Recruiters	Micheline Denis
	Patrick Kenniff
Contact	Micheline Denis

Description Kenniff Denis Inc. is an executive search firm committed to personalized and professional research and recruitment for senior and intermediate management positions.

KENT LEGAL PERSONNEL
2 Lombard Street, Suite 301
Toronto, ON M5C 1M1

Telephone	416-363-8304
Fax	416-363-6125
E-mail	kentlegal@on.aibn.com
Website	www.kent
	personnel.com
Founded	1970
Specialties	Law
Level	Mid-Level
	Junior
Recruiters	Susan Bennett
	Jayne Parish
	Kelly Smith
	Kelly Zarek
Contact	Susan Bennett

Description Kent Legal Personnel specializes in the recruitment of legal staff, including lawyers, paralegals and legal secretaries.

KEY EXECUTIVE CONSULTANTS
47A Collier Street
Barrie, ON L4M 1G7

Telephone	705-737-5603
Fax	705-737-5793
E-mail	csadler@keyexecutive.
	com
Website	www.keyexecutive.com
Founded	1989
Employees	8
Specialties	Automotive
	Design
	Management
	Plastics
	Quality Control
	Human Resource
	Accounting
	Operations
Level	Mid-Level
	Senior
Min. Salary	$60,000
Fee Basis	Retainer Only
Contact	Chris Sadler

Description Specialists in the recruitment and placement of manufacturing, operations, engineering, information systems, sales and financial management professionals.

KEY EXECUTIVE CONSULTANTS
1550 Kingston Road, Suite 215
Pickering, ON L1V 1C3

Telephone	905-831-6788
Fax	905-831-5202
E-mail	keyexec@keyexec.com
Founded	1989
Employees	3

Specialties	Engineering
	Consulting
	Automotive
	Accounting
	Human Resource
	Plastics
	Operations
Level	Mid-Level
	Senior
Fee Basis	Sometimes contingent
Recruiters	Neil McCarthy
	Murray McNeely
	Alan Tomlinson
Contact	Neil McCarthy

Description Specialists in the recruitment and placement of manufacturing, operations, engineering, information systems, sales and financial management professionals.

KEYSTONE SELECT / M.A. HAGGITH CONSULTANTS LTD.
5160 Yonge Street, Suite 810
Toronto, ON M2N 6L9

Telephone	416-229-2527
Fax	416-229-2527
E-mail	jobs@haggith.com
Website	www.haggith.com
Founded	1979
Employees	8
Specialties	Operations
	Marketing
	Pharmaceutical
	General Practice
	Insurance
Level	Mid-Level
	Senior
Min. Salary	$40,000
Fee Basis	Retainer Only
Recruiters	Marvin A. Haggith
	R. Vijh
Contact	R. Vijh

Description Keystone Select / M.A. Haggith Consultants Ltd. provides executive and outplacement services and HR management training.

KFORCE.CA
100 Wellington St. West, Suite 2110
Toronto, ON M5K 1J5

Telephone	416-907-8400
Fax	416-495-6809
E-mail	ooawdo@kforce.com
Website	www.kforce.com
Founded	1962
Employees	12
Specialties	Computing
	Human Resource
	Telecom
Level	Mid-Level
	Senior
Min. Salary	$40,000
Fee Basis	Always contingent
Contact	Michael Mancuso,
	General Manager

Description Kforce is one of North Americas largest IT recruitment and staffing service providers.

KHORASANEE & PARTNERS
48 Longboat Avenue
Toronto, ON M5A 4E3

Telephone	416-350-9684
E-mail	morejobs@
	pathcom.com
Website	www.topechelon.com/
	morejobs
Founded	1991
Specialties	Computing
Level	Mid-Level
	Senior
Contact	Jay Khorasanee,
	Managing Partner

Description K & P specializes in placing candidates regionally, nationally or internationally, rather than locally. Send resumes by email only.

KING MANAGEMENT SEARCH GROUP
11 Nobert Road
Toronto, ON M1T 1C2

Telephone	416-499-8875
Specialties	Accounting
	Finance
Level	Mid-Level
Contact	Stan King

KINGSLEY ALLEN IT SEARCH INC.
2 Bloor Street West
Suite 1720
Toronto, ON M4W 3E2

Telephone	416-969-9001
Fax	416-969-9443
E-mail	jobs@kitsearch.com
Website	www.kitsearch.com
Founded	1995
Employees	4
Specialties	General Practice
	Direct Mktng.
	Management
	Marketing
	Sales
	Telecom
Level	Senior
	Mid-Level
Min. Salary	$70,000
Fee Basis	Retainer Only
Contact	Richard Bélanger

Description Kingsley Allen IT Search specializes in the recruitment of information technology professionals.

KINGSLEY AND ASSOCIATES
145 King Street West
Suite 1000
Toronto, ON M5H 3X6

Telephone	866-444-0114
E-mail	pspencer11@
	hotmail.com
Specialties	Management
Level	Mid-Level
	Senior
Contact	Pauline Spencer

KINGSTON ROSS PASNAK
10104 - 103rd Avenue
3000 Canada Trust Tower
Edmonton, AB T5J 3S4

Telephone	780-424-3000
Fax	780-429-4817
E-mail	brosser@krpgroup.com
Website	www.krpgroup.com
Specialties	Accounting
	Management
	Finance
Level	Mid-Level
Contact	Harold Kingston CA

Description Kingston Ross Pasnak is
a chartered accounting firm that also
does search work for clients.

KIRKPATRICK PERSONNEL LTD.
990 Homer Street , Suite 205
Vancouver, BC V6B 2W7

Telephone	604-682-1171
Fax	604-682-1194
E-mail	get-a-job@
	kirkpatrick.ca
Website	www.kirkpatrick.ca
Specialties	Administrative
	Accounting
	Finance
	Marketing
Level	Senior
	Mid-Level
Fee Basis	Always contingent
Recruiters	Stacey Cecconi
	Karin Kirkpatrick
	Janice MacLean
	Alandra Rayner
	Nancy Temple
Contact	Karin Kirkpatrick

Description Kirkpatrick Personnel
Ltd. is an employment agency serving Vancouver and its surrounding
communities.

KISCHI KONSULTING INC.
1530 Merivale Road
Ottawa, ON K2G 3J7

Telephone	613-231-2777
E-mail	hr@kischi.com
Website	www.kischi.com
Specialties	Computing
Level	Mid-Level
Contact	Maria Mancini

Description Kischi Konsulting Inc. is
an IT consulting firm that also recruits computing professionals for
assignments with the federal government and private sector organizations.

KITCHENER EXECUTIVE
CONSULTANTS
1601 River Road East, Suite 12
Kitchener, ON N2A 3Y4

Telephone	519-894-3030
Fax	519-894-5196
E-mail	kec@golden.net
Website	www.kitchener
	executive.com
Founded	1976
Employees	9
Specialties	Aerospace
	Automotive
	Engineering
	Finance
	Human Resource
	Management
	Operations
	Computing
Level	Senior
	Mid-Level
Min. Salary	$50,000
Fee Basis	Always contingent
Recruiters	Kevin Alger
	Jim Fairfax
	Dave Gent
	Steve Johnston
	Doug MacEachern
	Dave Porter
	Dan Scott
Contact	Stacy Breckles,
	Administrator

Description Kitchener Executive
Consultants are manufacturing industry specialists.

KLASSEN & COMPANY
294 Portage Avenue, Suite 607
Winnipeg, MB R3C 0B8

Telephone	204-949-0755
Specialties	Accounting
	Finance
Level	Mid-Level

Description Klassen & Company is
an accounting firm that does occasional search work for clients.

KNIPPER & ASSOCIATES
852 Purcell Crescent
Kingston, ON K7P 1B9

Telephone	613-634-2476
Fax	613-634-2647
E-mail	cknipper@home.com
Founded	1986
Employees	4
Specialties	Computing
	Engineering
	Health/Medical
	Marketing
	Operations
	Sales
	Pharmaceutical
Level	Mid-Level
	Senior
Min. Salary	$60,000
Fee Basis	Retainer Only
Contact	Carol Knipper

Description Knipper & Associates is
a generalist firm offering personalized attention to every client. Specialists in the US market.

KNV RESULTS MANAGEMENT INC.
15261 Russell Avenue, Suite 300
White Rock, BC V4B 2P7

Telephone	604-536-7614
Fax	604-538-5356
E-mail	results@knv.com
Website	www.knv.com
Founded	1973
Specialties	Accounting
	Finance
Level	Mid-Level
	Senior

Description KNV is an accounting
and consulting firm that also provides recruitment services to clients.

KOCH & ASSOCIATES
5246 Columbia Avenue
Hamburg, NY 14075   USA

Telephone	716-627-5350
Fax	716-627-7545
E-mail	phyrecr@aol.com
Founded	1992
Employees	5
Specialties	Health/Medical
	International
Level	Mid-Level
	Junior
Fee Basis	Sometimes contingent
Contact	Leonard Koch, MBA

Description Specializing in the permanent and locum tenens placement of physicians in all specialties
across the US and Canada.

KONKIN & ASSOCIATES INC.
18415 - 55th Avenue NW
Edmonton, AB T6M 1Y8

Telephone	780-496-3507
Fax	780-496-3511
E-mail	konkin.assoc@
	v-wave.com
Specialties	Management
	Hospitality
Contact	Alan Konkin

Description Konkin & Associates Inc.
is a management consulting firm
that also does recruitment work, often in the gaming industry.

KORN / FERRY INTERNATIONAL
1055 Dunsmuir Street
Four Bentall Centre
Suite 3300, PO Box 49206
Vancouver, BC V7X 1K8

Telephone	604-684-1834
Fax	604-684-1884
E-mail	resumes.vancouver@
	kornferry.com
Website	www.kornferry.com
Founded	1988
Employees	15
Specialties	Computing
	Finance
	Human Resource
	International
	Law
	Marketing
	Govt/Nonprofit
Level	Mid-Level
	Senior
Min. Salary	$90,000
Fee Basis	Retainer Only

Recruiters	Chris J. Bloomer
	Marilyn Crawford
	Kelly Gayford
	W. Michael M. Honey
	W. John McKay
	Terry K. O'Callaghan
	Joanna O'Callaghan
	Martine L. Parent
	Grant Spitz
	Angela Winter
Contact	Grant Spitz

Description Korn / Ferry, with more than 71 offices in over 41 countries, maintains specialty practices in financial services, advanced technology, telecommunications, industrial, life sciences, health care, consumer and professional services.

KORN / FERRY INTERNATIONAL
181 Bay Street, Suite 3320, Box 763
Bay Wellington Tower
Toronto, ON M5J 2T3

Telephone	416-365-1841
Fax	416-365-0851
E-mail	pratzer@pratzer.com
Website	www.pratzer.com
Founded	1989
Employees	21
Specialties	General Practice
	Finance
	Computing
	Real Estate
	Banking
	Telecom
Level	Senior
	Mid-Level
Fee Basis	Retainer Only
Recruiters	Peter Cooper
	Adina Gwartzman
	Valerie Johnson
	John Mealia
	Elan Pratzer
	Jay Rosenzweig
	Tom Summers
	Dov Zevy
Contact	Elan Pratzer

Description Korn / Ferry, with more than 71 offices in over 41 countries, maintains specialty practices in financial services, advanced technology, telecommunications, industrial, life sciences, health care, consumer and professional services.

KORN / FERRY INTERNATIONAL
420, rue McGill, Bureau 400
Montréal, QC H2Y 2G1

Telephone	514-397-9655
Fax	514-397-0410
Website	www.kornferry.com
Founded	1992
Employees	27
Specialties	Management
	Engineering
	Finance
	Human Resource
	Pharmaceutical
	Telecom
	International
Level	Mid-Level
	Senior

Min. Salary	$65,000
Recruiters	Jean-Pierre Bourbonnais
	Yves Champoux
	Ronald Drennan
	François Durand
	Jean-Pierre Lefebvre
	Michel Pinsonneault
Contact	Jean-Pierre Bourbonnais, Managing Director, Quebec

Description Korn/Ferry, with more than 71 offices in over 41 countries, maintains specialty practices in financial services, advanced technology, telecommunications, industrial, life sciences, health care, consumer and professional services.

KORN / FERRY INTERNATIONAL
2102-2106 Gloucester Tower
The Landmark, Central
Hong Kong   CHINA

Telephone	852-2521-5457
Fax	852-2810-1632
E-mail	andrew.tsui@kornferry.com
Website	www.kornferry.com
Specialties	International
	Education
Level	Senior
Contact	Andrew Tsui, Managing Director

Description Korn/Ferry, with more than 71 offices in over 41 countries, maintains specialty practices in financial services, advanced technology, telecommunications, industrial, life sciences, health care, consumer and professional services.

KORN / FERRY INTERNATIONAL
123 Buckingham Palace Road
London, SW1 W9DZ
UNITED KINGDOM

Telephone	44-20-7312-3100
Fax	44-20-7312-3130
E-mail	kfs-london@kornferry.com
Website	www.kornferry.com
Specialties	Management
	International
	Finance
Level	Senior
Recruiters	Kenneth MacLennan
	Mitchell Metin
Contact	Kenneth MacLennan

Description Korn/Ferry, with more than 71 offices in over 41 countries, maintains specialty practices in financial services, advanced technology, telecommunications, industrial, life sciences, health care, consumer and professional services.

KPMG EXECUTIVE SEARCH AND SELECTION
1 Stokes Place, St. Stephen's Green
Dublin 2   IRELAND

Telephone	353-1-410-1000
Fax	353-1-412-1122

E-mail	hr@kpmg.ie
Website	www.kpmg.ie
Specialties	International
	Management
	Govt/Nonprofit
	General Practice
Level	Senior
	Mid-Level
Fee Basis	Retainer Only
Recruiters	Ray Carolan
	John McCullogh
	Jo-Anne Sexton
	Alison Taylor
Contact	John McCullough, Director

Description KPMG Executive Search and Selection works in partnership with clients, to assist them in the successful recruitment and selection of their executives and senior management professionals, across all industry sectors.

KRECKLO CONSULTANTS INTERNATIONAL INC.
2 Bloor Street West, Suite 700
Toronto, ON M4W 3R1

Telephone	800-573-2556
E-mail	toronto@krecklo.com
Website	www.krecklo.com
Specialties	Computing
Level	Mid-Level
Fee Basis	Retainer Only
Recruiters	Wayne Hussey
	Vijay P. Mathur
Contact	Wayne Hussey, Senior Consultant

Description Krecklo Consultants International Inc. is a retained search firm focusing on the information technology and information systems sectors.

KRECKLO CONSULTANTS INTERNATIONAL INC.
1250 Rene-Levesque W., Suite 2200
Montréal, QC H3B 4W8

Telephone	514-281-9999
E-mail	montreal@krecklo.com
Website	www.krecklo.com
Founded	2000
Employees	2
Specialties	Computing
Level	Senior
	Mid-Level
Min. Salary	$45,000
Fee Basis	Retainer Only
Contact	Brian Douglas Krecklo, Managing Director

Description Krecklo Consultants is a retained search firm focusing on the information technology and information systems sectors.

L.S. NOEL CONSULTING LIMITED
162 Mill Pond Court
Richmond Hill, ON L4C 4W5

Telephone	905-770-1517
Fax	905-884-9433
E-mail	lesnoel@home.com
Website	members.home.net/ lesnoel
Founded	1995
Employees	4
Specialties	Computing
Level	Senior Mid-Level
Fee Basis	Sometimes contingent
Contact	Les Noel, President

Description L.S. Noel Consulting Limited is an executive search firm specializing in information technology career placement.

LAB SUPPORT
26651 West Agoura Road
Calabasas, CA 91302 USA

Telephone	800-998-3332
Fax	818-880-5021
E-mail	recruit@ labsupport.com
Website	www.labsupport.com
Founded	1985
Specialties	Scientific International
Level	Mid-Level

Description Lab Support is a scientific staffing company that places professionals in short and long-term assignments to companies nationwide.

LAB SUPPORT CANADA
4170 Still Creek Drive, Suite 200
Burnaby, BC V5C 6C6

Telephone	604-570-0511
Website	www.labsupport.com
Founded	1985
Specialties	Scientific
Level	Mid-Level

Description Lab Support is a scientific staffing company that places professionals in short and long-term assignments to companies nationwide.

LAB SUPPORT CANADA
105 Lexington
Waterloo, ON N2J 4R7

Telephone	519-883-7586
Website	www.labsupport.com
Founded	1985
Specialties	Scientific
Level	Mid-Level

Description Lab Support is a scientific staffing company that places professionals in short and long-term assignments to companies nationwide.

LAB SUPPORT CANADA
2 Sheppard Ave. East., Suite 900
Toronto, ON M2N 5Y7

Telephone	416-221-8914
Website	www.labsupport.com
Founded	1985
Specialties	Scientific
Level	Mid-Level

Description Lab Support is a scientific staffing company that places professionals in short and long-term assignments to companies nationwide.

LAB SUPPORT CANADA
6600 Trans-Canada Hwy.
Pointe-Claire, QC H9R 4S2

Telephone	514-630-2938
Website	www.labsupport.com
Founded	1985
Specialties	Scientific
Level	Mid-Level

Description Lab Support is a scientific staffing company that places professionals in short and long-term assignments to companies nationwide.

LABOR TEK PERSONNEL SERVICES LTD.
1370 Triole Street
Ottawa, ON K1B 3M4

Telephone	613-741-1128
Fax	613-741-1130
E-mail	industrial@ labortek.com
Website	www.labortek.com
Specialties	Trades/Technicians
Level	Mid-Level Junior
Recruiters	Denis Chennette Julie Meilleur Donald Tardif
Contact	Donald Tardif, President

Description Labor Tek Personnel Services Ltd. recruits for positions in the industrial, commercial, institutional (ICI) sector.

LABOUR SOURCE
4140 Steeles Avenue West, Unit 3
Woodbridge, ON L4L 4V3

Telephone	905-264-9675
Fax	905-264-1733
E-mail	general@ laboursource.com
Website	www.laboursource.com
Employees	5
Specialties	Operations Logistics Trades/Technicians
Level	Mid-Level Junior
Contact	George Wittgenstein

Description Labour Source places skilled tradespeople in industrial assignments.

LAING & ASSOCIATES
57 Leuty Avenue
Toronto, ON M4E 2R2

Telephone	416-694-1703
Fax	416-694-2965
E-mail	janice@laingjobs.com
Website	www.laingjobs.com
Specialties	Computing Sales
Contact	Janice Laing

Description Laing & Associates is an executive recruiting firm specializing in software sales.

LALIBERTÉ & ASSOCIÉS RECHERCHE DE CADRES INC.
59, rue St-Charles Ouest
Longueuil, QC J4H 1C5

Téléphone	450-677-3388
Télécopieur	450-677-1630
Spécialités	Généralistes Gestion
Échelon	Direction Intermédiaire

LAMON + STUART + MICHAELS INC.
335 Bay Street, Suite 701
Toronto, ON M5H 2R3

Telephone	416-361-7033
Fax	416-361-0728
E-mail	info@lsm consulting.com
Website	www.lsm consulting.com
Founded	1995
Employees	20
Specialties	General Practice Engineering Finance Actuarial Insurance Management Pharmaceutical
Level	Mid-Level Senior
Fee Basis	Retainer Only
Recruiters	Wayne Lamon Elaine Litwin Bob Stuart
Contact	Bob Stuart

Description LSM is a consulting firm helping companies design more effective workplaces through search, organizational development, workplace learning, outplacement and technology.

LANDMARK CONSULTING GROUP INC.
25 Main Street West, Suite 2225
Hamilton, ON L8P 1H1

Telephone	905-570-8882
E-mail	resumes@landmark consulting.org
Founded	1990
Employees	4
Specialties	General Practice Education

Level   Senior
Min. Salary $100,000
Fee Basis   Retainer Only
Recruiters   Tom Holmes
              Jim Lundy
              Kathy Niziol
              Scott Rowand
Contact   Jim Lundy

LANDON MORGAN INC.
3350 Merrittville Highway
Suite 12, Schmon Place
Thorold, ON L2V 4Y6

Telephone   905-641-2476
Fax   905-641-2735
E-mail   team@landon
              morgan.com
Website   www.landon
              morgan.com

Founded   1992
Employees   5
Specialties   Accounting
              Computing
              Engineering
              Finance
              Operations
              Purchasing
              Automotive
Level   Senior
              Mid-Level
Min. Salary $25,000
Recruiters   Heather Chandler
              Don Hetherington
              Charlie Nalezinski
              Traci Polak
              Vince Polce
Contact   Don Hetherington

Description Landon Morgan screens and recruits salaried staff for their clients.

LANNICK ASSOCIATES
20 Queen Street West, Suite 1500
Toronto, ON M5H 3R3

Telephone   416-340-1500
Fax   416-340-1344
E-mail   lannick@lannick.com
Website   www.lannick.com

Employees   17
Specialties   Accounting
              Finance
Level   Senior
              Mid-Level
Recruiters   Bob Campkin
              Marilyn Eddy
              Joanne Elek
              Celia Featherby
              Daphne Fernandes
              Janet McAlpine
              Lance Osborne
              Lynn Stivaletti
              Janet Webb
Contact   Lance Osborne,
              President

Description Lannick Associates is an executive search firm specializing in the recruitment of financial professionals and executives, with particular emphasis on chartered accountants.

LARKIN GROUP, THE
10 Kingsbridge Garden Circle
Suite 704
Mississauga, ON L5R 3K6

Telephone   905-502-3475
Fax   905-502-3461
E-mail   slarkin@interlog.com

Founded   1998
Employees   4
Specialties   Accounting
              Finance
Level   Senior
              Mid-Level
Min. Salary $55,000
Fee Basis   Always contingent
Recruiters   Tracy Creelman
              Susan Larkin
Contact   Susan Larkin, CA, MBA

Description The Larkin Group is an executive search firm specializing in placing accounting and finance professionals in the $55,000 - $125,000 annual salary range.

LAROUCHE & ASSOCIATES
1405 TransCanada Hwy., Suite 200
Dorval, QC H9P 2V9

Telephone   514-683-4303
Fax   514-683-8644
E-mail   r.larouche@qc.aira.com

Specialties   Accounting
              Computing
Contact   Rene Larouche

LARSON & ASSOCIATES RECRUITMENT SERVICES
250 - 6th Avenue SW
Suite 600, Bow Valley Square IV
Calgary, AB T2P 3H7

Telephone   403-705-5377
Fax   403-705-5366
E-mail   submit-resume@
              your-headhunter.com
Website   www.your-
              headhunter.com
Founded   1991
Specialties   Administrative
Level   Mid-Level
              Junior
Fee Basis   Always contingent
Contact   Colleen M. Larson

Description Larson & Associates is a recruiting agency specializing in permanent placement in the areas of customer service, administration, office clerical, accounting, finance, sales, marketing and management.

LAURA REID & ASSOCIATES LTD.
808 Nelson Street, Suite 1730
Vancouver, BC V6Z 2H2

Telephone   604-684-8447
Fax   604-685-8993
Specialties   Law
Level   Mid-Level
              Senior
Contact   Laura Reid

LAWRENCE ASSOCIATES EXECUTIVE SEARCH INC.
145 King Street West, Suite 1000
Toronto, ON M5H 1J8

Telephone   416-941-9371
Fax   416-941-1086
E-mail   phil@lawrence-
              search.com
Founded   1988
Employees   3
Specialties   Finance
              Banking
              Geology/Geography
              Human Resource
              Mining
Level   Senior
              Mid-Level
Fee Basis   Sometimes contingent
Contact   Phillip Lawrence

Description Lawrence Associates Executive Search Inc. is a search practice focused on recruiting professional staff and senior management for the financial services industry.

LAWRENCE JOE CONSULTANTS INC.
271 Finch Avenue E.
Toronto, ON M2N 4S3

Telephone   416-250-5677
Fax   416-250-6119
Employees   2
Specialties   Computing
              Sales
              Marketing
Contact   Lawrence Joe

Description Placements in software and electronics, technical sales and marketing.

LEADER SEARCH INC.
44 Barclay Walk SW
Calgary, AB T2P 4V9

Telephone   403-262-8545
Fax   403-262-8549
E-mail   recruiting@
              leadersearch.com
Website   www.leadersearch.com
Founded   1991
Employees   7
Specialties   Oil & Gas
              Operations
              Finance
              Geology/Geography
              Management
              Accounting
              General Practice
Level   Mid-Level
Fee Basis   Retainer Only
Recruiters   R.W. (Bob) Johnson
              Maureen Kelsey
              Kendra Koss
              Todd Reed
              Dickson Wood
Contact   R.W. (Bob) Johnson,
              President

Description Leader Search Inc. is a retainer firm specializing in fitting right character candidates to the right culture organization.

LECOURS WOLFSON LIMITED
116 Spadina Avenue, Suite 700
Toronto, ON M5V 2K6

Telephone	416-703-5482
Fax	416-703-5486
E-mail	jobs@lecours wolfson.com
Website	www.lecours wolfson.com
Founded	1979
Specialties	Hospitality Retail
Level	Mid-Level Senior
Recruiters	Brent Alkema Jeff Canning Peter Danakas Douglas Harb Peter Howley John Labun Sharon Lee Angelo Panousis Jordan Romoff Norm Wolfson
Contact	Norm Wolfson

Description Lecours, Wolfson is North America's leading recruiter of hospitality managers, chefs and executives.

LEFCORT ENGEL
5165 Queen Mary Road, Suite 400
Montréal, QC H3W 1X7

Telephone	514-481-1121
Fax	514-481-1411
E-mail	rengel@lefcortengel.ca
Specialties	Accounting Finance
Level	Mid-Level
Contact	R. Engel, CA

Description Lefcort Engel is an accounting firm that also does occasional search work for clients.

LEGAL FREELANCE CENTRE
900 West Georgia Street
Suite 1607, Hotel Vancouver
Vancouver, BC V6C 2W6

Telephone	604-689-5476
Fax	604-689-5171
E-mail	legalfreelance@ datapark.com
Website	www.mybc.com/ legal_freelance
Specialties	Law
Level	Mid-Level Junior
Contact	Betty Garbutt, CHRP

Description Legal Freelance Centre specializes in the placement of legal assistants and paralegals.

LEGAL PERSONNEL CONSULTANTS INC.
20 Adelaide Street East, Suite 920
Toronto, ON M5C 2T6

Telephone	416-955-9035
Fax	416-955-9204
Founded	1969
Specialties	Law
Level	Mid-Level
Contact	Lila Kaegi

Description Legal Personnel Consultants Inc. is a recruitment agency for legal support staff.

LEHMOR ASSOCIATES
1745 Edouard Laurin
Saint-Laurent, QC H4L 5E9

Telephone	514-856-1109
Fax	514-856-1139
E-mail	ldl@total.net
Specialties	Accounting Finance
Level	Mid-Level

Description Lehmor Associates is an accounting firm that also does search work for clients.

LENARD KAY & ASSOCIATES (1993) INC.
2154 Brays Lane
Oakville, ON L6M 3J7

Telephone	905-847-3778
Fax	905-847-8824
E-mail	lenkay@home.com
Founded	1987
Specialties	Computing
Level	Senior Mid-Level
Fee Basis	Always contingent
Contact	Lenard Kay

Description Lenard Kay & Associates places AS/400 professionals (programmer/analysts, systems analysts, business analysts, managers) on a permanent and contract basis.

LENVIL INDUSTRIES LTD.
2102 Dalecroft Cr.
Burlington, ON L7M 4B3

Telephone	905-331-2691
E-mail	lenvil@idirect.com
Founded	1988
Employees	2
Specialties	Plastics
Level	Senior Mid-Level
Min. Salary	$40,000
Fee Basis	Sometimes contingent
Contact	Dr. Leno Braida, P.Eng.

Description Lenvil Industries Ltd. places technical personnel within the plastics industry.

LEPAGE INTERNATIONAL INC.
800, boul. René-Lévesque O.
Bureau 2450
Montréal, QC H3B 4V7

Téléphone	514-876-9876
Télécopieur	514-879-0797
Courriel	resume@ lepageintl.com
Site Internet	www.jacques lepage.com
Fondée	1990
Employés	6
Spécialités	Comptabilité Aérospatial Biotechnologie/biologie Ingénierie Finance Métaux Exploitation Pharmaceutique Papeterie Télécommunications
Échelon	Direction Intermédiaire
Salaire min.	60 000 $
Frais	Honoraire seulement
Contact	Jacques LePage, President

LESLEY VARGA AND ASSOCIATES
100 Adelaide Street West, Suite 410
Toronto, ON M5H 1S3

Telephone	416-865-9944
Fax	416-693-2550
E-mail	l.varga@sympatico.ca
Specialties	Computing
Level	Senior Mid-Level
Fee Basis	Sometimes contingent
Recruiters	Julie Tuer Lesley Varga
Contact	Lesley Varga, President

Description Lesley Varga and Associates recruits mid and high-level IT positions.

LESLIE CORPORATION, THE
10700 North Freeway, Suite 670
Houston, TX 77037
USA

Telephone	281-591-0915
Fax	281-591-0921
E-mail	tlc@lesliecorp.com
Website	www.lesliecorp.com
Founded	1977
Specialties	International Oil & Gas Engineering
Level	Mid-Level

Description The Leslie Corporation specializes in oil & gas placements in the Middle East.

LETZLER & ASSOCIATES
10 King Street E., Suite 1400
Toronto, ON M5C 1C3

Telephone	416-366-8100
Fax	416-366-7086
Specialties	Insurance
Contact	Helene Letzler

LEVEL A INC.
277 George Street North, Suite 212
Peterborough, ON K9J 3G9

Telephone	705-749-1919
Fax	705-749-5494
E-mail	levela@cgocable.net
Founded	1988
Employees	4
Specialties	Quality Control
	Packaging
	Engineering
	Computing
	Logistics
	Govt/Nonprofit
	Trades/Technicians
	Administrative
Level	Mid-Level
	Senior
Fee Basis	Sometimes contingent
Recruiters	Nancy Flatt
	Kathy Pyle
Contact	Kathy Pyle, President

Description Level A Inc., a licensed distributor and facilitator of Carlson and TTI Performance Systems DiSC profiles, performs prequalification, behaviour profiling and placement services.

LEVERT PERSONNEL RESOURCES INC.
119 Pine Street, Suite 1
Timmins, ON P4N 2K3

Telephone	705-268-0808
Fax	705-268-3773
E-mail	info@levert.ca
Website	www.levert.ca
Specialties	Mining
	Govt/Nonprofit
	Engineering
Level	Mid-Level
Contact	Paul Laverdière

Description Levert Personnel (formerly Nortemp Staffing Services) has been providing staffing and recruitment services to northern Ontario mining and government businesses for over 16 years.

LEVERT PERSONNEL RESOURCES INC.
1771 Old Falconbridge Road
PO Box 2727, Station A
Sudbury, ON P3A 5J2

Telephone	705-525-8367
Fax	705-525-2451
E-mail	info@levert.ca
Website	www.levert.ca
Specialties	Engineering
	Mining
	Govt/Nonprofit
Level	Mid-Level
Recruiters	Rich Harper
	Julie Lacroix
	Mark Landry
	Mark J. Leclair
	Richard Levert
	Roger Levert
	Judy Polano
	Victor Richer
	Barb Young
Contact	Richard Levert

Description Levert Personnel (formerly Nortemp Staffing Services) has been providing staffing and recruitment services to northern Ontario mining and government businesses for over 16 years.

LEVTON GROUP INC., THE
140 Symington Avenue
Toronto, ON M6P 3W4

Telephone	416-532-0161
Fax	416-532-5832
E-mail	info@levton.com
Website	www.levton.com
Founded	1989
Employees	3
Specialties	Computing
	Accounting
	Management
	Operations
	Sales
	Health/Medical
	Multimedia
Level	Senior
	Mid-Level
Fee Basis	Sometimes contingent
Recruiters	K. Nick Breaks
	Wayne Lewis
	Don McLeod
Contact	K. Nick Breaks, Principal

Description Levton Group Inc. is a full-service human resource bureau providing consultant services, including recruitment, salary administration, outplacement and employee relations.

LEVY PILOTTE
5250 Decarie Blvd., 7th Floor
Montréal, QC H3X 3Z6

Telephone	514-487-1566
Fax	514-488-5145
E-mail	rguirgui@levypilotte.com
Website	www.levypilotte.com
Specialties	Accounting
	Finance
Level	Mid-Level
Recruiters	Johnny Colonna CA
	Raouf Guirguis CA
	Martin Rohr CA
Contact	Raouf Guirguis, CA

Description Levy Pilotte is an accounting firm that occasionally does search work for clients.

LEWIS & ASSOCIATES
777 Dunsmuir Street, Suite 1850
Vancouver, BC V5K 2B0

Telephone	604-683-6400
Fax	604-683-6440
E-mail	lewis@tdgstaff.com
Website	www.tdgstaff.com/pgc/lewis.html
Specialties	General Practice
Level	Mid-Level
	Junior

Description Lewis & Associates is a general placement agency recruiting both administrative and technical positions for office and manufacturing clients.

LEWIS COMPANIES INC.
162 Cumberland Street, Suite 305
Toronto, ON M5R 3N5

Telephone	416-929-1506
Fax	416-929-8470
E-mail	info@lewiscos.com
Website	www.lewiscos.com
Founded	1989
Employees	14
Specialties	Engineering
	Finance
	Telecom
	Operations
	Govt/Nonprofit
	Health/Medical
	Human Resource
Level	Senior
Min. Salary	$80,000
Fee Basis	Retainer Only
Recruiters	Anita Bhalla
	Ann Curran
	Chantal Haas
	Michelle Hughes
	Lorraine Lewis
	Rhonda Robillard
Contact	Lorraine Lewis, Managing Partner

Description Lewis Companies Inc. is an executive search practice, with clients representing some of the world's foremost employers and an international network of corporate contacts and professional affiliations.

LICARI & VITANZA ASSOCIATES INC.
16 Elm Place
Rye, NY 10580 USA

Fax	914-921-0078
E-mail	mv@lv123.com
Website	www.lv123.com
Specialties	International
	Accounting
	Finance
Level	Mid-Level
	Senior
Contact	Michael Vitanza

Description Licari & Vitanza Associates is a full-service recruiting firm specializing in accounting and finance professionals within Fairfield County, Westchester County and New York City.

LIFE AFTER LAW
355 Burrard Street
Suite 1000, Marine Building
Vancouver, BC V6C 2G8

Telephone	604-216-6785
Fax	604-216-6787
E-mail	info@lifeafterlaw.com
Website	www.lifeafterlaw.com
Specialties	Law

Level Mid-Level
Senior

Description Life After Law specializes in placing former lawyers in
careers outside the traditional practice of law.

LIFE AFTER LAW
2 St. Clair Avenue East, Suite 800
Toronto, ON M4T 2T5

Telephone 416-789-1444
Fax 416-789-4114
E-mail info@lifeafterlaw.com
Website www.lifeafterlaw.com

Founded 2000

Specialties Law

Level Mid-Level
Senior

Fee Basis Always contingent

Contact Randi Bean, Director

Description Life After Law specializes in placing former lawyers in
careers outside the traditional practice of law.

LINDA WALTER & ASSOCIÉS
291 Montée Sagala
Île-Perrot, QC J7V 3C8

Telephone 514-425-7000
E-mail cicson@total.net

Founded 1983

Specialties Finance
Accounting
Computing
Management
Engineering
Marketing
Administrative

Level Mid-Level
Senior

Contact Linda Cicuta

LINE 1000 PLACEMENT SERVICES
1355 Bank Street, Suite 209
Ottawa, ON K1H 8K7

Telephone 613-526-1000
Fax 613-731-3510
E-mail placement@line1000.ca
Website www.line1000.ca

Founded 1979
Employees 14

Specialties Disabled

Level Mid-Level
Junior

Fee Basis Retainer Only

Recruiters Rob Daly
Denise Kelly

Contact Madeline Kelly

Description Provides employment
services for people with disabilities,
including case management, job development and employment support.

LINK CONSULTING
1275 - 6th Avenue West, Suite 302
Vancouver, BC V6H 1A6

Telephone 604-732-5012
Fax 604-738-7134
E-mail sunnyk@link
consulting.com
Website www.link
consulting.com

Founded 1986
Employees 2

Specialties Computing

Level Mid-Level
Senior

Recruiters Andrew J. Fitzpatrick
Sunny L. Kae

Contact Andrew J. Fitzpatrick

Description Link Consulting specializes in placing IT professionals in
contract opportunities with clients
in British Columbia.

LINK RESOURCE PARTNERS
225 Sheppard Avenue West
Toronto, ON M2N 1N2

Telephone 416-224-5465
Fax 416-224-5450
E-mail resume@
linksearch.com
Website www.linksearch.com

Specialties Sales
Marketing
Computing

Level Senior

Recruiters Blake Atto
Jack Buzaglo
Roy Murad
Lemore Naveh
George Scodras
Sonja Sellors

Contact Roy Murad

Description Link Resource Partners
is a leader among Canada's executive recruitment firms, providing
quality service for clients and candidates through a professional, innovative and ethical approach.

LINTEX COMPUTER GROUP INC.
1280 Finch Avenue West, Suite 312
Toronto, ON M3J 3K6

Telephone 416-663-0900
Fax 416-663-7315
E-mail jobs@lintexgroup.com
Website www.lintexgroup.com

Founded 1981

Specialties Computing

Level Senior
Mid-Level

Fee Basis Always contingent

Contact Jas Mann, President &
CEO

Description Lintex Computer Group
Inc. specializes in placing IT professionals in contract assignments and
permanent positions across Ontario.

LIPTON WISEMAN
245 Fairview Mall Drive, Suite 600
Toronto, ON M2J 4T1

Telephone 416-496-2900
Fax 416-496-0559
E-mail fred@lwap.com
Website www.liptonca.com

Employees 48

Specialties Accounting
Finance

Level Mid-Level

Recruiters Stephen Altbaum
Fred Arshoff
Mel Leiderman

Contact Stephen Altbaum,
Partner

Description Lipton Wiseman is a
chartered accounting firm that also
does occasional recruitment work
for clients.

LITTLE GROUP, THE
442 Grey Street, Ste F
Brantford, ON N3S 7N3

Telephone 519-758-2663
Fax 519-758-2667
E-mail apply@littlegroup.com
Website www.littlegroup.com

Founded 1993
Employees 4

Specialties Accounting
Human Resource
Management
Operations
Administrative
Finance
Quality Control

Level Mid-Level

Recruiters Laura Davis
Angela McCarron CPC

Contact Angela McCarron, CPC,
Branch Manager

Description The Little Group is a
staffing and human resource specialist for executive search, permanent,
contract and opportunities.

LITTLE GROUP, THE
720 Guelph Line, Suite LL104
Burlington, ON L7R 4E2

Telephone 905-333-5901
Fax 905-333-5887
E-mail info@littlegroup.com
Website www.littlegroup.com

Founded 1993
Employees 4

Specialties Accounting
Human Resource
Management
Operations
Administrative
Finance
Quality Control

Level Mid-Level

Recruiters Karen Blackburn
David Booth
Gail F. Citroen
Marilyn Dalgleish
Judy Dulovic
Jim Giddens
Peggy Martens
Dave Martens
Larry Potter

Ben Scipione
Leslie Young

Contact Gail Citroen CPC CIPC, President

Description The Little Group is a staffing and human resource specialist for executive search, permanent, contract and opportunities.

LIZ YORKE & ASSOCIATES
96 Sherwood Avenue, Suite 202
Toronto, ON M4P 2A7

Telephone 416-481-4096
Fax 416-487-4048
E-mail lizyorke@interlog.com
Specialties Health/Medical
Level Mid-Level

Description Liz Yorke & Associates is a consulting firm that recruits people in the healthcare field.

LJB & COMPANY
144 Liverpool Road, The Maples
London N1 1LA
UNITED KINGDOM

Telephone 44-207-609-7769
Fax 44-207-607-7378
E-mail andy@ljbrecruit.com
Specialties Construction
International
Contact John Harris

Description LJB & Company are construction recruitment specialists.

LMR CONSULTANTS
180 Steeles Avenue West, Suite 223
Thornhill, ON L4J 2L1

Telephone 905-889-3445
Fax 905-889-9552
E-mail marcie@lmr consultantsinc.com
Founded 1985
Employees 4
Specialties Sales
Marketing
Administrative
Accounting
Contact Marcie Pollack

Description LMR Consultants is an HR consulting firm.

LOBO CONSULTING SERVICES INC.
2070 The Chase
Mississauga, ON L5N 2V7

Telephone 905-820-9970
Specialties Govt/Nonprofit

LOCK & ASSOCIATES
1040 West Georgia Street
Suite 1770, Grosvenor Building
Vancouver, BC V6E 4H1

Telephone 604-669-8806
Fax 604-669-5385
E-mail mpalmer@lock-associates.com
Website www.lock-associates.com

Founded 1983
Employees 6
Specialties Sales
Marketing
Operations
Level Mid-Level
Senior
Fee Basis Sometimes contingent
Recruiters Andrew Jones
Bruce MacDonald
Dan O'Day
Mike Palmer
Debbie Popeniuk
Allan Welyk
Melanie Winch
Contact Mike Palmer

Description Lock & Associates is Western Canada's largest recruitment firm, specializing primarily in sales and marketing.

LOCK & ASSOCIATES
10180 - 101st Street
Suite 1810, Manulife Place
Edmonton, AB T5J 3S4

Telephone 780-429-9044
Fax 780-424-1806
E-mail gjohnson@lock-associates.com
Website www.lock-associates.com
Specialties Sales
Marketing
Level Mid-Level
Senior
Fee Basis Sometimes contingent
Recruiters Greig Johnson
Glenn W.J. Lesko
Contact Greig Johnson

Description Lock & Associates is Western Canada's leading sales, marketing, finance and management search firm.

LOCK & ASSOCIATES
400 - 3rd Ave. SW, Suite 1500
Calgary, AB T2P 4H2

Telephone 403-234-8500
Fax 403-234-8503
E-mail crusynyk@lock-associates.com
Website www.lock-associates.com
Specialties Marketing
Sales
Level Mid-Level
Senior
Recruiters David McCorkill
Chris Rusynyk
Peter Sheehan
Contact David McCorkill

Description Lock & Associates is a leading sales, marketing and management search firm in Canada.

LOCK & ASSOCIATES
410 - 22nd Street East, Suite 480
Saskatoon, SK S7K 5T6

Telephone 306-244-2000
Fax 306-244-0087
E-mail gmattocks@lock-associates.com
Website www.lock-associates.com
Specialties Sales
Marketing
Level Mid-Level
Senior
Fee Basis Sometimes contingent
Contact Gary Mattocks

Description Lock & Associates is Western Canada's leading sales, marketing, finance and management search firm.

LOCK & ASSOCIATES
201 Portage Avenue
Suite 1106, TD Centre
Winnipeg, MB R3B 3K6

Telephone 204-987-3744
Fax 204-987-3745
E-mail gmattocks@ lock-associates.com
Website www.lock-associates.com
Employees 2
Specialties Management
Marketing
Sales
Level Mid-Level
Senior
Fee Basis Sometimes contingent
Recruiters Ray Beaudry
Gary Mattocks
Contact Gary Mattocks

Description Lock & Associates is Western Canada's premier executive search firm specializing in the placement of sales and marketing professionals at all levels.

LOCK & ASSOCIATES
10 Four Seasons Place, Suite 902
Toronto, ON M9B 6H7

Telephone 416-626-8383
Fax 416-626-6609
E-mail emead@ lock-associates.com
Website www.lock-associates.com
Specialties Sales
Marketing
Management
Level Senior
Mid-Level
Recruiters Andy Bennett
Todd Bourgon
Kristy Boyd
Richard Lock
Steven Marshall
Ed Mead
David Mitchell
Karen Paquette
Peter Zukow
Contact Richard Lock

Description Lock & Associates is Canada's only national executive search firm specializing in the placement of sales, marketing and management professionals.

LOCK & ASSOCIATES
1800 McGill College Ave., 30th Fl.
Montréal, QC H3A 3J6

Telephone	514-866-2121
Fax	514-866-5257
E-mail	dnadeau@lock-associates.com
Website	www.lock-associates.com
Specialties	Sales
	Marketing
Level	Mid-Level
	Senior
Fee Basis	Sometimes contingent
Contact	Denis Nadeau

Description Lock & Associates is Canada's only national executive search firm specializing in the placement of sales, marketing and management professionals.

LOCK & ASSOCIATES
633 Main Street, Suite 650
Moncton, NB E1C 9X9

Telephone	506-389-7835
Fax	506-389-7801
E-mail	gobrien@ lock-associates.com
Website	www.lock-associates.com
Specialties	Sales
	Marketing
Level	Mid-Level
	Senior
Fee Basis	Sometimes contingent
Contact	Greg O'Brien

Description Lock & Associates is Western Canada's premier executive search firm specializing in the placement of sales and marketing professionals at all levels.

LOCK & ASSOCIATES
1969 Upper Water St., Suite 2200
Halifax, NS B3J 3R7

Telephone	902-491-4491
Fax	902-429-4327
E-mail	gobrien@lock-associates.com
Website	www.lock-associates.com
Specialties	Sales
	Marketing
Level	Mid-Level
	Senior
Fee Basis	Sometimes contingent
Contact	Greg O'Brien

Description Lock & Associates is Western Canada's premier executive search firm specializing in the placement of sales and marketing professionals at all levels.

LOCUM GROUP, THE
56 Glen Manor Drive
Toronto, ON M4E 2X2

Telephone	416-690-2755
Fax	416-690-2755
E-mail	jobs@locumgroup.com
Website	www.locumgroup.com
Specialties	Education
	Health/Medical
	International
Contact	Larry MacNeil

Description The Locum Group places professionals in the UK in the following fields: nurses, doctors, physiotherapists, scientists, social workers and teachers.

LOGISTIC SOLUTIONS, INC.
200 Centennial Avenue
Piscataway, NJ 08854
USA

Telephone	732-457-0015
Fax	732-457-0016
E-mail	info@ logistic-solutions.com
Website	www.logistic-solutions.com
Founded	1990
Specialties	Telecom
	Finance
	Pharmaceutical
	International
Level	Mid-Level

Description Logistic Solutions, Inc. is a staffing services firm that provides contract and permanent placement services for the telecom, finance, pharmaceutical and wireless markets.

LONDON EXECUTIVE CONSULTANTS
380 Wellington Street, Suite 1420
London, ON N6A 5B5

Telephone	519-434-9167
Fax	519-434-6318
E-mail	info@london executive.com
Website	www.london executive.com
Founded	1976
Employees	7
Specialties	Automotive
	Engineering
	Metals
	Plastics
	Human Resource
	Management
	Accounting
	Finance
	Computing
	Purchasing
	Operations
Level	Senior
	Mid-Level
Min. Salary	$40,000
Fee Basis	Sometimes contingent
Recruiters	Daniel Bennett
	David Irons
	Michael Marshman

Paul R. Nelson
Ted Wilson

Contact	Michael Marshman,
	Senior Consultant

Description A division of O.E.M. Search International, London Executive Consultants specializes in the search and placement of candidates for the manufacturing and engineering sectors.

LORNE SEAMAN & ASSOCIATES
10611 - 90 Avenue NW
Suite 1002, Park Plaza
Edmonton, AB T5K 2P7

Telephone	780-420-0799
Fax	780-424-0199
E-mail	lorne@oanet.com
Founded	1985
Specialties	Management
	Operations
Level	Mid-Level
Contact	Dr. Lorne Seaman

LOUISE ROBINSON PLACEMENT SERVICES / LRPS
RR #2
Keene, ON K0L 2G0

Telephone	705-295-4464
Fax	705-295-6100
E-mail	lrps@recruitersnet.com
Website	www.recruitersnet.com
Founded	1976
Specialties	Engineering
	Operations
	Management
	Purchasing
	Scientific
	Pharmaceutical
	Packaging
Level	Mid-Level
	Senior
Min. Salary	$40,000
Fee Basis	Always contingent
Contact	Louise Robinson

Description For over 20 years, LRPS has specialized in recruiting manufacturing and engineering professionals for Canada's leading food and pharmaceutical firms.

LOUISE SIDKY & ASSOCIATES
7 Valleyanna Drive
Toronto, ON M4N 1J7

Telephone	416-488-8100
Fax	416-486-5300
E-mail	lsidky@msn.com
Specialties	General Practice
Contact	Louise Sidky, President

Description Louise Sidky & Assoc. is a management consulting firm that also does recruitment work.

LTV & ASSOCIATES INC.
26 Renova Drive
Toronto, ON M9C 3E9

Telephone	416-626-1437

Fax	416-695-2689
E-mail	ltvinc@ltvinc.com
Founded	1991
Employees	4
Specialties	Printing
	Graphic Arts
	Packaging
	Advertising
	Design
	Publishing/Media
	Multimedia
Level	Senior
	Mid-Level
Min. Salary	$36,000
Fee Basis	Sometimes contingent
Recruiters	Gerald A. Fruehwirth
	Linda Turnbull-Vezina
Contact	Linda Turnbull-Vezina

Description LTV & Associates Inc. specializes in placements in the graphic arts industry.

LUCIE DOMINGUE ET ASSOCIÉS INC.
3845, La Vérendrye
Sherbrooke, QC J1L 1W8

Telephone	819-823-8939
Fax	819-823-2357
E-mail	lucied@microtec.net
Founded	1990
Employees	2
Specialties	Human Resource
	Management
	Administrative
Contact	Marie-Andrée Houle

Description Lucie Domingue et associés specializes in human resources management, organizational development and executive and administrative recruitment.

LUDLOW PROJECT SERVICES, INC. / LPS
603 Argus Road, Suite 202
Oakville, ON L6J 6G6

Telephone	905-338-0064
Fax	905-338-0758
E-mail	projects@ludlowtec.com
Website	www.ludlowtec.com
Founded	1993
Employees	4
Specialties	Construction
	Consulting
	Engineering
	Management
	Metals
	Oil & Gas
	Pulp & Paper
Level	Senior
	Mid-Level
Min. Salary	$40,000
Fee Basis	Sometimes contingent
Recruiters	Cheri Brown
	Maurice Hunt CCE
Contact	Maurice Hunt, CCE, President

Description LPS specializes in providing staffing in project control, cost estimating, cost control, planning and scheduling in heavy industries.

LUNA SOURCE, INC.
2801 Southwest 31st Avenue
Suite 2B
Coconut Grove, FL 33133
USA

Telephone	305-774-6088
Fax	305-774-6087
E-mail	recruiting@lunasource.com
Website	www.lunasource.com
Specialties	Computing
	Multimedia
	International
Level	Mid-Level

Description Luna Source, Inc. is a full service search, recruiting and professional placement firm that focuses on technology placements for the South Florida marketplace.

LUSSIER EXECUTIVE SEARCH INC.
Exchange Tower, Suite 1800
130 King Street West, PO Box 427
Toronto, ON M5X 1E3

Telephone	416-860-6236
Fax	416-945-6604
E-mail	helene.lussier@sympatico.ca
Founded	1999
Specialties	Finance
	Banking
	Accounting
	Insurance
Level	Senior
	Mid-Level
Min. Salary	$65,000
Fee Basis	Sometimes contingent
Contact	Hélène P. Lussier

Description Lussier Executive Search specializes in finance and risk management recruitment for various industry sectors.

LYNNE MILETTE & ASSOCIATES LTD.
PO Box 9
Chapeau, QC J0X 1M0

Telephone	819-689-5202
Fax	819-689-2825
Founded	1979
Specialties	Sales
	Engineering
	Management
	Marketing
Level	Mid-Level
Min. Salary	$25,000
Fee Basis	Sometimes contingent
Contact	Lynne C. Milette

Description Lynne Milette & Associates has a 20 year track record in recruiting sales / management professionals, with emphasis on Ontario, Quebec, USA and start-ups.

LYNX CAREER CONSULTANTS INC.
4283 Village Centre Court
Mississauga, ON L4Z 1S2

Telephone	905-897-5969
Fax	905-897-5995
E-mail	opportunities@lynxcareers.com
Website	www.lynxcareers.com
Specialties	Accounting
	Finance
	Sales
	Marketing
	Human Resource
	Computing
	Administrative
Level	Mid-Level
	Junior
Recruiters	Nina Adamo
	Krista Dolbec
	Lianne Hall
Contact	Lianne Hall

Description Lynx Career Consultants Inc. is an employment agency focusing on permanent career opportunities throughout the Ontario region.

LYONS, BLACK + ASSOCIATES
666 Burrard Street, Suite 1300
Vancouver, BC V6C 2X8

Telephone	604-638-2561
Fax	604-241-4259
E-mail	alyons@lyonsblack.com
Website	www.lyonsblack.com
Founded	1992
Employees	2
Specialties	General Practice
	Management
Level	Senior
Fee Basis	Retainer Only
Contact	Arthur Lyons

Description Lyons, Black + Associates is an executive search firm that recruits positions from technical roles to Presidential and Board of Directors searches, with salaries ranging from $50,000 to $500,000.

M.E. MONEY & ASSOCIATES, INC.
3080 Yonge Street
Suite 5004, PO Box 60
Toronto, ON M4N 3N1

Telephone	416-221-7117
Fax	416-221-7462
E-mail	money@interlog.com
Founded	1986
Employees	3
Specialties	Human Resource
	Management
	Marketing
	Sales
	Govt/Nonprofit
	Finance
Level	Senior
	Mid-Level
Fee Basis	Retainer Only
Contact	Margaret E. Money

M.I.S. CONSULTANTS
55 Eglinton Avenue East, Suite 701
Toronto, ON M4P 1G8

Telephone	416-489-4334
Fax	416-489-0918
E-mail	jobs@misconsult.com
Website	www.misconsult.com
Founded	1978
Specialties	Computing
Level	Senior
	Mid-Level
Contact	Eric Winters, President

Description M.I.S. Consultants recruits for IT positions across Canada and the USA.

M.I.S. CONSULTANTS
3190 Steeles Ave. West, Suite 120
Markham, ON L3R 1G9

Telephone	905-305-1455
Fax	905-305-0033
E-mail	jobs@misconsult.com
Website	www.misconsult.com
Specialties	Computing
Contact	Eric Winters, President

Description M.I.S. Consultants recruits for IT positions across Canada and the USA.

M.J. JANSSEN & ASSOCIATES INC.
190 Robert Speck Parkway
Suite 105
Mississauga, ON L4Z 3K3

Telephone	905-272-1335
Fax	905-272-9396
E-mail	janssen@trends.ca
Employees	2
Specialties	Logistics
Level	Mid-Level
Recruiters	Mary J. Janssen
	Trish O'Quinn
	Arch Walsh
Contact	Mary J. Janssen

Description M.J. Janssen & Associates is one of Canada's leading executive search firms, specializing in all aspects of logistics.

M.J. MICHAELS CONSULTING GROUP
1395 Pineway Court, Suite 101
Oakville, ON L6M 2H3

Fax	905-847-2985
E-mail	kilkenny@cgocable.net
Specialties	Banking

M.R. GOODMAN CONSULTING INC.
400 - 5th Avenue SW, Suite 300
Calgary, AB T2P 0L6

Telephone	403-262-4506
Fax	403-264-9218
E-mail	goodman@ internode.net
Specialties	Oil & Gas
	Engineering

	Operations
	Accounting
Level	Senior
	Mid-Level
Contact	R.E. (Ruby) Goodman

M. TREW & ASSOCIATES
1 Dundas Street West
Suite 2500, PO Box 84
Toronto, ON M5G 1Z3

Telephone	416-593-3783
Fax	416-593-3798
E-mail	mtrew@idirect.com
Specialties	Accounting
	Finance
Level	Mid-Level
Contact	Margaret Trew, Owner

Description M. Trew & Associates specializes in placements in the brokerage industry.

MACDONALD & BRISSON PERSONNEL SERVICES LTD.
234 Nepean Street
Ottawa, ON K2P 0B8

Telephone	613-233-4055
Fax	613-233-2166
E-mail	macbri@comnet.ca
Founded	1976
Employees	7
Specialties	Computing
	Administrative
	Govt/Nonprofit
	Engineering
	Telecom
	Bilingual
Level	Mid-Level
	Junior
Contact	Gerry Brisson, Director

Description MacDonald & Brisson Personnel Services Ltd. strives to offer the best possible service in order to assist employers in obtaining their objectives.

MACGREGOR RAE MANAGEMENT INC.
93 Coachwood Road
Lethbridge, AB T1K 6B4

Telephone	403-381-0611
Fax	403-381-2667
E-mail	macgregor.rae@ telusplanet.net
Specialties	Govt/Nonprofit
Level	Mid-Level
	Senior

MACKENZIE GRAY MANAGEMENT INC.
444 - 5th Avenue SW, Suite 1500
Calgary, AB T2P 2T8

Telephone	403-264-8906
Fax	403-264-8907
E-mail	macgray@ cadvision.com
Founded	1996
Employees	3

Specialties	Finance
	Human Resource
	Mining
	Oil & Gas
	Agriculture/Fisheries
	Food Processing
	Engineering
	Real Estate
	Construction
Level	Senior
Fee Basis	Retainer Only
Recruiters	Douglas G. MacKenzie
	Anna Martin
	Mary O'Neill
	Peter Stack
Contact	Douglas G. MacKenzie

MACLEAN & ASSOCIATES
190 Robert Speck Parkway
Suite 203
Mississauga, ON L4Z 3K3

Telephone	905-279-7744
Fax	905-279-7747
E-mail	recruiting@maclean-associates.com
Website	www.maclean-associates.com
Founded	1988
Employees	5
Specialties	Computing
	Management
	Finance
	Accounting
	Sales
	Human Resource
	Trades/Technicians
Fee Basis	Sometimes contingent
Recruiters	Ted Maclean
	Anita Wydooghe
Contact	Ted Maclean, President

Description Maclean & Associates provides cost-effective recruiting solutions to their client companies while ensuring the best fit for candidates.

MACLEAN HAY CONSULTING
1219 Willowbrook Drive
Oakville, ON L6L 2J9

Telephone	905-469-8873
Fax	905-469-9238
E-mail	machay@cgocable.net
Founded	1980
Employees	3
Specialties	Aerospace
	Biotech/Biology
	Telecom
	Plastics
	Computing
	Engineering
	Management
Level	Senior
	Mid-Level
Min. Salary	$90,000
Fee Basis	Sometimes contingent
Recruiters	Ian Hay
	Allistair Maclean
Contact	Ian Hay

MACRAE ATWOOD MANAGEMENT
1235 Bay Street, Suite 400
Toronto, ON M5R 3K4

Telephone	416-966-4559
Fax	416-969-8916
E-mail	lmacrae@interlog.com
Employees	1
Specialties	Finance
	Geology/Geography
	Human Resource
	Metals
	Mining
	Publishing/Media
	Real Estate
Level	Mid-Level
	Senior
Fee Basis	Retainer Only
Contact	Linda MacRae

MADELEINE MARTEL INC.
2075, rue University, Bureau 1112
Montréal, QC H3A 2M3

Telephone	514-288-3178
Fax	514-288-2264
E-mail	madeleine@
	madeleinemartel-inc.ca
Website	www.madeleinemartel-inc.ca
Founded	1982
Employees	6
Specialties	Administrative
	Bilingual
	Insurance
Échelon	Mid-Level
Fee Basis	Retainer Only
Recruiters	Shirley Blainey
	Jo-Anne Gagnon
	Carole Gagnon
	Madeleine Martel
Contact	Madeleine Martel,
	President

Description Madeleine Martel Inc. recruits and places permanent or contractual employees.

MADISON MACARTHUR INC.
33 Madison Avenue
Toronto, ON M5R 2S2

Telephone	416-920-0092
Fax	416-920-0099
E-mail	resumes@
	mmsearch.com
Website	www.macarthursearch.com
Founded	1992
Employees	9
Specialties	Marketing
	Advertising
	Finance
	Sales
	Management
	Operations
	Direct Mktng.
Level	Senior
	Mid-Level
Min. Salary	$40,000
Fee Basis	Retainer Only
Contact	R. Ian MacArthur,
	Director

Description Madison MacArthur is an executive search firm specializing in the communications, marketing, advertising, financial services, manufacturing, e-commerce and internet related business sectors.

MAINTENANCE PLUS INC.
405 Riverview Drive
RR #5, Suite 301
Chatham, ON N7M 5J5

Telephone	519-354-5111
Fax	519-354-5189
E-mail	mainplus@
	ciaccess.com
Founded	1992
Specialties	Operations
	Engineering
	Automotive
	Trades/Technicians
Level	Junior
	Mid-Level
Contact	Glenn Markham

Description Maintenance Plus Inc. is a skilled trades personnel depot committed to providing unique, high-quality service in the maintenance world.

MAIZIS & MILLER CONSULTANTS
5405 Eglinton Ave. West, Suite 109
Toronto, ON M9C 5K6

Telephone	416-620-5111
Fax	416-620-5216
E-mail	inquire@
	maizisandmiller.com
Website	www.maizisandmiller.com
Founded	1988
Specialties	Administrative
	General Practice
	Computing
	Telecom

Description Founded in 1988, Maizis & Miller Consultants provides recruitment services in 3 operating divisions: office support; permanent staffing for office, administrative and IT support; and executive / specialized search.

MALLINOS DENTAL PERSONNEL
1074 Sandhurst Circle
Toronto, ON M1V 3R3

Telephone	416-297-8983
Fax	416-299-0466
Specialties	Health/Medical
Level	Mid-Level
	Junior
Contact	Helen Mallinos

MANAGEMENT ADVICE INTERNATIONAL LTD.
6 Adelaide Street East, Suite 400
Toronto, ON M5C 1H6

Telephone	416-916-6800
Fax	416-916-7543
E-mail	resume@managementadvice.com

Founded	1988
Employees	3
Specialties	Finance
	Marketing
	Management
Level	Mid-Level
Min. Salary	$60,000
Fee Basis	Retainer Only
Recruiters	Peter Crawford
	David Sprague
Contact	Peter Crawford

MANAGEMENT CONNECTIONS INCORPORATED
999 Canada Place, Suite 404
Vancouver, BC V6C 3E2

Telephone	604-685-5110
Fax	604-685-5112
E-mail	mcisearch@telus.net
Founded	1987
Employees	6
Specialties	Health/Medical
	Education
	Govt/Nonprofit
	Management
Level	Senior
	Mid-Level
Min. Salary	$65,000
Fee Basis	Retainer Only
Recruiters	Christopher M. Davies
	Kathleen Mahoney
	Alan L. Rehner CMC
Contact	Christopher Davies

MANAGEMENT ONE CONSULTANTS
1200 Bay Street, Suite 501
Toronto, ON M5R 2A5

Telephone	416-961-6100
Fax	416-961-7018
E-mail	management-one@
	sympatico.ca
Founded	1976
Specialties	Marketing
	Sales
	Finance
	Direct Mktng.
	Advertising
	Retail
Level	Mid-Level
	Senior
Min. Salary	$50,000
Recruiters	Frank Edelberg
	Dana Stewart
Contact	Frank Edelberg

Description Management One Consultants is a recruitment firm specializing in marketing, sales, finance, advertising, market research, direct marketing and sales promotion positions.

MANAGEMENT PLUS CONSULTING SERVICES
Sami El-Solh Ave., Rahal Building
3rd Floor, PO Box 13-6392
Beirut LEBANON

Telephone	961-1-396309
Fax	961-1-382713
E-mail	mplus@management plus.com.lb
Website	www.mgtplus.com
Founded	1993
Employees	15
Specialties	Management Accounting International Computing Oil & Gas Construction Health/Medical
Fee Basis	Always contingent
Contact	Ms Hasmig Tatoolian

Description Management Plus Consulting Services places candidates in Lebanon, Saudi Arabia and the Gulf region.

MANAGEMENT RECRUITERS OF KANNAPOLIS
1787 Dale Earnhardt Blvd.
Kannapolis, NC 28081   USA

Telephone	800-868-6177
Fax	704-938-3480
E-mail	kay.allison@ mrkannapolis.com
Website	www.computer-jobs-careers.com
Founded	1981
Employees	20
Specialties	Computing International
Level	Senior Mid-Level
Min. Salary	$35,000
Fee Basis	Sometimes contingent
Recruiters	Christi Bradford Andrew Bridges Allen Burnett Caroline Cagle Brenda Luck Gene Powell Jim Rothwell Joni Whitaker Tom Whitley
Contact	Andrew Bridges

Description Management Recruiters specializes in recruiting information systems professionals for top-level client companies throughout the USA.

MANAGEMENT SOLUTIONS CONSULTING INC.
190 Robert Speck Pkwy., Suite 107
Mississauga, ON L4Z 3K3

Telephone	905-276-7856
Fax	905-897-8385
E-mail	klachine@msci.net
Website	www.msci.net
Founded	1977
Specialties	Computing Human Resource Management Marketing Multimedia Telecom
Recruiters	Robyn Brookes Ken Lachine Charles Mitchell
Contact	Ken Lachine, President

Description For over 24 years, Management Solutions has specialized in human resources consulting, including IT and executive searches and contracting services.

MANCOMIT INTERNATIONAL INC.
456 Main Street, 3rd Floor
Winnipeg, MB R3B 1B6

Telephone	204-943-6411
Fax	204-943-8603
E-mail	ghauser@ mancomit.com
Website	www.mancomit.com
Specialties	Computing
Contact	Greg Hauser

Description Mancomit International Inc. provides information technology personnel on a contract basis to assist clients with the construction, implementation and support of information systems and associated technologies.

MANDRAKE GROUPE CONSEIL
1155 boul Rene Levesque Ouest
Bureau 2500
Montréal, QC H3B 2K4

Telephone	514-878-4224
Fax	514-878-4222
E-mail	nlebeau@mandrake.ca
Website	www.mandrake.ca
Specialties	General Practice Management
Level	Senior Mid-Level
Contact	Norman Labeau, Executive VP

Description Mandrake, Canada's largest privately held search firm, is a generalist firm with well-developed practice in marketing, communications and sales.

MANDRAKE MANAGEMENT CONSULTANTS
400 - 3rd Avenue SW, Suite 1400
Calgary, AB T2P 4H2

Telephone	403-303-3207
Fax	403-303-3208
E-mail	gelinas@mandrake.ca
Website	www.mandrake.ca
Specialties	General Practice Management
Level	Mid-Level Senior
Contact	André Gelinas, Director, Western Canada

Description Mandrake, Canada's largest privately held search firm, is a generalist firm with well-developed practice in marketing, communications and sales.

MANDRAKE MANAGEMENT CONSULTANTS
55 St. Clair Avenue West, Suite 401
Toronto, ON M4V 2Y7

Telephone	416-922-5400
Fax	416-922-1356
E-mail	info@mandrake.ca
Website	www.mandrake.ca
Founded	1970
Employees	28
Specialties	Finance Govt/Nonprofit Management Marketing Sales General Practice Advertising Banking Pharmaceutical Publishing/Media Telecom Consulting Design Retail
Level	Senior Mid-Level
Min. Salary	$60,000
Fee Basis	Retainer-Only
Recruiters	Mark Atkins Ron Brooks Daphne Bykerk James Coburn Louise Daigneault Stéfan Danis Terence Donnelly Angela Eckford Heidi Ehlers Michael Gates Lisa Gonzales William Holland James Kemble Normand Lebeau Paul Lintner Hector Marsilis Stephen Milic Harold Perry Bruce Powell
Contact	Bill Holland, Executive Vice-President

Description Mandrake, Canada's largest privately held search firm, is a generalist firm with well-developed practice in marketing, communications and sales.

MANPOWER PROFESSIONAL
1207 Douglas Street, Suite 303
Victoria, BC V8W 2E7

Telephone	250-389-6200
Fax	250-389-6255
Website	www.manpower professional.com
Founded	1947
Specialties	Computing Engineering Management Marketing Purchasing Scientific Telecom
Level	Mid-Level

Description The fastest-growing segment of the world's largest staffing service, Manpower Professional provides technical staffing for almost 95% of the Fortune 500.

MANPOWER PROFESSIONAL
1290 Hornby Street, Suite 304
Vancouver, BC V6Z 1W2

Telephone	604-682-7176
Fax	604-682-3594
E-mail	vancouver.bc-professional@na.manpower.com
Website	www.manpowerprofessional.com
Founded	1947
Specialties	Computing Engineering Management Marketing Purchasing Scientific Telecom
Level	Mid-Level

Description The fastest-growing segment of the world's largest staffing service, Manpower Professional provides technical staffing for almost 95% of the Fortune 500.

MANPOWER PROFESSIONAL
5611 Cooney Road, Suite 220
Richmond Professional Bldg.
Richmond, BC V6X 3J5

Telephone	604-270-9633
Fax	604-270-8775
Website	www.manpowerprofessional.com
Founded	1947
Specialties	Computing Engineering Management Marketing Purchasing Scientific Telecom
Level	Mid-Level

Description The fastest-growing segment of the world's largest staffing service, Manpower Professional provides technical staffing for almost 95% of the Fortune 500.

MANPOWER PROFESSIONAL
3495 North Road, Suite 202
Burnaby, BC V3J 7T8

Telephone	604-444-3339
Fax	604-444-3307
E-mail	burnaby@direct.ca
Website	www.manpowerprofessional.com
Founded	1947
Specialties	Computing Engineering Management Marketing Purchasing Scientific Telecom
Level	Mid-Level

Contact Brenda Cathy

Description The fastest-growing segment of the world's largest staffing service, Manpower Professional provides technical staffing for almost 95% of the Fortune 500.

MANPOWER PROFESSIONAL
10088 - 102nd Avenue
2101 Toronto Dominion Tower
Edmonton, AB T5J 2Z1

Telephone	780-420-0110
Fax	780-424-0807
E-mail	edmonton.ab@na.manpower.ca
Website	www.manpowerprofessional.com
Founded	1947
Employees	22
Specialties	Computing Engineering Management Marketing Purchasing Scientific Telecom
Level	Mid-Level
Contact	Terry Huculak

Description The fastest-growing segment of the world's largest staffing service, Manpower Professional provides technical staffing for almost 95% of the Fortune 500.

MANPOWER PROFESSIONAL
4919 - 59 Street, Suite 266
Red Deer, AB T4N 6C9

Telephone	403-342-2166
Fax	403-342-1405
E-mail	reddeer.ab-professional@na.manpower.com
Website	www.manpowerprofessional.com
Founded	1947
Specialties	Computing Engineering Management Marketing Purchasing Scientific Telecom
Level	Mid-Level

Description The fastest-growing segment of the world's largest staffing service, Manpower Professional provides technical staffing for almost 95% of the Fortune 500.

MANPOWER PROFESSIONAL
734 - 7th Avenue SW, Suite 360
Calgary, AB T2P 3P8

Telephone	403-269-6936
Fax	403-265-4063
E-mail	calgary.ab-supportcenter@na.manpower.com
Website	www.manpowerprofessional.com
Founded	1947

Specialties Computing Engineering Management Marketing Purchasing Scientific Telecom

Level Mid-Level

Contact Leona Watts

Description The fastest-growing segment of the world's largest staffing service, Manpower Professional provides technical staffing for almost 95% of the Fortune 500.

MANPOWER PROFESSIONAL
2103 - 11th Avenue, Suite 850
Regina, SK S4P 3Z8

Telephone	306-791-8730
Fax	306-525-2518
Website	www.manpowerprofessional.com
Founded	1947
Specialties	Computing Engineering Management Marketing Purchasing Scientific Telecom
Level	Mid-Level
Contact	Nancy Russell

Description The fastest-growing segment of the world's largest staffing service, Manpower Professional provides technical staffing for almost 95% of the Fortune 500.

MANPOWER PROFESSIONAL
201 Portage Avenue, Suite 1005
Toronto Dominion Centre
Winnipeg, MB R3B 3K6

Telephone	204-949-7800
Fax	204-942-8870
E-mail	prairie.mb.tech@na.manpower.ca
Website	www.manpowerprofessional.com
Founded	1947
Specialties	Computing Engineering Management Marketing Purchasing Scientific Telecom
Level	Mid-Level
Contact	Nancy Russell

Description The fastest-growing segment of the world's largest staffing service, Manpower Professional provides technical staffing for almost 95% of the Fortune 500.

MANPOWER PROFESSIONAL
1205 Amber Drive, Suite 106
Edinborough Office Centre
Thunder Bay, ON P7B 6M4

Telephone 807-346-8367

Fax 807-346-8888
Website www.manpower
professional.com

Founded 1947

Specialties Computing
Engineering
Management
Marketing
Purchasing
Scientific
Telecom

Level Mid-Level

Description The fastest-growing segment of the world's largest staffing service, Manpower Professional provides technical staffing for almost 95% of the Fortune 500.

MANPOWER PROFESSIONAL
1901 Lasalle Blvd.
Sudbury, ON P3A 2A3

Telephone 705-525-4357
Fax 705-524-6368
Website www.manpower
professional.com

Founded 1947

Specialties Computing
Engineering
Management
Marketing
Purchasing
Scientific
Telecom

Level Mid-Level

Description The fastest-growing segment of the world's largest staffing service, Manpower Professional provides technical staffing for almost 95% of the Fortune 500.

MANPOWER PROFESSIONAL
3155 Howard Avenue
Suite 215, The Roundhouse Centre
Windsor, ON N8X 3Y9

Telephone 519-966-9360
Fax 519-966-9569
Website www.manpower
professional.com

Founded 1947

Specialties Computing
Engineering
Management
Marketing
Purchasing
Scientific
Telecom

Level Mid-Level

Description The fastest-growing segment of the world's largest staffing service, Manpower Professional provides technical staffing for almost 95% of the Fortune 500.

MANPOWER PROFESSIONAL
395 Wellington Road S.
Suite 216, Victoria Place
London, ON N6C 5Z6

Telephone 519-680-0100
Fax 519-680-7577

Website www.manpower
professional.com

Founded 1947

Specialties Computing
Engineering
Management
Marketing
Purchasing
Scientific
Telecom

Level Mid-Level

Description The fastest-growing segment of the world's largest staffing service, Manpower Professional provides technical staffing for almost 95% of the Fortune 500.

MANPOWER PROFESSIONAL
55 Cork Street, Suite 206
Guelph, ON N1H 2W7

Telephone 519-822-6667
Fax 519-822-9926
Website www.manpower
professional.com

Founded 1947

Specialties Computing
Engineering
Management
Marketing
Purchasing
Scientific
Telecom

Level Mid-Level

Description The fastest-growing segment of the world's largest staffing service, Manpower Professional provides technical staffing for almost 95% of the Fortune 500.

MANPOWER PROFESSIONAL
3300 Bloor Street W., Suite 3070
10th Floor, Centre Tower
Toronto, ON M8X 2X3

Telephone 416-231-6523
Fax 416-231-4549
Website www.manpower
professional.com

Founded 1947

Specialties Computing
Engineering
Management
Marketing
Purchasing
Scientific
Telecom

Level Mid-Level

Description The fastest-growing segment of the world's largest staffing service, Manpower Professional provides technical staffing for almost 95% of the Fortune 500.

MANPOWER PROFESSIONAL
20 Queen Street West, Suite 1010
Toronto, ON M5H 3R3

Telephone 416-977-1748
Fax 416-977-0947
Website www.manpower
professional.com

Founded 1947

Specialties Computing
Education
Management
Marketing
Purchasing
Scientific
Telecom

Level Mid-Level

Description The fastest-growing segment of the world's largest staffing service, Manpower Professional provides technical staffing for almost 95% of the Fortune 500.

MANPOWER PROFESSIONAL
1090 Don Mills Road, Suite 402
Toronto, ON M3C 3R6

Telephone 416-510-1211
Fax 416-510-1216
Website www.manpower
professional.com

Founded 1947

Specialties Computing
Engineering
Management
Marketing
Purchasing
Scientific
Telecom

Level Mid-Level

Description The fastest-growing segment of the world's largest staffing service, Manpower Professional provides technical staffing for almost 95% of the Fortune 500.

MANPOWER PROFESSIONAL
4950 Yonge Street, Suite 900
Toronto, ON M2N 6K1

Telephone 416-225-5599
Fax 416-225-9096
E-mail torontotechnical.
ontario@na.manpower.com
Website www.manpower
professional.com

Founded 1947

Specialties Computing
Engineering
Management
Marketing
Purchasing
Scientific
Telecom

Level Mid-Level

Recruiters Nadine Isaacs
Chandan Singh

Contact Leigh Austin

Description The fastest-growing segment of the world's largest staffing service, Manpower Professional provides technical staffing for almost 95% of the Fortune 500.

MANPOWER PROFESSIONAL
5650 Yonge Street, Suite 204
Toronto, ON M2M 4G3

Telephone 416-733-1440
Fax 416-733-2429

Website   www.manpower
             professional.com
Founded   1947
Specialties Computing
             Engineering
             Management
             Marketing
             Purchasing
             Scientific
             Telecom
Level   Mid-Level
Contact   Erin Brodie

Description The fastest-growing segment of the world's largest staffing service, Manpower Professional provides technical staffing for almost 95% of the Fortune 500.

MANPOWER PROFESSIONAL
21 King Street West, Suite 525
Hamilton, ON L8P 4W7

Telephone   905-527-1534
Fax   905-527-1478
E-mail   hamilton.on@
             na.manpower.com
Website   www.manpower
             professional.com
Founded   1947
Specialties Computing
             Engineering
             Management
             Marketing
             Purchasing
             Scientific
             Telecom
Level   Mid-Level
Contact   Liz Toth

Description The fastest-growing segment of the world's largest staffing service, Manpower Professional provides technical staffing for almost 95% of the Fortune 500.

MANPOWER PROFESSIONAL
3060 Mainway Drive, Suite 106
Burlington, ON L7M 1A3

Telephone   905-336-9868
Fax   905-336-5727
Website   www.manpower
             professional.com
Founded   1947
Specialties Computing
             Engineering
             Management
             Marketing
             Purchasing
             Scientific
             Telecom
Level   Mid-Level

Description The fastest-growing segment of the world's largest staffing service, Manpower Professional provides technical staffing for almost 95% of the Fortune 500.

MANPOWER PROFESSIONAL
2 County Court Blvd., Suite 335
Brampton, ON L6W 3W8

Telephone   905-454-3331

Fax   905-454-4964
Website   www.manpower
             professional.com
Founded   1947
Specialties Computing
             Engineering
             Management
             Marketing
             Purchasing
             Scientific
             Telecom
Level   Mid-Level

Description The fastest-growing segment of the world's largest staffing service, Manpower Professional provides technical staffing for almost 95% of the Fortune 500.

MANPOWER PROFESSIONAL
1 City Centre Drive, Suite 810
Mississauga, ON L5B 1M2

Telephone   905-276-2000
Fax   905-276-2596
Website   www.manpower
             professional.com
Founded   1947
Specialties Computing
             Engineering
             Management
             Marketing
             Purchasing
             Scientific
             Telecom
Level   Mid-Level
Contact   Karoline

Description The fastest-growing segment of the world's largest staffing service, Manpower Professional provides technical staffing for almost 95% of the Fortune 500.

MANPOWER PROFESSIONAL
64 Cedar Point Drive, Unit 1405
Barrie, ON L4N 5R7

Telephone   705-728-1191
Fax   705-734-9857
Website   www.manpower
             professional.com
Founded   1947
Specialties Computing
             Engineering
             Management
             Marketing
             Purchasing
             Scientific
             Telecom
Level   Mid-Level

Description The fastest-growing segment of the world's largest staffing service, Manpower Professional provides technical staffing for almost 95% of the Fortune 500.

MANPOWER PROFESSIONAL
16775 Yonge Street, Suite 211
Newmarket, ON L3Y 8J4

Telephone   800-567-6443
Fax   905-715-7725

Website   www.manpower
             professional.com
Founded   1947
Specialties Computing
             Engineering
             Management
             Marketing
             Purchasing
             Scientific
             Telecom
Level   Mid-Level

Description The fastest-growing segment of the world's largest staffing service, Manpower Professional provides technical staffing for almost 95% of the Fortune 500.

MANPOWER PROFESSIONAL
7030 Woodbine Avenue, Suite 205
Markham, ON L3R 6G2

Telephone   905-948-1235
Fax   905-948-1271
Website   www.manpower.ca
Specialties Direct Mktng.
             Human Resource
             Trades/Technicians
             Sales
             Computing
Level   Mid-Level

Description The fastest-growing segment of the world's largest staffing service, Manpower Professional provides technical staffing for almost 95% of the Fortune 500.

MANPOWER PROFESSIONAL
80 King Street
2nd Floor, Corbloc Building
St. Catharines, ON L2R 7G1

Telephone   905-688-6080
Fax   905-688-3967
Website   www.manpower
             professional.com
Founded   1947
Specialties Computing
             Engineering
             Management
             Marketing
             Purchasing
             Scientific
             Telecom
Level   Mid-Level

Description The fastest-growing segment of the world's largest staffing service, Manpower Professional provides technical staffing for almost 95% of the Fortune 500.

MANPOWER PROFESSIONAL
4342 Queen Street
Niagara Falls, ON L2E 7J7

Telephone   905-356-0777
Fax   905-356-6604
Website   www.manpower
             professional.com
Founded   1947
Specialties Computing
             Engineering
             Management

Marketing
Purchasing
Scientific
Telecom

Level   Mid-Level

Description The fastest-growing segment of the world's largest staffing service, Manpower Professional provides technical staffing for almost 95% of the Fortune 500.

MANPOWER PROFESSIONAL
1305 Pickering Parkway, Suite 201
Pickering, ON L1V 3P2

Telephone	905-831-7683
Fax	905-831-8134
Website	www.manpower professional.com
Founded	1947
Specialties	Computing Engineering Management Marketing Purchasing Scientific Telecom
Level	Mid-Level

Description The fastest-growing segment of the world's largest staffing service, Manpower Professional provides technical staffing for almost 95% of the Fortune 500.

MANPOWER PROFESSIONAL
340 George Street North
Suite 312, Peterborough Square
Peterborough, ON K9H 7E8

Telephone	705-743-5871
Fax	705-743-3460
Website	www.manpower professional.com
Founded	1947
Specialties	Computing Engineering Management Marketing Purchasing Scientific Telecom
Level	Mid-Level

Description The fastest-growing segment of the world's largest staffing service, Manpower Professional provides technical staffing for almost 95% of the Fortune 500.

MANPOWER PROFESSIONAL
253 Division Street, Suite 107
Cobourg, ON K9A 3P9

Telephone	905-373-0967
Fax	905-373-8329
Website	www.manpower professional.com
Founded	1947
Specialties	Computing Engineering Management Marketing Purchasing

Scientific
Telecom

Level   Mid-Level

Description The fastest-growing segment of the world's largest staffing service, Manpower Professional provides technical staffing for almost 95% of the Fortune 500.

MANPOWER PROFESSIONAL
179 Pinnacle Street
Belleville, ON K8N 3A5

Telephone	613-968-3455
Fax	613-968-2764
Website	www.manpower professional.com
Founded	1947
Specialties	Computing Engineering Management Marketing Purchasing Scientific Telecom
Level	Mid-Level

Description The fastest-growing segment of the world's largest staffing service, Manpower Professional provides technical staffing for almost 95% of the Fortune 500.

MANPOWER PROFESSIONAL
King Street & Portsmouth Avenue
St. Lawrence College, ATI Building
Kingston, ON K7L 5A6

Telephone	613-546-2693
Fax	613-546-5980
Website	www.manpower professional.com
Founded	1947
Specialties	Computing Engineering Management Marketing Purchasing Scientific Telecom
Level	Mid-Level

Description The fastest-growing segment of the world's largest staffing service, Manpower Professional provides technical staffing for almost 95% of the Fortune 500.

MANPOWER PROFESSIONAL
2288 Parkdale Avenue
Brockville, ON K6V 5X3

Telephone	613-342-0250
Fax	613-342-0252
Website	www.manpower professional.com
Founded	1947
Specialties	Computing Engineering Management Marketing Purchasing Scientific Telecom

Level   Mid-Level

Description The fastest-growing segment of the world's largest staffing service, Manpower Professional provides technical staffing for almost 95% of the Fortune 500.

MANPOWER PROFESSIONAL
700 - 14th Street West, Suite 12
Cornwall, ON K6J 5M2

Telephone	613-938-1818
Fax	905-938-1067
Website	www.manpower professional.com
Founded	1947
Specialties	Computing Engineering Management Marketing Purchasing Sales Scientific
Level	Mid-Level

Description The fastest-growing segment of the world's largest staffing service, Manpower Professional provides technical staffing for almost 95% of the Fortune 500.

MANPOWER PROFESSIONAL
301 Moodie Drive, Suite 101
Nepean, ON K2H 9C4

Telephone	613-820-1493
Fax	613-820-3392
E-mail	nepean.ontario@ na.manpower.com
Website	www.manpower professional.com
Founded	1947
Specialties	Computing Engineering Management Marketing Purchasing Scientific Telecom
Level	Mid-Level

Description The fastest-growing segment of the world's largest staffing service, Manpower Professional provides technical staffing for almost 95% of the Fortune 500.

MANPOWER PROFESSIONAL
55 Metcalfe Street, Suite 800
Ottawa, ON K1P 6L5

Telephone	613-237-9070
Fax	613-563-9735
E-mail	ottawa.ontario@ na.manpower.com
Website	www.manpower professional.com
Founded	1947
Specialties	Computing Engineering Management Marketing Purchasing Scientific Telecom

Level	Mid-Level
Contact	W. Mallon

Description The fastest-growing segment of the world's largest staffing service, Manpower Professional provides technical staffing for almost 95% of the Fortune 500.

MANPOWER PROFESSIONAL
8, rue Langlois
Granby, ON J2G 6J4

Telephone	450-776-6630
Fax	450-776-7730
Website	www.manpower professional.com
Founded	1947
Specialties	Computing Engineering Management Marketing Purchasing Scientific Telecom
Level	Mid-Level

Description The fastest-growing segment of the world's largest staffing service, Manpower Professional provides technical staffing for almost 95% of the Fortune 500.

MANPOWER PROFESSIONAL
455 rue King Ouest, Bureau 330
Sherbrooke, QC J1H 6E9

Telephone	819-821-2427
Fax	819-821-3799
Website	www.manpower professional.com
Founded	1947
Specialties	Computing Engineering Management Marketing Purchasing Scientific Telecom
Level	Mid-Level

Description The fastest-growing segment of the world's largest staffing service, Manpower Professional provides technical staffing for almost 95% of the Fortune 500.

MANPOWER PROFESSIONAL
1800, avenue McGill College
Bureau 900
Montréal, QC H3A 3J6

Telephone	514-848-9922 ext 238
Fax	514-848-1962
E-mail	montreal.pq.tech@ na.manpower.com
Website	www.manpower professional.com
Founded	1947
Specialties	Computing Engineering Management Marketing Purchasing Scientific Telecom

Level	Mid-Level
Min. Salary	$30,000
Contact	David Guerette, Directeur

Description The fastest-growing segment of the world's largest staffing service, Manpower Professional provides technical staffing for almost 95% of the Fortune 500.

MANPOWER PROFESSIONAL
880, chemin Ste-Foy, Bureau 860
Québec, QC G1S 2L2

Telephone	418-681-6244
Fax	418-687-1339
E-mail	quebec@manpower.ca
Website	www.manpower professional.com
Founded	1947
Specialties	Computing Engineering Management Marketing Purchasing Scientific Telecom
Level	Mid-Level
Contact	Thérèse Monette

Description The fastest-growing segment of the world's largest staffing service, Manpower Professional provides technical staffing for almost 95% of the Fortune 500.

MANPOWER PROFESSIONAL
364 York Street
Fredericton, NB E3B 3P7

Telephone	506-458-9172
Fax	506-458-0841
Website	www.manpower professional.com
Founded	1947
Specialties	Computing Engineering Management Marketing Purchasing Scientific Telecom
Level	Mid-Level

Description The fastest-growing segment of the world's largest staffing service, Manpower Professional provides technical staffing for almost 95% of the Fortune 500.

MANPOWER PROFESSIONAL
15 Market Square
Suite 1503, City Hall Bldg.
Saint John, NB E2L 1E8

Telephone	506-672-2000
Fax	506-652-6729
E-mail	pro@manpower.ca
Website	www.manpower professional.com
Founded	1947
Specialties	Computing Engineering Management

	Marketing Purchasing Scientific Telecom
Level	Mid-Level
Recruiters	Brenda Cummings David Kirkpatrick
Contact	Brenda Cummings, Recruiter

Description The fastest-growing segment of the world's largest staffing service, Manpower Professional provides technical staffing for almost 95% of the Fortune 500.

MANPOWER PROFESSIONAL
18 Queen Street, Suite 103
Charlottetown, PE C1A 4A1

Telephone	902-566-4147
Fax	902-368-1918
Website	www.manpower professional.com
Founded	1947
Specialties	Computing Engineering Management Marketing Purchasing Scientific Telecom
Level	Mid-Level

Description The fastest-growing segment of the world's largest staffing service, Manpower Professional provides technical staffing for almost 95% of the Fortune 500.

MANPOWER PROFESSIONAL
1969 Upper Water Street
Suite 1009, Box 41
Halifax, NS B3J 3R7

Telephone	902-422-1373
Fax	902-484-0841
E-mail	pro@manpower.ca
Website	www.manpower professional.com
Founded	1947
Specialties	Computing Engineering Management Marketing Purchasing Scientific Telecom
Level	Mid-Level

Description The fastest-growing segment of the world's largest staffing service, Manpower Professional provides technical staffing for almost 95% of the Fortune 500.

MANPOWER PROFESSIONAL
500 Kings Road
Suite 114, Cabot Complex
Sydney, NS B1S 1B1

Telephone	902-564-6616
Fax	902-564-6262
Website	www.manpower professional.com

Founded   1947

Specialties   Computing
Engineering
Management
Marketing
Purchasing
Scientific
Telecom

Level   Mid-Level

Description The fastest-growing segment of the world's largest staffing service, Manpower Professional provides technical staffing for almost 95% of the Fortune 500.

MANPOWER PROFESSIONAL
139 Water St., Suite 903
Fortis Building
St. John's, NF A1C 1B2

Telephone   709-737-1692
Fax   709-737-1651
E-mail   manpower@
nf.sympatico.ca
Website   www.manpower
professional.com
Founded   1947

Specialties   Computing
Engineering
Management
Marketing
Purchasing
Scientific
Telecom

Level   Mid-Level

Description The fastest-growing segment of the world's largest staffing service, Manpower Professional provides technical staffing for almost 95% of the Fortune 500.

MANPOWER SERVICES CANADA LIMITED
4950 Yonge Street, Suite 700
Toronto, ON M2N 6K1

Telephone   416-225-4455
Fax   416-225-6217
E-mail   tanya.macmillan@
na.manpower.com
Website   www.ca.manpower.com
Founded   1947

Specialties   Computing
Engineering
Management
Marketing
Purchasing
Scientific
Telecom

Level   Mid-Level
Junior

Recruiters   Melissa Harju
Tanya Macmillan
Samantha O'Brien

Contact   Tanya Macmillan

Description The fastest-growing segment of the world's largest staffing service, Manpower Services Canada Limited provides technical staffing for almost 95% of the Fortune 500.

MANPOWER, TORONTO HEALTH SECTOR
101 College Street, Room 807
Charlie Conacher Research Wing
Toronto, ON M5G 1L7

Telephone   416-971-8575
Fax   416-971-7135
Website   www.manpower.ca

Specialties   Health/Medical
Trades/Technicians

Level   Mid-Level

Description Manpower is a leader in the staffing industry.

MARANOVA RESOURCES CORPORATION
202 Hoylake Crescent
Orleans, ON K1E 2M8

Telephone   613-837-5565
Fax   613-837-9507
E-mail   opportunities@
maranova.com
Website   www.maranova.com
Founded   1997

Specialties   Telecom
Engineering
Computing

Level   Mid-Level

Contact   Ronald D. Ralph,
President and CEO

Description Maranova Resources Corporation recruits personnel for the telecommunications and high-tech industries.

MARBERG & ASSOCIATES
390 Bay Street, Suite 601
Toronto, ON M5H 2Y2

Telephone   416-363-6442
Fax   416-363-7966
E-mail   resumes@marberg.com
Website   www.marberg.com
Founded   1980
Employees   10

Specialties   Banking
Bilingual
Finance
Govt/Nonprofit
Insurance
Law

Level   Mid-Level
Senior

Contact   Jerry Fisch

Description A full-service search firm catering to the Greater Toronto employers in the financial, legal, customer service and public service communities.

MARCOBELLI GROUP
55 Cosburn Avenue, Suite 1110
Toronto, ON M4K 2E9

Telephone   416-467-7477
Fax   416-467-7477
E-mail   marcobelliproinc@
sprint.ca

Specialties   General Practice

Contact   Mona Marcobelli

MARCON MANAGEMENT CONSULTANTS INC.
555, boul. René-Lévesque O.
Bureau 750
Montréal, QC H2Z 1B1

Telephone   514-393-1378
Fax   514-875-7505
E-mail   info@marcon.qc.ca
Website   www.marcon.qc.ca
Founded   1986

Specialties   Marketing
Sales

Level   Senior
Mid-Level

Contact   Ian H. Moodie CMC,
Chairman

Description Marcon is a management consulting firm specializing in all aspects of the marketing industry. Their services occasionally include recruitment work for clients.

MARINA SIRRAS & ASSOCIATES LLC
420 Lexington Avenue, Suite 2545
New York, NY 10170 USA

Telephone   212-490-0333
Fax   212-490-2074
E-mail   info@lawseek.com
Website   www.lawseek.com
Founded   1987

Specialties   Law
International

Level   Senior
Mid-Level

Fee Basis   Sometimes contingent

Recruiters   Marina Sirras
Jennifer Ivana Sirras

Contact   Marina Sirras

Description Marina Sirras & Associates LLC specializes in the placement of attorneys at all levels of experience in law firms and corporations in the USA and internationally.

MARK PROFESSIONAL SERVICES INC.
734 - 7th Avenue SW, Suite 730
Calgary, AB T2P 3P8

Telephone   403-263-5120
Fax   403-266-5691
E-mail   info@markpersonnel.
com
Website   www.markpersonnel.
com
Founded   1990
Employees   18

Specialties   Administrative

Level   Mid-Level
Junior

Fee Basis   Always contingent

Contact   Beverley Hughes

Description Mark Professional Services Inc. provides organizations with creative, flexible and quality staffing solutions.

MARKENT PERSONNEL, INC.
PO Box 423
Portage, WI 53901   USA

Telephone	608-742-7300
Fax	413-280-5674
E-mail	contactus@markentpersonnel.com
Website	www.markentpersonnel.com
Specialties	Accounting
	Computing
	Design
	Management
	Metals
	Plastics
	Pulp & Paper
	International
Level	Mid-Level
Min. Salary	$30,000
Fee Basis	Sometimes contingent
Recruiters	Bonnie Stroede
	Tom Udulutch
	Mark Udulutch
	Janet Van Epps
	Kelly Zahn
Contact	Tom Udulutch

Description 20 years experience recruiting for manufacturing companies in Wisconsin, Minnesota and U.P. of Michigan.

MARLENE BILODEAU CONSEILS
255, rue Racine Est, Bureau 555
Chicoutimi, QC G7H 7L2

Téléphone	418-543-6655
Télécopieur	418-693-5919
Courriel	marlene.bilodeau@videotron.net
Spécialités	Comptabilité
	Ingénierie
	Ressources humaines
	Gestion
	Papeterie
	Ventes
Échelon	Intermédiaire
Contact	Marlene Bilodeau

Description Gestion des processus de sélection pour combler des postes. Développement organisationnel. Développement du potential humain.

MARR ROY GROUP, THE / MRG
8 Stavebank Road North, Suite 402
Toronto, ON L5G 2T4

Telephone	905-271-2710
Fax	905-271-2783
E-mail	info@webmrg.com
Website	www.webmrg.com
Founded	1992
Employees	5
Specialties	Computing
Level	Senior
	Mid-Level
Fee Basis	Always contingent
Recruiters	Laurie Marr
	Steve Roy
Contact	Laurie Marr, President

Description MRG specializes in the recruitment and placement of permanent and contract professionals exclusively for the Information Technology industry.

MARSDEN NAGATA LEGAL SEARCH
8 King Street East, Suite 1110
Toronto, ON M5C 1B5

Telephone	416-214-9881
Fax	416-214-1989
E-mail	info@marsdennagata.com
Specialties	Law
Level	Mid-Level
	Senior
Recruiters	Jonathan Marsden
	Lorene Nagata LL.B.
Contact	Jonathan Marsden

Description Marsden Nagata is a high-end search firm dedicated to the legal profession.

MARTIN RANDOLPH & ASSOCIÉS
3470, rue Stanley, Bureau 1901
Montréal, QC H3A 1R9

Telephone	514-286-9559
Employees	1
Specialties	Purchasing
	Logistics
	Transport
Level	Mid-Level
	Senior
Contact	Martin Randolph

Description Specializing in the distribution industry.

MASCAREN INTERNATIONAL INC.
500 Danforth Avenue
Toronto, ON M4K 1P6

Telephone	416-465-6690
Fax	905-787-1648
E-mail	heather_mascaren@yahoo.com
Website	www.mascaren.com
Founded	1987
Specialties	Retail
	Sales
Level	Mid-Level
	Junior
Contact	Heather Mascaren

Description Specializing in training and placing sales staff for the cosmetic and fragrance industries.

MASTER PERFORMERS
55 Livingston Road, Suite 109
Toronto, ON M1E 1K9

Telephone	416-266-3143
Fax	416-266-3048
E-mail	info@masterperformers.com
Website	www.masterperformers.com
Founded	1995
Employees	5
Specialties	Computing
	Direct Mktng.
	Management
	Marketing
	Sales
	Telecom
	Multimedia
Level	Senior
Min. Salary	$80,000
Fee Basis	Retainer Only
Contact	Karen Kammer Meier

Description Master Performers is a retainer-based management consulting firm specializing in search and advisory services and human potential assessments of senior-level specialists, with an e-business market focus.

MATCHPOINT EXECUTIVE PLACEMENT SERVICES
1370 Don Mills Road, Suite 300
Toronto, ON M3B 3N7

Telephone	416-391-3300
Fax	416-391-3523
E-mail	match@interlog.com
Website	www.matchpointeps.com
Employees	2
Specialties	Marketing
	Sales
Level	Mid-Level
	Senior
Recruiters	Robert Bernstein
	Andrew Czerwinski
	Ashley Winick
Contact	Andrew Czerwinski

Description Matchpoint Executive Placement Services places sales and marketing professionals at all levels.

MATCHTECH ENGINEERING LTD.
1590 Parkway, Fareham
Solent Business Park
Hampshire, PO15 7AG
UNITED KINGDOM

Telephone	44-1489-575111
Fax	44-1489-575883
E-mail	marine@matchtech.co.uk
Website	www.matchtech.co.uk
Founded	1990
Employees	16
Specialties	Engineering
	International
	Design
	Oil & Gas
	Pharmaceutical
	Pulp & Paper
	Transport
Level	Mid-Level
	Senior
Recruiters	Alex Bizzey
	Mike Bowler
	Andrew Bradshaw
	Kelly Brocklehurst
	Mark Butter
	Debbie Cox
	Nick Day
	Elric Heslop

Iain Howard
Jake Jessey
Alex Jones
Keith Lewis
Paul Raine
John Stead
Will Winfield
Ed Wright

Contact   Paul Raine,
           Managing Director

Description Matchtech Engineering
Ltd. is one of the UK's most successful technical recruitment consultan-
cies in engineering recruitment.

MATTE GROUPE CONSEIL INC.
1010, rue Sherbrooke Ouest
Bureau 1200
Montréal, QC H3A 2R7

Telephone	514-848-1008
Fax	514-848-9157
E-mail	jbenoit@matteiic.com
Website	www.matteiic.com
Founded	1988
Employees	12
Specialties	Engineering
	Finance
	Health/Medical
	Management
	Operations
	Pharmaceutical
Level	Senior
	Mid-Level
Min. Salary	$50,000
Recruiters	Isabelle Girard
	Danielle Laurinaitis
	Marie-Andrea Longtin
	Richard M. Matte
	Michel St-Louis
Contact	Richard M. Matte,
	Managing Partner

Description The Matte Group is an
international executive search firm.
Affiliated internationally with the
IIC Partners Group.

MATTESON MANAGEMENT INC.
1200 Bay Street, Suite 405
Toronto, ON M5R 2A5

Telephone	416-960-8600
Fax	416-960-8602
E-mail	sm@matteson
	management.com
Website	www.matteson
	management.com
Founded	1995
Employees	5
Specialties	Finance
	Human Resource
	Marketing
	Pharmaceutical
	Retail
	Sales
	Public Relations
Level	Senior
Min. Salary	$75,000
Fee Basis	Retainer Only
Recruiters	Patrick Bruneteau
	Peter Laurence
	Deborah Magidson

Sandra Matteson
Kathy Moloney

Contact   Kathy Moloney

Description Matteson Management
Inc. is a competency-based retained
executive search practice specializing in mid-to-senior level roles in
communications, public relations,
sales, marketing and finance.

MATTHEWS MANAGEMENT
33 Arnold Crescent
Richmond Hill, ON L4C 3R6

Telephone	905-884-6970
Fax	905-884-6716
E-mail	mattman1@
	sympatico.ca
Founded	1967
Specialties	Automotive
	Engineering
	Plastics
	Metals
	Operations
	Purchasing
Level	Senior
	Mid-Level
Min. Salary	$40,000
Recruiters	Faith Bartley
	Angela K. Matthews
	Myrna Pavlin
Contact	Angela K. Matthews
	CPC CIPC, President

Description Matthews Management
specializes in technical and engineering recruiting for the automotive industry.

MAUREEN SINDEN EXECUTIVE SEARCH
440 Laurier Ave. West, Suite 200
Ottawa, ON K1R 7X6

Telephone	613-233-6866
Fax	613-257-2806
E-mail	sinden@intranet.ca
Specialties	Management
	Finance
	Health/Medical
	Sales
	Scientific
	Govt/Nonprofit
	Public Relations
Level	Senior
	Mid-Level
Contact	Maureen Sinden

MAXIM GROUP
13700 International Place
Suite 250
Richmond, BC V5V 2X8

Telephone	604-232-2570
Fax	604-232-7001
E-mail	maximgroup@
	maximgroup.com
Website	www.maximgroup.com
Founded	1987
Specialties	Management
Level	Senior
	Mid-Level

Fee Basis	Always contingent
Recruiters	Darren Butterworth
	Damon Harbert
	Brad Mackenzie
Contact	Ada Ip

Description An IT consulting firm
that also provides technical staffing
and executive search services. Call
toll-free 1-800-688-0725.

MAYDAY PERSONNEL (1992) INC.
475 Provencher Blvd., Suite 107
Winnipeg, MB R2J 4A7

Telephone	204-942-3733
Fax	204-942-3756
E-mail	mayday1@
	mb.sympatico.ca
Specialties	General Practice
Contact	Geoff Campbell

MAYFAIR PERSONNEL NORTHERN LTD.
9804 - 100 Avenue, Suite 305
Grande Prairie, AB T8V 0T8

Telephone	780-539-5090
Fax	780-539-7089
E-mail	mayfair@
	telusplanet.net
Website	www.grp-biz.com/
	mayfairpersonnel
Specialties	Accounting
	Administrative
Level	Mid-Level
	Junior
Contact	Irene Logan

Description Mayfair Personnel is a
multi-service employment agency
supplying administrative and bookkeeping staff throughout the Grande
Prairie area.

MBL GROUP LLC
1220 SW Morrison, Suite 900
Portland, OR 97205 USA

Telephone	503-224-7249
Fax	503-224-6707
E-mail	info@mblgroup.com
Website	www.mblgroup.com
Founded	1992
Specialties	Oil & Gas
	Finance
	Human Resource
	Computing
	Operations
	Engineering
	International
Recruiters	Paul Barber
	Dianne Burt-Green
	Brian Keegan
	Sean Madian
	Jim Morris
	Amy Sinclair
	Liz Wong
Contact	Paul Barber,
	Managing Principal

Description MBL Group is an HR
consulting firm that also provides
recruitment services for clients.

MCCRACKEN/LABBETT EXECUTIVE SEARCH

145 King Street West, Suite 1000
Toronto, ON M5H 1J8

Telephone	416-363-4749
E-mail	keith@gary mccracken.com
Website	www.gary mccracken.com
Specialties	Real Estate Sales Marketing Construction
Level	Mid-Level Senior
Fee Basis	Retainer Only
Contact	Keith J. Labbett

Description McCracken/Labbett Executive Search is a retained, mid- to senior-level executive search practice, operating within GaryMcCracken Executive Search Inc.

MCDONALD-GREEN PERSONNEL

215 Holiday Inn Drive
Cambridge, ON N3C 3T2

Telephone	519-654-9388
Fax	519-654-9362
E-mail	info@mcdonald green.com
Website	www.mcdonald green.com
Founded	1994
Employees	7
Specialties	Administrative Computing Engineering Human Resource Bilingual Purchasing Sales
Level	Mid-Level Junior
Fee Basis	Always contingent
Recruiters	Kim J. Cameron Grace Frias Erin Gratton Helen Jowett CHRP Jennifer P. Sietsma Toni Vieledal
Contact	Helen Jowett CHRP, President

Description MGP is a full-service human resource agency that specializes in all areas of recruitment, including administrative, industrial, IT and executive placements.

MCGUIRE MANAGEMENT

124 Centre Street West
Richmond Hill, ON L4C 3P7

Fax	905-884-6082
E-mail	mcguiremanagement@ iprimus.ca
Specialties	Accounting
Level	Mid-Level

MCINTYRE MANAGEMENT RESOURCES

1030 Upper James Street, Suite 301
Hamilton, ON L9C 6X6

Telephone	905-574-6765
Fax	905-574-5025
E-mail	jobs@mcintyrejobs.com
Website	www.mcintyre mgmt.com
Founded	1990
Employees	2
Specialties	Management Computing Operations Engineering Human Resource Accounting Sales
Level	Senior Mid-Level
Min. Salary	$40,000
Fee Basis	Sometimes contingent
Contact	Marlene McIntyre, CPC

Description McIntyre Management is a search and contract firm, with assignments throughout North America and global assignments through NPA. Member ACSESS.

MCKINNON GROUPE CONSEIL INC.

5253, avenue du Parc, Bureau 600
Montréal, QC H2V 4P2

Téléphone	514-948-0025
Télécopieur	514-948-4127
Courriel	mckmtl@ mckinnon.qc.ca
Site Internet	www.aseproteck.com/ mckinnon.htm
Fondée	1988
Employés	4
Spécialités	Ressources humaines Droit Gestion Marketing Ventes
Échelon	Direction Intermédiaire
Salaire min.	45 000 $
Contact	Michel McKinnon, President

Description Entreprise specialisée dans la recherche de cadres de professionnels de la vente et d'associes. Les secteurs d'activites sont: les services, les manufactures et les commerces de detail partout au Québec.

MCKINNON MANAGEMENT GROUP INC.

5160 Yonge Street, Suite 700
Toronto, ON M2N 6L9

Telephone	416-250-6763
Fax	416-250-6916
E-mail	info@mckinnon.com
Website	www.mckinnon.com
Founded	1992
Employees	14
Specialties	Management Marketing Sales

	Multimedia Pharmaceutical Direct Mktng. Health/Medical Govt/Nonprofit
Level	Mid-Level Senior
Min. Salary	$50,000
Fee Basis	Sometimes contingent
Contact	Sylvia Lisi

Description McKinnon Management Group Inc. is a search firm that focuses on leading-edge businesses, placing sales, marketing and healthcare professionals throughout North America.

MCLEAN & ASSOCIATES

600 Ellis Street
North Vancouver, BC V7H 2G9

Fax	604-929-1694
E-mail	donmcleanis@ home.com
Specialties	Mining Transport
Contact	Don McLean

Description McLean & Associates is a consulting firm that often does placements in heavy industries and transport.

MCLEAN EXECUTIVE CONSULTANTS LTD.

250 - 6th Avenue SW
Suite 1200, Bow Valley Square IV
Calgary, AB T2P 3H7

Telephone	403-265-7715
Fax	403-265-7730
E-mail	bdielissen@mac.com
Founded	1968
Employees	4
Specialties	Computing Engineering Sales Accounting Oil & Gas
Level	Mid-Level Senior
Min. Salary	$35,000
Fee Basis	Sometimes contingent
Recruiters	Gordon Burton Bruce Dielissen Lloyd Gordon Jan Mah Dick Thomas
Contact	Bruce Dielissen

MCM SELEZIONE SRL

Via Zamboni 7
Bologna 40126 ITALY

Telephone	39-051-233768
Fax	39-051-235458
E-mail	bo@mcmselezione.it
Website	www.mcmselezione.it
Specialties	Management International
Level	Senior

Description MCM Selezione SRL does senior-level management placements throughout Italy.

MCNEILL NAKAMOTO RECRUITMENT GROUP INC.
401 West Georgia Street, Suite 1620
Vancouver, BC V6B 5A1

Telephone	604-662-8920
Fax	604-662-8927
E-mail	jobs@peoplebuzz.com
Website	www.peoplebuzz.com
Specialties	Management
	Banking
	Finance
	Computing
	Marketing
	Sales
Level	Mid-Level
	Senior
Contact	Cheryl Nakamoto, CPC

Description McNeill Nakamoto is a boutique-style recruitment firm that personalizes all aspects of the recruitment process for clients and applicants.

MCO BUSINESS GROUP INC.
1505 Laperrière Avenue
Ottawa, ON K1Z 7T1

Telephone	613-728-2188
Fax	613-728-5298
E-mail	mco@mco.ca
Website	www.mco.ca
Founded	1992
Specialties	General Practice
	Computing
Level	Mid-Level
Recruiters	Bernie O'Reilly
	Marie Ormandy
Contact	Marie Ormandy, President

Description MCO Business Group Inc. provides public and private sector clients with outplacement, executive assessment and recruitment services for all levels of employees.

MCQ INTERNATIONAL SERVICES
12 Market St., Progressive House
Portadown, County Armagh
Northern Ireland, BT62 3JY
UNITED KINGDOM

Telephone	44-1762-339121
Fax	44-1762-338837
E-mail	mcq@mcqinter.co.uk
Website	www.mcqinter.co.uk
Specialties	International
	Engineering
	Telecom
	Oil & Gas
	Construction

Description McQ International Services provides placement services to international contractors in the civil engineering, building, telecommunications and oil & gas industries.

MED-EMERG INTERNATIONAL INC.
2550 Argentia Road, Suite 205
Mississauga, ON L5N 5R1

Telephone	905-858-1368
Fax	905-858-1399
E-mail	info@med-emerg.com
Website	www.med-emerg.com
Specialties	Health/Medical
Contact	Shannon MacGillivray

Description Med-Emerg International Inc. is a publicly-traded Canadian healthcare company providing healthcare-related services, including physician and nurse recruitment.

MEDA GROUP
1575 Lauzon Road
Windsor, ON N8S 3N4

Telephone	519-944-6459
Fax	519-944-6862
E-mail	meda@medagroup.com
Website	www.medagroup.com
Founded	1970
Employees	100
Specialties	Automotive
	Design
	Engineering
	Computing
	Plastics
	Telecom
	Management
Level	Mid-Level
	Senior
Min. Salary	$30,000
Fee Basis	Sometimes contingent
Recruiters	Sam Dragich
	Donna Duckett
	Paula Hale
	Frank Hupalo
	David Lawn
	Serena Quick
	Richard Rosenthal
	Chris Uszynski
Contact	Richard Rosenthal

Description With offices in Ontario, Michigan, Arizona and the United Kingdom, Meda Group specializes in permanent and contract positions for high-technology specialists.

MEDFALL INC.
6453 Morrison Street, Suite 103
Niagara Falls, ON L2E 7H1

Telephone	905-304-7176
Fax	905-357-2601
E-mail	ktremblay@medfall.com
Website	www.medfall.com
Specialties	Health/Medical
Level	Senior
	Mid-Level
Min. Salary	$60,000
Fee Basis	Sometimes contingent
Recruiters	Laurie Fulcher RN
	Joan Hatcher
	Barbara Monaghan
	Joan Stoll RN
	Ken Tremblay
Contact	Ken Tremblay, MHSc, CHE

Description MedFall Inc. is an search and consulting firm specializing in placing healthcare professionals.

MEDHUNTERS.COM
180 Dundas Street West, Suite 2403
Toronto, ON M5G 1Z8

Telephone	416-977-5777
Fax	416-977-2869
E-mail	info@medhunters.com
Website	www.medhunters.com
Specialties	Health/Medical
Recruiters	Danielle Keir RN
	Moira McIntyre
	Adele Mirabelli
	Kathy Wheeler
Contact	Kathy Wheeler, Director of Operations & Marketing

Description Medhunters specializes in recruiting professionals for healthcare jobs.

MEDICAL PD BUREAU
330 Bay Street, Suite 1304
Toronto, ON M5H 2S8

Telephone	416-368-1844
Specialties	Health/Medical
Level	Mid-Level
	Junior
Contact	Lynne D. Delfs

MEDISTAFF
12555 High Bluff Drive, Suite 180
San Diego, CA 92130 USA

Telephone	858-793-4901
Fax	858-793-4909
E-mail	medistaff@earthlink.net
Website	www.medistaff.com
Founded	1995
Employees	12
Specialties	Health/Medical
	International
Level	Mid-Level
Fee Basis	Always contingent
Recruiters	Christine August
	Nadia Gruzd
	Gary Gruzd
	Susan Hempler
	Shannon Kehl
	Andrea Marcus
	Anita Marhsall
	Sally Panzer
	Tracy Preston
	Kirk Rentschler
	Keith Rentschler
	Sharon Williams
Contact	Nadia Gruzd

Description MediStaff specializes in placing Canadian medical professionals, primarily registered nurses, in full-time positions across the USA. call toll-free: 1-800-548-2428.

MEDISTAFF
1345 Broadway
El Cajon, CA 92021 USA

Telephone	619-440-8110
Fax	619-440-8120
E-mail	nursesandiego@ earthlink.net
Website	www.medistaff.com
Specialties	Health/Medical International

Description MediStaff specializes in placing Canadian medical professionals, primarily registered nurses, in full-time positions across the USA. call toll-free: 1-866-440-8110. This office does placements in San Diego.

MEECH PARTNERS LLP
40 King St. W., Suite 4900
Toronto, ON M5H 4A2

Telephone	416-367-5656
Fax	416-367-4104
E-mail	saipatel@idirect.com
Specialties	Actuarial Insurance Finance Banking
Contact	Sai Patel, Partner & Principal Search Consultant

Description Specializing in the placement of actuarial personnel.

MEGASEARCH INTERNATIONAL INC.
PO Box 428
Hudson, QC J0P 1H0

Telephone	450-458-4342
Fax	450-458-7741
E-mail	djoseph@videotron.ca
Specialties	Computing Engineering Health/Medical Logistics Purchasing
Level	Mid-Level

MELMAK CONSULTANTS LTD.
235 Yorkland Boulevard, Suite 300
Toronto, ON M2J 4Y8

Telephone	416-492-4101
Fax	416-491-2757
E-mail	melmakconsultants@ sympatico.ca
Website	www.melmak.net
Specialties	Marketing Sales
Level	Mid-Level Senior
Contact	Stuart R. McCormack

Description Melmak Consultants specializes in placing people in sales and marketing careers.

MERIDIA RECRUITMENT SERVICES INC.
Barrington Tower, Scotia Square
10th Floor, PO Box 2166
Halifax, NS B3J 3C4

Telephone	902-424-1125
Fax	902-425-1108
E-mail	info@meridia.ca
Website	www.meridia.ca
Specialties	Engineering Finance Marketing Purchasing Sales Telecom Accounting Direct Mktng.
Level	Senior Mid-Level
Fee Basis	Always contingent
Recruiters	Rob Faloon Jeff Forbes Holly McKinnon Nicole Simpson Bruce Snow Kevin Stoddart
Contact	Charlotte Rockwell, Search Coordinator

Description Meridia specializes in placements in IT, sales, marketing, accounting, finance, human resources and call centre management.

MERIT VENDOR PERSONNEL INC.
64 Charles Street East
Toronto, ON M4Y 1T1

Telephone	416-392-9226
Fax	416-928-2298
E-mail	jobs@meritvp.com
Website	www.meritvp.com
Specialties	Sales Computing
Level	Mid-Level
Recruiters	Irvin Bennett Peter Cliffe Merissa Preston John Shanks
Contact	Irving Bennett

Description Merit Vendor Personnel Inc. specializes in placing software personnel for vendors, including pre-sales technical support, sales, marketing, management and post-sales positions.

MESTEL & COMPANY
575 Madison Avenue
New York, NY 10022 USA

Telephone	212-605-0340
Fax	212-605-0137
E-mail	jspeede@mestel.com
Website	www.mestel.com
Founded	1987
Specialties	Law International
Level	Mid-Level Senior
Contact	Joyce Speede, Director, General Counsel & Partner Placements

Description Mestel & Company specializes in the permanent attorney placement industry. Offices in New York, Washington and London.

MÉTIVIER GROUPE CONSEIL INC.
1 Place Ville-Marie, Bureau 2821
Montréal, QC H3B 4R7

Telephone	514-398-9345
Fax	514-683-4063
E-mail	metivier@videotron.ca
Founded	1993
Employees	3
Specialties	General Practice Management Operations
Level	Senior Mid-Level
Min. Salary	$60,000
Fee Basis	Retainer Only
Contact	Jean Métivier

Description Métivier Groupe Conseil Inc. provides placements in all areas of manufacturing and service industries, except IT fields.

MEYERS NORRIS PENNY
808 - 4th Avenue SW, Suite 600
Calgary, AB T2P 3E8

Telephone	403-263-3385
Fax	403-263-3511
E-mail	morgans@mnp.ca
Website	www.mnp.ca
Founded	1997
Employees	5
Specialties	Accounting Finance Management Oil & Gas Administrative Marketing
Level	Mid-Level Senior
Fee Basis	Retainer Only
Contact	Jane Grant, CHRP

Description Meyers Norris Penny (formerly Barr Shelley Stuart) provides accounting, consulting and financial services.

MEYERS NORRIS PENNY / MNP
711 - 10th Street
Wainwright, AB T9W 1P3

Telephone	780-842-4171
Fax	780-842-4169
E-mail	isamand@mnp.ca
Website	www.mnp.ca
Employees	6
Specialties	Accounting Finance
Level	Mid-Level
Contact	Don Isaman, CA

Description MNP is one of Western Canada's largest regional accounting firms. This office occasionally does recruitment work for clients.

MEYERS NORRIS PENNY / MNP
5019 - 49th Avenue, Suite 200
Leduc, AB T9E 6T5

Telephone	780-986-2626
Fax	780-986-2621

E-mail	sarneckid@mnp.ca
Website	www.mnp.ca
Employees	21
Specialties	Accounting Finance
Level	Mid-Level
Contact	Deborah A. Sarnecki

Description MNP is one of Western Canada's largest regional accounting firms. This office occasionally provides recruitment services for clients.

MEYERS NORRIS PENNY / MNP
9909 - 102 Street
7th Floor, 214 Place
Grande Prairie, AB T8V 2V4

Telephone	780-831-1700
Fax	780-539-9600
E-mail	hennigarb@mnp.ca
Website	www.mnp.ca
Employees	38
Specialties	Accounting Finance
Level	Mid-Level
Contact	Bridget Hennigar, CA

Description MNP is one of Western Canada's largest regional accounting firms. This office occasionally provides recruitment services for clients.

MEYERS NORRIS PENNY / MNP
4922 - 53rd Street, Suite 102
Red Deer, AB T4N 2E9

Telephone	403-346-8878
Fax	403-341-5599
E-mail	rumbergerr@mnp.ca
Website	www.mnp.ca
Employees	45
Specialties	Accounting Finance
Level	Mid-Level
Contact	Rick Rumberger, CA

Description MNP is one of Western Canada's largest regional accounting firms. This office occasionally provides recruitment services for clients.

MEYERS NORRIS PENNY / MNP
4923 - 50th Street
Innisfail, AB T4G 1S7

Telephone	403-227-3763
Fax	403-227-2388
E-mail	rumberger@mnp.ca
Website	www.mnp.ca
Employees	6
Specialties	Accounting Finance
Level	Mid-Level
Contact	Rick Rumberger, CA

Description MNP is one of Western Canada's largest regional accounting firms. This office occasionally does recruitment work for clients.

MEYERS NORRIS PENNY / MNP
14310 - 111th Avenue, 500 WT
Edmonton, AB T3M 3Z7

Telephone	780-451-4406
Fax	780-454-1908
E-mail	llewellynj@mnp.ca
Website	www.mnp.ca
Employees	53
Specialties	Accounting Finance
Level	Mid-Level
Contact	Jeff Llewellyn, CA

Description MNP is one of Western Canada's largest regional accounting firms, and provides a complete range of financial, management and business advisory services, including recruitment.

MEYERS NORRIS PENNY / MNP
808 - 4th Avenue SW, Suite 600
Calgary, AB T2P 3E8

Telephone	403-263-3385
Fax	403-263-3511
E-mail	morgans@mnp.ca
Website	www.mnp.ca
Employees	67
Specialties	Accounting Finance
Level	Mid-Level
Contact	David Stuart, CA

Description MNP is one of Western Canada's largest regional accounting firms, and provides a complete range of financial, management and business advisory services, including recruitment.

MEYERS NORRIS PENNY / MNP
528 - 6th Street South, Box 1232
Lethbridge, AB T1J 4A4

Telephone	403-329-1552
Fax	403-329-1540
E-mail	taitg@mnp.ca
Website	www.mnp.ca
Employees	45
Specialties	Accounting Finance
Level	Mid-Level
Contact	Gord Tait, CA

Description MNP is one of Western Canada's largest regional accounting firms, and provides a complete range of financial, management and business advisory services, including recruitment.

MEYERS NORRIS PENNY / MNP
666 - 4th Street SE
Medicine Hat, AB T1A 7G5

Telephone	403-527-4441
Fax	403-526-6218
E-mail	keckm@mnp.ca
Website	www.mnp.ca
Employees	27
Specialties	Accounting Finance

Level	Mid-Level
Contact	Michael Keck, CA

Description MNP is one of Western Canada's largest regional accounting firms. This office occasionally does recruitment work for clients.

MEYERS NORRIS PENNY / MNP
Box 2138
Rocky Mountain House, AB
T0M 1T0

Telephone	403-845-2422
Fax	403-845-3794
E-mail	porterg@mnp.ca
Website	www.mnp.ca
Employees	3
Specialties	Accounting Finance
Level	Mid-Level
Contact	Gary Porter, CA

Description MNP is one of Western Canada's largest regional accounting firms. This office occasionally provides recruitment services for clients.

MEYERS NORRIS PENNY / MNP
697 Main Street
Pincher Creek, AB T0K 1W0

Telephone	403-627-3313
Fax	403-627-5259
E mail	vandenheuvelt@ mnp.ca
Website	www.mnp.ca
Employees	16
Specialties	Accounting Finance
Level	Mid-Level
Contact	Tony Vanden Heuvel, CA

Description MNP is one of Western Canada's largest regional accounting firms. This office occasionally provides recruitment services for clients.

MEYERS NORRIS PENNY / MNP
Box 119
Milk River, AB T0K 1M0

Telephone	403-647-3882
Fax	403-320-5066
E-mail	hornfordd@mnp.ca
Website	www.mnp.ca
Specialties	Accounting Finance
Level	Mid-Level
Contact	Don Hornford

Description MNP is one of Western Canada's largest regional accounting firms. This office occasionally provides recruitment services for clients.

MEYERS NORRIS PENNY / MNP
102 - 2nd Avenue West
Foremost, AB T0K 0X0

Telephone	403-382-3688
Fax	403-320-5066

E-mail	stromsmoe@mnp.ca
Website	www.mnp.ca
Specialties	Accounting Finance
Level	Mid-Level
Contact	Ed Stromsmoe

Description MNP is one of Western Canada's largest regional accounting firms. This office occasionally provides recruitment services for clients.

MEYERS NORRIS PENNY / MNP
706 Centre Street
Bow Island, AB T0K 0G0

Telephone	403-545-6309
Fax	403-320-5066
E-mail	grossh@mnp.ca
Website	www.mnp.ca
Specialties	Accounting Finance
Level	Mid-Level
Contact	Harry Gross

Description MNP is one of Western Canada's largest regional accounting firms. This office occasionally provides recruitment services for clients.

MEYERS NORRIS PENNY / MNP
365 - 2nd Street East
Drumheller, AB T0J 0Y0

Telephone	403-823-7800
Fax	403-823-8914
E-mail	wileyde@mnp.ca
Website	www.mnp.ca
Employees	8
Specialties	Accounting Finance
Level	Mid-Level
Contact	Delia L. Wiley

Description MNP is one of Western Canada's largest regional accounting firms. This office occasionally provides recruitment services for clients.

MEYERS NORRIS PENNY / MNP
4714 - 50th Avenue, Box 1480
Rimbey, AB T0C 2J0

Telephone	403-843-4666
Fax	403-843-4616
E-mail	stewarttarneyr@ mnp.ca
Website	www.mnp.ca
Employees	4
Specialties	Accounting Finance
Level	Mid-Level
Contact	Rhonda Rae Stewart- Tarney, CA

Description MNP is one of Western Canada's largest regional accounting firms. This office occasionally provides recruitment services for clients.

MEYERS NORRIS PENNY / MNP
140 - 2nd Avenue NW
Swift Current, SK S9H 3X4

Telephone	306-773-8375
Fax	306-773-7735
E-mail	lightfoota@mnp.ca
Website	www.mnp.ca
Employees	39
Specialties	Accounting Finance
Level	Mid-Level
Contact	Al Lightfoot, CA

Description MNP is one of Western Canada's largest regional accounting firms. This office occasionally provides recruitment services for clients.

MEYERS NORRIS PENNY / MNP
366 - 3rd Avenue South
Saskatoon, SK S7K 1M5

Telephone	306-665-6766
Fax	306-665-9910
E-mail	bernakevitchk@mnp.ca
Website	www.mnp.ca
Employees	48
Specialties	Accounting Finance
Level	Mid-Level
Contact	Kelly Bernakevitch, FCA

Description MNP is one of Western Canada's largest regional accounting firms, and provides a complete range of financial, management and business advisory services, including recruitment.

MEYERS NORRIS PENNY / MNP
25 - 11th Street East
Prince Albert, SK S6V 0Z8

Telephone	306-764-6873
Fax	306-763-0766
E-mail	reid@mnp.ca
Website	www.mnp.ca
Employees	15
Specialties	Accounting Finance
Level	Mid-Level
Contact	Gordon Reid, CA

Description MNP is one of Western Canada's largest regional accounting firms. This office occasionally provides recruitment services for clients.

MEYERS NORRIS PENNY / MNP
438 Victoria Ave. E., Suite 200
Regina, SK S4N 0N7

Telephone	306-525-8157
Fax	306-525-8159
E-mail	cochrane@mnp.ca
Website	www.mnp.ca
Employees	18
Specialties	Accounting Finance
Level	Mid-Level

Recruiters	Neil Cochrane CA Roy Spear
Contact	Neil Cochrane, CA

Description MNP is one of Western Canada's largest regional accounting firms, and provides a complete range of financial, management and business advisory services, including recruitment.

MEYERS NORRIS PENNY / MNP
701 - 9th Street
Humboldt, SK S0K 2A0

Telephone	306-682-2673
Fax	306-682-5910
E-mail	kunamand@mnp.ca
Website	www.mnp.ca
Employees	25
Specialties	Accounting Finance
Level	Mid-Level
Contact	Donald R. Kunaman, FCA

Description MNP is one of Western Canada's largest regional accounting firms. This office occasionally does recruitment work for clients.

MEYERS NORRIS PENNY / MNP
715 Main Street
Moosomin, SK S0G 3N0

Telephone	306-435-3347
Fax	306-435-2494
E-mail	mcfarlanel@mnp.ca
Website	www.mnp.ca
Employees	17
Specialties	Accounting Finance
Level	Mid-Level
Contact	Layne McFarlane, CA

Description MNP is one of Western Canada's largest regional accounting firms. This office occasionally does recruitment work for clients.

MEYERS NORRIS PENNY / MNP
609 Main Street
Melfort, SK S0E 1A0

Telephone	306-752-5800
Fax	306-752-5933
E-mail	harderj@mnp.ca
Website	www.mnp.ca
Employees	28
Specialties	Accounting Finance
Level	Mid-Level
Contact	John E. Harder, CA

Description MNP is one of Western Canada's largest regional accounting firms. This office occasionally does recruitment work for clients.

MEYERS NORRIS PENNY / MNP
103 Churchill Street
Hudson Bay, SK S0E 0Y0

Telephone	306-752-5800

Fax   306-752-5933
E-mail   ogrenm@mnp.ca
Website   www.mnp.ca

Employees 3

Specialties Accounting
             Finance

Level   Mid-Level

Contact   Milt Ogren, CA

Description MNP is one of Western Canada's largest regional accounting firms. This office occasionally provides recruitment services for clients.

MEYERS NORRIS PENNY / MNP

32 - 2nd Avenue SW
Dauphin, MB R7N 2V5

Telephone 204-638-6767
Fax   204-638-8634
E-mail   museyg@mnp.ca
Website   www.mnp.ca

Employees 20

Specialties Accounting
             Finance

Level   Mid-Level

Contact   Gerry Musey, CA

Description MNP is one of Western Canada's largest regional accounting firms, and provides a complete range of financial, management and business advisory services, including recruitment.

MEYERS NORRIS PENNY / MNP

1401 Princess Avenue
Brandon, MB R7A 7L7

Telephone 204-727-0661
Fax   204-726-1543
E-mail   motiuk@mnp.ca
Website   www.mnp.ca
Founded   1945
Employees 97

Specialties Accounting
             Finance

Level   Mid-Level

Fee Basis Retainer Only

Recruiters Tim Dekker CA
             Jim Foster
             Terry Motiuk
             Bob Twerdun

Contact   Terry Motiuk, CMA, CGA, MBA

Description MNP is one of Western Canada's largest regional accounting firms, and provides a complete range of financial, management and business advisory services, including recruitment work for clients.

MEYERS NORRIS PENNY / MNP

1661 Portage Avenue, Suite 500
Winnipeg, MB R3J 3T7

Telephone 204-775-4531
Fax   204-987-4846
E-mail   search@mnp.ca
Website   www.mnp.ca

Specialties Accounting

Finance
Sales
Management

Level   Mid-Level
             Senior

Recruiters Carolyn Bensky
             Barbara Bowes CHRP
             Diane Chomichuk
             Leslie Dornan
             Maureen Drummond
             Josée Lemoine
             Liane MacIntosh
             Sherry Phaneuf CHRP
             David Rushforth
             Jennifer Sitarz

Contact   Sherry Phaneuf CHRP, Partner

Description MNP (formerly The Bentley Consulting Group Ltd.) is an accounting and consulting firm that also does recruitment work for clients.

MEYERS NORRIS PENNY / MNP

14 Tupper Street S.
Portage La Prairie, MB R1N 1W6

Telephone 204-239-6117
Fax   204-857-3972
E-mail   ronaldk@mnp.ca
Website   www.mnp.ca

Employees 54

Specialties Accounting
             Finance

Level   Mid-Level

Contact   Keith Ronald, CA

Description MNP is one of Western Canada's largest regional accounting firms. This office occasionally does recruitment work for clients.

MEYERS NORRIS PENNY / MNP

233 Queen Street West
Virden, MB R0M 2C0

Telephone 204-748-1340
Fax   204-748-3294
E-mail   kirkupt@mnp.ca
Website   www.mnp.ca

Employees 12

Specialties Accounting
             Finance

Level   Mid-Level

Contact   Tom Kirkup, CA

Description MNP is one of Western Canada's largest regional accounting firms. This office occasionally does recruitment work for clients.

MEYERS NORRIS PENNY / MNP

207 North Railway West
Deloraine, MB R0M 0M0

Telephone 204-747-3111
Fax   204-747-2989
E-mail   galvinj@mnp.ca
Website   www.mnp.ca

Employees 5

Specialties Accounting
             Finance

Level   Mid-Level

Contact   Julee Galvin, CA

Description MNP is one of Western Canada's largest regional accounting firms. This office occasionally does recruitment work for clients.

MEYERS NORRIS PENNY / MNP

501 Broadway
Kilarney, MB R0K 1G0

Telephone 204-523-4633
Fax   204-523-4538
E-mail   schultzr@mnp.ca
Website   www.mnp.ca

Employees 8

Specialties Accounting
             Finance

Level   Mid-Level

Contact   Ron Schultz, CA

Description MNP is one of Western Canada's largest regional accounting firms. This office occasionally does recruitment work for clients.

MEYERS NORRIS PENNY / MNP

251 Davidson Street
Neepawa, MB R0J 1H0

Telephone 204-476-2326
Fax   204-476-3663
E-mail   henlisia@mnp.ca
Website   www.mnp.ca

Employees 13

Specialties Accounting
             Finance

Level   Mid-Level

Contact   Dave Henlisia, CA

Description MNP is one of Western Canada's largest regional accounting firms. This office occasionally does recruitment work for clients.

MICHAEL FOLLETT CONSULTING INC.

650 Riverbend Drive, Suite A1
Kitchener, ON N2K 3S2

Telephone 519-742-8700
Fax   519-742-9298
E-mail   info@follett consulting.com
Website   www.follett consulting.com

Specialties Govt/Nonprofit
             Management

Level   Senior

Recruiters April-Dawn Blackwell
             Michael Follett CMC

Contact   Michael Follett CMC

Description Michael Follett Consulting is a management consulting firm active in all areas of human resources consulting, including executive and board-level recruitment.

MICHAEL J. CAVANAGH & ASSOCIATES

60 St. Clair Ave. East, Suite 905
Toronto, ON M4T 1N5

Telephone	416-324-9661
Fax	416-324-0958
E-mail	cavsearch@ sympatico.ca
Founded	1989
Employees	2
Specialties	Operations Purchasing Telecom Logistics Management
Level	Senior Mid-Level
Min. Salary	$70,000
Fee Basis	Retainer Only
Contact	Michael J. Cavanaugh , President

MICHAEL MARMUR & ASSOCIATES
4950 Yonge Street
Suite 2200, Madison Centre
Toronto, ON M2N 6K1

Telephone	416-410-3311
E-mail	search@marmur.ca
Founded	1992
Employees	3
Specialties	Computing Telecom
Level	Mid-Level Senior
Min. Salary	$90,000
Fee Basis	Retainer Only
Contact	Michael J. Marmur, MBA, CMC

Description Michael Marmur & Associates specializes in the recruitment of senior managers and executives for IT positions across all industry sectors.

MICHAEL PAGE FINANCE
One Pacific Place
Suite 601, 88 Queensway
Hong Kong   CHINA

Telephone	852-2530-2000
Fax	852-2530-2255
E-mail	hkbanking@ michaelpage.com.hk
Website	www.michael page.com.hk
Founded	1994
Employees	30
Specialties	International Finance Banking Accounting Sales Marketing
Level	Mid-Level Senior
Recruiters	Dan Chavasse Guy Day Hugh Everard Richard Letcher Andrew Oliver
Contact	Dan Chavasse, Director

Description Michael Page Finance specializes in executive recruitment in the finance, banking and sales and marketing sectors, as well as contract assignments.

MICHAEL PAGE INTERNATIONAL
405 Lexington Avenue
The Chrysler Building
New York, NY 10174   USA

Telephone	212-661-4800
Fax	212-661-6622
E-mail	lorrycrecco@ michaelpage.com
Website	www.michaelpage.com
Specialties	Finance Accounting Banking International
Level	Mid-Level Senior
Recruiters	Lorry Crecco Chantal Phillipps

Description Michael Page International is a leader in the recruitment industry.

MICHAEL STERN ASSOCIATES INC.
70 University Avenue, Suite 370
Toronto, ON M5J 2M4

Telephone	416-593-0100
Fax	416-593-5716
E-mail	search@ michaelstern.com
Website	www.michaelstern.com
Founded	1982
Employees	6
Specialties	Computing Hospitality Management Marketing Retail Sales Telecom
Level	Senior
Min. Salary	$70,000
Fee Basis	Retainer Only
Recruiters	Glenda Hirvela Dane MacCarthy James Parr Michael Stern Bob Sturgess Margaret Vanwyck
Contact	Michael Stern, President

Description Michael Stern Associates Inc. specializes in executive search from a strategic point of view.

MICHEL PAUZÉ ET ASSOCIÉS
1470, rue Peel, bur. 1000, Tour A
Montréal, QC H3A 1T1

Téléphone	514-845-2128
Télécopieur	514-845-8687
Courriel	michel.pauze@ sympatico.ca
Fondée	1977
Employés	15
Spécialités	Publicité Marketing direct International Marketing Multimédia Emballage Imprimerie Édition/média
Échelon	Direction Intermédiaire
Recruteurs	Hervé Benoit Denis Carter Louise Hudon Isabelle Larivière Michel Pauzé Louise Pauzé Sylvie Roy
Contact	Michel Pauzé

MIDLYN ADVERTISING INC.
2458 Haywood Avenue West
PO Box 86097
North Vancouver, BC V7V 1Y1

Telephone	604-926-2987
Fax	604-926-6478
E-mail	jobs@ canadacareers.com
Website	www.canadacareers. com
Specialties	General Practice

Description Midlyn Advertising Inc. is a BC-owned and operated recruitment advertising agency.

MILAGROW TECHNOLOGY SOLUTIONS
470 Granville Street, Suite 930
Vancouver, BC V6C 1V5

Telephone	604-606-7106
Fax	604-683-4010
E-mail	info@milagrow.com
Website	www.milagrow.com
Specialties	Computing
Level	Mid-Level Senior
Contact	Marnie Franklin

Description Milagrow Technology Solutions is an IT recruiting firm.

MILES PARTNERSHIP, THE
54 St. James Street, Bennet House
London SW1A 1JT
UNITED KINGDOM

Telephone	44-20-7495-7772
Fax	44-20-7495-7773
E-mail	postbox@miles-partnership.com
Website	www.miles-partnership.com
Specialties	International
Level	Senior
Fee Basis	Retainer Only
Recruiters	Nigel Backwith Guy Beresford Miles Broadbent Chris Stainton
Contact	Miles Broadbent

Description Miles Partnership provides executive search services to UK and international clients across a range of sectors.

MILGRAM & ASSOCIATES

100 Adelaide St. W., Suite 502
Toronto, ON M5H 1S3

Telephone   416-366-2256

Founded   1980
Employees   5

Specialties   Insurance
            Banking
            Marketing
            Accounting
            Actuarial
            Finance

Level   Senior
            Mid-Level

Min. Salary $60,000
Fee Basis   Retainer Only

Contact   David Milgram, M.Sc.,
            MSW

Description Milgram & Associates
works on retainer to meet the personality profiles of clients.

MILLAR WALKER & GAY

379 Dundas Street East, 2nd Floor
Toronto, ON M5A 2A6

Telephone   416-365-7818
Fax   416-368-6716
E-mail   mwgmt@idirect.com

Specialties   Accounting
            Finance

Contact   Jim Millar

MILLER & ASSOCIATES LTD.

2085 Hurontario Street, Suite 300
Mississauga, ON L5A 4G1

Telephone   905-281-3090
Fax   905-281-9641
E-mail   resume@
            itcareermatch.com
Website   www.itcareer
            match.com

Founded   1989
Employees   4

Specialties   Computing
Level   Mid-Level
            Senior

Min. Salary $40,000
Fee Basis   Always contingent

Recruiters   Donna Hawkins CPC
            Marcus Miller

Contact   Marcus Miller

Description Miller & Associates provides IT recruitment services to
companies throughout the Greater
Toronto Area.

MILLER RECRUITMENT SOLUTIONS INC.

33 Ochterloney Street
Suite 250, Quaker Landing
Halifax, NS B2Y 4P5

Telephone   902-466-2255
Fax   902-466-0009
E-mail   careers@careers
            bythesea.com
Website   www.careers
            bythesea.com
Founded   1999

Employees   2

Specialties   General Practice
            Accounting
            Engineering
            Logistics
            Management
            Marketing
            Sales

Level   Senior
            Mid-Level

Fee Basis   Always contingent

Contact   Scott E. Miller,
            President

Description Professional recruiters
working with a select clintele requiring the services of proactive, discre-
tionary recruitment.

MINDBANK CONSULTING GROUP

8500 Leesburg Pike, Suite 602
Vienna, VA 22182   USA

Telephone   703-893-4700
Fax   703-761-3038
E-mail   info@mindbank.com
Website   www.mindbank.com

Founded   1986

Specialties   Computing
            International

Recruiters   Peter Brooks
            Kathy Cox
            Neal Grunstra
            Donna Merryman
            Randy Michael
            Judy Perrault

Contact   Neal Grunstra,
            President

Description Mindbank Consulting
Group provides IT professionals to
a range of clients including Fortune
500 companies, defense contractors
and government agencies nationwide.

MINTZ & PARTNERS, LLP

1446 Don Mills Road, Suite 100
Toronto, ON M3B 3N6

Telephone   416-391-2900
Fax   416-644-4341
E-mail   hr@mintzca.com
Website   www.mintzca.com

Specialties   Accounting
            Real Estate
            Finance

Level   Mid-Level

Recruiters   Jacqueline McDonald
            Annette Plorins

Contact   Annette Plorins

Description Mintz & Partners LLP is
a chartered accounting firm providing a complete range of professional
services to national and international clients, including search and
recruiting work.

MIS RESOURCES INTERNATIONAL, INC.

801 Brickell Avenue, 9th Floor
Miami, FL 33131
USA

Telephone   305-860-9133
E-mail   jobs@mis-resources.
            com
Website   www.mis-resources.
            com

Specialties   Computing
            International

Description Originally founded in
Montreal, MIS-Resources places IT
professionals on contracts throughout the southeast USA.

MIS RESOURCES INTERNATIONAL, INC.

7380 Sand Lake Road, 5th Floor
Orlando, FL 32819
USA

Telephone   407-352-5281
E-mail   jobs@mis-resources.
            com
Website   www.mis-resources.
            com

Specialties   Computing
            International

Description Originally founded in
Montreal, MIS-Resources places IT
professionals on contracts throughout the southeast USA.

MIS RESOURCES INTERNATIONAL, INC.

570 Colonial Park Drive, Suite 301
Roswell, GA 30075
USA

Telephone   770-594-7500
Fax   770-587-1932
E-mail   jobs@mis-
            resources.com
Website   www.mis-
            resources.com

Founded   1985

Specialties   International
            Computing

Description Originally founded in
Montreal, MIS-Resources places IT
professionals on contracts throughout the southeast USA.

MISS HALL'S PERSONNEL SERVICES LTD.

56 Sparks Street, Suite 300
Ottawa, ON K1P 5A9

Telephone   613-233-8469
Fax   613-233-5280
E-mail   misshalls@cyberus.ca

Specialties   Librarians
            Administrative

Level   Mid-Level
            Senior

Recruiters   Kitty Cocks
            Nathalie Gauthier
            Hélène Martin

Contact   Nathalie Gauthier

MISSION CRITICAL RECRUITMENT

10256 - 112th Street, Suite 301
Edmonton, AB T5K 1M4

Telephone   780-497-7707

Fax	780-497-7700
E-mail	target@mcrwork.com
Website	www.mcrwork.com

Specialties	Sales
	General Practice
	Management
Level	Mid-Level
Contact	Susan Hazelwood

Description Mission Critical Recruitment is a Canadian-based search firm that places only the top 20% of potential candidates in diverse fields from management to administration.

MOLNAR & ASSOCIATES
330 Bay Street, Suite 1500
Toronto, ON M5H 2S8

Telephone	416-368-2233
Fax	416-368-0751
E-mail	dkm@molnarand associates.com
Founded	1986
Employees	7
Specialties	Accounting
	Banking
	Finance
Level	Mid-Level
Fee Basis	Always contingent
Contact	Dana Molnar

Description Molnar & Associates specializes in providing executive search for the financial services industry.

MONTGOMERY THOMASON & ASSOCIATES
53 Village Centre Place, Suite 203
Mississauga, ON L4Z 1V9

Telephone	905-896-7103
Fax	905-566-0177
E-mail	thomason@ compuserve.com
Founded	1988
Employees	2
Specialties	Sales
	Engineering
	Marketing
	Operations
	Finance
	Management
	Scientific
	Metals
	Plastics
	Pulp & Paper
Level	Senior
	Mid-Level
Fee Basis	Sometimes contingent
Contact	Ronald Thomason

Description Recruiting technical people who enjoy working in sales, engineering, manufacturing and research.

MOON OVER NIAGARA HOSPITALITY RESOURCES
195 King Street, Suite 201
St. Catharines, ON L2R 3J6

Telephone	905-688-3331
Fax	905-688-0247
E-mail	careercl@mergetel.com
Founded	1997
Specialties	Hospitality
	Management
	Retail
	Trade Shows
Fee Basis	Sometimes contingent
Recruiters	Heather Barber
	Mark Moon
Contact	Mark Moon, Co-Owner

Description Moon Over Niagara Hospitality Resources is a licensed recruiting and training firm providing staff and training to employers in the service, hospitality and tourism industries.

MORGAN & BANKS LTD.
26 Flinders Street, Level 15
Adelaide, SA 5000
AUSTRALIA

Telephone	61-8-8212-2677
Fax	61-8-8212-6233
E-mail	applyadl@ morganbanks.com.au
Website	www.morganbanks. com.au
Founded	1986
Employees	60
Specialties	Management
	International
	General Practice
Level	Mid-Level
	Senior
Fee Basis	Sometimes contingent
Recruiters	Sardi Calver
	Peter Goodwin
	Tony Hancock
	Greg May
	Phil Morton
	Geoff Qurban
	John Seaton
	Donny Walford
Contact	Geoff Qurban

Description An international human resources consultancy employing over 1,600 people worldwide. Now part of TMP Worldwide.

MORGAN & BANKS LTD.
26 St. Georges Terrace
6th Floor, International House
Perth, WA 6000
AUSTRALIA

Telephone	61-8-9323-0222
Fax	61-8-9323-0202
E-mail	applyper@ morganbanks.com.au
Website	www.morganbanks. com.au
Founded	1985
Specialties	Management
	International
Level	Mid-Level
	Senior

Description An international human resources consultancy employing

over 1,600 people worldwide. Now part of TMP Worldwide.

MORGAN EXECUTIVE SEARCH GROUP LTD.
35 Kilbarry Road
Toronto, ON M5P 1K4

Telephone	416-485-9192
Fax	416-485-7481
E-mail	morgansearchgrp@ sprint.ca
Founded	1970
Employees	5
Specialties	Accounting
	Engineering
	Marketing
	Purchasing
	Management
	Operations
	Sales
	Advertising
	Packaging
	Plastics
Level	Senior
	Mid-Level
Fee Basis	Sometimes contingent
Contact	Maureen Donaldson

MORGAN PALMER SEARCH DIRECTIVES INC.
10 King Street East, Suite 810
Toronto, ON M5C 1C3

Telephone	416-360-7788
Fax	416-360-3818
E-mail	jmaiste@interlog.com
Employees	4
Specialties	Finance
	Accounting
	Sales
	Marketing
	Management
	Operations
	Plastics
Level	Senior
	Mid-Level
Fee Basis	Retainer Only
Recruiters	Jeff Maiste
	Marvin Peck
	Doug Wallace
Contact	Jeff Maiste

MORRIS PERVIN GROUP INC.
90 Eglinton Avenue East, Suite 620
Toronto, ON M4P 2T3

Telephone	416-440-8434
Fax	416-503-3938
E-mail	resume@ morrispervin.com
Website	www.morrispervin.com
Founded	1999
Specialties	Advertising
	Multimedia
	Finance
	Marketing
	Direct Mktng.
	Sales
	Pharmaceutical
Recruiters	Martin Kingston

Barbara Morris
Timothy Pervin
Cornel Stander
Jennifer Stephenson

Contact   Timothy Pervin,
President

MOSCOE & COMPANY
5000 Dufferin Street, Suite 205
Toronto, ON M3H 5T5

Telephone   416-665-9559
Fax   416-665-9357

Specialties   Accounting
Finance

Level   Mid-Level

Description   Moscoe & Company is
an accounting firm that also does
search work for clients.

MOSOR SEARCH GROUP
201 City Centre Drive, Suite 900
Mississauga, ON L5B 2T4

Telephone   905-272-8984
Fax   905-272-9232
E-mail   samosor@hotmail.com

Specialties   Sales
Transport
Marketing

Level   Mid-Level

MOUNT ROYAL PERSONNEL
933 - 17th Avenue SW, Suite 400
Calgary, AB T2T 5R6

Telephone   403-228-4243
Fax   403-245-6227
E-mail   katemckenzie@
mrpcalgary.com

Specialties   Finance
Accounting

Level   Mid-Level

Contact   Kate McKenzie

MOXON DOLPHIN KERBY INTERNATIONAL
178 - 202 Great Portland Street
London W1W 5AD
UNITED KINGDOM

Telephone   44-20-323-0681
Fax   44-20-636-4977
E-mail   pshrigley@mdk.co.u

Specialties   International
Mining

Level   Senior
Mid-Level

Contact   Paul Shrigley

Description   Moxon Dolphin Kerby
specializes in international search
and selection.

MOXON PERSONNEL LTD.
701 West Georgia Street, Suite 1500
Vancouver, BC V7Y 1A1

Telephone   604-688-5100
Fax   604-688-0342
E-mail   moxon@
execcentre.com

Website   www.moxon
personnel.com

Founded   1988

Specialties   Accounting
Finance

Level   Mid-Level
Senior

Recruiters   Joanne Carroll
Ben Moxon CA
Tracy Ring
Marnie Ward-Whate
Audrey Zidle

Contact   Ben Moxon, CA

Description   Moxon Personnel is the
leading accounting placement
agency in British Columbia.

MPA RECHERCHE DE CADRES INC.
7900, boul. Taschereau O.
Bureau A-204
Brossard, QC J4X 1C2

Téléphone   514-875-3996
Télécopieur   450-465-9215
Courriel   courrier@m-p-a.qc.ca
Site Internet www.m-p-a.qc.ca

Fondée   1996
Employés   5

Spécialités   Automobile
Santé/médical
Logistique
Métaux
Emballage
Papeterie
Télécommunications

Échelon   Direction
Intermédiaire

Salaire min.   40 000 $
Frais   Honoraire seulement

Contact   Marc Paquet

Description   Recherche de cadres
intermé diaires et supérieurs.

MQS EXECUTIVE SEARCH
PO Box 824, Station B
Toronto, ON M2K 2R1

Telephone   416-497-5070
Fax   416-496-8899
E-mail   mqsjones@total.net
Website   www.miningjobs.com

Founded   1989

Specialties   Mining
Computing
Telecom
Sales

Level   Mid-Level

Fee Basis   Sometimes contingent

Contact   Fred Jones

Description   MQS provides local, national and international search services for the telecommunications and
mining industries.

MRK CONSULTING LTD.
1 School Lane, Bagshot
Surrey GU19 5BP
UNITED KINGDOM

Telephone   44-1276-476866

Fax   44-1276-479666
E-mail recruit@mrk-
consulting.co.uk
Website www.mrk-
consulting.co.uk

Founded   1988

Specialties   International
Computing
Telecom

Level   Senior
Mid-Level

Min. Salary $30,000
Fee Basis   Always contingent

Recruiters   Roger Hayes
Michael Ketley
Beverly Moss
Ann Young

Contact   Michael Ketley,
Principal

Description   MRK Consulting Ltd. is
a global IT recruitment specialist
with ability to secure scarce IT skills.

MSX INTERNATIONAL, INC.
2916 South Sheridan Way
Suite 100
Oakville, ON L6J 7J8

Telephone   905-829-0719
Fax   905-829-2437
Website   www.msxi.com

Specialties   Computing
Automotive
Engineering

Level   Senior
Mid-Level

Fee Basis   Sometimes contingent

Description   Based in Auburn Hills,
Michigan, MSX International is an
IT consulting and staffing firm for
the engineering and technology sectors.

MSX INTERNATIONAL, INC.
275 Rex Blvd.
Auburn Hills, MI 48326   USA

Telephone   248-299-1000
Fax   248-844-4115
Website   www.msxi.com

Founded   1967
Employees   1000

Specialties   Automotive
International
Computing
Engineering

Level   Senior
Mid-Level

Fee Basis   Sometimes contingent

Description   Based in Auburn Hills,
Michigan, MSX International is an
IT consulting and staffing firm for
the engineering and technology sectors.

MSX INTERNATIONAL, INC.
19855 West Outer Drive
Suites 300 & 500
Dearborn, MI 48124   USA

Telephone   248-304-7500

Fax	248-304-7505
Website	www.msxi.com
Founded	1967
Employees	1000
Specialties	Automotive
	International
	Computing
	Engineering
Level	Senior
	Mid-Level
Fee Basis	Sometimes contingent

Description Based in Auburn Hills, Michigan, MSX International is an IT consulting and staffing firm for the engineering and technology sectors.

MSX INTERNATIONAL, INC.
17425 Federal Drive
Allen Park, MI 48101-3614   USA

Telephone	313-203-6300
Fax	313-203-6310
E-mail	rabessinio@msxi.com
Website	www.msxi.com
Specialties	Engineering
	Automotive
	Computing
	International
Level	Mid-Level
	Senior
Recruiters	Rocco Abessinio
	Jennifer Bandurski
	Marcus Kirkland
Contact	Marcus Kirkland,
	Senior Lead Recruiter

Description Based in Auburn Hills, Michigan, MSX International is an IT consulting and staffing firm for the engineering and technology sectors.

MSX INTERNATIONAL, INC.
1100 East Mandoline, Suite B
Madison Heights, MI 48071   USA

Telephone	248-829-6390
Fax	248-829-6332
E-mail	jblair@msxi.com
Website	www.msxi.com
Founded	1967
Employees	1000
Specialties	Automotive
	International
	Computing
	Engineering
Level	Senior
	Mid-Level
Fee Basis	Sometimes contingent
Contact	Lori Kurek, Technical
	Recruiter

Description Based in Auburn Hills, Michigan, MSX International is an IT consulting and staffing firm for the engineering and technology sectors.

MULTEC CANADA LTD.
200 Ronson Drive, Suite 314
Toronto, ON M9W 5Z9

Telephone	416-244-2402
Fax	416-244-6883
E-mail	toronto@multec.ca
Website	www.multec.ca
Specialties	Engineering
	Computing
	Sales
	Management
Level	Mid-Level
Contact	Rick Randell, President

Description Multec Canada is a partner with Brunel International, a worldwide source for highly qualified engineers and managers.

MULTEC CANADA LTD.
38 Aurega Drive, Suite 266
Nepean, ON K2E 8A5

Telephone	613-228-8411
Fax	613-228-0303
E-mail	ottawa@multec.ca
Website	www.multec.ca
Specialties	Engineering
	Computing
	Sales
	Management
Level	Mid-Level
Contact	Kent E. Baston

Description Multec Canada is a partner with Brunel International, a worldwide source for highly qualified engineers and managers.

MULTEC CANADA LTD.
2000 Peel Street, Suite 888
Montréal, QC H3A 2W5

Telephone	514-396-7890
Fax	514-396-7144
E-mail	montreal@multec.ca
Website	www.multec.ca
Specialties	Engineering
	Computing
	Sales
	Management
Contact	Catharine Boyer

Description Multec Canada is a partner of Brunel International, a worldwide source for highly qualified engineers and managers.

MULTI-RESSOURCES
1510 boul. Rene-Levesque O.
Québec, QC G1S 1X5

Téléphone	418-681-7733
Télécopieur	418-681-1989
Courriel	jlabrie@
	multiressources.com
Spécialités	Finance
	Gestion
Échelon	Direction
	Intermédiaire
Recruteurs	Chantal Turcotte
	Marie Turmel
Contact	Chantal Turcotte

MULTIPERSONNEL INTERNATIONAL
9501, avenue Ryan, Bureau 201
Dorval, QC H9P 1A2

Telephone	514-636-3240
Fax	514-676-3388
E-mail	cv@multipersonnel.
	com
Specialties	Accounting
	Bilingual
	Engineering
	Finance
	Human Resource
	Administrative
	Transport
Level	Senior
	Mid-Level
Min. Salary	$40,000
Fee Basis	Sometimes contingent
Contact	André Allard

Description MultiPersonnel International recruits senior managers and professionals in all sectors.

MULTIPRO SERVICES CONSEILS
1253, avenue McGill College
Bureau 540
Montréal, QC H3B 2Y5

Telephone	514-874-0124
Fax	514-574-0622
E-mail	multipro@multipro-
	mtl.com
Website	www.multipro-mtl.com
Specialties	Computing
	Consulting

Description Multipro specializes in the recruitment of business consultants, management consultants and information technology specialists.

MUSKOKA STAFFING COMPANY LTD., THE
295 Wellington Street
Bracebridge, ON P1L 1P3

Telephone	705-645-0099
Fax	705-645-0009
E-mail	muskstaf@
	muskoka.com
Website	www.j2group.com/
	MuskokaStaffing
Specialties	Hospitality
	Health/Medical
Level	Mid-Level
	Junior
Recruiters	Jennifer Kingshott
	Leslie Larkin
	Kerri Murray
	Jim Stewart
	Jinty Stewart
Contact	Jim Stewart

Description The Muskoka Staffing Company is a placement firm that serves over 100 employers in Ontario's cottage country.

MVC ASSOCIATES INTERNATIONAL
36 Toronto Street, Suite 850
Toronto, ON M5C 2C5

Telephone	416-489-1917
Fax	416-489-2573
E-mail	kris@mvc
	international.com

Website	www.mvc international.com
Founded	1988
Employees	5
Specialties	General Practice Management Engineering Finance
Level	Senior
Fee Basis	Retainer Only
Contact	Mark Van Clieaf, Managing Director

Description MVC Associates completes board and executive-level searches using a "complexity based" candidate selection process.

NAP EXECUTIVE SERVICES (CANADA) INC., RETAIL DIVISION
3101 Bathurst Street, Suite 300
Toronto, ON M6A 2A6

Telephone	416-949-8896
E-mail	toronto@fashion-career.com
Website	www.fashion-career.com
Founded	1994
Employees	2
Specialties	Apparel Retail
Level	Senior Mid-Level
Min. Salary	$40,000
Fee Basis	Sometimes contingent
Contact	Steve Rothstein

Description NAP is a professional personnel recruiting firm servicing medium to large size apparel and retail businesses across the country.

NAP EXECUTIVE SERVICES INC., APPAREL & TEXTILE DIVISON
1230 Dr. Penfield, Suite 904
Montréal, QC H3G 1B5

Telephone	514-592-8896
Fax	514-592-5228
E-mail	montreal@fashion-career.com
Website	www.fashion-career.com
Founded	1974
Employees	3
Specialties	Apparel Retail
Level	Senior Mid-Level
Min. Salary	$40,000
Fee Basis	Sometimes contingent
Contact	Janet Presser

Description NAP is a professional personnel recruiting firm servicing medium to large size apparel and retail businesses across the country.

NARAMI EXECUTIVE SEARCH
191 The West Mall, Suite 500
Toronto, ON M9C 5K8

Telephone	416-626-8072
Fax	416-695-0246
E-mail	narami@home.com
Founded	1991
Specialties	Health/Medical Computing Marketing Sales
Min. Salary	$25,000
Fee Basis	Sometimes contingent
Contact	Corinna Ammoser, President

Description Narami specializes in sales, marketing and senior management positions in the healthcare and high tech industries.

NATIONAL COMPUTER PROFESSIONALS / NCP
4950 Yonge Street, Suite 2222
Toronto, ON M2N 6K1

Telephone	416-221-0881
Fax	416-221-7273
E-mail	ncp95@ncp95.com
Website	www.ncp95.com
Specialties	Computing
Recruiters	Carmen Furtado Darlene Harryott Adrian Lombardi
Contact	Attilio A. Lombardi, President

Description NCP is a dynamic search firm, providing a full range of human resources consulting services to the IT industry.

NATIONAL EXECUTIVE
3200 Dufferin Street, Suite 305
Toronto, ON M6A 3B2

Telephone	416-256-0300
Fax	416-256-0035
E-mail	resume@national-executive.com
Website	www.national-executive.com
Founded	1984
Employees	12
Specialties	Computing Engineering Management Aerospace Telecom
Level	Mid-Level Senior
Min. Salary	$30,000
Fee Basis	Always contingent
Recruiters	Don Cormier Peter Ferrante
Contact	Don Cormier

Description High tech specialists working on permanent and contract placements. Specialties include electronic / software engineering and information technology.

NATIONAL SYSTEMS INC.
8131 LBJ Freeway, Suite 800
Dallas, TX 75251 USA

Telephone	972-997-7260
Fax	972-997-7261
E-mail	nsi@nsiamerica.com
Website	www.nsiamerica.com
Founded	1996
Employees	35
Specialties	Computing Telecom International
Level	Senior Mid-Level
Fee Basis	Sometimes contingent
Contact	Hari Patro

Description National Systems Inc. specializes in placing experienced IT consultants, especially DBAs (Oracle, SQL Server, DB2), Unix administrators, ERP experts (JD Edwards, SAP, BaaN) and Oracle experts.

NATIONWIDE ADVERTISING SERVICE / NAS
1185 West Georgia Street, Suite 910
Vancouver, BC V6E 4E6

Telephone	604-683-4461
Fax	604-689-5886
E-mail	nas.vc@hrads.com
Website	www.hrads.com
Founded	1947
Specialties	General Practice Hospitality

Description NAS is the largest and oldest independent, full-service agency specializing in human resource advertising, communications and promotions.

NATIONWIDE ADVERTISING SERVICE / NAS
119 Spadina Avenue
Suite 901, Balfour Building
Toronto, ON M5V 2L1

Telephone	416-971-7866
Fax	416-971-9139
E-mail	nas.to@hrads.com
Website	www.hrads.com
Founded	1947
Specialties	General Practice Sales Marketing

Description NAS is the largest and oldest independent, full-service agency specializing in human resource advertising, communications and promotions.

NATIONWIDE ADVERTISING SERVICE / NAS
280 Albert Street, Suite 703
Ottawa, ON K1P 5G8

Telephone	613-236-5839
Fax	613-236-7423
E-mail	nas.ot@hrads.com
Website	www.hrads.com
Founded	1947
Specialties	General Practice

Description NAS is the largest and oldest independent, full-service agency specializing in Human Resource advertising, communications and promotions.

NATIONWIDE ADVERTISING SERVICE / NAS
1023 Executive Parkway, Suite 16
St. Louis, MO 63141   USA

Telephone	314-579-0050
Fax	314-579-0575
E-mail	nas.st@hrads.com
Website	www.hrads.com
Founded	1947
Specialties	General Practice International

Description NAS is the largest and oldest independent, full-service agency specializing in Human Resource advertising, communications and promotions.

NCL PERSONNEL INC.
10458, avenue des Recollets
Montréal, QC H1H 4E7

Téléphone	514-329-7008
Spécialités	Imprimerie Transport
Échelon	Intermédiaire
Contact	Claude Lamoureaux, Directeur

NCR ASSOCIATES
130 Albert St., Suite 605
Ottawa, ON K1P 5G4

Telephone	613-234-5686
Fax	819-643-4878
E-mail	ncr.rcn@qc.aira.com
Specialties	Banking Govt/Nonprofit Human Resource

NELSON KRYNICKI & ASSOCIATES INC
1084 Queen Street West, Suite 24B
Mississauga, ON L5H 4K4

Telephone	905-274-1917
Fax	905-271-0759
E-mail	recruit@nkait.com
Founded	1998
Specialties	Computing Telecom
Level	Senior Mid-Level
Fee Basis	Sometimes contingent
Recruiters	Margaret Krynicki Tim Nelson
Contact	Tim Nelson

Description NK&A recruits executives and IT personnel for permanent and contract positions.

NES OVERSEAS LTD.
Station House
Stamford New Road, Altrincham
Cheshire WA14 1EP
UNITED KINGDOM

Telephone	44-161-929-1313
Fax	44-161-926-9867
E-mail	admin@nes overseas.com
Website	www.nes.co.uk
Specialties	Oil & Gas Construction International

Description NES Overseas Ltd., a division of NES Group, specializes in the management and engineering resource demands of worldwide clients in the hydrocarbon, power, water and construction market sectors in the Middle East, Asia, Africa, the Americas and Europe.

NESMA INTERNATIONAL SERVICES LIMITED
39A Lower Brook Street
Unit 1, Merchants Court
Ipswich IP4 1AQ
UNITED KINGDOM

Telephone	44-1473-281700
Fax	44-1473-216473
Website	www.nesma.com
Specialties	International Telecom Engineering

Description NESMA provides large-scale technical staffing services for demanding technical and industrial projects in Saudi Arabia, particularly in communications.

NET-TEMPS INC.
55 Middlesex Street, Suite 220
North Chelmsford, MA 01863
USA

Telephone	800-307-0062
Fax	978-251-7250
E-mail	service@net-temps.com
Website	www.net-temps.com
Founded	1996
Specialties	General Practice International
Contact	Gregory A. Booth, President

Description Net-Temps Inc. is a leading Internet-based recruitment site for placement agencies to advertise their own contract and permanent opportunities.

NETGAIN PARTNERS INC.
390 Bay Street, Suite 701
Toronto, ON M5H 2Y2

Telephone	416-367-2385
Fax	416-956-7754
E-mail	netgain.reed@ on.aibn.com
Website	www.netgain partners.com
Specialties	Govt/Nonprofit
Level	Mid-Level Senior
Recruiters	Clark Reed Rod Smith
Contact	Clark Reed

Description Netgain Partners Inc. is a consulting firm that specializes in the cultural and non-profit sector. Their services include executive search and staff recruitment in this field.

NETWORK CORPORATE SEARCH PERSONNEL INC.
500 - 4th Avenue SW, Suite 1515
Calgary, AB T2P 2V6

Telephone	403-262-6630
Fax	403-262-5150
E-mail	network@ cadvision.com
Specialties	Computing Insurance Oil & Gas Sales
Level	Mid-Level
Fee Basis	Always contingent
Recruiters	Kim McKay Pat Riddell
Contact	Pat Riddell

Description Network Corporate Search specializes in the recruitment of professionals in the computer, insurance, and oil & gas industries, with focus on permanent career positions in Canada and USA.

NEW WORLD INTERNATIONAL CONSULTANTS
267 Pelissier Street
Suite 501, Security Building
Windsor, ON N9A 4K4

Telephone	519-252-0559
Fax	519-252-5153
E-mail	newworld@mnsi.net
Website	www.go2rsite.com/ newworld
Founded	1994
Specialties	Computing Health/Medical Engineering International Trades/Technicians
Level	Senior Mid-Level
Fee Basis	Always contingent
Contact	Susan Techko, President

Description New World International Consultants and its parent company, MIR Consultants Ltd., provide professional immigration and recruitment services in the healthcare, computer, engineering and manufacturing fields.

NEW ZEALAND SKILLS EXPORT LTD.
Wellesley Street, PO Box 6120
Auckland, NEW ZEALAND

Telephone	64-9-360-1156
Fax	64-9-376-1523
E-mail	nzskills@ paradise.net.nz
Specialties	International Oil & Gas

Contact   Petra Niermann

Description New Zealand Skills Export Ltd. specializes in placing oil and gas staff in the Middle East and India.

NEWFOUNDLAND PERSONNEL INC.
3 Queens Street, 2nd Floor
PO Box 1840, Station C
St. John's, NF A1C 5R2

Telephone	709-579-3400
Fax	709-579-0464
E-mail	info@nfpersonnel.nf.net
Website	www.nfpersonnel.nf.net
Founded	1983
Employees	3
Specialties	Administrative
	Computing
	Direct Mktng.
	Human Resource
	Oil & Gas
Level	Mid-Level
	Senior
Fee Basis	Always contingent
Recruiters	Kelly Critch
	Judy English
	Doug Haynes
	Jonathan Pearce
Contact	Judy English, President

Description Newfoundland-owned agency that does placements at all levels, including executive search.

NEWORK CORP.
21 St. Clair Avenue East, Suite 400
Toronto, ON M4T 1L9

Telephone	416-323-0944
Fax	416-323-0230
E-mail	jobs@neworkcorp.com
Website	www.neworkcorp.com
Founded	1998
Employees	25
Specialties	Multimedia
	Computing
	Design
	Finance
Level	Senior
	Mid-Level
Min. Salary	$50,000
Fee Basis	Always contingent
Recruiters	Cherene Bajin
	Kelli Cera
	Dorothy Charbonneau
	Audrey Clydesdale
	Tim Cromwell
	Ron Goldson
	Sandi Marques
	Laura Mitchell
	Rob Munday
	Steve Opena
	Dan Patel
	Peter Townsend
	Chris Volum
Contact	Sandi Marques, Director of Operations

Description Nework Corp. operates in three areas: new media, information technology and financial serv-ices. Nework sources talent for each of these vertical markets.

NEWSOURCE MANAGEMENT LTD.
145 King Street West, Suite 1000
Toronto, ON M5H 1J8

Telephone	416-368-2333
Fax	905-275-5677
E-mail	info@newsource.ca
Website	www.newsource.ca
Specialties	Management
	Finance
	Accounting
	Human Resource
	Sales
	Marketing
	Computing
Level	Senior
	Mid-Level
Recruiters	Tom Bell
	Gary Busteed
	Bruce Heslip MBA
	Rod Howland
	Andy Silman
Contact	Bruce Heslip, Partner

Description NewSource Management specializes in placing senior-level candidates in technology, finance, accounting, human resources and sales and marketing.

NEX CANADA INC.
55 University Avenue
Suite 305, PO Box 35
Toronto, ON M5J 2H7

Telephone	416-867-1162
Fax	416-867-1369
E-mail	pasonajh@echo-on.net
Website	www.nex-usa.com
Founded	1992
Employees	4
Specialties	International
	Administrative
	Automotive
	Management
	Engineering
	Finance
	Marketing
	Bilingual
Fee Basis	Always contingent
Recruiters	Sawako Fukami
	Joy Haywood
	Fumie Wada
Contact	Joy Haywood

Description Next Canada Inc. (formerly Pasona Canada, Inc.) is an employment agency serving all industries and levels. Strong focus on Japanese bilingual placements.

NEXSTAF IT RECRUITMENT
116 Spadina Avenue, Suite 300
Toronto, ON M5V 2K6

Telephone	416-203-1711
Fax	416-203-1577
E-mail	resumes@nexstaf.com
Website	www.nexstaf.com
Specialties	Computing
Level	Mid-Level
Recruiters	Brian Edmunds
	Dennis Miller
	Scott O'Donoghue
	Paul Paterson
	Prentice Smith
	Ryan Sutherland
Contact	Scott O'Donoghue

Description Nexstaf is an IT recruitment firm.

NONPROFIT CAREER QUEST
34 Robertson Street
Fergus, ON N1M 3P6

Telephone	519-787-1443
Fax	519-787-2728
E-mail	careerquest@on.aibn.com
Website	www.nonprofitcareerquest.com
Specialties	Govt/Nonprofit
Level	Mid-Level

Description Nonprofit Career Quest is a centralized resource centre for the employment and volunteer needs of the non-profit sector in Canada.

NORAMTEC CONSULTANTS INC.
1382 Main Street North, 2nd Floor
North Vancouver, BC V7J 1C6

Telephone	604-983-3551
Fax	604-983-3551
E-mail	noramtec@westcad.com
Website	www.gsa-search.com
Founded	1964
Specialties	Engineering
	Design
	Trades/Technicians
Level	Mid-Level
Contact	Harvey Fishman

Description Noramtec Consultants, recently merged with GSA Search Consultants, offers flexible staffing solutions to premier organizations on contract, contract-to-hire or a full-time basis.

NORAMTEC CONSULTANTS INC.
10506 Jasper Avenue
Suite 1006, 10th Floor
Edmonton, AB T5J 2W9

Telephone	780-448-9364
Fax	780-428-4831
E-mail	jobs@gsa-search.com
Website	www.gsa-search.com
Specialties	Engineering
	Computing
Level	Mid-Level
	Junior
Contact	Kiran Garbaria

Description Noramtec Consultants, now part of GSA Search Consultants, offers flexible staffing solutions to premier organizations on contract, contract-to-hire or a full-time basis.

NORAMTEC CONSULTANTS INC.
6 Gurdwara Road
Nepean, ON K2G 3J2

Telephone	613-727-3997
Fax	613-727-5116
E-mail	andrew@noramtec.com
Website	www.gsa-search.com
Specialties	Trade Shows
	Engineering
	Design
	Computing
Level	Mid-Level
Contact	Andrew Charles

Description Noramtec Consultants, recently merged with GSA Search Consultants, offers flexible staffing solutions to premier organizations on contract, contract-to-hire or a full-time basis.

NORAMTEC CONSULTANTS INC.
19 Heritage Drive, PO Box 331
Bath, ON K0H 1G0

Telephone	613-352-7599
Fax	613-352-5985
E-mail	jobs@gsa-search.com
Website	www.gsa-search.com
Specialties	Engineering
	Computing
Level	Mid-Level
	Junior
Contact	Les Guest

Description Noramtec Consultants, recently merged with GSA Search Consultants, offers flexible staffing solutions to premier organizations on contract, contract-to-hire or a full-time basis.

NORAMTEC CONSULTANTS INC.
180 Rene-Levesque Boulevard East
Suite 112
Montréal, QC H2X 1N5

Telephone	514-861-6678
Fax	514-861-0307
E-mail	mda@noramtec.com
Website	www.gsa-search.com
Specialties	Engineering
	Oil & Gas
	International
Level	Mid-Level
Recruiters	Morie-Josée Binda
	André Boudeau
	Mike McDuff
Contact	John Kubinski

Description Noramtec Consultants, recently merged with GSA Search Consultants, offers flexible staffing solutions to premier organizations on contract, contract-to-hire or a full-time basis.

NORMATECH EXECUTIVE TECHNICAL MANAGEMENT
2350 Dundas Street West, Suite 421
Toronto, ON M6P 4B1

Telephone	416-535-7566
Fax	416-802-8945
E-mail	normatech@
	accglobal.net
Specialties	Aerospace
	Automotive
	Design
	Engineering
	Management
	Oil & Gas
	Telecom
Level	Senior
	Mid-Level
Min. Salary	$50,000
Fee Basis	Sometimes contingent
Contact	Alicja Wlodek

Description Normatech Executive provides comprehensive technical search services, from senior executive management positions to engineering, consulting, marketing and manufacturing professionals.

NORRELL SERVICES CANADA LTD.
4940 No 3 Road, Suite 305
Richmond, BC V6X 3A5

Telephone	604-273-5474
Fax	604-273-4042
E-mail	smurphy@
	norrellrichmond.com
Website	www.norrell.com
Specialties	Administrative
	Accounting
	Finance
Level	Mid-Level
	Junior

Description Norrell Services Canada Ltd. is a workforce management company specializing in managing vendor partnering, call centre management, financial staffing, executive projects and information technology.

NORRELL SERVICES CANADA LTD.
1166 Alberni Street, Suite 1201
Vancouver, BC V6E 3Z2

Telephone	604-688-9556
Fax	604-682-0955
E-mail	zarina@norrellvan.com
Website	www.norrell.com
Specialties	Administrative
	Accounting
	Forestry
Level	Mid-Level
	Junior
Contact	Zarina Jan Mohamed,
	Area Manager

Description Norrell Services Canada Ltd. is a workforce management company specializing in managing vendor partnering, call centre management, financial staffing, executive projects and information technology.

NORRELL SERVICES CANADA LTD.
2 Bloor Street West, Suite 1802
Toronto, ON M4W 3E2

Telephone	416-923-9801
Fax	416-923-1064
Website	www.norrell.com

Specialties	General Practice
	Accounting
	Administrative
	Finance
	Computing
Level	Mid-Level
	Junior

Description Norrell Services Canada Ltd. is a workforce management company specializing in managing vendor partnering, call centre management, financial staffing, executive projects and information technology.

NORTEC INFORMATION CONSULTANTS INC.
155 Queen Street, Suite 1302
Ottawa, ON K1P 6L1

Telephone	613-786-3290
Fax	613-786-3291
E-mail	jobs@nortec.on.ca
Website	www.nortec.on.ca
Founded	1993
Specialties	Computing
Level	Mid-Level
Contact	Courtney Klein,
	President

Description Nortec Information Consultants Inc. recruits experienced and qualified information systems consultants for the National Capital Region's high-technology sector.

NORTH AMERICAN SEARCH GROUP INC.
145 King Street W., Suite 1000
Toronto, ON M5H 3Z6

Telephone	416-861-9301
Fax	416-861-0433
Employees	2
Specialties	Insurance
	Actuarial
Level	Mid-Level
	Senior
Contact	Iqbal Shaw

Description North American Search Group specializes in actuarial placements.

NORTH YORK PERSONNEL INC.
5799 Yonge Street, Suite 404
Toronto, ON M2M 3V3

Telephone	416-226-2244
Fax	416-226-4244
E-mail	enquiries@
	northyorkpersonnel.com
Website	www.northyork
	personnel.com
Specialties	Bilingual
	Administrative
	Accounting
	Banking
Level	Mid-Level
	Junior
Contact	Paula Arnold, Owner

Description NYP is an owner operated, Canadian-based agency.

NORTHEAST TEACHER PERSONNEL SERVICES
34 Glendale Avenue
Mount Pearl, NF A1N 1M9

Fax 709-834-8603
Specialties Education
Description Northeast Teacher Personnel Services is a company dedicated to placing Newfoundland teachers in Northeastern and Northwestern Ontario schools.

NORTHWIND CONSULTING ALLIANCE
Box 276
King City, ON L7B 1A6

Fax 905-833-0321
E-mail bjm@northwind alliance.com
Specialties Sales
Packaging
Level Mid-Level
Contact B.J. Marshall

NOVARA COMP SERVICES INC.
1025 Old Country Road
Westbury, NY 11590
USA

Telephone 516-780-2000
Fax 516-512-6139
E-mail info@novaratech.com
Website www.novaratech.com
Founded 1993
Employees 120
Specialties Computing
International
Contact Miheer Shah, President
Description Novara Comp Services is an IT consulting firm with offices in New York, Florida and India that places IT consultants.

NU-TECH RECRUITERS INC.
4211 Yonge Street, Suite 323
Toronto, ON M2P 2A9

Telephone 416-224-8324
Fax 416-224-8844
E-mail jobs@itrecruiter.net
Website www.itrecruiter.net
Specialties Computing
Level Mid-Level
Contact Harry Benz
Description Nu-Tech Recruiters Inc. is a technical recruitment agency that specializes in Information Technology staffing.

NUGGET GROUP INC., THE / TNG GLOBAL
4115 Sherbrooke St. West, Suite 320
Westmount, QC H3Z 1K9

Telephone 514-931-8542
Fax 514-931-8310
E-mail inquiries@ tngglobal.com
Website www.tngglobal.com
Founded 1995
Specialties Computing
Management
Level Senior
Contact Norman Gold
Description TNG Global is a leading provider of packaged software implementation consultants.

NURSEFINDERS, INC.
1701 East Lamar Blvd., Suite 200
Arlington, TX 76006
USA

Telephone 817-460-1181
Fax 817-462-9146
E-mail info@nursefinders.com
Website www.nursefinders.com
Specialties Health/Medical
International
Level Mid-Level
Senior
Description Nursefinders, Inc. provides high-level nursing and allied health personnel services to hospitals, nursing homes, clinics and other healthcare facilities.

NURSES RX CANADA
9800 West Kincey Ave., Suite 150
Huntersville, NC 28078
USA

Telephone 800-733-9354
Fax 800-408-9227
E-mail nursesrx@ nursesrx.com
Website www.nursesrx.com
Founded 1990
Specialties Health/Medical
International
Level Mid-Level
Recruiters Melissa Bessent
Christine Brown
Donna Flynn
Meredith McKee
Contact Donna Flynn
Description Nurses Rx Canada offers career opportunities to Canadian nurses exploring career opportunities in the USA.

NURSING & HOME HEALTH CARE INC. / NHI
120 Adelaide St. West, Suite 1201
Toronto, ON M5H 1L1

Telephone 416-368-9871
Fax 416-368-9034
E-mail nhihealthcare@ canscape.com
Website www.nhi healthcare.com
Founded 1984
Specialties Accounting
Health/Medical
International
Level Mid-Level
Junior
Contact Delores Lawrence, President
Description NHI is a long standing provider of quality health care professionals for placement in private homes, institutions and industries.

NURSING MANAGEMENT SERVICES (USA) INC.
2400 Herodian Way SE, Suite 110
Smyrna, GA 30080 USA

Telephone 770-952-5382
Fax 770-956-1894
E-mail meales@gonms.com
Website www.gonms.com/ newsletter.html
Specialties Health/Medical
International
Level Mid-Level
Junior
Contact Chris Eales, CEO
Description Nursing Management Services (USA) Inc. specializes in placing nurses in the USA and the United Kingdom.

O'SULLIVAN SEARCH INC.
2300 Yonge Street
Suite 401, Box 2427
Toronto, ON M4P 1E4

Telephone 416-481-2992
Fax 416-481-3424
E-mail osullivansearch@ on.aibn.com
Website www.joes.com/home/ osullivan
Specialties Insurance
Computing
Telecom
Contact Tanya Gerson
Description O'Sullivan Search Inc. is a professional organization with over 20 years recruitment experience.

OBJECTIF EMPLOI 40 ANS PLUS
1900, rue Sauve Est, Bureau 300
Montréal, QC H2B 3A8

Téléphone 514-381-1171
Spécialités Généralistes
Échelon Intermédiaire
Contact Yves Deslauriers, Directeur
Description Orientation et recherche d'emploi pour les 40 ans et plus.

OBJECTSEARCH
1930 Yonge Street, Suite 1100
Toronto, ON M4S 1Z4

Telephone 416-421-1940
Fax 416-421-9244
E-mail lori@objectsearch.com
Website www.objectsearch.com
Founded 1994
Employees 4
Specialties Computing
Engineering
Telecom
Level Senior
Mid-Level

Fee Basis   Always contingent

Contact   Donald Lascelle

Description ObjectSearch delivers object-oriented technology expertise for large-scale projects. They provide clients with contract consulting, mentoring, training, permanent and contract staffing.

OCC COMPUTER PERSONNEL
108 Welsh Row, Nantwich
Cheshire   CW5 5EY
UNITED KINGDOM

Telephone   44-1270-627206
Fax   44-1270-629168
E-mail   jane@occ.u-net.com
Website   www.occ.u-net.com

Specialties   Computing
International
Telecom
Engineering
Trades/Technicians

Level   Mid-Level

Contact   Jane Birchall

Description OCC supplies IT, telecom and technical staff for British and European companies.

OFFICE TEAM ADMINISTRATIVE STAFFING
10180 - 101 Street, Suite 1280
Edmonton, AB   T5J 3S4

Telephone   780-423-1466
Fax   780-423-1581
E-mail   edmonton@officeteam.com
Website   www.officeteam.com

Specialties   Administrative

Level   Junior
Mid-Level

Description Office Team, a division of Robert Half International, has annual sales of $3 billion and over 300 offices worldwide.

OFFICE TEAM ADMINISTRATIVE STAFFING
181 Bay St., PO Box 824, Suite 820
Toronto, ON   M5J 2T3

Telephone   416-350-2010
Fax   416-350-3573
E-mail   toronto@officeteam.com
Website   www.officeteam.com

Specialties   Administrative

Level   Junior
Mid-Level

Contact   Stephen Mill,
Branch Manager

Description OfficeTeam is a world leader in specialized administrative staffing.

OFFICE TEAM ADMINISTRATIVE STAFFING
5140 Yonge Street, Suite 1500
Toronto, ON   M2N 6L7

Telephone   416-226-1051
Fax   416-226-4498
E-mail   north.york@officeteam.com
Website   www.officeteam.com

Specialties   Administrative

Level   Junior
Mid-Level

Description OfficeTeam is a world leader in specialized administrative staffing.

OFFICE TEAM ADMINISTRATIVE STAFFING
755 blvd. St. Jean, Bureau 404
Pointe-Claire, QC   H9R 5M9

Telephone   514-694-9609
Fax   514-694-3346
E-mail   carole.viger@officeteam.com
Website   www.officeteam.com

Specialties   Administrative

Level   Junior
Mid-Level

Fee Basis   Always contingent

Contact   Carole Viger

Description OfficeTeam is a world leader in specialized administrative staffing.

OKA COMPUTER SYSTEMS LTD. / GESTION INFORMATIQUE OKA LTÉE
2075 University Street, Suite 750
Montréal, QC   H3A 2L1

Telephone   514-282-9334
Fax   514-282-8060
E-mail   oka@oka-info.com
Website   www.oka-info.com

Specialties   Computing

Level   Mid-Level

Recruiters   Isabelle Courville
Sylvie Godin
Catharine Le Capitaine

Contact   Isabelle Courville

Description OKA Computer Systems Ltd. provides quality professional services in information technology, turnkey systems, senior consulting and personnel recruitment.

OMNICOM PROFESSIONAL LANGUAGE INC.
2 Sheppard Avenue East, Suite 503
Toronto, ON   M2N 5Y7

Telephone   416-224-0754
Fax   416-224-1641
Website   www.omnicomtranslations.com

Founded   1974

Specialties   Bilingual

Contact   Bill Metham

Description Omnicom Professional Language Inc. specializes in placing multilingual candidates.

ON-SITE PLACEMENT SERVICES LTD.
9707 - 110 Street NW, Suite 802
Edmonton, AB   T5K 2L9

Telephone   780-488-8122

Specialties   Disabled

ONICO SOLUTIONS
55 Direzze Court
Richmond Hill, ON   L4C 0C6

Telephone   416-657-4464
Fax   416-657-4492
E-mail   jamie@onicosolutions.com
Website   www.onicosolutions.com

Specialties   Computing

Description Onico Solutions in an industry leader in providing helpdesk staffing to Fortune 500 companies.

ONWEGO PERSONNEL INC.
1630 Star Top Road, Suite 200
Gloucester, ON   K1B 3W6

Telephone   613-742-0811
Fax   613-749-9037
E-mail   b.dick@lavignetrucklines.com

Specialties   Transport

Contact   Suzanne Fox

Description Onwego Personnel Inc. supplies professional transport drivers.

OPENSOFT INC.
322 King Street West, Suite 201
Toronto, ON   M5V 1J2

Telephone   416-260-2656
Fax   416-260-5973
E-mail   info@osft.com
Website   www.osft.com

Specialties   Computing

Description Opensoft Inc. is a consulting and recruitment firm which specializes in solving business problems using a system integration approach called Distributed Object Technology.

OPTIMUM LTÉE
3073 boul. des Sources
Les Galeries des Sources
Dorval, QC   H9B 1Z6

Telephone   514-683-1057
Fax   514-683-1858
E-mail   info@optimumpersonnel.com
Website   www.optimumpersonnel.com

Founded   1979

Specialties   General Practice

Level   Mid-Level
Junior

Contact   Kelly Loiseau

Description Optimum Personnel has successfully placed thousands of candidates in executive, permanent and contract positions.

OPTIONS OUTREACH EMPLOYMENT INC.
61 Union Street, Suite 1430
Saint John, NB E2L 1A2

Telephone	506-652-3977
Fax	506-658-1452
E-mail	options@fundy.net
Specialties	Disabled
Contact	Karen MacFarlane, Manager

Description Options Outreach Employment Inc. assists disabled people in the Saint John area in finding employment.

OPTIONS PERSONNEL
80 Bloor Street West, Suite 1003
Toronto, ON M5S 2V1

Telephone	416-926-8820
Fax	416-926-1977
E-mail	shummell@ optionspersonnel.com
Specialties	Law
Level	Junior
Recruiters	Sarah Hummell Antoinette King
Contact	Sarah Hummell

OREXX MANAGEMENT SERVICES INC.
4699 rue Beneche
Montréal, QC H9J 3R1

Telephone	514-696-1813
Fax	514-696-1814
Specialties	General Practice
Contact	John Bezpalok

ORGANIZATION CONSULTING LTD.
156 Duncan Mill Road, Suite 5
Toronto, ON M3B 3N2

Telephone	416-385-9972
Fax	416-385-9977
E-mail	resumes@ organizationconsulting.ca
Founded	1981
Specialties	General Practice
Contact	Robert F. Johnson

ORILLIA WORKS
17 Colborne Street East, Unit 101
Orillia, ON L3V 7A3

Telephone	705-327-1717
Fax	705-327-0727
E-mail	oriworks@bconnex.net
Specialties	Administrative Construction
Level	Mid-Level Junior
Contact	Erna Collins, President

Description A full-service staffing agency.

ORION EXECUTIVE RESEARCH
6965 Lambeth Walk
London, ON N6P 1A5

Telephone	519-652-2581
Fax	519-652-6428
E-mail	orion.exec@ sympatico.ca
Specialties	Scientific Health/Medical Management
Level	Mid-Level Senior
Contact	Mike Kuzmanovich

Description Specializing in high-end scientific placements.

ORION RESOURCE GROUP INC.
405 Riverview Drive
Chatham, ON N7M 5J5

Telephone	519-354-3506
Fax	519-354-5189
Specialties	Trades/Technicians
Level	Mid-Level Junior

OSBORNE GROUP, THE
1111 West Georgia St., Suite 1700
Vancouver, BC V6C 3E8

Telephone	604-688-4960
Fax	604-683-0687
E-mail	vancouver@ osborne-group.com
Website	www. osborne-group.com
Founded	1993
Employees	30
Specialties	Operations Management Engineering Finance Accounting Aerospace Computing Human Resource Logistics
Level	Mid-Level Senior
Fee Basis	Retainer Only

Description The Osborne Group provides contract executives for senior management assignments in all major disciplines.

OSBORNE GROUP, THE
602 - 11th Avenue SW, Suite 303
Calgary, AB T2R 1J8

Telephone	403-264-8195
Fax	403-264-4113
E-mail	alberta@ osborne-group.com
Website	www. osborne-group.com
Specialties	Operations Management Engineering Finance Accounting Aerospace Computing Logistics Human Resource
Level	Senior Mid-Level
Fee Basis	Retainer Only
Recruiters	George Jones Ted Pound
Contact	Ted Pound, Executive Director

Description The Osborne Group provides contract executives for senior management assignments in all major disciplines.

OSBORNE GROUP, THE
10665 Jasper Avenue
Suite 900, First Edmonton Place
Edmonton, AB T2J 3S9

Telephone	780-451-4698
Fax	780-421-8400
E-mail	alberta@ osborne-group.com
Website	www. osborne-group.com
Specialties	Accounting Aerospace Computing Engineering Finance Human Resource Logistics Management Operations
Level	Senior Mid-Level
Fee Basis	Retainer Only

Description The Osborne Group provides contract executives for senior management assignments in all major disciplines.

OSBORNE GROUP, THE
505 Consumers Road, Suite 901
Toronto, ON M2J 4V8

Telephone	416-498-1550
Fax	416-498-6928
E-mail	toronto@ osborne-group.com
Website	www. osborne-group.com
Founded	1993
Employees	30
Specialties	Operations Management Engineering Finance Accounting Aerospace Computing Human Resource Logistics
Level	Mid-Level Senior
Fee Basis	Retainer Only
Contact	John Stewardson, Vice-President

Description The Osborne Group provides contract executives for senior management assignments in all major disciplines.

OSBORNE GROUP, THE
1080 Beaver Hall Hill, Suite 1525
Montréal, QC H2Z 1S8

Telephone	514-989-2213
Fax	451-466-4912
E-mail	montreal@ osborne-group.com
Website	www. osborne-group.com
Specialties	Accounting Aerospace Computing Engineering Finance Human Resource Logistics Management Operations
Level	Senior Mid-Level
Fee Basis	Retainer Only

Description The Osborne Group provides contract executives for senior management assignments in all major disciplines.

OT&T INFORMATION SYSTEMS
6081 No. 3 Road
Richmond, BC V6Y 2B2

Telephone	604-271-8603
Fax	604-271-8203
E-mail	vancouver@ottinf.com
Website	www.ottinf.com
Specialties	Computing
Level	Mid-Level

Description OT&T Information Systems specializes in recruiting IT personnel for the high-tech industry.

OTTAWA VALLEY PERSONNEL INC.
1179 Pembroke Street East
Pembroke, ON K8A 7R6

Telephone	613-735-1034
Fax	613-732-4998
E-mail	ovp@nrtco.net
Founded	1986
Specialties	Computing Education Management Human Resource Administrative
Level	Mid-Level Junior
Contact	Liliane Leclerc-Roesner, CSO

Description Ottawa Valley Personnel Inc. is an employment agency that also provides computer training.

OUTSOURCING CONNECTION INC., THE
2300 Yonge Street, Suite 2401
Toronto, ON M4P 1E4

Telephone	416-932-3339
Fax	416-932-8662
Website	www.outsourcing connection.com
Founded	1996

Employees	6
Specialties	Bilingual Direct Mktng. Administrative
Level	Junior Mid-Level
Recruiters	Gisele Da Costa Rebecca Dworkin Mindi Klein Dan McDonald Janet Orr
Contact	Dan McDonald

Description The Outsourcing Connection Inc. is a full-service recruitment agency for administrative to executive-level positions.

OVER 55 INC.
78 Riverside Drive
London, ON N6H 1B4

Telephone	519-433-5427
Fax	519-433-6097
E-mail	over55@lon.hookup.net
Website	www.crm.mb.ca/ options45+/bureau/ london.html
Founded	1985
Employees	2
Specialties	Management
Level	Mid-Level
Contact	Emilie Dudley-Jones, Admin. Secretary

Description Over 55 Inc. specializes in placing people over 55 years of age.

P.R.Y.
20 Carlton Street, Suite 123
Toronto, ON M5B 2H5

Telephone	416-599-0929
Fax	416-599-4708
E-mail	pryresource@ idirect.com
Founded	1995
Employees	7
Specialties	Computing Engineering Accounting Bilingual Human Resource Insurance Management Sales
Level	Mid-Level Senior
Fee Basis	Always contingent
Contact	Harry Yong

Description P.R.Y., a division of P.R.Y. Resources Inc., specializes in permanent and contract placements.

P.W. ROURKE & ASSOCIATES
1255 Laird Blvd., Suite 371
Mount Royal, QC H3P 2T1

Telephone	514-739-3113
Fax	514-739-5377
E-mail	prourke@axess.com
Specialties	Management

	Operations
Level	Mid-Level Senior
Contact	Patrick Rourke

Description PWR & Associates is a consulting firm in human resources.

PACE PERSONNEL LTD.
2096 - 41st Avenue West, Suite 113
Vancouver, BC V6M 1Y9

Telephone	604-207-9262
Fax	604-207-9263
E-mail	paceltd@ intergate.bc.ca
Founded	1987
Employees	4
Specialties	Computing International Law Scientific Education Health/Medical Human Resource
Level	Senior Mid-Level
Fee Basis	Sometimes contingent
Contact	S.M. Singh, Director Personnel Services

Description Pace Personnel Ltd. is a national and international medical, dental, technical, educational and legal search firm.

PACIFIC FIRST SYSTEMS
8 King Street East, Suite 201
Toronto, ON M5C 1B5

Telephone	416-350-2050
Fax	416-350-2047
E-mail	pfsgroup@netcom.ca
Website	www.pacificfirst.com
Founded	1991
Specialties	Computing
Contact	Roger Rajkuman

Description Pacific First Systems is an independent, Canadian-owned recruitment and consulting firm based in downtown Toronto.

PAL PERSONNEL SERVICES
200 Consumers Road, Suite 300
Toronto, ON M2J 4R4

Telephone	416-497-8200
Fax	416-497-8352
E-mail	toronto@ pal.stivers.com
Website	www.pal.stivers.com
Founded	1977
Specialties	Administrative Accounting
Level	Mid-Level Junior
Contact	L. Shannon

Description Pal Personnel is a full-service placement agency and a division of Chicago-based Stivers Staffing Services, Inc., the oldest national personnel service in the USA.

PALMER & ASSOCIATES
556 O'Connor Drive
Kingston, ON K7P 1N3

Telephone	613-389-1108
Fax	613-389-2080
E-mail	pbpalmer@kingston.net
Website	www.whatsonkingston. com/busdir/ palmerassoc
Founded	1993
Specialties	Engineering Human Resource Marketing Sales Operations General Practice Computing
Level	Mid-Level Senior
Min. Salary	$60,000
Fee Basis	Sometimes contingent
Recruiters	Angela Morin Brenda Palmer
Contact	Angela Morin

Description Palmer & Associates, with offices in Kanata and Kingston, specializes in national searches in computing, engineering, HR, marketing, operations and sales industries.

PALMER & COMPANY EXECUTIVE RECRUITMENT
69 Bloor Street East
Suite 310
Toronto, ON M4W 1A9

Telephone	416-975-9595
Fax	416-975-9068
E-mail	execsearch@ palmerco.on.ca
Website	www.palmerco.ca
Founded	1990
Employees	6
Specialties	General Practice Finance Management
Level	Senior
Min. Salary	$75,000
Fee Basis	Retainer Only
Recruiters	John Johnston Mark Palmer Elaine Sigurdsen
Contact	Mark Palmer, President

Description Palmer & Company performs searches spanning most sectors and industries at the senior or officer level.

PALMER REED
439 University Avenue
Suite 1550
Toronto, ON M5G 1Y8

Telephone	416-599-9186
Fax	416-599-9189
Specialties	General Practice Accounting Finance
Contact	Ted Masters

PAMENTER, PAMENTER, BREZER & DEGANIS LTD.
4 Eva Road, Suite 400
Toronto, ON M9C 2A8

Telephone	416-620-5980
Fax	416-620-5074
E-mail	FHCraig@msn.com
Specialties	Management Education
Level	Mid-Level
Contact	Fred Pamenter, President

Description Pamenter, Pamenter, Brezer & Deganis Ltd. is a human resources consulting firm that also does search work.

PAQUETTE & ASSOCIATES LTD.
1040 West Georgia St., Suite 1770
Vancouver, BC V6E 4H1

Telephone	604-688-7266
Fax	604-688-3542
E-mail	positions@paquette personnel.com
Website	www.paquette personnel.com
Specialties	Marketing Administrative Accounting
Level	Mid-Level Junior
Contact	Karen Paquette

PAQUETTE CONSULTING
729 Morin Street
Ottawa, ON K1K 3G8

Telephone	613-749-8503
Fax	613-749-8622
E-mail	philemon@magma.ca
Website	www.paquette consulting.com
Specialties	General Practice
Recruiters	Brian Beyer Philémon Paquette
Contact	Philémon Paquette

Description Paquette Consulting is a generalist HR consulting firm that also does selection and recruitment work for clients.

PARADIGM CONSULTING GROUP INC.
1874 Scarth Street, Suite 1700
Regina, SK S4P 4B3

Telephone	306-522-8588
Fax	306-352-3051
E-mail	headoffice@ paradigm.sk.ca
Website	www.paradigm.sk.ca
Founded	1990
Specialties	Computing
Level	Mid-Level
Contact	Ken Gerhardt, CEO

Description Paradigm is an IT consulting firm that also places contract software professionals.

PARADIGM MANAGEMENT SOLUTIONS INC.
21 St. Clair Avenue East
Penthouse Suite
Toronto, ON M4T 2T7

Telephone	416-515-2904
E-mail	keythinkers@axxent.ca
Website	www.pathcom.com/ ~paradigm
Specialties	Finance Accounting
Level	Mid-Level Senior
Contact	Coralee Sheridan, President

Description Paradigm Management Solutions Inc. identifies and recommends top performers for corporate clients.

PARAGON CONSULTING
20 Bay Street, Suite 1205
Toronto, ON M5J 2N8

Telephone	416-364-1515
Fax	416-214-2043
Founded	1992
Employees	3
Specialties	Computing Sales Telecom
Level	Senior Mid-Level
Min. Salary	$40,000
Contact	John Anderson

Description Paragon Consulting places intermediate- and senior-level data and telecom professionals, concentrating on sales and technical positions.

PARKWOOD ASSOCIATES INC.
5200 Dixie Road, Suite 112
Mississauga, ON L4W 1E4

Telephone	905-624-5887
Fax	905-624-3141
E-mail	parkwood@ican.net
Employees	5
Specialties	Scientific Accounting Computing Finance Engineering Marketing Operations Purchasing
Level	Mid-Level Senior
Contact	Ihor Cherkas

Description Parkwood Associates Inc. is a recruiting firm specializing in full-time career opportunities, mainly in the IT field.

PARTNERS EMPLOYMENT GROUP
145 Wellington Street W., Suite 600
Toronto, ON M5J 1H8

Telephone	416-977-4697
Fax	416-977-5076

Employees	15
Specialties	Accounting
	Banking
	Computing
	Finance
	Engineering
	Marketing
	Sales
Level	Mid-Level
	Senior
Contact	Ted Bennett

Description Partners Employment Group specializes in permanent and contract placements, domestically and internationally.

PARTNERS IN EMPLOYMENT
52 East Street
Goderich, ON N7A 1N3

Telephone	519-524-8624
E-mail	pie@partnersin
	employment.on.ca
Website	www.partnersin
	employment.on.ca
Specialties	General Practice
Level	Mid-Level
	Junior

Description Partners in Employment is a non-profit organization that assists people in Perth and Huron counties who have difficulty finding employment.

PARTNERS IN EMPLOYMENT
100 Albert Street
Stratford, ON N5A 3K4

Telephone	519-272-1946
Fax	519-272-1299
E-mail	pie@ partnersin
	employment.on.ca
Website	www.partnersin
	employment.on.ca
Specialties	Disabled

Description Partners In Employment is a non-profit organization that assists people in Perth and Huron counties who have difficulty finding employment.

PARTNERS IN EMPLOYMENT
210 Main Street East
Listowel, ON N4W 2B7

Telephone	519-291-2726
Fax	519-272-1299
E-mail	pie@partnersin
	employment.on.ca
Website	www.partnersin
	employment.on.ca
Specialties	Disabled
Contact	Deb Hotchkiss

Description Partners in Employment is a non-profit organization that assists people in Perth and Huron counties who have difficulty finding employment.

PARTNERS IN SEARCH
120 Eglinton Ave. East, Suite 500
Toronto, ON M4P 1E2

Telephone	416-480-0322
Fax	416-480-1219
E-mail	psearch@idirect.com
Founded	1998
Employees	1
Specialties	Accounting
	Finance
	Human Resource
	Management
	Telecom
	Sales
	Marketing
Level	Senior
	Mid-Level
Min. Salary	$30,000
Fee Basis	Always contingent
Contact	Donna Cook

Description Partners in Search works with clients to find staffing solutions.

PARTNERVISION CONSULTING GROUP INC.
1 Yonge Street, Suite 2406
Toronto, ON M5E 1E5

Telephone	416-360-6688
Fax	416-955-0251
E-mail	info@partnervision.net
Website	www.partnervision.net
Founded	1991
Employees	7
Specialties	Human Resource
	Management
	Finance
	Consulting
	Banking
	Insurance
	Real Estate
Level	Senior
	Mid-Level
Min. Salary	$60,000
Fee Basis	Retainer Only
Recruiters	Peter Flynn
	Diane Kenton
	Lynn Lefebre
	Kelly McGregor
	Dennis Mogg
	Chris Ronneseth
Contact	Dianne Kenton

Description Partnervision are specialists in senior- to middle-management searches, with proven expertise in human resources, corporate services and finance recruiting.

PATH EMPLOYMENT SERVICES
140 King Street East, Suite 7
Hamilton, ON L8N 1B2

Telephone	905-528-6611
Fax	905-528-2181
E-mail	path1@worldchat.com
Website	www.path
	employment.com
Specialties	Disabled
Level	Mid-Level
Contact	Aznive Mallett,
	Executive Director

Description PATH provides employment services for the disabled.

PATHFINDER PERSONNEL LIMITED
161 Eglinton Avenue E., Suite 504
Toronto, ON M4P 1J5

Telephone	416-440-1056
Fax	416-484-6587
E-mail	topathfinder@sprint.ca
Founded	1973
Specialties	Insurance
Level	Mid-Level
	Senior
Recruiters	Patrick Duffy
	Michael W. Duffy
Contact	Michael E. Duffy

Description Pathfinder Personnel Limited specializes in insurance placements.

PATTY SHAPIRO & ASSOCIATES
333 Chabanel West, Suite 333
Montréal, QC H2N 2E7

Telephone	514-389-5627
Fax	514-389-9969
E-mail	patty@psacanada.com
Website	www.psacanada.com
Founded	1992
Specialties	Apparel
	Retail
Recruiters	Julie Albert
	Patty Shapiro
Contact	Julie Albert

Description Patty Shapiro & Associates is a consulting and training firm that also does recruitment in the fashion and apparel industry.

PAZIUK PROFESSIONAL PLACEMENTS / P3
10250 - 101st Street
Suite 1040, AT&T Canada Tower
Edmonton, AB T5J 3P4

Telephone	780-414-5558
Fax	780-414-5556
E-mail	dian@paziuk
	placements.com
Website	www.paziuk
	placements.com
Specialties	Administrative
	Accounting
	Human Resource
Level	Mid-Level
	Junior
Recruiters	Theresa J. Antolick
	Carla Perry
Contact	Dian G. Paziuk, CPC,
	President

Description P3 provides permanent and contract human resources staffing services.

PDQ PERSONNEL INC.
1133 Dundas St. East, Units 7 & 8
Mississauga, ON L4Y 2C3

Telephone	905-949-6050
Fax	905-949-6201
Specialties	Administrative
	Trades/Technicians

Level	Mid-Level
	Junior
Recruiters	William Jones
	Al Terpstra
Contact	Al Terpstra

PEAK ASSOCIATES INC.
170 University Avenue, Suite 901
Toronto, ON M5H 3B3

Telephone	416-979-7303 ext. 203
Fax	416-979-7457
E-mail	resumes@
	peakassociates.com
Website	www.peak
	associates.com
Founded	1992
Employees	16
Specialties	Accounting
	Insurance
	Real Estate
	Finance
	Banking
	Administrative
Level	Mid-Level
Min. Salary	$50,000
Fee Basis	Always contingent
Recruiters	Robert Baron
	Jennifer Williamson
Contact	Robert Baron, Partner

PEAPELL & ASSOCIATES
5251 Duke Street, Suite 1206
Halifax, NS B3J 1P3

Telephone	902-421-1523
Fax	902-425-8559
E-mail	peapell@
	ns.sympatico.ca
Website	www3.ns.
	sympatico.ca/peapell
Founded	1989
Employees	7
Specialties	Accounting
	Management
	Marketing
	Computing
	Hospitality
	Pharmaceutical
Level	Mid-Level
	Senior
Min. Salary	$30,000
Fee Basis	Sometimes contingent
Recruiters	Georgina DeWitt CPC
	Theo Mitchell
	Jill Peapell
	Philip Peapell
Contact	Jill Peapell

Description Peapell & Assoc. is an executive search / placement firm serving the Atlantic provinces.

PEGASUS CONSULTING INC.
55 Eglinton Avenue East, Suite 208
Toronto, ON M4P 1G8

Telephone	416-488-7007
Fax	416-488-7337
E-mail	pegasus@pegsoft.com
Website	www.pegsoft.com
Founded	1987

Specialties	Computing
Level	Mid-Level
	Senior
Recruiters	Seana Bingham
	Jon Blackburn
	John Goldsmith
	Neil Goldsmith
	Leslie Graham-Williams
	Greg Habros
	Mark Healy
	Chris McIntosh
Contact	Leslie Graham-
	Williams, President

Description Pegasus Consulting Inc. is a professional computer systems consulting company specializing in consulting assignments throughout Canada, USA, Europe and the UK.

PEI OFFICE OF THE FUTURE
93 Pownal Street, PO Box 1474
Charlottetown, PE C1A 7N1

Telephone	902-892-9484
Fax	902-566-3352
E-mail	peioffice@isn.net
Website	www.virtuo.com/
	peioffice
Specialties	Administrative
	General Practice
Level	Mid-Level
	Junior
Contact	Sharon Elderkin,
	Owner/Manager

Description PEI Office of the Future is a PEI-owned and operated employment agency.

PENNOX EXPRESS LTD.
2220 Midland Avenue
Toronto, ON M1P 3E6

Telephone	416-321-9030
Fax	416-321-9422
Specialties	Administrative
	Trades/Technicians
Level	Junior
	Mid-Level
Contact	Andrew Webber

Description Pennox Express Ltd. is a general personnel agency that specializes in industrial placements.

PEOPLE +
2323 Yonge Street, Suite 203
Toronto, ON M4P 2C9

Telephone	416-484-8408
Fax	416-484-0151
E-mail	pshrive@
	cambridgemgmt.com
Founded	1998
Specialties	Retail
	Human Resource
	Sales
	Operations
	Franchising
	Management
	General Practice
Level	Mid-Level
Min. Salary	$30,000

Fee Basis	Retainer Only
Contact	Peter Shrive, Prinicipal

Description People + is a cost-effective alternative to a full-scale search that is still conducted by an executive recruiter.

PEOPLE BANK, THE
800 - 6th Avenue SW, Suite 1420
Calgary, AB T2P 3G3

Telephone	403-266-6328
Fax	403-266-6388
E-mail	tgivens@
	thepeoplebank.com
Website	www.the
	peoplebank.com
Specialties	Administrative
	Computing
	Finance
Level	Mid-Level
	Junior

Description People Bank is a permanent placement service, specializing in administrative, technical, financial, call centre and light industrial placements.

PEOPLE BANK, THE
715 Portage Avenue
Winnipeg, MB R3G 0M8

Telephone	204-772-5040
Fax	204-772-5747
E-mail	plaurin@
	thepeoplebank.com
Website	www.thepeople
	bank.com
Specialties	Sales
	Marketing
	Management
	Accounting
	Computing
	Finance
Level	Mid-Level
Contact	Linda Beaudry,
	Manager

Description People Bank is a permanent placement service, specializing in administrative, technical, financial, call centre and light industrial placements.

PEOPLE BANK, THE
140 Fullarton Street
Suite 408, Talbot Centre
London, ON N6A 5P2

Telephone	519-672-6888
Fax	519-672-6444
E-mail	kkindree@
	thepeoplebank.com
Website	www.thepeople
	bank.com
Specialties	Administrative
	Computing
	Finance
Level	Mid-Level
	Junior

Description People Bank is a permanent placement service, specializing in administrative, technical, financial, call centre and light industrial placements.

PEOPLE BANK, THE
220 Yonge St., Box 603
Suite 211, Eaton Centre Galleria
Toronto, ON M5B 2H1

Telephone	416-343-9109
Fax	416-340-0447
E-mail	kmugford@ thepeoplebank.com
Website	www.thepeople bank.com
Specialties	Computing Accounting
Level	Mid-Level Junior
Recruiters	Londa Burke CPC Mary Calladine CPC Marnie Davis CPC Steve Jones CPC Mary Milevski CPC Karen Mugford CPC Ingrid Singer CPC Sherri Strong CPC Michelle Torre CPC Judith Walker CPC Deborah Wurster CPC
Contact	Karen Mugford

Description People Bank is a permanent placement service, specializing in administrative, technical, financial, call centre and light industrial placements.

PEOPLE BANK, THE
10 Kingsbridge Garden Circle
Suite 103, Ground Floor
Mississauga, ON L5K 3K6

Telephone	905-890-0093
Fax	905-890-0094
E-mail	rhollingsworth@ thepeoplebank.com
Website	www.thepeople bank.com
Specialties	Computing Engineering
Level	Mid-Level Junior
Contact	Don O'Hanlon, Technical Consultant

Description People Bank is a permanent placement service, specializing in administrative, technical, financial, call centre and light industrial placements.

PEOPLE BANK, THE
3000 Steeles Ave. East, Suite 307
Markham, ON L3R 4T9

Telephone	905-470-3111
Fax	905-470-5822
E-mail	vtrpkovski@ thepeoplebank.com
Website	www.thepeople bank.com
Specialties	Administrative Computing Finance
Level	Mid-Level

Description People Bank is a permanent placement service, specializing in administrative, technical, financial, call centre and light industrial placements.

PEOPLE BANK, THE
275 Bank Street, Suite 303
Ottawa, ON K2P 2L6

Telephone	613-234-8118
Fax	613-234-7365
E-mail	mchallenger@ thepeoplebank.com
Website	www.thepeople bank.com
Specialties	Computing Sales Human Resource Administrative Govt/Nonprofit
Level	Mid-Level
Contact	Diane Cinkant

Description People Bank is a permanent placement service, specializing in administrative, technical, financial, call centre and light industrial placements.

PEOPLE BANK, THE
2020 University Street, Suite 427
Montréal, QC H3A 2A5

Telephone	514-286-9700
Fax	514-286-1008
E-mail	pmantzioros@ thepeoplebank.com
Website	www.thepeople bank.com
Specialties	Administrative Computing Finance
Level	Mid-Level Junior
Recruiters	Diane Cinkant Peter Mantzioros
Contact	Peter Mantzioros

Description People Bank is a permanent placement service, specializing in administrative, technical, financial, call centre and light industrial placements.

PEOPLE FIRST SOLUTIONS INC.
675 West Hastings Street, Suite 415
Vancouver, BC V6B 1N2

Telephone	604-684-2288
Fax	604-684-2265
E-mail	resume@ peoplefirstsolutions.com
Website	www.peoplefirst solutions.com
Founded	1998
Employees	25
Specialties	Accounting General Practice Finance Insurance Management Sales Computing
Level	Mid-Level
Fee Basis	Sometimes contingent
Recruiters	Paul Gibbons Shayda Kassam
Contact	Paul Gibbons

Description People First Solutions Inc. is a full-service human resources consulting firm, with 25 HR professionals available on a project or contract basis.

PEOPLE MANAGEMENT GROUP
65 Springbank Ave. North, Suite 1
Woodstock, ON N4S 8V8

Fax	519-539-9348
E-mail	peoplemg@ execulink.com
Specialties	Trades/Technicians Plastics Human Resource Accounting
Level	Mid-Level

PEOPLE PLACERS PERSONNEL AGENCY
111 Isley Avenue, Suite 200
Halifax, NS B3B 1S8

Telephone	902-468-5552
Fax	902-468-4626
Specialties	Accounting Administrative
Level	Mid-Level Junior
Contact	Tammy Burke

Description A personnel firm serving employers in the Dartmouth area.

PEOPLEFIND INC.
7030 Woodbine Avenue, Suite 500
Markham, ON L3T 6X6

Telephone	905-477-9330
Fax	905-771-0273
E-mail	infopeoplefind@ aol.com
Website	www.ipeoplefind.com
Founded	1999
Specialties	Accounting Advertising Human Resource Management Marketing Retail
Level	Mid-Level
Fee Basis	Sometimes contingent
Recruiters	Harvey Glasner Charles Grossner Carolyn Wiseman
Contact	Charles Grossner, President

Description PeopleFind is dedicated to providing corporate clients with pre-qualified job candidates who consistently meet and exceed the expectations of their employer.

PEOPLEWEB INC.
120 Eglinton Ave. East, Suite 500
Toronto, ON M4P 1E2

Telephone   416-483-5615
Fax   416-483-6211
E-mail   contactus@
thepeoplewebinc.com
Website   www.thepeople
webinc.com

Specialties   Computing
Multimedia

Contact   Kathy Hughey

Description   PeopleWeb Inc. is a full-service technology recruiting firm, providing placements in all areas of technology, from entry-level to senior management.

PERCEPTIVE EDGE
1370 Don Mills Road, Suite 300
Toronto, ON   M3B 3N7

Telephone   416-490-0529
Fax   416-490-6690
E-mail   epdersen@
perceptiveedge.com
Website   www.perceptive
edge.com

Founded   1991
Employees   2

Specialties   Management
Engineering
Marketing
Operations
Sales

Level   Mid-Level

Min. Salary $30,000

Contact   Else Pedersen,
Consultant

Description   Perceptive Edge offers non-traditional, in-house human resources, consulting and recruiting services.

PERFORMANCE HOUSE LTD.
1601 River East, PO Box 456
Waterloo, ON   N2J 4B4

Telephone   519-893-5520
Fax   519-746-0027
E-mail   inquiry@performance
house.com
Website   www.performance
house.com

Specialties   Operations
Management
Accounting

Level   Mid-Level
Senior

Contact   Adele Ostfield,
President

Description   Performance House Ltd. is a consultant in the management of human resources.

PERMANENT SEARCH GROUP INC. / PSG
190 Robert Speck Pkwy., Suite 109
Mississauga, ON   L4Z 3K3

Telephone   905-276-2006
Fax   905-276-0258
E-mail   jobs@permanent
search.com

Website   www.permanent
search.com
Founded   1978
Employees   8

Specialties   Sales
Human Resource
Management
Finance
Accounting
Marketing

Level   Mid-Level
Senior

Fee Basis   Always contingent

Recruiters   Chris Boyd
Janet Chappell
Lorrie Clark
Rachelle Cushing
Magdalena Duleba
Renée Fisher
Lori Forcione
Krista McLean
Lisa Price
Shannon Terpstra
Grainne Walsh

Contact   Lisa Price, Partner

Description   PSG is a Canadian personnel consulting firm with over 16 years in the permanent placement industry. The firm specializes in national account management, sales management and sales team building within a variety of industries.

PERMANENT SOLUTIONS INC.
201 City Centre Drive, Suite 608
Mississauga, ON   L5B 2T4

Telephone   905-566-5950
Fax   905-566-5991
E-mail   resumes@permanent
solutions.com
Website   www.permanent
solutions.com

Founded   1988
Employees   10

Specialties   Accounting
Finance
General Practice
Bilingual
Consulting
Human Resource
Logistics
Management
Marketing
Administrative
Operations
Purchasing
Sales

Level   Mid-Level
Senior

Fee Basis   Always contingent

Recruiters   Cari Bragg
Catherine Crawford
Dara Eisner
Nicole McMullen
Lilly Montalbano
Lisa Ranger
Sue Taylor
Tracy Webber

Contact   Catherine Crawford,
President

Description   Permanent Solutions Inc. is a customer service-oriented

recruitment firm placing management, junior management and support staff in all areas.

PERRY MARTEL INTERNATIONAL INC. / PMI
451 Daily Avenue
Ottawa, ON   K1N 6H6

Telephone   613-236-6995
Fax   613-236-8240
E-mail   dperry@
perrymartel.com
Website   www.perrymartel.com

Founded   1988

Specialties   Computing
Engineering
Management
Marketing
Sales

Level   Senior
Mid-Level

Min. Salary $75,000
Fee Basis   Retainer Only

Contact   David Perry,
Managing Partner

Description   PMI offers three-dimensional, value-based search services developed exclusively to meet the needs of the high-technology sector.

PERSONNEL ALTER EGO INC.
6600 Transcanada Hwy, Suite 501
Pointe-Claire, QC   H9R 4S2

Téléphone   514-426-8511
Télécopieur   514-426-9169
Courriel   pointeclaire@
persalterego.com
Site Internet   www.persalterego.com

Fondée   1989

Spécialités   Comptabilité
Administratif
Aérospatial
Ingénierie
Ressources humaines
Droit
Exploitation

Échelon   Intermédiaire

Recruteurs   Isabelle Arrivault
Saby Bergeron
Louise Bernatchez
Julie Brais
Brenda Everitt
Austin Francis
Josée Lapierre
Sylvia Neumann
Caroline Paquin

Contact   Caroline Paquin

PERSONNEL ALTER EGO INC.
2055 Peel Street, Suite 300
Montréal, QC   H3A 1V4

Téléphone   514-939-7177
Fax   514-939-7176
E-mail   montreal@
persalterego.com
Website   www.persalterego.com

Specialties   Administrative
Accounting
Aerospace
Engineering

Human Resource
Law
Operations

Level Mid-Level

Recruiters Nicole Giguere
Sophie Malet

Contact Sophie Malet

PERSONNEL BY PRO-STAFF
360 Eugenie Street E., Unit 211
Windsor, ON N8X 2Y1

Telephone 519-250-9403
Fax 519-250-9407
E-mail churst@personnelby
prostaff.com
Website wnd-biz.com/
personnelbyprostaff

Specialties Management
Administrative
Accounting
Computing
Sales

Level Mid-Level
Junior

Contact Colleen Hurst

PERSONNEL CLÉ INC.
515, Grande Allée est
Québec, QC G1R 1J5

Téléphone 418-647-3775
Télécopieur 418-525-8632
Courriel admin@
personnelcle.com
Site Internet www.personnelcle.com

Fondée 1993
Employés 6

Spécialités Comptabilité
Informatique
Ingénierie
Finance
Santé/médical
Hospitalité
Ressources humaines

Échelon Intermédiaire
Débutant

Frais Parfois relative

Contact Marie Fortier

Description Personnel Clé Inc.
spécialise surtout dans trois grandes
divisions: administration; l'industrie; et santé.

PERSONNEL DENTAIRE DIANE SOUCY
2401, avenue West Hill
Montréal, QC H4B 2S3

Telephone 514-488-6855
Fax 514-488-6855
E-mail personnel.dentaire@
qc.aira.com

Founded 1983

Specialties Health/Medical

Level Mid-Level
Junior

Contact Diane Soucy

Description Personnel dentaire Diane Soucy specializes in placing dental support personnel (secretaries,

dental assistants, dental hygienists)
in Greater Montreal.

PERSONNEL DEPARTMENT, THE
595 Howe Street, Suite 1205
Vancouver, BC V6C 2T5

Telephone 604-685-3530
Fax 604-688-5636
E-mail info@goodstaff.com
Website www.goodstaff.com

Specialties General Practice

Level Mid-Level

Recruiters Deborah Kitson
Nicole Postiener

Contact Deborah Kitson

Description In addition to staffing
services, clients receive news articles, personality inventories (e.g.
Myers-Briggs Type Indicator), online
skills testing, and a 360-degree peer
quality review system.

PERSONNEL DEPARTMENT, THE
10250 - 101st Street NW, Suite 1806
Edmonton, AB T5J 3P4

Telephone 780-421-1811
E-mail edmonton@
goodstaff.com
Website www.goodstaff.com

Specialties General Practice

Level Mid-Level

Contact Edith Dubois

Description In addition to staffing
services, clients receive news articles, personality inventories (e.g.
Myers-Briggs Type Indicator), online
skills testing, and a 360-degree peer
quality review system.

PERSONNEL DEPARTMENT, THE
444 - 5th Avenue SW, Suite 300
Calgary, AB T2P 2T8

Telephone 403-266-7030
E-mail calgary@goodstaff.com
Website www.goodstaff.com

Specialties General Practice

Level Mid-Level

Description In addition to staffing
services, clients receive news articles, personality inventories (e.g.
Myers-Briggs Type Indicator), online
skills testing, and a 360-degree peer
quality review system.

PERSONNEL FORCE
350 Sparks Street, Suite 701
Ottawa, ON K1R 7S8

Telephone 613-237-9798
Fax 613-237-7752
E-mail pforce@storm.ca

Specialties Computing

Contact Paul Gillissie

PERSONNEL HÉLÈNE TOBIN INC.
315, avenue Dorval, Bureau 105
Dorval, QC H9S 3H

Téléphone 514-633-8111
Télécopieur 514-633-8226

Spécialités Comptabilité

Échelon Intermédiaire
Débutant

Contact Helène Tobin

PERSONNEL MANAGEMENT CONSULTANTS
540 - 5th Avenue SW, Suite 1850
Calgary, AB T2P 0M2

Telephone 403-232-1234
Fax 403-232-1244
E-mail pmc2@cadvision.com

Specialties Management
Retail

Level Senior
Mid-Level

Description Personnel Management
Consultants specializes in executive
searches.

PERSONNEL MANAGEMENT GROUP
209 Notre Dame Avenue, Suite 300
Winnipeg, MB R3B 1M9

Telephone 204-982-1100
Fax 204-943-9535
E-mail yvonne@pmg.mb.ca
Website www.pmg.mb.ca

Founded 1981

Specialties Computing
Engineering
Accounting
Transport
Construction
Logistics
Management

Level Mid-Level
Senior

Min. Salary $45,000
Fee Basis Always contingent

Recruiters Yvonne Baert
Robert Baert
Danielle Baert PEng
Cynthia Wharton

Contact Yvonne Baert

Description Personnel Management
Group are technical, transportation,
logistics and manufacturing recruiters with 23 years experience. Local
and national placements.

PERSONNEL MENEN
4480, boul. Côte-de-Liesse
Bureau 110
Mount Royal, QC H4N 2R1

Telephone 514-344-8545
Fax 514-626-3748

Specialties Finance
Banking
Insurance
Accounting
Marketing
Sales

Recruiters Karin Menendyan
Najda Menendyan

Contact Karin Menendyan

PERSONNEL OPPORTUNITIES LTD.
70 Yorkville Avenue, Suite 8
Toronto, ON M5R 1B9

Telephone	416-515-7727
Fax	416-515-8351
E-mail	nqureshi@idirect.ca
Website	www.personnel opportunities.com
Employees	13
Specialties	Computing Accounting
Level	Mid-Level Junior
Recruiters	Nellie Draper Linda Foster
Contact	Nellie Draper

Description Our centrally-situated Bloor/Bay location enables Personnel Opportunities Ltd. to service clients and represent candidates in all of the Greater Toronto Area.

PERSONNEL OPTIONS
320 Main Street
PO Box 398, Crocus Place
Winkler, MB R6W 4A6

Telephone	204-325-6933
Fax	204-325-0930
Specialties	General Practice
Level	Mid-Level

PERSONNEL OUTAOUAIS
72, rue Laval
Hull, QC J8X 3H3

Telephone	819-778-7020
Fax	819-778-6534
E-mail	emploi@ personneloutaouais.com
Website	www.personnel outaouais.com
Founded	1987
Employees	4
Specialties	Accounting Banking Bilingual Computing Construction Finance Govt/Nonprofit Librarians Management
Level	Junior Mid-Level
Fee Basis	Always contingent
Contact	Bernard Grenier, President

Description Over 25 years of experience in human resources recruitment.

PERSONNEL SEARCH LTD.
53 King Street, Suite 300
Saint John, NB E2L 1G5

Telephone	506-652-4728
Fax	506-674-2836
E-mail	psearch@ nb.sympatico.ca
Website	www.personnel-search.com
Founded	2000
Employees	13
Specialties	Management Engineering Accounting Computing Finance Health/Medical Hospitality Human Resource International Marketing Sales Oil & Gas
Level	Mid-Level Senior
Recruiters	Sheri Killam Jennifer Myles
Contact	Jennifer Myles, Branch Manager

Description Personnel Search represents some of the most successful and respected corporations in Atlantic Canada.

PERSONNEL SEARCH LTD.
883 Main Street
Moncton, NB E1C 1G5

Telephone	506-857-2156
Fax	506-857-9172
E-mail	pscareer@nbnet.nb.ca
Website	www.personnel-search.com
Founded	1978
Employees	13
Specialties	Management Engineering Accounting Computing Finance Health/Medical Hospitality Human Resource International Marketing Sales Oil & Gas
Level	Mid-Level Senior
Recruiters	Jennifer Batog Lynn Breau Steven Love
Contact	Lynn Breau

Description Personnel Search represents some of the most successful and respected corporations in Atlantic Canada.

PERSONNEL SOLUTIONS
PO Box 485
Westmount Postal Station
Westmount, QC H3Z 2T6

Telephone	450-458-7618
Fax	450-458-9927
E-mail	solper@total.net
Specialties	Administrative
Level	Mid-Level
Contact	Maria Pagani

PERSONNEL STAR AVON FJ INC.
6280, boulevard Decarie, Bureau 1006
Montréal, QC H3X 2K1

Telephone	514-739-5906
Specialties	Engineering Accounting
Level	Mid-Level Junior
Contact	Fred Avon

PETER GLASER & ASSOCIATES
PO Box 55, Bodmin
Cornwall, PL30 4YH
UNITED KINGDOM

Telephone	44-7071-221155
Fax	44-7071-221166
E-mail	pglaser@pga.co.uk
Website	www.pga.co.uk
Founded	1991
Employees	6
Specialties	Construction Design Engineering Geology/Geography International Sales Transport Environmental
Level	Senior Mid-Level
Fee Basis	Always contingent
Recruiters	Peter Glaser Cathy Glaser
Contact	Peter Glaser

Description International search specialists in the construction, water, environmental, power and transportation industries. Recruiting from technician- to board-level appointments.

PETER LEONARD & ASSOCIATES
924 Lake Emerald Place SE
Calgary, AB T2J 7C9

Telephone	403-278-4122
Fax	403-271-5476
E-mail	peterleonard@ home.com
Founded	1981
Specialties	International Engineering Construction Biotech/Biology Aerospace Oil & Gas Scientific
Level	Senior Mid-Level
Min. Salary	$40,000
Fee Basis	Sometimes contingent
Contact	Peter Leonard

Description Peter Leonard & Associates specializes in international project recruiting and staffing.

PETRO MIDDLE EAST RECRUITMENT

National Cinema Building
PO Box 7743, 1st Floor, Office 108
Abu Dhabi,
UNITED ARAB EMIRATES

Telephone	971-2-710300
Fax	971-2-710660
E-mail	
	sundus@emirates.net.ae
Website	www.petrome.com
Specialties	International
	Oil & Gas
	Engineering

Description Petro Middle East Recruitment specializes in the recruitment of oilfield engineers, skilled senior onshore and offshore professionals.

PETRO STAFF INTERNATIONAL HUMAN RESOURCE ADVISORS LTD.

444 - 5th Avenue SW, Suite 1250
Calgary, AB T2P 2T8

Telephone	403-266-8988
Fax	403-262-1310
E-mail	resumes@ petro-staff.com
Website	www.petro-staff.com
Founded	1983
Employees	8
Specialties	Engineering
	Management
	Accounting
	Purchasing
	Operations
	Computing
	Oil & Gas
Level	Senior
	Mid-Level
Fee Basis	Sometimes contingent
Contact	Iqbal E. Ali

Description Petro Staff is an international recruitment specialist, handling overseas recruitment in engineering, computer systems, accounting, medical, oil & gas and telecommunications.

PETTITT GROUP INC., THE

4145 North Service Road, Suite 200
Burlington, ON L7L 6A3

Telephone	905-336-8922
Fax	905-332-0261
E-mail	info@pettittgroup.com
Website	www.pettittgroup.com
Founded	1991
Specialties	Engineering
	Automotive
	Actuarial
	Management
	Metals
	Purchasing
	Plastics

Level	Mid-Level
	Senior
Min. Salary	$50,000
Fee Basis	Sometimes contingent
Contact	Sue Pettitt, CPC

Description The Pettitt Group Inc. specializes in recruiting mid- and senior-level professionals within the manufacturing sector.

PG CONSULTANTS

82 Leah Crescent
Toronto, ON L4J 8C3

Telephone	905-889-7345
E-mail	pgconsultants@home.com
Specialties	Real Estate
Level	Mid-Level
Contact	Pat Gladman

PHASE II AGENCE DE PERSONNEL

6600 route Transcanadienne
Bureau 140
Pointe-Claire, QC H9R 4S2

Telephone	514-697-5424
Fax	514-697-7352
Specialties	General Practice
Contact	Ruby Catz

PHEE FARRER JONES LTD.

10 Alfred Place, 1st Floor
London, WC1E 7EB
UNITED KINGDOM

Telephone	44-20-785-8800
Fax	44-20-7854-8885
E-mail	enquiries@pfj.co.uk
Website	www.pheefarrerjones.co.uk
Employees	140
Specialties	Advertising
	International
	Direct Mktng.
	Librarians
	Multimedia
	Publishing/Media
	Sales
Level	Senior
	Mid-Level
Min. Salary	$50,000
Fee Basis	Sometimes contingent
Recruiters	Paul Farrer
	Alan Phee
Contact	Paul Farrer, Managing Director

Description Phee Farrer Jones Ltd. specializes in searches in the media, publishing, advertising, information and new media markets. The company also offers HR consultancy, employee benefits and psychometric profiling.

PHELPS STAFFING RESOURCE CENTRE

920 Tungsten Street, Suite 105

Thunder Bay, ON P7B 5Z6

Telephone	807-345-9638
Fax	807-345-9638
E-mail	career@phelpsstaffing.com
Website	www.psrc.ca
Founded	1986
Specialties	Management
	Computing
	Accounting
	Sales
	Engineering
Level	Mid-Level
Recruiters	Cathy LeBrun
	Kellie Petrik
	Heather Phelps CPC
	Valerie Phelps
	Gina Poulin CPC
Contact	Heather Phelps

Description Phelps Staffing Resource is a licensed full-service employment agency and member of Canadian Personnel Services Inc. (CPS Inc.), Association of Canadian Search, Employment and Staffing Services (ACSESS), and TempNet.

PHIPPS CONSULTING ENTERPRISES INC. / PCE

99 Fifth Avenue, Suite 187
Ottawa, ON K1S 5P5

Telephone	613-234-0849
Fax	613-234-3826
E-mail	pce@magma.ca
Website	www.magma.ca/ ~ pce
Specialties	Computing
Contact	Susan N. Phipps

Description PCE specializes in the recruitment of computer personnel for long- and short-term contracts, and full-time positions.

PHOENIX INFORMATION SYSTEMS LTD.

156 Front Street West, Suite 305
Toronto, ON M5J 2L6

Telephone	416-593-8886
Fax	416-593-9793
E-mail	consulting@phoenixltd.com
Website	www.phoenixltd.com
Founded	1984
Specialties	Computing
Contact	Bettyanne Maloughney

Description Phoenix Information Systems is an IT consulting firm that places computing professionals in project management, systems integration, development and consulting assignments.

PHOENIX SEARCH GROUP INC.

112 Sheppard Avenue West
Suite 730
Toronto, ON M2N 1M5

Telephone	416-221-5077
Fax	416-221-5059

E-mail	bruce@phoenixsearch.on.ca
Specialties	Management
	Engineering
	Human Resource
	Accounting
	Banking
	Finance
	Transport
Level	Mid-Level
	Senior
Recruiters	Ian Farooque
	Bruce Sturley
Contact	Bruce Sturley

PIERRE H. DELISLE CONSEIL EN RESSOURCES HUMAINES INC.
1 Place Ville-Marie, Bureau 2821
Montréal, QC H3B 4R4

Telephone	514-861-7100
Fax	514-879-3281
E-mail	phdelisle@videotron.ca
Website	pages.infinit.net/phdrh
Founded	1988
Employees	1
Specialties	Computing
	Management
	Sales
Level	Mid-Level
	Senior
Min. Salary	$55,000
Contact	Pierre H. Delisle

Description Selection and recruitment of managers and highly-skilled professionals in IT and sales of IT.

PILA RECRUITING & ASSOCIATES INC.
8580 Dakota Place
Richmond, BC V7C 4Y6

Telephone	604-275-7436
Fax	604-275-7437
E-mail	jobs@pilarecruiting.com
Website	www.pilarecruiting.com
Founded	1997
Employees	1
Specialties	Engineering
	Telecom
	Computing
	Management
	Multimedia
	Sales
	Logistics
Level	Senior
	Mid-Level
Min. Salary	$40,000
Contact	Esther Pila

Description Pila Recruiting & Associates Inc. specializes in recruiting professionals for the high-tech industry throughout Canada.

PINSTRIPE PERSONNEL INC.
100 Wellington Street, Suite 301
London, ON N6B 2K6

Telephone	519-858-5851
Fax	519-433-0837
E-mail	london@pinstripegroup.net
Website	www.pinstripegroup.net
Specialties	Administrative
	Accounting
	Banking
	Computing
Level	Mid-Level
	Junior

Description Pinstripe Personnel Inc. is an integrated employment solutions leader specializing in the areas of general office, financial service, call centre operations and information technology.

PINSTRIPE PERSONNEL INC.
1 Adelaide Street East
One Financial Place
Suite 2330, PO Box 188
Toronto, ON M5C 2V9

Telephone	416-777-9675
Fax	416-863-5008
E-mail	mail@pinstripegroup.net
Website	www.pinstripegroup.net
Founded	1985
Specialties	Banking
	Computing
	Finance
	Operations
	Purchasing
Level	Mid-Level
	Junior
Fee Basis	Always contingent
Recruiters	Nicala Farwell
	Greg George CPC
	Susan Riddell
Contact	Linda Wylie

Description Pinstripe Personnel Inc. is an integrated employment solutions leader specializing in the areas of general office, financial service, call centre operations and information technology.

PINSTRIPE PERSONNEL INC.
55 Town Centre Court, Suite 640
Toronto, ON M1P 4X4

Telephone	416-279-1043
Fax	416-279-1050
E-mail	scarboro@pinstripegroup.net
Website	www.pinstripegroup.net
Specialties	Administrative
	Accounting
	Banking
	Computing
Level	Mid-Level
	Junior

Description Pinstripe Personnel Inc. is an integrated employment solutions leader specializing in the areas of general office, financial service, call centre operations and information technology.

PINSTRIPE PERSONNEL INC.
33 City Centre Drive, Suite 576
Mississauga, ON L4Z 2N5

Telephone	905-306-0568
Fax	905-306-0579
E-mail	sfg@pinstripegroup.net
Website	www.pinstripegroup.net
Specialties	Administrative
	Accounting
	Banking
	Computing
Level	Mid-Level
	Junior
Contact	Susan Foster

Description Pinstripe Personnel Inc. is an integrated employment solutions leader specializing in the areas of general office, financial service, call centre operations and information technology.

PINTON FORREST & MADDEN / EMA PARTNERS INTERNATIONAL
1055 West Hastings Street
Suite 2020, Guinness Tower
Vancouver, BC V6E 2E9

Telephone	604-689-9970
Fax	604-689-9943
E-mail	pfm@pfmsearch.com
Website	www.pfmsearch.com
Founded	1992
Employees	10
Specialties	Management
	Marketing
	Finance
	Operations
	Forestry
	Pulp & Paper
	Education
Level	Senior
	Mid-Level
Min. Salary	$70,000
Fee Basis	Retainer Only
Recruiters	Shaun Carpenter
	Trish Eng
	Shelina Esmail
	Casey Forrest
	Seema Kanwal
	George Madden
	Melissa Mueller
	Garth Pinton
	Allison Shepard
	Tracey Vopni
Contact	Garth Pinton

Description Pinton Forrest & Madden specializes in the recruitment and placement of executives and management in the private, public, education and non-profit sectors.

PIONEER EXECUTIVE CONSULTANTS
936 The East Mall, Suite 201
Toronto, ON M9B 6J9

Telephone	416-620-5563
Fax	416-620-5648
E-mail	pioneer.executive@sympatico.ca
Website	www.pioneerexecutive.com

Founded	1970
Employees	3
Specialties	Engineering Accounting Management Sales Scientific Logistics Quality Control
Level	Mid-Level Senior
Fee Basis	Sometimes contingent
Recruiters	Edward Gres Paul Sinclair
Contact	Paul Sinclair, Senior Consultant

Description Pioneer Executive Consultants is a multi-disciplinary search firm handling positions in management, sales, manufacturing, engineering and coatings.

PIPER-MORGAN ASSOCIATES
3355 West Alabama, Suite 1100
Houston, TX 77098 USA

Telephone	713-840-9922
Fax	713-840-9931
E-mail	info@ pipermorgan-aei.com
Website	www. pipermorgan-aei.com
Employees	1977
Specialties	Oil & Gas International
Level	Mid-Level Senior
Recruiters	Cindy Carter Will Darroh Dick Darroh Gladney Darroh Steve Emshoff Dan Gibbons Kristi Madison Mike Ryerson
Contact	Will Darroh, Senior Partner

Description Piper-Morgan Associates is a professional / technical personnel search firm, specialized to meet the staffing needs of the energy industry with emphasis in exploration and production, refining and petrochemical and energy transmission.

PITSEL & ASSOCIATES
1609 - 14th Street SW, Suite 212
Calgary, AB T3C 1E3

Telephone	403-245-0550
Fax	403-244-2018
E-mail	pitselp@nucleus.com
Website	www.4imago.com/ pitsel/pindex.htm
Founded	1984
Specialties	General Practice
Recruiters	Angeline Fitch PhD Gregory Folk Patricia Pitsel PhD
Contact	Patricia Pitsel

Description Pitsel & Associates Ltd. is an HR consulting firm that also does occasional recruitment work.

PKF HILL LLP
41 Valleybrook Drive, Suite 200
Toronto, ON M3B 2S6

Telephone	416-449-9171
Fax	416-449-7401
E-mail	wendy.macdonald@ pkfhill.com
Website	www.pkfhill.com
Specialties	Accounting Finance
Level	Mid-Level Senior
Contact	Ronald Kretchman, CA

Description PKF Hill LLP is a chartered accounting firm that also does some search work for clients.

PLACEMENT DE PERSONNEL LOUISE BOLDUC INC.
2320, rue Real-Angers
Sillery, QC G1T 1N1

Téléphone	418-527-7331
Télécopieur	418-527-6756
Spécialités	Généralistes
Contact	Louise Bolduc

PLACEMENT GROUP PERSONNEL SERVICES INC., THE
10117 Jasper Avenue, Suite 1508
Edmonton, AB T5J 1W8

Telephone	780-421-7702
Fax	780-426-3427
E-mail	info@ placementgroup.ab.ca
Website	www.placementgroup. ab.ca
Specialties	Human Resource Health/Medical
Level	Junior Mid-Level
Contact	Sandra Steele, Manager

Description The Placement Group Personnel Services Inc. is an ISO-certified, full service staffing agency and is a division of The Design Group.

PLACEMENT QUALI-TECH
655 Jean-Paul Vincent, Bureau 15
Longueuil, QC J4G 1R3

Téléphone	450-928-3838
Télécopieur	450-928-1264
Courriel	info@placementquali- tech.com
Site Internet	www.placementquali- tech.com
Spécialités	Métiers/techniciens
Échelon	Intermédiaire

Description Quali-Tech, une division de Gestsec Inc., offre à ses clients des services de placement professionel de personnel qualifié dans l'industrie.

PLACEMENT TESTART INC.
5252, boul. de Maisonneuve Ouest
Bureau 309
Westmount , QC H4A 3S5

Téléphone	514-489-8484
Télécopieur	514-489-8486
Courriel	cv@testart.com
Site Internet	www.testart.com
Fondée	1981
Employés	5
Spécialités	Informatique Ingénierie Télécommunications
Échelon	Direction Intermédiaire
Frais	Toujours relative
Contact	Marion Testart

Description Spécialisée dans le recrutement de professionels en haute technologie, informatique et électronique, existe depuis 15 ans.

PLANET PERSONNEL AGENCY INC.
55 Yonge Street, Suite 603
Toronto, ON M5E 1J4

Telephone	416-363-9888
Fax	416-363-9899
E-mail	planet@planet4it.com
Website	www.planet4it.com
Specialties	Computing
Level	Mid-Level
Recruiters	Jim Carlson Nadine Christie Ed Johnson
Contact	Ed Johnson

Description Planet Personnel serves the IT community with respect and fairness by employing best practices in recruitment.

PLANIGESTION A. CHOQUETTE INC.
2810, boul. Saint-Martin E.
Bureau 203
Duvernay, QC H7E 4Y6

Téléphone	450-664-3804
Fax	450-664-3707
E-mail	plani-ac@dsuper.net
Founded	1988
Employees	5
Specialties	Engineering Management Marketing Operations Sales Pulp & Paper Retail
Level	Senior Mid-Level
Min. Salary	$50,000
Fee Basis	Retainer Only
Recruiters	André Choquette Claude Choquette Jacques Daigle
Contact	André Choquette, President

Description Senior- and mid-level recruiting in all fields except computing.

PLEIAD CANADA INC.
560 Churchill Avenue North
Ottawa, ON K1Z 5E5

Telephone	613-722-9902
Fax	613-728-4542
E-mail	corporate@pleiad.ca
Website	www.pleiad.ca
Specialties	Computing
	Management
Level	Mid-Level
Recruiters	Blake Armitage
	Laurie Morin
	Andrée Riffou
Contact	Blake Armitage,
	Office Manager

Description Pleiad Canada Inc. is a management and IT consulting firm that recruits for positions in the private sector and government.

PME PARTENAIRES CONSULTANTS
11535 - 1e Avenue, Bureau 301
Saint-Georges, QC G5Y 7H5

Téléphone	418-228-2055
Télécopieur	418-228-1886
Courriel	pmeparte@
	globetrotter.net
Site Internet	www.pme
	partenaires.com
Fondée	1988
Employés	10
Spécialités	Comptabilité
	Informatique
	Éducation
	Ingénierie
	Finance
	Gouvt/OSBL
	Santé/médical
	Hospitalité
	Gestion
	Marketing
	Exploitation
	Achat
	Ventes
Échelon	Intermédiaire
	Débutant
Frais	Toujours relative
Recruteurs	Yvan Landry
	Jean-Claude Langevin
	Thomas Quirion
Contact	Yvan Landry

Description PME Partenaires offre evaluation de potentiel, sélection de personnel (cols blancs: cadres — intermédiaires — junior), et services en GRH et en formation de personnel.

POLARIS EMPLOYMENT SERVICES
5066 Kingsway, Suite 205
Burnaby, BC V5H 2E7

Telephone	604-430-1557
Fax	604-430-8693
E-mail	polaris_employment@
	bc.sympatico.ca
Founded	1977
Employees	10
Specialties	Disabled
Level	Junior
Contact	Linda Delparte,
	Executive Director

Description Polaris Employment provides quality services for job-seekers with developmental disabilities.

POLLACK GROUP, THE
176 Bronson Avenue, Pollack Place
Ottawa, ON K1R 6H4

Telephone	613-238-2233
Fax	613-238-4407
E-mail	tpg@pollackgroup.com
Website	www.pollackgroup.com
Founded	1973
Employees	10
Specialties	Computing
	Engineering
	Govt/Nonprofit
	Management
	Sales
Level	Mid-Level
Recruiters	Charles Durning
	Cindy Larocque CPC
	Debbie McRae
	Paul Peter Pollack
	Karen Pollack
Contact	Paul P. Pollack,
	President

Description The Pollack Group (formerly Paul Pollack Personnel Ltd.) is a full-service professional management consulting firm specializing in recruitment, staffing, outplacement and counseling.

POMMEN & ASSOCIATES LIMITED
9358 - 49th Street, Suite 201
Edmonton, AB T6B 2L7

Telephone	780-496-7707
Fax	780-461-7700
E-mail	dpommen@
	pommen.com
Website	www.pommen.com
Founded	1991
Employees	3
Specialties	Finance
	Health/Medical
	Operations
	Govt/Nonprofit
	Accounting
	Consulting
	Management
Level	Mid-Level
	Senior
Min. Salary	$45,000
Fee Basis	Sometimes contingent
Recruiters	Dennis W. Pommen
	Elizabeth Rucki
Contact	Dennis Pommen

Description Pommen & Associates Limited is a management consulting firm providing human resources services to public and private clients.

POWELL JONES MANAGEMENT SERVICES
121 Anne Street South
Barrie, ON L4N 7B6

Telephone	705-728-7461
Fax	705-728-8317
E-mail	pjones@barint.on.ca
Specialties	Operations
	Accounting
	Finance
Level	Mid-Level
Contact	Jeff Maize

Description Powell Jones is a chartered accounting firm that does occasional search work for clients.

PRAGMATIZM
106 Front Street East, Suite 300
Toronto, ON M5A 1E1

Telephone	416-868-4767
Fax	416-868-6002
E-mail	info@pragmatizm.com
Website	www.pragmatizm.com
Specialties	Computing
	Law
	Insurance
	Finance
	Advertising
	Accounting
Level	Mid-Level
	Senior

Description Pragmatizm is a staffing and human resources consulting firm that recruits professionals at all levels for positions in the high-tech, legal, insurance, financial services, advertising and communications industries.

PRECISION RESOURCES LIMITED
100 New Kings Road
London House
London SW6 4LX
UNITED KINGDOM

Telephone	44-20-731-8199
Fax	44-20-371-7200
E-mail	precision.resources@
	virgin.net
Specialties	Oil & Gas
	International
	Engineering

PRECISION STAFFING INC.
779 The Queensway
Toronto, ON M8Z 1N4

Telephone	416-233-4003
Fax	416-251-3334
Specialties	General Practice
Contact	Paul Mangion

PREFERRED HEALTHCARE STAFFING
100 West Cyprus Creek Road
Suite 750
Fort Lauderdale, FL 33309   USA

Telephone	800-735-4774
Fax	888-329-2411
E-mail	travel@preferred
	healthcare.com
Website	www.preferred
	healthcare.com
Specialties	Health/Medical
	International

Recruiters	Janet Alford
	Rachelle Berla
	Joe Borras
	Lana Braunstein
	Staci Culligan
	Miriam Domash
Contact	Kathy Kohnke, VP Sales

Description Preferred Healthcare Staffing (formerly Hospital Staffing Services) places Canadian nurses in the USA.

PREMIER PERSONNEL LIMITED
25 - 29 High Street, Leatherhead
Surrey, KT22 8AB
UNITED KINGDOM

Telephone	44-1372-379183
Fax	44-1372-372301
E-mail	pjd@ prem-per.demon.co.uk
Website	www.premier personnel.co.uk
Founded	1981
Employees	6
Specialties	Engineering
	International
	Construction
	Oil & Gas
Level	Mid-Level
Fee Basis	Sometimes contingent
Recruiters	Philip Dee
	Richard Holmes
	Paul O'Bryan
Contact	Philip Dee

Description Premier Personnel Limited is an international company recruiting for the construction, oil and gas, process and general engineering industries.

PREMIER PERSONNEL MANANGEMENT
192 Jarvis Street
Toronto, ON M5B 2J9

Telephone	416-364-2175
Specialties	Direct Mktng.
	Insurance
Level	Junior
	Mid-Level
Fee Basis	Always contingent
Contact	Kimberley Stephenson

Description Premier Personnel recruits for corporate call centres in Ontario.

PRICEWATERHOUSECOOPERS
7 Church St. W., Dorchester House
Hamilton HM 11
BERMUDA

Telephone	441-295-2000
Fax	441-295-1242
E-mail	susan.darrell@ bm.pwcglobal.com
Website	www.pwcglobal.com
Specialties	Finance
	Accounting
	Management
	International

Level	Mid-Level
	Senior
Fee Basis	Retainer Only
Contact	Jan Landwehr, Executive Search and Selection

Description PricewaterhouseCoopers is an accounting and professional services firm that occasionally does search work for clients.

PRICEWATERHOUSECOOPERS EXECUTIVE SEARCH
1111 West Hastings Street
Vancouver West Tower
Vancouver, BC V6E 3R2

Telephone	604-806-7000
Fax	604-806-7806
E-mail	execsearch.vancouver@ ca.pwcglobal.com
Website	www.pwcglobal.com/ executive/ca
Founded	1961
Employees	800
Specialties	Mining
	Engineering
	General Practice
Level	Mid-Level
	Senior
Min. Salary	$70,000
Fee Basis	Retainer Only
Recruiters	Robert A. McMillan
	Grant Smith
Contact	Michelle Meakin

Description A national firm founded in 1961 with a generalist practice which recruits middle and senior management for private and not-for-profit organizations.

PRICEWATERHOUSECOOPERS EXECUTIVE SEARCH
10088 - 102 Avenue, Suite 1501
Toronto Dominion Tower
Edmonton, AB T5J 2Z1

Telephone	780-441-6700
Fax	780-441-6776
E-mail	edm.execsearch@ ca.pwcglobal.com
Website	www.pwcglobal.com/ executive/ca
Founded	1961
Employees	300
Specialties	Management
	Marketing
	Sales
	Health/Medical
	Govt/Nonprofit
	Finance
Level	Senior
	Mid-Level
Min. Salary	$70,000
Fee Basis	Retainer Only
Recruiters	Enid Bradley
	Rose Mary Holland
Contact	Rose Mary Holland, Director

Description PricewaterhouseCoopers, a national firm founded in 1961,

is a generalist practice which recruits middle and senior management for private and not-for-profit organizations.

PRICEWATERHOUSECOOPERS EXECUTIVE SEARCH
425 - 1st Street SW, Suite 1200
Calgary, AB T2P 3V7

Telephone	403-509-7500
Fax	403-781-1825
E-mail	calgary.resumes@ ca.pwcglobal.com
Website	www.pwcglobal.com/ executive/ca
Founded	1961
Employees	150
Specialties	General Practice
	Management
	Accounting
	Govt/Nonprofit
	Engineering
	Finance
Level	Senior
	Mid-Level
Min. Salary	$70,000
Fee Basis	Retainer Only
Recruiters	Rollie Hearn
	Diane Wilding
Contact	Diane Wilding

Description A national firm founded in 1961 with a generalist practice which recruits middle and senior management for private and not-for-profit organizations.

PRICEWATERHOUSECOOPERS EXECUTIVE SEARCH
2010 - 11th Avenue, Suite 900
Regina, SK S4P 0J3

Telephone	306-790-7900
Fax	306-790-7990
E-mail	merrill.brinton@ ca.pwcglobal.com
Website	www.pwcglobal.com/ executive/ca
Founded	1961
Specialties	Management
	Computing
	Finance
	Health/Medical
	Hospitality
	Operations
Level	Senior
	Mid-Level
Min. Salary	$50,000
Contact	Merrill Brinton

Description PricewaterhouseCoopers, a national firm founded in 1961, is a generalist practice which recruits middle and senior management for private and not-for-profit organizations.

PRICEWATERHOUSECOOPERS EXECUTIVE SEARCH
One Lombard Place
Suite 2300, Richardson Building
Winnipeg, MB R3B 0X6

Telephone	204-926-2400
Fax	204-944-1020
E-mail	execsearch.winnipeg@ca.pwcglobal.com
Website	www.pwcglobal.com/executive/ca
Founded	1993
Employees	140
Specialties	General Practice
	Finance
	Management
	Computing
	Banking
	Human Resource
	Law
Level	Mid-Level
	Senior
Fee Basis	Retainer Only
Contact	Karen Swystun

Description A national firm founded in 1961 with a generalist practice which recruits middle and senior management for private and not-for-profit organizations.

PRICEWATERHOUSECOOPERS EXECUTIVE SEARCH
145 King Street West, 23rd Floor
Toronto, ON M5H 1V8

Telephone	416-869-1130
Fax	416-814-5733
E-mail	execsearch.toronto@ca.pwcglobal.com
Website	www.pwcglobal.com/executive/ca
Founded	1961
Employees	11
Specialties	Management
	Accounting
	Finance
	Computing
	Education
Level	Mid-Level
	Senior
Min. Salary	$70,000
Fee Basis	Retainer Only
Recruiters	Paul F. Crath
	Charles M. Lennox
	Jordene S. Lyttle
	B. Keith McLean
	Barbara Nixon
	Margaret Pelton
	Tom Sinclair
	Elizabeth Zucchiatti
Contact	Keith McLean

Description A national firm founded in 1961 with a generalist practice which recruits middle and senior management for private and not-for-profit organizations.

PRICEWATERHOUSECOOPERS EXECUTIVE SEARCH
1250 Rene-Levesque Blvd. West
Suite 3500
Montréal, QC H3B 2G4

Telephone	514-205-5000
Fax	514-938-5709
E-mail	pwcmtl-es.rc@ca.pwcglobal.com
Website	www.pwcglobal.com/executive/ca
Founded	1961
Specialties	General Practice
	Management
	International
	Marketing
	Sales
	Accounting
	Consulting
Level	Senior
	Mid-Level
Min. Salary	$70,000
Recruiters	Joseph M.B. Beaupré
	Claude Daigneault
Contact	Joseph M.B. Beaupré

Description PricewaterhouseCoopers, a national firm founded in 1961, is a generalist practice that recruits middle and senior management for private and not-for-profit organizations.

PRICEWATERHOUSECOOPERS EXECUTIVE SEARCH
900 Rene-Levesque Boulevard East
Suite 500
Québec, QC G1R 2B5

Téléphone	418-522-7001
Télécopieur	418-522-5663
Courriel	michel.chalifour@ca.pwcglobal.com
Site Internet	www.pwcglobal.com/executive/ca
Fondée	1961
Spécialités	Comptabilité
	Éducation
	Ingénierie
	Finance
	Santé/médical
	Ressources humaines
	International
	Gestion
	Exploitation
	Ventes
Échelon	Direction
	Intermédiaire
Salaire min.	50 000 $
Frais	Honoraire seulement
Contact	Michel Chalifour

Description PricewaterhouseCoopers offre des services diversifiés: vérification fiscalité, financement, litiges, conseils en gestion avec emphase sur la reingenierie et les ressources humaines, particulierement le recrutement de cadres.

PRICEWATERHOUSECOOPERS EXECUTIVE SEARCH
GPO Box 150, Waterfront Place
Brisbane, Queensland 4001
AUSTRALIA

Telephone	61-7-3257-5000
Fax	61-7-3257-599
Website	www.pwcglobal.com
Specialties	Scientific
	Engineering
	International

Level	Mid-Level
	Senior
Contact	Steve Laney

PRICEWATERHOUSECOOPERS EXECUTIVE SEARCH
Prince's Building, 22nd Floor
GPO Box 390
Hong Kong   CHINA

Telephone	852-2289-8888
Fax	852-2869-4410
E-mail	Executive_Recruitment@Hong-Kong.notes.PW.com
Website	www.pwcglobal.com
Specialties	General Practice
	Engineering
	Management
	International
Level	Senior
	Mid-Level

Description PricewaterhouseCoopers is a generalist practice which recruits middle and senior management for private and not-for-profit organizations.

PRICEWATERHOUSECOOPERS EXECUTIVE SEARCH
Kosmodamianskaya
Naberezhnaya 52, Building 5
Moscow 113054   RUSSIA

Telephone	7-095-9676000
Fax	7-095-9676001
Website	www.pwcglobal.com
Specialties	General Practice
	International
Contact	O. Novikova

Description PricewaterhouseCoopers is a generalist practice which recruits middle and senior management for private and not-for-profit organizations.

PRICEWATERHOUSECOOPERS LLP
777 Broughton Street
Victoria, BC V8W 1E3

Telephone	250-384-4131
Fax	250-360-5400
E-mail	vict.dhw@sun.vic.cooperslybrand.ca
Website	www.pwcglobal.com
Specialties	Finance
	Accounting
Contact	David H. Williams, CMC

Description PricewaterhouseCoopers LLP is an accounting and professional services firm that occasionally does search work.

PRICEWATERHOUSECOOPERS LLP
123 - 2nd Avenue South
Suite 200, The Princeton Tower
Saskatoon, SK S7K 7E6

Telephone	306-668 5900
Fax	306-652-1315
Website	www.pwcglobal.com
Founded	1955

Specialties	Finance
	Management
	Accounting
Level	Mid-Level
	Senior
Min. Salary	$50,000
Contact	Monte Gorchinski CA

Description PricewaterhouseCoopers LLP is an accounting and professional services firm that occasionally does search work.

PRICEWATERHOUSECOOPERS LLP
275 Dundas Street, Suite 1500
London, ON N6B 3L1

Telephone	519-640-7907
Fax	519-640-8015
E-mail	robert.eaton@
	ca.pwcglobal.com
Website	www.pwcglobal.com/ca
Founded	1961
Employees	50
Specialties	General Practice
	Administrative
	Automotive
	Management
	Human Resource
	Finance
	Operations
Level	Senior
	Mid-Level
Min. Salary	$60,000
Fee Basis	Retainer Only
Contact	Robert E. Eaton,
	Director HR Consulting

Description PricewaterhouseCoopers LLP is an accounting and professional services firm that occasionally does search work.

PRICEWATERHOUSECOOPERS LLP
55 King Street West
Suite 900, Canada Trust Centre
Kitchener, ON N2G 4W1

Telephone	519-570-5700
Website	www.pwcglobal.com
Specialties	Accounting
	Finance
Contact	Linda Monkman

Description PricewaterhouseCoopers LLP is an accounting and professional services firm that occasionally does search work.

PRICEWATERHOUSECOOPERS LLP
21 King Street West, Main Floor
Hamilton, ON L8P 4W7

Telephone	905-777-7000
Fax	905-777-7060
E-mail	pv.c.hamilton.
	recruiting@ca.pwcglobal.
	com
Website	www.pwcglobal.com
Founded	1955
Specialties	Accounting
	Finance
	Management
	Human Resource

	Operations
	Non-Profit
Level	Senior
	Mid-Level
Min. Salary	$50,000
Contact	Rita Bishop

Description PricewaterhouseCoopers LLP is an accounting and professional services firm that occasionally does search work.

PRICEWATERHOUSECOOPERS LLP
1 Robert Speck Parkway
Suite 1100
Mississauga Executive Centre
Mississauga, ON L4Z 3M3

Telephone	905-949-7400
Fax	905-949-7550
E-mail	kerry.v.kessler@
	ca.pwcglobal.com
Website	www.pwcglobal.com
Specialties	General Practice
Contact	Kerry Kessler

Description PricewaterhouseCoopers LLP is an accounting and professional services firm that occasionally does search work.

PRICEWATERHOUSECOOPERS LLP
99 Bank Street, Suite 800
Ottawa, ON K1P 1E4

Telephone	613-237-3702
Fax	613-237-3963
E-mail	libby.e.cantwell@
	ca.pwcglobal.com
Website	www.pwcglobal.com
Specialties	General Practice
Level	Mid-Level
Contact	Libby Cantwell

Description PricewaterhouseCoopers LLP is an accounting and professional services firm that occasionally does search work.

PRICEWATERHOUSECOOPERS LLP
44 Chipman Hill
P.O. Box 789 Brunswick House
Saint John, NB E2L 4B9

Telephone	506-632-1810
Fax	506-632-8997
E-mail	claude.j.maillet@
	ca.pwcglobal.com
Website	www.pwcglobal.com
Specialties	Accounting
	Finance
	Consulting
	Human Resource
	Management
	Marketing
Level	Mid-Level
	Senior
Fee Basis	Sometimes contingent
Contact	Martina MacDougall

Description PricewaterhouseCoopers LLP is an accounting and professional services firm that occasionally does search work for clients.

PRICEWATERHOUSECOOPERS LLP
18 Queen Street
Suite 100, Prince Edward Place
Charlottetown, PE C1A 4A2

Telephone	902-368-3100
Fax	902-566-5074
Website	www.pwcglobal.com
Specialties	Accounting
	Finance
Level	Mid-Level
Contact	Mary Best, CA

Description PricewaterhouseCoopers LLP is an accounting and professional services firm that occasionally does search work for clients.

PRICEWATERHOUSECOOPERS LLP
1809 Barrington Street, Suite 600
Halifax, NS B3J 3K8

Telephone	902-425-6190
Fax	902-422-1166
E-mail	elsie.e.collins@
	ca.pwcglobal.com
Website	www.pwcglobal.com
Founded	1955
Specialties	Govt/Nonprofit
	Management
	Finance
	Consulting
	Education
	Human Resource
Level	Senior
	Mid-Level
Min. Salary	$50,000
Fee Basis	Retainer Only
Contact	Donald C. Moore

Description PricewaterhouseCoopers LLP is an accounting and professional services firm that occasionally does search work for clients.

PRICEWATERHOUSECOOPERS LLP
215 Water Street, Box 75
Suite 802, Atlantic Place
St. John's, NF A1C 6C9

Telephone	709-722-3883
Fax	709-722-5874
Website	www.pwcglobal.com
Specialties	Accounting
	Finance
Level	Mid-Level
Contact	Ron Walsh CA, Partner

Description PricewaterhouseCoopers LLP is an accounting and professional services firm that occasionally does search work for clients.

PRICEWATERHOUSECOOPERS MANAGEMENT CONSULTANTS LIMITED
13 Victoria Avenue
Suite 11, PO Box 550
Port of Spain   TRINIDAD

Telephone	868-623-1361
Fax	868-624-7831
E-mail	nicolyn.wyke@
	tt.pwcglobal.com
Website	www.pwcglobal.com

Specialties	General Practice
	Management
	International
Level	Senior
	Mid-Level
Fee Basis	Retainer Only
Contact	Nicolyn Wyke

Description PricewaterhouseCoopers Management Consultants Limited recruits middle and senior management for private and not-for-profit organizations.

PRICHARD KYMEN INC. / PKI
12204 - 106th Avenue, Suite 302
Edmonton, AB T5M 0T2

Telephone	780-448-0128
Fax	780-453-5246
E-mail	pkymen@
	telusplanet.net
Website	pkymen.cjb.net
Founded	1984
Employees	2
Specialties	Management
	Engineering
	Sales
	Banking
	Human Resource
	Marketing
	Operations
	Purchasing
	Mining
Level	Mid-Level
	Senior
Fee Basis	Retainer Only
Contact	Pat McKinney,
	Principal

Description PKI are certified human resources professionals and consultants to management for executive search, recruitment and career transition counselling services.

PRIDE IN PERSONNEL INC.
11 Allstate Parkway, Suite 420
Oakland Corporate Centre
Markham, ON L3R 9T8

Telephone	905-470-7011
Fax	905-470-0259
E-mail	pdubois@pridein
	personnel.com
Website	www.pridein
	personnel.com
Founded	1990
Employees	10
Specialties	Engineering
	Operations
	Marketing
	Sales
	Management
	Pharmaceutical
	Automotive
	Aerospace
	Telecom
Level	Mid-Level
Min. Salary	$40,000
Fee Basis	Sometimes contingent
Recruiters	Nelson Abreu
	Phil Dubois
Contact	Nelson Abreu

Description Specialists in recruiting technical professionals in all facets of manufacturing, engineering, sales and marketing. Industry focus in pharmaceutical, data / telecommunications, automation / robotics, automotive and aerospace.

PRIME MANAGEMENT GROUP INC.
365 Queens Avenue
London, ON N6B 1X5

Telephone	519-672-7710
Fax	519-672-5155
E-mail	jobs@pmg.on.ca
Website	www.pmg.on.ca
Founded	1990
Employees	10
Specialties	Accounting
	Computing
	Engineering
	Finance
	Human Resource
	Insurance
	Management
	Marketing
	Sales
Level	Mid-Level
	Senior
Min. Salary	$45,000
Recruiters	Kimberley Chesney
	Paul Coleman CPC
	Linda Gauld CPC
	Joanne L. Glendenning
	Jodie Harper
	Gisele Lavigne
	Jay McKillop CPC
	Loretta Smith
Contact	Kimberley Chesney,
	President

Description Prime specializes in placing professionals for positions in computing, manufacturing, healthcare, sales, retail, human resources, accounting and finance, engineering and earth sciences.

PRIME MANAGEMENT GROUP INC.
260 Holiday Inn Drive, Suite 26
Cambridge, ON N3C 4E8

Telephone	519-220-0310
Fax	519-220-0327
E-mail	jobs2@pmg.on.ca
Website	www.pmg.on.ca
Specialties	Accounting
	Computing
	Engineering
	Finance
	Human Resource
	Insurance
	Management
	Marketing
	Sales
Level	Mid-Level
	Senior
Min. Salary	$45,000
Fee Basis	Sometimes contingent
Recruiters	Juliette Hunter
	Carol Parnall CPC
	Colleen Young
Contact	Juliette Hunter, Recruitment Coordinator

Description Prime places professionals for positions in computing, manufacturing, health-care, sales, retail, HR, accounting and finance, engineering and earth sciences.

PRIME SOURCE MANAGEMENT INC.
40 King Street W.
Suite 4900, Scotia Plaza
Toronto, ON M5H 4A2

Telephone	416-362-6222
Fax	416-362-4506
E-mail	careers@primesource
	mgmt.com
Website	www.primesource
	mgmt.com
Founded	1982
Employees	45
Specialties	Engineering
	Computing
	Aerospace
	Telecom
Level	Mid-Level
	Senior
Min. Salary	$50,000
Contact	Michael Morris

Description Prime Source is dedicated to engineering placement specializing in the aerospace and electronics industries.

PRINCE ARTHUR ADVERTISING
64 Prince Arthur Avenue
Toronto, ON M5R 1B4

Telephone	416-920-7730
Fax	416-922-8646
Specialties	General Practice
	Management
Level	Senior
Fee Basis	Retainer Only

Description Prince Arthur Advertising is a recruitment advertising agency affiliated with The Caldwell Partners, a major retained executive search firm.

PRIOR RESOURCE GROUP INC., THE
50 Queen Street North, Suite 800
Kitchener, ON N2M 6P4

Telephone	519-570-1100
Fax	519-570-1144
E-mail	priorkw@
	priorresource.com
Website	www.priorresource.com
Founded	1974
Employees	20
Specialties	Accounting
	Computing
	Engineering
	Management
	Marketing
	Operations
	Sales
Level	Mid-Level
	Senior
Recruiters	Bob Cecil
	Angela Mackay
Contact	Bob Cecil

Description Prior is a staffing, search and consulting company serving the Kitchener-Waterloo tech triangle.

PRISM ASSOCIATES, THE
PO Box 3418, WECSC
Edmonton, AB T5L 3B2

Fax	780-451-3082
Specialties	General Practice
Level	Mid-Level
	Junior

PRO MED NATIONAL STAFFING OF WICHITA FALLS, INC.
1501 Brook Avenue, Suite B
Wichita Falls, TX 76301   USA

Telephone	940-723-0372
Fax	940-723-0375
E-mail	promed@wf.net
Website	www.promedjobs.com
Specialties	Health/Medical
	Management
	International
Fee Basis	Always contingent
Contact	Colleen Mills, CEO

Description Pro Med specializes in placing medical professionals in the USA, concentrating on nurses, physicians, therapists and technicians.

PRO TEC GLOBAL STAFFING SERVICES
8500 Leslie Street, Suite 600
Thornhill, ON L3T 7M8

Telephone	905-707-2300
Fax	905-707-0332
E-mail	protec@protecstaff.com
Website	www.protecstaff.com
Founded	1982
Employees	20
Specialties	Engineering
	Computing
	Aerospace
	Automotive
	Scientific
	Pharmaceutical
	Plastics
Level	Senior
	Mid-Level
Min. Salary	$25,000
Fee Basis	Sometimes contingent
Recruiters	R.J. (Reg) Baraniuk
	John Chrobak
	Dave Clark
	Glen Collard
	Bill Johnson
	Iain Purves
	Michael Slimkowich
Contact	R.J. (Reg) Baraniuk

Description Pro Tec Global Staffing is a global engineering, construction, manufacturing and information technology employment service.

PRO TEC SERVICES TECHNIQUES
5525, rue Varin
Brossard, QC J4W 1E2

Téléphone	450-923-2680

Fax	450-923-2851
E-mail	jpbelan@neuronet.net
Specialties	General Practice
	Engineering
	Trades/Technicians
Contact	Jean-Pierre Bélanger

PRO-ACTION PERSONNEL
4020, boul. Le Corbusier, bur. 200
Chomedey, QC H7L 5R2

Téléphone	450-963-3399
Télécopieur	450-963-2510
Fondée	1992
Spécialités	Généralistes
	Comptabilité
	Informatique
	Ingénierie
	Marketing
	Plastique
	Télécommunications
Échelon	Intermédiaire
	Débutant
Frais	Toujours relative
Contact	Sylvie Gosselin

Description Pro-Action Personnel specialise dans le recrutement et placement de personnel.

PROACTIVE MANAGEMENT DEVELOPMENT INC.
800 West Pender Street, Suite 220
Vancouver, BC V6C 2V6

Telephone	604-685-8889
Fax	604-685-6597
E-mail	proact@uniserve.com
Specialties	Management
Level	Senior
Contact	David Terry

PROBANK SERVICES INC.
6295 Mississauga Road, Suite 222
Mississauga, ON L5N 1A5

Telephone	905-286-0642
Fax	905-274-2051
E-mail	resumes@probank services.com.
Website	www.probank services.com
Specialties	Hospitality
	Administrative
Level	Mid-Level
	Junior

PROBEN MANAGEMENT LTD.
2075, rue University, Bureau 1610
Montréal, QC H3A 2L1

Telephone	514-288-7161
Fax	514-843-4095
E-mail	proben@proben.com
Website	www.proben.com
Specialties	Computing
Level	Senior
	Mid-Level
Recruiters	Laurent Benattar
	Michel Moquin
	Daniel Pelletier
	Normand Tremblay

Contact	Michel Moquin

Description Proben Management Ltd. is an IT consulting firm that also places computing professionals in contract assignments.

PROCOM / PROFESSIONAL COMPUTER CONSULTANTS GROUP LTD.
250 - 6th Avenue SW
Suite 1200, Bow Valley Square IV
Calgary, AB T2P 3H7

Telephone	403-571-7241
Fax	403-571-7195
E-mail	wendym@procom.ca
Website	www.procom.ca
Founded	1978
Specialties	Computing
	Engineering
	Telecom
Level	Mid-Level
	Senior
Fee Basis	Always contingent
Recruiters	Sandy Drysdale
	Karen Jefferson
	Jennifer MacGregor
	Wendy Mah
	Lynn Wilsack
Contact	Wendy Mah

Description Procom is a leading supplier of computer and IT personnel on a contract and full-time basis.

PROCOM / PROFESSIONAL COMPUTER CONSULTANTS GROUP LTD.
405 King Street North, Suite 106
Waterloo, ON N2J 2Z4

Telephone	519-885-4331
Fax	519-885-5308
E-mail	mail@procom.ca
Website	www.procom.ca
Founded	1978
Specialties	Computing
Level	Senior
	Mid-Level
Fee Basis	Always contingent
Contact	Luke Morrison

Description Procom is a leading supplier of computer and IT personnel on a contract and full-time basis.

PROCOM / PROFESSIONAL COMPUTER CONSULTANTS GROUP LTD.
2323 Yonge Street, Suite 605
Toronto, ON M4P 2C9

Telephone	416-483-0766
Fax	416-483-8102
E-mail	mail@procom.ca
Website	www.procom.ca
Founded	1978
Employees	40
Specialties	Computing
Level	Senior
	Mid-Level
Fee Basis	Always contingent

Recruiters   John Csatri
Eric Descoteaux
Lisa Elliot
Mark Galloway
Kevin Jaques
Jennifer Lacka
Michael Low
Alex MacKenzie
Dave Mahood
John Mahood
Lisa Manahan
Jeff Nugent

Contact   Frank McCrea

Description   Procom is a leading supplier of computer and IT personnel on a contract and full-time basis.

PROCOM / PROFESSIONAL COMPUTER CONSULTANTS GROUP LTD.
300 March Road, Suite 600
Kanata, ON   K2K 2E2

Telephone   613-270-9339
Fax   613-270-9449
E-mail   shawnm@procom.ca
Website   www.procom.ca
Founded   1978
Specialties   Computing
Level   Senior
Mid-Level
Fee Basis   Always contingent
Recruiters   Maggie Alves
Paul Brown
Keith Carter
Moodie Cheikh
Lesley Collins
Kim Hodge
Jane McElligott
Shawn Mountain
Daria Sangiovanni
Derek Weber

Contact   Shawn Mountain,
Manager of
Professional Services

Description   Procom is a leading supplier of computer and IT personnel on a contract and full-time basis.

PROCOM / PROFESSIONAL COMPUTER CONSULTANTS GROUP LTD.
1260 Crescent, Suite 210
Montréal, QC H3G 2A9

Telephone   514-731-7224
Fax   514-731-7244
E-mail   mail@procom.ca
Website   www.procom.ca
Founded   1978
Specialties   Computing
Level   Senior
Mid-Level
Fee Basis   Always contingent
Recruiters   André Couillard
Annaliza Evans
Joe Kerub
Christopher Paget

Description   Procom is a leading supplier of computer and IT personnel on a contract and full-time basis.

PROCOM SERVICES
275 Battery Street, Suite 950
San Francisco, CA 94111-3050
USA

Telephone   415-773-1873
Fax   415-773-1833
E-mail   mail@procom.ca
Website   www.procom.ca
Founded   1978
Specialties   Computing
International
Recruiters   Roberta D'Alois
Sylvia Herczku
Annie Yee

Contact   Roberta D'Alois

Description   Procom is a leading supplier of computer and IT personnel on a contract and full-time basis.

PROCOM SERVICES
801 East Campbell Road, Suite 375
Richardson, TX 75081-1890
USA

Telephone   972-234-6055
Fax   972-234-5661
E-mail   mail@procom.ca
Website   www.procom.ca
Founded   1978
Specialties   Computing
International
Level   Mid-Level
Fee Basis   Always contingent
Recruiters   Amy Askins
Neil Brooks
Ron Hunt
Jeet Sikdar
Gregg Wright

Contact   Amy Askins

Description   Procom is a leading supplier of computer and IT personnel on a contract and full-time basis.

PROCOM SERVICES
3000 RDU Center Drive
Suite 114, Research Triangle Park
Morrisville, NC 27560
USA

Telephone   919-840-0606
Fax   919-840-0777
E-mail   mail@procom.ca
Website   www.procom.ca
Founded   1978
Specialties   Computing
International
Level   Senior
Mid-Level
Fee Basis   Always contingent
Recruiters   Rosemarie S. Brady
Dan Colby
Michelle Harrelson
Rich Kviring
Jon Michalec
Donna Rose
Donna Stainback
Stacey Young
Joe Zuchlewski

Contact   Dan Colby

Description   Procom is a leading supplier of computer and IT personnel on a contract and full-time basis.

PROFESSIONAL DEVELOPMENT ASSOCIATES
2892 South Sheridan Way
Suite 100, Lower Level
Oakville, ON   L6J 7L4

Telephone   905-829-9959
Fax   905-829-9927
E-mail   drtracy@home.com
Specialties   Human Resource
Sales
Computing
Contact   Dr. Shayne Tracy,
Associate

PROFESSIONAL ENVIRONMENTAL RECREATION CONSULTANTS LTD.
6751 Westview Drive
North Delta, BC V4E 2L7

Telephone   604-596-4433
Fax   604-596-4473
Website   www.perconline.com
Specialties   Govt/Nonprofit
Education
Forestry
Environmental
Level   Mid-Level
Recruiters   Brian Johnston
Kevan Tisshaw
William D. (Bill) Webster
Contact   William D. (Bill) Webster

Description   PERC specializes in placing people in the environmental and recreational fields.

PROFESSIONAL EXECUTIVE SERVICES
333 - 5th Avenue SW, Suite 390
Calgary, AB T2P 1H4

Telephone   403-266-7350
Fax   403-265-5024
Specialties   Computing
Sales
Level   Mid-Level
Contact   Maureen A. Robertson

Description   Professional Executive Services is a Calgary-based recruitment firm specializing in placing professionals in Canada and around the world.

PROFESSIONAL PERSONNEL
45 Barrie Street
Cambridge, ON N1S 3A8

Telephone   519-623-2437
Fax   519-623-4543
Specialties   General Practice
Level   Mid-Level
Junior
Contact   Sue Hutchinson

PROFESSIONAL STAFFING RESOURCES, INC.
PO Box 15093
Savannah, GA 31416-5093 USA

Telephone 800-455-8041
Fax 912-352-1926
E-mail psrnurses@aol.com
Website www.psrnurses.com
Founded 1978
Specialties Health/Medical
International
Contact Shirley Permenter, RN

Description Professional Staffing Resources, Inc. is a global staffing company specializing in healthcare professionals.

PROFILE PERSONNEL CONSULTANTS
65 Queen Street West, Suite 1504
Toronto, ON M5H 2M5

Telephone 416-363-1488
E-mail profile@netcom.ca
Website www.profile
consultants.com
Founded 1985
Employees 7
Specialties Management
Finance
Bilingual
Administrative
Level Mid-Level
Fee Basis Always contingent
Contact Ann Turner

Description Profile Personnel Consultants specializes in contract and permanent placements in office support, administration, management, investment, financial and bilingual areas.

PROFILE SEARCH INTERNATIONAL LTD.
805 - 5th Avenue SW, Suite 120
Calgary, AB T2J 0S2

Telephone 403-231-2727
Fax 403-231-2724
E-mail darryl@profile
search.com
Website www.profilesearch.com
Founded 1992
Employees 7
Specialties Management
Engineering
Finance
Geology/Geography
Mining
Oil & Gas
Computing
Design
Level Mid-Level
Fee Basis Sometimes contingent
Contact David J . Lee

Description Profile takes a scientific approach to recruitment by using advanced tools, processes and scrutiny in selecting candidates to fill well-defined positions.

PROGESTIC GROUP INC.
4950 Yonge Street, Suite 2200
Toronto, ON M2N 6K1

Telephone 416-218-0665
Fax 416-218-0669
E-mail hr@progestic-group.com
Website www.progestic-group.com
Founded 1982
Specialties Computing
Level Mid-Level
Contact Don Gutoski,
Marketing Manager

Description Progestic is an IT consulting firm that also places computer professionals with clients on a contract basis.

PROGESTIC GROUP INC.
95 Camirand Street, Suite 100
Sherbrooke, QC J1H 4J6

Telephone 819-829-2715
Fax 819-564-3058
E-mail hr@progestic-group.com
Website www.progestic-group.com
Specialties Computing
Level Mid-Level
Contact André Malo, President

Description Progestic is an IT consulting firm that also places computer professionals with clients on a contract basis.

PROGESTIC GROUP INC.
360 St. Jacques Street, Bureau 400
Montréal, QC H2Y 1P5

Telephone 514-842-7995
Fax 514-842-1602
E-mail hr@progestic-group.com
Website www.progestic-group.com
Founded 1982
Specialties Computing
Level Mid-Level
Recruiters Johanne Allaire
Paul Benoit
Liane Landry
Éric Lefebvre
André Malo
Anthony E. Stamatakis
Contact André Malo, President

Description Progestic is an IT consulting firm that also places computer professionals with clients on a contract basis.

PROGROUPE RESSOURCES HUMAINES INC.
120, rue du Portage
Hull, QC J8X 2K1

Telephone 819-770-6833
Fax 819-770-4335
E-mail hull@progroupe.ca
Website www.progroupe.ca
Specialties General Practice
Level Mid-Level

Description Progroupe Ressources Humaines Inc. provides human resource management services, including staffing, organizational analysis and position evaluation.

PROGROUPE RESSOURCES HUMAINES INC.
4886 St-Charles North, Suite 500
Pierrefonds, QC H9H 3E4

Telephone 519-626-6834
Fax 514-626-0519
E-mail montreal@progroupe.ca
Website www.progroupe.ca
Specialties General Practice
Level Mid-Level
Contact Silvie Beluse

Description Progroupe Ressources Humaines Inc. provides human resource management services, including staffing, organizational analysis and position evaluation.

PROJECT MANAGEMENT RECRUITING INC.
208 Evans Avenue
Toronto, ON M8Z 1J7

Telephone 416-201-9118
Fax 905-812-8331
E-mail info@pmrecruiting.com
Website www.pmrecruiting.com
Specialties Operations
Computing
Telecom
Multimedia
Recruiters David Barrett
Terry Clark
Pat McCallas
Contact David Barrett,
President

Description Project Management Recruiting Inc. provides qualified personnel for the full range of project management needs for virtually any size project in IT, web-based and telecommunications environments.

PROKOSCH GROUP, THE
421 - 7th Avenue SW, Suite 1200
Calgary, AB T2P 4K9

Telephone 403-269-7767
Fax 403-269-7848
E-mail rprokosch@telusplanet.net
Founded 1998
Specialties Human Resource
Accounting
Sales
Marketing
Oil & Gas
Management
Consulting
Level Senior
Mid-Level
Min. Salary $50,000

Fee Basis   Retainer Only

Contact   Ron Prokosch

PROLET INC.
25 Adelaide Street East, Suite 1310
Toronto, ON M5C 3A1

Telephone   416-222-7099
Fax   416-222-1577
E-mail   engineers@prolet.com
Website   www.prolet.com

Specialties   Engineering
Trades/Technicians

Level   Mid-Level
Senior

Description   Prolet Inc. specializes in placing engineering and technical personnel.

PROLET INC.
2333 Wyecroft Road, Unit 9
Oakville, ON L6L 6L4

Telephone   905-825-0697
Fax   905-825-0716
E-mail   engineers@prolet.com
Website   www.prolet.com

Specialties   Engineering
Trades/Technicians

Level   Mid-Level
Senior

Description   Prolet Inc. specializes in placing engineering and technical personnel.

PROLINK CONSULTING INC.
45 Sheppard Ave. East, Suite 409
Toronto, ON M2N 5W9

Telephone   416-225-9900
Fax   416-225-9104
E-mail   mail@prolink
consulting.com
Website   www.prolink
consulting.com

Founded   1997
Employees   18

Specialties   Computing
Telecom

Level   Mid-Level

Min. Salary $40,000
Fee Basis   Always contingent

Recruiters   Craig Allen
Mark Bachman

Contact   Mark Bachman

Description   Prolink Consulting Inc. is a full-service search firm linking IT professionals with dynamic, leading-edge Fortune 500 corporations across North America.

PROLOGIC SYSTEMS LTD.
75 Albert Street, Suite 206
Ottawa, ON K1P 5E7

Telephone   613-238-1376
Fax   613-238-2347
E-mail   prologic@intranet.com
Website   www.comsearch-can.com/prolog.htm

Founded   1975

Specialties   Computing
Engineering
Management
Marketing

Level   Mid-Level
Senior

Fee Basis   Always contingent

Recruiters   Keith Langley
Liz Pereira-Silva

Contact   Keith Langley,
President

PROSEARCH ASSOCIATES
5004 Natkarni Cr.
Mississauga, ON L5V 1L2

Telephone   905-567-6497
Fax   905-567-8068
E-mail   info@prosearch.on.ca
Website   www.prosearch.on.ca

Founded   1999
Employees   1

Specialties   Automotive
Engineering
Management
Marketing
Operations
Purchasing
Sales

Level   Senior
Mid-Level

Fee Basis   Always contingent

Contact   Daniel Duquette

Description   Prosearch Associates serves the manufacturing community in North America, with particular expertise in the automotive OEM and parts sector.

PROSOURCE MANAGEMENT CONSULTANTS INC.
1 Director Court, Suite 201
Woodbridge, ON L4L 4S5

Telephone   905-264-1663
Fax   905-264-1773
E-mail   prosorce@
pathcom.com

Founded   1996
Employees   3

Specialties   Engineering
Finance
Management
Marketing
Pharmaceutical
Printing
Sales

Level   Senior
Mid-Level

Min. Salary $40,000
Fee Basis   Sometimes contingent

Contact   Marvin Kalchman

PROSPECTS PLUS INC.
3549, boul. St-Charles
Kirkland, QC H9H 3C4

Telephone   514-697-4240
Fax   514-697-7806
E-mail   info@prospectplus.com
Website   www.prospectplus.com

Founded   1987

Specialties   Accounting
Banking
Computing
Engineering
Finance
Health/Medical
Human Resource
Management
Marketing
Operations
Purchasing
Sales
Scientific

Level   Mid-Level

Fee Basis   Sometimes contingent

Recruiters   Manon Boileau CPC
Vaughan Reid CPC
Monique Vigue CPC

Contact   Manon Boileau

Description   Prospects Plus Inc. is a full-service placement agency.

PROTEMPS CANADA INC.
10011 - 109th Street, Suite 101
Edmonton, AB T5J 3S8

Telephone   780-425-9000
Fax   780-426-3413
E-mail   edmonton@
protempscanada.com
Website   www.protemps
edmonton.com

Founded   1985

Specialties   Administrative
Logistics
Trades/Technicians

Level   Mid-Level
Junior

Recruiters   Cheryl Brandt
Janine Jeworski
Maureen Kempster
Tracy Loveridge

Contact   Cheryl Brandt

Description   ProTemps Canada Inc. is a full-service personnel placement agency specializing in office and general labour needs.

PROTEMPS CANADA INC.
824 - 5th Avenue SW
Calgary, AB T2P 0N3

Telephone   403-264-9000
Fax   403-261-4766
E-mail   calgary@
protempscanada.com
Website   www.protemps
calgary.com

Founded   1985

Specialties   Administrative
Logistics
Trades/Technicians

Level   Mid-Level
Junior

Recruiters   Bonnie Higgins
Karen Hildebrandt
Jennie Ogilvie
Kris Robertson
Paul Stout
Christy Stout

Contact   Paul Stout, President,
Affiliate Office

Description ProTemps Canada Inc. is
a full-service personnel placement
agency specializing in office and
general labour needs.

PROTEMPS CANADA INC.
40 Eglinton Avenue East, Suite 304
Toronto, ON M4P 3A2

Telephone	416-488-2022
Fax	416-488-8124
E-mail	toronto@ protempscanada.com
Website	www.protemps canada.com
Founded	1985
Specialties	Administrative Logistics Trades/Technicians
Level	Mid-Level Junior
Recruiters	Sandy Field Raj Gurung Janet Tomsic
Contact	Janet Tomsic, Senior Consultant

Description ProTemps Canada Inc. is
a full-service personnel placement
agency specializing in office and
general labour needs.

PROTEMPS CANADA INC.
151 City Centre Drive, Suite 300
Mississauga, ON L5B 1M7

Telephone	905-270-0022
Fax	905-270-4222
E-mail	mississauga@ protempscanada.com
Website	www.protemps canada.com
Founded	1985
Specialties	Administrative Logistics Trades/Technicians
Level	Mid-Level Junior
Recruiters	Shirley Gajdemski Heather McKay-Prinn Beverly Service Fran Spooner
Contact	Beverly Service, Founder / Owner

Description ProTemps Canada Inc. is
a full-service personnel placement
agency specializing in office and
general labour needs.

PROTOCOLE
2155, rue Guy, Bureau 740
Montréal, QC H3H 2R9

Telephone	514-846-1878
Fax	514-846-9395
E-mail	info@birch- protocole.com
Website	www.birch- protocole.com
Founded	1990
Employees	6

Specialties	Computing Engineering Multimedia Telecom
Level	Senior Mid-Level
Contact	Jerry Birch, President

Description Protocole, a division of
Birch & Associes, provides recruitment in technical and high tech industries.

PROTRANS PERSONNEL SERVICES INC.
909 Champlain Street
Dieppe, NB E1A 5T6

Telephone	506-858-7727
Fax	506-858-7732
E-mail	sinclair.keith@ jdirving.com
Specialties	Purchasing Transport Administrative
Level	Mid-Level
Recruiters	Audrie Elderkin Keith Sinclair W.C. Wilson
Contact	W.C. Wilson, General Manager

Description Protrans Personnel Services recruits driver positions, as well
as light industrial and clerical jobs.

PROVENCE CONSULTING INC.
1555 Marine Drive, Suite 202
Vancouver, BC V7V 1H9

Telephone	604-913-7768
Fax	604-913-8356
E-mail	search@provence consulting.com
Website	www.provence consulting.com
Founded	1999
Employees	4
Specialties	Arts & Culture Education Govt/Nonprofit Management Health/Medical
Level	Senior
Recruiters	Kanya Adam Libby Dybikowski Maureen Geldart Sandi Johnston Lynn Penrod Laverne Smith
Contact	Sandi Johnston

Description Provence assists public
sector (universities and colleges)
and not-for-profit organizations with
senior searches across Canada.

PRUD'HOMME GROUPE-CONSEIL EN PSYCHOLOGIE ORGANISATIONNELLE INC.
2020, rue Universite, Bureau 2190
Montréal, QC H3A 2A5

Telephone	514-840-1090
Fax	514-840-1099

E-mail	contact@ prud-homme.com
Website	www.prud-homme.com
Founded	1980
Specialties	Accounting Computing Engineering Finance Human Resource Insurance Management Marketing Operations Purchasing Sales
Level	Senior Mid-Level
Contact	Marteal Prud'homme

Description Prud'Homme Groupe-
Conseil en Psychologie Organisationnelle is a human resource team
specializing in four fields: recruitment; relocation; psychological
evaluation; and training.

PSISEARCH
5151 Beltline Road, Suite 455
Dallas, TX 75254   USA

Telephone	972-448-7070
Fax	972-448-7059
E-mail	jleonard@ psisearch.com
Website	www.psisearch.com
Specialties	Computing International
Contact	Jason Leonard

Description psiSearch specializes in
recruitment for computer professionals.

PTACK SCHNARCH BASEVITZ
3333 Graham Blvd., Suite 400
Montréal, QC H3R 3L5

Telephone	514-341-5511
Fax	514-342-0589
E-mail	cwills@psb.qc.ca
Website	www.psb.qc.ca
Founded	1966
Specialties	Accounting Finance
Contact	Caroline Wills

Description PSB is a mid-sized, full-
service accounting firm that does
occasional search work for clients.

PTC - FINANCIAL STAFFING INC.
1600 Steeles Ave. West, Suite 300
Concord, ON L4K 4M2

Telephone	905-660-9550
Fax	905-660-1051
E-mail	info@ptcstaffing.com
Website	www.ptcstaffing.com
Founded	1992
Employees	25
Specialties	Accounting Finance
Level	Mid-Level Senior

Min. Salary $30,000
Fee Basis   Retainer Only
Recruiters Howard Maritzer
            Bruce Singer CA
            Ken Sugar CGA
Contact   Ken Sugar CGA

Description PTC - Financial Staffing Inc. (formerly Part Time Controllers Co.) places senior-level accounting professionals in southern Ontario in assignments from $30K - 300K.

PUBLICIS TANDEM
111 Queen Street East, Suite 200
Toronto, ON M5C 1S2

Telephone   416-925-7733
Fax   416-925-7341
E-mail   tandem@publicis.ca
Website   www.publicis.ca

Specialties Public Relations
            Marketing
            General Practice
            Pharmaceutical
Level   Mid-Level
Contact   Serge Rancourt,
            President and COO

Description Publicis Tandem is a large advertising and communications firm that also does recruitment advertising.

PUBLICITÉ DAY INC.
60 St. Jacques Street, 7th Floor
Montréal, QC H2Y 1L5

Telephone   514-845-7777
Fax   514-849-2202
E-mail   pubday@citenet.net

Specialties General Practice
            Govt/Nonprofit
            Management
Level   Senior
            Mid-Level

Description Publicité Day Inc. is a recruitment advertising agency.

PUBLIFACTUM INC.
385 Place d'Youville, Suite 200
Montréal, QC H2Y 2B7

Telephone   514-284-2221
Fax   514-284-2333
E-mail   info@publifactum.com
Website   www.publifactum.com

Specialties General Practice

Description PubliFactum Inc. is an advertising agency whose services include recruitment advertising.

PUGLISEVICH CREWS AND SERVICES LIMITED
611 Torbay Road, Suite 1
St. John's, NF A1C 6E6

Telephone   709-739-1030
Fax   709-722-3208
E-mail   philw@puglisevich.com
Website   www.puglisevich.
            nfnet.com/pcsl.html
Founded   1979
Employees   8

Specialties Oil & Gas
            Construction
            Mining
            Transport
            International
Recruiters Frances Boland
            Theresa Borg
            Philip, F. Whelan
Contact   Philip F. Whelan

Description Puglisevich Crews & Services has been providing offshore personnel in Canada and internationally for the past twenty years.

PURCELL TECHNICAL STAFFING
6309 Fern Valley Pass
Louisville, KY 40228 USA

Telephone   502-968-5022
Fax   502-968-4912
E-mail   jbasu@
            purcellstaffing.com
Website   www.purcell
            staffing.com

Specialties International
            Engineering
            Oil & Gas
Contact   Recruitment Manager

PYA SOLUTIONS INC.
2449 Oregon Avenue
Victoria, BC V8R 3V8

Telephone   250-383-6350
Fax   250-383-6370
E-mail   info@pya.ca
Website   www.pya.ca
Founded   1992
Employees   20

Specialties Computing
Level   Mid-Level
Fee Basis   Sometimes contingent
Contact   Lawrence M. Young,
            President

Description PYA Solutions Inc. (formerly Ptack Young & Associates) is an IT consulting firm that also places computing professionals on contract assignments with clients.

PYA SOLUTIONS INC.
11 Sims Crescent, Unit 2
Toronto, ON L4B 1C9

Telephone   905-764-9696
Fax   905-882-2116
E-mail   info@pya.ca
Website   www.pya.ca
Founded   1992
Employees   20

Specialties Computing
Level   Mid-Level
Fee Basis   Sometimes contingent
Contact   Lawrence M. Young,
            President

Description PYA Solutions Inc. (formerly Ptack Young & Associates) is an IT consulting firm that also places computing professionals on contract assignments with clients.

PYA SOLUTIONS INC.
3333 Graham Boulevard, Suite 300
Montréal, QC H3R 3L5

Telephone   514-341-5512
Fax   514-341-9934
E-mail   info@pya.ca
Website   www.pya.ca
Founded   1992
Employees   20

Specialties Computing
Level   Mid-Level
Fee Basis   Sometimes contingent
Contact   Lawrence M. Young,
            President

Description PYA Solutions Inc. (formerly Ptack Young & Associates) is an IT consulting firm that also places computing professionals on contract assignments with clients.

PYA SOLUTIONS INC.
1 Southeast Third Ave., 10th Floor
Miami, FL 33131 USA

Telephone   305-416-2425
Fax   305-377-8331
E-mail   info@rchtg.com
Website   www.pya.ca

Specialties Computing
            International
Contact   Lawrence M. Young,
            President

Description PYA Solutions Inc. (formerly Ptack Young & Associates) is an IT consulting firm that also places computing professionals on contract assignments with clients.

QBYTE SERVICES LTD.
639 - 5th Avenue SW, Suite 2100
Calgary, AB T2P 0M9

Telephone   403-509-7333
Fax   403-232-1010
E-mail   mike.r.fielding@
            ca.pwcglobal.com
Website   www.qbyte.com
Founded   1984
Employees   130

Specialties Computing
            Oil & Gas
Level   Junior
            Mid-Level
Contact   Mike Fielding, Vice-
            President

Description QByte, a subsidiary of PriceWaterhouseCoopers LLP, is an IT consulting firm specializing in the oil and gas industry. Their services include placing computing professionals on contracts with client companies.

QUAD SEARCH INC.
8 King Street East, Suite 812
Toronto, ON M5C 1B5

Telephone   416-362-2630
Fax   416-362-0496

Specialties Finance
            Insurance

Level   Mid-Level
              Senior

Contact   Mr. C.R. (Roly) Rowatt

Description Quad Search Inc. specializes in placing insurance and finance staff.

QUALI-TECH INC.
655 Jean-Paul Vincent, Bureau 15
Longueuil, QC J4G 1R3

Téléphone   450-928-3838
Télécopieur 450-928-1264
Courriel   info@placementquali-
              tech.com
Site Internet www.placementquali-
              tech.com

Spécialités Généralistes
Échelon   Intermédiaire
Contact   Sean Williard

Description Quali-Tech Inc. est une division de Gestsec Inc.

QUALICUM CONSULTING LIMITED
150 Isabella Street, Suite 1205
Ottawa, ON K1S 1V7

Telephone   613-233-1366
Fax   613-233-0847
E-mail   jobs@qualicum.com
Website   www.qualicum.com

Specialties Computing
              Engineering
              Telecom

Recruiters   Monty O'Callaghan
              Gerry Piche

Contact   Monty O'Callaghan,
              President

Description Qualicum Consulting Limited specializes in providing hi-tech human resources candidates.

QUALITY PERSONNEL INC.
45 Bramalea Road, Suite 101
Brampton, ON L6T 2W4

Telephone   905-792-0088
Fax   905-792-7115

Founded   1985
Employees   8

Specialties Accounting
              Engineering
              Automotive
              Bilingual
              Computing
              Management
              Administrative

Level   Mid-Level
Fee Basis   Sometimes contingent
Contact   H.J. Sobottka

Description Office and technical personnel generalists. Permanent and contract placements.

QUANTUM
2000 McGill College Avenue
Bureau 1800
Montréal, QC H3A 3H3

Téléphone   514-842-5555

Fax   514-849-6786
E-mail   nikik@quantum.ca
Website   www.quantum.ca
Founded   1968

Specialties Accounting
              Administrative
              Marketing
              Sales
              Finance
              Human Resource
              Banking

Level   Mid-Level

Recruiters   Julie Maltby
              Cindy Poulin
              Connie Roy

Contact   Stacey Kemp

Description Quantum is an international firm, serving the professional recruitment needs of businesses through a network of 13 branch offices.

QUANTUM CONSULTING LTD.
703 - 6 Avenue SW, Suite 320
Calgary, AB T2P 0T9

Telephone   403-232-8811
Fax   403-232-8861
E-mail   quantumc@
              cadvision.com

Specialties General Practice
Contact   Anne Chippendale

QUANTUM EDP RECRUITING SERVICES LTD.
55 University Avenue, Suite 301
Toronto, ON M5J 2H7

Telephone   416-366-3660
Fax   416-366-4363
E-mail   toronto@
              quantum-qtr.com
Website   www.quantum-qtr.com
Founded   1968
Employees   16

Specialties Computing
              Consulting
              Engineering
              Telecom

Level   Mid-Level
              Senior

Fee Basis   Always contingent

Recruiters   Christina Green
              Kyra Kendall
              Leonard Kuek
              Kevin McCloskey
              Greg Portelance
              Alison Ripley
              Marc Roginsky
              Jon Sato
              Margaret Szarek
              Sudha Variya
              Steve Vrbancic
              Christine Wall
              Christopher Welsh

Contact   Louis Camus

Description Quantum Technology Recruiting is the permanent, technical recruiting firm in the Quantum Group, representing growing, leading-edge clients in Canada and USA.

QUANTUM EDP RECRUITING SERVICES LTD.
45 O'Connor Street, Suite 1860
Ottawa, ON K1P 1A4

Telephone   613-237-8888
Fax   613-565-7329
E-mail   ottawa@quantum-
              qtr.com
Website   www.qedp.com
Founded   1968

Specialties Computing
              Engineering
              Marketing
              Sales

Level   Senior
              Mid-Level

Contact   Louis Camus,
              General Manager

Description The permanent, technical recruiting firm in the Quantum Group of Companies, representing growing, leading-edge clients in Canada and the USA.

QUANTUM EDP RECRUITING SERVICES LTD.
8601 Six Forks Road, Suite 428
Raleigh, NC 27615   USA

Telephone   919-676-5311
Fax   919-676-5313
E-mail   raleigh@quantum-
              qtr.com
Website   www.qedp.com

Specialties Computing
              Marketing
              Sales
              Telecom
              Engineering
              International

Level   Senior
              Mid-Level

Contact   Louis Camus

Description Quantum EDP Recruiting Services Ltd. is the permanent, technical recruiting firm in the Quantum Group of Companies, representing growing, leading-edge clients in Canada and the USA.

QUANTUM, LES SERVICES DE GESTION
1010 rue de Sérigny, Ground Floor
Complexe Metro Longueuil
Longueuil, QC J4K 5B1

Telephone   450-651-1313
Fax   450-651-9769
Website   www.quantum.ca

Specialties Accounting
              Administrative
              Marketing
              Sales
              Finance
              Human Resource

Contact   Carol-Anne Wade,
              Manager

Description Les services de gestion Quantum is the permanent, technical recruiting firm in the Quantum Group, representing growing, leading-edge clients in Canada and USA.

QUANTUM, LES SERVICES DE GESTION

1 Holiday Rd., Ste. 250, West Tower
Pointe-Claire, QC H9R 5N3

Telephone	514-694-9994
Fax	514-694-0269
E-mail	cgiguere@quantum.ca
Website	www.quantum.ca
Specialties	Accounting
	Administrative
	Marketing
	Sales
	Finance
	Human Resource
Contact	Marlene Carroll,
	Manager

Description Les services de gestion Quantumk is the permanent, technical recruiting firm in the Quantum Group of Companies, representing growing, leading-edge clients in Canada and the USA.

QUANTUM, LES SERVICES DE GESTION

3090, boul. le Carrefour
Bureau 205
Laval, QC H7T 2J7

Telephone	450-973-3332
Fax	450-973-1148
E-mail	aarchambault@quantum.ca
Website	www.qedp.com
Specialties	Accounting
	Administrative
	Marketing
	Sales
	Hospitality
	Finance
Level	Mid-Level
	Senior
Contact	Annie Archambault

Description Les services de gestion Quantum is the permanent, technical recruiting firm in the Quantum Group of Companies, representing growing, leading-edge clients in Canada and the USA.

QUANTUM, LES SERVICES DE GESTION

5500, boulevard des Galeries
Bureau 102
Complexe de la Capitale III
Québec, QC G2K 2E2

Téléphone	418-621-8800
Télécopieur	418-621-8855
Site Internet	www.quantum.ca
Fondée	1968
Spécialités	Comptabilité
	Administratif
Échelon	Intermédiaire
	Débutant
Contact	Josée Moreau

QUANTUM MANAGEMENT SERVICES

420 Lexington Avenue, Suite 2221
New York, NY 10170-2299
USA

Telephone	212-972-1313
Fax	212-983-7087
Website	www.qedp.com
Specialties	Computing
	International
Level	Mid-Level
	Senior

Description Quantum is the permanent, technical recruiting firm in the Quantum Group of Companies, representing growing, leading-edge clients in Canada and the USA.

QUANTUM MANAGEMENT SERVICES LIMITED

55 University Avenue, Suite 950
Toronto, ON M5J 2H7

Telephone	416-366-3660
Fax	416-366-4363
E-mail	rgeringer@quantum.ca
Website	www.quantum.ca
Founded	1968
Employees	33
Specialties	Marketing
	Sales
	Accounting
	Banking
	Administrative
	Finance
	Logistics
Fee Basis	Always contingent
Recruiters	Kim Benedict
	Marie DiMarco-Brace
	Joanne Fretwell
	Ramona King
	Angela Lombardi
	Kristina Ramanauskas
	Lauren Shaw
	Carolina Toscano
Contact	Rona Geringer

Description Quantum Management Services Limited is the permanent, technical recruiting firm in the Quantum Group of Companies, representing growing, leading-edge clients in Canada and the USA.

QUANTUM MANAGEMENT SERVICES LTD.

5160 Yonge Street, Suite 1825
Toronto, ON M2N 6L9

Telephone	416-226-5685
Fax	416-226-0364
E-mail	dmaclean@quantum.ca
Website	www.qedp.com
Specialties	Computing
	Accounting
	Banking
	Engineering
	Finance
	Health/Medical
	Human Resource
	Insurance
	Marketing
	Operations
	Purchasing
	Sales
Level	Mid-Level
	Senior
Contact	Diana McLean

Description The permanent, technical recruiting firm in the Quantum Group of Companies, representing growing, leading-edge clients in Canada and the USA.

QUANTUM MANAGEMENT SERVICES LTD.

305 Milner Ave, Suite 311
Toronto, ON M1B 3V4

Telephone	416-292-2282
Fax	416-292-8947
Website	www.qedp.com
Founded	1968
Specialties	Clerical
	Office Support
	Accounting
	Administrative
	Sales
Level	Mid-Level
Contact	Lana Rupke

Description The permanent, technical recruiting firm in the Quantum Group of Companies, representing growing, leading-edge clients in Canada and the USA.

QUANTUM MANAGEMENT SERVICES LTD.

33 City Centre Drive, Suite 660
Mississauga, ON L5B 2N5

Telephone	905-276-8611
Fax	905-276-7739
E-mail	alombardi@quantum.ca
Website	www.qedp.com
Founded	1968
Specialties	Accounting
	Finance
	Human Resource
	Marketing
	Sales
	Computing
Level	Mid-Level
Contact	Sandy Roberts

Description Quantum Management Services Ltd. is a permanent, technical recruiting firm in the Quantum Group of Companies, representing growing, leading-edge clients in Canada and the USA.

QUANTUM MANAGEMENT SERVICES LTD.

50 O'Connor Street, Suite 1410
Ottawa, ON K1P 6L2

Telephone	613-237-8888
Fax	613-230-7711
E-mail	kwoo@quantum.ca
Website	www.qedp.com
Founded	1968
Specialties	Office Support
	Administrative
	Finance
	Sales
	Marketing
	Computing
	Industrial
Level	Mid-Level
	Senior

Recruiters	Anne Côté
	Bonnie Rae
Contact	Anne Côté, Branch Manager

Description Quantum is the permanent, technical recruiting firm in the Quantum Group of Companies, representing growing, leading-edge clients in Canada and the USA.

QUEST CONSULTANTS
2323 Yonge Street, Suite 302
Toronto, ON M4P 2C9

Telephone	416-489-6411
Fax	416-489-7542
E-mail	questcon@netcom.ca
Founded	1986
Employees	5
Specialties	Administrative
	Accounting
Level	Mid-Level
	Junior
Fee Basis	Always contingent
Contact	Nicky Perry

Description Quest Consultants is a boutique search firm dedicated to excellence, placing permanent staff in all areas of office administration.

QUEST EXECUTIVE RECRUITMENT PROFESSIONALS INC.
100 Richmond St. West, Suite 330
Toronto, ON M5H 3M9

Telephone	416-861-9244
Fax	416-861-9290
E-mail	quester@interlog.com
Website	www.quest executive.com
Founded	1996
Employees	5
Specialties	Accounting
	Finance
	Marketing
	Hospitality
	Human Resource
	Administrative
	Logistics
Level	Senior
	Mid-Level
Min. Salary	$40,000
Fee Basis	Always contingent
Recruiters	Wendy Melvin
	Clint Scott
	Jocelyn Yacoub
Contact	Jocelyn Yacoub, Principal

Description Quest is a search firm with a focus on financial services and accounting, business process re-engineering, project management, marketing and human resources.

QUEST RESOURCE GROUP
2600 Skymark Avenue
Suite 202, Building 6
Mississauga, ON L4W 5B2

Telephone	905-602-8701
Fax	905-629-8639
E-mail	quest@ questresource.com
Website	www.quest resource.com
Specialties	Accounting
	Administrative
Level	Junior
	Mid-Level
Fee Basis	Sometimes contingent
Contact	Anthony Plut, CPC

Description Quest specializes in recruiting for accounting, payroll and customer service positions throughout the Greater Toronto Area.

QUESTUS RECRUITMENT
1015 - 4th Street SW, Suite 1060
Calgary, AB T2R 1J4

Telephone	403-232-1333
Fax	403-263-4893
E-mail	mail@questus.ca
Website	www.questus.ca
Employees	5
Specialties	Sales
	Marketing
	Management
Level	Senior
	Mid-Level
Recruiters	Morgan Arndt
	Todd Cochlan
	Dave Elliott
	Mike Johnson
	Keli Sandford
	Bob Scott
	Barry Wroe
Contact	Morgan Arndt, President

Description Questus Recruitment (formerly Schell Personnel Services) is one of Western Canada's leading specialists in the recruitment of sales, marketing and management professionals.

QUEUE SYSTEMS INC.
600 Alden Road, Suite 606
Markham, ON L3R 0E7

Telephone	905-940-8132
Fax	905-940-9234
E-mail	agency@ queuesystems.net
Website	www.queuesystems.net
Founded	1992
Specialties	Computing
	Multimedia
	Telecom
Level	Mid-Level
	Junior
Contact	Kyu Lee

Description Queue Systems Inc. is a full-service technology consulting firm providing placement services to their select clientele.

QUINTAL & ASSOCIATES HR CONSULTANTS INC.
133, de La Commune Ouest,
Bureau 301
Montréal, QC H2Y 2C7

Téléphone	514-284-7444
Télécopieur	514-284-9290
Courriel	quintal@total.net
Site Internet	www.quintal.ca
Fondée	1991
Employés	6
Spécialités	Biotechnologie/biologie
	Santé/médical
	Gestion
	Pharmaceutique
	Ventes
Échelon	Direction
	Intermédiaire
Salaire min.	40 000 $
Frais	Parfois relative
Recruteurs	Hélène Dickenson
	Danielle Fontaine
	Marcel Lahaie
	Yves Quintal
	Elise St-Jean
Contact	Yves Quintal, President

Description Quintal & Associates HR specialise dans la dotation, recrutement, formation et développment professionnel dans les secteurs des sciences de la sante tels que pharmaceutique.

R. JACQUES PLANTE & ASSOCIÉS
1135, chemin St-Louis, Bureau 300
Sillery, QC G1S 1E7

Téléphone	418-527-1300
Télécopieur	418-681-4190
Courriel	pt@ perspectivetravail.com
Site Internet	www.perspective travail.com
Fondée	1977
Employés	6
Spécialités	Comptabilité
	Informatique
	Éducation
	Ingénierie
	Finance
	Assurance
	Marketing
Échelon	Direction
	Intermédiaire
Recruteurs	Marcel Bérubé
	Frederic Briere
	Richard Marchessault
	Fernand Matte
	R. Jacques Plante
	Suzanne C. Tardif
Contact	Marcel Bérubé

Description R. Jacques Plante & Associés est une firme spécialisée dans la recherche de cadres, la sélection et l'évaluation du personnel.

R.K. CHENGKALATH PROFESSIONAL CORPORATION
1144 - 29 Avenue NE, Suite 104
Calgary, AB T2E 7P1

Telephone	403-234 - 7133
Fax	403-735-4995
E-mail	rmchngklth@aol.com
Website	www.punjabicenter. com/rkchengkalath
Founded	1980

Specialties   Accounting
                Finance

Level   Mid-Level

Contact   R.K. Chengkalath

Description   R.K. Chengkalath Professional Corporation (formerly Bharwani & Company) is accounting firm that also hires accounting personnel for clients.

RAINMAKER GROUP
1 Adelaide Street East
One Financial Place
Suite 2330, PO Box 188
Toronto, ON M5C 2V9

Telephone   416-863-9543
Fax   416-863-9757
E-mail   rmaker@
              pinestripegroup.net
Website   www.rainmaker
              group.net

Specialties   Law

Level   Senior
                Mid-Level

Recruiters   Carrie Heller
                Kim Lacey
                Adam Lepofsky
                Jamie Rampersad
                Lillian Sversky

Contact   Adam Lepofsky,
                Director

Description   RainMaker Group is a recruitment and placement company that specializes in placing legal professionals.

RANDAL CUNNINGHAM ENTERPRISES LTD.
1190 Melville St., Suite 504
Vancouver, BC V6E 3W1

Telephone   604-321-3203
Fax   604-321-4744
E-mail   randy_cunningham@
              telus.net
Website   randalcunningham.com

Specialties   Engineering

Level   Senior
                Mid-Level

Contact   Randy Cunningham

Description   Randal Cunningham Enterprises Ltd. is a specialist recruiter in the engineering field.

RANDSTAD INTERIM INC.
2 Sheppard Avenue East, Suite 210
Toronto, ON M2N 5Y7

Telephone   416-221-5799
Fax   416-221-9916
Website   www.randstadna.com

Specialties   Administrative

Level   Mid-Level
                Junior

Description   Randstad Interim is a wholly-owned subsidiary of Randstad Holding, the third-largest staffing service in the world.

RANDSTAD INTERIM INC.
6020 Hurontario Street, Suite 2
Mississauga, ON L5R 4B3

Telephone   905-501-7117
Website   www.randstadna.com

Specialties   Administrative

Level   Mid-Level
                Junior

Description   Randstad Interim is a wholly-owned subsidiary of Randstad Holding, the third-largest staffing service in the world.

RANDSTAD INTERIM INC.
99 Bank Street, Main Floor
Ottawa, ON K1P 6B9

Telephone   613-564-2555
Fax   613-569-2666
E-mail   ottawa@
              randstadna.com
Website   www.randstadna.com

Specialties   Administrative

Level   Mid-Level
                Junior

Contact   Tara Burley

Description   Randstad Interim is a wholly-owned subsidiary of Randstad Holding, the third-largest staffing service in the world.

RANDSTAD INTERIM INC.
3100 Côte-Vertu
Saint-Laurent, QC H4R 2J8

Telephone   514-332-1055
Fax   514-332-8208
E-mail   ken.louise@randstad.ca
Website   www.randstadna.com

Specialties   Apparel
                Operations
                Administrative

Level   Mid-Level
                Junior

Contact   Ken Louise

Description   Randstad Interim is a wholly-owned subsidiary of Randstad Holding, the third largest staffing service in the world.

RANDSTAD INTERIM INC.
1800 McGill College Avenue
Suite 2420
Montréal, QC H3A 3J6

Telephone   514-350-0033
Fax   514-350-0034
E-mail   lyne.levasseur@
              randstad.ca
Website   www.randstadna.com

Specialties   Administrative

Level   Mid-Level
                Junior

Contact   Lyne Levasseur,
                Senior Market Manager

Description   Randstad Interim is a wholly-owned subsidiary of Randstad Holding, the third-largest staffing service in the world.

RAY & BERNDTSON
234 Park Avenue, 33rd Floor
New York, NY 10167-0001
USA

Telephone   212-370-1316
Fax   212-370-1462
E-mail   marketing@
              rayberndtson.com
Website   www.rayberndtson.com

Specialties   International
                Management

Level   Senior

Fee Basis   Retainer Only

Recruiters   Jacques P. André
                Pammy Brooks
                Kevin Chase
                Abram Claude
                Frederic M. Comins
                Patrick A. Delhougne
                Mary Helen Dunn
                Ellery Gordon
                G. Angela Henry
                Lisa C. Hooker
                Peter Kaplan
                Catherine McNamara
                Kenneth M. Rich
                Penny Simon
                Judy K. Weddle
                William H. Weed

Contact   Abram Claude Jr.,
                Partner

Description   Ray & Berndtson is a premier international executive search firm, specializing in recruiting services for top-level executives.

RAY & BERNDTSON A/S
Nyhavn 63C, DK-1051
Copenhagen, K
DENMARK

Telephone   45-33-14-36-36
Fax   45-33-32-43-32
E-mail   rb@rbcph.dk
Website   www.rayberndtson.com

Specialties   International

Level   Senior

Fee Basis   Retainer Only

Recruiters   Kurt Bruusgaard
                Christian Joergensen
                Lis Knudsen

Contact   Kurt Bruusgaard

Description   Ray & Berndtson is a premier international executive search firm, specializing in recruiting services for top-level executives.

RAY & BERNDTSON / LAURENDEAU LABRECQUE
1250, boul. René-Lévesque O.
Bureau 3925
Montréal, QC H3B 4W8

Telephone   514-937-1000
Fax   514-937-1264
E-mail   managingdirector@
              ray-berndtson.ca
Website   www.rayberndtson.com

Founded   1989
Employees   12

Specialties   Finance
                Operations

Management
Computing
Scientific
Biotech/Biology
Human Resource
Pharmaceutical
Telecom

Level	Senior
Min. Salary	$70,000
Fee Basis	Retainer Only
Recruiters	Bernard F. Labrecque
	Roger Lachance
	Jean E. Laurendeau
Contact	Bernard F. Labrecque,
	Partner

Description Recruiting senior executives who will integrate well with client organizations and achieve the client's corporate objectives and growth ambitions.

RAY & BERNDTSON / LOVAS STANLEY

200 Bay Street, Royal Bank Plaza
Suite 3150, South Tower
Toronto, ON M5J 2J3

Telephone	416-366-1990
Fax	416-366-7353
E-mail	toronto@raybern.ca
Website	www.rayberndtson.com
Founded	1990
Employees	40
Specialties	Management
	Marketing
	Govt/Nonprofit
	Finance
	Pharmaceutical
	Sales
	Telecom
Level	Senior
Fee Basis	Retainer Only
Recruiters	Sue Banting
	Margaret Campbell
	Cathy Graham
	W. Carl Lovas
	David R. Murray
	Chris Pantelidis
	Larry Ross
	Paul Stanley
	Jim Stonehouse
	Christine Thomas
	Betsy Wright
	Joe Zinner
Contact	W. Carl Lovas,
	Managing Partner

Description Ray & Berndtson provides leadership staffing services worldwide through its 47 offices.

RAY & BERNDTSON / ROBERTSON SURRETTE

29 Beechwood Avenue, Suite 200
Ottawa, ON K1M 1M2

Telephone	613-749-9909
Fax	613-749-9599
E-mail	ottawa@rsottawa.com
Website	www.rayberndtson.com
Founded	1975
Specialties	Management
	Engineering

Govt/Nonprofit

Level	Senior
Min. Salary	$75,000
Fee Basis	Retainer Only
Recruiters	Donna Drummond
	James Harmon
	Richard S. (Rick)
	Morgan
	Michael Naufal
	Michelle Richard
	Brenda Robertson
	Robert Robertson
Contact	Ronald Robertson,
	Managing Partner

Description Ray & Berndtson / Robertson Surrette has assessed thousands of senior managers for key leadership roles in every sector.

RAY & BERNDTSON / ROBERTSON SURRETTE

100 Cameron Street, Suite 1003
Moncton, NB E1C 5Y6

Telephone	506-384-4923
Fax	506-854-8464
E-mail	moncton@robsur.com
Website	www.robsur.com
Specialties	General Practice
Level	Senior
Fee Basis	Retainer Only
Contact	Pierre Battah,
	Managing Partner

Description Ray & Berndtson / Robertson Surrette (formerly Robertson Surrette Executive Search) is an executive search firm.

RAY & BERNDTSON / ROBERTSON SURRETTE

1894 Barrington St., Scotia Square
10th Floor, Barrington Tower
Box 2166
Halifax, NS B3J 3C4

Telephone	902-421-1330
Fax	902-425-1108
E-mail	info@robsur.com
Website	www.rayberndtson.com
Founded	1975
Employees	14
Specialties	General Practice
	Management
	Engineering
	Govt/Nonprofit
	Health/Medical
	Marketing
Level	Senior
Min. Salary	$40,000
Fee Basis	Retainer Only
Recruiters	Jamie Baillie CA
	Lindsey Clark
	Dan Shaw
	Mark J. Surette
Contact	Mark J. Surrette,
	Managing Partner

Description Founded in 1975, Robertson Surrette has assessed thousands of senior managers for key leadership roles in every sector.

RAY & BERNDTSON / TANTON MITCHELL

1050 West Pender Street, Suite 710
Vancouver, BC V6E 3S7

Telephone	604-685-0261
Fax	604-684-7988
E-mail	vancouver@raybern.ca
Website	www.rayberndtson.com
Founded	1970
Employees	25
Specialties	Management
	Govt/Nonprofit
	Education
	Marketing
	Human Resource
	Finance
	Forestry
Level	Senior
Min. Salary	$60,000
Fee Basis	Retainer Only
Recruiters	Brent Cameron
	Wendy Carter
	Craig Hemer
	Caroline Jellinck
	Lisa Kershaw CMC
	Annika Lofstrand
	Kyle R. Mitchell
	Patrick Reynolds
	John E. Tanton
	Catherine Van Alstine
	Alec Wallace
	Kathryn Young
Contact	John E. Tanton,
	Co-Managing Partner

Description Ray & Berndtson is one of the largest search firms in Canada and is the seventh-largest executive search firm worldwide.

RAYMOND CHABOT HUMAN RESOURCES INC.

200 Bay Street, 19th Floor
Toronto, ON M5J 2P9

Telephone	416-366-0100
Fax	416-360-4949
Website	www.recrutement.ca
Specialties	Finance
	Accounting
Level	Senior
	Mid-Level
Recruiters	Janette Kramer
	Michel LaRue
Contact	Michel LaRue, Director,
	Executive Search

Description Raymond Chabot Human Resources Inc., the recruitment division of the accounting firm Raymond Chabot Grant Thorton, has over 70,000 candidates on file in accounting and finance.

RAYMOND CHABOT HUMAN RESOURCES INC.

15, boul. Gamelin, Bureau 400
Hull, QC J8Y 1V4

Telephone	819-770-9833
Fax	819-770-5398
Website	www.recrutement.ca
Specialties	Accounting
	Finance

Level   Mid-Level
           Senior

Contact   André Houle, Manager

Description Raymond Chabot Human Resources Inc., the recruitment division of the accounting firm Raymond Chabot Grant Thorton, has over 70,000 candidates on file in accounting and finance.

RAYMOND CHABOT HUMAN RESOURCES INC.
600 de la Gauchetière Street West
Suite 1900, National Bank Tower
Montréal, QC H3B 4L8

Telephone   514-878-2691
Fax   514-878-2127
E-mail   info@rcgt.com
Website   www.recrutement.ca

Founded   1981
Employees   19

Specialties Accounting
              Finance

Level   Senior
              Mid-Level

Contact   Benoit Lague,
              Communication
              Advisor

Description Raymond Chabot Human Resources Inc., the recruitment division of the accounting firm Raymond Chabot Grant Thorton, has over 70,000 candidates on file in accounting and finance.

RAYMOND CHABOT HUMAN RESOURCES INC.
888 Saint-Jean Street, Suite 200
Québec, QC G1R 5H6

Telephone   418-647-3151
Fax   418-647-3241
E-mail   mondou.cecile@
              rcgt.com
Website   www.recrutement.ca

Specialties Finance
              Accounting

Level   Mid-Level

Contact   Cecile Mondou

Description Raymond Chabot Human Resources Inc., the recruitment division of the accounting firm Raymond Chabot Grant Thorton, has over 70,000 candidates on file in accounting and finance.

RBA INTERNATIONAL HR CONSULTANTS INC.
4999, rue St-Catherine O.
Bureau 231
Westmount, QC H3Z 1T3

Telephone   514-481-6488
Fax   514-481-2088
E-mail   teross@rbaintl.ca

Founded   1987
Employees   2

Specialties Engineering
              Management
              Consulting
              Marketing

              International
              Construction
              Pulp & Paper

Level   Senior
Min. Salary $70,000
Fee Basis   Sometimes contingent

Contact   T.E. Ross

Description RBA International provides the consulting engineering market with senior project-related personnel, in Canada or overseas.

RCM TECHNOLOGIES
6620 Kitimat Road, Unit 5A
Mississauga, ON L5N 2B8

Telephone   905-812-3868
Fax   905-812-6585
E-mail   ron.kondrat@rcmt.com
Website   www.rcmt.com

Founded   1971
Employees   15

Specialties Computing
              Engineering
              Management
              Banking
              Automotive
              Govt/Nonprofit

Level   Senior
              Mid-Level

Fee Basis   Sometimes contingent

Recruiters Ron Kondrat
              Tim Tottenham

Contact   E.P. (Gene) Wasylciw,
              Vice President

Description RCM is an IT consulting firm that specializes in micro, mini, mainframe, client server and Web-based projects. The also place IT professionals on contracts with clients.

RECAREER.COM
3500 Dufferin Street, Suite 401
Toronto, ON M3K 1N2

Telephone   416-630-7771
Fax   416-631-8144
E-mail   info@recareer.com
Website   www.recareer.com

Founded   1999
Employees   6

Specialties General Practice

Level   Mid-Level
              Junior

Fee Basis   Sometimes contingent

Contact   Greg Arbitman

Description Recareer arranges the pairing of companies and candidates from their resume database. Recareer provides candidates for contract projects and permanent placement.

RECHERCHES EN RECRUTEMENT LYN JOHNSON
5515 Plamondon Boulevard,
Bureau 313
Saint-Lambert, QC J4S 1W4

Telephone   450-672-6060

Fax   450-671-1463
E-mail   lj@r2lj.com

Founded   2000

Specialties Accounting
              Computing
              Finance
              Human Resource
              Multimedia
              Telecom

Level   Senior
Min. Salary $100,000
Fee Basis   Retainer Only

Contact   Lyn Johnson

RECORDS & INFORMATION MANAGEMENT SERVICES INC.
740 Huron Street
Toronto, ON M4V 2W3

Telephone   416-968-1357
Fax   416-968-9577
E-mail   caroline@rim-inc.com
Website   www.rim-inc.com

Specialties Librarians

Level   Mid-Level
              Senior

Contact   Carolyn Werle CRM,
              President

Description RIM specializes in placing librarians and records management personnel.

RECRU SCIENCE, INC.
32 St. Charles West
Suite 370
Longueuil, QC J4H 1C6

Telephone   450-463-0903
Fax   450-463-0324
E-mail   info@recruscience.com
Website   www.recruscience.com

Specialties Scientific

Level   Mid-Level

Recruiters Denis R. Arseneau
              Martin J. Groleau

Contact   Denis R. Arseneau,
              BScChem, CTox

Description Recru Science, Inc. specializes in recruiting scientific professionals and executives.

RECRUITAD CONFIDENTIAL REPLY
1090 West Georgia Street
Suite 420
Vancouver, BC V6E 3V7

Telephone   604-687-0825
Fax   604-687-5397
E-mail   vancouver@
              recruitad.com
Website   www.recruitad.com

Founded   1981

Specialties General Practice

Level   Mid-Level
              Junior

Description RecruitAd, part of the CNC Global Companies, provides clients with a broad range of recruitment services.

RECRUITAD CONFIDENTIAL REPLY
700 - 9th Avenue SW
Western Canadian Place
Suite 2910, South Tower
Calgary, AB T2P 3V4

Telephone	403-205-2422
Fax	403-263-4502
E-mail	calgary@recruitad.com
Website	www.recruitad.com
Founded	1981
Specialties	General Practice
Level	Mid-Level Junior

Description RecruitAd, part of the CNC Global Companies, provides clients with a broad range of recruitment services.

RECRUITAD CONFIDENTIAL REPLY
60 Bloor Street West, Suite 1400
Toronto, ON M4W 3B8

Telephone	416-962-8133
Fax	416-962-9709
E-mail	info@recruitad.com
Website	www.recruitad.com
Founded	1981
Specialties	General Practice
Level	Mid-Level Senior

Description RecruitAd, part of the CNC Global Companies, provides clients with a broad range of recruitment services.

RECRUITMENT ENHANCEMENT SERVICES / RES
2445 West 41st Avenue
Vancouver, BC V6M 2A5

Telephone	604-266-7350
Fax	604-266-7420
Website	www.resjobs.com
Specialties	General Practice
Contact	Lisa Benjamin

Description Created in 1984, RES is the applicant management and recruitment outsourcing division of Bernard Hodes Group, a world leader in human resource communications.

RECRUITMENT ENHANCEMENT SERVICES / RES
2 Adelaide Street West, 4th Floor
Toronto, ON M5H 1L6

Telephone	416-362-7999
Fax	416-367-9895
E-mail	camail@to.hodes.com
Website	www.resjobs.com
Founded	1984
Specialties	General Practice
Contact	Helen Tom

Description Created in 1984, RES is the applicant management and recruitment outsourcing division of Bernard Hodes Group, a world leader in human resource communications.

RECRUITMENT INTERNATIONAL LTD.
International House, PO Box 300
Harrogate   HG1 5XL
UNITED KINGDOM

Telephone	44-1423-530533
Fax	44-1423-530558
E-mail	ri_group@ compuserve.com
Founded	1981
Specialties	Oil & Gas International
Contact	Dean Culshaw

Description Recruitment International Ltd. places oil and gas professionals in the Middle East.

REID MANAGEMENT CONSULTANTS INC.
313 Oriole Parkway
Toronto, ON M5P 2H6

Fax	416-544-8064
Specialties	Accounting Administrative
Level	Mid-Level Junior
Contact	William Reid

RELATIONAL RESOURCES INC.
236 King Street East, Suite 301
Toronto, ON M5A 1K1

Telephone	416-921-3600
Fax	416-921-0017
E-mail	relres@interlog.com
Founded	1984
Specialties	Telecom Engineering Computing

Description Relatinal Resources Inc. specializes in recruitment of S/W engineers, firmware engineers, H/W engineers, engineering management and marketing management specifically for the communications industry.

RENAISSANCE PERSONNEL
1575 Lauzon Road
Windsor, ON N8S 3N4

Telephone	519-944-1066
Fax	519-944-2075
E-mail	windsor@ renaperson.com
Website	www.renaperson.com
Specialties	Engineering Trades/Technicians Administrative Management Automotive
Level	Mid-Level Junior

Description Renaissance Personnel recruits for engineering, skilled trades, administration and management positions throughout Southern Ontario.

RENAISSANCE PERSONNEL
300 Grand Avenue West
Chatham, ON N7L 1C1

Telephone	519-351-1957
Fax	519-351-5254
E-mail	rena@ciaccess.com
Website	www.renaperson.com
Founded	1997
Employees	6
Specialties	Engineering Trades/Technicians Administrative Management Automotive
Level	Mid-Level
Fee Basis	Sometimes contingent
Recruiters	Chris Bechard Brock Bechard Meredith Cadotte Cheryl Caldwell Jackie Dean-Couture Tracy Hoffman Ray Morris Marjorie Walsh
Contact	Chris Bechard

Description Renaissance recruits for engineering, skilled trades, administration and management positions throughout Southern Ontario.

RENARD HOSPITALITY SEARCH CONSULTANTS
121 Richmond St. West, Suite 500
Toronto, ON M5H 2K1

Telephone	416-364-8325
Fax	416-364-4924
E-mail	consultants@ renard-international.com
Website	www.renard-international.com
Founded	1971
Employees	30
Specialties	Hospitality
Level	Mid-Level Senior
Fee Basis	Sometimes contingent
Recruiters	Michel Aquarone Erik Buckland Shashi Chitnis Louis-Philippe D'Orleans Bernard Lenouvel Christian Mayr Stephen Renard Hyacinth Robinson Christine Sanson Robin Sheardown Dorothy Thomson Hengi von Rohr Sherwin Waldman June Waldman Lary Willows
Contact	Stephen Renard

Description Renard is a leading recruitment firm for the hospitality industry.

RENAUD FOSTER MANAGEMENT CONSULTANTS
100 Sparks Street, Suite 550
Ottawa, ON K1P 5B7

Telephone	613-231-6666
Fax	613-231-6663
E-mail	documents@ renaudfoster.com
Website	www.renaudfoster.com
Founded	1986
Employees	9
Specialties	Finance
	Management
	Govt/Nonprofit
	Computing
	Education
	Public Relations
	Scientific
Level	Senior
	Mid-Level
Fee Basis	Retainer Only
Recruiters	Buffy Bill
	Jean-Marie David
	Thomas C. Foster
	Kirsten Giles
	Andrea Hughes
	Monique Lafreniére
	Marie Larocque
	Liliane (Lil) Lê
	Heather Perry
	R. Alastair Sinclair
	Jim B. Stephen
Contact	Tom Foster

Description Renaud Foster Management Consultants specializes in executive search services, executive coaching and corporate governance.

RENNICK, HOPPE & ASSOC., INC.
4 Milldock Drive
Toronto, ON M1C 4R2

Telephone	416-281-7816
Fax	416-281-7836
E-mail	info@rennick hoppe.com
Website	www.rennick hoppe.com
Specialties	Govt/Nonprofit
Level	Mid-Level
Recruiters	Peter Hoppe
	Lee Rennick
Contact	Peter Hoppe, CEO

Description Rennick, Hoppe & Associates, Inc. provides innovative marketing solutions and executive recruitment services for clients in the non-profit industry.

RESEARCH ASSOCIATES LTD.
17704 - 103 Avenue
Suite 103, Plaza West
Edmonton, AB T5S 1J9

Telephone	780-451-4700
Fax	780-451-4317
E-mail	raltd@telusplanet.net
Founded	1997
Employees	3
Specialties	Management
	Operations
	Human Resource
	Oil & Gas
	Health/Medical
	Consulting
	Finance

Level	Senior
	Mid-Level
Min. Salary	$80,000
Fee Basis	Retainer Only
Recruiters	Yvette Carlyle
	Beverley Kelly
Contact	Beverley Kelly

Description Research Associates Ltd. provides research services to search firms and recruiters throughout Canada.

RESEARCH PERSONNEL CONSULTANTS
335 Bay Street, Suite 810
Toronto, ON M5H 2R3

Telephone	416-726-8000
Fax	905-272-3900
E-mail	respers@interlog.com
Website	www.research personnel.com
Founded	1992
Employees	1
Specialties	Marketing
	Direct Mktng.
Level	Senior
	Mid-Level
Fee Basis	Sometimes contingent
Contact	Robert E. Capel, President

Description Research Personnel Consultants are executive search consultants to database, marketing and market research professionals.

RESOURCE 7 INC.
9440 - 49 Street NW, Suite 207
Edmonton, AB T6B 2M9

Telephone	780-413-0015
Fax	780-413-0063
E-mail	r7@connect.ab.ca
Employees	3
Specialties	Engineering
	Purchasing
	Design
Level	Mid-Level
Contact	Joe Gheran

Description Resource 7 is an employee-owned placement agency.

RESOURCE CONCEPTS
4 Oxen Pond Place
St. John's, NF A1B 4E1

Telephone	709-753-3263
Fax	709-753-2317
E-mail	johnfleming@ roadrunner.nf.net
Specialties	Govt/Nonprofit
	Environmental
	Oil & Gas
Contact	John M. Fleming, President

Description Resource Concepts Inc. offers consulting and recruitment services focusing on natural resources and environmental management.

RESOURCE CORPORATION, THE
2025 Sheppard Avenue East
Suite 2114
Toronto, ON M2J 1V7

Telephone	416-498-7800
Fax	416-498-9650
E-mail	info@resource corporation.com
Website	www.resource corporation.com
Founded	1986
Specialties	Administrative
	Sales
	Accounting
	Management
	Bilingual
	Marketing
	Operations
	Engineering
Level	Mid-Level
	Junior
Fee Basis	Retainer Only
Contact	Rick Dogen

Description The Resource Corporation provides a complete range of HR consulting services, including recruitment.

RESOURCE MANAGEMENT GROUP INC.
500 Richmond St. West, Suite 125
Toronto, ON M5V 1Y2

Telephone	416-822-5279
E-mail	resume@whatis rmg.com
Website	www.whatisrmg.com
Founded	1998
Employees	2
Specialties	Computing
	Consulting
	Human Resource
	Management
	Marketing
	Operations
	Sales
Level	Senior
	Mid-Level
Fee Basis	Always contingent
Recruiters	Lazzlo Kovari
	Peter Uzunov
Contact	Lazzlo Kovari

Description Resource Management Group offers strategic recruitment consulting, recruiting process reengineering, resource management, organizational change management and advice on retention and compensation issues.

RESOURCE PROFESSIONALS INC.
736 - 6th Avenue SW, Suite 1020
Calgary, AB T2P 3T7

Telephone	403-269-3044
Fax	403-264-8509
E-mail	rpi@resourceprof.com
Website	www.resourceprof.com
Founded	1987
Employees	12
Specialties	Oil & Gas

Engineering
Geology/Geography
Computing
Operations
Accounting
International

Level	Mid-Level
	Senior
Min. Salary	$40,000
Fee Basis	Retainer Only
Recruiters	David Banks
	Barrie Burch
	Edwin (Win) Fraser
	Terri Fraser
	Darcy Frey
	Blair Killen
	J.D. (Jack) Melnyk
Contact	David Banks, President

Description Resource Professionals is a professional / technical staffing company serving domestic and international oil and gas industries.

RESOURCE RECRUITERS LTD.
90A Isabella Street
Toronto, ON M4Y 1N4

Telephone	416-967-0045
Fax	416-921-3237
E-mail	mparsons@
	interlog.com
Employees	7
Specialties	Sales
	Marketing

RESOURCES CONNECTION
95 Wellington Street West
Suite 1800
Toronto, ON M5J 2N7

Telephone	416-364-3360
Fax	416-364-3362
E-mail	rctoronto@
	resources-us.com
Website	www.resources
	connection.com
Specialties	Finance
	Accounting
Level	Mid-Level
Contact	Lee Ann Skulsky

Description Resources Connection, founded by the US firm of Deloitte & Touche LLP, is a project-based professional services firm. The firm recruits specialists in finance, accounting and tax.

RESSOURCES 3000
1 Westmount Square, Suite 1350
Westmount, QC H3Z 2P9

Telephone	514-931-9992
Fax	514-931-9949
E-mail	info@
	ressources3000.net
Website	www.ressources
	3000.net
Specialties	Computing
	Engineering
	Administrative
	Management
Level	Mid-Level

Contact	Gabriella Cohen

Description Ressources 3000 is a full-service agency specializing in technical and administrative placements.

RESULTS MANAGEMENT CANADA INC.
151 Frobisher Road
Suite 202, Building A
Waterloo, ON N2V 2C9

Telephone	519-884-3330
Fax	519-884-2767
E-mail	info@winwin
	results.com
Website	www.winwin
	results.com
Founded	1994
Specialties	Finance
	Accounting
	General Practice
	Human Resource
Level	Mid-Level
	Senior
Fee Basis	Retainer Only
Recruiters	Adel Joone
	Len Luksa CHRP
Contact	Len Luksa, BA CHRP

Description Results Management Canada Inc. is an HR consulting firm that also does recruitment work for clients.

RESULTS SEEKERS HUMAN RESOURCES SERVICES
660 Speedvale Avenue West
Suite 101
Guelph, ON N1K 1E5

Telephone	519-822-0723
Fax	519-651-6666
E-mail	results@ionline.net
Specialties	Marketing
	Sales
Level	Mid-Level
Contact	Marnie Porcellato,
	Consultant

RHI CONSULTING
1055 Dunsmuir Street, Suite 1274
Vancouver, BC V7X 1L4

Telephone	604-688-5256
Fax	604-687-7533
E-mail	vancouver.bc@rhic.com
Website	www.rhic.com
Specialties	Computing
Level	Mid-Level
Fee Basis	Always contingent

Description RHI Consulting specializes in the placement of contract and full-time information technology professionals.

RHI CONSULTING
10180 - 101 Street, Suite 1280
Edmonton, AB T5J 3S4

Telephone	780-426-6642
Fax	780-423-1581

E-mail	edmonton@rhic.com
Website	www.rhic.com
Specialties	Computing
Level	Mid-Level
Fee Basis	Always contingent

Description RHI Consulting specializes in the placement of contract and full-time information technology professionals.

RHI CONSULTING
888 - 3rd Street SW, Suite 4200
Calgary, AB T2P 5C5

Telephone	403-237-7500
Fax	403-264-0934
E-mail	calgary@rhic.com
Website	www.rhic.com
Specialties	Computing
Level	Mid-Level
Fee Basis	Always contingent

Description RHI Consulting specializes in the placement of contract and full-time information technology professionals.

RHI CONSULTING
181 Bay Street
PO Box 824, Suite 820
Toronto, ON M5J 2T3

Telephone	416-350-8143
Fax	416-350-3573
E-mail	toronto@rhic.com
Website	www.rhic.com
Specialties	Computing
Level	Mid-Level
Fee Basis	Always contingent
Contact	David Tighe, Area
	Manager

Description RHI Consulting specializes in the placement of contract and full-time information technology professionals.

RHI CONSULTING
5140 Yonge Street, Suite 1500
Toronto, ON M2N 6L7

Telephone	416-227-0581
Fax	416-226-4498
E-mail	north.york@rhic.com
Website	www.rhic.com
Specialties	Computing
Level	Mid-Level
Fee Basis	Always contingent
Contact	Antje Wittholz

Description RHI Consulting specializes in the placement of contract and full-time information technology professionals.

RHI CONSULTING
1 Robert Speck Parkway, Suite 940
Mississauga, ON L4Z 3M3

Telephone	905-273-6524
Fax	905-273-6217
E-mail	mississauga@rhic.com

Website   www.rhic.com

Specialties   Computing

Level   Mid-Level

Fee Basis   Always contingent

Description RHI Consulting specializes in the placement of contract and full-time information technology professionals.

RHI CONSULTING
427 Laurier Ave. West, Suite 1400
Ottawa, ON K1R 7Y2

Telephone   613-236-7442
Fax   613-236-8301
E-mail   ottawa@rhic.com
Website   www.rhic.com

Founded   1948
Employees   25

Specialties   Computing

Level   Mid-Level

Fee Basis   Always contingent

Contact   Sandra Lavoy

Description RHI Consulting specializes in the placement of contract and full-time information technology professionals.

RHI CONSULTING
1 Place Ville Marie, Suite 2838
Montréal, QC H3B 4R4

Téléphone   514-875-8588
Télécopieur   514-875-8066
Courriel   montreal@rhic.com
Site Internet www.rhic.com

Fondée   1948
Employés   12

Spécialités   Informatique

Échelon   Intermédiaire

Frais   Toujours relative

Contact   Michel LeBoeuf, VP

Description RHI Consulting specializes in the placement of contract and full-time information technology professionals.

RHI CONSULTING
245 Park Avenue, 25th Floor
New York, NY 10167-2596   USA

Telephone   212-687-7072
Fax   212-973-0818
E-mail   new.york.midtown@
rhic.com
Website   www.rhic.com

Specialties   Computing
International

Level   Mid-Level

Fee Basis   Always contingent

Description RHI Consulting specializes in the placement of contract and full-time information technology professionals.

RHI MANAGEMENT RESOURCES
888 - 3rd Street SW, Suite 4200
Calgary, AB T2P 5C5

Telephone   403-264-5301
Fax   403-264-0934
E-mail   calgary@rhimr.com
Website   www.rhimr.com

Specialties   Accounting
Consulting
Finance
Management

Level   Mid-Level

Fee Basis   Always contingent

Recruiters   Brenda J. Banda CMA
David Stamper CMA
Terry G. Stein
Janalee F. Woods CA

Contact   Janalee F. Woods, CA

Description RHI places senior-level accounting and financial professionals on a project basis.

RHI MANAGEMENT RESOURCES
181 Bay Street
Suite 820, PO Box 824
Toronto, ON M5J 2T3

Telephone   416-350-5201
Fax   416-350-3983
E-mail   sara.loconte@rhi.com
Website   www.rhimr.com

Founded   1948

Specialties   Accounting
Banking
Consulting
Finance
Management

Level   Mid-Level

Fee Basis   Always contingent

Recruiters   Donald Ness CA
Antje Wittholz

Contact   Antje Wittholz

Description RHI Management Resources, a division of Robert Half International, is North America's largest consulting firm providing senior-level accounting and finance professionals on a project basis.

RICE / DRUMMOND PERSONNEL SERVICES LTD.
1209 - 6th Street SW, Suite 705
Calgary, AB T2R 0Z5

Telephone   403-531-0085
Fax   403-531-0089
E-mail   ricedrummond@
home.com

Specialties   Administrative

Level   Mid-Level
Junior

Recruiters   Cindy Drummond
Lisa Rice

Contact   Lisa Rice

Description Rice / Drummond Personnel Services places administrative and support staff at all levels.

RICHARD FOSTER COMPANY LTD., THE
1200 Bay Street, Suite 1005
Toronto, ON M5R 2A5

Telephone   416-963-5900
Fax   416-963-4911

Specialties   General Practice

Contact   Richard S. Foster

RICHARD LÉVESQUE & ASSOCIÉS INC
4949 Metropolitain E., Bur. 100
Saint-Léonard, QC H1R 1Z6

Téléphone   514-955-6638
Télécopieur   514-955-9254
Courriel   consultrh@
hotmail.com
Site Internet www.homestead.com/
jobsinformatik

Spécialités   Informatique

Échelon   Intermédiaire

Contact   Richard Lévesque

Description Specialisé en emplois en informatique.

RICHARD MAJOR & ASSOCIATES
145 King Street West, Suite 10002
Toronto, ON M5H 3X6

Telephone   416-365-0312

Founded   1988
Employees   1

Specialties   Accounting
Finance

Level   Mid-Level
Senior

Min. Salary $45,000
Fee Basis   Sometimes contingent

Contact   Rick Major

RICHARDSON PERSONNEL
120 Eglinton Avenue East
Toronto, ON M4P 1E2

Telephone   416-482-2363
Fax   416-482-3518
E-mail   richardson@
on.aibn.com

Specialties   Sales
Administrative

Level   Mid-Level

RICHMARK GROUP, THE
1200 Bay Street, Suite 903
Toronto, ON M5R 2A5

Telephone   416-934-9730
Fax   416-934-9732
E-mail   shara@
therichmarkgroup.com

Specialties   Law
Administrative
Accounting
Finance
Real Estate

Level   Mid-Level
Senior

Contact   Shara Stone

RICHTER CONSULTING
90 Eglinton Avenue East, Suite 700
Toronto, ON M4P 2Y3

Telephone	416-932-8000
Fax	416-932-6200
E-mail	torinfo@richter.ca
Website	www.richter.ca
Founded	1926
Specialties	Accounting Finance
Level	Mid-Level
Recruiters	Leonard Borer Caroline Freedman Sara Knill
Contact	Leonard Borer

Description Richter is one of the largest independent accounting, business advisory and consulting firms in Canada. They occasionally recruit accounting and finance staff for clients.

RICHTER RAYMOND GROUP, THE
1155 North Service Rd. W., Suite 11
Glen Abbey Executive Suites
Oakville, ON L6M 3E3

Telephone	905-825-9144
Fax	905-465-3793
E-mail	richray@sympatico.ca
Specialties	Operations Purchasing Sales Retail
Level	Mid-Level Senior
Min. Salary	$50,000
Fee Basis	Retainer Only
Contact	Paul R. Richter CHRP, Principal

RICHTER & RICHTER HUMAN RESOURCES CONSULTANTS INC.
43 Gibson Lake Drive, PO Box 54
Palgrave, ON L0N 1P0

Telephone	905-880-7356
Fax	905-880-3704
E-mail	rgrgr@interlog.com
Website	www.interlog.com/~rgrgr
Specialties	Human Resource Management
Level	Mid-Level
Recruiters	Bob Richter Gloria Richter
Contact	Bob Richter

Description Specialists in providing organizations with cost-effective human resources expertise. Call toll-free 1-888-896-6630.

RICHTER, USHER & VINEBERG
2 Place Alexis Nihon, Suite 2230
Montréal, QC H3Z 3C2

Telephone	514-934-3400
Fax	514-934-3539
E-mail	mtlhr@richter.ca
Website	www.richter.ca
Founded	1926
Specialties	Accounting Finance

	Apparel Computing
Level	Mid-Level
Recruiters	Lyn Lalonde Benoît Lemelin Marisa Rezzara
Contact	Marisa Rezzara

Description Richter, Usher & Vineberg is a large accounting firm that also does occasional search work for clients.

RIDEAU MANAGEMENT GROUP LTD.
9 Erinlea Court
Nepean, ON K2E 7C8

Telephone	613-762-5074
E-mail	hr@rmgltd.com
Website	www.rmgltd.com
Founded	1993
Specialties	Computing Telecom Aerospace Engineering
Level	Senior Mid-Level
Contact	Bruce MacRae, Partner

Description Rideau Management Group Ltd. provides consulting, contracting and technical recruiting services to clients in the telecommunications, aerospace and defense markets.

RJ PROFESSIONALS
65 Queen Street West
Suite 1602, PO Box 94
Toronto, ON M5H 2M5

Telephone	416-363-4238
Fax	416-363-4239
E-mail	rjpro@rjprofessional.com
Website	www.rjprofessionals.com
Founded	1992
Employees	10
Specialties	Accounting Management Finance Engineering Direct Mktng. Hospitality Printing Retail Metals
Level	Senior Mid-Level
Min. Salary	$85,000
Fee Basis	Retainer Only
Contact	Natasha David

Description RJ Professionals (formerly Rushmore Judge Inc.) is a retainer-based firm that provides senior-level recruitment services for corporations and non-profit organizations.

RJK & ASSOCIATES
7270 Woodbine Avenue, Suite 200
Markham, ON L3R 4B9

Telephone	905-947-8454
Fax	905-947-8439
E-mail	robert.kahler@home.com
Founded	1996
Employees	2
Specialties	Engineering Automotive Design Operations Logistics
Level	Mid-Level
Min. Salary	$35,000
Fee Basis	Sometimes contingent
Recruiters	Glenn Agnew Bob Kahler
Contact	Bob Kahler

Description RJK & Associates specializes in searches relating to manufacturing. Call toll-free: 1-877-353-0330.

RJS ASSOCIATES INC.
55 Town Centre Court, Suite 700
Toronto, ON M1P 4X4

Telephone	416-291-4417
Fax	416-291-5819
E-mail	info@rjscanada.com
Website	www.rjscanada.com
Specialties	Computing
Level	Senior Mid-Level
Recruiters	Vivian Chen Jim Heels Joshua Soon Ruth Tan
Contact	Ruth Tan

Description RJS Associates Inc. is a full-service consulting firm specializing in the recruitment and placement of IT professionals, especially for the software industry.

RLP CONSULTING
2810 Matheson Boulevard East
Suite 515
Mississauga, ON L4W 4X7

Telephone	905-238-9400
Fax	905-238-3414
E-mail	mread@cuco.on.ca
Website	www.cuco.on.ca
Specialties	Banking Finance
Level	Mid-Level
Contact	Alan G. Small, Partner

Description RLP Consulting is affiliated with Credit Union Central of Ontario and recruits banking, finance and IT staff for credit unions across the province.

ROAN INTERNATIONAL INC.
2155 Dunwin Drive, Unit 4
Mississauga, ON L5L 4M1

Telephone	905-820-3511
Fax	905-820-0679
E-mail	resume@roan.ca
Website	www.roan.ca

Specialties Computing
Engineering
Automotive
Oil & Gas
Mining
Aerospace
Construction

Level Mid-Level
Senior

Contact Pete Curran

Description Roan International Inc. provides engineering and technical personnel to companies operating in Canada and the USA.

ROBERT B. CHANNING CONSULTING
1099 Rebecca Street
Oakville, ON L6L 1Y6

Telephone 905-338-9981
Fax 905-338-9982
E-mail rbcc@globalserve.net

Specialties General Practice
Management

Level Senior

Fee Basis Retainer Only

Contact Robert B. Channing

Description Robert B. Channing is a former partner of Korn / Ferry International and ex-head of the KPMG Peat Marwick Executive Search practice.

ROBERT CONNELLY & ASSOCIATES, INC.
5200 Willson Road, Suite 150
Minneapolis, MN 55424   USA

Telephone 612-925-3039
E-mail robtconn@aol.com

Founded 1976
Employees 5

Specialties General Practice
Real Estate
Construction
Architecture
Design
Engineering
Agriculture/Fisheries
International

Level Senior

Min. Salary $80,000
Fee Basis Retainer Only

Contact Robert F. Olsen,
President

ROBERT HALF CANADA INC.
10180 - 101st Street, Suite 1280
Edmonton, AB T5J 3S4

Telephone 780-423-1466
Fax 780-423-1581
E-mail edmonton@
roberthalf.com
Website www.roberthalf.com

Specialties Accounting
Administrative

Level Mid-Level
Junior

Fee Basis Always contingent

Contact Karen Vonkeman,
Branch Manager

Description Robert Half Canada is part of Robert Half International, a leading specialized staffing services with 290 offices worldwide.

ROBERT HALF CANADA INC.
888 - 3rd Street SW, Suite 4200
Calgary, AB T2P 5C5

Telephone 403-237-9363
Fax 403-264-0934
E-mail calgary@roberthalf.com
Website www.rhii.com

Founded 1948

Specialties Accounting
Banking
Finance
Computing

Level Mid-Level
Junior

Fee Basis Always contingent

Recruiters Barry Carlyle
Toni Guido

Contact Toni Guido

Description Robert Half Canada is part of Robert Half International, a leading specialized staffing services with 290 offices worldwide.

ROBERT HALF CANADA INC.
181 Bay St., Suite 820, PO Box 824
Toronto, ON M5J 2T3

Telephone 416-350-2330
Fax 416-350-3573
E-mail toronto@roberthalf.com
Website www.roberthalf.com

Founded 1948

Specialties Accounting
Finance
Management

Level Mid-Level
Junior

Fee Basis Always contingent

Recruiters Sara Loconte
Trevor Zigelstein

Contact Sara Loconte, District
Staffing Recruiter

Description Robert Half Canada is part of Robert Half International, a leading specialized staffing services with 290 offices worldwide.

ROBERT HALF CANADA INC.
5140 Yonge Street, Suite 2500
Toronto, ON M2N 6L7

Telephone 416-226-2538
Fax 416-226-4498
E-mail north.york@
roberthalf.com
Website www.roberthalf.com

Founded 1948
Employees 21

Specialties Management
Engineering
Accounting

Finance
Sales

Level Mid-Level
Junior

Fee Basis Always contingent

Contact Tammy Turner,
Manager

Description Robert Half Canada is part of Robert Half International, a leading specialized staffing services with 290 offices worldwide.

ROBERT HALF CANADA INC.
1 Robert Speck Parkway, Suite 940
Mississauga, ON L4Z 3M3

Telephone 905-273-4229
Fax 905-273-6217
E-mail mississauga@
roberthalf.com
Website www.roberthalf.com

Founded 1948
Employees 20

Specialties Accounting
Finance
Management

Level Mid-Level
Junior

Fee Basis Always contingent

Contact Christine Lucy, Branch
Manager

Description Robert Half Canada is part of Robert Half International, a leading specialized staffing services with 290 offices worldwide.

ROBERT HALF CANADA INC.
427 Laurier Ave. West, Suite 1400
Ottawa, ON K1R 7Y2

Telephone 613-236-4253
Fax 613-236-2159
E-mail ottawa@roberthalf.com
Website www.roberthalf.com

Founded 1948
Employees 15

Specialties Accounting
Banking
Finance
Govt/Nonprofit
Sales
Consulting

Level Mid-Level
Junior

Contact Avalee Prehogan,
Branch Manager

Description Robert Half Canada is part of Robert Half International, a leader in specialized staffing services with 290 offices worldwide.

ROBERT HALF CANADA INC.
1 Place Ville-Marie, Bureau 2838
Montréal, QC H3B 4G4

Telephone 514-875-8585
Fax 514-875-8066
E-mail montreal@
roberthalf.com
Website www.roberthalf.com

Specialties Accounting

Administrative
Bilingual
Banking

Level   Mid-Level
        Junior

Fee Basis   Always contingent

Description Robert Half Canada is part of Robert Half International, a leading specialized staffing services with 290 offices worldwide.

ROBERT HALF FINANCIAL RECRUITING

1055 Dunsmuir Street, Suite 1274
Vancouver, BC V7X 1L4

Telephone 604-688-7572
Fax   604-687-7533
E-mail   vancouver.bc@
        roberthalf.com
Website   www.roberthalf.com
Founded 1948
Specialties Accounting
        Finance
        Management
Level   Mid-Level
        Junior
Fee Basis Always contingent
Contact Geri Ramsay,
        Division Director

Description Robert Half Canada is part of Robert Half International, a leading specialized staffing services with 290 offices worldwide.

ROBERT L. HOLMES PROFESSIONAL PLACEMENT SERVICES INC.

264-266 Water Street N.
Cambridge, ON N1R 3C2

Telephone 519-621-4373
Fax   519-621-4084
E-mail   careers@
        robertlholmes.com
Website   www.robertlholmes.
        com
Founded 1987
Employees 4
Specialties Management
        Plastics
        Metals
        Accounting
        Engineering
        Finance
Level   Mid-Level
        Senior
Recruiters Gina Bowerman
        Robert L. (Bob) Holmes
        Zoë Holmes
Contact Robert L. (Bob) Holmes

Description Robert L Holmes Placement has provided clients in the plastics, rubber and metal industries in Ontario with the best candidates since 1987.

ROBERT LAMARRE & ASSOCIATES INC.

937 Boissy
Saint-Lambert, QC J4R 1K1

Telephone 450-671-5736
Fax   450-671-2962
E-mail   gcrl@attglobal.net
Website   pws.prserv.net/
        cainet.rlamarr
Founded 1991
Employees 9
Specialties Purchasing
        Logistics
Contact Robert Lamarre

Description Robert Lamarre & Associates Inc. is a management consulting firm specializing in supply chain logistics. They occasionally do search work for clients.

ROBERT M. LECAVALIER, EXECUTIVE SEARCH CONSULTANTS

4150, rue Ste-Catherine Ouest
Bureau 225
Montréal, QC H3Z 2Y5

Telephone 514-934-3944
Fax   514-934-6232
E-mail   ccrml@sympatico.ca
Website   pages.infinit.net/
        pdperfo/pageweb.htm
Specialties General Practice
Level   Senior
Contact Robert M. Lecavalier

Description Robert M. Lecavalier is a firm of executive search consultants.

ROBERT PAQUET & ASSOCIÉS

2600, boul. Laurier
Bureau 2265, Place de la Cité
Sainte-Foy, QC G1V 4M6

Téléphone 418-657-1357
Télécopieur 418-657-2196
Courriel rob.paquet@
        sympatico.ca
Fondée 1974
Employés 1
Spécialités Généralistes
        Marketing
        Ventes
Échelon Intermédiaire
Frais   Parfois relative
Contact Robert Paquet

Description Conseillers en recrutement, sélection et réaffectation de ressources humaines.

ROBERT R. SCURFIELD & ASSOC.

238 Oxford Street
Winnipeg, MB R3M 3J6

Telephone 204-489-9372
Fax   204-489-6204
Website   www.hkdesigngroup.
        com/rrs/contact/
        contact.html
Specialties Management
        Human Resource
        Accounting
        Finance
Level   Senior
        Mid-Level
Contact Robert R. Scurfield

ROBERT T. KEEGAN & ASSOCIATES INC.

700 Dorval Drive, Suite 503
Oakville, ON L6K 3V3

Telephone 905-339-1479
Fax   905-821-3800
E-mail   careers@rtkeegan.com
Website   www.rtkeegan.com
Founded 1971
Employees 1
Specialties Engineering
        Operations
        Purchasing
        Management
        Logistics
Level   Senior
        Mid-Level
Min. Salary $40,000
Contact Robert T. Keegan

Description Robert T. Keegan & Associates Inc. specializes in production, materials, engineering and human resources management in the manufacturing sector.

ROBERT W. DINGMAN COMPANY, INC.

650 Hampshire Road, Suite 116
Westlake Village, CA 91361
USA

Telephone 805-778-1777
Fax   805-778-9288
E-mail   info@dingman.com
Website   www.dingman.com
Specialties International
        General Practice
        Govt/Nonprofit
Level   Senior
Fee Basis Retainer Only
Recruiters Bret Dalton
        H. Bruce Dingman
        Robert A. Dingman
        Fleming Jones
Contact H. Bruce Dingman,
        President

Description Robert W. Dingman Co., Inc. is a retained executive search firm devoted exclusively to the process of consulting with clients on matters of executive selection.

ROBERTSON HANCOCK LTD.

1200 Bay Street, Suite 1104
Toronto, ON M5R 2A5

Telephone 416-924-0226
Fax   416-929-5549
E-mail   assign@idirect.com
Specialties Accounting
        Banking
        Consulting
        Law
        Direct Mktng.
        Human Resource
        Telecom
        Finance
Level   Mid-Level
        Junior
Fee Basis Sometimes contingent
Contact Dave Robertson

ROBERTSON HUMAN ASSET MANAGEMENT
1455 Lakeshore Rd. S., Suite 204
Burlington, ON L7S 2J1

Telephone	905-333-9188
Fax	905-333-9153
E-mail	robertso@netcom.ca

Specialties	Pharmaceutical
	Health/Medical
	Biotech/Biology
	Finance
	Management
	Marketing
	Packaging
	Sales
Level	Mid-Level
	Senior
Contact	Linda Robertson

Description Robertson Human Asset Management specializes in human resource consulting for the pharmaceutical, healthcare and consumer industries.

ROBINSON & ASSOCIATES PERSONNEL INC.
666 Burrard St., Suite 1300
Vancouver, BC V6C 3J8

Telephone	604-684-9663
Fax	604-684-9664
E-mail	resume@ robinsonp.com

Specialties	Pulp & Paper
	Forestry
Level	Mid-Level
	Senior
Contact	Barbara Scammell, Manager

ROBINSON, FRASER GROUP LTD.
13 Clarence Square
Toronto, ON M5V 1H1

Telephone	416-977-9174
Fax	416-977-7600
E-mail	es@robinsonfraser.com

Specialties	Telecom
	Operations
	Finance
	Publishing/Media
	Computing
Level	Senior
Min. Salary	$100,000
Fee Basis	Retainer Only
Contact	Stephen A. Robinson, President

Description RFG is an international executive search firm specializing in building executive teams for the telecommunications, high technology, financial and media sectors.

ROBINSON ROSE ASSOCIATES LTD.
2 Robert Speck Parkway, Suite 750
Mississauga, ON L4Z 1H8

Telephone	905-277-3232
Fax	905-277-5505
E-mail	dmosdell@ robinsonrose.com
Website	www.robinsonrose.com

Specialties	Engineering
	Sales
Level	Mid-Level
Contact	Doug Mosdell

ROCHON PARTNERS CORP.
121 Richmond St. West, Suite 903
Toronto, ON M5H 2K1

Telephone	416-359-9444
Fax	416-359-9420
E-mail	jrochon@sympatico.ca
Employees	4
Specialties	Management
Level	Senior
Contact	Joel Rochon, Partner

Description Rochon Partners is a reputable executive search and management consulting company.

ROCKWELL PLACEMENT AGENCIES
4940 No. 3 Road, Suite 212
Richmond, BC V6X 3A5

Telephone	604-278-3077
Fax	604-278-3005
E-mail	staff@rockwell placement.com
Website	www.rockwell placement.com

Specialties	Sales
	Accounting
	Marketing
Level	Mid-Level
	Junior
Recruiters	Lyle Babcock
	Chaouen Bragg
	Tammy Danforth
	Ruth Jennings
Contact	Karla Rockwell, President

Description For over 20 years, Rockwell Placement Agencies has been providing companies in the Lower Mainland with highly skilled professional personnel.

ROD TURPIN & ASSOCIATES
10216 - 124th Street, Suite 502
Edmonton, AB T5N 4A3

Telephone	780-944-0824
Fax	780-452-2576
E-mail	jobs@rtastaffing.com
Website	www.rtastaffing.com
Founded	1989

Specialties	Oil & Gas
	Pulp & Paper
	Construction
	Engineering
	Design
Level	Mid-Level
	Senior
Recruiters	Niki Melnyk
	Rod Turpin
Contact	Rod Turpin

Description Rod Turpin & Associates is a firm of staffing specialists providing services to clients in Alberta's heavy industry sector.

ROEVIN TECHNICAL PEOPLE LTD.
1480 Marine Drive, Suite 8
North Vancouver, BC V7P 1T6

Telephone	604-987-5627
Fax	604-987-5602
E-mail	vancouver@roevin.ca
Website	www.roevin.ca

Specialties	Engineering
	Computing
	Mining
	Forestry
	Pulp & Paper
Level	Mid-Level
	Senior
Contact	Dalton Grady

Description Roevin has been in business for over two decades, providing technical people at all levels to industries worldwide.

ROEVIN TECHNICAL PEOPLE LTD.
10303 Jasper Avenue
Suite 1160, Metropolitan Place
Edmonton, AB T5J 3N6

Telephone	780-420-6232
Fax	780-428-0580
E-mail	edmonton@roevin.ca
Website	www.roevin.ca
Founded	1969
Employees	4

Specialties	Engineering
	Computing
	Design
	Mining
	Oil & Gas
	Pulp & Paper
Level	Mid-Level
	Senior
Contact	David Shea

Description Roevin has been in business for over two decades, providing technical people at all levels to industries worldwide.

ROEVIN TECHNICAL PEOPLE LTD.
505 - 3rd Street SW, Suite 1710
Calgary, AB T2P 3E6

Telephone	403-264-3283
Fax	403-264-3298
E-mail	calgary@roevin.ca
Website	www.roevin.ca

Specialties	Engineering
	Oil & Gas
	Computing
	Design
	Mining
	Pulp & Paper

Description Roevin has been in business for over two decades, providing technical people at all levels to industries worldwide.

ROEVIN TECHNICAL PEOPLE LTD.
265 North Front Street, Suite 411
Sarnia, ON N7T 7X1

Telephone	519-383-6630
Fax	519-383-6631
E-mail	sarnia@roevin.ca
Website	www.roevin.ca
Founded	1968

Specialties	Automotive
	Aerospace
	Engineering
	Trades/Technicians
	Quality Control
	Design
	Computing
	Oil & Gas
Level	Senior
	Mid-Level
Recruiters	Melanie Andrew
	Steve Thomson
Contact	Steve Thomson

Description Roevin has been in business for over two decades, providing technical people at all levels to industries worldwide.

ROEVIN TECHNICAL PEOPLE LTD.
148 Bedford Road, Unit 3
Kitchener, ON N2G 3A4

Telephone	519-578-8446
Fax	519-578-6550
E-mail	kitchener@roevin.ca
Website	www.roevin.ca
Founded	1968
Specialties	Automotive
	Aerospace
	Engineering
	Trades/Technicians
	Quality Control
	Design
	Computing
	Mining
Level	Senior
	Mid-Level

Description Roevin has been in business for over two decades, providing technical people at all levels to industries worldwide.

ROEVIN TECHNICAL PEOPLE LTD.
2500 Meadowpine Blvd., Suite 201
Mississauga, ON L5N 6C4

Telephone	905-826-4155
Fax	905-826-5336
E-mail	resumes@roevin.ca
Website	www.roevin.ca
Founded	1981
Specialties	Engineering
	Trades
	Aerospace
	Automotive
	Computing
	Construction
	Design
Level	Mid-Level
	Senior
Recruiters	David Lamond
	Ian Wright
Contact	Ian Wright

Description Roevin has been in business for over two decades, providing technical people at all levels to industries worldwide.

ROEVIN TECHNICAL PEOPLE LTD.
80F Centurian Drive, Suite 210
Markham, ON L3R 8C1

Telephone	905-258-6325
Fax	905-258-6328
E-mail	toronto@roevin.ca
Website	www.roevin.ca
Founded	1968
Specialties	Automotive
	Aerospace
	Engineering
	Trades/Technicians
	Quality Control
	Design
	Computing
Level	Senior
	Mid-Level

Description Roevin has been in business for over two decades, providing technical people at all levels to industries worldwide.

ROEVIN TECHNICAL PEOPLE LTD.
1117 St. Catherine Ouest
Bureau 1101
Montréal, QC H3B 1H9

Telephone	514-849-7701
Fax	514-849-5258
E-mail	montreal@roevin.ca
Website	www.roevin.ca
Specialties	Mining
	Operations
	Pulp & Paper
	Engineering
	Design
	Aerospace
Recruiters	Nicolla Coppin
	Angela Giorgio
	Joëlle Messier
Contact	Joëlle Messier, Manager

Description Roevin has been in business for over two decades, providing technical people at all levels to industries worldwide.

ROLFE, BENSON
900 West Hastings St., Suite 1400
Vancouver, BC V6C 1E3

Telephone	604-684-7937
Fax	604-684-7937
E-mail	admin@
	rolfebenson.com
Website	www.rolfebenson.com
Specialties	Accounting
	Finance
Level	Mid-Level
Contact	David R.L. Rolfe, FCA

Description Rolfe, Benson is an accounting firm that occasionally places accounting and finance staff with its Vancouver-area clients.

ROLL HARRIS & ASSOCIATES
4141 Sherbrooke St. W., Suite 550
Montréal, QC H3Z 1B9

Telephone	514-933-2791
Fax	514-933-2470
E-mail	info@rha.ca
Website	www.rha.ca
Specialties	Accounting
	Finance

Description Roll Harris is an accounting firm that also does search work.

ROLLAND GROUPE CONSEIL INC.
1 Square Westmount, Bureau 1405
Westmount, QC H3Z 2P9

Telephone	514-937-7112
Fax	514-937-9738
E-mail	rgc@videotron.ca
Employees	5
Specialties	Accounting
	Biotech/Biology
	Finance
	Forestry
	Human Resource
	Marketing
	Operations
Level	Senior
Min. Salary	$80,000
Recruiters	Jasmine Asselin
	Mireille Audibert
	Denise Rolland
Contact	Denise Rolland,
	President

ROLLAND RESSOURCES HUMAINES INC.
560, boul. Henri-Bourassa O.
Bureau 202
Montréal, QC H3L 1P4

Téléphone	514-333-6619
Télécopieur	514-334-5985
Fondée	1987
Employés	3
Spécialités	Comptabilité
	Affaires de banque
	Ingénierie
	Finance
	Ressources humaines
	Gestion
	Marketing
	Exploitation
	Achat
	Ventes
Échelon	Direction
	Intermédiaire
Salaire min.	50 000 $
Frais	Honoraire seulement
Contact	Guy Rolland, MSc

Description Recherche de cadres. Services flexibles et professionels. Clientele parmi les grandes entreprises et les PME (banques, télécom, manufacturier, haute technologie, etc.).

ROPER AND ASSOCIATES INC.
550 - 6th Avenue SW, Suite 900
Calgary, AB T2P 0S2

Telephone	403-263-0937
Fax	403-264-7127
E-mail	recruiters@
	roper-assoc.com
Founded	1975
Employees	5
Specialties	Oil & Gas
	Geology/Geography
	Engineering
Level	Senior

Min. Salary $50,000
Fee Basis Sometimes contingent
Contact Bruce Roper

ROSSCAM EXECUTIVE SEARCH GROUP LTD. / UNIVERSAL SUPPORT SYSTEMS LTD.
1501 Danforth Avenue
Toronto, ON M4J 5C3

Telephone 416-405-8389
Fax 416-405-8399
E-mail rosscam@rosscam.com
Website www.rosscam.com

Founded 1981

Specialties Computing

Description Rosscam Executive Search Group Ltd. is a professional IT recruitment firm. Universal Support Systems Ltd. is their contract placements division.

ROSSI & ASSOCIATES INC.
1500 West Georgia St., Suite 1400
Vancouver, BC V6G 2Z6

Telephone 604-683-3755
Fax 604-683-3721
E-mail rossi@execcentre.com
Website www.rossipeople.com

Founded 1982
Employees 4

Specialties Sales
Management
Marketing
Printing
Telecom
Human Resource

Level Mid-Level

Min. Salary $30,000
Fee Basis Always contingent

Contact Donna Rossi

Description Rossi & Associates provides sales and sales management professionals to a broad range of business-to-business industries.

ROSTIE & ASSOCIATES INC.
20 Bay Street
Suite 1205, Waterpark Place
Toronto, ON M5J 2N8

Telephone 416-777-0780
Fax 416-777-0451
E-mail rostie@rostie.com
Website www.rostie.com

Founded 1991

Specialties Computing
Engineering
Finance

Level Mid-Level

Fee Basis Sometimes contingent

Recruiters Ben Coniglio
Craig Darlington
Cynthia Rostie
Judy White

Contact Cynthia Rostie

Description Rostie & Associates Inc. offers expertise in recruiting for progressive careers in the high technology industry.

ROSTIE & ASSOCIATES INC.
625 Michigan Avenue
Chicago, IL 60601 USA

Telephone 312-867-8875
E-mail rostie@rostie.com
Website www.rostie.com

Specialties Computing
International

Description Rostie & Associates Inc. offers expertise in recruiting for progressive careers in the high technology industry.

ROSTIE & ASSOCIATES INC.
20 Park Plaza, Suite 628
Boston, MA 02116 USA

Telephone 617-350-6350
Fax 617-350-6354
E-mail rostie@rostie.com
Website www.rostie.com

Specialties Computing
International

Description Rostie & Associates Inc. offers expertise in recruiting for progressive careers in the high technology industry.

ROYAL VALVET PERSONNEL INC.
2 Robert Speck Parkway, Suite 750
Mississauga, ON L4Z 1H8

Telephone 905-848-3990
Fax 905-848-3991
E-mail royalvalvet@sprint.ca

Specialties Administrative
Bilingual

Level Junior
Mid-Level

RUDL INTERNATIONAL
327 Mountbatten Avenue
Ottawa, ON K1H 5W2

Telephone 613-591-0440
Fax 613-733-6828

Employees 3

Specialties Computing
Engineering
International
Marketing
Sales
Operations

Level Mid-Level
Senior

Min. Salary $40,000

Contact John Rudl

Description Rudl International specializes in recruiting quality professionals for high tech industries, including engineering, sales, project management and senior management.

RUSSELL & ASSOCIATES
215 Lawrence Avenue, Suite 100
Kelowna, BC V1Y 6L2

Telephone 250-763-6464
Fax 250-763-4688

Specialties Insurance

Accounting
Banking
Finance
Operations

Level Mid-Level

Contact Trevor West

RUSSELL REYNOLDS ASSOCIATES, INC.
202 - 6th Avenue SW
630 Bow Valley Square 1
Calgary, AB T2P 2R9

Telephone 403-205-3640
Fax 403-205-4888
E-mail awiebe@
russellreynolds.com
Website www.russellreynolds.
com

Founded 1997
Employees 5

Specialties Agriculture/Fisheries
Banking
Computing
Education
Geology/Geography
Oil & Gas
Telecom

Level Senior
Mid-Level

Fee Basis Retainer Only

Recruiters Paul Gregus
Irene E. Pfeiffer
Laird Willson

Contact Irene E. Pfeiffer,
Managing Director

Description Founded in New York, Russell Reynolds is one of the world's leading executive recruiting services, with 300 + recruiting professionals working in 35 offices worldwide.

RUSSELL REYNOLDS ASSOCIATES, INC.
40 King Street West
Suite 3500, Scotia Plaza
Toronto, ON M5H 3Y2

Telephone 416-364-3355
Fax 416-364-5174
E-mail pcantor@
russellreynolds.com
Website www.russellreynolds.
com

Founded 1969
Employees 4

Specialties Banking
Finance
Management

Level Senior

Fee Basis Retainer Only

Recruiters Laura Brannan
Paul Cantor
Shawn Cooper
Mark Derbyshire
Patrick Galpin
Paul Hudson
Tony van Straubenzee

Contact Paul Cantor,
Managing Director

Description Russell Reynolds is one of the world's leading providers of executive recruiting services, with more than 300 recruiting professionals working in 35 offices worldwide.

RUSSELL REYNOLDS ASSOCIATES, INC.

50 Bridge Street
Suite 1902, AMP Centre
Sydney,   NSW 2000
AUSTRALIA

Telephone	61-2-9 364 3100
Fax	61-2-9 233 3471
Website	www.russellreynolds.com
Specialties	Govt/Nonprofit Management International
Level	Senior
Fee Basis	Retainer Only
Contact	Mr. Lynn R. Anderson

Description Founded in New York, Russell Reynolds is one of the world's leading providers of executive recruiting services, with more than 300 recruiting professionals working in 35 offices worldwide.

RUSSELL REYNOLDS ASSOCIATES, INC.

7, Place Vendôme
Paris,   75001
FRANCE

Telephone	33-1-49-26-13-00
Fax	33-1-42-60-03-85
E-mail	blemercier@russellreynolds.com
Website	www.russellreynolds.com
Specialties	International General Practice
Level	Senior
Fee Basis	Retainer Only
Recruiters	Caroline Apffel Lucia F. Archambeaud Carl Azar Bruno-Luc Banton Natalie Behar Olivier Blin Bruno Bolzan Henry De Montebello Brigitte Lemercier Nicolas Manset Gilles Nobécourt Sophie Noir Christophe Tellier Laurence Viénot
Contact	Brigette Lemercier

Description Founded in New York, Russell Reynolds is one of the world's leading providers of executive recruiting services, with more than 300 recruiting professionals working in 35 offices worldwide.

RUSSELL REYNOLDS ASSOCIATES, INC.

6 Battery Road, #16-08
SINGAPORE   049909

Telephone	65-225-1811
Fax	65-224-4058
E-mail	cchew@russreyn.com
Website	www.russellreynolds.com
Specialties	International General Practice
Level	Senior
Fee Basis	Retainer Only
Contact	Choon Soo Chew

Description Founded in New York, Russell Reynolds is one of the world's leading providers of executive recruiting services, with more than 300 recruiting professionals working in 35 offices worldwide.

RUSSELL REYNOLDS ASSOCIATES, INC.

Castellana, 51
Madrid   28046   SPAIN

Telephone	34-91-319-7100
Fax	34-91-310-4470
E-mail	elegorburu@russellreynolds.com
Website	www.russellreynolds.com
Specialties	International General Practice
Level	Senior
Fee Basis	Retainer Only
Recruiters	Javier Anitua Edurardo R. Legorburu
Contact	Eduardo R. Legorburu

Description Founded in New York, Russell Reynolds is one of the world's leading providers of executive recruiting services, with more than 300 recruiting professionals working in 35 offices worldwide.

RUSSELL REYNOLDS ASSOCIATES, INC.

200 Park Avenue, Suite 2300
New York, NY 10166-0002   USA

Telephone	212-351-2000
Fax	212-370-0896
E-mail	jbagley@russellreynolds.com
Website	www.russellreynolds.com
Specialties	International General Practice
Level	Senior
Fee Basis	Retainer Only
Recruiters	James M. Bagley Joseph A. Bailey III Hobson Brown Jr. James J. Carpenter Richard S. Lannamann
Contact	James M. Bagley

Description Founded in New York, Russell Reynolds is one of the world's leading providers of executive recruiting services, with more than 300 recruiting professionals working in 35 offices worldwide.

RUTHERFORD INTERNATIONAL EXECUTIVE SEARCH GROUP INC.

390 Bay Street, Suite 2000
Toronto, ON M2H 2Y2

Telephone	416-250-6300
Fax	416-250-8191
E-mail	rutherford@rutherfordinternational.com
Website	www.rutherfordinternational.com
Founded	1990
Employees	3
Specialties	Real Estate Finance Health/Medical International Biotech/Biology
Level	Senior
Min. Salary	$75,000
Fee Basis	Retainer Only
Contact	Forbes J. Rutherford

Description Rutherford International is a management consulting firm, which specializes in retained executive search, career management and selected areas of HR advisory work.

RWJ & ASSOCIATES

150 Dufferin Avenue
Suite 702, Richmond Court
London, ON N6A 5N6

Telephone	519-672-2795
Fax	519-672-8870
E-mail	recruit@rwj.com
Website	www.rwjcanada.com
Founded	1980
Employees	6
Specialties	Engineering Accounting Purchasing Computing Human Resource Sales Quality Control
Level	Mid-Level Senior
Fee Basis	Always contingent
Recruiters	Tracy Cross Tamara Dahl Tracey Johns Jim Sefeldas Jane Vickers
Contact	Jim Sefeldas, Senior Manager

Description RWJ & Associates, the permanent search and contract staffing arm of Express Services Inc., specializes in placements for the engineering, manufacturing / technical, accounting / finance, human resources and IT sectors.

RWJ & ASSOCIATES

50 Queen Street N.
Suite 704, Commerce House
Kitchener, ON N2H 6P4

Telephone	519-578-9030
Fax	519-578-1121
E-mail	kitchener@rwj.com
Website	www.rwjcanada.com

Founded   1980
Employees   9
Specialties Computing
              Engineering
              Human Resource
              Finance
              Purchasing
              Packaging
              Plastics
              Quality Control
Level   Senior
              Mid-Level
Min. Salary $30,000
Recruiters   Ann Derry
              Mark Macleod
              Carol Marttini CPC
              Ann Ryan
              Sanjeev Verma
Contact   Carol Marttini, CPC
              Manager

Description RWJ & Associates, the permanent search and contract staffing arm of Express Services Inc., specializes in placements for the engineering, manufacturing / technical, accounting / finance, human resources and IT sectors.

RWM MANAGEMENT RESOURCES LTD.
250 - 6th Avenue SW, Suite 1500
Calgary, AB T2P 3H7

Telephone   403-233-2757
Fax   403-264-1262
E-mail   mgmt.resources@
              cadvision.com
Specialties Management
              Engineering
              Finance
Level   Mid-Level
              Senior
Contact   R.W. Michael CMC,
              President

RWS CONSULTING GROUP
700 Wonderland Road North
Suite 201
London, ON N6H 4V3

Telephone   519-474-2112
Fax   519-474-1475
E-mail   rsopo@rwsgroup.com
Founded   1977
Employees   3
Specialties General Practice
              Management
              Operations
Level   Mid-Level
              Senior
Min. Salary $50,000
Fee Basis   Retainer Only
Contact   Robert W. Sopo

Description An international firm, RWS Consulting provides extensive search services for executive and management-level personnel.

RXLPRO
30 rue Belioz, Suite 804
Île-des-Soeurs, QC H3E 1L3

Telephone   514-762-1947
Fax   514-879-8385
E-mail   cv@rxlpro.qc.ca
Website   www.rxlpro.qc.ca
Founded   1991
Specialties Computing
Level   Mid-Level
Contact   René Laporte

Description RXLPRO is a computer recruitment service providing technical personnel to more than 200 companies in the greater Montreal area.

S.I. SYSTEMS LTD.
1111 West Hastings St., Suite 520
Vancouver, BC V6E 2J3

Telephone   604-669-1387
Fax   604-669-2576
E-mail   tkearney@si
              systems.com
Website   www.sisystems.com
Founded   1994
Employees   10
Specialties Computing
Level   Senior
              Mid-Level
Fee Basis   Always contingent
Contact   Thaddeus Kearney,
              Account Manager

Description This office of S.i. Systems Ltd. (formerly West Point Integrated Technologies Inc.) provides IT consulting and recruiting services.

S.I. SYSTEMS LTD.
10130 - 103 Street, Suite 1350
Edmonton, AB T5J 3N9

Telephone   780-424-3999
Fax   780-426-0626
E-mail   arlene@sisystems.com
Website   www.sisystems.com
Specialties Computing
Contact   Arlene Breitkreuz,
              Senior Account
              Manager

Description S.i. Systems Ltd. matches IT professionals with client projects, specializing in software development.

S.I. SYSTEMS LTD.
202 - 6th Avenue SW, Suite 1000
Calgary, AB T2P 2R9

Telephone   403-264-4343
Fax   403-264-0929
E-mail   supportforce_calgary@
              sisystems.com
Website   www.sisystems.com
Specialties Computing
Level   Mid-Level
Recruiters   Larry Henderson
              Joanne Shaver
Contact   Larry Henderson,
              Branch Manager

Description S.i. Systems Ltd. matches IT professionals with client projects, specializing in software development.

S. TANNER & ASSOCIATES INC.
700 Dorval Drive, Suite 503
Oakville Corporate Centre
Oakville, ON L6K 3V3

Telephone   905-339-2233
Fax   905-339-2230
E-mail   stanner@
              globalserve.net
Website   www.globalserve.net/
              ~stanner
Founded   1986
Employees   2
Specialties Packaging
              Engineering
              Pharmaceutical
              Automotive
              Purchasing
              Logistics
Level   Mid-Level
Min. Salary $35,000
Fee Basis   Sometimes contingent
Contact   Steve Tanner

Description S. Tanner & Associates Inc. recruits professionals in the fields of engineering, operations management and logistics.

SAG RESSOURCES HUMAINES INC.
353, rue Saint-Nicolas, Bureau 310
Montréal, QC H2Y 2P1

Telephone   514-842-7171
Fax   514-842-0200
E-mail   info@sagrh.com
Website   www.sagrh.com
Founded   1987
Employees   6
Specialties Accounting
              Actuarial
              Computing
              Engineering
              Management
              Operations
              Telecom
Level   Mid-Level
              Senior
Fee Basis   Retainer Only
Recruiters   Nathalie Blouin
              Simon Gentile
              Gilles Rouleau
              Mathieu Simard
              Lorraine St-Cyr
              Sara Catherine St-Laurent
Contact   Gilles Rouleau

Description SAG ressources humaines inc. specializes in executive and professional searches.

SAI SOFTWARE CONSULTANTS, INC.
90 Snowshoe Crescent
Toronto, ON L3T 4M6

E-mail   toronto@saisoft.com
Website   www.saisoft.com
Founded   1986

Specialties Computing
International
Level Senior
Mid-Level
Description SAI Software Consultants, Inc. is a US-based provider of IT staffing services to Fortune 1000 companies.

SAI SOFTWARE CONSULTANTS, INC.
2313 Timber Shadows Dr., Suite 200
Kingwood, TX 77339 USA

Telephone 281-358-1858
Fax 281-358-8952
E-mail info@saisoft.com
Website www.saisoft.com
Founded 1986
Specialties Computing
International
Level Senior
Mid-Level
Contact Rao Tayi
Description SAI Software Consultants, Inc. is a US-based provider of IT staffing services to Fortune 1000 companies.

SAI SOFTWARE CONSULTANTS, INC.
222 - 3rd Avenue SE, Suite 506
Cedar Rapids, IA 52401 USA

Telephone 319-369-0484
Fax 319-363-5882
E-mail cedar.rapids@saisoft.com
Website www.saisoft.com
Founded 1984
Specialties Construction
International
Level Mid-Level
Senior
Contact Jeff Jackson
Description SAI Software Consultants, Inc. is a US-based provider of IT staffing services to Fortune 1000 companies.

SALESFORCE DEVELOPMENT LTD.
245, avenue Victoria, Bureau 520
Westmount, QC H3Z 2M6

Telephone 514-931-4201
Fax 514-939-3499
E-mail dtimmons@total.net
Specialties Sales
Marketing
Level Mid-Level
Contact Dennis Timmons

SALESSEARCH
17 Goodwill Avenue
Toronto, ON M3H 1V5

Telephone 416-636-3660
Fax 416-638-9997
E-mail ssearch@ionsys.com
Website www.salessearch-toronto.com

Founded 1969
Employees 2
Specialties Sales
Management
Marketing
Level Mid-Level
Min. Salary $25,000
Fee Basis Sometimes contingent
Contact Bob Glassberg, Manager
Description SalesSearch specializes in sales, marketing and related management recruitment.

SAM PERRI & ASSOCIATES
420 Britannia Road East
Mississauga, ON L4Z 3L5

Telephone 905-339-2237
Fax 905-339-2232
Specialties Automotive
Plastics
Engineering
Operations
Sales
Marketing
Level Mid-Level
Senior
Fee Basis Always contingent
Contact Sam Perri

SAPPHIRE TECHNOLOGIES
2323 Yonge Street, Suite 700
Toronto, ON M4P 2C9

Telephone 416-322-0930
Fax 416-322-3462
E-mail teena.shea@sapphireca.com
Website www.sapphireca.com
Specialties Computing
Description Sapphire Technologies places IT professionals in both contract and full-time positions.

SAULT & DISTRICT PERSONNEL SERVICES
1719 Trunk Road
Sault Ste. Marie, ON P6A 6X9

Telephone 705-759-6191
Fax 705-945-9678
Founded 1987
Specialties Administrative
Level Mid-Level
Junior
Contact R.H. Collins

SAUNDERS COMPANY, THE
477 Richmond St. West, Suite 509
Toronto, ON M5V 3E7

Telephone 416-703-0007
Fax 416-703-2045
E-mail djsco@idirect.com
Founded 1972
Specialties General Practice
Level Mid-Level
Senior
Fee Basis Retainer Only

Contact David Saunders, President

SAVAGE CONSULTANTS INC.
1066 West Hastings St., Suite 2000
Vancouver, BC V6E 3X2

Telephone 604-601-8222
Fax 604-669-3844
Founded 1991
Employees 5
Specialties Engineering
Accounting
Forestry
Human Resource
Management
Operations
Pulp & Paper
Level Senior
Mid-Level
Fee Basis Retainer Only
Recruiters A. Bill Calder
Jack D. MacDonald
John W. Savage
Contact John W. Savage
Description Savage Consultants Inc. provides a full range of search, human resources and labour relations consulting services.

SAYLER'S EMPLOYMENT & CONSULTING LTD.
10109 - 106th Street
Suite 703, Energy Square Building
Edmonton, AB T5J 3L7

Telephone 780-414-0990
Fax 780-414-0994
E-mail sayler@v-wave.com
Website www.saylersemployment.com
Founded 1993
Employees 6
Specialties Accounting
Finance
Level Mid-Level
Senior
Fee Basis Sometimes contingent
Recruiters Stacey Sayler
Judy Sayler
Contact Stacey Sayler
Description Sayler's Employment & Consulting specializes in recruiting, testing and placing qualified individuals in accounting positions.

SCARROW & DONALD
5 Donald Street, Suite 100
Winnipeg, MB R3L 2T4

Telephone 204-982-9809
Fax 204-474-2886
E-mail sd@scarrowdonald.mb.ca
Website www.scarrowdonald.mb.ca
Specialties Accounting
Finance
Level Mid-Level
Contact Peter J. Donald

Description Scarrow & Donald is an accounting firm that also provides occasional search services for clients.

SCHLESINGER NEWMAN GOLDMAN
625 René-Levesque Blvd. West
Suite 1600
Montréal, QC H3B 1R2

Telephone 514-866-8553
Fax 514-866-8469
E-mail cv@sng.ca
Website www.sng.ca

Specialties Accounting
Finance
Level Mid-Level
Recruiters Howard Berish
Jeffrey Greenburg
Stanley Hitzig
Stuart Ladd
Sonia Medvescek
Abe Zylberlicht
Contact Howard Berish

Description In business for over 60 years, Schlesinger Newman Goldman is a mid-sized accounting firm that also performs search services.

SCHOALES & ASSOCIATES INC.
145 King Street West, Suite 1000
Toronto, ON M5H 1J8

Telephone 416-863-9978
Fax 416-491-1223

Founded 1981
Employees 4
Specialties Marketing
Sales
Finance
Banking
Insurance
Level Senior
Mid-Level

Min. Salary $50,000
Fee Basis Sometimes contingent
Contact Michael Schoales

Description Schoales & Associates is one of Canada's leading executive search firms, specializing in recruiting for the brokerage and financial industries.

SCHWARTZ LEVITSKY FELDMAN
1167 Caledonia Road
Toronto, ON M6A 2X1

Telephone 416-785-5353
Fax 416-785-5663
E-mail eric.gollant@slf.ca
Website www.slf.ca

Specialties Accounting
Finance
Level Mid-Level
Contact Eric Gollant, Partner

Description SLF is an accounting firm that also does occasional search work for clients.

SCHWARTZ LEVITSKY FELDMAN
1980 Sherbrooke Street West
10th Floor
Montréal, QC H3H 1E8

Telephone 514-937-6392
Fax 514-933-9710
E-mail bernard.jeanty@slf.ca
Website www.slf.ca

Specialties Accounting
Finance
Level Mid-Level
Recruiters Farhat Ahmad
Luciano D'Ignazio
Morty Zafran FCA
Contact Luciano D'Ignazio

Description SLF is an accounting firm that also does search work for clients and has offices in Montreal, Toronto and Ottawa.

SCIENTIFIC PLACEMENT, INC.
PO Box 202676
Austin, TX 78720-2676
USA

Telephone 512-331-0302
Fax 512-331-1828
E-mail tml@scientific.com
Website www.scientific.com

Founded 1996
Specialties Scientific
Computing
Engineering
International
Level Mid-Level
Recruiters Beth Folmar
Tracy Lebel
Ryan Stockwell
Contact Tracy Lebel, Branch Manager

Description Scientific Placement, Inc. is a high-technology recruitment firm.

SCOTT, BATENCHUK & CO. LLP
3600 Billings Court, Suite 301
Burlington, ON L7N 3N6

Telephone 905-632-5978
Fax 905-632-9068
E-mail rwydryk@
scottbat.on.ca
Website www.scottbat.on.ca

Specialties Accounting
Finance
Level Mid-Level
Recruiters Glen Taylor CA
Robin J. Wydryk CA
Contact Robin J. Wydryk, CA

Description Scott, Batenchuk & Co. is an entrepreneurial firm of chartered accountants that also does search work for clients.

SCOTT HUBAND CONSULTING GROUP INC.
700 Dorval Drive, Suite 503
Oakville Corporate Centre
Oakville, ON L6K 3V3

Telephone 905-339-2145
Fax 905-339-2232
E-mail shcgi@globalserve.net
Specialties Management
Operations
Engineering
Automotive
Level Mid-Level
Senior
Contact Scott Huband

SCOTT WOLFE MANAGEMENT INC.
5423 Portage Avenue
Headingly, MB R4H 1E5

Telephone 204-987-7700
Fax 204-987-7705
E-mail wolfe@mb.
sympatico.ca
Founded 1992
Employees 7
Specialties Agriculture/Fisheries
Management
Scientific
Marketing
Biotech/Biology
Level Senior
Mid-Level
Min. Salary $45,000
Fee Basis Retainer Only
Contact Bob Hyde, CMC

Description Scott Wolfe Management Inc. provides a range of management consulting services to the agriculture and food sectors, including occasional recruitment.

SEARCH AHEAD LIMITED
12 Birch Avenue, Suite 200
Toronto, ON M4V 1C8

Telephone 416-975-8281
Fax 416-975-9841
E-mail recruit@
searchahead.com
Website www.searchahead.com
Specialties Computing
Level Mid-Level
Senior
Contact Lisa Orenbach, Owner

Description Search Ahead Limited is a leading-edge recruitment and placement agency for information systems professionals.

SEARCH ASSOCIATES
R.R. #5
Belleville, ON K8N 4Z5

Telephone 613-967-4902
Fax 613-967-8981
E-mail rbarlas@reach.net
Website www.
search-associates.com
Founded 1995
Specialties Education
International
Level Senior
Mid-Level
Fee Basis Sometimes contingent

Contact   Bob Barlas

Description Search Associates is an
educational recruitment agency specializing in the placement of qualified elementary and secondary
school teachers in international
schools overseas.

SEARCH COMPANY, THE
8 Oriole Gardens
Toronto, ON M4V 1V7

Telephone   416-972-9400
Fax   416-972-9460

Founded   1996
Employees   3

Specialties Public Relations
            General Practice
            Govt/Nonprofit
            Advertising
            Marketing

Level   Mid-Level
            Senior

Min. Salary $50,000
Fee Basis   Retainer Only

Contact   George Nutter, Partner

Description The Search Company, a
division of Strategic Search, specializes in senior and intermediate level
recruiting for public affairs, corporate communications, research and
marketing positions.

SEARCH EXCELLENCE INC.
2040 Sheppard Ave. East, Suite 208
Toronto, ON M2J 4B3

Telephone   416-756-1717
Fax   416-756-1371

Specialties Computing

Level   Mid-Level

Contact   Joseph Mak

Description Search Excellence Inc.
specializes in the Greater Toronto
Area information technology job
market.

SEARCH JUSTIFIED SELECTION INC.
40 King Street West
Suite 4900, Scotia Plaza
Toronto, ON M5H 4A2

Telephone   416-236-9944
E-mail   sjs@interlog.com

Founded   1992
Employees   2

Specialties Computing
            International
            Marketing
            Sales
            Management
            Telecom

Level   Mid-Level
            Senior

Min. Salary $70,000
Fee Basis   Retainer Only

Contact   Barbara Snow

Description Search Justified Selection Inc. specializes in recruiting for
the IT industry in Canada and the
USA.

SEARCHCORP INTERNATIONAL
550 - 17th Avenue SW, Main Floor
Calgary, AB T2S 0B1

Telephone   403-228-3071
Fax   403-228-5533
E-mail   info@
            baldwinstaffing.com
Website   www.baldwin
            staffing.com

Founded   1987
Employees   10

Specialties Computing
            Engineering
            Finance
            Oil & Gas
            Sales
            Marketing

Level   Mid-Level
            Senior

Contact   Steve Baldwin,
            President

Description SearchCorp International is a full-service recruitment
firm specializing in national and international IT, financial, engineering and sales opportunities.

SEARCHS / SASKATOON EMPLOY-MENT ACCESS RESOURCE CENTRE FOR HUMAN SERVICES
505 - 23rd Street East
Saskatoon, SK S7K 4K7

Telephone   306-343-3463
Fax   306-343-3460
E-mail   searchs@
            sk.sympatico.ca
Website   www.searchssask.com
Founded   1997
Employees   4

Specialties Disabled
Level   Junior
Recruiters Janice Brotheridge
            Brian Campbell
            Launel Scott
            Shari Thompson

Contact   Launel Scott,
            Coordinator

Description SEARCHs is a community-based organization helping people with disabilities find work.

SEARCHWEST INC.
595 Howe Street
Suite 1125
Vancouver, BC V6C 2T5

Telephone   604-684-4237
Fax   604-684-4240
E-mail   terry@searchwest.ca
Website   www.searchwest.ca
Founded   1991
Employees   2

Specialties Marketing
            Pharmaceutical
            Sales
            Telecom

Level   Mid-Level
            Junior

Min. Salary $30,000
Fee Basis   Sometimes contingent

Recruiters Jeff Abram
            Terry Vanderkruyk
Contact   Terry Vanderkruyk,
            Partner

Description SearchWest Inc. is a recruitment firm specializing in sales
and marketing professionals. Practice areas include consumer, medical, pharmaceutical, technical, high-
tech, telecom and business-to-business services.

SEGALL & ASSOCIATES INC.
235 Yorkland Blvd., Suite 300
Toronto, ON M2J 4Y8

Telephone   416-492-7333
Fax   416-492-7413
E-mail   ronas@netcom.ca

Specialties Sales
            Marketing
            Telecom

Level   Senior
            Mid-Level

Fee Basis   Sometimes contingent
Recruiters Helene Brown
            Claire Pressman
            Rona Segall
Contact   Rona Segall

Description Segall & Associates Inc.
specializes in sales and marketing
specialists serving the telecommunications and IT industries.

SELECTION GROUP MANAGEMENT SERVICES
2800 Skymark Avenue, Suite 32
Mississauga, ON L4W 5A6

Telephone   905-238-1300
Fax   905-238-0753

Specialties Engineering
            Finance
            Management

Level   Mid-Level
Contact   Susan Strickland

SELECTIVE PERSONNEL
14 Irwin Avenue, Suite 300
Toronto, ON M4Y 1K9

Telephone   416-962-5153
Fax   416-922-6983
E-mail   selective@direct.com

Specialties Health/Medical
Level   Mid-Level
            Junior

Contact   Hana Havlicek

Description Selective Personnel provides homecare staffing.

SELLUTIONS INC.
39 Robertson Road
Suite 205
Nepean, ON K2H 8R2

Telephone   613-820-2422
Fax   613-248-4830
E-mail   djohnson@
            sellutions4success.com

Website   www.sellutions4
            success.com
Founded   1996
Specialties Sales
            Marketing
Level   Mid-Level
Contact   Diane Johnson

Description Sellutions Inc. is an HR consulting firm specializing in sales force training. They occasionally provide recruitment services for clients.

SENAC PERSONNEL SERVICES
5200 Finch Avenue East, Suite 311
Toronto, ON M1S 4Z4

Telephone 416-321-3730
Fax   416-321-8144
E-mail   info@senacc.com
Website   www.senacc.com
Specialties Administrative
            Law
Level   Mid-Level
            Junior

Description Senac Personnel places employees with administrative, legal, computer and customer service experience.

SENIORS FOR BUSINESS
55 Eglinton Avenue East, Suite 311
Toronto, ON M4P 1G8

Telephone 416-481-4579
Fax   416-481-6752
Specialties Management
Level   Mid-Level
Contact   Peter Cook

Description Seniors for Business specializes in placing people 55 years old and over.

SERECON MANAGEMENT CONSULTING INC.
10665 Jasper Avenue
Suite 600, First Edmonton Place
Edmonton, AB T5J 3S9

Telephone 780-448-7440
Fax   780-421-1270
E-mail   info@serecon.ca
Website   www.serecon.ca
Specialties Agriculture/Fisheries
Contact   Ann Boyda

Description Serecon is a management consulting firm active in the agricultural industry that occasionally does search work for clients.

SERVICE DB INC.
2543, rue Centre
Montréal, QC H3K 1J9

Téléphone 514-934-5681
Télécopieur 514-939-6458
Spécialités Transport
Échelon   Intermédiaire
             Débutant

Contact   François B. Amour,
             Directeur

SERVICE DE PERSONNEL EXPRESS
170, rue Beaubien Est
Montréal, QC H2S 1R2

Téléphone 514-277-3175
Télécopieur 514-270-8576
Spécialités Transport
Échelon   Intermédiaire
             Débutant

Contact   Jaclyne Charland

SERVOCRAFT LIMITED
325 Lesmill Road
Toronto, ON M3B 2V1

Telephone 416-391-2229
Fax   416-391-4998
E-mail   scl@servocraft.com
Website   www.servocraft.com
Founded   1982
Employees 6
Specialties Engineering
            International
            Construction
            Management
            Oil & Gas
            Purchasing
Level   Mid-Level
            Senior
Fee Basis Retainer Only
Contact   Vazken Terzian,
            Vice-President

Description Servocraft Limited is a consulting engineering firm that also assists with technical placements in the fields of engineering and procurement.

SHANNON HUMAN RESOURCES
120 Sheppard Avenue West
Toronto, ON M2N 1M5

Telephone 416-224-5884
Fax   416-224-2827
Specialties Administrative
            Banking
Level   Mid-Level
            Junior
Contact   Shannon Doyle

Description Shannon Human Resources recruits a full range of administrative and office personnel.

SHARED VISION MANAGEMENT SEARCH INC.
548 King Street West, Suite 202
Toronto, ON M5V 1M3

Telephone 416-703-9768
Fax   416-703-9774
E-mail   confidential@
            sharedvision.on.ca
Website   www.shared
            vision.on.ca
Founded   1999
Employees 20
Specialties Advertising
            Banking
            Direct Mktng.
            Govt/Nonprofit
            Graphic Arts
            Insurance
            International
Level   Senior
Min. Salary $70,000
Fee Basis Sometimes contingent
Contact   Cyril Plummer,
            President and Founder

Description Shared Vision accepts assignments only within their industry expertise, and practices the Executive Recruiter Association's code of ethics.

SHELDON RECRUITING
40 Eglinton Avenue East, Suite 306
Toronto, ON M4P 3A2

Telephone 416-489-6969
Founded   1977
Specialties Retail
            Apparel
Level   Senior
            Mid-Level
Min. Salary $65,000
Fee Basis Retainer Only
Contact   Barbara L. Sheldon,
            President

Description Sheldon Recruiting places senior managers with specialty retailers and their suppliers.

SHELDON RESNICK ASSOCIATES
145 King Street W., Suite 1000
Toronto, ON M5H 1J8

Telephone 416-360-5518
Fax   416-360-6436
Employees 1
Specialties Banking
            Finance
Level   Senior
            Mid-Level
Min. Salary $70,000
Contact   Sheldon Resnick

SHERWOOD ENGINEERING RECRUITMENT
Sherwood House, Aldwarke Road
Parkgate, Rotherham
South Yorkshire S62 6BU
UNITED KINGDOM

Telephone 44-1709-710800
Fax   44-1709-710880
E-mail   robert@sherwoodrec.
            force9.co.uk
Website   www.sherwood
            rec.force9.co.uk
Specialties International
            Engineering
Contact   Robert Sykes

Description Sherwood Engineering Recruitment is an engineering recruitment consultancy run by engineers for engineers.

SHL GROUP
10 Bay Street, Suite 600
Waterpark Place
Toronto, ON M5J 2N8

Telephone	416-361-3454
Fax	416-361-1114
E-mail	resume-can@shlgroup.com
Website	www.shlgroup.com
Founded	1977
Specialties	General Practice
Level	Senior Mid-Level

Description SHL is a UK-based consultancy that offers a full range of HR services, including selection and recruitment.

SHL GROUP
275 Slater Street, Suite 2004
Ottawa, ON K1P 5H9

Telephone	613-569-1110
Fax	613-569-1118
E-mail	resume-can@shlgroup.com
Website	www.shlgroup.com
Specialties	General Practice
Level	Senior Mid-Level

Description SHL is a UK-based consultancy that offers a full range of HR services, including selection and recruitment.

SHORE & FITZWILLIAM
1155 University Street, Suite 1414
Montréal, QC H3B 3A7

Telephone	514-940-5353
Fax	514-878-2473
E-mail	info@shorefitzwilliam.com
Website	www.shorefitzwilliam.com
Founded	1993
Specialties	Law
Level	Mid-Level Senior
Min. Salary	$65,000
Fee Basis	Retainer Only
Recruiters	Peter Bateman Carol A. Fitzwilliam Barbara Shore M.A.
Contact	Barbara Shore

Description Shore & Fitzwilliam is a dedicated legal recruitment practice and is a preferred supplier to the Canadian Bar Association, Quebec Division.

SILICON EXECUTIVE SEARCH INC.
4214 Dundas Street West
Toronto, ON M8X 1Y6

Telephone	416-232-0600
E-mail	josie_erent@hotmail.com
Founded	2000
Employees	1
Specialties	Computing Telecom Sales
Level	Mid-Level Senior
Min. Salary	$75,000
Fee Basis	Always contingent
Contact	Josie Erent

Description Silicon Executive Search is an IT recruitment company that focuses on the IT vendor market.

SILICON NETWORK, THE
40 King Street W.
Suite 4900, Scotia Plaza
Toronto, ON M5H 4A2

Telephone	416-777-6746
Fax	416-777-6748
E-mail	silicon@passport.ca
Founded	1989
Employees	5
Specialties	Computing Sales Telecom Engineering
Level	Mid-Level
Fee Basis	Sometimes contingent
Recruiters	Lucy Cunningham Mike Fernandez Rolph Larson
Contact	Mike Fernandez

Description The Silicon Network specializes in placing data and telecom professionals in positions such as systems engineers, project management, marketing and sales.

SIMMONS GROUP INC.
4316 - 117th Street NW
Edmonton, AB T6J 1T8

Telephone	780-944-1711
Specialties	General Practice
Level	Mid-Level

SIMON A. BULL & ASSOCIATES
Cambridge Centre, PO Box 20046
Cambridge, ON N1R 8C8

Telephone	519-622-9000
Fax	519-740-3439
E-mail	careers@simonbull.com
Website	www.simonbull.com
Founded	1978
Specialties	Automotive
Level	Mid-Level Senior
Min. Salary	$50,000
Contact	Simon A. Bull

Description Simon A. Bull & Associates specializes in recruitment in automotive OEM, automotive parts manufacturing, automotive systems integration and capital equipment design and build.

SIMON-TECH INC.
2075, rue University, Bureau 1710
Montréal, QC H3A 2L1

Téléphone	514-845-6800
Télécopieur	514-845-9090
Courriel	simon-tech@jobsimon.com
Site Internet	www.jobsimon.com
Spécialités	Aérospatial International
Échelon	Intermédiaire
Contact	Guy Pendleton

SIMPSON MCGRATH INC.
1780 Wellington Avenue, Suite 99
Winnipeg, MB R3H 1B3

Telephone	204-940-3420
Fax	204-940-3429
E-mail	smi@mim.ca
Specialties	Finance Management Human Resource Operations Scientific
Level	Mid-Level Senior
Contact	Leslie A. Johnson CMC

SINCLAIR SMITH & ASSOCIATES LTD.
3607 Elie Auclair
Sainte-Polycarpe, QC J0P 1X0

Telephone	450-265-3539
Fax	450-265-4018
E-mail	sinclair@rocler.qc.ca
Website	www.sinclair-smithassoc.com
Founded	1968
Specialties	Engineering
Level	Mid-Level Senior
Contact	Michael Sinclair-Smith

Description Sinclair Smith & Associates Ltd. specializes in engineering and executive engineering recruitment.

SIRIUS PERSONNEL INC.
2001, rue University, Bureau 810
Montréal, QC H3A 2A6

Telephone	514-844-8449
Fax	514-844-0004
E-mail	info@siriuspersonne.com
Website	www.siriuspersonnel.com
Founded	1998
Specialties	Sales Retail
Level	Mid-Level
Contact	Pascal Becotte

Description Sirius Personnel specializes exclusively in the recruitment of sales professionals for all industry sectors in Quebec and Eastern Ontario.

SKILL TECH
3500 Fairview Street, Unit B5
Burlington, ON L7N 2R5

Telephone	905-333-4424
Fax	905-333-9585
E-mail	info@skilltech.net
Website	www.skilltech.net
Founded	1986
Specialties	Trades/Technicians
Level	Mid-Level

Description Skill Tech is a professional employment agency specializing in the placement of professional tradespeople for industry.

SKOTT/EDWARDS CONSULTANTS
1776 On the Green
Morristown, NJ 07960
USA

Telephone	973-644-0900
Fax	973-644-0991
E-mail	search@skottedwards.com
Website	www.skottedwards.com
Founded	1974
Specialties	Pharmaceutical International Health/Medical Bilingual Computing
Level	Senior
Fee Basis	Retainer Only
Recruiters	Frank Barbosa Skott B. Burkland Julie Burkland Charlie Grebenstein Lee Moldock Joe Ryan
Contact	Skott B. Burkland

Description Skott/Edwards is a retained executive search service specializing in corporate governance, pharmaceuticals, biotechnology, medical devices, healthcare and IT services.

SLANEY MANAGEMENT CONSULTING
332 Queensway West, PO Box 367
Simcoe, ON N3Y 2N1

Telephone	519-426-9842
Fax	519-426-9039
E-mail	slaneyomac@on.aibn.com
Specialties	Health/Medical Insurance Govt/Nonprofit
Level	Mid-Level
Contact	Bryan Slaney

Description Slaney Management Consulting is a consulting firm that also does regular recruitment work for clients.

SLATE GROUP, THE
10130 - 103rd Street, Suite 950
Edmonton, AB T5J 3N9

Telephone	780-424-7528
Fax	780-426-7528
E-mail	info@slate.ab.ca
Website	www.slate.ab.ca
Founded	1964
Employees	12
Specialties	Accounting Computing Insurance Administrative
Level	Mid-Level
Contact	Jake Rust, Agency Manager

Description The Slate Group has been active in the Edmonton personnel, employment and training scene for over 30 years.

SMC MANAGEMENT SERVICES
161 Briston Private
Ottawa, ON K1G 5R3

Telephone	613-247-9327
Fax	613-247-1781
E-mail	toby@web.net
Specialties	Govt/Nonprofit
Contact	Toby Rabinovitz

Description SMC is a management consulting firm that does occasional recruitment work for the nonprofit sector.

SMITH, NIXON & CO.
320 Bay Street, Suite 1600
Toronto, ON M5H 4A6

Telephone	416-361-1622
Fax	416-367-1238
E-mail	info@smith-nixon.com
Website	www.smith-nixon.com
Founded	1962
Specialties	Accounting Finance
Level	Mid-Level

Description Smith, Nixon & Co. is a full-service accounting firm that also does occasional search work for clients.

SMYTHE RATCLIFFE
355 Burrard Street
Suite 700
Vancouver, BC V6C 2G8

Telephone	604-687-1231
Fax	604-688-4675
E-mail	johnson@smytheratcliffe.com
Website	www.smytheratcliffe.com
Specialties	Accounting Finance
Level	Mid-Level
Recruiters	Anita Johnson CA Norman Ratcliffe Stacey Werboweski W.R. (Bill) Wright
Contact	Norman Ratcliffe

Description Smythe Ratcliffe is an accounting firm that regularly does search work for clients.

SNELGROVE PERSONNEL CONSULTANTS
107 George Street
Hamilton, ON L8P 1E3

Telephone	905-522-5200
Fax	905-522-5506
Employees	4
Specialties	Computing Finance Accounting Sales Bilingual Management Marketing
Level	Mid-Level Senior
Recruiters	Janet Snelgrove Graham Snelgrove
Contact	Janet Snelgrove

SOBOT STONE CONSULTANTS
2550 Argentia Road, Suite 119
Mississauga, ON L5N 5R1

Telephone	905-821-2033
Fax	905-821-4890
Specialties	General Practice

SOCIÉTÉ JEAN PIERRE BRISE-BOIS INDUSTRIAL / ORGANIZATIONAL PSYCHOLOGY INC.
2015 Peel Street, Suite 1015
Montréal, QC II3A 1T8

Telephone	514-987-0202
Fax	514-987-0204
E-mail	admin@societejpb.com
Website	www.societejpb.com
Employees	4
Specialties	Management Bilingual Finance Human Resource International Operations
Level	Senior
Min. Salary	$80,000
Fee Basis	Retainer Only
Recruiters	Jean-Pierre Brisebois Sylvie Marchand
Contact	Pauline St-Pierre

Description Société Jean Pierre Brisebois specializes in executive recruitment, as well as career pathing, organizational development, succession planning and change management.

SOCIÉTÉ PIERRE BOUCHER / SPB BUSINESS PSYCHOLOGY
375 Roland-Therrien Boulevard
Suite 501
Longueuil, QC J4H 4A6

Telephone	450-646-1022
Fax	450-646-5184
E-mail	recherchecadres@spb.ca
Website	www.spb.ca
Specialties	General Practice

Level	Mid-Level
	Senior
Contact	Pierre Boucher

Description SPB offers value-added recruitment services in the field of organizational / industrial psychology.

SOFTCOM CONSULTING INC.
30 East Beaver Creek Road
Suite 212
Richmond Hill, ON L4B 1J2

Telephone	905-771-9650
Fax	905-707-6889
Founded	1994
Specialties	Computing
Level	Senior
	Mid-Level
Fee Basis	Always contingent
Contact	Mabel Yu

Description Softcom Consulting Inc. is an IT consulting firm that places computing professionals on contract assignments.

SOLUTIONS
225 Pitt Street
Cornwall, ON K6J 3P8

Telephone	613-936-2728
Fax	613-936-6685
E-mail	bryan@solutions.on.ca
Website	www.solutions.on.ca
Founded	1990
Employees	9
Specialties	Accounting
	Bilingual
	Computing
	Govt/Nonprofit
	Health/Medical
	Insurance
	Law
	Packaging
	Administrative
Fee Basis	Sometimes contingent
Recruiters	Sue Crites
	Bryan Merkley
Contact	Bryan Merkley

Description SOLUTIONS, a member of the Association of Canadian Search, Employment and Staffing Services (ACSESS), offers professional, attentive service backed by years of experience.

SOS PERSONNEL INC.
189 Wellington Street, Unit 2
Sarnia, ON N7T 1G6

Telephone	519-336-6620
Fax	519-336-7531
E-mail	sos@wwdc.com
Website	www.front.net/qsinc/
	sos
Founded	1963
Employees	4
Specialties	Trades/Technicians
	Administrative
	Engineering

Level	Mid-Level
	Junior
Contact	Lilly DiRezze CGA,
	President

Description Sarnia's first employment agency, providing professional and effective service to businesses of all sizes.

SOURCECO EXECUTIVE SEARCH
10665 Jasper Avenue
Suite 900, First Edmonton Place
Edmonton, AB T5J 3S9

Telephone	780-439-3502
Fax	780-439-3499
E-mail	sourceco@ican.net
Founded	1998
Employees	3
Specialties	Telecom
	Sales
	Management
	Engineering
	Marketing
	Direct Mktng.
	Computing
Level	Mid-Level
	Senior
Fee Basis	Sometimes contingent
Contact	Peter Simpson, Partner

Description Sourceco Executive Search are recruiting and search professionals in datacom/telecom, broadband, wireless, WAN / LAN and fibre optics for national carriers, CLECs and service providers.

SOURCECO EXECUTIVE SEARCH
245, avenue Victoria, Bureau 520
Westmount, QC H3Z 2M6

Telephone	514-939-3502
Fax	514-939-3499
E-mail	sourceco@ican.net
Founded	1998
Employees	3
Specialties	Telecom
	Sales
	Management
	Engineering
	Marketing
	Direct Mktng.
	Computing
Level	Senior
	Mid-Level
Fee Basis	Sometimes contingent

Description Sourceco Executive Search are recruiting and search professionals in datacom / telecom, broadband, wireless, WAN / LAN and fibre optics for national carriers, CLECs and service providers.

SOUTHWEST HUMAN RESOURCES CENTRE LTD.
2050 Cornwall Street, Suite 110
Regina, SK S4P 2K5

Telephone	306-569-9945
Fax	306-569-3533
Specialties	Govt/Nonprofit
	Disabled

Contact	Kim LaLiberte

Description Southwest Human Resources is a nonprofit employment agency that specializes in finding employment for people who face barriers to finding employment.

SPECIAL NEEDS EMPLOYMENT SERVICES / SNES
265 Front Street North, Suite 405
Sarnia, ON N7T 7X1

Telephone	519-337-7377
Fax	519-337-9040
E-mail	snes@ebtech.net
Website	www.specialneeds
	employment.com
Specialties	Disabled
Contact	Kelly Adams

Description SNES is a non-profit, charitable organization that provides career counselling and consulting services to assist adults with employment barriers.

SPECTRUM & ASSOCIATES EXECUTIVE SEARCH
3800 Steeles Avenue West, Suite 2
Woodbridge, ON L4L 4G9

Telephone	905-856-3954
Fax	905-856-9463
Specialties	General Practice
Level	Senior
Contact	Frances Vaianisi

SPECTRUM COMPUTER PERSONNEL INC.
1071 King Street West, Suite 327
Toronto, ON M6K 3K2

Telephone	416-345-8043
Fax	416-490-0566
E-mail	headhntr@interlog.com
Website	www.interlog.com/
	~hedhntr
Founded	1994
Specialties	Computing
Contact	John Papish, President

Description Spectrum Computer Personnel Inc. is a Toronto-based agency specializing in contract and permanent jobs for computer professionals in the Greater Toronto Area and in the USA.

SPECTRUM HEALTH CARE
180 Bloor Street West, Suite 1000
Toronto, ON M5S 2V6

Telephone	416-964-0322
Fax	416-964-0912
E-mail	admin-spectrum@
	spectrumhealthcare.com
Website	www.spectrum
	healthcare.com
Founded	1977
Specialties	Health/Medical
Level	Mid-Level
	Junior

Contact   Mitchell Gallinger,
            President

Description Spectrum Health Care
provides community nursing and
home support services.

SPENCER STUART

Alameda Santos, 1787, 10th Floor
São Paolo, SP, 01419-010
BRAZIL

Telephone   55-11-284-0349
Fax   55-11-289-1159
E-mail   gdale@
            spencerstuart.com
Website   www.spencer
            stuart.com

Specialties International
            General Practice
Level   Senior
Fee Basis   Retainer Only
Recruiters Guilherme de Noronha Dale
            Rudolf Mayer-Sinqule
            Zoila Pinto

Contact   Guilherme de Noronha Dale

Description Operating 50 offices
across 24 countries, Spencer Stuart
specializes in leadership appointments in a broad range of industries.

SPENCER STUART

Schaumainkai 69
Frankfurt, 60596
GERMANY

Telephone   49-69-610-9270
Fax   49-69-610-92750
E-mail   yramm@
            spencerstuart.com
Website   www.spencer
            stuart.com

Specialties International
            General Practice
Level   Senior
Fee Basis   Retainer Only
Recruiters Otto Obermaier
            Uwe Pavel
            Yvonne Ramm
            Lutz Tilker

Contact   Yvonne Ramm,
            Office Manager

Description Operating 50 offices
across 24 countries, Spencer Stuart
specializes in leadership appointments in a broad range of industries.

SPENCER STUART

12, Via Visconti di Modrone
Milan, 20122   ITALY

Telephone   39-02-771251
Fax   39-02-782452
E-mail   bcolumbo@
            spencerstuart.com
Website   www.spencer
            stuart.com

Specialties International
            General Practice
Level   Senior
Fee Basis   Retainer Only

Recruiters Mauro Capriata
            Bruno Columbo
            Umberto B. Dell'Orto
            Maurizia L. Leto di Priolo
            Simone Maggioni
            Luca Pacces
            Maurizio Pozzetti
            Luciana Sommaruga

Contact   Bruno Columbo

Description Operating 50 offices
across 24 countries, Spencer Stuart
specializes in leadership appointments in a broad range of industries.

SPENCER STUART

401 N. Michigan Ave., Suite 3400
Chicago, IL 60611   USA

Telephone   312-822-0080
Fax   312-822-0116
E-mail   kconnelly@
            spencerstuart.com
Website   www.spencer
            stuart.com

Specialties International
            General Practice
Level   Senior
Fee Basis   Retainer Only
Recruiters Karl Aavik
            Richard Brennen
            Virginia Clarke
            Kevin Connelly
            James J. Drury III
            Paul Earle
            J. Curtis Fee
            Amanda Fox
            Joseph Kopsick
            Christopher Nadherny
            John Puisis
            Don Render
            Robert Shields
            Toni Smith
            Thomas Snyder
            Gilbert Stenholm
            H. Alvan Turner
            Peter Urbain
            Gail Vergara
            Patrick Walsh
            Gregory Welch

Contact   Kevin Connelly,
            Office Manager

Description Operating 50 offices
across 24 countries, Spencer Stuart
specializes in leadership appointments in a broad range of industries.

SPENCER STUART

2005 Market St., Suite 2350
1 Commerce Square
Philadelphia, PA 19103   USA

Telephone   215-851-6201
Fax   215-963-0181
E-mail   cmccann@
            spencerstuart.com
Website   www.spencer
            stuart.com

Specialties International
            General Practice
Level   Senior
Fee Basis   Retainer Only
Recruiters Jeffrey Bell
            Dennis Carey

            Peter Goossens
            Jennifer Herrmann
            Frank Marsteller
            Connie McCann
            Jeffrey Wierichs

Contact   Connie McCann,
            Office Manager

Description Operating 50 offices
across 24 countries, Spencer Stuart
specializes in leadership appointments in a broad range of industries.

SPENCER STUART & ASSOCIATES (CANADA) LTD.

1 University Avenue, Suite 801
Toronto, ON M5J 2P1

Telephone   416-361-0311
Fax   416-361-6118
E-mail   jhauswirth@
            spencerstuart.com
Website   www.spencer
            stuart.com

Founded   1956
Employees   20
Specialties Management
            Computing
            Finance
            Banking
            Biotech/Biology
            Health/Medical
            Real Estate
            Telecom
            Insurance
            Publishing/Media
            Engineering
            Public Relations
Level   Senior
Min. Salary $100,000
Fee Basis   Retainer Only
Recruiters Tori Barton
            Gerald W. Bliley
            Roger M. Clarkson
            Noel Desautels
            Jeffrey M. Hauswirth
            David MacEachern
            Andrew McDougall
            Michelle M. Morin
            Sharon Rudy

Contact   Jeffrey Hauswirth,
            Office Manager

Description Operating 50 offices
across 24 countries, Spencer Stuart
specializes in leadership appointments in a broad range of industries.

SPENCER STUART & ASSOCIATES (CANADA) LTD.

1981, avenue McGill College
Bureau 1430
Montréal, QC H3A 2Y1

Telephone   514-288-3777
Fax   514-288-4626
E-mail   rnadeau@
            spencerstuart.com
Website   www.spencer
            stuart.com

Employees   7
Specialties Engineering
            Management
            Human Resource
            Law

	Computing
Level	Senior
Min. Salary	$100,000
Fee Basis	Retainer Only
Recruiters	Robert Nadeau
	Jerome Piche
	Manon Vennat
Contact	Robert Nadeau, Office
	Manager

Description Operating 50 offices across 24 countries, Spencer Stuart specializes in leadership appointments in a broad range of industries.

SPENCER STUART & ASSOCIATES / SELECTOR PACIFIC

10 Des Voeux Road, Central
17th Floor, Bank of East Asia Bldg.
Hong Kong   CHINA

Telephone	852-2521-8373
Fax	852-2810-5246
E-mail	mtang@
	spencerstuart.com
Website	www.spencer
	stuart.com
Specialties	Management
	International
	General Practice
Level	Senior
Fee Basis	Retainer Only
Recruiters	Timothy Hoffman
	Margaret Lee
	Martin Tang
	Janet Tung
Contact	Martin Tang,
	Office Manager

Description Operating 50 offices across 24 countries, Spencer Stuart specializes in leadership appointments in a broad range of industries.

SPHERION WORKFORCE ARCHITECTS

880 Douglas Street, Suite 204
Victoria, BC V8W 2B7

Telephone	250-383-1389
Fax	250-360-1685
Website	www.spherion.com
Specialties	Accounting
	Govt/Nonprofit
	Sales
	Administrative
	Banking
Level	Mid-Level

Description Spherion Workforce Architects (formerly Bradson Staffing) is a $3.8 billion global human capital management company with more than 1000 offices around the world.

SPHERION WORKFORCE ARCHITECTS

1166 Alberni Street, Suite 1201
Vancouver, BC V6E 3Z3

Telephone	604-688-9556
Fax	604-682-0955
E-mail	lnovak@spherion.ca

Website	www.spherion.com
Specialties	Accounting
	Administrative
	Banking
	Govt/Nonprofit
	Sales
Level	Mid-Level

Description Spherion Workforce Architects (formerly Bradson Staffing) is a $3.8 billion global human capital management company with more than 1000 offices around the world.

SPHERION WORKFORCE ARCHITECTS

14907 - 111th Avenue
Edmonton, AB T5M 2P6

Telephone	780-444-6677
Fax	780-489-2399
Website	www.spherion.com
Specialties	Accounting
	Banking
	Sales
	Administrative
	Govt/Nonprofit
Level	Mid-Level
Contact	Wendy Tchir,
	Operations Manager

Description Spherion Workforce Architects (formerly Bradson Staffing) is a $3.8 billion global human capital management company with more than 1000 offices around the world.

SPHERION WORKFORCE ARCHITECTS

10025 Jasper Avenue, Main Floor
Edmonton, AB T5J 1S6

Telephone	780-426-6666
Fax	780-424-8115
Website	www.spherion.com
Specialties	Accounting
	Administrative
	Govt/Nonprofit
	Banking
	Sales
Level	Mid-Level
Fee Basis	Always contingent
Recruiters	Stephen Routhier
	Allan Wong
Contact	Stephen Routhier

Description Spherion Workforce Architects (formerly Bradson Staffing) is a $3.8 billion global human capital management company with more than 1000 offices around the world.

SPHERION WORKFORCE ARCHITECTS

736 - 8th Avenue SW, Suite 1040
Calgary, AB T2P 1H4

Telephone	403-266-1082
Fax	403-265-5024
Website	www.spherion.com
Specialties	Accounting

	Administrative
	Banking
	Govt/Nonprofit
	Sales
Level	Mid-Level

Description Spherion Workforce Architects (formerly Bradson Staffing) is a $3.8 billion global human capital management company with more than 1000 offices around the world.

SPHERION WORKFORCE ARCHITECTS

294 Portage Avenue, Suite 300
Winnipeg, MB R3C 0B9

Telephone	204-943-5211
Fax	204-953-0954
E-mail	winnipeg@spherion.ca
Website	www.spherion.com
Founded	1986
Employees	4
Specialties	Accounting
	Administrative
	Govt/Nonprofit
	Banking
	Sales
Level	Mid-Level
Fee Basis	Always contingent
Recruiters	Pat Ferens
	Berniece Johnson
	Carol Rebeck
	Terri Tysowski
Contact	Berniece Johnson,
	Branch Manager

Description Spherion Workforce Architects (formerly Bradson Staffing) is a $3.8 billion global human capital management company with more than 1000 offices around the world.

SPHERION WORKFORCE ARCHITECTS

171 Queens Avenue, Suite 409
London, ON N6A 5J7

Telephone	519-673-5574
Fax	519-673-6939
E-mail	jdecosse@spherion.ca
Website	www.bradson.com
Specialties	Administrative
	Direct Mktng.
Level	Mid-Level
Fee Basis	Always contingent

Description Spherion Workforce Architects (formerly Bradson Tele-Staffing) is a $3 billion human capital management organization that helps companies enhance workforce performance.

SPHERION WORKFORCE ARCHITECTS

655 Bay Street, Suite 13
Toronto, ON M5G 2K4

Telephone	416-596-3434
Fax	416-596-8150
E-mail	telestaffing@
	spherion.ca

Website	www.spherion.com
Founded	1959
Employees	6
Specialties	Sales Accounting Administrative Banking Govt/Nonprofit
Level	Mid-Level Junior
Fee Basis	Always contingent
Contact	Rupinder Ahluwalia

Description Spherion Workforce Architects (formerly Bradson Staffing) is a $3.8 billion global human capital management company with more than 1000 offices around the world.

SPHERION WORKFORCE ARCHITECTS
235 Yorkland Blvd., Suite 109
Toronto, ON   M2J 4Y8

Telephone	416-494-3434
Fax	416-494-2887
Website	www.spherion.com
Specialties	Accounting Govt/Nonprofit Sales Administrative Banking
Level	Mid-Level
Fee Basis	Always contingent
Contact	Ishbel Wilkie

Description Spherion Workforce Architects (formerly Bradson Staffing) is a $3.8 billion global human capital management company with more than 1000 offices around the world.

SPHERION WORKFORCE ARCHITECTS
20 Commander Boulevard
Toronto, ON   M1S 3L9

Telephone	416-295-5393
Website	www.spherion.com
Specialties	Accounting Administrative Banking Govt/Nonprofit Sales
Level	Mid-Level
Fee Basis	Always contingent

Description Spherion Workforce Architects (formerly Bradson Staffing) is a $3.8 billion global human capital management company with more than 1000 offices around the world.

SPHERION WORKFORCE ARCHITECTS
2100 Ellesmere Road
Toronto, ON   M1H 3B7

Telephone	416-431-6077
Website	www.spherion.com
Specialties	Accounting

	Administrative Banking Govt/Nonprofit Sales
Level	Mid-Level
Fee Basis	Always contingent

Description Spherion Workforce Architects (formerly Bradson Staffing) is a $3.8 billion global human capital management company with more than 1000 offices around the world.

SPHERION WORKFORCE ARCHITECTS
16 Harlowe Road, Unit 1
Hamilton, ON   L8W 3R6

Telephone	888-851-8494
Fax	905-387-0504
Website	www.spherion.com
Specialties	Accounting Administrative Banking Govt/Nonprofit Sales
Level	Mid-Level
Fee Basis	Always contingent

Description Spherion Workforce Architects (formerly Bradson Staffing) is a $3.8 billion global human capital management company with more than 1000 offices around the world.

SPHERION WORKFORCE ARCHITECTS
253 Queen Street East, Unit 5
Brampton, ON   L6W 2B8

Telephone	905-452-7110
Fax	905-452-7663
Website	www.spherion.com
Founded	1957
Specialties	Accounting Trades/Technicians Logistics Packaging Pharmaceutical Plastics
Level	Mid-Level
Fee Basis	Sometimes contingent
Recruiters	Josie Agostino John Barrie Sam Gough Crystal Paulitzki
Contact	John Barrie, Branch Manager

Description Spherion Workforce Architects (formerly Bradson Staffing) is a $3.8 billion global human capital management company with over 1000 offices around the world.

SPHERION WORKFORCE ARCHITECTS
4 Robert Speck Parkway, Suite 210
Mississauga, ON   L4Z 1S1

Telephone	905-896-1055
Fax	905-896-1035

Website	www.spherion.com
Founded	1957
Specialties	Accounting Banking Computing Engineering Govt/Nonprofit Insurance Marketing
Level	Mid-Level Junior
Fee Basis	Always contingent
Recruiters	Andrea Favreau Judy Lindenbach
Contact	Judy Lindenbach, Vice President

Description Spherion Workforce Architects (formerly Bradson Staffing) is a $3.8 billion global human capital management company with more than 1000 offices around the world.

SPHERION WORKFORCE ARCHITECTS
2700 Matheson Blvd. East
Mississauga, ON   L4W 4V9

Telephone	905-361-1550
Website	www.spherion.com
Specialties	Accounting Administrative Banking Govt/Nonprofit Sales
Level	Mid-Level
Fee Basis	Always contingent

Description Spherion Workforce Architects (formerly Bradson Staffing) is a $3.8 billion global human capital management company with more than 1000 offices around the world.

SPHERION WORKFORCE ARCHITECTS
64 Cedar Pointe Drive, Unit 1411
Barrie, ON   L4N 5R7

Telephone	705-735-1106
Fax	705-735-6346
Website	www.spherion.com
Specialties	Accounting Administrative Banking Govt/Nonprofit Sales
Level	Mid-Level
Fee Basis	Always contingent

Description Spherion Workforce Architects (formerly Bradson Staffing) is a $3.8 billion global human capital management company with more than 1000 offices around the world.

SPHERION WORKFORCE ARCHITECTS
1125 Squires Beach Road
Pickering, ON   L1W 3T9

Telephone	905-426-6332
Website	www.spherion.com
Specialties	Accounting
	Administrative
	Banking
	Govt/Nonprofit
	Sales
Level	Mid-Level
Fee Basis	Always contingent

Description Spherion Workforce Architects (formerly Bradson Staffing) is a $3.8 billion global human capital management company with more than 1000 offices around the world.

SPHERION WORKFORCE ARCHITECTS
111 Consumers Drive
Whitby, ON L1N 1C4

Telephone	905-430-4258
Website	www.spherion.com
Specialties	Accounting
	Administrative
	Banking
	Govt/Nonprofit
	Sales
Level	Mid-Level
Fee Basis	Always contingent

Description Spherion Workforce Architects (formerly Bradson Staffing) is a $3.8 billion global human capital management company with more than 1000 offices around the world.

SPHERION WORKFORCE ARCHITECTS
419 King Street, Suite 604
Oshawa, ON L1J 2K5

Telephone	905-579-2911
Website	www.spherion.com
Specialties	Accounting
	Administrative
	Banking
	Govt/Nonprofit
	Sales
Level	Mid-Level
Fee Basis	Always contingent

Description Spherion Workforce Architects (formerly Bradson Staffing) is a $3.8 billion global human capital management company with more than 1000 offices around the world.

SPHERION WORKFORCE ARCHITECTS
50 Colchester Square
Kanata, ON K2K 2Z9

Telephone	613-270-8282
Website	www.spherion.com
Specialties	Accounting
	Administrative
	Banking
	Govt/Nonprofit
	Sales
Level	Mid-Level

Fee Basis	Always contingent

Description Spherion Workforce Architects (formerly Bradson Staffing) is a $3.8 billion global human capital management company with more than 1000 offices around the world.

SPHERION WORKFORCE ARCHITECTS
440 Laurier Ave. West, Suite 120
Ottawa, ON K1R 7X6

Telephone	613-782-2333
Fax	613-782-2434
E-mail	lmcdougall@ spherion.ca
Website	www.spherion.com
Founded	1957
Employees	92
Specialties	Accounting
	Administrative
	Banking
	Govt/Nonprofit
	Sales
Level	Mid-Level
Fee Basis	Always contingent
Contact	Wendy Windle

Description Spherion Workforce Architects (formerly Bradson Staffing) is a $3.8 billion global human capital management company with more than 1000 offices around the world.

SPHERION WORKFORCE ARCHITECTS
112 Nelson Street
Ottawa, ON K1N 7R5

Telephone	613-782-2400
Website	www.spherion.com
Specialties	Accounting
	Administrative
	Banking
	Govt/Nonprofit
	Sales
Level	Mid-Level
Fee Basis	Always contingent

Description Spherion Workforce Architects (formerly Bradson Staffing) is a $3.8 billion global human capital management company with more than 1000 offices around the world.

SPHERION WORKFORCE ARCHITECTS
800 René-Lévesque Blvd. Ouest
Bureau 2450
Montréal, QC H3B 4V7

Telephone	514-874-8014
Fax	514-861-1441
Website	www.spherion.com
Specialties	Bilingual
	Accounting
	Administrative
	Banking
	Govt/Nonprofit
	Sales
Level	Mid-Level

Fee Basis	Always contingent
Contact	Jacqueline Gilbert

Description Spherion Workforce Architects (formerly Bradson Staffing) is a $3.8 billion global human capital management company with more than 1000 offices around the world.

SPHERION WORKFORCE ARCHITECTS
1791 Barrington Street, Suite 1130
Halifax, NS B3J 3K9

Telephone	902-422-9675
Fax	902-420-0156
Website	www.spherion.com
Specialties	Health/Medical
	Sales
	Accounting
	Administrative
	Banking
Level	Mid-Level
Fee Basis	Always contingent
Contact	Angela Jefferies

Description Spherion Workforce Architects (formerly Bradson Staffing) is a $3.8 billion global human capital management company with more than 1000 offices around the world.

SPI EXECUTIVE SEARCH
170 Laurier Avenue W., Suite 1200
Ottawa, ON K1P 5V5

Telephone	613-234-8503
Fax	613-234-2593
E-mail	general@spi.ca
Website	www.spi.ca
Founded	1985
Employees	6
Specialties	Operations
	Management
	Computing
	Human Resource
	Sales
Level	Mid-Level
	Senior
Fee Basis	Always contingent
Contact	Jeremy Ingle, Managing Partner

SQUIRES RESOURCES INC.
301 Bryne Drive, Unit 6
Barrie, ON L4N 8V4

Telephone	705-725-7660
Fax	705-725-7665
E-mail	resume@ squiresresources.com
Website	www.squires resources.com
Founded	1992
Employees	6
Specialties	Accounting
	Computing
	International
Level	Mid-Level
Min. Salary	$40,000
Fee Basis	Sometimes contingent

Recruiters   Rebecca d'Amboise
              Frank Squires
              Jason Squires
              Jocelyn Squires
              Dave Squires
              David White

Contact   Frank Squires

Description Squires Resources Inc. is a recruitment company specializing in placing IT professionals in Canada, Bermuda and the Caribbean.

SSA SERVICES CONSEILS
2075, rue University, Bureau 450
Montréal, QC H3A 2L1

Telephone   514-288-6388
Fax   514-288-5947
E-mail   info1@ssacons.qc.ca

Founded   1994
Employees   16

Specialties Logistics
             Marketing
             Multimedia
             Telecom
             Direct Mktng.
             Computing
             Engineering
             Sales

Level   Senior
             Mid-Level

Fee Basis   Sometimes contingent

Recruiters   Joceline Lemieux
             Lucy Martineau

Contact   Joceline Lemieux,
             Managing Partner

Description SSA is an executive search firm specializing in telecommunications and call centres, with an extensive network of contacts and in-depth niche market knowledge.

ST-AMOUR & ASSOCIATES
191 The West Mall, Suite 1010
Toronto, ON M9C 5K8

Telephone   416-626-6151
Fax   416-620-7189
E-mail   careers@st-amour.com
Website   www.st-amour.com

Specialties Marketing
             Sales
             Management
             Scientific
             Engineering

Level   Mid-Level
             Senior

Recruiters   Charles Benham
             Paul Bichler
             Paul Copcutt
             Jeff Courey
             Kevin Desjardins
             Ron Fine
             Marcus Garrison
             John Pallidino
             Steve Sampson
             David Street
             Brian Vickery

Contact   Jeff Courey

Description With offices in Montreal and Toronto, St-Amour & Associates is one of Canada's leaders in personnel recruitment, particularly for sales and marketing positions.

ST-AMOUR & ASSOCIATES
666 Sherbrooke Street West
Suite 2000
Montréal, QC H3A 1E7

Telephone   514-288-7400
Fax   514-288-6745
E-mail   info@st-amour.com
Website   www.st-amour.com

Founded   1975
Employees   18

Specialties Sales
             Marketing
             Management
             Scientific
             Engineering
             Computing

Level   Mid-Level
             Senior

Recruiters   Stephane Beauchemin
             Marc Beaudoin
             Jacques Bédard
             Steve Bélanger
             Benoît Charlebois
             Michel Guay
             Stéphane Kubic
             Michel LeBoeuf
             Pierre Lussier
             Robert Myers
             Jean Perreault
             Emmauelle Pocreau
             Fernand Poltrini
             Alain Renaud
             Luc Samson
             Leslie St-Amour

Contact   Michel Guay, Vice
             President

Description With offices in Montreal and Toronto, St-Amour & Associates is one of Canada's leaders in personnel recruitment, particularly for sales and marketing positions.

STAFF BUREAU EMPLOYMENT GROUP
10020 - 101A Avenue NW, Suite 650
Phipps-McKinnon Building
Edmonton, AB T5J 3G2

Telephone   780-420-6083
Fax   780-423-2431
E-mail   staffbur@
             telusplanet.net
Website   www.telusplanet.net/
             public/staffbur

Founded   1981
Employees   7

Specialties Management
             Marketing
             Sales
             Pharmaceutical
             Finance
             Oil & Gas
             Accounting

Level   Mid-Level

Fee Basis   Always contingent

Recruiters   Lucille Barton CPC

             Christine Chater
             Diane Dawson
             Connie Duguid CPC
             Pat Lover CHRP

Contact   Christine Chater

Description Staff Bureau Employment Group is a full-service placement firm specializing in recruiting for sales / marketing, accounting / finance, information technology, senior management and engineering positions.

STAFF PLUS
6 Lansing Square, Suite 221
Toronto, ON M2J 1T5

Telephone   416-495-0900
Fax   416-495-0941
E-mail   dgosseli@netcom.ca

Specialties Administrative
             Accounting
             Banking

Level   Mid-Level

Fee Basis   Always contingent

Contact   Derek Gosselin

Description Staff Plus specializes in recruiting for administrative positions. Call toll-fgree: 1-888-509-3222.

STAFFING STRATEGIES LLC
2400 Augusta, Suite 248
Houston, TX 77057   USA

Telephone   281-646-1299
Fax   281-693-3094
E-mail   resumes@ staffing-
             strategies.com
Website   www.staffing
             strategies.com

Founded   1997

Specialties International
             Sales

Level   Mid-Level

Description Staffing Strategies LLC has recruited higher-level sales positions in Canada for clients in Houston. Call toll-free: 1-877-619-1180.

STAFFWORKS
1235 Bay Street, Suite 305
Toronto, ON M5R 3K4

Telephone   416-927-7575
Fax   416-927-7806
E-mail   leslyc@
             staffworkscanada.com
Website   www.staffworks
             canada.com

Specialties Administrative
             Accounting

Level   Junior
             Mid-Level

Recruiters   Lesly Carranza
             Palma Renaud
             Sandra Sears

Contact   Lesly Carranza

Description StaffWorks provides quality administrative personnel for contract and permanent assignments.

STAR SEARCH CONSULTANTS
211 Consumers Road, Suite 204
Toronto, ON M2J 4G8

Telephone	416-491-4440
Fax	416-491-4451
E-mail	star@searchstar.com
Website	www.searchstar.com

Employees 4

Specialties Administrative
Management
Engineering
Trades/Technicians
Finance
Computing
Sales

Level Senior
Mid-Level

Contact John Weiss, Manager

Description Star Search has provided quality service for over 25 years, recruiting the most important asset of small entrepreneurial and Fortune 500 companies alike — outstanding people.

STARDOT PRG INC.
808 Nelson St. Ste. 1700, Box 12148
Vancouver, BC V6Z 2H2

Telephone	604-838-1759
Fax	604-685-8993
E-mail	jobs@stardotprg.com
Website	www.stardotprg.com

Specialties Computing

Level Mid-Level

Contact Don M. Berard, VP
Finance

Description StarDot PRG Inc. specializes in the contract and permanent placement of quality information technology personnel.

STARDOT PRG INC.
10180 - 101 Street, Suite 1150
Edmonton, AB T5J 3S4

Telephone	780-424-8733
Fax	780-424-8732
E-mail	jobs@stardotprg.com
Website	www.stardotprg.ca

Specialties Computing

Level Mid-Level

Contact Don M. Berard, VP
Finance

Description StarDot PRG Inc. special izes in the contract and permanent placement of quality IT personnel.

STARDOT PRG INC.
633 - 6th Avenue SW, Suite 2020
Calgary, AB T2P 2Y5

Telephone	403-264-3897
Fax	403-264-3901
E-mail	jobs@stardotprg.com
Website	www.stardotprg.ca

Specialties Computing

Level Mid-Level

Recruiters Don M. Berard
Alice M. Matthews
Don Van Mierlo

Contact Don M. Berard, VP
Finance

Description StarDot PRG Inc. specializes in the contract and permanent placement of quality information technology personnel.

STARDOT PRG INC.
1 Yonge Street, Suite 1801
Toronto, ON M5E 1W7

Telephone	416-363-6822
Fax	416-369-0515
E-mail	jobs@stardotprg.com
Website	www.stardotprg.ca

Specialties Computing

Level Mid-Level

Contact Don M. Berard, VP
Finance

Description StarDot PRG Inc. specializes in the contract and permanent placement of quality information technology personnel.

STARDOT PRG INC.
416, rue Saint-Cloude
Montréal, QC H2Y 4A8

Telephone	514-871-0721
Fax	514-871-0724
E-mail	jobs@stardotprg.com
Website	www.stardotprg.ca

Specialties Computing

Contact Don M. Berard,
VP Finance

Description StarDot PRG Inc. specializes in the contract and permanent placement of quality information technology personnel.

STELLAR PERSONNEL PLACEMENT
500 Goyeau Street
Windsor, ON N9A 1H2

Telephone	519-977-5291
Fax	519-977-8864
E-mail	windsor@ stellarplacement.com
Website	www.stellar placement.com

Founded 1994

Specialties Computing
Management
Marketing
Sales
Engineering
Automotive
Administrative

Level Mid-Level
Junior

Contact Beth Kelly

Description Stellar serves a range of clients in the London-Windsor area.

STELLAR PERSONNEL PLACEMENT
2417 Main Street
PO Box 459, Lambeth Station
London, ON N6P 1P9

Telephone	519-652-2540
Fax	519-652-5683
E-mail	stellar@ stellarplacement.com
Website	www.stellar placement.com

Founded 1994

Specialties Administrative
Automotive
Computing
Engineering
Management
Marketing
Sales

Level Mid-Level
Junior

Contact Gord Peach

Description Stellar Personnel Placement serves a wide range of clients in the London-Windsor corridor.

STEPHEN ASHLEY ASSOCIATES
130 King Street West
Suite 1800, Exchange Tower
Toronto, ON M5X 1E3

Fax	416-947-0167
E-mail	sa@stephenashley.com
Website	www.stephen ashley.com

Specialties Finance

Level Senior

Contact Stephen Ashley

Description Stephen Ashley Associates is an executive search consulting firm.

STEPHEN GOLDSTEIN & ASSOCIATES
195 Clearview Avenue, Suite 1210
Ottawa, ON K1Z 6S1

Telephone	613-724-4844
Fax	613-724-1173
E-mail	golds@compmore.net

Specialties General Practice
Management
International
Govt/Nonprofit
Computing
Human Resource
Administrative

Min. Salary	$30,000
Fee Basis	Sometimes contingent

Contact Stephen Goldstein

Description Stephen Goldstein & Associates does general human resources consulting, including search and assessment.

STEPHEN LARAMEE & ASSOCIATES INC.
1 Yonge Street, Suite 1801
Toronto, ON M5E 1W7

Telephone	877-897-1474
Fax	416-369-0515
E-mail	slaramee@ compuserve.com
Website	www.laramee associates.com

Founded   1976
Employees   2
Specialties Accounting
              Engineering
              Management
              Marketing
              Operations
              Purchasing
              Sales

Level   Mid-Level
              Senior

Min. Salary $35,000
Fee Basis   Sometimes contingent

Contact   Stephen Laramee

Description Search assignments from coast to coast.

STERLING HOFFMAN
425 University Avenue, 8th Floor
Toronto, ON M5G 1T6

Telephone   416-979-6701
Fax   416-979-3030
E-mail   info@
              sterlinghoffman.com
Website   www.sterling
              hoffman.com

Specialties Computing
              Sales

Level   Senior

Description Sterling Hoffman recruits exclusively software CEOs and executives for venture capital companies and software companies. The firm also locates sales executives for mid-sized software companies.

STERLING HOFFMAN
2880 Zanker Road, Suite 203
San Jose, CA 95134   USA

Telephone   408-954-7310
Fax   408-432-7235
E-mail   info@sterling
              hoffman.com
Website   www.sterling
              hoffman.com

Specialties Computing
              International
              Sales

Description Sterling Hoffman recruits software CEOs and executives on behalf of venture capital companies and software companies. The firm also locates sales executives for mid-sized software companies.

STEVENS RESOURCE GROUP INC.
1071 Wellington Road, Suite 200
London, ON N6E 1W4

Telephone   519-668-7702
Fax   519-668-6859
E-mail   london@stevens
              resourcegroup.com
Website   www.stevens
              resourcegroup.com

Specialties Trades/Technicians
              Operations
              Administrative

Level   Mid-Level
              Junior

Description Stevens Resource Group (formerly 9 To 5 Personnel Services Inc.) specializes in training and development, human resources, staffing and executive search services.

STEVENS RESOURCE GROUP INC.
368 Cambria Street, Suite 205
Stratford, ON N5A 1J4

Telephone   519-273-7000
Fax   519-273-9395
E-mail   stratford@stevens
              resourcegroup.com
Website   www.stevens
              resourcegroup.com

Specialties Administrative
              Operations
              Trades/Technicians

Description Stevens Resource Group (formerly 9 To 5 Personnel Services Inc.) specializes in training and development, human resources, staffing and executive search services.

STEVENS RESOURCE GROUP INC.
496 Adelaide Street
Woodstock, ON N4S 4B4

Telephone   519-421-9556
Fax   519-421-0237
E-mail   woodstock@stevens
              resourcegroup.com
Website   www.stevens
              resourcegroup.com

Specialties Administrative
              Operations
              Trades/Technicians

Level   Mid-Level
              Junior

Description Stevens Resource Group (formerly 9 To 5 Personnel Services Inc.) specializes in training and development, human resources, staffing and executive search services.

STEVENS RESOURCE GROUP INC.
185 Broadway Street
Tillsonburg, ON N4G 3P9

Telephone   519-842-7003
Fax   519-842-4887
E-mail   tillsonburg@stevens
              resourcegroup.com
Website   www.stevens
              resourcegroup.com

Specialties General Practice
              Administrative
              Operations
              Trades/Technicians

Level   Mid-Level
              Junior

Description Stevens Resource Group (formerly 9 To 5 Personnel Services Inc.) specializes in training and development, human resources, staffing and executive search services.

STEVENS RESOURCE GROUP INC.
325 West Street, Suite 203A
Brantford, ON N3R 6B7

Telephone   519-751-7707
Fax   519-751-2373

E-mail   brantford@stevens
              resourcegroup.com
Website   www.stevens
              resourcegroup.com

Specialties Administrative
              Operations
              Trades/Technicians

Level   Mid-Level
              Junior

Description Stevens Resource Group (formerly 9 To 5 Personnel Services Inc.) specializes in training and development, human resources, staffing and executive search services.

STEVENS RESOURCE GROUP INC.
260 Holiday Inn Drive, Suite 25
Cambridge, ON N3C 4E8

Telephone   519-249-0077
Fax   519-249-0309
E-mail   cambridge@stevens
              resourcegroup.com
Website   www.stevens
              resourcegroup.com

Specialties Administrative
              Operations
              Trades/Technicians

Level   Mid-Level
              Junior

Contact   Sherri Stevens,
              President

Description Stevens Resource Group (formerly 9 To 5 Personnel Services Inc.) specializes in training and development, human resources, staffing and executive search services.

STEVENSON & WHITE INC.
2301 Carling Avenue, Suite 201
Ottawa, ON K2B 7G3

Telephone   613-225-5417
Fax   613-225-0913
E-mail   info@stevenson
              andwhite.com
Website   www.stevenson
              andwhite.com

Specialties Finance
              Accounting

Level   Mid-Level
              Senior

Recruiters Anne Stevenson
              Trevor White

Contact   Anne Stevenson

Description Stevenson & White specializes in the recruitment and placement of full-time financial and accounting professionals.

STOAKLEY-DUDLEY CONSULTANTS LTD.
6547 Mississauga Road N., Unit A
Mississauga, ON L5N 1A6

Telephone   905-821-3455
Fax   905-821-3467
E-mail   stoakley@stoakley.com
Website   www.stoakley.com

Founded   1978
Employees   9

Specialties	Telecom
	Engineering
	Sales
	Management
	Automotive
	Accounting
	Plastics
Level	Senior
	Mid-Level
Min. Salary	$30,000
Fee Basis	Sometimes contingent
Recruiters	Don Christensen
	Susan Clarke
	Patrick Laforet
	Deborah Milo
	Reg Shortt
	Ernie Stoakley CPC
	Steven Watts
Contact	Ernie Stoakley, CPC

Description Specializes in placing hardware and software developers, electronics, engineering, manufacturing, sales, marketing, senior-management, finance and executive positions. Member ACSESS, NPA.

STOKES ASSOCIATES
1874 Parkside Drive
Pickering, ON L1V 3R2

Telephone	416-580-2159
E-mail	stokesinc@
	sympatico.ca
Website	www.davestokes.com
Founded	1977
Specialties	Printing
	Packaging
	Graphic Arts
Level	Senior
	Mid-Level
Min. Salary	$40,000
Fee Basis	Sometimes contingent
Contact	H. David Stokes

Description Stokes Associates specializes in the pre-press, printing and packaging industries.

STONE LEGAL RESOURCES GROUP
50 Milk Street, 5th Floor
Boston, MA 02109 USA

Telephone	617-482-1400
Fax	617-482-6018
E-mail	info@stonelegal.com
Website	www.stonelegal.com
Specialties	International
	Law
Level	Senior
Contact	Peter Twining

Description Stone Legal Resources Group provides search and consulting services to lawyers, paralegals and administrative professionals.

STONEWOOD GROUP
330 Bay Street, Suite 1100
Toronto, ON M5H 2S8

Telephone	416-365-9494
Fax	416-365-7081
E-mail	info@stonewood
	group.com
Website	www.stonewood
	group.com
Founded	1991
Employees	8
Specialties	Management
	Engineering
	Aerospace
	Telecom
	Computing
	Multimedia
	Scientific
Level	Senior
Min. Salary	$100,000
Fee Basis	Retainer Only
Recruiters	Robert Hebert
	Sal Rocco
	Larry Sartor
	Leigh Walsh
Contact	Robert Hebert

Description Stonewood Group offers a full range of assessment and executive search services to aid organizations in making key selection and hiring decisions.

STONEWOOD GROUP
34 Birchdale Avenue
Ottawa, ON K2H 5A1

Telephone	613-282-3038
Fax	613-829-7759
E-mail	info@stonewood
	group.com
Website	www.stonewood
	group.com
Specialties	Aerospace
	Computing
	Engineering
	Management
	Multimedia
	Scientific
	Telecom
Level	Senior
Fee Basis	Retainer Only
Contact	Greg Boyle, Partner

Description Stonewood Group offers a full range of assessment and executive search services to aid organizations in making key selection and hiring decisions.

STONEWOOD GROUP
64, de la Plage Riviera
Sainte-Geneviève, QC H9H 4T9

Telephone	514-696-3968
Fax	514-696-3480
E-mail	info@stonewood
	group.com
Website	www.stonewood
	group.com
Specialties	Aerospace
	Computing
	Engineering
	Management
	Multimedia
	Scientific
	Telecom
Level	Senior
Fee Basis	Retainer Only

Contact	Gerard Benchetrit,
	Partner

Description Stonewood Group offers a full range of assessment and executive search services to aid organizations in making key selection and hiring decisions.

STOP THE WORLD INC.
347 Bay Street, Suite 1000
Toronto, ON M5M 2R7

Telephone	416-366-3844
Fax	416-366-5705
E-mail	kirsten@stopthe
	world.com
Website	www.stoptheworld.com
Specialties	Computing
Contact	Kirsten Barr

Description Stop The World Inc. is a Canadian placement agency specializing in contract and permanent opportunities in the IT sector.

STOPKA & ASSOCIATES
65 Queen Street West, Suite 2110
Toronto, ON M5H 2M5

Telephone	416-203-2266
Fax	416-203-1622
E-mail	toronto@stopka.com
Website	www.stopka.com
Founded	1995
Specialties	Computing
Contact	Bruce Stopka, President

Description Stopka & Associates provides competent and ethical technical staff to the world's most successful companies.

STOREY & ASSOCIATES
67 Yonge Street, Suite 700
Toronto, ON M5E 1J8

Telephone	416-366-1212
Fax	416-366-4100
E-mail	mail@storey.on.ca
Website	www.storey.on.ca
Founded	1991
Employees	16
Specialties	Marketing
	Multimedia
	Finance
Level	Mid-Level
	Senior
Min. Salary	$60,000
Fee Basis	Sometimes contingent
Recruiters	John Brownlee
	Andrew Gartha
	Matt Rivers
	Susan Rogers
	Glen Schultz
	Catherine Storey
	Roy Storey
	Dave Walls
Contact	Anthony Smith

Description Storey & Associates specializes in marketing placements in several fields, including consumer packaged goods, finance, database marketing, market research and multimedia.

STRATEGIC RESOURCES INTERNATIONAL INC.
299 Roehampton Ave., Suite 1125
Toronto, ON M4P 1S2

Telephone	416-487-6053
Fax	416-487-6292
E-mail	dkettle@istar.ca
Specialties	Computing
	Engineering
	Management
	Multimedia
	Quality Control
	Sales
	Telecom
Level	Mid-Level
	Senior
Min. Salary	$50,000
Fee Basis	Always contingent
Contact	Dave Kettle

Description Specializing in the telecom and information technology arena, including software and hardware development, engineering sales and management.

SUMMIT PERSONNEL SERVICES INC.
6630 Tecumseh Road East
Windsor, ON N8T 1E6

Telephone	519-944-6070
Specialties	Accounting
	Administrative
	Automotive
	Engineering
	Human Resource
	Management
	Quality Control
Level	Mid-Level
	Junior
Fee Basis	Sometimes contingent
Recruiters	Richard Fox
	Karen Haycox
	Kim Ryan
Contact	Kim Ryan

Description Summit Personnel Services is a full-service personnel agency specializing in cost-effective staffing solutions for client placement needs.

SUMMIT SEARCH GROUP
400 - 5th Avenue SW, Suite 300
Calgary, AB T2P 0L6

Telephone	403-303-2727
Fax	403-303-2728
E-mail	mail@summit searchgroup.com
Website	www.summit searchgroup.com
Specialties	Health/Medical
	Management
	Oil & Gas
	Sales
	Telecom
	Transport
Level	Mid-Level
Fee Basis	Sometimes contingent
Recruiters	Darrell Dvorak
	Gareon Fox
	Bruce Proctor

Contact	Bruce Proctor

Description Summit Search Group is a recruitment firm specializing in sales, marketing and management positions.

SURPRENANT RESSOURCES MÉDIA INC.
1100, rue de la Gauchetière Ouest
Bureau 246
Montréal, QC H3B 2S2

Téléphone	514-394-1002
Télécopieur	514-394-1097
Courriel	nathalie@surprenant-ressources-media.com
Site Internet	www.surprenant-ressources-media.com
Fondée	1998
Spécialités	Marketing
	Multimédia
	Affaires publiques
Échelon	Direction
	Intermédiaire
Contact	Nathalie Surprenant

Description Depuis plus de 3 ans, Surprenant ressources média s'est spécialisée dans le recrutement et le placement de personnel en communication, marketing, multimédia et publicité.

SUSAN CRAIG ASSOCIATES INC.
371 Berkeley Street
Toronto, ON M5A 2X8

Telephone	416-960-5062
Fax	416-960-6467
E-mail	susan@susancraig.com
Website	www.susancraig.com
Founded	1996
Employees	6
Specialties	Health/Medical
	International
Level	Senior
Fee Basis	Sometimes contingent
Contact	Susan J. Craig

Description Susan Craig Associates is dedicated to successfully relocating eligible doctors, nurses, health care executives and professionals in the US, Canada and overseas.

SUSSEX RETAIL MANAGEMENT
1550 Enterprise Road, Suite 300
Mississauga, ON L4W 4P4

Telephone	905-795-1988
Fax	519-742-3282
E-mail	jan@sussexretail.com
Website	www.sussexretail.com
Specialties	Retail
Level	Mid-Level
	Senior
Recruiters	Jan Ciuciura
	Kevin Graff
Contact	Jan Ciuciura

Description Sussex is a management consulting firm specializing in the retail sector. Their services include

recruiting management candidates for clients.

SYDELLE ASSOCIATES
PO Box 146
Georgetown, ON L7G 4T1

Telephone	905-702-8229
Fax	905-702-8296
E-mail	sydelle@attcanada.ca
Founded	1999
Employees	2
Specialties	Administrative
	Finance
	Logistics
	Marketing
	Purchasing
	Sales
	Bilingual
	Accounting
Level	Mid-Level
	Junior
Min. Salary	$35,000
Fee Basis	Sometimes contingent
Contact	Michelle Elliott

Description Sydelle Associates are specialists in providing professional, finance and administrative candidates.

SYMMETRY SEARCH GROUP INC.
250 Consumers Road, Suite 502
Toronto, ON M2J 4V6

Telephone	416-756-9077
Fax	416-756-9080
E-mail	stu@symmetry search.com
Website	www.symmetry search.com
Specialties	Computing
	Finance
	Accounting
	Engineering
	Logistics
	Management
	Pharmaceutical
Level	Mid-Level
Fee Basis	Retainer Only
Contact	Jim McRae

Description Symmetry Search Group is a full-service search firm.

SYNAGENT INC.
5412 Torbolton Ridge Road
Woodlawn, ON K0A 3M0

Telephone	613-832-1122
Fax	613-832-1227
E-mail	john.bickerstaff@synagent.com
Website	www.synagent.com
Founded	1986
Employees	2
Specialties	Banking
	Finance
	Sales
	Automotive
Level	Senior
	Mid-Level
Min. Salary	$50,000

Fee Basis	Sometimes contingent
Recruiters	Julie Bédard
	John Bickerstaff
Contact	John Bickerstaff,
	President

Description Synagent Inc. is an executive search firm specializing in equipment and vehicle leasing, inventory financing, banking and financial services for clients in the US and Canada.

SYNAPTUIT GROUP
318 Homer Street, Suite 401
Vancouver, BC V6B 2V2

Telephone	604-602-4388
Fax	604-602-7511
E-mail	brenda@synaptuit.com
Website	www.synaptuit.com
Specialties	Public Relations
	Marketing
Recruiters	Angela Harris
	Brenda Plowman
	Bonnie Plowman
	Diana Ross
Contact	Brenda Plowman

Description SynapTuit Group is a new management consulting firm that also does recruitment work for clients in the field of marketing and public relations.

SYNERGIES RESSOURCES HUMAINES
181 rue Bonaventure, CP 788
Trois-Rivières, QC G9A 5J9

Téléphone	819-691-2505
Télécopieur	819-691-2496
Courriel	srh@tr.cgocable.ca
Fondée	1991
Employés	8
Spécialités	Consultatif
	Ressources humaines
	Gestion
Échelon	Direction
	Intermédiaire
Contact	Carole Menguy

SYNERGY SEARCH CONSULTANTS
100 Lombard Street, Suite 105
Toronto, ON M5C 1M3

Telephone	416-365-1891
Fax	416-367-0068
E-mail	dave@synergy
	search.on.ca
Founded	2000
Employees	5
Specialties	Computing
Level	Senior
	Mid-Level
Min. Salary	$30,000
Fee Basis	Sometimes contingent
Recruiters	Dave Clements
	Wally Follett
	Marc Roberts
Contact	Dave Clements

Description Synergy Search specializes recruiting IT professionals for full-time and contract assignments.

SYNERSOFT DISTRIBUTION INC.
204 rue St-Sacrement, 7ièm Étage
Montreal, QC H2Y 1W8

Téléphone	514-858-6333
Télécopieur	514-858-6334
Courriel	jpesetti@synersoft.ca
Site Internet	www.synersoft.ca
Fondée	1996
Spécialités	Gestion
Échelon	Direction
	Intermédiaire

Description Depuis 1996, Synersoft offre à ses clients des services d'impartition en matière de gestion du recrutement.

SYNTECH PLACEMENTS INC.
5650 Yonge Street, Suite 1500
Toronto, ON M2M 4G3

Telephone	416-512-2525
Fax	416-512-8304
E-mail	lnoorden@syntech-employment.com
Website	www.syntech-employment.com
Founded	1987
Employees	10
Specialties	Retail
	Management
	Engineering
	Aerospace
	Automotive
	Human Resource
	International
Level	Senior
	Mid-Level
Fee Basis	Sometimes contingent
Recruiters	Gord Lyons
	Louis Noorden
	Tim Robert
	Tim Ryan
	Dan Yolleck
Contact	Louis Noorden

Description Syntech Placements Inc. specializes in permanent and contract employment, testing, coaching and consulting services.

SYSTEMATIX INFORMATION TECHNOLOGY CONSULTANTS INC.
555 West - 8th Avenue, Suite 401
Vancouver, BC V5Z 1C6

Telephone	604-872-0038
Fax	604-872-0089
E-mail	scivan@systematix.com
Website	www.systematix.com
Founded	1975
Employees	500
Specialties	Computing
Level	Mid-Level
Recruiters	Annette Albrecht
	Dennis Duggan
Contact	Annette Albrecht,
	Recruiter

Description Systematix is a leading IT consulting firm that works with over 500 consultants in seven offices across Canada.

SYSTEMATIX INFORMATION TECHNOLOGY CONSULTANTS INC.
10405 Jasper Avenue
Suite 120
Edmonton, AB T5J 3N4

Telephone	780-421-7767
Fax	780-428-1775
E-mail	sciedm@systematix.com
Website	www.systematix.com
Founded	1975
Specialties	Computing
Level	Mid-Level
Recruiters	Lyle Dahl
	Janice Fernie
	Don Hughes
Contact	Janice Fernie, Recruiter

Description Systematix is a leading IT consulting firm that works with over 500 consultants in seven offices across Canada.

SYSTEMATIX INFORMATION TECHNOLOGY CONSULTANTS INC.
815 - 8th Avenue SW
Suite 1410
Calgary, AB T2P 3P2

Telephone	403-237-8990
Fax	403-233-0036
E-mail	sciclg@systematix.com
Website	www.systematix.com
Founded	1975
Employees	500
Specialties	Computing
Level	Mid-Level
Recruiters	Siania Biehl
	Henry Nizynski
Contact	Siania Biehl, Recruiter

Description Systematix is a leading IT consulting firm that works with over 500 consultants in seven offices across Canada.

SYSTEMATIX INFORMATION TECHNOLOGY CONSULTANTS INC.
320 Front Street West
Suite 830
Toronto, ON M5V 3B6

Telephone	416-595-5331
Fax	416-595-1525
E-mail	scitor@systematix.com
Website	www.systematix.com
Specialties	Computing
Level	Mid-Level
Recruiters	Henk Oudman
	Eric Pitters
	Brent Zions
Contact	Lisa Silva, Recruiter

Description Systematix is a leading IT consulting firm that works with over 500 consultants in seven offices across Canada.

SYSTEMATIX INFORMATION TECHNOLOGY CONSULTANTS INC.
141 Laurier Ave. West, Suite 366
Ottawa, ON K1P 5J3

Telephone	613-567-8939
Fax	613-567-1916
E-mail	sciott@systematix.com
Website	www.systematix.com
Founded	1975
Specialties	Computing
Level	Mid-Level
Recruiters	Laury Dacre
	Lucie Huneault
	Carolyn Mitchell
	Heather Penney
	Les Templeton
	Marilyn Theriault
Contact	Heather Penney, Recruiter

Description Systematix is a leading IT consulting firm that works with over 500 consultants in seven offices across Canada.

SYSTEMATIX INFORMATION TECHNOLOGY CONSULTANTS INC.
1 Place Ville Marie, Bureau 1601
Montréal, QC H3B 2B6

Telephone	514-393-1313
Fax	514-393-8997
E-mail	scimtl@systematix.com
Website	www.systematix.com
Founded	1975
Specialties	Computing
Level	Mid-Level
Recruiters	Jocelyne Alaire
	Richard Charpentier
	Tom Cummings
	Tony Del Duca
	Daniel Deschênes
	Valerie Deschênes
	Anne-Marie Dinelle
	Pasquale Falocco
	Yvan Hoste
	Marc Lapierre
	Liem Nguyen
	Daryl Roberts
	Michel St-Gelais
Contact	Daniel Deschênes, President

Description Systematix is a leading IT consulting firm that works with over 500 consultants in seven offices across Canada.

SYSTEMATIX INFORMATION TECHNOLOGY CONSULTANTS INC.
830, ave Ernest Gagnon
Bureau 201, Édifice 4
Québec, QC G1S 3R3

Telephone	418-681-0151
Fax	418-681-4061
E-mail	scique@systematix.com
Website	www.systematix.com
Founded	1975
Specialties	Computing
Level	Mid-Level
Recruiters	Michel Belley
	Sabin Blais

Marie-Josée Bleau
Normand Fortier
Jean Gagné
Noël Leclerc

Contact	Jean Gagné, President

Description Systematix is a leading IT consulting firm that works with over 500 consultants in seven offices across Canada.

SYSTEMS CAREER GROUP
55 Town Centre Court, Suite 521
Toronto, ON M1P 4X4

Telephone	416-296-7441
Fax	416-296-7064
E-mail	gmoffatt@interlog.com
Specialties	Computing
Level	Senior
Contact	Geoff Moffatt, Senior Consultant

Description Systems Career Group is a Scarborough-based computer-related employment agency.

SYSTEMS ONTIME INC.
20 Holly Street, Suite 202
Toronto, ON M4S 3B1

Telephone	416-410-8984
Fax	416-485-2252
E-mail	jobs@systems ontime.com
Website	www.systems ontime.com
Founded	1996
Specialties	Computing
Level	Mid-Level

Description Systems OnTime supplies clients with IT resources and personnel in computer systems development, maintenance and consulting.

SYSTEMSEARCH CONSULTING SERVICES INC.
3300 Bloor St. W., Suite 540, Box 38
Toronto, ON M8X 2X3

Telephone	416-233-4440
Fax	416-233-3119
E-mail	sysearch@interlog.com
Website	web.idirect.com/~sysearch
Specialties	Telecom
	Computing
	Finance
	Govt/Nonprofit
	Insurance
	Law
Level	Mid-Level
Contact	Tim Powell

Description Systemsearch is a full-service employment agency offering recruitment opportunities in the Greater Toronto Area.

T.J. SEATON MANAGEMENT INC.
144 - 4th Avenue SW, Suite 1260
Calgary, AB T2P 2J1

Telephone	403-261-6000
Fax	403-261-6060
E-mail	seaton@cadvision.com
Founded	1983
Employees	3
Specialties	International
	Oil & Gas
	Finance
	Management
Level	Senior
Min. Salary	$80,000
Fee Basis	Retainer Only
Contact	Tom Seaton

Description T.J. Seaton Management Inc. specializes in senior-level searches, with a focus on the energy industry.

T.L.W. ENTERPRISE INC.
255 Duncan Mill Road, Suite 312
Toronto, ON M3B 3H9

Telephone	416-510-3011
Fax	416-510-8993
E-mail	hr@tlwenterprise.com
Website	www.tlwenterprise.com
Founded	1985
Specialties	Computing

Description T.L.W. Enterprise Inc. is an IT consulting and career placement company that services a number of major corporations and government organizations.

TAD CANADA
505 - 3rd Street SW, Suite 1710
Calgary, AB T2P 3E6

Telephone	403-589-0759
Fax	403-215-1280
E-mail	calgary@tadcanada.com
Website	www.tadcanada.com
Founded	1989
Employees	2
Specialties	Consulting
	Engineering
	Management
	Operations
	Telecom
	Trades/Technicians
Level	Mid-Level
	Junior
Fee Basis	Always contingent
Recruiters	Ken Kyswaty
	Sharon Wastle
Contact	Julia Gdowski

Description TAD Canada, a division of TAD Telecom, recruits technical personnel primarily in the telecom field.

TAD CANADA
446 Grey Bay Street
Brantford, ON N3S 7L6

Telephone	519-753-5769
Fax	519-753-5146
E-mail	jgdowski@tadcanada.com
Website	www.tadcanada.com

Founded	1989
Employees	1
Specialties	Consulting
	Engineering
	Management
	Operations
	Telecom
	Trades/Technicians
Level	Mid-Level
	Junior
Fee Basis	Always contingent
Contact	Julia Gdowski

Description TAD Canada, a division of TAD Telecom, recruits technical personnel primarily in the telecom field.

TAD CANADA
50 Burnhamthorpe Road West
Suite 704
Mississauga, ON L5B 3C2

Telephone	905-848-0087
Fax	905-848-0087
E-mail	toronto@
	tadcanada.com
Website	www.tadcanada.com
Founded	1989
Employees	16
Specialties	Consulting
	Engineering
	Management
	Operations
	Telecom
	Trades/Technicians
Level	Mid-Level
	Junior
Fee Basis	Always contingent
Recruiters	Chrystal Gaffar
	Angela Martins
Contact	Julia Gdowski

Description TAD Canada, a division of TAD Telecom, recruits technical personnel primarily in the telecom field.

TAD CANADA
60 Queen Street, Suite 200
Ottawa, ON K1P 5Y7

Telephone	613-232-4744
Fax	613-232-1199
E-mail	work@tadcanada.com
Website	www.tadcanada.com
Founded	1989
Employees	20
Specialties	Consulting
	Engineering
	Management
	Operations
	Telecom
	Trades/Technicians
Level	Mid-Level
	Junior
Fee Basis	Always contingent
Recruiters	Paula Cowan
	Andrea Standing
	Angie Turpin
Contact	Julia Gdowski

Description TAD Canada, a division of TAD Telecom, recruits technical personnel primarily in the telecom field.

TAD CANADA
4025, boul. Industriel, Suite 100
Laval, QC H7L 3S4

Telephone	450-628-6677
Fax	450-628-9714
E-mail	montreal@
	tadcanada.com
Website	www.tadcanada.com
Founded	1989
Employees	10
Specialties	Consulting
	Engineering
	Management
	Operations
	Telecom
	Trades/Technicians
Level	Mid-Level
	Junior
Fee Basis	Always contingent
Contact	Julia Gdowski

Description TAD Canada, a division of TAD Telecom, recruits technical personnel primarily in the telecom field.

TAD CANADA
134 - 1600 Bedford Hwy., Suite 100
Bedford, NS B4A 1E8

Telephone	902-832-0306
Fax	902-832-9289
E-mail	halifax@tadcanada.com
Website	www.tadcanada.com
Founded	1989
Employees	1
Specialties	Consulting
	Engineering
	Management
	Operations
	Telecom
	Trades/Technicians
Level	Junior
	Mid-Level
Fee Basis	Always contingent
Contact	Julia Gdowski

Description TAD Canada, a division of TAD Telecom, recruits technical personnel, primarily in telecom.

TAG PERSONNEL CONSULTANTS INC.
1253, avenue McGill College
Bureau 980
Montréal, QC H3B 2Y5

Telephone	514-878-1005
Fax	514-878-9925
E-mail	tagpersonnel@
	qc.aira.com
Specialties	Real Estate
	Human Resource
	General Practice
Recruiters	Michele Amcarelli
	Philip Magder
Contact	Michele Amcarelli

TAL GROUP
372 Richmond St. West, Suite 306
Toronto, ON M5V 1X6

Telephone	416-599-1825
Fax	416-599-8251
E-mail	talent@talgroup.net
Website	www.talgroup.net
Founded	1999
Employees	8
Specialties	Multimedia
	Computing
	Telecom
	Management
	Sales
Level	Senior
	Mid-Level
Fee Basis	Always contingent
Contact	Farad Amirkhani

Description TAL Group specializes in brokering technology professionals.

TALENT CONSULTING SERVICES, INC.
21 New Britain Avenue, Suite 204
Rocky Hill, CT 06067   USA

Telephone	860-563-4441
Fax	860-563-4440
E-mail	conniec@talentsys.com
Website	www.talentsys.com
Specialties	Computing
	Telecom
	Engineering
	International
Level	Mid-Level
	Senior

Description Talent Consulting Services, Inc. is one of the fastest-growing IT consulting firms in the USA, specializing in recruiting for the telecom, datacom and wireless industries.

TALENTLAB
49 Wellington Street East
Unit 5W, Flatiron Building
Toronto, ON M5E 1C9

Telephone	416-728-2229
Fax	416-203-8119
E-mail	toronto@talentlab.com
Website	www.talentlab.com
Specialties	Engineering
	Multimedia
	Computing
Level	Mid-Level
Recruiters	Scott Landgraff
	Stephen McColgan
Contact	Stephen McColgan

Description TalentLab recruits technology stars.

TALENTLAB
173 Princess Street, Unit 5
Kingston, ON K7L 1A9

Telephone	613-540-3700
E-mail	kingston@
	talentlab.com
Website	www.talentlab.com
Specialties	Engineering

Description TAD Canada, a division of TAD Telecom, recruits technical personnel primarily in the telecom field.

Multimedia
Computing

Level   Mid-Level

Description TalentLab recruits technology stars.

TALENTLAB
4048 Carling Avenue
Kanata, ON K2K 1V1

Telephone   613-271-0955
Fax   613-271-0816
E-mail   info@talentlab.com
Website   www.talentlab.com

Specialties Engineering
Multimedia
Computing

Level   Mid-Level

Recruiters Les Banks
Andrea Bird
Jonathan Buick
Christina Christenson
Aaron Del Duca
Barclay Easton
Frank Hall
Sue Kavanagh
Alan Kearns
Tami LeBlanc
Erika MacPhee
Doug Martin
Stuart Musson
Megan Paterson
Rob Pritchard
Warren Robinson
Teri Theoret
Jill Wall

Contact   Les Banks,
Practice Manager

Description TalentLab recruits technology stars.

TALENTLAB
4445 Eastgate Mall, Second Floor
San Diego, CA 92121   USA

Telephone   858-812-3045
Fax   858-812-2001
E-mail   sandiego@
talentlab.com
Website   www.talentlab.com

Specialties Computing
International

Description TalentLab recruits technology stars.

TAMM COMMUNICATIONS INC. / TCI CONFIDENTIAL
250 The Esplanade
Suite 402, Berkeley Hall
Toronto, ON M5A 1J2

Telephone   416-304-0188
Fax   416-304-0181
E-mail   resumes@
tcicanada.com
Website   www.tcicanada.com

Specialties General Practice

Level   Mid-Level

Contact   Pam Sexsmith,
Special Projects

Description TCI Confidential is a recruitment advertising agency. They do not accept unsolicited resumes.

TANAKA ASSOCIATES
40 King Street West
Suite 4900, Scotia Plaza
Toronto, ON M5H 4A2

Telephone   416-410-8262
Fax   416-777-6720
E-mail   tanaka@sympatico.ca

Specialties Accounting
Banking
Computing
Finance
Insurance
Law

Level   Mid-Level
Senior

Min. Salary $60,000
Fee Basis   Sometimes contingent

Contact   Rod Tanaka, CA

Description Tanaka Associates recruits professionals in a variety of fields, including taxation.

TANCREDI CONSULTING
65 Scadding Avenue, Suite 980
Toronto, ON M5A 4L1

Telephone   416-931-4292
Fax   416-365-6602
E-mail   frank@frankhrc.com

Specialties Accounting

Fee Basis   Retainer Only

Contact   Frank Tancredi

Description Tancredi is a management consulting firm that does occasional recruitment work in the accounting field.

TAPP CONSULTING SERVICES
RR #3
Merrickville, ON K0G 1N0

Telephone   613-269-4255
Fax   613-224-3457
E-mail   richcomb@comnet.ca

Founded   1995
Employees   1

Specialties Govt/Nonprofit
Finance
Consulting
Human Resource
Management
International
Education

Level   Mid-Level
Senior

Fee Basis   Sometimes contingent

Contact   Richard Combley,
President

Description TAPP Consulting Services provides government and companies with executives and senior managers.

TAPSCOTT ASSOCIATES
133 King Street East, 2nd Floor
Toronto, ON M5C 1G6

Telephone   416-367-7300
Fax   416-367-7333
E-mail   bill@tapscott.com
Website   www.tapscott.com

Founded   1983
Employees   18

Specialties Engineering
Architecture
Computing

Level   Mid-Level
Senior

Min. Salary $60,000

Contact   William K. Tapscott,
Owner

Description Tapscott Associates specializes in recruiting senior-level IT candidates for firms in financial services and technology-driven businesses.

TARAN VIRTUAL ASSOCIATES
100 Fullarton Street
London, ON N6A 1K1

Telephone   519-432-8626
Fax   519-663-1165
E-mail   taran@
virtualassociates.ca
Website   www.virtual
associates.ca

Specialties Law

Level   Mid-Level
Junior

Contact   Stephen Taran,
President

Description Taran Virtual Assoc. provides contract lawyers (and even law students) on an outsourcing basis to law firms, corporate law departments and government law offices.

TAYLOR, LOW & ASSOCIATES INC.
1200 Sheppard Ave. East, Suite 406
Toronto, ON M2K 2S5

Telephone   416-494-3315
Fax   416-491-5301
E-mail   kathy@taylorlow.com
Website   www.taylorlow.com

Founded   1987

Specialties Computing

Level   Senior
Mid-Level

Min. Salary $40,000
Fee Basis   Always contingent

Contact   Kathy Low

Description Taylor, Low & Associates Inc. provides full-time and contract personnel to AS/400, SAP, networking and client-server clients.

TAYLOR PERSONNEL LIMITED
1207 Douglas Street, Suite 517
Victoria, BC V8W 2E7

Telephone   250-480-0700
Fax   250-480-1446
E-mail   resumes@taylor
personnel.net
Website   www.taylor
personnel.net

Founded   1983
Employees   4

Specialties Accounting
Computing

Marketing
Purchasing
Govt/Nonprofit
Bilingual

Level Junior
Mid-Level

Recruiters Sheenagh Beadell
Karen Russell
Hillary Samson

Contact Sheenagh Beadell,
Branch Manager

Description Taylor Personnel Limited provides general staffing services to all areas of private sector and government.

TAYLOR PERSONNEL LIMITED
10104 - 103rd Avenue
Suite 2360, Canada Trust Tower
Edmonton, AB

Telephone 780-426-6887
Fax 780-428-0256
E-mail taylor@supernet.ab.ca
Website www.taylor
personnel.net

Founded 1983
Employees 8

Specialties Accounting
Computing
Marketing
Purchasing
Bilingual
Oil & Gas

Level Mid-Level
Junior

Fee Basis Always contingent

Contact Gillian Taylor

Description Taylor provides general staffing services to all areas of private sector and government.

TAYLOR RECRUITMENT LTD.
2 Chalk Road, Godalming
Harcros Building
Surrey GU7 3HH
UNITED KINGDOM

Telephone 44-1483-418383
Fax 44-1483-418989
E-mail jobs@taylorrec.
freeserve.co.uk
Website www.taylorrec.
freeserve.co.uk

Founded 1994
Employees 8

Specialties Oil & Gas
Construction
Engineering
Computing
International

Level Senior
Mid-Level

Min. Salary $70,000
Fee Basis Sometimes contingent

Recruiters Edward Bradley
Peter Fairfax
Peter Lewer

Contact Peter Lewer

Description Taylor Recruitment Ltd. specializes in recruiting for the construction of petrochemical, oil and gas plants, together with the civil works incorporated in the construction, and maintenance of the plants when finished.

TAYLOR ROOT
25 Farrington St., Fleetway House
London EC4A 4SR
UNITED KINGDOM

Telephone 44-20-7415-2828
Fax 44-20-7332-9054
E-mail nickroot@
taylor-root.co.uk
Website www.taylor-root.com

Founded 1984
Employees 9

Specialties Law
International

Level Senior
Mid-Level

Fee Basis Always contingent

Recruiters Andy Curtis
Caroline Frizzell
Darryn Hale
Richard Hanks
Alison Harvey
Jo Heron
Jenny Isaacs
Gill Jones
Lynnsey McCall
Jamie Newbold
Ed O'Brien
Sara-Beth O'Farrell
Nick Root

Contact Nick Root, Partner

Description Taylor Root is an international legal recruitment consultancy recruiting lawyers into the major UK and US law firms, corporations and international banking groups.

TAYLOR TOMAS CONSULTING INC.
2883 Nash Drive
Coquitlam, BC V3B 6P9

Telephone 604-941-0684
Fax 604-941-0674
E-mail grant_sutherland@
telus.net
Website www.taylortomas.com

Founded 1998
Employees 2

Specialties Consulting
Accounting
Computing
Forestry
Human Resource
Management

Level Senior
Mid-Level

Fee Basis Sometimes contingent

Contact Grant Sutherland

Description TTCI provides recruitment and consulting services in various sectors to firms seeking critical staff to grow their business.

TAYLORMADE CAREERS, INC.
1 Old Country Road, Suite 297
Carle Place, NY 11514 USA

Telephone 516-873-7300
Fax 516-873-9317
E-mail hr@taylormade
careers.com
Website www.taylor
madecareers.com

Specialties Accounting
Administrative
Engineering
Computing
Sales
International

Level Mid-Level

Contact Maxine Taylor,
President

Description TaylorMade Careers, Inc. is a full-service placement firm.

TDM TECHNICAL SERVICES
3 Church Street, Suite 300
Toronto, ON M5E 1M2

Telephone 416-777-0007
Fax 416-777-1117
E-mail tdm@tdm.ca
Website www.tdm.ca

Founded 1967
Employees 15

Specialties Consulting
Engineering
Aerospace
Architecture
Automotive
Design
Metals
Mining
Packaging
Plastics
Pulp & Paper
Scientific

Level Senior
Mid-Level

Fee Basis Always contingent

Recruiters Lynn Albin
Tony Burgess
Warren Carey
George Halliwell
Chris Halliwell
Greg McGean
Dale Ohirko
Val Slastnikov
Mandy Stenzler
Iris Walker

Contact Dale Ohirko, Manager

Description TDM Technical Services specializes in contract employment for engineers, designers, analysts, technologists and technicians.

TDR HUMAN RESOURCES SERVICES LTD.
4401 Albert Street, Suite 201
Regina, SK S4S 6B4

Telephone 306-721-4114
Fax 306-543-5592
E-mail kbrehm@sk.
sympatico.ca

Specialties Govt/Nonprofit
Management
Agriculture/Fisheries

Level Mid-Level

Recruiters   Ken Brehm
              Ron Dedman

Contact   Ken Brehm

Description TDR is an HR management consulting firm that also provides recruitment services for clients.

TEAM POWER EXECUTIVE SEARCH
181 Whitehall Drive
Markham, ON L3R 9T1

Telephone   905-475-6800
Fax   905-475-8702
E-mail   sales@team-power.com

Founded   1997
Employees   4

Specialties   Actuarial
              Administrative
              Banking
              Consulting
              Finance
              Insurance
              Management

Level   Senior

Min. Salary $75,000
Fee Basis   Retainer Only

Recruiters   Gerold Roberts
              Allan Turowetz

Contact   Gerold Roberts, VP &
              General Manager

Description Team-Power Executive Search is a leadership consulting firm committed to the identification, evaluation and recommendation of justified candidates for senior executive level positions.

TECH FORCE SEARCH GROUP
1 Yonge Street, Suite 1801
Toronto, ON M5E 1W7

Telephone   416-777-0070
Fax   416-777-0070
E-mail   tekforce@interlog.com
Website   www.biznet.
              maximizer.com/
              techforcesearch

Specialties   Computing

Level   Mid-Level

Min. Salary $35,000

Contact   Michael Weir

Description Tech Force Search Group specializes in the placement of computing professionals.

TECH HI CONSULTANTS LIMITED
22 Frederick Street, Suite 200
Kitchener, ON N2H 6M6

Telephone   519-749-1020
Fax   519-749-1070
E-mail   employment@
              techhi.com
Website   www.techhi.com

Founded   1982

Specialties   Computing
              Engineering

Level   Mid-Level
              Senior

Recruiters   John Peters
              Suzanne Voteary

Contact   J. Harris, President

Description Since 1982, TechHi Consultants has serviced the needs of some of the most recognized corporations throughout North America.

TECH-PRO, INC.
3000 Centre Pointe Drive
Roseville, MN 55113   USA

Telephone   651-634-1400
Fax   651-634-1499
E-mail   web@tech-pro.com
Website   www.tech-pro.com

Specialties   Computing
              International

Recruiters   Tiffany Bethel
              Dave Vadis

Contact   Dave Vadis, President

Description Tech-Pro, Inc. is a computer consulting services company providing experienced computer professionals to their clients.

TECHAID INC.
5165, ch. Queen-Mary, Bureau 401
Montréal, QC H3W 1X7

Telephone   514-482-6790
Fax   514-482-0324
E-mail   info@techaid.ca
Website   www.techaid.ca

Founded   1962
Employees   38

Specialties   Engineering
              Computing
              Operations
              Telecom
              Management
              International

Level   Mid-Level
              Senior

Fee Basis   Always contingent

Recruiters   William F. Allen
              Andre Chitayat
              Sandrine Faucher
              Philip Handyside
              John Romvary
              Marie Stabler

Contact   William F. Allen

Description Techaid specializes in permanent and contract recruiting for the engineering, software, technical and manufacturing sectors.

TECHNICAL CONNECTIONS INC.
11400 Olympic Blvd., Suite 700
Los Angeles, CA 90064-1550 USA

Telephone   310-479-8830
Fax   310-445-8726
E-mail   info@tci-la.com
Website   www.tci-la.com

Founded   1984
Employees   25

Specialties   Computing
              International

Level   Senior
              Mid-Level

Fee Basis   Always contingent

Recruiters   Shelly Beard
              Brenda Bukowski-Green
              Celine Bundy
              Scott Connelly
              Janine Davis
              Peggy Kinney
              Helen MacKinnon
              Peter MacKinnon
              Nattineque McClain
              Raquel Neidhold
              Nola Quinn
              Marc Rafferty
              Karen Renner
              Timothy Schwarz
              Douglas Stuart
              Glenn Yoshimura

Contact   Celine Bundy, Senior
              Recruitment Counselor

Description Technical Connections is a recruitment firm specializing in placing technology, professional services and Internet professionals on a permanent and contract basis.

TECHNICAL MANAGEMENT RESOURCES INC.
110 Dunlop Street East, Suite 304
Barrie, ON L4M 1A5

Telephone   705-727-7678
Fax   705-727-7989
E-mail   tmr@techmgmt
              resources.com

Founded   1998
Employees   12

Specialties   Aerospace
              Automotive
              Computing
              Management
              Operations
              Packaging
              Quality Control
              Engineering

Level   Senior
              Mid-Level

Min. Salary $50,000
Fee Basis   Sometimes contingent

Recruiters   Wendell Brewster
              Paul Catling
              Brian Deck
              Michael Fisher
              Michael Flook
              Ann Griffiths
              Michael Groh
              Dave Kehoe
              Doug McMillan
              Michael O'Brien
              Robert Rice
              Margo Van Muyen

Contact   Margo Van Muyen

Description Technical Management Resources Inc. is a full-service recruitment firm specializing in the permanent placement of technical, engineering and management professionals across Canada.

TECHNICAL RESOURCE NETWORK
2091 West Broadway, Suite 200
Vancouver, BC V6J 1Z6

Telephone   604-739-1711
Fax   604-739-1710

E-mail   jobs@vanjobs.com
Website   www.vanjobs.com
Founded   1971
Employees   10
Specialties Computing
               Engineering
               Scientific
               Telecom
Level   Senior
               Mid-Level
Min. Salary $50,000
Contact   Mark S. Strong
Description Technical Resource Network specializes in R&D recruitment for data / telecommunications and IT as well as senior technical sales and systems engineers.

TECHNICAL SERVICE CONSULTANTS INC. / TSC WEST
10767 - 148th Street
Surrey, BC V3R 0S4

Telephone   604-951-8814
Fax   604-585-2790
E-mail   sdavies@asttbc.org
Website   www.asttbc.org/xc/
               tscwest.html
Specialties General Practice
               Construction
               Operations
               Design
               Engineering
               Plastics
               Scientific
Level   Senior
               Mid-Level
Fee Basis   Sometimes contingent
Contact   Wendell Sanford
Description TSC provides experienced recruiting and placement services, maintaining a comprehensive database of highly skilled professional and technical people across Canada.

TECHNICAL SERVICE CONSULTANTS OF MANITOBA LTD. / TSC
125 Garry Street, Suite 890
Winnipeg, MB R3C 3P2

Telephone   204-987-8080
Fax   204-987-8086
E-mail   tsc@escape.ca
Specialties Engineering
               Operations
               Metals
Level   Mid-Level
               Senior
Contact   Brian Hayes,
               General Manager
Description TSC specializes in executive search, recruitment and outplacement services for the manufacturing and engineering sectors.

TECHNICAL SERVICES CONSULTANTS ONTARIO LTD. / TSC GROUP
6 Lansing Square, Suite 226
Toronto, ON M2J 1T5

Telephone   416-494-6868
Fax   416-494-6171
E-mail   tscgroup@sprint.ca
Founded   1994
Employees   6
Specialties Engineering
               Architecture
               Aerospace
               Pharmaceutical
               Scientific
               Operations
               Human Resource
Level   Mid-Level
               Senior
Fee Basis   Sometimes contingent
Recruiters   Bob Carro
               Eugene Henry
               Joe Somer
               Gary Thompson
               Lesley Wieser
Contact   Lesley Wieser, Director
Description TSC specializes in the placement of technical and professional personnel.

TECHNICAL SKILLS CONSULTING INC.
220 Yonge Street, Box 507
Toronto, ON M5B 2H1

Telephone   416-586-7971
Fax   416-586-0416
E-mail   tscinc@tscinc.on.ca
Website   www.tscinc.on.ca
Employees   4
Specialties Engineering
               Operations
               Sales
               Design
               Automotive
               Pulp & Paper
               Mining
Level   Senior
               Mid-Level
Min. Salary $50,000
Fee Basis   Always contingent
Recruiters   Sonya Lockhart
               Paul MacBean
               Roxanne Mars
               Don Phaneuf
Contact   Paul MacBean
Description Technical Skills Consulting Inc. specializes in the recruitment of engineering, technology and science professionals for Canadian manufacturers.

TECHNICAL SOLUTIONS INC.
1817 Golden Mile Highway
Pittsburgh, PA 15239   USA

Telephone   724-733-2100
Fax   724-733-2099
E-mail   techical@tsiwork.com
Website   www.tsiwork.com
Founded   1991
Specialties Engineering
               Computing
               Metals
               Operations
               Scientific
               International
Level   Mid-Level
Description Technical Solutions Inc. provides technical personnel to clients on a contract, temporary-to-permanent and direct-hire basis.

TECHNISOLUTIONS EXECUTIVE INC.
1210 chemin Perry
Aylmer, QC J9H 5C9

Telephone   819-684-2777
E-mail   technisolutions.com@
               sympatico.ca
Founded   1994
Specialties Pulp & Paper
               Forestry
               Engineering
Level   Mid-Level
               Senior
Min. Salary $35,000
Fee Basis   Sometimes contingent
Contact   Yvonne Pascual
Description Technisolutions Executive Inc. places engineers with specialty chemical or water treatment backgrounds in the pulp and paper industry.

TECHNISOURCE, INC.
555 Legget Drive
Suite 304, Tower A
Kanata, ON K2K 2X3

Telephone   613-271-2130
Fax   613-271-2136
E-mail   ottawa@
               technisource.com
Website   www.tsrc.net
Specialties Computing
Level   Mid-Level
               Senior
Recruiters   Todd Black
               Chad Clost
               Michelle Morrice
Contact   Todd Black,
               Regional Manager
Description Technisource is an international, publicly-traded IT consulting company that provides the best in technical personnel to meet client project specifications and staffing requirements.

TECHNISOURCE, INC.
1901 W. Cypress Creek Rd., Ste. 202
Fort Lauderdale, FL 33309   USA

Telephone   954-493-8701
Fax   954-493-8603
E-mail   ftl@tsrc.net
Website   www.tsrc.net
Founded   1987
Specialties Computing
               Engineering
               Telecom
               Aerospace
               International
Level   Mid-Level
Description Technisource, Inc. is an international, publicly-traded IT

consulting company that provides the best in technical personnel to meet client project specifications and staffing requirements.

TECHNIX INC.
100 Esgore Drive
Toronto, ON M5M 3S2

Telephone	416-250-9195
Fax	416-485-7964
E-mail	tnixon@technix.on.ca
Website	www.technix.on.ca
Founded	1990
Specialties	Sales
	Marketing
	Computing
	Telecom
	Public Relations
Level	Mid-Level
	Senior
Min. Salary	$50,000
Fee Basis	Sometimes contingent
Contact	Ted Nixon

Description Specializing in sales, marketing and technical positions for vendors of information technology. Also recruits public relations and investor relations personnel.

TECHNOLOGY PLUS
PO Box 26420
Adliya   BAHRAIN

Telephone	973-554-469
Fax	973-554-528
E-mail	lgd@technoplus.com
Website	www.technoplus.com
Founded	1993
Employees	80
Specialties	Computing
	Telecom
	Banking
	Hospitality
	Biotech/Biology
	International
	Health/Medical
Level	Mid-Level
	Senior
Min. Salary	$50,000
Fee Basis	Sometimes contingent
Contact	Luc G. Dallaire

Description Technology Plus specializes in placements in the Middle East, including IT professionals, Internet / intranet experts for telecom, banking and government clients, medical and hospitality staffing.

TECHNOLOGY SEARCH GROUP
49 Ventris Drive
Ajax, ON L1T 1W6

Telephone	905-427-1706
Fax	905-427-8856
E-mail	jobs@thetsg.com
Website	www.thetsg.com
Specialties	Computing
Recruiters	Drew Markle
	Tyrone Phipps
Contact	Tyrone Phipps, President

Description TSG locates, identifies, and places only those I/T professionals with a reputation for being the best at what they do.

TEK-SEARCH CORPORATION
400 Walmer Road
Suite 1728, East Tower
Toronto, ON M5P 2X7

Telephone	416-979-7500
Fax	416-979-0108
E-mail	careers@teksearch.net
Website	www.teksearch.net
Founded	1995
Specialties	Computing
	Management
Level	Senior
	Mid-Level
Fee Basis	Always contingent
Recruiters	Bonnie Gough
	Felicia Shao
Contact	Bonnie Gough

Description Tek-Search specializes in placing information technology professionals in all industries in the greater Toronto area.

TEKMARK COMPUTER SERVICES LLC
100 Metroplex Drive, Suite 102
Edison, NJ 08817   USA

Telephone	732-572-5400
Fax	732-572-7117
E-mail	tekmark@tekmarkinc.com
Website	www.tekmarkinc.com
Founded	1979
Specialties	Computing
	International
Level	Senior
	Mid-Level
Contact	Mr. Powers

Description Tekmark Global Solutions is a nationwide provider of information technology consultants.

TEKNICA (UK) LTD.
137 High Holborn, Holborn Tower
London WC1V 6PW
UNITED KINGDOM

Telephone	44-207-413-9600
Fax	44-207-413-9777
E-mail	info@teknica-uk.co.uk
Website	www.teknica-uk.co.uk
Specialties	Engineering
	International
	Oil & Gas

Description Teknica is a fully integrated engineering contractor capable of providing a wide range of services in the energy sector.

TEKSYSTEMS
13711 International Place
Building 2, Suite 250
Richmond, BC V6V 2X8

Telephone	604-233-8700

Fax	604-233-8740
E-mail	adaip@aerotek.com
Website	www.aerotek.com
Founded	1983
Specialties	Computing
	Engineering
	Administrative
Level	Mid-Level
	Junior
Recruiters	Ada Ip
	Bryan Toffey
Contact	Ada Ip

Description TEKsystems (formerly Aerotek) provides a range of consulting services, including staffing for the technical and administrative fields. Call us toll-free at 1-800-688-6948.

TEKSYSTEMS
5975 Whittle Road
Mississauga, ON L4Z 3N1

Telephone	905-712-8666
Fax	905-712-8667
E-mail	stricci@aerotek.com
Website	www.aerotek.com
Founded	1983
Specialties	Engineering
	Computing
	Scientific
	Automotive
	Administrative

Description TEKsystems (formerly Aerotek) provides a range of consulting services, including staffing for the technical and administrative fields. Call us toll-free at 1-800-688-6948.

TEKSYSTEMS
2650 Queensview Drive, Suite 110
Ottawa, ON K2B 8H6

Telephone	613-721-6670
Fax	613-721-6683
E-mail	sczerlau@teksystems.com
Website	www.teksystems.com
Specialties	Administrative
	Engineering
	Automotive
	Computing
	Scientific

Description TEKsystems (formerly Aerotek) provides a range of consulting services, including staffing for the technical and administrative fields. Call toll-free at 1-800-264-8217.

TELE-RESSOURCES LTÉE
2021, avenue Union, Bureau 915
Montréal, QC H3A 2C1

Telephone	514-842-0066
Fax	514-842-8797
E-mail	fbedard@teleressources.com
Website	www.teleressources.com
Founded	1985
Employees	65

Specialties	Administrative
	Accounting
	Banking
	Bilingual
	Multimedia
	Telecom
	Aerospace
Level	Mid-Level
	Junior
Recruiters	Françoise Bédard
	Johanne Berry
	Liette Languerand
Contact	Francoise Bédard

Description Tele-Ressources specializes in the recruitment and placement of personnel, outsourcing and payroll services.

TEMPLEMAN CONSULTING GROUP INC.
173 Brock Street North
Whitby, ON L1N 4H3

Telephone	905-666-4500
Fax	905-668-8552
E-mail	tafw@templeman consulting.com
Website	www.templeman consulting.com
Specialties	General Practice
Contact	Terrence A.F. Whyte

Description Templeman Consulting Group Inc. provides general human resources consulting services, including recruitment.

TEMPLEMAN CONSULTING GROUP INC.
205 Dundas Street East
Suite 200, PO Box 234
Belleville, ON K8N 5A2

Telephone	613-966-2620
Fax	613-966-2866
E-mail	tafw@templeman consulting.com
Website	www.templeman consulting.com
Specialties	General Practice
Contact	Terrence A.F. Whyte

Description Templeman Consulting Group Inc. provides general human resources consulting services, including recruitment.

TEMPLEMAN CONSULTING GROUP INC.
115 Clarence Street
Suite 203, Gore Building
Kingston, ON K7L 5N6

Telephone	613-542-1889
Fax	613-542-8202
E-mail	tafw@templeman consulting.com
Website	www.templeman consulting.com
Specialties	General Practice
Recruiters	Deborah Hall
	Erin Nieradka
	Terrence A.F. Whyte
Contact	Terrence A.F. Whyte

Description Templeman Consulting Group Inc. provides general human resources consulting services, including recruitment.

TENNEN PERSONNEL SERVICES LIMITED
1000 Finch Avenue West, Suite 510
Toronto, ON M3J 2V5

Telephone	416-663-0610
Fax	416-663-0750
E-mail	info@tennenjobs.com
Website	www.tennenjobs.com
Founded	1978
Specialties	Engineering
Level	Mid-Level
	Senior
Fee Basis	Sometimes contingent
Contact	Lanny Tennen, Owner

Description Tennen Personnel Services Limited specializes in placement within the high-technology electronics industry.

TERHAM MANAGEMENT CONSULTANTS LTD.
2 Bloor Street West, Suite 1805
Toronto, ON M4W 3E2

Telephone	416-968-3636
Fax	416-968-6617
E-mail	consultants@ terham.com
Website	www.terham.com
Founded	1987
Employees	6
Specialties	Marketing
	Advertising
	Direct Mktng.
	Multimedia
	Publishing/Media
	Public Relations
Level	Senior
	Mid-Level
Min. Salary	$40,000
Fee Basis	Retainer Only
Contact	Terry Hammond

Description TERHAM specializes in mid/senior-level searches in advertising, marketing, direct marketing, communications and new media.

TES, THE EMPLOYMENT SOLUTION
40 Holly St., Suite 500, Box 2315
Toronto, ON M4S 3C3

Telephone	416-482-2420
Fax	416-482-8076
E-mail	jacobb@tes.net
Website	www.tes.net
Founded	1975
Employees	36
Specialties	Computing
	Engineering
	Administrative
	Accounting
	Trades/Technicians
Level	Mid-Level
	Junior
Fee Basis	Sometimes contingent
Recruiters	Jacob Baker
	Kent Burns
	Steve Cook
	Sergio Greco CPC
	Serge Lucchetto
	Raymond Moscoe
	Len Speck
	Alex Welsh
	Frank A. Wilson CPC
	Barbi Wilson
Contact	Jacob Baker

Description TES provides contract and permanent placements in engineering, information technology and office support industries.

TES, THE EMPLOYMENT SOLUTION
2021 James Street
Burlington, ON L7R 1H2

Telephone	905-639-2600
Fax	905-639-4998
E-mail	billd@tes.net
Website	www.tes.net
Founded	1975
Employees	9
Specialties	Computing
	Engineering
Recruiters	Bill Docherty
	Michael Fitzpatrick
	Mary MacDonald
	Rita Smith
Contact	Bill Docherty

Description TES provides contract and permanent placements in engineering, information technology and office support industries.

TES, THE EMPLOYMENT SOLUTION
1 City Centre Drive, Suite 705
Mississauga, ON L5B 1M2

Telephone	905-272-4296
Fax	905-272-1068
E-mail	chrisr@tes.net
Website	www.tes.net
Founded	1975
Employees	9
Specialties	Engineering
	Architecture
	Administrative
	Design
	Pharmaceutical
	Telecom
	Computing
Fee Basis	Always contingent
Recruiters	Sandra Allmark
	Tamera Johnson
	Yolanda Malcolm
	Bruno Rizzuto
	Chris Roach CPC
	Graham Wilson
Contact	Chris Roach, Vice President

Description TES provides contract and permanent placements in engineering, information technology and office support industries.

Description Templeman Consulting Group Inc. provides general human resources consulting services, including recruitment.

TES, THE EMPLOYMENT SOLUTION
301 Moodie Drive, Suite 410
Ottawa, ON K2H 9C4

Telephone	613-828-7887
Fax	613-828-2729
E-mail	ottreply@tes.net
Website	www.tes.net
Founded	1975
Employees	7
Specialties	Computing Engineering
Contact	Frank A. Wilson

Description TES provides contract and permanent placements in engineering, information technology and office support industries.

TES, THE EMPLOYMENT SOLUTION
1425 Rene-Levesque Blvd. West
Suite 1101
Montréal, QC H3G 1T7

Telephone	514-866-2493
Fax	514-866-6488
E-mail	marianan@tes.net
Website	www.tes.net
Founded	1975
Employees	7
Specialties	Computing Engineering
Recruiters	Yvan Michon Hans Witte
Contact	Yvan Michon, VP Executive Search

Description TES provides contract and permanent placements in engineering, information technology and office support industries.

TES, THE EMPLOYMENT SOLUTION
101 East Park Boulevard, Suite 875
Plano, TX 75074   USA

Telephone	972-398-8900
Fax	972-398-8904
E-mail	yvanm@tes.net
Website	www.tes.net
Specialties	Accounting Administrative Computing Engineering Trades/Technicians International
Contact	Yvan Michon, VP Executive Search

Description TES provides contract and permanent placements in engineering, information technology and office support industries.

TES, THE EMPLOYMENT SOLUTION
4000 West Chase Blvd., Suite 390
Raleigh, NC 27607   USA

Telephone	919-832-8900
Fax	919-832-8905
E-mail	yvanm@tes.net
Website	www.tes.net

Specialties	Accounting Administrative Computing Engineering International Trades/Technicians
Contact	Yvan Michon, VP Executive Search

Description TES provides contract and permanent placements in engineering, information technology and office support industries.

THINKPATH.COM INC.
3300 Bloor Street West
Suite 540, PO Box 38
Toronto, ON M8X 2X3

Telephone	416-233-4440
Fax	416-233-3119
E-mail	torontowest@ thinkpath.com
Website	www.thinkpath.com
Founded	1984
Specialties	Computing Design Engineering
Contact	John Wilson, Branch Manager

Description IT Staffing Ltd. and CAD CAM Inc. have merged into Thinkpath.com Inc., a global provider of IT and engineering recruiting, consulting and recruitment services.

THINKPATH.COM INC.
55 University Avenue, Suite 505
Toronto, ON M5J 2H7

Telephone	416-364-8767
Fax	416-364-2424
E-mail	headoffice@ thinkpath.com
Website	www.thinkpath.com
Founded	1995
Employees	45
Specialties	Computing Engineering Sales Management Telecom Design
Level	Mid-Level Senior
Fee Basis	Sometimes contingent
Recruiters	Maureen Neglia CPC Carm Sukhabut
Contact	Carm Sukhabut

Description IT Staffing Ltd. and CAD CAM Inc. have merged into Thinkpath.com Inc., a global provider of IT and engineering recruiting, consulting and recruitment technologies.

THINKPATH.COM INC.
38 Auriga Drive, Suite 245
Ottawa, ON K2E 8A5

Telephone	613-226-9292
Fax	613-226-7907
E-mail	ottawa@thinkpath.com

Website	www.thinkpath.com
Founded	1995
Specialties	Computing Engineering Design Telecom
Contact	Tony French, Branch Manager

Description IT Staffing Ltd. and CAD CAM Inc. have merged into Thinkpath.com Inc., a global provider of IT and engineering recruiting, consulting and recruitment technologies.

THINKPATH.COM INC.
1 World Trade Centre, Suite 7847
New York, NY 10048   USA

Telephone	212-912-1169
Fax	212-912-1189
E-mail	newyork@ thinkpath.com
Website	www.thinkpath.com
Founded	1997
Specialties	Computing International Engineering
Level	Mid-Level
Contact	Grace Piscopo, Branch Manager

Description IT Staffing Ltd. and CAD CAM Inc. have merged into Thinkpath.com Inc., a global provider of IT and engineering recruiting, consulting and recruitment technologies.

THINKPATH.COM INC.
375 Totten Pond Road, Suite 200
Waltham, MA 02451   USA

Telephone	781-890-6444
Fax	781-890-3355
E-mail	boston@thinkpath.com
Website	www.thinkpath.com
Founded	1997
Specialties	Computing International Engineering
Level	Mid-Level
Contact	Denise Dunne, Branch Manager

Description IT Staffing Ltd. and CAD CAM Inc. have merged into Thinkpath.com Inc., a global provider of IT and engineering recruiting, consulting and recruitment technologies.

THOMAS & DESSAIN
16 Vine St., Vine Street Chambers
St. Helier, Jersey
Channel Islands JE2 4WB
UNITED KINGDOM

Telephone	44-1534-888-345
Fax	44-1534-618-585
E-mail	enquiries@ thomasdessain.com
Website	www.thomas dessain.com

Specialties	International Banking Finance Law
Level	Senior
Recruiters	Rosy Dessain Clare Fenwick Sarah Hazzard ACA David Hunter Karen Mars Fiona Ruane Jonathan Stratford Ian Thomas MA
Contact	Rosy Dessain

Description Thomas & Dessain specialises in sourcing senior staff in the offshore banking and financial services industry and in the accountancy and legal professions offshore.

THOMAS E. HEDEFINE ASSOCIATES
21 Ardagh Street
Toronto, ON M6S 1Y2

Telephone	416-604-9444
Fax	416-604-8995
E-mail	hedefine@sprint.ca
Specialties	Banking Finance
Level	Mid-Level Senior
Fee Basis	Always contingent
Recruiters	Thomas E. Hedefine Philip Stoddart
Contact	Thomas E. Hedefine, CPC

Description Thomas E. Hedefine provides professional staffing requirements for retail / commercial banking as well as asset-based lending industries.

THOMAS GROUP, THE
190 Robert Speck Pkwy, Suite 322
Mississauga, ON L4Z 3K3

Telephone	905-273-4040
Fax	905-273-6659
E-mail	camthom@ interlog.com
Specialties	Finance Management Logistics Sales
Level	Mid-Level Senior
Recruiters	Heather Nadler Catherine Thomas
Contact	Catherine Thomas, Owner

THOMAS MINING ASSOCIATES
PO Box 2010, Lancing
West Sussex, BN15 8HZ
UNITED KINGDOM

Telephone	44-1903-753511
Fax	44-1903-753510
E-mail	chris@thomasmining. prestel.co.uk

Website	www.thomasmining. com
Founded	1987
Employees	3
Specialties	Mining International
Level	Senior Mid-Level
Fee Basis	Sometimes contingent
Recruiters	Christopher Humphreys Dennis Thomas
Contact	Chris Humphreys

Description TMA provides technical back-up to the mining and quarrying industries in personnel and management consultancy.

THOMAS & RAYMENT INC.
3950 - 14th Avenue, Suite 301
Markham, ON L3R 0A9

Telephone	905-470-0548
Fax	905-470-0871
E-mail	info@tandr.com
Website	www.tandr.com
Founded	1981
Employees	25
Specialties	Computing
Level	Mid-Level
Min. Salary	$30,000
Recruiters	Chris Frame Greg Frame Mike Frame Dan Watts
Contact	Chris Frame

Description Thomas & Rayment is an IT consulting firm that also provides recruitment services to over 100 clients in Canada and the USA.

THOMAS-MITCHELL ASSOCIATES INC., THE
Box 89
Niagara-on-the-Lake, ON L0S 1J0

Telephone	416-926-1860
Fax	416-960-3921
Founded	1985
Specialties	Management Sales
Level	Mid-Level Senior
Contact	Meg Mitchell

THOMPSON ASSOCIATES CAREER CONSULTING
1969 Upper Water Street
Suite 1701, Purdy's Wharf II
Halifax, NS B3J 3R7

Telephone	902-422-2099
Fax	902-492-1824
E-mail	thompson.assoc@ ns.sympatico.ca
Employees	10
Specialties	Management Health/Medical Finance Marketing

	Human Resource Govt/Nonprofit Education
Level	Senior Mid-Level
Fee Basis	Retainer Only
Recruiters	Brian Duggan Bernice Finley Joanne Lefebre Diane Peters Mildred Royer Judy A. Slade
Contact	Judy A. Slade

Description Thompson Associates does senior- and mid-level recruitment for a variety of local and national clients, including many in the education and non-profit fields.

THOMPSON ELLIOTT GROUP, THE
12 Alcina Avenue
Toronto, ON M6G 2E8

Telephone	416-654-7911
Fax	416-654-1720
E-mail	thompsonelliott@ sympatico.ca
Specialties	Law
Level	Mid-Level Senior
Contact	Barbara Thompson

Description Thompson Elliott Group specializes in recruiting lawyers.

THOMPSON RESOURCES
323 Mississauga Street, PO Box 778
Niagara-on-the-Lake, ON L0S 1J0

Telephone	905-468-4137
Specialties	Management Govt/Nonprofit
Level	Mid-Level
Contact	Colin K. Thompson

THOMSON TREMBLAY INC.
1250 Mansfield Street
Montréal, QC H3B 2Y3

Telephone	514-861-9971
Fax	514-861-5639
E-mail	thomson-tremblay@ thomson-tremblay.com
Website	www.thomson- tremblay.com
Founded	1971
Specialties	Trades/Technicians Management Human Resource Hospitality
Level	Mid-Level Junior
Recruiters	Rita Amato Frank Bertucci George Gawrych
Contact	Rita Amato

Description TTI is a recruitment and placement firm, offering services in industrial / technical, management consulting, payroll, permanent and contract placements.

THOREK / SCOTT AND PARTNERS
67 Yonge Street, Suite 601
Toronto, ON M5E 1J8

Telephone	416-365-7561
Fax	416-365-3240
E-mail	thorek@netcom.ca
Website	www.thorekscott.com
Specialties	Law
	Finance
	Banking
Level	Senior
	Mid-Level
Recruiters	Elaine Franklin
	Josh Israeli
	Aimee Lavallee
	Barry Reid
	Liane Silver
	Michael Thorek
	Faye Thorek
	Paul Weinberg
	Salina Williams
Contact	Faye Thorek

Description Specializes in the banking, legal and finance sectors.

TIS SERVICE INDUSTRIEL
4865 Jean Talon West, Suite 220
Montréal, QC H4P 1W7

Telephone	514-733-2114
Fax	514-733-0031
Founded	1974
Specialties	Trades/Technicians
Level	Mid-Level
	Junior

Description TIS has been a leader in the industrial personnel placement industry since 1974.

TMP QD LEGAL RECRUITMENT
3 Church Street, Suite 601
Toronto, ON M5E 1M2

Telephone	416-955-4783
Fax	416-955-0428
E-mail	human.resources@ tmp.com
Website	www.tmp.com
Employees	6
Specialties	Law
Level	Senior
	Mid-Level
Recruiters	Melissa Firth
	Emma Fitzgerald
	Karen MacKay
	Christopher S. Pang
	Ted Remillard
Contact	Ted Remillard

Description TMP QD Legal Recruitment, a Canadian and international legal recruitment specialist, is the preferred supplier of lawyer recruitment services to the Canadian Corporate Counsel Association.

TMP WORLDWIDE ADVERTISING & COMMUNICATIONS
475 West Georgia Street, Suite 450
Vancouver, BC V6B 4M9

Telephone	604-688-2441
Fax	604-688-1885
Website	www.tmp.com
Specialties	General Practice
Contact	Sandra Higgins

Description TMP Worldwide Advertising & Communications is a recruitment company with a unique suite of global career solutions and a client base that includes more than 90 of the Fortune 100 and more than 480 of the Fortune 500.

TMP WORLDWIDE ADVERTISING & COMMUNICATIONS
152 King Street East, Third Floor
Toronto, ON M5A 1J3

Telephone	416-861-8679
Fax	416-861-1171
E-mail	employment@ recruitmentsolutions.com
Website	www.tmp.com
Specialties	General Practice
Contact	Carline O'Meally

Description TMP Worldwide Advertising is a recruitment company with a unique suite of global career solutions and a client base that includes more than 90 of the Fortune 100 and more than 480 of the Fortune 500.

TMP WORLDWIDE ADVERTISING & COMMUNICATIONS
63 rue de Brésoles, 4th Floor
Montréal, QC H2Y 1V7

Telephone	514-288-9004
Fax	514-288-1689
Website	www.tmp.com
Specialties	General Practice

Description TMP Worldwide is a recruitment advertising company.

TMP WORLDWIDE EXECUTIVE SEARCH
475 West Georgia , Suite 450
Vancouver, BC V6B 4M9

Telephone	604-688-2441
Fax	604-688-1885
E-mail	resumes@tmp.ca
Website	www.tmp.com
Specialties	General Practice
	Management
Level	Senior

Description TMP Worldwide Executive Search is a recruitment company with a unique suite of global career solutions and a client base that includes more than 90 of the Fortune 100 and more than 480 of the Fortune 500.

TMP WORLDWIDE EXECUTIVE SEARCH
237 - 8th Avenue SE
Suite 700, The Burns Building
Calgary, AB T2G 5C3

Telephone	403-262-8055
Fax	403-262-8120
E-mail	cc2@tmp.ca

TMP WORLDWIDE EXECUTIVE SEARCH
40 King Street West
Suite 3200, Scotia Plaza
Toronto, ON M5H 3Y2

Telephone	416-862-1273
Fax	416-363-5720
E-mail	research@tmp.com
Website	www.tmp.com
Founded	199
Employees	35
Specialties	Management
	Finance
	Insurance
	Pharmaceutical
	Telecom
Level	Senior
Min. Salary	$100,000
Fee Basis	Retainer Only
Recruiters	Hugh G. Illsley
	Eva Kaufman
	Lisa Knight
	Philip Lefebvre
	Marcelo MacKinlay
	Rick Moore
	Sandra Paynter
	William W. Probert
	Derek J. Roberts
	Sheila L. Ross
	Bernadette Testani
	Denise Tobin-McCarthy
	Tanya van Biesen
	John Wallace
Contact	Stephanie Hancock-Kuhn, Librarian

Description TMP Worldwide Executive Search is a recruitment company with a unique suite of global career solutions and a client base that includes more than 90 of the Fortune 100 and more than 480 of the Fortune 500.

TMP WORLDWIDE EXECUTIVE SEARCH
1 Nicholas Street, Suite 1208
Ottawa, ON K1N 7B7

Telephone	613-241-5335
Fax	613-241-5995
E-mail	cc2@tmp.ca
Website	www.tmp.com
Specialties	General Practice
	Management
Level	Senior
Contact	Valerie Hill

Description TMP Worldwide Executive Search is a recruitment company with a unique suite of global career solutions and a client base that includes more than 90 of the Fortune 100 and more than 480 of the Fortune 500.

TMP WORLDWIDE INTERACTIVE / MONSTER.CA
276 St-Jacques Street West
10th Floor
Montréal, QC H2Y 1N3

Telephone	514-350-0700
Fax	514-350-0727
E-mail	jlt@monster.ca
Website	www.monster.ca
Specialties	General Practice
Contact	Jennifer-Lee Thomas

Description TMP Worldwide Interactive operates Monster.ca, a recruitment advertising site that is among the two largest recruitment advertising websites in Canada.

TODAYS STAFFING, INC.
360 Main Street, Suite 1630
Winnipeg, MB R3C 3Z3

Telephone	204-956-5600
Fax	204-947-9672
Website	www.todays.com
Specialties	Administrative
	Banking
	Insurance
	Law
Level	Mid-Level
	Junior

Description Todays Staffing, Inc., provides staffing support services in professional, legal and financial skill categories.

TODAYS STAFFING, INC.
148 Fullerton Street, Suite 1704
London, ON N6A 5P3

Telephone	519-679-9910
Fax	519-679-2933
Website	www.todays.com
Specialties	Administrative
	Banking
	Insurance
	Law
Level	Mid-Level
	Junior

Description Todays Staffing, Inc., provides staffing support services in professional, legal and financial skill categories.

TODAYS STAFFING, INC.
171 Colborne St., Holstein Place
Suite 202, Main Floor
Brantford, ON N3T 6C9

Telephone	519-758-1511
Fax	519-758-8153
Website	www.todays.com
Specialties	Administrative
	Banking
	Insurance
	Law

Level	Mid-Level
	Junior

Description Todays Staffing, Inc., provides staffing support services in professional, legal and financial skill categories.

TODAYS STAFFING, INC.
1315 Bishop Street, Unit 160
Cambridge, ON N1R 6Z2

Telephone	519-740-6944
Fax	519-740-2467
Website	www.todays.com
Specialties	Administrative
	Banking
	Insurance
	Law
Level	Mid-Level
	Junior

Description Todays Staffing, Inc., provides staffing support services in professional, legal and financial skill categories.

TODAYS STAFFING, INC.
450 Speedvale Ave. West, Suite 103
Guelph, ON N1H 7Y6

Telephone	519-763-7775
Fax	519-763-2369
Website	www.todays.com
Specialties	Administrative
	Banking
	Insurance
	Law
Level	Mid-Level
	Junior

Description Todays Staffing, Inc., provides staffing support services in professional, legal and financial skill categories.

TODAYS STAFFING, INC.
3300 Bloor St. West, Suite 162
Toronto, ON M8X 2W8

Telephone	416-231-1851
Fax	416-231-2154
E-mail	sarah.coomber@todays.com
Website	www.todays.com
Specialties	Administrative
	Banking
	Insurance
	Law
Level	Mid-Level
	Junior
Contact	Sarah Coomber

Description Todays Staffing, Inc., provides staffing support services in professional, legal and financial skill categories.

TODAYS STAFFING, INC.
3300 Bloor Street West, Unit 162
Etobicoke, ON M8X 2W8

Telephone	416-231-1851
Fax	416-231-2154
Website	www.todays.com
Specialties	Administrative

	Banking
	Insurance
	Law
Level	Mid-Level
	Junior

Description Todays Staffing, Inc., provides staffing support services in professional, legal and financial skill categories.

TODAYS STAFFING, INC.
145 King Street West, Suite 1710
Toronto, ON M5H 1J8

Telephone	416-360-7700
Fax	416-360-7524
Website	www.todays.com
Specialties	Administrative
	Banking
	Insurance
	Law
Level	Mid-Level
	Junior

Description Todays Staffing, Inc., provides staffing support services in professional, legal and financial skill categories.

TODAYS STAFFING, INC.
2001 Sheppard Ave. East, Suite 118
Toronto, ON M2J 4Z8

Telephone	416-496-1844
Fax	416-491-9030
Website	www.todays.com
Specialties	Advertising
	Banking
	Insurance
	Law
Level	Mid-Level
	Junior

Description Todays Staffing, Inc., provides staffing support services in professional, legal and financial skill categories.

TODAYS STAFFING, INC.
One King Street West, Suite 1502
Hamilton, ON L8P 1A4

Telephone	905-528-3400
Fax	905-528-7211
Website	www.todays.com
Specialties	Administrative
	Banking
	Insurance
	Law
Level	Mid-Level
	Junior

Description Todays Staffing, Inc., provides staffing support services in professional, legal and financial skill categories.

TODAYS STAFFING, INC.
2319 Fairview Street, Unit 603
Burlington, ON L7R 2E3

Telephone	905-681-2000
Fax	905-681-0827
Website	www.todays.com
Specialties	Administrative

Banking
Insurance
Law

Level Mid-Level
Junior

Description Todays Staffing, Inc., provides staffing support services in professional, legal and financial skill categories.

TODAYS STAFFING, INC.
33 City Centre Drive, Suite 543
Mississauga, ON L5B 2N5

Telephone 905-848-5900
Fax 905-848-8828
Website www.todays.com

Specialties Administrative
Banking
Insurance
Law

Level Mid-Level
Junior

Description Todays Staffing, Inc., provides staffing support services in professional, legal and financial skill categories.

TOLFREY GROUP
PO Box 1982
El Cerrito, CA 94530   USA

Telephone 510-234-0090
Fax 510-234-0097
E-mail resumes@tolfrey.com
Website www.tolfrey.com

Founded 1997
Employees 2

Specialties Computing
International
Finance
Human Resource

Level Senior
Mid-Level

Min. Salary $60,000
Fee Basis Sometimes contingent

Recruiters Grant Du Plooy
Ybella Hofstede

Contact Grant Du Plooy

Description Tolfrey Group focuses on the recruitment and placement of ERP specialists in the PeopleSoft, Oracle, SAP and BaaN markets, primarily in the west.

TOLSTOY RESOURCES
R.R. 1
Bolton, ON L7E 5R7

Telephone 905-880-0804
Fax 905-880-2671
E-mail dtolstoy@inforamp.net
Website www.
tolstoy-resources.com

Founded 1990
Employees 1

Specialties Banking
Direct Mktng.
Finance
Management

Level Senior
Mid-Level

Min. Salary $60,000
Fee Basis Retainer Only

Recruiters Lorraine Henderson
Stan Janes
Diane Tolstoy

Contact Diane Tolstoy

Description Tolstoy Resources are career brokers specializing in database mining, risk management, predictive modelling and scorecard development in the credit and collections field.

TOMA & BOUMA
10328 - 81 Avenue, Suite 305
Edmonton, AB T6E 1X2

Telephone 780-413-9262
Fax 780-431-9262
E-mail dtoma@
junctionnet.com

Specialties Agriculture/Fisheries

Contact Darrell Toma

Description Toma & Bouma are management consultants specializing in agribusiness. They occasionally do search work for clients.

TONY CURTIS & ASSOCIATES
45 Sheppard Avenue E., Suite 900
Toronto, ON M2N 5Y7

Telephone 416-224-0500
Fax 905-294-3349

Founded 1980
Employees 5

Specialties Apparel
Retail

Level Mid-Level
Senior

Recruiters Tony Curtis
Howard Curtis

Contact Tony Curtis

Description Tony Curtis & Associates specializes in all levels of recruiting pertaining to the clothing industry.

TORONTO EXECUTIVE CONSULTANTS
20 Bay Street, Suite 1205
Toronto, ON M5J 2N8

Telephone 416-366-6120
Fax 416-366-6117
E-mail info@toronto
executive.com
Website www.toronto
executive.com

Founded 1976

Specialties Computing
Engineering
Accounting
Finance
Sales
Marketing

Level Senior

Fee Basis Sometimes contingent

Description Since its inception, TEC has provided professional recruitment services to some of the most recognized firms in the nation.

TORSTAFF PERSONNEL
67 Yonge Street, Suite 503
Toronto, ON M5E 1J8

Telephone 416-866-8855
Fax 416-866-8126
E-mail jobs@torstaff.com
Website www.torstaff.com

Founded 1989

Specialties Accounting
Finance
Human Resource
Administrative

Level Mid-Level
Junior

Fee Basis Always contingent

Contact Kathy Reynolds,
Partner

Description Torstaff Personnel provides candidates and challenging positions in accounting, finance, administration, human resources and customer service.

TOSI PLACEMENT SERVICES INC.
40 University Avenue, Suite 900
Toronto, ON M5J 1T1

Telephone 416-362-7454
Fax 416-362-7414
E-mail services@tosi.com
Website www.tosi.com

Founded 1967

Specialties Computing
Finance
Administrative
Accounting
Direct Mktng.

Level Mid-Level

Recruiters Barb Allen
Loni Attrell
Brian Dawson
Mark Dyett
Michele Knezaurek
Sophia Shaw
Kim Villecco

Contact Barb Allen,
General Manager

Description For over 34 years, TOSI Placement Services has provided permanent and contract staffing services to the Canadian business community.

TOTTEN & ASSOCIATES INC.
392 Eastcastle Place
London, ON N6G 3W5

Telephone 519-471-6152
Fax 519-471-2309
E-mail bobtotten@home.com
Website www.tottenassoc.com

Founded 1985
Employees 2

Specialties General Practice
Administrative
Automotive
Finance
Human Resource
Management
Sales

Level Mid-Level

Min. Salary $40,000
Fee Basis   Retainer Only

Contact   Bob Totten

Description Totten & Associates is an independent Canadian firm offering professional human resources consulting services to business, industry and the public sector.

TOWNGATE PERSONNEL
3 Alum Chine Road, Bournemouth
Dorset   BH4 8DT
UNITED KINGDOM

Telephone 44-1202-752955
Fax   44-1202-752954

Specialties Hospitality
             International

Contact   James Tucker,
             Operations Manager

Description Towngate Personnel specializes in placing people in the UK hotel and catering industry.

TPS UNIMECS
Malledijk 18, 3208 LA
Spijkenisse   2517 KR
THE NETHERLANDS

Telephone 31-181-694-111
Fax   31-181-693-550
E-mail   nl.tps@sgs.com
Website   www.tps.co.uk

Specialties International
             Management
             Oil & Gas

Description TPS Unimecs recruits for the oil and gas, chemicals, power and utilities sectors.

TRACK INTERNATIONAL LTD.
PO Box 1
Perranporth   TR6 0YG
UNITED KINGDOM

Telephone 44-187-257-3937
Fax   44-870-164-0764
E-mail   register@
             track.demon.co.uk
Website   www.trackint.com

Specialties Computing
             International

Description Track International is a British employment agency specializing in placing IT professionals throughout Europe.

TRANS-UNITED CONSULTANTS LTD.
3228 South Service Road, Suite 110
Burlington, ON   L7N 3H8

Telephone 905-632-7176
Fax   905-632-5777
E-mail   tuc@trans-united.net
Website   www.trans-united.net

Founded   1980

Specialties Engineering
             Design
             Technical Support
             Architecture
             Aerospace
             Automotive
             Packaging
             Plastics

Level   Mid-Level
             Senior

Fee Basis Always contingent

Recruiters Brian deLottinville
             Bob Fletcher
             Robert Fratric
             Alice Giglio
             Jacob Grobbelaar
             Maria Kinsella
             Gary Koblik
             Michael Neill
             Philip O'Neill
             Arne Suutari
             John Train

Contact   Brian deLottinville

Description Trans-United recruits CADD drafters, engineers and other design professionals.

TRANSPERSONNEL DRIVER STAFFING AND ALLIED SERVICES
10088 - 102nd Ave., Suite 2101
Edmonton, AB   T5J 2Z1

Telephone 780-420-0110
Fax   780-424-0807
E-mail   info@trans
             personnel.com
Website   www.trans
             personnel.com

Founded   1943
Employees 14

Specialties Transport
             Logistics

Level   Mid-Level
             Junior

Fee Basis Always Contingent

Recruiters Bert Boutin
             Cathie Henderson
             Audrey Luft
             Brian McRae
             Travis Whenham

Contact   Cathie Henderson

Description Transpersonnel, a subsidiary of Manpower Inc., places professional drivers, warehousemen and office staff with private and contract carriers.

TRANSPERSONNEL DRIVER STAFFING AND ALLIED SERVICES
6910 - 6th Street SE, Suite 102
Calgary, AB   T2W 6E4

Telephone 403-255-0882
Fax   403-569-0870
E-mail   info@trans
             personnel.com
Website   www.trans
             personnel.com

Founded   1943
Employees 14

Specialties Transport
             Logistics

Fee Basis Always Contingent

Recruiters Joe Hebert
             Brian MacRae

Contact   Joe Hebert,
             Calgary Operations

Description Transpersonnel, a subsidiary of Manpower Inc., places professional drivers, warehousemen and office staff with private and contract carriers.

TRANSPERSONNEL DRIVER STAFFING AND ALLIED SERVICES
6 - 295 Queen St. E., Suite 375
Brampton, ON   L6W 4S6

Telephone 416-434-5309
Fax   519-372-0080
E-mail   info@trans
             personnel.com
Website   www.trans
             personnel.com

Specialties Transport
             Logistics

Level   Mid-Level

Fee Basis Always Contingent

Contact   John McQueen

Description Transpersonnel, a subsidiary of Manpower Inc., places professional drivers, warehousemen and office staff with private and contract carriers.

TRANSPORT HELP DRIVER SERVICE
161 Main Street
Thunder Bay, ON   P7B 6S5

Telephone 807-346-4370
Fax   807-346-4416
E-mail   thelp@air.on.ca
Website   www.transport
             help.com

Specialties Transport

Level   Mid-Level

Contact   Lou Hebert

Description We are a transportation training and personnel recruiting operation devoted to trucks.

TRANSPORT HELP DRIVER SERVICE
25 Vagnini Crescent
Lively, ON   P3Y 1K8

Telephone 705-692-9215
Fax   705-692-9256
E-mail   thelp@vianet.on.ca
Website   www.transport
             help.com

Specialties Transport

Level   Mid-Level

Contact   Raymond Lendt

Description We are a transportation training and personnel recruiting operation devoted to trucks.

TRANSPORT HELP DRIVER SERVICE
790 Industrial Road
Cambridge, ON   N3H 4W1

Telephone 519-653-1770
Fax   519-653-4132
E-mail   thelp@vianet.on.ca
Website   www.transporthelp.com

Specialties Transport

Level Mid-Level

Description We are a transportation training and personnel recruiting operation devoted to trucks.

TRANSPORT HELP DRIVER SERVICE

1335 Shawson Drive
Mississauga, ON L4W 1C4

Telephone 905-670-8239
Fax 905-670-1329
E-mail thelp@vianet.on.ca
Website www.transport
help.com

Specialties Transport

Level Mid-Level

Description We are a transportation training and personnel recruiting operation devoted to trucks.

TRANSPORT HELP DRIVER SERVICE

4120 Belgreen Drive
Gloucester, ON K1G 3N2

Telephone 613-739-9455
Fax 613-739-3881
E-mail thelp@vianet.on.ca
Website www.transport
help.com

Specialties Transport

Level Mid-Level

Contact Bob Garton

Description We are a transportation training and personnel recruiting operation devoted to trucks.

TRAVEL JOBS

120 Eglinton Avenue East
Suite 1000
Toronto, ON M4P 1E2

Telephone 416-483-1893
Fax 416-322-6371

Specialties Hospitality

Contact Jack Cliff

Description Travel Jobs specializes in placing people in the travel and hospitality industry.

TREAT & ASSOCIATES EXECUTIVE RECRUITERS

40 King Street West
Suite 4900, Scotia Plaza
Toronto, ON M5H 4A2

Telephone 416-777-6679
Fax 416-366-8759
E-mail treatandassoc@
home.com

Specialties Accounting
Finance
Management
International

Level Senior
Mid-Level

Contact Harvey Rosenthal

TREBOR PERSONNEL INC.

5 Manitou Drive, Suite 101
Kitchener, ON N2C 2J6

Telephone 519-894-1337
Fax 519-894-5364
E-mail kitchener@
tpipersonnel.com
Website www.tpipersonnel.com

Specialties Trades/Technicians
Transport
Administrative

Level Mid-Level
Junior

Description Trebor Personnel Inc. is one of the largest suppliers of industrial help and drivers in southern Ontario.

TREBOR PERSONNEL INC.

1680 Jane Street, Suite 202
Toronto, ON M9N 2S2

Telephone 416-244-5693
Fax 416-244-3659
E-mail janest@
tpipersonnel.com
Website www.tpipersonnel.com

Founded 1985

Specialties Trades/Technicians
Transport

Level Senior

Description Trebor Personnel Inc. is one of the largest suppliers of industrial help and drivers in southern Ontario.

TREBOR PERSONNEL INC.

3875 Keele Street, Suite 310
Toronto, ON M3J 1N6

Telephone 416-630-9536
Fax 416-630-8154
E-mail keelest@
tpipersonnel.com
Website www.tpipersonnel.com

Founded 1985

Specialties Trades/Technicians
Transport

Level Senior

Description Trebor Personnel Inc. is one of the largest suppliers of industrial help and drivers in southern Ontario.

TREBOR PERSONNEL INC.

2312 Eglinton Ave. East, Suite 201
Toronto, ON M1K 2M2

Telephone 416-750-4291
Fax 416-750-4292
E-mail scarborough@
tpipersonnel.com
Website www.tpipersonnel.com

Founded 1985

Specialties Trades/Technicians
Transport

Level Mid-Level
Junior

Contact Derek James

TREBOR PERSONNEL INC.

Description Trebor Personnel Inc. is one of the largest suppliers of industrial help and drivers in southern Ontario.

TREBOR PERSONNEL INC.

460 Brant Street, Unit 9
Burlington, ON L7R 4B6

Telephone 905-631-0100
Fax 905-631-1221
E-mail burlington@
tpipersonnel.com
Website www.tpipersonnel.com

Founded 1985

Specialties Trades/Technicians
Transport

Level Mid-Level
Junior

Description Trebor Personnel Inc. is one of the largest suppliers of industrial help and drivers in southern Ontario.

TREBOR PERSONNEL INC.

153 Queen Street West
Brampton, ON L6Y 1M4

Telephone 905-457-1326
Fax 905-457-8213
E-mail brampton@
tpipersonnel.com
Website www.tpipersonnel.com

Founded 1985

Specialties Trades/Technicians
Transport

Level Mid-Level
Junior

Description Trebor Personnel Inc. is one of the largest suppliers of industrial help and drivers in southern Ontario.

TREBOR PERSONNEL INC.

1090 Dundas Street East, Suite 203
Mississauga, ON L4Y 2B8

Telephone 905-566-0922
Fax 905-566-0925
E-mail mississauga@
tpipersonnel.com
Website www.tpipersonnel.com

Founded 1985

Specialties Trades/Technicians
Transport

Level Mid-Level
Junior

Description Trebor is one of the largest suppliers of industrial help and drivers in southern Ontario.

TRELLA & ASSOCIATES INC.

2 Bloor Street West, Suite 700
Toronto, ON M4W 3R1

Telephone 416-967-6759
Fax 416-967-1131

Founded 1977

Specialties Pharmaceutical
Health/Medical
Scientific

Level Senior
Mid-Level

Fee Basis Sometimes contingent

Contact Gordon Trella, President

Description An owner-managed company specializing in the pharmaceutical / healthcare industry with over 20 years experience. No entry-level positions.

TREMBLAY ET ASSOCIÉS INC.
8352, de Marseille
Montréal, QC H1L 1P7

Téléphone 514-353-2300
Télécopieur 514-353-2437

Employés 6

Spécialités Généralistes

Échelon Intermédiaire

Contact Réal Tremblay

TRENDLINE CONSULTING SERVICES
1100C Memorial Avenue, Suite 154
Thunder Bay, ON P7B 4A3

Telephone 807-623-3766
Fax 807-623-0706
E-mail trendlin@tbaytel.net

Specialties Management

Contact Gail Lawrence, President

Description Trendline Consulting Services provides search services for their corporate clients on a limited basis.

TRETIAK, HOLOWKA
1155, boul. René-Lévesque Ouest
Bureau 2020
Montréal, QC H3B 2J8

Telephone 514-954-0740
Fax 514-954-0743
E-mail th@sympatico.ca

Employees 5

Specialties Accounting
Finance

Level Mid-Level
Junior

Fee Basis Retainer Only

Contact Helen Holowka, CA

Description Tretiak, Holowka is an accounting firm that also provides occasional search work for clients.

TRI TECHRES INC.
25 Laurier, Suite 460
Hull, QC J8X 4C8

Telephone 819-595-5055
Fax 819-595-4647
E-mail jobs@tri-techres.com
Website www.tri-techres.com

Specialties Computing

Level Mid-Level

Contact President

Description TRI TechRes Inc. is a computer consulting firm specializ-

ing in system development, consulting and IT recruiting.

TRI-TEC INTERNATIONAL RESOURCES / TTIR
100 South Citrus Avenue, Suite 203
Covina, CA 91723 USA

Telephone 626-332-8006
Fax 626-323-7767
E-mail admin@ttir.com
Website www.ttir.com

Founded 1996

Specialties Computing
International

Description TTIR is a global resourcing company focusing on IT placements.

TRIDENT TECHNOLOGY SERVICES INC.
456 Main Street, 3rd Floor
Winnipeg, MB R3B 1B6

Telephone 204-943-6411
Fax 204-943-8603
E-mail pkostiuk@
mancomit.com
Website www.mancomit.com

Specialties Computing

Contact Peter Kostiuk

Description Trident Technology Services Inc. provides information technology personnel on a contract basis to assist clients with the construction, implementation and support of information systems and associated technologies.

TRILLIUM TALENT RESOURCE INC.
99 Main Street, Suite 204A
Cambridge, ON N1R 1W1

Telephone 519-620-9683
Fax 519-620-9686
E-mail thr@trilliumhr.com
Website www.trilliumhr.com

Founded 1988
Employees 4

Specialties Health/Medical
International

Fee Basis Always contingent

Recruiters Beryl A. Collingwood
Sabina Di Nino BBA

Contact Beryl A. Collingwood

Description This office of Trillium Talent Resource Inc. specializes in the placement of healthcare professionals in the USA, UK and Canada.

TRILLIUM TALENT RESOURCE INC.
150 Consumers Road, Suite 210
Toronto, ON M2J 1P9

Telephone 416-497-2624
Fax 416-497-8491
E-mail ttr@trilliumhr.com
Website www.trilliumhr.com

Specialties Health/Medical

Computing
Logistics

Recruiters Mark Byles MBA
Poonam Kathuria
Robert Masters
Bhagat Taggar

Contact Poonam Kathuria,
President

Description Trillium Talent Resource Group has over 15 years experience in the recruitment, retention and training of technical and management professionals for the healthcare, technology and supply chain sectors.

TRINET EMPLOYMENT GROUP
45 Sheppard Ave. East, Suite 900
Toronto, ON M2N 5W9

Telephone 416-221-2274
Fax 416-221-9176
E-mail canada@trinet.com
Website www.trinet.com

Specialties General Practice

Level Mid-Level

Description TriNet offers a full set of HR services to employers, including staffing and recruitment.

TRINET EMPLOYMENT GROUP
101 Callan Avenue
San Leandro, CA 94577 USA

Telephone 510-352-5000
Fax 510-352-6480
E-mail sanleandro@trinet.com
Website www.trinet.com

Specialties General Practice
International

Level Mid-Level

Contact Glen Glazar

Description TriNet offers a full set of HR services to employers, including staffing and recruitment.

TRISER CORP
121 John Street
Toronto, ON M5V 2E2

Telephone 416-977-1010
Fax 416-977-2455
E-mail info@triser.com
Website www.triser.com

Specialties Computing

Level Mid-Level

Contact Peter Sargautis

Description Triser Corp. is an IT consulting firm that also provides contract recruitment services for computing professionals.

TRS STAFFING SOLUTIONS (CANADA) INC.
355 - 4th Avenue SW, Suite 590
Calgary, AB T2P 0J1

Telephone 403-571-4775
Fax 403-571-4795
E-mail calgary@
trsstaffing.com

Website	www.trsstaffing.com
Employees	10
Specialties	Engineering Design Computing
Level	Mid-Level Senior
Min. Salary	$35,000
Fee Basis	Retainer Only
Recruiters	S. Gordon D. Lane P. Miller K. Olansen J. Schmidt
Contact	S. Gordon, Regional Manager

Description TRS, a subsidiary of Fluor Corporation, specializes in the sourcing and placement of information technology, engineering and design staff.

TRUE NORTH EXECUTIVE SEARCH
67 Yonge Street, Suite 900
Toronto, ON M5E 1J8

Telephone	416-304-0022
Fax	416-304-0029
E-mail	bnorth@truenorth search.com
Website	www.truenorth search.com
Founded	1995
Employees	5
Specialties	Telecom Engineering Publishing/Media Retail
Level	Senior
Contact	Bruce North

Description True North Executive Search is a full-service executive search firm with expertise in the technology and telecommunications, entertainment/media, and retail industries.

TSI GROUP / TSI STAFFING SERVICES
2630 Skymark Avenue, Suite 301
Mississauga, ON L4W 5A4

Telephone	905-629-3701
Fax	905-629-0799
E-mail	tsi@tsigroup.com
Website	www.tsigroup.com
Founded	1990
Employees	5
Specialties	Transport Logistics Purchasing Operations
Level	Junior Mid-Level
Min. Salary	$29,000
Recruiters	Stacy Agnos Shaun Elson Elizabeth Galli Donna Kelly Annette McDonough

Robyn Phillips
Pamela Ruebusch

Contact	Pamela Ruebusch, Senior Partner

Description Specializes in providing human resource solutions in supply chain management, including all areas of logistics, transportation, purchasing, customs and production planning.

TURNER DICKINSON & PARTNERS
666 Burrard Street
Suite 3400, Park Place
Vancouver, BC V6C 2X8

Telephone	604-408-4101
Fax	604-224-7795
E-mail	search@ turnerdickinson.com
Specialties	Management Marketing Finance
Level	Mid-Level Senior
Contact	John Dickinson

ULTIMATE STAFFING
143 James Street South, Suite 500
Hamilton, ON L8P 3A1

Telephone	905-529-4887
Fax	905-528-8840
E-mail	ultimatestaffing@ execushare.com
Founded	1989
Employees	5
Specialties	Accounting Finance Engineering Human Resource Insurance Operations
Level	Mid-Level
Fee Basis	Sometimes contingent
Recruiters	Len Falco Tony Meeker Elka Rombaor
Contact	Len Falco, President

Description Ultimate Staffing provides all levels of staff, including executive / professional, technical / skilled trades, accounting / clerical, specialty skills, to truck drivers and labour.

UNIQUE PERSONNEL CANADA INC.
400 Creditstone Road, Unit 5
Concord, ON L4K 3Z3

Telephone	905-660-8835
Fax	905-660-7581
E-mail	robertarossi@ uniquepersonnel.com
Specialties	Sales Marketing Transport Administrative
Level	Mid-Level Junior

UNIQUE PERSONNEL SERVICES INC.
11450 Cote-de-Liesse
Dorval, QC H9P 1A9

Telephone	514-631-3341
E-mail	pascalt@ uniquepersonnel.com
Specialties	Sales Marketing Transport Administrative
Level	Mid-Level Junior
Contact	Pascal Trepanier

UNIXEL RECRUTEMENT EN INFORMATIQUE
38, place du Commerce
Bureau 200
Île-des-Soeurs, QC H3T 1T8

Téléphone	514-362-1234
Télécopieur	514-362-8270
Courriel	info@unixel.com
Site Internet	www.unixel.com
Fondée	1993
Spécialités	Informatique
Échelon	Intermédiaire
Recruteurs	François Angrignon Jacques Morel Isabelle Peloquin
Contact	Francois Angrignon

Description Unixel specialise en recrutement et en placement de ressources spécialisées en technologies de l'information.

URENTIA
1176 Bishop, S-300
Montréal, QC H3G 2E3

Telephone	514-396-0011
Fax	514-396-0012
E-mail	dfournier@urentia.com
Website	www.urentia.com
Specialties	Computing Sales Telecom
Level	Mid-Level Senior
Min. Salary	$40,000
Fee Basis	Sometimes contingent
Recruiters	Florent Coache Daniel Fournier Eugenette Morin
Contact	Daniel Fournier, Senior Partner

Description Urentia is the result of the merger of Henderson-Fournier Inc. and Gestion Florent Coache Inc. These two firms combine over 15 years of expertise in the recruiting of IT professionals.

URQUHART MANAGEMENT INC.
41 Shanley Street, Suite 7
Toronto, ON M6H 1S2

Telephone	416-516-8611
Fax	416-536-1846
E-mail	umi@istar.ca
Founded	1978

Specialties Actuarial
Level Mid-Level
Senior
Fee Basis Retainer Only
Contact Dave Urquhart
Description Urquhart Management Inc. specializes in placing actuarial professionals.

VAN BIESEN GROUP INC.
505 Third Street SW
Suite 950
Calgary, AB T2P 3E6
Telephone 403-292-0950
Fax 403-292-0959
E-mail cbell@vanbiesen
group.com
Website www.vanbiesen
group.com
Founded 1988
Employees 5
Specialties Management
Oil & Gas
Construction
Finance
International
Engineering
Level Senior
Min. Salary $100,000
Fee Basis Retainer Only
Recruiters Catherine Bell
Jacques A.H. van
Biesen
Contact Jacques van Biesen
Description Van Biesen Group are specialists in national and worldwide searches at senior executive and specialist levels.

VAN HEES PERSONNEL INC.
115 King Street West
Dundas, ON L9H 1V1
Telephone 905-627-5472
Fax 905-627-5473
E-mail info@
vanheespersonnel.ca
Website www.vanhees
personnel.ca
Founded 1975
Specialties Engineering
Finance
Logistics
Quality Control
Human Resource
Sales
Marketing
Level Mid-Level
Senior
Contact Tony Van Hees,
President
Description Van Hees Personnel specializes in recruiting professionals for manufacturing and assembly (including engineering), finance, MIS, senior management, quality assurance, human resources, materials management and sales / marketing assignments.

VAN KLAVEREN LITHERLAND & COMPANY
1 Toronto Street, Suite 802
Toronto, ON M2C 2W3
Telephone 416-868-4888
Fax 416-868-6882
E-mail ltl@searchmgmt.com
Specialties Management
Marketing
Finance
Health/Medical
Operations
Agriculture/Fisheries
Level Mid-Level
Senior
Min. Salary $60,000
Recruiters Paul Cudmore
Lori Litherland
David Van Klaveren
Contact Lori Litherland
Description Van Klaveren Litherland & Company specializes in recruiting financial management and agricultural candidates.

VANTEC CONSULTANTS LTD.
1275 - 6th Avenue West, Suite 300
Vancouver, BC V6H 1A6
Telephone 604-738-8836
Specialties Engineering
Insurance
Level Mid-Level
Contact Leslie Richardson

VECTOR TECHNICAL SERVICES
330 Bay Street, Suite 820
Toronto, ON M5H 2S8
Telephone 416-865-0086
Fax 416-366-8512
E-mail jobs@vector-tech.com
Website www.vector-tech.com
Founded 1984
Specialties Computing
Description Vector Technical Services is a professional information technology employment organization.

VEGA CONSULTING SOLUTIONS, INC.
99 Cherry Hill Road, Suite 112
Parsippany, NJ 07054 USA
Telephone 201-335-7800
Fax 201-335-1677
E-mail vegaconsul@aol.com
Website www.vegaconsulting.com
Specialties Computing
International
Level Mid-Level
Recruiters Kim Shand
Gregory Shand
Lawrence Sullivan
Contact Kim Shand
Description VEGA places IT consultants in assignments across the USA.

VENATUS CONSEIL LTÉE
485 rue McGill, Bureau 601
Montréal, QC H2Y 2H4
Téléphone 514-992-1713
Télécopieur 514-993-1713
Courriel info@venatus.com
Site Internet www.venatus.com
Spécialités Aérospatial
Agriculture/pêches
Affaires de banque
Ingénierie
Finance
Pharmaceutique
Télécommunications
Échelon Direction
Intermédiaire
Recruteurs Jacqueline Dahan
Nathalie Francisci
Manuel Francisci
Lyne Groulx
Natacha McCrea
Contact Nathalie Francisci,
President
Description Venatus Conseil Ltée est une entreprise de services conseil en ressources humaines dont la spécialisation concerne la recherche de cadres et professionnels pour de grandes ou de moyennes entreprises.

VENPRO CONSULTING INC.
37 Rainbow Creekway
Toronto, ON M2K 2T9
Telephone 416-223-3341
E-mail venpro@sympatico.ca
Founded 1990
Employees 1
Specialties Sales
Marketing
Computing
Level Senior
Mid-Level
Min. Salary $60,000
Fee Basis Always contingent
Contact Brian Campbell
Description Venpro specializes in placing computer vendor professionals, particularly sales representatives, pre-sales systems engineers and sales and marketing managers.

VERELLI ARRIZZA
3680, avenue du Musée
Bureau 200
Montréal, QC H3G 2C9
Telephone 514-849-8007
Fax 514-849-7060
Specialties Accounting
Finance
Operations
Level Mid-Level
Contact Adriano Arrizza, CA
Description Verelli Arrizza is an accounting firm that also does occasional search work for clients.

VERES PICTON & CO.
10339 - 124th Street, Suite 400
Edmonton, AB T5N 3W1

Telephone	780-482-2349
Fax	780-452-9060
E-mail	veres@planet.eon.net
Website	www.accountantsca.com/vpk/vpk-home.html

Employees	26
Specialties	Accounting Finance
Level	Mid-Level
Recruiters	J.W. Bruce Picton John R. Veres CA
Contact	John R. Veres, Partner

Description Veres Picton & Co. is an accounting firm that also does occasional search work for clients.

VERRIEZ GROUP INC., THE
205 John Street
London, ON N6A 1N9

Telephone	519-673-3463
Fax	519-673-4748
E-mail	verriez@verriez.com
Website	www.verriez.com
Founded	1985
Employees	6
Specialties	Marketing Sales Management Accounting Finance Engineering International
Level	Mid-Level Senior
Min. Salary	$65,000
Fee Basis	Sometimes contingent
Recruiters	Tara Forster Melissa Machan Lynn Sveinbjornson Paul Verriez
Contact	Paul Verriez

Description Verriez Group is an executive search practice, with emphasis on accounting / finance professionals in Canada, USA, Mexico and United Kingdom.

VEZINA GOODMAN EXECUTIVE SEARCH
417, rue Saint-Nicolas, Bureau 100
Montréal, QC H2Y 2P4

Telephone	514-849-2333
Fax	514-849-5619
E-mail	vg@ergonet.com
Website	www.emapartners.com
Founded	1986
Employees	5
Specialties	Management
Level	Senior Mid-Level
Min. Salary	$70,000
Recruiters	Michael Goodman Claude Vézina

Contact	Claude Vézina, President

Description Vezina Goodman Executive Search is a member of EMA Partners Worldwide.

VICKERY BOARDMAN & ASSOCIATES INC.
604 Brock Street S.
Whitby, ON L1N 4K9

Telephone	905-666-9990
Fax	905-666-5275
Founded	1980
Specialties	Marketing Sales Health/Medical General Practice Biotech/Biology Pharmaceutical
Level	Mid-Level Senior
Contact	Valerie Vickery

VICTOR & GOLD
759, square Victoria, Bureau 400
Montréal, QC H2Y 2J7

Telephone	514-282-1836
Fax	514-282-6640
E-mail	info@victorgold.com
Founded	1932
Specialties	Accounting Finance Real Estate
Level	Mid-Level
Fee Basis	Retainer Only
Recruiters	Edward Victor Gary Wechsler CA
Contact	Edward Victor, CMC

Description Victor & Gold is a chartered accounting firm in downtown Montreal that occasionally provides search work for clients.

VILLOR CONSULTANTS INC.
759 Square Victoria, Bureau 400
Montréal, QC H2Y 2J7

Telephone	514-282-0561
Fax	514-282-6640
E-mail	vg@total.net
Specialties	Accounting
Level	Mid-Level

VINCENT-ENGLEHART LIMITED
1358 Queen Street
PO Box 3698, Park Lane Centre
Halifax, NS B3J 2H5

Telephone	902-423-7291
Fax	902-423-7293
E-mail	dbm.atlantic@ns.sympatico.ca
Employees	4
Specialties	Govt/Nonprofit Management Finance Marketing Sales

Level	Mid-Level Senior
Contact	Miriam Englehart

VOLT HUMAN RESOURCES INC.
1055 Dunsmuir Street
Suite 2684, PO Box 49288
Vancouver, BC V7X 1L3

Telephone	604-408-0422
Fax	604-685-6175
E-mail	vancouverbcjobs@volt.com
Website	www.volt.com
Specialties	Computing Engineering
Level	Mid-Level
Recruiters	Vito deCandia David Desormeaux
Contact	David Desormeaux

Description VHRI is a Fortune 1000 company and a leader in the technical staffing industry.

VOLT HUMAN RESOURCES INC.
130 King Street West, Suite 1305
Toronto, ON M5X 1A4

Telephone	416-306-3390
Fax	416-306-1449
E-mail	torontotechjubs@volt.com
Website	www.volt.com
Specialties	Computing Engineering
Level	Mid-Level
Contact	Michelle Laughlin

Description VHRI is a Fortune 1000 company and a leader in the technical staffing industry.

VTRAC IT CONSULTANTS CORP.
121 Willowdale Ave., Suite 301
Toronto, ON M2N 6A3

Telephone	416-227-9293
Fax	416-227-9299
E-mail	admin@vtrac.com
Website	www.vtrac.com
Specialties	Sales Computing
Level	Senior Mid-Level
Fee Basis	Always contingent

Description VTRAC is a recruitment and consulting firm specializing in placing IT professionals in the e-commerce, telecommunications and financial markets.

W.G. MELDRUM LIMITED
938 Howe Street, Suite 318
Vancouver, BC V6Z 1N9

Telephone	604-929-8342
Fax	604-929-8392
E-mail	lboyd@telus.net
Website	www.wgmeldrum.com
Specialties	Computing Sales Marketing

Level	Senior
	Mid-Level
Fee Basis	Sometimes contingent
Contact	Lesley Boyd

Description W.G. Meldrum Limited is an information technology recruitment firm specializing in sales, marketing and management placement for the computer industry.

W.G. MELDRUM LIMITED
400 - 3rd Avenue SW, Suite 500
Calgary, AB T2P 4H2

Telephone	403-244-9828
Fax	403-294-0765
E-mail	alwson@ab.imag.net
Website	www.wgmeldrum.com
Founded	1980
Employees	2
Specialties	Sales
	Computing
	Marketing
Level	Senior
	Mid-Level
Min. Salary	$50,000
Fee Basis	Sometimes contingent
Recruiters	Rebecca Bailer
	Alayna Christie
	Sandra Fournier
	Mari Anne Lawson
Contact	Alayna Christie

Description W.G. Meldrum Limited is an information technology recruitment firm specializing in sales, marketing and management placement for the computer industry.

W.G. MELDRUM LIMITED
3080 Yonge Street, Suite 4062
Toronto, ON M4N 3N1

Telephone	416-480-0036
Fax	416-482-3737
E-mail	wgmeldrum@
	sympatico.ca
Website	www.wgmeldrum.com
Founded	1982
Specialties	Sales
	Marketing
	Computing
Level	Senior
	Mid-Level
Fee Basis	Sometimes contingent
Recruiters	Bruce McIsaac
	William G. Meldrum
	Laurie Mountford
	Marianne Romak
Contact	Bill Meldrum

Description W.G. Meldrum Limited is an information technology recruitment firm specializing in sales, marketing and management placement for the computer industry.

W.H. JACKSON & ASSOCIATES
1 Cuthbert Crescent
Toronto, ON M4S 2G9

Telephone	416-480-0809
Fax	416-480-0073
E-mail	hayesjackson@
	attcanada.net
Specialties	Finance
Level	Senior
	Mid-Level
Contact	W.H. Jackson

W. HUTT MANAGEMENT RESOURCES LTD.
2349 Fairview Street, Suite 110
Burlington, ON L7R 2E3

Telephone	905-637-3800
Fax	905-637-3221
E-mail	whuttmgt@skyline.net
Website	www.whutt
	management.com
Founded	1982
Employees	6
Specialties	Operations
	Management
	Engineering
	Accounting
	Purchasing
	Automotive
	Metals
Level	Mid-Level
	Senior
Fee Basis	Retainer Only
Recruiters	Wayne Hutt
	Grant Parsons
Contact	Wayne Hutt

Description WHMR performs retained searches only.

W.R. LONDON CONSULTANTS INC.
2 Bloor Street West, Suite 700
Toronto, ON M4W 3R1

Telephone	416-975-0520
Fax	416-975-9241
E-mail	wlondon@on.aibn.com
Specialties	Public Relations
	General Practice
	Govt/Nonprofit
Level	Mid-Level
	Senior
Contact	Wendy R. London

W5 RESOURCES, INC.
325 Renfrew Drive, Suite 302
Markham, ON L3R 9S8

Telephone	905-940-0989
Fax	905 940 0258
E-mail	info@w5.net
Website	www.w5.net
Specialties	Computing
Level	Mid-Level
	Junior

Description W5 Resources, Inc. is an IT consulting company that places computing professionals in consulting and help-desk assignments.

WACE & ASSOCIATES
151 City Centre Drive, Suite 301
Mississauga, ON L5B 1M7

Telephone	905-281-0111
Fax	905-281-0144
E-mail	wace@idirect.com
Founded	1989
Employees	4
Specialties	Human Resource
	Govt/Nonprofit
	Finance
	Administrative
	Accounting
	Sales
	Management
Level	Senior
	Mid-Level
Min. Salary	$50,000
Fee Basis	Retainer Only
Recruiters	Judith E. Henry CMC
	Steve Wace
Contact	Steve Wace

Description Wace & Associates provides recruiting services and consulting on strategic, organizational, pay and incentive systems, executive coaching, human resource and labour relations issues.

WADE & PARTNERS
3190 Harvester Road, 2nd Floor
Burlington, ON L7N 3T1

Telephone	905-333-9888
Fax	905-333-9583
E-mail	ca@wadepartners.com
Website	www.wade
	partners.com
Founded	1968
Specialties	Accounting
	Finance
Level	Mid-Level

Description Wade & Partners is an accounting firm that also provides occasional recruitment services for clients in the Hamilton-Wentworth and Halton regions.

WAGNER ET ASSOCIÉS
360, rue Saint-Francois-Xavier
Bureau 200
Montréal, QC H2Y 2S8

Telephone	514-842-5494
Fax	514-842-4529
E-mail	cv@wagner.ca
Founded	1983
Employees	3
Specialties	Computing
	Management
Level	Senior
	Mid-Level
Fee Basis	Always contingent
Contact	Gabriel Wagner,
	President

Description Wagner et Associés specializes in placing high-specialty IT professionals, technical service and management personnel.

WALBROOK APPOINTMENTS ENGLAND
330 Bay Street, Suite 1304
Toronto, ON M5H 2S8

Telephone	416-364-4477
Specialties	Accounting
	Computing
	Govt/Nonprofit
	Health/Medical
	Management
Level	Mid-Level
Contact	Lynne D. Delfs

WALKER FOREST
992 Old Eagle School Road
Suite 913
Wayne, PA 19087-1803 USA

Telephone	610-989-8500
Fax	610-989-8501
E-mail	pdl@walkerforest.com
Website	www.walkerforest.com
Founded	1995
Employees	7
Specialties	Computing
	Sales
	Telecom
	International
	Banking
	Logistics
	Management
	Marketing
	Multimedia
Level	Senior
	Mid-Level
Min. Salary	$80,000
Fee Basis	Sometimes contingent
Recruiters	Terri Evans
	Philip Gardiner
	Jacqueline Grant
	Jeffrey L. Kozol
	Jaclyn Lairson
	Peter Levitt
	Jack Mahon
	Lauren Nassau
	Michael O'Gara
	James J. Sperduto
Contact	Peter Levitt

Description Walker Forest (formerly Sales Consultants of King of Prussia) is an executive search firm providing a full range of services and specializing in the telecommunications, e-commerce and banking technology industries.

WALKER-DAVIES CONSULTANTS LTD.
470 Granville Street, Suite 818
Vancouver, BC V6C 1V5

Telephone	604-687-7646
Specialties	Law
Level	Mid-Level
	Junior
Contact	Barbara Davies

Description Specializing in the placement of legal assistants and paralegals.

WALLACE & PARTNERS INC.
151 Yonge Street, Suite 1400
Toronto, ON M5C 2W7

Telephone	416-368-6886
Fax	416-368-3464
E-mail	info@
	wallacepartners.on.ca
Website	www.wgroupinc.com
Specialties	General Practice
Level	Senior
Recruiters	Peter Armstrong
	Lynn Jessop
	Graeme Wallace PhD
Contact	Graeme Wallace,
	Senior Partner

Description Wallace & Partners Inc. provides a range of human resources consulting services including executive search.

WALSH KING
595 Howe Street, 14th Floor
Vancouver, BC V6C 2T5

Telephone	604-687-2003
Fax	604-687-2066
E-mail	rwalsh@walshking.com
Website	www.walshking.com
Specialties	Accounting
	Forestry
	Real Estate
Level	Mid-Level
Recruiters	Jill Guthrie CA
	Ron Walsh FCA
Contact	Ron Walsh, Partner

Description Walsh King is an accounting firm that occasionally provides recruitment services for clients, particularly in the forestry field.

WALTER P. MILLER & COMPANY
108 LeMarchant Road, Box 8505
St. John's, NF A1B 3N9

Telephone	709-579-2161
Fax	709-738-2391
E-mail	steve@
	walterpmiller.com
Website	www.walterpmiller.com
Specialties	Accounting
	Finance
	Agriculture/Fisheries
Level	Mid-Level
Contact	Steve Belanger, Partner

Description Walter P. Miller & Company is an accounting firm that occasionally provides recruitment services for clients, particularly in the seafood industry.

WARD VINGE & ASSOCIATES
10909 Jasper Avenue, Suite 100
Edmonton, AB T5J 3L9

Telephone	780-429-9058
Fax	780-425-7419
E-mail	dssedm@
	diversifiedstaffing.com
Website	www.diversified staffing.com
Founded	1978
Employees	70
Specialties	Engineering
	Construction
	Geology/Geography
	Oil & Gas
	Plastics
	Real Estate
	Transport
Level	Mid-Level
Min. Salary	$30,000
Fee Basis	Sometimes contingent
Contact	Ken Vinge

Description Ward Vinge & Associates is the permanent and executive staffing division of Diversified Staffing Services.

WARD VINGE & ASSOCIATES
805 - 5th Avenue SW
Calgary, AB T2P 0N6

Telephone	403-237-5577
Fax	403-269-1428
E-mail	dsscal@
	diversifiedstaffing.com
Website	www.wardvinge.com
Founded	1978
Employees	70
Specialties	Engineering
	Construction
	Geology/Geography
	Oil & Gas
	Plastics
	Real Estate
	Transport
Level	Mid-Level
Min. Salary	$30,000
Fee Basis	Sometimes contingent
Recruiters	Jane Campbell
	Roberta Clement
	Nick Hudson
	Laurie Kozicki
Contact	Laurie Kozicki

Description Ward Vinge & Associates is the permanent and executive staffing division of Diversified Staffing Services.

WASSERMAN, STOTLAND, BRATT, GROSSBAUM/WSBG
1155 René-Levesque Blvd. West
Suite 2010
Montréal, QC H3B 2J8

Telephone	514-861-9724
Fax	514-861-9446
E-mail	wsbg@wsbg.com
Specialties	Accounting
	Finance
Level	Mid-Level
Contact	Murray Pinsky

Description WSBG is an accounting, auditing, management advisory services and taxation services firm that also does search work for clients.

WATSON WYATT WORLDWIDE
401 West Georgia Street, Suite 700
Vancouver, BC V6B 5A1

Telephone	604-688-6211
Fax	604-688-3202
E-mail	david_m_harris@
	watsonwyatt.com

Website	www.watsonwyatt.com
Specialties	Govt/Nonprofit
	Human Resource
	Management
Level	Senior
	Mid-Level
Contact	David M. Harris

Description Specializes in human resources consulting, particularly in the fields of compensation, pensions and benefits. Sometimes also provides senior-level recruitment services to clients.

WATSON WYATT WORLDWIDE
1 Queen Street East, Suite 1100
Toronto, ON M5C 2Y4

Telephone	416-862-0393
Fax	416-366-9691
E-mail	martin_brown@
	watsonwyatt.com
Website	www.watsonwyatt.com
Specialties	Management
	Govt/Nonprofit
	Human Resource
Level	Mid-Level
	Senior
Contact	Martin Brown

Description Specializes in HR consulting, particularly in the fields of compensation, pensions and benefits. Sometimes provides senior-level recruitment services to clients.

WAYNE PERRY & ASSOCIATES
335 Bay Street, Suite 701
Toronto, ON M5H 2R3

Telephone	416-214-2010
Fax	416-361-0728
E-mail	wperry@
	wayne-perry.com
Website	www.wayne-perry.com
Founded	1996
Employees	5
Specialties	Accounting
	Computing
	Engineering
	Finance
	Logistics
	Operations
Level	Senior
	Mid-Level
Fee Basis	Retainer Only
Contact	Wayne B. Perry

Description Wayne Perry & Associates is a general recruitment practice that does retainer searches only.

WAYNE THOMAS & ASSOCIATES
2428 Wyndale Crescent
Ottawa, ON K1H 7A6

Telephone	613-738-9324
Fax	603-807-7926
E-mail	waynethomas@
	ottawa.com
Founded	1977
Specialties	Engineering
	Computing

	Sales
Level	Mid-Level
	Senior
Min. Salary	$50,000
Fee Basis	Always contingent
Contact	Wayne Thomas

Description Wayne Thomas specializes in placing technology sales and systems engineering personnel.

WEIR ASSOCIATES INC.
2200 Yonge Street, Suite 1210
Toronto, ON M4S 2C9

Telephone	416-440-1033
Fax	416-440-1957
E-mail	reception@
	weirassociates.com
Website	www.weir
	associates.com
Founded	1987
Employees	4
Specialties	Computing
	Sales
	General Practice
Level	Senior
	Mid-Level
Min. Salary	$75,000
Fee Basis	Retainer Only
Recruiters	Jane Stewart
	Jon Stungevicius
	Douglas Weir
Contact	Douglas Weir, President

Description Weir Associates recruits senior management talent for organizations that build, sell or use information technology.

WELLINGTON PARTNERS INTERNATIONAL INC.
625 King Street East, Suite 1C
Kitchener, ON N2G 4V4

Telephone	519-744-2444
Fax	519-744-0913
E-mail	info@
	wellingtonpartners.com
Website	www.wellington
	partners.com
Founded	1991
Employees	15
Specialties	Engineering
	Management
	Sales
	Operations
	Accounting
	Finance
	Marketing
	Purchasing
	Automotive
	Mining
Level	Senior
	Mid-Level
Min. Salary	$45,000
Fee Basis	Sometimes contingent
Recruiters	Bryan East
	Don Fildey
	John Holmes
	Byrle Klink
	Steve Machowski
Contact	Don Fildey

Description Dedicated to providing highly professional and ethical services to companies in the areas of executive search and career transition management.

WENJE MANAGEMENT LTD.
4315 Major MacKenzie Drive East
Markham, ON L6C 1K4

Telephone	905-887-0840
Fax	905-887-0841
E-mail	resumes@wenje.com
Website	www.wenje.com
Founded	1986
Employees	7
Specialties	Computing
	Engineering
	Marketing
	Sales
	Telecom
	Finance
	General Practice
Level	Senior
	Mid-Level
Fee Basis	Retainer Only
Contact	Jennifer Chamberlain,
	President

Description Global in scope, Wenje Management offers research services to both executive search firms and corporate clients directly.

WESTCOTT, THOMAS & ASSOCIATES LTD. / PSA INTERNATIONAL
75 Main Street West, Suite 9
Huntsville, ON P1H 1X1

Telephone	705-789-2220
E-mail	westcott@vianet.on.ca
Website	www.westcott-thomas.com
Founded	1997
Specialties	General Practice
	Management
Level	Senior
	Mid-Level
Min. Salary	$50,000
Contact	Michael J. Thomas,
	President & CEO

Description Westcott, Thomas & Associates Limited is a member of PSA International.

WESTCOTT, THOMAS & ASSOCIATES LTD. / PSA INTERNATIONAL
5650 Yonge Street, Suite 1500
Toronto, ON M2M 4G3

Telephone	416-481-4471
Fax	416-481-4473
E-mail	westcott@vianet.on.ca
Website	www.westcott-thomas.com
Founded	1969
Employees	5
Specialties	General Practice
	Management
	Govt/Nonprofit
Level	Senior
	Mid-Level

Min. Salary	$50,000
Fee Basis	Retainer Only
Contact	Michael J. Thomas, President & CEO

Description Westcott, Thomas & Associates Limited is a member of PSA International, a global search firm.

WESTERN HR CONSULTING LTD.
5920 Macleod Trail SW, Suite 610
Calgary, AB T2H 0K2

Telephone	403-215-2150
Fax	403-215-2151
E-mail	careers@westernhr.com
Website	www.westernhr.com
Founded	1996
Employees	4
Specialties	Agriculture/Fisheries Logistics Hospitality Management Marketing Operations Sales
Level	Mid-Level Senior
Fee Basis	Sometimes contingent
Recruiters	Steve Morrison Don Murchie
Contact	Steve Morrison, President

Description Western HR Consulting Ltd. provides a full range of human resource services, including recruitment services, to any size organization.

WESTERN MANAGEMENT CONSULTANTS
1188 West Georgia St., Suite 2000
Vancouver, BC V6E 4A2

Telephone	604-687-0391
Fax	604-687-2315
E-mail	vancouver@wmc.ca
Website	www.wmc.ca
Founded	1975
Employees	35
Specialties	Management Marketing Operations Finance Human Resource General Practice Sales
Level	Senior Mid-Level
Min. Salary	$80,000
Fee Basis	Retainer Only
Recruiters	Janet David CMC Brian Morrison CMC Adrian J. Palmer Richard Savage CMC Roger Welch CMC
Contact	Brian Morrison CMC, Director

Description Western Management Consultants provides 25 years executive search experience in local, national and international manage-

ment for corporate, government and non-profit sectors.

WESTERN MANAGEMENT CONSULTANTS
10250 - 101st Street, Suite 1500
Edmonton, AB T5J 3P4

Telephone	780-428-1501
Fax	780-429-0256
E-mail	edmonton@wmc.ca
Website	www.wmc.ca
Founded	1975
Specialties	Management Govt/Nonprofit Banking Biotech/Biology Computing Construction Engineering
Level	Senior Mid-Level
Min. Salary	$50,000
Fee Basis	Retainer Only
Recruiters	Rick L. Harvey CMC John E. Steffensen
Contact	John E. Steffensen FCMC, Director

Description Western Management Consultants provides a wide range of management consulting services, including executive search.

WESTERN MANAGEMENT CONSULTANTS
333 - 5th Avenue SW, Suite 800
Calgary, AB T2P 3B6

Telephone	403-531-8200
Fax	403-531-8218
E-mail	calgary@wmc.ca
Website	www.wmc.ca
Founded	1975
Specialties	Accounting Management Scientific Oil & Gas
Level	Mid-Level Senior
Min. Salary	$50,000
Contact	Jeannie Wexler

Description Western Management Consultants is dedicated to providing a wide range of management consulting services to clients in public and private sectors.

WESTERN MANAGEMENT CONSULTANTS
1004 University Drive
Saskatoon, SK S7N 0K3

Telephone	306-242-6191
Fax	306-665-0025
E-mail	saskatoon@wmc.ca
Website	www.wmc.ca
Founded	1975
Specialties	Management
Level	Senior Mid-Level

Min. Salary	$50,000
Contact	Brian Pratt, CMC

Description Western Management Consultants is dedicated to providing a wide range of management consulting services, including executive search.

WESTERN MANAGEMENT CONSULTANTS
65 Queen Street West, Suite 800
Toronto, ON M5H 2M5

Telephone	416-362-6863
Fax	416-362-0761
E-mail	toronto@wmc.on.ca
Website	www.wmc.on.ca
Founded	1975
Employees	8
Specialties	Management Finance Operations
Level	Mid-Level Senior
Min. Salary	$50,000
Fee Basis	Retainer Only
Recruiters	Mary Baetz Jim Carlisle Kathy Dempster Leo Gotlieb Ron Knowles Anne-Marie Stewart George Toner Allan Young-Pugh
Contact	Karen Degan

Description Western Management Consultants is dedicated to providing a wide range of management consulting services, including executive search.

WIDMAN ASSOCIATES INC.
555 West Hastings Street, Suite 700
Vancouver, BC V6B 4N5

Telephone	604-443-5087
Fax	604-443-5097
E-mail	crwidman@widman.com
Founded	1993
Specialties	Forestry
Contact	Charles Widman

Description Widman Associates Inc. is a management consulting firm specializing in the solid wood products industry. They also do regular recruitment work for clients.

WIGHTMAN & ASSOCIATES
PO Box 72037
Kanata, ON K2K 2P4

Telephone	613-591-8630
Fax	613-591-8501
E-mail	wightmanju@aol.com
Founded	1993
Specialties	General Practice
Level	Mid-Level Senior
Min. Salary	$50,000

Fee Basis Retainer Only
Contact Judith Wightman

Description Wightman & Assoc. does professional national and international searches for a broad range of mid- to senior-level positions in public, private and para-public sector.

WILKIE GROUP INTERNATIONAL, THE
1 First Canadian Place
PO Box 408, Suite 815
Toronto, ON M5X 1E3

Specialties Retail
Finance
Logistics
Health/Medical

Level Senior

Min. Salary $125,000
Fee Basis Always contingent

Contact Glenn Wilkie, Owner

WILLIAM LEE & ASSOCIATES, INC.
885 West Georgia Street, Suite 1500
Vancouver, BC V6C 3E8

Telephone 604-689-7893
Fax 604-689-7882
E-mail info@wlee.com
Website www.wlee.com

Specialties Computing
Level Senior
Mid-Level

Recruiters William Lee
Anna Vasques

Contact William Lee

Description William Lee & Associates, Inc. is an executive search firm specializing in recruiting IT professionals.

WILLIAM SQUIBB & ASSOCIATES
48 St. Francis Street North
Kitchener, ON N2H 5B5

Telephone 519-570-2515
Fax 519-585-0720
E-mail information@wsquibb.com
Website www.wsquibb.com
Founded 1988

Specialties Health/Medical
International

Contact Lisa Filipowitsch

Description William Squibb & Associates is active in nursing and physician recruitment for positions in Canada, USA and Saudi Arabia.

WILLIAMS & ASSOCIATES INC.
96 Cowley Avenue
Toronto, ON M9B 2E5

Telephone 416-626-9100
Fax 416-622-3205
E-mail consultant@williamsandassociates.net
Website www.williamsandassociates.net
Founded 1986

Specialties Trade Shows
Design
Retail
Level Mid-Level
Min. Salary $30,000
Fee Basis Sometimes contingent
Contact Jasmin Chandler, General Manager

Description Williams & Assoc. recruits for the exhibit/display, point-of-sale and store fixture industry.

WILLING PLUS PERSONNEL CORPORATION
1056 Wilson Avenue, Suite 100
Toronto, ON M3K 1G6

Telephone 416-398-8770
Fax 416-398-8431

Specialties Trades/Technicians

WINDOWPANE MANAGEMENT INC.
1414 - 8th Avenue SW, Suite 340
Calgary, AB T2R 1J6

Telephone 403-262-2660
Fax 403-229-3778
E-mail dneumann@windowpanemanagement.com
Website www.windowpanemanagement.com

Specialties Engineering
Management
Health/Medical
Oil & Gas
Level Mid-Level
Contact Donna Neumann, President

WINDSOR PERSONNEL & EXECUTIVE CENTER
1319 Ouellette Avenue
Windsor, ON N8X 1J6

Telephone 519-258-9500
Fax 519-258-6478

Specialties Management
Engineering
Sales
Trades/Technicians
Computing
Level Mid-Level
Junior
Contact Colleen Hurst

Description Windsor Personnel & Executive recruits in a range of fields, including management, technical, administration, clerical, sales, IT, accounting and skilled trades.

WINTERS TECHNICAL STAFFING SERVICES
2025 Sheppard Ave. E., Suite 4110
Toronto, ON M2J 1V7

Telephone 416-495-7422
Fax 416-495-8479
E-mail winters@ionsys.com

Specialties Engineering
Level Senior
Mid-Level

Contact Brian Taverner

WITHEY ADDISON
1865 Lakeshore Road W., Suite 201
Mississauga, ON L5J 4P1

Telephone 905-822-1226
Fax 905-822-0372
E-mail mississauga@witheyaddison.com
Website www.witheyaddison.com

Founded 1970
Employees 12

Specialties Accounting
Finance
Fee Basis Retainer Only
Contact Richard Withey

Description Withey Addison is an accounting firm that also does some search work for clients.

WOLF GUGLER & ASSOCIATES LIMITED
1370 Don Mills Road, Suite 300
Toronto, ON M3B 3N7

Telephone 416-386-1719
Fax 416-386-1719
E-mail admin@wolfgugler.com
Website www.wolfgugler.com

Founded 1985
Employees 3

Specialties Logistics
Marketing
Management
Retail
Sales
Level Senior
Mid-Level
Min. Salary $50,000
Fee Basis Retainer Only
Contact Wolf Gugler, President

Description Wolf Gugler & Associates provides executive search and management appraisals to retailers and their suppliers, with particular expertise in the home improvement and housewares industries.

WOLFER-HALE & ASSOCIATES
1700 Varsity Estates Drive NW
Varsity ExecuCentre
Calgary, AB T3B 2W9

Telephone 403-247-2654
Fax 403-286-1407

Founded 1970
Employees 3

Specialties Sales
Oil & Gas
Engineering
Geology/Geography
Operations
Level Mid-Level
Senior
Fee Basis Sometimes contingent
Contact Morley Wolfer

WOLVERINE TECHNICAL SERVICES
315 North Main Street
Ann Arbor, MI 48104   USA

Telephone	734-996-8367
Fax	734-996-3105
E-mail	kari@mich.com
Website	www.wolverine tech.com
Specialties	Multimedia Computing International
Level	Mid-Level

Description Wolverine Technical Services supplies IT and Internet professionals to the Michigan marketplace.

WOOD WEST & PARTNERS INC.
1281 West Georgia Street, Suite 700
Vancouver, BC V6E 3J7

Telephone	604-682-3141
Fax	604-688-5749
E-mail	fwest@wood-west.com
Website	www.wood-west.com
Founded	1982
Employees	7
Specialties	Computing Engineering Mining Pulp & Paper Sales Telecom
Level	Senior Mid-Level
Min. Salary	$35,000
Recruiters	Fred West PEng, MCP Ron Wood
Contact	Fred West, PEng, MCP

Description Wood West & Partners Inc. specializes in the high tech engineering, telecom and sales industries in Western Canada, USA and the Far East.

WOODRIDGE ASSOCIATES
The Ridge House
The Ridge, Broad Blunsdon
Swindon SN2 4AD
UNITED KINGDOM

Telephone	44-1793-721500
Fax	44-1793-721700
E-mail	info@woodridge.co.uk
Website	www.woodridge.co.uk
Founded	1993
Specialties	International Engineering Computing Geology/Geography Telecom Mining Construction
Level	Senior Mid-Level
Fee Basis	Sometimes contingent
Contact	Michael C. Nott

Description Woodridge Associates are international recruitment consultants for the mining and miner-

als, power generation, waste disposal, petrochemical, oil, construction, tunnelling, telecom and IT industries.

WORK ABLE SERVICES INC.
1 James St. South, 2nd Floor
Hamilton, ON L8P 4R5

Telephone	905-546-2696
Fax	905-546-2835
Specialties	Disabled
Contact	Dawn Cunningham

Description Work Able Services Inc. sources and pre-screens for their employer clients from the entire community, specializing in candidates with disablties and disadvantages.

WORKCENTRAL CSI
46 Elgin Street, Suite 110
Central Chambers Building
Ottawa, ON K1P 5K6

Telephone	613-235-6398
Fax	613-235-9675
E-mail	work@workcentral.com
Website	www.workcentral.com
Specialties	Computing
Level	Mid-Level
Recruiters	Stephane Dagenais John Healy Christopher Healy Gurpreet Singh Kanwar Phil Laberge Will Poho Peter Sheehan Kim Tapp
Contact	Stephane Dagenais, Manager, Outbound Sales

Description WorkCentral CSI specializes in recruiting IT professionals for contract placements.

WORKING WELL CONSULTING INC.
2612 Leonard Street
Innisfil, ON L9S 3T9

Telephone	705-431-2933
Fax	705-431-9234
E-mail	wrkwell@ planeteer.com
Website	www.workingwell inc.com
Specialties	General Practice Management
Level	Mid-Level
Recruiters	B.J. McCabe Joan Oickle
Contact	Joan Oickle

Description Working Well Consulting Inc. is an HR consulting firm that also offers recruitment and selection services.

WORKPLACE COMPETENCE INTERNATIONAL
5903 Third Line
Erin, ON N0B 1Z0

Telephone	519-855-4041
Fax	519-855-6759
E-mail	recruit@wciltd.com
Founded	1986
Employees	3
Specialties	Computing
Level	Senior
Min. Salary	$80,000
Fee Basis	Retainer Only
Contact	Roelf Wolding

Description Workplace Competence International uses competency-based methods to recruit professionals for their clients.

WORLDWIDE HEALTHCARE EXCHANGE
601 West Broadway, Suite 400
Vancouver, BC V5Z 4C2

Telephone	604-629-1900
Fax	604-629-1901
E-mail	info@whecan.com
Website	www.whe.co.uk
Specialties	Health/Medical International
Level	Mid-Level
Recruiters	Anne Kuleta Elizabeth Lewis
Contact	Anne Kuleta

Description Worldwide Healthcare Exchange recruits healthcare professionals for assignments in the United Kingdom.

WORTH PERSONNEL GROUP
20 Eglinton Avenue West
Suite 1905, Yonge-Eglinton Centre
Toronto, ON M4R 1K8

Telephone	416-489-3900
Fax	416-489-8900
E-mail	resumes@ worthpersonnel.com
Website	www.worth personnel.com
Founded	1979
Specialties	Retail Trades/Technicians Computing Engineering
Level	Mid-Level
Contact	Shelley Worth

Description Worth Personnel is a human resource services firm that provides permanent and contract personnel to Ontario businesses.

WORTH PERSONNEL GROUP
33 City Centre Drive, Suite 375
Mississauga, ON L5B 2N5

Telephone	905-277-4800
Fax	905-277-4900
E-mail	resumes@ worthpersonnel.com
Website	www.worth personnel.com
Founded	1979
Specialties	Retail

Computing
Engineering
Trades/Technicians

Level Mid-Level

Contact Shelley Worth

Description Worth Personnel is a human resource services firm that provides permanent and contract personnel to Ontario businesses.

WYNNE CHISHOLM & ASSOCIATES INC.
7 Tumbleweed Point NW
Calgary, AB T3Z 3B7

Telephone 403-547-0568
Fax 403-547-2850
E-mail wynnec@attglobal.net

Founded 1986

Specialties Management
Computing
Human Resource

Level Mid-Level

Contact Wynne L. Chisholm, CMC

Description Wynne Chisholm is a management consulting firm that does occasional search business. Practice areas include executive coaching, human resource and organizational strategy.

WYPICH INTERNATIONAL
84 Avenue Road
Toronto, ON M5R 2H2

Telephone 416-966-0875
Fax 416-966-4527

Founded 1988
Employees 4

Specialties Engineering
Finance
Operations
Scientific
General Practice

Level Senior
Mid-Level

Min. Salary $80,000
Fee Basis Retainer Only

Contact Martha White

Description Wypich International is a leading Canadian practice comprised of a unique combination of 45 years of executive search and consulting experience in conducting senior management searches.

XENOTEC CONSULTING SERVICES INC.
1119 Harrison Way
PO Box 35025, Sherwood
Regina, SK S4X 4C6

Telephone 306-949-9113
Fax 306-775-1035
E-mail xenotec@
cableregina.com
Website www.mancomit.com

Specialties Computing

Level Mid-Level

Contact Marianne Hofmeister

Description Xenotec provides IT personnel on a contract basis to clients in the construction, implementation and support of information systems and associated technologies.

XYCORP INC.
365 Bloor Street E., Suite 2001
Toronto, ON M4W 3L4

Telephone 416-923-4344
Fax 416-923-0120
E-mail info@xycorp.com
Website www.xycorp.com

Founded 1974

Specialties Computing
Sales

Level Mid-Level

Recruiters Roy Cope
Ron Ellingson
David Smith
Frank Switt
Mark Wells

Contact Ron Ellingson,
President

Description Xycorp places experienced IT professionals looking for permanent or contract positions in all operating system environments.

YORKLAND SEARCH TECHNOLOGIES
5925 Airport Road, Suite 200
Mississauga, ON L4V 1W1

Telephone 905-405-6210
Fax 905-405-6228
E-mail yst98@globalserve.net

Founded 1989
Employees 6

Specialties Engineering
Management
Marketing
Operations
Sales
Scientific

Level Mid-Level
Senior

Contact Steve Joakim

Description Recruits high-calibre individuals with good credentials in the areas of engineering, manufacturing, sales, marketing, operations, customer service, chemists and all types of managers.

YOUR ADVANTAGE STAFFING CONSULTANTS INC.
426 Queen Street West
Cambridge, ON N3C 1H1

Telephone 519-651-2120
Fax 519-651-2780
E-mail info@yasci.com
Website www.yasci.com

Founded 1997
Employees 5

Specialties Transport

Level Mid-Level
Junior

Contact Lori Van Opstal,
President

Description Your Advantage Staffing specializes in providing contract and permanent placement services to the ground transporation industry.

YVES BÉLIVEAU RECHERCHE DE CADRES
31, boul. Desaulniers
Saint-Lambert, QC J4P 1L7

Téléphone 450-922-0088
Télécopieur 450-922-0099

Spécialités Gestion
Télécommunications

Échelon Direction
Intermédiaire

Contact Yves Béliveau,
President

YVES ELKAS INC.
485, rue McGill, Bureau 601
Montréal, QC H2Y 2H4

Téléphone 514-845-0088
Télécopieur 514-845-2518
Courriel elkas@total.net

Fondée 1989
Employés 7

Spécialités Ingénierie
Finance
Ressources humaines
Marketing
Exploitation
Vente au détail
Transport

Échelon Direction
Intermédiaire

Salaire min. 50 000 $
Frais Honoraire seulement

Recruteurs Jean-Pierre Hurtubise
Jacques E. Ouellet
Sumon Parisien
Isabelle Roy

Contact Yves Elkas c.r.i.

Description Yves Elkas Inc. propose des services professionels bilingues en matière de recherche et de location de personnel cadre et professionnel.

YVES PLOUFFE ET ASSOCIÉS
5 Place du Commerce, Suite 103
Île-des-Soeurs, QC H3E 1M8

Téléphone 514-769-9997
Télécopieur 514-769-9666
Courriel ypa@qc.aira.com
Site Internet www.bottindu
quartier.com/ypa

Fondée 1986

Spécialités Généralistes
Sylviculture
Gestion
Mines
Exploitation
Papeterie
Télécommunications

Échelon Direction
Intermédiaire

Salaire min. 75 000 $
Frais Honoraire seulement
Recruteurs Gilles Charest MBA
Ghislaine Cimon
Yves J. Plouffe
Suzanne Trepanier
Contact Yves J. Plouffe,
Président

Description Yves Plouffe et associés est une firme établie depuis 1986. Spécialités: telecom, services aux entreprises, manufacturiers, miniers canadiens et internationaux, et ressources naturelles (produits forestiers).

ZEIDEL, GREGORY & ASSOCIATES
45 Sheppard Ave. East, Suite 900
Toronto, ON M2N 5W9

Telephone 416-229-2525
Fax 416-229-6111

Specialties Accounting
Finance
Real Estate
Administrative
Level Mid-Level
Fee Basis Sometimes contingent
Recruiters Zoya Gregory
Jerry Zeidel
Contact Jerry Zeidel

Description Zeidel, Gregory & Associates is a recruitment firm that specializes in all levels of accounting and finance placements.

ZEN ZEN INTERNATIONAL INC.
456 Main Street, 3rd Floor
Winnipeg, MB R3B 1B6

Telephone 204-837-7943
Fax 204-943-8603
E-mail zenzenmy@
mb.sympatico.ca
Website www.mancomit.com
Founded 1997
Employees 4
Specialties Accounting
Computing
Engineering
Human Resource
Management
Sales
Telecom
Level Mid-Level
Senior
Recruiters Craig McLean
Michael Yakimishyn
Contact Michael Yakimishyn

Description Zen Zen International Inc. provides executive, mid-level management and technical search services for information technology and business professionals.

ZENZEN PIERCE & ASSOCIATES
1200 Bay Street, Suite 303
Toronto, ON M5R 2X5

Telephone 416-924-7790
Fax 416-924-8522

Founded 1988
Specialties Retail
Marketing
Apparel
Advertising
Finance
Management
Sales
Level Senior
Mid-Level
Fee Basis Retainer Only
Contact Julia Zenzen

Description Specialists in senior-level searches for progressive, retail-related international companies.

ZSA LEGAL RECRUITMENT
1055 West Hastings St., Suite 300
Vancouver, BC V6E 2E9

Telephone 604-681-0706
Fax 604-681-0566
E-mail cshaw@zsa.ca
Website www.zsa.ca
Specialties Law
Level Senior
Mid-Level
Fee Basis Always contingent
Recruiters Stephanie Hacksel
Catherine Shaw
Contact Catherine Shaw

Description ZSA Legal Recruitment is Canada's only national and international legal recruitment firm, staffed exclusively by lawyers with offices across Canada.

ZSA LEGAL RECRUITMENT
444 - 5th Avenue SW, Suite 1110
Calgary, AB T2P 2T8

Telephone 403-205-3444
Fax 403-205-3428
E-mail bjorn@zsa.ca
Website www.zsa.ca
Specialties Law
Level Senior
Recruiters Bjorn Harsanyi
Tina Pick
Contact Bjorn Harsanyi

Description ZSA is Canada's premier legal recruitment firm, staffed exclusively by lawyers.

ZSA LEGAL RECRUITMENT
20 Richmond Street East, Suite 315
Toronto, ON M5C 2R9

Telephone 416-368-2051
Fax 416-368-5699
E-mail csweeney@zsa.ca
Website www.zsa.ca
Founded 1996
Specialties Law
Level Senior
Mid-Level
Recruiters Cheryl Berger
Carolyn Berger
Warren Bongard

Caroline Carnerie
Sheila Hepworth
Susan Kennedy
Nancie Lataille
Rosi Zirger
Contact Christopher Sweeney,
Director

Description ZSA Legal Recruitment is a leading legal recruitment firm staffed exclusively by lawyers.

ZSA LEGAL RECRUITMENT
1200 McGill College Avenue
Suite 1100
Montréal, QC H3B 4G7

Telephone 514-390-2300
Fax 514-390-2320
E-mail chaney@zsa.ca
Website www.zsa.ca
Specialties Law
Contact Maitre Caroline Haney

Description ZSA Legal Recruitment is Canada's premier legal recruitment firm, staffed exclusively by lawyers.

ZSA LEGAL RECRUITMENT
630 Fifth Avenue, 20th Floor
45 Rockefeller Plaza
New York, NY 10111 USA

Telephone 212-332-3440
Fax 212-332-3436
E-mail csweeney@
lawrecruit.com
Website www.zsa.com
Specialties Law
International
Level Senior
Mid-Level
Contact Christopher Sweeney,
Director

Description ZSA Legal Recruitment is staffed exclusively by lawyers.

INDEXES

֍

INDEXES

DETAILED LIST OF OCCUPATIONS
LISTE DÉTAILLÉE DES OCCUPATIONS

Here are more detailed descriptions of the occupational categories used in this directory:

Accounting (p. 282) includes chartered accountants (CAs, CGAs, CMAs), controllers, comptrollers, auditors, cost accountants, tax specialists, accounting supervisors, bookkeepers and students in professional training programs. *See also: Finance, Actuarial, Consulting.*

Actuarial (p. 287) includes actuaries, statisticians, statistical process control (SPC) personnel, biostatisticians and other positions requiring actuarial or statistical training. *See also: Insurance, Quality Control.*

Administrative (p. 287) includes executive assistants, office managers, secretarial staff, call centre personnel, data entry staff, receptionists, collection officers and clerks.

Advertising (p. 289) includes creative directors, advertising managers, media buyers, copy writers and advertising sales representatives. *See also: Graphic Arts, Public Relations, Marketing, Publishing/Media.*

Aerospace (p. 290) includes aerospace engineers, propulsion engineers, avionics technicians, aircraft maintenance engineers, simulator engineers, airport managers, airworthness inspectors, pilots and airline staff. *See also: Engineering, Transport, Trades/Technicians.*

Agriculture / Fisheries (p. 290) includes agricultural scientists, agronomists, veterinarians, crop insurance managers, feed sales personnel, farm equipment personnel and farm managers. *See also: Biotech/Biology, Scientific.*

Apparel (p. 290) includes buyers, designers and marketers of clothing and footwear. *See also: Retail, Design.*

Architecture (p. 291) includes architects, architectural technologists, interior designers and structural technologists. *See also: Construction, Real Estate, Design, Trades/Technicians.*

Arts & Culture (p. 291) includes anyone working for a museum, gallery, theatre company, orchestra or other cultural organization. *See also: Govt./Nonprofit, Hospitality, Public Relations.*

Automotive (p. 291) includes automotive engineers, designers and technologists, tooling engineers, leasing managers, parts managers, service managers, warranty administrators and dealership staff. *See also: Engineering, Transport, Trades/Technicians.*

Banking (p. 292) includes anyone working for a bank, credit union or trust company, including branch managers, loan officers, mortgage specialists, private banking representatives, credit analysts, RRSP administrators and customer service representatives. *See also: Finance, Insurance, Accounting.*

Bilingual (p. 293) includes translators, interpreters and other positions where the ability to speak

Voici des descriptions plus détaillées des spécialités professionnelles se trouvant en cette répertoire:

Achat (p. 337) comprend les directeurs des achats, les acheteurs, les directeurs de l'acquisition, les administrateurs des contrats, les estimateurs, les administrateurs des devis estimatifs, les marchands de produits de base et tout emploi exigeant la désignation d'Acheteur Professionnel Certifié (CPP) ou l'achèvement du cours PMAC. Voir aussi: Logistique, Exploitation.

Actuariel (p. 287) comprend les actuaires, les statisticiens, le personnel-contrôleur du processus statistique (SPC), les biostatisticiens et autres postes exigeant une formation actuarielle ou statistique. Voir aussi: Assurance, Contrôle de qualité.

Administratif (p. 287) comprend les exécutifs adjoints, les directeurs de bureau, le personnel-secrétaire, le personnel de centre d'appels, le personnel traiteur des données, les réceptionnistes, les responsables du recouvrement et les clercs.

Aérospatial (p. 290) comprend les ingénieurs aérospatiaux, les ingénieurs de propulsion, les techniciens de l'avionique, les ingénieurs de maintien des avions, les ingénieurs simulateurs, les directeurs d'aéroport, les inspecteurs de navigabilité, les pilotes et le personnel de ligne aérienne. Voir aussi: Ingénierie, Transport, Métiers/Techniciens.

Affaires publiques (p. 336) comprend les chargés des relations avec le public, les directeurs des communications, les directeurs des relations médiatiques, les chargés des affaires publiques, les directeurs des relations communautaires, les auteurs de matériel corporatif et les consultants en affaires gouvernementales. Voir aussi: Publicité, Marketing, Gouvernement/Organisations sans but lucratif.

Agriculture / pêches (p. 290) comprend les scientifiques agronomes, les agronomes, les vétérinaires, les chargés de l'assurance des cultures, le personnel de vente de fourrage, le personnel d'équipement de ferme et les directeurs de ferme. Voir aussi: Biotechnologie/biologie, Scientifique.

Architecture (p. 291) comprend les architectes, les technologues architecturaux, les dessinateurs d'intérieurs et les technologues de construction. Voir aussi: Construction, Immobilier, Design, Métiers/Techniciens.

Arts et culture (p. 291) comprend toute personne qui travaille pour un musée, une galerie, une compagnie de théâtre, un orchestre ou autre organisation culturelle. Voir aussi: Gouvernement/Organisations sans but lucratif, Hospitalité, Affaires publiques.

Assurance (p. 318) comprend les souscripteurs (membres d'un syndicat de garantie), les ajusteurs, les courtiers, les professionnels de gestion de risque, les négociateurs de traité, le personnel superviseur des demandes d'indemnité, le personnel investigateur des demandes d'indemnité de la Commission de Compensation des Travailleurs (WCB), les investigateurs et les vendeurs d'assurance. Voir aussi: Actuariel, Banque, Gouvernement/OSBL.

Automobile (p. 291) comprend les ingénieurs de l'automobile, les créateurs et technologues, les ingénieurs d'usinage, les chargés de location, les chargés du service, les administrateurs de garantie et le personnel de centre de distribution. Voir aussi: Ingénierie, Transport, Métiers/Techniciens.

Banque, affaires de, (p. 292) comprend toute personne travaillant pour une banque, caisse populaire ou société fiduciaire, y compris les chefs de filiale, les chargés des prêts, les spécialistes en hypothèques-logement, les

a second language is the principal requirement of the position. *See also: International, Education, Administrative.*

Biotech / Biology (p. 293) includes biologists, biomedical engineers, biotechnology developers, biological scientists and other positions relating to the commercial development of biological, life sciences and genetic technologies. *See also: Pharmaceutical, Scientific, Health/Medical.*

Computing (p. 294) includes programmers, analysts, software developers, hardware engineers, MIS directors, CIOs, LAN administrators, database administrators, technical writers, software testers, technical support personnel and other information technology positions. *See also: Multimedia, Engineering, Telecom, Design.*

Construction (p. 300) includes project managers, site supervisors, surveyors, building inspectors, builders and other personnel required for construction projects. *See also: Real Estate, Architecture, Trades/Technicians.*

Consulting (p. 301) includes management consultants, policy advisors and personnel working for management consulting firms. Does not include consulting and contract positions in information technology, which are listed under "Computing". *See also: Management, Computing, Human Resource, Govt./Nonprofit.*

Design (p. 301) includes draftspersons, designers, product designers, circuit designers, electrical designers, mechanical designers, design technicians and technologist positions requiring specialized CAD and AUTOCad training. *See also: Architects, Engineering, Graphic Arts, Publishing/Media.*

Direct Marketing (p. 302) includes direct mail managers, outbound call specialists, call centre supervisors, telemarketing staff and all positions that involve marketing by direct mail, telephone, fax or email. *See also: Sales, Marketing, Advertising, Graphic Arts, Printing.*

Disabled (p. 302) includes positions working with physically or mentally challenged people. *See also: Health/Medical, Education, Govt./Nonprofit.*

Education (p. 302) includes teachers, principals, instructors, superintendents, school inspectors, professors, deans, education directors, ESL teachers, admission directors and administrative positions at schools, universities and colleges. Does not include training positions, which are listed under "Human Resource". *See also: Librarians, Govt./Nonprofit.*

Engineering (p. 303) includes electrical engineers, mechanical engineers, structural engineers, civil engineers, chemical engineers, engineering managers and other positions requiring a university engineering degree or membership in a provincial engineering association. Does not include engineering technologists and non-university trained engineers (see "Trades/Technicians") or software engineers (see "Computing"). *See also: Aerospace, Automotive, Design, Quality Control, Telecom.*

Environmental (p. 308) includes environmental compliance specialists, environmental engi-

représentants des comptes en banque personnels, les analystes de crédit, les administrateurs de régime enregistré d'épargne-retraite (REÉR) et les chargés du service à la clientèle. Voir aussi: Finance, Assurance, Comptabilité.

Bibliothécaires *(p. 322) comprend les bibliothécaires, les archivistes et les techniciens des données de santé. Voir aussi: Éducation, Santé/Médical.*

Bilingue *(p. 293) comprend les traducteurs, les interprètes et autres postes où l'aptitude à parler une deuxième langue est le besoin principal de l'emploi. Voir aussi: International, Éducation, Administratif.*

Biotechnologie / biologie *(p. 293) comprend les biologistes, les ingénieurs biomédicaux, les créateurs de biotechnologie, les scientifiques biologistes et autres postes relatifs à l'exploitation commerciale des technologies des sciences biologiques, naturelles et génétiques. Voir aussi: Pharmaceutique, Scientifique, Santé/Médical.*

Comptabilité *(p. 282) comprend les comptables agréés (CA, CGA, CMA), les vérificateurs, les contrôleurs, les experts-comptables, les comptables d'affaires en partie simple, les spécialistes des taxes, les comptables surveillants, les teneurs de livres et les étudiants en cours de formation professionnelle. Voir aussi: Finance, Actuariel, Consultatif.*

Construction *(p. 300) comprend les directeurs de projet, les surveillants de chantier, les experts arpenteurs, les inspecteurs des bâtiments, les constructeurs et autres emplois dont on a besoin pour les projets de construction. Voir aussi: Immobilier, Architecture, Métiers/Tech-niciens.*

Consultatif *(p. 301) comprend les consultants en gestion, les conseillers politiques et le personnel travaillant pour les compagnies de consultation en gestion. Ne comprend pas les postes consultatifs ou à forfait dans la technologie informatique, qui se trouvent sous "Informatique". Voir aussi: Gestion, Informatique, Ressources humaines, Gouvernement/OSBL.*

Design *(p. 301) comprend les dessinateurs, les créateurs, les créateurs de produits et de circuits, les dessinateurs électriciens, les dessinateurs mécaniciens et techniciens et autres postes technologiques exigeant une formation en CAO (conception assistée par ordinateur) ou en AUTO-CAO. (anglais AUTOCad). Voir aussi: Architecture, Ingénierie, Dessin graphique, Édition/média.*

Dessin graphique, arts du, *(p. 314) comprend les artistes, les dessinateurs en arts graphiques, les gérants de la création, les directeurs artistiques, les illustrateurs, les artistes Macintosh, les opérateurs prépresse, les techniciens en création d'images et autres emplois exigeant une connaissance des logiciels en arts graphiques tels que QuarkXpress, Photoshop, Illustrator ou PageMaker. Ne comprend pas les créateurs de site Web, qui se trouvent séparément sous "Multimédia". Voir aussi: Multimédia, Imprimerie, Publicité, Édition/média, Emballage.*

Détail, vente au, *(p. 338) comprend les gérants de magasin, les analystes des ventes au détail, les planificateurs de magasin, les spécialistes en prévention des pertes, les directeurs adjoints, les cadres stagiaires et les vendeurs adjoints. Voir aussi: Ventes, Franchise, Habillement, Hospitalité.*

Droit *(p. 321) comprend les avocats, les procureurs, les postes d'avocat général, les avocats spécialisés qui conseillent en matière juridique et défendent des causes en justice, les juges, les arbitres, les médiateurs, les professeurs de droit, les agents de brevets et de marques déposées, les administrateurs de bureau d'avocat, les clercs de notaires, liés par le contrat d'apprentissage, les paralégaux, les secrétaires d'avocat, les agents de police et le personnel de mise en application du droit. Voir aussi: Gouvernement/OSBL.*

Édition / média *(p. 336) comprend les éditeurs, les écrivains, les rédacteurs, les journalistes, les reporters, les*

neers, hydrogeologists, wastewater technicians, environmental technicians, pollution control officers, conservation officers. *See also: Engineering, Agriculture/Fisheries, Govt/Nonprofit.*

Finance (p. 308) includes finance directors, controllers, CFOs, credit managers, treasurers, budget directors, financial analysts, investment bankers, investment advisors, economists, stockbrokers, traders, securities regulators, compliance officers, portfolio managers, mutual fund administrators and any position requiring a CFA or completion of a securities course. *See also: Accounting, Banking.*

Forestry (p. 312) includes foresters, lumber traders, forest practices officers, arborists and other positions relating to tree planting, harvesting and sawmills. Does not include positions in papermaking, which are listed separately under "Pulp & Paper". *See also: Pulp & Paper, Govt./Nonprofit.*

Franchising (p. 313) includes franchise recruiters, territory managers and all other positions involved in developing new retail franchises. Does not include positions in franchisees' stores, which are listed separately under "Retail". *See also: Retail, Hospitality, Real Estate.*

Geology / Geography (p. 313) includes geologists, geophysicists, hydrogeologists, geodesists, geotechnical engineers, geological technicans and GIS mapping technicians. *See also: Mining, Oil & Gas, Engineering, Scientific.*

Govt./Nonprofit (p. 313) includes deputy ministers, executive directors of nonprofit organizations, town administrators, city planners and other positions working for government bodies, charities or nonprofit organizations. Does not include healthcare positions, which are listed under "Health/Medical", or arts opportunities listed under "Arts & Culture". *See also: Education, Health/Medical, International, Arts & Culture.*

Graphic Arts (p. 314) includes artists, graphic designers, creative directors, art directors, illustrators, Mac artists, prepress operators, imaging technicians and other positions requiring knowledge of graphic design software such as QuarkXpress, Photoshop, Illustrator or PageMaker. Does not include website designers, which are listed separately under "Multimedia". *See also: Multimedia, Printing, Advertising, Publishing/Media, Packaging.*

Health/Medical (p. 314) includes nurses, therapists, medical doctors, health officers, hospital administrators, physiotherapists, rehabilitation counsellors, occupational therapists, kinesiologists, anaesthesiologists, ultrasound technicians, epidemiologists, dietitians, ophthalmologists, dentists, dental hygienists, pathologists, psychologists, psychiatrists, mental health workers, social workers, health data analysts, medical sales representatives, nursing assistants, medical technologists and medical secretaries. *See also: Pharmaceutical, Biotech/Biology, Govt./Nonprofit.*

Hospitality (p. 315) includes anyone working in the tourism, foodservice, entertainment or travel industries, including hotel managers, catering managers, film theater managers, travel

gérants de publication, les rédacteurs adjoints, les auteurs techniques et les rédacteurs publicitaires. Voir aussi: *Imprimerie, Multimédia, Dessin graphique, Publicité.*

Éducation (p. 302) *comprend les enseignants, les directeurs, les professeurs, les chefs de département, les inspecteurs d'école, les professeurs de niveau collégial ou universitaire, les doyens, les directeurs de l'éducation, les professeurs d'anglais langue seconde (ESL), les directeurs d'admission et les postes administratifs aux écoles, universités et collèges. Ne comprend pas les postes de formation, qui se trouvent sous "Ressources humaines".* Voir aussi: *Bibliothécaires, Gouvernement/OSBL.*

Emballage (p. 334) *comprend les postes dans l'industrie de l'emballage, y compris les ingénieurs de l'emballage, les créateurs d'étiquettes, les surveillants de rayon d'emballage, les pressiers, les opérateurs de machine à étiquettes, les spécialistes en boîtes et les techniciens de l'emballage.* Voir aussi: *Dessin graphique, Imprimerie, Métiers/Techniciens.*

Environnementaux (p. 308) *comprend tous les positions concernant l'environnement et la protection de l'eau potable.*

Exploitation (p. 332) *comprend les gérants d'usine, les chargés des opérations, les chefs de la production, les gérants de manufacture, les surveillants de relais, les surveillants de rayon et les technologues engagés dans la production.* Voir aussi: *Logistique, Contrôle de qualité, Métiers/Techniciens.*

Expositions (p. 345) *comprend les gérants d'exposition, les vendeurs d'objets exposés, le personnel d'exposition et les réalisateurs de conférence.* Voir aussi: *Marketing, Ventes, Hospitalité.*

Finance (p. 308) *comprend les directeurs de finance, les contrôleurs, les administrateurs en chef (CFO), les directeurs du crédit, les trésoriers, les analystes financiers, les banquiers d'investissement, les conseillers aux investisseurs, les économistes, les agents de change, les commerçants, les régulateurs des valeurs, les directeurs de l'acquiescement, les chargés de portefeuilles, les administrateurs de fonds mutuels et tout emploi exigeant l'obtention de la désignation CFA (analyste financier certifié) ou la réussite d'un cours en valeurs.* Voir aussi: *Comptabilité, Banque.*

Franchise (p. 313) *comprend les recruteurs de franchises, les gérants de territoire et tout autre emploi engagé dans l'exploitation de nouveaux permis de vente. Ne comprend pas les postes dans les magasins des détenteurs de permis, qui se trouvent séparément sous "Détail".* Voir aussi: *Détail, Hospitalité, Immobilier.*

Géologie / géographie (p. 313) *comprend les géologues, les géophysiciens, les hydrogéologues, les spécialistes en géodésie, les ingénieurs géotechnologues, les techniciens géologiques et les techniciens de dessin MIS (système d'informatique géographique).* Voir aussi: *Mines, Pétrole et gaz, Ingénierie, Scientifique.*

Gestion (p. 323) *comprend les postes exécutifs et directoriaux pas autrement classifiés, y compris les présidents, les PDG, les directeurs généraux, les vice-présidents, les gérants d'entreprise. Les postes de direction dans les métiers particuliers se trouvent sous le métier en question (un vice-président du marketing se trouverait, p.ex., sous "Marketing" plutôt que sous "Gestion").* Voir aussi: *Consultatif.*

Gouvernement / Organisations sans but lucratif (p. 313) *comprend les ministres adjoints, les directeurs généraux des organisations sans but lucratif, les administrateurs municipaux, les urbanistes et autres emplois travaillant pour les corps gouvernementaux, les charités ou les organisations sans but lucratif. Ne comprend pas les postes en soins de santé, qui se trouvent sous "Santé/Médical", ni les débouchés en beaux-arts, qui se trouvent sous "Arts et Culture".* Voir aussi: *Éducation, Santé et médical, International, Arts et Culture.*

agents, lodge and resort managers, chefs, food and beverage directors, nightclub managers and restaurant managers. *See also: Retail, Franchising, Govt./Nonprofit.*

Human Resources (p. 316) includes human resource managers, personnel managers, compensation and benefits specialists, labour relations officers, HRIS specialists, pension administrators, payroll officers, career counsellors, outplacement consultants, employee development personnel, trainers, recruiters, executive search staff. *See also: "Public Relations".*

Insurance (p. 318) includes underwriters, adjusters, brokers, risk management professionals, treaty negotiators, claims supervisors, WCB claims personnel, investigators and insurance sales representatives. *See also: Actuarial, Banking, Govt./Nonprofit.*

International (p. 319) includes positions based outside Canada or requiring significant international experience, foreign language skills or travel outside Canada. *See also: Consulting, Oil & Gas, Govt./Nonprofit, Bilingual.*

Law (p. 321) includes lawyers, prosecutors, general counsel positions, barristers and solicitors, judges, arbitrators, mediators, law professors, patent and trade mark agents, law office administrators, articling clerks, paralegals, legal secretaries, police officers and law enforcement personnel. *See also: Govt./Nonprofit.*

Librarians (p. 322) includes librarians, archivists and health record technicians. *See also: Education, Health/Medical.*

Logistics (p. 322) includes material managers, distribution managers, inventory supervisors, traffic managers, material resource planning (MRP) specialists, production schedulers, supply chain managers, order administrators, shippers, customs brokers and warehouse supervisors. *See also: Purchasing, Transport, Operations, Actuarial.*

Management (p. 323) includes executive and managerial positions not otherwise classified including presidents, CEOs, managing directors, vice-presidents, general managers. Managerial positions in particular occupations are listed under the occupation (e.g. a Vice President of Marketing would be found under "Marketing" not "Management"). *See also: Consulting.*

Marketing (p. 328) includes marketing managers, product managers, brand managers, marketing analysts, merchandisers, competitive analysts and market researchers. *See also: Sales, Direct Mktng., Advertising, Public Relations.*

Metals (p. 330) includes metallurgists, metallurgical engineers, metal traders, foundry supervisors, metallurgical technologists, metal fabricators, sheet metal personnel and metal stamping staff. *See also: Mining, Trades/Technicians, Automotive.*

Mining (p. 331) includes mine superintendents, prospectors, underground shift bosses, mine inspectors and all positions requiring specialized knowledge of mines and minerals. *See also: Geology/Geography, Metals, Oil & Gas, Engineering.*

Habillement *(p. 290) comprend les acheteurs, les créateurs et les metteurs en vente de vêtements et chaussures. Voir aussi: Détail, Design.*

Handicapé/Infirme *(p. 302) comprend tous les emplois travaillant avec les personnes physiquement handicapées ou à débilité mentale. Voir aussi: Santé et médical, Éducation, Gouvernement/OSBL.*

Hospitalité *(p. 315) comprend toute personne travaillant dans les industries du tourisme, du service de ravitaillement ou du divertissement, y compris les gérants d'hôtel, les chargés de l'approvisionnement, les gérants de cinéma, les agents de tourisme, les gérants de cottage, de pavillon de chasse ou de station, les chefs de cuisine, les chargés de la nourriture et des boissons, les gérants de boîte de nuit et de restaurant. Voir aussi: Détail, Franchise, Gouvernement/OSBL.*

Immobilier *(p. 338) comprend les directeurs de location, les ingénieurs exploitateurs des terres, les administrateurs des terres, les chefs des facilités, les travailleurs agricoles, les courtiers, les agents de vente de nouveaux foyers, les agents de location, les inspecteurs de zonage, les gérants de centre d'achat, les gérants des biens de la propriété, les chefs de l'entretien du bâtiment, les concierges, le personnel de sécurité du bâtiment et les planificateurs d'espace. Voir aussi: Construction, Franchise, Architecture.*

Imprimerie *(p. 336) comprend tous les postes dans l'industrie papetière, y compris les directeurs d'usine, les opérateurs de presse, les vendeurs d'articles d'imprimerie et les exploitateurs d'atelier de reliure. Voir aussi: Édition/média, Dessin graphique, Emballage, Métiers/Techniciens.*

Informatique *(p. 294) comprend les programmeurs, les analystes, les créateurs de logiciels, les ingénieurs du matériel informatique, les directeurs du système informatique MIS, les chargés de l'information (CIO), les administrateurs de réseau informatique local (LAN), les administrateurs de base de données, les auteurs techniques, les vérificateurs de logiciels, le personnel de soutien technique et autres emplois en technologie informatique. Voir aussi: Multimédia, Ingénierie, Télécommunication, Design.*

Ingénierie *(p. 303) comprend les ingénieurs électriques, les ingénieurs mécaniques, les ingénieurs ponts et chaussées et en génie civil, les ingénieurs chimiques, les administrateurs d'ingénierie et autres postes exigeant un grade universitaire ou l'adhésion à une société provinciale d'ingénierie. Ne comprend pas les ingénieurs technologues ni les ingénieurs sans formation universitaire (voir "Métiers/Techniciens") ni les ingénieurs des logiciels (voir "Informatique"). Voir aussi: Aérospatial, Automobile, Design, Contrôle de qualité, Télécommunication.*

International *(p. 319) comprend les postes basés à l'extérieur du Canada ou exigeant une expérience internationale considérable, de l' habileté en langues étrangères ou des voyages à l'extérieur du Canada. Voir aussi: Consultatif, Pétrole et Gaz, Gouvernement/OSBL, Bilingue.*

Logistique *(p. 322) comprend les chargés du matériel, les gérants de la distribution, les surveillants de l'inventaire, les directeurs de la circulation, les spécialistes en planification des ressources en matériel (MRP), les programmeurs de la production, les chargés du convoi de ravitaillement, les administrateurs des commandes, les expéditeurs, les courtiers en douanes et les surveillants d'entrepôt. Voir aussi: Achat, Transport, Exploitation, Actuariel.*

Marketing *(étude des marchés) (p. 328) comprend les gérants de la mise en vente, les directeurs de produit, les chefs de marque, les analystes du marché, les spécialistes des techniques marchandes, les consultants en compétition et les étudiants du marché. Voir aussi: Ventes, Marketing direct, Publicité, Affaires publiques.*

Multimedia (p. 331) includes web site designers, webmasters, Internet content developers, new media specialists, CD-ROM designers, HTML programmers and games programmers. *See also: Graphic Arts, Computing, Publishing/Media, Printing.*

Oil & Gas (p. 332) includes exploration engineers, drilling engineers, reservoir engineers, pipeline engineers, petroleum chemists, crude oil marketing analysts, gas marketing specialists, oil and gas traders, gas plant personnel and wellhead operators. *See also: Geology/Geography, Engineering, International, Trades/Technicians.*

Operations (p. 332) includes plant managers, operations managers, production managers, manufacturing managers, shift supervisors, maintenance supervisors, line supervisors and production-related technologists. *See also: Logistics, Quality Control, Trades/Technicians.*

Packaging (p. 334) includes positions in the packaging industry, including packaging engineers, label designers, packaging line supervisors, pressmen, label machine operators, box specialists and packaging technicians. *See also: Graphic Arts, Printing, Trades/Technicians.*

Pharmaceutical (p. 335) includes pharmacists, pharmaceutical sales representatives, medicinal chemists, clinical trial administrators, toxicology study managers, clinical research associates, regulatory affairs specialists and drug approval officers. Does not include pure research positions (see "Scientific") or life science opportunities outside the drug industry (see "Biotech/Biology"). *See also: Biotech/Biology, Health/Medical, Scientific.*

Plastics (p. 335) includes all positions in the plastics industry, including plant managers, project engineers, line managers, injection molding managers, mold makers, fixture builders and plastics traders. *See also: Operations, Engineering, Trades/Technicians.*

Printing (p. 336) includes all positions in the printing industry, including plant managers, press operators, printing sales representatives and bindery operators. *See also: Publishing/Media, Graphic Arts, Packaging, Trades/Technicians.*

Public Relations (p. 336) includes public relations officers, communications managers, media relations managers, public affairs managers, community relations officers, corporate writers and government affairs consultants. *See also: Advertising, Marketing, Govt./Nonprofit.*

Publishing / Media (p. 336) includes publishers, writers, editors, journalists, reporters, publication managers, editorial assistants, technical writers and copy writers. *See also: Printing, Multimedia, Graphic Arts, Advertising.*

Pulp & Paper (p. 336) includes all positions in the papermaking industry, including pulp mill managers, woodyard superintendents, pulp chemists, environmental compliance specialists, pulp line personnel, pulp sales representatives, pulp transport specialists, paper mill supervisors and paper sales personnel. *See also: Forestry, Printing, Engineering.*

Marketing direct (p. 302) comprend les chefs des ventes par correspondance, les spécialistes des appels sortants, les directeurs de centre d'appels, le personnel de télémarketing et tout emploi engagé dans le marketing par correspondance, par téléphone, fax ou courrier électronique (email). Voir aussi: Ventes, Marketing, Publicité, Dessin graphique, Imprimerie.

Métaux (p. 330) comprend tous les positions concernant les métaux et la métallurgie.

Métiers/Techniciens (p. 345) comprend les installateurs de moulins, les ingénieurs de machines fixes, les mécaniciens, les outilleurs-graveurs, les électriciens, les soudeurs, les machinistes et autres métiers qualifiés exigeant une désignation comme apprenti, ouvrier ou maître fournisseur. Comprend également les technologues et les techniciens. Ne comprend pas les ingénieurs à formation universitaire, qui se trouvent sous "Ingénierie". Voir aussi: Exploitation, Ingénierie.

Mines, exploitation des, (p. 331) comprend les directeurs de mine, les prospecteurs, les chefs de relais souterrain, les inspecteurs de mines et tout emploi exigeant une connaissance spéciale des mines et des minéraux. Voir aussi: Géologie/géographie, Métaux, Pétrole et gaz, Ingénierie.

Multimédia (p. 331) comprend les créateurs de site Web, les maîtres Web, les créateurs de contenu Internet, les spécialistes en nouveaux médias, les créateurs de DOC (disque optique compact à mémoire-lecture), les programmeurs HTML (code électronique pour la rédaction) et les programmeurs de jeux. Voir aussi: Dessin graphique, Informatique, Édition/média, Imprimerie.

Papeterie (p. 336) comprend tous les emplois dans l'industrie papetière, y compris les directeurs de papeterie, les surveillants de chantier de bois de charpente, les chimistes papetiers, les spécialistes de la conformité environnementale, le personnel travaillant à la chaîne de production de pâte à papier, les vendeurs de pâte à papier, les spécialistes du transport de pâte à papier, les surveillants de papeterie et le personnel de vente de papier. Voir aussi: Sylviculture, Imprimerie, Ingénierie.

Pétrole et gaz (p. 332) comprend les ingénieurs de l'exploration, les ingénieurs de forage, les ingénieurs de réservoir, les ingénieurs-oléoduc, les chimistes pétroliers, les analystes de marché du pétrole brut, les spécialistes de la mise en vente du gaz, les marchands de pétrole et de gaz, le personnel d'usine de gaz et les opérateurs de source. Voir aussi: Géologie/géographie, Ingénierie, International, Métiers/Techniciens.

Pharmaceutique (p. 335) comprend les pharmaciens, les vendeurs d'articles pharmaceutiques, les chimistes médicinaux, les administrateurs des essais cliniques, les chefs d'études toxicologiques, les associés en recherches cliniques, les spécialistes en affaires régulatrices et les chargés de l'approbation des médicaments. Ne comprend pas les postes en recherche pure (voir "Scientifique") ni les débouchés hors de l'industrie pharmaceutique (voir "Biotechnologie/biologie"). Voir aussi: Biotechnologie/biologie, Santé et médical, Scientifique.

Plastique (p. 335) comprend tous les emplois dans l'industrie plastique, y compris les directeurs d'usine, les ingénieurs de projet, les chefs de rayon, les directeurs de moulage par injection, les fabricants de moules, les constructeurs d'installations et les commerçants en plastique. Voir aussi: Exploitation, Ingénierie, Métiers/Techniciens.

Publicité (p. 289) comprend les gérants de la création, les administrateurs de la réclame, les acheteurs des médias, les rédacteurs publicitaires et les vendeurs de publicité. Voir aussi: Dessin graphique, Affaires publiques, Marketing, Édition/média.

Qualité, contrôle de, (p. 338) comprend les ingénieurs de qualité, les vérificateurs de qualité, les coordinateurs

Purchasing (p. 337) includes purchasing managers, buyers, purchasing agents, procurement managers, contract administrators, estimators, quotation administrators, commodity traders and any position requiring a Certified Professional Purchaser (CPP) designation or completion of the PMAC course. *See also: Logistics, Operations.*

Quality Control (p. 338) includes quality engineers, quality auditors, statistical process control (SPC) coordinators, test engineers, reliability managers, quality assurance technicians, TQM consultants, continuous improvement coordinators, testers and ISO 9000 inspectors. *See also: Actuarial, Logistics, Operations, Engineering.*

Real Estate (p. 338) includes leasing managers, land development engineers, land administrators, facilities managers, landmen, real estate agents, brokers, new home sales representatives, rental agents, zoning inspectors, shopping mall managers, property managers, building maintenance managers, superintendants, building security staff and space planners. *See also: Construction, Franchising, Architecture.*

Retail (p. 338) includes store managers, retail analysts, store planners, loss prevention specialists, assistant managers, management trainees and sales associates. *See also: Sales, Franchising, Apparel, Hospitality.*

Sales (p. 339) includes sales managers, account executives, area supervisors, territory managers, sales representatives and customer service representatives. *See also: Marketing, Direct Mktng.*

Scientific (p. 342) includes scientists, chemists, research associates, anthropologists, physicists, ecologists, regulatory affairs associates, laboratory managers and any position requiring a BSc, MSc or PhD in science. *See also: Biotech/Biology, Pharmaceutical, Health/Medical.*

Telecom (p. 343) includes network managers, telecommunications engineers, telephony analysts, switch technicians, network engineers, SONET software engineers, network support analysts, TCP/IP engineers and ATM/Frame Relay engineers. *See also: Engineering, Computing, Trades/Technicians.*

Trade Shows (p. 345) includes trade show managers, exhibit sales representatives, exposition staff and conference producers. *See also: Marketing, Sales, Hospitality.*

Trades/Technicians (p. 345) includes millwrights, stationary engineers, mechanics, tool and die makers, electricians, welders, machinists and other skilled trades requiring an apprentice, journeyman or master tradesman designation. Also includes technologists and technicians. Does not include university-trained engineers, which are listed under "Engineering". *See also: Operations, Engineering.*

Transport (p. 345) includes transportation managers, transit planners, transport analysts, traffic study engineers, terminal managers, fleet managers, rail traffic coordinators, dispatchers, tractor-trailer drivers, coach drivers, ships pilots and AZ drivers. *See also: Logistics, Operations, Aerospace.*

du processus de contrôle statistique (SPC), les ingénieurs-contrôleurs, les chargés de la fiabilité, les techniciens de l'assurance de qualité, les consultants en gestion de qualité entière (TQM), les coordinateurs de perfectionnement continu, les vérificateurs et les inspecteurs selon la norme ISO 9000 (désignation internationale de normalisation). Voir aussi: Actuariel, Logistique, Exploitation, Ingénierie.

Ressources humaines *(p. 316) comprend les directeurs des ressources humaines, les chargés du personnel, les spécialistes en rémunération, les chargés des relations du travail, les spécialistes des informations sur les ressources humaines (HRIS), les administrateurs de pensions, les chargés de la paie, les conseillers d'orientation professionnelle, les consultants en redéploiement, le personnel de développement des employés, les entraîneurs, les recruteurs, le personnel à la recherche des exécutifs. Voir aussi: Affaires publiques.*

Santé et médical *(p. 314) comprend les infirmières, les thérapeutes, les médecins, les chargés de la santé, les administrateurs d'hôpital, les physiothérapeutes, les conseillers en réadaptation, les ergothérapeutes, les kinésiologues, les anesthésiologues, les techniciens-ultrason, les épidémiologues, les diététiens, les ophthamologues, les dentistes, les hygiénistes dentaires, les pathologistes, les psychologues, les psychiatres, les travailleurs en santé mentale, les assistants sociaux, les analystes des données de santé, les vendeurs d'articles médicaux, les aides soignantes, les technologues médicaux et les secrétaires médicales. Voir aussi: Pharmaceutique, Biotechnologie/biologie, Gouvernement/OSBL.*

Scientifique et recherche *(p. 342) comprend les scientifiques, les chimistes, les chercheurs adjoints, les anthropologues, les physiciens, les écologues, les adjoints des affaires régulatrices, les directeurs de laboratoire et tout emploi exigeant une licence ès sciences (BSc), une maîtrise (MSc) ou un doctorat (PhD) en sciences. Voir aussi: Biotechnologie/biologie, Pharmaceutique, Santé et médical.*

Sylviculture *(p. 312) comprend les forestiers, les marchands en bois de charpente, les chargés de la pratique forestière, les arboriculteurs et autres emplois relatifs à la plantation et la récolte des arbres et aux scieries. Ne comprend pas les postes dans l'industrie papetière, qui se trouvent séparément sous "Papeterie". Voir aussi: Papeterie, Gouvernement/OSBL.*

Télécommunications *(p. 343) comprend les chefs de réseau, les ingénieurs en télécommunications, les analystes téléphoniques, les techniciens d'interrupteur, les ingénieurs de réseau, les ingénieurs du logiciel SONET, les analystes de support-réseau, les ingénieurs du protocol Internet TCP/IP et les ingénieurs du mode de transmission asynchrone (ATM/Frame Relay). Voir aussi: Ingénierie, Informatique, Métiers/Techniciens.*

Transport *(p. 345) comprend les directeurs des transports, les planificateurs de transit, les analystes des transports, les ingénieurs d'études de circulation, les gérants de terminus, les chefs de flotte, les coordinateurs de trafic ferroviaire, les expéditeurs, les chauffeurs de tracteur à remorque, les chauffeurs d'autobus, les pilotes de navire et les chauffeurs de désignation ontarienne AZ (sans restriction). Voir aussi: Logistique, Exploitation, Aérospatial.*

Ventes *(p. 339) comprend les directeurs commerciaux, les administrateurs de la comptabilité, les surveillants de région, les gérants du territoire, les vendeurs et les chargés du service à la clientèle. Voir aussi: Marketing, Marketing direct.*

OCCUPATIONAL INDEX
INDEX OCCUPATIONNEL

GENERAL PRACTICE (Cont.)
GÉNÉRALISTES (Suivre)

Jonathan .... Québec, QC
JWT Special Communications .... Toronto, ON
Keith Bagg & Associates .... Toronto, ON
Keith-Murray Partners .... Toronto, ON
Keystone Select/MA Haggith .... Toronto, ON
Kingsley Allen IT Search .... Toronto, ON
Korn/Ferry Intl .... Toronto, ON
KPMG Executive Search .... IRELAND
Laliberté assoc cadres .... Longueuil, QC
Lamon + Stuart + Michaels .... Toronto, ON
Landmark Consulting Group .... Hamilton, ON
Leader Search Inc .... Calgary, AB
Lewis & Assoc .... Vancouver, BC
Louise Sidky & Assoc .... Toronto, ON
Lyons Black + Associates .... Vancouver, BC
Maizis & Miller Consultants .... Toronto, ON
Mandrake Groupe Conseil .... Montréal, QC
Mandrake Mgmt Consult .... Calgary, AB
Mandrake Mgmt Consult .... Toronto, ON
Marcobelli Group .... Toronto, ON
MayDay Personnel .... Winnipeg, MB
MCO Business Group Inc .... Ottawa, ON
Métivier Groupe Conseil .... Montréal, QC
Midlyn Advertising .... North Vancouver, BC
Miller Recruitment Solutions .... Halifax, NS
Mission Critical Recruit .... Edmonton, AB
Morgan & Banks Ltd .... AUSTRALIA
MVC Associates Intl .... Toronto, ON
Nationwide Advertising Svc .... Vancouver, BC
Nationwide Advertising Svc .... Toronto, ON
Nationwide Advertising Svc .... Ottawa, ON
Nationwide Advertising Svc .... USA
Net-Temps Inc. .... USA
Norrell Services .... Toronto, ON
Objectif Emploi 40+ .... Montréal, QC
Optimum Ltée .... Dorval, QC
Orexx Management Svcs .... Montréal, QC
Organization Consulting .... Toronto, ON
Palmer & Associates .... Kingston, ON
Palmer & Company Executive .... Toronto, ON
Palmer Reed .... Toronto, ON
Paquette Consulting .... Ottawa, ON
Partners in Employment .... Goderich, ON
PEI Office of Future .... Charlottetown, PE
People + ... Toronto, ON
People First Solutions .... Vancouver, BC
Permanent Solutions .... Mississauga, ON
Personnel Department, The .... Vancouver, BC
Personnel Department, The .... Edmonton, AB
Personnel Department, The .... Calgary, AB
Personnel Options .... Winkler, MB
Phase II Personnel .... Pointe-Claire, QC
Pitsel & Assoc .... Calgary, AB
Placement personnel Bolduc .... Sillery, QC
Precision Staffing .... Toronto, ON
PricewaterhouseCoopers .... Vancouver, BC
PricewaterhouseCoopers .... Calgary, AB
PricewaterhouseCoopers .... Winnipeg, MB
PricewaterhouseCoopers .... London, ON
PricewaterhouseCoopers .... Mississauga, ON
PricewaterhouseCoopers .... Ottawa, ON
PricewaterhouseCoopers .... Montréal, QC
PricewaterhouseCoopers .... CHINA
PricewaterhouseCoopers .... RUSSIA
PricewaterhouseCoopers .... TRINIDAD
Prince Arthur Advertising .... Toronto, ON
Prism Associates, The .... Edmonton, AB

Pro Tec Services Techniques .... Brossard, QC
Pro-Action Personnel .... Chomedey, QC
Professional Personnel .... Cambridge, ON
Progroupe Ress Humaines .... Hull, QC
Progroupe Ress Humaines .... Pierrefonds, QC
Publicis Tandem .... Toronto, ON
Publicité Day .... Montréal, QC
PubliFactum Inc .... Montréal, QC
Quali-Tech Inc. .... Longueuil, QC
Quantum Consulting .... Calgary, AB
Ray & Berndtson/Robertson .... Moncton, NB
Ray & Berndtson/Robertson .... Halifax, NS
Recareer.com .... Toronto, ON
RecruitAd Confidential .... Vancouver, BC
RecruitAd Confidential .... Calgary, AB
RecruitAd Confidential .... Toronto, ON
Recruitment Enhancement .... Vancouver, BC
Recruitment Enhancement .... Toronto, ON
Results Management Canada .... Waterloo, ON
Richard Foster Company .... Toronto, ON
Robert Channing Consulting .... Oakville, ON
Robert Connelly & Associates .... USA
Robert Lecavalier Executive .... Montréal, QC
Robert Paquet & Assoc .... Sainte-Foy, QC
Robert W. Dingman Company .... USA
Russell Reynolds Assoc .... FRANCE
Russell Reynolds Assoc .... SINGAPORE
Russell Reynolds Assoc .... SPAIN
Russell Reynolds Assoc .... USA
RWS Consulting Group .... London, ON
Saunders Company .... Toronto, ON
Search Company, The .... Toronto, ON
SHL Group .... Toronto, ON
SHL Group .... Ottawa, ON
Simmons Group .... Edmonton, AB
Sobot Stone Consultants .... Mississauga, ON
Société Pierre Boucher .... Longueuil, QC
Spectrum Assoc Executive .... Woodbridge, ON
Spencer Stuart .... BRAZIL
Spencer Stuart .... CHINA
Spencer Stuart .... GERMANY
Spencer Stuart .... ITALY
Spencer Stuart .... USA
Spencer Stuart .... USA
Stephen Goldstein Associates .... Ottawa, ON
Stevens Resource Group .... Tillsonburg, ON
TAG Personnel Consultants .... Montréal, QC
Tamm Communications .... Toronto, ON
Technical Service Consult .... Surrey, BC
Templeman Consulting .... Whitby, ON
Templeman Consulting .... Belleville, ON
Templeman Consulting .... Kingston, ON
TMP Worldwide Advertising .... Vancouver, BC
TMP Worldwide Advertising .... Toronto, ON
TMP Worldwide Advertising .... Montréal, QC
TMP Worldwide Exec .... Ottawa, ON
TMP Worldwide Exec Search .... Vancouver, BC
TMP Worldwide Exec Search .... Calgary, AB
TMP Worldwide Interactive .... Montréal, QC
Totten & Associates .... London, ON
Tremblay & Assoc .... Montréal, QC
TriNet Employment Group .... Toronto, ON
TriNet Employment Group .... USA
Vickery Boardman Assoc .... Whitby, ON
W.R. London Consultants .... Toronto, ON
Wallace & Partners .... Toronto, ON
Weir Associates .... Toronto, ON
Wenje Management Ltd .... Markham, ON
Westcott Thomas Assoc .... Huntsville, ON
Westcott Thomas Assoc .... Toronto, ON

GENERAL PRACTICE (Cont.)
GÉNÉRALISTES (Suivre)

Western Mgmnt Consultants .... Vancouver, BC
Wightman & Associates .... Kanata, ON
Working Well Consulting .... Innisfil, ON
Wypich International .... Toronto, ON
Yves Plouffe et assoc .... Île-des-Soeurs, QC

ACCOUNTING
COMPTABILITÉ

1st Choice Personnel .... USA
500 Services de Selection .... Val-d'Or, QC
A. Lawrence Abrams Assoc .... Waterloo, ON
Abel Placement Consult .... Markham, ON
Access Career Solutions .... Brampton, ON
Account Ability .... Toronto, ON
Accountants on Call .... Vancouver, BC
Accountants on Call .... Toronto, ON
Accountemps Financial .... Vancouver, BC
Accountemps Financial .... Surrey, BC
Accountemps Financial ....Edmonton, AB
Accountemps Financial .... Calgary, AB
Accountemps Financial .... Winnipeg, MB
Accountemps Financial .... Toronto, ON
Accountemps Financial .... Toronto, ON
Accountemps Financial .... Burlington, ON
Accountemps Financial .... Mississauga, ON
Accountemps Financial .... Markham, ON
Accountemps Financial .... Ottawa, ON
Accountemps Financial .... Montréal, QC
Accounting Machine Personnel .... Toronto, ON
Action Personnel Svcs .... Peace River, AB
Adecco Canada .... Victoria, BC
Adecco Canada .... Vancouver, BC
Adecco Canada .... Richmond, BC
Adecco Canada .... Burnaby, BC
Adecco Canada .... Langley, BC
Adecco Canada .... Calgary, AB
Adecco Canada .... Saskatoon, SK
Adecco Canada .... Regina, SK
Adecco Canada .... Winnipeg, MB
Adecco Canada .... Guelph, ON
Adecco Canada .... Toronto, ON
Adecco Canada .... Toronto, ON
Adecco Canada .... Toronto, ON
Adecco Canada .... Brampton, ON
Adecco Canada .... Oakville, ON
Adecco Canada .... Markham, ON
Adecco Canada .... Ottawa, ON
Adecco / Compaq .... Toronto, ON
Adecco LPI .... Saint-Laurent, QC
Adecco Personnel Technique .... Sherbrooke, QC
Adecco Québec .... Laval, QC
Adecco Québec ....Chicoutimi, QC
Adecco Québec .... Québec, QC
Adirect Recruiting Corp .... Toronto, ON
Administration Gespro .... Montréal, QC
AES Recruitment .... Toronto, ON
Agence de personnel Abitibi .... Val-d'Or, QC
Aim Personnel Svcs .... Ottawa, ON
Allen Austin Lowe & Powers .... USA
Allen Personnel Svcs .... London, ON
Allen Personnel Svcs .... Cambridge, ON
Altis Human Resources .... Toronto, ON
Alumni-Network Recruit .... Mississauga, ON
Andersen .... Vancouver, BC

Andersen .... Winnipeg, MB
Andersen .... Toronto, ON
Andersen .... Toronto, ON
Andersen .... Mississauga, ON
Andersen .... Ottawa, ON
Andersen .... Montréal, QC
Andersen .... Sainte-Foy, QC
Apple Management Corp .... Toronto, ON
Apple One Employment .... Toronto, ON
Applicants Inc. .... Kitchener, ON
Archer Assoc .... Toronto, ON
Argentus Inc. .... Toronto, ON
Arlyn Personnel Agencies .... Vancouver, BC
Armor Personnel .... Orangeville, ON
Armor Personnel .... Brampton, ON
Armor Personnel ....Mississauga, ON
Armor Personnel .... Vaughan, ON
Associates Group .... Ottawa, ON
ASTRA Management Corp .... Vancouver, BC
Ayrshire Group .... Toronto, ON
Baines Gwinner Ltd .... UNITED KINGDOM
Baldock Associates .... Toronto, ON
Baldwin Staffing Group .... Calgary, AB
Barry Blostein Recruitment .... Thornhill, ON
Barry Hults Consultants .... Markham, ON
Bay Street Placement .... Richmond Hill, ON
BDO Dunwoody & Assoc .... Kitchener, ON
BDO Dunwoody & Assoc .... Hamilton, ON
BDO Dunwoody & Assoc .... Markham, ON
BDO Dunwoody Exec Search .... Winnipeg, MB
BDO Dunwoody LLP .... Winnipeg, MB
BDO Dunwoody LLP .... Sarnia, ON
BDO Dunwoody LLP .... Toronto, ON
BDO Dunwoody LLP .... Uxbridge, ON
BDO Dunwoody LLP .... Kingston, ON
BDO Dunwoody LLP .... Nepean, ON
BDO Dunwoody LLP .... Winchester, ON
BDO Dunwoody LLP .... Montréal, QC
Beallor & Partners .... Toronto, ON
Bessner Gallay Kreisman .... Westmount, QC
Bondwell Staffing .... Toronto, ON
Booke & Partners .... Winnipeg, MB
Bosworth Field Assoc .... Toronto, ON
Bouris Wilson LLP .... Ottawa, ON
Bower Ng Staff Systems .... Vancouver, BC
Boyd-Laidler Assoc .... Toronto, ON
Bray Larouche et Assoc .... Montréal, QC
Brownlow Associates .... Ancaster, ON
Bruce R. Duncan Assoc .... Toronto, ON
Bryan Jason Assoc .... Toronto, ON
Business&Prof Appointmnts .... UNITED KINGDOM
C.G. Thomson & Co .... Toronto, ON
C.N. Taylor Consulting .... Bedford, NS
C. Price & Associates .... Toronto, ON
C. Snow & Associates .... Toronto, ON
Cadillac Career Centre .... Toronto, ON
Cambridge Mgmnt Planning .... Toronto, ON
Cameron Consulting Group .... Brampton, ON
Cameron Mgmnt Svcs ....Edmonton, AB
Cameron Mgmnt Svcs .... Calgary, AB
Canadian Exec Consultants .... Toronto, ON
Capital Executive .... Calgary, AB
CAPP Employment Svcs ....Mississauga, ON
Career Partners/Harrison .... Hamilton, ON
Careers & Professions .... Montréal, QC
Carion Resource Group .... Mississauga, ON
Catherine Thomas Partners .... Toronto, ON
CCG Mgmnt Consultants ....Mississauga, ON
Central Mgmnt Consultants .... Toronto, ON
Centre for Corp Resources .... Toronto, ON

ACCOUNTING (Cont.)
COMPTABILITÉ (Suivre)

Centrex HR Centre .... Hamilton, ON
Chad Management Group .... Toronto, ON
Charter Mgmnt Group .... Winnipeg, MB
Chase Consultants .... Mississauga, ON
Cheryl Craig Careers .... Burlington, ON
Chisholm & Partners Intl .... Toronto, ON
Christmas McIvor Assoc .... Mississauga, ON
Christopher Vincent & Assoc .... Calgary, AB
Churchill Group, The .... Toronto, ON
CLA Personnel .... Ottawa, ON
Clarendon Parker ME .... UNITED ARAB EMIRATES
Clark Pollard & Gagliardi .... Waterloo, ON
Clarke Henning LLP .... Toronto, ON
Classic Consulting Group .... Calgary, AB
Classified Canada .... Mississauga, ON
Claude Guedj Assoc .... Montréal, QC
CMP Select .... Toronto, ON
Coakwell Crawford Cairns .... High River, AB
Coape Staffing Network .... Vancouver, BC
Coape Staffing Network .... Burnaby, BC
Coape Staffing Network .... Edmonton, AB
Coape Staffing Network .... Calgary, AB
Coast Personnel Svcs .... Nanaimo, BC
Collins Barrow .... Calgary, AB
Conestoga Personnel .... Kitchener, ON
Connors Lovell Assoc .... Cambridge, ON
Connors Lovell Assoc .... Mississauga, ON
Conseillers Jacques Cartier .... Montréal, QC
Contemporary Personnel .... Vancouver, BC
Core-Staff Inc. .... Toronto, ON
Corporate & Career Develop .... Vancouver, BC
Corporate Consultants .... Toronto, ON
Corporate Controllers Inc .... Halifax, NS
Corporate Expressions .... Toronto, ON
Corporate HR Communicat .... Winnipeg, MB
Corporate Res (Hertford) .... UNITED KINGDOM
Corporate Resources .... Toronto, ON
Courtney Personnel .... Brampton, ON
Cowan & Associates .... Calgary, AB
Cowan Personnel .... Montréal, QC
Cox Merritt & Co .... Kanata, ON
Craig Davies Collins .... Red Deer, AB
Creative Financial Staff .... Vancouver, BC
Creative Financial Staff .... Toronto, ON
Creative Financial Staff .... Toronto, ON
Creative Financial Staff .... Mississauga, ON
Cyberna Associates .... Montréal, QC
D & H Group .... Vancouver, BC
D.P. Group, The .... UNITED KINGDOM
Daniluck & Associates .... Edmonton, AB
Dare Human Resources .... Ottawa, ON
David Aplin & Assoc .... Edmonton, AB
David Aplin & Assoc .... Calgary, AB
David Warwick Kennedy Assoc .... Vancouver, BC
Davies Kidd .... UNITED KINGDOM
Davies Park .... Edmonton, AB
Davies Park .... Calgary, AB
Davis Daignault Schick & Co .... Calgary, AB
Dean & Associates .... Toronto, ON
Deloitte Consulting .... Toronto, ON
Deloitte Consulting .... Montréal, QC
Delorme et Assoc .... Québec, QC
Design Group Staffing .... Calgary, AB
Design Group Staffing .... Toronto, ON
Dial Staffing Solutions .... Calgary, AB
Dick Cook Schulli .... Calgary, AB
Doré Liaison .... Greenfield Park, QC

Dotemtex Executive Search .... Montréal, QC
Drake Executive .... Burnaby, BC
Drake Executive .... Winnipeg, MB
Drake Executive .... Sudbury, ON
Drake Executive .... London, ON
Drake Executive .... Toronto, ON
Drake Executive .... Montréal, QC
Drake International .... Edmonton, AB
Drake International .... North Bay, ON
Drake International .... London, ON
Drake International .... Toronto, ON
Drake International .... Hamilton, ON
Drake International .... Oakville, ON
Drake International .... Barrie, ON
Drake International .... Belleville, ON
Drake International .... Kingston, ON
Drake International .... Ottawa, ON
Drake International .... Montréal, QC
Drake International .... Québec, QC
Drake International .... Moncton, NB
Drake International .... Halifax, NS
Drakkar Human Resources .... Montréal, QC
Drakkar Human Resources .... Québec, QC
Ducharme Group .... Toronto, ON
Dunhill Consultants N York .... Toronto, ON
Dunhill Personnel London .... London, ON
E.H. Scissons & Associates .... Saskatoon, SK
E-Search Consulting .... Toronto, ON
Eastleigh Personnel .... Langley, BC
Edan Search Group .... Toronto, ON
Edie Bench Personnel .... Toronto, ON
Élan Personnel .... Calgary, AB
Ellis Foster .... Vancouver, BC
Employment Partnership .... Saint John, NB
ePersonnel Inc .... Montréal, QC
Erie Personnel Corp .... Thorold, ON
Erie Personnel Corp .... Fort Erie, ON
Ernst & Young .... Kitchener, ON
Ernst & Young .... SAUDI ARABIA
Eureka Recruitment .... Calgary, AB
Euro-West Consulting .... Vancouver, BC
Evancic Perrault EPR .... Drayton Valley, AB
Evans Search Group .... Toronto, ON
Everest Mgmnt Network .... Toronto, ON
Excel Personnel .... Kamloops, BC
ExecuCounsel Inc .... Toronto, ON
Executive Assistance .... Toronto, ON
Executive Network .... Victoria, BC
Executive Source .... Regina, SK
Executives Available .... Pointe-Claire, QC
Executrade Consultants .... Edmonton, AB
Expert Recruiters Inc .... Vancouver, BC
Expertech Personnel Svcs .... Montréal, QC
Fifth Option .... Burnaby, BC
Finacc Executive Search .... Toronto, ON
Finance Department Ltd .... Toronto, ON
First Choice Personnel .... Toronto, ON
Freelandt Caldwell Reilly .... Sudbury, ON
Friday Personnel Inc .... Vancouver, BC
Friday Personnel Inc .... Calgary, AB
Friedman & Friedman .... Montréal, QC
Fromm & Assoc Personnel .... Toronto, ON
Fuller Landau .... Montréal, QC
Future Executive Personnel .... Toronto, ON
Future Executive Personnel .... USA
Futurestep .... Toronto, ON
G.L. Penney & Associates .... Edmonton, AB
G-P Personnel .... Chicoutimi, QC
Galt Global Recruiting .... Vancouver, BC
Galt Global Recruiting .... Calgary, AB

ACCOUNTING (Cont.)
COMPTABILITÉ (Suivre)

Gardner & Coombs .... St. John's, NF
Garrison Group, The .... Toronto, ON
Gaspar & Associates .... Toronto, ON
Gauthier Conseils .... Montréal, QC
Genesis Corporate Search .... Calgary, AB
Georgian Staffing Svcs .... Collingwood, ON
Gerald Walsh Recruitment .... Halifax, NS
Geri Ramsay & Associates .... Vancouver, BC
Gestion Conseils DLT Inc .... Manotick, ON
Gestion Orion Ltée .... Montréal, QC
Ginsberg Gluzman Fage .... Ottawa, ON
Girardin & Associates .... Winnipeg, MB
Givens Hamilton Lain .... Edmonton, AB
Global Personnel .... Toronto, ON
Global Placement Svcs .... Mississauga, ON
Goldsmith Miller Hersh .... Montréal, QC
Graduate Consulting Svcs .... Montréal, QC
Graham Matthew & Partners .... Cambridge, ON
Grand River Personnel .... Kitchener, ON
Grant Thornton Intl .... Victoria, BC
Grant Thornton Intl .... Richmond, BC
Grant Thornton Intl .... Vancouver, BC
Grant Thornton Intl .... New Westminster, BC
Grant Thornton Intl .... Langley, BC
Grant Thornton Intl .... Kelowna, BC
Grant Thornton Intl .... Wetaskiwin, AB
Grant Thornton Intl .... Peace River, AB
Grant Thornton Intl .... Edmonton, AB
Grant Thornton Intl .... Calgary, AB
Grant Thornton Intl .... Winnipeg, MB
Grant Thornton Intl .... Sault Ste. Marie, ON
Grant Thornton Intl .... North Bay, ON
Grant Thornton Intl .... New Liskeard, ON
Grant Thornton Intl .... London, ON
Grant Thornton Intl .... Toronto, ON
Grant Thornton Intl .... Toronto, ON
Grant Thornton Intl .... Hamilton, ON
Grant Thornton Intl .... Mississauga, ON
Grant Thornton Intl .... Barrie, ON
Grant Thornton Intl .... Orillia, ON
Grant Thornton Intl .... Markham, ON
Grant Thornton Intl .... Port Colborne, ON
Grant Thornton Intl .... St. Catharines, ON
Grant Thornton Intl .... Fredericton, NB
Grant Thornton Intl .... Saint John, NB
Grant Thornton Intl .... Bathurst, NB
Grant Thornton Intl .... Miramichi, NB
Grant Thornton Intl .... Moncton, NB
Grant Thornton Intl .... Summerside, PE
Grant Thornton Intl .... Charlottetown, PE
Grant Thornton Intl .... Yarmouth, NS
Grant Thornton Intl .... Bridgewater, NS
Grant Thornton Intl .... Kentville, NS
Grant Thornton Intl .... Halifax, NS
Grant Thornton Intl .... Dartmouth, NS
Grant Thornton Intl .... Truro, NS
Grant Thornton Intl .... New Glasgow, NS
Grant Thornton Intl .... Antigonish, NS
Grant Thornton Intl .... Sydney, NS
Grant Thornton Intl .... Digby, NS
Grant Thornton Intl .... Corner Brook, NF
Grant Thornton Intl .... Grand Falls-Windsor, NF
Grant Thornton Intl .... St. John's, NF
Grant Thornton Intl .... Marystown, NF
GRH Consultants Inc .... Québec, QC
Group Four Mgmnt Consultants .... Toronto, ON
Groupe conseil Lamarche .... Granby, QC

Groupe SFP .... Trois-Rivières, QC
Groupe Tele Ressources .... Montréal, QC
Harcourt & Assoc .... Edmonton, AB
Harcourt & Assoc .... Calgary, AB
Harcourt Matthews Group .... Edmonton, AB
Harris Consulting Corp .... Winnipeg, MB
Harrison Carlson .... Burlington, ON
Hayhurst Consulting .... London, ON
HEC Group .... Ancaster, ON
Heighway Personnel .... London, ON
Hein & Company .... Ottawa, ON
Hemmerich Flanagan & Assoc .... Waterloo, ON
Heywood Holmes Partners .... Red Deer, AB
High Road Personnel .... Burlington, ON
Higher Vision Recruitment .... Toronto, ON
Holloway Schulz & Partners .... Vancouver, BC
Horizon Resources Intl .... Calgary, AB
Horwath Appel .... Montréal, QC
Houston Personnel Group .... Winnipeg, MB
HR Business Partners .... Calgary, AB
HR Vision Corporation .... Oakville, ON
Hughes LeBel .... Ottawa, ON
Human Resources Consult .... Mississauga, ON
Hunt Technical Personnel .... Vancouver, BC
Hunt Technical Personnel .... Calgary, AB
Hunt Technical Personnel .... Toronto, ON
Hunt Technical Personnel .... Toronto, ON
Hunt Technical Personnel .... Mississauga, ON
Hunt Technical Personnel .... Saint-Laurent, QC
Hunt Technical Personnel .... Montréal, QC
ICAP Management Inc .... Fredericton, NB
Ideal Personnel .... Mississauga, ON
Impact Staffing .... Windsor, ON
Integrated Data Svcs .... Ottawa, ON
Interchange Personnel .... Calgary, AB
Interim Plus .... Granby, QC
Intermark Mgmt Inc. .... Mississauga, ON
International Staffing .... UNITED KINGDOM
InterSearch Canada/Staffing .... Halifax, NS
J.O. Bush & Associates .... Mindemoya, ON
James Boyce Associates .... Toronto, ON
James E. Thomas & Assoc .... London, ON
James Partnership .... BERMUDA
Jan Howard & Associates .... Toronto, ON
Jenereaux & Associates .... Mississauga, ON
Jerry Adel & Company .... Toronto, ON
Job Born Candidate Select .... Hamilton, ON
JSG Group Mgmnt Consult .... Unionville, ON
K-International Group .... Toronto, ON
KAS Personnel Svcs .... North Bay, ON
KAS Personnel Svcs .... Kitchener, ON
KAS Personnel Svcs .... Guelph, ON
KAS Personnel Svcs .... Toronto, ON
KAS Personnel Svcs .... Toronto, ON
KAS Personnel Svcs .... Hamilton, ON
KAS Personnel Svcs .... Burlington, ON
KAS Personnel Svcs .... Brampton, ON
KAS Personnel Svcs .... Mississauga, ON
KAS Personnel Svcs .... Barrie, ON
KAS Personnel Svcs .... Belleville, ON
Kaymac & Associates .... Toronto, ON
Keeley Consulting .... Toronto, ON
Keith Bagg & Associates .... Toronto, ON
Keith Bagg Regional .... Thornhill, ON
Keith Bagg Staffing .... Toronto, ON
Kelly, Les svcs .... Granby, QC
Kelly, Les svcs .... Pointe-Claire, QC
Kelly, Les svcs .... Québec, QC
Kelly Permanent Recruit .... Toronto, ON
Kelly Permanent Recruit .... Toronto, ON

ACCOUNTING (Cont.)
COMPTABILITÉ (Suivre)

Kelly Permanent Recruit .... Mississauga, ON
Kelly Professional & Tech .... Victoria, BC
Kelly Professional & Tech .... Vancouver, BC
Kelly Professional & Tech .... Windsor, ON
Kelly Professional & Tech .... Chatham, ON
Kelly Professional & Tech .... London, ON
Kelly Professional & Tech .... St. Thomas, ON
Kelly Professional & Tech .... Brantford, ON
Kelly Professional & Tech .... Kitchener, ON
Kelly Professional & Tech .... Cambridge, ON
Kelly Professional & Tech .... Guelph, ON
Kelly Professional & Tech .... Hamilton, ON
Kelly Professional & Tech .... Burlington, ON
Kelly Professional & Tech .... Brampton, ON
Kelly Professional & Tech .... Oakville, ON
Kelly Professional & Tech .... St. Catharines, ON
Kelly Professional & Tech .... Oakville, ON
Kelly Professional & Tech .... Belleville, ON
Kelly Professional & Tech .... Kingston, ON
Kelly Professional & Tech .... Fredericton, NB
Kelly Professional & Tech .... Saint John, NB
Kelly Professional & Tech .... Moncton, NB
Kelly Professional & Tech .... Halifax, NS
Kenneth Murphy & Assoc .... Halifax, NS
Key Executive Consultants .... Barrie, ON
Key Executive Consultants .... Pickering, ON
King Mgmnt Search Group .... Toronto, ON
Kingston Ross Pasnak .... Edmonton, AB
Kirkpatrick Personnel .... Vancouver, BC
Klassen & Company .... Winnipeg, MB
KNV Results Management .... White Rock, BC
Landon Morgan Inc .... Thorold, ON
Lannick Associates .... Toronto, ON
Larkin Group .... Mississauga, ON
Larouche & Associates .... Dorval, QC
Leader Search Inc .... Calgary, AB
Lefcort Engel .... Montréal, QC
Lehmor Associates .... Saint-Laurent, QC
LePage International .... Montréal, QC
Levton Group .... Toronto, ON
Levy Pilotte .... Montréal, QC
Licari & Vitanza Associates .... USA
Linda Walter & Assoc .... Île-Perrot, QC
Lipton Wiseman .... Toronto, ON
Little Group, The .... Brantford, ON
Little Group, The .... Burlington, ON
LMR Consultants .... Thornhill, ON
London Executive Consultants .... London, ON
Lussier Executive Search .... Toronto, ON
Lynx Career Consultants .... Mississauga, ON
M.R. Goodman Consulting .... Calgary, AB
M. Trew & Associates .... Toronto, ON
Maclean & Assoc .... Mississauga, ON
Management Plus Consulting .... LEBANON
Markent Personnel Inc .... USA
Marlene Bilodeau Conseils .... Chicoutimi, QC
Mayfair Personnel .... Grande Prairie, AB
McGuire Management .... Richmond Hill, ON
McIntyre Mgmnt Resources .... Hamilton, ON
McLean Exec Consultants .... Calgary, AB
Meridia Recruitment Svcs .... Halifax, NS
Meyers Norris Penny .... Wainwright, AB
Meyers Norris Penny .... Leduc, AB
Meyers Norris Penny .... Grande Prairie, AB
Meyers Norris Penny .... Red Deer, AB
Meyers Norris Penny .... Innisfail, AB
Meyers Norris Penny .... Edmonton, AB
Meyers Norris Penny .... Calgary, AB
Meyers Norris Penny .... Calgary, AB
Meyers Norris Penny .... Lethbridge, AB
Meyers Norris Penny .... Medicine Hat, AB
Meyers Norris Penny .... Rocky Mountain House, AB
Meyers Norris Penny .... Pincher Creek, AB
Meyers Norris Penny .... Milk River, AB
Meyers Norris Penny .... Foremost, AB
Meyers Norris Penny .... Bow Island, AB
Meyers Norris Penny .... Drumheller, AB
Meyers Norris Penny .... Rimbey, AB
Meyers Norris Penny .... Swift Current, SK
Meyers Norris Penny .... Saskatoon, SK
Meyers Norris Penny .... Prince Albert, SK
Meyers Norris Penny .... Regina, SK
Meyers Norris Penny .... Humboldt, SK
Meyers Norris Penny .... Moosomin, SK
Meyers Norris Penny .... Melfort, SK
Meyers Norris Penny .... Hudson Bay, SK
Meyers Norris Penny .... Dauphin, MB
Meyers Norris Penny .... Brandon, MB
Meyers Norris Penny .... Winnipeg, MB
Meyers Norris Penny .... Portage La Prairie, MB
Meyers Norris Penny .... Virden, MB
Meyers Norris Penny .... Deloraine, MB
Meyers Norris Penny .... Kilarney, MB
Meyers Norris Penny .... Neepawa, MB
Michael Page Finance .... CHINA
Michael Page International .... USA
Milgram & Associates .... Toronto, ON
Millar Walker & Gay .... Toronto, ON
Miller Recruitment Solutions .... Halifax, NS
Mintz & Partners .... Toronto, ON
Molnar & Associates .... Toronto, ON
Morgan Exec Search Group .... Toronto, ON
Morgan Palmer Search .... Toronto, ON
Moscoe & Company .... Toronto, ON
Mount Royal Personnel .... Calgary, AB
Moxon Personnel .... Vancouver, BC
MultiPersonnel International .... Dorval, QC
NewSource Management .... Toronto, ON
Norrell Services .... Toronto, ON
Norrell Staffing Services .... Richmond, BC
Norrell Staffing Services .... Vancouver, BC
North York Personnel .... Toronto, ON
Nursing & Home Health Care .... Toronto, ON
Osborne Group .... Vancouver, BC
Osborne Group .... Calgary, AB
Osborne Group .... Edmonton, AB
Osborne Group .... Toronto, ON
Osborne Group .... Montréal, QC
P.R.Y. .... Toronto, ON
Pal Personnel Svcs .... Toronto, ON
Palmer Reed .... Toronto, ON
Paquette & Associates .... Vancouver, BC
Paradigm Mgmnt Solutions .... Toronto, ON
Parkwood Associates .... Mississauga, ON
Partners Employment Group .... Toronto, ON
Partners in Search .... Toronto, ON
Paziuk Professional Placements .... Edmonton, AB
Peak Associates Inc .... Toronto, ON
Peapell & Associates .... Halifax, NS
People Bank, The .... Winnipeg, MB
People Bank, The .... Toronto, ON
People First Solutions .... Vancouver, BC
People Management Group .... Woodstock, ON
People Placers Personnel .... Halifax, NS
PeopleFind Inc. .... Markham, ON
Performance House .... Waterloo, ON
Permanent Search Group .... Mississauga, ON

ACCOUNTING (Cont.)
COMPTABILITÉ (Suivre)

Permanent Solutions	Mississauga, ON
Personnel Alter Ego	Pointe-Claire, QC
Personnel Alter Ego	Montréal, QC
Personnel by Pro-Staff	Windsor, ON
Personnel Clé	Québec, QC
Personnel Hélène Tobin	Dorval, QC
Personnel Menen	Mount Royal, QC
Personnel Mgmnt Group	Winnipeg, MB
Personnel Opportunities	Toronto, ON
Personnel Outaouais	Hull, QC
Personnel Search	Saint John, NB
Personnel Search	Moncton, NB
Personnel Star Avon FJ	Montréal, QC
Petro Staff Intl HR Advisors	Calgary, AB
Phelps Staffing Resource	Thunder Bay, ON
Phoenix Search Group	Toronto, ON
Pinstripe Personnel	London, ON
Pinstripe Personnel	Toronto, ON
Pinstripe Personnel	Mississauga, ON
Pioneer Exec Consultants	Toronto, ON
PKF Hill LLP	Toronto, ON
PME Partenaire Consult	Saint-Georges, QC
Pommen & Associates	Edmonton, AB
Powell Jones Mgmnt Services	Barrie, ON
Pragmatizm	Toronto, ON
PricewaterhouseCoopers	Victoria, BC
PricewaterhouseCoopers	Calgary, AB
PricewaterhouseCoopers	Saskatoon, SK
PricewaterhouseCoopers	Kitchener, ON
PricewaterhouseCoopers	Toronto, ON
PricewaterhouseCoopers	Hamilton, ON
PricewaterhouseCoopers	Montréal, QC
PricewaterhouseCoopers	Québec, QC
PricewaterhouseCoopers	Saint John, NB
PricewaterhouseCoopers	Charlottetown, PE
PricewaterhouseCoopers	St. John's, NF
PricewaterhouseCoopers	BERMUDA
Prime Management Group	London, ON
Prime Management Group	Cambridge, ON
Prior Resource Group	Kitchener, ON
Pro-Action Personnel	Chomedey, QC
Prokosch Group, The	Calgary, AB
Prospects Plus	Kirkland, QC
Prud'Homme Groupe-Conseil	Montréal, QC
Ptack Schnarch Basevitz	Montréal, QC
PTC - Financial Staffing	Concord, ON
Quality Personnel	Brampton, ON
Quantum	Montréal, QC
Quantum, Les services	Longueuil, QC
Quantum, Les services	Pointe-Claire, QC
Quantum, Les services	Laval, QC
Quantum, Les services	Québec, QC
Quantum Mgmnt Services	Toronto, ON
Quantum Mgmnt Services	Toronto, ON
Quantum Mgmnt Services	Mississauga, ON
Quantum Mgmt Services	Toronto, ON
Quest Consultants	Toronto, ON
Quest Exec Recruitment	Toronto, ON
Quest Resource Group	Mississauga, ON
R. Jacques Plante & Assoc	Sillery, QC
R.K. Chengkalath PC	Calgary, AB
Raymond Chabot HR Inc	Toronto, ON
Raymond Chabot HR Inc	Hull, QC
Raymond Chabot HR Inc	Montréal, QC
Raymond Chabot HR Inc	Québec, QC
Recherches Johnson	Saint-Lambert, QC
Reid Management Consultants	Toronto, ON
Resource Corporation, The	Toronto, ON
Resource Professionals	Calgary, AB
Resources Connection	Toronto, ON
Results Management Canada	Waterloo, ON
RHI Management Resources	Calgary, AB
RHI Management Resources	Toronto, ON
Richard Major & Assoc	Toronto, ON
Richmark Group, The	Toronto, ON
Richter Consulting	Toronto, ON
Richter Usher Vineberg	Montréal, QC
RJ Professionals	Toronto, ON
Robert Half Canada	Edmonton, AB
Robert Half Canada	Calgary, AB
Robert Half Canada	Toronto, ON
Robert Half Canada	Toronto, ON
Robert Half Canada	Mississauga, ON
Robert Half Canada	Ottawa, ON
Robert Half Canada	Montréal, QC
Robert Half Financial	Vancouver, BC
Robert L Holmes Placement	Cambridge, ON
Robert R. Scurfield & Assoc	Winnipeg, MB
Robertson Hancock Ltd	Toronto, ON
Rockwell Placement Agencies	Richmond, BC
Rolfe, Benson	Vancouver, BC
Roll Harris & Associates	Montréal, QC
Rolland Groupe Conseil	Westmount, QC
Rolland ressources humaines	Montréal, QC
Russell & Associates	Kelowna, BC
RWJ & Associates	London, ON
SAG ressources humaines	Montréal, QC
Savage Consultants	Vancouver, BC
Sayler's Employment Consult	Edmonton, AB
Scarrow & Donald	Winnipeg, MB
Schlesinger Newman Goldman	Montréal, QC
Schwartz Levitsky Feldman	Toronto, ON
Schwartz Levitsky Feldman	Montréal, QC
Scott Batenchuk & Co	Burlington, ON
Slate Group, The	Edmonton, AB
Smith Nixon & Co	Toronto, ON
Smythe Ratcliffe	Vancouver, BC
Snelgrove Personnel	Hamilton, ON
SOLUTIONS	Cornwall, ON
Spherion Workforce	Victoria, BC
Spherion Workforce	Vancouver, BC
Spherion Workforce	Edmonton, AB
Spherion Workforce	Edmonton, AB
Spherion Workforce	Calgary, AB
Spherion Workforce	Winnipeg, MB
Spherion Workforce	Toronto, ON
Spherion Workforce	Toronto, ON
Spherion Workforce	Toronto, ON
Spherion Workforce	Hamilton, ON
Spherion Workforce	Brampton, ON
Spherion Workforce	Mississauga, ON
Spherion Workforce	Mississauga, ON
Spherion Workforce	Barrie, ON
Spherion Workforce	Pickering, ON
Spherion Workforce	Whitby, ON
Spherion Workforce	Oshawa, ON
Spherion Workforce	Kanata, ON
Spherion Workforce	Ottawa, ON
Spherion Workforce	Ottawa, ON
Spherion Workforce	Montréal, QC
Spherion Workforce	Halifax, NS
Squires Resources	Barrie, ON
Staff Bureau Employment	Edmonton, AB
Staff Plus	Toronto, ON
Staffworks	Toronto, ON
Stephen Laramee Associates	Toronto, ON

ACCOUNTING (Cont.)
COMPTABILITÉ (Suivre)

Stevenson & White Inc	Ottawa, ON
Stoakley-Dudley Consult	Mississauga, ON
Summit Personnel Services	Windsor, ON
Sydelle Associates	Georgetown, ON
Symmetry Search Group	Toronto, ON
Tanaka Associates	Toronto, ON
Tancredi Consulting	Toronto, ON
Taylor Personnel	Victoria, BC
Taylor Personnel	Edmonton, AB
Taylor Tomas Consulting	Coquitlam, BC
TaylorMade Careers	USA
Tele-Ressources Ltée	Montréal, QC
TES Employment Solution	Toronto, ON
TES Employment Solution	USA
TES Employment Solution	USA
Toronto Exec Consultants	Toronto, ON
Torstaff Personnel	Toronto, ON
Tosi Placement Services	Toronto, ON
Treat & Associates Executive	Toronto, ON
Tretiak Holowka	Montréal, QC
Ultimate Staffing	Hamilton, ON
Verelli Arrizza	Montréal, QC
Veres Picton & Co	Edmonton, AB
Verriez Group Inc	London, ON
Victor & Gold	Montréal, QC
Villor Consultants	Montréal, QC
W. Hutt Mgmnt Resources	Burlington, ON
Wace & Assoc	Mississauga, ON
Wade & Partners	Burlington, ON
Walbrook Appointment England	Toronto, ON
Walsh King	Vancouver, BC
Walter P. Miller Company	St. John's, NF
Wasserman Stotland Bratt	Montréal, QC
Wayne Perry & Associates	Toronto, ON
Wellington Partners Intl	Kitchener, ON
Western Mgmnt Consultants	Calgary, AB
Withey Addison	Mississauga, ON
Zeidel Gregory Associates	Toronto, ON
Zen Zen International	Winnipeg, MB

ACTUARIAL
ACTUARIEL

Austin Marlowe Intl	Toronto, ON
Delta Management Options	Toronto, ON
Executrade Consultants	Edmonton, AB
Lamon + Stuart + Michaels	Toronto, ON
Meech Partners	Toronto, ON
Milgram & Associates	Toronto, ON
North American Search Group	Toronto, ON
Pettitt Group Inc., The	Burlington, ON
SAG ressources humaines	Montréal, QC
Team Power Exec Search	Markham, ON
Urquhart Management Inc	Toronto, ON

ADMINISTRATIVE
ADMINISTRATIF

1st Choice Personnel	USA
1st Choice Staffing	Mississauga, ON
Abel Placement Consult	Markham, ON
Action Info-Travail	Mont-Laurier, QC
Adecco Canada	Edmonton, AB

Adecco Canada	Saskatoon, SK
Adecco Canada	Regina, SK
Adecco Canada	Kitchener, ON
Adecco Canada	Toronto, ON
Adecco Canada	Toronto, ON
Adecco Canada	Toronto, ON
Adecco Canada	Toronto, ON
Adecco Canada	Halifax, NS
Adecco / Compaq	Toronto, ON
Adecco LPI	Saint-Laurent, QC
Adecco Québec	Laval, QC
Adecco Québec	Québec, QC
Adecco Québec (Vieux-Mtl)	Montréal, QC
Administrative Fundamentals	Toronto, ON
Affordable Personnel	Concord, ON
Agence de place H Roy	Saint-Hyacinthe, QC
Agence de place H Roy	Montréal, QC
Agence de place H Roy	Sainte-Foy, QC
Agence place	Notre-Dame-des-Prairies, QC
Aimco Personnel	Mississauga, ON
Aimco Staffing Solutions	Toronto, ON
Aimco Staffing Solutions	Toronto, ON
Aimco Staffing Solutions	Burlington, ON
Aimco Staffing Solutions	Brampton, ON
Aimco Staffing Solutions	Mississauga, ON
Allen Personnel Svcs	London, ON
Alliance Personnel Group	Edmonton, AB
Alliance Personnel Group	Oakville, ON
Altis Human Resources	Toronto, ON
Apple One Employment	Toronto, ON
Armor Personnel	Orangeville, ON
Armor Personnel	Brampton, ON
Armor Personnel	Mississauga, ON
Armor Personnel	Vaughan, ON
Association Resource Centre	Toronto, ON
Associum Consultants	Toronto, ON
Augment Prestige Svcs	Point Edward, ON
B.B. Consultants Group	Point Edward, ON
Baldwin Staffing Group	Calgary, AB
Barry Hults Consultants	Markham, ON
BCB Candidates Bank	Lasalle, QC
Bilingual Source	Toronto, ON
Bongard Marsh Assoc	Toronto, ON
Bourassa Brodeur Assoc	Trois-Rivières, QC
Bower Ng Staff Systems	Vancouver, BC
BP Floater Staffing	Calgary, AB
Brainhunter.com	Toronto, ON
Brainhunter.com	Ottawa, ON
Brant & Associates	Winnipeg, MB
Bray Larouche et Assoc	Montréal, QC
Brock Placement Group	Toronto, ON
Bruce R. Duncan Assoc	Toronto, ON
Bryan Jason Assoc	Toronto, ON
Bureau de placement d'Anjou	Montréal, QC
Burke Group	Hamilton, ON
Burke Group	St. Catharines, ON
Business Rescue Associates	Ottawa, ON
Cadillac Career Centre	Toronto, ON
Calian Technology Svcs	Mississauga, ON
Calian Technology Svcs	Ottawa, ON
Calian Technology Svcs	Kanata, ON
Canadian Exec Consultants	Toronto, ON
Career Advance Employment	Burlington, ON
Career Centre, The	Toronto, ON
Career Partners/Harrison	Hamilton, ON
Centrex HR Centre	Hamilton, ON
Cheryl Craig Careers	Burlington, ON
CLA Personnel	Ottawa, ON
Coape Staffing Network	Vancouver, BC
Coape Staffing Network	Burnaby, BC

ADMINISTRATIVE (Cont.)
ADMINISTRATIF (Suivre)

Coape Staffing Network	Edmonton, AB
Coape Staffing Network	Calgary, AB
Concept II Employment Svcs	Moncton, NB
Contemporary Personnel	Vancouver, BC
Contemporary Personnel	Toronto, ON
Contemporary Personnel	Brampton, ON
Contemporary Personnel	Barrie, ON
Contemporary Personnel	Newmarket, ON
Core-Staff Inc.	Toronto, ON
Dare Human Resources	Ottawa, ON
Dean & Associates	Toronto, ON
Dial Staffing Solutions	Calgary, AB
Dotemtex Executive Search	Montréal, QC
Drake Executive	Toronto, ON
Drake Executive	Montréal, QC
Drake International	Burnaby, BC
Drake International	Mississauga, ON
Drake Medox	Powell River, BC
Drake Office Overload	Burnaby, BC
Drake Office Overload	Toronto, ON
Drake Office Overload	Toronto, ON
Drake Office Overload	Toronto, ON
Drakkar Human Resources	Montréal, QC
Drakkar Human Resources	Québec, QC
Dynamic Employment Solution	Brampton, ON
Dynamic Employment Solution	Brampton, ON
Dynamic Personnel	Ottawa, ON
Edie Bench Personnel	Toronto, ON
EDS Executive Staffing	Vancouver, BC
Élan Personnel	Victoria, BC
Élan Personnel	Vancouver, BC
Emplois Competences	Granby, QC
Emplois Competences	Sherbrooke, QC
Employer's Choice	Brampton, ON
Employer's Overload	Toronto, ON
Employment Network	Regina, SK
Eric Turner & Associates	Mississauga, ON
Evans Search Group	Toronto, ON
Excel Human Resources	Ottawa, ON
Excel Personnel	Kamloops, BC
Excel Personnel	Montréal, QC
Execusearch	Lethbridge, AB
Executrade Consultants	Edmonton, AB
Expert Recruiters Inc	Vancouver, BC
Express Personnel Svcs	Port Coquitlam, BC
Express Personnel Svcs	Windsor, ON
Express Personnel Svcs	London, ON
Express Personnel Svcs	Kitchener, ON
Express Personnel Svcs	Guelph, ON
Express Personnel Svcs	Hamilton, ON
Express Personnel Svcs	Burlington, ON
Express Personnel Svcs	Ottawa, ON
First Choice Personnel	Toronto, ON
Force Recruiting Services	Calgary, AB
Friday Personnel Inc	Vancouver, BC
Friday Personnel Inc	Calgary, AB
Fromm & Assoc Personnel	Toronto, ON
Gens Inc., La	Laval, QC
Georgian Staffing Svcs	Collingwood, ON
Grand River Personnel	Kitchener, ON
Groom & Assoc	Pointe-Claire, QC
Group Four Mgmnt Consultants	Toronto, ON
Groupe conseil Lamarche	Granby, QC
Groupe Pluridis	Montréal, QC
Groupe SFP	Trois-Rivières, QC
Groupe Tele Ressources	Montréal, QC
Hallmark Personnel	Oakville, ON
Harrington Staffing Services	Ottawa, ON
Heighway Personnel	London, ON
High Road Personnel	Burlington, ON
Higher Vision Recruitment	Toronto, ON
Hire Choice	Toronto, ON
Human Resource Mgmt Group	Unionville, ON
Hunt Technical Personnel	Toronto, ON
Hunt Technical Personnel	Ottawa, ON
In Place Select Recruitment	Toronto, ON
Jan Howard & Associates	Toronto, ON
Keith Bagg Regional	Mississauga, ON
Keith Bagg Regional	Thornhill, ON
Keith Bagg Staffing	Toronto, ON
Kelly, Les svcs	Pointe-Claire, QC
Kelly, Les svcs	Montréal, QC
Kelly, Les svcs	Montréal, QC
Kelly Permanent Recruit	Toronto, ON
Kelly Permanent Recruit	Toronto, ON
Kelly Permanent Recruit	Mississauga, ON
Kelly Professional & Tech	Edmonton, AB
Kelly Professional & Tech	Ottawa, ON
Kirkpatrick Personnel	Vancouver, BC
Larson & Associates	Calgary, AB
Level A Inc	Peterborough, ON
Linda Walter & Assoc	Île-Perrot, QC
Little Group, The	Brantford, ON
Little Group, The	Burlington, ON
LMR Consultants	Thornhill, ON
Luccie Domingue et assoc	Sherbrooke, QC
Lynx Career Consultants	Mississauga, ON
Macdonald & Brisson Personnel	Ottawa, ON
Madeleine Martel Inc.	Montréal, QC
Maizis & Miller Consultants	Toronto, ON
Mark Professional Services	Calgary, AB
Mayfair Personnel	Grande Prairie, AB
McDonald-Green Personnel	Cambridge, ON
Meyers Norris Penny	Calgary, AB
Miss Hall's Personnel Svcs	Ottawa, ON
MultiPersonnel International	Dorval, QC
Newfoundland Personnel	St. John's, NF
Nex Canada	Toronto, ON
Norrell Services	Toronto, ON
Norrell Staffing Services	Richmond, BC
Norrell Staffing Services	Vancouver, BC
North York Personnel	Toronto, ON
Office Team Staffing	Edmonton, AB
Office Team Staffing	Toronto, ON
Office Team Staffing	Toronto, ON
Office Team Staffing	Pointe-Claire, QC
Orillia Works	Orillia, ON
Ottawa Valley Personnel	Pembroke, ON
Outsourcing Connection	Toronto, ON
Pal Personnel Svcs	Toronto, ON
Paquette & Associates	Vancouver, BC
Paziuk Professional Placements	Edmonton, AB
PDQ Personnel	Mississauga, ON
Peak Associates Inc	Toronto, ON
PEI Office of Future	Charlottetown, PE
Pennox Express	Toronto, ON
People Bank, The	Calgary, AB
People Bank, The	London, ON
People Bank, The	Markham, ON
People Bank, The	Ottawa, ON
People Bank, The	Montréal, QC
People Placers Personnel	Halifax, NS
Permanent Solutions	Mississauga, ON
Personnel Alter Ego	Pointe-Claire, QC
Personnel Alter Ego	Montréal, QC
Personnel by Pro-Staff	Windsor, ON
Personnel Solutions	Westmount, QC

ADMINISTRATIVE (Cont.)
ADMINISTRATIF (Suivre)

Pinstripe Personnel .... London, ON
Pinstripe Personnel .... Toronto, ON
Pinstripe Personnel .... Mississauga, ON
PricewaterhouseCoopers .... London, ON
Probank Services .... Mississauga, ON
Profile Personnel Consult .... Toronto, ON
ProTemps Canada .... Edmonton, AB
ProTemps Canada .... Calgary, AB
ProTemps Canada .... Toronto, ON
ProTemps Canada .... Mississauga, ON
Protrans Personnel Svcs .... Dieppe, NB
Quality Personnel .... Brampton, ON
Quantum .... Montréal, QC
Quantum, Les services .... Longueuil, QC
Quantum, Les services .... Pointe-Claire, QC
Quantum, Les services .... Laval, QC
Quantum, Les services .... Québec, QC
Quantum Mgmt Services .... Toronto, ON
Quantum Mgmt Services .... Ottawa, ON
Quantum Mgmt Services .... Toronto, ON
Quest Consultants .... Toronto, ON
Quest Exec Recruitment .... Toronto, ON
Quest Resource Group .... Mississauga, ON
Randstad Interim .... Toronto, ON
Randstad Interim .... Mississauga, ON
Randstad Interim .... Ottawa, ON
Randstad Interim .... Saint-Laurent, QC
Randstad Interim .... Montréal, QC
Reid Management Consultants .... Toronto, ON
Renaissance Personnel .... Windsor, ON
Renaissance Personnel .... Chatham, ON
Resource Corporation, The .... Toronto, ON
Ressources 3000 .... Westmount, QC
Rice / Drummond Personnel .... Calgary, AB
Richardson Personnel .... Toronto, ON
Richmark Group, The .... Toronto, ON
Robert Half Canada .... Edmonton, AB
Robert Half Canada .... Montréal, QC
Royal Valvet Personnel .... Mississauga, ON
Sault Personnel .... Sault Ste. Marie, ON
Senac Personnel Services .... Toronto, ON
Shannon Human Resources .... Toronto, ON
Slate Group, The .... Edmonton, AB
SOLUTIONS .... Cornwall, ON
SOS Personnel .... Sarnia, ON
Spherion Workforce .... Victoria, BC
Spherion Workforce .... Vancouver, BC
Spherion Workforce .... Edmonton, AB
Spherion Workforce .... Edmonton, AB
Spherion Workforce .... Calgary, AB
Spherion Workforce .... Winnipeg, MB
Spherion Workforce .... London, ON
Spherion Workforce .... Toronto, ON
Spherion Workforce .... Toronto, ON
Spherion Workforce .... Toronto, ON
Spherion Workforce .... Toronto, ON
Spherion Workforce .... Hamilton, ON
Spherion Workforce .... Mississauga, ON
Spherion Workforce .... Barrie, ON
Spherion Workforce .... Pickering, ON
Spherion Workforce .... Whitby, ON
Spherion Workforce .... Oshawa, ON
Spherion Workforce .... Kanata, ON
Spherion Workforce .... Ottawa, ON
Spherion Workforce .... Ottawa, ON
Spherion Workforce .... Montréal, QC
Spherion Workforce .... Halifax, NS

Staff Plus .... Toronto, ON
Staffworks .... Toronto, ON
Star Search Consultants .... Toronto, ON
Stellar Personnel Placement .... Windsor, ON
Stellar Personnel Placement .... London, ON
Stephen Goldstein Associates .... Ottawa, ON
Stevens Resource Group .... London, ON
Stevens Resource Group .... Stratford, ON
Stevens Resource Group .... Woodstock, ON
Stevens Resource Group .... Tillsonburg, ON
Stevens Resource Group .... Brantford, ON
Stevens Resource Group .... Cambridge, ON
Summit Personnel Services .... Windsor, ON
Sydelle Associates .... Georgetown, ON
TaylorMade Careers .... USA
Team Power Exec Search .... Markham, ON
TEKsystems .... Richmond, BC
TEKsystems .... Mississauga, ON
TEKsystems .... Ottawa, ON
Tele-Ressources Ltée .... Montréal, QC
TES Employment Solution .... Toronto, ON
TES Employment Solution .... Mississauga, ON
TES Employment Solution .... USA
TES Employment Solution .... USA
Todays Staffing Inc .... Winnipeg, MB
Todays Staffing Inc .... London, ON
Todays Staffing Inc .... Brantford, ON
Todays Staffing Inc .... Cambridge, ON
Todays Staffing Inc .... Guelph, ON
Todays Staffing Inc .... Toronto, ON
Todays Staffing Inc .... Etobicoke, ON
Todays Staffing Inc .... Toronto, ON
Todays Staffing Inc .... Hamilton, ON
Todays Staffing Inc .... Burlington, ON
Todays Staffing Inc .... Mississauga, ON
Torstaff Personnel .... Toronto, ON
Tosi Placement Services .... Toronto, ON
Totten & Associates .... London, ON
Trebor Personnel .... Kitchener, ON
Unique Personnel Canada .... Concord, ON
Unique Personnel Services .... Dorval, QC
Wace & Assoc .... Mississauga, ON
Zeidel Gregory Associates .... Toronto, ON

ADVERTISING
PUBLICITÉ

Allen Austin Lowe & Powers .... USA
Chad Management Group .... Toronto, ON
Creative Force Network .... Toronto, ON
Dial A-1 Resources .... Toronto, ON
Fred Litman & Associates .... Toronto, ON
Freelancers Unlimited .... Toronto, ON
FWJ Communications .... Calgary, AB
Global Personnel .... Toronto, ON
Grapevine Exec Recruiters .... Toronto, ON
Henry Hill & Associates .... Mississauga, ON
HumanEtics Inc .... Mississauga, ON
InterCom Recruitment .... Toronto, ON
LTV & Associates .... Toronto, ON
Madison MacArthur Inc .... Toronto, ON
Management One Consultants .... Toronto, ON
Mandrake Mgmt Consult .... Toronto, ON
Michel Pauzé et Assoc .... Montréal, QC
Morgan Exec Search Group .... Toronto, ON
Morris Pervin Group .... Toronto, ON
PeopleFind Inc. .... Markham, ON
Phee Farrer Jones Ltd .... UNITED KINGDOM

ADVERTISING (Cont.)
PUBLICITÉ (Suivre)

Pragmatizm .... Toronto, ON
Search Company, The .... Toronto, ON
Shared Vision Mgmt Search .... Toronto, ON
TERHAM Mgmnt Consulting .... Toronto, ON
Todays Staffing Inc .... Toronto, ON
Zenzen Pierce Assoc .... Toronto, ON

AEROSPACE
AÉROSPATIAL

ADV Advanced Tech Svcs .... Toronto, ON
AeroPersonnel Intl .... Dorval, QC
Alan Davis Assoc .... Ottawa, ON
Alan Davis Assoc .... Hudson Heights, QC
Allen Ballach Assoc .... Whitby, ON
Angus Employment .... Burlington, ON
Archer Resource Solutions .... Mississauga, ON
ATS Reliance Industrial .... Toronto, ON
ATS Reliance Tech Group .... Vancouver, BC
ATS Reliance Tech Group .... Edmonton, AB
ATS Reliance Tech Group .... Calgary, AB
ATS Reliance Tech Group .... Toronto, ON
ATS Reliance Tech Group .... Burlington, ON
Aviation Personnel Support .... Toronto, ON
Aztech Recruitment .... USA
Berlys Personnel .... Saint-Laurent, QC
BMA International .... Montréal, QC
BMA International .... Montréal, QC
Bruce Ward Partners .... Toronto, ON
Can-Tech Services .... Brooklin, ON
Can-Tech Services .... Saint-Laurent, QC
ComFact Corp .... Oakville, ON
Conseillers en Admin FORMA .... Montréal, QC
Corporate Consultants .... Toronto, ON
CTS International .... USA
Dotemtex Executive Search .... Montréal, QC
Dotemtex Executive Search .... Sillery, QC
Drake Executive .... Toronto, ON
Drakkar Human Resources .... Saint-Laurent, QC
E.L. Shore & Associates .... Toronto, ON
Erie Personnel Corp .... Thorold, ON
Erie Personnel Corp .... Fort Erie, ON
Future Executive Personnel .... Toronto, ON
GR Search Inc .... Toronto, ON
Groupe Ranger .... Montréal, QC
Harris Consulting Corp .... Winnipeg, MB
Heenan Consulting IT .... Toronto, ON
Herman Smith Search Inc .... Toronto, ON
Human Edge Consulting .... Richmond Hill, ON
Ian Martin Ltd .... Montréal, QC
Interim Mgmt Resources .... Mississauga, ON
Kitchener Exec Consultants .... Kitchener, ON
LePage International .... Montréal, QC
MacLean Hay Consulting .... Oakville, ON
National Executive .... Toronto, ON
Normatech Executive .... Toronto, ON
Osborne Group .... Vancouver, BC
Osborne Group .... Calgary, AB
Osborne Group .... Edmonton, AB
Osborne Group .... Toronto, ON
Osborne Group .... Montréal, QC
Personnel Alter Ego .... Pointe-Claire, QC
Personnel Alter Ego .... Montréal, QC
Peter Leonard & Assoc .... Calgary, AB
Pride in Personnel .... Markham, ON

Prime Source Management .... Toronto, ON
Pro Tec Global Staffing .... Thornhill, ON
Rideau Management Group .... Nepean, ON
Roan International .... Mississauga, ON
Roevin Tech People .... Sarnia, ON
Roevin Tech People .... Kitchener, ON
Roevin Tech People .... Mississauga, ON
Roevin Tech People .... Markham, ON
Roevin Tech People .... Montréal, QC
Simon-Tech Inc .... Montréal, QC
StoneWood Group .... Toronto, ON
StoneWood Group .... Ottawa, ON
StoneWood Group .... Sainte-Geneviève, QC
Syntech Placements .... Toronto, ON
TDM Technical Services .... Toronto, ON
Technical Mgmnt Resources .... Barrie, ON
Technical Service Consult .... Toronto, ON
Technisource .... USA
Tele-Ressources Ltée .... Montréal, QC
Trans-United Consultants .... Burlington, ON
Venatus Conseil Ltée .... Montréal, QC

AGRICULTURE/FISHERIES
AGRICULTURE/PÊCHES

AgCall Human Resources .... Calgary, AB
AgCall Human Resources .... St. Jean, MB
AgCall Human Resources .... Markham, ON
Bestard Agricultural .... St. Marys, ON
Coakwell Crawford Cairns .... High River, AB
Conseillers en Admin FORMA .... Montréal, QC
Employment Network .... Regina, SK
Ernst David International .... Winnipeg, MB
Executive Resources Intl .... Montréal, QC
Grasslands Group .... Medicine Hat, AB
Grasslands Group .... Swift Current, SK
Harrison Jones Assoc .... UNITED KINGDOM
Hodgins Koenig & Assoc .... Saskatoon, SK
MacKenzie Gray Mgmnt .... Calgary, AB
Robert Connelly & Associates .... USA
Russell Reynolds Assoc .... Calgary, AB
Scott Wolfe Management .... Headingly, MB
Serecon Mgmnt Consulting .... Edmonton, AB
TDR Human Resource Svcs .... Regina, SK
Toma & Bouma .... Edmonton, AB
Van Klaveren Litherland Co .... Toronto, ON
Venatus Conseil Ltée .... Montréal, QC
Walter P. Miller Company .... St. John's, NF
Western HR Consulting .... Calgary, AB

APPAREL
HABILLEMENT

Allen Etcovitch Assoc .... Montréal, QC
Campbell Edgar Inc .... Richmond, BC
Campbell Edgar Inc .... Delta, BC
Canpro Executive Search .... Markham, ON
Colintex Agencies .... Toronto, ON
Dumont & Associates .... Vancouver, BC
Dumont & Associates .... North Vancouver, BC
ePersonnel Inc .... Montréal, QC
NAP Executive Apparel .... Montréal, QC
NAP Executive Retail .... Toronto, ON
Patty Shapiro & Assoc .... Montréal, QC
Randstad Interim .... Saint-Laurent, QC
Richter Usher Vineberg .... Montréal, QC

APPAREL (Cont.)
HABILLEMENT (Suivre)

Sheldon Recruiting .... Toronto, ON
Tony Curtis & Associates .... Toronto, ON
Zenzen Pierce Assoc .... Toronto, ON

ARCHITECTURE
ARCHITECTURE

BeyondTech Solutions .... Vancouver, BC
C.J. Stafford & Assoc .... Toronto, ON
Coles Associates .... Charlottetown, PE
Corporate Resources .... Toronto, ON
F.J. Galloway & Assoc .... London, ON
Robert Connelly & Associates .... USA
Tapscott Associates .... Toronto, ON
TDM Technical Services .... Toronto, ON
Technical Service Consult .... Toronto, ON
TES Employment Solution .... Mississauga, ON
Trans-United Consultants .... Burlington, ON

ARTS & CULTURE
ARTS ET CULTURE

Erland International .... Toronto, ON
Genovese Vanderhoof & Assoc .... Toronto, ON
Janet Wright & Associates .... Toronto, ON
Provence Consulting .... Vancouver, BC

AUTOMOTIVE
AUTOMOBILE

Accu-Staff Resource Systems .... Windsor, ON
Allen Ballach Assoc .... Whitby, ON
Allen Personnel Svcs .... London, ON
Alumni-Network Recruit .... Mississauga, ON
Angus Employment .... Burlington, ON
Archer Resource Solutions .... Mississauga, ON
Ashlar-Stone Consultants .... Mississauga, ON
ATS Reliance Industrial .... Toronto, ON
ATS Reliance Tech Group .... London, ON
ATS Reliance Tech Group .... Toronto, ON
Augment Prestige Svcs .... Point Edward, ON
B & L Consultants .... Toronto, ON
Berlys Personnel .... Saint-Laurent, QC
Bongard Marsh Assoc .... Toronto, ON
Braun-Valley Associates .... Sarnia, ON
Bruce Ward Partners .... Toronto, ON
C. Wolfe & Assoc .... Toronto, ON
CAMPA & Associates .... Toronto, ON
Can-Tech Services .... Brooklin, ON
Can-Tech Services .... Saint-Laurent, QC
Canadian Exec Recruitmnt .... Mississauga, ON
Carion Resource Group .... Mississauga, ON
Caron Executive Search .... London, ON
Central Mgmt Consultants .... Toronto, ON
Centre for Corp Resources .... Toronto, ON
Christmas McIvor Assoc .... Mississauga, ON
Churchill Group, The .... Toronto, ON
Connors Lovell Assoc .... Cambridge, ON
Connors Lovell Assoc .... Mississauga, ON
Contemporary Personnel .... Newmarket, ON
Cowan & Associates .... Calgary, AB
Crawford de Munnik Executive .... Toronto, ON

Cromark International .... Mississauga, ON
Direct Career Concepts .... Woodbridge, ON
Drakkar Human Resources .... Mississauga, ON
Eagle Prof Resources .... Vancouver, BC
ERC Management Group .... Kelowna, BC
Execusource Staffing Intl .... Windsor, ON
Executive House Inc .... Chatham, ON
First Choice Personnel .... Toronto, ON
Future Executive Personnel .... USA
G-Tech Professional Staffing .... USA
Gallant Search Group .... London, ON
GBL Resources .... USA
Grand River Personnel .... Kitchener, ON
Grant Martin & Assoc .... Richmond Hill, ON
Hains & Associates .... Victoria, BC
Hayhurst Consulting .... London, ON
HEC Group .... Ancaster, ON
Herman Smith Search Inc .... Toronto, ON
International Tech Recruit .... Windsor, ON
J.R. Bechtle & Company .... USA
Jerry Adel & Company .... Toronto, ON
JSG Group Mgmnt Consult .... Unionville, ON
Kellman Mgmnt Resources .... Markham, ON
Kelly Professional & Tech .... Kitchener, ON
Key Executive Consultants .... Barrie, ON
Key Executive Consultants .... Pickering, ON
Kitchener Exec Consultants .... Kitchener, ON
Landon Morgan Inc .... Thorold, ON
London Executive Consultants .... London, ON
Maintenance Plus .... Chatham, ON
Matthews Management .... Richmond Hill, ON
Meda Group .... Windsor, ON
MPA Recherche de Cadres .... Brossard, QC
MSX International .... Oakville, ON
MSX International .... USA
MSX International .... USA
MSX International .... USA
MSX International .... USA
Nex Canada .... Toronto, ON
Normatech Executive .... Toronto, ON
Pettitt Group Inc., The .... Burlington, ON
PricewaterhouseCoopers .... London, ON
Pride in Personnel .... Markham, ON
Pro Tec Global Staffing .... Thornhill, ON
Prosearch Associates .... Mississauga, ON
Quality Personnel .... Brampton, ON
RCM Technologies .... Mississauga, ON
Renaissance Personnel .... Windsor, ON
Renaissance Personnel .... Chatham, ON
RJK & Associates .... Markham, ON
Roan International .... Mississauga, ON
Roevin Tech People .... Sarnia, ON
Roevin Tech People .... Kitchener, ON
Roevin Tech People .... Mississauga, ON
Roevin Tech People .... Markham, ON
S. Tanner & Associates .... Oakville, ON
Sam Perri & Associates .... Mississauga, ON
Scott Huband Consulting .... Oakville, ON
Simon Bull Associates .... Cambridge, ON
Stellar Personnel Placement .... Windsor, ON
Stellar Personnel Placement .... London, ON
Stoakley-Dudley Consult .... Mississauga, ON
Summit Personnel Services .... Windsor, ON
Synagent Inc .... Woodlawn, ON
Syntech Placements .... Toronto, ON
TDM Technical Services .... Toronto, ON
Technical Mgmt Resources .... Barrie, ON
Technical Skills Consulting .... Toronto, ON
TEKsystems .... Mississauga, ON
TEKsystems .... Ottawa, ON

AUTOMOTIVE (Cont.)
AUTOMOBILE (Suivre)

Totten & Associates .... London, ON
Trans-United Consultants .... Burlington, ON
W. Hutt Mgmnt Resources .... Burlington, ON
Wellington Partners Intl .... Kitchener, ON

BANKING
AFFAIRES DE BANQUE

Ad-Link Advertising .... Toronto, ON
Adecco Canada .... Regina, SK
Adecco LPI .... Saint-Laurent, QC
Agence de place H Roy .... Saint-Hyacinthe, QC
Agence de place H Roy .... Montréal, QC
Agence de place H Roy .... Sainte-Foy, QC
Al-Khaleej Computers .... SAUDI ARABIA
Allen Austin Lowe & Powers .... USA
Ambridge Management .... Toronto, ON
Andrew Duncan Assoc .... UNITED KINGDOM
Associates Group .... Ottawa, ON
Association Resource Centre .... Toronto, ON
Austin Park Mgmnt Group .... Toronto, ON
Baldock Associates .... Toronto, ON
Bedford Consulting Group .... Toronto, ON
Bedford Consulting Group .... Oakville, ON
Bilingual Source .... Toronto, ON
Boyd-Laidler Assoc .... Toronto, ON
Brendan Wood International .... Toronto, ON
C. Price & Associates .... Toronto, ON
C. Scott & Associates .... Toronto, ON
Cadillac Career Centre .... Toronto, ON
Calvin Partners Intl .... Toronto, ON
CCG Mgmnt Consultants .... Mississauga, ON
CDM & Associates .... Toronto, ON
Chase Consultants .... Mississauga, ON
Christopher Vincent & Assoc .... Calgary, AB
CLA Personnel .... Ottawa, ON
Contemporary Personnel .... Vancouver, BC
Corporate HR Communicat .... Winnipeg, MB
D.P. Group, The .... UNITED KINGDOM
D.R. Nolan Assoc .... Toronto, ON
Dave White Personnel .... Ottawa, ON
Dingle & Associates .... Toronto, ON
Doré Liaison .... Greenfield Park, QC
Dotemtex Executive Search .... Montréal, QC
Dynamic Employment Solution .... Brampton, ON
Dynamic Employment Solution .... Brampton, ON
Eastgate Consultants .... Toronto, ON
ERC Management Group .... Kelowna, BC
Everest Mgmnt Network .... Toronto, ON
Excel HR Consultants .... Toronto, ON
Executrade Consultants .... Edmonton, AB
Future Executive Personnel .... Toronto, ON
Futurestep .... Toronto, ON
Gauthier Conseils .... Montréal, QC
George Stewart Consultants .... Toronto, ON
Gibson Kennedy & Company .... Toronto, ON
Gilligan & Associates .... Toronto, ON
Global Personnel .... Toronto, ON
Groupe consult affaire .... Québec, QC
Harcourt & Assoc .... Edmonton, AB
Harcourt & Assoc .... Calgary, AB
Harris Consulting Corp .... Winnipeg, MB
Hastings Group .... Toronto, ON
Herman Smith Search Inc .... Toronto, ON
Hunt Technical Personnel .... Vancouver, BC

Hunt Technical Personnel .... Calgary, AB
Hunt Technical Personnel .... Toronto, ON
Hunt Technical Personnel .... Ottawa, ON
Hunt Technical Personnel .... Saint-Laurent, QC
Hunt Technical Personnel .... Montréal, QC
ICAP Management Inc .... Fredericton, NB
In Place Select Recruitment .... Toronto, ON
International Agency Group .... Toronto, ON
IT Resources .... Markham, ON
James Partnership .... BERMUDA
JSL Search Leaders .... Toronto, ON
K-International Group .... Toronto, ON
Keeley Consulting .... Toronto, ON
Keith Bagg Regional .... Thornhill, ON
Keith Bagg Staffing .... Toronto, ON
Kenniff Denis Inc. .... Montréal, QC
Korn/Ferry Intl .... Toronto, ON
Lawrence Assoc Exec Search .... Toronto, ON
Lussier Executive Search .... Toronto, ON
M.J. Michaels Consulting .... Oakville, ON
Mandrake Mgmt Consult .... Toronto, ON
Marberg & Associates .... Toronto, ON
McNeill Nakamoto Recruit .... Vancouver, BC
Meech Partners .... Toronto, ON
Michael Page Finance .... CHINA
Michael Page International .... USA
Milgram & Associates .... Toronto, ON
Molnar & Associates .... Toronto, ON
NCR Associates .... Ottawa, ON
North York Personnel .... Toronto, ON
Partners Employment Group .... Toronto, ON
Partnervision Consulting .... Toronto, ON
Peak Associates Inc .... Toronto, ON
Personnel Menen .... Mount Royal, QC
Personnel Outaouais .... Hull, QC
Phoenix Search Group .... Toronto, ON
Pinstripe Personnel .... London, ON
Pinstripe Personnel .... Toronto, ON
Pinstripe Personnel .... Toronto, ON
Pinstripe Personnel .... Mississauga, ON
PricewaterhouseCoopers .... Winnipeg, MB
Prichard Kymen Inc .... Edmonton, AB
Prospects Plus .... Kirkland, QC
Quantum .... Montréal, QC
Quantum Mgmnt Services .... Toronto, ON
Quantum Mgmt Services .... Toronto, ON
RCM Technologies .... Mississauga, ON
RHI Management Resources .... Toronto, ON
RLP Consulting .... Mississauga, ON
Robert Half Canada .... Calgary, AB
Robert Half Canada .... Ottawa, ON
Robert Half Canada .... Montréal, QC
Robertson Hancock Ltd .... Toronto, ON
Rolland ressources humaines .... Montréal, QC
Russell & Associates .... Kelowna, BC
Russell Reynolds Assoc .... Calgary, AB
Russell Reynolds Assoc .... Toronto, ON
Schoales & Associates .... Toronto, ON
Shannon Human Resources .... Toronto, ON
Shared Vision Mgmt Search .... Toronto, ON
Sheldon Resnick Associates .... Toronto, ON
Spencer Stuart .... Toronto, ON
Spherion Workforce .... Victoria, BC
Spherion Workforce .... Vancouver, BC
Spherion Workforce .... Edmonton, AB
Spherion Workforce .... Edmonton, AB
Spherion Workforce .... Calgary, AB
Spherion Workforce .... Winnipeg, MB
Spherion Workforce .... Toronto, ON
Spherion Workforce .... Toronto, ON

BANKING (Cont.)
AFFAIRES DE BANQUE (Suivre)

Spherion Workforce .... Toronto, ON
Spherion Workforce .... Toronto, ON
Spherion Workforce .... Hamilton, ON
Spherion Workforce .... Mississauga, ON
Spherion Workforce .... Mississauga, ON
Spherion Workforce .... Barrie, ON
Spherion Workforce .... Pickering, ON
Spherion Workforce .... Whitby, ON
Spherion Workforce .... Oshawa, ON
Spherion Workforce .... Kanata, ON
Spherion Workforce .... Ottawa, ON
Spherion Workforce .... Ottawa, ON
Spherion Workforce .... Montréal, QC
Spherion Workforce .... Halifax, NS
Staff Plus .... Toronto, ON
Synagent Inc .... Woodlawn, ON
Tanaka Associates .... Toronto, ON
Team Power Exec Search .... Markham, ON
Technology Plus .... BAHRAIN
Tele-Ressources Ltée .... Montréal, QC
Thomas & Dessain .... UNITED KINGDOM
Thomas E. Hedefine Assoc .... Toronto, ON
Thorek/Scott Partners .... Toronto, ON
Todays Staffing Inc .... Winnipeg, MB
Todays Staffing Inc .... London, ON
Todays Staffing Inc .... Brantford, ON
Todays Staffing Inc .... Cambridge, ON
Todays Staffing Inc .... Guelph, ON
Todays Staffing Inc .... Toronto, ON
Todays Staffing Inc .... Etobicoke, ON
Todays Staffing Inc .... Toronto, ON
Todays Staffing Inc .... Toronto, ON
Todays Staffing Inc .... Hamilton, ON
Todays Staffing Inc .... Burlington, ON
Todays Staffing Inc .... Mississauga, ON
Tolstoy Resources .... Bolton, ON
Venatus Conseil Ltée .... Montréal, QC
Walker Forest .... USA
Western Mgmnt Consultants .... Edmonton, AB

BILINGUAL
BILINGUE

Adecco Canada .... Victoria, BC
Adecco Canada .... Calgary, AB
Adecco Canada .... Regina, SK
Adecco Canada .... Toronto, ON
Adecco Québec .... Longueuil, QC
Adecco Québec .... Québec, QC
Agence de personnel Abitibi .... Val-d'Or, QC
Aim Personnel Svcs .... Ottawa, ON
Altis Human Resources .... Toronto, ON
Anne Whitten Bilingual HR .... Toronto, ON
Bilingual Source .... Toronto, ON
Bilingual-Jobs.com .... Vancouver, BC
BMA International .... Montréal, QC
BMA International .... Montréal, QC
Bryan Jason Assoc .... Toronto, ON
C. Wolfe & Assoc .... Toronto, ON
Cadillac Career Centre .... Toronto, ON
Cameron Consulting Group .... Brampton, ON
Canadian Findings .... Toronto, ON
CLA Personnel .... Ottawa, ON
Conseillers Jacques Cartier .... Montréal, QC
Core-Staff Inc. .... Toronto, ON

Courtney Personnel .... Brampton, ON
Drake Executive .... Toronto, ON
Duo Mega Inc .... Montréal, QC
Dynamic Employment Solution .... Brampton, ON
Dynamic Employment Solution .... Brampton, ON
Evans Search Group .... Toronto, ON
Executives Available .... Pointe-Claire, QC
Express Personnel Svcs .... Ottawa, ON
F.E.R. Executive Search .... Vancouver, BC
First Choice Personnel .... Toronto, ON
Future Executive Personnel .... Toronto, ON
Global Consulting Group .... Markham, ON
Harrington Staffing Services .... Ottawa, ON
Heale & Associates .... Toronto, ON
Hire Choice .... Toronto, ON
Hunt Technical Personnel .... Mississauga, ON
Hunt Technical Personnel .... Ottawa, ON
Hunt Technical Personnel .... Saint-Laurent, QC
ICAP Management Inc .... Fredericton, NB
InterSearch Canada/Corso .... Toronto, ON
J.R. Bechtle & Company .... USA
Jan Howard & Associates .... Toronto, ON
Keith Bagg Regional .... Thornhill, ON
Keith Bagg Staffing .... Toronto, ON
Macdonald & Brisson Personnel .... Ottawa, ON
Madeleine Martel Inc. .... Montréal, QC
Marberg & Associates .... Toronto, ON
McDonald-Green Personnel .... Cambridge, ON
MultiPersonnel International .... Dorval, QC
Nex Canada .... Toronto, ON
North York Personnel .... Toronto, ON
Omnicom Prof Language .... Toronto, ON
Outsourcing Connection .... Toronto, ON
P.R.Y. .... Toronto, ON
Permanent Solutions .... Mississauga, ON
Personnel Outaouais .... Hull, QC
Profile Personnel Consult .... Toronto, ON
Quality Personnel .... Brampton, ON
Resource Corporation, The .... Toronto, ON
Robert Half Canada .... Montréal, QC
Royal Valvet Personnel .... Mississauga, ON
Skott/Edwards Consult .... USA
Snelgrove Personnel .... Hamilton, ON
Société Jean P. Brisebois .... Montréal, QC
SOLUTIONS .... Cornwall, ON
Spherion Workforce .... Montréal, QC
Sydelle Associates .... Georgetown, ON
Taylor Personnel .... Victoria, BC
Taylor Personnel .... Edmonton, AB
Tele-Ressources Ltée .... Montréal, QC

BIOTECH/BIOLOGY
BIOTECHNOLOGIE/BIOLOGIE

Archer Resource Solutions .... Mississauga, ON
Brethet Barnum Associates .... Toronto, ON
Btsn inc. .... St. George, ON
CanMed Consultants .... Mississauga, ON
Christian & Timbers .... USA
ConsulPro .... Westmount, QC
Corporate Consultants .... Toronto, ON
Cortex HR .... Toronto, ON
CV Theque .... Laval, QC
Davitech Consulting .... Calgary, AB
Derhak Ireland Partners .... Toronto, ON
Dion Mgmnt Exec Search .... Toronto, ON
Dion Mgmnt Groupe Conseil .... Sainte-Foy, QC
Dotemtex Executive Search .... Sillery, QC

BIOTECH/BIOLOGY (Cont.)
BIOTECHNOLOGIE/BIOLOGIE (Suivre)

Drakkar Human Resources .... Saint-Laurent, QC
Executive Resources Intl .... Montréal, QC
GAAP Inc .... Montréal, QC
Groupe Primacor .... Longueuil, QC
Henry Hill & Associates .... Mississauga, ON
Hess Associates Exec Search .... Toronto, ON
InterSearch Canada/Western .... Vancouver, BC
Kelly Scientific .... Mississauga, ON
Kelly Scientifique .... Montréal, QC
LePage International .... Montréal, QC
MacLean Hay Consulting .... Oakville, ON
Peter Leonard & Assoc .... Calgary, AB
Quintal & Associates HR .... Montréal, QC
Ray & Berndtson/Laurendeau .... Montréal, QC
Robertson Human Asset .... Burlington, ON
Rolland Groupe Conseil .... Westmount, QC
Rutherford Intl Exec Search .... Toronto, ON
Scott Wolfe Management .... Headingly, MB
Spencer Stuart .... Toronto, ON
Technology Plus .... BAHRAIN
Vickery Boardman Assoc .... Whitby, ON
Western Mgmnt Consultants .... Edmonton, AB

COMPUTING
INFORMATIQUE

180 Consulting .... Toronto, ON
180 Consulting .... Thornhill, ON
1st Choice Personnel .... USA
Abane & Associates .... Newmarket, ON
Abel Placement Consult .... Markham, ON
Accenture .... Toronto, ON
Acorn Consulting Group .... Concord, ON
Addmore Personnel .... Toronto, ON
Adecco Canada .... Victoria, BC
Adecco Canada .... Edmonton, AB
Adecco Canada .... Winnipeg, MB
Adecco Canada .... Toronto, ON
Adecco Canada .... Brampton, ON
Adecco Canada .... Oakville, ON
Adecco Canada .... Markham, ON
Adecco Canada .... Pickering, ON
Adecco Canada .... Ottawa, ON
Adecco Canada .... Ottawa, ON
Adecco / Compaq .... Toronto, ON
Adecco Personnel Technique .... Sherbrooke, QC
Adecco Québec .... Longueuil, QC
Adecco Québec .... Laval, QC
Adecco Québec ....Chicoutimi, QC
ADV Advanced Tech Svcs .... Toronto, ON
Advanced Tech Partners .... Vancouver, BC
Advanced Tech Partners ....Edmonton, AB
Advanced Tech Partners .... Calgary, AB
Advanced Tech Partners .... Toronto, ON
Advantage Tech .... Calgary, AB
Aginove Inc. .... Dorval, QC
Aide Technique .... Longueuil, QC
Aim Personnel Svcs .... Ottawa, ON
AIME Consultants .... Vancouver, BC
Ajilon Canada .... Vancouver, BC
Ajilon Canada .... Calgary, AB
Ajilon Canada .... Toronto, ON
Ajilon Canada .... Toronto, ON
Ajilon Canada .... Markham, ON
Ajilon Canada .... Ottawa, ON

Ajilon Canada .... Montréal, QC
Ajilon Canada .... Halifax, NS
Ajilon Canada .... St. John's, NF
Ajilon Canada International .... Toronto, ON
AJJA Information Technology .... Ottawa, ON
Al-Khaleej Computers .... SAUDI ARABIA
Alan Davis Assoc .... Hudson Heights, QC
Allegiance Group .... USA
Allen Austin Lowe & Powers .... USA
Allen Ballach Assoc .... Whitby, ON
Allen Personnel Svcs .... London, ON
Allen Personnel Svcs .... Cambridge, ON
Alliance Search .... Vancouver, BC
Alliance Search Group .... Toronto, ON
Alpha Job Consulting .... Toronto, ON
Alphasource Inc. .... Toronto, ON
Alternative Resources Corp .... Toronto, ON
Altis Human Resources .... Toronto, ON
Alumni-Network Recruit .... Mississauga, ON
Andersen .... Montréal, QC
Anderson Associates .... Toronto, ON
Angus Employment .... Burlington, ON
Angus One Pro Recruitment .... Vancouver, BC
Apex Search .... Toronto, ON
Apple One Employment .... Toronto, ON
Applicants Inc. .... Kitchener, ON
Applied Technology Solutions .... Toronto, ON
Aquent Partners .... Vancouver, BC
Aquent Partners .... Toronto, ON
Aquent Partners .... Montréal, QC
Arabian Careers .... UNITED KINGDOM
ARES Consulting Svcs .... Toronto, ON
Argentus Inc. .... Toronto, ON
Argus Group Corporation .... Toronto, ON
Arie Shenkar Assoc .... Toronto, ON
Armitage Associates .... Vancouver, BC
Armitage Associates .... Toronto, ON
Armitage Associates .... Rosmere, QC
Ashton Computer Pros .... North Vancouver, BC
Asset Computer Personnel .... Toronto, ON
Assoc de dessins mecaniques .... Montréal, QC
Associates Group .... Ottawa, ON
ASTRA Management Corp .... Vancouver, BC
ATS Reliance Industrial .... Toronto, ON
ATS Reliance Tech Group .... Vancouver, BC
ATS Reliance Tech Group ....Edmonton, AB
ATS Reliance Tech Group .... Calgary, AB
ATS Reliance Tech Group .... London, ON
ATS Reliance Tech Group .... Toronto, ON
ATS Reliance Tech Group .... Burlington, ON
Atticus Resources .... Calgary, AB
Austin Park Mgmnt Group .... Toronto, ON
Axxes Technologies .... Saint-Laurent, QC
Axxes Technologies .... Sillery, QC
Ayrshire Group .... Toronto, ON
Aztech Recruitment .... USA
B.B. Consultants Group .... Point Edward, ON
B Wyze Inc. .... Richmond Hill, ON
Bach Associates .... Vancouver, BC
Bailey Professional Search .... Calgary, AB
Baldock Associates .... Toronto, ON
Baldwin Staffing Group .... Calgary, AB
Barrett Rose & Lee .... Toronto, ON
Bassett Laudi Partners .... Toronto, ON
Bedford Consulting Group .... Toronto, ON
Bedford Consulting Group ....Oakville, ON
Belanger Partners .... Thornhill, ON
Bernard Frigon & Assoc .... Montréal, QC
Bernier & Assoc .... Montréal, QC
Bertrand Elbaz C.R.H. .... Montréal, QC

COMPUTING (Cont.)
INFORMATIQUE (Suivre)

Bevertec CST Inc.	Toronto, ON
BeyondTech Solutions	Vancouver, BC
Black Talon Svcs	Edmonton, AB
Blackshire Recruiting	New Westminster, BC
BMB / MaxSys	Ottawa, ON
Booth International Mgmnt	Toronto, ON
Boscan Consultants	Marysville, ON
Bosworth Field Assoc	Toronto, ON
Botrie Associates	Toronto, ON
Bourassa Brodeur Assoc	Trois-Rivières, QC
Bower Ng Staff Systems	Vancouver, BC
Boyden Global Exec Search	Calgary, AB
Brad Lake Consulting	Orleans, ON
Bradson Tech Professionals	Toronto, ON
Bradson Tech Professionals	Halifax, NS
Bradson Tech Professionals	USA
Brainhunter.com	Toronto, ON
Brainhunter.com	Ottawa, ON
Brant & Associates	Winnipeg, MB
Braun-Valley Associates	Sarnia, ON
Bray Larouche et Assoc	Montréal, QC
Bridge Info Technology	Vancouver, BC
Bridgemount Solutions	Ottawa, ON
Bruce Cowan Assoc	Toronto, ON
Btsn inc.	St. George, ON
C.N. Taylor Consulting	Bedford, NS
C. Scott & Associates	Toronto, ON
Cadillac Career Centre	Toronto, ON
Cadman Consulting Group	Vancouver, BC
Calian Technical Svcs	Ottawa, ON
Calian Technology Svcs	Mississauga, ON
Calian Technology Svcs	Ottawa, ON
Calian Technology Svcs	Kanata, ON
Cameron Consulting Group	Brampton, ON
Can-Tech Services	Brooklin, ON
Can-Tech Services	Saint-Laurent, QC
CanadaIT Ventures	Surrey, BC
Canadian Exec Consultants	Toronto, ON
Canatrade International	Candiac, QC
Candidatech placement	Sainte-Julie, QC
Capital Consulting & Research	USA
Capital Executive	Calgary, AB
Career Management Solutions	Toronto, ON
Career Partners/Harrison	Hamilton, ON
Carrières Avenir	Montréal, QC
CCT Inc	London, ON
CCT Inc	Burlington, ON
CCT Inc	Mississauga, ON
CDI Technical Svcs	Calgary, AB
CDI Technical Svcs	Oakville, ON
CDI Technical Svcs	Pointe-Claire, QC
Centre for Corp Resources	Toronto, ON
Centrex HR Centre	Hamilton, ON
CFT Training and HR	Montréal, QC
CG Consulting Group	Toronto, ON
Chacra Belliveau & Assoc	Montréal, QC
Chase Consultants	Mississauga, ON
Christian & Timbers	USA
Christmas McIvor Assoc	Mississauga, ON
Christopher Vincent & Assoc	Calgary, AB
Clarendon Parker ME	UNITED ARAB EMIRATES
Classic Consulting Group	Calgary, AB
CM Inc	Markham, ON
CNC Global	Vancouver, BC
CNC Global	Edmonton, AB
CNC Global	Calgary, AB
CNC Global	Toronto, ON

CNC Global	Mississauga, ON
CNC Global	Richmond Hill, ON
CNC Global	Ottawa, ON
CNC Global	Montréal, QC
CNC Global	USA
Coape Staffing Network	Vancouver, BC
Coape Staffing Network	Burnaby, BC
Coape Staffing Network	Edmonton, AB
Coape Staffing Network	Calgary, AB
Coast Personnel Svcs	Nanaimo, BC
Coffey & Associates	Hamilton, ON
CompuForce Inc	Calgary, AB
Computer Action Co	Calgary, AB
Computer Action Co	London, ON
Computer Action Co	Toronto, ON
Computer Consultants Inc	Toronto, ON
Computer Horizons ISG	Calgary, AB
Computer Horizons ISG	Mississauga, ON
Computer Horizons ISG	Ottawa, ON
Computer People Company	Toronto, ON
Computer Task Group	Toronto, ON
ComUnity Systems Consultants	Calgary, AB
Connectstaff Solutions	Calgary, AB
Connors Lovell Assoc	Mississauga, ON
Conseillers Jacques Cartier	Montréal, QC
ConsulPRO Executive Search	Ottawa, ON
Consultant's Choice	USA
Consultation Delan	Saint-Laurent, QC
Contemporary Personnel	Toronto, ON
Core Group, The	Toronto, ON
Cornell Consulting Corp	Burlington, ON
Corporate & Career Develop	Vancouver, BC
Corporate Consultants	Toronto, ON
Corporate Recruiters	Vancouver, BC
Croden Personnel	Vancouver, BC
CrossLink Consulting	Vancouver, BC
CSI Consulting	Toronto, ON
CTC Computer-Tech Consult	Vancouver, BC
CTC Computer-Tech Consult	Edmonton, AB
CTC Computer-Tech Consult	Calgary, AB
CTC Computer-Tech Consult	Regina, SK
CTC Computer-Tech Consult	Winnipeg, MB
CTS International	USA
CV Theque	Laval, QC
D.J. Macadam & Assoc	North Vancouver, BC
D.P. Group, The	UNITED KINGDOM
Danette Milne Corp Search	Markham, ON
Daniluck & Associates	Edmonton, AB
Datalist	Toronto, ON
Dataware Consulting	Toronto, ON
Datpro Personnel	Toronto, ON
David Aplin & Assoc	Edmonton, AB
David Aplin & Assoc	Calgary, AB
David Warwick Kennedy Assoc	Vancouver, BC
Davis Search Group	Toronto, ON
DDP Consulting Group	Vancouver, BC
Deevan Technology Mgmt	Richmond Hill, ON
Design Group Staffing	Vancouver, BC
Design Group Staffing	Edmonton, AB
Design Group Staffing	Red Deer, AB
Design Group Staffing	Calgary, AB
Design Group Staffing	London, ON
Design Group Staffing	Toronto, ON
Dial Staffing Solutions	Calgary, AB
Digital Power Corp	Calgary, AB
Digital Staffing	USA
Dilbert Group, The	Toronto, ON
Donald L Hart & Assoc	Toronto, ON
Doré Liaison	Greenfield Park, QC
Dotemtex Executive Search	Sillery, QC

COMPUTING (Cont.)
INFORMATIQUE (Suivre)

COMPUTING (Cont.)
INFORMATIQUE (Suivre)

Ian Martin Ltd .... USA
ICAP Management Inc .... Fredericton, NB
IMS Innovative Mgmnt .... Toronto, ON
INFO-TEK Consulting .... Edmonton, AB
Infocybex .... Brampton, ON
Information Bus Consulting .... Edmonton, AB
Information Resources Ctr .... SAUDI ARABIA
Information Systems Consult .... Edmonton, AB
Information Tech Recruiting .... Toronto, ON
Information Tech Resources .... Toronto, ON
Information Technologies .... USA
InGenius Engineering Inc .... Ottawa, ON
Insight Technology Corp .... Calgary, AB
Intec Recruitment Svcs .... UNITED KINGDOM
Integra IT Partners .... Toronto, ON
Intelligent Tech Solutions .... Ottawa, ON
Inter-Tek Inc. .... USA
Interactive Business Systems .... Toronto, ON
Interchange Personnel .... Calgary, AB
International Bus Search .... Richmond Hill, ON
International Career Special .... Toronto, ON
International Search Assoc .... Toronto, ON
International Staffing .... UNITED KINGDOM
International Tech Recruit .... Windsor, ON
Interstate Technical Services .... USA
InviTech Corporation .... Toronto, ON
Isomeric Inc. .... Toronto, ON
IT People Ltd .... Calgary, AB
IT Prospects .... Toronto, ON
IT Resources .... Markham, ON
IT Select .... Toronto, ON
ITbanx Technology Recruit .... Toronto, ON
ITECC Consulting .... Toronto, ON
ITnmotion .... Toronto, ON
ITPlacements.com .... Markham, ON
ITSuperstars Recruiting .... Toronto, ON
ITSuperstars Recruiting .... Hamilton, ON
J. Edgar & Associates .... Toronto, ON
J.G. Flynn & Associates .... Vancouver, BC
J.P. Anderson & Assoc .... Burlington, ON
James Partnership .... BERMUDA
Jamich Technology Group .... Ottawa, ON
Jan Howard & Associates .... Toronto, ON
Jenereaux & Associates .... Mississauga, ON
JENEX Technology Placement .... Vancouver, BC
John Doucette Mgmnt .... Richmond Hill, ON
Johnstone Assoc Pro Search .... Calgary, AB
JSG Group Mgmnt Consult .... Unionville, ON
JSL Search Leaders .... Toronto, ON
Juno Systems .... CHINA
K-International Group .... Toronto, ON
Karabus Management .... Toronto, ON
KAS Personnel Svcs .... North Bay, ON
KAS Personnel Svcs .... Kitchener, ON
KAS Personnel Svcs .... Toronto, ON
KAS Personnel Svcs .... Toronto, ON
KAS Personnel Svcs .... Hamilton, ON
KAS Personnel Svcs .... Burlington, ON
KAS Personnel Svcs .... Brampton, ON
KAS Personnel Svcs .... Mississauga, ON
KAS Personnel Svcs .... Barrie, ON
KAS Personnel Svcs .... Belleville, ON
Keith Bagg IT Search .... Toronto, ON
Keith Bagg Regional .... Thornhill, ON
Keith Bagg Staffing .... Toronto, ON
Kelly, Les svcs .... Granby, QC
Kelly, Les svcs .... Montréal, QC

Kelly Professional & Tech .... Victoria, BC
Kelly Professional & Tech .... Vancouver, BC
Kelly Professional & Tech .... Edmonton, AB
Kelly Professional & Tech .... Saskatoon, SK
Kelly Professional & Tech .... Regina, SK
Kelly Professional & Tech .... Winnipeg, MB
Kelly Professional & Tech .... Windsor, ON
Kelly Professional & Tech .... Chatham, ON
Kelly Professional & Tech .... St. Thomas, ON
Kelly Professional & Tech .... Brantford, ON
Kelly Professional & Tech .... Kitchener, ON
Kelly Professional & Tech .... Guelph, ON
Kelly Professional & Tech .... Toronto, ON
Kelly Professional & Tech .... Toronto, ON
Kelly Professional & Tech .... Downsview, ON
Kelly Professional & Tech .... Toronto, ON
Kelly Professional & Tech .... Burlington, ON
Kelly Professional & Tech .... Bolton, ON
Kelly Professional & Tech .... Brampton, ON
Kelly Professional & Tech .... Oakville, ON
Kelly Professional & Tech .... Newmarket, ON
Kelly Professional & Tech .... Markham, ON
Kelly Professional & Tech .... St. Catharines, ON
Kelly Professional & Tech .... Oakville, ON
Kelly Professional & Tech .... Belleville, ON
Kelly Professional & Tech .... Ottawa, ON
Kelly Professional & Tech .... Fredericton, NB
Kelly Professional & Tech .... Saint John, NB
Kelly Professional & Tech .... Moncton, NB
Kelly Professional & Tech .... Halifax, NS
Kelly Services .... Calgary, AB
Kenneth Murphy & Assoc .... Halifax, NS
Kforce.ca .... Toronto, ON
Khorasanee & Partners .... Toronto, ON
Kischi Konsulting .... Ottawa, ON
Kitchener Exec Consultants .... Kitchener, ON
Knipper & Associates .... Kingston, ON
Korn/Ferry Intl .... Vancouver, BC
Korn/Ferry Intl .... Toronto, ON
Krecklo Consultants .... Toronto, ON
Krecklo Consultants .... Montréal, QC
L.S. Noel Consulting .... Richmond Hill, ON
Laing & Associates .... Toronto, ON
Landon Morgan Inc .... Thorold, ON
Larouche & Associates .... Dorval, QC
Lawrence Joe Consultants .... Toronto, ON
Lenard Kay & Associates .... Oakville, ON
Lesley Varga & Assoc .... Toronto, ON
Level A Inc .... Peterborough, ON
Levton Group .... Toronto, ON
Linda Walter & Assoc .... Île-Perrot, QC
Link Consulting .... Vancouver, BC
Link Resource Partners .... Toronto, ON
Lintex Computer Group .... Toronto, ON
London Executive Consultants .... London, ON
Luna Source .... USA
Lynx Career Consultants .... Mississauga, ON
M.I.S. Consultants .... Toronto, ON
M.I.S. Consultants .... Markham, ON
Macdonald & Brisson Personnel .... Ottawa, ON
Maclean & Assoc .... Mississauga, ON
MacLean Hay Consulting .... Oakville, ON
Maizis & Miller Consultants .... Toronto, ON
Management Plus Consulting .... LEBANON
Management Recruiters Kannapolis .... USA
Management Solutions .... Mississauga, ON
Mancomit International .... Winnipeg, MB
Manpower Professional .... Victoria, BC
Manpower Professional .... Vancouver, BC
Manpower Professional .... Richmond, BC

COMPUTING (Cont.)
INFORMATIQUE (Suivre)

COMPUTING (Cont.)
INFORMATIQUE (Suivre)

COMPUTING (Cont.)
INFORMATIQUE (Suivre)

StarDot PRG Inc .... Toronto, ON
StarDot PRG Inc .... Montréal, QC
Stellar Personnel Placement .... Windsor, ON
Stellar Personnel Placement .... London, ON
Stephen Goldstein Associates .... Ottawa, ON
Sterling Hoffman .... Toronto, ON
Sterling Hoffman .... USA
StoneWood Group .... Toronto, ON
StoneWood Group .... Ottawa, ON
StoneWood Group .... Sainte-Geneviève, QC
Stop the World Inc .... Toronto, ON
Stopka & Associates .... Toronto, ON
Strategic Resources Intl .... Toronto, ON
Symmetry Search Group .... Toronto, ON
Synergy Search Consultants .... Toronto, ON
Systematix IT Consultants .... Vancouver, BC
Systematix IT Consultants .... Edmonton, AB
Systematix IT Consultants .... Calgary, AB
Systematix IT Consultants .... Toronto, ON
Systematix IT Consultants .... Ottawa, ON
Systematix IT Consultants .... Montréal, QC
Systematix IT Consultants .... Québec, QC
Systems Career Group .... Toronto, ON
Systems OnTime .... Toronto, ON
Systemsearch Consulting Svcs .... Toronto, ON
T.L.W. Enterprise Inc .... Toronto, ON
TAL Group .... Toronto, ON
Talent Consulting Services .... USA
TalentLab .... Toronto, ON
TalentLab .... Kingston, ON
TalentLab .... Kanata, ON
TalentLab .... USA
Tanaka Associates .... Toronto, ON
Tapscott Associates .... Toronto, ON
Taylor Low & Associates .... Toronto, ON
Taylor Personnel .... Victoria, BC
Taylor Personnel .... Edmonton, AB
Taylor Recruitment .... UNITED KINGDOM
Taylor Tomas Consulting .... Coquitlam, BC
TaylorMade Careers .... USA
Tech Force Search Group .... Toronto, ON
Tech Hi Consultants Ltd .... Kitchener, ON
Tech-Pro Inc .... USA
Techaid Inc .... Montréal, QC
Technical Connections Inc .... USA
Technical Mgmnt Resources .... Barrie, ON
Technical Resource Network .... Vancouver, BC
Technical Solutions Inc .... USA
Technisource .... Kanata, ON
Technisource .... USA
TechNix Inc .... Toronto, ON
Technology Plus .... BAHRAIN
Technology Search Group / TSG .... Ajax, ON
Tek-Search Corp .... Toronto, ON
Tekmark Computer Services .... USA
TEKsystems .... Richmond, BC
TEKsystems .... Mississauga, ON
TEKsystems .... Ottawa, ON
TES Employment Solution .... Toronto, ON
TES Employment Solution .... Burlington, ON
TES Employment Solution .... Mississauga, ON
TES Employment Solution .... Ottawa, ON
TES Employment Solution .... Montréal, QC
TES Employment Solution .... USA
TES Employment Solution .... USA
Thinkpath.com Inc .... Toronto, ON
Thinkpath.com Inc. .... Toronto, ON

Thinkpath.com Inc. .... Ottawa, ON
Thinkpath.com Inc .... USA
Thinkpath.com Inc. .... USA
Thomas & Rayment .... Markham, ON
Tolfrey Group .... USA
Toronto Exec Consultants .... Toronto, ON
Tosi Placement Services .... Toronto, ON
Track International Ltd .... UNITED KINGDOM
TRI TechRes Inc .... Hull, QC
Tri-Tec International Resources .... USA
Trident Technology Svcs .... Winnipeg, MB
Trillium Talent Resource .... Toronto, ON
Triser Corp .... Toronto, ON
TRS Staffing Solutions .... Calgary, AB
Unixel recrutement .... Île-des-Soeurs, QC
Urentia .... Montréal, QC
Vector Technical Services .... Toronto, ON
VEGA Consulting Solutions .... USA
Venpro Consulting .... Toronto, ON
Volt Human Resources .... Vancouver, BC
Volt Human Resources .... Toronto, ON
VTRAC IT Consultants .... Toronto, ON
W.G. Meldrum Ltd .... Vancouver, BC
W.G. Meldrum Ltd .... Calgary, AB
W.G. Meldrum Ltd .... Toronto, ON
W5 Resources .... Markham, ON
Wagner et Assoc .... Montréal, QC
Walbrook Appointment England .... Toronto, ON
Walker Forest .... USA
Wayne Perry & Associates .... Toronto, ON
Wayne Thomas & Associates .... Ottawa, ON
Weir Associates .... Toronto, ON
Wenje Management Ltd .... Markham, ON
Western Mgmnt Consultants .... Edmonton, AB
William Lee Associates .... Vancouver, BC
Windsor Personnel & Exec .... Windsor, ON
Wolverine Technical Services .... USA
Wood West & Partners .... Vancouver, BC
Woodridge Associates .... UNITED KINGDOM
WorkCentral CSI .... Ottawa, ON
Workplace Competence Intl .... Erin, ON
Worth Personnel Group .... Toronto, ON
Worth Personnel Group .... Mississauga, ON
Wynne Chisholm Associates .... Calgary, AB
Xenotec Consulting Services .... Regina, SK
Xycorp Inc. .... Toronto, ON
Zen Zen International .... Winnipeg, MB

CONSTRUCTION
CONSTRUCTION

A.W. Fraser Assoc .... Edmonton, AB
ABC Corries (Canada) .... Calgary, AB
Adecco Canada .... Victoria, BC
Allen Austin Lowe & Powers .... USA
Ashtead Mgmnt Consultants .... UNITED KINGDOM
B.B. Consultants Group .... Point Edward, ON
C.J. Stafford & Assoc .... Toronto, ON
CDI Technical Svcs .... Calgary, AB
Central Mgmnt Consultants .... Toronto, ON
Contracts Consultancy Ltd .... UNITED KINGDOM
Design Group Staffing .... Vancouver, BC
Design Group Staffing .... Calgary, AB
Design Group Staffing .... Toronto, ON
Diversified Staffing Svcs .... Edmonton, AB
Diversified Staffing Svcs .... Calgary, AB
Don Miles Personnel .... Toronto, ON
Drakkar Human Resources .... Mississauga, ON

CONSTRUCTION (Cont.)
CONSTRUCTION (Suivre)

Edie Bench Personnel .... Toronto, ON
G-Tech Professional Staffing .... USA
J.G. Flynn & Associates .... Vancouver, BC
KAS Personnel Svcs .... Guelph, ON
Katherine Holt Enterprises .... Toronto, ON
LJB & Company .... UNITED KINGDOM
Ludlow Project Services .... Oakville, ON
MacKenzie Gray Mgmnt .... Calgary, AB
Management Plus Consulting .... LEBANON
McCracken/Labbett Exec Search .... Toronto, ON
McQ International Svcs .... UNITED KINGDOM
NES Overseas Ltd .... UNITED KINGDOM
Orillia Works .... Orillia, ON
Personnel Mgmnt Group .... Winnipeg, MB
Personnel Outaouais .... Hull, QC
Peter Glaser Assoc .... UNITED KINGDOM
Peter Leonard & Assoc .... Calgary, AB
Premier Personnel .... UNITED KINGDOM
Puglisevich Crews & Svcs .... St. John's, NF
RBA Intl HR Consultants .... Westmount, QC
Roan International .... Mississauga, ON
Robert Connelly & Associates .... USA
Rod Turpin & Assoc .... Edmonton, AB
Roevin Tech People .... Mississauga, ON
SAI Software Consultants .... USA
Servocraft Limited .... Toronto, ON
Taylor Recruitment .... UNITED KINGDOM
Technical Service Consult .... Surrey, BC
Van Biesen Group .... Calgary, AB
Ward Vinge & Associates .... Edmonton, AB
Ward Vinge & Associates .... Calgary, AB
Western Mgmnt Consultants .... Edmonton, AB
Woodridge Associates .... UNITED KINGDOM

CONSULTING
CONSULTATIF

Adecco Canada .... Calgary, AB
Audax Corporation .... Toronto, ON
Bill Kellie Consulting .... Norwich, ON
BMB / MaxSys .... Ottawa, ON
Burke Group .... Hamilton, ON
Burke Group .... St. Catharines, ON
Canatrade International .... Candiac, QC
CCG Mgmnt Consultants .... Mississauga, ON
CCT Inc .... Kitchener, ON
Claude Guedj Assoc .... Montréal, QC
Dion Mgmnt Groupe Conseil .... Montréal, QC
Dion Mgmnt Groupe Conseil .... Sainte-Foy, QC
Drake International .... Edmonton, AB
Drake International .... Belleville, ON
Drake Medox .... Powell River, BC
Drakkar Human Resources .... Mississauga, ON
Drakkar Human Resources .... Saint-Laurent, QC
Driver Carrier Placement .... Toronto, ON
Ducharme Group .... Toronto, ON
Eagle Prof Resources .... Vancouver, BC
Eagle Prof Resources .... Calgary, AB
Eagle Prof Resources .... Toronto, ON
Eagle Prof Resources .... Toronto, ON
Eagle Prof Resources .... Ottawa, ON
Eagle Prof Resources .... Montréal, QC
Eagle Prof Resources .... Halifax, NS
Ernst & Young .... SAUDI ARABIA
Everest Systems Network .... Toronto, ON

Excel HR Consultants .... Toronto, ON
Grant Thornton Intl .... Saint John, NB
Groupe consult affaire .... Québec, QC
GSI International Consult .... Toronto, ON
Information Systems Consult .... Edmonton, AB
Kelly Professional & Tech .... Vancouver, BC
Key Executive Consultants .... Pickering, ON
Ludlow Project Services .... Oakville, ON
Mandrake Mgmt Consult .... Toronto, ON
Multipro Services Conseils .... Montréal, QC
Partnervision Consulting .... Toronto, ON
Permanent Solutions .... Mississauga, ON
Pommen & Associates .... Edmonton, AB
PricewaterhouseCoopers .... Montréal, QC
PricewaterhouseCoopers .... Saint John, NB
PricewaterhouseCoopers .... Halifax, NS
Prokosch Group, The .... Calgary, AB
Quantum EDP Recruiting Svcs .... Toronto, ON
RBA Intl HR Consultants .... Westmount, QC
Research Associates .... Edmonton, AB
Resource Management Group .... Toronto, ON
RHI Management Resources .... Calgary, AB
RHI Management Resources .... Toronto, ON
Robert Half Canada .... Ottawa, ON
Robertson Hancock Ltd .... Toronto, ON
Synergies res humaine .... Trois-Rivières, QC
TAD Canada .... Calgary, AB
TAD Canada .... Brantford, ON
TAD Canada .... Mississauga, ON
TAD Canada .... Ottawa, ON
TAD Canada .... Laval, QC
TAD Canada .... Bedford, NS
TAPP Consulting Svcs .... Merrickville, ON
Taylor Tomas Consulting .... Coquitlam, BC
TDM Technical Services .... Toronto, ON
Team Power Exec Search .... Markham, ON

DESIGN
DESIGN

Adecco Canada .... Ottawa, ON
Advanced Design&Drafting .... Mississauga, ON
Applicants Inc. .... Kitchener, ON
Aquent Partners .... Vancouver, BC
Aquent Partners .... Toronto, ON
Aquent Partners .... Montréal, QC
Archer Resource Solutions .... Mississauga, ON
Assoc de dessins mecaniques .... Montréal, QC
ASTRA Management Corp .... Vancouver, BC
ATS Reliance Industrial .... Toronto, ON
ATS Reliance Tech Group .... Vancouver, BC
ATS Reliance Tech Group .... Edmonton, AB
ATS Reliance Tech Group .... Calgary, AB
ATS Reliance Tech Group .... London, ON
ATS Reliance Tech Group .... Burlington, ON
Aztech Recruitment .... USA
B.B. Consultants Group .... Point Edward, ON
BeyondTech Solutions .... Vancouver, BC
Bongard Marsh Assoc .... Toronto, ON
Braun-Valley Associates .... Sarnia, ON
CAMPA & Associates .... Toronto, ON
Capital Executive .... Calgary, AB
CCT Inc .... London, ON
CCT Inc .... Kitchener, ON
CCT Inc .... Burlington, ON
CCT Inc .... Mississauga, ON
CDI Technical Svcs .... Calgary, AB
CDI Technical Svcs .... Oakville, ON

DESIGN (Cont.)
DESIGN (Suivre)

CDI Technical Svcs .... Pointe-Claire, QC
Coffey & Associates .... Hamilton, ON
Colintex Agencies .... Toronto, ON
ComFact Corp .... Oakville, ON
Comtech Prof Services .... Windsor, ON
Cornell Consulting Corp .... Burlington, ON
Creative Force Network .... Toronto, ON
Design Group Staffing .... Vancouver, BC
Design Group Staffing .... Edmonton, AB
Design Group Staffing .... Red Deer, AB
Design Group Staffing .... Calgary, AB
Design Group Staffing .... London, ON
Design Group Staffing .... Toronto, ON
Design Team Inc .... Richmond Hill, ON
Employment Network .... Regina, SK
Expertech Personnel Svcs .... Montréal, QC
Gallant Search Group .... London, ON
Graphic Assistants .... Toronto, ON
Grove Personnel Ltd .... UNITED KINGDOM
Horizon Resources Intl .... Calgary, AB
Hunt Technical Personnel .... Mississauga, ON
Information Bus Consulting .... Edmonton, AB
Interstate Technical Services .... USA
JCOR Human Resource Svcs .... Calgary, AB
Key Executive Consultants .... Barrie, ON
LTV & Associates .... Toronto, ON
Mandrake Mgmt Consult .... Toronto, ON
Markent Personnel Inc .... USA
Matchtech Engineering .... UNITED KINGDOM
Meda Group .... Windsor, ON
Nework Corp .... Toronto, ON
Noramtec Consultants .... North Vancouver, BC
Noramtec Consultants .... Nepean, ON
Normatech Executive .... Toronto, ON
Peter Glaser Assoc .... UNITED KINGDOM
Profile Search International .... Calgary, AB
Resource 7 Inc .... Edmonton, AB
RJK & Associates .... Markham, ON
Robert Connelly & Associates .... USA
Rod Turpin & Assoc .... Edmonton, AB
Roevin Tech People .... Edmonton, AB
Roevin Tech People .... Calgary, AB
Roevin Tech People .... Sarnia, ON
Roevin Tech People .... Kitchener, ON
Roevin Tech People .... Mississauga, ON
Roevin Tech People .... Markham, ON
Roevin Tech People .... Montréal, QC
TDM Technical Services .... Toronto, ON
Technical Service Consult .... Surrey, BC
Technical Skills Consulting .... Toronto, ON
TES Employment Solution .... Mississauga, ON
Thinkpath.com Inc .... Toronto, ON
Thinkpath.com Inc. .... Toronto, ON
Thinkpath.com Inc. .... Ottawa, ON
Trans-United Consultants .... Burlington, ON
TRS Staffing Solutions .... Calgary, AB
Williams Associates .... Toronto, ON

DIRECT MARKETING
MARKETING DIRECT

ABP Personnel Consult .... Westmount, QC
Adecco Québec .... Longueuil, QC
Colintex Agencies .... Toronto, ON
Dymar Mgmnt Consultants .... Mississauga, ON

First Choice Personnel .... Toronto, ON
Freelancers Unlimited .... Toronto, ON
Grant Search Group .... Toronto, ON
Grapevine Exec Recruiters .... Toronto, ON
InterCom Recruitment .... Toronto, ON
Interim Mgmt Resources .... Mississauga, ON
Jenereaux & Associates .... Mississauga, ON
Jerry Adel & Company .... Toronto, ON
Keith-Murray Partners .... Toronto, ON
Kingsley Allen IT Search .... Toronto, ON
Madison MacArthur Inc .... Toronto, ON
Management One Consultants .... Toronto, ON
Manpower Professional .... Markham, ON
Master Performers .... Toronto, ON
McKinnon Mgmnt Group .... Toronto, ON
Meridia Recruitment Svcs .... Halifax, NS
Michel Pauzé et Assoc .... Montréal, QC
Morris Pervin Group .... Toronto, ON
Newfoundland Personnel .... St. John's, NF
Outsourcing Connection .... Toronto, ON
Phee Farrer Jones Ltd .... UNITED KINGDOM
Premier Personnel Mgmt .... Toronto, ON
Research Personnel Consult .... Toronto, ON
RJ Professionals .... Toronto, ON
Robertson Hancock Ltd .... Toronto, ON
Shared Vision Mgmt Search .... Toronto, ON
Sourceco Exec Search .... Edmonton, AB
Sourceco Exec Search .... Westmount, QC
Spherion Workforce .... London, ON
SSA Services Conseils .... Montréal, QC
TERHAM Mgmnt Consulting .... Toronto, ON
Tolstoy Resources .... Bolton, ON
Tosi Placement Services .... Toronto, ON

DISABLED
HANDICAPÉ/INFIRME

Alder Centre, The .... Toronto, ON
Blooming Humans .... Victoria, BC
Career Connections .... Brandon, MB
Community Living Muskoka .... Bracebridge, ON
D.C. Powers & Assoc .... Vancouver, BC
Fairview Management .... Prince Rupert, BC
Interlake Employment Svcs .... Stonewall, MB
Line 1000 Placement Svcs .... Ottawa, ON
On-Site Placement Svcs .... Edmonton, AB
Options Outreach Emplmnt .... Saint John, NB
Partners in Employment .... Stratford, ON
Partners in Employment .... Listowel, ON
PATH Employment Svcs .... Hamilton, ON
Polaris Employment Svcs .... Burnaby, BC
SEARCHs .... Saskatoon, SK
Southwest HR Centre .... Regina, SK
Special Needs Employment Svcs .... Sarnia, ON
Work Able Services .... Hamilton, ON

EDUCATION
ÉDUCATION

Al-Khaleej Computers .... SAUDI ARABIA
Arabian Careers .... UNITED KINGDOM
Bilingual-Jobs.com .... Vancouver, BC
Bourassa Brodeur Assoc .... Trois-Rivières, QC
Brian Hetherington & Assoc .... Edmonton, AB
Bruce Hill Assoc .... Toronto, ON
Bruce Ward Partners .... Toronto, ON

EDUCATION (Cont.)
ÉDUCATION (Suivre)

Cathryn Lohrisch & Co .... Toronto, ON
Chris Green & Assoc .... Vancouver, BC
Conseillers en Admin FORMA .... Montréal, QC
Davies Park .... Calgary, AB
Diversified Staffing Svcs .... Edmonton, AB
Diversified Staffing Svcs .... Calgary, AB
Executive Network .... Victoria, BC
Executive Source .... Regina, SK
Fiala Consulting Group .... Vancouver, BC
Gordon Welch Consult .... Sherwood Park, AB
GRH Consultants Inc .... Québec, QC
Heidrick & Struggles Canada .... Toronto, ON
Heidrick & Struggles Canada .... Montréal, QC
Hodgins Koenig & Assoc .... Saskatoon, SK
Initial Education Personnel .... Markham, ON
InterSearch Canada/Western .... Vancouver, BC
Janet Wright & Associates .... Toronto, ON
Korn/Ferry Intl .... CHINA
Landmark Consulting Group .... Hamilton, ON
Locum Group, The .... Toronto, ON
Management Connections Inc .... Vancouver, BC
Manpower Professional .... Toronto, ON
Northeast Teacher Svcs .... Mount Pearl, NF
Ottawa Valley Personnel .... Pembroke, ON
Pace Personnel Ltd .... Vancouver, BC
Pamenter Pamenter Brezer .... Toronto, ON
Pinton Forrest & Madden .... Vancouver, BC
PME Partenaire Consult .... Saint-Georges, QC
PricewaterhouseCoopers .... Toronto, ON
PricewaterhouseCoopers .... Québec, QC
PricewaterhouseCoopers .... Halifax, NS
Professional Environment .... North Delta, BC
Provence Consulting .... Vancouver, BC
R. Jacques Plante & Assoc .... Sillery, QC
Ray Berndtson/Tanton .... Vancouver, BC
Renaud Foster Mgmt .... Ottawa, ON
Russell Reynolds Assoc .... Calgary, AB
Search Associates .... Belleville, ON
TAPP Consulting Svcs .... Merrickville, ON
Thompson Associates .... Halifax, NS

ENGINEERING
INGÉNIERIE

A.B. Schwartz Assoc .... Toronto, ON
A.W. Fraser Assoc .... Edmonton, AB
A.W. Fraser Assoc .... Calgary, AB
Abane & Associates .... Newmarket, ON
ABC Corries (Canada) .... Calgary, AB
Abecassis recherches cadres .... Montréal, QC
Access Career Solutions .... Brampton, ON
Accu-Staff Resource Systems .... Windsor, ON
Adecco Canada .... Victoria, BC
Adecco Canada .... Vancouver, BC
Adecco Canada .... Richmond, BC
Adecco Canada .... Burnaby, BC
Adecco Canada .... Langley, BC
Adecco Canada .... Calgary, AB
Adecco Canada .... Guelph, ON
Adecco Canada .... Toronto, ON
Adecco Canada .... Brampton, ON
Adecco Canada .... Oakville, ON
Adecco Canada .... Markham, ON
Adecco Canada .... Pickering, ON
Adecco Canada .... Ottawa, ON

Adecco Personnel Technique .... Sherbrooke, QC
Adecco Québec .... Laval, QC
Adecco Québec .... Chicoutimi, QC
Adecco Québec .... Québec, QC
Adler Recruitment .... UNITED KINGDOM
ADV Advanced Tech Svcs .... Toronto, ON
Advanced Design&Drafting .... Mississauga, ON
Advanced Tech Partners .... Vancouver, BC
Advanced Tech Partners .... Edmonton, AB
Advanced Tech Partners .... Calgary, AB
Advanced Tech Partners .... Toronto, ON
Aginove Inc. .... Dorval, QC
Aide Technique .... Longueuil, QC
Aim Personnel Svcs .... Ottawa, ON
Alan Davis Assoc .... Hudson Heights, QC
Allen Ballach Assoc .... Whitby, ON
Allen Personnel Svcs .... London, ON
Allen Personnel Svcs .... Cambridge, ON
Alumni-Network Recruit .... Mississauga, ON
Anderson Associates .... Toronto, ON
Angus Employment .... Burlington, ON
Applicants Inc. .... Kitchener, ON
Aramco Services Company .... USA
Archer Resource Solutions .... Mississauga, ON
Ariel Group Intl .... Toronto, ON
Ashtead Mgmnt Consultants .... UNITED KINGDOM
Assistance Teknica .... UNITED KINGDOM
Assoc de dessins mecaniques .... Montréal, QC
Associates Group .... Ottawa, ON
ASTRA Management Corp .... Vancouver, BC
ATS Reliance Industrial .... Toronto, ON
ATS Reliance Tech Group .... Vancouver, BC
ATS Reliance Tech Group .... Edmonton, AB
ATS Reliance Tech Group .... Calgary, AB
ATS Reliance Tech Group .... London, ON
ATS Reliance Tech Group .... Toronto, ON
ATS Reliance Tech Group .... Burlington, ON
Augment Prestige Svcs .... Point Edward, ON
Austin Park Mgmnt Group .... Toronto, ON
Axxes Technologies .... Sillery, QC
Aztech Recruitment .... USA
B.B. Consultants Group .... Point Edward, ON
Bailey Professional Search .... Calgary, AB
Baldwin Staffing Group .... Calgary, AB
BDS Challenge International .... AUSTRALIA
Beechwood Recruitment .... UNITED KINGDOM
Beresford Blake Thomas .... UNITED KINGDOM
Bertrand Elbaz C.R.H. .... Montréal, QC
Best Personnel Services .... Sarnia, ON
Best Personnel Services .... Strathroy, ON
BeyondTech Solutions .... Vancouver, BC
Blackshire Recruiting .... New Westminster, BC
BMA International .... Montréal, QC
BMA International .... Montréal, QC
BMB / MaxSys .... Ottawa, ON
Bongard Marsh Assoc .... Toronto, ON
Boscan Consultants .... Marysville, ON
Bourassa Brodeur Assoc .... Trois-Rivières, QC
Boyden Global Exec Search .... Calgary, AB
Brainhunter.com .... Toronto, ON
Brainhunter.com .... Ottawa, ON
Braun-Valley Associates .... Sarnia, ON
Bray Larouche et Assoc .... Montréal, QC
Bridge Info Technology .... Vancouver, BC
Btsn inc. .... St. George, ON
Burke Group .... Hamilton, ON
Burke Group .... St. Catharines, ON
C.G. Thomson & Co .... Toronto, ON
C.J. Stafford & Assoc .... Toronto, ON
C.N. Taylor Consulting .... Bedford, NS

ENGINEERING (Cont.)
INGÉNIERIE (Suivre)

C.W. Clasen Recruiting .... Coquitlam, BC
C. Wolfe & Assoc .... Toronto, ON
Cadman Consulting Group .... Vancouver, BC
Calian Technology Svcs .... Mississauga, ON
Calian Technology Svcs .... Ottawa, ON
Calian Technology Svcs .... Kanata, ON
CAMPA & Associates .... Toronto, ON
Campbell Morden Inc .... Toronto, ON
Can-Tech Services .... Brooklin, ON
Can-Tech Services .... Saint-Laurent, QC
Canadian Exec Recruitmnt .... Mississauga, ON
Canpro Executive Search .... Markham, ON
Capital Executive .... Calgary, AB
Career Advance Employment .... Burlington, ON
Career Partners/Harrison .... Hamilton, ON
Carion Resource Group .... Mississauga, ON
Caron Executive Search .... London, ON
CCT Inc .... London, ON
CCT Inc .... Kitchener, ON
CCT Inc .... Burlington, ON
CCT Inc .... Mississauga, ON
CDI Technical Svcs .... Calgary, AB
CDI Technical Svcs .... Oakville, ON
CDI Technical Svcs .... Pointe-Claire, QC
CFT Training and HR .... Montréal, QC
Chacra Belliveau & Assoc .... Montréal, QC
Chapman & Associates .... Vancouver, BC
Chase Consultants .... Mississauga, ON
Christmas McIvor Assoc .... Mississauga, ON
Churchill Group, The .... Toronto, ON
Clarendon Parker ME .... UNITED ARAB EMIRATES
Classic Consulting Group .... Calgary, AB
Coast Personnel Svcs .... Nanaimo, BC
Coffey & Associates .... Hamilton, ON
Coles Associates .... Charlottetown, PE
ComFact Corp .... Oakville, ON
Communication Dynamique .... Beaconsfield, QC
Comtech Prof Services .... Windsor, ON
Conestoga Personnel .... Kitchener, ON
Connectstaff Solutions .... Calgary, AB
Connors Lovell Assoc .... Cambridge, ON
Connors Lovell Assoc .... Mississauga, ON
Conseillers Jacques Cartier .... Montréal, QC
ConsulPRO Executive Search .... Ottawa, ON
Contemporary Personnel .... Toronto, ON
Contempra Personnel .... Pointe-Claire, QC
Contracts Consultancy Ltd .... UNITED KINGDOM
Core Group, The .... Toronto, ON
Cornell Consulting Corp .... Burlington, ON
Corporate Consultants .... Toronto, ON
Corporate HR Communicat .... Winnipeg, MB
Corporate Recruiters .... Vancouver, BC
Cosier Associates .... Calgary, AB
Cowan Personnel .... Montréal, QC
CV Theque .... Laval, QC
Cyberna Associates .... Montréal, QC
D.J. Macadam & Assoc .... North Vancouver, BC
Dan McNamara & Assoc .... Woodstock, ON
Danette Milne Corp Search .... Markham, ON
Daniluck & Associates .... Edmonton, AB
David Aplin & Assoc .... Edmonton, AB
David Aplin & Assoc .... Calgary, AB
David Taylor Mfg Search .... Toronto, ON
Delorme et Assoc .... Québec, QC
Derhak Ireland Partners .... Toronto, ON
Derkitt Herbert Exec Search .... Calgary, AB
Design Group Staffing .... Vancouver, BC

Design Group Staffing .... Edmonton, AB
Design Group Staffing .... Red Deer, AB
Design Group Staffing .... Calgary, AB
Design Group Staffing .... London, ON
Design Group Staffing .... Toronto, ON
Design Team Inc .... Richmond Hill, ON
DHR Canada .... Mississauga, ON
Doré Liaison .... Greenfield Park, QC
Dotemtex Executive Search .... Montréal, QC
Drake International .... Belleville, ON
Drakkar Human Resources .... Montréal, QC
Drakkar Human Resources .... Québec, QC
Duke Blakey Inc .... Toronto, ON
Dunhill Professional Search .... Vancouver, BC
Employment Partnership .... Saint John, NB
ENS Group Inc. .... Ottawa, ON
Erie Personnel Corp .... Thorold, ON
Erie Personnel Corp .... Fort Erie, ON
ExecuPlace Inc .... Kirkland, QC
Execusource Staffing Intl .... Windsor, ON
Executives Available .... Pointe-Claire, QC
Executrade Consultants .... Edmonton, AB
F.J. Galloway & Assoc .... London, ON
Fifth Option .... Burnaby, BC
First Choice Personnel .... Toronto, ON
Friday Personnel Inc .... Vancouver, BC
Friday Personnel Inc .... Calgary, AB
FSK Associates Inc .... USA
Future Executive Personnel .... Toronto, ON
Future Executive Personnel .... USA
G.L. Penney & Associates .... Edmonton, AB
G.W. Goudreau Personnel .... Windsor, ON
G-P Personnel .... Chicoutimi, QC
G-Tech Professional Staffing .... USA
Gallant Search Group .... London, ON
Gaudry Shink Levasseur .... Montréal, QC
Gauthier Conseils .... Montréal, QC
GBL Resources .... USA
Genesis Corporate Search .... Calgary, AB
Génisa Conseil Inc .... Montréal, QC
Girardin & Associates .... Winnipeg, MB
Glen Abbey Exec Search .... Oakville, ON
Global Consulting Group .... Markham, ON
Global Placement Svcs .... Mississauga, ON
Graduate Consulting Svcs .... Montréal, QC
Grand River Personnel .... Kitchener, ON
Grant Martin & Assoc .... Richmond Hill, ON
Grasslands Group .... Medicine Hat, AB
Grasslands Group .... Swift Current, SK
GRH Consultants Inc .... Québec, QC
Groupe LJL .... Pierrefonds, QC
Groupe Pluridis .... Montréal, QC
Groupe SFP .... Trois-Rivières, QC
GSA Search Consultants .... Bedford, NS
Gulco International Recruiting .... USA
Hallmark Personnel .... Oakville, ON
Harcourt & Assoc .... Edmonton, AB
Harcourt & Assoc .... Calgary, AB
Harrington Staffing Services .... Ottawa, ON
Hayhurst Consulting .... London, ON
HEC Group .... Ancaster, ON
High Road Personnel .... Burlington, ON
Horizon Resources Intl .... Calgary, AB
HR Business Partners .... Calgary, AB
HR Recruiting & Employment .... Red Deer, AB
Human Capital Solutions .... Mississauga, ON
Human Edge Consulting .... Richmond Hill, ON
Human Resources Mgmnt Canada .... Toronto, ON
Hunt Technical Personnel .... Vancouver, BC
Hunt Technical Personnel .... Calgary, AB

ENGINEERING (Cont.)
INGÉNIERIE (Suivre)

Hunt Technical Personnel	Toronto, ON
Hunt Technical Personnel	Toronto, ON
Hunt Technical Personnel	Mississauga, ON
Hunt Technical Personnel	Ottawa, ON
Hunt Technical Personnel	Saint-Laurent, QC
Hunt Technical Personnel	Montréal, QC
Huntech Consultants	Toronto, ON
Huntech Consultants	Ottawa, ON
Ian Martin Ltd	Vancouver, BC
Ian Martin Ltd	Calgary, AB
Ian Martin Ltd	London, ON
Ian Martin Ltd	Kitchener, ON
Ian Martin Ltd	Toronto, ON
Ian Martin Ltd	Hamilton, ON
Ian Martin Ltd	Oakville, ON
Ian Martin Ltd	Ottawa, ON
Ian Martin Ltd	Montréal, QC
Ian Martin Ltd	Sainte-Foy, QC
Ian Martin Ltd	USA
Ian Martin Ltd	USA
Impact Staffing	Windsor, ON
INFO-TEK Consulting	Edmonton, AB
Information Bus Consulting	Edmonton, AB
Information Resources Ctr	SAUDI ARABIA
InGenius Engineering Inc	Ottawa, ON
Intec Recruitment Svcs	UNITED KINGDOM
Intelligent Tech Solutions	Ottawa, ON
Interchange Personnel	Calgary, AB
Interim Plus	Granby, QC
International Bus Partners	Toronto, ON
International Staffing	UNITED KINGDOM
International Tech Recruit	Windsor, ON
Interocean Personnel Svcs	UNITED KINGDOM
InterSearch Canada/Staffing	Halifax, NS
Interstate Technical Services	USA
IT Resources	Markham, ON
J.E. Coulter Associates	Toronto, ON
J. Edgar & Associates	Toronto, ON
J.G. Flynn & Associates	Vancouver, BC
J.O. Bush & Associates	Mindemoya, ON
J.P. Anderson & Assoc	Burlington, ON
J.R. Bechtle & Company	USA
James E. Thomas & Assoc	London, ON
Jan Howard & Associates	Toronto, ON
Jawaby Oil Service	UNITED KINGDOM
JCOR Human Resource Svcs	Calgary, AB
Jerry Adel & Company	Toronto, ON
Job Born Candidate Select	Hamilton, ON
K.B. Lye & Associates	Toronto, ON
KAS Personnel Svcs	North Bay, ON
KAS Personnel Svcs	Kitchener, ON
KAS Personnel Svcs	Guelph, ON
KAS Personnel Svcs	Toronto, ON
KAS Personnel Svcs	Toronto, ON
KAS Personnel Svcs	Hamilton, ON
KAS Personnel Svcs	Burlington, ON
KAS Personnel Svcs	Brampton, ON
KAS Personnel Svcs	Mississauga, ON
KAS Personnel Svcs	Barrie, ON
KAS Personnel Svcs	Belleville, ON
Keith Bagg & Associates	Toronto, ON
Kellman Mgmnt Resources	Markham, ON
Kelly, Les svcs	Granby, QC
Kelly, Les svcs	Pointe-Claire, QC
Kelly, Les svcs	Montréal, QC
Kelly, Les svcs	Québec, QC
Kelly Professional & Tech	Victoria, BC
Kelly Professional & Tech	Vancouver, BC
Kelly Professional & Tech	Edmonton, AB
Kelly Professional & Tech	Saskatoon, SK
Kelly Professional & Tech	Regina, SK
Kelly Professional & Tech	Winnipeg, MB
Kelly Professional & Tech	Chatham, ON
Kelly Professional & Tech	London, ON
Kelly Professional & Tech	St. Thomas, ON
Kelly Professional & Tech	Brantford, ON
Kelly Professional & Tech	Kitchener, ON
Kelly Professional & Tech	Cambridge, ON
Kelly Professional & Tech	Guelph, ON
Kelly Professional & Tech	Toronto, ON
Kelly Professional & Tech	Downsview, ON
Kelly Professional & Tech	Toronto, ON
Kelly Professional & Tech	Hamilton, ON
Kelly Professional & Tech	Burlington, ON
Kelly Professional & Tech	Bolton, ON
Kelly Professional & Tech	Brampton, ON
Kelly Professional & Tech	Oakville, ON
Kelly Professional & Tech	Newmarket, ON
Kelly Professional & Tech	Markham, ON
Kelly Professional & Tech	St. Catharines, ON
Kelly Professional & Tech	Oakville, ON
Kelly Professional & Tech	Kingston, ON
Kelly Professional & Tech	Ottawa, ON
Kelly Professional & Tech	Fredericton, NB
Kelly Professional & Tech	Saint John, NB
Kelly Professional & Tech	Moncton, NB
Kelly Professional & Tech	Halifax, NS
Kelly Services	Calgary, AB
Key Executive Consultants	Pickering, ON
Kitchener Exec Consultants	Kitchener, ON
Knipper & Associates	Kingston, ON
Korn/Ferry Intl	Montréal, QC
Lamon + Stuart + Michaels	Toronto, ON
Landon Morgan Inc	Thorold, ON
LePage International	Montréal, QC
Leslie Corporation	USA
Level A Inc	Peterborough, ON
Levert Personnel Resources	Timmins, ON
Levert Personnel Resources	Sudbury, ON
Lewis Companies	Toronto, ON
Linda Walter & Assoc	Île-Perrot, QC
London Executive Consultants	London, ON
Louise Robinson Placement	Keene, ON
Ludlow Project Services	Oakville, ON
Lynne Milette & Associates	Chapeau, QC
M.R. Goodman Consulting	Calgary, AB
Macdonald & Brisson Personnel	Ottawa, ON
MacKenzie Gray Mgmnt	Calgary, AB
MacLean Hay Consulting	Oakville, ON
Maintenance Plus	Chatham, ON
Manpower Professional	Victoria, BC
Manpower Professional	Vancouver, BC
Manpower Professional	Richmond, BC
Manpower Professional	Burnaby, BC
Manpower Professional	Edmonton, AB
Manpower Professional	Red Deer, AB
Manpower Professional	Calgary, AB
Manpower Professional	Regina, SK
Manpower Professional	Winnipeg, MB
Manpower Professional	Thunder Bay, ON
Manpower Professional	Sudbury, ON
Manpower Professional	Windsor, ON
Manpower Professional	London, ON
Manpower Professional	Guelph, ON
Manpower Professional	Toronto, ON
Manpower Professional	Toronto, ON
Manpower Professional	Toronto, ON

ENGINEERING (Cont.)
INGÉNIERIE (Suivre)

Manpower Professional .... Toronto, ON
Manpower Professional .... Hamilton, ON
Manpower Professional .... Burlington, ON
Manpower Professional .... Brampton, ON
Manpower Professional .... Mississauga, ON
Manpower Professional .... Barrie, ON
Manpower Professional .... Newmarket, ON
Manpower Professional .... St. Catharines, ON
Manpower Professional .... Niagara Falls, ON
Manpower Professional .... Pickering, ON
Manpower Professional .... Peterborough, ON
Manpower Professional .... Cobourg, ON
Manpower Professional .... Belleville, ON
Manpower Professional .... Kingston, ON
Manpower Professional .... Brockville, ON
Manpower Professional .... Cornwall, ON
Manpower Professional .... Nepean, ON
Manpower Professional .... Ottawa, ON
Manpower Professional .... Granby, ON
Manpower Professional .... Sherbrooke, QC
Manpower Professional .... Montréal, QC
Manpower Professional .... Québec, QC
Manpower Professional .... Fredericton, NB
Manpower Professional .... Saint John, NB
Manpower Professional .... Charlottetown, PE
Manpower Professional .... Halifax, NS
Manpower Professional .... Sydney, NS
Manpower Professional .... St. John's, NF
Manpower Services Canada .... Toronto, ON
Maranova Resources Corp .... Orleans, ON
Marlene Bilodeau Conseils .... Chicoutimi, QC
Matchtech Engineering .... UNITED KINGDOM
Matte Groupe Conseil .... Montréal, QC
Matthews Management .... Richmond Hill, ON
MBL Group LLC .... USA
McDonald-Green Personnel .... Cambridge, ON
McIntyre Mgmnt Resources .... Hamilton, ON
McLean Exec Consultants .... Calgary, AB
McQ International Svcs .... UNITED KINGDOM
Meda Group .... Windsor, ON
Megasearch International .... Hudson, QC
Meridia Recruitment Svcs .... Halifax, NS
Miller Recruitment Solutions .... Halifax, NS
Montgomery Thomason Assoc .... Mississauga, ON
Morgan Exec Search Group .... Toronto, ON
MSX International .... Oakville, ON
MSX International .... USA
MSX International .... USA
MSX International .... USA
MSX International .... USA
Multec Canada .... Toronto, ON
Multec Canada .... Nepean, ON
Multec Canada .... Montréal, QC
MultiPersonnel International .... Dorval, QC
MVC Associates Intl .... Toronto, ON
National Executive .... Toronto, ON
Nesma International Svcs .... UNITED KINGDOM
New World Intl Consultants .... Windsor, ON
Nex Canada .... Toronto, ON
Noramtec Consultants .... North Vancouver, BC
Noramtec Consultants .... Edmonton, AB
Noramtec Consultants .... Nepean, ON
Noramtec Consultants .... Bath, ON
Noramtec Consultants .... Montréal, QC
Normatech Executive .... Toronto, ON
ObjectSearch .... Toronto, ON
OCC Computer Personnel .... UNITED KINGDOM

Osborne Group .... Vancouver, BC
Osborne Group .... Calgary, AB
Osborne Group .... Edmonton, AB
Osborne Group .... Toronto, ON
Osborne Group .... Montréal, QC
P.R.Y. .... Toronto, ON
Palmer & Associates .... Kingston, ON
Parkwood Associates .... Mississauga, ON
Partners Employment Group .... Toronto, ON
People Bank, The .... Mississauga, ON
Perceptive Edge .... Toronto, ON
Perry Martel International .... Ottawa, ON
Personnel Alter Ego .... Pointe-Claire, QC
Personnel Alter Ego .... Montréal, QC
Personnel Clé .... Québec, QC
Personnel Mgmnt Group .... Winnipeg, MB
Personnel Search .... Saint John, NB
Personnel Search .... Moncton, NB
Personnel Star Avon FJ .... Montréal, QC
Peter Glaser Assoc .... UNITED KINGDOM
Peter Leonard & Assoc .... Calgary, AB
Petro Middle East .... UNITED ARAB EMIRATES
Petro Staff Intl HR Advisors .... Calgary, AB
Pettitt Group Inc., The .... Burlington, ON
Phelps Staffing Resource .... Thunder Bay, ON
Phoenix Search Group .... Toronto, ON
Pila Recruiting & Assoc .... Richmond, BC
Pioneer Exec Consultants .... Toronto, ON
Placement Testart .... Westmount, QC
Planigestion A. Choquette .... Duvernay, QC
PME Partenaire Consult .... Saint-Georges, QC
Pollack Group, The .... Ottawa, ON
Precision Resources Ltd .... UNITED KINGDOM
Premier Personnel .... UNITED KINGDOM
PricewaterhouseCoopers .... Vancouver, BC
PricewaterhouseCoopers .... Calgary, AB
PricewaterhouseCoopers .... Québec, QC
PricewaterhouseCoopers .... AUSTRALIA
PricewaterhouseCoopers .... CHINA
Prichard Kymen Inc .... Edmonton, AB
Pride in Personnel .... Markham, ON
Prime Management Group .... London, ON
Prime Management Group .... Cambridge, ON
Prime Source Management .... Toronto, ON
Prior Resource Group .... Kitchener, ON
Pro Tec Global Staffing .... Thornhill, ON
Pro Tec Services Techniques .... Brossard, QC
Pro-Action Personnel .... Chomedey, QC
Procom .... Calgary, AB
Profile Search International .... Calgary, AB
Prolet Inc. .... Toronto, ON
Prolet Inc. .... Oakville, ON
Prologic Systems .... Ottawa, ON
Prosearch Associates .... Mississauga, ON
ProSource Mgmnt Consult .... Woodbridge, ON
Prospects Plus .... Kirkland, QC
Protocole .... Montréal, QC
Prud'Homme Groupe-Conseil .... Montréal, QC
Purcell Technical Staffing .... USA
Qualicum Consulting .... Ottawa, ON
Quality Personnel .... Brampton, ON
Quantum EDP Recruiting Svcs .... Toronto, ON
Quantum EDP Recruiting Svcs .... Ottawa, ON
Quantum EDP Recruiting Svcs .... USA
Quantum Mgmnt Services .... Toronto, ON
R. Jacques Plante & Assoc .... Sillery, QC
Randal Cunningham Enr .... Vancouver, BC
Ray & Berndtson/Robertson .... Ottawa, ON
Ray & Berndtson/Robertson .... Halifax, NS
RBA Intl HR Consultants .... Westmount, QC

ENGINEERING (Cont.)
INGÉNIERIE (Suivre)

RCM Technologies .... Mississauga, ON
Relational Resources .... Toronto, ON
Renaissance Personnel .... Windsor, ON
Renaissance Personnel .... Chatham, ON
Resource 7 Inc .... Edmonton, AB
Resource Corporation, The .... Toronto, ON
Resource Professionals .... Calgary, AB
Ressources 3000 .... Westmount, QC
Rideau Management Group .... Nepean, ON
RJ Professionals .... Toronto, ON
RJK & Associates .... Markham, ON
Roan International .... Mississauga, ON
Robert Connelly & Associates .... USA
Robert Half Canada .... Toronto, ON
Robert L Holmes Placement .... Cambridge, ON
Robert T. Keegan & Assoc .... Oakville, ON
Robinson Rose Associates .... Mississauga, ON
Rod Turpin & Assoc .... Edmonton, AB
Roevin Tech People .... North Vancouver, BC
Roevin Tech People .... Edmonton, AB
Roevin Tech People .... Calgary, AB
Roevin Tech People .... Sarnia, ON
Roevin Tech People .... Kitchener, ON
Roevin Tech People .... Mississauga, ON
Roevin Tech People .... Markham, ON
Roevin Tech People .... Montréal, QC
Rolland ressources humaines .... Montréal, QC
Roper and Assoc .... Calgary, AB
Rostie & Associates .... Toronto, ON
Rudl International .... Ottawa, ON
RWJ & Associates .... London, ON
RWJ & Associates .... Kitchener, ON
RWM Management Resources .... Calgary, AB
S. Tanner & Associates .... Oakville, ON
SAG ressources humaines .... Montréal, QC
Sam Perri & Associates .... Mississauga, ON
Savage Consultants .... Vancouver, BC
Scientific Placement .... USA
Scott Huband Consulting .... Oakville, ON
SearchCorp International .... Calgary, AB
Selection Group Mgmnt .... Mississauga, ON
Servocraft Limited .... Toronto, ON
Sherwood Engineer Recruit .... UNITED KINGDOM
Silicon Network .... Toronto, ON
SinclairSmith Assoc .... Sainte-Polycarpe, QC
SOS Personnel .... Sarnia, ON
Sourceco Exec Search .... Edmonton, AB
Sourceco Exec Search .... Westmount, QC
Spencer Stuart .... Toronto, ON
Spencer Stuart .... Montréal, QC
Spherion Workforce .... Mississauga, ON
SSA Services Conseils .... Montréal, QC
St-Amour & Assoc .... Toronto, ON
St-Amour & Assoc .... Montréal, QC
Star Search Consultants .... Toronto, ON
Stellar Personnel Placement .... Windsor, ON
Stellar Personnel Placement .... London, ON
Stephen Laramee Associates .... Toronto, ON
Stoakley-Dudley Consult .... Mississauga, ON
StoneWood Group .... Toronto, ON
StoneWood Group .... Ottawa, ON
StoneWood Group .... Sainte-Geneviève, QC
Strategic Resources Intl .... Toronto, ON
Summit Personnel Services .... Windsor, ON
Symmetry Search Group .... Toronto, ON
Syntech Placements .... Toronto, ON
TAD Canada .... Calgary, AB
TAD Canada .... Brantford, ON
TAD Canada .... Mississauga, ON
TAD Canada .... Ottawa, ON
TAD Canada .... Laval, QC
TAD Canada .... Bedford, NS
Talent Consulting Services .... USA
TalentLab .... Toronto, ON
TalentLab .... Kingston, ON
TalentLab .... Kanata, ON
Tapscott Associates .... Toronto, ON
Taylor Recruitment .... UNITED KINGDOM
TaylorMade Careers .... USA
TDM Technical Services .... Toronto, ON
Tech Hi Consultants Ltd .... Kitchener, ON
Techaid Inc .... Montréal, QC
Technical Mgmnt Resources .... Barrie, ON
Technical Resource Network .... Vancouver, BC
Technical Service Consult .... Surrey, BC
Technical Service Consult .... Winnipeg, MB
Technical Service Consult .... Toronto, ON
Technical Skills Consulting .... Toronto, ON
Technical Solutions Inc .... USA
Technisolutions Executive .... Aylmer, QC
Technisource .... USA
Teknica (UK) Ltd .... UNITED KINGDOM
TEKsystems .... Richmond, BC
TEKsystems .... Mississauga, ON
TEKsystems .... Ottawa, ON
Tennen Personnel Services .... Toronto, ON
TES Employment Solution .... Toronto, ON
TES Employment Solution .... Burlington, ON
TES Employment Solution .... Mississauga, ON
TES Employment Solution .... Ottawa, ON
TES Employment Solution .... Montréal, QC
TES Employment Solution .... USA
TES Employment Solution .... USA
Thinkpath.com Inc .... Toronto, ON
Thinkpath.com Inc. .... Toronto, ON
Thinkpath.com Inc. .... Ottawa, ON
Thinkpath.com Inc .... USA
Thinkpath.com Inc. .... USA
Toronto Exec Consultants .... Toronto, ON
Trans-United Consultants .... Burlington, ON
TRS Staffing Solutions .... Calgary, AB
True North Exec Search .... Toronto, ON
Ultimate Staffing .... Hamilton, ON
Van Biesen Group .... Calgary, AB
Van Hees Personnel .... Dundas, ON
Vantec Consultants .... Vancouver, BC
Venatus Conseil Ltée .... Montréal, QC
Verriez Group Inc .... London, ON
Volt Human Resources .... Vancouver, BC
Volt Human Resources .... Toronto, ON
W. Hutt Mgmnt Resources .... Burlington, ON
Ward Vinge & Associates .... Edmonton, AB
Ward Vinge & Associates .... Calgary, AB
Wayne Perry & Associates .... Toronto, ON
Wayne Thomas & Associates .... Ottawa, ON
Wellington Partners Intl .... Kitchener, ON
Wenje Management Ltd .... Markham, ON
Western Mgmnt Consultants .... Edmonton, AB
Windowpane Mgmnt .... Calgary, AB
Windsor Personnel & Exec .... Windsor, ON
Winters Technical Staffing .... Toronto, ON
Wolfer-Hale & Associates .... Calgary, AB
Wood West & Partners .... Vancouver, BC
Woodridge Associates .... UNITED KINGDOM
Worth Personnel Group .... Toronto, ON
Worth Personnel Group .... Mississauga, ON
Wypich International .... Toronto, ON

ENGINEERING (Cont.)
INGÉNIERIE (Suivre)

Yorkland Search Tech .... Mississauga, ON
Yves Elkas Inc .... Montréal, QC
Zen Zen International .... Winnipeg, MB

ENVIRONMENTAL
ENVIRONNEMENTAUX

Career Advance Employment .... Burlington, ON
Peter Glaser Assoc .... UNITED KINGDOM
Professional Environment .... North Delta, BC
Resource Concepts .... St. John's, NF

FINANCE
FINANCE

1st Choice Personnel .... USA
A. Lawrence Abrams Assoc .... Waterloo, ON
A.W. Fraser Assoc .... Calgary, AB
Abecassis recherches cadres .... Montréal, QC
Account Ability .... Toronto, ON
Accountants on Call .... Vancouver, BC
Accountants on Call .... Toronto, ON
Accountemps Financial .... Vancouver, BC
Accountemps Financial .... Surrey, BC
Accountemps Financial .... Edmonton, AB
Accountemps Financial ....Calgary, AB
Accountemps Financial .... Winnipeg, MB
Accountemps Financial .... Toronto, ON
Accountemps Financial .... Toronto, ON
Accountemps Financial .... Burlington, ON
Accountemps Financial .... Mississauga, ON
Accountemps Financial .... Markham, ON
Accountemps Financial .... Ottawa, ON
Accountemps Financial .... Montréal, QC
Accounting Machine Personnel .... Toronto, ON
Adecco Canada .... Vancouver, BC
Adecco Canada .... Richmond, BC
Adecco Canada .... Langley, BC
Adecco Canada .... Kitchener, ON
Adecco Canada .... Ottawa, ON
Adecco Québec .... Longueuil, QC
Adecco Québec ....Chicoutimi, QC
Adirect Recruiting Corp .... Toronto, ON
Administration Gespro .... Montréal, QC
Administrative Fundamentals .... Toronto, ON
Agence de place H Roy .... Saint-Hyacinthe, QC
Agence de place H Roy .... Montréal, QC
Agence de place H Roy .... Sainte-Foy, QC
Aldonna Barry Mgmnt Consult .... Bolton, ON
Allen Austin Lowe & Powers .... USA
Allen Etcovitch Assoc .... Montréal, QC
Allmat & Associates ....Cobourg, ON
Ambridge Management .... Toronto, ON
Andersen .... Vancouver, BC
Andersen .... Winnipeg, MB
Andersen .... Toronto, ON
Andersen .... Toronto, ON
Andersen .... Mississauga, ON
Andersen .... Ottawa, ON
Andersen .... Montréal, QC
Andersen .... Sainte-Foy, QC
Anderson Associates .... Toronto, ON
Andrew Duncan Assoc .... UNITED KINGDOM

Angus Employment .... Burlington, ON
Angus One Pro Recruitment .... Vancouver, BC
Apple Management Corp .... Toronto, ON
Archer Assoc .... Toronto, ON
Argentus Inc. .... Toronto, ON
Armitage Associates .... Vancouver, BC
Armitage Associates .... Toronto, ON
Armitage Associates .... Rosmere, QC
Ashlar-Stone Consultants .... Mississauga, ON
Associates Group .... Ottawa, ON
Association Resource Centre .... Ottawa, ON
ASTRA Management Corp .... Vancouver, BC
AT Kearney Executive .... Toronto, ON
Audax Corporation .... Toronto, ON
Austin Marlowe Intl .... Toronto, ON
Austin Park Mgmnt Group .... Toronto, ON
Ayrshire Group .... Toronto, ON
Baines Gwinner Ltd .... UNITED KINGDOM
Baldock Associates .... Toronto, ON
Barry Blostein Recruitment .... Thornhill, ON
Bay Street Placement .... Richmond Hill, ON
BDO Dunwoody & Assoc .... Kitchener, ON
BDO Dunwoody & Assoc .... Hamilton, ON
BDO Dunwoody & Assoc .... Markham, ON
BDO Dunwoody Exec Search .... Winnipeg, MB
BDO Dunwoody LLP .... Winnipeg, MB
BDO Dunwoody LLP .... Sarnia, ON
BDO Dunwoody LLP .... Uxbridge, ON
BDO Dunwoody LLP .... Kingston, ON
BDO Dunwoody LLP .... Nepean, ON
BDO Dunwoody LLP .... Winchester, ON
BDO Dunwoody LLP .... Montréal, QC
Beallor & Partners .... Toronto, ON
Bernhard Consulting .... Winnipeg, MB
Bessner Gallay Kreisman .... Westmount, QC
Bialecki Inc. .... USA
Bilingual Source .... Toronto, ON
Birch & Assoc .... Montréal, QC
BMA International .... Montréal, QC
BMA International .... Montréal, QC
Bondwell Staffing .... Toronto, ON
Booke & Partners .... Winnipeg, MB
Bosworth Field Assoc .... Toronto, ON
Botrie Associates .... Toronto, ON
Bouris Wilson LLP .... Ottawa, ON
Bower Ng Staff Systems .... Vancouver, BC
Boyd-Laidler Assoc .... Toronto, ON
Brainhunter.com .... Toronto, ON
Brainhunter.com .... Ottawa, ON
Bray Larouche et Assoc .... Montréal, QC
Brendan Wood International .... Toronto, ON
Brownlow Associates .... Ancaster, ON
Bruce R. Duncan Assoc .... Toronto, ON
Bruce Ward Partners .... Toronto, ON
Bryan Jason Assoc .... Toronto, ON
Burke Group .... Hamilton, ON
Burke Group .... St. Catharines, ON
Business&Prof Appointmnts .... UNITED KINGDOM
C.N. Taylor Consulting .... Bedford, NS
C. Price & Associates .... Toronto, ON
C. Scott & Associates .... Toronto, ON
C. Snow & Associates .... Toronto, ON
Caldwell Partners .... Vancouver, BC
Calvin Partners Intl .... Toronto, ON
Cameron Consulting Group .... Brampton, ON
Campbell Morden Inc .... Toronto, ON
Canadian Exec Consultants .... Toronto, ON
Canadian Findings .... Toronto, ON
Canatrade International .... Candiac, QC

FINANCE (Cont.)
FINANCE (Suivre)

Canpro Executive Search .... Markham, ON
Career Advance Employment .... Burlington, ON
Career Partners/Harrison .... Hamilton, ON
Careers & Professions .... Montréal, QC
Carion Resource Group .... Mississauga, ON
Cathryn Lohrisch & Co .... Toronto, ON
CCG Mgmnt Consultants .... Mississauga, ON
CDM & Associates .... Toronto, ON
Central Mgmnt Consultants .... Toronto, ON
Centre for Corp Resources .... Toronto, ON
Centrex HR Centre .... Hamilton, ON
Chad Management Group .... Toronto, ON
Chapman & Associates .... Vancouver, BC
Chisholm & Partners Intl .... Toronto, ON
Christian & Timbers .... USA
Christmas McIvor Assoc .... Mississauga, ON
CLA Personnel .... Ottawa, ON
Clarendon Parker ME .... UNITED ARAB EMIRATES
Clark Pollard & Gagliardi .... Waterloo, ON
Clarke Henning LLP .... Toronto, ON
Classic Consulting Group .... Calgary, AB
Classified Canada .... Mississauga, ON
Claude Guedj Assoc .... Montréal, QC
Coakwell Crawford Cairns .... High River, AB
Coe & Company Intl .... Calgary, AB
Collins Barrow .... Calgary, AB
Connors Lovell Assoc .... Mississauga, ON
Conroy Partners .... Calgary, AB
Contemporary Personnel .... Toronto, ON
Core Group, The .... Toronto, ON
Corporate Consultants .... Toronto, ON
Corporate Controllers Inc .... Halifax, NS
Corporate HR Communicat .... Winnipeg, MB
Corporate Recruiters .... Toronto, ON
Corporate Res (Hertford) .... UNITED KINGDOM
Corporate Resources .... Toronto, ON
Cosier Associates .... Calgary, AB
Courtney Personnel .... Brampton, ON
Cox Merritt & Co .... Kanata, ON
Craig Davies Collins .... Red Deer, AB
Crawford de Munnik Executive .... Toronto, ON
Creative Financial Staff .... Vancouver, BC
Creative Financial Staff .... Toronto, ON
Creative Financial Staff .... Toronto, ON
Cyberna Associates .... Montréal, QC
Cyr & Assoc .... Campbellville, ON
D & H Group .... Vancouver, BC
D.R. Nolan Assoc .... Toronto, ON
Danette Milne Corp Search .... Markham, ON
Dave White Personnel .... Ottawa, ON
David Aplin & Assoc .... Edmonton, AB
David Warwick Kennedy Assoc .... Vancouver, BC
Davies Kidd .... UNITED KINGDOM
Davis Daignault Schick & Co .... Calgary, AB
Dean & Associates .... Toronto, ON
Deloitte Consulting .... Toronto, ON
Deloitte Consulting .... Montréal, QC
Delorme et Assoc .... Québec, QC
Derkitt Herbert Exec Search .... Calgary, AB
Dick Cook Schulli .... Calgary, AB
Dingle & Associates .... Toronto, ON
Dion Mgmnt Exec Search .... Toronto, ON
Dion Mgmnt Groupe Conseil .... Montréal, QC
Dion Mgmnt Groupe Conseil .... Sainte-Foy, QC
Doré Liaison .... Greenfield Park, QC
Dotemtex Executive Search .... Montréal, QC
Drake Executive .... Burnaby, BC

Drake Executive .... Winnipeg, MB
Drake Executive .... Sudbury, ON
Drake Executive .... London, ON
Drake Executive .... Toronto, ON
Drake Executive .... Montréal, QC
Drake International .... Edmonton, AB
Drake International .... North Bay, ON
Drake International .... London, ON
Drake International .... Toronto, ON
Drake International .... Hamilton, ON
Drake International .... Oakville, ON
Drake International .... Barrie, ON
Drake International .... Kingston, ON
Drake International .... Ottawa, ON
Drake International .... Montréal, QC
Drake International .... Québec, QC
Drake International .... Moncton, NB
Drake International .... Halifax, NS
Drakkar Human Resources .... Saint-Laurent, QC
Drummond & Associates .... USA
Ducharme Group .... Toronto, ON
Dunhill Consultants N York .... Toronto, ON
Dunhill Professional Search .... Vancouver, BC
Dymar Mgmnt Consultants .... Mississauga, ON
E.H. Scissons & Associates .... Saskatoon, SK
E.L. Shore & Associates .... Toronto, ON
E-Search Consulting .... Toronto, ON
Eastgate Consultants .... Toronto, ON
Edan Search Group .... Toronto, ON
EDS Executive Staffing .... Vancouver, BC
Élan Personnel .... Victoria, BC
Élan Personnel .... Vancouver, BC
Élan Personnel .... Calgary, AB
Ellis Foster .... Vancouver, BC
Employment Network .... Regina, SK
Enns Hever Inc .... Toronto, ON
ePersonnel Inc .... Montréal, QC
Ernst David International .... Winnipeg, MB
Ernst & Young .... Kitchener, ON
Ernst & Young .... SAUDI ARABIA
Euro-West Consulting .... Vancouver, BC
Evancic Perrault EPR .... Drayton Valley, AB
Everest Mgmnt Network .... Toronto, ON
Excel HR Consultants .... Toronto, ON
ExecuCounsel Inc .... Toronto, ON
Executive Assistance .... Toronto, ON
Expert Recruiters Inc .... Vancouver, BC
Farley Law & Assoc .... Thornhill, ON
Feldman Gray Associates .... Toronto, ON
Fifth Option .... Burnaby, BC
Finacc Executive Search .... Toronto, ON
Finance Department Ltd .... Toronto, ON
Fisher Group Exec Search .... Calgary, AB
Force Recruiting Services .... Calgary, AB
Fountainhealth Recruitment .... Toronto, ON
Friday Personnel Inc .... Vancouver, BC
Friday Personnel Inc .... Calgary, AB
Friedman & Friedman .... Montréal, QC
Fromm & Assoc Personnel .... Toronto, ON
Fuller Landau .... Montréal, QC
Future Executive Personnel .... Toronto, ON
Future Executive Personnel .... USA
Futurestep .... Toronto, ON
GAAP Inc .... Montréal, QC
Gardner & Coombs .... St. John's, NF
Garrison Group, The .... Toronto, ON
Gaspar & Associates .... Toronto, ON
Gaudry Shink Levasseur .... Montréal, QC
Gauthier Conseils .... Montréal, QC
Genesis Corporate Search .... Calgary, AB

FINANCE (Cont.)
FINANCE (Suivre)

FINANCE (Cont.)
FINANCE (Suivre)

Mandrake Mgmt Consult	Toronto, ON
Marberg & Associates	Toronto, ON
Matte Groupe Conseil	Montréal, QC
Matteson Management	Toronto, ON
Maureen Sinden Exec Search	Ottawa, ON
MBL Group LLC	USA
McNeill Nakamoto Recruit	Vancouver, BC
Meech Partners	Toronto, ON
Meridia Recruitment Svcs	Halifax, NS
Meyers Norris Penny	Wainwright, AB
Meyers Norris Penny	Leduc, AB
Meyers Norris Penny	Grande Prairie, AB
Meyers Norris Penny	Red Deer, AB
Meyers Norris Penny	Innisfail, AB
Meyers Norris Penny	Edmonton, AB
Meyers Norris Penny	Calgary, AB
Meyers Norris Penny	Calgary, AB
Meyers Norris Penny	Lethbridge, AB
Meyers Norris Penny	Medicine Hat, AB
Meyers Norris Penny	Rocky Mountain House, AB
Meyers Norris Penny	Pincher Creek, AB
Meyers Norris Penny	Milk River, AB
Meyers Norris Penny	Foremost, AB
Meyers Norris Penny	Bow Island, AB
Meyers Norris Penny	Drumheller, AB
Meyers Norris Penny	Rimbey, AB
Meyers Norris Penny	Swift Current, SK
Meyers Norris Penny	Saskatoon, SK
Meyers Norris Penny	Prince Albert, SK
Meyers Norris Penny	Regina, SK
Meyers Norris Penny	Humboldt, SK
Meyers Norris Penny	Moosomin, SK
Meyers Norris Penny	Melfort, SK
Meyers Norris Penny	Hudson Bay, SK
Meyers Norris Penny	Dauphin, MB
Meyers Norris Penny	Brandon, MB
Meyers Norris Penny	Winnipeg, MB
Meyers Norris Penny	Portage La Prairie, MB
Meyers Norris Penny	Virden, MB
Meyers Norris Penny	Deloraine, MB
Meyers Norris Penny	Kilarney, MB
Meyers Norris Penny	Neepawa, MB
Michael Page Finance	CHINA
Michael Page International	USA
Milgram & Associates	Toronto, ON
Millar Walker & Gay	Toronto, ON
Mintz & Partners	Toronto, ON
Molnar & Associates	Toronto, ON
Montgomery Thomason Assoc	Mississauga, ON
Morgan Palmer Search	Toronto, ON
Morris Pervin Group	Toronto, ON
Moscoe & Company	Toronto, ON
Mount Royal Personnel	Calgary, AB
Moxon Personnel	Vancouver, BC
Multi-Ressources	Québec, QC
MultiPersonnel International	Dorval, QC
MVC Associates Intl	Toronto, ON
Nework Corp	Toronto, ON
NewSource Management	Toronto, ON
Nex Canada	Toronto, ON
Norrell Services	Toronto, ON
Norrell Staffing Services	Richmond, BC
Osborne Group	Vancouver, BC
Osborne Group	Calgary, AB
Osborne Group	Edmonton, AB
Osborne Group	Toronto, ON
Osborne Group	Montréal, QC

Palmer & Company Executive	Toronto, ON
Palmer Reed	Toronto, ON
Paradigm Mgmnt Solutions	Toronto, ON
Parkwood Associates	Mississauga, ON
Partners Employment Group	Toronto, ON
Partners in Search	Toronto, ON
Partnervision Consulting	Toronto, ON
Peak Associates Inc	Toronto, ON
People Bank, The	Calgary, AB
People Bank, The	Winnipeg, MB
People Bank, The	London, ON
People Bank, The	Markham, ON
People Bank, The	Montréal, QC
People First Solutions	Vancouver, BC
Permanent Search Group	Mississauga, ON
Permanent Solutions	Mississauga, ON
Personnel Clé	Québec, QC
Personnel Menen	Mount Royal, QC
Personnel Outaouais	Hull, QC
Personnel Search	Saint John, NB
Personnel Search	Moncton, NB
Phoenix Search Group	Toronto, ON
Pinstripe Personnel	Toronto, ON
Pinton Forrest & Madden	Vancouver, BC
PKF Hill LLP	Toronto, ON
PME Partenaire Consult	Saint-Georges, QC
Pommen & Associates	Edmonton, AB
Powell Jones Mgmnt Services	Barrie, ON
Pragmatizm	Toronto, ON
PricewaterhouseCoopers	Victoria, BC
PricewaterhouseCoopers	Edmonton, AB
PricewaterhouseCoopers	Calgary, AB
PricewaterhouseCoopers	Saskatoon, SK
PricewaterhouseCoopers	Regina, SK
PricewaterhouseCoopers	Winnipeg, MB
PricewaterhouseCoopers	London, ON
PricewaterhouseCoopers	Kitchener, ON
PricewaterhouseCoopers	Toronto, ON
PricewaterhouseCoopers	Hamilton, ON
PricewaterhouseCoopers	Québec, QC
PricewaterhouseCoopers	Saint John, NB
PricewaterhouseCoopers	Charlottetown, PE
PricewaterhouseCoopers	Halifax, NS
PricewaterhouseCoopers	St. John's, NF
PricewaterhouseCoopers	BERMUDA
Prime Management Group	London, ON
Prime Management Group	Cambridge, ON
Profile Personnel Consult	Toronto, ON
Profile Search International	Calgary, AB
ProSource Mgmnt Consult	Woodbridge, ON
Prospects Plus	Kirkland, QC
Prud'Homme Groupe-Conseil	Montréal, QC
Ptack Schnarch Basevitz	Montréal, QC
PTC - Financial Staffing	Concord, ON
Quad Search Inc.	Toronto, ON
Quantum	Montréal, QC
Quantum, Les services	Longueuil, QC
Quantum, Les services	Pointe-Claire, QC
Quantum, Les services	Laval, QC
Quantum Mgmnt Services	Toronto, ON
Quantum Mgmnt Services	Mississauga, ON
Quantum Mgmnt Services	Ottawa, ON
Quantum Mgmnt Services	Toronto, ON
Quest Exec Recruitment	Toronto, ON
R. Jacques Plante & Assoc	Sillery, QC
R.K. Chengkalath PC	Calgary, AB
Ray & Berndtson/Laurendeau	Montréal, QC
Ray Berndtson/Lovas Stanley	Toronto, ON
Ray Berndtson/Tanton	Vancouver, BC
Raymond Chabot HR Inc	Toronto, ON

FINANCE (Cont.)
FINANCE (Suivre)

Raymond Chabot HR Inc .... Hull, QC
Raymond Chabot HR Inc .... Montréal, QC
Raymond Chabot HR Inc .... Québec, QC
Recherches Johnson .... Saint-Lambert, QC
Renaud Foster Mgmnt .... Ottawa, ON
Research Associates .... Edmonton, AB
Resources Connection .... Toronto, ON
Results Management Canada .... Waterloo, ON
RHI Management Resources .... Calgary, AB
RHI Management Resources .... Toronto, ON
Richard Major & Assoc .... Toronto, ON
Richmark Group, The .... Toronto, ON
Richter Consulting .... Toronto, ON
Richter Usher Vineberg .... Montréal, QC
RJ Professionals .... Toronto, ON
RLP Consulting .... Mississauga, ON
Robert Half Canada .... Calgary, AB
Robert Half Canada .... Toronto, ON
Robert Half Canada .... Toronto, ON
Robert Half Canada .... Mississauga, ON
Robert Half Canada .... Ottawa, ON
Robert Half Financial .... Vancouver, BC
Robert L Holmes Placement .... Cambridge, ON
Robert R. Scurfield & Assoc .... Winnipeg, MB
Robertson Hancock Ltd .... Toronto, ON
Robertson Human Asset .... Burlington, ON
Robinson Fraser Group .... Toronto, ON
Rolfe, Benson .... Vancouver, BC
Roll Harris & Associates .... Montréal, QC
Rolland Groupe Conseil .... Westmount, QC
Rolland ressources humaines .... Montréal, QC
Rostie & Associates .... Toronto, ON
Russell & Associates .... Kelowna, BC
Russell Reynolds Assoc .... Toronto, ON
Rutherford Intl Exec Search .... Toronto, ON
RWJ & Associates .... Kitchener, ON
RWM Management Resources .... Calgary, AB
Sayler's Employment Consult .... Edmonton, AB
Scarrow & Donald .... Winnipeg, MB
Schlesinger Newman Goldman .... Montréal, QC
Schoales & Associates .... Toronto, ON
Schwartz Levitsky Feldman .... Toronto, ON
Schwartz Levitsky Feldman .... Montréal, QC
Scott Batenchuk & Co .... Burlington, ON
SearchCorp International .... Calgary, AB
Selection Group Mgmnt .... Mississauga, ON
Sheldon Resnick Associates .... Toronto, ON
Simpson McGrath Inc .... Winnipeg, MB
Smith Nixon & Co .... Toronto, ON
Smythe Ratcliffe .... Vancouver, BC
Snelgrove Personnel .... Hamilton, ON
Société Jean P. Brisebois .... Montréal, QC
Spencer Stuart .... Toronto, ON
Staff Bureau Employment .... Edmonton, AB
Star Search Consultants .... Toronto, ON
Stephen Ashley Associates .... Toronto, ON
Stevenson & White Inc .... Ottawa, ON
Storey & Associates .... Toronto, ON
Sydelle Associates .... Georgetown, ON
Symmetry Search Group .... Toronto, ON
Synagent Inc .... Woodlawn, ON
Systemsearch Consulting Svcs .... Toronto, ON
T.J. Seaton Management .... Calgary, AB
Tanaka Associates .... Toronto, ON
TAPP Consulting Svcs .... Merrickville, ON
Team Power Exec Search .... Markham, ON
Thomas & Dessain .... UNITED KINGDOM

Thomas E. Hedefine Assoc .... Toronto, ON
Thomas Group, The .... Mississauga, ON
Thompson Associates .... Halifax, NS
Thorek/Scott Partners .... Toronto, ON
TMP Worldwide Exec Search .... Toronto, ON
Tolfrey Group .... USA
Tolstoy Resources .... Bolton, ON
Toronto Exec Consultants .... Toronto, ON
Torstaff Personnel .... Toronto, ON
Tosi Placement Services .... Toronto, ON
Totten & Associates .... London, ON
Treat & Associates Executive .... Toronto, ON
Tretiak Holowka .... Montréal, QC
Turner Dickinson Partners .... Vancouver, BC
Ultimate Staffing .... Hamilton, ON
Van Biesen Group .... Calgary, AB
Van Hees Personnel .... Dundas, ON
Van Klaveren Litherland Co .... Toronto, ON
Venatus Conseil Ltée .... Montréal, QC
Verelli Arrizza .... Montréal, QC
Veres Picton & Co .... Edmonton, AB
Verriez Group Inc .... London, ON
Victor & Gold .... Montréal, QC
Vincent-Englehart Ltd .... Halifax, NS
W.H. Jackson Associates .... Toronto, ON
Wace & Assoc .... Mississauga, ON
Wade & Partners .... Burlington, ON
Walter P. Miller Company .... St. John's, NF
Wasserman Stotland Bratt .... Montréal, QC
Wayne Perry & Associates .... Toronto, ON
Wellington Partners Intl .... Kitchener, ON
Wenje Management Ltd .... Markham, ON
Western Mgmnt Consultants .... Vancouver, BC
Western Mgmnt Consultants .... Toronto, ON
Wilkie Group International .... Toronto, ON
Withey Addison .... Mississauga, ON
Wypich International .... Toronto, ON
Yves Elkas Inc .... Montréal, QC
Zeidel Gregory Associates .... Toronto, ON
Zenzen Pierce Assoc .... Toronto, ON

FORESTRY
SYLVICULTURE

A.W. Fraser Assoc .... Edmonton, AB
Adecco Canada .... Burnaby, BC
Berlys Personnel .... Saint-Laurent, QC
C.W. Clasen Recruiting .... Coquitlam, BC
Caldwell Partners .... Vancouver, BC
Christopher Vincent & Assoc .... Calgary, AB
Coast Personnel Svcs .... Nanaimo, BC
David Warwick Kennedy Assoc .... Vancouver, BC
Forest People Intl Search .... Vancouver, BC
G.L. Penney & Associates .... Edmonton, AB
Groupe LJL .... Pierrefonds, QC
Groupe Ranger .... Montréal, QC
Groupe Ressources DGO .... Trois-Rivières, QC
Norrell Staffing Services .... Vancouver, BC
Pinton Forrest & Madden .... Vancouver, BC
Professional Environment .... North Delta, BC
Ray Berndtson/Tanton .... Vancouver, BC
Robinson Assoc Personnel .... Vancouver, BC
Roevin Tech People .... North Vancouver, BC
Rolland Groupe Conseil .... Westmount, QC
Savage Consultants .... Vancouver, BC
Taylor Tomas Consulting .... Coquitlam, BC
Technisolutions Executive .... Aylmer, QC
Walsh King .... Vancouver, BC

FORESTRY (Cont.)
SYLVICULTURE (Suivre)

Widman Associates .... Vancouver, BC
Yves Plouffe et assoc .... Île-des-Soeurs, QC

FRANCHISING
FRANCHISE

Allen Austin Lowe & Powers .... USA
Coke & Associates .... Toronto, ON
Euro-West Consulting .... Vancouver, BC
FHG International .... Toronto, ON
People + ... Toronto, ON

GEOLOGY/GEOGRAPHY
GÉOLOGIE/GÉOGRAPHIE

Advantage Tech .... Calgary, AB
Allen Austin Lowe & Powers .... USA
Boyd PetroSearch .... Calgary, AB
Classic Consulting Group .... Calgary, AB
Conroy Partners .... Calgary, AB
Cosier Associates .... Calgary, AB
Cowan Personnel .... Montréal, QC
Davies Park .... Calgary, AB
Derkitt Herbert Exec Search .... Calgary, AB
Executive Resources Intl .... Montréal, QC
Genesis Corporate Search .... Calgary, AB
Horizon Resources Intl .... Calgary, AB
Interchange Personnel .... Calgary, AB
Jawaby Oil Service .... UNITED KINGDOM
Lawrence Assoc Exec Search .... Toronto, ON
Leader Search Inc .... Calgary, AB
MacRae Atwood Mgmnt .... Toronto, ON
Peter Glaser Assoc .... UNITED KINGDOM
Profile Search International .... Calgary, AB
Resource Professionals .... Calgary, AB
Roper and Assoc .... Calgary, AB
Russell Reynolds Assoc .... Calgary, AB
Ward Vinge & Associates .... Edmonton, AB
Ward Vinge & Associates .... Calgary, AB
Wolfer-Hale & Associates .... Calgary, AB
Woodridge Associates .... UNITED KINGDOM

GOVERNMENT & NONPROFIT
GOUVERNEMENT ET OSBL

A.O. Management Svcs .... Edmonton, AB
Adecco Canada .... Calgary, AB
Adecco Canada .... Ottawa, ON
Adecco Canada .... Ottawa, ON
Adecco Québec .... Chicoutimi, QC
Agence de personnel Abitibi .... Val-d'Or, QC
Al-Khaleej Computers .... SAUDI ARABIA
Altis Human Resources .... Toronto, ON
Associates Group .... Ottawa, ON
Association Mgmnt Consult .... Vancouver, BC
Association Resource Centre .... Toronto, ON
Association Strategy Group .... Ottawa, ON
Associum Consultants .... Toronto, ON
ATI Consulting Corp .... Halifax, NS
AZUR Ressources Humaines .... Hull, QC

Barcon Consulting Inc. .... New Hamburg, ON
Berkeley Consulting Group .... Markham, ON
Betty Steinhauer & Assoc .... Toronto, ON
Bradford Bachinski Ltd .... Ottawa, ON
Bridges Consulting .... Ottawa, ON
Caldwell Partners .... Vancouver, BC
Cathryn Lohrisch & Co .... Toronto, ON
Centre for Aboriginal HR .... Winnipeg, MB
CES & Associates .... Calgary, AB
Chancellor Partners .... Vancouver, BC
Chris Green & Assoc .... Vancouver, BC
CLA Personnel .... Ottawa, ON
Classified Canada .... Mississauga, ON
D.J. Macadam & Assoc .... North Vancouver, BC
Dana Stehr & Assoc .... Toronto, ON
Davies Park .... Edmonton, AB
Day Advertising Group .... Toronto, ON
Denise Walters & Assoc .... Edmonton, AB
DHR Canada .... Mississauga, ON
Diversified Staffing Svcs .... Edmonton, AB
Diversified Staffing Svcs .... Calgary, AB
Dotemtex Executive Search .... Sillery, QC
Ducharme Group .... Toronto, ON
Dymar Mgmnt Consultants .... Mississauga, ON
Excel HR Consultants .... Toronto, ON
Excel Human Resources .... Ottawa, ON
Excel Personnel .... Kamloops, BC
Execusearch .... Lethbridge, AB
Executive Source .... Regina, SK
Geddes Jefferson & Assoc .... Victoria, BC
Genesis Group .... Yellowknife, NT
Genovese Vanderhoof & Assoc .... Toronto, ON
Global Recruitment Specialists .... USA
GR Search Inc .... Toronto, ON
GSI International Consult .... Toronto, ON
Hawn & Associates .... Sault Ste. Marie, ON
Heidrick & Struggles Canada .... Toronto, ON
Heidrick & Struggles Canada .... Montréal, QC
Herman Smith Search Inc .... Toronto, ON
Human Resource Group Mgmnt .... Edmonton, AB
Hunt Technical Personnel .... Ottawa, ON
Hutchinson Group .... Toronto, ON
ICAP Management Inc .... Fredericton, NB
InGenius Engineering Inc .... Ottawa, ON
InterSearch Canada/Corso .... Toronto, ON
InterSearch Canada/Western .... Vancouver, BC
James E. Thomas & Assoc .... London, ON
Janet Wright & Associates .... Toronto, ON
Kelly Professional & Tech .... Ottawa, ON
Korn/Ferry Intl .... Vancouver, BC
KPMG Executive Search .... IRELAND
Level A Inc .... Peterborough, ON
Levert Personnel Resources .... Timmins, ON
Levert Personnel Resources .... Sudbury, ON
Lewis Companies .... Toronto, ON
Lobo Consulting Svcs .... Mississauga, ON
M.E. Money & Associates .... Toronto, ON
Macdonald & Brisson Personnel .... Ottawa, ON
MacGregor Rae Management .... Lethbridge, AB
Management Connections Inc .... Vancouver, BC
Mandrake Mgmnt Consult .... Toronto, ON
Marberg & Associates .... Toronto, ON
Maureen Sinden Exec Search .... Ottawa, ON
McKinnon Mgmnt Group .... Toronto, ON
Michael Follett Consulting .... Kitchener, ON
NCR Associates .... Ottawa, ON
Netgain Partners Inc .... Toronto, ON
NonProfit Career Quest .... Fergus, ON
People Bank, The .... Ottawa, ON

GOVERNMENT & NONPROFIT(Cont.)
GOUVERNEMENT ET OSBL (Suivre)

Personnel Outaouais	Hull, QC
PME Partenaire Consult	Saint-Georges, QC
Pollack Group, The	Ottawa, ON
Pommen & Associates	Edmonton, AB
PricewaterhouseCoopers	Edmonton, AB
PricewaterhouseCoopers	Calgary, AB
PricewaterhouseCoopers	Halifax, NS
Professional Environment	North Delta, BC
Provence Consulting	Vancouver, BC
Publicité Day	Montréal, QC
Ray Berndtson/Lovas Stanley	Toronto, ON
Ray & Berndtson/Robertson	Ottawa, ON
Ray & Berndtson/Robertson	Halifax, NS
Ray Berndtson/Tanton	Vancouver, BC
RCM Technologies	Mississauga, ON
Renaud Foster Mgmnt	Ottawa, ON
Rennick Hoppe Associates	Toronto, ON
Resource Concepts	St. John's, NF
Robert Half Canada	Ottawa, ON
Robert W. Dingman Company	USA
Russell Reynolds Assoc	AUSTRALIA
Search Company, The	Toronto, ON
Shared Vision Mgmt Search	Toronto, ON
Slaney Mgmnt Consulting	Simcoe, ON
SMC Management Services	Ottawa, ON
SOLUTIONS	Cornwall, ON
Southwest HR Centre	Regina, SK
Spherion Workforce	Victoria, BC
Spherion Workforce	Vancouver, BC
Spherion Workforce	Edmonton, AB
Spherion Workforce	Edmonton, AB
Spherion Workforce	Calgary, AB
Spherion Workforce	Winnipeg, MB
Spherion Workforce	Toronto, ON
Spherion Workforce	Toronto, ON
Spherion Workforce	Toronto, ON
Spherion Workforce	Toronto, ON
Spherion Workforce	Hamilton, ON
Spherion Workforce	Mississauga, ON
Spherion Workforce	Mississauga, ON
Spherion Workforce	Barrie, ON
Spherion Workforce	Pickering, ON
Spherion Workforce	Whitby, ON
Spherion Workforce	Oshawa, ON
Spherion Workforce	Kanata, ON
Spherion Workforce	Ottawa, ON
Spherion Workforce	Ottawa, ON
Spherion Workforce	Montréal, QC
Stephen Goldstein Associates	Ottawa, ON
Systemsearch Consulting Svcs	Toronto, ON
TAPP Consulting Svcs	Merrickville, ON
Taylor Personnel	Victoria, BC
TDR Human Resource Svcs	Regina, SK
Thompson Associates	Halifax, NS
Thompson Resources	Niagara-on-the-Lake, ON
Vincent-Englehart Ltd	Halifax, NS
W.R. London Consultants	Toronto, ON
Wace & Assoc	Mississauga, ON
Walbrook Appointment England	Toronto, ON
Watson Wyatt Worldwide	Vancouver, BC
Watson Wyatt Worldwide	Toronto, ON
Westcott Thomas Assoc	Toronto, ON
Western Mgmnt Consultants	Edmonton, AB

GRAPHIC ARTS
DESSIN GRAPHIQUE

Aquent Partners	Vancouver, BC
Aquent Partners	Toronto, ON
Aquent Partners	Montréal, QC
Chad Management Group	Toronto, ON
CLA Personnel	Ottawa, ON
Creative Force Network	Toronto, ON
Dial A-1 Resources	Toronto, ON
First Choice Personnel	Toronto, ON
Fred Litman & Associates	Toronto, ON
Freelancers Unlimited	Toronto, ON
Grapevine Exec Recruiters	Toronto, ON
Graphic Assistants	Toronto, ON
In Place Select Recruitment	Toronto, ON
Interim Mgmt Resources	Mississauga, ON
LTV & Associates	Toronto, ON
Shared Vision Mgmt Search	Toronto, ON
Stokes Associates	Pickering, ON

HEALTH & MEDICAL
SANTÉ ET MÉDICAL

A.R. Beadle Assoc	Kelowna, BC
Adecco Canada	Victoria, BC
Adecco LPI	Saint-Laurent, QC
AES Recruitment	Toronto, ON
AIME Consultants	Vancouver, BC
All Health Svcs	Toronto, ON
Alumni-Network Recruit	Mississauga, ON
Applied Mgmnt Consultants	Toronto, ON
Applied Mgmnt Consultants	Fredericton, NB
Arabian Careers	UNITED KINGDOM
Aramco Services Company	USA
ATI Consulting Corp	Halifax, NS
BC Health Services	Vancouver, BC
BDO Dunwoody LLP	Winnipeg, MB
Beresford Blake Thomas	UNITED KINGDOM
Botrie Associates	Toronto, ON
Bradson Home Health Care	Kanata, ON
Bradson Home Health Care	Ottawa, ON
Bradson Home Health Care	Gloucester, ON
Brethet Barnum Associates	Toronto, ON
Brock Placement Group	Toronto, ON
C.G. Thomson & Co	Toronto, ON
C.N. Taylor Consulting	Bedford, NS
Campbell Morden Inc	Toronto, ON
Canadian Exec Consultants	Toronto, ON
Canadian Medical Placement	London, ON
Canadian Nurse & Physician	Kitchener, ON
CanMed Consultants	Mississauga, ON
CLA Personnel	Ottawa, ON
ComFact Corp	Oakville, ON
Comidic Inc	Montréal, QC
Connors Lovell Assoc	Cambridge, ON
Connors Lovell Assoc	Mississauga, ON
Corporate Consultants	Toronto, ON
Corporate HR Communicat	Winnipeg, MB
Courtney Personnel	Brampton, ON
Croden Personnel	Vancouver, BC
Cross Country TravCorps	USA
Dana Stehr & Assoc	Toronto, ON
Dare Human Resources	Ottawa, ON
Davies Park	Edmonton, AB
Davies Park	Calgary, AB

HEALTH / MEDICAL (Cont.)
SANTÉ / MÉDICAL(Suivre)

HOSPITALITY
HOSPITALITÉ

HOSPITALITY (Cont.)
HOSPITALITÉ (Suivre)

Decisionaide Canada	Magog, QC
Execusearch	Lethbridge, AB
Executive Network	Victoria, BC
FHG International	Toronto, ON
Glazin / Sisco Exec Search	Vancouver, BC
Glazin / Sisco Exec Search	Toronto, ON
Global Hospitality Search	Mississauga, ON
Global Hospitality Search	Montréal, QC
Global Hospitality Search	Halifax, NS
Global Hospitality Search	USA
Grant Thornton Intl	Victoria, BC
Groupe Conseil Stante	Saint-Léonard, QC
Harcourt & Assoc	Edmonton, AB
Harcourt & Assoc	Calgary, AB
Harcourt Matthews Group	Edmonton, AB
Hospitality Canada Inc	Toronto, ON
Hospitality Personnel	Toronto, ON
Hotel & Restaurant Mgmnt	Toronto, ON
Houston Personnel Group	Winnipeg, MB
Hunter International Exec	Toronto, ON
Ian Scott & Associates	Mississauga, ON
Jankar Human Resources	Burlington, ON
Kelly Professional & Tech	Windsor, ON
Konkin & Associates	Edmonton, AB
Lecours Wolfson Ltd	Toronto, ON
Michael Stern Associates	Toronto, ON
Moon Over Niagara	St. Catharines, ON
Muskoka Staffing Co	Bracebridge, ON
Nationwide Advertising Svc	Vancouver, BC
Peapell & Associates	Halifax, NS
Personnel Clé	Québec, QC
Personnel Search	Saint John, NB
Personnel Search	Moncton, NB
PME Partenaire Consult	Saint-Georges, QC
PricewaterhouseCoopers	Regina, SK
Probank Services	Mississauga, ON
Quantum, Les services	Laval, QC
Quest Exec Recruitment	Toronto, ON
Renard Hospitality Search	Toronto, ON
RJ Professionals	Toronto, ON
Technology Plus	BAHRAIN
Thomson Tremblay Inc	Montréal, QC
Towngate Personnel	UNITED KINGDOM
Travel Jobs	Toronto, ON
Western HR Consulting	Calgary, AB

HUMAN RESOURCE
RESSOURCES HUMAINES

500 Services de Selection	Val-d'Or, QC
A.W. Fraser Assoc	Edmonton, AB
Abecassis recherches cadres	Montréal, QC
Accountemps Financial	Vancouver, BC
Accountemps Financial	Surrey, BC
Accountemps Financial	Edmonton, AB
Accountemps Financial	Calgary, AB
Accountemps Financial	Winnipeg, MB
Accountemps Financial	Toronto, ON
Accountemps Financial	Toronto, ON
Accountemps Financial	Burlington, ON
Accountemps Financial	Mississauga, ON
Accountemps Financial	Markham, ON
Accountemps Financial	Ottawa, ON
Accountemps Financial	Montréal, QC
Action Info-Travail	Mont-Laurier, QC

Adecco Canada	Edmonton, AB
Adecco Canada	Calgary, AB
Adecco Canada	Saskatoon, SK
Adecco Canada	Regina, SK
Adecco Canada	Toronto, ON
Adecco Canada	Ottawa, ON
Adecco LPI	Saint-Laurent, QC
Adecco Québec	Longueuil, QC
Adecco Québec	Chicoutimi, QC
Adecco Québec	Québec, QC
Adirect Recruiting Corp	Toronto, ON
Advantage Tech	Calgary, AB
AES Recruitment	Toronto, ON
Al-Khaleej Computers	SAUDI ARABIA
Altura Group	Toronto, ON
Andrew Duncan Assoc	UNITED KINGDOM
Apple One Employment	Toronto, ON
Ashlar-Stone Consultants	Mississauga, ON
Associum Consultants	Toronto, ON
AT Kearney Executive	Toronto, ON
Audax Corporation	Toronto, ON
Austin Marlowe Intl	Toronto, ON
Axxes Technologies	Sillery, QC
Barry Blostein Recruitment	Thornhill, ON
Bertrand Elbaz C.R.H.	Montréal, QC
Bilingual Source	Toronto, ON
Bill Kellie Consulting	Norwich, ON
Booth International Mgmnt	Toronto, ON
Bourassa Brodeur Assoc	Trois-Rivières, QC
Boyden Global Exec Search	Calgary, AB
Bradford Bachinski Ltd	Ottawa, ON
Brainhunter.com	Toronto, ON
Brainhunter.com	Ottawa, ON
Brant & Associates	Winnipeg, MB
Braun-Valley Associates	Sarnia, ON
Bray Larouche et Assoc	Montréal, QC
Bruce Ward Partners	Toronto, ON
Bryan Jason Assoc	Toronto, ON
Burke Group	Hamilton, ON
Burke Group	St. Catharines, ON
C.G. Thomson & Co	Toronto, ON
C. Price & Associates	Toronto, ON
C. Stevenson Consult	Pointe-Claire, QC
C.W. Clasen Recruiting	Coquitlam, BC
Cadman Consulting Group	Vancouver, BC
Caldwell Partners	Vancouver, BC
Caldwell Partners	Calgary, AB
Cameron Mgmnt Svcs	Edmonton, AB
Cameron Mgmnt Svcs	Calgary, AB
Campbell Clark Inc	Mississauga, ON
Campbell Edgar Inc	Richmond, BC
Campbell Edgar Inc	Delta, BC
Canadian Exec Consultants	Toronto, ON
Canpro Executive Search	Markham, ON
Career Path Personnel	Toronto, ON
Catherine Thomas Partners	Toronto, ON
Cathryn Lohrisch & Co	Toronto, ON
CCG Mgmnt Consultants	Mississauga, ON
Centrex HR Centre	Hamilton, ON
Chapman & Associates	Vancouver, BC
Cheryl Craig Careers	Burlington, ON
Chisholm & Partners Intl	Toronto, ON
Christopher Vincent & Assoc	Calgary, AB
Churchill Group, The	Toronto, ON
Claude Guedj Assoc	Montréal, QC
CM Inc	Markham, ON
Coe & Company Intl	Calgary, AB
Coke & Associates	Toronto, ON
CompuForce Inc	Calgary, AB
Connectstaff Solutions	Calgary, AB

HUMAN RESOURCE (Cont.)
RESSOURCES HUMAINES (Suivre)

Connors Lovell Assoc .... Cambridge, ON
Connors Lovell Assoc .... Mississauga, ON
Conseillers en Admin FORMA .... Montréal, QC
Core-Staff Inc. .... Toronto, ON
Corporate Expressions .... Toronto, ON
Corporate HR Communicat .... Winnipeg, MB
Cowan Personnel .... Montréal, QC
Cyberna Associates .... Montréal, QC
D.R. Nolan Assoc .... Toronto, ON
Danek Anthony Inc .... White Rock, BC
Danek Anthony Inc .... Toronto, ON
Danette Milne Corp Search .... Markham, ON
David Aplin & Assoc .... Calgary, AB
Davies Park .... Edmonton, AB
Davies Park .... Calgary, AB
Delorme et Assoc .... Québec, QC
DHR Canada .... Mississauga, ON
Dion Mgmnt Exec Search .... Toronto, ON
Dion Mgmnt Groupe Conseil .... Montréal, QC
Dion Mgmnt Groupe Conseil .... Sainte-Foy, QC
Dotemtex Executive Search .... Montréal, QC
Drake Executive .... Toronto, ON
Drake International .... Edmonton, AB
Drake International .... Montréal, QC
Drakkar Human Resources .... Mississauga, ON
Drakkar Human Resources .... Saint-Laurent, QC
Driver Carrier Placement .... Toronto, ON
Ducharme Group .... Toronto, ON
Dumont & Associates .... North Vancouver, BC
E.H. Scissons & Associates .... Saskatoon, SK
E.L. Shore & Associates .... Toronto, ON
E-Search Consulting .... Toronto, ON
Enns Hever Inc .... Toronto, ON
Erie Personnel Corp .... Thorold, ON
Erie Personnel Corp .... Fort Erie, ON
Ernst & Young .... SAUDI ARABIA
Everest Mgmnt Network .... Toronto, ON
Excel Personnel .... Kamloops, BC
ExecuCounsel Inc .... Toronto, ON
Executive Network .... Victoria, BC
Executive Source .... Regina, SK
Executives Available .... Pointe-Claire, QC
Executrade Consultants .... Edmonton, AB
Express Personnel Svcs .... Port Coquitlam, BC
Express Personnel Svcs .... Windsor, ON
Express Personnel Svcs .... London, ON
Express Personnel Svcs .... Kitchener, ON
Express Personnel Svcs .... Guelph, ON
Express Personnel Svcs .... Hamilton, ON
Express Personnel Svcs .... Burlington, ON
Express Personnel Svcs .... Ottawa, ON
FCM Inc .... Montréal, QC
Feldman Gray Associates .... Toronto, ON
Fifth Option .... Burnaby, BC
First Choice Personnel .... Toronto, ON
First Step Recruitment .... Toronto, ON
Friday Personnel Inc .... Vancouver, BC
Friday Personnel Inc .... Calgary, AB
G-P Personnel .... Chicoutimi, QC
GAAP Inc .... Montréal, QC
Gallant Search Group .... London, ON
Gaudry Shink Levasseur .... Montréal, QC
Gauthier Conseils .... Montréal, QC
Geode Consulting Group .... Vancouver, BC
Gerald Walsh Recruitment .... Halifax, NS
Girardin & Associates .... Winnipeg, MB
Glazin / Sisco Exec Search .... Vancouver, BC

Glazin / Sisco Exec Search .... Toronto, ON
Glen Abbey Exec Search .... Oakville, ON
Godbout Martin Godbout Assoc .... Hull, QC
Goldbeck Recruiting .... Vancouver, BC
Golden Mile Mgmnt Consulting .... Toronto, ON
GR Search Inc .... Toronto, ON
Graduate Consulting Svcs .... Montréal, QC
GRH Consultants Inc .... Québec, QC
Group Four Mgmnt Consultants .... Toronto, ON
Groupe conseil Lamarche .... Granby, QC
Hamilton & Sherwood Employment .... USA
Hayhurst Consulting .... London, ON
HaysZMB .... UNITED KINGDOM
He@d2Head.com Inc .... Toronto, ON
HEC Group .... Ancaster, ON
Herman Smith Search Inc .... Toronto, ON
High Road Personnel .... Burlington, ON
Higher Vision Recruitment .... Toronto, ON
Holloway Schulz & Partners .... Vancouver, BC
Houston Personnel Group .... Winnipeg, MB
HR Business Partners .... Calgary, AB
HR / RH Inc. .... Montréal, QC
Human Edge Consulting .... Richmond Hill, ON
Human Resource Mgmt Group .... Unionville, ON
Human Resources Consult .... Mississauga, ON
In Place Select Recruitment .... Toronto, ON
InGenius Engineering Inc .... Ottawa, ON
Interim Plus .... Granby, QC
Intermark Mgmt Inc. .... Mississauga, ON
InterSearch Canada/Lennox .... Calgary, AB
InterSearch Canada/Western .... Vancouver, BC
J.O. Bush & Associates .... Mindemoya, ON
James Boyce Associates .... Toronto, ON
James E. Thomas & Assoc .... London, ON
Janet Wright & Associates .... Toronto, ON
Job Born Candidate Select .... Hamilton, ON
Keith-Murray Partners .... Toronto, ON
Kelly Permanent Recruit .... Toronto, ON
Kelly Permanent Recruit .... Toronto, ON
Kelly Permanent Recruit .... Mississauga, ON
Kelly Professional & Tech .... Windsor, ON
Kelly Professional & Tech .... Kitchener, ON
Key Executive Consultants .... Barrie, ON
Key Executive Consultants .... Pickering, ON
Kforce.ca .... Toronto, ON
Kitchener Exec Consultants .... Kitchener, ON
Korn/Ferry Intl .... Vancouver, BC
Korn/Ferry Intl .... Montréal, QC
Lawrence Assoc Exec Search .... Toronto, ON
Lewis Companies .... Toronto, ON
Little Group, The .... Brantford, ON
Little Group, The .... Burlington, ON
London Executive Consultants .... London, ON
Luccie Domingue et assoc .... Sherbrooke, QC
Lynx Career Consultants .... Mississauga, ON
M.E. Money & Associates .... Toronto, ON
MacKenzie Gray Mgmnt .... Calgary, AB
Maclean & Assoc .... Mississauga, ON
MacRae Atwood Mgmnt .... Toronto, ON
Management Solutions .... Mississauga, ON
Manpower Professional .... Markham, ON
Marlene Bilodeau Conseils .... Chicoutimi, QC
Matteson Management .... Toronto, ON
MBL Group LLC .... USA
McDonald-Green Personnel .... Cambridge, ON
McIntyre Mgmnt Resources .... Hamilton, ON
McKinnon Groupe Conseil .... Montréal, QC
MultiPersonnel International .... Dorval, QC
NCR Associates .... Ottawa, ON
Newfoundland Personnel .... St. John's, NF

HUMAN RESOURCE (Cont.)
RESSOURCES HUMAINES (Suivre)

NewSource Management .... Toronto, ON
Osborne Group .... Vancouver, BC
Osborne Group .... Calgary, AB
Osborne Group .... Edmonton, AB
Osborne Group .... Toronto, ON
Osborne Group .... Montréal, QC
Ottawa Valley Personnel .... Pembroke, ON
P.R.Y. .... Toronto, ON
Pace Personnel Ltd .... Vancouver, BC
Palmer & Associates .... Kingston, ON
Partners in Search .... Toronto, ON
Partnervision Consulting .... Toronto, ON
Paziuk Professional Placements .... Edmonton, AB
People + ... Toronto, ON
People Bank, The .... Ottawa, ON
People Management Group .... Woodstock, ON
PeopleFind Inc. .... Markham, ON
Permanent Search Group .... Mississauga, ON
Permanent Solutions .... Mississauga, ON
Personnel Alter Ego .... Pointe-Claire, QC
Personnel Alter Ego .... Montréal, QC
Personnel Clé .... Québec, QC
Personnel Search .... Saint John, NB
Personnel Search .... Moncton, NB
Phoenix Search Group .... Toronto, ON
Placement Group Personnel .... Edmonton, AB
PricewaterhouseCoopers .... Winnipeg, MB
PricewaterhouseCoopers .... London, ON
PricewaterhouseCoopers .... Hamilton, ON
PricewaterhouseCoopers .... Québec, QC
PricewaterhouseCoopers .... Saint John, NB
PricewaterhouseCoopers .... Halifax, NS
Prichard Kymen Inc .... Edmonton, AB
Prime Management Group .... London, ON
Prime Management Group .... Cambridge, ON
Professional Develop Assoc .... Oakville, ON
Prokosch Group, The .... Calgary, AB
Prospects Plus .... Kirkland, QC
Prud'Homme Groupe-Conseil .... Montréal, QC
Quantum .... Montréal, QC
Quantum, Les services .... Longueuil, QC
Quantum, Les services .... Pointe-Claire, QC
Quantum Mgmnt Services .... Toronto, ON
Quantum Mgmnt Services .... Mississauga, ON
Quest Exec Recruitment .... Toronto, ON
Ray & Berndtson/Laurendeau .... Montréal, QC
Ray Berndtson/Tanton .... Vancouver, BC
Recherches Johnson .... Saint-Lambert, QC
Research Associates .... Edmonton, AB
Resource Management Group .... Toronto, ON
Results Management Canada .... Waterloo, ON
Richter & Richter HR .... Palgrave, ON
Robert R. Scurfield & Assoc .... Winnipeg, MB
Robertson Hancock Ltd .... Toronto, ON
Rolland Groupe Conseil .... Westmount, QC
Rolland ressources humaines .... Montréal, QC
Rossi & Associates .... Vancouver, BC
RWJ & Associates .... London, ON
RWJ & Associates .... Kitchener, ON
Savage Consultants .... Vancouver, BC
Simpson McGrath Inc .... Winnipeg, MB
Société Jean P. Brisebois .... Montréal, QC
Spencer Stuart .... Montréal, QC
SPI Executive Search .... Ottawa, ON
Stephen Goldstein Associates .... Ottawa, ON
Summit Personnel Services .... Windsor, ON
Synergies res humaine .... Trois-Rivières, QC

Syntech Placements .... Toronto, ON
TAG Personnel Consultants .... Montréal, QC
TAPP Consulting Svcs .... Merrickville, ON
Taylor Tomas Consulting .... Coquitlam, BC
Technical Service Consult .... Toronto, ON
Thompson Associates .... Halifax, NS
Thomson Tremblay Inc .... Montréal, QC
Tolfrey Group .... USA
Torstaff Personnel .... Toronto, ON
Totten & Associates .... London, ON
Ultimate Staffing .... Hamilton, ON
Van Hees Personnel .... Dundas, ON
Wace & Assoc .... Mississauga, ON
Watson Wyatt Worldwide .... Vancouver, BC
Watson Wyatt Worldwide .... Toronto, ON
Western Mgmnt Consultants .... Vancouver, BC
Wynne Chisholm Associates .... Calgary, AB
Yves Elkas Inc .... Montréal, QC
Zen Zen International .... Winnipeg, MB

INSURANCE
ASSURANCE

Adecco Canada .... London, ON
Adecco Canada .... Kitchener, ON
AMAC Consultants .... Vancouver, BC
Associates Group .... Ottawa, ON
Austin Park Mgmnt Group .... Toronto, ON
Ayrshire Group .... Toronto, ON
Bilingual Source .... Toronto, ON
Bongard Marsh Assoc .... Toronto, ON
Bray Larouche et Assoc .... Montréal, QC
C. Scott & Associates .... Toronto, ON
Cadillac Career Centre .... Toronto, ON
Campbell Morden Inc .... Toronto, ON
Coffey & Associates .... Hamilton, ON
Conestoga Personnel .... Kitchener, ON
Conlin Personnel .... Vancouver, BC
Corporate Recruiters .... Toronto, ON
Cowan Wright Ltd .... Waterloo, ON
D.C. Powers & Assoc .... Vancouver, BC
Delta Management Options .... Toronto, ON
Descheneaux Recruitment .... Vancouver, BC
Devonwood Partners .... Mississauga, ON
Donald Givelos & Assoc .... Toronto, ON
Duncan & Associates .... Toronto, ON
Dynamic Employment Solution .... Brampton, ON
Dynamic Employment Solution .... Brampton, ON
Emplois plus pre-sélection .... Lasalle, QC
ExecuCounsel Inc .... Toronto, ON
Feldman Gray Associates .... Toronto, ON
First Choice Personnel .... Toronto, ON
GAAP Inc .... Montréal, QC
George Stewart Consultants .... Toronto, ON
Global Personnel .... Toronto, ON
GRH Consultants Inc .... Québec, QC
Harcourt & Assoc .... Edmonton, AB
Harcourt & Assoc .... Calgary, AB
Harris Consulting Corp .... Winnipeg, MB
Heale & Associates .... Toronto, ON
Impact Staffing .... Windsor, ON
Insurance Consulting Group .... Toronto, ON
Insurance Overload Systems .... Toronto, ON
Insurance Overload Systems .... USA
InsuranceWorks.com .... Toronto, ON
James Partnership .... BERMUDA
Joanne Starr Consultants .... Toronto, ON
Job Born Candidate Select .... Hamilton, ON

INSURANCE (Cont.)
ASSURANCE (Suivre)

INTERNATIONAL
INTERNATIONAL

INTERNATIONAL (Cont.)
INTERNATIONAL (Suivre)

INTERNATIONAL (Cont.)
INTERNATIONAL (Suivre)

Ray & Berndtson .... DENMARK
Ray & Berndtson .... USA
RBA Intl HR Consultants .... Westmount, QC
Recruitment International .... UNITED KINGDOM
Resource Professionals .... Calgary, AB
RHI Consulting .... USA
Robert Connelly & Associates .... USA
Robert W. Dingman Company .... USA
Rostie & Associates .... USA
Rostie & Associates .... USA
Rudl International .... Ottawa, ON
Russell Reynolds Assoc .... AUSTRALIA
Russell Reynolds Assoc .... FRANCE
Russell Reynolds Assoc .... SINGAPORE
Russell Reynolds Assoc .... SPAIN
Russell Reynolds Assoc .... USA
Rutherford Intl Exec Search .... Toronto, ON
SAI Software Consultants .... Toronto, ON
SAI Software Consultants .... USA
SAI Software Consultants .... USA
Scientific Placement .... USA
Search Associates .... Belleville, ON
Search Justified Selection .... Toronto, ON
Servocraft Limited .... Toronto, ON
Shared Vision Mgmt Search .... Toronto, ON
Sherwood Engineer Recruit .... UNITED KINGDOM
Simon-Tech Inc .... Montréal, QC
Skott/Edwards Consult .... USA
Société Jean P. Brisebois .... Montréal, QC
Spencer Stuart .... BRAZIL
Spencer Stuart .... CHINA
Spencer Stuart .... GERMANY
Spencer Stuart .... ITALY
Spencer Stuart .... USA
Spencer Stuart .... USA
Squires Resources .... Barrie, ON
Staffing Strategies .... USA
Stephen Goldstein Associates .... Ottawa, ON
Sterling Hoffman .... USA
Stone Legal Resources Group .... USA
Susan Craig Associates .... Toronto, ON
Syntech Placements .... Toronto, ON
T.J. Seaton Management .... Calgary, AB
Talent Consulting Services .... USA
TalentLab .... USA
TAPP Consulting Svcs .... Merrickville, ON
Taylor Recruitment .... UNITED KINGDOM
Taylor Root .... UNITED KINGDOM
TaylorMade Careers .... USA
Tech-Pro Inc .... USA
Techaid Inc .... Montréal, QC
Technical Connections Inc .... USA
Technical Solutions Inc .... USA
Technisource .... USA
Technology Plus .... BAHRAIN
Tekmark Computer Services .... USA
Teknica (UK) Ltd .... UNITED KINGDOM
TES Employment Solution .... USA
TES Employment Solution .... USA
Thinkpath.com Inc .... USA
Thinkpath.com Inc .... USA
Thomas & Dessain .... UNITED KINGDOM
Thomas Mining Associates .... UNITED KINGDOM
Tolfrey Group .... USA
Towngate Personnel .... UNITED KINGDOM
TPS Unimecs .... THE NETHERLANDS
Track International Ltd .... UNITED KINGDOM

Treat & Associates Executive .... Toronto, ON
Tri-Tec International Resources .... USA
Trillium Talent Resource .... Cambridge, ON
TriNet Employment Group .... USA
Van Biesen Group .... Calgary, AB
VEGA Consulting Solutions .... USA
Verriez Group Inc .... London, ON
Walker Forest .... USA
William Squibb Associates .... Kitchener, ON
Wolverine Technical Services .... USA
Woodridge Associates .... UNITED KINGDOM
Worldwide Healthcare .... Vancouver, BC
ZSA Legal Recruitment .... USA

LAW
DROIT

Advocate Placement .... Toronto, ON
Advocate Placement .... Markham, ON
Affiliates, The .... Calgary, AB
Affiliates, The .... Toronto, ON
Affiliates, The .... Ottawa, ON
Affiliates, The .... Montréal, QC
Allen Austin Lowe & Powers .... USA
Apple Management Corp .... Toronto, ON
Applicant Testing Services .... London, ON
Associates Group .... Ottawa, ON
Baldwin Staffing Group .... Calgary, AB
Barr Legal Personnel .... Toronto, ON
Bruce Ward Partners .... Toronto, ON
Caldwell Partners .... Calgary, AB
Cameron Mgmnt Svcs .... Edmonton, AB
Cameron Mgmnt Svcs .... Calgary, AB
Cartel Inc .... Toronto, ON
Catalyst Consulting .... Vancouver, BC
Catalyst Consulting .... Toronto, ON
Catalyst Consulting .... Montréal, QC
Counsel Network .... Vancouver, BC
Counsel Network .... Calgary, AB
Counsel Network .... USA
Dare Human Resources .... Ottawa, ON
Diversified Staffing Svcs .... Edmonton, AB
Diversified Staffing Svcs .... Calgary, AB
Doré Liaison .... Greenfield Park, QC
Employer's Choice .... Brampton, ON
Employment Partnership .... Saint John, NB
Excel Personnel .... Kamloops, BC
Executive Registry .... Montréal, QC
Gerald Walsh Recruitment .... Halifax, NS
Gibson Kennedy & Company .... Toronto, ON
Global Personnel .... Toronto, ON
Group Four Mgmnt Consultants .... Toronto, ON
Gruber Associates .... Orleans, ON
GSG Partners .... Toronto, ON
HaysZMB .... UNITED KINGDOM
Heale & Associates .... Toronto, ON
Hoffman Legal Search .... USA
ICAP Management Inc .... Fredericton, NB
Jurissec Inc. .... Montréal, QC
Karabus Management .... Toronto, ON
Kathy Jackson Associates .... Vancouver, BC
Kenniff Denis Inc. .... Montréal, QC
Kent Legal Personnel .... Toronto, ON
Korn/Ferry Intl .... Vancouver, BC
Laura Reid & Associates .... Vancouver, BC
Legal Freelance Centre .... Vancouver, BC
Legal Personnel Consultants .... Toronto, ON
Life After Law .... Vancouver, BC

LAW (Cont.)
DROIT (Suivre)

Life After Law	Toronto, ON
Marberg & Associates	Toronto, ON
Marina Sirras & Associates	USA
Marsden Nagata Legal Search	Toronto, ON
McKinnon Groupe Conseil	Montréal, QC
Mestel & Company	USA
Options Personnel	Toronto, ON
Pace Personnel Ltd	Vancouver, BC
Personnel Alter Ego	Pointe-Claire, QC
Personnel Alter Ego	Montréal, QC
Pragmatizm	Toronto, ON
PricewaterhouseCoopers	Winnipeg, MB
RainMaker Group	Toronto, ON
Richmark Group, The	Toronto, ON
Robertson Hancock Ltd	Toronto, ON
Senac Personnel Services	Toronto, ON
Shore & Fitzwilliam	Montréal, QC
SOLUTIONS	Cornwall, ON
Spencer Stuart	Montréal, QC
Stone Legal Resources Group	USA
Systemsearch Consulting Svcs	Toronto, ON
Tanaka Associates	Toronto, ON
Taran Virtual Associates	London, ON
Taylor Root	UNITED KINGDOM
Thomas & Dessain	UNITED KINGDOM
Thompson Elliott Group	Toronto, ON
Thorek/Scott Partners	Toronto, ON
TMP QD Legal Recruitment	Toronto, ON
Todays Staffing Inc	Winnipeg, MB
Todays Staffing Inc	London, ON
Todays Staffing Inc	Brantford, ON
Todays Staffing Inc	Cambridge, ON
Todays Staffing Inc	Guelph, ON
Todays Staffing Inc	Toronto, ON
Todays Staffing Inc	Etobicoke, ON
Todays Staffing Inc	Toronto, ON
Todays Staffing Inc	Toronto, ON
Todays Staffing Inc	Hamilton, ON
Todays Staffing Inc	Burlington, ON
Todays Staffing Inc	Mississauga, ON
Walker-Davies Consultants	Vancouver, BC
ZSA Legal Recruitment	Vancouver, BC
ZSA Legal Recruitment	Calgary, AB
ZSA Legal Recruitment	Toronto, ON
ZSA Legal Recruitment	Montréal, QC
ZSA Legal Recruitment	USA

LIBRARIANS
BIBLIOTHÉCAIRES

Hunt Technical Personnel	Ottawa, ON
Miss Hall's Personnel Svcs	Ottawa, ON
Personnel Outaouais	Hull, QC
Phee Farrer Jones Ltd	UNITED KINGDOM
Records & Information Mgmnt	Toronto, ON

LOGISTICS
LOGISTIQUE

1st Choice Staffing	Mississauga, ON
Abecassis recherches cadres	Montréal, QC
Action Manutention Lasalle	Lasalle, QC
Adecco Québec	Longueuil, QC

Allen Austin Lowe & Powers	USA
Allen Personnel Svcs	London, ON
Alliance Personnel Group	Edmonton, AB
Alliance Personnel Group	Oakville, ON
Applicants Inc.	Kitchener, ON
Archer Resource Solutions	Mississauga, ON
Ashlar-Stone Consultants	Mississauga, ON
ATS Reliance Tech Group	London, ON
Barry Blostein Recruitment	Thornhill, ON
BMA International	Montréal, QC
BMA International	Montréal, QC
Braun-Valley Associates	Sarnia, ON
Buckley Search	Toronto, ON
Campbell Edgar Inc	Richmond, BC
Campbell Edgar Inc	Delta, BC
Can-Tech Services	Brooklin, ON
Can-Tech Services	Saint-Laurent, QC
Canadian Exec Recruitmnt	Mississauga, ON
Canadian Logistics Recruit	Burlington, ON
Canpro Executive Search	Markham, ON
CAPP Employment Svcs	Mississauga, ON
Christmas McIvor Assoc	Mississauga, ON
Cyberna Associates	Montréal, QC
Daniluck & Associates	Edmonton, AB
Derkitt Herbert Exec Search	Calgary, AB
Direct Career Concepts	Woodbridge, ON
Drakkar Human Resources	Mississauga, ON
Drakkar Human Resources	Montréal, QC
Drakkar Human Resources	Québec, QC
Driver Carrier Placement	Toronto, ON
Dynamic Employment Solution	Brampton, ON
Dynamic Employment Solution	Brampton, ON
E.L. Shore & Associates	Toronto, ON
ERP Staffing Solutions	Calgary, AB
ERP Staffing Solutions	Brampton, ON
Evans Search Group	Toronto, ON
Executive Source	Regina, SK
First Choice Personnel	Toronto, ON
G-Tech Professional Staffing	USA
GAAP Inc	Montréal, QC
Gallant Search Group	London, ON
Groves & Partners Intl	Mississauga, ON
Hallmark Personnel	Oakville, ON
Harris Consulting Corp	Winnipeg, MB
Hayhurst Consulting	London, ON
Herman Smith Search Inc	Toronto, ON
Hire Purpose	Burlington, ON
HR / RH Inc.	Montréal, QC
HT Search Company	Nepean, ON
HumanEtics Inc	Mississauga, ON
International Bus Partners	Toronto, ON
J.P. Anderson & Assoc	Burlington, ON
JSL Search Leaders	Toronto, ON
Kenniff Denis Inc.	Montréal, QC
Labour Source	Woodbridge, ON
Level A Inc	Peterborough, ON
M.J. Janssen Associates	Mississauga, ON
Martin Randolph Assoc	Montréal, QC
Megasearch International	Hudson, QC
Michael J. Cavanagh Assoc	Toronto, ON
Miller Recruitment Solutions	Halifax, NS
MPA Recherche de Cadres	Brossard, QC
Osborne Group	Vancouver, BC
Osborne Group	Calgary, AB
Osborne Group	Edmonton, AB
Osborne Group	Toronto, ON
Osborne Group	Montréal, QC
Permanent Solutions	Mississauga, ON
Personnel Mgmnt Group	Winnipeg, MB
Pila Recruiting & Assoc	Richmond, BC

LOGISTICS (Cont.)
LOGISTIQUE (Suivre)

Pioneer Exec Consultants .... Toronto, ON
ProTemps Canada .... Edmonton, AB
ProTemps Canada .... Calgary, AB
ProTemps Canada .... Toronto, ON
ProTemps Canada .... Mississauga, ON
Quantum Mgmt Services .... Toronto, ON
Quest Exec Recruitment .... Toronto, ON
RJK & Associates.. Markham, ON
Robert Lamarre & Assoc .... Saint-Lambert, QC
Robert T. Keegan & Assoc .... Oakville, ON
S. Tanner & Associates .... Oakville, ON
Spherion Workforce .... Brampton, ON
SSA Services Conseils .... Montréal, QC
Sydelle Associates .... Georgetown, ON
Symmetry Search Group .... Toronto, ON
Thomas Group, The .... Mississauga, ON
Transpersonnel Driver Staff .... Edmonton, AB
Transpersonnel Driver Staff .... Calgary, AB
Transpersonnel Driver Staff .... Brampton, ON
Trillium Talent Resource .... Toronto, ON
TSI Group / TSI Staffing .... Mississauga, ON
Van Hees Personnel .... Dundas, ON
Walker Forest .... USA
Wayne Perry & Associates .... Toronto, ON
Western HR Consulting .... Calgary, AB
Wilkie Group International .... Toronto, ON
Wolf Gugler & Associates .... Toronto, ON

MANAGEMENT
GESTION

500 Services de Selection .... Val-d'Or, QC
A. Lawrence Abrams Assoc .... Waterloo, ON
A.W. Fraser Assoc .... Edmonton, AB
A.W. Fraser Assoc .... Calgary, AB
Abecassis recherches cadres .... Montréal, QC
Abel Placement Consult............................... Markham, ON
Adecco Canada .... Edmonton, AB
Adecco Canada .... Calgary, AB
Adecco Canada .... Saskatoon, SK
Adecco Canada .... Regina, SK
Adecco Canada .... London, ON
Adecco Canada .... Kitchener, ON
Adecco Canada .... Toronto, ON
Adecco Canada .... Toronto, ON
Adecco Canada .... Ottawa, ON
Adecco Québec .... Chicoutimi, QC
Adecco Québec .... Québec, QC
Adirect Recruiting Corp .... Toronto, ON
Aim Personnel Svcs .... Ottawa, ON
Alan Davis Assoc .... Hudson Heights, QC
Aldonna Barry Mgmnt Consult .... Bolton, ON
Allen Austin Lowe & Powers .... USA
Allen Ballach Assoc .... Whitby, ON
Allen Etcovitch Assoc .... Montréal, QC
Allen Personnel Svcs .... London, ON
Andersen .... Vancouver, BC
Andersen .... Calgary, AB
Andersen .... Winnipeg, MB
Andersen .... Toronto, ON
Andersen .... Toronto, ON
Andersen .... Mississauga, ON
Andersen .... Ottawa, ON
Andersen .... Montmagny, QC

Andersen .... Sainte-Foy, QC
Anderson Associates .... Toronto, ON
Andrew Campbell Assoc .... Oakville, ON
Angus Employment .... Burlington, ON
Angus One Pro Recruitment .... Vancouver, BC
Apple Management Corp .... Toronto, ON
Applied Technology Solutions .... Toronto, ON
Argentus Inc. .... Toronto, ON
Ariel Group Intl .... Toronto, ON
Armitage Associates .... Vancouver, BC
Armitage Associates .... Toronto, ON
Armitage Associates .... Rosmere, QC
Aron Printz Assoc .... Vancouver, BC
Ashton Computer Pros .... North Vancouver, BC
Associates Group .... Ottawa, ON
Association Resource Centre .... Toronto, ON
AT Kearney Executive .... Toronto, ON
ATI Consulting Corp .... Halifax, NS
Audax Corporation .... Toronto, ON
Austin Marlowe Intl .... Toronto, ON
Axxes Technologies .... Sillery, QC
B.B. Consultants Group .... Point Edward, ON
Bailey Professional Search .... Calgary, AB
Baldock Associates .... Toronto, ON
Barrett Rose & Lee .... Toronto, ON
Bassett Laudi Partners .... Toronto, ON
BDO Dunwoody & Assoc .... Kitchener, ON
BDO Dunwoody LLP .... Winnipeg, MB
Becky Jones & Assoc .... Toronto, ON
Belanger Partners .... Thornhill, ON
Bernard Frigon & Assoc .... Montréal, QC
Bernhard Consulting .... Winnipeg, MB
Birch & Assoc .... Montréal, QC
Boscan Consultants .... Marysville, ON
Botrie Associates .... Toronto, ON
Bourassa Brodeur Assoc .... Trois-Rivières, QC
Bowen Staffing .... Calgary, AB
Bower Ng Staff Systems .... Vancouver, BC
Bradford Bachinski Ltd .... Ottawa, ON
Brant & Associates .... Winnipeg, MB
Bray Larouche et Assoc .... Montréal, QC
Brendan Wood International .... Toronto, ON
Brethet Barnum Associates .... Toronto, ON
Brock Placement Group .... Toronto, ON
Bruce Cowan Assoc .... Toronto, ON
Bruce Ward Partners .... Toronto, ON
Buckley Search .... Toronto, ON
Burke Group .... Hamilton, ON
Burke Group .... St. Catharines, ON
C.N. Taylor Consulting .... Bedford, NS
C.W. Clasen Recruiting .... Coquitlam, BC
Cadillac Career Centre .... Toronto, ON
Caldwell Intl., La Societé .... Montréal, QC
Caldwell Partners .... Vancouver, BC
Caldwell Partners .... Calgary, AB
Caldwell Partners .... Toronto, ON
CAMPA & Associates .... Toronto, ON
Campbell Edgar Inc .... Richmond, BC
Campbell Edgar Inc .... Delta, BC
Campbell Morden Inc .... Toronto, ON
Canadian Exec Recruitmnt .... Mississauga, ON
Canatrade International .... Candiac, QC
Canpro Executive Search .... Markham, ON
CAPP Employment Svcs .... Mississauga, ON
Career Advance Employment .... Burlington, ON
Career Partners/Harrison .... Hamilton, ON
Carmichael Birrell & Co .... Toronto, ON
Cathryn Lohrisch & Co .... Toronto, ON
CCG Mgmnt Consultants .... Mississauga, ON
Central Mgmnt Consultants .... Toronto, ON

MANAGEMENT (Cont.)
GESTION (Suivre)

Centrex HR Centre	Hamilton, ON
Chacra Belliveau & Assoc	Montréal, QC
Chancellor Partners	Vancouver, BC
Chase Consultants	Mississauga, ON
Chisholm & Partners Intl	Toronto, ON
Christmas McIvor Assoc	Mississauga, ON
Churchill Group, The	Toronto, ON
Classified Canada	Mississauga, ON
Claude Guedj Assoc	Montréal, QC
CM Inc	Markham, ON
CMP Select	Toronto, ON
Coakwell Crawford Cairns	High River, AB
Coast Personnel Svcs	Nanaimo, BC
Coke & Associates	Toronto, ON
Compton Graham Intl	Toronto, ON
Comtech Prof Services	Windsor, ON
Connors Lovell Assoc	Mississauga, ON
Conroy Partners	Calgary, AB
Conseillers en Admin FORMA	Montréal, QC
Conseillers Jacques Cartier	Montréal, QC
ConsulPRO Executive Search	Ottawa, ON
Corporate Consultants	Toronto, ON
Courtney Personnel	Brampton, ON
Cowan Personnel	Montréal, QC
Cyr & Assoc	Campbellville, ON
D.J. Simpson Assoc	Mississauga, ON
D.P. Group, The	UNITED KINGDOM
D.R. Nolan Assoc	Toronto, ON
Dana Stehr & Assoc	Toronto, ON
Danek Anthony Inc	White Rock, BC
Danek Anthony Inc	Toronto, ON
Daniluck & Associates	Edmonton, AB
Datalist	Toronto, ON
David Aplin & Assoc	Calgary, AB
David Taylor Mfg Search	Toronto, ON
Davies Park	Edmonton, AB
Davies Park	Calgary, AB
Davis Daignault Schick & Co	Calgary, AB
Davitech Consulting	Calgary, AB
Day Advertising Group	Toronto, ON
Dean Tower & Associates	Ottawa, ON
Decisionaide Canada	Magog, QC
Deloitte Touche Tohmatsu	AUSTRALIA
Delorme et Assoc	Québec, QC
Derhak Ireland Partners	Toronto, ON
Design Group Staffing	Toronto, ON
Dial Staffing Solutions	Calgary, AB
Digital Power Corp	Calgary, AB
Dingle & Associates	Toronto, ON
Dion Mgmnt Groupe Conseil	Montréal, QC
Dion Mgmnt Groupe Conseil	Sainte-Foy, QC
Direct Career Concepts	Woodbridge, ON
Donald L Hart & Assoc	Toronto, ON
Donati & Associates	Maple, ON
Doré Liaison	Greenfield Park, QC
Drake Executive	Vancouver, BC
Drake Executive	Burnaby, BC
Drake Executive	Winnipeg, MB
Drake Executive	Sudbury, ON
Drake Executive	London, ON
Drake Executive	Toronto, ON
Drake Executive	Toronto, ON
Drake Executive	Montréal, QC
Drake International	Edmonton, AB
Drake International	North Bay, ON
Drake International	London, ON
Drake International	Toronto, ON

Drake International	Hamilton, ON
Drake International	Oakville, ON
Drake International	Barrie, ON
Drake International	Belleville, ON
Drake International	Kingston, ON
Drake International	Ottawa, ON
Drake International	Montréal, QC
Drake International	Québec, QC
Drake International	Moncton, NB
Drake International	Halifax, NS
Drakkar Human Resources	Saint-Laurent, QC
Ducharme Group	Toronto, ON
Dunhill Personnel London	London, ON
Dunhill Professional Search	Vancouver, BC
Dymar Mgmnt Consultants	Mississauga, ON
E.H. Scissons & Associates	Saskatoon, SK
E.L. Shore & Associates	Toronto, ON
Eastleigh Personnel	Langley, BC
Edie Bench Personnel	Toronto, ON
Egon Zehnder International	Toronto, ON
Egon Zehnder International	Montréal, QC
Employment Network	Regina, SK
Employment Partnership	Saint John, NB
Enns & Enns Consulting	Winnipeg, MB
ERC Management Group	Kelowna, BC
Erie Personnel Corp	Thorold, ON
Erie Personnel Corp	Fort Erie, ON
Ernst David International	Winnipeg, MB
Ernst & Young	St. John's, NF
Ernst & Young	SAUDI ARABIA
Eureka Recruitment	Calgary, AB
Evans Search Group	Toronto, ON
Excel HR Consultants	Toronto, ON
Excel Personnel	Kamloops, BC
Execusearch	Lethbridge, AB
Executive Facts	Toronto, ON
Executive Network	Victoria, BC
Executive Recruiters	London, ON
Executive Registry	Montréal, QC
Executive Resources Intl	Montréal, QC
Executive Services Plus	Saint John, NB
Executive Source	Regina, SK
Executrade Consultants	Edmonton, AB
F.E.R. Executive Search	Vancouver, BC
F.J. Galloway & Assoc	London, ON
Feldman Gray Associates	Toronto, ON
Fenton Lockhart Assoc	Calgary, AB
Fifth Option	Burnaby, BC
First Choice Personnel	Toronto, ON
Fisher Group Exec Search	Calgary, AB
Frappier St-Denis et Assoc	Montréal, QC
Friedman & Friedman	Montréal, QC
Future Executive Personnel	Toronto, ON
Futurestep	Toronto, ON
G.L. Penney & Associates	Edmonton, AB
G-P Personnel	Chicoutimi, QC
Gallant Search Group	London, ON
Galt Global Recruiting	Vancouver, BC
Galt Global Recruiting	Calgary, AB
Gauthier Conseils	Montréal, QC
Genesis Corporate Search	Calgary, AB
Genesis Group	Yellowknife, NT
George Preger & Associates	Toronto, ON
George Stewart Consultants	Toronto, ON
Gerald Walsh Recruitment	Halifax, NS
Gibson Kennedy & Company	Toronto, ON
Girardin & Associates	Winnipeg, MB
Glazin / Sisco Exec Search	Vancouver, BC
Glazin / Sisco Exec Search	Toronto, ON
Glen Abbey Exec Search	Oakville, ON

MANAGEMENT (Cont.)
GESTION (Suivre)

MANAGEMENT (Cont.)
GESTION (Suivre)

Manpower Professional	Burlington, ON
Manpower Professional	Brampton, ON
Manpower Professional	Mississauga, ON
Manpower Professional	Barrie, ON
Manpower Professional	Newmarket, ON
Manpower Professional	St. Catharines, ON
Manpower Professional	Niagara Falls, ON
Manpower Professional	Pickering, ON
Manpower Professional	Peterborough, ON
Manpower Professional	Cobourg, ON
Manpower Professional	Belleville, ON
Manpower Professional	Kingston, ON
Manpower Professional	Brockville, ON
Manpower Professional	Cornwall, ON
Manpower Professional	Nepean, ON
Manpower Professional	Ottawa, ON
Manpower Professional	Granby, ON
Manpower Professional	Sherbrooke, QC
Manpower Professional	Montréal, QC
Manpower Professional	Québec, QC
Manpower Professional	Fredericton, NB
Manpower Professional	Saint John, NB
Manpower Professional	Charlottetown, PE
Manpower Professional	Halifax, NS
Manpower Professional	Sydney, NS
Manpower Professional	St. John's, NF
Manpower Services Canada	Toronto, ON
Markent Personnel Inc	USA
Marlene Bilodeau Conseils	Chicoutimi, QC
Master Performers	Toronto, ON
Matte Groupe Conseil	Montréal, QC
Maureen Sinden Exec Search	Ottawa, ON
Maxim Group	Richmond, BC
McIntyre Mgmnt Resources	Hamilton, ON
McKinnon Groupe Conseil	Montréal, QC
McKinnon Mgmnt Group	Toronto, ON
MCM Selezione SRL	ITALY
McNeill Nakamoto Recruit	Vancouver, BC
Meda Group	Windsor, ON
Métivier Groupe Conseil	Montréal, QC
Meyers Norris Penny	Calgary, AB
Meyers Norris Penny	Winnipeg, MB
Michael Follett Consulting	Kitchener, ON
Michael J. Cavanagh Assoc	Toronto, ON
Michael Stern Associates	Toronto, ON
Miller Recruitment Solutions	Halifax, NS
Mission Critical Recruit	Edmonton, AB
Montgomery Thomason Assoc	Mississauga, ON
Moon Over Niagara	St. Catharines, ON
Morgan & Banks	AUSTRALIA
Morgan & Banks Ltd	AUSTRALIA
Morgan Exec Search Group	Toronto, ON
Morgan Palmer Search	Toronto, ON
Multec Canada	Toronto, ON
Multec Canada	Nepean, ON
Multec Canada	Montréal, QC
Multi-Ressources	Québec, QC
MVC Associates Intl	Toronto, ON
National Executive	Toronto, ON
NewSource Management	Toronto, ON
Nex Canada	Toronto, ON
Normatech Executive	Toronto, ON
Nugget Group Inc.	Westmount, QC
Orion Executive Search	London, ON
Osborne Group	Vancouver, BC
Osborne Group	Calgary, AB
Osborne Group	Edmonton, AB
Osborne Group	Toronto, ON
Osborne Group	Montréal, QC
Ottawa Valley Personnel	Pembroke, ON
Over 55 Inc	London, ON
P.R.Y.	Toronto, ON
P.W. Rourke & Associates	Mount Royal, QC
Palmer & Company Executive	Toronto, ON
Pamenter Pamenter Brezer	Toronto, ON
Partners in Search	Toronto, ON
Partnervision Consulting	Toronto, ON
Peapell & Associates	Halifax, NS
People +	Toronto, ON
People Bank, The	Winnipeg, MB
People First Solutions	Vancouver, BC
PeopleFind Inc.	Markham, ON
Perceptive Edge	Toronto, ON
Performance House	Waterloo, ON
Permanent Search Group	Mississauga, ON
Permanent Solutions	Mississauga, ON
Perry Martel International	Ottawa, ON
Personnel by Pro-Staff	Windsor, ON
Personnel Mgmnt Consultants	Calgary, AB
Personnel Mgmnt Group	Winnipeg, MB
Personnel Outaouais	Hull, QC
Personnel Search	Saint John, NB
Personnel Search	Moncton, NB
Petro Staff Intl HR Advisors	Calgary, AB
Pettitt Group Inc., The	Burlington, ON
Phelps Staffing Resource	Thunder Bay, ON
Phoenix Search Group	Toronto, ON
Pierre H. Delisle conseil	Montréal, QC
Pila Recruiting & Assoc	Richmond, BC
Pinton Forrest & Madden	Vancouver, BC
Pioneer Exec Consultants	Toronto, ON
Planigestion A. Choquette	Duvernay, QC
Pleiad Canada	Ottawa, ON
PME Partenaire Consult	Saint-Georges, QC
Pollack Group, The	Ottawa, ON
Pommen & Associates	Edmonton, AB
PricewaterhouseCoopers	Edmonton, AB
PricewaterhouseCoopers	Calgary, AB
PricewaterhouseCoopers	Saskatoon, SK
PricewaterhouseCoopers	Regina, SK
PricewaterhouseCoopers	Winnipeg, MB
PricewaterhouseCoopers	London, ON
PricewaterhouseCoopers	Toronto, ON
PricewaterhouseCoopers	Hamilton, ON
PricewaterhouseCoopers	Montréal, QC
PricewaterhouseCoopers	Québec, QC
PricewaterhouseCoopers	Saint John, NB
PricewaterhouseCoopers	Halifax, NS
PricewaterhouseCoopers	BERMUDA
PricewaterhouseCoopers	CHINA
PricewaterhouseCoopers	TRINIDAD
Prichard Kymen Inc	Edmonton, AB
Pride in Personnel	Markham, ON
Prime Management Group	London, ON
Prime Management Group	Cambridge, ON
Prince Arthur Advertising	Toronto, ON
Prior Resource Group	Kitchener, ON
Pro Med National Staffing	USA
Proactive Mgmnt Developmnt	Vancouver, BC
Profile Personnel Consult	Toronto, ON
Profile Search International	Calgary, AB
Prokosch Group, The	Calgary, AB
Prologic Systems	Ottawa, ON
Prosearch Associates	Mississauga, ON
ProSource Mgmnt Consult	Woodbridge, ON
Prospects Plus	Kirkland, QC
Provence Consulting	Vancouver, BC

MANAGEMENT (Cont.)
GESTION (Suivre)

MANAGEMENT (Cont.)
GESTION (Suivre)

Yves Plouffe et assoc .... Île-des-Soeurs, QC
Zen Zen International .... Winnipeg, MB
Zenzen Pierce Assoc .... Toronto, ON

MARKETING
MARKETING

1st Choice Personnel .... USA
500 Services de Selection .... Val-d'Or, QC
A.E. Harrison Partners .... Mississauga, ON
A.W. Fraser Assoc .... Edmonton, AB
A.W. Fraser Assoc .... Calgary, AB
Abecassis recherches cadres .... Montréal, QC
Abel Placement Consult .... Markham, ON
ABP Personnel Consult .... Westmount, QC
Addition 2000 .... Montréal, QC
Adecco Canada .... Ottawa, ON
Adecco LPI .... Saint-Laurent, QC
Adirect Recruiting Corp .... Toronto, ON
AIME Consultants .... Vancouver, BC
Aldonna Barry Mgmnt Consult .... Bolton, ON
Allemby Mgmnt Group .... Toronto, ON
Allen Austin Lowe & Powers .... USA
Allen Ballach Assoc .... Whitby, ON
Allen Etcovitch Assoc .... Montréal, QC
Allen Personnel Svcs .... Cambridge, ON
Argus Group Corporation .... Toronto, ON
Ariel Group Intl .... Toronto, ON
Ashlar-Stone Consultants .... Mississauga, ON
Associates Group .... Ottawa, ON
Association Resource Centre .... Toronto, ON
AT Kearney Executive .... Toronto, ON
Audax Corporation .... Toronto, ON
Austin Marlowe Intl .... Toronto, ON
Axxes Technologies .... Sillery, QC
Bailey Professional Search .... Calgary, AB
Baldock Associates .... Toronto, ON
Barrett Rose & Lee .... Toronto, ON
Bassett Laudi Partners .... Toronto, ON
Belanger Partners .... Thornhill, ON
Bernhard Consulting .... Winnipeg, MB
Birch & Assoc .... Montréal, QC
Bongard Marsh Assoc .... Toronto, ON
Boscan Consultants .... Marysville, ON
Boyden Global Exec Search .... Calgary, AB
Brainhunter.com .... Toronto, ON
Brainhunter.com .... Ottawa, ON
Bray Larouche et Assoc .... Montréal, QC
Brethet Barnum Associates .... Toronto, ON
Brock Placement Group .... Toronto, ON
Bruce Cowan Assoc .... Toronto, ON
Bruce R. Duncan Assoc .... Toronto, ON
C.G. Thomson & Co .... Toronto, ON
C. Snow & Associates .... Toronto, ON
C. Wolfe & Assoc .... Toronto, ON
Caldwell Intl., La Societé .... Montréal, QC
Caldwell Partners .... Calgary, AB
Cameron Consulting Group .... Brampton, ON
Campbell Clark Inc .... Mississauga, ON
Campbell Edgar Inc .... Richmond, BC
Campbell Edgar Inc .... Delta, BC
Campbell Morden Inc .... Toronto, ON
Canatrade International .... Candiac, QC
Canpro Executive Search .... Markham, ON
CDM & Associates .... Toronto, ON

Centrex HR Centre .... Hamilton, ON
Chad Management Group .... Toronto, ON
Chapman & Associates .... Vancouver, BC
Chase Consultants .... Mississauga, ON
Chisholm & Partners Intl .... Toronto, ON
Christmas McIvor Assoc .... Mississauga, ON
Claude Guedj Assoc .... Montréal, QC
Coe & Company Intl .... Calgary, AB
Colintex Agencies .... Toronto, ON
Connor Clark Assoc .... Dundas, ON
Connors Lovell Assoc .... Cambridge, ON
Connors Lovell Assoc .... Mississauga, ON
ConsulPro .... Westmount, QC
ConsulPRO Executive Search .... Ottawa, ON
Corporate Consultants .... Toronto, ON
Corporate Recruiters .... Vancouver, BC
Courtney Personnel .... Brampton, ON
Cyberna Associates .... Montréal, QC
Daniluck & Associates .... Edmonton, AB
Davies Park .... Edmonton, AB
Davies Park .... Calgary, AB
Delorme et Assoc .... Québec, QC
Derhak Ireland Partners .... Toronto, ON
Derkitt Herbert Exec Search .... Calgary, AB
Dial Staffing Solutions .... Calgary, AB
Digital Power Corp .... Calgary, AB
Dion Mgmnt Exec Search .... Toronto, ON
Dion Mgmnt Groupe Conseil .... Montréal, QC
Dion Mgmnt Groupe Conseil .... Sainte-Foy, QC
Donald L Hart & Assoc .... Toronto, ON
Donati & Associates .... Maple, ON
Doré Liaison .... Greenfield Park, QC
Drake International .... Edmonton, AB
Drake International .... Toronto, ON
Drakkar Human Resources .... Montréal, QC
Drakkar Human Resources .... Québec, QC
Ducharme Group .... Toronto, ON
Dumont & Associates .... North Vancouver, BC
Dymar Mgmnt Consultants .... Mississauga, ON
E.L. Shore & Associates .... Toronto, ON
E-Search Consulting .... Toronto, ON
Edie Bench Personnel .... Toronto, ON
Elliot Associates .... Toronto, ON
Enns Hever Inc .... Toronto, ON
Ernst David International .... Winnipeg, MB
Ernst & Young .... SAUDI ARABIA
Evans Search Group .... Toronto, ON
Excalibur Careers .... Markham, ON
Execusearch .... Lethbridge, AB
Execusource Staffing Intl .... Windsor, ON
Executive Recruiters .... London, ON
Executives Available .... Pointe-Claire, QC
Executrade Consultants .... Edmonton, AB
Express Personnel Svcs .... Port Coquitlam, BC
Express Personnel Svcs .... Windsor, ON
Express Personnel Svcs .... London, ON
Express Personnel Svcs .... Kitchener, ON
Express Personnel Svcs .... Guelph, ON
Express Personnel Svcs .... Hamilton, ON
Express Personnel Svcs .... Burlington, ON
Express Personnel Svcs .... Ottawa, ON
Farley Law & Assoc .... Thornhill, ON
Feldman Gray Associates .... Toronto, ON
Fifth Option .... Burnaby, BC
First Choice Personnel .... Toronto, ON
Frappier St-Denis et Assoc .... Montréal, QC
Freelancers Unlimited .... Toronto, ON
Friday Personnel Inc .... Vancouver, BC
Friday Personnel Inc .... Calgary, AB
Futurestep .... Toronto, ON

MARKETING (Cont.)
MARKETNG (Suivre)

G-P Personnel .... Chicoutimi, QC
Galloway and Associates .... Toronto, ON
Galt Global Recruiting .... Vancouver, BC
Galt Global Recruiting .... Calgary, AB
Gaudry Shink Levasseur .... Montréal, QC
Gauthier Conseils .... Montréal, QC
Gerald Walsh Associates .... Halifax, NS
Glazin / Sisco Exec Search .... Vancouver, BC
Glazin / Sisco Exec Search .... Toronto, ON
Glen Abbey Exec Search .... Oakville, ON
Global Consulting Group .... Markham, ON
Global Placement Svcs .... Mississauga, ON
Goldbeck Recruiting .... Vancouver, BC
Grant Search Group .... Toronto, ON
Grapevine Exec Recruiters .... Toronto, ON
GRH Consultants Inc .... Québec, QC
Groupe Primacor .... Longueuil, QC
Groupe SFP .... Trois-Rivières, QC
Guay Labelle & Assoc .... Montréal, QC
Harcourt & Assoc .... Edmonton, AB
Harcourt & Assoc .... Calgary, AB
Harris Consulting Corp .... Winnipeg, MB
Hart & Associates .... Winnipeg, MB
HaysZMB .... UNITED KINGDOM
Heale & Associates .... Toronto, ON
Holloway Schulz & Partners .... Vancouver, BC
HR Business Partners .... Calgary, AB
HR Impact .... Toronto, ON
HR / RH Inc. .... Montréal, QC
Human Edge Consulting .... Richmond Hill, ON
Human Resources Consult .... Mississauga, ON
Hunt Technical Personnel .... Mississauga, ON
Ideal Personnel .... Mississauga, ON
IMS Innovative Mgmt .... Toronto, ON
In Place Select Recruitment .... Toronto, ON
Interchange Personnel .... Calgary, AB
InterCom Recruitment .... Toronto, ON
Interim Mgmt Resources .... Mississauga, ON
International Bus Partners .... Toronto, ON
InterSearch Canada/Corso .... Toronto, ON
InterSearch Canada/Lennox .... Calgary, AB
InterSearch Canada/Western .... Vancouver, BC
James Boyce Associates .... Toronto, ON
Jan Howard & Associates .... Toronto, ON
Jerry Adel & Company .... Toronto, ON
JSG Group Mgmt Consult .... Unionville, ON
Keith Bagg & Associates .... Toronto, ON
Keith Bagg Regional .... Thornhill, ON
Keith-Murray Partners .... Toronto, ON
Kelly Professional & Tech .... Windsor, ON
Kelly Professional & Tech .... Belleville, ON
Keystone Select/MA Haggith .... Toronto, ON
Kingsley Allen IT Search .... Toronto, ON
Kirkpatrick Personnel .... Vancouver, BC
Knipper & Associates .... Kingston, ON
Korn/Ferry Intl .... Vancouver, BC
Lawrence Joe Consultants .... Toronto, ON
Linda Walter & Assoc .... Île-Perrot, QC
Link Resource Partners .... Toronto, ON
LMR Consultants .... Thornhill, ON
Lock & Associates .... Vancouver, BC
Lock & Associates .... Edmonton, AB
Lock & Associates .... Calgary, AB
Lock & Associates .... Saskatoon, SK
Lock & Associates .... Winnipeg, MB
Lock & Associates .... Toronto, ON
Lock & Associates .... Montréal, QC

Lock & Associates .... Moncton, NB
Lock & Associates .... Halifax, NS
Lynne Milette & Associates .... Chapeau, QC
Lynx Career Consultants .... Mississauga, ON
M.E. Money & Associates .... Toronto, ON
Madison MacArthur Inc .... Toronto, ON
Management Advice Intl .... Toronto, ON
Management One Consultants .... Toronto, ON
Management Solutions .... Mississauga, ON
Mandrake Mgmt Consult .... Toronto, ON
Manpower Professional .... Victoria, BC
Manpower Professional .... Vancouver, BC
Manpower Professional .... Richmond, BC
Manpower Professional .... Burnaby, BC
Manpower Professional .... Edmonton, AB
Manpower Professional .... Red Deer, AB
Manpower Professional .... Calgary, AB
Manpower Professional .... Regina, SK
Manpower Professional .... Winnipeg, MB
Manpower Professional .... Thunder Bay, ON
Manpower Professional .... Sudbury, ON
Manpower Professional .... Windsor, ON
Manpower Professional .... London, ON
Manpower Professional .... Guelph, ON
Manpower Professional .... Toronto, ON
Manpower Professional .... Toronto, ON
Manpower Professional .... Toronto, ON
Manpower Professional .... Toronto, ON
Manpower Professional .... Hamilton, ON
Manpower Professional .... Burlington, ON
Manpower Professional .... Brampton, ON
Manpower Professional .... Mississauga, ON
Manpower Professional .... Barrie, ON
Manpower Professional .... Newmarket, ON
Manpower Professional .... St. Catharines, ON
Manpower Professional .... Niagara Falls, ON
Manpower Professional .... Pickering, ON
Manpower Professional .... Peterborough, ON
Manpower Professional .... Cobourg, ON
Manpower Professional .... Belleville, ON
Manpower Professional .... Kingston, ON
Manpower Professional .... Brockville, ON
Manpower Professional .... Cornwall, ON
Manpower Professional .... Nepean, ON
Manpower Professional .... Ottawa, ON
Manpower Professional .... Granby, ON
Manpower Professional .... Sherbrooke, QC
Manpower Professional .... Montréal, QC
Manpower Professional .... Québec, QC
Manpower Professional .... Fredericton, NB
Manpower Professional .... Saint John, NB
Manpower Professional .... Charlottetown, PE
Manpower Professional .... Halifax, NS
Manpower Professional .... Sydney, NS
Manpower Professional .... St. John's, NF
Manpower Services Canada .... Toronto, ON
MARCON Mgmt Consultants .... Montréal, QC
Master Performers .... Toronto, ON
Matchpoint Exec Placement .... Toronto, ON
Matteson Management .... Toronto, ON
McCracken/Labbett Exec Search .... Toronto, ON
McKinnon Groupe Conseil .... Montréal, QC
McKinnon Mgmt Group .... Toronto, ON
McNeill Nakamoto Recruit .... Vancouver, BC
Melmak Consultants Ltd .... Toronto, ON
Meridia Recruitment Svcs .... Halifax, NS
Meyers Norris Penny .... Calgary, AB
Michael Page Finance .... CHINA
Michael Stern Associates .... Toronto, ON

MARKETING (Cont.)
MARKETNG (Suivre)

Michel Pauzé et Assoc .... Montréal, QC
Milgram & Associates .... Toronto, ON
Miller Recruitment Solutions .... Halifax, NS
Montgomery Thomason Assoc .... Mississauga, ON
Morgan Exec Search Group .... Toronto, ON
Morgan Palmer Search .... Toronto, ON
Morris Pervin Group .... Toronto, ON
Mosor Search Group .... Mississauga, ON
Narami Executive Search .... Toronto, ON
Nationwide Advertising Svc .... Toronto, ON
NewSource Management .... Toronto, ON
Nex Canada .... Toronto, ON
Palmer & Associates .... Kingston, ON
Paquette & Associates .... Vancouver, BC
Parkwood Associates .... Mississauga, ON
Partners Employment Group .... Toronto, ON
Partners in Search .... Toronto, ON
Peapell & Associates .... Halifax, NS
People Bank, The .... Winnipeg, MB
PeopleFind Inc. .... Markham, ON
Perceptive Edge .... Toronto, ON
Permanent Search Group .... Mississauga, ON
Permanent Solutions .... Mississauga, ON
Perry Martel International .... Ottawa, ON
Personnel Menen .... Mount Royal, QC
Personnel Search .... Saint John, NB
Personnel Search .... Moncton, NB
Pinton Forrest & Madden .... Vancouver, BC
Planigestion A. Choquette .... Duvernay, QC
PME Partenaire Consult .... Saint-Georges, QC
PricewaterhouseCoopers .... Edmonton, AB
PricewaterhouseCoopers .... Montréal, QC
PricewaterhouseCoopers .... Saint John, NB
Prichard Kymen Inc .... Edmonton, AB
Pride in Personnel .... Markham, ON
Prime Management Group .... London, ON
Prime Management Group .... Cambridge, ON
Prior Resource Group .... Kitchener, ON
Pro-Action Personnel .... Chomedey, QC
Prokosch Group, The .... Calgary, AB
Prologic Systems .... Ottawa, ON
Prosearch Associates .... Mississauga, ON
ProSource Mgmnt Consult .... Woodbridge, ON
Prospects Plus .... Kirkland, QC
Prud'Homme Groupe-Conseil .... Montréal, QC
Publicis Tandem .... Toronto, ON
Quantum .... Montréal, QC
Quantum EDP Recruiting Svcs .... Ottawa, ON
Quantum EDP Recruiting Svcs .... USA
Quantum, Les services .... Longueuil, QC
Quantum, Les services .... Pointe-Claire, QC
Quantum, Les services .... Laval, QC
Quantum Mgmnt Services .... Toronto, ON
Quantum Mgmnt Services .... Mississauga, ON
Quantum Mgmnt Services .... Ottawa, ON
Quantum Mgmt Services .... Toronto, ON
Quest Exec Recruitment .... Toronto, ON
Questus Recruitment .... Calgary, AB
R. Jacques Plante & Assoc .... Sillery, QC
Ray Berndtson/Lovas Stanley .... Toronto, ON
Ray & Berndtson/Robertson .... Halifax, NS
Ray Berndtson/Tanton .... Vancouver, BC
RBA Intl HR Consultants .... Westmount, QC
Research Personnel Consult .... Toronto, ON
Resource Corporation, The .... Toronto, ON
Resource Management Group .... Toronto, ON
Resource Recruiters .... Toronto, ON

Results Seekers HR Svcs .... Guelph, ON
Robert Paquet & Assoc .... Sainte-Foy, QC
Robertson Human Asset .... Burlington, ON
Rockwell Placement Agencies .... Richmond, BC
Rolland Groupe Conseil .... Westmount, QC
Rolland ressources humaines .... Montréal, QC
Rossi & Associates .... Vancouver, BC
Rudl International .... Ottawa, ON
Salesforce Development .... Westmount, QC
SalesSearch .... Toronto, ON
Sam Perri & Associates .... Mississauga, ON
Schoales & Associates .... Toronto, ON
Scott Wolfe Management .... Headingly, MB
Search Company, The .... Toronto, ON
Search Justified Selection .... Toronto, ON
SearchCorp International .... Calgary, AB
SearchWest Inc .... Vancouver, BC
Segall & Associates .... Toronto, ON
Sellutions Inc. .... Nepean, ON
Snelgrove Personnel .... Hamilton, ON
Sourceco Exec Search .... Edmonton, AB
Sourceco Exec Search .... Westmount, QC
Spherion Workforce .... Mississauga, ON
SSA Services Conseils .... Montréal, QC
St-Amour & Assoc .... Toronto, ON
St-Amour & Assoc .... Montréal, QC
Staff Bureau Employment .... Edmonton, AB
Stellar Personnel Placement .... Windsor, ON
Stellar Personnel Placement .... London, ON
Stephen Laramee Associates .... Toronto, ON
Storey & Associates .... Toronto, ON
Surprenant ressources média .... Montréal, QC
Sydelle Associates .... Georgetown, ON
SynapTuit Group .... Vancouver, BC
Taylor Personnel .... Victoria, BC
Taylor Personnel .... Edmonton, AB
TechNix Inc .... Toronto, ON
TERHAM Mgmnt Consulting .... Toronto, ON
Thompson Associates .... Halifax, NS
Toronto Exec Consultants .... Toronto, ON
Turner Dickinson Partners .... Vancouver, BC
Unique Personnel Canada .... Concord, ON
Unique Personnel Services .... Dorval, QC
Van Hees Personnel .... Dundas, ON
Van Klaveren Litherland Co .... Toronto, ON
Venpro Consulting .... Toronto, ON
Verriez Group Inc .... London, ON
Vickery Boardman Assoc .... Whitby, ON
Vincent-Englehart Ltd .... Halifax, NS
W.G. Meldrum Ltd .... Vancouver, BC
W.G. Meldrum Ltd .... Calgary, AB
W.G. Meldrum Ltd .... Toronto, ON
Walker Forest .... USA
Wellington Partners Intl .... Kitchener, ON
Wenje Management Ltd .... Markham, ON
Western HR Consulting .... Calgary, AB
Western Mgmnt Consultants .... Vancouver, BC
Wolf Gugler & Associates .... Toronto, ON
Yorkland Search Tech .... Mississauga, ON
Yves Elkas Inc .... Montréal, QC
Zenzen Pierce Assoc .... Toronto, ON

METALS
MÉTAUX

Assistance Teknica .... UNITED KINGDOM
C.J. Stafford & Assoc .... Toronto, ON
CAMPA & Associates .... Toronto, ON

METALS (Cont.)
MÉTAUX (Suivre)

Caron Executive Search .... London, ON
Christmas McIvor Assoc .... Mississauga, ON
Direct Career Concepts .... Woodbridge, ON
Guildwood Group .... Ajax, ON
LePage International .... Montréal, QC
London Executive Consultants .... London, ON
Ludlow Project Services .... Oakville, ON
MacRae Atwood Mgmnt .... Toronto, ON
Markent Personnel Inc .... USA
Matthews Management .... Richmond Hill, ON
Montgomery Thomason Assoc .... Mississauga, ON
MPA Recherche de Cadres .... Brossard, QC
Pettitt Group Inc., The .... Burlington, ON
RJ Professionals .... Toronto, ON
Robert L Holmes Placement .... Cambridge, ON
TDM Technical Services .... Toronto, ON
Technical Service Consult .... Winnipeg, MB
Technical Solutions Inc .... USA
W. Hutt Mgmnt Resources .... Burlington, ON

MINING
MINES

Agence de personnel Abitibi .... Val-d'Or, QC
Bedford Consulting Group .... Toronto, ON
Bedford Consulting Group .... Oakville, ON
Bruce Ward Partners .... Toronto, ON
C.J. Stafford & Assoc .... Toronto, ON
Caldwell Partners .... Vancouver, BC
Christopher Vincent & Assoc .... Calgary, AB
Contracts Consultancy Ltd .... UNITED KINGDOM
Cowan Personnel .... Montréal, QC
Crawford de Munnik Executive .... Toronto, ON
David Warwick Kennedy Assoc .... Vancouver, BC
Design Group Staffing .... Vancouver, BC
GR Search Inc .... Toronto, ON
Groupe LJL .... Pierrefonds, QC
Groupe Ranger .... Montréal, QC
Groupe Ressources DGO .... Trois-Rivières, QC
Guildwood Group .... Ajax, ON
J.G. Flynn & Associates .... Vancouver, BC
J.O. Bush & Associates .... Mindemoya, ON
Keith-Murray Partners .... Toronto, ON
Kenniff Denis Inc. .... Montréal, QC
Lawrence Assoc Exec Search .... Toronto, ON
Levert Personnel Resources .... Timmins, ON
Levert Personnel Resources .... Sudbury, ON
MacKenzie Gray Mgmnt .... Calgary, AB
MacRae Atwood Mgmnt .... Toronto, ON
McLean & Associates .... North Vancouver, BC
Moxon Dolphin Kerby Intl .... UNITED KINGDOM
MQS Executive Search .... Toronto, ON
PricewaterhouseCoopers .... Vancouver, BC
Prichard Kymen Inc .... Edmonton, AB
Profile Search International .... Calgary, AB
Puglisevich Crews & Svcs .... St. John's, NF
Roan International .... Mississauga, ON
Roevin Tech People .... North Vancouver, BC
Roevin Tech People .... Edmonton, AB
Roevin Tech People .... Calgary, AB
Roevin Tech People .... Kitchener, ON
Roevin Tech People .... Montréal, QC
TDM Technical Services .... Toronto, ON
Technical Skills Consulting .... Toronto, ON

Thomas Mining Associates .... UNITED KINGDOM
Wellington Partners Intl .... Kitchener, ON
Wood West & Partners .... Vancouver, BC
Woodridge Associates .... UNITED KINGDOM
Yves Plouffe et assoc .... Île-des-Soeurs, QC

MULTIMEDIA
MULTIMÉDIA

Adecco Canada .... Ottawa, ON
Alliance Search Group .... Toronto, ON
Aquent Partners .... Vancouver, BC
Aquent Partners .... Toronto, ON
Aquent Partners .... Montréal, QC
ARES Consulting Svcs .... Toronto, ON
Axxes Technologies .... Sillery, QC
Bach Associates .... Vancouver, BC
BeyondTech Solutions .... Vancouver, BC
BMA International .... Montréal, QC
BMA International .... Montréal, QC
Bradford Bachinski Ltd .... Ottawa, ON
CanadaIT Ventures .... Surrey, BC
CDM & Associates .... Toronto, ON
CG Consulting Group .... Toronto, ON
ComUnity Systems Consultants .... Calgary, AB
Creative Force Network .... Toronto, ON
Dial A-1 Resources .... Toronto, ON
Duo Mega Inc .... Montréal, QC
E-Search Consulting .... Toronto, ON
Eastridge Infotech Tech Staffing .... USA
eTalent Group .... Toronto, ON
Freelancers Unlimited .... Toronto, ON
Grant Search Group .... Toronto, ON
Groupe MCS .... Montréal, QC
GSI International Consult .... Toronto, ON
Levton Group .... Toronto, ON
LTV & Associates .... Toronto, ON
Luna Source .... USA
Management Solutions .... Mississauga, ON
Master Performers .... Toronto, ON
McKinnon Mgmnt Group .... Toronto, ON
Michel Pauzé et Assoc .... Montréal, QC
Morris Pervin Group .... Toronto, ON
Nework Corp .... Toronto, ON
PeopleWeb Inc. .... Toronto, ON
Phee Farrer Jones Ltd .... UNITED KINGDOM
Pila Recruiting & Assoc .... Richmond, BC
Project Mgmnt Recruiting .... Toronto, ON
Protocole .... Montréal, QC
Queue Systems .... Markham, ON
Recherches Johnson .... Saint-Lambert, QC
SSA Services Conseils .... Montréal, QC
StoneWood Group .... Toronto, ON
StoneWood Group .... Ottawa, ON
StoneWood Group .... Sainte-Geneviève, QC
Storey & Associates .... Toronto, ON
Strategic Resources Intl .... Toronto, ON
Surprenant ressources média .... Montréal, QC
TAL Group .... Toronto, ON
TalentLab .... Toronto, ON
TalentLab .... Kingston, ON
TalentLab .... Kanata, ON
Tele-Ressources Ltée .... Montréal, QC
TERHAM Mgmnt Consulting .... Toronto, ON
Walker Forest .... USA
Wolverine Technical Services .... USA

OIL & GAS
PÉTROLE ET GAZ

ABC Corries (Canada) .... Calgary, AB
Advantage Tech .... Calgary, AB
Al-Khaleej Computers .... SAUDI ARABIA
Alberta Recruiting Group .... Calgary, AB
Alconsult International .... Calgary, AB
Arabian Careers .... UNITED KINGDOM
Aramco Services Company .... USA
Ashtead Mgmnt Consultants .... UNITED KINGDOM
ATS Reliance Tech Group .... Vancouver, BC
ATS Reliance Tech Group .... Edmonton, AB
ATS Reliance Tech Group .... Calgary, AB
ATS Reliance Tech Group .... London, ON
ATS Reliance Tech Group .... Toronto, ON
ATS Reliance Tech Group .... Burlington, ON
Bailey Professional Search .... Calgary, AB
Baldwin Staffing Group .... Calgary, AB
Bowen Staffing .... Calgary, AB
Boyd PetroSearch .... Calgary, AB
Boyden Global Exec Search .... Calgary, AB
Brant & Associates .... Winnipeg, MB
Braun-Valley Associates .... Sarnia, ON
C.N. Taylor Consulting .... Bedford, NS
Caldwell Partners .... Calgary, AB
Canadian Career Partners .... Calgary, AB
Capital Executive .... Calgary, AB
CBM Projects .... Calgary, AB
CDI Technical Svcs .... Calgary, AB
Christian & Timbers .... USA
Christopher Vincent & Assoc .... Calgary, AB
Clarendon Parker ME .... UNITED ARAB EMIRATES
Classic Consulting Group .... Calgary, AB
Coe & Company Intl .... Calgary, AB
ComFact Corp .... Oakville, ON
Conroy Partners .... Calgary, AB
Contracts Consultancy Ltd .... UNITED KINGDOM
Corporate Res (Hertford) .... UNITED KINGDOM
Cosier Associates .... Calgary, AB
Crawford de Munnik Executive .... Toronto, ON
David Aplin & Assoc .... Edmonton, AB
Davies Park .... Calgary, AB
Delton Personnel .... UNITED KINGDOM
Derkitt Herbert Exec Search .... Calgary, AB
Design Group Staffing .... Vancouver, BC
Design Group Staffing .... Edmonton, AB
Design Group Staffing .... Calgary, AB
Diversified Staffing Svcs .... Edmonton, AB
Diversified Staffing Svcs .... Calgary, AB
Doug Morley & Associates .... Calgary, AB
Duke Blakey Inc .... Toronto, ON
Executive Resources Intl .... Montréal, QC
Fisher Group Exec Search .... Calgary, AB
G.L. Penney & Associates .... Edmonton, AB
Genesis Corporate Search .... Calgary, AB
Grasslands Group .... Medicine Hat, AB
Grasslands Group .... Swift Current, SK
Gulco International Recruiting .... USA
Horizon Resources Intl .... Calgary, AB
HR Business Partners .... Calgary, AB
Information Resources Ctr .... SAUDI ARABIA
Interchange Personnel .... Calgary, AB
Interocean Personnel Svcs .... UNITED KINGDOM
InterSearch Canada/Staffing .... Halifax, NS
Jawaby Oil Service .... UNITED KINGDOM
Johnstone Assoc Pro Search .... Calgary, AB
Leader Search Inc .... Calgary, AB

Leslie Corporation .... USA
Ludlow Project Services .... Oakville, ON
M.R. Goodman Consulting .... Calgary, AB
MacKenzie Gray Mgmnt .... Calgary, AB
Management Plus Consulting .... LEBANON
Matchtech Engineering .... UNITED KINGDOM
MBL Group LLC .... USA
McLean Exec Consultants .... Calgary, AB
McQ International Svcs .... UNITED KINGDOM
Meyers Norris Penny .... Calgary, AB
NES Overseas Ltd .... UNITED KINGDOM
Network Corporate Search .... Calgary, AB
New Zealand Skills Export .... NEW ZEALAND
Newfoundland Personnel .... St. John's, NF
Noramtec Consultants .... Montréal, QC
Normatech Executive .... Toronto, ON
Personnel Search .... Saint John, NB
Personnel Search .... Moncton, NB
Peter Leonard & Assoc .... Calgary, AB
Petro Middle East .... UNITED ARAB EMIRATES
Petro Staff Intl HR Advisors .... Calgary, AB
Piper-Morgan Associates .... USA
Precision Resources Ltd .... UNITED KINGDOM
Premier Personnel .... UNITED KINGDOM
Profile Search International .... Calgary, AB
Prokosch Group, The .... Calgary, AB
Puglisevich Crews & Svcs .... St. John's, NF
Purcell Technical Staffing .... USA
Qbyte Services .... Calgary, AB
Recruitment International .... UNITED KINGDOM
Research Associates .... Edmonton, AB
Resource Concepts .... St. John's, NF
Resource Professionals .... Calgary, AB
Roan International .... Mississauga, ON
Rod Turpin & Assoc .... Edmonton, AB
Roevin Tech People .... Edmonton, AB
Roevin Tech People .... Calgary, AB
Roevin Tech People .... Sarnia, ON
Roper and Assoc .... Calgary, AB
Russell Reynolds Assoc .... Calgary, AB
SearchCorp International .... Calgary, AB
Servocraft Limited .... Toronto, ON
Staff Bureau Employment .... Edmonton, AB
Summit Search Group .... Calgary, AB
T.J. Seaton Management .... Calgary, AB
Taylor Personnel .... Edmonton, AB
Taylor Recruitment .... UNITED KINGDOM
Teknica (UK) Ltd .... UNITED KINGDOM
TPS Unimecs .... THE NETHERLANDS
Van Biesen Group .... Calgary, AB
Ward Vinge & Associates .... Edmonton, AB
Ward Vinge & Associates .... Calgary, AB
Western Mgmnt Consultants .... Calgary, AB
Windowpane Mgmnt .... Calgary, AB
Wolfer-Hale & Associates .... Calgary, AB

OPERATIONS
EXPLOITATION

A. Lawrence Abrams Assoc .... Waterloo, ON
A.W. Fraser Assoc .... Calgary, AB
Access Career Solutions .... Brampton, ON
Ad-Link Advertising .... Toronto, ON
Adecco Canada .... London, ON
Adecco Canada .... Kitchener, ON
Adecco Québec .... Laval, QC
Adecco Québec .... Chicoutimi, QC
AES Recruitment .... Toronto, ON

OPERATIONS (Cont.)
EXPLOITATION (Suivre)

Allen Etcovitch Assoc	Montréal, QC
Alliance Personnel Group	Edmonton, AB
Alliance Personnel Group	Oakville, ON
Andrew Campbell Assoc	Oakville, ON
Angus One Pro Recruitment	Vancouver, BC
Apple One Employment	Toronto, ON
Applicants Inc.	Kitchener, ON
Aron Printz Assoc	Vancouver, BC
Ashlar-Stone Consultants	Mississauga, ON
Audax Corporation	Toronto, ON
Ayrshire Group	Toronto, ON
Barry Blostein Recruitment	Thornhill, ON
Bay3000 Consulting	Markham, ON
Bernhard Consulting	Winnipeg, MB
Best Personnel Services	Sarnia, ON
Best Personnel Services	Strathroy, ON
Botrie Associates	Toronto, ON
Bourassa Brodeur Assoc	Trois-Rivières, QC
Bray Larouche et Assoc	Montréal, QC
Brock Placement Group	Toronto, ON
Bruce Ward Partners	Toronto, ON
C.G. Thomson & Co	Toronto, ON
Caldwell Intl., La Societé	Montréal, QC
Cambridge Mgmnt Planning	Toronto, ON
CAMPA & Associates	Toronto, ON
Campbell Clark Inc	Mississauga, ON
Campbell Morden Inc	Toronto, ON
Can-Tech Services	Saint-Laurent, QC
Canadian Exec Recruitmnt	Mississauga, ON
Canpro Executive Search	Markham, ON
CAPP Employment Svcs	Mississauga, ON
Carion Resource Group	Mississauga, ON
Central Mgmnt Consultants	Toronto, ON
Centre for Corp Resources	Toronto, ON
Centrex HR Centre	Hamilton, ON
Chase Consultants	Mississauga, ON
CMP Select	Toronto, ON
Coe & Company Intl	Calgary, AB
Conestoga Personnel	Kitchener, ON
Connors Lovell Assoc	Cambridge, ON
Connors Lovell Assoc	Mississauga, ON
Contemporary Personnel	Brampton, ON
Contemporary Personnel	Barrie, ON
Corporate Consultants	Toronto, ON
Courtney Personnel	Brampton, ON
Dan McNamara & Assoc	Woodstock, ON
Dana Consultants	Saint-Laurent, QC
David Taylor Mfg Search	Toronto, ON
Delorme et Assoc	Québec, QC
Design Group Staffing	Calgary, AB
Design Group Staffing	Toronto, ON
Dion Mgmnt Exec Search	Toronto, ON
Dion Mgmnt Groupe Conseil	Montréal, QC
Dion Mgmnt Groupe Conseil	Sainte-Foy, QC
Direct Career Concepts	Woodbridge, ON
Doré Liaison	Greenfield Park, QC
Drake International	Toronto, ON
Drake International	Montréal, QC
Drakkar Human Resources	Saint-Laurent, QC
Dynamic Employment Solution	Brampton, ON
Dynamic Employment Solution	Brampton, ON
Emplois plus pre-sélection	Lasalle, QC
Enns Hever Inc	Toronto, ON
ERC Management Group	Kelowna, BC
Erie Personnel Corp	Thorold, ON
Erie Personnel Corp	Fort Erie, ON
Ernst David International	Winnipeg, MB
ERP Staffing Solutions	Calgary, AB
ERP Staffing Solutions	Brampton, ON
Everest Mgmnt Network	Toronto, ON
Executive Facts	Toronto, ON
Executive House Inc	Chatham, ON
Executive Registry	Montréal, QC
Executrade Consultants	Edmonton, AB
Feldman Gray Associates	Toronto, ON
Fifth Option	Burnaby, BC
First Choice Personnel	Toronto, ON
G.L. Penney & Associates	Edmonton, AB
G-P Personnel	Chicoutimi, QC
Galloway and Associates	Toronto, ON
Gaudry Shink Levasseur	Montréal, QC
Gauthier Conseils	Montréal, QC
Genesis Corporate Search	Calgary, AB
George Stewart Consultants	Toronto, ON
Gerald Walsh Recruitment	Halifax, NS
Girardin & Associates	Winnipeg, MB
Godbout Martin Godbout Assoc	Hull, QC
Goldbeck Recruiting	Vancouver, BC
Golden Mile Mgmnt Consulting	Toronto, ON
GR Search Inc	Toronto, ON
Grant Thornton Intl	Saint John, NB
Grasslands Group	Medicine Hat, AB
Grasslands Group	Swift Current, SK
GRH Consultants Inc	Québec, QC
Groupe conseil Lamarche	Granby, QC
Groupe Pluridis	Montréal, QC
Groupe SFP	Trois-Rivières, QC
Hallmark Personnel	Oakville, ON
Harcourt & Assoc	Edmonton, AB
Harcourt & Assoc	Calgary, AB
Harris Consulting Corp	Winnipeg, MB
Hayhurst Consulting	London, ON
HEC Group	Ancaster, ON
Heidrick & Struggles Canada	Montréal, QC
Herman Smith Search Inc	Toronto, ON
High Road Personnel	Burlington, ON
Hire Purpose	Burlington, ON
Holloway Schulz & Partners	Vancouver, BC
HR / RH Inc.	Montréal, QC
Human Capital Solutions	Mississauga, ON
Human Resource Group Mgmnt	Edmonton, AB
Interim Plus	Granby, QC
International Tech Recruit	Windsor, ON
InterSearch Canada/Lennox	Calgary, AB
J. Edgar & Associates	Toronto, ON
J.P. Anderson & Assoc	Burlington, ON
J.R. Bechtle & Company	USA
James E. Thomas & Assoc	London, ON
Jan Howard & Associates	Toronto, ON
Jerry Adel & Company	Toronto, ON
JSG Group Mgmnt Consult	Unionville, ON
K.B. Lye & Associates	Toronto, ON
KAS Personnel Svcs	North Bay, ON
KAS Personnel Svcs	Kitchener, ON
KAS Personnel Svcs	Guelph, ON
KAS Personnel Svcs	Toronto, ON
KAS Personnel Svcs	Toronto, ON
KAS Personnel Svcs	Hamilton, ON
KAS Personnel Svcs	Burlington, ON
KAS Personnel Svcs	Brampton, ON
KAS Personnel Svcs	Mississauga, ON
KAS Personnel Svcs	Barrie, ON
KAS Personnel Svcs	Belleville, ON
Kelly Professional & Tech	Chatham, ON
Kelly Professional & Tech	London, ON
Kelly Professional & Tech	St. Thomas, ON
Kelly Professional & Tech	Kitchener, ON

OPERATIONS (Cont.)
EXPLOITATION (Suivre)

Kelly Professional & Tech .... Cambridge, ON
Kelly Professional & Tech .... Guelph, ON
Kelly Professional & Tech .... Hamilton, ON
Kelly Professional & Tech .... St. Catharines, ON
Kelly Professional & Tech .... Kingston, ON
Kelly Select .... Woodstock, ON
Kenneth Murphy & Assoc .... Halifax, NS
Key Executive Consultants .... Barrie, ON
Key Executive Consultants .... Pickering, ON
Keystone Select/MA Haggith .... Toronto, ON
Kitchener Exec Consultants .... Kitchener, ON
Knipper & Associates .... Kingston, ON
Labour Source .... Woodbridge, ON
Landon Morgan Inc .... Thorold, ON
Leader Search Inc .... Calgary, AB
LePage International .... Montréal, QC
Levton Group .... Toronto, ON
Lewis Companies .... Toronto, ON
Little Group, The .... Brantford, ON
Little Group, The .... Burlington, ON
Lock & Associates .... Vancouver, BC
London Executive Consultants .... London, ON
Lorne Seaman & Associates .... Edmonton, AB
Louise Robinson Placement .... Keene, ON
M.R. Goodman Consulting .... Calgary, AB
Madison MacArthur Inc .... Toronto, ON
Maintenance Plus .... Chatham, ON
Matte Groupe Conseil .... Montréal, QC
Matthews Management .... Richmond Hill, ON
MBL Group LLC .... USA
McIntyre Mgmnt Resources .... Hamilton, ON
Métivier Groupe Conseil .... Montréal, QC
Michael J. Cavanagh Assoc .... Toronto, ON
Montgomery Thomason Assoc .... Mississauga, ON
Morgan Exec Search Group .... Toronto, ON
Morgan Palmer Search .... Toronto, ON
Osborne Group .... Vancouver, BC
Osborne Group .... Calgary, AB
Osborne Group .... Edmonton, AB
Osborne Group .... Toronto, ON
Osborne Group .... Montréal, QC
P.W. Rourke & Associates .... Mount Royal, QC
Palmer & Associates .... Kingston, ON
Parkwood Associates .... Mississauga, ON
People + ... Toronto, ON
Perceptive Edge .... Toronto, ON
Performance House .... Waterloo, ON
Permanent Solutions .... Mississauga, ON
Personnel Alter Ego .... Pointe-Claire, QC
Personnel Alter Ego .... Montréal, QC
Petro Staff Intl HR Advisors .... Calgary, AB
Pinstripe Personnel .... Toronto, ON
Pinton Forrest & Madden .... Vancouver, BC
Planigestion A. Choquette .... Duvernay, QC
PME Partenaire Consult .... Saint-Georges, QC
Pommen & Associates .... Edmonton, AB
Powell Jones Mgmnt Services .... Barrie, ON
PricewaterhouseCoopers .... Regina, SK
PricewaterhouseCoopers .... London, ON
PricewaterhouseCoopers .... Hamilton, ON
PricewaterhouseCoopers .... Québec, QC
Prichard Kymen Inc .... Edmonton, AB
Pride in Personnel .... Markham, ON
Prior Resource Group .... Kitchener, ON
Project Mgmnt Recruiting .... Toronto, ON
Prosearch Associates .... Mississauga, ON
Prospects Plus .... Kirkland, QC

Prud'Homme Groupe-Conseil .... Montréal, QC
Quantum Mgmnt Services .... Toronto, ON
Randstad Interim .... Saint-Laurent, QC
Ray & Berndtson/Laurendeau .... Montréal, QC
Research Associates .... Edmonton, AB
Resource Corporation, The .... Toronto, ON
Resource Management Group .... Toronto, ON
Resource Professionals .... Calgary, AB
Richter Raymond Group .... Oakville, ON
RJK & Associates .... Markham, ON
Robert T. Keegan & Assoc .... Oakville, ON
Robinson Fraser Group .... Toronto, ON
Roevin Tech People .... Montréal, QC
Rolland Groupe Conseil .... Westmount, QC
Rolland ressources humaines .... Montréal, QC
Rudl International .... Ottawa, ON
Russell & Associates .... Kelowna, BC
RWS Consulting Group .... London, ON
SAG ressources humaines .... Montréal, QC
Sam Perri & Associates .... Mississauga, ON
Savage Consultants .... Vancouver, BC
Scott Huband Consulting .... Oakville, ON
Simpson McGrath Inc .... Winnipeg, MB
Société Jean P. Brisebois .... Montréal, QC
SPI Executive Search .... Ottawa, ON
Stephen Laramee Associates .... Toronto, ON
Stevens Resource Group .... London, ON
Stevens Resource Group .... Stratford, ON
Stevens Resource Group .... Woodstock, ON
Stevens Resource Group .... Tillsonburg, ON
Stevens Resource Group .... Brantford, ON
Stevens Resource Group .... Cambridge, ON
TAD Canada .... Calgary, AB
TAD Canada .... Brantford, ON
TAD Canada .... Mississauga, ON
TAD Canada .... Ottawa, ON
TAD Canada .... Laval, QC
TAD Canada .... Bedford, NS
Techaid Inc .... Montréal, QC
Technical Mgmnt Resources .... Barrie, ON
Technical Service Consult .... Surrey, BC
Technical Service Consult .... Winnipeg, MB
Technical Service Consult .... Toronto, ON
Technical Skills Consulting .... Toronto, ON
Technical Solutions Inc .... USA
TSI Group / TSI Staffing .... Mississauga, ON
Ultimate Staffing .... Hamilton, ON
Van Klaveren Litherland Co .... Toronto, ON
Verelli Arrizza .... Montréal, QC
W. Hutt Mgmnt Resources .... Burlington, ON
Wayne Perry & Associates .... Toronto, ON
Wellington Partners Intl .... Kitchener, ON
Western HR Consulting .... Calgary, AB
Western Mgmnt Consultants .... Vancouver, BC
Western Mgmnt Consultants .... Toronto, ON
Wolfer-Hale & Associates .... Calgary, AB
Wypich International .... Toronto, ON
Yorkland Search Tech .... Mississauga, ON
Yves Elkas Inc .... Montréal, QC
Yves Plouffe et assoc .... Île-des-Soeurs, QC

PACKAGING
EMBALLAGE

Adecco Canada .... Toronto, ON
Adecco Québec .... Longueuil, QC
Adecco Québec .... Chicoutimi, QC
Advantage Tech .... Calgary, AB

PACKAGING (Cont.)
EMBALLAGE (Suivre)

Boyden Global Exec Search .... Calgary, AB
Canadian Findings .... Toronto, ON
Canpro Executive Search .... Markham, ON
Future Executive Personnel .... USA
G-Tech Professional Staffing .... USA
Harris Consulting Corp .... Winnipeg, MB
Level A Inc .... Peterborough, ON
Louise Robinson Placement .... Keene, ON
LTV & Associates .... Toronto, ON
Michel Pauzé et Assoc .... Montréal, QC
Morgan Exec Search Group .... Toronto, ON
MPA Recherche de Cadres .... Brossard, QC
Northwind Consulting .... King City, ON
Robertson Human Asset .... Burlington, ON
RWJ & Associates .... Kitchener, ON
S. Tanner & Associates .... Oakville, ON
SOLUTIONS .... Cornwall, ON
Spherion Workforce .... Brampton, ON
Stokes Associates .... Pickering, ON
TDM Technical Services .... Toronto, ON
Technical Mgmnt Resources .... Barrie, ON
Trans-United Consultants .... Burlington, ON

PHARMACEUTICAL
PHARMACEUTIQUE

Adirect Recruiting Corp .... Toronto, ON
Alan Davis Assoc .... Hudson Heights, QC
AT Kearney Executive .... Toronto, ON
Bedard Ressources .... Montréal, QC
Bedford Consulting Group .... Toronto, ON
Bedford Consulting Group .... Oakville, ON
Bilingual Source .... Toronto, ON
Botrie Associates .... Toronto, ON
Braun-Valley Associates .... Sarnia, ON
Brethet Barnum Associates .... Toronto, ON
Brock Placement Group .... Toronto, ON
C.J. Stafford & Assoc .... Toronto, ON
Cameron Consulting Group .... Brampton, ON
CanMed Consultants .... Mississauga, ON
Canpro Executive Search .... Markham, ON
Career Path Personnel .... Toronto, ON
Carion Resource Group .... Mississauga, ON
Caron Executive Search .... London, ON
Centre for Corp Resources .... Toronto, ON
Chisholm & Partners Intl .... Toronto, ON
ConsulPro .... Westmount, QC
Contempra Personnel .... Pointe-Claire, QC
Cortex HR .... Toronto, ON
Cyberna Associates .... Montréal, QC
David Aplin & Assoc .... Edmonton, AB
Derhak Ireland Partners .... Toronto, ON
Dion Mgmnt Groupe Conseil .... Sainte-Foy, QC
Direct Career Concepts .... Woodbridge, ON
Dotemtex Executive Search .... Sillery, QC
Dynamic Employment Solution .... Brampton, ON
Dynamic Employment Solution .... Brampton, ON
Fisher Group Exec Search .... Calgary, AB
Graduate Consulting Svcs .... Montréal, QC
Grapevine Exec Recruiters .... Toronto, ON
Groom & Assoc .... Pointe-Claire, QC
Groupe Primacor .... Longueuil, QC
Harris Consulting Corp .... Winnipeg, MB
Hart & Associates .... Winnipeg, MB
Henry Hill & Associates .... Mississauga, ON

Hess Associates Exec Search .... Toronto, ON
Kelly Scientific .... Mississauga, ON
Kelly Scientifique .... Montréal, QC
Kenniff Denis Inc. .... Montréal, QC
Keystone Select/MA Haggith .... Toronto, ON
Knipper & Associates .... Kingston, ON
Korn/Ferry Intl .... Montréal, QC
Lamon + Stuart + Michaels .... Toronto, ON
LePage International .... Montréal, QC
Logistic Solutions .... USA
Louise Robinson Placement .... Keene, ON
Mandrake Mgmt Consult .... Toronto, ON
Matchtech Engineering .... UNITED KINGDOM
Matte Groupe Conseil .... Montréal, QC
Matteson Management .... Toronto, ON
McKinnon Mgmnt Group .... Toronto, ON
Morris Pervin Group .... Toronto, ON
Peapell & Associates .... Halifax, NS
Pride in Personnel .... Markham, ON
Pro Tec Global Staffing .... Thornhill, ON
ProSource Mgmnt Consult .... Woodbridge, ON
Publicis Tandem .... Toronto, ON
Quintal & Associates HR .... Montréal, QC
Ray & Berndtson/Laurendeau .... Montréal, QC
Ray Berndtson/Lovas Stanley .... Toronto, ON
Robertson Human Asset .... Burlington, ON
S. Tanner & Associates .... Oakville, ON
SearchWest Inc .... Vancouver, BC
Skott/Edwards Consult .... USA
Spherion Workforce .... Brampton, ON
Staff Bureau Employment .... Edmonton, AB
Symmetry Search Group .... Toronto, ON
Technical Service Consult .... Toronto, ON
TES Employment Solution .... Mississauga, ON
TMP Worldwide Exec Search .... Toronto, ON
Trella & Associates .... Toronto, ON
Venatus Conseil Ltée .... Montréal, QC
Vickery Boardman Assoc .... Whitby, ON

PLASTICS
PLASTIQUE

Adecco Québec .... Chicoutimi, QC
ATS Reliance Tech Group .... Edmonton, AB
ATS Reliance Tech Group .... Calgary, AB
ATS Reliance Tech Group .... Toronto, ON
ATS Reliance Tech Group .... Burlington, ON
Berlys Personnel .... Saint-Laurent, QC
Bongard Marsh Assoc .... Toronto, ON
Canadian Exec Recruitmnt .... Mississauga, ON
Canadian Findings .... Toronto, ON
Carion Resource Group .... Mississauga, ON
Caron Executive Search .... London, ON
Direct Career Concepts .... Woodbridge, ON
Drakkar Human Resources .... Mississauga, ON
Dynamic Employment Solution .... Brampton, ON
Dynamic Employment Solution .... Brampton, ON
Future Executive Personnel .... Toronto, ON
Future Executive Personnel .... USA
Gallant Search Group .... London, ON
Godbout Martin Godbout Assoc .... Hull, QC
Harris Consulting Corp .... Winnipeg, MB
HCR Personnel Solutions .... Toronto, ON
HCR Personnel Solutions .... Toronto, ON
HCR Personnel Solutions .... Newmarket, ON
Human Resources Consult .... Mississauga, ON
Key Executive Consultants .... Barrie, ON
Key Executive Consultants .... Pickering, ON

PLASTICS (Cont.)
PLASTIQUE (Suivre)

Lenvil Industries .... Burlington, ON
London Executive Consultants .... London, ON
MacLean Hay Consulting .... Oakville, ON
Markent Personnel Inc .... USA
Matthews Management .... Richmond Hill, ON
Meda Group .... Windsor, ON
Montgomery Thomason Assoc .... Mississauga, ON
Morgan Exec Search Group .... Toronto, ON
Morgan Palmer Search .... Toronto, ON
People Management Group .... Woodstock, ON
Pettitt Group Inc., The .... Burlington, ON
Pro Tec Global Staffing .... Thornhill, ON
Pro-Action Personnel .... Chomedey, QC
Robert L Holmes Placement .... Cambridge, ON
RWJ & Associates .... Kitchener, ON
Sam Perri & Associates .... Mississauga, ON
Spherion Workforce .... Brampton, ON
Stoakley-Dudley Consult .... Mississauga, ON
TDM Technical Services .... Toronto, ON
Technical Service Consult .... Surrey, BC
Trans-United Consultants .... Burlington, ON
Ward Vinge & Associates .... Edmonton, AB
Ward Vinge & Associates .... Calgary, AB

PRINTING
IMPRIMERIE

Aquent Partners .... Vancouver, BC
Aquent Partners .... Toronto, ON
Aquent Partners .... Montréal, QC
C. Wolfe & Assoc .... Toronto, ON
Carscarp Consulting .... Gloucester, ON
Core-Staff Inc. .... Toronto, ON
Fisher Group Exec Search .... Calgary, AB
Hunt Technical Personnel .... Ottawa, ON
Interim Mgmt Resources .... Mississauga, ON
Jenereaux & Associates .... Mississauga, ON
LTV & Associates .... Toronto, ON
Michel Pauzé et Assoc .... Montréal, QC
NCL Personnel .... Montréal, QC
ProSource Mgmt Consult .... Woodbridge, ON
RJ Professionals .... Toronto, ON
Rossi & Associates .... Vancouver, BC
Stokes Associates .... Pickering, ON

PUBLIC RELATIONS
AFFAIRES PUBLIQUES

Berlys Personnel .... Saint-Laurent, QC
Bridges Consulting .... Ottawa, ON
Caldwell Partners .... Calgary, AB
CDM & Associates .... Toronto, ON
Chad Management Group .... Toronto, ON
Communication Dynamique .... Beaconsfield, QC
David Bell Executive Search .... Toronto, ON
FWJ Communications .... Calgary, AB
GAAP Inc .... Montréal, QC
Grapevine Exec Recruiters .... Toronto, ON
InterCom Recruitment .... Toronto, ON
Jeffery Group .... Toronto, ON
Jenereaux & Associates .... Mississauga, ON
Matteson Management .... Toronto, ON
Maureen Sinden Exec Search .... Ottawa, ON

Publicis Tandem .... Toronto, ON
Renaud Foster Mgmnt .... Ottawa, ON
Search Company, The .... Toronto, ON
Spencer Stuart .... Toronto, ON
Surprenant ressources média .... Montréal, QC
SynapTuit Group .... Vancouver, BC
TechNix Inc .... Toronto, ON
TERHAM Mgmnt Consulting .... Toronto, ON
W.R. London Consultants .... Toronto, ON

PUBLISHING/MEDIA
ÉDITION/MÉDIA

Adirect Recruiting Corp .... Toronto, ON
CDM & Associates .... Toronto, ON
Crawford de Munnik Executive .... Toronto, ON
Ernst David International .... Winnipeg, MB
First Choice Personnel .... Toronto, ON
Freelancers Unlimited .... Toronto, ON
Herman Smith Search Inc .... Toronto, ON
Information Bus Consulting .... Edmonton, AB
LTV & Associates .... Toronto, ON
MacRae Atwood Mgmnt .... Toronto, ON
Mandrake Mgmt Consult .... Toronto, ON
Michel Pauzé et Assoc .... Montréal, QC
Phee Farrer Jones Ltd .... UNITED KINGDOM
Robinson Fraser Group .... Toronto, ON
Spencer Stuart .... Toronto, ON
TERHAM Mgmnt Consulting .... Toronto, ON
True North Exec Search .... Toronto, ON

PULP & PAPER
PAPETERIE

Allen Ballach Assoc .... Whitby, ON
Bedford Consulting Group .... Toronto, ON
Bedford Consulting Group .... Oakville, ON
C.N. Taylor Consulting .... Bedford, NS
C.W. Clasen Recruiting .... Coquitlam, BC
Caldwell Partners .... Vancouver, BC
Christopher Vincent & Assoc .... Calgary, AB
Coast Personnel Svcs .... Nanaimo, BC
Cowan Personnel .... Montréal, QC
Design Group Staffing .... Vancouver, BC
Executive Resources Intl .... Montréal, QC
Forest People Intl Search .... Vancouver, BC
G.L. Penney & Associates .... Edmonton, AB
Groupe LJL .... Pierrefonds, QC
Groupe Ressources DGO .... Trois-Rivières, QC
Guildwood Group .... Ajax, ON
J.G. Flynn & Associates .... Vancouver, BC
J.O. Bush & Associates .... Mindemoya, ON
LePage International .... Montréal, QC
Ludlow Project Services .... Oakville, ON
Markent Personnel Inc .... USA
Marlene Bilodeau Conseils .... Chicoutimi, QC
Matchtech Engineering .... UNITED KINGDOM
Montgomery Thomason Assoc .... Mississauga, ON
MPA Recherche de Cadres .... Brossard, QC
Pinton Forrest & Madden .... Vancouver, BC
Planigestion A. Choquette .... Duvernay, QC
RBA Intl HR Consultants .... Westmount, QC
Robinson Assoc Personnel .... Vancouver, BC
Rod Turpin & Assoc .... Edmonton, AB
Roevin Tech People .... North Vancouver, BC
Roevin Tech People .... Edmonton, AB

PULP & PAPER (Cont.)
PAPETERIE (Suivre)

Roevin Tech People .... Calgary, AB
Roevin Tech People .... Montréal, QC
Savage Consultants .... Vancouver, BC
TDM Technical Services .... Toronto, ON
Technical Skills Consulting .... Toronto, ON
Technisolutions Executive .... Aylmer, QC
Wood West & Partners .... Vancouver, BC
Yves Plouffe et assoc .... Île-des-Soeurs, QC

PURCHASING
ACHAT

500 Services de Selection .... Val-d'Or, QC
A.W. Fraser Assoc .... Edmonton, AB
Access Career Solutions .... Brampton, ON
Ad-Link Advertising .... Toronto, ON
Adecco Canada .... Ottawa, ON
Adecco LPI .... Saint-Laurent, QC
Adecco Québec .... Laval, QC
Adler Recruitment .... UNITED KINGDOM
Allen Austin Lowe & Powers .... USA
Alliance Personnel Group .... Edmonton, AB
Alliance Personnel Group .... Oakville, ON
Applicants Inc. .... Kitchener, ON
Audax Corporation .... Toronto, ON
Barry Blostein Recruitment .... Thornhill, ON
Bray Larouche et Assoc .... Montréal, QC
Canadian Findings .... Toronto, ON
CAPP Employment Svcs .... Mississauga, ON
Centrex HR Centre .... Hamilton, ON
Chapman & Associates .... Vancouver, BC
Christmas McIvor Assoc .... Mississauga, ON
Connors Lovell Assoc .... Cambridge, ON
Connors Lovell Assoc .... Mississauga, ON
Corporate Consultants .... Toronto, ON
Courtney Personnel .... Brampton, ON
Delorme et Assoc .... Québec, QC
Doré Liaison .... Greenfield Park, QC
Dumont & Associates .... Vancouver, BC
Dumont & Associates .... North Vancouver, BC
E-Search Consulting .... Toronto, ON
Emplois plus pre-sélection .... Lasalle, QC
First Choice Personnel .... Toronto, ON
Gallant Search Group .... London, ON
Gaudry Shink Levasseur .... Montréal, QC
Gauthier Conseils .... Montréal, QC
Gestion-Conseil Gilles Richer .... Montréal, QC
GR Search Inc .... Toronto, ON
GRH Consultants Inc .... Québec, QC
Groupe SFP .... Trois-Rivières, QC
Harcourt & Assoc .... Edmonton, AB
Harcourt & Assoc .... Calgary, AB
Harris Consulting Corp .... Winnipeg, MB
HT Search Company .... Nepean, ON
Human Edge Consulting .... Richmond Hill, ON
Human Resource Group Mgmnt .... Edmonton, AB
InterSearch Canada/Staffing .... Halifax, NS
Kelly Permanent Recruit .... Toronto, ON
Kelly Permanent Recruit .... Toronto, ON
Kelly Permanent Recruit .... Mississauga, ON
Landon Morgan Inc .... Thorold, ON
London Executive Consultants .... London, ON
Louise Robinson Placement .... Keene, ON
Manpower Professional .... Victoria, BC
Manpower Professional .... Vancouver, BC

Manpower Professional .... Richmond, BC
Manpower Professional .... Burnaby, BC
Manpower Professional .... Edmonton, AB
Manpower Professional .... Red Deer, AB
Manpower Professional .... Calgary, AB
Manpower Professional .... Regina, SK
Manpower Professional .... Winnipeg, MB
Manpower Professional .... Thunder Bay, ON
Manpower Professional .... Sudbury, ON
Manpower Professional .... Windsor, ON
Manpower Professional .... London, ON
Manpower Professional .... Guelph, ON
Manpower Professional .... Toronto, ON
Manpower Professional .... Toronto, ON
Manpower Professional .... Toronto, ON
Manpower Professional .... Toronto, ON
Manpower Professional .... Toronto, ON
Manpower Professional .... Hamilton, ON
Manpower Professional .... Burlington, ON
Manpower Professional .... Brampton, ON
Manpower Professional .... Mississauga, ON
Manpower Professional .... Barrie, ON
Manpower Professional .... Newmarket, ON
Manpower Professional .... St. Catharines, ON
Manpower Professional .... Niagara Falls, ON
Manpower Professional .... Pickering, ON
Manpower Professional .... Peterborough, ON
Manpower Professional .... Cobourg, ON
Manpower Professional .... Belleville, ON
Manpower Professional .... Kingston, ON
Manpower Professional .... Brockville, ON
Manpower Professional .... Cornwall, ON
Manpower Professional .... Nepean, ON
Manpower Professional .... Ottawa, ON
Manpower Professional .... Granby, ON
Manpower Professional .... Sherbrooke, QC
Manpower Professional .... Montréal, QC
Manpower Professional .... Québec, QC
Manpower Professional .... Fredericton, NB
Manpower Professional .... Saint John, NB
Manpower Professional .... Charlottetown, PE
Manpower Professional .... Halifax, NS
Manpower Professional .... Sydney, NS
Manpower Professional .... St. John's, NF
Manpower Services Canada .... Toronto, ON
Martin Randolph Assoc .... Montréal, QC
Matthews Management .... Richmond Hill, ON
McDonald-Green Personnel .... Cambridge, ON
Megasearch International .... Hudson, QC
Meridia Recruitment Svcs .... Halifax, NS
Michael J. Cavanagh Assoc .... Toronto, ON
Morgan Exec Search Group .... Toronto, ON
Parkwood Associates .... Mississauga, ON
Permanent Solutions .... Mississauga, ON
Petro Staff Intl HR Advisors .... Calgary, AB
Pettitt Group Inc., The .... Burlington, ON
Pinstripe Personnel .... Toronto, ON
PME Partenaire Consult .... Saint-Georges, QC
Prichard Kymen Inc .... Edmonton, AB
Prosearch Associates .... Mississauga, ON
Prospects Plus .... Kirkland, QC
Protrans Personnel Svcs .... Dieppe, NB
Prud'Homme Groupe-Conseil .... Montréal, QC
Quantum Mgmnt Services .... Toronto, ON
Resource 7 Inc .... Edmonton, AB
Richter Raymond Group .... Oakville, ON
Robert Lamarre & Assoc .... Saint-Lambert, QC
Robert T. Keegan & Assoc .... Oakville, ON
Rolland ressources humaines .... Montréal, QC
RWJ & Associates .... London, ON

PURCHASING (Cont.)
ACHAT (Suivre)

RWJ & Associates .... Kitchener, ON
S. Tanner & Associates .... Oakville, ON
Servocraft Limited .... Toronto, ON
Stephen Laramee Associates .... Toronto, ON
Sydelle Associates .... Georgetown, ON
Taylor Personnel .... Victoria, BC
Taylor Personnel .... Edmonton, AB
TSI Group / TSI Staffing .... Mississauga, ON
W. Hutt Mgmnt Resources .... Burlington, ON
Wellington Partners Intl .... Kitchener, ON

QUALITY CONTROL
CONTRÔL DE QUALITÉ

Applicants Inc. .... Kitchener, ON
ATS Reliance Tech Group .... London, ON
Axxes Technologies .... Sillery, QC
C.W. Clasen Recruiting .... Coquitlam, BC
Drake International .... Edmonton, AB
Excel HR Consultants .... Toronto, ON
Grand River Personnel .... Kitchener, ON
Information Bus Consulting .... Edmonton, AB
Kelly Scientific .... Mississauga, ON
Kelly Scientifique .... Montréal, QC
Key Executive Consultants .... Barrie, ON
Level A Inc .... Peterborough, ON
Little Group, The .... Brantford, ON
Little Group, The .... Burlington, ON
Pioneer Exec Consultants .... Toronto, ON
Roevin Tech People .... Sarnia, ON
Roevin Tech People .... Kitchener, ON
Roevin Tech People .... Markham, ON
RWJ & Associates .... London, ON
RWJ & Associates .... Kitchener, ON
Strategic Resources Intl .... Toronto, ON
Summit Personnel Services .... Windsor, ON
Technical Mgmnt Resources .... Barrie, ON
Van Hees Personnel .... Dundas, ON

REAL ESTATE
IMMOBILIER

Associated Recruitment .... Toronto, ON
Bower Ng Staff Systems .... Vancouver, BC
Bryan Jason Assoc .... Toronto, ON
CAPP Employment Svcs .... Mississauga, ON
D & H Group .... Vancouver, BC
Diversified Staffing Svcs .... Edmonton, AB
Diversified Staffing Svcs .... Calgary, AB
Edie Bench Personnel .... Toronto, ON
Everest Mgmnt Network .... Toronto, ON
Glazin / Sisco Exec Search .... Vancouver, BC
Glazin / Sisco Exec Search .... Toronto, ON
Global Personnel .... Toronto, ON
Godbout Martin Godbout Assoc .... Hull, QC
Interchange Personnel .... Calgary, AB
Katherine Holt Enterprises .... Toronto, ON
Korn/Ferry Intl .... Toronto, ON
MacKenzie Gray Mgmnt .... Calgary, AB
MacRae Atwood Mgmnt .... Toronto, ON
McCracken/Labbett Exec Search .... Toronto, ON
Mintz & Partners .... Toronto, ON
Partnervision Consulting .... Toronto, ON

Peak Associates Inc .... Toronto, ON
PG Consultants .... Toronto, ON
Richmark Group, The .... Toronto, ON
Robert Connelly & Associates .... USA
Rutherford Intl Exec Search .... Toronto, ON
Spencer Stuart .... Toronto, ON
TAG Personnel Consultants .... Montréal, QC
Victor & Gold .... Montréal, QC
Walsh King .... Vancouver, BC
Ward Vinge & Associates .... Edmonton, AB
Ward Vinge & Associates .... Calgary, AB
Zeidel Gregory Associates .... Toronto, ON

RETAIL
VENTE AU DÉTAIL

Allen Etcovitch Assoc .... Montréal, QC
Bedford Consulting Group .... Toronto, ON
Bedford Consulting Group .... Oakville, ON
Birch & Assoc .... Montréal, QC
Bruce Ward Partners .... Toronto, ON
Campbell Edgar Inc .... Richmond, BC
Campbell Edgar Inc .... Delta, BC
Canadianretail.ca .... Vancouver, BC
Claude Guedj Assoc .... Montréal, QC
Coke & Associates .... Toronto, ON
Colintex Agencies .... Toronto, ON
Cromark International .... Mississauga, ON
Dotemtex Executive Search .... Sillery, QC
Drake International .... Toronto, ON
Dumont & Associates .... Vancouver, BC
Dumont & Associates .... North Vancouver, BC
Dynamic Employment Solution .... Brampton, ON
Dynamic Employment Solution .... Brampton, ON
E.L. Shore & Associates .... Toronto, ON
ePersonnel Inc .... Montréal, QC
Executive 2000 Institute .... Toronto, ON
Executive Network .... Victoria, BC
FHG International .... Toronto, ON
Gestion Conseils DLT Inc .... Manotick, ON
Glazin / Sisco Exec Search .... Vancouver, BC
Glazin / Sisco Exec Search .... Toronto, ON
Hunt Technical Personnel .... Vancouver, BC
Hunt Technical Personnel .... Calgary, AB
Hunt Technical Personnel .... Toronto, ON
Hunt Technical Personnel .... Montréal, QC
Karabus Management .... Toronto, ON
Lecours Wolfson Ltd .... Toronto, ON
Management One Consultants .... Toronto, ON
Mandrake Mgmt Consult .... Toronto, ON
Mascaren International .... Toronto, ON
Matteson Management .... Toronto, ON
Michael Stern Associates .... Toronto, ON
Moon Over Niagara .... St. Catharines, ON
NAP Executive Apparel .... Montréal, QC
NAP Executive Retail .... Toronto, ON
Patty Shapiro & Assoc .... Montréal, QC
People + ... Toronto, ON
PeopleFind Inc. .... Markham, ON
Personnel Mgmt Consultants .... Calgary, AB
Planigestion A. Choquette .... Duvernay, QC
Richter Raymond Group .... Oakville, ON
RJ Professionals .... Toronto, ON
Sheldon Recruiting.. Toronto, ON
Sirius Personnel .... Montréal, QC
Sussex Retail Management .... Mississauga, ON
Syntech Placements .... Toronto, ON
Tony Curtis & Associates .... Toronto, ON

RETAIL (Cont.)
VENTE AU DÉTAIL (Suivre)

True North Exec Search .... Toronto, ON
Wilkie Group International .... Toronto, ON
Williams Associates .... Toronto, ON
Wolf Gugler & Associates .... Toronto, ON
Worth Personnel Group .... Toronto, ON
Worth Personnel Group .... Mississauga, ON
Yves Elkas Inc .... Montréal, QC
Zenzen Pierce Assoc .... Toronto, ON

SALES
VENTES

1st Choice Personnel .... USA
500 Services de Selection .... Val-d'Or, QC
A.E. Harrison Partners .... Mississauga, ON
A.W. Fraser Assoc .... Calgary, AB
Abel Placement Consult .... Markham, ON
ABP Personnel Consult .... Westmount, QC
Addition 2000 .... Montréal, QC
Adecco Canada .... Victoria, BC
Adecco Canada .... Saskatoon, SK
Adecco Canada .... Toronto, ON
Adecco Canada .... Markham, ON
Adecco Canada .... Pickering, ON
Adecco Canada .... Ottawa, ON
Adecco / Compaq .... Toronto, ON
Adecco Personnel Technique .... Sherbrooke, QC
Adecco Québec .... Chicoutimi, QC
Adecco Québec .... Québec, QC
AES Recruitment .... Toronto, ON
AIME Consultants .... Vancouver, BC
Aldonna Barry Mgmnt Consult .... Bolton, ON
Allen Austin Lowe & Powers .... USA
Allen Personnel Svcs .... Cambridge, ON
Alternative Resources Corp .... Toronto, ON
Altura Group .... Toronto, ON
Anderson Associates .... Toronto, ON
Angus One Pro Recruitment .... Vancouver, BC
Apple One Employment .... Toronto, ON
Argus Group Corporation .... Toronto, ON
Ariel Group Intl .... Toronto, ON
Armor Personnel .... Orangeville, ON
Armor Personnel .... Brampton, ON
Armor Personnel .... Mississauga, ON
Armor Personnel .... Vaughan, ON
Ashlar-Stone Consultants .... Mississauga, ON
Austin Marlowe Intl .... Toronto, ON
Bailey Professional Search .... Calgary, AB
Baldwin Staffing Group .... Calgary, AB
Barrett Rose & Lee .... Toronto, ON
Barry Hults Consultants .... Markham, ON
Belanger Partners .... Thornhill, ON
Bernard Frigon & Assoc .... Montréal, QC
Bilingual Source .... Toronto, ON
Birch & Assoc .... Montréal, QC
Botrie Associates .... Toronto, ON
Boyden Global Exec Search .... Calgary, AB
Brainhunter.com .... Toronto, ON
Brainhunter.com .... Ottawa, ON
Brant & Associates .... Winnipeg, MB
Bray Larouche et Assoc .... Montréal, QC
Brethet Barnum Associates .... Toronto, ON
Brock Placement Group .... Toronto, ON
Bruce Cowan Assoc .... Toronto, ON
C.G. Thomson & Co .... Toronto, ON

C.N. Taylor Consulting .... Bedford, NS
C. Wolfe & Assoc .... Toronto, ON
Cambridge Mgmnt Planning .... Toronto, ON
Cameron Consulting Group .... Brampton, ON
Campbell Clark Inc .... Mississauga, ON
Campbell Edgar Inc .... Richmond, BC
Campbell Edgar Inc .... Delta, BC
Campbell Morden Inc .... Toronto, ON
Canadian Exec Consultants .... Toronto, ON
Canpro Executive Search .... Markham, ON
CAPP Employment Svcs .... Mississauga, ON
Career Advance Employment .... Burlington, ON
Career Partners/Harrison .... Hamilton, ON
Carscarp Consulting .... Gloucester, ON
Central Mgmnt Consultants .... Toronto, ON
Centrex HR Centre .... Hamilton, ON
Chacra Belliveau & Assoc .... Montréal, QC
Chad Management Group .... Toronto, ON
Chapman & Associates .... Vancouver, BC
Chase Consultants .... Mississauga, ON
Chisholm & Partners Intl .... Toronto, ON
Christmas McIvor Assoc .... Mississauga, ON
Claymore Search Group .... London, ON
Clements Consulting Group .... Calgary, AB
CMP Select .... Toronto, ON
Coape Staffing Network .... Vancouver, BC
Coape Staffing Network .... Burnaby, BC
Coape Staffing Network .... Edmonton, AB
Coape Staffing Network .... Calgary, AB
Coast Personnel Svcs .... Nanaimo, BC
Coe & Company Intl .... Calgary, AB
Coke & Associates .... Toronto, ON
Colintex Agencies .... Toronto, ON
Connor Clark Assoc .... Dundas, ON
Connors Lovell Assoc .... Cambridge, ON
Connors Lovell Assoc .... Mississauga, ON
Conseillers Jacques Cartier .... Montréal, QC
ConsulPro .... Westmount, QC
ConsulPRO Executive Search .... Ottawa, ON
Contempra Personnel .... Pointe-Claire, QC
Core Group, The .... Toronto, ON
Corporate & Career Develop .... Vancouver, BC
Corporate Consultants .... Toronto, ON
Corporate Recruiters .... Vancouver, BC
Danette Milne Corp Search .... Markham, ON
Daniluck & Associates .... Edmonton, AB
Dare Human Resources .... Ottawa, ON
David Aplin & Assoc .... Calgary, AB
David Warwick Kennedy Assoc .... Vancouver, BC
Delorme et Assoc .... Québec, QC
Derhak Ireland Partners .... Toronto, ON
Dial Staffing Solutions .... Calgary, AB
Digital Power Corp .... Calgary, AB
Donald L Hart & Assoc .... Toronto, ON
Donati & Associates .... Maple, ON
Doré Liaison .... Greenfield Park, QC
Drake International .... Toronto, ON
Drakkar Human Resources .... Montréal, QC
Drakkar Human Resources .... Québec, QC
Duncan & Associates .... Toronto, ON
Dunhill Professional Search .... Vancouver, BC
Elliot Associates .... Toronto, ON
Emplois plus pre-sélection .... Lasalle, QC
Eureka Recruitment .... Calgary, AB
Everest Mgmnt Network .... Toronto, ON
Excalibur Careers .... Markham, ON
Execusource Staffing Intl .... Windsor, ON
Executive Network .... Victoria, BC
Executive Recruiters .... London, ON
Executive Registry .... Montréal, QC

SALES (Cont.)
VENTES (Suivre)

Executives Available .... Pointe-Claire, QC
Executrade Consultants .... Edmonton, AB
Express Personnel Svcs .... Port Coquitlam, BC
Express Personnel Svcs .... Windsor, ON
Express Personnel Svcs .... London, ON
Express Personnel Svcs .... Kitchener, ON
Express Personnel Svcs .... Guelph, ON
Express Personnel Svcs .... Hamilton, ON
Express Personnel Svcs .... Burlington, ON
Express Personnel Svcs .... Ottawa, ON
Farley Law & Assoc .... Thornhill, ON
Feldman Gray Associates .... Toronto, ON
Fiala Consulting Group .... Vancouver, BC
Fifth Option .... Burnaby, BC
First Choice Personnel .... Toronto, ON
Fisher Group Exec Search .... Calgary, AB
Future Executive Personnel .... Toronto, ON
Futurestep .... Toronto, ON
G.L. Penney & Associates .... Edmonton, AB
G-P Personnel .... Chicoutimi, QC
Galloway and Associates .... Toronto, ON
Galt Global Recruiting .... Vancouver, BC
Galt Global Recruiting .... Calgary, AB
Gaudry Shink Levasseur .... Montréal, QC
Gauthier Conseils .... Montréal, QC
Georgian Staffing Svcs .... Collingwood, ON
Glen Abbey Exec Search .... Oakville, ON
Global Consulting Group .... Markham, ON
Global Placement Svcs .... Mississauga, ON
Goldbeck Recruiting .... Vancouver, BC
Golden Mile Mgmnt Consulting .... Toronto, ON
Graham Elliott & Assoc .... Toronto, ON
GRH Consultants Inc .... Québec, QC
Groupe conseil Lamarche .... Granby, QC
Groupe Conseil Stante .... Saint-Léonard, QC
Groupe Primacor .... Longueuil, QC
GSA Search Consultants .... Bedford, NS
Guay Labelle & Assoc .... Montréal, QC
Hains & Associates ...., Victoria, BC
Harcourt & Assoc .... Edmonton, AB
Harcourt & Assoc .... Calgary, AB
Harrington Staffing Services .... Ottawa, ON
Hart & Associates .... Winnipeg, MB
Hayhurst Consulting .... London, ON
HEC Group .... Ancaster, ON
Herman Smith Search Inc .... Toronto, ON
Holloway Schulz & Partners .... Vancouver, BC
Houston Personnel Group .... Winnipeg, MB
HR Business Partners .... Calgary, AB
HR / RH Inc. .... Montréal, QC
Human Edge Consulting .... Richmond Hill, ON
Human Resource Mgmt Group .... Unionville, ON
Human Resources Consult .... Mississauga, ON
HumanEtics Inc .... Mississauga, ON
Hunt Technical Personnel .... Vancouver, BC
Hunt Technical Personnel .... Calgary, AB
Hunt Technical Personnel .... Toronto, ON
Hunt Technical Personnel .... Toronto, ON
Hunt Technical Personnel .... Saint-Laurent, QC
Hunt Technical Personnel .... Montréal, QC
Hutchinson Group .... Toronto, ON
Ideal Personnel .... Mississauga, ON
Impact Staffing .... Windsor, ON
IMS Innovative Mgmnt .... Toronto, ON
In Place Select Recruitment .... Toronto, ON
International Staffing .... UNITED KINGDOM
J. Edgar & Associates .... Toronto, ON

J.O. Bush & Associates .... Mindemoya, ON
J.R. Bechtle & Company .... USA
Jenereaux & Associates .... Mississauga, ON
Jerry Adel & Company .... Toronto, ON
Job Born Candidate Select .... Hamilton, ON
Keith Bagg & Associates .... Toronto, ON
Kelly Permanent Recruit .... Toronto, ON
Kelly Permanent Recruit .... Toronto, ON
Kelly Permanent Recruit .... Mississauga, ON
Kelly Professional & Tech .... Belleville, ON
Kenneth Murphy & Assoc .... Halifax, NS
Kingsley Allen IT Search .... Toronto, ON
Knipper & Associates .... Kingston, ON
Laing & Associates .... Toronto, ON
Lawrence Joe Consultants .... Toronto, ON
Levton Group .... Toronto, ON
Link Resource Partners .... Toronto, ON
LMR Consultants .... Thornhill, ON
Lock & Associates .... Vancouver, BC
Lock & Associates .... Edmonton, AB
Lock & Associates .... Calgary, AB
Lock & Associates .... Saskatoon, SK
Lock & Associates .... Winnipeg, MB
Lock & Associates .... Toronto, ON
Lock & Associates .... Montréal, QC
Lock & Associates .... Moncton, NB
Lock & Associates .... Halifax, NS
Lynne Milette & Associates .... Chapeau, QC
Lynx Career Consultants .... Mississauga, ON
M.E. Money & Associates .... Toronto, ON
Maclean & Assoc .... Mississauga, ON
Madison MacArthur Inc .... Toronto, ON
Management One Consultants .... Toronto, ON
Mandrake Mgmt Consult .... Toronto, ON
Manpower Professional .... Markham, ON
Manpower Professional .... Cornwall, ON
MARCON Mgmnt Consultants .... Montréal, QC
Marlene Bilodeau Conseils .... Chicoutimi, QC
Mascaren International .... Toronto, ON
Master Performers .... Toronto, ON
Matchpoint Exec Placement .... Toronto, ON
Matteson Management .... Toronto, ON
Maureen Sinden Exec Search .... Ottawa, ON
McCracken/Labbett Exec Search .... Toronto, ON
McDonald-Green Personnel .... Cambridge, ON
McIntyre Mgmnt Resources .... Hamilton, ON
McKinnon Groupe Conseil .... Montréal, QC
McKinnon Mgmnt Group .... Toronto, ON
McLean Exec Consultants .... Calgary, AB
McNeill Nakamoto Recruit .... Vancouver, BC
Melmak Consultants Ltd .... Toronto, ON
Meridia Recruitment Svcs .... Halifax, NS
Merit Vendor Personnel .... Toronto, ON
Meyers Norris Penny .... Winnipeg, MB
Michael Page Finance .... CHINA
Michael Stern Associates .... Toronto, ON
Miller Recruitment Solutions .... Halifax, NS
Mission Critical Recruit .... Edmonton, AB
Montgomery Thomason Assoc .... Mississauga, ON
Morgan Exec Search Group .... Toronto, ON
Morgan Palmer Search .... Toronto, ON
Morris Pervin Group .... Toronto, ON
Mosor Search Group .... Mississauga, ON
MQS Executive Search .... Toronto, ON
Multec Canada .... Toronto, ON
Multec Canada .... Nepean, ON
Multec Canada .... Montréal, QC
Narami Executive Search .... Toronto, ON
Nationwide Advertising Svc .... Toronto, ON
Network Corporate Search .... Calgary, AB

SALES (Cont.)
VENTES (Suivre)

NewSource Management .... Toronto, ON
Northwind Consulting .... King City, ON
P.R.Y. .... Toronto, ON
Palmer & Associates .... Kingston, ON
Paragon Consulting .... Toronto, ON
Partners Employment Group .... Toronto, ON
Partners in Search .... Toronto, ON
People + ... Toronto, ON
People Bank, The .... Winnipeg, MB
People Bank, The .... Ottawa, ON
People First Solutions .... Vancouver, BC
Perceptive Edge .... Toronto, ON
Permanent Search Group .... Mississauga, ON
Permanent Solutions .... Mississauga, ON
Perry Martel International .... Ottawa, ON
Personnel by Pro-Staff .... Windsor, ON
Personnel Menen .... Mount Royal, QC
Personnel Search .... Saint John, NB
Personnel Search .... Moncton, NB
Peter Glaser Assoc .... UNITED KINGDOM
Phee Farrer Jones Ltd .... UNITED KINGDOM
Phelps Staffing Resource .... Thunder Bay, ON
Pierre H. Delisle conseil .... Montréal, QC
Pila Recruiting & Assoc .... Richmond, BC
Pioneer Exec Consultants .... Toronto, ON
Planigestion A. Choquette .... Duvernay, QC
PME Partenaire Consult .... Saint-Georges, QC
Pollack Group, The .... Ottawa, ON
PricewaterhouseCoopers .... Edmonton, AB
PricewaterhouseCoopers .... Montréal, QC
PricewaterhouseCoopers .... Québec, QC
Prichard Kymen Inc .... Edmonton, AB
Pride in Personnel .... Markham, ON
Prime Management Group .... London, ON
Prime Management Group .... Cambridge, ON
Prior Resource Group .... Kitchener, ON
Professional Develop Assoc .... Oakville, ON
Professional Exec Services .... Calgary, AB
Prokosch Group, The .... Calgary, AB
Prosearch Associates .... Mississauga, ON
ProSource Mgmnt Consult .... Woodbridge, ON
Prospects Plus .... Kirkland, QC
Prud'Homme Groupe-Conseil .... Montréal, QC
Quantum .... Montréal, QC
Quantum EDP Recruiting Svcs .... Ottawa, ON
Quantum EDP Recruiting Svcs .... USA
Quantum, Les services .... Longueuil, QC
Quantum, Les services .... Pointe-Claire, QC
Quantum, Les services .... Laval, QC
Quantum Mgmnt Services .... Toronto, ON
Quantum Mgmnt Services .... Toronto, ON
Quantum Mgmnt Services .... Mississauga, ON
Quantum Mgmnt Services .... Ottawa, ON
Quantum Mgmt Services .... Toronto, ON
Questus Recruitment .... Calgary, AB
Quintal & Associates HR .... Montréal, QC
Ray Berndtson/Lovas Stanley .... Toronto, ON
Resource Corporation, The .... Toronto, ON
Resource Management Group .... Toronto, ON
Resource Recruiters .... Toronto, ON
Results Seekers HR Svcs .... Guelph, ON
Richardson Personnel .... Toronto, ON
Richter Raymond Group .... Oakville, ON
Robert Half Canada .... Toronto, ON
Robert Half Canada .... Ottawa, ON
Robert Paquet & Assoc .... Sainte-Foy, QC
Robertson Human Asset .... Burlington, ON

Robinson Rose Associates .... Mississauga, ON
Rockwell Placement Agencies .... Richmond, BC
Rolland ressources humaines .... Montréal, QC
Rossi & Associates .... Vancouver, BC
Rudl International .... Ottawa, ON
RWJ & Associates .... London, ON
Salesforce Development .... Westmount, QC
SalesSearch .... Toronto, ON
Sam Perri & Associates .... Mississauga, ON
Schoales & Associates .... Toronto, ON
Search Justified Selection .... Toronto, ON
SearchCorp International .... Calgary, AB
SearchWest Inc .... Vancouver, BC
Segall & Associates .... Toronto, ON
Sellutions Inc. .... Nepean, ON
Silicon Executive Search .... Toronto, ON
Silicon Network .... Toronto, ON
Sirius Personnel .... Montréal, QC
Snelgrove Personnel .... Hamilton, ON
Sourceco Exec Search .... Edmonton, AB
Sourceco Exec Search .... Westmount, QC
Spherion Workforce .... Victoria, BC
Spherion Workforce .... Vancouver, BC
Spherion Workforce .... Edmonton, AB
Spherion Workforce .... Edmonton, AB
Spherion Workforce .... Calgary, AB
Spherion Workforce .... Winnipeg, MB
Spherion Workforce .... Toronto, ON
Spherion Workforce .... Toronto, ON
Spherion Workforce .... Toronto, ON
Spherion Workforce .... Toronto, ON
Spherion Workforce .... Hamilton, ON
Spherion Workforce .... Mississauga, ON
Spherion Workforce .... Barrie, ON
Spherion Workforce .... Pickering, ON
Spherion Workforce .... Whitby, ON
Spherion Workforce .... Oshawa, ON
Spherion Workforce .... Kanata, ON
Spherion Workforce .... Ottawa, ON
Spherion Workforce .... Ottawa, ON
Spherion Workforce .... Montréal, QC
Spherion Workforce .... Halifax, NS
SPI Executive Search .... Ottawa, ON
SSA Services Conseils .... Montréal, QC
St-Amour & Assoc .... Toronto, ON
St-Amour & Assoc .... Montréal, QC
Staff Bureau Employment .... Edmonton, AB
Staffing Strategies .... USA
Star Search Consultants .... Toronto, ON
Stellar Personnel Placement .... Windsor, ON
Stellar Personnel Placement .... London, ON
Stephen Laramee Associates .... Toronto, ON
Sterling Hoffman .... Toronto, ON
Sterling Hoffman .... USA
Stoakley-Dudley Consult .... Mississauga, ON
Strategic Resources Intl .... Toronto, ON
Summit Search Group .... Calgary, AB
Sydelle Associates .... Georgetown, ON
Synagent Inc .... Woodlawn, ON
TAL Group .... Toronto, ON
TaylorMade Careers .... USA
Technical Skills Consulting .... Toronto, ON
TechNix Inc .... Toronto, ON
Thinkpath.com Inc. .... Toronto, ON
Thomas Group, The .... Mississauga, ON
Thomas-Mitchell .... Niagara-on-the-Lake, ON
Toronto Exec Consultants .... Toronto, ON
Totten & Associates .... London, ON
Unique Personnel Canada .... Concord, ON
Unique Personnel Services .... Dorval, QC

SALES (Cont.)
VENTES (Suivre)

SCIENTIFIC & RESEARCH
SCIENTIFIQUE ET RECHERCHE

SCIENTIFIC & RESEARCH (Cont.)
SCIENTIFIQUE ET RECHERCHE (Suivre)

Technical Service Consult .... Surrey, BC
Technical Service Consult .... Toronto, ON
Technical Solutions Inc .... USA
TEKsystems .... Mississauga, ON
TEKsystems .... Ottawa, ON
Trella & Associates .... Toronto, ON
Western Mgmnt Consultants .... Calgary, AB
Wypich International .... Toronto, ON
Yorkland Search Tech .... Mississauga, ON

TELECOM
TÉLÉCOMMUNICATIONS

A.B. Schwartz Assoc .... Toronto, ON
Abecassis recherches cadres .... Montréal, QC
Adecco Canada .... Ottawa, ON
ADV Advanced Tech Svcs .... Toronto, ON
Advanced Tech Partners .... Vancouver, BC
Advanced Tech Partners .... Edmonton, AB
Advanced Tech Partners .... Calgary, AB
Advanced Tech Partners .... Toronto, ON
Advantage Tech .... Calgary, AB
Aim Personnel Svcs .... Ottawa, ON
Al-Khaleej Computers .... SAUDI ARABIA
Alan Davis Assoc .... Hudson Heights, QC
Allen Ballach Assoc .... Whitby, ON
Alumni-Network Recruit .... Mississauga, ON
Angus Employment .... Burlington, ON
Argus Group Corporation .... Toronto, ON
Ashton Computer Pros .... North Vancouver, BC
Assoc de dessins mecaniques .... Montréal, QC
ASTRA Management Corp .... Vancouver, BC
AT Kearney Executive .... Toronto, ON
Austin Park Mgmnt Group .... Toronto, ON
Axxes Technologies .... Saint-Laurent, QC
Axxes Technologies .... Sillery, QC
Aztech Recruitment .... USA
Bailey Professional Search .... Calgary, AB
Barry Blostein Recruitment .... Thornhill, ON
Bassett Laudi Partners .... Toronto, ON
Bedford Consulting Group .... Toronto, ON
Bedford Consulting Group .... Oakville, ON
Belanger Partners .... Thornhill, ON
Berlys Personnel .... Saint-Laurent, QC
Bernard Frigon & Assoc .... Montréal, QC
BMA International .... Montréal, QC
BMA International .... Montréal, QC
Boscan Consultants .... Marysville, ON
Botrie Associates .... Toronto, ON
Boyden Global Exec Search .... Calgary, AB
Bradford Bachinski Ltd .... Ottawa, ON
Bridge Info Technology .... Vancouver, BC
Bruce Cowan Assoc .... Toronto, ON
Btsn inc. .... St. George, ON
C.N. Taylor Consulting .... Bedford, NS
C. Snow & Associates .... Toronto, ON
C. Wolfe & Assoc .... Toronto, ON
Calian Technology Svcs .... Mississauga, ON
Calian Technology Svcs .... Ottawa, ON
Calian Technology Svcs .... Kanata, ON
Cameron Consulting Group .... Brampton, ON
Candidatech placement .... Sainte-Julie, QC
CDI Technical Svcs .... Calgary, AB
Centre for Corp Resources .... Toronto, ON
CG Consulting Group .... Toronto, ON

Chase Consultants .... Mississauga, ON
Chisholm & Partners Intl .... Toronto, ON
Churchill Group, The .... Toronto, ON
Coe & Company Intl .... Calgary, AB
ComFact Corp .... Oakville, ON
Connor Clark Assoc .... Dundas, ON
Conroy Partners .... Calgary, AB
Corporate Recruiters .... Vancouver, BC
CTS International .... USA
D.P. Group, The .... UNITED KINGDOM
David Aplin & Assoc .... Edmonton, AB
David Aplin & Assoc .... Calgary, AB
Davis Search Group .... Toronto, ON
DDP Consulting Group .... Vancouver, BC
Distinct Directions .... Mississauga, ON
Dotemtex Executive Search .... Montréal, QC
Dunhill Professional Search .... Vancouver, BC
Duo Mega Inc .... Montréal, QC
Dynamic Employment Solution .... Brampton, ON
Dynamic Employment Solution .... Brampton, ON
EAE Info Staff Ltd .... UNITED KINGDOM
Eastridge Infotech Tech Staffing .... USA
ENS Group Inc. .... Ottawa, ON
ERC Management Group .... Kelowna, BC
ERP Staffing Solutions .... Brampton, ON
Executive Source .... Regina, SK
First Choice Personnel .... Toronto, ON
Fisher Group Exec Search .... Calgary, AB
Florio Gosset Group .... Mississauga, ON
FSK Associates Inc .... USA
Global Personnel .... Toronto, ON
Global Placement Svcs .... Mississauga, ON
Grant Search Group .... Toronto, ON
Groom & Assoc .... Pointe-Claire, QC
Groupe Primacor .... Longueuil, QC
Groupe Ranger .... Montréal, QC
GSG Partners .... Toronto, ON
Harrington Staffing Services .... Ottawa, ON
Heenan Consulting IT .... Toronto, ON
Hire Choice .... Toronto, ON
Hire Technology .... Toronto, ON
Human Resources Consult .... Mississauga, ON
HumanEtics Inc .... Mississauga, ON
IBISKA Telecom .... Ottawa, ON
INFO-TEK Consulting .... Edmonton, AB
Information Resources Ctr .... SAUDI ARABIA
InGenius Engineering Inc .... Ottawa, ON
Interim Mgmt Resources .... Mississauga, ON
InterSearch Canada/Staffing .... Halifax, NS
InterSearch Canada/Western .... Vancouver, BC
IT Resources .... Markham, ON
Jenereaux & Associates .... Mississauga, ON
JENEX Technology Placement .... Vancouver, BC
JSG Group Mgmnt Consult .... Unionville, ON
JSL Search Leaders .... Toronto, ON
Kelly Professional & Tech .... Toronto, ON
Kenniff Denis Inc. .... Montréal, QC
Kforce.ca .... Toronto, ON
Kingsley Allen IT Search .... Toronto, ON
Korn/Ferry Intl .... Toronto, ON
Korn/Ferry Intl .... Montréal, QC
LePage International .... Montréal, QC
Lewis Companies .... Toronto, ON
Logistic Solutions .... USA
Macdonald & Brisson Personnel .... Ottawa, ON
MacLean Hay Consulting .... Oakville, ON
Maizis & Miller Consultants .... Toronto, ON
Management Solutions .... Mississauga, ON
Mandrake Mgmt Consult .... Toronto, ON
Manpower Professional .... Victoria, BC

TELECOM (Cont.)
TÉLÉCOMMUNICATIONS (Suivre)

Manpower Professional .... Vancouver, BC
Manpower Professional .... Richmond, BC
Manpower Professional .... Burnaby, BC
Manpower Professional .... Edmonton, AB
Manpower Professional .... Red Deer, AB
Manpower Professional .... Calgary, AB
Manpower Professional .... Regina, SK
Manpower Professional .... Winnipeg, MB
Manpower Professional .... Thunder Bay, ON
Manpower Professional .... Sudbury, ON
Manpower Professional .... Windsor, ON
Manpower Professional .... London, ON
Manpower Professional .... Guelph, ON
Manpower Professional .... Toronto, ON
Manpower Professional .... Toronto, ON
Manpower Professional .... Toronto, ON
Manpower Professional .... Toronto, ON
Manpower Professional .... Hamilton, ON
Manpower Professional .... Burlington, ON
Manpower Professional .... Brampton, ON
Manpower Professional .... Mississauga, ON
Manpower Professional .... Barrie, ON
Manpower Professional .... Newmarket, ON
Manpower Professional .... St. Catharines, ON
Manpower Professional .... Niagara Falls, ON
Manpower Professional .... Pickering, ON
Manpower Professional .... Peterborough, ON
Manpower Professional .... Cobourg, ON
Manpower Professional .... Belleville, ON
Manpower Professional .... Kingston, ON
Manpower Professional .... Brockville, ON
Manpower Professional .... Nepean, ON
Manpower Professional .... Ottawa, ON
Manpower Professional .... Granby, ON
Manpower Professional .... Sherbrooke, QC
Manpower Professional .... Montréal, QC
Manpower Professional .... Québec, QC
Manpower Professional .... Fredericton, NB
Manpower Professional .... Saint John, NB
Manpower Professional .... Charlottetown, PE
Manpower Professional .... Halifax, NS
Manpower Professional .... Sydney, NS
Manpower Professional .... St. John's, NF
Manpower Services Canada .... Toronto, ON
Maranova Resources Corp .... Orleans, ON
Master Performers .... Toronto, ON
McQ International Svcs .... UNITED KINGDOM
Meda Group .... Windsor, ON
Meridia Recruitment Svcs .... Halifax, NS
Michael J. Cavanagh Assoc .... Toronto, ON
Michael Marmur & Assoc .... Toronto, ON
Michael Stern Associates .... Toronto, ON
MPA Recherche de Cadres .... Brossard, QC
MQS Executive Search .... Toronto, ON
MRK Consulting .... UNITED KINGDOM
National Executive .... Toronto, ON
National Systems Inc .... USA
Nelson Krynicki Assoc .... Mississauga, ON
Nesma International Svcs .... UNITED KINGDOM
Normatech Executive .... Toronto, ON
O'Sullivan Search .... Toronto, ON
ObjectSearch .... Toronto, ON
OCC Computer Personnel .... UNITED KINGDOM
Paragon Consulting .... Toronto, ON

Partners in Search .... Toronto, ON
Pila Recruiting & Assoc .... Richmond, BC
Placement Testart .... Westmount, QC
Pride in Personnel .... Markham, ON
Prime Source Management .... Toronto, ON
Pro-Action Personnel .... Chomedey, QC
Procom .... Calgary, AB
Project Mgmnt Recruiting .... Toronto, ON
Prolink Consulting .... Toronto, ON
Protocole .... Montréal, QC
Qualicum Consulting .... Ottawa, ON
Quantum EDP Recruiting Svcs .... Toronto, ON
Quantum EDP Recruiting Svcs .... USA
Queue Systems .... Markham, ON
Ray & Berndtson/Laurendeau .... Montréal, QC
Ray Berndtson/Lovas Stanley .... Toronto, ON
Recherches Johnson .... Saint-Lambert, QC
Relational Resources .... Toronto, ON
Rideau Management Group .... Nepean, ON
Robertson Hancock Ltd .... Toronto, ON
Robinson Fraser Group .... Toronto, ON
Rossi & Associates .... Vancouver, BC
Russell Reynolds Assoc .... Calgary, AB
SAG ressources humaines .... Montréal, QC
Search Justified Selection .... Toronto, ON
SearchWest Inc .... Vancouver, BC
Segall & Associates .... Toronto, ON
Silicon Executive Search .... Toronto, ON
Silicon Network .... Toronto, ON
Sourceco Exec Search .... Edmonton, AB
Sourceco Exec Search .... Westmount, QC
Spencer Stuart .... Toronto, ON
SSA Services Conseils .... Montréal, QC
Stoakley-Dudley Consult .... Mississauga, ON
StoneWood Group .... Toronto, ON
StoneWood Group .... Ottawa, ON
StoneWood Group .... Sainte-Geneviève, QC
Strategic Resources Intl .... Toronto, ON
Summit Search Group .... Calgary, AB
Systemsearch Consulting Svcs .... Toronto, ON
TAD Canada .... Calgary, AB
TAD Canada .... Brantford, ON
TAD Canada .... Mississauga, ON
TAD Canada .... Ottawa, ON
TAD Canada .... Laval, QC
TAD Canada .... Bedford, NS
TAL Group .... Toronto, ON
Talent Consulting Services .... USA
Techaid Inc .... Montréal, QC
Technical Resource Network .... Vancouver, BC
Technisource .... USA
TechNix Inc .... Toronto, ON
Technology Plus .... BAHRAIN
Tele-Ressources Ltée .... Montréal, QC
TES Employment Solution .... Mississauga, ON
Thinkpath.com Inc. .... Toronto, ON
Thinkpath.com Inc. .... Ottawa, ON
TMP Worldwide Exec Search .... Toronto, ON
True North Exec Search .... Toronto, ON
Urentia .... Montréal, QC
Venatus Conseil Ltée .... Montréal, QC
Walker Forest .... USA
Wenje Management Ltd .... Markham, ON
Wood West & Partners .... Vancouver, BC
Woodridge Associates .... UNITED KINGDOM
Yves Béliveau recherch .... Saint-Lambert, QC
Yves Plouffe et assoc .... Île-des-Soeurs, QC
Zen Zen International .... Winnipeg, MB

TRADE SHOWS
EXPOSITIONS

TRADES/TECHNICIANS
MÉTIERS/TECHNICIENS

TRANSPORT
TRANSPORT

TRANSPORT (Cont.)
TRANSPORT (Suivre)

GEOGRAPHIC INDEX
INDEX GÉOGRAPHIQUE

NEWFOUNDLAND
TERRE-NEUVE

Corner Brook .... Grant Thornton Intl
Grand Falls-Windsor .... Grant Thornton Intl
Marystown .... Grant Thornton Intl
Mount Pearl .... Northeast Teacher Svcs
St. John's .... Advantage Group
St. John's .... Ajilon Canada
St. John's .... Ernst & Young
St. John's .... Gardner & Coombs
St. John's .... Grant Thornton Intl
St. John's .... Manpower Professional
St. John's .... Newfoundland Personnel
St. John's .... PricewaterhouseCoopers
St. John's .... Puglisevich Crews & Svcs
St. John's .... Resource Concepts
St. John's .... Walter P. Miller Company

NOVA SCOTIA
NOUVELLE-ÉCOSSE

Antigonish .... Grant Thornton Intl
Bedford .... C.N. Taylor Consulting
Bedford .... GSA Search Consultants
Bedford .... TAD Canada
Bridgewater .... Grant Thornton Intl
Dartmouth .... Advantage Group
Dartmouth .... Grant Thornton Intl
Digby .... Grant Thornton Intl
Halifax .... Adecco Canada
Halifax .... Ajilon Canada
Halifax .... ATI Consulting Corp
Halifax .... Bradson Tech Professionals
Halifax .... Caldwell Partners
Halifax .... Corporate Controllers Inc
Halifax .... Drake International
Halifax .... Eagle Prof Resources
Halifax .... Gerald Walsh Recruitment
Halifax .... Global Hospitality Search
Halifax .... Grant Thornton Intl
Halifax .... Hirepower
Halifax .... InterSearch Canada/Staffing
Halifax .... Kelly Professional & Tech
Halifax .... Kenneth Murphy & Assoc
Halifax .... Lock & Associates
Halifax .... Manpower Professional
Halifax .... Meridia Recruitment Svcs
Halifax .... Miller Recruitment Solutions
Halifax .... Peapell & Associates
Halifax .... People Placers Personnel
Halifax .... PricewaterhouseCoopers
Halifax .... Ray & Berndtson/Robertson
Halifax .... Spherion Workforce
Halifax .... Thompson Associates
Halifax .... Vincent-Englehart Ltd
Kentville .... Grant Thornton Intl
New Glasgow .... Grant Thornton Intl
Sydney .... Grant Thornton Intl
Sydney .... Manpower Professional
Truro .... Grant Thornton Intl
Yarmouth .... Grant Thornton Intl

PRINCE EDWARD ISLAND
ÎLE-DU-PRINCE-EDOUARD

Charlottetown .... Baker Consulting
Charlottetown .... Coles Associates
Charlottetown .... Grant Thornton Intl
Charlottetown .... Manpower Professional
Charlottetown .... PEI Office of Future
Charlottetown .... PricewaterhouseCoopers
Summerside .... Grant Thornton Intl

NEW BRUNSWICK
NOUVEAU-BRUNSWICK

Bathurst .... Grant Thornton Intl
Dieppe .... Protrans Personnel Svcs
Fredericton .... Applied Mgmnt Consultants
Fredericton .... Grant Thornton Intl
Fredericton .... ICAP Management Inc
Fredericton .... Kelly Professional & Tech
Fredericton .... Manpower Professional
Miramichi .... Grant Thornton Intl
Moncton .... Advantage Group
Moncton .... Concept II Employment Svcs
Moncton .... Drake International
Moncton .... Grant Thornton Intl
Moncton .... Kelly Professional & Tech
Moncton .... Lock & Associates
Moncton .... Personnel Search
Moncton .... Ray & Berndtson/Robertson
Saint John .... Advantage Group
Saint John .... Employment Partnership
Saint John .... Executive Services Plus
Saint John .... Grant Thornton Intl
Saint John .... Irving Personnel Plus
Saint John .... Kelly Professional & Tech
Saint John .... Manpower Professional
Saint John .... Options Outreach Emplmnt
Saint John .... Personnel Search
Saint John .... PricewaterhouseCoopers

QUEBEC
QUÉBEC

Aylmer .... Technisolutions Executive
Beaconsfield .... Communication Dynamique
Brossard .... MPA Recherche de Cadres
Brossard .... Pro Tec Services Techniques
Candiac .... Canatrade International
Chapeau .... Lynne Milette & Associates
Charlesbourg .... Groupe Gagne-Langevin
Chicoutimi .... Adecco Québec
Chicoutimi .... G-P Personnel
Chicoutimi .... Marlene Bilodeau Conseils
Chomedey .... Pro-Action Personnel
Dorval .... AeroPersonnel Intl
Dorval .... Aginove Inc.
Dorval .... Larouche & Associates
Dorval .... MultiPersonnel International
Dorval .... Optimum Ltée

QUEBEC (Cont.)
QUÉBEC (Suivre)

QUEBEC (Cont.)
QUÉBEC (Suivre)

Montréal .... Levy Pilotte
Montréal .... Lock & Associates
Montréal .... Madeleine Martel Inc.
Montréal .... Mandrake Groupe Conseil
Montréal .... Manpower Professional
Montréal .... MARCON Mgmnt Consultants
Montréal .... Martin Randolph Assoc
Montréal .... Matte Groupe Conseil
Montréal .... McKinnon Groupe Conseil
Montréal .... Métivier Groupe Conseil
Montréal .... Michel Pauzé et Assoc
Montréal .... Multec Canada
Montréal .... Multipro Services Conseils
Montréal .... NAP Executive Apparel
Montréal .... NCL Personnel
Montréal .... Noramtec Consultants
Montréal .... Objectif Emploi 40+
Montréal .... OKA Computer Systems
Montréal .... Orexx Management Svcs
Montréal .... Osborne Group
Montréal .... Patty Shapiro & Assoc
Montréal .... People Bank, The
Montréal .... Personnel Alter Ego
Montréal .... Personnel dentaire D. Soucy
Montréal .... Personnel Star Avon FJ
Montréal .... Pierre H. Delisle conseil
Montréal .... PricewaterhouseCoopers
Montréal .... Proben Management
Montréal .... Procom
Montréal .... Progestic Group
Montréal .... Protocole
Montréal .... Prud'Homme Groupe-Conseil
Montréal .... Ptack Schnarch Basevitz
Montréal .... Publicité Day
Montréal .... PubliFactum Inc
Montréal .... PYA Solutions
Montréal .... Quantum
Montréal .... Quintal & Associates HR
Montréal .... Randstad Interim
Montréal .... Ray & Berndtson/Laurendeau
Montréal .... Raymond Chabot HR Inc
Montréal .... RHI Consulting
Montréal .... Richter Usher Vineberg
Montréal .... Robert Half Canada
Montréal .... Robert Lecavalier Executive
Montréal .... Roevin Tech People
Montréal .... Roll Harris & Associates
Montréal .... Rolland ressources humaines
Montréal .... SAG ressources humaines
Montréal .... Schlesinger Newman Goldman
Montréal .... Schwartz Levitsky Feldman
Montréal .... Service DB Inc
Montréal .... Service de Personnel
Montréal .... Shore & Fitzwilliam
Montréal .... Simon-Tech Inc
Montréal .... Sirius Personnel
Montréal .... Société Jean P. Brisebois
Montréal .... Spencer Stuart
Montréal .... Spherion Workforce
Montréal .... SSA Services Conseils
Montréal .... St-Amour & Assoc
Montréal .... StarDot PRG Inc
Montréal .... Surprenant ressources média
Montréal .... Synersoft Distribution
Montréal .... Systematix IT Consultants
Montréal .... TAG Personnel Consultants
Montréal .... Techaid Inc

Montréal .... Tele-Ressources Ltée
Montréal .... TES Employment Solution
Montréal .... Thomson Tremblay Inc
Montréal .... TIS Service Industriel
Montréal .... TMP Worldwide Advertising
Montréal .... TMP Worldwide Interactive
Montréal .... Tremblay & Assoc
Montréal .... Tretiak Holowka
Montréal .... Urentia
Montréal .... Venatus Conseil Ltée
Montréal .... Verelli Arrizza
Montréal .... Vezina Goodman Exec Search
Montréal .... Victor & Gold
Montréal .... Villor Consultants
Montréal .... Wagner et Assoc
Montréal .... Wasserman Stotland Bratt
Montréal .... Yves Elkas Inc
Montréal .... ZSA Legal Recruitment
Mount Royal .... P.W. Rourke & Associates
Mount Royal .... Personnel Menen
Notre-Dame-des-Prairies .... Agence place
Pierrefonds .... Groupe LJL
Pierrefonds .... Progroupe Ress Humaines
Pointe-Claire .... C. Stevenson Consult
Pointe-Claire .... CDI Technical Svcs
Pointe-Claire .... Contempra Personnel
Pointe-Claire .... Executives Available
Pointe-Claire .... Groom & Assoc
Pointe-Claire .... Kelly, Les svcs
Pointe-Claire .... Lab Support Canada
Pointe-Claire .... Office Team Staffing
Pointe-Claire .... Personnel Alter Ego
Pointe-Claire .... Phase II Personnel
Pointe-Claire .... Quantum, Les services
Québec .... Adecco Québec
Québec .... Défi-Changement
Québec .... Delorme et Assoc
Québec .... Drake International
Québec .... Drakkar Human Resources
Québec .... GRH Consultants Inc
Québec .... Groupe consult affaire
Québec .... Jonathan
Québec .... Kelly, Les svcs
Québec .... Manpower Professional
Québec .... Multi-Ressources
Québec .... Personnel Clé
Québec .... PricewaterhouseCoopers
Québec .... Quantum, Les services
Québec .... Raymond Chabot HR Inc
Québec .... Systematix IT Consultants
Rimouski .... Ficelles
Rosmere .... Armitage Associates
Saint-Georges .... PME Partenaire Consult
Saint-Hyacinthe .... Agence de place H Roy
Saint-Lambert .... Recherches Johnson
Saint-Lambert .... Robert Lamarre & Assoc
Saint-Lambert .... Yves Béliveau recherch
Saint-Laurent .... Adecco LPI
Saint-Laurent .... Advantage Group
Saint-Laurent .... Axxes Technologies
Saint-Laurent .... Berlys Personnel
Saint-Laurent .... Can-Tech Services
Saint-Laurent .... Consultation Delan
Saint-Laurent .... Dana Consultants
Saint-Laurent .... Drakkar Human Resources
Saint-Laurent .... GenerationJobs.com
Saint-Laurent .... Hunt Technical Personnel
Saint-Laurent .... Lehmor Associates
Saint-Laurent .... Randstad Interim
Saint-Léonard .... Agence de personnel Routier

ONTARIO (Cont.)
ONTARIO (Suivre)

Cambridge	Todays Staffing Inc
Cambridge	Transport Help Driver
Cambridge	Trillium Talent Resource
Cambridge	Your Advantage Staffing
Campbellville	Cyr & Assoc
Chatham	Executive House Inc
Chatham	Kelly Professional & Tech
Chatham	Maintenance Plus
Chatham	Orion Resource Group
Chatham	Renaissance Personnel
Cobourg	Allmat & Associates
Cobourg	Manpower Professional
Collingwood	Georgian Staffing Svcs
Concord	Acorn Consulting Group
Concord	Affordable Personnel
Concord	PTC - Financial Staffing
Concord	Unique Personnel Canada
Cornwall	Drake International
Cornwall	Manpower Professional
Cornwall	SOLUTIONS
Downsview	Kelly Professional & Tech
Dundas	Connor Clark Assoc
Dundas	Van Hees Personnel
Elora	EPW & Associates
Erin	Workplace Competence Intl
Etobicoke	Todays Staffing Inc
Fergus	NonProfit Career Quest
Fort Erie	Erie Personnel Corp
Georgetown	Sydelle Associates
Gloucester	Bradson Home Health Care
Gloucester	Carscarp Consulting
Gloucester	Onwego Personnel
Gloucester	Transport Help Driver
Goderich	Partners in Employment
Granby	Manpower Professional
Guelph	Adecco Canada
Guelph	Canjobs.com
Guelph	Express Personnel Svcs
Guelph	KAS Personnel Svcs
Guelph	Kelly Professional & Tech
Guelph	Manpower Professional
Guelph	Results Seekers HR Svcs
Guelph	Todays Staffing Inc
Hamilton	BDO Dunwoody & Assoc
Hamilton	Burke Group
Hamilton	Career Partners/Harrison
Hamilton	Centrex HR Centre
Hamilton	Coffey & Associates
Hamilton	Drake International
Hamilton	Express Personnel Svcs
Hamilton	Grant Thornton Intl
Hamilton	Ian Martin Ltd
Hamilton	ITSuperstars Recruiting
Hamilton	Job Born Candidate Select
Hamilton	KAS Personnel Svcs
Hamilton	Kelly Professional & Tech
Hamilton	Landmark Consulting Group
Hamilton	Manpower Professional
Hamilton	McIntyre Mgmnt Resources
Hamilton	PATH Employment Svcs
Hamilton	PricewaterhouseCoopers
Hamilton	Snelgrove Personnel
Hamilton	Spherion Workforce
Hamilton	Todays Staffing Inc
Hamilton	Ultimate Staffing
Hamilton	Work Able Services
Huntsville	Westcott Thomas Assoc
Innisfil	Working Well Consulting
Kanata	Bradson Home Health Care
Kanata	Calian Technology Svcs
Kanata	Cox Merritt & Co
Kanata	Procom
Kanata	Spherion Workforce
Kanata	TalentLab
Kanata	Technisource
Kanata	Wightman & Associates
Keene	Louise Robinson Placement
King City	Northwind Consulting
Kingston	BDO Dunwoody LLP
Kingston	Drake International
Kingston	Kelly Professional & Tech
Kingston	Knipper & Associates
Kingston	Manpower Professional
Kingston	Palmer & Associates
Kingston	TalentLab
Kingston	Templeman Consulting
Kitchener	55 Plus Personnel
Kitchener	Adecco Canada
Kitchener	Applicants Inc.
Kitchener	BDO Dunwoody & Assoc
Kitchener	Canadian Nurse & Physician
Kitchener	CCT Inc
Kitchener	CEO Inc
Kitchener	Conestoga Personnel
Kitchener	Ernst & Young
Kitchener	Express Personnel Svcs
Kitchener	Grand River Personnel
Kitchener	Ian Martin Ltd
Kitchener	KAS Personnel Svcs
Kitchener	Kelly Professional & Tech
Kitchener	Kitchener Exec Consultants
Kitchener	Michael Follett Consulting
Kitchener	PricewaterhouseCoopers
Kitchener	Prior Resource Group
Kitchener	Roevin Tech People
Kitchener	RWJ & Associates
Kitchener	Tech Hi Consultants Ltd
Kitchener	Trebor Personnel
Kitchener	Wellington Partners Intl
Kitchener	William Squibb Associates
Lakefield	Hiland Research Consultant
Listowel	Partners in Employment
Lively	Transport Help Driver
London	Adecco Canada
London	Allen Personnel Svcs
London	Applicant Testing Services
London	ATS Reliance Tech Group
London	Canadian Medical Placement
London	Caron Executive Search
London	CCT Inc
London	Claymore Scarch Group
London	Competitive Edge
London	Computer Action Co
London	Design Group Staffing
London	Drake Executive
London	Drake International
London	Dunhill Personnel London
London	Executive Recruiters
London	Express Personnel Svcs
London	F.J. Galloway & Assoc
London	Gallant Search Group
London	Grant Thornton Intl
London	Hayhurst Consulting
London	Heighway Personnel
London	Ian Martin Ltd
London	ISG International
London	James E. Thomas & Assoc

ONTARIO (Cont.)
ONTARIO (Suivre)

ONTARIO (Cont.)
ONTARIO (Suivre)

ONTARIO (Cont.)
ONTARIO (Suivre)

Toronto	St-Amour & Assoc
Toronto	Staff Plus
Toronto	Staffworks
Toronto	Star Search Consultants
Toronto	StarDot PRG Inc
Toronto	Stephen Ashley Associates
Toronto	Stephen Laramee Associates
Toronto	Sterling Hoffman
Toronto	StoneWood Group
Toronto	Stop the World Inc
Toronto	Stopka & Associates
Toronto	Storey & Associates
Toronto	Strategic Resources Intl
Toronto	Susan Craig Associates
Toronto	Symmetry Search Group
Toronto	Synergy Search Consultants
Toronto	Syntech Placements
Toronto	Systematix IT Consultants
Toronto	Systems Career Group
Toronto	Systems OnTime
Toronto	Systemsearch Consulting Svcs
Toronto	T.L.W. Enterprise Inc
Toronto	TAL Group
Toronto	TalentLab
Toronto	Tamm Communications
Toronto	Tanaka Associates
Toronto	Tancredi Consulting
Toronto	Tapscott Associates
Toronto	Taylor Low & Associates
Toronto	TDM Technical Services
Toronto	Tech Force Search Group
Toronto	Technical Service Consult
Toronto	Technical Skills Consulting
Toronto	TechNix Inc
Toronto	Tek-Search Corp
Toronto	Tennen Personnel Services
Toronto	TERHAM Mgmnt Consulting
Toronto	TES Employment Solution
Toronto	Thinkpath.com Inc.
Toronto	Thinkpath.com Inc
Toronto	Thomas E. Hedefine Assoc
Toronto	Thompson Elliott Group
Toronto	Thorek/Scott Partners
Toronto	TMP QD Legal Recruitment
Toronto	TMP Worldwide Advertising
Toronto	TMP Worldwide Exec Search
Toronto	Todays Staffing Inc
Toronto	Todays Staffing Inc
Toronto	Todays Staffing Inc
Toronto	Tony Curtis & Associates
Toronto	Toronto Exec Consultants
Toronto	Torstaff Personnel
Toronto	Tosi Placement Services
Toronto	Travel Jobs
Toronto	Treat & Associates Executive
Toronto	Trebor Personnel
Toronto	Trebor Personnel
Toronto	Trebor Personnel
Toronto	Trella & Associates
Toronto	Trillium Talent Resource
Toronto	TriNet Employment Group
Toronto	Triser Corp
Toronto	True North Exec Search
Toronto	Urquhart Management Inc
Toronto	Van Klaveren Litherland Co
Toronto	Vector Technical Services
Toronto	Venpro Consulting
Toronto	Volt Human Resources
Toronto	VTRAC IT Consultants
Toronto	W.G. Meldrum Ltd
Toronto	W.H. Jackson Associates
Toronto	W.R. London Consultants
Toronto	Walbrook Appointment England
Toronto	Wallace & Partners
Toronto	Watson Wyatt Worldwide
Toronto	Wayne Perry & Associates
Toronto	Weir Associates
Toronto	Westcott Thomas Assoc
Toronto	Western Mgmnt Consultants
Toronto	Wilkie Group International
Toronto	Williams Associates
Toronto	Willing Plus Personnel
Toronto	Winters Technical Staffing
Toronto	Wolf Gugler & Associates
Toronto	Worth Personnel Group
Toronto	Wypich International
Toronto	Xycorp Inc.
Toronto	Zeidel Gregory Associates
Toronto	Zenzen Pierce Assoc
Toronto	ZSA Legal Recruitment
Unionville	Human Resource Mgmt Group
Unionville	JSG Group Mgmnt Consult
Uxbridge	BDO Dunwoody LLP
Vaughan	Ace Recruiters Canada
Vaughan	Armor Personnel
Waterloo	A. Lawrence Abrams Assoc
Waterloo	Clark Pollard & Gagliardi
Waterloo	Cowan Wright Ltd
Waterloo	Hemmerich Flanagan & Assoc
Waterloo	Lab Support Canada
Waterloo	Performance House
Waterloo	Procom
Waterloo	Results Management Canada
Whitby	Advantage Group
Whitby	Allen Ballach Assoc
Whitby	Spherion Workforce
Whitby	Templeman Consulting
Whitby	Vickery Boardman Assoc
Winchester	BDO Dunwoody LLP
Windsor	Accu-Staff Resource Systems
Windsor	Comtech Prof Services
Windsor	Execusource Staffing Intl
Windsor	Express Personnel Svcs
Windsor	G.W. Goudreau Personnel
Windsor	Impact Staffing
Windsor	International Tech Recruit
Windsor	Kelly Professional & Tech
Windsor	Manpower Professional
Windsor	Meda Group
Windsor	New World Intl Consultants
Windsor	Personnel by Pro-Staff
Windsor	Renaissance Personnel
Windsor	Stellar Personnel Placement
Windsor	Summit Personnel Services
Windsor	Windsor Personnel & Exec
Woodbridge	Direct Career Concepts
Woodbridge	HIRElogix Inc.
Woodbridge	Labour Source
Woodbridge	ProSource Mgmnt Consult
Woodbridge	Spectrum Assoc Executive
Woodlawn	Synagent Inc
Woodstock	Dan McNamara & Assoc
Woodstock	Kelly Select
Woodstock	People Management Group
Woodstock	Stevens Resource Group

ALBERTA (Cont.)
ALBERTA (Suivre)

BRITISH COLUMBIA
COLOMBIE-BRITANNIQUE

BRITISH COLUMBIA (Cont.)
COLOMBIE-BRITANNIQUE (Suivre)

MINIMUM SALARY INDEX
INDEX SALAIRE MINIMUM

$100,000 plus

AT Kearney Executive .... Toronto, ON
Compton Graham Intl .... Toronto, ON
Egon Zehnder International .... Montréal, QC
Egon Zehnder International .... Toronto, ON
Enns Hever Inc .... Toronto, ON
FHG International .... Toronto, ON
GaryMcCracken Exec Search .... Toronto, ON
Glazin / Sisco Exec Search .... Toronto, ON
Glazin / Sisco Exec Search .... Vancouver, BC
Goldjobs.com .... UNITED KINGDOM
Heidrick & Struggles Canada .... Montréal, QC
Heidrick & Struggles Canada .... Toronto, ON
Hiland Research Consultant .... Lakefield, ON
Hutchinson Group .... Toronto, ON
J.R. Bechtle & Company .... USA
Landmark Consulting Group .... Hamilton, ON
Recherches Johnson .... Saint-Lambert, QC
Robinson Fraser Group .... Toronto, ON
Spencer Stuart .... Montréal, QC
Spencer Stuart .... Toronto, ON
StoneWood Group .... Toronto, ON
TMP Worldwide Exec Search .... Toronto, ON
Van Biesen Group .... Calgary, AB
Wilkie Group International .... Toronto, ON

$75,000 - $99,999

Allen Ballach Assoc .... Whitby, ON
Armitage Associates .... Rosmere, QC
Armitage Associates .... Toronto, ON
Armitage Associates .... Vancouver, BC
Austin Marlowe Intl .... Toronto, ON
Bach Associates .... Vancouver, BC
Boyden Global Exec Search .... Montréal, QC
Bruce Ward Partners .... Toronto, ON
Caldwell Intl., La Societé .... Montréal, QC
Caldwell Partners .... Calgary, AB
Caldwell Partners .... Toronto, ON
Caldwell Partners .... Vancouver, BC
Cambridge Mgmnt Planning .... Toronto, ON
CAMPA & Associates .... Toronto, ON
CMP Select .... Toronto, ON
Coe & Company Intl .... Calgary, AB
Conroy Partners .... Calgary, AB
Crawford de Munnik Executive .... Toronto, ON
D.P. Group, The .... UNITED KINGDOM
D.R. Nolan Assoc .... Toronto, ON
E.L. Shore & Associates .... Toronto, ON
Futurestep .... Toronto, ON
HR Business Partners .... Calgary, AB
InterSearch Canada/Corso .... Toronto, ON
InterSearch Canada/Staffing .... Halifax, NS
InterSearch Canada/Western .... Vancouver, BC
J.G. Flynn & Associates .... Vancouver, BC
Korn/Ferry Intl .... Vancouver, BC
Lewis Companies .... Toronto, ON
MacLean Hay Consulting .... Oakville, ON
Master Performers .... Toronto, ON
Matteson Management .... Toronto, ON
Michael Marmur & Assoc .... Toronto, ON
Palmer & Company Executive .... Toronto, ON

Perry Martel International .... Ottawa, ON
Ray & Berndtson/Robertson .... Ottawa, ON
Research Associates .... Edmonton, AB
RJ Professionals .... Toronto, ON
Robert Connelly & Associates .... USA
Rolland Groupe Conseil .... Westmount, QC
Rutherford Intl Exec Search .... Toronto, ON
Silicon Executive Search .... Toronto, ON
Société Jean P. Brisebois .... Montréal, QC
T.J. Seaton Management .... Calgary, AB
Team Power Exec Search .... Markham, ON
Walker Forest .... USA
Weir Associates .... Toronto, ON
Western Mgmnt Consultants .... Vancouver, BC
Workplace Competence Intl .... Erin, ON
Wypich International .... Toronto, ON
Yves Plouffe et assoc .... Île-des-Soeurs, QC

$50,000 - $74,999

Adirect Recruiting Corp .... Toronto, ON
Advocate Placement .... Markham, ON
Advocate Placement .... Toronto, ON
Allen Austin Lowe & Powers .... USA
Ambridge Management .... Toronto, ON
Ashlar-Stone Consultants .... Mississauga, ON
Association Resource Centre .... Toronto, ON
ASTRA Management Corp .... Vancouver, BC
Audax Corporation .... Toronto, ON
Barrett Rose & Lee .... Toronto, ON
Bedford Consulting Group .... Oakville, ON
Bedford Consulting Group .... Toronto, ON
Botrie Associates .... Toronto, ON
Bradford Bachinski Ltd .... Ottawa, ON
Brassard & Assoc .... Montréal, QC
Bruce Cowan Assoc .... Toronto, ON
C.N. Taylor Consulting .... Bedford, NS
Calvin Partners Intl .... Toronto, ON
CanMed Consultants .... Mississauga, ON
Carmichael Birrell & Co .... Toronto, ON
Catalyst Consulting .... Montréal, QC
CCG Mgmnt Consultants .... Mississauga, ON
Chisholm & Partners Intl .... Toronto, ON
Christopher Vincent & Assoc .... Calgary, AB
Claude Guedj Assoc .... Montréal, QC
Coakwell Crawford Cairns .... High River, AB
Connaught Clark Company .... Mississauga, ON
Connor Clark Assoc .... Dundas, ON
Cosier Associates .... Calgary, AB
Cyberna Associates .... Montréal, QC
David Taylor Mfg Search .... Toronto, ON
David Warwick Kennedy Assoc .... Vancouver, BC
Davies Park .... Calgary, AB
Davies Park .... Edmonton, AB
Derkitt Herbert Exec Search .... Calgary, AB
Dion Mgmnt Exec Search .... Toronto, ON
Dion Mgmnt Groupe Conseil .... Montréal, QC
Dion Mgmnt Groupe Conseil .... Sainte-Foy, QC
Direct Career Concepts .... Woodbridge, ON
Don Miles Personnel .... Toronto, ON
Drake International .... Toronto, ON
Ducharme Group .... Toronto, ON
Dunhill Professional Search .... Vancouver, BC
Ernst David International .... Winnipeg, MB

$50,000 - $74,999 (Cont. / *Suivre*)

Ernst & Young .... St. John's, NF
ERP Staffing Solutions .... Brampton, ON
Excalibur Careers .... Markham, ON
Executive Network .... Victoria, BC
Feldman Gray Associates .... Toronto, ON
Fisher Group Exec Search .... Calgary, AB
Future Executive Personnel .... Toronto, ON
Galloway and Associates .... Toronto, ON
Gaspar & Associates .... Toronto, ON
Gaudry Shink Levasseur .... Montréal, QC
Genesis Corporate Search .... Calgary, AB
George Preger & Associates .... Toronto, ON
Gilligan & Associates .... Toronto, ON
GR Search Inc .... Toronto, ON
Groupe Primacor .... Longueuil, QC
Groupe Ranger .... Montréal, QC
Harris Consulting Corp .... Winnipeg, MB
Herman Smith Search Inc .... Toronto, ON
Herrmann Group, The .... Toronto, ON
HR / RH Inc. .... Montréal, QC
Interim Mgmt Resources .... Mississauga, ON
InterSearch Canada/Lennox .... Calgary, AB
J.O. Bush & Associates .... Mindemoya, ON
John Doucette Mgmnt .... Richmond Hill, ON
JSL Search Leaders .... Toronto, ON
Kenniff Denis Inc. .... Montréal, QC
Key Executive Consultants .... Barrie, ON
Kingsley Allen IT Search .... Toronto, ON
Kitchener Exec Consultants .... Kitchener, ON
Knipper & Associates .... Kingston, ON
Korn/Ferry Intl .... Montréal, QC
Larkin Group .... Mississauga, ON
LePage International .... Montréal, QC
Lussier Executive Search .... Toronto, ON
Management Advice Intl .... Toronto, ON
Management Connections Inc .... Vancouver, BC
Management One Consultants .... Toronto, ON
Mandrake Mgmt Consult .... Toronto, ON
Matte Groupe Conseil .... Montréal, QC
McKinnon Mgmnt Group .... Toronto, ON
Medfall Inc .... Niagara Falls, ON
Métivier Groupe Conseil .... Montréal, QC
Michael J. Cavanagh Assoc .... Toronto, ON
Michael Stern Associates .... Toronto, ON
Milgram & Associates .... Toronto, ON
Nework Corp .... Toronto, ON
Normatech Executive .... Toronto, ON
Palmer & Associates .... Kingston, ON
Partnervision Consulting .... Toronto, ON
Peak Associates Inc .... Toronto, ON
Pettitt Group Inc., The .... Burlington, ON
Phee Farrer Jones Ltd .... UNITED KINGDOM
Pierre H. Delisle conseil .... Montréal, QC
Pinton Forrest & Madden .... Vancouver, BC
Planigestion A. Choquette .... Duvernay, QC
PricewaterhouseCoopers .... Calgary, AB
PricewaterhouseCoopers .... Edmonton, AB
PricewaterhouseCoopers .... Halifax, NS
PricewaterhouseCoopers .... Hamilton, ON
PricewaterhouseCoopers .... London, ON
PricewaterhouseCoopers .... Montréal, QC
PricewaterhouseCoopers .... Québec, QC
PricewaterhouseCoopers .... Regina, SK
PricewaterhouseCoopers .... Saskatoon, SK
PricewaterhouseCoopers .... Toronto, ON
PricewaterhouseCoopers .... Vancouver, BC
Prime Source Management .... Toronto, ON
Prokosch Group, The .... Calgary, AB

Ray & Berndtson/Laurendeau .... Montréal, QC
Ray Berndtson/Tanton .... Vancouver, BC
RBA Intl HR Consultants .... Westmount, QC
Richter Raymond Group .... Oakville, ON
Rolland ressources humaines .... Montréal, QC
Roper and Assoc .... Calgary, AB
RWS Consulting Group .... London, ON
Schoales & Associates .... Toronto, ON
Search Company, The .... Toronto, ON
Search Justified Selection .... Toronto, ON
Shared Vision Mgmt Search .... Toronto, ON
Sheldon Recruiting .... Toronto, ON
Sheldon Resnick Associates .... Toronto, ON
Shore & Fitzwilliam .... Montréal, QC
Simon Bull Associates .... Cambridge, ON
Storey & Associates .... Toronto, ON
Strategic Resources Intl .... Toronto, ON
Synagent Inc .... Woodlawn, ON
Tanaka Associates .... Toronto, ON
Tapscott Associates .... Toronto, ON
Taylor Recruitment .... UNITED KINGDOM
Technical Mgmnt Resources .... Barrie, ON
Technical Resource Network .... Vancouver, BC
Technical Skills Consulting .... Toronto, ON
TechNix Inc .... Toronto, ON
Technology Plus .... BAHRAIN
Tolfrey Group .... USA
Tolstoy Resources .... Bolton, ON
Van Klaveren Litherland Co .... Toronto, ON
Venpro Consulting .... Toronto, ON
Verriez Group Inc .... London, ON
Vezina Goodman Exec Search .... Montréal, QC
W.G. Meldrum Ltd .... Calgary, AB
Wace & Assoc .... Mississauga, ON
Wayne Thomas & Associates .... Ottawa, ON
Westcott Thomas Assoc .... Huntsville, ON
Westcott Thomas Assoc .... Toronto, ON
Western Mgmnt Consultants .... Calgary, AB
Western Mgmnt Consultants .... Edmonton, AB
Western Mgmnt Consultants .... Saskatoon, SK
Western Mgmnt Consultants .... Toronto, ON
Wightman & Associates .... Kanata, ON
Wolf Gugler & Associates .... Toronto, ON
Yves Elkas Inc .... Montréal, QC

$25,000 - $49,999

A.W. Fraser Assoc .... Edmonton, AB
Abel Placement Consult .... Markham, ON
Accountants on Call .... Toronto, ON
Accountants on Call .... Vancouver, BC
ADV Advanced Tech Svcs .... Toronto, ON
AeroPersonnel Intl .... Dorval, QC
AgCall Human Resources .... Calgary, AB
AgCall Human Resources .... Markham, ON
Aginove Inc. .... Dorval, QC
Allen Etcovitch Assoc .... Montréal, QC
Allen Personnel Svcs .... London, ON
Altura Group .... Toronto, ON
Applicants Inc. .... Kitchener, ON
Applied Technology Solutions .... Toronto, ON
Ashton Computer Pros .... North Vancouver, BC
Austin Park Mgmnt Group .... Toronto, ON
Aztech Recruitment .... USA
Bailey Professional Search .... Calgary, AB
Barr Legal Personnel .... Toronto, ON
Bassett Laudi Partners .... Toronto, ON
Belanger Partners .... Thornhill, ON

$25,000 - $49,999 (Cont. / Suivre)

Bilingual Source .... Toronto, ON
Bilingual-Jobs.com .... Vancouver, BC
BMA International .... Montréal, QC
BMA International .... Montréal, QC
Boscan Consultants .... Marysville, ON
Braun-Valley Associates .... Sarnia, ON
Brethet Barnum Associates .... Toronto, ON
C & E Conn Associates .... Mississauga, ON
C.G. Thomson & Co .... Toronto, ON
C. Scott & Associates .... Toronto, ON
Cadman Consulting Group .... Vancouver, BC
Cameron Consulting Group .... Brampton, ON
Campbell Edgar Inc .... Delta, BC
Campbell Edgar Inc .... Richmond, BC
Canadian Exec Recruitmnt .... Mississauga, ON
Canpro Executive Search .... Markham, ON
Career Advance Employment .... Burlington, ON
Career Partners/Harrison .... Hamilton, ON
Carion Resource Group .... Mississauga, ON
Central Mgmnt Consultants .... Toronto, ON
Centre for Corp Resources .... Toronto, ON
Chacra Belliveau & Assoc .... Montréal, QC
Chapman & Associates .... Vancouver, BC
Coast Personnel Svcs .... Nanaimo, BC
Coke & Associates .... Toronto, ON
Connors Lovell Assoc .... Cambridge, ON
Connors Lovell Assoc .... Mississauga, ON
ConsulPRO Executive Search .... Ottawa, ON
Corporate Recruiters .... Vancouver, BC
Counsel Network .... Calgary, AB
Counsel Network .... USA
Counsel Network .... Vancouver, BC
CTEW Executive Personnel .... Vancouver, BC
D & H Group .... Vancouver, BC
Danette Milne Corp Search .... Markham, ON
David Aplin & Assoc .... Calgary, AB
David Aplin & Assoc .... Edmonton, AB
Dotemtex Executive Search .... Montréal, QC
Driver Carrier Placement .... Toronto, ON
Dumont & Associates .... North Vancouver, BC
Dumont & Associates .... Vancouver, BC
Dunhill Consultants N York .... Toronto, ON
Dunhill Personnel London .... London, ON
Duo Mega Inc .... Montréal, QC
Eagle Prof Resources .... Calgary, AB
Eagle Prof Resources .... Halifax, NS
Eagle Prof Resources .... Montréal, QC
Eagle Prof Resources .... Ottawa, ON
Eagle Prof Resources .... Toronto, ON
Eagle Prof Resources .... Toronto, ON
Eagle Prof Resources .... Vancouver, BC
Evans Search Group .... Toronto, ON
Executive Assistance .... Toronto, ON
Executive Resources Intl .... Montréal, QC
Finney-Taylor Consulting .... Calgary, AB
Gallant Search Group .... London, ON
Gauthier Conseils .... Montréal, QC
Girardin & Associates .... Winnipeg, MB
Glen Abbey Exec Search .... Oakville, ON
Global Consulting Group .... Markham, ON
Global Hospitality Search .... Mississauga, ON
Grant Martin & Assoc .... Richmond Hill, ON
Grant Search Group .... Toronto, ON
Grant Thornton Intl .... Saint John, NB
Grapevine Exec Recruiters .... Toronto, ON
Group Four Mgmnt Consultants .... Toronto, ON
GSI International Consult .... Toronto, ON
Harcourt & Assoc .... Calgary, AB

Harcourt & Assoc .... Edmonton, AB
Hayhurst Consulting .... London, ON
HEC Group .... Ancaster, ON
Higher Vision Recruitment .... Toronto, ON
Hire Choice .... Toronto, ON
Hotel & Restaurant Mgmnt .... Toronto, ON
Human Edge Consulting .... Richmond Hill, ON
Ian Martin Ltd .... Toronto, ON
ICAP Management Inc .... Fredericton, NB
IMS Innovative Mgmnt .... Toronto, ON
In Place Select Recruitment .... Toronto, ON
INFO-TEK Consulting .... Edmonton, AB
Infocybex .... Brampton, ON
InGenius Engineering Inc .... Ottawa, ON
Insight Technology Corp .... Calgary, AB
Interchange Personnel .... Calgary, AB
InterCom Recruitment .... Toronto, ON
IT People Ltd .... Calgary, AB
J.P. Anderson & Assoc .... Burlington, ON
James Partnership .... BERMUDA
Jenereaux & Associates .... Mississauga, ON
Jerry Adel & Company .... Toronto, ON
K-International Group .... Toronto, ON
Katherine Holt Enterprises .... Toronto, ON
Kaymac & Associates .... Toronto, ON
Keith Bagg & Associates .... Toronto, ON
Kelly Permanent Recruit .... Mississauga, ON
Kelly Permanent Recruit .... Toronto, ON
Kelly Permanent Recruit .... Toronto, ON
Kenneth Murphy & Assoc .... Halifax, NS
Keystone Select/MA Haggith .... Toronto, ON
Kforce.ca .... Toronto, ON
Krecklo Consultants .... Montréal, QC
Landon Morgan Inc .... Thorold, ON
Lenvil Industries .... Burlington, ON
London Executive Consultants .... London, ON
Louise Robinson Placement .... Keene, ON
LTV & Associates .... Toronto, ON
Ludlow Project Services .... Oakville, ON
Lynne Milette & Associates .... Chapeau, QC
Madison MacArthur Inc .... Toronto, ON
Management Recruiters Kannapolis .... USA
Manpower Professional .... Montréal, QC
Markent Personnel Inc .... USA
Matthews Management .... Richmond Hill, ON
McIntyre Mgmnt Resources .... Hamilton, ON
McKinnon Groupe Conseil .... Montréal, QC
McLean Exec Consultants .... Calgary, AB
Meda Group .... Windsor, ON
Miller & Associates .... Mississauga, ON
MPA Recherche de Cadres .... Brossard, QC
MRK Consulting .... UNITED KINGDOM
MultiPersonnel International .... Dorval, QC
NAP Executive Apparel .... Montréal, QC
NAP Executive Retail .... Toronto, ON
Narami Executive Search .... Toronto, ON
National Executive .... Toronto, ON
Paragon Consulting .... Toronto, ON
Partners in Search .... Toronto, ON
Peapell & Associates .... Halifax, NS
People + ... Toronto, ON
Perceptive Edge .... Toronto, ON
Personnel Mgmnt Group .... Winnipeg, MB
Peter Leonard & Assoc .... Calgary, AB
Pila Recruiting & Assoc .... Richmond, BC
Pommen & Associates .... Edmonton, AB
Pride in Personnel .... Markham, ON
Prime Management Group .... Cambridge, ON
Prime Management Group .... London, ON
Pro Tec Global Staffing .... Thornhill, ON

$25,000 - $49,999 (Cont. / *Suivre*)

Prolink Consulting .... Toronto, ON
ProSource Mgmnt Consult .... Woodbridge, ON
PTC - Financial Staffing .... Concord, ON
Quest Exec Recruitment .... Toronto, ON
Quintal & Associates HR .... Montréal, QC
Ray & Berndtson/Robertson .... Halifax, NS
Resource Professionals .... Calgary, AB
Richard Major & Assoc .... Toronto, ON
RJK & Associates .... Markham, ON
Robert T. Keegan & Assoc .... Oakville, ON
Rossi & Associates .... Vancouver, BC
Rudl International .... Ottawa, ON
RWJ & Associates .... Kitchener, ON
S. Tanner & Associates .... Oakville, ON
SalesSearch .... Toronto, ON
Scott Wolfe Management .... Headingly, MB
SearchWest Inc .... Vancouver, BC
Squires Resources .... Barrie, ON
Stephen Goldstein Associates .... Ottawa, ON
Stephen Laramee Associates .... Toronto, ON
Stoakley-Dudley Consult .... Mississauga, ON
Stokes Associates .... Pickering, ON
Sydelle Associates .... Georgetown, ON
Synergy Search Consultants .... Toronto, ON
Taylor Low & Associates .... Toronto, ON
Tech Force Search Group .... Toronto, ON
Technisolutions Executive .... Aylmer, QC
TERHAM Mgmnt Consulting .... Toronto, ON
Thomas & Rayment .... Markham, ON
Totten & Associates .... London, ON
TRS Staffing Solutions .... Calgary, AB
TSI Group / TSI Staffing .... Mississauga, ON
Urentia .... Montréal, QC
Ward Vinge & Associates .... Calgary, AB
Ward Vinge & Associates .... Edmonton, AB
Wellington Partners Intl .... Kitchener, ON
Williams Associates .... Toronto, ON
Wood West & Partners .... Vancouver, BC

FEE BASIS INDEX
INDEX FRAIS

RETAINER ONLY
HONORAIRE SEULEMENT

A.E. Harrison Partners .... Mississauga, ON
A.W. Fraser Assoc .... Edmonton, AB
A.W. Fraser Assoc .... Calgary, AB
Abecassis recherches cadres .... Montréal, QC
Adirect Recruiting Corp .... Toronto, ON
Alan Davis Assoc .... Ottawa, ON
Alan Davis Assoc .... Hudson Heights, QC
Allemby Mgmnt Group .... Toronto, ON
Allen Austin Lowe & Powers .... USA
Amrop International .... BRAZIL
Amrop International .... SWITZERLAND
Armitage Associates .... Vancouver, BC
Armitage Associates .... Toronto, ON
Armitage Associates .... Rosmere, QC
Ashlar-Stone Consultants .... Mississauga, ON
AT Kearney Executive .... Toronto, ON
Audax Corporation .... Toronto, ON
Austin Marlowe Intl .... Toronto, ON
Aztech Recruitment .... USA
Bach Associates .... Vancouver, BC
Baldock Associates .... Toronto, ON
Bedford Consulting Group .... Toronto, ON
Bedford Consulting Group .... Oakville, ON
Belle Isle Djandji Brunet .... Montréal, QC
Booth International Mgmnt .... Toronto, ON
Botrie Associates .... Toronto, ON
Boyden Global Exec Search .... Calgary, AB
Boyden Global Exec Search .... Montréal, QC
Bradford Bachinski Ltd .... Ottawa, ON
Brassard & Assoc .... Montréal, QC
Brendan Wood International .... Toronto, ON
Bruce Ward Partners .... Toronto, ON
Cadman Consulting Group .... Vancouver, BC
Caldwell Intl., La Societé .... Montréal, QC
Caldwell Partners .... Toronto, ON
Caldwell Partners .... Halifax, NS
Cambridge Mgmnt Planning .... Toronto, ON
CAMPA & Associates .... Toronto, ON
Canadian Career Partners .... Calgary, AB
Canpro Executive Search .... Markham, ON
Carmichael Birrell & Co .... Toronto, ON
Cathryn Lohrisch & Co .... Toronto, ON
CCG Mgmnt Consultants .... Mississauga, ON
Christopher Vincent & Assoc .... Calgary, AB
Claude Guedj Assoc .... Montréal, QC
CMP Select .... Toronto, ON
Coakwell Crawford Cairns .... High River, AB
Coe & Company Intl .... Calgary, AB
Compton Graham Intl .... Toronto, ON
Connaught Clark Company .... Mississauga, ON
Conroy Partners .... Calgary, AB
Conseillers en Admin FORMA .... Montréal, QC
Crawford de Munnik Executive .... Toronto, ON
D & H Group .... Vancouver, BC
D.R. Nolan Assoc .... Toronto, ON
Dana Stehr & Assoc .... Toronto, ON
Danek Anthony Inc .... White Rock, BC
Danek Anthony Inc .... Toronto, ON
Daniluck & Associates .... Edmonton, AB
David Taylor Mfg Search .... Toronto, ON
David Warwick Kennedy Assoc .... Vancouver, BC
Davies Park .... Edmonton, AB

Davies Park .... Calgary, AB
Derhak Ireland Partners .... Toronto, ON
Derkitt Herbert Exec Search .... Calgary, AB
Dingle & Associates .... Toronto, ON
Dion Mgmnt Exec Search .... Vancouver, BC
Dion Mgmnt Exec Search .... Toronto, ON
Dion Mgmnt Groupe Conseil .... Montréal, QC
Dion Mgmnt Groupe Conseil .... Sainte-Foy, QC
Dotemtex Executive Search .... Montréal, QC
Drakkar Human Resources .... Mississauga, ON
Drakkar Human Resources .... Saint-Laurent, QC
Drakkar Human Resources .... Montréal, QC
Drakkar Human Resources .... Québec, QC
Ducharme Group .... Toronto, ON
Dymar Mgmnt Consultants .... Mississauga, ON
E.L. Shore & Associates .... Toronto, ON
Egon Zehnder International .... Toronto, ON
Egon Zehnder International .... Montréal, QC
Enns Hever Inc .... Toronto, ON
Erie Personnel Corp .... Thorold, ON
Erie Personnel Corp .... Fort Erie, ON
Erland International .... Toronto, ON
Ernst & Young .... St. John's, NF
ExecuCounsel Inc .... Toronto, ON
Execusearch .... Lethbridge, AB
Executive Network .... Victoria, BC
Express Personnel Svcs .... Ottawa, ON
Facilité Informatique .... Montréal, QC
Feldman Gray Associates .... Toronto, ON
Futurestep .... Toronto, ON
G-P Personnel .... Chicoutimi, QC
G-Tech Professional Staffing .... USA
GAAP Inc .... Montréal, QC
GaryMcCracken Exec Search .... Toronto, ON
Gaspar & Associates .... Toronto, ON
Gaudry Shink Levasseur .... Montréal, QC
Genesis Corporate Search .... Calgary, AB
George Preger & Associates .... Toronto, ON
George Stewart Consultants .... Toronto, ON
Glazin Group, The .... Calgary, AB
Glazin / Sisco Exec Search .... Vancouver, BC
Glazin / Sisco Exec Search .... Toronto, ON
GR Search Inc .... Toronto, ON
Grant Thornton Intl .... Saint John, NB
Groupe conseil Lamarche .... Granby, QC
Groupe Pluridis .... Montréal, QC
Groves & Partners Intl .... Mississauga, ON
GSA Search Consultants .... Bedford, NS
GSG Partners .... Toronto, ON
Harris Consulting Corp .... Winnipeg, MB
Hayhurst Consulting .... London, ON
Heidrick & Struggles .... USA
Heidrick & Struggles Canada .... Toronto, ON
Heidrick & Struggles Canada .... Montréal, QC
Heidrick & Struggles Intl .... ITALY
Heidrick & Struggles Intl .... JAPAN
Heidrick & Struggles Intl .... USA
Heidrick & Struggles Intl .... USA
Heidrick & Struggles Intl .... VENEZUELA
Herman Smith Search Inc .... Toronto, ON
Herrmann Group, The .... Toronto, ON
Heywood Holmes Partners .... Red Deer, AB
HR Business Partners .... Calgary, AB
HR / RH Inc. .... Montréal, QC
Hutchinson Group .... Toronto, ON
InterSearch Canada/Corso .... Toronto, ON

RETAINER ONLY (Cont.)
HONORAIRE SEULEMENT (Suivre)

InterSearch Canada/Lennox	Calgary, AB
J.G. Flynn & Associates	Vancouver, BC
J.R. Bechtle & Company	USA
Janet Wright & Associates	Toronto, ON
Jerry Adel & Company	Toronto, ON
John Stoten Consulting	Edmonton, AB
JSG Group Mgmnt Consult	Unionville, ON
Keeley Consulting	Toronto, ON
Keith-Murray Partners	Toronto, ON
Kenniff Denis Inc.	Montréal, QC
Key Executive Consultants	Barrie, ON
Keystone Select/MA Haggith	Toronto, ON
Kingsley Allen IT Search	Toronto, ON
Knipper & Associates	Kingston, ON
Korn/Ferry Intl	Vancouver, BC
Korn/Ferry Intl	Toronto, ON
KPMG Executive Search	IRELAND
Krecklo Consultants	Toronto, ON
Krecklo Consultants	Montréal, QC
Lamon + Stuart + Michaels	Toronto, ON
Landmark Consulting Group	Hamilton, ON
Leader Search Inc	Calgary, AB
LePage International	Montréal, QC
Lewis Companies	Toronto, ON
Line 1000 Placement Svcs	Ottawa, ON
Lyons Black + Associates	Vancouver, BC
M.E. Money & Associates	Toronto, ON
MacKenzie Gray Mgmnt	Calgary, AB
MacRae Atwood Mgmnt	Toronto, ON
Madeleine Martel Inc.	Montréal, QC
Madison MacArthur Inc	Toronto, ON
Management Advice Intl	Toronto, ON
Management Connections Inc	Vancouver, BC
Mandrake Mgmt Consult	Toronto, ON
Master Performers	Toronto, ON
Matteson Management	Toronto, ON
McCracken/Labbett Exec Search	Toronto, ON
Métivier Groupe Conseil	Montréal, QC
Meyers Norris Penny	Calgary, AB
Meyers Norris Penny	Brandon, MB
Michael J. Cavanagh Assoc	Toronto, ON
Michael Marmur & Assoc	Toronto, ON
Michael Stern Associates	Toronto, ON
Miles Partnership	UNITED KINGDOM
Milgram & Associates	Toronto, ON
Morgan Palmer Search	Toronto, ON
MPA Recherche de Cadres	Brossard, QC
MVC Associates Intl	Toronto, ON
Osborne Group	Vancouver, BC
Osborne Group	Calgary, AB
Osborne Group	Edmonton, AB
Osborne Group	Toronto, ON
Osborne Group	Montréal, QC
Palmer & Company Executive	Toronto, ON
Partnervision Consulting	Toronto, ON
People +	Toronto, ON
Perry Martel International	Ottawa, ON
Pinton Forrest & Madden	Vancouver, BC
Planigestion A. Choquette	Duvernay, QC
PricewaterhouseCoopers	Vancouver, BC
PricewaterhouseCoopers	Edmonton, AB
PricewaterhouseCoopers	Calgary, AB
PricewaterhouseCoopers	Winnipeg, MB
PricewaterhouseCoopers	London, ON
PricewaterhouseCoopers	Toronto, ON
PricewaterhouseCoopers	Québec, QC
PricewaterhouseCoopers	Halifax, NS
PricewaterhouseCoopers	BERMUDA
PricewaterhouseCoopers	TRINIDAD
Prichard Kymen Inc	Edmonton, AB
Prince Arthur Advertising	Toronto, ON
Prokosch Group, The	Calgary, AB
PTC - Financial Staffing	Concord, ON
Ray & Berndtson	DENMARK
Ray & Berndtson	USA
Ray & Berndtson/Laurendeau	Montréal, QC
Ray Berndtson/Lovas Stanley	Toronto, ON
Ray & Berndtson/Robertson	Ottawa, ON
Ray & Berndtson/Robertson	Moncton, NB
Ray & Berndtson/Robertson	Halifax, NS
Ray Berndtson/Tanton	Vancouver, BC
Recherches Johnson	Saint-Lambert, QC
Renaud Foster Mgmnt	Ottawa, ON
Research Associates	Edmonton, AB
Resource Corporation, The	Toronto, ON
Resource Professionals	Calgary, AB
Results Management Canada	Waterloo, ON
Richter Raymond Group	Oakville, ON
RJ Professionals	Toronto, ON
Robert Channing Consulting	Oakville, ON
Robert Connelly & Associates	USA
Robert W. Dingman Company	USA
Robinson Fraser Group	Toronto, ON
Rolland ressources humaines	Montréal, QC
Russell Reynolds Assoc	Calgary, AB
Russell Reynolds Assoc	Toronto, ON
Russell Reynolds Assoc	AUSTRALIA
Russell Reynolds Assoc	FRANCE
Russell Reynolds Assoc	SINGAPORE
Russell Reynolds Assoc	SPAIN
Russell Reynolds Assoc	USA
Rutherford Intl Exec Search	Toronto, ON
RWS Consulting Group	London, ON
SAG ressources humaines	Montréal, QC
Saunders Company	Toronto, ON
Savage Consultants	Vancouver, BC
Scott Wolfe Management	Headingly, MB
Search Company, The	Toronto, ON
Search Justified Selection	Toronto, ON
Servocraft Limited	Toronto, ON
Sheldon Recruiting	Toronto, ON
Shore & Fitzwilliam	Montréal, QC
Skott/Edwards Consult	USA
Société Jean P. Brisebois	Montréal, QC
Spencer Stuart	Toronto, ON
Spencer Stuart	Montréal, QC
Spencer Stuart	BRAZIL
Spencer Stuart	CHINA
Spencer Stuart	GERMANY
Spencer Stuart	ITALY
Spencer Stuart	USA
Spencer Stuart	USA
StoneWood Group	Toronto, ON
StoneWood Group	Ottawa, ON
StoneWood Group	Sainte-Geneviève, QC
Symmetry Search Group	Toronto, ON
T.J. Seaton Management	Calgary, AB
Tancredi Consulting	Toronto, ON
Team Power Exec Search	Markham, ON
TERHAM Mgmnt Consulting	Toronto, ON
Thompson Associates	Halifax, NS
TMP Worldwide Exec Search	Toronto, ON
Tolstoy Resources	Bolton, ON
Totten & Associates	London, ON
Tretiak Holowka	Montréal, QC
TRS Staffing Solutions	Calgary, AB
Urquhart Management Inc	Toronto, ON

RETAINER ONLY (Cont.)
HONORAIRE SEULEMENT (Suivre)

Van Biesen Group .... Calgary, AB
Victor & Gold .... Montréal, QC
W. Hutt Mgmnt Resources .... Burlington, ON
Wace & Assoc .... Mississauga, ON
Wayne Perry & Associates .... Toronto, ON
Weir Associates .... Toronto, ON
Wenje Management Ltd .... Markham, ON
Westcott Thomas Assoc .... Toronto, ON
Western Mgmnt Consultants .... Vancouver, BC
Western Mgmnt Consultants .... Edmonton, AB
Western Mgmnt Consultants .... Toronto, ON
Wightman & Associates .... Kanata, ON
Withey Addison .... Mississauga, ON
Wolf Gugler & Associates .... Toronto, ON
Workplace Competence Intl .... Erin, ON
Wypich International .... Toronto, ON
Yves Elkas Inc .... Montréal, QC
Yves Plouffe et assoc .... Île-des-Soeurs, QC
Zenzen Pierce Assoc .... Toronto, ON

SOMETIMES CONTINGENT
PARFOIS RELATIVE

A.B. Schwartz Assoc .... Toronto, ON
ADV Advanced Tech Svcs .... Toronto, ON
Advantage Tech .... Calgary, AB
Advocate Placement .... Toronto, ON
AeroPersonnel Intl .... Dorval, QC
AgCall Human Resources .... Calgary, AB
AgCall Human Resources .... Markham, ON
Aim Personnel Svcs .... Ottawa, ON
Allen Etcovitch Assoc .... Montréal, QC
Altura Group .... Toronto, ON
Ambridge Management .... Toronto, ON
Angus Employment .... Burlington, ON
ASTRA Management Corp .... Vancouver, BC
Austin Park Mgmnt Group .... Toronto, ON
Axxes Technologies .... Sillery, QC
B & L Consultants .... Toronto, ON
Bailey Professional Search .... Calgary, AB
Baldwin Staffing Group .... Calgary, AB
Barrett Rose & Lee .... Toronto, ON
Barry Blostein Recruitment .... Thornhill, ON
BDO Dunwoody LLP .... Winnipeg, MB
Belanger Partners .... Thornhill, ON
Berlys Personnel .... Saint-Laurent, QC
BMA International .... Montréal, QC
BMA International .... Montréal, QC
Brethet Barnum Associates .... Toronto, ON
Brock Placement Group .... Toronto, ON
Bruce Cowan Assoc .... Toronto, ON
Buckley Search .... Toronto, ON
Burke Group .... Hamilton, ON
Burke Group .... St. Catharines, ON
C.J. Stafford & Assoc .... Toronto, ON
C.N. Taylor Consulting .... Bedford, NS
Calvin Partners Intl .... Toronto, ON
Cameron Consulting Group .... Brampton, ON
Canadian Exec Consultants .... Toronto, ON
Canadian Exec Recruitmnt .... Mississauga, ON
Canadian Findings .... Toronto, ON
Canadian Medical Placement .... London, ON
Candidatech placement .... Sainte-Julie, QC
CanMed Consultants .... Mississauga, ON
Career Partners/Harrison .... Hamilton, ON

Central Mgmnt Consultants .... Toronto, ON
Centre for Corp Resources .... Toronto, ON
Centrex HR Centre .... Hamilton, ON
Chacra Belliveau & Assoc .... Montréal, QC
Chapman & Associates .... Vancouver, BC
Chase Consultants .... Mississauga, ON
Chisholm & Partners Intl .... Toronto, ON
Churchill Group, The .... Toronto, ON
Coast Personnel Svcs .... Nanaimo, BC
Coke & Associates .... Toronto, ON
Connectstaff Solutions .... Calgary, AB
Connor Clark Assoc .... Dundas, ON
Connors Lovell Assoc .... Cambridge, ON
Connors Lovell Assoc .... Mississauga, ON
ConsulPro .... Westmount, QC
Corporate Consultants .... Toronto, ON
Corporate Recruiters .... Vancouver, BC
Cosier Associates .... Calgary, AB
Counsel Network .... Vancouver, BC
Cowan Personnel .... Montréal, QC
CTC Computer-Tech Consult .... Winnipeg, MB
Cyberna Associates .... Montréal, QC
D.P. Group, The .... UNITED KINGDOM
Deevan Technology Mgmt .... Richmond Hill, ON
Descheneaux Recruitment .... Vancouver, BC
Design Group Staffing .... Vancouver, BC
Direct Career Concepts .... Woodbridge, ON
Distinct Directions .... Mississauga, ON
Drake Executive .... Toronto, ON
Drake International .... Edmonton, AB
Drake International .... Toronto, ON
Driver Carrier Placement .... Toronto, ON
Dumont & Associates .... Vancouver, BC
Dumont & Associates .... North Vancouver, BC
Dunhill Professional Search .... Vancouver, BC
Duo Mega Inc .... Montréal, QC
EPW & Associates .... Elora, ON
ERP Staffing Solutions .... Brampton, ON
Everest Mgmnt Network .... Toronto, ON
Excalibur Careers .... Markham, ON
Excel Personnel .... Kamloops, BC
Execusource Staffing Intl .... Windsor, ON
Executive Assistance .... Toronto, ON
Executive Resources Intl .... Montréal, QC
Executrade Consultants .... Edmonton, AB
Expertech Personnel Svcs .... Montréal, QC
Farley Law & Assoc .... Thornhill, ON
Fifth Option .... Burnaby, BC
Fisher Group Exec Search .... Calgary, AB
Fred Litman & Associates .... Toronto, ON
Galloway and Associates .... Toronto, ON
Gilligan & Associates .... Toronto, ON
Glen Abbey Exec Search .... Oakville, ON
Global Consulting Group .... Markham, ON
Godbout Martin Godbout Assoc .... Hull, QC
Grant Search Group .... Toronto, ON
Grasslands Group .... Medicine Hat, AB
Grasslands Group .... Swift Current, SK
Groupe LJL .... Pierrefonds, QC
Groupe Primacor .... Longueuil, QC
HCR Personnel Solutions .... Newmarket, ON
HEC Group .... Ancaster, ON
Heenan Consulting IT .... Toronto, ON
Higgins International .... Winnipeg, MB
Horizon Resources Intl .... Calgary, AB
Human Resources Consult .... Mississauga, ON
Ian Martin Ltd .... Toronto, ON
ICAP Management Inc .... Fredericton, NB
Impact Staffing .... Windsor, ON
In Place Select Recruitment .... Toronto, ON

SOMETIMES CONTINGENT (Cont.)
PARFOIS RELATIVE (Suivre)

ALWAYS CONTINGENT (Cont.)
TOUJOURS RELATIVE (Suivre)

Groupe PCA Inc .... Montréal, QC
GSI International Consult .... Toronto, ON
Heale & Associates .... Toronto, ON
Higher Vision Recruitment .... Toronto, ON
Hire Choice .... Toronto, ON
Holloway Schulz & Partners .... Vancouver, BC
HT Search Company .... Nepean, ON
Human Edge Consulting .... Richmond Hill, ON
Hunt Technical Personnel .... Toronto, ON
Hunt Technical Personnel .... Mississauga, ON
Hunt Technical Personnel .... Montréal, QC
Ian Martin Ltd .... Oakville, ON
IMS Innovative Mgmnt .... Toronto, ON
Information Resources Ctr .... SAUDI ARABIA
InGenius Engineering Inc .... Ottawa, ON
Insight Technology Corp .... Calgary, AB
International Search Assoc .... Toronto, ON
International Staffing .... UNITED KINGDOM
IT Resources .... Markham, ON
J. Edgar & Associates .... Toronto, ON
J.P. Anderson & Assoc .... Burlington, ON
James Boyce Associates .... Toronto, ON
Jan Howard & Associates .... Toronto, ON
Jenereaux & Associates .... Mississauga, ON
JENEX Technology Placement .... Vancouver, BC
JSL Search Leaders .... Toronto, ON
Juno Systems .... CHINA
Kate Cowhig Intl Recruitment .... IRELAND
Keith Bagg Staffing .... Toronto, ON
Kelly Permanent Recruit .... Toronto, ON
Kelly Permanent Recruit .... Toronto, ON
Kelly Permanent Recruit .... Mississauga, ON
Kenneth Murphy & Assoc .... Halifax, NS
Kforce.ca .... Toronto, ON
Kirkpatrick Personnel .... Vancouver, BC
Kitchener Exec Consultants .... Kitchener, ON
Larkin Group .... Mississauga, ON
Larson & Associates .... Calgary, AB
Lenard Kay & Associates .... Oakville, ON
Life After Law .... Toronto, ON
Lintex Computer Group .... Toronto, ON
Louise Robinson Placement .... Keene, ON
Management Plus Consulting .... LEBANON
Mark Professional Services .... Calgary, AB
Marr Roy Group .... Toronto, ON
Maxim Group .... Richmond, BC
McDonald-Green Personnel .... Cambridge, ON
MediStaff .... USA
Meridia Recruitment Svcs .... Halifax, NS
Miller & Associates .... Mississauga, ON
Miller Recruitment Solutions .... Halifax, NS
Molnar & Associates .... Toronto, ON
MRK Consulting .... UNITED KINGDOM
National Executive .... Toronto, ON
Network Corporate Search .... Calgary, AB
New World Intl Consultants .... Windsor, ON
Newfoundland Personnel .... St. John's, NF
Nework Corp .... Toronto, ON
Nex Canada .... Toronto, ON
ObjectSearch .... Toronto, ON
Office Team Staffing .... Pointe-Claire, QC
P.R.Y. .... Toronto, ON
Partners in Search .... Toronto, ON
Peak Associates Inc .... Toronto, ON
Permanent Search Group .... Mississauga, ON
Permanent Solutions .... Mississauga, ON
Personnel Mgmnt Group .... Winnipeg, MB

Personnel Outaouais .... Hull, QC
Peter Glaser Assoc .... UNITED KINGDOM
Pinstripe Personnel .... Toronto, ON
Placement Testart .... Westmount, QC
PME Partenaire Consult .... Saint-Georges, QC
Premier Personnel Mgmt .... Toronto, ON
Pro Med National Staffing .... USA
Pro-Action Personnel .... Chomedey, QC
Procom .... Calgary, AB
Procom .... Waterloo, ON
Procom .... Toronto, ON
Procom .... Kanata, ON
Procom .... Montréal, QC
Procom Services .... USA
Procom Services .... USA
Profile Personnel Consult .... Toronto, ON
Prolink Consulting .... Toronto, ON
Prologic Systems .... Ottawa, ON
Prosearch Associates .... Mississauga, ON
Quantum EDP Recruiting Svcs .... Toronto, ON
Quantum Mgmt Services .... Toronto, ON
Quest Consultants .... Toronto, ON
Quest Exec Recruitment .... Toronto, ON
Resource Management Group .... Toronto, ON
RHI Consulting .... Vancouver, BC
RHI Consulting .... Edmonton, AB
RHI Consulting .... Calgary, AB
RHI Consulting .... Toronto, ON
RHI Consulting .... Toronto, ON
RHI Consulting .... Mississauga, ON
RHI Consulting .... Ottawa, ON
RHI Consulting .... Montréal, QC
RHI Consulting .... USA
RHI Management Resources .... Calgary, AB
RHI Management Resources .... Toronto, ON
Robert Half Canada .... Edmonton, AB
Robert Half Canada .... Calgary, AB
Robert Half Canada .... Toronto, ON
Robert Half Canada .... Toronto, ON
Robert Half Canada .... Mississauga, ON
Robert Half Canada .... Montréal, QC
Robert Half Financial .... Vancouver, BC
Rossi & Associates .... Vancouver, BC
RWJ & Associates .... London, ON
S.i. Systems .... Vancouver, BC
Sam Perri & Associates .... Mississauga, ON
Silicon Executive Search .... Toronto, ON
Softcom Consulting .... Richmond Hill, ON
Spherion Workforce .... Edmonton, AB
Spherion Workforce .... Winnipeg, MB
Spherion Workforce .... London, ON
Spherion Workforce .... Toronto, ON
Spherion Workforce .... Toronto, ON
Spherion Workforce .... Toronto, ON
Spherion Workforce .... Toronto, ON
Spherion Workforce .... Hamilton, ON
Spherion Workforce .... Mississauga, ON
Spherion Workforce .... Mississauga, ON
Spherion Workforce .... Barrie, ON
Spherion Workforce .... Pickering, ON
Spherion Workforce .... Whitby, ON
Spherion Workforce .... Oshawa, ON
Spherion Workforce .... Kanata, ON
Spherion Workforce .... Ottawa, ON
Spherion Workforce .... Ottawa, ON
Spherion Workforce .... Montréal, QC
Spherion Workforce .... Halifax, NS
SPI Executive Search .... Ottawa, ON
Staff Bureau Employment .... Edmonton, AB
Staff Plus .... Toronto, ON

ALWAYS CONTINGENT (Cont.)
TOUJOURS RELATIVE (Suivre)

"WHO'S WHO" INDEX
PERSONNES-RESSOURCES

AAVIK - ANDERSON

ANDERSON - BACHMAN

Anderson, David .... BDO Dunwoody LLP (Winnipeg, MB)
Anderson, Doug .... Corporate Recruiters Ltd. (Vancouver, BC)
Anderson, Jeff .... J.P. Anderson & Associates Inc. (Burlington, ON)
Anderson, Jim .... Fountainhealth Recruitment (Toronto, ON)
Anderson, Mr. Lynn R. .... Russell Reynolds Associates, Inc. (AUSTRALIA)
Andrade, Roy .... Alliance Search Group Inc. (Toronto, ON)
Andras, Tony .... Fountainhealth Recruitment (Toronto, ON)
André, Jacques P. .... Ray & Berndtson (USA)
Andrew, Melanie .... Roevin Technical People Ltd. (Sarnia, ON)
Andrews, Julie .... Brock Placement Group Inc. (Toronto, ON)
Andrews, Robert L. .... Allen Austin Lowe & Powers (USA)
Angrignon, François .... Unixel recrutement en informatique (Île-des-Soeurs, QC)
Anitua, Javier .... Russell Reynolds Associates, Inc. (SPAIN)
Anthony, Derrick .... Grant Thornton International (Grand Falls-Windsor, NF)
Anthony, Simon K. .... HRmax (Toronto, ON)
Antolick, Theresa J. .... Paziuk Professional Placements / P3 (Edmonton, AB)
Antonel, Elaine .... Drakkar Human Resources (Mississauga, QC)
Apablaza, Raul .... Godbout Martin Godbout & Associates (Hull, QC)
Apffel, Caroline .... Russell Reynolds Associates, Inc. (FRANCE)
Aplin, David .... David Aplin & Associates (Edmonton, AB)
Apple, Lawrie .... Apple Management Corporation (Toronto, ON)
April, Frederic .... Candidatech Inc., service de placement (Sainte-Julie, QC)
April, Jean-Paul .... Candidatech Inc., service de placement (Sainte-Julie, QC)
Aquarone, Michel .... Renard Hospitality Search Consultants (Toronto, ON)
Arbic, Nancy .... Freelancers Unlimited Inc. (Toronto, ON)
Arbitman, Greg .... Recareer.com (Toronto, ON)
Arcand, Claude P. .... Groupe Pluridis Inc. (Montréal, QC)
Archambault, Annie .... Quantum, Les services de gestion (Laval, QC)
Archambealt, Jean-Luc .... CV Theque (Laval, QC)
Archambeaud, Lucia Ferreira .... Russell Reynolds Associates, Inc. (FRANCE)
Archer, Diane .... Datalist (Toronto, ON)
Ardito, Lisa .... Asset Computer Personnel Ltd. (Toronto, ON)
Arkell, Jennifer .... Eagle Professional Resources Inc. (Ottawa, ON)
Armitage, Blake .... Pleiad Canada Inc. (Ottawa, ON)
Armitage, John D. .... Armitage Associates Ltd. (Toronto, ON)
Armstrong, Diane .... Bosworth Field Associates (Toronto, ON)
Armstrong, Lynn .... Chapman & Associates (Vancouver, BC)
Armstrong, Nicholas .... Harvey Nash plc (UNITED KINGDOM)
Armstrong, Peter .... Wallace & Partners Inc. (Toronto, ON)
Armstrong, Shawn .... Applied Technology Solutions Inc. / ATS (Toronto, ON)
Arndt, Morgan .... Questus Recruitment (Calgary, AB)
Arnold, Paula .... North York Personnel Inc. (Toronto, ON)
Arrivault, Isabelle .... Personnel Alter Ego Inc. (Pointe-Claire, QC)
Arseneau, Denis R. .... Recru Science, Inc. (Longueuil, QC)
Arshoff, Fred .... Lipton Wiseman (Toronto, ON)
Arthur, Frances .... Futurestep (Toronto, ON)
Arts, Beverly .... Adecco Canada Inc. (Victoria, BC)
Ashley, Stephen .... Stephen Ashley Associates (Toronto, ON)
Ashton, Barbara L. .... Ashton Computer Professionals Inc. / ACP (North Vancouver, BC)
Askins, Amy .... Procom Services (USA)
Assad, Helen .... Day Advertising Group Inc. (Toronto, ON)
Assargard, Ulf .... Amrop International (SWEDEN)
Asselin, Jasmine .... Rolland Groupe Conseil Inc. (Westmount, QC)
Atkins, Mark .... Mandrake Management Consultants (Toronto, ON)
Attard, Frank .... Connors, Lovell & Associates Inc. (Mississauga, ON)
Atto, Blake .... Link Resource Partners (Toronto, ON)
Attrell, Loni .... Tosi Placement Services Inc. (Toronto, ON)
Audet, Christine .... Harrington Staffing Services and Informatics Resources (Ottawa, ON)
Audibert, Mireille .... Rolland Groupe Conseil Inc. (Westmount, QC)
August, Christine .... MediStaff (USA)
Austin, Brad .... ATS Reliance Technical Group (Toronto, ON)
Averbach, Jay .... Canadian Executive Consultants Inc. (Toronto, ON)
Avon, Fred .... Personnel Star Avon FJ Inc. (Montréal, QC)
Azar, Carl .... Russell Reynolds Associates, Inc. (FRANCE)
Azulay, Tara .... Altis Human Resources (Toronto, ON)
Azure, Doralee .... Jenereaux & Associates Inc. (Mississauga, ON)
Babcock, Dick .... Allen Austin Lowe & Powers (USA)
Babcock, Lyle .... Rockwell Placement Agencies (Richmond, BC)
Babin, Lyn .... Dotemtex Executive Search (Montréal, QC)
Babinger, Kevin .... Connors, Lovell & Associates Inc. (Mississauga, ON)
Bacchus, Mike .... David Aplin & Associates (Edmonton, AB)
Bach, Leora .... Bach Associates (Vancouver, BC)
Bachinski, Anne .... Bradford Bachinski Limited (Ottawa, ON)
Bachman, Mark .... Prolink Consulting Inc. (Toronto, ON)

BACHNER - BATHURST

BATIUK - BENSKY

Batiuk, Janice .... Cameron Management Services Group / CMSG (Edmonton, AB)
Batog, Jennifer .... Personnel Search Ltd. (Moncton, NB)
Battah, Pierre .... Ray & Berndtson / Robertson Surrette (Moncton, NB)
Baynton, Karen .... Adecco Canada Inc. (Saskatoon, SK)
Baz, Jennifer .... Drakkar Human Resources (Mississauga, ON)
Bazinet, Sophie .... Adecco Québec Inc. (Québec, QC)
Beadell, Sheenagh .... Taylor Personnel Limited (Victoria, BC)
Beadle, Art .... A.R. Beadle & Associates Ltd. (Kelowna, BC)
Beallor, Morley .... Beallor & Partners LLP (Toronto, ON)
Bean, Randi .... Life After Law (Toronto, ON)
Beard, Shelly .... Technical Connections Inc. (USA)
Bearss, Steve .... Genesis Group Ltd., The (Yellowknife, NT)
Beauchamp, Joe .... Express Personnel Services (Ottawa, ON)
Beauchemin, Stephane .... St-Amour & Associates (Montréal, QC)
Beaudoin, Marc .... St-Amour & Associates (Montréal, QC)
Beaudoin, Marie-Andrée .... Groupe Tele Ressources (Montréal, QC)
Beaudry, Ray .... Lock & Associates (Winnipeg, MB)
Beaudry, Rick .... B Wyze Inc. (Richmond Hill, ON)
Beaulieu, Benoît .... Dotemtex Executive Search (Montréal, QC)
Beaupré, Cathy .... Impact Staffing Inc. (Windsor, ON)
Beaupré, Joseph M.B. .... PricewaterhouseCoopers Executive Search (Montréal, QC)
Bebby, Evelyn .... Feldman Gray & Associates Inc. (Toronto, ON)
Bechard, Brock .... Renaissance Personnel (Chatham, ON)
Bechard, Chris .... Renaissance Personnel (Chatham, ON)
Becotte, Pascal .... Sirius Personnel Inc. (Montréal, QC)
Bédard, Carole .... Bedard Ressources Inc. (Montréal, QC)
Bédard, Françoise .... Tele-Ressources Ltée (Montréal, QC)
Bédard, Jacques .... St-Amour & Associates (Montréal, QC)
Bédard, Julie .... Synagent Inc. (Woodlawn, ON)
Bedard, Kim .... AgCall Human Resources (Calgary, AB)
Bédard, Yvonne .... Bedard Ressources Inc. (Montréal, QC)
Beechey, Lynn .... Connors, Lovell & Associates Inc. (Mississauga, ON)
Beet, Coralee .... About Staffing (Edmonton, AB)
Behar, Natalie .... Russell Reynolds Associates, Inc. (FRANCE)
Beidas, Ramzi .... Information Resources Center (SAUDI ARABIA)
Bélanger, Jean-Pierre .... Pro Tec Services Techniques (Brossard, QC)
Bélanger, Richard .... Kingsley Allen IT Search Inc. (Toronto, ON)
Belanger, Rick .... Belanger Partners Limited (Thornhill, ON)
Bélanger, Steve .... St-Amour & Associates (Montréal, QC)
Belanger, Steve .... Walter P. Miller & Company / WPM (St. John's, NF)
Belcourt, Clint .... Coape Staffing Network (Calgary, AB)
Belgrave, Catherine .... CDI Technical Services Ltd. (Oakville, ON)
Beliveau, JoAnn .... David Aplin & Associates (Edmonton, AB)
Béliveau, Yves .... Yves Béliveau recherche de cadres (Saint-Lambert, QC)
Bell, Barbara .... Drake Executive (Montréal, QC)
Bell, Catherine .... Van Biesen Group Inc. (Calgary, AB)
Bell, David .... David Bell Executive Search (Toronto, ON)
Bell, Ellen .... Adecco Canada Inc. (Brampton, ON)
Bell, Gordon .... Global Options Inc. / IT Intellect, Inc. (USA)
Bell, Jeffrey .... Spencer Stuart (USA)
Bell, Lynn .... Executive Services Plus Ltd. (Saint John, NB)
Bell, M.E. .... Drake Executive (Toronto, ON)
Bell, Tom .... NewSource Management Ltd. (Toronto, ON)
Belle Isle, Charles .... Belle Isle Djandji Brunet, Inc. (Montréal, QC)
Belley, Michel .... Systematix Information Technology Consultants Inc. (Québec, QC)
Bellis, Kyra .... Computer Action Company (Toronto, ON)
Bellmore-Donaldson, Marianne .... HR / RH Inc. (Montréal, QC)
Beluse, Silvie .... Progroupe Ressources Humaines Inc. (Pierrefonds, QC)
Benattar, Laurent .... Proben Management Ltd. (Montréal, QC)
Bench, Edie .... Edie Bench Personnel Consultants (Toronto, ON)
Benchetrit, Gérard .... StoneWood Group (Sainte-Geneviève, QC)
Benedict, Kim .... Quantum Management Services Limited (Toronto, ON)
Benham, Charles .... St-Amour & Associates (Toronto, ON)
Benidir, Omar .... Executive 2000 Institute (Toronto, ON)
Benjamin, Lisa .... Recruitment Enhancement Services / RES (Vancouver, BC)
Bennett, Andy .... Lock & Associates (Toronto, ON)
Bennett, Daniel .... London Executive Consultants (London, ON)
Bennett, Fiona .... HaysZMB (UNITED KINGDOM)
Bennett, Irvin .... Merit Vendor Personnel Inc. (Toronto, ON)
Bennett, Susan .... Kent Legal Personnel (Toronto, ON)
Bennett, Val .... Deloitte Consulting (Toronto, ON)
Benoit, Hervé .... Michel Pauzé et Associés (Montréal, QC)
Benoit, Paul .... Progestic Group Inc. (Montréal, QC)
Bensky, Carolyn .... Meyers Norris Penny / MNP (Winnipeg, MB)

BENTON - BLIN

BLONDIE - BRADSHAW

Blondie, Nicole	Adecco Canada Inc. (Calgary, AB)
Bloomer, Chris J.	Korn / Ferry International (Vancouver, BC)
Blostein, Barry	Barry Blostein Recruitment (Thornhill, ON)
Blouin, Nathalie	SAG ressources humaines inc. (Montréal, QC)
Bloye, Joanne	Apex Search Inc. (Toronto, ON)
Blue, Jim	Clarke, Henning LLP (Toronto, ON)
Blumenthal, Peggy	Hunt Technical Personnel (Vancouver, BC)
Blunt, Antoinette	Ironside Consulting Services Inc. (Sault Ste. Marie, ON)
Boal, Marie	Aquent Partners (Toronto, ON)
Bobeldyk, Lisa	Drake Executive (Toronto, ON)
Bodman, W.D. "Bill"	BDO Dunwoody LLP (Winnipeg, MB)
Bodnaryk, David	Grant Search Group Inc., The (Toronto, ON)
Bohm, Charles	Aztech Recruitment Co. (USA)
Boileau, Manon	Prospects Plus Inc. (Kirkland, QC)
Bois, Simon E.	Keith Bagg & Associates Inc. (Toronto, ON)
Boivin, Maude	Kelly, Les services (Montréal, QC)
Boland, Frances	Puglisevich Crews and Services Limited (St. John's, NF)
Bolduc, Louise	Placement de personnel Louise Bolduc inc. (Sillery, QC)
Bolduc, Serge	Groupe Ranger (Montréal, QC)
Bolivar, Tim	Grant Thornton International (Wetaskiwin, AB)
Bollman, Myles	Canadian Career Partners (Calgary, AB)
Bolzan, Bruno	Russell Reynolds Associates, Inc. (FRANCE)
Bonar, Tamara	InterCom Recruitment Ltd. (Toronto, ON)
Bongard, Susan	Bongard Marsh Associates Inc. (Toronto, ON)
Bongard, Warren	ZSA Legal Recruitment (Toronto, ON)
Boniface, Lisa	HCCA Canada Inc. (Mississauga, ON)
Bonnell, Robert	Ashlar-Stone Management Consultants Inc. (Mississauga, ON)
Booth, David	Little Group, The (Burlington, ON)
Booth, Gregory A.	Net-Temps Inc. (USA)
Booth, Lisa	Forbes & Gunn Consultants Ltd. (USA)
Booth, Richard W.	Booth International Management Consultants (Toronto, ON)
Borer, Leonard	Richter Consulting (Toronto, ON)
Borg, Theresa	Puglisevich Crews and Services Limited (St. John's, NF)
Borras, Joe	Preferred Healthcare Staffing (USA)
Bossio, Mike	Boscan Consultants Inc. (Marysville, ON)
Botrie, James	Botrie Associates / Stanton Chase International (Toronto, ON)
Boucher, Marie-Josée	Adecco Québec (Longueuil, QC)
Boucher, Pierre	Société Pierre Boucher / SPB Business Psychology (Longueuil, QC)
Boudeau, André	Noramtec Consultants Inc. (Montréal, QC)
Bourbeau, Paul J.	Boyden Global Executive Search (Montréal, QC)
Bourbonnais, Jean-Pierre	Korn / Ferry International (Montréal, QC)
Bourdeau, Marc	Effective Personnel Solutions, Inc. (Calgary, AB)
Bourelle, Jade	Armitage Associates Ltd. (Vancouver, BC)
Bourgon, Todd	Lock & Associates (Toronto, ON)
Boutin, Bert	Transpersonnel Driver Staffing and Allied Services (Edmonton, AB)
Bowen, Larry	Keith Bagg & Associates Inc. (Toronto, ON)
Bowen-Smed, Shannon	Bowen Staffing (Calgary, AB)
Bower, Darcia	Expert Recruiters Inc. (Vancouver, BC)
Bower, Jamie	Bower Ng Staff Systems Inc. (Vancouver, BC)
Bowerman, Gina	Robert L. Holmes Professional Placement Services Inc. (Cambridge, ON)
Bowers, Joanne	Keith Bagg & Associates Inc. (Toronto, ON)
Bowes, Barbara	Meyers Norris Penny / MNP (Winnipeg, MB)
Bowler, Mike	Matchtech Engineering Ltd. (UNITED KINGDOM)
Bownes, Ed	Canadian Career Partners (Calgary, AB)
Boyce, James T. (Jim)	James T. Boyce & Associates (Toronto, ON)
Boyd, Chris	Permanent Search Group Inc. / PSG (Mississauga, ON)
Boyd, John P.	Boyd PetroSearch (Calgary, AB)
Boyd, Kristy	Lock & Associates (Toronto, ON)
Boyd, Lesley	W.G. Meldrum Limited (Vancouver, BC)
Boyd, Robert	Administrative Fundamentals Inc. (Toronto, ON)
Boyda, Ann	Serecon Management Consulting Inc. (Edmonton, AB)
Boyea, Wendy	Burke Group, The (Hamilton, ON)
Boyer, Catharine	Multec Canada Ltd. (Montréal, QC)
Boyle, Art	Canpro Executive Search (Markham, ON)
Boyle, Greg	StoneWood Group (Ottawa, ON)
Boyle, Kimberly	Human Resource Initiatives (Mississauga, ON)
Bozek, Gary	Connectstaff Solutions Corp. (Calgary, AB)
Bradford, Christi	Management Recruiters of Kannapolis (USA)
Bradford, David	Harvey Nash plc (UNITED KINGDOM)
Bradley, Edward	Taylor Recruitment Ltd. (UNITED KINGDOM)
Bradley, Enid	PricewaterhouseCoopers Executive Search (Edmonton, AB)
Bradley, Janis	Accountemps Financial Staffing (Calgary, AB)
Bradshaw, Andrew	Matchtech Engineering Ltd. (UNITED KINGDOM)
Bradshaw, Dianne	Alan Davis & Associates Inc. (Hudson Heights, QC)

BRADY - BRUNELLE

BRUNET - CAMERON

Brunet, Michel S. .... Belle Isle Djandji Brunet, Inc. (Montréal, QC)
Brunet, Micheline .... BMA International (Montréal, QC)
Bruneteau, Patrick .... Matteson Management Inc. (Toronto, ON)
Bruntjen, Cindy .... HR Business Partners (Calgary, AB)
Brushett, Bill .... Grant Thornton International (St. John's, NF)
Bruusgaard, Kurt .... Ray & Berndtson A/S (DENMARK)
Bryan, Fiona .... Asset Computer Personnel Ltd. (Toronto, ON)
Bryan, Rickie .... Bryan Jason & Associates Inc. (Toronto, ON)
Bryski, Kerry .... Datalist (Toronto, ON)
Bucher, Irene .... Harrison, Carlson, Criminisi (Burlington, ON)
Buckland, Erik .... Renard Hospitality Search Consultants (Toronto, ON)
Buckland, G. Russell .... Bedford Consulting Group Inc., The (Toronto, ON)
Buckley, Anna .... Buckley Search Inc. (Toronto, ON)
Buckley, Kevin .... Buckley Search Inc. (Toronto, ON)
Budworth, Mark .... Forbes & Gunn Consultants Ltd. (Vancouver, BC)
Buick, Jonathan .... TalentLab (Kanata, ON)
Bukowski-Green, Brenda .... Technical Connections Inc. (USA)
Bull, Mary K. .... Canadian Career Partners (Calgary, AB)
Bull, Simon A. .... Simon A. Bull & Associates (Cambridge, ON)
Bullen, Tim .... Keith Bagg Information Technology Search Inc. / KBITS (Toronto, ON)
Bundy, Celine .... Technical Connections Inc. (USA)
Burch, Barrie .... Resource Professionals Inc. (Calgary, AB)
Burdon, Ed .... Canadian Career Partners (Calgary, AB)
Burgess, Douglas C. .... Computer Task Group / CTG (Toronto, ON)
Burgess, Tony .... TDM Technical Services (Toronto, ON)
Burke, Londa .... People Bank, The (Toronto, ON)
Burke, Randy .... Connors, Lovell & Associates Inc. (Mississauga, ON)
Burkey, David .... Drake International (Kingston, ON)
Burkland, Julie .... Skott/Edwards Consultants (USA)
Burkland, Skott B. .... Skott/Edwards Consultants (USA)
Burley, Tara .... Randstad Interim Inc. (Ottawa, ON)
Burnett, Allen .... Management Recruiters of Kannapolis (USA)
Burns, Alan .... Enns Hever Inc. (Toronto, ON)
Burns, Kent .... TES, The Employment Solution (Toronto, ON)
Bursey, Tom .... Alan Davis & Associates Inc. (Ottawa, ON)
Burt-Green, Dianne .... MBL Group LLC (USA)
Burton, Gordon .... McLean Executive Consultants Ltd. (Calgary, AB)
Bush, Jim .... J.O. Bush & Associates (Mindemoya, ON)
Bussey, Louisa .... James Partnership, The (BERMUDA)
Busteed, Gary .... NewSource Management Ltd. (Toronto, ON)
Butcher, Gordon .... AgCall Human Resources (Calgary, AB)
Butler, Gary .... Facilité Informatique (Montréal, QC)
Butler, Kasey .... Kelly Scientific Resources / KSR (Mississauga, ON)
Butler, Lisa .... Futurestep (Toronto, ON)
Butler, Marina .... Erie Personnel Corporation (Fort Erie, ON)
Butler, Ron .... Erie Personnel Corporation (Fort Erie, ON)
Butter, Mark .... Matchtech Engineering Ltd. (UNITED KINGDOM)
Butterworth, Darren .... Maxim Group (Richmond, BC)
Buxton, Gary .... Initial Healthcare (Markham, ON)
Buzaglo, Jack .... Link Resource Partners (Toronto, ON)
Bykerk, Daphne .... Mandrake Management Consultants (Toronto, ON)
Byles, Mark .... Trillium Talent Resource Inc. (Toronto, ON)
Byrne, Allister .... Grant Thornton International (Markham, ON)
Byrne, Miles .... CBM Projects Inc. (Calgary, AB)
Byrne, Patricia M. .... Catalyst Consulting (Vancouver, BC)
Byrne, Suzanne .... Ian Martin Limited (Toronto, ON)
Byun, Thomas .... Accountants on Call / AOC Financial Executive Search (Toronto, ON)
Cadman, Gary .... Cadman Consulting Group Inc. (Vancouver, BC)
Cadotte, Meredith .... Renaissance Personnel (Chatham, ON)
Cagle, Caroline .... Management Recruiters of Kannapolis (USA)
Calder, A. Bill .... Savage Consultants Inc. (Vancouver, BC)
Caldwell, C. Douglas .... Caldwell Partners, The (Toronto, ON)
Caldwell, Cheryl .... Renaissance Personnel (Chatham, ON)
Caldwell, Gordon B. .... Grant Thornton International (Kentville, NS)
Caley, Timothy .... Cambridge Management Planning Inc. (Toronto, ON)
Calladine, Mary .... People Bank, The (Toronto, ON)
Callaghan, Bruce .... Armor Personnel (Mississauga, ON)
Callocchia, Fiorella .... HR Impact (Toronto, ON)
Calver, Sardi .... Morgan & Banks Ltd. (AUSTRALIA)
Calver, Simon .... HaysZMB (UNITED KINGDOM)
Calvert, Victoria .... Canadian Career Partners (Calgary, AB)
Cameron, Brent .... Ray & Berndtson / Tanton Mitchell (Vancouver, BC)
Cameron, H. Allen .... Cameron Management Services Group / CMSG (Calgary, AB)
Cameron, Jack .... Cameron Consulting Group (Brampton, ON)

CAMERON - CHAMBERS

CHAMBERS - CLARK

Chambers, Patricia .... Global Consulting Group Inc. (Markham, ON)
Chamerland, Carol .... Calian Technology Services Ltd. (Kanata, ON)
Champoux, Yves .... Korn / Ferry International (Montréal, QC)
Chan, Alan .... CBM Projects Inc. (Calgary, AB)
Chan, Anita .... JENEX Technology Placement Inc. (Vancouver, BC)
Chan, Arnold .... Kelly Professional & Technical Services (Toronto, ON)
Chanchlani, Dave .... Applied Technology Solutions Inc. / ATS (Toronto, ON)
Chandler, Heather .... Landon Morgan Inc. (Thorold, ON)
Chandler, Jasmin .... Williams & Associates Inc. (Toronto, ON)
Channing, Robert B. .... Robert B. Channing Consulting (Oakville, ON)
Chapatis, John .... CNC Global (Ottawa, ON)
Chapdelaine, Joanne .... Experts Conseils 2000 (Montréal, QC)
Chapman, Claude .... Ernst David International (Winnipeg, MB)
Chappell, Janet .... Permanent Search Group Inc. / PSG (Mississauga, ON)
Charbonneau, Dorothy .... Nework Corp. (Toronto, ON)
Charest, Gilles .... Yves Plouffe et associés (Île-des-Soeurs, QC)
Charette, Anne .... Burke Group, The (St. Catharines, ON)
Charfeddine, Kamel .... ePersonnel Inc. (Montréal, QC)
Charlebois, Benoît .... St-Amour & Associates (Montréal, QC)
Charles, Andrew .... Noramtec Consultants Inc. (Nepean, ON)
Charpentier, Richard .... Systematix Information Technology Consultants Inc. (Montréal, QC)
Chase, Kevin .... Ray & Berndtson (USA)
Chastney, Helen .... Harvey Nash plc (UNITED KINGDOM)
Chater, Christine .... Staff Bureau Employment Group (Edmonton, AB)
Chaterji, Raj .... Drake International (Toronto, ON)
Chavasse, Dan .... Michael Page Finance (CHINA)
Cheikh, Moodie .... Procom / Professional Computer Consultants Group Ltd. (Kanata, ON)
Chelew, Robert D. .... Central Management Consultants Inc. (Toronto, ON)
Chen, Monica .... Computer Task Group / CTG (Toronto, ON)
Chen, Peter .... FAS Resources (Markham, ON)
Chen, Vivian .... RJS Associates Inc. (Toronto, ON)
Cheng, Aimée .... Harrington Staffing Services and Informatics Resources (Ottawa, ON)
Chengkalath, R.K. .... R.K. Chengkalath Professional Corporation (Calgary, AB)
Chennette, Denis .... Labor Tek Personnel Services Ltd. (Ottawa, ON)
Chesney, Kimberley .... Prime Management Group Inc. (London, ON)
Chew, Choon Soo .... Russell Reynolds Associates, Inc. (SINGAPORE)
Chiles, John .... Drake International (Barrie, ON)
Chillcott, Gordon .... CM Inc. (Markham, ON)
Chilton, Liz .... B Wyze Inc. (Richmond Hill, ON)
Chippendale, Anne .... Quantum Consulting Ltd. (Calgary, AB)
Chisholm, Debbie .... Canadian Career Partners (Calgary, AB)
Chisholm, Robert .... Ashlar-Stone Management Consultants Inc. (Mississauga, ON)
Chisholm, Sherilynn .... Chisholm & Partners International Inc. (Toronto, ON)
Chisholm, Timothy J. .... Chisholm & Partners International Inc. (Toronto, ON)
Chisholm, Wynne L. .... Wynne Chisholm & Associates Inc. (Calgary, AB)
Chiswell, Fred .... Advantage Group, The (Moncton, NB)
Chitayat, Andre .... Techaid Inc. (Montréal, QC)
Chitnis, Shashi .... Renard Hospitality Search Consultants (Toronto, ON)
Cho, Peter .... Alliance Search Group Inc. (Toronto, ON)
Chomichuk, Diane .... Meyers Norris Penny / MNP (Winnipeg, MB)
Chondon, David .... Employer's Choice, The (Brampton, ON)
Choquet, Celine .... Deloitte Consulting (Montréal, QC)
Choquette, André .... Planigestion A. Choquette Inc. (Duvernay, QC)
Choquette, Claude .... Planigestion A. Choquette Inc. (Duvernay, QC)
Chorney, Jenn .... ATS Reliance Technical Group (Toronto, ON)
Chorney, Marilyn .... Executrade Consultants Ltd. (Edmonton, AB)
Chouier, Caroline .... Bernier & Associés Recherche et Selection (Montréal, QC)
Christensen, Don .... Stoakley-Dudley Consultants Ltd. (Mississauga, ON)
Christenson, Christina .... TalentLab (Kanata, ON)
Christian, Jeffrey E. .... Christian & Timbers (USA)
Christie, Alayna .... W.G. Meldrum Limited (Calgary, AB)
Christie, Nadine .... Planet Personnel Agency Inc. (Toronto, ON)
Chrobak, John .... Pro Tec Global Staffing Services (Thornhill, ON)
Chrzan, Phyllis .... Brethet, Barnum & Associates Inc. (Toronto, ON)
Chua, Jacqueline .... Keith Bagg Staffing Resources Inc. (Toronto, ON)
Chun, David .... Hospitality Personnel Consultants (Toronto, ON)
Cicciarella, Katherine .... Accountants on Call / AOC Financial Executive Search (Toronto, ON)
Cimon, Ghislaine .... Yves Plouffe et associés (Île-des-Soeurs, QC)
Cinkant, Diane .... People Bank, The (Montréal, QC)
Citroen, Gail F. .... Little Group, The (Burlington, ON)
Ciuciura, Jan .... Sussex Retail Management (Mississauga, ON)
Clairoux, Jacques .... Dion Management Executive Search (Toronto, ON)
Clark, Arthur .... Barrett Rose & Lee Inc. (Toronto, ON)
Clark, Blair .... Grasslands Group Inc. (Swift Current, SK)

CLARK - CONNELLY

Clark, Bob .... Clark, Pollard & Gagliardi (Waterloo, ON)
Clark, Dave .... Pro Tec Global Staffing Services (Thornhill, ON)
Clark, Jane .... Connor Clark & Associates (Dundas, ON)
Clark, Julie .... Corporate Recruiters Ltd. (Vancouver, BC)
Clark, Lindsey .... Ray & Berndtson / Robertson Surrette (Halifax, NS)
Clark, Lorrie .... Permanent Search Group Inc. / PSG (Mississauga, ON)
Clark, Michael .... David Aplin & Associates (Edmonton, AB)
Clark, Ruth .... Ajilon Canada (Vancouver, BC)
Clark, Terry .... Project Management Recruiting Inc. (Toronto, ON)
Clarke, Brad .... Clarke Management Services, Inc. (Calgary, AB)
Clarke, David .... Drake International (Kingston, ON)
Clarke, Jim .... Ian Martin Limited (Oakville, ON)
Clarke, Murray W. .... Derhak Ireland & Partners Ltd. (Toronto, ON)
Clarke, Susan .... Stoakley-Dudley Consultants Ltd. (Mississauga, ON)
Clarke, Virginia .... Spencer Stuart (USA)
Clarkson, Roger M. .... Spencer Stuart & Associates (Canada) Ltd. (Toronto, ON)
Clasen, Colin .... C.W. Clasen Recruiting Services (Coquitlam, BC)
Claude, Abram .... Ray & Berndtson (USA)
Clemens, Randy .... Asset Computer Personnel Ltd. (Toronto, ON)
Clement, Roberta .... Ward Vinge & Associates (Calgary, AB)
Clements, Dave .... Synergy Search Consultants (Toronto, ON)
Clements, Sharon .... Accountants on Call / AOC Financial Executive Search (Toronto, ON)
Clements, Wayne .... Clements Consulting Group (Calgary, AB)
Cliffe, Peter .... Merit Vendor Personnel Inc. (Toronto, ON)
Clinton, Debra .... Cambridge Management Planning Inc. (Toronto, ON)
Clost, Chad .... Technisource, Inc. (Kanata, ON)
Clydesdale, Audrey .... Nework Corp. (Toronto, ON)
Coache, Florent .... Urentia (Montréal, QC)
Coburn, James .... Mandrake Management Consultants (Toronto, ON)
Cochlan, Todd .... Questus Recruitment (Calgary, AB)
Cochrane, Dianne .... Advantage Group, The (Saint John, NB)
Cochrane, Neil .... Meyers Norris Penny / MNP (Regina, SK)
Cocks, Kitty .... Miss Hall's Personnel Services Ltd. (Ottawa, ON)
Coe, Karen J. .... Coe & Company International Inc. (Calgary, AB)
Coffey, Tommy Joe .... Coffey & Associates (Hamilton, ON)
Coghlan, George .... Fifth Option, The (Burnaby, BC)
Cohen, Gabriella .... Ressources 3000 (Westmount, QC)
Cohen, Lisa .... Canadian Executive Consultants Inc. (Toronto, ON)
Cohen, Mark .... Computer Horizons ISG (Ottawa, ON)
Cohen, Sheri .... Alder Centre, The (Toronto, ON)
Cohen, Tamara .... HaysZMB (UNITED KINGDOM)
Colbert, Brad .... Executive Network, The (Victoria, BC)
Colborne, Rick .... Hunt Technical Personnel (Vancouver, BC)
Colby, Dan .... Procom Services (USA)
Coleman, Paul .... Prime Management Group Inc. (London, ON)
Coles, Howard .... Coles Associates Ltd. (Charlottetown, PE)
Coll, Kathryn .... Baker Consulting Inc. (Charlottetown, PE)
Collard, Glen .... Pro Tec Global Staffing Services (Thornhill, ON)
Collett, Christie .... Drake International (Toronto, ON)
Colley, Laura .... Asset Computer Personnel Ltd. (Toronto, ON)
Collier, Jeff .... ATS Reliance Technical Group (London, ON)
Colling, Doug .... DHR Canada Inc. (Mississauga, ON)
Collingwood, Beryl A. .... Trillium Talent Resource Inc. (Cambridge, ON)
Collins, Erna .... Orillia Works (Orillia, ON)
Collins, Lesley .... Procom / Professional Computer Consultants Group Ltd. (Kanata, ON)
Collis, Marty .... E.L. Shore & Associates (Toronto, ON)
Colombe, Jeannie .... Advantage Group, The (St. John's, NF)
Colonna, Johnny .... Levy Pilotte (Montréal, QC)
Columbo, Bruno .... Spencer Stuart (ITALY)
Combley, Richard .... TAPP Consulting Services (Merrickville, ON)
Comer, Michael L. .... International Staffing Consultants, Europe (UNITED KINGDOM)
Comins, Frederic M. .... Ray & Berndtson (USA)
Compagnon, Alice .... Fairview Management (Prince Rupert, BC)
Compton, Graham .... Design Group Staffing Services Inc., The (Vancouver, BC)
Compton, Jo Ann L. .... Compton Graham International Inc. (Toronto, ON)
Conde, Luis .... Amrop International / Seeliger y Condé (SPAIN)
Coniglio, Ben .... Rostie & Associates Inc. (Toronto, ON)
Conn, Charles .... C & E Conn & Associates Ltd. (Mississauga, ON)
Conn, Erika .... C & E Conn & Associates Ltd. (Mississauga, ON)
Connell, Nigel .... D.P. Group, The (UNITED KINGDOM)
Connelly, Ann .... Adecco Canada Inc. (Edmonton, AB)
Connelly, Heather .... Heidrick & Struggles Canada Inc. (Toronto, ON)
Connelly, Kevin .... Spencer Stuart (USA)
Connelly, Scott .... Technical Connections Inc. (USA)

CONNOR - CRODEN

Connor, Carolyn .... Connor Clark & Associates (Dundas, ON)
Connors, Barry .... Connors, Lovell & Associates Inc. (Cambridge, ON)
Connors, Brian J. .... Canadian Executive Recruitment (Mississauga, ON)
Conroy, M.J. (Jim) .... Conroy Partners Limited (Calgary, AB)
Constant, Linda .... Alan Davis & Associates Inc. (Hudson Heights, QC)
Conway, Colleen .... Drake International (Halifax, NS)
Conway, Julie-Anne .... Groom & Associés Ltée (Pointe-Claire, QC)
Cook, Donna .... Partners in Search (Toronto, ON)
Cook, Peter .... Seniors for Business (Toronto, ON)
Cook, Steve .... TES, The Employment Solution (Toronto, ON)
Cooke, Brenda .... First Choice Personnel (Toronto, ON)
Coomber, Sarah .... Todays Staffing, Inc. (Toronto, ON)
Cooper, Michael L. .... Group Four Management Consultants (Toronto, ON)
Cooper, Peter .... Korn / Ferry International (Toronto, ON)
Cooper, Sara .... Accountants on Call / AOC Financial Executive Search (Toronto, ON)
Cooper, Shawn .... Russell Reynolds Associates, Inc. (Toronto, ON)
Copcutt, Paul .... St-Amour & Associates (Toronto, ON)
Cope, Roy .... Xycorp Inc. (Toronto, ON)
Copeland, Isabelle .... Harrington Staffing Services and Informatics Resources (Ottawa, ON)
Copp, Bob .... Adirect Recruiting Corporation (Toronto, ON)
Coppin, Nicolla .... Roevin Technical People Ltd. (Montréal, QC)
Corazzola, Susan .... Archer Resource Solutions Inc. (Mississauga, ON)
Corbett, Mike .... David Aplin & Associates (Edmonton, AB)
Corlett, Ray .... Asset Computer Personnel Ltd. (Toronto, ON)
Cormier, Don .... National Executive (Toronto, ON)
Cornell, Gerald .... Cornell Consulting Corporation (Burlington, ON)
Corso, John J. .... InterSearch Canada / Corso, Mizgala + French (Toronto, ON)
Cosgrove, Leah .... Eagle Professional Resources Inc. (Toronto, ON)
Cosier, Brian L. .... Cosier Associates, Inc. (Calgary, AB)
Costin, Richard C. .... Allen Austin Lowe & Powers (USA)
Côté, Anne .... Quantum Management Services Ltd. (Ottawa, ON)
Cotterill, John .... Advantage Group, The (Dartmouth, NS)
Couillard, André .... Procom / Professional Computer Consultants Group Ltd. (Montréal, QC)
Couillard, Jill .... Coe & Company International Inc. (Calgary, AB)
Coulter, John .... J.E. Coulter Associates Limited (Toronto, ON)
Coulter, Penny .... Dunhill Personnel of London (London, ON)
Courey, Jeff .... St-Amour & Associates (Toronto, ON)
Court, Lorna .... Holloway Schulz & Partners Inc. (Vancouver, BC)
Courville, Isabelle .... OKA Computer Systems Ltd. / Gestion Informatique OKA Ltée (Montréal, QC)
Couturier, Alain .... Heidrick & Struggles International, Inc. (VENEZUELA)
Couzens, Gary .... Horizon Resources International Inc. (Calgary, AB)
Cowan, Bruce .... Bruce Cowan & Associates (Toronto, ON)
Cowan, Elaine .... Anokiiwin Employment Solutions, Inc. (Winnipeg, MB)
Cowan, Gordon .... Cowan & Associates (Calgary, AB)
Cowan, Marge .... Bruce Cowan & Associates (Toronto, ON)
Cowan, Paula .... TAD Canada (Ottawa, ON)
Cowhig, Kate .... Kate Cowhig International Recruitment Ltd. (IRELAND)
Cowie, Brenda .... Armor Personnel (Brampton, ON)
Cox, Carl E. .... James T. Boyce & Associates (Toronto, ON)
Cox, Debbie .... Matchtech Engineering Ltd. (UNITED KINGDOM)
Cox, Kathy .... Mindbank Consulting Group (USA)
Crabtree, Lionel .... Galloway and Associates (Toronto, ON)
Craig, Susan J. .... Susan Craig Associates Inc. (Toronto, ON)
Cramer, Roxanne .... David Bell Executive Search (Toronto, ON)
Crane, Penny .... Advantage Group, The (Mississauga, ON)
Crath, Paul F. .... PricewaterhouseCoopers Executive Search (Toronto, ON)
Crawford, Cam .... Coakwell Crawford Cairns (High River, AB)
Crawford, Catherine .... Permanent Solutions Inc. (Mississauga, ON)
Crawford, John D. .... Crawford de Munnik Executive Search (Toronto, ON)
Crawford, Marilyn .... Korn / Ferry International (Vancouver, BC)
Crawford, Michael .... Austin Park Management Group Inc. (Toronto, ON)
Crawford, Peter .... Management Advice International Ltd. (Toronto, ON)
Crawford, Susan .... Employer's Choice, The (Brampton, ON)
Crawley, Judith .... Core-Staff Incorporated (Toronto, ON)
Creber, Lara .... Altis Human Resources (Toronto, ON)
Crecco, Lorry .... Michael Page International (USA)
Creelman, Tracy .... Larkin Group, The (Mississauga, ON)
Creighton, Elaine .... Communication Dynamique Inc. (Beaconsfield, QC)
Creighton, G.P. .... Executive Resources International (Montréal, QC)
Criminisi, Carm .... Harrison, Carlson, Criminisi (Burlington, ON)
Cristofoli, Gabriella .... Argentus Inc. (Toronto, ON)
Critch, Kelly .... Newfoundland Personnel Inc. (St. John's, NF)
Crites, Sue .... SOLUTIONS (Cornwall, ON)
Croden, Irene .... Croden Personnel Consulting Services Inc. (Vancouver, BC)

CROGHAN - DAVIES

DAVIES - DEXTER

Davies, Gordon .... Intec Recruitment Services (UNITED KINGDOM)
Davies, Huw .... Canadian Findings Ltd. (Toronto, ON)
Davies, Veronica .... Becky Jones & Associates Ltd. (Toronto, ON)
Davis, Alan .... Alan Davis & Associates Inc. (Hudson Heights, QC)
Davis, Alison .... Access Human Resources Inc. / AccessHR (Ottawa, ON)
Davis, Alison .... Interocean Personnel Services (UK) Ltd. (UNITED KINGDOM)
Davis, Betty-Anne .... A.E. Harrison & Partners Inc. (Mississauga, ON)
Davis, Bruce .... Interocean Personnel Services (UK) Ltd. (UNITED KINGDOM)
Davis, Charlene .... Heidrick & Struggles Canada Inc. (Toronto, ON)
Davis, Ethel .... Health Match BC (Vancouver, BC)
Davis, Graeme .... Grant Thornton International (Langley, BC)
Davis, Jane .... TES, The Employment Solution (Ottawa, ON)
Davis, Janine .... Technical Connections Inc. (USA)
Davis, Jason .... Davis Search Group (Toronto, ON)
Davis, Laura .... Little Group, The (Brantford, ON)
Davis, Marnie .... People Bank, The (Toronto, ON)
Davis, Valerie .... Can-Tech Services (Brooklin, ON)
Dawson, Brian .... Tosi Placement Services Inc. (Toronto, ON)
Dawson, Diane .... Staff Bureau Employment Group (Edmonton, AB)
Daxon, Corey .... Feldman Gray & Associates Inc. (Toronto, ON)
Day, Guy .... Michael Page Finance (CHINA)
Day, Nick .... Matchtech Engineering Ltd. (UNITED KINGDOM)
De Gannes, Simonne .... Drake International (Toronto, ON)
de la Torre, Marcela .... Canadian Findings Ltd. (Toronto, ON)
De Montebello, Henry .... Russell Reynolds Associates, Inc. (FRANCE)
de Munnik, N. Lynne .... Crawford de Munnik Executive Search (Toronto, ON)
de Noronha Dale, Guilherme .... Spencer Stuart (BRAZIL)
De Oliveira, Peggy .... Campbell Morden Inc. (Toronto, ON)
De Piero, Randy .... Botrie Associates / Stanton Chase International (Toronto, ON)
de Vries, Nanno J.H. .... Amrop International (SWITZERLAND)
Dean, Peggy .... Dean & Associates (Toronto, ON)
Dean-Couture, Jackie .... Renaissance Personnel (Chatham, ON)
deCandia, Vito .... Volt Human Resources Inc. / VHRI (Vancouver, BC)
Deck, Brian .... Technical Management Resources Inc. (Barrie, ON)
Dedman, Ron .... TDR Human Resources Services Ltd. (Regina, SK)
Dee, Philip .... Premier Personnel Limited (UNITED KINGDOM)
Deegan, Nadia .... Berlys Inc., Service de Personnel (Saint-Laurent, QC)
Dekker, Tim .... Meyers Norris Penny / MNP (Brandon, MB)
Del Duca, Aaron .... TalentLab (Kanata, ON)
Del Duca, Tony .... Systematix Information Technology Consultants Inc. (Montréal, QC)
Delaney, David .... InterSearch Canada / Staffing Strategists International (Halifax, NS)
Delhougne, Patrick A. .... Ray & Berndtson (USA)
Deligianis, Louie .... ATS Reliance Technical Group (Toronto, ON)
Delisle, Pierre H. .... Pierre H. Delisle conseil en ressources humaines Inc. (Montréal, QC)
Dell'Orto, Umberto Bussolati .... Spencer Stuart (ITALY)
Delorme, Pierre .... Delorme et Associés inc. (Québec, QC)
deLottinville, Brian .... Trans-United Consultants Ltd. (Burlington, ON)
Delparte, Linda .... Polaris Employment Services (Burnaby, BC)
Delville, Jan .... Ideal Personnel (Mississauga, ON)
Demers, Marie-Josée .... Allen Etcovitch Associates Ltd. / PSA International (Montréal, QC)
Demmery, Andrew .... Eagle Professional Resources Inc. (Toronto, ON)
Dempster, Kathy .... Western Management Consultants (Toronto, ON)
Denhoff, Eric .... InterSearch Canada / Western Executive Selection Inc. (Vancouver, BC)
Denis, Micheline .... Kenniff Denis Inc. (Montréal, QC)
Deodhar, Amit .... InviTech Corporation (Toronto, ON)
Derbyshire, Mark .... Russell Reynolds Associates, Inc. (Toronto, ON)
Dereveanko, Sophie .... Aquent Partners (Montréal, QC)
Derhak, Allen R. .... Derhak Ireland & Partners Ltd. (Toronto, ON)
Derhak, William M. .... Derhak Ireland & Partners Ltd. (Toronto, ON)
Derkitt, Robert J. .... Derkitt & Herbert Executive Search Inc. (Calgary, AB)
Derry, Ann .... RWJ & Associates (Kitchener, ON)
Desautels, Noel .... Spencer Stuart & Associates (Canada) Ltd. (Toronto, ON)
Desautels, Sylvie .... HR / RH Inc. (Montréal, QC)
Descheneaux, Pat .... Descheneaux Recruitment Services Ltd. (Vancouver, BC)
Deschênes, Daniel .... Systematix Information Technology Consultants Inc. (Montréal, QC)
Deschênes, Valerie .... Systematix Information Technology Consultants Inc. (Montréal, QC)
Descoteaux, Eric .... Procom / Professional Computer Consultants Group Ltd. (Toronto, ON)
Desjardins, Kevin .... St-Amour & Associates (Toronto, ON)
Deslauriers, Anne-Marie .... Consultation Delan Inc. (Saint-Laurent, QC)
Deslisle, Jean-François .... Cyberna Associates Limited (Montréal, QC)
Desormeaux, David .... Volt Human Resources Inc. / VHRI (Vancouver, BC)
Dessain, Rosy .... Thomas & Dessain (UNITED KINGDOM)
DeWitt, Georgina .... Peapell & Associates (Halifax, NS)
Dexter, Dave .... IBISKA Telecom Inc. (Ottawa, ON)

DEYOUNG - DU TOIT

DeYoung, Lisa .... Adecco Canada Inc. (Halifax, NS)
Di Biase, Fiorenzo .... Datalist (Toronto, ON)
Di Domenico, Andrea .... Eagle Professional Resources Inc. (Montréal, QC)
Di Natale, Rachel .... Datalist (Toronto, ON)
Di Nino, Sabina .... Trillium Talent Resource Inc. (Cambridge, ON)
di Priolo, Maurizia Lachino Leto .... Spencer Stuart (ITALY)
Diamond, Hela .... Drake Executive (Montréal, QC)
Diardichuk, Tim .... Applied Technology Solutions Inc. / ATS (Toronto, ON)
Dickenson, Hélène .... Quintal & Associates HR Consultants Inc. (Montréal, QC)
Dickin, Noranne .... Conroy Partners Limited (Calgary, AB)
Dickinson, John .... Turner Dickinson & Partners (Vancouver, BC)
Dickinson, Michael .... Aviation Personnel Support Inc. / APS (Toronto, ON)
Dicks, Jan .... Ernst & Young (St. John's, NF)
Dicks, Richard .... Helix Management Consulting Services Inc. / HMCS Inc. (Orleans, ON)
Dickson, William B. .... Advocate Placement Ltd. (Toronto, ON)
Dielissen, Bruce .... McLean Executive Consultants Ltd. (Calgary, AB)
DiMarco-Brace, Marie .... Quantum Management Services Limited (Toronto, ON)
Dimitropoulos, Jim .... Allen Personnel Services (London, ON)
Dimond, Jack .... Janet Wright & Associates Inc. / JWA (Toronto, ON)
Dinelle, Anne-Marie .... Systematix Information Technology Consultants Inc. (Montréal, QC)
Dingman, H. Bruce .... Robert W. Dingman Company, Inc. (USA)
Dingman, Robert A. .... Robert W. Dingman Company, Inc. (USA)
Dion, Nancy .... Dotemtex Executive Search (Montréal, QC)
DiRezze, Lilly .... SOS Personnel Inc. (Sarnia, ON)
Disik, Linda .... Allen Personnel Services (London, ON)
Disspain, Vanessa .... Everest Management Network Inc. (Toronto, ON)
Diver, Gordon .... Centre for Corporate Resources, The (Toronto, ON)
Dixon, Sam .... Bay Street Placement (Richmond Hill, ON)
Djandji, Guy N. .... Belle Isle Djandji Brunet, Inc. (Montréal, QC)
Dmyterko, Sherri .... Datalist (Toronto, ON)
Dobson, Karin .... Kenneth Murphy & Associates / KMA (Halifax, NS)
Docherty, Bill .... TES, The Employment Solution (Burlington, ON)
Dodd, Paul .... He@d2Head.com Inc. (Toronto, ON)
Dodd-Jones, Barbara .... Canadian Career Partners (Calgary, AB)
Dogra, Paul .... InGenius Engineering Inc. (Ottawa, ON)
Doherty, Heather .... ICAP Management Inc. (Fredericton, NB)
Doiron, Richard .... IBISKA Telecom Inc. (Ottawa, ON)
Dolan, Keren .... Protocole (Montréal, QC)
Dolbec, Krista .... Lynx Career Consultants Inc. (Mississauga, ON)
Domash, Miriam .... Preferred Healthcare Staffing (USA)
Dominczuk, Don .... Danek Anthony Inc. (White Rock, BC)
Domingue, Lucie .... Lucie Domingue et associés inc. (Sherbrooke, QC)
Donald, Peter J. .... Scarrow & Donald (Winnipeg, MB)
Donald, Walter .... Executive Network, The (Victoria, BC)
Donaldson, Marianne B. .... HR / RH Inc. (Montréal, QC)
Donati, Morris .... Donati & Associates (Maple, ON)
Donnelly, Terence .... Mandrake Management Consultants (Toronto, ON)
Dooley, Mark .... Asset Computer Personnel Ltd. (Toronto, ON)
Doomernik, Cathy .... Adecco Canada Inc. (Toronto, ON)
Doré, André H.J. .... Doré Liaison Inc. (Greenfield Park, QC)
Doré, Joseph L. .... Doré Liaison Inc. (Greenfield Park, QC)
Doré, Sylvie .... TMP Worldwide Executive Search (Calgary, AB)
Doré, Vincent .... Doré Liaison Inc. (Greenfield Park, QC)
Dornan, Leslie .... Meyers Norris Penny / MNP (Winnipeg, MB)
Dorval, Lucie .... Action Info-Travail Inc. (Mont-Laurier, QC)
Dorval, Suzanne .... Adecco Québec Inc. (Laval) (Laval, QC)
Doucette, John .... John Doucette Management Services (Richmond Hill, ON)
Doupe, Scott S. .... Conroy Partners Limited (Calgary, AB)
Dowhanick, Kim .... CAMPA & Associates (Toronto, ON)
Downer, Karen .... Advantage Group, The (Whitby, ON)
Doyle, Ian .... Galt Global Recruiting (Vancouver, BC)
Doyle, Shannon .... Shannon Human Resources (Toronto, ON)
Dragich, Sam .... Meda Group (Windsor, ON)
Draper, Nellie .... Personnel Opportunities Ltd. (Toronto, ON)
Drennan, Ronald .... Korn / Ferry International (Montréal, QC)
Drolet, Jacques .... Action Info-Travail Inc. (Mont-Laurier, QC)
Drummond, Cindy .... Rice / Drummond Personnel Services Ltd. (Calgary, AB)
Drummond, Donna .... Ray & Berndtson / Robertson Surrette (Ottawa, ON)
Drummond, Maureen .... Meyers Norris Penny / MNP (Winnipeg, MB)
Drury III, James J. .... Spencer Stuart (USA)
Drysdale, Sandy .... Procom / Professional Computer Consultants Group Ltd. (Calgary, AB)
Du Plooy, Grant .... Tolfrey Group (USA)
Du Sablon, François .... Axxes Technologies Inc. (Sillery, QC)
Du Toit, Amanda .... Corporate Recruiters Ltd. (Vancouver, BC)

DUBOIS - EMOND

Dubois, Edith .... Personnel Department, The (Edmonton, AB)
Dubois, Louis-Stephane .... Groupe Ranger (Montréal, QC)
Dubois, Phil .... Pride in Personnel Inc. (Markham, ON)
Ducharme, Lynda .... Ducharme Group Inc. (Toronto, ON)
Duckett, Donna .... Meda Group (Windsor, ON)
Dudney, Sarah .... Baines Gwinner Limited (UNITED KINGDOM)
Duff, Rosemary .... AT Kearney Executive Search (Toronto, ON)
Duffy, Michael W. .... Pathfinder Personnel Limited (Toronto, ON)
Duffy, Patrick .... Pathfinder Personnel Limited (Toronto, ON)
Duggan, Brian .... Thompson Associates Career Consulting (Halifax, NS)
Duggan, Dennis .... Systematix Information Technology Consultants Inc. (Vancouver, BC)
Dugré, Richard .... Hunt Technical Personnel (Saint-Laurent, QC)
Dugrosprez, Stéphan .... Action Info-Travail Inc. (Mont-Laurier, QC)
Duguid, Connie .... Staff Bureau Employment Group (Edmonton, AB)
Duleba, Magdalena .... Permanent Search Group Inc. / PSG (Mississauga, ON)
Dulong, Diane .... TAD Canada (Laval, QC)
Dulovic, Judy .... Little Group, The (Burlington, ON)
Dumont, Brenda .... Canadianretail.ca (Vancouver, BC)
Dumontet, Mireille .... Adecco Québec Inc. (Laval) (Laval, QC)
Dunn, Mary Helen .... Ray & Berndtson (USA)
Dunne, Denise .... Thinkpath.com Inc. (USA)
Dunnigan, Sean .... Counsel Network, The (Calgary, AB)
Dunscombe, Bryon .... Anderson Associates (Toronto, ON)
Duquette, Daniel .... Prosearch Associates (Mississauga, ON)
Durand, François .... Korn / Ferry International (Montréal, QC)
Durning, Charles .... Pollack Group, The (Ottawa, ON)
Durocher, Keeley .... Calian Technology Services Ltd. (Kanata, ON)
Dusome, Terry .... Holloway Schulz & Partners Inc. (Vancouver, BC)
Dvorak, Darrell .... Summit Search Group (Calgary, AB)
Dwan, Rosalyn .... Goldjobs.com (UNITED KINGDOM)
Dworkin, Rebecca .... Outsourcing Connection Inc., The (Toronto, ON)
Dworkin, Stephen .... CTS International, Inc. (USA)
Dybikowski, Libby .... Provence Consulting Inc. (Vancouver, BC)
Dyer, Graham .... Canjobs.com Inc. (Guelph, ON)
Dyett, Mark .... Tosi Placement Services Inc. (Toronto, ON)
Dykes, Beth .... Houston Personnel Group, The (Winnipeg, MB)
Dykler, Leon .... ForeFront Information Strategies Group, Inc. (Ottawa, ON)
Eales, Chris .... Nursing Management Services (USA) Inc. (USA)
Earle, Paul .... Spencer Stuart (USA)
East, Bryan .... Wellington Partners International Inc. (Kitchener, ON)
Easton, Barclay .... TalentLab (Kanata, ON)
Eaton, David .... Global Hospitality Search Consultants (Mississauga, ON)
Eburne, Linda .... Harrington Staffing Services and Informatics Resources (Ottawa, ON)
Eckford, Angela .... Mandrake Management Consultants (Toronto, ON)
Eddis, Hugo .... Baines Gwinner Limited (UNITED KINGDOM)
Eddy, Marilyn .... Lannick Associates (Toronto, ON)
Edelberg, Frank .... Management One Consultants (Toronto, ON)
Edgar, Jason .... J. Edgar & Associates Inc. (Toronto, ON)
Edmond, Bruce .... Corporate Recruiters Ltd. (Vancouver, BC)
Edmunds, Brian .... Nexstaf IT Recruitment (Toronto, ON)
Edwards, Caroline .... Harvey Nash plc (UNITED KINGDOM)
Edwards, Dean .... Isomeric Inc. (Toronto, ON)
Edwards, Glenna .... Adecco Canada Inc. (Richmond, BC)
Edwards, Peter .... Conroy Partners Limited (Calgary, AB)
Edwards, Thérèse .... Glen Abbey Executive Search Inc. (Oakville, ON)
Eertmans, Vanessa .... Baines Gwinner Limited (UNITED KINGDOM)
Egan, Ron .... Executrade Consultants Ltd. (Edmonton, AB)
Egui, Tony .... Heidrick & Struggles International, Inc. (VENEZUELA)
Ehlers, Heidi .... Mandrake Management Consultants (Toronto, ON)
Einarson, Doug .... BDO Dunwoody LLP (Winnipeg, MB)
Eisner, Dara .... Permanent Solutions Inc. (Mississauga, ON)
Elderkin, Audrie .... Protrans Personnel Services Inc. (Dieppe, NB)
Elderkin, Sharon .... PEI Office of the Future (Charlottetown, PE)
Elek, Joanne .... Lannick Associates (Toronto, ON)
Ellingson, Ron .... Xycorp Inc. (Toronto, ON)
Elliot, Joanne .... Elliot Associates (Toronto, ON)
Elliot, Lisa .... Procom / Professional Computer Consultants Group Ltd. (Toronto, ON)
Elliott, Dave .... Questus Recruitment (Calgary, AB)
Elliott, Michelle .... Sydelle Associates (Georgetown, ON)
Ellis, Glen .... Ian Martin Limited (USA)
Ellis, Phyllis .... Jenereaux & Associates Inc. (Mississauga, ON)
Elridge, Chris .... Harvey Nash plc (UNITED KINGDOM)
Elson, Shaun .... TSI Group / TSI Staffing Services (Mississauga, ON)
Emond, Peggy .... Advantage Group, The (Nepean, ON)

EMSHOFF - FISHER

FISHER - FRENCH

Fisher, Mel V. .... Fisher Group Executive Search (Calgary, AB)
Fisher, Michael .... Technical Management Resources Inc. (Barrie, ON)
Fisher, Renée .... Permanent Search Group Inc. / PSG (Mississauga, ON)
Fishman, Harvey .... Noramtec Consultants Inc. (North Vancouver, BC)
Fisico, Ken .... Anderson Associates (Toronto, ON)
Fitch, Angeline .... Pitsel & Associates (Calgary, AB)
Fitz-Gerald, Adrian .... Interactive Business Systems, Inc. / IBS Inc. (Toronto, ON)
Fitzgerald, Emma .... TMP QD Legal Recruitment (Toronto, ON)
Fitzpatrick, Andrew J. .... Link Consulting (Vancouver, BC)
Fitzpatrick, Michael .... TES, The Employment Solution (Burlington, ON)
Fitzwilliam, Carol A. .... Shore & Fitzwilliam (Montréal, QC)
Flatt, Nancy .... Level A Inc. (Peterborough, ON)
Fletcher, Bob .... Trans-United Consultants Ltd. (Burlington, ON)
Flewwelling, David .... Corporate Controllers Inc. (Halifax, NS)
Flint, Kent .... Futurestep (Toronto, ON)
Flook, Michael .... Technical Management Resources Inc. (Barrie, ON)
Florio, John G. .... Florio Gosset Group Inc. (Mississauga, ON)
Flynn, Donna .... Nurses Rx Canada (USA)
Flynn, Jerry G. .... J.G. Flynn & Associates Inc. (Vancouver, BC)
Flynn, Peter .... Partnervision Consulting Group Inc. (Toronto, ON)
Flynn, Rob .... Grant Thornton International (Corner Brook, NF)
Fobert, Eric .... Brock Placement Group Inc. (Toronto, ON)
Folk, Gregory .... Pitsel & Associates (Calgary, AB)
Follett, Michael .... Michael Follett Consulting Inc. (Kitchener, ON)
Follett, Wally .... Synergy Search Consultants (Toronto, ON)
Folmar, Beth .... Scientific Placement, Inc. (USA)
Fontaine, Danielle .... Quintal & Associates HR Consultants Inc. (Montréal, QC)
Forbes, Jeff .... Meridia Recruitment Services Inc. (Halifax, NS)
Forbes, Susan .... Trebor Personnel Inc. (Kitchener, ON)
Forcione, Lori .... Permanent Search Group Inc. / PSG (Mississauga, ON)
Ford, Julia .... Eagle Professional Resources Inc. (Vancouver, BC)
Ford, Linda .... Access Career Solutions Inc. (Brampton, ON)
Forrest, Casey .... Pinton Forrest & Madden / EMA Partners International (Vancouver, BC)
Forrestall, Vince .... Deevan Technology Management (Richmond Hill, ON)
Forster, Tara .... Verriez Group Inc., The (London, ON)
Fortier, Normand .... Systematix Information Technology Consultants Inc. (Québec, QC)
Fortin, Latifa B. .... Godbout Martin Godbout & Associates (Hull, QC)
Fortin, Roch .... Godbout Martin Godbout & Associates (Hull, QC)
Foster, Jim .... Meyers Norris Penny / MNP (Brandon, MB)
Foster, Linda .... Personnel Opportunities Ltd. (Toronto, ON)
Foster, Richard S. .... Richard Foster Company Ltd., The (Toronto, ON)
Foster, Sharon .... Interim Management Resources Inc. / IMR (Mississauga, ON)
Foster, Susan .... Pinstripe Personnel Inc. (Mississauga, ON)
Foster, Thomas C. .... Renaud Foster Management Consultants (Ottawa, ON)
Fournier, Daniel .... Urentia (Montréal, QC)
Fournier, Sandra .... W.G. Meldrum Limited (Calgary, AB)
Fox, Amanda .... Spencer Stuart (USA)
Fox, Gareon .... Summit Search Group (Calgary, AB)
Fox, Laurie Kathleen .... Careers & Professions Inc. (Montréal, QC)
Fox, Mary Francis .... Becky Jones & Associates Ltd. (Toronto, ON)
Fox, Richard .... Summit Personnel Services Inc. (Windsor, ON)
Fox, Suzanne .... Onwego Personnel Inc. (Gloucester, ON)
Fradera, Joan .... Adecco Canada Inc. (Vancouver, BC)
Frame, Chris .... Thomas & Rayment Inc. (Markham, ON)
Frame, Greg .... Thomas & Rayment Inc. (Markham, ON)
Frame, Mike .... Thomas & Rayment Inc. (Markham, ON)
Francis, Austin .... Personnel Alter Ego Inc. (Pointe-Claire, QC)
Francisci, Manuel .... Venatus Conseil Ltée (Montréal, QC)
Francisci, Nathalie .... Venatus Conseil Ltée (Montréal, QC)
Francoeur, Joanne .... AeroPersonnel International (Dorval, QC)
Franklin, Elaine .... Thorek / Scott and Partners (Toronto, ON)
Franklin, Kevin .... Melmak Consultants Ltd. (Toronto, ON)
Franklin, Marnie .... Milagrow Technology Solutions (Vancouver, BC)
Fraresso, Marianne .... Contemporary Personnel Inc. (Brampton, ON)
Fraser, Daunine G. .... Cameron Management Services Group / CMSG (Calgary, AB)
Fraser, Edwin (Win) .... Resource Professionals Inc. (Calgary, AB)
Fraser, Karen .... Angus One Professional Recruitment Ltd. (Vancouver, BC)
Fraser, Terri .... Resource Professionals Inc. (Calgary, AB)
Fratric, Robert .... Trans-United Consultants Ltd. (Burlington, ON)
Fredette, Caroline .... Adecco Personnel Technique (Sherbrooke, QC)
Freedman, Caroline .... Richter Consulting (Toronto, ON)
Freedman, Val .... Datalist (Toronto, ON)
French, Guy P. .... InterSearch Canada / Corso, Mizgala + French (Toronto, ON)
French, Tony .... Thinkpath.com Inc. (Ottawa, ON)

FRETWELL - GIBSON

GIDDENS - GOWANS

Giddens, Jim .... Little Group, The (Burlington, ON)
Gies, Graham .... ATS Reliance Technical Group (Toronto, ON)
Giglio, Alice .... Trans-United Consultants Ltd. (Burlington, ON)
Giguere, Cathy .... Quantum, Les services de gestion (Pointe-Claire, QC)
Giguere, Nicole .... Personnel Alter Ego Inc. (Montréal, QC)
Gilbert, Julie .... G-P Personnel Inc. (Chicoutimi, QC)
Gilbert, Mandy .... Aquent Partners (Toronto, ON)
Gilchrist, Jim .... Career Advancement Employment Services Inc. / CAES (Burlington, ON)
Gilcrist, Carol .... Adecco Canada Inc. (London, ON)
Giles, David .... Contracts Consultancy Limited (UNITED KINGDOM)
Giles, Kirsten .... Renaud Foster Management Consultants (Ottawa, ON)
Gill, Lyn .... Canadian Executive Consultants Inc. (Toronto, ON)
Gillies, Mark .... ATS Reliance Technical Group (London, ON)
Gillissie, Paul .... Personnel Force (Ottawa, ON)
Gilmour, Dave .... ATS Reliance Technical Group (Toronto, ON)
Gilmour, John .... ATS Reliance Technical Group (Toronto, ON)
Giorgio, Angela .... Roevin Technical People Ltd. (Montréal, QC)
Girard, Hélène .... Kelly, Les services (Granby, QC)
Girard, Isabelle .... Matte Groupe Conseil Inc. (Montréal, QC)
Girard, Marie .... Adecco LPI (Saint-Laurent, QC)
Girard, Nicole .... Adecco Québec Inc. (Chicoutimi, QC)
Giroux, Richard .... G-P Personnel Inc. (Chicoutimi, QC)
Givelos, Don .... Donald Givelos & Associates Inc. / DGA (Toronto, ON)
Gladman, Pat .... PG Consultants (Toronto, ON)
Glaser, Cathy .... Peter Glaser & Associates (UNITED KINGDOM)
Glaser, Peter .... Peter Glaser & Associates (UNITED KINGDOM)
Glasner, Harvey .... PeopleFind Inc. (Markham, ON)
Glassberg, Bob .... SalesSearch (Toronto, ON)
Glazar, Glen .... TriNet Employment Group (USA)
Glazin, Lynne .... Glazin / Sisco Executive Search Consultants Inc. (Vancouver, BC)
Glendenning, Joanne L. .... Prime Management Group Inc. (London, ON)
Gloyd, Barbara J. .... Jankar Human Resources Inc. (Burlington, ON)
Godbout, Alain J. .... Godbout Martin Godbout & Associates (Hull, QC)
Godbout, Guillaume .... Godbout Martin Godbout & Associates (Hull, QC)
Godbout, Johannes .... Godbout Martin Godbout & Associates (Hull, QC)
Godin, Sylvie .... OKA Computer Systems Ltd. / Gestion Informatique OKA Ltée (Montréal, QC)
Goffe, Peter .... FHG International Inc. (Toronto, ON)
Gold, Norman .... Nugget Group Inc., The / TNG Global (Westmount, QC)
Goldbeck, Henry .... Goldbeck Recruiting Inc. (Vancouver, BC)
Goldberg, Erin .... Group Four Management Consultants (Toronto, ON)
Goldsmith, John .... Pegasus Consulting Inc. (Toronto, ON)
Goldsmith, Neil .... Pegasus Consulting Inc. (Toronto, ON)
Goldson, Ron .... Nework Corp. (Toronto, ON)
Goldstein, Stephen .... Stephen Goldstein & Associates (Ottawa, ON)
Goldwater, Sherri .... Group Four Management Consultants (Toronto, ON)
Gollant, Eric .... Schwartz Levitsky Feldman / SLF (Toronto, ON)
Goncalves, Zeta .... Deloitte Touche Tohmatsu (AUSTRALIA)
Gonnet, Nathalie .... Facilité Informatique (Montréal, QC)
Gonthier, Jean-Yves .... 500 Services de Selection Ltée (Val-d'Or, QC)
Gonzales, Lisa .... Mandrake Management Consultants (Toronto, ON)
Good, Carol .... Apple Management Corporation (Toronto, ON)
Goodchild, Alison .... Capital Executive Ltd. (Calgary, AB)
Goode, Jan .... Health Match BC (Vancouver, BC)
Goodman, Glenda .... Futurestep (Toronto, ON)
Goodman, Michael .... Vezina Goodman Executive Search (Montréal, QC)
Goodman, R.E. (Ruby) .... M.R. Goodman Consulting Inc. (Calgary, AB)
Goodwin, Peter .... Morgan & Banks Ltd. (AUSTRALIA)
Goossens, Peter .... Spencer Stuart (USA)
Gordon, Ellery .... Ray & Berndtson (USA)
Gordon, Jim .... Bruce R. Duncan & Associates Ltd. (Toronto, ON)
Gordon, Lloyd .... McLean Executive Consultants Ltd. (Calgary, AB)
Gordon, S. .... TRS Staffing Solutions (Canada) Inc. (Calgary, AB)
Gornak, Ed .... Canadian Findings Ltd. (Toronto, ON)
Goshulak, Gayla .... Applied Technology Solutions Inc. / ATS (Toronto, ON)
Gosselin, Benoît .... Berlys Inc., Service de Personnel (Saint-Laurent, QC)
Gosselin, Derek .... Staff Plus (Toronto, ON)
Gosselin, Sylvie .... Pro-Action Personnel (Chomedey, QC)
Gotlieb, Leo .... Western Management Consultants (Toronto, ON)
Goudreau, Gary W. .... G.W. Goudreau Personnel Services Ltd. (Windsor, ON)
Gougeon, Gilbert G. .... Godbout Martin Godbout & Associates (Hull, QC)
Gough, Bonnie .... Tek-Search Corporation (Toronto, ON)
Gough, Sam .... Spherion Workforce Architects (Brampton, ON)
Gouin, Heather .... CNC Global (Toronto, ON)
Gowans, Janine .... Classic Consulting Group Inc. (Calgary, AB)

GOWDAR - HABERMAN

Gowdar, Michelle .... Adecco Canada Inc. (Winnipeg, MB)
Grady, Dalton .... Roevin Technical People Ltd. (North Vancouver, BC)
Grady, Michael P. .... IMS / Innovative Management Solutions Group (Toronto, ON)
Graff, Kevin .... Sussex Retail Management (Mississauga, ON)
Graham, Bob .... Graham, Elliott & Associates (Toronto, ON)
Graham, Cathy .... Ray & Berndtson / Lovas Stanley (Toronto, ON)
Graham, Margie .... David Aplin & Associates (Edmonton, AB)
Graham-Williams, Leslie .... Pegasus Consulting Inc. (Toronto, ON)
Grant, Brad .... Centre for Corporate Resources, The (Toronto, ON)
Grant, Jacqueline .... Walker Forest (USA)
Grant, Jane .... Meyers Norris Penny (Calgary, AB)
Grant, Virginia .... Connors, Lovell & Associates Inc. (Cambridge, ON)
Gratix, Everett .... Canadian Career Partners (Calgary, AB)
Gratton, Erin .... McDonald-Green Personnel (Cambridge, ON)
Gravel, Sandra .... In Place Selective Recruitment Services (Toronto, ON)
Gravel, Suzette .... Dotemtex Executive Search (Montréal, QC)
Gray, Beverly .... Freelancers Unlimited Inc. (Toronto, ON)
Gray, Frank .... Feldman Gray & Associates Inc. (Toronto, ON)
Gray, James .... Freelancers Unlimited Inc. (Toronto, ON)
Gray, Tim .... Anderson Associates (Toronto, ON)
Grayevsky, Eli .... CTS International, Inc. (USA)
Grebenstein, Charlie .... Skott/Edwards Consultants (USA)
Greco, Sergio .... TES, The Employment Solution (Toronto, ON)
Greco, Victoria .... IT Resources Ltd. (Markham, ON)
Green, Bruce .... Canadian Career Partners (Calgary, AB)
Green, Christina .... Quantum EDP Recruiting Services Ltd. (Toronto, ON)
Greenburg, Dan .... Allegiance Group, The (USA)
Greenburg, Jeffrey .... Schlesinger Newman Goldman (Montréal, QC)
Greer, Wayne .... International Search Associates Inc. (Toronto, ON)
Grega, Glenn .... Godbout Martin Godbout & Associates (Hull, QC)
Gregg, Gary .... Apple One Employment Services (Toronto, ON)
Gregoire, Sandra .... Argus Group Corporation, The (Toronto, ON)
Gregory, Zoya .... Zeidel, Gregory & Associates (Toronto, ON)
Gregus, Paul .... Russell Reynolds Associates, Inc. (Calgary, AB)
Grenier, Bernard .... Personnel Outaouais (Hull, QC)
Grenier, Sylvie .... Kelly Scientifique (Montréal, QC)
Gres, Edward .... Pioneer Executive Consultants (Toronto, ON)
Gribben, Joanne .... Harvey Nash plc (UNITED KINGDOM)
Griffiths, Ann .... Technical Management Resources Inc. (Barrie, ON)
Griffiths, Ruth .... Kelly Permanent Recruitment (Toronto, ON)
Grigonis, Alex .... Canadian Findings Ltd. (Toronto, ON)
Grobbelaar, Jacob .... Trans-United Consultants Ltd. (Burlington, ON)
Groh, Michael .... Technical Management Resources Inc. (Barrie, ON)
Groleau, Martin J. .... Recru Science, Inc. (Longueuil, QC)
Groom De Mizio, Susie .... Groom & Associés Ltée (Pointe-Claire, QC)
Gross, Harry .... Meyers Norris Penny / MNP (Bow Island, AB)
Grossner, Charles .... PeopleFind Inc. (Markham, ON)
Groulx, Lyne .... Venatus Conseil Ltée (Montréal, QC)
Groves, Barry .... Groves & Partners International (Mississauga, ON)
Gruber, Gerald P. .... Gruber Associates (Orleans, ON)
Grunstra, Neal .... Mindbank Consulting Group (USA)
Gruzd, Gary .... MediStaff (USA)
Gruzd, Nadia .... MediStaff (USA)
Grzela, Hugh .... Drake International (Toronto, ON)
Guay, Michel .... St-Amour & Associates (Montréal, QC)
Guest, Les .... Noramtec Consultants Inc. (Bath, ON)
Guest, Patrick .... Ajilon Canada (Montréal, QC)
Gugler, Wolf .... Wolf Gugler & Associates Limited (Toronto, ON)
Guido, Toni .... Robert Half Canada Inc. (Calgary, AB)
Guinn, Andrea .... Computer Horizons ISG (Calgary, AB)
Guirguis, Raouf .... Levy Pilotte (Montréal, QC)
Guld, Allison ...... JENEX Technology Placement Inc. (Vancouver, BC)
Gullo, Rod .... Gulco International Recruiting Services (USA)
Gunn, Doug .... Hire Choice Inc. (Toronto, ON)
Gunn, Lesley .... Affiliates, The (Toronto, ON)
Guns, Bob .... Aron Printz & Associates Ltd. (Vancouver, BC)
Gurung, Raj .... ProTemps Canada Inc. (Toronto, ON)
Gushev, Ted .... Chase Consultants Inc. (Mississauga, ON)
Guthrie, Jill .... Walsh King (Vancouver, BC)
Gutsoski, Don .... Progestic Group Inc. (Toronto, ON)
Gwartzman, Adina .... Korn / Ferry International (Toronto, ON)
Gynp, Russell .... Excel Human Resources Consultants (Toronto, ON)
Haas, Chantal .... Lewis Companies Inc. (Toronto, ON)
Haberman, Carol .... Canadian Executive Consultants Inc. (Toronto, ON)

HABROS - HAUSWIRTH

Habros, Greg .... Pegasus Consulting Inc. (Toronto, ON)
Hacksel, Stephanie .... ZSA Legal Recruitment (Vancouver, BC)
Hacquard, Rheo .... Grant Thornton International (New Liskeard, ON)
Haggith, Marvin A. .... Keystone Select / M.A. Haggith Consultants Ltd. (Toronto, ON)
Hale, Darryn .... Taylor Root (UNITED KINGDOM)
Hale, Paula .... Meda Group (Windsor, ON)
Haley, Nidal .... CTC Computer-Tech Consultants Ltd. (Vancouver, BC)
Halferty, Pat .... Insurance Consulting Group (Toronto, ON)
Hall, Arlene .... CNC Global (Ottawa, ON)
Hall, Deborah .... Templeman Consulting Group Inc. (Kingston, ON)
Hall, Frank .... TalentLab (Kanata, ON)
Hall, George .... ATI Consulting Corporation Inc. (Halifax, NS)
Hall, Lianne .... Lynx Career Consultants Inc. (Mississauga, ON)
Hall, Sue .... Glazin / Sisco Executive Search Consultants Inc. (Vancouver, BC)
Hall, Suzanne .... Computer Horizons ISG (Calgary, AB)
Hall, Vera .... Becky Jones & Associates Ltd. (Toronto, ON)
Hallard, Chris .... Allen Austin Lowe & Powers (USA)
Halliwell, Chris .... TDM Technical Services (Toronto, ON)
Halliwell, George .... TDM Technical Services (Toronto, ON)
Hamersak, Stan .... He@d2Head.com Inc. (Toronto, ON)
Hamilton, Carl .... Canadian Findings Ltd. (Toronto, ON)
Hamilton, John .... Cameron Management Services Group / CMSG (Calgary, AB)
Hamilton, Peter .... Dunhill Professional Search (Vancouver, BC)
Hamilton, Sheryl .... Datalist (Toronto, ON)
Hamilton, Timothy J. .... Caldwell Partners, The (Calgary, AB)
Hammond, Terry .... TERHAM Management Consultants Ltd. (Toronto, ON)
Hancock, Tony .... Morgan & Banks Ltd. (AUSTRALIA)
Handyside, Philip .... Techaid Inc. (Montréal, QC)
Haney, Caroline .... ZSA Legal Recruitment (Montréal, QC)
Hanka, Terry .... Express Personnel Services (Burlington, ON)
Hanks, Richard .... Taylor Root (UNITED KINGDOM)
Hanner, Marilyn .... Corporate Coach, The (Calgary, AB)
Hanniman, Bill .... Eagle Professional Resources Inc. (Calgary, AB)
Hansen, Ralph G. .... InterSearch Canada / Corso, Mizgala + French (Toronto, ON)
Harb, Douglas .... Lecours Wolfson Limited (Toronto, ON)
Harbert, Damon .... Maxim Group (Richmond, BC)
Harcourt, Judy .... Harcourt & Associates (Edmonton, AB)
Harcourt, Peter .... Harcourt & Associates (Edmonton, AB)
Harder, John E. .... Meyers Norris Penny / MNP (Melfort, SK)
Harding, Kathleen .... Kelly, Les services (Québec, QC)
Hargreaves, Janine .... People Bank, The (Winnipeg, MB)
Harju, Melissa .... Manpower Services Canada Limited (Toronto, ON)
Harlein, Rebecca .... Allen Austin Lowe & Powers (USA)
Harlick, Martin J. .... Applicants Inc. (Kitchener, ON)
Harmon, James .... Ray & Berndtson / Robertson Surrette (Ottawa, ON)
Harper, Jodie .... Prime Management Group Inc. (London, ON)
Harper, Rich .... Levert Personnel Resources Inc. (Sudbury, ON)
Harrelson, Michelle .... Procom Services (USA)
Harrington, Garry .... Harrington Staffing Services and Informatics Resources (Ottawa, ON)
Harrington, Julie .... D.P. Group, The (UNITED KINGDOM)
Harris, Andrew .... Cowan Personnel Consultants Ltd. (Montréal, QC)
Harris, Angela .... SynapTuit Group (Vancouver, BC)
Harris, Cathy .... Cowan Personnel Consultants Ltd. (Montréal, QC)
Harris, Daphne .... David Aplin & Associates (Calgary, AB)
Harris, David M. .... Watson Wyatt Worldwide (Vancouver, BC)
Harris, Jack .... AT Kearney Executive Search (Toronto, ON)
Harris, Lee .... Capital Executive Ltd. (Calgary, AB)
Harris, Marlene .... Dion Management Groupe Conseil Inc. (Montréal, QC)
Harris, Pauline .... Advantage Group, The (Toronto, ON)
Harris, Sharon .... Cameron Management Services Group / CMSG (Calgary, AB)
Harrison, Colette .... D.P. Group, The (UNITED KINGDOM)
Harrison, Don .... Career Partners / Harrison Associates (Hamilton, ON)
Harrison, Joe .... Harrison, Carlson, Criminisi (Burlington, ON)
Harrison, Rick .... A.E. Harrison & Partners Inc. (Mississauga, ON)
Harryott, Darlene .... National Computer Professionals / NCP (Toronto, ON)
Harsanyi, Bjorn .... ZSA Legal Recruitment (Calgary, AB)
Hart, Beverley I. .... Expert Recruiters Inc. (Vancouver, BC)
Hart, Donald L. .... Donald L. Hart & Associates / Talent in Motion (Toronto, ON)
Hartley, Karen .... Insight Technology Corporation (Calgary, AB)
Harvey, Alison .... Taylor Root (UNITED KINGDOM)
Harvey, Rick L. .... Western Management Consultants (Edmonton, AB)
Hatcher, Joan .... MedFall Inc. (Niagara Falls, ON)
Hauser, Greg .... Mancomit International Inc. (Winnipeg, MB)
Hauswirth, Jeffrey M. .... Spencer Stuart & Associates (Canada) Ltd. (Toronto, ON)

HAWKINS - HIGGINS

HIGGINS - HOUSTON

Higgins, Brenda .... Higgins International Inc. (Winnipeg, MB)
Higgins, Sandra .... TMP Worldwide Advertising & Communications (Vancouver, BC)
Highgate, Jennifer .... Executive House Inc. (Chatham, ON)
Hiland, Rick .... Hiland Research Consultants Inc. (Lakefield, ON)
Hildebrandt, Karen .... ProTemps Canada Inc. (Calgary, AB)
Hill, Bruce .... Bruce Hill & Associates / International Education Consultants Inc. (Toronto, ON)
Hill, Henry .... Henry Hill & Associates Inc. (Mississauga, ON)
Hill, Larry .... Drake Executive (Burnaby, BC)
Hill, Paul Guy .... ADV Advanced Technical Services Inc. (Toronto, ON)
Hill, Ross .... A.W. Fraser & Associates / PSA International (Edmonton, AB)
Hill, Shawna .... Initial Education Personnel (Markham, ON)
Hill, Susan .... Health Match BC (Vancouver, BC)
Hill, Valerie .... TMP Worldwide Executive Search (Ottawa, ON)
Hillman, Hart .... Heidrick & Struggles Canada Inc. (Toronto, ON)
Hills, Rose .... Adecco Canada Inc. (Toronto, ON)
Hime, Stephen .... Ian Martin Limited (Oakville, ON)
Hindley-Smith, Sharon .... Affiliates, The (Toronto, ON)
Hines, Darrell .... Argentus Inc. (Toronto, ON)
Hines, P.F. (Trish) .... Genesis Corporate Search Ltd. (Calgary, AB)
Hines, Robert .... Heidrick & Struggles Canada Inc. (Toronto, ON)
Hirvela, Glenda .... Michael Stern Associates Inc. (Toronto, ON)
Hitzig, Stanley .... Schlesinger Newman Goldman (Montréal, QC)
Hnatiuk, Ivan .... Corporate Recruiters Ltd. (Vancouver, BC)
Hodge, Jeff .... Heidrick & Struggles International, Inc. (USA)
Hodge, Kim .... Procom / Professional Computer Consultants Group Ltd. (Kanata, ON)
Hodges, Stephen .... Aquent Partners (Toronto, ON)
Hodgins, George .... Dan McNamara & Associates (Woodstock, ON)
Hoeppner, Ben .... Charter Management Group / CMG (Winnipeg, MB)
Hoffman, Dan .... Hoffman Legal Search (USA)
Hoffman, Timothy .... Spencer Stuart & Associates / Selector Pacific (CHINA)
Hoffman, Tracy .... Renaissance Personnel (Chatham, ON)
Hoffmann, Susanne .... David Aplin & Associates (Edmonton, AB)
Hofmeister, Marianne .... Xenotec Consulting Services Inc. (Regina, SK)
Hofstede, Ybella .... Tolfrey Group (USA)
Hogan, Brian .... BDO Dunwoody LLP (Kingston, ON)
Hogan, Cindy .... Eagle Professional Resources Inc. (Vancouver, BC)
Hogg, Ron .... Forest People International Search Ltd. (Vancouver, BC)
Hogya, Nick .... Interim Management Resources Inc. / IMR (Mississauga, ON)
Holder, Jutta .... Emex Systems Inc. (Toronto, ON)
Holla, Shylee .... CSI Consulting (Toronto, ON)
Holland, Brian .... Associes de dessins mecaniques (Montréal, QC)
Holland, Glen .... Associes de dessins mecaniques (Montréal, QC)
Holland, Rose Mary .... PricewaterhouseCoopers Executive Search (Edmonton, AB)
Holland, William .... Mandrake Management Consultants (Toronto, ON)
Hollander, Paula .... Accountants on Call / AOC Financial Executive Search (Vancouver, BC)
Holloway, Clive .... Holloway Schulz & Partners Inc. (Vancouver, BC)
Hollyer, Elizabeth .... FHG International Inc. (Toronto, ON)
Holmes, John .... Wellington Partners International Inc. (Kitchener, ON)
Holmes, Richard .... Premier Personnel Limited (UNITED KINGDOM)
Holmes, Robert L. (Bob) .... Robert L. Holmes Professional Placement Services Inc. (Cambridge, ON)
Holmes, Tom .... Landmark Consulting Group Inc. (Hamilton, ON)
Holmes, Zoë .... Robert L. Holmes Professional Placement Services Inc. (Cambridge, ON)
Holowka, Helen .... Tretiak, Holowka (Montréal, QC)
Holst, Kathleen .... Integrated Data Services Inc. (Ottawa, ON)
Holt, Katherine .... Katherine Holt Enterprises Ltd. (Toronto, ON)
Holtom, Susan .... Bouris, Wilson LLP (Ottawa, ON)
Holz, Christopher .... Jeffery Group Ltd., The (Toronto, ON)
Honey, W. Michael M. .... Korn / Ferry International (Vancouver, BC)
Hooker, Lisa C. .... Ray & Berndtson (USA)
Hopkins, Mark .... Conroy Partners Limited (Calgary, AB)
Hopkinson, Fred .... Career Partners / Harrison Associates (Hamilton, ON)
Hoppe, Charles .... CTC Computer-Tech Consultants Ltd. (Regina, SK)
Hoppe, Peter .... Rennick, Hoppe & Associates, Inc. (Toronto, ON)
Horn, Deborah .... CTC Computer-Tech Consultants Ltd. (Edmonton, ON)
Hornford, Don .... Meyers Norris Penny / MNP (Milk River, AB)
Hornsby, Geoff .... Harvey Nash plc (UNITED KINGDOM)
Horodyskj, Christine .... Accountants on Call / AOC Financial Executive Search (Vancouver, BC)
Horton, Andrew .... David Aplin & Associates (Calgary, AB)
Hoste, Yvan .... Systematix Information Technology Consultants Inc. (Montréal, QC)
Hotchkiss, Deb .... Partners in Employment (Listowel, ON)
Houde, Lucie .... Consultation Delan Inc. (Saint-Laurent, QC)
Houston, Dana .... Allen Austin Lowe & Powers (USA)
Houston, Jean .... Excalibur Careers Inc. (Markham, ON)
Houston, Marilyn .... Houston Personnel Group, The (Winnipeg, MB)

HOWARD - JAMES

JAMIESON - JOWETT

Jamieson, Roland .... Grant Thornton International (Dartmouth, NS)
Janes, Stan .... Tolstoy Resources (Bolton, ON)
Jansen, Christine .... Canadian Career Partners (Calgary, AB)
Janssen, Mary J. .... M.J. Janssen & Associates Inc. (Mississauga, ON)
Jaques, Kevin .... Procom / Professional Computer Consultants Group Ltd. (Toronto, ON)
Jasek, Adam .... AJJA Information Technology Consultants Inc. (Ottawa, ON)
Jason, Bonnie .... Bryan Jason & Associates Inc. (Toronto, ON)
Jaye, John .... ASTRA Management Corp. (Vancouver, BC)
Jefferson, Karen .... Procom / Professional Computer Consultants Group Ltd. (Calgary, AB)
Jefferson, Larry .... Geddes Jefferson & Associates (Victoria, BC)
Jeffery, Pam .... Jeffery Group Ltd., The (Toronto, ON)
Jellinck, Caroline .... Ray & Berndtson / Tanton Mitchell (Vancouver, BC)
Jenereaux, Catherine .... Jenereaux & Associates Inc. (Mississauga, ON)
Jennings, Ruth .... Rockwell Placement Agencies (Richmond, BC)
Jennings, Susan .... Interim Management Resources Inc. / IMR (Mississauga, ON)
Jerome, Chuck .... BDO Dunwoody & Associates Limited (Hamilton, ON)
Jessey, Jake .... Matchtech Engineering Ltd. (UNITED KINGDOM)
Jessome, Stacey .... Altis Human Resources (Toronto, ON)
Jessop, Lynn .... Wallace & Partners Inc. (Toronto, ON)
Jetté, François .... Axxes Technologies Inc. (Sillery, QC)
Jeworski, Janine .... ProTemps Canada Inc. (Edmonton, AB)
Jhu, Yvonne .... Design Team Incorporated (Richmond Hill, ON)
Jimenez, Maria .... Kelly Professional & Technical Services (Saint John, NB)
Joanisse, Carole B. .... CLA Personnel (Ottawa, ON)
Joanisse, Eric .... CLA Personnel (Ottawa, ON)
Joe, Lawrence .... Lawrence Joe Consultants Inc. (Toronto, ON)
Joergensen, Christian .... Ray & Berndtson A/S (DENMARK)
John, Chris .... Aztech Recruitment Co. (USA)
John, Lidia .... Aztech Recruitment Co. (USA)
Johns, Tracey .... RWJ & Associates (London, ON)
Johnson, Adrian C. .... Associum Consultants (Toronto, ON)
Johnson, Anita .... Smythe Ratcliffe (Vancouver, BC)
Johnson, Berniece .... Spherion Workforce Architects (Winnipeg, MB)
Johnson, Bill .... Pro Tec Global Staffing Services (Thornhill, ON)
Johnson, Diane .... Sellutions Inc. (Nepean, ON)
Johnson, Ed .... Planet Personnel Agency Inc. (Toronto, ON)
Johnson, Greig .... Lock & Associates (Edmonton, AB)
Johnson, Jennifer .... Feldman Gray & Associates Inc. (Toronto, ON)
Johnson, Kurt .... Coape Staffing Network (Calgary, AB)
Johnson, Leslie A. .... Simpson McGrath Inc. (Winnipeg, MB)
Johnson, Lyn .... Recherches en recrutement Lyn Johnson (Saint-Lambert, QC)
Johnson, Mike .... Questus Recruitment (Calgary, AB)
Johnson, Phil .... Ian Martin Limited (Vancouver, BC)
Johnson, R.W. (Bob) .... Leader Search Inc. (Calgary, AB)
Johnson, Tamera .... TES, The Employment Solution (Mississauga, ON)
Johnson, Valerie .... Korn / Ferry International (Toronto, ON)
Johnston, Brian .... Professional Environmental Recreation Consultants Ltd. / PERC (North Delta, BC)
Johnston, George .... Distinct Directions Inc. (Mississauga, ON)
Johnston, John .... Palmer & Company Executive Recruitment (Toronto, ON)
Johnston, Sandi .... Provence Consulting Inc. (Vancouver, BC)
Johnston, Steve .... Kitchener Executive Consultants (Kitchener, ON)
Johnstone, Debra .... Canadian Career Partners (Calgary, AB)
Johnstone, Pat .... Blooming Humans (Victoria, BC)
Johnstone, Stephen .... Everest Systems Network (Toronto, ON)
Johnstone, Steve .... GAAP Inc. (Montréal, QC)
Johnstone, Trevor .... Johnstone Associates Professional Search Inc. (Calgary, AB)
Jolopara, Bhavisha .... HaysZMB (UNITED KINGDOM)
Joly, Michele .... Contempra Personnel (Pointe-Claire, QC)
Jones, Alex .... Matchtech Engineering Ltd. (UNITED KINGDOM)
Jones, Allan .... ComUnity Systems Consultants Inc. (Calgary, AB)
Jones, Andrew .... Lock & Associates (Vancouver, BC)
Jones, Becky .... Becky Jones & Associates Ltd. (Toronto, ON)
Jones, David .... D.P. Group, The (UNITED KINGDOM)
Jones, Dianne .... Dymar Management Consultants Inc. (Mississauga, ON)
Jones, Fleming .... Robert W. Dingman Company, Inc. (USA)
Jones, Fred .... MQS Executive Search (Toronto, ON)
Jones, George .... Osborne Group, The (Calgary, AB)
Jones, Gill .... Taylor Root (UNITED KINGDOM)
Jones, Neal .... Canadian Career Partners (Calgary, AB)
Jones, Steve .... People Bank, The (Toronto, ON)
Jones, William .... PDQ Personnel Inc. (Mississauga, ON)
Joone, Adel .... Results Management Canada Inc. (Waterloo, ON)
Joosse, Carl .... Alliance Personnel Group, The (Edmonton, AB)
Jowett, Helen .... McDonald-Green Personnel (Cambridge, ON)

JULL - KHAWAJA

KHORASANEE - KYSWATY

Khorasanee, Jay .... Khorasanee & Partners (Toronto, ON)
Killam, Sheri .... Personnel Search Ltd. (Saint John, NB)
Killen, Blair .... Resource Professionals Inc. (Calgary, AB)
Kim, Sandra .... Keith Bagg Information Technology Search Inc. / KBITS (Toronto, ON)
King, Antoinette .... Options Personnel (Toronto, ON)
King, Arlene .... IT Prospects (Toronto, ON)
King, Daniel .... Canadian Findings Ltd. (Toronto, ON)
King, Eric .... Canadian Executive Consultants Inc. (Toronto, ON)
King, Neil .... Brainhunter.com (Toronto, ON)
King, Ramona .... Quantum Management Services Limited (Toronto, ON)
King, Terry .... Datalist (Toronto, ON)
Kingshott, Jennifer .... Muskoka Staffing Company Ltd., The (Bracebridge, ON)
Kingston, Harold .... Kingston Ross Pasnak (Edmonton, AB)
Kingston, Martin .... Morris Pervin Group Inc. (Toronto, ON)
Kinley, David .... Christian & Timbers (USA)
Kinney, Peggy .... Technical Connections Inc. (USA)
Kinsella, Maria .... Trans-United Consultants Ltd. (Burlington, ON)
Kinzie, George A. .... Coke & Associates Ltd. Franchise Recruiters Ltd. (Toronto, ON)
Kirk, Margaret .... Godbout Martin Godbout & Associates (Hull, QC)
Kirkland, Marcus .... MSX International, Inc. (USA)
Kirkpatrick, David .... Manpower Professional (Saint John, NB)
Kirkpatrick, Karin .... Kirkpatrick Personnel Ltd. (Vancouver, BC)
Kirkup, Tom .... Meyers Norris Penny / MNP (Virden, MB)
Kirlew, Cynthia .... Armor Personnel (Brampton, ON)
Kitson, Deborah .... Personnel Department, The (Vancouver, BC)
Kleiman, Howard .... Derhak Ireland & Partners Ltd. (Toronto, ON)
Klein, Courtney .... Nortec Information Consultants Inc. (Ottawa, ON)
Klein, Mindi .... Outsourcing Connection Inc., The (Toronto, ON)
Klemchuck, Darlene .... Adecco Canada Inc. (Markham, ON)
Klians, Caroline .... Canadian Executive Consultants Inc. (Toronto, ON)
Klink, Byrle .... Wellington Partners International Inc. (Kitchener, ON)
Klock, Leah A. .... Alberta Recruiting Group (Calgary, AB)
Knezaurek, Michele .... Tosi Placement Services Inc. (Toronto, ON)
Knight, David .... Baker Consulting Inc. (Charlottetown, PE)
Knight, John .... Canadian Career Partners (Calgary, AB)
Knight, Lisa .... TMP Worldwide Executive Search (Toronto, ON)
Knight, Sherry .... Canadian Career Partners (Calgary, AB)
Knill, Lynda .... Baines Gwinner Limited (UNITED KINGDOM)
Knill, Sara .... Richter Consulting (Toronto, ON)
Knipper, Carol .... Knipper & Associates (Kingston, ON)
Knopf, Gaye .... InterSearch Canada / Lennox Partnership, The (Calgary, AB)
Knowles, Ron .... Western Management Consultants (Toronto, ON)
Knudsen, Lis .... Ray & Berndtson A/S (DENMARK)
Knudson, Kirsty .... Genesis Group Ltd., The (Yellowknife, NT)
Koblik, Gary .... Trans-United Consultants Ltd. (Burlington, ON)
Koch, Leonard .... Koch & Associates (USA)
Kondrat, Ron .... RCM Technologies (Mississauga, ON)
Konkin, Alan .... Konkin & Associates Inc. (Edmonton, AB)
Koopman, John .... Heidrick & Struggles Canada Inc. (Toronto, ON)
Kopelowitz, Justin .... HaysZMB (UNITED KINGDOM)
Kopsick, Joseph .... Spencer Stuart (USA)
Koss, Kendra .... Leader Search Inc. (Calgary, AB)
Kostiuk, Peter .... Trident Technology Services Inc. (Winnipeg, MB)
Kotsopoulos, Daphne .... Canadian Findings Ltd. (Toronto, ON)
Kouchlev, Luben .... Advantage Group, The (Mississauga, ON)
Kovari, Lazzlo .... Resource Management Group Inc. (Toronto, ON)
Kozicki, Laurie .... Ward Vinge & Associates (Calgary, AB)
Kozol, Jeffrey L. .... Walker Forest (USA)
Krahn, Lorraine .... David Aplin & Associates (Edmonton, AB)
Kramer, Janette .... Raymond Chabot Human Resources Inc. (Toronto, ON)
Krecklo, Brian Douglas .... Krecklo Consultants International Inc. (Montréal, QC)
Kretchman, Ronald .... PKF Hill LLP (Toronto, ON)
Krueger, Rudy .... InterSearch Canada / Lennox Partnership, The (Calgary, AB)
Kruszynski, Darren .... Grapevine Executive Recruiters Inc. (Toronto, ON)
Kruszynski, Ray .... Grapevine Executive Recruiters Inc. (Toronto, ON)
Krynicki, Margaret .... Nelson Krynicki & Associates Inc (Mississauga, ON)
Kubic, Stéphane .... St-Amour & Associates (Montréal, QC)
Kuek, Leonard .... Quantum EDP Recruiting Services Ltd. (Toronto, ON)
Kuleta, Anne .... Worldwide Healthcare Exchange (Vancouver, BC)
Kunaman, Donald R. .... Meyers Norris Penny / MNP (Humboldt, SK)
Kurach, Mr. Lynn .... G.L. Penney & Associates Inc. (Edmonton, AB)
Kuse, Kendra .... Hodgins Koenig & Associates (Saskatoon, SK)
Kviring, Rich .... Procom Services (USA)
Kyswaty, Ken .... TAD Canada (Calgary, AB)

LA - LAROCHE

LAROCQUE - LEHOUILLIER

Larocque, Cindy .... Pollack Group, The (Ottawa, ON)
Larocque, Marie .... Renaud Foster Management Consultants (Ottawa, ON)
Larouche, Rene .... Larouche & Associates (Dorval, QC)
Larson, Colleen M. .... Larson & Associates Recruitment Services (Calgary, AB)
Larson, Rolph .... Silicon Network, The (Toronto, ON)
LaRue, Michel .... Raymond Chabot Human Resources Inc. (Toronto, ON)
Lascelle, Donald .... ObjectSearch (Toronto, ON)
Lataille, Nancie .... ZSA Legal Recruitment (Toronto, ON)
Lattimore, Mike .... ExecuPlace Inc. (Kirkland, QC)
Latuplie, Manon .... Carrières Avenir Inc. (Montréal, QC)
Lau, Hayley .... CTEW Executive Personnel Services Inc. (Vancouver, BC)
Lau, Nancy .... GSI International Consulting Group (Toronto, ON)
Laughlin, Michelle .... Volt Human Resources Inc. / VHRI (Toronto, ON)
Laurence, Peter .... Matteson Management Inc. (Toronto, ON)
Laurendeau, Jean E. .... Ray & Berndtson / Laurendeau Labrecque (Montréal, QC)
Laurich, Carol .... Canadian Career Partners (Calgary, AB)
Laurinaitis, Danielle .... Matte Groupe Conseil Inc. (Montréal, QC)
Lauterbach, Aaron .... Caron Executive Search (London, ON)
Lauterbach, Carrie .... Caron Executive Search (London, ON)
Lauterbach, Ed .... Caron Executive Search (London, ON)
Lauzon, Jacques .... Godbout Martin Godbout & Associates (Hull, QC)
Lavalée, Patricia .... Dotemtex Executive Search (Montréal, QC)
Lavallee, Aimee .... Thorek / Scott and Partners (Toronto, ON)
Lavallee, Daniel .... Advantage Group, The (Nepean, ON)
Laver, Anne .... BP Floater Staffing Inc. (Calgary, AB)
Laverdière, Paul .... Levert Personnel Resources Inc. (Timmins, ON)
Lavigne, Gisele .... Prime Management Group Inc. (London, ON)
Law, Bill .... Farley Law & Associates (Thornhill, ON)
Law, Peter .... Farley Law & Associates (Thornhill, ON)
Lawler, Shawn .... Design Group Staffing Services Inc., The (Calgary, AB)
Lawn, David .... Meda Group (Windsor, ON)
Lawrence, Gail .... Trendline Consulting Services (Thunder Bay, ON)
Lawrence, Phillip .... Lawrence Associates Executive Search Inc. (Toronto, ON)
Lawrie, Brad .... Ian Martin Limited (Oakville, ON)
Laws, David .... GSG Partners (Toronto, ON)
Lawson, Mari Anne .... W.G. Meldrum Limited (Calgary, AB)
Laye, Bernard .... Facilité Informatique (Montréal, QC)
Layton, Lori .... Colintex Agencies Ltd. (Toronto, ON)
Le Capitaine, Catharine .... OKA Computer Systems Ltd. / Gestion Informatique OKA Ltée (Montréal, QC)
Lê, Liliane (Lil) .... Renaud Foster Management Consultants (Ottawa, ON)
Leatherman, Jerry .... Allen Austin Lowe & Powers (USA)
Lebeau, Normand .... Mandrake Management Consultants (Toronto, ON)
Lebel, Chantal .... Bryan Jason & Associates Inc. (Toronto, ON)
Lebel, Dany .... Groupe Primacor, Le (Longueuil, QC)
Lebel, Tracy .... Scientific Placement, Inc. (USA)
Leblanc, Danielle .... Gestion Conseils DLT Inc. (Manotick, ON)
Leblanc, Joyce .... Advantage Group, The (Moncton, NB)
LeBlanc, Karen .... Advantage Group, The (Toronto, ON)
LeBlanc, Leona .... Drake International (Moncton, NB)
LeBlanc, Tami .... TalentLab (Kanata, ON)
LeBoeuf, Michel .... St-Amour & Associates (Montréal, QC)
LeBrun, Cathy .... Phelps Staffing Resource Centre (Thunder Bay, ON)
Lecavalier, Robert M. .... Robert M. Lecavalier, Executive Search Consultants (Montréal, QC)
Leckie, Jacqueline A. .... Jacqueline A. Leckie Medical Consultants, Inc. (Calgary, AB)
LeClair, Christopher .... Association Strategy Group (Ottawa, ON)
Leclair, Mark J. .... Levert Personnel Resources Inc. (Sudbury, ON)
Leclerc, Noël .... Systematix Information Technology Consultants Inc. (Québec, QC)
Leclerc-Roesner, Liliane .... Ottawa Valley Personnel Inc. (Pembroke, ON)
LeComte, Andre .... Egon Zehnder International Inc. (Montréal, QC)
Leduc, Raymond .... HR / RH Inc. (Montréal, QC)
Lee, Andrea .... Eureka Recruitment (Calgary, AB)
Lee, Margaret .... Spencer Stuart & Associates / Selector Pacific (CHINA)
Lee, Sharon .... Lecours Wolfson Limited (Toronto, ON)
Lee, William .... William Lee & Associates, Inc. (Vancouver, BC)
Lefebre, Joanne .... Thompson Associates Career Consulting (Halifax, NS)
Lefebre, Lynn .... Partnervision Consulting Group Inc. (Toronto, ON)
Lefebvre, Éric .... Progestic Group Inc. (Montréal, QC)
Lefebvre, Jean-Pierre .... Korn / Ferry International (Montréal, QC)
Lefebvre, Jeanne .... CTC Computer-Tech Consultants Ltd. (Calgary, AB)
Lefebvre, Johanne .... Action Info-Travail Inc. (Mont-Laurier, QC)
Lefebvre, Philip .... TMP Worldwide Executive Search (Toronto, ON)
Leggett, Doreen .... Classic Consulting Group Inc. (Calgary, AB)
Legorburu, Edurardo Rodriguez .... Russell Reynolds Associates, Inc. (SPAIN)
Lehouillier, Johanne .... Delorme et Associés inc. (Québec, QC)

LEHOUILLIER - LONG

LONG - MACKINLAY

Long, Dr. Gerald .... A.W. Fraser & Associates / PSA International (Edmonton, AB)
Long, J. Alan .... Grant Thornton International (Charlottetown, PE)
Longley, Rebecca .... Baines Gwinner Limited (UNITED KINGDOM)
Longshaw, Dawn .... Holloway Schulz & Partners Inc. (Vancouver, BC)
Longsworth, Jerry .... Consultant's Choice, Inc. (USA)
Longtin, Marie-Andrea .... Matte Groupe Conseil Inc. (Montréal, QC)
Longworth, Kieran .... David Aplin & Associates (Calgary, AB)
Lor, Caroline .... Baines Gwinner Limited (UNITED KINGDOM)
Lorrain, Chantal .... CLA Personnel (Ottawa, ON)
Lorte, Christian .... Adecco Québec Inc. (Québec, QC)
Louchard, Michael .... Adecco Québec Inc. (Québec, QC)
Louie, Michael E. .... D & H Group (Vancouver, BC)
Louis, Laniel .... Consultation Delan Inc. (Saint-Laurent, QC)
Louis, Mervyn .... Grant Thornton International (Richmond, BC)
Lovas, W. Carl .... Ray & Berndtson / Lovas Stanley (Toronto, ON)
Love, Steven .... Personnel Search Ltd. (Moncton, NB)
Lovell, Andrée .... Connors, Lovell & Associates Inc. (Mississauga, ON)
Lover, Pat .... Staff Bureau Employment Group (Edmonton, AB)
Loveridge, Tracy .... ProTemps Canada Inc. (Edmonton, AB)
Lovesey, Rob .... Grant Thornton International (Bathurst, NB)
Low, Kathy .... Taylor, Low & Associates Inc. (Toronto, ON)
Low, Michael .... Procom / Professional Computer Consultants Group Ltd. (Toronto, ON)
Lown, Michele .... Keith Bagg Staffing Resources Inc. (Toronto, ON)
Luby, Patrick .... Clarendon Parker Middle East (UNITED ARAB EMIRATES)
Lucchetto, Serge .... TES, The Employment Solution (Toronto, ON)
Luck, Brenda .... Management Recruiters of Kannapolis (USA)
Luft, Audrey .... Transpersonnel Driver Staffing and Allied Services (Edmonton, AB)
Lukish, Dawn .... Angus Employment Limited (Burlington, ON)
Luksa, Len .... Results Management Canada Inc. (Waterloo, ON)
Lundy, Jim .... Landmark Consulting Group Inc. (Hamilton, ON)
Lundy, Warren M. .... Feldman Gray & Associates Inc. (Toronto, ON)
Lunnen, Harvey .... Grant Thornton International (Marystown, NF)
Lussier, Hélène P. .... Lussier Executive Search Inc. (Toronto, ON)
Lussier, Pierre .... BDO Dunwoody LLP (Montréal, QC)
Lussier, Pierre .... St-Amour & Associates (Montréal, QC)
Lydiatt, Jay .... IT People Ltd. (Calgary, AB)
Lyons, Arthur .... Lyons, Black + Associates (Vancouver, BC)
Lyons, Gord .... Syntech Placements Inc. (Toronto, ON)
Lyons, Marlene .... Adecco Canada Inc. (Langley, BC)
Lyttle, Jordene S. .... PricewaterhouseCoopers Executive Search (Toronto, ON)
Macadam, Deborah .... D.J. Macadam & Associates Inc. (North Vancouver, BC)
MacArthur, Mary .... Drake Executive (Montréal, QC)
MacArthur, R. Ian .... Madison MacArthur Inc. (Toronto, ON)
MacBean, Paul .... Technical Skills Consulting Inc. (Toronto, ON)
MacBeath, Alex .... Grant Thornton International (Port Colborne, ON)
MacCarthy, Dane .... Michael Stern Associates Inc. (Toronto, ON)
MacDonald, Bruce .... Lock & Associates (Vancouver, BC)
MacDonald, Jack D. .... Savage Consultants Inc. (Vancouver, BC)
MacDonald, Mary .... TES, The Employment Solution (Burlington, ON)
MacDougall, Allison .... Baker Consulting Inc. (Charlottetown, PE)
MacDougall, J. Robert .... Carscarp Consulting (Gloucester, ON)
MacDougall, Jennifer .... Adecco Canada Inc. (Langley, BC)
MacEachern, David .... Spencer Stuart & Associates (Canada) Ltd. (Toronto, ON)
MacEachern, Doug .... Kitchener Executive Consultants (Kitchener, ON)
Macfarlane, Elaine .... Canadian Career Partners (Calgary, AB)
MacFarlane, Karen .... Options Outreach Employment Inc. (Saint John, NB)
MacGillivray, Shannon .... Med-Emerg International Inc. (Mississauga, ON)
MacGregor, Jennifer .... Procom / Professional Computer Consultants Group Ltd. (Calgary, AB)
Machan, Melissa .... Verriez Group Inc., The (London, ON)
Machowski, Steve .... Wellington Partners International Inc. (Kitchener, ON)
Macht, Darci .... G.L. Penney & Associates Inc. (Edmonton, AB)
MacIntosh, Liane .... Meyers Norris Penny / MNP (Winnipeg, MB)
MacIntosh, Wayne .... Grant Thornton International (Sydney, NS)
Mackay, Angela .... Prior Resource Group Inc., The (Kitchener, ON)
Mackay, Jason .... M.I.S. Consultants (Toronto, ON)
MacKay, Karen .... TMP QD Legal Recruitment (Toronto, ON)
MacKellar, Allison .... Austin Marlowe International Inc. (Toronto, ON)
MacKenzie, Alex .... Procom / Professional Computer Consultants Group Ltd. (Toronto, ON)
Mackenzie, Brad .... Maxim Group (Richmond, BC)
MacKenzie, Bruce J. .... Chapman & Associates (Vancouver, BC)
Mackenzie, Diana .... Consultation Delan Inc. (Saint-Laurent, QC)
MacKenzie, Douglas G. .... MacKenzie Gray Management Inc. (Calgary, AB)
MacKenzie, Jamie .... Genesis Group Ltd., The (Yellowknife, NT)
MacKinlay, Marcelo .... TMP Worldwide Executive Search (Toronto, ON)

MACKINNON - MARCHESSAULT

MARCOS - MCATEER

Marcos, Lisa .... Argus Group Corporation, The (Toronto, ON)
Marcus, Andrea .... MediStaff (USA)
Marcus, Barry .... Everest Management Network Inc. (Toronto, ON)
Marhsall, Anita .... MediStaff (USA)
Marion, Denise .... Bureau de placement d'Anjou (Montréal, QC)
Maritzer, Howard .... PTC - Financial Staffing Inc. (Concord, ON)
Markesini, Karen .... Accountants on Call / AOC Financial Executive Search (Toronto, ON)
Markham, Garda .... Executive House Inc. (Chatham, ON)
Markham, Glenn .... Maintenance Plus Inc. (Chatham, ON)
Markle, Drew .... Technology Search Group / TSG (Ajax, ON)
Marklinger, Karyn K. .... Andersen (Calgary, AB)
Marks, Julie .... Global Hospitality Search Consultants (Halifax, NS)
Marleau, Joanne .... Drakkar Human Resources (Montréal, QC)
Marlowe, Edward .... Galloway and Associates (Toronto, ON)
Marmur, Michael J. .... Michael Marmur & Associates (Toronto, ON)
Marques, Sandi .... Nework Corp. (Toronto, ON)
Marr, John F. .... Allen Austin Lowe & Powers (USA)
Marr, Laurie .... Marr Roy Group, The / MRG (Toronto, ON)
Mars, Karen .... Thomas & Dessain (UNITED KINGDOM)
Mars, Roxanne .... Technical Skills Consulting Inc. (Toronto, ON)
Marsden, Jonathan .... Marsden Nagata Legal Search (Toronto, ON)
Marsh, Barb .... Interim Management Resources Inc. / IMR (Mississauga, ON)
Marsh, Malcolm .... Bongard Marsh Associates Inc. (Toronto, ON)
Marshall, B.J. .... Northwind Consulting Alliance (King City, ON)
Marshall, Fiona .... Canadian Executive Consultants Inc. (Toronto, ON)
Marshall, Steven .... Lock & Associates (Toronto, ON)
Marshman, Michael .... London Executive Consultants (London, ON)
Marsilis, Hector .... Mandrake Management Consultants (Toronto, ON)
Marsland, Darren .... Canjobs.com Inc. (Guelph, ON)
Marsteller, Frank .... Spencer Stuart (USA)
Martel, Madeleine .... Madeleine Martel Inc. (Montréal, QC)
Martens, Dave .... Little Group, The (Burlington, ON)
Martens, Peggy .... Little Group, The (Burlington, ON)
Martin, Anna .... MacKenzie Gray Management Inc. (Calgary, AB)
Martin, Doug .... TalentLab (Kanata, ON)
Martin, Ed .... InterCom Recruitment Ltd. (Toronto, ON)
Martin, Hélène .... Miss Hall's Personnel Services Ltd. (Ottawa, ON)
Martin, Paul .... B & L Consultants Inc. / Autorecruit Inc. (Toronto, ON)
Martin, Stan J. .... Cameron Management Services Group / CMSG (Calgary, AB)
Martineau, Lucy .... SSA Services Conseils (Montréal, QC)
Martins, Angela .... TAD Canada (Mississauga, ON)
Marttini, Carol .... RWJ & Associates (Kitchener, ON)
Marty, Dick .... ExecuCounsel Inc (Toronto, ON)
Mascaren, Heather .... Mascaren International Inc. (Toronto, ON)
Massey, Sharlene .... About Staffing Ltd. (Calgary, AB)
Masters, Robert .... Trillium Talent Resource Inc. (Toronto, ON)
Masters, Ted .... Palmer Reed (Toronto, ON)
Masterson, Paul .... ICAP Management Inc. (Fredericton, NB)
Mateus, Sergio .... CNC Global (Richmond Hill, ON)
Mathew, Richard .... Graham Matthew & Partners LLP (Cambridge, ON)
Mathews, Maria .... Drake Executive (Winnipeg, MB)
Mathews, Seandra .... Drake International (Toronto, ON)
Mathur, Amit .... Global Softech Inc. (Toronto, ON)
Mathur, Vijay P. .... Krecklo Consultants International Inc. (Toronto, ON)
Matte, Fernand .... R. Jacques Plante & Associés (Sillery, QC)
Matte, Richard M. .... Matte Groupe Conseil Inc. (Montréal, QC)
Matteson, Sandra .... Matteson Management Inc. (Toronto, ON)
Matthews, Alice M. .... StarDot PRG Inc. (Calgary, AB)
Matthews, Angela K. .... Matthews Management (Richmond Hill, ON)
Mattice, Kelly .... IBISKA Telecom Inc. (Ottawa, ON)
Mattocks, Gary .... Lock & Associates (Winnipeg, MB)
Maurer, Kelly .... Canadian Career Partners (Calgary, AB)
May, Anthony .... Baines Gwinner Limited (UNITED KINGDOM)
May, E.J. .... Cambridge Management Planning Inc. (Toronto, ON)
May, Greg .... Morgan & Banks Ltd. (AUSTRALIA)
May, Lori .... Harris Consulting Corporation, The (Winnipeg, MB)
May, Russell .... Harris Consulting Corporation, The (Winnipeg, MB)
Mayer-Sinqule, Rudolf .... Spencer Stuart (BRAZIL)
Maynard, Dave .... ATS Reliance Technical Group (Toronto, ON)
Mayr, Christian .... Renard Hospitality Search Consultants (Toronto, ON)
Mcaleer, Wendy .... Drake International (Mississauga, ON)
McAlpine, Janet .... Lannick Associates (Toronto, ON)
McArthur, John C. .... AMAC Consultants Inc. (Vancouver, BC)
McAteer, Tara .... Health Match BC (Vancouver, BC)

MCCABE - MCLEAN

MCLEOD - MILLER

McLeod, Don .... Levton Group Inc., The (Toronto, ON)
McLeod, Kim .... B & L Consultants Inc. / Autorecruit Inc. (Toronto, ON)
McLeod, Kirsty .... HaysZMB (UNITED KINGDOM)
McLure, Patsy .... Action Personnel Services (Peace River, AB)
McMahon, Barb .... Higgins International Inc. (Winnipeg, MB)
McMillan, Doug .... Technical Management Resources Inc. (Barrie, ON)
McMillan, John .... ITECC Consulting (Toronto, ON)
McMillan, Robert A. .... PricewaterhouseCoopers Executive Search (Vancouver, BC)
McMullen, Nicole .... Permanent Solutions Inc. (Mississauga, ON)
McNamara, Catherine .... Ray & Berndtson (USA)
McNamara, Dan .... Dan McNamara & Associates (Woodstock, ON)
McNamara, Shannon .... Dan McNamara & Associates (Woodstock, ON)
McNeely, Murray .... Key Executive Consultants (Pickering, ON)
McNeil, Greg .... Adecco Canada Inc. (Edmonton, AB)
McPherson, A. .... Corporate & Career Development Inc. (Vancouver, BC)
McPherson, Cindy .... Allen Personnel Services (London, ON)
McQueen, John .... Transpersonnel Driver Staffing and Allied Services (Brampton, ON)
McRae, Brian .... Transpersonnel Driver Staffing and Allied Services (Edmonton, AB)
McRae, Cam .... Canadian Career Partners (Calgary, AB)
McRae, Darren .... Advanced Design & Drafting (Mississauga, ON)
McRae, Debbie .... Pollack Group, The (Ottawa, ON)
McRae, Jim .... Symmetry Search Group Inc. (Toronto, ON)
Mead, Ed .... Lock & Associates (Toronto, ON)
Mead, Gayle .... Executive Assistance Inc. (Toronto, ON)
Mealia, John .... Korn / Ferry International (Toronto, ON)
Medeirda, Anne-Marie .... Abecassis conseil en recherches de cadres Inc. (Montréal, QC)
Medvescek, Sonia .... Schlesinger Newman Goldman (Montréal, QC)
Meeker, Tony .... Ultimate Staffing (Hamilton, ON)
Meier, Karen Kammer .... Master Performers (Toronto, ON)
Meier, Peter .... Grant Thornton International (Saint John, NB)
Meilleur, Julie .... Labor Tek Personnel Services Ltd. (Ottawa, ON)
Meingast, Peter .... Galt Global Recruiting (Vancouver, BC)
Meksula, Stan .... Caron Executive Search (London, ON)
Meldrum, William G. .... W.G. Meldrum Limited (Toronto, ON)
Melnychuk, Ken .... CDI Technical Services Ltd. (Calgary, AB)
Melnyk, J.D. (Jack) .... Resource Professionals Inc. (Calgary, AB)
Melnyk, Niki .... Rod Turpin & Associates (Edmonton, AB)
Melvin, Wendy .... Quest Executive Recruitment Professionals Inc. (Toronto, ON)
Mendes, Tony .... C.G. Thomson & Company (Toronto, ON)
Menendyan, Karin .... Personnel Menen (Mount Royal, QC)
Menendyan, Najda .... Personnel Menen (Mount Royal, QC)
Menguy, Carole .... Synergies ressources humaines (Trois-Rivières, QC)
Menna, Teresa .... Hunt Technical Personnel (Mississauga, ON)
Mensah, Jennifer .... Drake International (Toronto, ON)
Menzies, Al .... Grant Thornton International (Calgary, AB)
Meredith, Karen .... Drake International (Toronto, ON)
Merizzi, Robyn .... Integra IT Partners Inc. (Toronto, ON)
Merk, Sandra .... Executive Source, The (Regina, SK)
Merkley, Bryan .... SOLUTIONS (Cornwall, ON)
Merryman, Donna .... Mindbank Consulting Group (USA)
Messier, Joëlle .... Roevin Technical People Ltd. (Montréal, QC)
Methot, Christine .... InGenius Engineering Inc. (Ottawa, ON)
Metin, Mitchell .... Korn / Ferry International (UNITED KINGDOM)
Métivier, Jean .... Métivier Groupe Conseil Inc. (Montréal, QC)
Meyers, Ron .... Feldman Gray & Associates Inc. (Toronto, ON)
Michael, R.W. .... RWM Management Resources Ltd. (Calgary, AB)
Michael, Randy .... Mindbank Consulting Group (USA)
Michaelis, Paul .... Dana Stehr & Associates Inc. (Toronto, ON)
Michaels, Bonnie .... Davies Park (Calgary, AB)
Michalec, Jon .... Procom Services (USA)
Michaud, Lyn .... Manpower Professional (Sherbrooke, QC)
Michon, Yvan .... TES, The Employment Solution (Montréal, QC)
Middleton, Anne .... Apple One Employment Services (Toronto, ON)
Miggiani, Roberta .... Anderson Associates (Toronto, ON)
Milan, Frank .... Grant Thornton International (Kelowna, BC)
Milczynski, Jack .... Canadian Findings Ltd. (Toronto, ON)
Miles, Don .... Don Miles Personnel Consultants Inc. (Toronto, ON)
Miles, Hughes .... Don Miles Personnel Consultants Inc. (Toronto, ON)
Milette, Lynne C. .... Lynne Milette & Associates Ltd. (Chapeau, QC)
Milevski, Mary .... People Bank, The (Toronto, ON)
Milgram, David .... Milgram & Associates (Toronto, ON)
Milic, Stephen .... Mandrake Management Consultants (Toronto, ON)
Mill, Stephen .... Office Team Administrative Staffing (Toronto, ON)
Miller, Dennis .... Nexstaf IT Recruitment (Toronto, ON)

MILLER - MORRISON

MORRISON - NELSON

Morrison, Steve .... Western HR Consulting Ltd. (Calgary, AB)
Morrissette, Jean F. .... HR / RH Inc. (Montréal, QC)
Morton, Phil .... Morgan & Banks Ltd. (AUSTRALIA)
Moscoe, Raymond .... TES, The Employment Solution (Toronto, ON)
Mosdell, Doug .... Robinson Rose Associates Ltd. (Mississauga, ON)
Mosher, Charles .... CTS International, Inc. (USA)
Moss, Beverly .... MRK Consulting Ltd. (UNITED KINGDOM)
Moss, John .... GSI International Consulting Group (Toronto, ON)
Motiuk, Terry .... Meyers Norris Penny / MNP (Brandon, MB)
Mouchet, Dave .... Helix Management Consulting Services Inc. / HMCS Inc. (Orleans, ON)
Mountain, Shawn .... Procom / Professional Computer Consultants Group Ltd. (Kanata, ON)
Mountford, Laurie .... W.G. Meldrum Limited (Toronto, ON)
Moxon, Ben .... Moxon Personnel Ltd. (Vancouver, BC)
Moyer, Jan .... Drake International (Oakville, ON)
Mrozek, Elly .... Kelly Professional & Technical Services (Toronto, ON)
Mudie, Rick .... Grant Thornton International (New Westminster, BC)
Mueller, Melissa .... Pinton Forrest & Madden / EMA Partners International (Vancouver, BC)
Mueller, Trish .... Capital Executive Ltd. (Calgary, AB)
Muenchrath, Kerry .... CDI Technical Services Ltd. (Calgary, AB)
Mugford, Karen .... People Bank, The (Toronto, ON)
Mukerjee, Amanda .... HaysZMB (UNITED KINGDOM)
Mullen, Francine .... Employer's Choice, The (Brampton, ON)
Munday, Rob .... Nework Corp. (Toronto, ON)
Munger, Julie .... Adecco Québec (Longueuil, QC)
Munro, Steve .... Cromark International Inc. (Mississauga, ON)
Munro, Victor .... Applied Technology Solutions Inc. / ATS (Toronto, ON)
Munroe, Crystal .... Canadian Career Partners (Calgary, AB)
Munroe, Victor .... Datalist (Toronto, ON)
Murad, Roy .... Link Resource Partners (Toronto, ON)
Murani, Almas .... Information Business Consulting (IBC) Group Inc. (Edmonton, AB)
Murchie, Don .... Western HR Consulting Ltd. (Calgary, AB)
Murphy, Dan .... CNC Global (Ottawa, ON)
Murphy, Kenneth .... Kenneth Murphy & Associates / KMA (Halifax, NS)
Murphy, Krista .... Advantage Group, The (Dartmouth, NS)
Murphy, Meta .... Ian Martin Limited (USA)
Murray, Cris .... J. Edgar & Associates Inc. (Toronto, ON)
Murray, David R. .... Ray & Berndtson / Lovas Stanley (Toronto, ON)
Murray, Gord .... GSI International Consulting Group (Toronto, ON)
Murray, Ian .... BMB / MaxSys (Ottawa, ON)
Murray, John .... Harvey Nash plc (UNITED KINGDOM)
Murray, Kerri .... Muskoka Staffing Company Ltd., The (Bracebridge, ON)
Murray, L. Byron .... Grant Thornton International (Summerside, PE)
Murray, Michelle .... Eagle Professional Resources Inc. (Halifax, NS)
Murray, Scott .... International Technical Recruiting (Windsor, ON)
Murray, Virginia .... AT Kearney Executive Search (Toronto, ON)
Musey, Gerry .... Meyers Norris Penny / MNP (Dauphin, MB)
Musgrove, Sheila .... Kelly Services (Calgary, AB)
Mussell, Connie .... High Road Personnel (Burlington, ON)
Musson, Stuart .... TalentLab (Kanata, ON)
Musthill, Don .... Global Consulting Group Inc. (Markham, ON)
Myers, Robert .... St-Amour & Associates (Montréal, QC)
Myles, Jennifer .... Personnel Search Ltd. (Saint John, NB)
Nachon, Julie .... Adecco Québec (Longueuil, QC)
Nadeau, Denis .... Lock & Associates (Montréal, QC)
Nadeau, Leslie .... HR Business Partners (Calgary, AB)
Nadeau, Louis .... BMB / MaxSys (Ottawa, ON)
Nadeau, Robert .... Spencer Stuart & Associates (Canada) Ltd. (Montréal, QC)
Nadherny, Christopher .... Spencer Stuart (USA)
Nadler, Heather .... Thomas Group, The (Mississauga, ON)
Nagata, Lorene .... Marsden Nagata Legal Search (Toronto, ON)
Naidu, Sarita .... Forbes & Gunn Consultants Ltd. (Vancouver, BC)
Nakamoto, Cheryl .... McNeill Nakamoto Recruitment Group Inc. (Vancouver, BC)
Nalezinski, Charlie .... Landon Morgan Inc. (Thorold, ON)
Nallli, Luciane .... Accountants on Call / AOC Financial Executive Search (Toronto, ON)
Nash, Stephen .... Counsel Network, The (Calgary, AB)
Nassau, Lauren .... Walker Forest (USA)
Naufal, Michael .... Ray & Berndtson / Robertson Surrette (Ottawa, ON)
Naveh, Lemore .... Link Resource Partners (Toronto, ON)
Navidad, Ramil .... Core Group, The (Toronto, ON)
Nederpelt, Jack .... Heidrick & Struggles Canada Inc. (Toronto, ON)
Neglia, Maureen .... Thinkpath.com Inc. (Toronto, ON)
Neidhold, Raquel .... Technical Connections Inc. (USA)
Neill, Michael .... Trans-United Consultants Ltd. (Burlington, ON)
Nelson, Allan C. .... Davies Park (Calgary, AB)

NELSON - O'NEILL

Nelson, Desrine .... Adecco Canada Inc. (Toronto, ON)
Nelson, Paul R. .... London Executive Consultants (London, ON)
Nelson, Tim .... Nelson Krynicki & Associates Inc (Mississauga, ON)
Nemeth, Shelley .... Galt Global Recruiting (Calgary, AB)
Ness, Donald .... RHI Management Resources (Toronto, ON)
Nettleton, Gary .... Executive House Inc. (Chatham, ON)
Neumann, Donna .... Windowpane Management Inc. (Calgary, AB)
Neumann, Sylvia .... Personnel Alter Ego Inc. (Pointe-Claire, QC)
Nevard, Sharon .... First Step Recruitment (Toronto, ON)
Neville, Keltie .... Altis Human Resources (Toronto, ON)
Newbold, Jamie .... Taylor Root (UNITED KINGDOM)
Newton, David .... Drake International (Toronto, ON)
Newton, Paul .... Georgian Staffing Services (Collingwood, ON)
Ng, Pauline .... Bower Ng Staff Systems Inc. (Vancouver, BC)
Nguyen, Liem .... Systematix Information Technology Consultants Inc. (Montréal, QC)
Nguyen, Tram .... Advantage Group, The (Mississauga, ON)
Nicholas, Hoda .... Ian Martin Limited (Toronto, ON)
Nicholls, Peter .... Jawaby Oil Service (UNITED KINGDOM)
Nicholls, Robert J. (Bob) .... Interim Management Resources Inc. / IMR (Mississauga, ON)
Nicholson, Kevin A. .... Accu-Staff Resource Systems / Technical Group (Windsor, ON)
Nickerson, Harvey .... Grant Thornton International (Kentville, NS)
Nielsen, Caroline .... Canadian Executive Consultants Inc. (Toronto, ON)
Nieradka, Erin .... Templeman Consulting Group Inc. (Kingston, ON)
Niermann, Petra .... New Zealand Skills Export Ltd. (NEW ZEALAND)
Nighswander, Jan .... Canadian Career Partners (Calgary, AB)
Nimmo, Bryce K. .... Cameron Management Services Group / CMSG (Calgary, AB)
Nirenberg, David .... Botrie Associates / Stanton Chase International (Toronto, ON)
Nish, Gillian .... Execusearch, a division of Execuserve Plus Inc. (Lethbridge, AB)
Nixon, Barbara .... PricewaterhouseCoopers Executive Search (Toronto, ON)
Nixon, Drina .... Canadian Career Partners (Calgary, AB)
Nixon, Geoff .... Can-Tech Services (Saint-Laurent, QC)
Nixon, Ted .... TechNix Inc. (Toronto, ON)
Niziol, Kathy .... Landmark Consulting Group Inc. (Hamilton, ON)
Nizynski, Henry .... Systematix Information Technology Consultants Inc. (Calgary, AB)
Nobécourt, Gilles .... Russell Reynolds Associates, Inc. (FRANCE)
Nobert, Terri .... David Aplin & Associates (Edmonton, AB)
Noble, Phil .... Grant Thornton International (Vancouver, BC)
Noel, Les .... L.S. Noel Consulting Limited (Richmond Hill, ON)
Nogas, Fred R. .... Feldman Gray & Associates Inc. (Toronto, ON)
Noir, Sophie .... Russell Reynolds Associates, Inc. (FRANCE)
Nolan, D.R. .... D.R. Nolan Associates Inc. (Toronto, ON)
Noon, Jason .... Eagle Professional Resources Inc. (Toronto, ON)
Noorden, Louis .... Syntech Placements Inc. (Toronto, ON)
Norman, Derek .... Canadian Career Partners (Calgary, AB)
Norraine, Judy .... CTC Computer-Tech Consultants Ltd. (Vancouver, BC)
North, Bruce .... True North Executive Search (Toronto, ON)
Nott, Michael C. .... Woodridge Associates (UNITED KINGDOM)
Nugent, Jeff .... Procom / Professional Computer Consultants Group Ltd. (Toronto, ON)
Nugent-Rooney, Sandra .... Burke Group, The (St. Catharines, ON)
O'Brian, Kieran .... Kee Transport Group Inc. (Mississauga, ON)
O'Brien, Ed .... Taylor Root (UNITED KINGDOM)
O'Brien, Greg .... Lock & Associates (Halifax, NS)
O'Brien, Michael .... Technical Management Resources Inc. (Barrie, ON)
O'Brien, Samantha .... Manpower Services Canada Limited (Toronto, ON)
O'Bryan, Paul .... Premier Personnel Limited (UNITED KINGDOM)
O'Callaghan, Joanna .... Korn / Ferry International (Vancouver, BC)
O'Callaghan, Monty .... Qualicum Consulting Limited (Ottawa, ON)
O'Callaghan, Terry K. .... Korn / Ferry International (Vancouver, BC)
O'Connell, Jennifer .... Baines Gwinner Limited (UNITED KINGDOM)
O'Connor, Helen .... Hire Choice Inc. (Toronto, ON)
O'Connor, Matthew .... Ian Martin Limited (Ottawa, ON)
O'Connor, Tom .... Genesis Group Ltd., The (Yellowknife, NT)
O'Day, Dan .... Lock & Associates (Vancouver, BC)
O'Donoghue, Scott .... Nexstaf IT Recruitment (Toronto, ON)
O'Dwyer, Conor .... D.P. Group, The (UNITED KINGDOM)
O'Farrell, Sara-Beth .... Taylor Root (UNITED KINGDOM)
O'Gara, Michael .... Walker Forest (USA)
O'Hare, Kathleen .... Canadian Career Partners (Calgary, AB)
O'Leary Collins, Susan .... Harvey Nash plc (UNITED KINGDOM)
O'Leary, Kevin .... Drake Executive (Winnipeg, MB)
O'Meally, Carline .... TMP Worldwide Advertising & Communications (Toronto, ON)
O'Neil-Taylor, Colette .... Computer Action Company (Toronto, ON)
O'Neill, Mary .... MacKenzie Gray Management Inc. (Calgary, AB)
O'Neill, Philip .... Trans-United Consultants Ltd. (Burlington, ON)

O'QUINN - PATTON

O'Quinn, Trish .... M.J. Janssen & Associates Inc. (Mississauga, ON)
O'Reilly, Bernie .... MCO Business Group Inc. (Ottawa, ON)
O'Reilly, Keith .... CNC Global (Ottawa, ON)
O'Rourke, F. Joseph .... BDO Dunwoody LLP (Sarnia, ON)
Oakley, Robert .... Grant Thornton International (Bridgewater, NS)
Obermaier, Otto .... Spencer Stuart (GERMANY)
Occhiboi, Emil .... Huntington Group, The (USA)
Ogilvie, Jennie .... ProTemps Canada Inc. (Calgary, AB)
Ogren, Milt .... Meyers Norris Penny / MNP (Hudson Bay, SK)
Ohirko, Dale .... TDM Technical Services (Toronto, ON)
Oickle, Joan .... Working Well Consulting Inc. (Innisfil, ON)
Olansen, K. .... TRS Staffing Solutions (Canada) Inc. (Calgary, AB)
Oldfield, Steve .... Kelly Professional & Technical Services (Toronto, ON)
Oliver, Andrew .... Michael Page Finance (CHINA)
Olivier, Linda .... Conseillers en Personnel Jacques Cartier, Les (Montréal, QC)
Olivito, Rita .... Impact Staffing Inc. (Windsor, ON)
Olo, Peter .... Anderson Associates (Toronto, ON)
Olsen, Robert F. .... Robert Connelly & Associates, Inc. (USA)
Opena, Steve .... Nework Corp. (Toronto, ON)
Ormandy, Marie .... MCO Business Group Inc. (Ottawa, ON)
Orr, Janet .... Outsourcing Connection Inc., The (Toronto, ON)
Osborne, Lance .... Lannick Associates (Toronto, ON)
Osler, Lawton .... First Choice Personnel (Toronto, ON)
Osman, A.B. .... Business & Professional Appointments (UNITED KINGDOM)
Ostfield, Adele .... Performance House Ltd. (Waterloo, ON)
Oudman, Henk .... Systematix Information Technology Consultants Inc. (Toronto, ON)
Ouellet, Jacques E. .... Yves Elkas Inc. (Montréal, QC)
Owen, Tom .... D.P. Group, The (UNITED KINGDOM)
Pacaud, Phil .... Goldbeck Recruiting Inc. (Vancouver, BC)
Pacces, Luca .... Spencer Stuart (ITALY)
Pace, Lorry .... Allen Personnel Services (London, ON)
Paddley, Robin .... Jenereaux & Associates Inc. (Mississauga, ON)
Pagani, Maria .... Personnel Solutions (Westmount, QC)
Page, Joan .... Kelly Professional & Technical Services (Vancouver, BC)
Paget, Christopher .... Procom / Professional Computer Consultants Group Ltd. (Montréal, QC)
Pairault, Denis .... Global Hospitality Search Consultants (Montréal, QC)
Pallascio, Francis .... Andersen (Montréal, QC)
Pallidino, John .... St-Amour & Associates (Toronto, ON)
Palmer, Adrian J. .... Western Management Consultants (Vancouver, BC)
Palmer, Brenda .... Palmer & Associates (Kingston, ON)
Palmer, Mark .... Palmer & Company Executive Recruitment (Toronto, ON)
Palmer, Mike .... Lock & Associates (Vancouver, BC)
Pamenter, Fred .... Pamenter, Pamenter, Brezer & Deganis Ltd. (Toronto, ON)
Pang, Christopher S. .... TMP QD Legal Recruitment (Toronto, ON)
Panousis, Angelo .... Lecours Wolfson Limited (Toronto, ON)
Pantelidis, Chris .... Ray & Berndtson / Lovas Stanley (Toronto, ON)
Panzer, Sally .... MediStaff (USA)
Papish, John .... Spectrum Computer Personnel Inc. (Toronto, ON)
Papps, Angela .... Keith Bagg Staffing (Regional) Inc. (Thornhill, ON)
Paquet, Marc .... MPA Recherche de Cadres Inc. (Brossard, QC)
Paquet, Robert .... Robert Paquet & Associés (Sainte-Foy, QC)
Paquette, Karen .... Lock & Associates (Toronto, ON)
Paquette, Karen .... Paquette & Associates Ltd. (Vancouver, BC)
Paquette, Philémon .... Paquette Consulting (Ottawa, ON)
Paquin, Caroline .... Personnel Alter Ego Inc. (Pointe-Claire, QC)
Parades, Pauline .... Edan Search Group (Toronto, ON)
Parent, Martine L. .... Korn / Ferry International (Vancouver, BC)
Parish, Jayne .... Kent Legal Personnel (Toronto, ON)
Parisien, Sumon .... Yves Elkas Inc. (Montréal, QC)
Park, K. Darwin .... Davies Park (Edmonton, AB)
Parnall, Carol .... Prime Management Group Inc. (Cambridge, ON)
Parr, James .... Michael Stern Associates Inc. (Toronto, ON)
Parslow, Harry .... J.G. Flynn & Associates Inc. (Vancouver, BC)
Parsons, Grant .... W. Hutt Management Resources Ltd. (Burlington, ON)
Parsons, Shawn .... Hire Choice Inc. (Toronto, ON)
Pasahow, David .... Heidrick & Struggles International, Inc. (USA)
Pascual, Yvonne .... Technisolutions Executive Inc. (Aylmer, QC)
Pask, David .... Futurestep (Toronto, ON)
Patel, Dan .... Nework Corp. (Toronto, ON)
Patel, Sai .... Meech Partners LLP (Toronto, ON)
Paterson, Megan .... TalentLab (Kanata, ON)
Paterson, Paul .... Nexstaf IT Recruitment (Toronto, ON)
Patterson, Merv .... GSI International Consulting Group (Ottawa, ON)
Patton, Dave .... Advantage Group, The (Dartmouth, NS)

PAUL - PHANEUF

PHEE - POWELL

Phee, Alan .... Phee Farrer Jones Ltd. (UNITED KINGDOM)
Phelps, Heather .... Phelps Staffing Resource Centre (Thunder Bay, ON)
Phelps, Valerie .... Phelps Staffing Resource Centre (Thunder Bay, ON)
Phillipps, Chantal .... Michael Page International (USA)
Phillips, Donald C. .... Coakwell Crawford Cairns (High River, AB)
Phillips, Jo Anne .... Higher Vision Recruitment Strategies Incorporated (Toronto, ON)
Phillips, Richard .... Baines Gwinner Limited (UNITED KINGDOM)
Phillips, Robyn .... TSI Group / TSI Staffing Services (Mississauga, ON)
Phipps, Susan N. .... Phipps Consulting Enterprises Inc. / PCE (Ottawa, ON)
Phipps, Tyrone .... Technology Search Group / TSG (Ajax, ON)
Piche, Gerry .... Qualicum Consulting Limited (Ottawa, ON)
Piche, Jerome .... Spencer Stuart & Associates (Canada) Ltd. (Montréal, QC)
Pick, Tina .... ZSA Legal Recruitment (Calgary, AB)
Pickersgill, Charlotte .... ATS Reliance Technical Group (London, ON)
Picton, J.W. Bruce .... Veres Picton & Co. (Edmonton, AB)
Pierce, Kim .... Advantage Group, The (Saint John, NB)
Pierotti, Bonnie .... Drake International (London, ON)
Pila, Esther .... Pila Recruiting & Associates Inc. (Richmond, BC)
Pinard, Armand .... ATI Consulting Corporation Inc. (Halifax, NS)
Pinsky, Murray .... Wasserman, Stotland, Bratt, Grossbaum / WSBG (Montréal, QC)
Pinsonneault, Michel .... Korn / Ferry International (Montréal, QC)
Pinto, Caroline .... Jeffery Group Ltd., The (Toronto, ON)
Pinto, Zoila .... Spencer Stuart (BRAZIL)
Pinton, Garth .... Pinton Forrest & Madden / EMA Partners International (Vancouver, BC)
Pitsel, Patricia .... Pitsel & Associates (Calgary, AB)
Pitters, Eric .... Systematix Information Technology Consultants Inc. (Toronto, ON)
Plante, R. Jacques .... R. Jacques Plante & Associés (Sillery, QC)
Plommer, Christopher .... Aquent Partners (Toronto, ON)
Plorins, Annette .... Mintz & Partners, LLP (Toronto, ON)
Plouffe, Yves J. .... Yves Plouffe et associés (Île-des-Soeurs, QC)
Plowman, Bonnie .... SynapTuit Group (Vancouver, BC)
Plowman, Brenda .... SynapTuit Group (Vancouver, BC)
Plummer, Cyril .... Shared Vision Management Search Inc. (Toronto, ON)
Plut, Anthony .... Quest Resource Group (Mississauga, ON)
Pocock, Martyn .... Baines Gwinner Limited (UNITED KINGDOM)
Pocreau, Emmauelle .... St-Amour & Associates (Montréal, QC)
Poho, Will .... WorkCentral CSI (Ottawa, ON)
Poirier, Madeleine .... G-P Personnel Inc. (Chicoutimi, QC)
Pojidaeff, Dimitri .... Human Resource Group Management Consultants (Edmonton, AB)
Polak, Traci .... Landon Morgan Inc. (Thorold, ON)
Polano, Judy .... Levert Personnel Resources Inc. (Sudbury, ON)
Polce, Vince .... Landon Morgan Inc. (Thorold, ON)
Poliakov, Igor .... Cambridge Management Planning Inc. (Toronto, ON)
Pollack, Karen .... Pollack Group, The (Ottawa, ON)
Pollack, Marcie .... LMR Consultants (Thornhill, ON)
Pollack, Paul Peter .... Pollack Group, The (Ottawa, ON)
Pollard, Jeff .... Grapevine Executive Recruiters Inc. (Toronto, ON)
Pollard, Mike .... Clark, Pollard & Gagliardi (Waterloo, ON)
Pollender, Louise .... Action Info-Travail Inc. (Mont-Laurier, QC)
Pollock, Peter .... Dunhill Consultants (North York) Ltd. (Toronto, ON)
Poltrini, Fernand .... St-Amour & Associates (Montréal, QC)
Pommen, Dennis W. .... Pommen & Associates Limited (Edmonton, AB)
Pon, Georgina .... BC Health Services Ltd. / BCHS (Vancouver, BC)
Pon, Marvin .... Corporate Recruiters Ltd. (Vancouver, BC)
Pond, Pat .... Executive Services Plus Ltd. (Saint John, NB)
Poole, C.J. (Chris) .... Cambridge Management Planning Inc. (Toronto, ON)
Poole, Ken .... Harris Consulting Corporation, The (Winnipeg, MB)
Pooley, Karen .... Adecco Canada Inc. (Winnipeg, MB)
Popeniuk, Debbie .... Lock & Associates (Vancouver, BC)
Popp, Gerry .... Grant Thornton International (Mississauga, ON)
Porcellato, Marnie .... Results Seekers Human Resources Services (Guelph, ON)
Portelance, Greg .... Quantum EDP Recruiting Services Ltd. (Toronto, ON)
Porter, Dave .... Kitchener Executive Consultants (Kitchener, ON)
Porter, Gary .... Meyers Norris Penny / MNP (Rocky Mountain House, AB)
Porter, Mitsy .... FSK Associates Inc. (USA)
Postiener, Nicole .... Personnel Department, The (Vancouver, BC)
Potter, Larry .... Little Group, The (Burlington, ON)
Pottie, Lynne .... Drake International (Halifax, NS)
Poulin, Cindy .... Quantum (Montréal, QC)
Poulin, Gina .... Phelps Staffing Resource Centre (Thunder Bay, ON)
Pound, Ted .... Osborne Group, The (Calgary, AB)
Pountney, Shannon .... Canadian Findings Ltd. (Toronto, ON)
Powell, Bruce .... Mandrake Management Consultants (Toronto, ON)
Powell, Gene .... Management Recruiters of Kannapolis (USA)

POWELL - READ

REAGEAR - ROBERTSON

Reagear, Melanie .... Design Group Staffing Services Inc., The (Red Deer, AB)
Rebeck, Carol .... Spherion Workforce Architects (Winnipeg, MB)
Reder, Sandra .... Accountemps Financial Staffing (Vancouver, BC)
Redlinghuys, Johann .... Heidrick & Struggles International, Inc. (UNITED KINGDOM)
Reed, Alec .... Argus Group Corporation, The (Toronto, ON)
Reed, Clark .... Netgain Partners Inc. (Toronto, ON)
Reed, Todd .... Leader Search Inc. (Calgary, AB)
Rees, Kaye .... First Choice Personnel (Toronto, ON)
Reeves, Michael .... Campbell Edgar Inc. (Delta, BC)
Reevie, Brian .... Becky Jones & Associates Ltd. (Toronto, ON)
Regnier, Marie-Andree .... Raymond Chabot Human Resources Inc. (Montréal, QC)
Rehner, Alan L. .... Management Connections Incorporated (Vancouver, BC)
Reid, Barry .... Thorek / Scott and Partners (Toronto, ON)
Reid, Gordon .... Meyers Norris Penny / MNP (Prince Albert, SK)
Reid, Gwen A. .... Higgins International Inc. (Winnipeg, MB)
Reid, Laura .... Laura Reid & Associates Ltd. (Vancouver, BC)
Reid, Tom .... Kathy Jackson Associates / KJA (Vancouver, BC)
Reid, Vaughan .... Prospects Plus Inc. (Kirkland, QC)
Reid, William .... Reid Management Consultants Inc. (Toronto, ON)
Remillard, Ted .... TMP QD Legal Recruitment (Toronto, ON)
Renard, Stephen .... Renard Hospitality Search Consultants (Toronto, ON)
Renaud, Alain .... St-Amour & Associates (Montréal, QC)
Renaud, Palma .... Staffworks (Toronto, ON)
Render, Don .... Spencer Stuart (USA)
Renner, Karen .... Technical Connections Inc. (USA)
Rennick, Lee .... Rennick, Hoppe & Associates, Inc. (Toronto, ON)
Rentschler, Keith .... MediStaff (USA)
Rentschler, Kirk .... MediStaff (USA)
Resnick, Sheldon .... Sheldon Resnick Associates (Toronto, ON)
Reyno, Shelley .... Eagle Professional Resources Inc. (Halifax, NS)
Reynolds, Kathy .... Torstaff Personnel (Toronto, ON)
Reynolds, Patrick .... Ray & Berndtson / Tanton Mitchell (Vancouver, BC)
Reynolds, Sarah .... James Partnership, The (BERMUDA)
Rezzara, Marisa .... Richter, Usher & Vineberg (Montréal, QC)
Rice, Lisa .... Rice / Drummond Personnel Services Ltd. (Calgary, AB)
Rice, Robert .... Technical Management Resources Inc. (Barrie, ON)
Rich, Kenneth M. .... Ray & Berndtson (USA)
Rich, Michele .... Drake Executive (Winnipeg, MB)
Richard, Michelle .... Ray & Berndtson / Robertson Surrette (Ottawa, ON)
Richards, Denise .... David Aplin & Associates (Calgary, AB)
Richards, Jayne .... Chisholm & Partners International Inc. (Toronto, ON)
Richards, Kate L. .... Andersen (Vancouver, BC)
Richards, Shalini .... Kelly Professional & Technical Services (Halifax, NS)
Richer, Victor .... Levert Personnel Resources Inc. (Sudbury, ON)
Richter, Bob .... Richter & Richter Human Resources Consultants Inc. (Palgrave, ON)
Richter, Gloria .... Richter & Richter Human Resources Consultants Inc. (Palgrave, ON)
Ricketts, Collett .... Donald Givelos & Associates Inc. / DGA (Toronto, ON)
Riddell, Pat .... Network Corporate Search Personnel Inc. (Calgary, AB)
Riddell, Susan .... Pinstripe Personnel Inc. (Toronto, ON)
Riffou, Andrée .... Pleiad Canada Inc. (Ottawa, ON)
Rigal, Jennifer .... JENEX Technology Placement Inc. (Vancouver, BC)
Rigby, Amanda .... Canadian Executive Consultants Inc. (Toronto, ON)
Ring, Tanya .... Capital Executive Ltd. (Calgary, AB)
Ring, Tracy .... Moxon Personnel Ltd. (Vancouver, BC)
Ripley, Alison .... Quantum EDP Recruiting Services Ltd. (Toronto, ON)
Ritchie, Debora .... Adecco Canada Inc. (Kitchener, ON)
Rivard, Arthur .... Glen Abbey Executive Search Inc. (Oakville, ON)
Rivard, Marc .... BDO Dunwoody Executive Search (Winnipeg, MB)
Rivers, Grace .... Adecco Canada Inc. (Toronto, ON)
Rivers, Matt .... Storey & Associates (Toronto, ON)
Rizzuto, Bruno .... TES, The Employment Solution (Mississauga, ON)
Rjeili, Eliane .... Express Personnel Services (Ottawa, ON)
Roach, Chris .... TES, The Employment Solution (Mississauga, ON)
Robert, Tim .... Syntech Placements Inc. (Toronto, ON)
Roberts, Charley .... Groom & Associés Ltée (Pointe-Claire, QC)
Roberts, Daryl .... Systematix Information Technology Consultants Inc. (Montréal, QC)
Roberts, Derek J. .... TMP Worldwide Executive Search (Toronto, ON)
Roberts, Gerold .... Team Power Executive Search (Markham, ON)
Roberts, Heidi .... Drake International (Edmonton, AB)
Roberts, Ian .... Connors, Lovell & Associates Inc. (Cambridge, ON)
Roberts, Marc .... Synergy Search Consultants (Toronto, ON)
Roberts, Melissa .... Executive Assistance Inc. (Toronto, ON)
Robertson, Brenda .... Ray & Berndtson / Robertson Surrette (Ottawa, ON)
Robertson, Christian .... Egon Zehnder International Inc. (Montréal, QC)

ROBERTSON - RUBIN

Robertson, Ken .... AgCall Human Resources (Calgary, AB)
Robertson, Kris .... ProTemps Canada Inc. (Calgary, AB)
Robertson, Linda .... Robertson Human Asset Management (Burlington, ON)
Robertson, Robert .... Ray & Berndtson / Robertson Surrette (Ottawa, ON)
Robidoux, Chantale .... Action Info-Travail Inc. (Mont-Laurier, QC)
Robillard, Rhonda .... Lewis Companies Inc. (Toronto, ON)
Robinson, Hyacinth .... Renard Hospitality Search Consultants (Toronto, ON)
Robinson, Lori .... Access Career Solutions Inc. (Brampton, ON)
Robinson, Moira .... Interim Management Resources Inc. / IMR (Mississauga, ON)
Robinson, Stephen .... Robinson, Fraser Group Ltd. / RFG (Toronto, ON)
Robinson, Warren .... TalentLab (Kanata, ON)
Robitaille, Jean-Marc .... Cyberna Associates Limited (Montréal, QC)
Rocco, Sal .... StoneWood Group (Toronto, ON)
Rocheleau, Ginette .... Adecco Québec (Longueuil, QC)
Rochon, Joel .... Rochon Partners Corp. (Toronto, ON)
Rock, Robert W.C. .... BDO Dunwoody LLP (Nepean, ON)
Rock, Vic .... Accountants on Call / AOC Financial Executive Search (Toronto, ON)
Rodrigue, Sylvie .... Adecco Québec Inc. (Laval) (Laval, QC)
Rodriguez, Susanna .... Access Human Resources Inc. / AccessHR (Ottawa, ON)
Roesch, Mickie .... Adecco Canada Inc. (Edmonton, AB)
Rogers, Bruce .... Advantage Group, The (Mississauga, ON)
Rogers, Kirsten .... Jenereaux & Associates Inc. (Mississauga, ON)
Rogers, Susan .... Storey & Associates (Toronto, ON)
Roginsky, Marc .... Quantum EDP Recruiting Services Ltd. (Toronto, ON)
Rohr, Martin .... Levy Pilotte (Montréal, QC)
Rolfe, David R.L. .... Rolfe, Benson (Vancouver, BC)
Rolin, Diane .... David Aplin & Associates (Edmonton, AB)
Rolland, Denise .... Rolland Groupe Conseil Inc. (Westmount, QC)
Rolland, Guy .... Rolland ressources humaines inc. (Montréal, QC)
Rolling, Brian .... Grant Thornton International (Peace River, AB)
Romak, Marianne .... W.G. Meldrum Limited (Toronto, ON)
Rombaor, Elka .... Ultimate Staffing (Hamilton, ON)
Romoff, Jordan .... Lecours Wolfson Limited (Toronto, ON)
Romvary, John .... Techaid Inc. (Montréal, QC)
Ronald, Keith .... Meyers Norris Penny / MNP (Portage La Prairie, MB)
Ronneseth, Chris .... Partnervision Consulting Group Inc. (Toronto, ON)
Rooke, Nancy .... Doré Liaison Inc. (Greenfield Park, QC)
Root, Nick .... Taylor Root (UNITED KINGDOM)
Rose, Donna .... Procom Services (USA)
Rose, John .... ATS Reliance Technical Group (London, ON)
Rosenblum, Iris .... InterCom Recruitment Ltd. (Toronto, ON)
Rosenthal, Harvey .... Treat & Associates Executive Recruiters (Toronto, ON)
Rosenthal, Jack .... Goldsmith Miller Hersh (Montréal, QC)
Rosenthal, Richard .... Meda Group (Windsor, ON)
Rosenzweig, Jay .... Korn / Ferry International (Toronto, ON)
Rosner, Shelley .... Brock Placement Group Inc. (Toronto, ON)
Ross, Diana .... SynapTuit Group (Vancouver, BC)
Ross, Jackie .... Dumont & Associates Retail Recruitment Ltd. (Vancouver, BC)
Ross, Jan .... Capital Executive Ltd. (Calgary, AB)
Ross, Larry .... Ray & Berndtson / Lovas Stanley (Toronto, ON)
Ross, Linsey .... Expert Recruiters Inc. (Vancouver, BC)
Ross, Mark .... Christian & Timbers (USA)
Ross, Sheila L. .... TMP Worldwide Executive Search (Toronto, ON)
Ross, T.E. .... RBA International HR Consultants Inc. (Westmount, QC)
Rossi, Donna .... Rossi & Associates Inc. (Vancouver, BC)
Rostie, Cynthia .... Rostie & Associates Inc. (Toronto, ON)
Rothstein, Steve .... NAP Executive Services (Canada) Inc., Retail Division (Toronto, ON)
Rothwell, Jim .... Management Recruiters of Kannapolis (USA)
Rouleau, Gilles .... SAG ressources humaines inc. (Montréal, QC)
Roulston, Ken .... Associated Recruitment Consultants (Toronto, ON)
Rourke, Patrick .... P.W. Rourke & Associates / PWR (Mount Royal, QC)
Routhier, Stephen .... Spherion Workforce Architects (Edmonton, AB)
Rowand, Scott .... Landmark Consulting Group Inc. (Hamilton, ON)
Rowe, Pamela .... Canadian Career Partners (Calgary, AB)
Rowe, Steve .... GSI International Consulting Group (Toronto, ON)
Rowland, Diane .... Fifth Option, The (Burnaby, BC)
Roy, Connie .... Quantum (Montréal, QC)
Roy, Isabelle .... Yves Elkas Inc. (Montréal, QC)
Roy, Steve .... Marr Roy Group, The / MRG (Toronto, ON)
Roy, Sylvie .... Michel Pauzé et Associés (Montréal, QC)
Royer, Mildred .... Thompson Associates Career Consulting (Halifax, NS)
Rozenberg, Elena .... Career Management Solutions Inc. / CMS (Toronto, ON)
Ruane, Fiona .... Thomas & Dessain (UNITED KINGDOM)
Rubin, Ron .... GR Search Inc. (Toronto, ON)

RUCKI - SCHULTZ

Rucki, Elizabeth .... Pommen & Associates Limited (Edmonton, AB)
Rudd, Trevor .... Ian Martin Limited (Oakville, ON)
Ruddy, Nancy .... Ian Martin Limited (Oakville, ON)
Rudl, John .... Rudl International (Ottawa, ON)
Rudy, Sharon .... Spencer Stuart & Associates (Canada) Ltd. (Toronto, ON)
Ruebusch, Pamela .... TSI Group / TSI Staffing Services (Mississauga, ON)
Rumberger, Rick .... Meyers Norris Penny / MNP (Red Deer, AB)
Rushforth, David .... Meyers Norris Penny / MNP (Winnipeg, MB)
Russell, Andrew .... HaysZMB (UNITED KINGDOM)
Russell, Karen .... Taylor Personnel Limited (Victoria, BC)
Russell, Suzanne .... John Stoten Consulting (Edmonton, AB)
Russo, Amy .... Baines Gwinner Limited (UNITED KINGDOM)
Rust, Jake .... Slate Group, The (Edmonton, AB)
Rusynyk, Chris .... Lock & Associates (Calgary, AB)
Rutherford, Forbes J. .... Rutherford International Executive Search Group Inc. (Toronto, ON)
Rutherford, Martin .... Grant Thornton International (Yarmouth, NS)
Rutland, Sharon .... Bradson Technology Professionals (Halifax, NS)
Ryan, Ann .... RWJ & Associates (Kitchener, ON)
Ryan, Craig .... Dan McNamara & Associates (Woodstock, ON)
Ryan, Joe .... Skott/Edwards Consultants (USA)
Ryan, Karen .... Classic Consulting Group Inc. (Calgary, AB)
Ryan, Kim .... Summit Personnel Services Inc. (Windsor, ON)
Ryan, Richard .... Chase Consultants Inc. (Mississauga, ON)
Ryan, Tim .... Syntech Placements Inc. (Toronto, ON)
Ryerson, Mike .... Piper-Morgan Associates (USA)
Sabourin, Mike .... Ajilon Canada (Halifax, NS)
Sadler, Chris .... Key Executive Consultants (Barrie, ON)
Safnuk, Don .... Corporate Recruiters Ltd. (Vancouver, BC)
Sagar, Pradeep K. .... Canatrade International Inc. (Candiac, QC)
Saint-Geours, Jean-Phillipe .... Heidrick & Struggles International, Inc. (FRANCE)
Sajous, Antoine .... Expert Recruiters Inc. (Vancouver, BC)
Salem, M. Daniel .... Dana Consultants (Saint-Laurent, QC)
Salmons, Dave .... Allen Austin Lowe & Powers (USA)
Sambey, Stephanie .... Drake International (Kingston, ON)
Sampson, Steve .... St-Amour & Associates (Toronto, ON)
Samson, Hillary .... Taylor Personnel Limited (Victoria, BC)
Samson, Luc .... St-Amour & Associates (Montréal, QC)
San, Matthew .... John Doucette Management Services (Richmond Hill, ON)
Sanderson, Patti .... Grapevine Executive Recruiters Inc. (Toronto, ON)
Sandford, Keli .... Questus Recruitment (Calgary, AB)
Sanford, Wendell .... Technical Service Consultants Inc. / TSC West (Surrey, BC)
Sangiovanni, Daria .... Procom / Professional Computer Consultants Group Ltd. (Kanata, ON)
Sanson, Christine .... Renard Hospitality Search Consultants (Toronto, ON)
Sargautis, Peter .... Triser Corp (Toronto, ON)
Sarne, Isabelle .... Dotemtex Executive Search (Montréal, QC)
Sarnecki, Deborah A. .... Meyers Norris Penny / MNP (Leduc, AB)
Sartor, Larry .... StoneWood Group (Toronto, ON)
Sassine, Joe .... Applied Technology Solutions Inc. / ATS (Toronto, ON)
Sato, Jon .... Quantum EDP Recruiting Services Ltd. (Toronto, ON)
Satoh, Tomoyuki .... Heidrick & Struggles International, Inc. (JAPAN)
Sauberli, Carol Lyn .... Career Partners / Harrison Associates (Hamilton, ON)
Saulnier, Jon .... Canadian Findings Ltd. (Toronto, ON)
Saulnier, Roxanne .... Drake Executive (Montréal, QC)
Saunders, David .... Saunders Company, The (Toronto, ON)
Saunders, Matt .... Advantage Group, The (Whitby, ON)
Saunderson, Patrick .... CTC Computer-Tech Consultants Ltd. (Calgary, AB)
Sauve, Stephanie .... Groupe MCS, Le (Montréal, QC)
Savage, John W. .... Savage Consultants Inc. (Vancouver, BC)
Savage, Richard .... Western Management Consultants (Vancouver, BC)
Savoy, Sandra .... Drakkar Human Resources (Saint-Laurent, QC)
Sayler, Judy .... Sayler's Employment & Consulting Ltd. (Edmonton, AB)
Sayler, Stacey .... Sayler's Employment & Consulting Ltd. (Edmonton, AB)
Schafer, Melissa .... Allemby Management Group Inc. (Toronto, ON)
Schallenberg, Ximena .... Grand River Personnel Ltd. / GRP (Kitchener, ON)
Scheelar, Andrea .... Canadian Career Partners (Calgary, AB)
Scheper, Bob .... GBL Resources Inc. (USA)
Schilling, Florian .... Heidrick & Struggles International / Mülder & Partner (GERMANY)
Schmidt, J. .... TRS Staffing Solutions (Canada) Inc. (Calgary, AB)
Schoales, Michael J. .... Schoales & Associates Inc. (Toronto, ON)
Schoenberg, Marilyn .... Global Personnel (Toronto, ON)
Schoenthaler, Mary .... About Staffing Ltd. (Calgary, AB)
Schroeder, Meagan .... Canadian Career Partners (Calgary, AB)
Schultz, Glen .... Storey & Associates (Toronto, ON)
Schultz, Ron .... Meyers Norris Penny / MNP (Kilarney, MB)

SCHULZ - SHORTT

SHOURIE - SMITH

Shourie, Anurag .... Davies Park (Edmonton, AB)
Shrigley, Paul .... Moxon Dolphin Kerby International (UNITED KINGDOM)
Shrive, Peter .... People + (Toronto, ON)
Shuster, Edward .... Ward Vinge & Associates (Edmonton, AB)
Sidhu, Sukhi .... Advantage Group, The (Mississauga, ON)
Sidky, Louise .... Louise Sidky & Associates (Toronto, ON)
Siemek, Willa .... 1st Choice Personnel (USA)
Sierra, Renée .... CTC Computer-Tech Consultants Ltd. (Winnipeg, MB)
Sietsma, Jennifer P. .... McDonald-Green Personnel (Cambridge, ON)
Sigurdsen, Elaine .... Palmer & Company Executive Recruitment (Toronto, ON)
Sikdar, Jeet .... Procom Services (USA)
Silbernagel, Shelly .... Glazin / Sisco Executive Search Consultants Inc. (Vancouver, BC)
Silbernagel, Valerie .... Coe & Company International Inc. (Calgary, AB)
Silman, Andy .... NewSource Management Ltd. (Toronto, ON)
Silver, Liane .... Thorek / Scott and Partners (Toronto, ON)
Siman, Sean .... Keith Bagg Information Technology Search Inc. / KBITS (Toronto, ON)
Simard, Mathieu .... SAG ressources humaines inc. (Montréal, QC)
Simon, Penny .... Ray & Berndtson (USA)
Simpson, Ali .... Genesis Group Ltd., The (Yellowknife, NT)
Simpson, Amy .... Genesis Group Ltd., The (Yellowknife, NT)
Simpson, David J. .... D.J. Simpson Associates Inc. (Mississauga, ON)
Simpson, Deb .... Genesis Group Ltd., The (Yellowknife, NT)
Simpson, Janet .... IT Resources Ltd. (Markham, ON)
Simpson, John .... Genesis Group Ltd., The (Yellowknife, NT)
Simpson, Nicole .... Meridia Recruitment Services Inc. (Halifax, NS)
Simpson, Peter .... Sourceco Executive Search (Edmonton, AB)
Sinclair, Amy .... MBL Group LLC (USA)
Sinclair, Keith .... Protrans Personnel Services Inc. (Dieppe, NB)
Sinclair, Paul .... Pioneer Executive Consultants (Toronto, ON)
Sinclair, R. Alastair .... Renaud Foster Management Consultants (Ottawa, ON)
Sinclair, Tom .... PricewaterhouseCoopers Executive Search (Toronto, ON)
Sinclair-Smith, Michael .... Sinclair Smith & Associates Ltd. (Sainte-Polycarpe, QC)
Sinden, Maureen .... Maureen Sinden Executive Search (Ottawa, ON)
Singer, Bruce .... PTC - Financial Staffing Inc. (Concord, ON)
Singer, Ingrid .... People Bank, The (Toronto, ON)
Singh, Chandan .... Manpower Professional (Toronto, ON)
Singh, G.V. (Jim) .... Higher Vision Recruitment Strategies Incorporated (Toronto, ON)
Singh, Raj .... Brainhunter.com (Toronto, ON)
Sinnett, Diane .... Cameron Consulting Group (Brampton, ON)
Sirras, Jennifer Ivana .... Marina Sirras & Associates LLC (USA)
Sirras, Marina .... Marina Sirras & Associates LLC (USA)
Sisco, Carol .... Glazin / Sisco Executive Search Consultants Inc. (Toronto, ON)
Sitarz, Jennifer .... Meyers Norris Penny / MNP (Winnipeg, MB)
Siversen, Brenda .... Drake Executive (Toronto, ON)
Skene, Suzanne .... Excel Personnel Inc. (Kamloops, BC)
Skiffington, Jane .... Gerald Walsh Recruitment Services Inc. (Halifax, NS)
Skillen, Emma .... Accountants on Call / AOC Financial Executive Search (Vancouver, BC)
Skode, David .... Finney-Taylor Consulting Group Ltd. (Calgary, AB)
Skrobecki, Marek .... InGenius Engineering Inc. (Ottawa, ON)
Skulsky, Lee Ann .... Resources Connection (Toronto, ON)
Slade, Judy A. .... Thompson Associates Career Consulting (Halifax, NS)
Slaney, Bryan .... Slaney Management Consulting (Simcoe, ON)
Slastnikov, Val .... TDM Technical Services (Toronto, ON)
Sleeth, Ron .... Human Resource Management Group (Unionville, ON)
Slimkowich, Michael .... Pro Tec Global Staffing Services (Thornhill, ON)
Small, Alan G. .... RLP Consulting (Mississauga, ON)
Smith, Betty .... Executive House Inc. (Chatham, ON)
Smith, Brad .... GSA Search Consultants Inc. (Bedford, NS)
Smith, David .... Xycorp Inc. (Toronto, ON)
Smith, Don .... Groupe Pluridis Inc. (Montréal, QC)
Smith, Grant .... PricewaterhouseCoopers Executive Search (Vancouver, BC)
Smith, Ian C. .... International Staffing Consultants, Europe (UNITED KINGDOM)
Smith, Janice .... David Aplin & Associates (Calgary, AB)
Smith, Kelly .... Kent Legal Personnel (Toronto, ON)
Smith, Laverne .... Provence Consulting Inc. (Vancouver, BC)
Smith, Loretta .... Prime Management Group Inc. (London, ON)
Smith, Nadiah .... Adecco Québec Inc. (Québec, QC)
Smith, Nancy .... Drakkar Human Resources (Mississauga, ON)
Smith, Neil .... Ian Martin Limited (Kitchener, ON)
Smith, Peter .... Advantage Group, The (Saint John, NB)
Smith, Philip J.W. .... Hutchinson Group Inc., The (Toronto, ON)
Smith, Prentice .... Nexstaf IT Recruitment (Toronto, ON)
Smith, Richard .... Datalist (Toronto, ON)
Smith, Rita .... TES, The Employment Solution (Burlington, ON)

SMITH - STANCER

STANDER - STRONG

Stander, Cornel .... Morris Pervin Group Inc. (Toronto, ON)
Standeven, Peter .... CanadaIT Ventures Inc. (Surrey, BC)
Standing, Andrea .... TAD Canada (Ottawa, ON)
Standish, Matthew J. .... Everest Management Network Inc. (Toronto, ON)
Staniloff, Rae .... Houston Personnel Group, The (Winnipeg, MB)
Stankova, Helen .... Applied Technology Solutions Inc. / ATS (Toronto, ON)
Stanley, Paul .... Ray & Berndtson / Lovas Stanley (Toronto, ON)
Stante, Michael .... Groupe Conseil Stante Inc. (Saint-Léonard, QC)
Starr, Joanne .... Joanne Starr Consultants Ltd. (Toronto, ON)
Stead, John .... Matchtech Engineering Ltd. (UNITED KINGDOM)
Steele, Jeff .... Brock Placement Group Inc. (Toronto, ON)
Steffensen, John E. .... Western Management Consultants (Edmonton, AB)
Stehr, Dana .... Dana Stehr & Associates Inc. (Toronto, ON)
Stein, Terry G. .... RHI Management Resources (Calgary, AB)
Stenholm, Gilbert .... Spencer Stuart (USA)
Stenzler, Mandy .... TDM Technical Services (Toronto, ON)
Stephen, Jim B. .... Renaud Foster Management Consultants (Ottawa, ON)
Stephenson, Jennifer .... Morris Pervin Group Inc. (Toronto, ON)
Stephenson, Kimberley .... Premier Personnel Manangement (Toronto, ON)
Stern, Michael .... Michael Stern Associates Inc. (Toronto, ON)
Stevens, Brad .... FWJ Communications Ltd. (Calgary, AB)
Stevens, Fern .... Fern Stevens & Associates (Toronto, ON)
Stevens, Sherri .... Stevens Resource Group Inc. (Cambridge, ON)
Stevenson, Anne .... Stevenson & White Inc. (Ottawa, ON)
Stevenson, C. .... C. Stevenson Consulting Inc. (Pointe-Claire, QC)
Stewart, Anne-Marie .... Western Management Consultants (Toronto, ON)
Stewart, Dana .... Management One Consultants (Toronto, ON)
Stewart, Evan .... Angus Employment Limited (Burlington, ON)
Stewart, George .... George Stewart Consultants Ltd. (Toronto, ON)
Stewart, Harvey N. .... Executive Registry / Ressources humaines ER (Montréal, QC)
Stewart, Jan J. .... Egon Zehnder International Inc. (Toronto, ON)
Stewart, Jane .... Weir Associates Inc. (Toronto, ON)
Stewart, Jim .... Muskoka Staffing Company Ltd., The (Bracebridge, ON)
Stewart, Jinty .... Muskoka Staffing Company Ltd., The (Bracebridge, ON)
Stewart, Joanne .... Adecco Canada Inc. (Ottawa, ON)
Stewart, John .... Angus Employment Limited (Burlington, ON)
Stewart, Julie .... Adecco Canada Inc. (Toronto, ON)
Stewart, Samantha .... Brownlow & Associates (Ancaster, ON)
Stewart-Tarney, Rhonda Rae .... Meyers Norris Penny / MNP (Rimbey, AB)
Sticlioff, Susan .... Heidrick & Struggles Canada Inc. (Toronto, ON)
Stilson, Jerry .... Canadian Career Partners (Calgary, AB)
Stinson, Dawn .... Kelly Permanent Recruitment (Mississauga, ON)
Stitt, Leigh-Anne .... Contemporary Personnel Inc. (Vancouver, BC)
Stivaletti, Lynn .... Lannick Associates (Toronto, ON)
Stoakley, Ernie .... Stoakley-Dudley Consultants Ltd. (Mississauga, ON)
Stober, Linda .... Argentus Inc. (Toronto, ON)
Stock, Richard G. .... Catalyst Consulting (Montréal, QC)
Stockwell, Ryan .... Scientific Placement, Inc. (USA)
Stoddart, Kevin .... Meridia Recruitment Services Inc. (Halifax, NS)
Stoddart, Philip .... Thomas E. Hedefine Associates (Toronto, ON)
Stokes, H. David .... Stokes Associates (Pickering, ON)
Stoll, Joan .... MedFall Inc. (Niagara Falls, ON)
Stone, Samantha .... Galt Global Recruiting (Vancouver, BC)
Stone, Shara .... Richmark Group, The (Toronto, ON)
Stonehouse, James (Jim) .... Ray & Berndtson / Lovas Stanley (Toronto, ON)
Stopka, Bruce .... Stopka & Associates (Toronto, ON)
Stoppler, Richard .... Executrade Consultants Ltd. (Edmonton, AB)
Stoppler, Scott .... Executrade Consultants Ltd. (Edmonton, AB)
Storey, Catherine .... Storey & Associates (Toronto, ON)
Storey, Roy .... Storey & Associates (Toronto, ON)
Stoten, John .... John Stoten Consulting (Edmonton, AB)
Stout, Christy .... ProTemps Canada Inc. (Calgary, AB)
Stout, Paul .... ProTemps Canada Inc. (Calgary, AB)
Strachan, Laura .... David Aplin & Associates (Calgary, AB)
Straka, Michelle .... Donald Givelos & Associates Inc. / DGA (Toronto, ON)
Stratford, Jonathan .... Thomas & Dessain (UNITED KINGDOM)
Strba, Kim .... David Aplin & Associates (Calgary, AB)
Street, David .... St-Amour & Associates (Toronto, ON)
Street, Joanne .... HaysZMB (UNITED KINGDOM)
Strickland, Scott .... Hire Choice Inc. (Toronto, ON)
Stroede, Bonnie .... Markent Personnel, Inc. (USA)
Stromsmoe, Ed .... Meyers Norris Penny / MNP (Foremost, AB)
Strong, Debra .... Canadian Career Partners (Calgary, AB)
Strong, Karen .... Eureka Recruitment (Calgary, AB)

STRONG - TAYLOR

TAYLOR - TOMKO

Taylor, Sue .... Permanent Solutions Inc. (Mississauga, ON)
Tchouanguem, Silvianne .... Emplois plus, service de pre-sélection (Lasalle, QC)
Teal, Gerri .... Allen Personnel Services (London, ON)
Techko, Susan .... New World International Consultants (Windsor, ON)
Teitelbaum, Harry .... InterCom Recruitment Ltd. (Toronto, ON)
Tellier, Christophe .... Russell Reynolds Associates, Inc. (FRANCE)
Temple, Nancy .... Kirkpatrick Personnel Ltd. (Vancouver, ON)
Temple, Todd .... Andersen (Winnipeg, MB)
Templeton, Les .... Systematix Information Technology Consultants Inc. (Ottawa, ON)
Tennant, Pamela .... Accountants on Call / AOC Financial Executive Search (Vancouver, BC)
Tennant, Stacey .... David Aplin & Associates (Calgary, AB)
Tennen, Lanny .... Tennen Personnel Services Limited (Toronto, ON)
Tennenbaum, Yvonne .... Kelly Professional & Technical Services (Kitchener, ON)
Teotico, Maria .... Keith Bagg Staffing (Regional) Inc. (Thornhill, ON)
Terpstra, Al .... PDQ Personnel Inc. (Mississauga, ON)
Terpstra, Shannon .... Permanent Search Group Inc. / PSG (Mississauga, ON)
Tessier, Catherine .... Drakkar Human Resources (Saint-Laurent, QC)
Testani, Bernadette .... TMP Worldwide Executive Search (Toronto, ON)
Testart, Marion .... Placement Testart Inc. (Westmount, QC)
Thacker, Ken .... Association Resource Centre Inc., The (Toronto, ON)
Themis, Chrisanthopoulos .... Expertech Personnel Services Inc. (Montréal, QC)
Theoret, Teri .... TalentLab (Kanata, ON)
Theriault, Marilyn .... Systematix Information Technology Consultants Inc. (Ottawa, ON)
Thiessen, Erin .... Grasslands Group Inc. (Swift Current, SK)
Thomas, Catherine .... Thomas Group, The (Mississauga, ON)
Thomas, Catherine M. .... Catherine M. Thomas & Partners Inc. (Toronto, ON)
Thomas, Christine .... Ray & Berndtson / Lovas Stanley (Toronto, ON)
Thomas, Dennis .... Thomas Mining Associates (UNITED KINGDOM)
Thomas, Dick .... McLean Executive Consultants Ltd. (Calgary, AB)
Thomas, Ian .... Thomas & Dessain (UNITED KINGDOM)
Thomas, James E. .... James E. Thomas & Associates Inc. (London, ON)
Thomas, Jeff .... Grant Thornton International (Winnipeg, MB)
Thomas, Jennifer-Lee .... TMP Worldwide Interactive / Monster.ca (Montréal, QC)
Thomas, Michael .... Westcott, Thomas & Associates Limited / PSA International (Toronto, ON)
Thomas, Sonia .... Baines Gwinner Limited (UNITED KINGDOM)
Thomas, Wayne .... Wayne Thomas & Associates (Ottawa, ON)
Thomason, Ronald .... Montgomery Thomason & Associates (Mississauga, ON)
Thomiak, Max .... J.R. Bechtle & Company (USA)
Thompson, Barbara .... Thompson Elliott Group, The (Toronto, ON)
Thompson, Colin K. .... Thompson Resources (Niagara-on-the-Lake, ON)
Thompson, Debbie .... Adecco Canada Inc. (Burnaby, BC)
Thompson, Gary .... Technical Services Consultants Ontario Ltd. / TSC Group (Toronto, ON)
Thompson, Glen .... Archer Resource Solutions Inc. (Mississauga, ON)
Thompson, Karen .... Geddes Jefferson & Associates (Victoria, BC)
Thompson, Paul .... Ian Martin Limited (Oakville, ON)
Thompson, Shari .... SEARCHs / Saskatoon Employment Access Resource Centre for Human Services (Saskatoon, SK)
Thomson, Dorothy .... Renard Hospitality Search Consultants (Toronto, ON)
Thomson, Sarah-Jane .... Expert Recruiters Inc. (Vancouver, BC)
Thomson, Steve .... Roevin Technical People Ltd. (Sarnia, ON)
Thorek, Faye .... Thorek / Scott and Partners (Toronto, ON)
Thorek, Michael .... Thorek / Scott and Partners (Toronto, ON)
Thorlakson, Alan .... Harris Consulting Corporation, The (Winnipeg, MB)
Thornton, Terry .... Galloway and Associates (Toronto, ON)
Thorp, Linda .... Aron Printz & Associates Ltd. (Vancouver, BC)
Tibbet, Brian J. .... Canadian Medical Placement Service (London, ON)
Tichbourne, Diane .... Applied Technology Solutions Inc. / ATS (Toronto, ON)
Tighe, David .... RHI Consulting (Toronto, ON)
Tiku, Deepak .... Applied Technology Solutions Inc. / ATS (Toronto, ON)
Tilker, Lutz .... Spencer Stuart (GERMANY)
Timmons, Dennis .... Salesforce Development Ltd. (Westmount, QC)
Tisshaw, Kevan .... Professional Environmental Recreation Consultants Ltd. / PERC (North Delta, BC)
Titian, Lisa .... Datalist (Toronto, ON)
Tizard, Mark .... Corporate Resources (Hertford) Ltd. (UNITED KINGDOM)
To, Raymond .... Corporate Recruiters Ltd. (Vancouver, BC)
Tobin, Hélène .... Personnel Hélène Tobin Inc. (Dorval, QC)
Tobin-McCarthy, Denise .... TMP Worldwide Executive Search (Toronto, ON)
Tod, Don .... AgCall Human Resources (Markham, ON)
Toffey, Bryan .... TEKsystems (Richmond, BC)
Toliver, Jennifer .... Archer Associates (Toronto, ON)
Tollefson, David .... Becky Jones & Associates Ltd. (Toronto, ON)
Tolstoy, Diane .... Tolstoy Resources (Bolton, ON)
Tom, Helen .... Recruitment Enhancement Services / RES (Toronto, ON)
Toma, Darrell .... Toma & Bouma (Edmonton, AB)
Tomko, Tony .... Aztech Recruitment Co. (USA)

TOMLINSON - VALADE

VALDSTYN - VONKEMAN

Valdstyn, Peter .... Advantage Group, The (Nepean, ON)
Valois, Glory Z. .... AeroPersonnel International (Dorval, QC)
Van Alstine, Catherine .... Ray & Berndtson / Tanton Mitchell (Vancouver, BC)
Van Andel, Connie .... Barcon Consulting Inc. (New Hamburg, ON)
van Biesen, Jacques A.H. .... Van Biesen Group Inc. (Calgary, AB)
van Biesen, Tanya .... TMP Worldwide Executive Search (Toronto, ON)
Van Clieaf, Mark .... MVC Associates International (Toronto, ON)
Van Epps, Janet .... Markent Personnel, Inc. (USA)
Van Hees, Tony .... Van Hees Personnel Inc. (Dundas, ON)
Van Klaveren, David .... Van Klaveren Litherland & Company (Toronto, ON)
Van Mierlo, Don .... StarDot PRG Inc. (Calgary, AB)
Van Muyen, Margo .... Technical Management Resources Inc. (Barrie, ON)
van Niekerk, Louisa .... Bridge Information Technology Inc. (Vancouver, BC)
Van Opstal, Lori .... Your Advantage Staffing Consultants Inc. (Cambridge, ON)
van Rensburg, Lourens .... Davies Park (Edmonton, AB)
Van Schalk, David E. .... Derhak Ireland & Partners Ltd. (Toronto, ON)
Van Slyck, Rob .... CCT Inc. (Mississauga, ON)
Van Slyck, Robert .... CCT Inc. (London, ON)
van Straubenzee, Tony .... Russell Reynolds Associates, Inc. (Toronto, ON)
van Veen, Charles .... Far West Group (Surrey, BC)
Vance, Deb .... Drakkar Human Resources (Mississauga, ON)
Vanden Heuvel, Tony .... Meyers Norris Penny / MNP (Pincher Creek, AB)
VanderBerg, Catherine .... Feldman Gray & Associates Inc. (Toronto, ON)
Vanderkruyk, Terry .... SearchWest Inc. (Vancouver, BC)
Vanderleeuw, Jim .... Connors, Lovell & Associates Inc. (Cambridge, ON)
Vanwyck, Margaret .... Michael Stern Associates Inc. (Toronto, ON)
Varga, Lesley .... Lesley Varga and Associates (Toronto, ON)
Varghese, Jane .... Computer Action Company (Toronto, ON)
Variya, Sudha .... Quantum EDP Recruiting Services Ltd. (Toronto, ON)
Vasilopoulos, Koula .... Affiliates, The (Calgary, AB)
Vasques, Anna .... William Lee & Associates, Inc. (Vancouver, BC)
Vaughn, Mary Ann .... Job Born Candidate Selection Bureau (Hamilton, ON)
Vell, Dora .... Heidrick & Struggles Canada Inc. (Toronto, ON)
Velloso, Guilherme .... Amrop International / PMC (BRAZIL)
Venderhoof, Dory .... Genovese Vanderhoof & Associates (Toronto, ON)
Veneranda, Jeanne .... Godbout Martin Godbout & Associates (Hull, QC)
Vennat, Manon .... Spencer Stuart & Associates (Canada) Ltd. (Montréal, QC)
Veres, John R. .... Veres Picton & Co. (Edmonton, AB)
Vergara, Gail .... Spencer Stuart (USA)
Verhallen, Mildred .... BDO Dunwoody LLP (Nepean, ON)
Verma, Sanjeev .... RWJ & Associates (Kitchener, ON)
Vernon, Donald .... Harris Consulting Corporation, The (Winnipeg, MB)
Verriez, Paul .... Verriez Group Inc., The (London, ON)
Verwagen, Christine .... ATS Reliance Technical Group (London, ON)
Vézina, Claude .... Vezina Goodman Executive Search (Montréal, QC)
Vickers, Jane .... RWJ & Associates (London, ON)
Vickers, Robert .... Canadian Pathfinder Consulting Services Inc. (Toronto, ON)
Vickery, Brian .... St-Amour & Associates (Toronto, ON)
Victor, Edward .... Victor & Gold (Montréal, QC)
Vieledal, Toni .... McDonald-Green Personnel (Cambridge, ON)
Viénot, Laurence .... Russell Reynolds Associates, Inc. (FRANCE)
Viger, Carole .... Office Team Administrative Staffing (Pointe-Claire, QC)
Vigue, Monique .... Prospects Plus Inc. (Kirkland, QC)
Vijh, R. .... Keystone Select / M.A. Haggith Consultants Ltd. (Toronto, ON)
Villa, Maurizia .... Heidrick & Struggles International, Inc. (ITALY)
Villecco, Kim .... Tosi Placement Services Inc. (Toronto, ON)
Villemure, Mariane .... Adecco Québec (Longueuil, QC)
Vincent, Christopher .... Christopher Vincent & Associates Ltd. (Calgary, AB)
Vineberg, Hanna .... Cyberna Associates Limited (Montréal, QC)
Vines, Murray .... Canadian Career Partners (Calgary, AB)
Vinet, Annick .... Adecco LPI (Saint-Laurent, QC)
Viola, Marc .... Accountants on Call / AOC Financial Executive Search (Toronto, ON)
Visconti, Victor .... DatPro Personnel Inc. (Toronto, ON)
Vitanza, Jocelyne .... Dare Human Resources Corporation (Ottawa, ON)
Vitanza, Michael .... Licari & Vitanza Associates Inc. (USA)
Vitols, Ivars .... GSI International Consulting Group (Toronto, ON)
Vo Buu, Cathy .... Groupe Ranger (Montréal, QC)
Voaklander, Vanore .... Daniluck & Associates International (Edmonton, AB)
Vohma, Kristina .... Feldman Gray & Associates Inc. (Toronto, ON)
Voigt, Rolf .... Graduate Consulting Services, The (Montréal, QC)
Voll, Lisa .... Ernst & Young (Kitchener, ON)
Volum, Chris .... Nework Corp. (Toronto, ON)
von Rohr, Hengi .... Renard Hospitality Search Consultants (Toronto, ON)
Vonkeman, Karen .... Robert Half Canada Inc. (Edmonton, AB)

VOPNI - WEBBER

WEBER - WILLIAMS

Weber, Derek .... Procom / Professional Computer Consultants Group Ltd. (Kanata, ON)
Webster, Janice .... CNC Global (Ottawa, ON)
Webster, William D. (Bill) .... Professional Environmental Recreation Consultants Ltd. / PERC (North Delta, BC)
Wechsler, Gary .... Victor & Gold (Montréal, QC)
Weckwerth, Glen .... Grant Thornton International (North Bay, ON)
Weddle, Judy K. .... Ray & Berndtson (USA)
Weed, William H. .... Ray & Berndtson (USA)
Weekes, Leslie .... Counsel Network, The (Calgary, AB)
Weeks, John .... Advantage Group, The (Mississauga, ON)
Weese, Roger .... Computer Action Company (London, ON)
Weinberg, Paul .... Thorek / Scott and Partners (Toronto, ON)
Weir, Douglas .... Weir Associates Inc. (Toronto, ON)
Weir, Michael .... Tech Force Search Group (Toronto, ON)
Weir, Shelley .... Braun-Valley Associates Ltd. (Sarnia, ON)
Weiss, John .... Star Search Consultants (Toronto, ON)
Welch, Gordon .... Gordon Welch Consulting Inc. (Sherwood Park, AB)
Welch, Gregory .... Spencer Stuart (USA)
Welch, Roger .... Western Management Consultants (Vancouver, BC)
Welling, Brenda .... Allen Austin Lowe & Powers (USA)
Wells, Mark .... Xycorp Inc. (Toronto, ON)
Wells, Wendy .... Adecco - Compaq Canada National Hiring Centre (Toronto, ON)
Welsh, Alex .... TES, The Employment Solution (Toronto, ON)
Welsh, Christopher .... Quantum EDP Recruiting Services Ltd. (Toronto, ON)
Welyk, Allan .... Lock & Associates (Vancouver, BC)
Werboweski, Stacey .... Smythe Ratcliffe (Vancouver, BC)
Werle, Carolyn .... Records & Information Management Services Inc. / RIM (Toronto, ON)
West, Fred .... Wood West & Partners Inc. (Vancouver, BC)
West, Kyle .... GSI International Consulting Group (Toronto, ON)
West, Trevor .... Russell & Associates (Kelowna, BC)
Wexler, Charles .... Integrated Data Services Inc. (Ottawa, ON)
Wexler, Jeannie .... Western Management Consultants (Calgary, AB)
Whalen, Diana H. .... ATI Consulting Corporation Inc. (Halifax, NS)
Wharton, Cynthia .... Personnel Management Group (Winnipeg, MB)
Wheeler, Kathy .... Medhunters.com (Toronto, ON)
Whelan, Philip, F. .... Puglisevich Crews and Services Limited (St. John's, NF)
Whenham, Travis .... Transpersonnel Driver Staffing and Allied Services (Edmonton, AB)
Whitaker, Joni .... Management Recruiters of Kannapolis (USA)
White, Dave .... Dave White Personnel Inc. (Ottawa, ON)
White, David .... Squires Resources Inc. (Barrie, ON)
White, Eric .... Chancellor Partners, The (Vancouver, BC)
White, Freyja .... Conlin Personnel (Vancouver, BC)
White, Judy .... Rostie & Associates Inc. (Toronto, ON)
White, King D. .... Allen Austin Lowe & Powers (USA)
White, Peter .... Consultant's Choice, Inc. (USA)
White, Phil .... GSI International Consulting Group (Toronto, ON)
White, Trevor .... Stevenson & White Inc. (Ottawa, ON)
Whitley, Tom .... Management Recruiters of Kannapolis (USA)
Whitten, Anne .... Anne Whitten Bilingual Human Resources Inc. (Toronto, ON)
Whittington, Rachel .... Datalist (Toronto, ON)
Whyte, Terrence A.F. .... Templeman Consulting Group Inc. (Kingston, ON)
Wicken, Mark .... InterCom Recruitment Ltd. (Toronto, ON)
Widman, Charles .... Widman Associates Inc. (Vancouver, BC)
Wierichs, Jeffrey .... Spencer Stuart (USA)
Wieser, Lesley .... Technical Services Consultants Ontario Ltd. / TSC Group (Toronto, ON)
Wiesner, Nancy .... Dynamic Employment Solution Inc. (Brampton, ON)
Wiethe, Britt .... Adecco Canada Inc. (Toronto, ON)
Wiggins, Ylonka .... Allen Austin Lowe & Powers (USA)
Wightman, Judith .... Wightman & Associates (Kanata, ON)
Wilding, C. .... Armor Personnel (Mississauga, ON)
Wilding, Diane .... PricewaterhouseCoopers Executive Search (Calgary, AB)
Wiles, Emily .... Applicants Inc. (Kitchener, ON)
Wiley, Delia L. .... Meyers Norris Penny / MNP (Drumheller, AB)
Wilins, Dan .... HaysZMB (UNITED KINGDOM)
Wilkie, Glenn .... Wilkie Group International, The (Toronto, ON)
Wilkie, Ishbel .... Spherion Workforce Architects (Toronto, ON)
Willcocks, Roy .... Belanger Partners Limited (Thornhill, ON)
Willden, Vincent G.B. .... Coast Personnel Services Ltd. (Nanaimo, BC)
Williams, Gary .... InterCom Recruitment Ltd. (Toronto, ON)
Williams, Glenn .... Grant Thornton International (Halifax, NS)
Williams, Kathryn .... Bialecki Inc. (USA)
Williams, Nick .... ExecuCounsel Inc (Toronto, ON)
Williams, Salina .... Thorek / Scott and Partners (Toronto, ON)
Williams, Sharon .... MediStaff (USA)
Williams, Todd .... Advantage Group, The (St. John's, NF)

WILLIAMSON - YASCHUK

YEE - ZYLBERLICHT

Yee, Annie .... Procom Services (USA)
Yee, Kam Sein .... Health Match BC (Vancouver, BC)
Yelle, Nelia .... Forest People International Search Ltd. (Vancouver, BC)
Yolleck, Dan .... Syntech Placements Inc. (Toronto, ON)
York, Andrea .... ASTRA Management Corp. (Vancouver, BC)
Yoshimura, Glenn .... Technical Connections Inc. (USA)
Young, Allison .... Descheneaux Recruitment Services Ltd. (Vancouver, BC)
Young, Ann .... MRK Consulting Ltd. (UNITED KINGDOM)
Young, Barb .... Levert Personnel Resources Inc. (Sudbury, ON)
Young, Colleen .... Prime Management Group Inc. (Cambridge, ON)
Young, Kathryn .... Ray & Berndtson / Tanton Mitchell (Vancouver, BC)
Young, L.A. .... Canadian Executive Recruitment (Mississauga, ON)
Young, Lawrence M. .... PYA Solutions Inc. (Montréal, QC)
Young, Leslie .... Little Group, The (Burlington, ON)
Young, Pam .... Dutton Group (Toronto, ON)
Young, Stacey .... Procom Services (USA)
Young-Pugh, Allan .... Western Management Consultants (Toronto, ON)
Youngberg, Laura .... Davies Park (Calgary, AB)
Youngs, Laura .... First Choice Personnel (Toronto, ON)
Yu, Mabel .... Softcom Consulting Inc. (Richmond Hill, ON)
Yuen-Pitre, Angeline .... Datalist (Toronto, ON)
Yurkoski, Leona .... Kelly Professional & Technical Services (Edmonton, AB)
Zaconni, Tony .... HT Search Company Ltd. (Nepean, ON)
Zafran, Morty .... Schwartz Levitsky Feldman / SLF (Montréal, QC)
Zahn, Kelly .... Markent Personnel, Inc. (USA)
Zarek, Kelly .... Kent Legal Personnel (Toronto, ON)
Zeidel, Jerry .... Zeidel, Gregory & Associates (Toronto, ON)
Zeller, Traci .... Finney-Taylor Consulting Group Ltd. (Calgary, AB)
Zevy, Dov .... Korn / Ferry International (Toronto, ON)
Zidle, Audrey .... Moxon Personnel Ltd. (Vancouver, BC)
Ziegler, Helen .... Helen Ziegler and Associates Inc. (Toronto, ON)
Zigelstein, Trevor .... Robert Half Canada Inc. (Toronto, ON)
Zinner, Joe .... Ray & Berndtson / Lovas Stanley (Toronto, ON)
Zions, Brent .... Systematix Information Technology Consultants Inc. (Toronto, ON)
Zirger, Rosi .... ZSA Legal Recruitment (Toronto, ON)
Ziziam, Robert .... Excel Personnel Inc. (Montréal, QC)
Zoffranieri, Domenic .... FHG International Inc. (Toronto, ON)
Zsebak, Deborah .... Express Personnel Services (Windsor, ON)
Zucchiatti, Elizabeth .... PricewaterhouseCoopers Executive Search (Toronto, ON)
Zuchlewski, Joe .... Procom Services (USA)
Zukauskas, John .... Graduate Consulting Services, The (Montréal, QC)
Zukow, Peter .... Lock & Associates (Toronto, ON)
Zupanic, Ivan .... Connors, Lovell & Associates Inc. (Cambridge, ON)
Zweep, Kelly .... Harvard Group, The (Markham, ON)
Zylberlicht, Abe .... Schlesinger Newman Goldman (Montréal, QC)

Also from the publishers of this directory...

Discover Canada's most amazing places to work

CANADA'S TOP 100 EMPLOYERS (2002 EDITION)

The first edition of this book was a runaway best-seller – The Globe and Mail named it Canada's #1 selling business book last year.

The new 2002 edition is bigger and better – competition by employers to make this year's list was fierce! The result is an amazing group of employers that lead their industries in attracting and retaining employees. These companies and organizations offer truly exceptional employee benefits, working conditions and perks.

This year's list includes employers from every region of the country and every major industry. Before you apply for a new job anywhere, discover what Canada's top employers offer employees.

"...a fountain of knowledge about Canadian workplaces, employers, workplace philosophies [and] perks," says The Vancouver Sun. This book "showcase[s] the employers that are doing the most interesting things to attract and keep good employees" adds The Ottawa Citizen. Trade paperback. 334 pages. ISBN 1-894450-05-1. **$18.95**

---

*To order by credit card, call **1-800-361-2580** or (416) 964-6069. Credit card orders can also be faxed to (416) 964-3202. View sample pages and order online at **www.mediacorp2.com**. Sold at bookstores everywhere.*

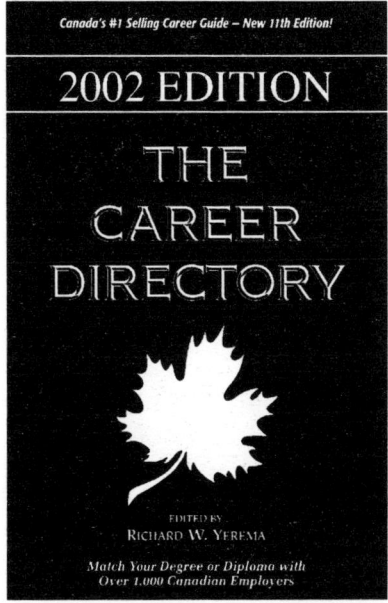

Also from the publishers of this directory...

See all the new jobs in your field every week

CANADA EMPLOYMENT WEEKLY

Every week, Canada Employment Weekly brings you over 1,000 of the best new job opportunities in the nation. No part-time, temporary, seasonal or agency jobs — just full-time careers with the companies and organziations that are succeeding in today's economy.

Our editors monitor recruitment at thousands of employers across Canada every week. Whenever a vacancy is announced in one of the occupations we track (see list at left), you'll read about it first in CEW. We do the legwork so you can spend your time applying for more and better positions.

In addition to leads on hundreds of unadvertised positions every week, you get valuable background information on employers that you won't see anywhere else. Best of all, 100% of the jobs in our paper are new every week — when you miss a single issue, you miss a lot!

All our subscriptions are sent via first-class mail to make sure each issue reaches you quickly. Subscription rates:

	Canada	USA	Overseas
12 issues (three months)	$55.80	$66.00	$103.50
50 issues (one year)	$232.50	$275.00	$431.25

Rates shown are in Canadian dollars. Canadian residents add 7% GST.

*To order by credit card, call **1-800-361-2580** or (416) 964-6069. Credit card orders can also be faxed to (416) 964-3202. View a sample issue and order online at **www.mediacorp2.com**. Sold at newsstands across Canada.*

Also from the publishers of this directory...

Get your copy of CEW before the ink is dry

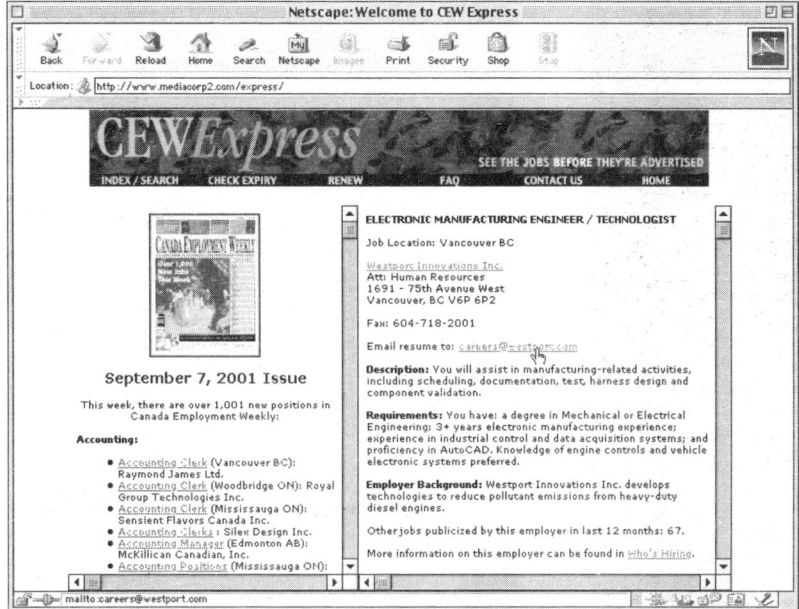

CEW*EXPRESS*

CEW*Express* is the fast online version of Canada Employment Weekly. It features exactly the same content as the newsprint edition, but offers the following advantages:

- ✔ **Instant Delivery.** A new issue is available to subscribers every Monday at 4:30 pm (Toronto time) – a full day before the paper appears on newsstands.

- ✔ **Searchable Text.** Job reports are searchable by keyword, so you can quickly find new opportunities in your field across different occupational categories.

- ✔ **Apply Faster.** Job listings include built-in links to employers' websites and recruiters' email addresses, so you can research hot prospects and apply for positions instantly.

- ✔ **Back Issues.** You can search the current week's issue plus the last three isssues.

Job reports in CEW*Express* are indexed under 61 major occupational categories, so you see all the vacancies in your field across Canada at once. And 100% of the positions are new every week, so you don't waste a moment reading outdated information.

A 12 week subscription to CEW*Express* **costs only $49** plus tax, regardless of where you live. To subscribe, complete the online subscription form at:

http://www.mediacorp2.com

You'll receive a password that lets you access the site for the duration of your subscription.

ACCOUNTING
ACTUARIAL
ADMINISTRATIVE
ADVERTISING
AEROSPACE
AGRICULTURE/FISHERIES
APPAREL
ARCHITECTURE
ARTS & CULTURE
AUTOMOTIVE
BANKING
BILINGUAL
BIOTECH/BIOLOGY
COMPUTING
CONSTRUCTION
CONSULTING
DESIGN
DIRECT MKTNG.
DISABLED
EDUCATION
ENGINEERING
ENVIRONMENTAL
FINANCE
FORESTRY
FRANCHISING
GEOLOGY/GEOGRAPHY
GOVT./NONPROFIT
GRAPHIC ARTS
HEALTH/MEDICAL
HOSPITALITY
HUMAN RESOURCE
INSURANCE
INTERNATIONAL
LAW
LIBRARIANS
LOGISTICS
MANAGEMENT
MARKETING
METALS
MINING
MULTIMEDIA
OIL & GAS
OPERATIONS
PACKAGING
PHARMACEUTICAL
PLASTICS
PRINTING
PUBLIC RELATIONS
PUBLISHING
PULP & PAPER
PURCHASING
QUALITY CONTROL
REAL ESTATE
RELIGIOUS
RETAIL
SALES
SCIENTIFIC
TELECOM
TRADE SHOWS
TRADES/TECHNICIANS
TRANSPORT

Also from the publishers of this directory...

See all the jobs reported in your field in the past year

OUR INDUSTRY REPORT SERVICE

Each week we publish Industry Reports in 61 major occupations showing:

✔ **The Top 25 Employers in the field**, based on the number of new positions each employer created in the field in the past 12 months.

✔ **All the new job opportunities that have been reported across Canada in the field in the past year.** You get full details of each position, the qualifications required, salary offered (if publicized), background information on the employer, and full contact information (HR contact name, employer address, email, fax and website). We also show you the date the vacancy was first reported.

Industry Reports are available in printed or electronic (PDF or text) formats. Reports vary in length from 25 pages to over 400 pages for larger categories (such as Computing and Engineering).

Our Industry Reports are used by:

❏ **Job-seekers** who want to discover the top employers in their field and see complete details on all the positions publicized in their field in the past year.

❏ **Human Resource Managers** who want to learn the current qualifications, duties and salary levels (where publicized) that are being offered by other employers in their industry.

❏ **Headhunters and recruitment professionals** who have an outstanding candidate and need to know all the employers that could use this candidate's skills and qualifications.

The price for one Industry Report is **$59.95** and there is a 15% discount if you receive your report by email. Categories are updated every Tuesday.

---

*To order by credit card, call **1-800-361-2580** or (416) 964-6069. Credit card orders can also be faxed to (416) 964-3202. View sample a sample Industry Report and order online at **www.mediacorp2.com**.*

COMMENTS &
CHANGES FORM

Please correct / add the following information
in the next edition of the Canadian Directory of
Search Firms:

AVIS DE CHANGEMENT
ET COMMENTAIRES

*Veuillez corriger / ajouter les reseignements suivants
à la prochaine édition du Répertoire canadien des
agences de placement:*

_____

NAME OF SEARCH FIRM

SUBMITTED BY

DATE   TELEPHONE

Send to: Canadian Directory of Search Firms, 21 New
Street, Toronto, ON M5R 1P7. Fax (416) 964-3202.
info@mediacorp2.com.

NOM D'AGENCE

SOUMIS PAR

DATE   TÉLÉPHONE

Envoyez à: *Répertoire canadien des agences de placement, 15 rue New, Toronto, ON M5R 1P7. Télécopieur
(416) 964-3202. info@mediacorp2.com.*

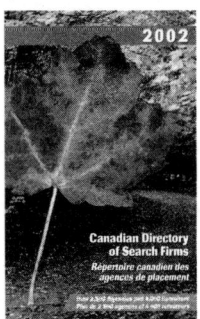

Canadian Directory of Search Firms

This directory is sold at major bookstores across Canada. You can also order directly from the publisher:

❏ **Telephone** your credit card order toll-free to 1-800-361-2580 or (416) 964-6069.

❏ **Fax** your credit card order to (416) 964-3202.

❏ **Mail this form** and your cheque or money order (payable to the "Canadian Directory of Search Firms") to the address below.

Orders within Canada and the USA are shipped by Expressmail and are delivered to you within two or three business days. Orders outside Canada are shipped by first class airmail.

Total charges per copy ordered are:

Shipped to	Directory	Shipping	GST	Total
Canada	$49.95	$5.00	$3.85	$58.80
USA	49.95	9.95	0.00	59.90
Overseas	49.95	18.96	0.00	68.91

GST # R134051515

Répertoire canadien des agences de placement

Ce répertoire est vendu dans les principales librairies partout au Canada. Vous pouvez aussi commander directement de l'éditeur:

❏ *Par téléphone, en utilisant votre carte et en composant le 1-800-361-2580 ou le (416) 964-6069.*

❏ *Par fax, en donnant votre numéro de carte au (416) 964-3202.*

❏ *Par la poste, en envoyant le bon de commande et votre paiement au Répertoire canadien des agences de placement à l'adresse indiquée ci-dessous.*

Les commandes à l'intérieur du Canada et É-U sont expédiées par livraison spéciale; vous devez prévoir deux ou trois jours pour la livraison. Les commandes à l'exterieur du Canada sont expédiées par avion en première classe.

Les frais totaux pour chaque exemplaire commandé sont:

Expédié au	Répertoire	Envoi	TPS	Total
Canada	49,95$	5,00$	3,85$	58,80$
États-Unis	49,95	9,95	0,00	59,90
Outre-mer	49,95	18,96	0,00	68,91

TPS # R134051515

ORDER FORM / *BON DE COMMANDE*

Number of copies ordered:
Nombre des copie(s) demandée(s):

NAME / *NOM*

ADDRESS / *ADRESSE*

CITY / *VILLE*   PROV.   POST. CODE

COUNTRY / *PAYS*

TÉLÉPHONE

Method of Payment:
Méthode de paiement:

❏ Visa
❏ MasterCard
❏ Amex
❏ Chèque

CREDIT CARD NUMBER / *NUMÉRO DE CARTE DE CRÉDIT*

/

EXP. *DATE D'EXPIRATION*   SIGNATURE

Send or fax to / *Envoyez à:*

Canadian Directory of Search Firms
Répertoire canadien des agences de placement
21 NEW STREET, TORONTO, ONTARIO M5R 1P7
TEL. (416) 964-6069 • FAX (416) 964-3202
TO ORDER, CALL TOLL-FREE 1-800-361-2580
http://www.mediacorp2.com